Also by Ron Chernow

Grant

Washington: A Life

Alexander Hamilton

Titan: The Life of John D. Rockefeller, Sr.

The Death of the Banker: The Decline and Fall of the Great Financial Dynasties and the Triumph of the Small Investor

The Warburgs: The Twentieth-Century Odyssey of a Remarkable Jewish Family

The House of Morgan: An American Banking Dynasty and the Rise of Modern Finance

Mark Twain

Ron Chernow

Penguin Press | New York | 2025

PENGUIN PRESS
An imprint of Penguin Random House LLC
1745 Broadway, New York, NY 10019
penguinrandomhouse.com

Copyright © 2025 by Ron Chernow

Penguin Random House values and supports copyright. Copyright fuels creativity, encourages diverse voices, promotes free speech, and creates a vibrant culture. Thank you for buying an authorized edition of this book and for complying with copyright laws by not reproducing, scanning, or distributing any part of it in any form without permission. You are supporting writers and allowing Penguin Random House to continue to publish books for every reader. Please note that no part of this book may be used or reproduced in any manner for the purpose of training artificial intelligence technologies or systems.

Photo credits appear on pages 1137–38.

Library of Congress Cataloging-in-Publication Data

Names: Chernow, Ron, author.
Title: Mark Twain / Ron Chernow.
Description: New York : Penguin Press, 2025. | Includes bibliographical references and index.
Identifiers: LCCN 2024044064 (print) | LCCN 2024044065 (ebook) | ISBN 9780525561729 (hardcover) | ISBN 9780525561736 (ebook)
Subjects: LCSH: Twain, Mark, 1835–1910. | Authors, American—19th century—Biography. | Humorists, American—19th century—Biography. | LCGFT: Biographies.
Classification: LCC PS1331 .C34 2025 (print) | LCC PS1331 (ebook) | DDC 818/.409 [B]—dc23
LC record available at https://lccn.loc.gov/2024044064
LC ebook record available at https://lccn.loc.gov/2024044065

Printed in Canada
1 3 5 7 9 10 8 6 4 2

Designed by Cassandra Garruzzo Mueller

The authorized representative in the EU for product safety and compliance is Penguin Random House Ireland, Morrison Chambers, 32 Nassau Street, Dublin D02 YH68, Ireland, https://eu-contact.penguin.ie.

*To my parents,
who somehow had a
crazy faith in their son's
quixotic dream of
becoming a writer*

Contents

PRELUDE: THE PILOT HOUSE   xiii

PART ONE: AFLOAT

One: **Loveless Marriage**   3
Two: **A Wild and Mischievous Boy**   19
Three: **Printer's Devil**   31
Four: **"Darling Existence"**   47
Five: **"A Ragged and Dirty Bunch"**   61
Six: **"The Most Lovable Scamp"**   73
Seven: **"Heaven on the Half Shell"**   91
Eight: **"Land of Indolence and Dreams"**   105
Nine: **"Grave of a Blood Relation"**   119
Ten: **A Branch of Hell**   137
Eleven: **"My Honored 'Sister'"**   153
Twelve: **Wedding Present**   167

PART TWO: FLOODTIDE

Thirteen: **Church of the Holy Speculators**   187
Fourteen: **Mississippi Steamboat and a Cuckoo Clock**   205

Fifteen: Chartering a Comet to Mars	223
Sixteen: "Invertebrate Without a Country"	239
Seventeen: Toast to the Babies	259
Eighteen: "Inspired Bugger of a Machine"	275
Nineteen: "Hallelujah Jennings"	291
Twenty: Twins of Genius	303
Twenty-One: "A Sound Heart & a Deformed Conscience"	325
Twenty-Two: Pure Mugwump	343
Twenty-Three: Reparation Due to Every Black Man	363
Twenty-Four: "No Pockets in the Armor"	383
Twenty-Five: "The Deriding of Shams"	399
Twenty-Six: Death and Delusion	413
Twenty-Seven: "One of the Vanderbilt Gang"	427

PART THREE: RAPIDS

Twenty-Eight: "Paradise of the Rheumatics"	445
Twenty-Nine: "A Lady Above Reproach"	461
Thirty: "Boss Machine of the World"	475
Thirty-One: "Too Much of a Human Being"	489
Thirty-Two: "Paris the Damnable"	509
Thirty-Three: "'Colossal' Is a Tame Word for Him"	525
Thirty-Four: "Clown of the Sea"	539
Thirty-Five: "Circumnavigation of This Great Globe"	559
Thirty-Six: "The Only Sad Voyage"	573
Thirty-Seven: "A Book Written in Blood & Tears"	587
Thirty-Eight: "Letters to Satan"	601

Thirty-Nine: "Stirring Times in Austria" — 617

Forty: "The European Edison" — 631

Forty-One: Dream Self — 643

Forty-Two: "A Hundred Capering Clowns" — 657

Forty-Three: "The Bastard Human Race" — 671

PART FOUR: WHIRLPOOL

Forty-Four: "The Ancient Mariner" — 685

Forty-Five: The Anti-Doughnut Party — 697

Forty-Six: "The United States of Lyncherdom" — 711

Forty-Seven: "Magnificent Panorama of the Mississippi" — 727

Forty-Eight: "Spirit of a Steam Engine" — 739

Forty-Nine: Divine Healing — 753

Fifty: The Dread Cavalcade of Death — 767

Fifty-One: "The War Prayer" — 781

Fifty-Two: "An Artist in Morals and Ink" — 793

Fifty-Three: "The Swindle of Life" — 807

Fifty-Four: Pier 70 — 817

Fifty-Five: Angelfish — 831

Fifty-Six: A Fan and a Halo — 843

Fifty-Seven: Wuthering Heights — 855

PART FIVE: SHIPWRECK

Fifty-Eight: Man in the White Clothes — 871

Fifty-Nine: "A Real American College Boy"	883
Sixty: "All the Wonders That Are Occurring"	897
Sixty-One: A Holiday from Life's Woes	909
Sixty-Two: Innocence at Home	925
Sixty-Three: "Mark Twain's Daughter"	935
Sixty-Four: The Death of Tammany	949
Sixty-Five: "An Insane Idea"	961
Sixty-Six: Grandpa Twain	987
Sixty-Seven: Letters from the Earth	999
Sixty-Eight: "An Old Bird of Paradise"	1009
Sixty-Nine: Halley's Comet	1019

ACKNOWLEDGMENTS	1035
ABBREVIATIONS	1041
NOTES	1045
BIBLIOGRAPHY	1121
ILLUSTRATION CREDITS	1137
INDEX	1139

PRELUDE

The Pilot House

From the time he was a small boy in Hannibal, Missouri, the Mississippi River had signified freedom for Samuel Langhorne Clemens (later known as Mark Twain), a place where he could toss aside worldly cares, indulge in high spirits, and find sanctuary from society's restraints. For a sheltered, small-town youth, the boisterous life aboard the steamboats plying the river, swarming with raffish characters, offered a gateway to a wider world. Pilots stood forth as undisputed royalty of this floating kingdom, and it was the pride of Twain's early years that, right before the Civil War, he had secured a license in just two years. However painstaking it was for a cub navigator to memorize the infinite details of a mutable river with its shifting snags, shoals, and banks, Twain had prized this demanding period of his life. Later he admitted that "I loved the profession far better than any I have followed since," the reason being quite simple: "a pilot, in those days, was the only unfettered and entirely independent human being that lived in the earth." In contrast, even kings and diplomats, editors and clergymen, felt muzzled by public opinion. "In truth, every man and woman and child has a master, and worries and frets in servitude; but in the day I write of, the Mississippi pilot had *none*."[1] That search for untrammeled truth and freedom would form a defining quest of Mark Twain's life.

For a man who immortalized Hannibal and the majestic river flowing past it, Twain had returned surprisingly few times to these youthful scenes, as if fearful that new impressions might intrude on cherished memories. In 1875, as he was about to turn forty, he had published in the *Atlantic Monthly* a seven-part series titled "Old Times on the Mississippi," which chronicled his days as an eager young pilot. Now, in April 1882, he rounded up his publisher, James R. Osgood, and a young Hartford stenographer, Roswell H. Phelps, and set out for a tour of the Mississippi that would allow him to elaborate those earlier articles into a full-length volume, *Life on the Mississippi,* that would fuse travel reportage with the earlier memoir. He had long fantasized about, but also long postponed, this momentous return to the river. "But when I come to write the Mississippi book," he promised his wife, Livy, "*then* look out! I will spend 2 months on the river & take notes, & I bet you I will make a standard work."[2]

Twain mapped out an ambitious six-week odyssey, heading first down the river from St. Louis to New Orleans, then retracing his steps as far north as St. Paul, Minnesota, stopping en route at Hannibal. The three men sped west by the Pennsylvania Railroad in a "joggling train," the very mode of transportation that already threatened the demise of the freewheeling steamboat culture Twain had treasured.[3] By journeying from east to west, he reversed the dominant trajectory of his life, enabling him to appraise his midwestern roots with fresh eyes. "All the R.R. station loafers west of Pittsburgh carry *both* hands in their pockets," he observed. "Further east one hand is sometimes out of doors."[4] Now accustomed to the genteel affluence of Hartford, Connecticut, where he had resided for a decade, he had grown painfully aware of the provinciality of his boyhood haunts. "The grace and picturesqueness of female dress seem to disappear as one travels west away from N. York."[5]

To secure candid glimpses of his old Mississippi world, Twain traveled under the incognito of "Mr. Samuel," but he underestimated his own renown. From St. Louis he informed Livy that he "got to meeting too many people who knew me. We swore them to secrecy, & left by the first boat."[6] After the three travelers boarded the steamer *Gold Dust*—"a vile, rusty old steamboat"—Twain was spotted by an old shipmate, his alias blown again. Henceforth his celebrity, which clung to him everywhere, would transform the atmosphere he sought to recapture. For all

THE PILOT HOUSE

his joy at being afloat, he carped at the ship's squalor, noting passageways "less than 2 inches deep in dirt" and spittoons "not particularly clean." He dispatched the vessel with a sarcasm: "This boat built by [Robert] Fulton; has not been repaired since." At many piers he noted that whereas steamers in his booming days had been wedged together "like sardines in a box," a paucity of boats now sat loosely strung along empty docks.[7]

Twain was saddened by the backward towns they passed, often mere collections of "tumble-down frame houses unpainted, looking dilapidated" or "a miserable cabin or two standing in [a] small opening on the gray and grassless banks of the river."[8] No less noticeable was how the river had reshaped a landscape he had once strenuously committed to memory. Hamlets that had fronted the river now stood landlocked, and when the boat stopped at a "God forsaken rocky point," disgorging passengers for an inland town, Twain stared mystified. "I couldn't remember that town; couldn't place it; couldn't call its name . . . couldn't imagine what the damned place might be." He guessed, correctly, that it was Ste. Genevieve, a onetime Missouri river town that in bygone days had stood "on high ground, handsomely situated," but had now been relocated by the river to a "town out in the country."[9]

Once Twain's identity was known—his voice and face, his nervous habit of running his hand through his hair, gave the game away—the pilots embraced this prodigal son as an honored member of their guild. In the ultimate compliment, they gave him the freedom to guide the ship alone—a dreamlike consummation. "Livy darling, I am in solitary possession of the pilot house of the steamer Gold Dust, with the familiar wheel & compass & bell ropes around me . . . I'm all alone, now (the pilot whose watch it is, told me to make myself entirely at home, & I'm doing it)." He seemed to expand in the solitary splendor of the wheelhouse and drank in the river's beauty. "It is a magnificent day, & the hills & levels are masses of shining green, with here & there a white-blossoming tree. I love you, sweetheart."[10]

Always a hypercritical personality, prone to disappointment, Mark Twain often felt exasperated in everyday life. By contrast, the return to

THE PILOT HOUSE

the pilot house cast a wondrous spell on him, retrieving precious moments of his past when he was still young and unencumbered by troubles. The river had altered many things beyond recognition. "Yet as unfamiliar as all the aspects have been to-day," he recorded in his copious notes, "I have felt as much at home and as much in my proper place in the pilot house as if I had never been out of the pilot house."[11] It was a pilot named Lem Gray who had allowed Twain to steer the ship himself. Lem "would lie down and sleep, and leave me there to dream that the years had not slipped away; that there had been no war, no mining days, no literary adventures; that I was still a pilot, happy and care-free as I had been twenty years before."[12] One morning he arose at 4 a.m. to watch "the day steal gradually upon this vast silent world . . . the marvels of shifting light & shade & color & dappled reflections that followed, were bewitching to see."[13] The paradox of Twain's life was that the older and more famous he became and the grander his horizons, the more he pined for the vanished paradise of his early years. His youth would remain the magical touchstone of his life, his memories preserved in amber.

Mark Twain has long been venerated as an emblem of Americana. Posterity has extracted a sanitized view of a humorous man in a white suit, dispensing witticisms with a twinkling eye, an avuncular figure sporting a cigar and a handlebar mustache. But far from being a soft-shoe, cracker-barrel philosopher, he was a waspish man of decided opinions delivering hard and uncomfortable truths. His wit was laced with vinegar, not oil. Some mysterious anger, some pervasive melancholy, fired his humor—the novelist William Dean Howells once told Twain "what a bottom of fury there is to your fun"—and his chronic dissatisfaction with society produced a steady stream of barbed denunciations.[14] Holding nothing sacred, he indulged in an unabashed irreverence that would easily create discomfort in our politically correct age. In a country that prides itself on can-do optimism, Mark Twain has always been an anomaly: a hugely popular but fiercely pessimistic man, the scourge of fools and frauds. On

THE PILOT HOUSE

the surface his humor can seem merely playful—the caprice of a bright, mischievous child—but the sources of his humor are deadly serious, rooted in a profound critique of society and human nature that gives his jokes their staying power.

Mark Twain discarded the image of the writer as a contemplative being, living a cloistered existence, and thrust himself into the hurly-burly of American culture, capturing the wild, uproarious energy throbbing in the heartland. Probably no other American author has led such an eventful life. A protean figure who played the role of printer, pilot, miner, journalist, novelist, platform artist, toastmaster, publisher, art patron, pundit, polemicist, inventor, crusader, investor, and maverick, he courted controversy and relished the limelight. A ferocious bargainer and shameless self-promoter, he sought fame and fortune without hesitation, and established the image of the author as celebrity. In fact, Mark Twain fairly invented our celebrity culture, seemingly anticipating today's world of social analysts and influencers.

With his inexhaustible commentary, he bestrode a larger stage than any other American writer, coining aphorisms that made him the country's most-quoted person. He created a literary voice that was wholly American, capturing the vernacular of western towns and small villages where a new culture had arisen, far from staid eastern precincts. Starting with an earthy brand of country humor, he mastered an astonishing variety of literary forms—the novel, short stories, essays, travelogues, burlesques, farces, political tracts, and historical romances—publishing thirty books and pamphlets plus thousands of newspaper and magazine articles. To that he added twelve thousand extant letters written by him or his immediate family, fifty notebooks crammed with ideas, and six hundred still-incomplete manuscripts.

Whether Twain was our greatest writer may be arguable, if not doubtful, but there's little question that he was our foremost talker. His oral output—recorded speeches, toasts, and interviews—is no less bountiful than his written record. A nonpareil among platform artists, he spent a lifetime perfecting a beguiling voice that elevated talk into an art form and made audiences yearn for more. For all his erudition, this many-sided

THE PILOT HOUSE

man employed a folksy charm and disarming wit that could appeal to mass audiences. He was so funny that people laughed in spite of themselves, his droll comments slipping past their defenses and shocking them into a recognition of their true beliefs. Even as he railed bitterly against the human race, kicking out the psychological props that sustained it, that race reveled in his biting depictions of its behavior. What any biography of Mark Twain demands is his inimitable voice, which sparkled even in his darkest moments.

No less essential for any life is to capture the massive breadth of Twain's interests and travels. Not simply the bard of America's heartland, he was a worldly, cosmopolitan figure who spent eleven years abroad, crossing the Atlantic twenty-nine times. His mind was broadened by an around-the-world lecture tour as well as years of enforced exile in Europe. One of our great autodidacts, he had a far-reaching intelligence that led him to consume history and biography and devour tomes on subjects ranging from astronomy to geology to entomology. Our contemporary recollection of Mark Twain—mostly a sketchy memory of *The Adventures of Tom Sawyer, Adventures of Huckleberry Finn,* and *Life on the Mississippi*—doesn't begin to encompass the scope of his interests.

Beyond literature, Mark Twain engaged in an active business life, which was a constant, often damaging, distraction. He raged against plutocrats even as he strove to become one. "All through my life I have been the easy prey of the cheap adventurer," he confessed sheepishly.[15] A compulsive speculator and a soft touch for swindlers, he spent a lifetime chasing harebrained schemes and failed business ventures. His mind would seize upon an idea with an obsessive tenacity that made him oblivious to contrary arguments. Again and again, he succumbed to money-mad schemes he might have satirized in one of his novels. He embodied the speculative bent of the Gilded Age (which he named) with its fondness for new inventions, quick killings, and high-pressure salesmanship.

After his early days in Hannibal, Nevada, and California, Twain reinvented himself as a northeastern liberal, even, at times, a radical. Preoccupied with the notion that only the dead dare speak the truth, he thought our need to make a living turned us all into cowards. There were some large, controversial topics, such as Reconstruction and the Ku Klux Klan, that he shamefully ducked for the most part. Nevertheless, one is struck by the number of intrepid stands he took. He expressed quite radical views on religion, slavery, monarchy, aristocracy, and colonialism; supported women's suffrage; contested anti-Semitism; and waged war on municipal corruption in New York. A foe of jingoism, he also took up an array of global issues, including American imperialism in the Philippines, the despotism of czarist Russia, and the depredations of Belgium's King Leopold II in Africa. Indifferent to politics as a young man, he increasingly emerged as a gadfly and a reformer, acting as a conscience of American society. Even as his novelistic powers faded, his polemical powers only strengthened.

Twain proved fierce in his loves and loyalties. Perhaps his one source of unalloyed happiness came from his intimate relations with his adored wife and three daughters. The cynicism he reserved for others was offset by his implicit faith in Livy—the linchpin of his life—and his deep, if often more complicated, love for his three offspring, Susy, Clara, and Jean. His family life was shadowed by a staggering number of calamities. The saga of the Clemens clan, so full of joy and heartache, lies at the very core of this narrative.

If exemplary in marriage, Twain could be implacable in his hatreds and grudges. A man who thrived on outrage, he had a tendency to lash out at people, often deservedly, but sometimes gratuitously and excessively. He once admitted to his sister that he was a man of "a fractious disposition & difficult to get along with."[16] A master of the vendetta, he would store up potent insults and unload them in full upon those who had disappointed him. He could never quite let things go or drop a quarrel. With his volcanic emotions and titanic tirades, he constantly threatened lawsuits and fired off indignant letters, settling scores in a life riddled with self-inflicted wounds. Faced with his frequent inability to govern his temper, the gentle, loving Livy tried gamely to tamp down his fury. Mark Twain was often rescued by his wife—she was the necessary ballast of his life—and, consequently, could never quite regain his equilibrium once she was gone.

THE PILOT HOUSE

In our own heightened time of racial reckoning, Twain poses special challenges to biographers and readers alike. Though perhaps the greatest antislavery novel in the English language, *Huck Finn* has been banned from most American secondary schools, and its repetitive use of the N-word has cast a shadow over Twain's reputation. Born into a slave-owning family, he transcended his southern roots to a remarkable degree, shaking off most, but never all, of his boyhood racism. No other white American writer in the nineteenth century engaged so fully with the Black community or saw its culture as so central to our national experience. From boyhood, he treated Black people with notable warmth, affection, and sympathy. He experienced tremendous growth in his attitudes, graduating from the crude racist gibes of his early letters and notebooks to a friendship with Frederick Douglass, financing a Black law student at Yale, promoting the Fisk Jubilee Singers, and denouncing racial bigotry in a wide variety of forms. William Dean Howells termed him "the most desouthernized southerner I ever met. No man more perfectly sensed and more entirely abhorred slavery."[17] "Perhaps the brightest side of his whole intellectual career is his progress away from racism," one scholar has noted, and the statement is true despite some significant lapses.[18] From unpromising beginnings, Twain's striking evolution in matters of racial tolerance will be traced throughout this book.

Twain's late-life fascination with teenage girls presents yet another disturbing topic for contemporary readers. In many ways a Victorian man, he tended to place women on a pedestal and treated his wife with unfailing reverence. There was never the least hint of scandal in his married life. Yet, after Livy's death, Twain pursued teenage girls with a strange passion that, while it always remained chaste, is likely to cause extreme discomfort nowadays. Like many geniuses, Twain had a large assortment of weird sides to his nature, and this account will try to make sense of his sometimes bizarre behavior toward girls and women.

To portray Mark Twain in his entirety, one must capture both the light and the shadow of a beloved humorist who could switch temper in a flash, changing from exhilarating joy to deep resentment. He is a fascinating, maddening puzzle to anyone trying to figure him out: charming,

THE PILOT HOUSE

funny, and irresistible one moment, paranoid and deeply vindictive the next. As he once observed ruefully, the "periodical and sudden changes of mood in me, from deep melancholy to half-insane tempests and cyclones of humor, are among the curiosities of my life."[19] Perhaps we should not be surprised that America's funniest man harbored ineffable sadness and displayed a host of contradictions. In a life of staggering variety, he managed to soar and plunge in emotional extremes. In the last analysis, Mark Twain's foremost creation—his richest and most complex gift to posterity—may well have been his own inimitable personality, the largest literary personality that America has produced.

PART ONE

Afloat

CHAPTER ONE

Loveless Marriage

Given the fine gusto with which Mark Twain flayed hereditary privilege, it seems fitting that he delighted in tracing his paternal ancestry to one Gregory Clement, who had served in the Parliament of England under Oliver Cromwell and joined in signing the death warrant of King Charles I. Twain confessed to being "wholly ignorant" of his forebears but applauded Gregory's action.[1] "He did what he could toward reducing the list of crowned shams of his day."[2] When the monarchy was restored, Gregory was declared guilty of regicide, his severed head posted as a warning atop Westminster Hall. Characteristically, Twain found pungent humor in his fate, declaring that Gregory was "much thought of by the family because he was the first of us that was hanged."[3] Unfortunately, Twain's descent from Gregory Clement was entirely fictitious, but it was hard to deprive him of a good story with such rich potential for laughter.

The earliest known English ancestor of Mark Twain was Richard Clements of Leicestershire, who lived in the early sixteenth century. In 1642 his great-grandson Robert boarded a ship for the American colonies and aided in founding the town of Haverhill, Massachusetts. Over the years the family drifted south to Pennsylvania and Virginia, where in 1770 it spawned Samuel B. Clemens, grandfather of our author. On October 29, 1797, he married Pamela Goggin in Bedford County in the Shenandoah Valley of Virginia. In 1742 her grandfather Stephen Goggin, Sr., had emigrated to Virginia from Queen's County, Ireland.

AFLOAT

Samuel and Pamela Clemens, a prosperous young couple, were fully enmeshed in slavery, their ten workers toiling on four hundred acres in Bedford County. The couple brought forth a brood of five children, the eldest being John Marshall Clemens. Born on August 11, 1798, and named after the future chief justice of the United States, John Marshall, he was destined to be the author's father. When he was seven, his father died in a freak accident—crushed by a falling log during a house-raising—and at some point before adulthood he labored in an iron foundry. Thus robbed of a carefree childhood, he developed a grim, driven personality, with little levity in his nature. He clung to pretensions of supposed descent from the "First Families of Virginia"; what his son labeled "a sumptuous legacy of pride in his fine Virginia stock." Having inherited three enslaved people, he settled in Columbia, Kentucky—his widowed mother had moved to Adair County, near the Tennessee border, and remarried—where he earned a license to practice law.

It was there that he met Jane Lampton, who had grown up in the town. On May 6, 1823, at twenty-four, he married Jane, who was pretty and gregarious, just shy of twenty, and brought a dowry of three more enslaved people. Her father, Benjamin Lampton, was a prominent local citizen, having served as a lieutenant colonel during the War of 1812. As a skilled brick mason, he had constructed many fine buildings in town. Jane's maternal grandfather, William Casey—Indian fighter extraordinaire and Kentucky legislator—was so illustrious that the state named an adjoining county after him. A lively young woman, Jane enjoyed the social opportunities available to the daughter of two prominent families. "During her girlhood Jane Lampton was noted for her vivacity and her beauty," her eldest son said.[4] "She was a great horsewoman when she was young and riding parties were a feature of Kentucky life . . . she was known as the best dancer in Kentucky," a descendant added.[5] Her famous son would inherit her wealth of red hair as well as her spunk, gift for language, and sprightly spirit.

Jane Lampton proudly claimed ancestry from the British Lambtons of Durham, giving her a dubious connection to a string of earls. As her famous son noted, "I knew that privately she was proud that the Lambtons, now Earls of Durham, had occupied the family lands for nine hundred years; that they were feudal lords of Lambton Castle and holding the high position of ancestors of hers" at the Norman Conquest.[6] Twain later poked fun at this family vanity, especially when one of Jane's relatives cooked up a preposterous claim to being the genuine Earl of Durham. Such genealogical pretensions would set up Mark Twain as a perfect satirist for big talkers, delusional dreamers, social climbers, and inflated windbags of every description.

The marriage of John Marshall Clemens and Jane Lampton was fated to be a loveless affair, and not solely because of strikingly dissimilar personalities. Jane had been jilted by a young doctor whom she loved and in retribution married John Marshall on the rebound. In a thinly veiled portrait of his father, Twain sketched the tragic consequences: "Stern, unsmiling, never demonstrated affection for wife or child. Had found out he had been married to spite another man."[7] Though his parents behaved in dignified fashion, making a point of mutual courtesy, Twain recalled no signs of outward affection, just a frosty arrangement that substituted handshakes for hugs at bedtime. This arid match would foster in Mark Twain a huge craving for affection in his own marriage.

After a year or two, the newlyweds moved across the border to Gainesboro in northeastern Tennessee. Plagued by headaches and a weak chest, John Marshall Clemens hoped the salubrious mountain air might strengthen his health. Their first son, Orion—pronounced *Or*-ee-on—was born in 1825, his astral name a reflection of Jane's taste for the occult. Although John Marshall was an ambitious man, it soon grew apparent that the backwoods hamlet lacked any hint of a future. When Orion visited the cheerless spot more than forty years later, he encountered the "melancholy spectacle of doors closed with signs over them indicating past business; windows broken; houses faded or guiltless of paint."[8]

The young family pushed forty miles farther east to Jamestown, in Fentress County, a scenic hinterland of low, rolling mountains called the Knobs, where the career of John Marshall Clemens seemed briefly to flourish. Unlike Gainesboro, this new town breathed an air of possibility, having recently been named the county seat, and John emerged as a model citizen, serving as the county commissioner and clerk of the circuit court and even taking a hand in building the county courthouse and jail. He erected an impressive house that set envious tongues wagging. With their future more secure, the Clemenses expanded their progeny to include two daughters—Pamela (pronounced Pa-*mee*-la) born in 1827 and Margaret in 1830—and another son, Benjamin, in 1832; a first son, named Pleasant, died in infancy.

As he strode about town in a blue coat with brass buttons, John Marshall seemed to have satisfied his hunger for respectability. He even branched out into land speculation, amassing virgin forest at a time when real estate could be acquired for less than a penny an acre. Of his total investment, his author son Sam would later bandy about a figure of seventy-five thousand acres, while Orion could only establish title to thirty thousand acres.[9] With an overheated imagination, John Marshall daydreamed that his forest of yellow pine would someday yield a cornucopia of iron ore, coal, copper, and timber. This inheritance of the "Tennessee land" would assume mythic proportions in his children's minds, alternately teasing and tormenting them with hopes of future grandeur. The beckoning mirage of phantom wealth would make ordinary riches seem paltry in comparison. For Sam Clemens, it would breed lifelong fantasies of king-size wealth and countless schemes to attain it. He later pronounced this grim epitaph on the Tennessee land: "It kept us hoping and hoping, during forty years . . . It put our energies to sleep and made visionaries of us—dreamers, and indolent. We were always going to be rich next year—no occasion to work."[10]

The time in Tennessee set a tragic pattern for John Marshall Clemens, who would attempt to scratch out a living as a lawyer and public servant only to be forced, for survival's sake, into the humdrum routine of keeping a store. When his business faltered, he was required to abandon the fine house in town—he was now land-rich but cash-poor—and move nine miles north to a secluded spot in the woods, Three Forks, where his family occupied a cramped log cabin, an abrupt comedown from their previous high status in town. This solitary place at the junction of three rivers preyed on his sociable young wife, who had grown accustomed to material comfort and a buoyant party life in Kentucky. "I had always been in society," Jane Clemens later complained, and was "very fond of company."[11] In this bleak backwater, John Marshall kept a store and served as the local postmaster at the nearby hamlet of Pall Mall.

In 1834 financial austerity brought on by Andrew Jackson's clash with the Second Bank of the United States snuffed out John Marshall Clemens's tenuous standing in Tennessee. Although Sam had not yet been born, the mood of that sudden wreckage must have formed the mental weather of his childhood; the specter of downward mobility shadowed his father, spawning constant status insecurity. As Twain recalled, "From being honored and envied as the most opulent citizen of Fentress county... he suddenly woke up and found himself reduced to less than one-fourth of that amount. He was a proud man, a silent, austere man, and not a person likely to abide among the scenes of his vanished grandeur."[12] Stymied by ill luck, battered by hardship, John Marshall became a dour, defeated character, his ambitions thwarted in the wilderness. As Mark Twain wrote, in a character patterned after his father in *The Gilded Age*, Squire Hawkins was "not more than thirty-five" but with "a worn look that made him seem older."[13] Between the two of them, John and Jane Clemens had inherited six enslaved people, but by the time they left Tennessee, austerity had thinned that number down to one—a young woman named Jennie.

Twice disappointed in Tennessee, John Marshall Clemens uprooted his family again in 1835, piled them into a two-horse carriage, and headed north to Louisville, Kentucky, where they boarded a steamer and rode down the Ohio River to St. Louis. "They had intended to settle in St. Louis, but when they got there they were horrified to hear that a Negro boy had recently been lynched," one Clemens descendant reported. "Moreover, there was cholera in the city. So they moved on to Florida [Missouri]."[14] A more likely story was that the Clemenses had planned to settle in Florida all along since Jane's brother-in-law, John A. Quarles, had warmly encouraged them to join him there. The new town of Florida, born four years earlier in the state's northeast corner, stood on the ragged edge of western settlement. The Missouri Compromise of 1820 had thrown the state wide open to slavery, spurring migration from Kentucky and Tennessee and lending the territory a southern character in the run-up to the Civil War.

Orion recalled their dismal first Florida residence as "a little white frame [house], one-story, with two small rooms, or a room and a shed under the same roof."[15] Since Jane Clemens was pregnant with Sam during the westward journey, Orion would tease his brother that this early "travel had something to do with your roving disposition."[16] With as sharp a tongue as her famous son, Jane Clemens later derided the frail house as "too small for a baby to be born in," yet she gave birth, two months prematurely, to Samuel Langhorne Clemens on November 30, 1835. The baby was named after his paternal grandfather, while John Marshall Clemens supplied the middle name in homage to a boon companion from his Virginia youth. With a flair for showmanship, mother and son converted Sam's birth into a cosmic event, marked by the appearance of Halley's Comet, which revisits the Earth at seventy-five-year intervals. Later endowed with a quip for every occasion, Twain remarked of his birth: "The village contained a hundred people and I increased the population by 1 per cent . . . There is no record of a person doing as much—not even Shakespeare."[17]

At a time of rampant infant mortality, the baby proved a runt with a sickly nature, and his parents grew concerned. "When I first saw him [I] could see no promise in him," Jane admitted in afteryears. "But I felt it my duty to do the best I could . . . But he was a poor-looking object to raise."[18] When she was in her eighties, her son asked about his troubled infancy. "I suppose that during all that time you were uneasy about me." "Yes, the whole time," she agreed. Twain persisted: "Afraid I wouldn't live?" With a perfect deadpan worthy of her son, Jane retorted, "No, afraid you would."[19]

Mark Twain would lampoon "the almost invisible village of Florida," evoking a settlement of two unpaved streets and scattered lanes. "Both the streets and the lanes were paved with the same material—tough black mud, in wet times, deep dust in dry." With flimsy houses made of logs, even the church was propped up on timber, allowing local hogs to root around underneath and squeal noisily during services. John Marshall entered into a partnership with John Quarles in a dry goods shop that sold a bit of everything: calico and coffee, shovels and brooms, hats and bonnets, even offering a swig of corn whiskey to every customer. Because John Marshall was a rigid man, he didn't cotton to the easygoing ways of John Quarles. Soon the partnership was dissolved and Clemens set up a rival store across the street.

As in Tennessee, John Marshall Clemens strove to lift a nascent town from obscurity and set it on the high road to progress. A political Whig, with an abiding faith in internal improvements, he was appointed president in 1837 of the Salt River Navigation Company, assembled to dredge the nearby river and open it to steamboat commerce from the Mississippi River. He was likewise made a commissioner of the Florida & Paris Railroad, both projects wiped out by the Panic of 1837 and a dearth of political support. John Marshall did land one coveted accolade: he was named a judge of the Monroe County Court, forever after bearing the proud title of Judge Clemens. He traded up to a larger house—three rooms and a kitchen—where Sam Clemens's beloved younger brother, Henry, was born in 1838.

The following year, Twain's sister Margaret died at age nine of a bilious fever. One day she returned from school in a delirious state and lay dead within a week. Jane Clemens always maintained that the girl "was in disposition & manner like Sam full of life" and enjoyed taunting her sister, Pamela.[20] As she lay dying, Sam glided fast asleep into her room one night and stroked her bedclothes, exhibiting the somnambulism that would mark his childhood. Perhaps, if informed of the episode, it was his first intimation that he harbored an inner self free from his conscious control—a spiritual twin—which would form a recurrent theme in his later writings.

The next year Judge Clemens concluded that the tiny village of Florida would never shake off its rustic slumber. Once again he had hitched his luckless fate to a dying town. In Mark Twain's mordant view, "He 'kept store' there several years, but had no luck, except that I was born to him."[21] When Sam was nearly four in 1839, the judge turned his eyes to the Mississippi port town of Hannibal, thirty-five miles to the northeast. Then a raw and relatively new country town with a vigorous, enterprising people and a diversified economy, Hannibal was a thriving metropolis compared to Florida. It already had the hallmarks of a genuine town, including sawmills, blacksmith shops, saloons, and a distillery. A fast-growing commercial hub, it exported wheat and tobacco harvested from inland farms while drovers herded swine through its streets to two slaughterhouses. As Orion later observed in the town paper, "Our people have a horrid aversion to the jury box and the witnesses' stand. They greatly prefer the study of pork and flour barrels, tape, cordwood, and the steamboat's whistle."[22] For Sam Clemens, the move to Hannibal was monumentally important, for it is impossible to picture his career without the front-row seat that Hannibal afforded for the abundant traffic steaming by on the Mississippi River.

After selling his farm acreage and house in Florida, Judge Clemens plowed the proceeds into purchasing a cluster of buildings in downtown Hannibal, including a corner hotel at the foot of sloping Hill Street, where his family first lived. He commenced yet another general store, facing the nearby Mississippi wharves, and stocked it with dry goods and groceries bought on credit from St. Louis merchants. The teenage Orion, clad in a brand-new suit of clothes, worked as a clerk. By autumn 1841, the judge's congenital bad luck and poor head for business ushered in yet another commercial collapse as economic conditions exhausted his credit in St. Louis. Orion remembered the store's chief creditor ruthlessly stripping the shelves bare for repayment—"all the dry goods, groceries, boots and shoes and hardware in his store"—so that his father "began his first acquaintance with poverty."[23] To help support the family, a resentful Orion was apprenticed to the *Hannibal Journal* before being shipped off to St. Louis to work as a printer.

The embarrassment of ingrained failure must have seeped deep into the pores of John Marshall Clemens. Snappish, moody, and temperamental, he wasn't the sort to be amused by the comic relief of his son Sam's compulsive pranks and mischief. His few surviving letters portray a man

LOVELESS MARRIAGE

riddled with anxiety and ground down by monetary stress; they are devoid of gaiety, charm, or humor. To raise cash in 1842, he traveled down the Mississippi and sent home a letter that reeked of desperation. "I do not know yet what I can commence at for a business in the spring. My brain is constantly on the rack with the study, and I can't relieve myself of it—The future taking its complexion from the state of my health, or mind, is alternately beaming in sunshine, or overshadowed with clouds; but mostly cloudy, as you will readily suppose."[24] When he got home and Jane berated him for the costly but fruitless trip, John Marshall pleaded that he meant well, saying plaintively, "I am not able to dig in the streets." Orion always remembered the "hopeless expression of his face."[25]

Adding to the fatalistic mood, Benjamin Clemens, nearly ten, died on May 12, 1842, and his parents' grief was so profound that Orion saw them kiss for the first time. The experience disclosed to Sam the depths of emotional pain bottled up inside Jane Clemens. As she and Sam knelt beside the dead boy stretched on the bed, she erupted in tears and moans of "dumb" sorrow that startled her son. "The mother made the children feel the cheek of the dead boy," Sam recalled, "and tried to make them understand the calamity that had befallen."[26] Childhood mortality, however commonplace, was still exquisitely painful for parents. This was the third child John Marshall and Jane Clemens had lost, and the harrowing scene was forever lodged in the memory of Sam Clemens, who, for some nameless reason, believed he had treacherously betrayed his dead brother.

There was both nobility and futility in the striving of Judge Clemens, who could never establish abiding security for his family and exhibited the bone-deep fatigue of a desperate man. Orion spoke of irritability from "disordered nerves" as he strained to find his elusive niche in the world.[27] His fortunes rebounded modestly as he picked up fees from practicing law, and around 1844 was named Justice of the Peace, which meant settling civil complaints and lawsuits over debt. He also oversaw slavery disputes and twice ordered lashes meted out to enslaved offenders. In his humble courtroom, he sat squarely on a three-legged stool, with dry goods boxes serving as his desk, rapping out decisions with a mallet and recording them with "his sharp pen," recalled Orion.[28] Though a respectable man, Judge Clemens could be forbiddingly humorless, the antithesis of the waggish Sam. One newspaper painted him thus: "He was a stern unbending man of splendid common-sense . . . the autocrat of the little dingy room on Bird Street, where he held his court . . . and preserved order as best he could in the village."[29] With his finances in somewhat better shape, Judge Clemens constructed a house for his family on the steeply inclined Hill Street, a two-story white frame, narrow but deep, with Sam likely occupying the last bedroom on the upper floor. Outside stood a certain fence that would be immortalized in *The Adventures of Tom Sawyer*.

From a fictional portrait Twain wrote of his father, we know that he was tall and lean with lank black hair drooping to his shoulders, showed "courtly, old-fashioned" manners, and was impeccably honest.[30] He scrupulously adhered to social convention and got precious little for it. Oppressed by worry, his face unsmiling, he walked the streets with such extreme formality that he cringed when someone accosted him and slapped his back. His scholarly bent made him a stickler for grammar— he shipped Orion an entire course of twenty lessons on the subject—and he presided as president of the Hannibal Library Institute. Hannibal's citizenry viewed him with respect, not warmth, and nicknamed him "Squire," suggestive of his superior airs. A local minister claimed he was "a grave, taciturn man, a foremost citizen in intelligence and wholesome influence." A local school principal called him "never a practical man, but an energetic dreamer . . . courteous, well-educated . . . a good conversationalist."[31] For all his moralistic zeal, Judge Clemens shied away from church attendance, and this may be the one trait that endeared him to Sam and influenced his later freethinking ways.

The father who found humor in nothing spawned a son who found humor in everything. It is easy to see how the aloof Judge Clemens, who hated disorder and was emotionally remote, produced a rebellious, devil-may-care son and left him with an enduring ambivalence toward authority figures. At thirty-four, Mark Twain recalled the "judicial frigidity" of a father who could discover no charm in his juvenile antics. Never cruel toward his children, John Marshall nonetheless threw a distinct chill in the air around him. As Twain said, he was "ungentle of manner toward his children," though he "never punished them—a look was enough, and more than enough." Father and son circled each other warily. "My father and I were always on the most distant terms when I was a boy—a sort of armed neutrality, so to speak."[32] Another time Twain said that "my own knowledge of him amounted to little more than an introduction."[33] He remembered only a single time when his father hazarded a joke. They had come upon a room full of loaves of bread moldy with blue cobwebs, and the startled boy asked where they came from. "From Noah's Ark," the judge responded.[34] Curiously enough, it is a very Mark Twain line. If there is a source of the rage that informed Mark Twain's career, it probably originated with a repressed fear of his father, whom he never dared to confront directly. Instead that rage expressed itself indirectly, played out in boyhood hijinks and a cynical defiance toward elders. Humor proved a survival strategy with a humorless father. Where Judge Clemens gravitated to the safety of courts, railroads, and libraries, his son would become a confirmed renegade against institutions and pride himself on a wild, lawless streak.

Luckily, with her joie de vivre, Jane Lampton Clemens provided compensatory warmth and brightness in her son's life. From her he derived all his emotional sustenance. Slim and pretty, with the erect carriage of a dancer and keen blue eyes, she moved through her day with good-humored energy and was a popular figure around town. If Sam carried the Clemens name, he clearly manifested the Lampton genes. "He is all 'Lampton,'" Orion's wife, Mollie, said, "and resembles his mother strongly in person as in mind."[35] Mother and son bore a comical resemblance, especially in their sharp but slightly melancholy eyes and exaggerated drawls. From his mother Sam inherited a storytelling passion and an insatiable curiosity about people. However kindly she was, Jane Clemens also exhibited a certain midwestern reserve, never kissing her children and maintaining a ladylike sense of propriety. Her puritanical side was observed by her son on a trip to New Orleans as a teenager. "Ma was delighted with her trip, but she was disgusted with the girls for allowing me to embrace and kiss them."[36]

With tender solicitude, Jane Clemens watched Sam perpetrate one outrageous prank after another. She adored but was bemused by this wayward son, taking an exasperated pride in his constant skylarking. He captured her ambivalence in his affectionate portrayal of Aunt Polly in *Tom Sawyer*. "My mother had a good deal of trouble with me," Mark Twain confessed, "but I think she enjoyed it."[37] Even as he got older, Twain relished prodding and teasing her, much like Tom with Aunt Polly. Whenever Jane, with a straight face, lectured Sam for some misdeed, he would rebut her with an unexpected witticism that made her break down in laughter. Early on she recognized his instinctive tendency to embellish the truth, and though she made an effort to quash it, she came to accept him on his own terms. "I discount him ninety per cent," she remarked of Sam's tall tales. "The rest is pure gold."[38] From his mother, Mark Twain learned that he could trust women and express a richer spectrum of emotion than with men. With his father, Sam had to suppress his personality; with his mother, he could flaunt it.

With her broad sympathies, Jane Clemens was likely to spy redeeming traits even in hardened sinners and outcasts. As her son expressed it, she had the "larger soul that God usually gives to women."[39] Despite struggles with her husband and the death of several children, she kept darkness at bay with a ready friendliness, her high-spirited and fun-loving nature reflected in her passion for the color red. "Grandma's room was always a perfect riot of red; carpets, chairs, ornaments, were all red," said a granddaughter. "She would have worn red, too, if she had not been restrained."[40] "She was of a sunshine disposition," agreed Twain, "and her long life was mainly a holiday for her. She always had the heart of a young girl."[41] Jane flocked to spectacles: circuses, Fourth of July parades, theatrical performances, and church revivals, and she boasted of never skipping a funeral. To those mystified by her fondness for funerals, she explained that "if she didn't go to other people's funerals they wouldn't go to hers!"[42] Sam's life would reflect his mother's love of pageantry. Her curiosity was also piqued by anything that savored of the occult, spirituality, or mysticism.

Another area where Jane Clemens left a profound imprint on her author son lay in the realm of language. She wasn't literary or sophisticated, and read little beyond Bibles and newspapers, yet she had a plainspoken eloquence when protesting injustice or indulging in pathos. She preferred short, simple words and flavored her conversation with banter in a way reminiscent of her son. A natural raconteur, she could spin large tales by embroidering scanty facts. When Twain later said his mother had "the ability to say a humorous thing with the perfect air of not knowing it to be humorous," he described his own trademark technique.[43] From her he also learned how the right manner could make the matter more affecting. In a story called "Hellfire Hotchkiss," he sketched this picture of Jane as a speaker, saying, "there was a subtle something in her voice and her manner that was irresistibly pathetic, and perhaps that was where a great part of the power lay; in that and in her moist eyes and trembling lip. I know now that she was the most eloquent person I have met in all my days, but I did not know it then."[44] Often Jane Clemens was inadvertently funny. When a distraught neighbor informed her that a man had died when a calf raced in front of him, throwing him from his horse, Jane responded unexpectedly, "What became of the calf?"[45]

Jane Clemens communicated to her son a deep love of animals, most notably cats. Unable to resist strays, she at one point had collected nineteen cats, a fondness for animals that moved her granddaughter to protest, "Grandma, I believe you like cats better than babies." A bit miffed, Jane defended her behavior: "When you're tired of a cat you can put it down."[46] She would never swat a fly, punished cats sneaking off with mice, and forbade caged pets in her household. As Twain put it, "An imprisoned creature was out of the question—my mother would not have allowed a rat to be restrained of its liberty."[47] This sympathy for living creatures would be amply reflected in the animal rights activism of her son and granddaughters.

Mark Twain retailed stories of his mother's bravery in standing up for the oppressed, how she blocked a Corsican father pursuing his grown daughter with a rope and scolded a St. Louis driver lashing his poor horse. She also showed sympathy for the enslaved of Hannibal that never extended to outright criticism of the institution itself. At one point, the

Clemenses hired for housework an enslaved boy, Sandy, whose incessant singing drove Sam (always hypersensitive to noise) to distraction. When he complained to his mother, she lectured him in terms of simple humanity. "Think; he is sold away from his mother; she is in Maryland, a thousand miles from here, and he will never see her again, poor thing. When he is singing it is a sign that he is not grieving . . . it would break my heart if Sandy should stop singing."[48]

Yet this same Jane Clemens could mistreat their house slave, Jennie, tended to badmouth "Yankees," and grumbled about "black Republicans."[49] When Twain attempted to trick Jane and her friend Betsey into staying at a Black minstrel show in St. Louis, saying they would hear African missionaries, the ladies were not amused by the stunt. Instead, they "began to question the propriety of their countenancing the industries of a company of negroes, no matter what their trade might be."[50] Because Hannibal was a slave-owning town, its institutions all conspired to certify the justice and legality of involuntary servitude. "Kindhearted and compassionate as she was," Twain reflected of his mother, "I think she was not conscious that slavery was a bald, grotesque, and unwarranted usurpation . . . As far as her experience went, the wise, the good, and the holy were unanimous in the belief that slavery was right, righteous, sacred, the peculiar pet of the Deity, and a condition which the slave himself ought to be daily and nightly thankful for."[51] Few, if any, contrary voices were heard on Hannibal's streets, and children were taught to dread abolitionists as sinister bogeymen who preyed on God-fearing, slave-owning folk. That the compassionate Jane Clemens could be trained to regard slavery as a humane system instead of a monstrosity would serve as an object lesson for Mark Twain in the terrifying power of environment to shape and distort human behavior.

While Twain maintained that his father opposed slavery in principle, deeming it "a great wrong," it is difficult to square that with his actions.[52] In September 1841, John Marshall Clemens served as foreman on a jury that convicted three abolitionists who had crossed the Mississippi to emancipate five slaves, and they were sentenced to twelve years' hard labor. The following year, during the Mississippi River trip that so upset

LOVELESS MARRIAGE

Jane Clemens, Judge Clemens tried to scrounge up money by selling a Black man named Charley for "whatever he will bring where I take water again, *viz*, at Louisville or Nashville."[53] Reading this letter late in life, Mark Twain was dismayed by the sickening way his father talked about the man as if he were "an ox—and somebody else's ox. It makes a body homesick for Charley, even after fifty years."[54] Even when Judge Clemens did not own enslaved people, he rented them from others.

As the years passed and darker truths about slavery surfaced in his memory, Twain remembered savage punishments inflicted upon the Black population and how such cruelty was so embedded in the society that nobody protested or even seemed to notice. In 1896, while traveling in India, Twain recorded how his father had struck him only twice in childhood, yet "he commonly cuffed our harmless slave boy Lewis for any little blunder or awkwardness, even gave him a lashing now & then, which terrified the poor thing nearly out of his wits. My father passed his life among the slaves from his cradle up, & his cuffings proceeded from the custom of the time, not from his nature."[55]

The following year, while summering in Switzerland, Twain had another flashback of how his father had brutalized the enslaved Jennie, who had nursed the Clemens children. As Jane Clemens was about to whip her for insubordination, Jennie dared to grab the whip from her hand, and Judge Clemens was promptly summoned. "Judge whipped her once, for impudence to his wife—whipped her with a bridle."[56] It may have been this notorious act of cruelty that led Jennie to plead for what was commonly seen as the worst punishment: to be sold down the river by a hated slave trader named William Beebe, who had, said Twain, beguiled "her with all sorts of fine and alluring promises."[57] Jane consented to this and persuaded her husband, who badly needed the money. Mark Twain remembered that the sale of Jennie was "a sore trial, for the woman was almost like one of the family."[58] Years later, he saw Jennie working as a chambermaid on a steamboat and she "cried and lamented."[59] Such barbarism toward Blacks was Hannibal's underlying reality, and Twain would spend the rest of his life seeking to acknowledge and understand how people could have accepted it.

In later years, yet another terrifying memory of slavery surged to the forefront of Mark Twain's mind: "When I was 10 I saw a man fling a lump of iron ore at a slaveman [*sic*] in anger—for merely doing something awkwardly, as if that were a crime. It bounded from his skull & the man fell & never spoke again. He was dead in an hour. I knew the man had a right to kill his slave if he wanted to, and yet it seemed a pitiful thing and somehow wrong ... Nobody in the village approved of that murder, but of course no one said much about it."[60] Mark Twain registered these fleeting impressions as a boy, but only with the benefit of hindsight would he fully fathom their true horror.

CHAPTER TWO

A Wild and Mischievous Boy

In his fiction, Mark Twain would memorably evoke Hannibal as "the white town drowsing in the sunshine of a summer's morning," a place where it never seemed to snow despite fierce Missouri winters.[1] He presented it as an earthly paradise where youngsters went barefoot in summer and gorged on cornmeal cakes and catfish. "Well, it was a beautiful life, a lovely life," he once told a dinner audience in his drollest vein. "There was no crime. Merely little things like pillaging orchards and watermelon patches and breaking the Sabbath—we didn't break the Sabbath often enough to signify—once a week perhaps."[2] The town's children may have been poor, but they didn't know it. "To get rich was no one's ambition—it was not in any young person's thoughts . . . It was an intensely sentimental age, but it took no sordid form."[3] He argued that the California gold rush in 1848, when he turned thirteen late in that year, introduced "the lust for money which is the rule of life to-day, and the hardness and cynicism which is the spirit of to-day."[4] He forever remembered the cavalcade of eager townspeople streaming westward in canvas-covered wagons—"We were all there to see and to envy"—and even the local schoolteacher, John D. Dawson, flocked to join the exodus with the money-hungry horde.[5]

That Twain could portray his boyhood in such sunlit terms shows the extent to which his frolics with friends enabled him to escape the grueling insecurity of family life and his father's financial woes. The carefree sprees stood in stark contrast to the gloom that enveloped his household, and he later traced his dread of debt to the monetary setbacks the Clemens clan endured. Fifty years later, he could still summon up, beneath the air of nostalgia, the "sordidness and hatefulness and humiliation" of those early days.[6]

Even as a boy, Sam Clemens had a pronounced streak of nonconformity—he hated being hemmed in by social rules—expressed in constant clowning as he mocked the conventional piety of the townspeople. "Sam was always full of fun," said one cousin. "He could play more pranks and escape with less punishment than anybody I ever knew."[7] With his intelligence concealed behind a mask of insouciance, he revolted against schoolhouse discipline and rote learning and Jane Clemens's valiant efforts to tame him. She recollected: "Sam was always a good-hearted boy, but he was a very wild and mischievous one, and do what we would we could never make him go to school. This used to trouble his father and me dreadfully, and we were convinced that he would never amount to as much in the world as his brothers, because he was not nearly so steady and sober-minded as they were . . . Finally his father and the teacher both said it was of no use trying to teach Sam anything, because he was determined not to learn."[8] In many ways, he was a lazy boy, disorganized and easily bored, always craving novelty, but he could focus intensely on things that dearly interested him—especially outside the schoolhouse.

In the manner of all autodidacts, Sam Clemens educated himself by reading from passion, not duty. He retained his boyhood fondness for *The Adventures of Robin Hood*, both the "quaint & simple . . . fragrant & woodsy England" as well as its characters, "the most darling sweet rascals that ever made crime graceful in this world."[9] He and close friend Will Bowen would "undress & play Robin Hood in our shirt-tails, with lath swords, in the woods on Holliday's Hill on those long summer days."[10] Confined in the remote little town, Sam escaped into the faraway exploits of *Robinson Crusoe*, *The Arabian Nights*, and *The Count of Monte Cristo*, which gave intimations of the boundless world "curtained away" beyond Hannibal.[11]

This willful boy had a penchant for doing shocking things, whether teasing girls with garter snakes or leaving dead bats for his mother to find. With his friends he rolled a giant boulder dangerously down Holliday's Hill, fed a tobacco plug to a visiting elephant, and jumped off a ferry into the river. With pardonable exaggeration, he claimed that he had nearly drowned nine times in the Mississippi River or Bear Creek, and on one occasion remembered an enslaved woman grasping his wriggling fingers and fishing him free from the water. Sam was a sweet burden to Jane Clemens, who nursed him back to health. "I guess there wasn't much danger," she warned him. "People born to be hanged are safe in water."[12]

Sam's reputation as a trickster and troublemaker likely came from a desire to be noticed; being funny was the best way to attract boys, impress girls, and ward off his father's looming presence. "Celebrity is what a boy or a youth longs for more than for any other thing," he observed in his *Autobiography*. "He would be a clown in a circus; he would be a pirate, he would sell himself to Satan, in order to attract attention and be talked about and envied."[13] Later on he came up with an aphorism: "There are no grades of vanity, there are only grades of ability in concealing it."[14] The naughty child grew up to be the naughty adult author, with the same ceaseless need to attract attention by spouting scandalous commentary. The older Mark Twain pointedly noted that the "appetite for notice and notoriety" had lingered in his adult life.[15]

Twain was fond of recounting a story about a measles epidemic that swept Hannibal when he was ten, killing many children. He was so steeped in fear that he decided to end the suspense by contracting the disease on purpose. So he sneaked into the bed of a friend with measles and duly came home with the disease. Far from suffering, Sam Clemens found the situation "most placid and tranquil and sweet and delightful ... I was the centre of all this emotional attention and was gratified by it and vain of it."[16]

Early on the boy learned that he could monopolize people's attention and cast a hypnotic spell thanks to his unusual facility with language. When her granddaughter once asked Jane Clemens what distinguished Sam from other children, she said that "when he had gone anywhere, if only downtown, when he came home all the children would gather around to hear what he had to tell. He knew even then how to make things interesting. She also said that when she saw a crowd running, she didn't ask what was the matter, but 'what has Sam done now?'"[17]

If Sam excelled at taunts, sometimes showing flashes of cruelty, he was also credited with a warm heart, a mixture of moods that persisted into adulthood. Orion praised his younger brother as "a rugged, brave, quick-tempered, generous-hearted fellow," with an outsize "capacity of enjoyment . . . and of suffering" who felt "the utmost extreme of every feeling."[18] Like Tom Sawyer and Huck Finn, Sam exhibited an outlaw spirit, preferring to tarry on the fringes of town, Holliday's Hill and McDowell's Cave, but most of all on the river with its mysterious, isolated islands, where he gloried in a sense of freedom. On Glasscock's Island, Sam and his comrades fished and swam, searched for turtle eggs, and smoked corncob pipes. He was especially enamored of a guttersnipe named Tom Blankenship, who resided a block from his home in a rude dwelling dark with poverty. A master of petty thefts, especially of turkeys and onions, Tom was scruffy and dirty, a stranger to baths and schools, and thoroughly happy despite being the son of the town drunkard. Tom's company was forbidden to Sam, which greatly enhanced his appeal. In Sam's view, Tom was "the only really independent person—boy or man—in the community."[19] This fascination with marginal and taboo figures previews the radical vision of Twain's fiction in which he found virtue in the low born and vice in the well bred, lending a dark glamour to boys who flouted parental strictures.

Mark Twain was born with a natural attraction for the disapproved thing. "There is a charm about the forbidden that makes it unspeakably desirable," he wrote. "It was not that A[dam] ate the apple for the apple's sake, but *because* it was forbidden."[20] A self-styled enfant terrible, he began to smoke by age eight, a habit that remained surreptitious while his father was alive. He believed devoutly in his later aphorism "Few things are harder to put up with than the annoyance of a good example."[21] He could never abide obedient, apple-polishing classmates who toadied to parents, teachers, and preachers, and he reserved a special animus for Theodore Dawson, the schoolteacher's son. "In fact he was inordinately good, extravagantly good, offensively good, detestably good—and he had pop-eyes—and I would have drowned him if I had had a chance."[22] His hatred for these model boys came from a feeling that they were priggish and empty, all show but no substance in their subservience.

If Hannibal was a sleepy town, it was galvanized into startling life twice daily by the arrival of a steamboat either traveling upriver from St. Louis or down from Keokuk, Iowa. The boat would paint a distant spot of black smoke in the sky that was usually noticed first by a Black drayman who uttered a jubilant cry: "S-t-e-a-m-boat a-comin'!" In *Life on the Mississippi,* Twain reported the tonic effect on the town. "The town drunkard stirs, the clerks wake up, a furious clatter of drays follows, every house and store pours out a human contribution, and all in a twinkling the dead town is alive and moving."[23] From the steamboat issued everything from carriages to traveling salesmen to minstrel shows to itinerant circuses. Sam Clemens enjoyed instant access to this excitement: he simply had to exit his Hill Street house, turn left, and there, just a block or two away, lay the vast, shining Mississippi, three-quarters of a mile wide, looking especially magnificent with a steamboat moored at the dock. From Holliday's Hill, three hundred feet up, he could obtain panoramic, unobstructed views of the river as it meandered through the rich flat farmland in northeast Missouri and western Illinois.

The daily advent of the steamboats planted the first ambition that took root in Sam Clemens: to be a pilot. He craved attention, and nobody drew more than the pilot, who wore fancy duds and enjoyed an "exalted respect" as he strutted about town.[24] Of no less interest was the "princely salary" that the pilot pocketed each month: "Two months of his wages would pay a preacher's salary for a year."[25] The river held many wonders beyond steamboats, especially the annual arrival of a massive fleet of rafts floating to markets downriver with "an acre or so of white, sweet-smelling boards in each craft," manned by "a crew of two dozen men or more."[26] Sam and his friends would plunge into the river, swim to the rafts, and hitch a thrilling ride.

In the meantime, the future author had to suffer through something called school, which he viewed as the centerpiece of an unspoken adult conspiracy to deprive children of fun. At age four he trudged off to a private school run by Elizabeth Horr, who commenced class with a prayer and a New Testament selection. On his first day, Sam, the class clown, got into trouble and was punished with strokes from a switch. He would attend three private schools, one a log schoolhouse with girls on one side, boys on the other, and wrote scornfully of "what passed for a school in those days: a place where tender young humanity devoted itself for eight or ten hours a day to learn incomprehensible rubbish by heart out of books and reciting it by rote, like parrots."[27] Restless in school, a born truant, he yearned on warm days for the barefoot freedom of the surrounding countryside. Perhaps this scanty education enabled him to develop a literary voice that was fresh and original, unspoiled by any European or Eastern Seaboard influences.

The most-perceptive observations of young Sam Clemens came from a very pretty girl named Laura Hawkins, who lived directly across Hill Street but in a more imposing house, which signaled a step up the economic ladder, her father having owned a large mill and slave plantation further inland. She would figure as the model for Becky Thatcher in *Tom Sawyer.* Twain sentimentalized her as his first sweetheart and never lost his soft spot for her. At age five, he said, "I had an apple, & fell in love with her & gave her the core."[28] Her first glimpse of her attention-grabbing young neighbor was indelible: a barefoot boy who "came out of his home, opposite mine, and started showing off, turning handsprings and cutting capers just as described in Tom Sawyer." Sam had "long golden curls hanging over his shoulders at the time."[29] His comic persona, she saw, concealed a sensitive boy of natural refinement, who was "gentle . . . and kind of quiet," with a conspicuous drawl reminiscent of his mother.[30] Even though Sam "played hooky from school" and "cared nothing at all for his books . . . I never heard a coarse word from him in all our childhood acquaintance."[31]

From his first encounter with the female sex, Sam Clemens was courtly and gallant, as in future years. "He used to carry my books to school every morning," recalled Laura, "bring them home for me in the afternoon, and occasionally he would treat me to apples, oranges and such

A WILD AND MISCHIEVOUS BOY

things, or divide his candy with me."[32] From Sam, she must have heard the family saga of past Virginia gentility—aristocrats down on their luck—for she noted that the Clemenses "came from very fine stock, but were very poor."[33] Appreciative of his special humor, she noted his ability to discern the absurdity in situations and said his success in telling a funny story lay not so much in its content than in his "drawling, appealing voice."[34]

School wasn't the only adult institution that Sam Clemens had to put up with: the Church also conspired against the pleasures coveted by small boys. In later years, Mark Twain came to believe that the creation of humanity, with its deeply flawed nature, was nothing for the Lord to boast about and would inveigh against "the superstitions in which I was born & mistrained."[35] That perspective came later. In Hannibal, atheists were about as popular as abolitionists, and Sam's boyhood was saturated with religious training. By age twelve he was steeped in the Old and New Testaments, which left their mark on his writings. While the skeptical John Marshall Clemens evaded church services, Jane Clemens was a fervent Presbyterian, and Sam was affected by all the fire-and-brimstone sermons about the afterlife. As he phrased it, "The Presbyterian hell is all misery; the heaven all happiness."[36] So far did early religious experience permeate his mind that heaven and hell became lifelong fixtures in his humorous repertoire, with Satan his best comic character. The only profession that ever vied with piloting in Sam Clemens's fantasy life was that of becoming a preacher, which seemed a sure way to forestall damnation. "It looked like a safe job," he confirmed.[37] Another time he confessed about being a preacher that he lacked "the necessary stock in trade—i.e., religion."[38]

Though he suffered through services in the Presbyterian church with its high pulpit, Bible on a red plush pillow, and congregants sitting in stiff pews, he still regarded himself as an incorrigible sinner, headed straight to hell. Every time a boy in town drowned, Sam chalked it up to an angry deity who was coming for him next. Although he consoled himself by day, saying God would be patient, dark fears of retribution sneaked up on him at night. "With the going down of the sun my faith failed, and the clammy fears gathered about my heart. It was then that I repented. Those were awful nights, nights of despair, nights charged with the bitterness of death."[39]

One thing, in retrospect, that weakened Mark Twain's faith in the church of his childhood was its unswerving endorsement of slavery. The evidence of slavery's misery stood scattered all around him—"the saddest faces" Sam Clemens ever saw were those of a dozen shackled slaves on Hannibal's dock awaiting shipment farther south—but he heard no condemnation from religious leaders.[40] Nearly half the families in Marion County held at least one person in bondage, almost invariably with a clear conscience. "In my schoolboy days," Twain said, "I had no aversion to slavery . . . the local pulpit taught us that God approved it, that it was a holy thing, and that the doubter need only look in the Bible if he wished to settle his mind."[41] Beyond preaching slavery, pastors practiced it unashamedly. Twain remembered one Methodist minister who sold an enslaved child to a fellow minister, who then profited by later selling the child downriver. As the steamboat departed with her offspring, the child's mother wept inconsolably at the dock.[42] As he got older and developed into an avid student of history, Twain came to believe that the Church had endorsed slavery for centuries and reformed its position only *after* congregants turned against it. Church complicity on slavery came to illustrate for him how social institutions could collude in a "lie of silent assertion . . . that nothing is going on which fair and intelligent men are aware of and are engaged by their duty to try to stop."[43]

When it came to slavery, the forces of repression were especially virulent in northern Missouri, settled mostly by people from slave states. Even though Missouri lay at the intersection of the free states of Illinois and Iowa and the mixed Kansas Territory, it had a heavily enslaved population in counties strung along the Mississippi River. In fact, the proximity of free Illinois right across the waterway only heightened the dread in Hannibal that dastardly abolitionists would sneak across and spirit slaves away. "In that day," Twain wrote, "for a man to speak out openly and proclaim himself an enemy of negro slavery was simply to proclaim

A WILD AND MISCHIEVOUS BOY

himself a madman. For he was blaspheming against the holiest thing known to a Missourian, and could *not* be in his right mind."[44]

As much as he had warmed to the lowly Tom Blankenship, Sam Clemens gravitated to the company of the enslaved, and for someone attracted to pariahs, the human chattel were the ultimate outcasts of society. For many years, his brain stuffed with early stereotypes, he would refer to Blacks in derogatory language—after all, he grew up in a town that still had slave auctions and minstrel shows with racist impersonations of Banjo and Bones—yet his boyish affection for Black people was also unmistakable. By some instinct he reveled in their company. Of having Black children as playmates, he contended that he preferred "their society to that of the elect, I being a person of low-down tastes from the start, notwithstanding my high birth."[45]

Sam spent two or three months of every summer at his uncle John Quarles's homestead, set on the crest of a beautiful hill, four miles outside of Florida. Populated by eight Quarles children and about a dozen enslaved people, it represented an emotional haven for the boy and would reappear as the Phelpses' farm in *Huck Finn*. "It was a heavenly place for a boy," Mark Twain recalled, "that farm of my uncle John's."[46] The meals served were hearty and irresistible—"the corn bread, the hot biscuits and wheatbread, and the fried chicken"—never to be surpassed in northern years.[47] Nor was it a small thing that, in contrast to his father's severity, John Quarles showed a winning geniality.

The plantation's foremost appeal lay in the smokehouse and a cluster of small log cabins that made up the "negro quarter," a place redolent with an atmosphere of magic, mystery, and folklore. Here the future novelist found figures of inexhaustible fascination, including "Aunt" Hannah, "a bedridden white-headed slave woman whom we visited daily, and looked upon with awe, for we believed she was upwards of a thousand years old and had talked with Moses."[48] It was thought "she had lost her health in the desert, coming out of Egypt. The bald spot on her head was caused by fright at seeing Pharaoh drowned."[49] The language, folkways, songs, and religion of the enslaved left lasting traces on Sam Clemens's imagination. He absorbed their dialects into his bloodstream and they became a part of him. Often the older Black children would chaperone younger whites, but, stepping outside their roles, they could also act as companions and co-conspirators. These unions, however pleasant, were illusory in nature. "We were comrades, and yet not comrades"; Twain remembered, "color and condition interposed a subtle line which both parties were conscious of, and which rendered complete fusion impossible."[50]

The high point each summer came at night by the kitchen fire, when the enslaved Old Uncle Dan'l would deliver a ghost story called the "Golden Arm" amid a flickering blaze. From Mark Twain's luminous memories of these performances, it grows clear that he encountered in the elderly Black man his first platform virtuoso, expert in tone and pacing. "We would huddle close about the old man, & begin to shudder with the first familiar words; & under the spell of his impressive delivery we always fell a prey to that climax at the end when the rigid black shape in the twilight sprang at us with a shout."[51] In his many years on the lecture circuit, Mark Twain would constantly reprise the Golden Arm story along with many tricks of delivery he had learned at the feet of his first mentor.

With his kindness, warmth, and intelligence, Uncle Dan'l would serve as inspiration for many characters in Mark Twain's fiction. As he admitted, "I . . . staged him in books under his own name and as 'Jim,' and carted him all around—to Hannibal, down the Mississippi on a raft, and even across the Desert of Sahara in a balloon—and he has endured it all with the patience and friendliness and loyalty which were his birthright."[52] Due to prolonged exposure to slavery at the Quarleses' farm, Twain had a fondness for Black people that didn't stem from polite tolerance or enforced familiarity. It was deep and personal, and he was never afraid to say so, distinguishing him from many white people of his era. "It was on the farm that I got my strong liking for [Uncle Dan'l's] race and my appreciation of certain of its fine qualities. This feeling and this estimate have stood the test of sixty years and more and have suffered no impairment. The black face is as welcome to me now as it was then."[53]

Sometimes it can be hard to reconcile Twain's varied memories of slavery in Hannibal, which he once termed "the mild domestic slavery, not the brutal plantation article. Cruelties were very rare, and exceedingly and wholesomely unpopular."[54] Of course, "mild domestic slavery," if such ever existed, was still slavery. Yet it was Twain himself who told the story of the lump of iron flung at a Black man that killed him and how his own parents had been corrupted by this system into cruel and unnatural behavior.

The situation that implicated the entire community in the crime of chattel slavery was the problem of runaway slaves. No white person who came into contact with a fugitive was spared responsibility. "To help steal a horse or a cow was a low crime," Mark Twain said, "but to help a hunted slave, or feed him or shelter him, or hide him, or comfort him, in his troubles, his terrors, his despair, or hesitate to promptly betray him to the slave-catcher . . . was a much baser crime, & carried with it a stain, a moral smirch which nothing could wipe away."[55] While Twain understood why slave owners pursued runaways in such ferocious fashion, he was always puzzled that "the loafers[,] the tag-rag & bobtail of the community" took up the hunt with equal zeal. "It shows that that strange thing, the conscience . . . can be trained to approve any wild thing you *want* it to approve if you begin its education early & stick to it."[56]

Sam Clemens experienced direct exposure to at least one fugitive slave, which became the genesis of *Huck Finn.* In the summer of 1847, Benson Blankenship, the older brother of Tom, happened upon a runaway from Missouri hiding in the swamp of an island on the Illinois side of the Mississippi River. Spurning the reward for returning runaways and defying the law, Benson smuggled food to the man and helped to sustain and safeguard him for several weeks. Then a band of woodcutters stumbled upon the Black man and gave chase until he disappeared and drowned. A few days later, Sam Clemens and his companions were present when the mutilated corpse, like some ghostly apparition, suddenly rose straight up from the water, scattering the boys in terror—a nightmarish moment that burned the episode into the future author's memory.

CHAPTER THREE

Printer's Devil

The fragile bark of John Marshall Clemens's career always seemed to struggle upstream against a heavy tide as his finances turned perilous again in 1845–46. To supplement his erratic, meager income as justice of the peace, he had been forced into an unwanted sideline, clerking at a local produce house. Mark Twain believed his father's final ruin came at the hands of a villain named Ira Stout, who defaulted on a loan of several thousand dollars guaranteed by his father. If the details remain murky, it seems clear that the straitened finances of the Clemens family forced them to relinquish their home and move across the street, occupying second-story rooms above Grant's Drug Store. This must have been a crushing blow to family pride: in lieu of rent, Jane Clemens, the erstwhile Kentucky belle, now had to cook for the family of Orville Grant.

Ever admirable in his civic projects, John Marshall Clemens cooperated on plans to build a railroad that would connect the Mississippi and Missouri Rivers and also lobbied for the creation of a state Masonic college in Hannibal. No project, however, materialized in time to pluck him from the depths of misfortune. His most promising prospect was a job as clerk of the circuit court, a position to be chosen at the next election in August 1847. Apart from its considerable prestige, the post would at last ensure the Clemens clan a steady income, with Judge Clemens considered a front-runner in the race. During the winter of 1846–47, he mounted his horse and rode from house to house to drum up support for his candidacy. In late February 1847, riding back twelve miles from Palmyra, the county seat north of Hannibal, he was drenched by sleet and rain, and in his chilled, sodden state succumbed to pleurisy and then pneumonia.

As the forty-eight-year-old patriarch lay dying, surrounded by his family, he uttered words that suggested he had learned little from his short, unhappy stay on earth. "I believe if I had stayed in Tennessee," he insisted, "I might have been worth twenty thousand dollars today."[1] He returned to the obsession that had cruelly beckoned for so many years: the Tennessee land, which he had insisted bulged with fabulous mineral deposits. "I shall not live to see these acres turn to silver and gold," he had prophesied, "but my children will."[2] "Cling to the land," he now urged them in a feeble voice. "Cling to the land, and wait. Let nothing beguile it away from you."[3] Instead of bequeathing a fortune to his children, he left them with the bane of imaginary riches. "He went to his grave in the full belief that he had done us a kindness," said Mark Twain. "It was a woeful mistake, but fortunately he never knew it."[4] At the end, he motioned to his daughter Pamela to approach, laced his arms around her neck, and gave her his first kiss in years. "Let me die" were his parting words on March 24, 1847.[5] Sam Clemens saw only a rebuke in his father's farewell kiss to Pamela: "He did not say good-bye to his wife, or to any but his daughter."[6] If Mark Twain became the quintessential American writer, it may have been because his father left such a poignant example of failure in a land obsessed with money and success. Twain would suffer the lifelong financial anxiety of someone whose family fortunes had crashed in early life.

With his father's death, the burden of family support now settled squarely on Orion, who yearned for a career as an orator or politician, but dutifully returned to his printing job in St. Louis. With more than a tincture of bitterness, he blamed his father for hastening his own demise. "He doctored himself from my earliest remembrance," he later said. "During the latter part of his life he bought Cook's pills by the box, and took some daily. He was very dexterous at throwing a pill to the root of his tongue, washing it down with a sip of water."[7] While it is impossible to verify Orion's suspicions, Cook's Pills were a blend of potent laxatives that included mercury chloride, which can have toxic effects on bodily organs. The pills were also used to treat syphilis. Sketchy evidence suggests that an autopsy was performed on Judge Clemens with Sam bending down to peer through a keyhole. At least one Mark Twain biographer has suggested that the autopsy disclosed shocking news: that Judge Clemens suffered from syphilis.[8] If so, the world knew nothing of this shame, and the local paper lauded Judge Clemens for his "public spirit" and "high sense of justice and moral rectitude."[9]

The whole troubled saga of John Marshall Clemens must have had a nightmarish quality for Sam, only eleven at the time of his father's death. The business failures, the harrowing plunge in social status, the ghastly fiscal strain, the early death perhaps brought on by bad habits, the keyhole autopsy—it was horror heaped on horror for the young boy, made especially galling by his father's cold, aloof attitude toward him. And it had all ended badly given that the judge's death condemned "his heirs to a long and discouraging struggle with the world for a livelihood."[10] So traumatic was his father's death that Mark Twain marked the date, sometimes with tears, for the rest of his life.[11]

The emotional toll was soon evident, for the night following his father's funeral and for several nights thereafter, Sam, cloaked in a sheet, reverted to sleepwalking—a sight that unnerved his mother and sister—as if all the nervous energy gathered by day exploded in his mind at night. His cousin Tabitha Quarles recalled Sam as "a pale, sickly boy" and said his sleepwalking proved an ongoing terror to his family, who feared he would harm himself in his nocturnal wanderings. One night at the Quarleses' farm, his uncle discovered Sam "out in the stable in his night gown. He was astride the old gray horse. He was yelling like a wild Indian and thought he was running a race, while old Gray just pricked up his ears and paid no more attention to Sam's tricks than the rest of us."[12]

That John Marshall Clemens had been so emotionally absent from his son's life only made it more difficult for Sam to accept his death since he no longer had a chance to repair relations and tortured himself with memories of disrespect toward his father. Jane Clemens escorted him into the room where the coffin rested, and as they stood on either side, she attempted to soothe him. "It is all right, Sammy. What's done is done, and it does not matter to him any more."[13] She used the occasion to broach the subject of his uncertain future. "I had some serious requests to make of him, and . . . I knew his word once given was never broken . . . He turned his streaming eyes upon me and cried out, 'Oh, mother, I will do anything, anything you ask of me except to go to school; I can't do that!' That was the very request I was going to make. Well, we afterward had a sober talk, and I concluded to let him go into a printing office to learn the trade, as I couldn't have him running wild."[14] Sam swore to his mother that he would behave himself and never break her heart.

After Judge Clemens's death, his family mostly survived on money Orion sent from St. Louis and income Pamela brought in from teaching piano and guitar. As it turned out, Sam wasn't immediately freed from homework and attended school part-time until John D. Dawson fled to California in 1849. In the meantime, he performed assorted part-time labor, including a stint as an apprentice printer at the *Hannibal Gazette* and an errand boy for the paper's owner, as well as short-term, menial assignments in a grocery, bookstore, and drugstore. Then he landed an apprentice job around May 1848 with the *Missouri Courier,* a Democratic paper headed by Joseph P. Ament, and by the next year he was sprung from hated schooling forever. With his shortened education, it is amazing how cultured, literate, and worldly Mark Twain would become as he continued to educate himself and far transcended his provincial upbringing.

An apprentice's job then stood only a notch above indentured servitude, entitling the occupant to no wages, only board in the owner's residence and two suits of cheap clothes. Mark Twain scoffed that he never saw the second suit and that the first, composed of worn garments discarded by the bigger Ament, made him feel "as if I had on a circus tent. I had to turn the trousers up to my ears to make them short enough."[15] Sometimes he slept on a pallet on the print shop floor, sometimes at Ament's house, and he dismissed his boss four years later as a "diminutive chunk of human meat."[16] Even though he was already hypercritical of people, others shared this derisory view of Ament, one editor railing at him as "the most fretful, peevish, cross-grained, ill-natured, sour-tempered, scolding obscure little brat we have met with."[17]

At the time no clear line demarcated the printing and editorial sides of a newspaper, which meant that Sam Clemens had now ventured, willy-nilly, into the writing world. This bleak existence was lightened by the uproarious company of apprentice Wales McCormick and journeyman printer Pet McMurry, who depicted Sam as "a little sandy-haired boy" who sat crooning ditties or smoked "a huge cigar or a diminutive pipe" as he sat "mounted upon a little box" setting type.[18] For all his self-deprecating jokes about his printing skills—"I had always been such a slow compositor that I looked with envy upon the achievements of apprentices of two years' standing"—he became quite agile at his craft.[19] The office factotum, he went around dunning subscribers and delivering newspapers at dawn. "The carrier was then an object of interest to all the dogs in town. If I had saved up all the bites I ever received, I could keep M. Pasteur busy for a year."[20] Sam stuck to his lazy, messy habits, as one old pressman learned when he tried to sweep around him. "He would rather die in the dust than uncross his legs."[21] Despite the fond feelings he had shown toward Blacks at the Quarleses' farm, he now resented being assigned to eat in the kitchen alongside an old enslaved cook and her mulatto daughter.

While working as a printer's devil, Twain betrayed his first spark of literary interest when he supposedly scooped up a scrap of paper lying in the street. This fugitive sheet came from a biography of Joan of Arc, and it blew open a window into another world. The passage in question chronicled Joan's imprisonment in a cage at Rouen and the two coarse English soldiers who mocked her and absconded with her clothes. The story spoke to Sam's chivalric side, his need to save young maidens in distress, especially those on the eve of womanhood, and he began to read eagerly about Joan. He found more mental nourishment reading on his own than in insipid school texts. For an author who would compose the classic ode to small-town American boyhood, it is also revealing that his first literary crush was a historical tale set on another continent in distant times. Sam was soon studying German, and within a few years, perhaps bewitched by Joan's mystique, he would be teaching himself French and filling notebooks with phrases.

Aside from reading, he also flirted briefly with the Cadets of Temperance, a group dedicated to stamping out drinking, smoking, and gambling—all pastimes dear to Mark Twain's heart. Sam's main attraction to the group was strictly sartorial: he liked the bright red merino scarves they sported during church parades. "I was clothed like a conflagration," he recalled. "I have never enjoyed any dress so much as I enjoyed that 'regalia.'"[22] Like Tom Sawyer, the proud, self-confessed sinner couldn't keep up the charade very long and lasted only three or four months in the group. Already wedded to his vices, Sam Clemens would forever nurse a healthy contempt for moral crusaders who tried to improve him.

In what proved a mixed blessing for Sam, Orion returned to Hannibal in the summer of 1850 and purchased a weekly newspaper, the *Western Union,* recruiting his brothers Sam and Henry as typesetters. Within a year he would purchase a second paper and merge it with the first, the resulting hybrid called the *Hannibal Journal.* When Orion worked in St. Louis as a journeyman printer, he had won a powerful patron in attorney Edward Bates, who advised him to study law and remembered him fondly as "a good boy, anxious to learn, using all means in his power to do so."[23] Studious and eager to improve himself, Orion led an austere life, poring over Benjamin Franklin's life in his boardinghouse, but he chafed at printing work as unsatisfying. While he dreamed of being a public orator, "that had been forbidden by my father who had placed me at the toil of printing and editing, because his own preference was in that direction."[24] Ten years older than Sam, Orion had been wounded more by Judge Clemens's severity, and the shadow of his father's hardship fell heavily across his life. Given the siblings' age difference and Orion's protracted stay in St. Louis, he arrived in Hannibal as something of an unknown entity to Sam.

Thanks to the sale of some Tennessee land and borrowed money, Orion was able to move the family from Grant's Drug Store back to the Hill Street frame house, where Jane took in boarders to bolster income. Like

PRINTER'S DEVIL

his deceased father, Orion was a confirmed Whig who penned editorials that protested talk of southern secession, even as he opposed the Free Soil movement and endorsed the Fugitive Slave Law. "We are entirely conservative," he reassured his readers, "and while our contempt for the Abolitionists of the North knows no bounds, we are loath to claim brotherhood with the 'Fire-eaters' of the South."[25] Newspapers were then expected to be highly partisan and opinionated, a hyperbolic style that would play to the strength of young Sam Clemens, who soon published "A Gallant Fireman," his first known piece, in which he mocked the antics of a printer's devil in his office when a fire broke out next door.

Like another famous apprentice printer, Ben Franklin, Sam squirmed under the arbitrary rule of his older brother. After starting work around January 1851, at fifteen, Sam awaited the handsome weekly wage of $3.50 that Orion promised him, only to discover that his older brother "never was able to pay me a single penny as long as I was with him."[26] Again he was reduced to involuntary servitude. Orion would admit that he only furnished Sam with "poor, shabby clothes," and Sam's anger toward his brother festered.[27] Perhaps in a case of sublimated rage, Sam taunted an apprentice, Jim Wolfe, until the latter retaliated and punched him in the nose.

Cruel pranks seemed to occupy a large portion of Sam Clemens's life. He was a wisecracking kid who never entirely shed that smart-alecky side of his personality. But where the young Sam Clemens could appear heartless in mocking people, the later Mark Twain would display a profound wit suffused with a much deeper humanity. The first known photo of Sam Clemens, taken in 1850 as he was turning fifteen and graduated from apprentice to printer, is striking for the turbulent gaze and the forceful intelligence of his expression. It is a mature look, as if this teenager were already somewhat hardened by experience. Whether as a joke or a form of bombastic self-promotion, he held the name "SAM," set up in the type of a "composing stick," at his belt.

Much like his father before him, Orion proved a hopeless businessman, who lowered the price of the *Journal* and its advertising rates until profits vanished and the paper had to operate from the Clemens home.

Not for the last time, his ambition far exceeded his reach, and he "began to yearn for a chance to get away from the office, and rest and breathe fresh air."[28] Both Orion and Sam were dreamers, but Sam had a tough, hardheaded practicality that would enable him to succeed, whereas Orion was an endearing oddball whose naivete would always serve as a whetstone that sharpened his younger brother's cynicism. In his frustration, Orion took out his bad humor on Sam. Basically fair and decent, Orion recognized belatedly that he had been a harsh taskmaster. "I was tyrannical and unjust to Sam. He was as swift and as clean as a good journeyman. I gave him tasks, and if he got through well I begrudged him the time and made him work more. He set a clean proof, and Henry a very dirty one . . . Once we were kept late, and Sam complained with tears of bitterness that he was held till midnight on Henry's dirty proofs."[29] Orion's tyranny left its lasting scars on Sam Clemens, who seldom resisted chances to exact revenge in later life.

Even though Sam entered printing with no literary ambitions, as a compositor "acres of good and bad literature" passed beneath his gaze daily and trained his eye to discriminate between the good stuff and the bad.[30] Almost by accident he crossed over from printer to writer. Short of money, Orion went to Tennessee to try to squeeze some money from the Tennessee land, leaving Sam as the paper's foreman. When Sam heard that the lovelorn editor of a rival paper had tramped down to the river in a botched effort to drown himself, he skewered him with the same irreverence that he had deployed throughout childhood. A skillful cartoonist, he drew the cautious editor creeping gingerly into the river and testing the water's depth. This was a natural step for Sam Clemens, who would take his schoolboy japes and convert them into literature. He would relish the combative image of the journalist as a gladiator battling opposing papers and trading insults with them.

The editor in question reacted with fury to the satire, and his newspaper upbraided Sam for not having "the decency of a gentleman nor the honor of a blackguard."[31] Orion wasn't amused when he returned from Tennessee. His impulse was always to pacify and conciliate whereas Sam's was to stir up and provoke. To placate the rival editor, Orion wrote of him as "a young man, recently come amongst us, with a design of occupying a respectable position in society, by industry and by propriety and straightforwardness of conduct."[32] Orion was so busy apologizing that he missed the cosmic significance of what had occurred: the birth of one of the premier literary talents in American history. For the first time, the future Mark Twain had served up a scathing portrait of human foibles. As Orion ruefully admitted later, "I could have distanced all competitors even then, if I had recognized Sam's ability and let him go ahead, merely keeping him from offending worthy persons."[33]

Sam would enjoy sporadic forays into print during his two years at Orion's paper. Perhaps still smarting from his father's treatment, he railed at one contribution against a husband guilty of "unmercifully beating and maltreating his wife and children" and opined that he ought "to be ducked, ridden on a rail, tarred and feathered, and politely requested to bundle up his 'duds' and make himself scarce."[34] The item was written in the chivalric mode that Mark Twain would develop to the brim with Joan of Arc. In another piece, he defended local culture from East Coast snobs who thought the interior peopled by philistines. "Your Eastern people seem to think this country is a barren, uncultivated region, with a population consisting of heathens."[35] If he gloried in the West's rough, lawless culture, he also wanted to show easterners they were dead wrong about it.

The paper sorely needed direction under the indecisive Orion, whom Sam likened to a human weathervane. Orion, rather pathetically, agreed: "I followed all the advice I received. If two or more persons conflicted with each other, I adopted the views of the last."[36] With this passive character, Orion lacked not only Sam's brash talent but also his instinctive sense of conviction. He couldn't settle on fixed prices for advertisements or subscriptions, and accepted everything from cabbages to cordwood as payment. Sam deplored the paper's amateur appearance, "a wretchedly printed little sheet, being very vague and pale in spots, and in other spots so caked with ink as to be hardly decipherable."[37]

By 1853 Orion realized that he had to cool off Sam's simmering discontent and so briefly gave him a slot in the paper called "Our Assistant's

Column"—a space Sam filled only three times. In one of his last efforts, he wrote a paean to redheaded people like himself, arguing that not only Thomas Jefferson but likely Jesus and Adam had been redheads. Then came the inevitable break with Orion. Sam asked him for money to purchase a used gun, and Orion flew into a rage at what he deemed an unreasonable request. Disgusted, Sam went to his mother, said Orion hated him, and announced he was leaving home. Fearing the sinful world beyond Hannibal, Jane Clemens made him swear on a Bible that he wouldn't "throw a card or drink a drop of liquor" while away. When he agreed, she planted a kiss, saying, "Remember that, Sam, and write to us."[38] Though he abided by his pledge, he later reflected, "The instant a person pledges himself not to drink, he feels the galling of the slavechain he has put upon himself; & if he be wise . . . he will go instantly and break that pledge."[39] We can roughly date Sam's departure from Hannibal because on May 27, 1853, Orion ran a notice: "Wanted! An Apprentice to the Printing Business. Apply Soon."[40]

As he contemplated future moves, Sam gave a clue as to a possible destination in his valedictory "Assistant's Column," referring to crowds "continually congregated around the new Crystal Palace in New York City," where "drunkenness and debauching are carried on to their fullest extent."[41] He narrowly missed a Hannibal lynching, when an accused slave, "a demon in human shape," according to Ament's paper, was hunted down by a mob and *"burned at the stake."*[42] Given Sam Clemens's budding interest in Joan of Arc, one wonders what he would have made of this modern example of medieval barbarity.

Sam left Hannibal bruised, not hopeful, later telling William Dean Howells that there was "not much satisfaction in it, even as a recollection."[43] For someone of his energy, Hannibal seemed a drowsy backwater. "Half the people were alive and the other half were dead," he later wrote. "A stranger could not tell them apart."[44] He must have felt that Orion had kept him in a state of peonage, of penniless labor and a threadbare existence, even as he awakened to a sense of his own proficiency as a printer and wordsmith. Orion, having bungled his relationship with Sam, understood in retrospect that Sam "went wandering in search of

PRINTER'S DEVIL

that comfort and that advancement and those rewards of industry which he had failed to find where I was—gloomy, taciturn, and selfish. I not only missed his labor; we all missed his bounding activity and merriment."[45] Sam's departure damaged the paper, and Orion had trouble getting it out after he left. Jane Clemens fumed at Sam's betrayal. Before the year was over, Orion packed up and traveled north to Muscatine, Iowa, where he bought a stake in a local paper, the *Muscatine Journal*, taking Jane and Henry Clemens with him.

When Sam Clemens departed from Hannibal, he bore a world of pain, but also a cargo of precious memories preserved intact in his mind, ready for future retrieval. The abrupt break with his boyhood had this advantage: there would be no overlay of later experience to mar the perfection of his recollections. Sam boarded a boat to St. Louis, as his first port of call, and stayed with Pamela, who had married a well-to-do commission merchant, William Moffett, and had a baby named Annie. Sam had a tendency to make fun of Pamela's piety and her "notorious Sunday school proclivities," but she was a true and loyal sister, and he owed her a great deal.[46]

At seventeen, Sam was fortunate to have a portable skill as a journeyman typesetter, affording him unusual freedom for an adolescent, and he soon obtained a job with the printing firm that had employed Orion. For a Hannibal boy, St. Louis shimmered as a teeming metropolis of one hundred thousand souls, with hospitals and libraries and fancy homes. As Mark Twain would observe, whenever anyone in those days traveled to St. Louis, "He talked St Louis, and nothing but SL and its wonders for months and months afterward."[47]

As far as Jane Clemens knew, Sam was to stay put in that town with Pamela. She didn't reckon on his restless, roving spirit; even as a teenager, he would embrace broad swaths of the country, as if soaking up all of the American experience for future use. "All I do know or feel," he later wrote his mother, "is that I am wild with impatience to move—move—Move!"[48] In a similar mood, he said, "I love stir & excitement; &

so the moment the spring birds begin to sing . . . I want to pack off somewhere where there's something going on."[49] Without telling Jane, the headstrong Sam decided to decamp to New York City in a personal declaration of independence. By breaking loose from his family, he was both asserting his autonomy and satisfying his innate, nomadic craving for adventure.

Traveling by rail to the city, he stopped in Syracuse, a hotbed of abolitionist fervor and a key stop in New York on the Underground Railroad. Two years earlier, a Hannibal man named John McReynolds had discovered in Syracuse his runaway slave Jerry, who had fled there years earlier, adopting the surname Henry. McReynolds sent slave-catchers to recapture him and, invoking the Fugitive Slave Act of 1850, enlisted local law enforcement to cooperate. When Jerry was held in the town courthouse, outraged abolitionists besieged the building and had the captive released in a notable victory for antislavery advocates. In Frederick Douglass's view, "the rescue of Jerry did most to bring the fugitive slave bill into contempt and to defeat its execution everywhere."[50]

Once in Syracuse, Sam Clemens immediately associated it with the McReynolds case. Not surprisingly, the racism of his boyhood society had not deserted him, and he exhibited all the nasty biases one might expect from a boy of his background. As he told his mother on August 24, 1853, "when I saw the Court House in Syracuse, it called to mind the time when it was surrounded with chains and companies of soldiers, to prevent the rescue of McReynolds' nigger, by the infernal abolitionists. I reckon I had better black my face, for in these Eastern States niggers are considerably better than white people."[51] Sam's first exposure to the North brought to the surface proslavery sympathies as yet untouched by residence outside Missouri. Hungry for copy after Sam's departure, Orion printed the letter in the *Hannibal Journal*, informing readers, "The free and easy impudence of the writer of the following letter will be appreciated by those who recognize him. We should be pleased to have more of his letters."[52]

Sam knew his mother would be furious that her footloose son at seventeen had traveled such a distance on his own. In effect, he had run away from home. "MY DEAR MOTHER: you will doubtless be a little surprised, and somewhat angry when you receive this, and find me so far from home"; he wrote, "but you must bear a little with me, for you know I was always the best boy you had, and perhaps you remember the people used to say to their children, 'Now don't do like Orion and Henry Clemens but take Samuel for your guide.'"[53] This last, of course, ironically inverted the truth. Once in New York City, he found in record time a room in a boardinghouse and a printing job at John A. Gray's at 97 Cliff Street, where he worked alongside forty compositors. He was enchanted by the vista from his fifth-floor office, where "from one window I have a pretty good view of the city, while another commands a view of the shipping beyond the Battery; and the 'forest of masts,' with all sorts of flags flying, is no mean sight."[54] After work, he frequented the free printers library at 3 Chambers Street, where he would settle in to "spend my evenings most pleasantly."[55]

However entranced by city views, Sam Clemens was still blinkered by small-town bias and revolted by the racial and ethnic mix in lower Manhattan. Shaped by Hannibal, he spewed forth prejudice. His daily stroll to work led him through the tough, immigrant neighborhood of Five Points, and he gazed with sheer loathing at the diverse inhabitants. "Niggers, mulattoes, quadroons, Chinese, and some the Lord no doubt originally intended to be white, but the dirt on whose faces leaves one uncertain as to that fact, block up the little, narrow street; and to wade through this mass of human vermin, would raise the ire of the most patient person that ever lived."[56] Such ugliness formed part of a youthful bravado that bespoke his own insecurity and provinciality. There was still a giant, unresolved conflict inside Sam between his warm feeling toward Blacks he knew personally in Hannibal and his fear-ridden antipathy toward Black strangers in the East.

Free of his father's disposition and his brother's despair, Sam Clemens sampled the city's murky charms. He had sufficient curiosity to attend a "model artist show" on Chatham Street, although prudery prevented him from savoring glimpses of female flesh provided by this early version of striptease. Even sixteen years later, he said how "everybody growled about it," denouncing it as "horrid" and "immoral."[57] Nonetheless, the city opened a wealth of new sights and sounds to his youthful curiosity, and his opinion of the town was revised favorably. "I have taken a liking to the abominable place," he confided to Pamela in October, "and every time I get ready to leave I put it off a day or so, from some unaccountable cause."[58]

Showing remarkable confidence in his own ability to earn a living, Sam pushed on to Philadelphia and obtained temporary work as a printer for the *Philadelphia Inquirer,* alerting Orion that, "unlike New York, I like this Philadelphia amazingly, and the people in it."[59] In his spare time he frequented art galleries and libraries, even though he still sounded like a hayseed in the metropolis. A massive tide of German and Irish immigration had spawned the nativist Know-Nothing Party in the 1850s, and Sam echoed their xenophobia, squawking to Orion that "there are so many abominable foreigners here (and among printers, too) who hate everything American."[60] He again voiced a lengthy litany of complaints. "I always thought the eastern people were patterns of uprightness; but I never before saw so many whisky-swilling, God-despising heathens as I find in this part of the country. I believe I am the only person in the Inquirer office that does not drink."[61] Nor did he shy away from further swipes at abolitionists and independent Black people. "How do you like 'free-soil?' I would like amazingly to see a good, old-fashioned negro."[62] Since Sam sent these letters with a view to having them reprinted by Orion, he was evolving, gradually, into a newspaper correspondent.

Before heading west again, Sam toured Independence Hall and recorded his feelings of "awe and reverence" as he entered the room where the Declaration of Independence was drafted.[63] He went on to Washington, D.C., where he marveled at the "fine specimens of architecture" and visited the halls of Congress, sending back vivid sketches of William Seward of New York and Thomas Hart Benton of Missouri. "Mr. Seward is a slim, dark, bony individual, and looks like a respectable wind would blow him out of the country . . . Mr. Benton sits silent and gloomy in the midst of the din, like a lion imprisoned in a cage of monkeys, who, feeling his superiority, disdains to notice their chattering."[64] Pretty good prose for an adolescent writer.

PRINTER'S DEVIL

One spring morning in 1854, Orion, Jane, and Henry Clemens were having breakfast when Sam suddenly materialized, brandishing a gun in a menacing fashion. "You wouldn't let me buy a gun," he exclaimed, "so I bought one myself, and I am going to use it, now, in self-defense."[65] Jane Clemens was alarmed by this threat until her son dissolved in typical laughter at his prank.

Orion tried to tempt Sam with a job at the *Muscatine Journal*. He accepted the offer for a few months then ended up back at his former printing job in St. Louis. It should be mentioned that Orion had undergone a political conversion in reaction to the Kansas-Nebraska Act, which repealed the Missouri Compromise and might open the western territories to slavery. Liberated by the free state atmosphere of Iowa, Orion editorialized in his paper that "the 'inevitable hour' for slavery has come . . . Slavery has culminated, and from the present, now, its decay may be dated."[66] Not yet an unabashed abolitionist, Orion was referred to locally as a "black Republican."

By his late teens, Sam Clemens had shown flashes of talent, intermixed with rank bigotry. Twenty years later he left a withering portrait of his youthful self as "a callow fool, a self-sufficient ass, a mere human tumble-bug, stern in air, heaving at his bit of dung and imagining that he is remodeling the world & is entirely capable of doing it right. Ignorance, intolerance, egotism, self-assertion, opaque perception, dense & pitiful chuckle-headedness—& an almost pathetic unconsciousness of it all. That is what I was at 19–20."[67] With hindsight he attributed these unattractive features to his southern upbringing.

Whatever his grievances with Orion, Sam happily sought his protection in moments of need. After leaving his printing post in St. Louis, he went to work with Orion again, this time in Keokuk, Iowa. In December 1854, Orion had married Mary Stotts—always referred to as "Mollie"—who bore him a daughter named Jennie. Mollie seems to have induced her husband to unload his half interest in the *Muscatine Journal* and move to Keokuk, her hometown, and he set up shop in June 1855.

Situated a bare fifty miles from Hannibal, Keokuk was a tiny town of 650 residents, with muddy streets and wooden plank sidewalks. From its third-floor office on Main Street, Orion's business, styled the Ben Franklin Book and Job Office, performed pretty banal work, printing business cards and forms—not something to set Sam's heart on fire. Sam was wooed with a promise of decent wages and a junior partnership, only to have it turn into a throwback to the bad times he had suffered with Orion in Hannibal.

Nor did the low-caliber work provide any offsetting satisfactions. With Henry Clemens and Dick Higham serving as his assistants, Sam worked on the Keokuk City Directory and other mundane projects, and blamed Orion for undermining his efforts. "They take Henry and Dick away from me too . . . they throw all my plans into disorder by taking my hands away from their work," he protested to his family. "I can't work blindly—without system."[68] By now an experienced typesetter, he had seen many professional print shops only to stumble back into the dreary tumult of working for the inept Orion.

Still, there were modest milestones to celebrate. As he sat up smoking in bed at night, Sam Clemens read voraciously and became acquainted with Charles Dickens and Edgar Allan Poe. On January 17, 1856—the 150th anniversary of Ben Franklin's birth—he stood up at Ivins House and debuted as a speaker at a printers' banquet, revealing a latent talent that must have surprised audience and speaker alike. "Blushing and slowly getting upon his feet, stammering in the start," one listener recollected, "he finally rallied his powers, and when he sat down, his speech was pronounced by all present a remarkable production of pathos and wit, with the latter, however, predominating, convulsing his hearers with round after round of applause."[69] Most significantly, Sam Clemens would soon publish three travel letters in a Keokuk paper under the pen name "Thomas Jefferson Snodgrass" and for the first time would be paid for his prose. The reading, the speaking, the writing—the faint outlines of a promising literary career were beginning to emerge.

CHAPTER FOUR

"Darling Existence"

Throughout his life, Sam Clemens would be attracted both to moneymaking ventures that promised to yield colossal fortunes and to nostrums that would rescue humankind from disease and suffering. Before he left Keokuk in October 1856 and went off to work for a Cincinnati printer, he happened upon a book, recently published, that held forth the possibility of accomplishing both miracles in one fell swoop. Written by William L. Herndon, it was titled *Exploration of the Valley of the Amazon, Made Under Direction of the Navy Department,* and it described a glorious four-thousand-mile trek that, Mark Twain recalled, passed "through the heart of an enchanted land, a land wastefully rich in tropical wonders, a romantic land where all the birds and flowers and animals were of the museum varieties, and where the alligator and the crocodile and the monkey seemed as much at home as if they were in the Zoo."[1]

The exotic beauty of this place, however, was not the book's chief draw so much as Herndon's discussion of how Incas in the Andes chewed coca leaves, rendering them "silent and patient" as they performed prodigious feats of labor in silver mines.[2] Sam came to believe that the coca plant held extraordinary powers that he could harness. Pretty soon, he had concocted a plan to sail to the Amazon's headwaters in a quest to monopolize the coca trade and ascend into the ranks of the global rich. He felt "a longing to open up a trade in coca with the world. During months I dreamed that dream, and tried to conjure ways to get to Pará [a Brazilian state] and spring that splendid enterprise upon an unsuspecting planet."³ The moment previewed much of Twain's future business career, with its grandiose schemes that often obscured practical pitfalls, treading a fine line between inspiration and pure folly.

The would-be coca mogul recruited two allies, a Keokuk physician named Martin and a youthful businessman named Ward. In August 1856, Sam told his brother Henry, in strictest confidence, that he and Ward would start for Brazil in six weeks. Sam had deliberately misled Orion, telling him Ward would venture alone to Brazil while he waited patiently in New York or New Orleans to receive a favorable report from him. "But that don't suit me," Sam confided to Henry. "My confidence in human nature does not extend quite that far. I won't depend upon Ward's judgment, or anybody's else—I want to see with my own eyes, and form my own opinion. But you know what Orion is. When he gets a notion into his head, and more especially if it is an erroneous one, the Devil can't get it out again . . . Ma knows my determination but *even she* counsels me to keep it from Orion." Orion had been talking "grandly about furnishing me with fifty or a hundred dollars in six weeks," but Sam, knowing his brother's changeable nature, did not trust a word of it.⁴

After a winter spent in Cincinnati and with only thirty dollars in his pocket, the cocksure Sam Clemens hopped a steamer to New Orleans on April 15, 1857, in an "ancient tub" christened the *Paul Jones*.⁵ By this time, Martin and Ward had jettisoned the project. Always careless with details, Sam was shocked to discover a critical flaw in his thinking. In New Orleans, he "inquired about ships leaving for Pará and discovered there weren't any and learned that there probably wouldn't be any during that century."⁶ Indeed, it turned out no ship had *ever* traveled from New Orleans to Pará. Looking back, Mark Twain blamed his own impulsive nature, plunging headlong into new projects, bedazzled by their supposed worth. "I have been punished many and many a time, and bitterly, for doing things and reflecting afterward, but these tortures have been of no value to me."⁷

As it happened, fate had more interesting things awaiting the twenty-one-year-old Sam Clemens than cornering the coca market. Onboard the *Paul Jones,* he became acquainted with its young pilot, Horace Bixby, who was so adept at his craft that he was licensed to work both the Mississippi and Missouri Rivers. Sam claimed he and Bixby hit it off and "pretty soon I was doing a lot of steering for him in his daylight watches."[8] Bixby would remember his first impression of Sam as "a big, shaggy-haired youth with a slow, drawling speech that was provoking to anyone that happened to be in a hurry."[9] When his Amazonian adventure proved a boondoggle, Sam begged Bixby to teach him the piloting trade on the lower Mississippi between St. Louis and New Orleans. Here lay the supreme ambition of any Hannibal boy—to be a riverboat pilot, with a salary equal to that of the U.S. vice president or a Supreme Court justice. Bixby agreed on the condition that Sam would pay him a hefty five hundred dollars, with one hundred laid out in advance, a sum Sam borrowed from his brother-in-law, William Moffett. This decision of Sam's disturbed Jane Clemens, who knew the disreputable types working the river and feared the worst for her son. "I gave him up then, for I always thought steamboating was a wicked business and was sure he would meet bad associates."[10] Jane extracted a fresh pledge that he would abstain from intoxicating liquors.

A blunt man who spat out rapid-fire instructions, the thirty-one-year-old Bixby immediately told Sam, "My boy, you must get a little memorandum-book, and every time I tell you a thing put it down right away. There's only one way to be a pilot, and that is to get this entire river by heart. You have to know it just like A B C."[11] For all his affection for Sam, he brooked no frivolity. "When I say I'll learn a man the river, I mean it," he warned Sam. "And you can depend on it, I'll learn him or kill him."[12]

Although Sam entered the job full of youthful bravado, it was a formidable undertaking: he had to master river sites and landmarks, both their nocturnal and daytime appearances, over twelve or thirteen hundred miles of broad, muddy river. He had to memorize innumerable shores, bends, reefs, snags, and sandbars, and study subtle shifts in the water's surface. "There is a light line of ripples, which no amateur can understand; a harmless-looking line of ripples, quiet and easy," which alerted the pilot to "the death of his ship if she gets there."[13] Nights were especially treacherous. As Bixby observed, "There were no signal-lights along the shore in those days . . . and on a dark, misty night . . . a pilot's judgment had to be founded on *absolute certainty*."[14]

Nobody had ever challenged Sam like this before. Overwhelmed with river details, he was awakened from his youthful slumber and thrust into a world of adult responsibility. The rigorous training gave structure and discipline to his vagabond character. An impossibly tough but understanding taskmaster, Bixby was impressed that Sam rose to the challenge. "Sam was always good-natured, and he had a natural taste for the river. He had a fine memory and never forgot anything I told him."[15] On another occasion, Bixby said of Sam, "In all my time I never knew a man who took to the labor of piloting with so little effort. He was born for it, just as some men are born to make poetry and some to paint pictures . . . Clemens kept on improving, and he went from one boat to another, getting better all the time."[16] This was the first time that Sam had ever really *stuck* to something. As river life weaned him from a lackadaisical adolescence, he was immeasurably proud of his progress, later boasting to Orion that "the young pilots who used to tell me, patronisingly, [sic] that I could never learn the river, cannot keep from showing a little of their chagrin at seeing me so far ahead of them. Permit me to 'blow my horn,' for I derive a *living* pleasure from these things."[17]

Such was the exalted status of a riverboat pilot that the Clemens clan basked in the glory of Sam becoming a cub pilot. Orion had sold his printing business in Keokuk and gone off to Tennessee with Mollie to study law and, if possible, unload some of the vaunted Tennessee land. Jane Clemens had moved in with Pamela and William Moffett in St. Louis, and Sam stayed with them whenever his boat docked there. Sam's niece Annie remembered the thrill they all felt about Sam's good fortune. "It seemed to me as if everyone was running up and down stairs and sitting on the steps to talk over the news. Piloting in those days was a dramatic and well-paid profession, and in a river town it was a great honor to have a pilot in the family."[18] Annie later told how Sam would thump the piano and sing by the hour. "He wore sideburns and had chestnut hair, though some call it red. It was very curly. My grandmother said that as a boy he would soak his hair in a tub of water and plaster it down to try and make it straight."[19]

Mark Twain always felt indebted to Pamela for her exceptional hospitality, for the "thousand affectionate kindnesses & services" she showed in his St. Louis days.[20] When the twenty-four-year-old Pamela married William, a man ten years her senior, he had scorned it as a match between an "old maid" and a "mouldy [sic] old bachelor" who was well-off.[21] A photo of Pamela shows a prim, matronly-looking woman with rimless glasses. Even when she became a semi-invalid late in life, Twain could never detect a blemish in her character, considered her incapable of deceit, and credited her with "a most kindly & gentle disposition."[22] A strict Presbyterian, she chided Sam for poaching on sacred topics and ridiculing the respectable things in life. Sam, an incorrigible tease, tried to tread gingerly with her, but often ended up upsetting her instead. On one occasion, in 1886, he wrote a revealing letter of apology. "I love you, & I am sorry for every time I have ever hurt you; but God Almighty knows I should keep on hurting you just the same if I were around; for I am built so, being merely in the image of God, but not otherwise resembling him enough to be mistaken for him by anybody but a very nearsighted person."[23] One clearly needed a rather thick skin to survive as Mark Twain's sister.

On the river Sam could escape family complications and fully emerge from Orion's shadow. With his restless soul, he found the mighty, rushing river his natural element and would long insist that his four years on the water were his life's most enjoyable. He began to perfect his deadpan storytelling style, letting punch lines explode in the listener's mind, not on the speaker's face, and his companions were often convulsed with laughter. "Piloting on the Mississippi River was not work to me; it was play—delightful play, vigorous play, adventurous play—and I loved it," he said.[24] The river never relinquished a drop of its romance. He spoke so nostalgically about it that his housekeeper later declared that "he loved the Mississippi almost as much as he loved a person, and he was always talking about it—what a wonderful river it was."[25] Those Mississippi years became the rapturous interlude of his life, distilling all the freedom of youth. "Oh! that was the darling existence," he pronounced forty years later. "There has been nothing comparable to it in my life since."[26]

This idyllic period left little time to spare for literary endeavors. "I cannot correspond with a newspaper," he explained to Orion and Mollie, "because when one is learning the river, he is not allowed to do or think of anything else."[27] He did manage, nonetheless, to publish some pieces in the St. Louis *Missouri Republican* and the New Orleans *Daily Crescent*. Commenting on the Lincoln-Douglas Senate race in Illinois, he leaned toward conservative positions, noting that Know-Nothings, ex-Whigs, and Democrats concurred that Stephen Douglas "ought to be" the winner.[28] He found time to read John Milton's *Paradise Lost* and was already taken with "the Arch-Fiend's terrible energy!"[29] After reading *The Age of Reason* by Thomas Paine, still a taboo volume, he began to toy with more unorthodox views on religion. "Disgusted by hypocrisy and bigotry," he later said of Paine, "he made war upon religion, fully believing that he was doing a good work."[30] Luckily for Twain, he befriended a pilot named George Ealer who "would read Shakespeare to me; not just casually but by the hour, when it was his watch, and I was steering."[31] Around this time, Sam Clemens also encountered the iconoclastic view of Delia Salter Bacon, expressed in her book *The Philosophy of the Plays of Shakespeare Unfolded,* that Francis Bacon and others had written the plays attributed to the actor William Shakespeare. He also ducked behind a barrel to read *The Fortunes of Nigel* by Sir Walter Scott— a writer he came to detest cordially.

First as a printer, then as a pilot, Sam Clemens had chosen two professions that promised to broaden his vision. With a true writer's instincts, he had already begun cramming a notebook with jottings that gave a glimpse into his busy mind. He had started tutoring himself in French, transcribing long lists of words and phrases. In a preview of his varied interests, he wrote out classifications of human appearance made by phrenologists, who believed that bodily constitutions conformed to psychological types. Describing the hot-blooded "sanguine" temperament, he penned a self-portrait of his own mercurial personality. "It is very sensitive and is first deeply hurt at a slight, the next emotion is violent rage, and in a few moments the cause and the result are both forgotten for the time being. It often forgives, but never entirely forgets an injury."[32]

Sam wasn't the only Clemens brother plying the Mississippi River: in 1858 he had wangled his brother Henry, almost twenty, a job as a "mud clerk"—a subordinate purser—on his sidewheeler, the *Pennsylvania*. However testy he could be toward Orion and Pamela, Sam lavished a selfless love on Henry. Three years younger than Sam, the witty Henry enjoyed reading, had a retentive memory, and exhibited a well-stocked mind. Docile, obedient, he was the adorable blue-eyed boy, the clear family favorite. Even though Henry sometimes tattled to their mother about Sam's misdeeds, when it came to Henry, Sam's usual cynicism seemed suspended. Henry was his confidant, his best comrade, and he later said that, except for his wife, Livy, he was never in such "entire sympathy" with a human being.[33] "He was the best boy in the whole region," Mark Twain recalled. "He never did harm to anybody, he never offended anybody. He was exasperatingly good. He had an overflowing abundance of goodness."[34] A model boy, but lovable. Orion noted the tight bond between his two younger brothers, describing Henry as "quiet, observing, thoughtful, leaning on Sam for protection."[35]

Sam's protective impulse toward Henry was palpable. In *Life on the Mississippi*, Twain tells how, on a trip aboard the *Pennsylvania*, the brutal pilot William Brown unfairly accused Henry of lying, grabbed a huge chunk of coal, and was ready to smash it over Henry's head when Sam rushed between them. According to Sam's account, he "hit Brown a good honest blow which stretched him out. I had committed the crime of crimes—I had lifted my hand against a pilot on duty . . . I stuck to him and pounded him with my fists a considerable time . . . but in the end he struggled free and jumped up and sprang to the wheel."[36] A contemporaneous letter Sam sent to Mollie Clemens gives a slightly different version of what happened on June 3. "Henry started out of the pilothouse—

Brown jumped up and collared him—turned him half way around and *struck him in the face!*—and him nearly six feet high—struck my little brother. I was wild from that moment."[37] Sam, though ordered off the boat, had made a point about the need for people to respect his younger brother. He would now take a different boat, hoping to rejoin the *Pennsylvania* when Brown left.

One night in New Orleans, before the *Pennsylvania* departed, the two brothers sat on a levee and discussed a topic never broached before—steamboat disasters. With brotherly solicitude, Sam advised Henry: "In case of accident, whatever you do, don't lose your head—the passengers will do that. Rush for the hurricane deck and to the life-boat . . . When the boat is launched, help the women and children into it. Don't get in yourself. The river is only a mile wide. You can swim ashore easily enough."[38] While the chief pilot bore the main responsibility for safeguarding passengers, the brothers agreed that subordinates should "at least stick to the boat, and give such minor service as chance might throw in the way."[39] Sam would soon wonder about the repercussions of this conversation as the *Pennsylvania,* with Henry aboard, began its journey upriver, while Sam followed in the *Alfred T. Lacey* two days later. Fifty years afterward, Twain reported that around the time of the voyage he had an eerie dream in St. Louis of amazing vividness: he saw Henry's corpse stretched out in a metal casket propped on two chairs, dressed in his clothing. A bouquet of white roses rested on his chest, with a lone crimson flower planted in the middle.

At dawn on June 13, 1858, the *Pennsylvania* blew up and burned near Helena, Arkansas. Three or four of its eight boilers exploded with such fierce intensity that the front part of the boat whirled into the sky, only to collapse back onto the stricken craft and set it aflame. The inferno claimed scores of lives, including that of pilot William Brown. Among those severely injured was Henry Clemens. Sam heard of the calamity when the *Alfred T. Lacey* reached Greenville, Mississippi, and someone hollered from the dock: "The *Pennsylvania* is blown up just below Memphis, at Ship Island! One hundred and fifty lives lost!"[40] That evening a shaken Sam Clemens learned from a Memphis paper that Henry was wounded but still alive. As he pieced together the story, he learned that Henry and a Mr. Wood had been blown into the water by the tremendous blast and had "struck out for shore, which was only a few hundred yards away; but Henry presently said he believed he was not hurt, . . . and therefore would swim back to the boat and help save the wounded. So they parted, and Henry returned."[41] Later on, Mark Twain tortured himself with the thought that Henry, by heading back to the disaster, had heeded his counsel and paid a terrible price.

But a letter that Sam wrote to Mollie Clemens five days afterward suggests that Henry could not possibly have returned to the burning craft. "Henry was asleep—was blown up—then fell back on the hot boilers, and I suppose that rubbish fell on him, for he is injured internally. He got into the water and swam to shore, and got into the flatboat with the other survivors. He had nothing on but his wet shirt, and he lay there burning up with a southern sun and freezing in the wind till the Kate Frisbee came along. His wounds were not dressed till he got to Memphis, 15 hours after the explosion. He was senseless and motionless for 12 hours after that."[42] There is no mention here of Henry heroically returning to the boat. Was this the accurate version, or did Sam Clemens alter the story to conceal his complicity in Henry's fate? Or did he later feel the need to find some redeeming feature and impose a heroic narrative on Henry?

By June 15, Sam reached the Cotton Exchange in Memphis, which had been turned into a makeshift hospital for the thirty-two scalded victims laid out on pallets on the floor. One observer recorded Twain's dramatic response to seeing his stricken brother, saying that as he "approached the bedside of the wounded man, his feelings so much overcame him, at the scalded and emaciated form before him, that he sunk [sic] to the floor overpowered."[43] Twain himself later wrote, "The sight I saw when I entered the large hall was new and strange to me. Two long rows of prostrate forms—more than forty, in all—and every face and head a shapeless wad of loose raw cotton. It was a grewsome [sic] spectacle. I watched there six days and nights, and a very melancholy experience it was . . . I saw many poor fellows removed to the 'death-room,' and saw them no more afterward."[44] With his lungs burned by steam, his body singed by flames, Henry had been brought to Memphis "in a senseless and almost lifeless condition."[45] Even though his face was not disfigured, the sight of his charred body unnerved his older brother. In the coming days, Henry would be only fitfully conscious and coherent, leaving Sam alone with his terrible thoughts.

Sam was impressed by the ministrations of Dr. Thomas Peyton—"What a magnificent man he was!"—who tended Henry with such devotion that, by the sixth night after the accident, it looked as if he might recover.[46] "I believe he is out of danger and will get well," he assured Sam before leaving for the evening.[47] Since he wanted Henry to sleep undisturbed and feared moaning patients might awaken him, Dr. Peyton entrusted Sam with a mission: if Henry woke up, he should have the doctor on duty give him an eighth of a grain of morphine. The scenario Dr. Peyton envisioned did occur, and Henry was roused from sleep by groans. When Sam approached the young medical student on duty, the latter grew flustered. "I have no way of measuring," he protested. "I don't know how much an eighth of a grain would be." As Henry's agitation worsened, Sam was beside himself. "If you have studied drugs," he told the medical student, "you ought to be able to judge an eighth of a grain of morphine."[48] Prodded by Sam, the young man measured a small amount of morphine onto the tip of a knife and administered it to Henry. Although Henry fell asleep, he was dead by morning, and Sam always suspected that an excessive morphine dose had hastened his brother's tragic demise.

Even before Henry died, an overwrought Sam poured out his grief to Mollie Clemens. "Long before this reaches you, my poor Henry,—my darling, my pride, my glory, my *all*, will have finished his blameless career, and the light of my life will have gone out in utter darkness," he wrote, sounding more like a father or lover than a brother. "The horrors of three days have swept over me—they have blasted my youth and left me an old man before my time. Mollie, there are grey hairs in my head to-night. For forty-eight hours I labored at the bedside of my poor burned and bruised, but uncomplaining brother, and then the star of my hope went out and left me in the gloom of despair." With aching sadness, he prayed to God to spare Henry and "to pour out the fulness of his just wrath upon my wicked head, but have mercy, mercy, mercy upon that unoffending boy."[49] Religious feeling still lay buried somewhere deep inside Sam Clemens, but such savage hurts as this would shake his faith.

In the immediate aftermath of his brother's death, Sam, exhausted from his harrowing vigil, slept for hours. Then he rose and went to view Henry's remains. Touched by his youthful beauty, some Memphis ladies had chipped in for a metal casket for Henry instead of the standard wooden model. Sam was startled to enter the room and see Henry just as he had pictured him in the dream, minus one detail: there were no white flowers on his chest. Then an elderly lady appeared with a large white bouquet, containing a red rose at its center, to complete the scene. The entire Clemens clan trooped back to Hannibal for the funeral at the First Presbyterian Church, and Henry was laid to rest beside Judge Clemens in the Old Baptist Cemetery. The stoical Jane Clemens had now suffered staggering losses: her husband and four of her seven children. In 1847 a Hannibal paper estimated that only half the children in town lived into adulthood, so her sad plight was not entirely atypical.

Of course, the story of Henry's death—his allegedly heroic but doomed behavior in returning to a burning ship, the uncanny dream and its realization—relies on Mark Twain's later and ever-fallible memory, yet it formed part of family lore. As Pamela's daughter Annie recalled, people in Memphis "had sent a young man up to St. Louis with Uncle Sam, who was so overcome with grief that they were afraid he would go insane. He was shadowed for years by the feeling that he was in a measure responsible for Henry's death." Twain expunged the dream story from *Life on the Mississippi* for fear of upsetting his mother, but Annie later testified that he needn't have worried. Sam had already told of the dream "before they started on the fatal trip," so that Jane Clemens knew of the dream "and often talked about it. He had told them about it before he went away but the family were not impressed; indeed they were amused that he took it so seriously."[50]

Mark Twain was never reconciled to his beloved brother's loss. As late as 1879 he even visited a medium and sought to communicate with

Henry. His reaction to the death revealed much about Sam Clemens at twenty-two: his melodramatic emotions, his capacity for guilt bordering on self-flagellation, his tendency to brood endlessly on past errors. Compounding his difficulty was that instead of his pure, loving feelings for Henry, he was left grappling with his ongoing psychodrama with Orion. The pangs of guilt never deserted him. In 1876 Twain published a story, "The Facts Concerning the Recent Carnival of Crime in Connecticut," in which a hideous dwarf, representing the narrator's conscience, torments him with sadistic glee and accuses him of betraying his younger brother's trust. "He always lovingly trusted in you with a fidelity that your manifold treacheries were not able to shake. He followed you about like a dog, content to suffer wrong and abuse if he might only be with you." The narrator, he says, had pushed his brother into an ice-covered brook, then roared with laughter as the boy struggled in freezing water. "Man, you will never forget the gentle, reproachful look he gave you as he struggled shivering out, if you live a thousand years!"[51] For Mark Twain, when it came to hellish torments of conscience, there existed no statute of limitations. In later years, he told a friend that his entire life was "one long apology," with him down on his knees pleading for forgiveness.[52]

Right before the steamboat debacle, Sam Clemens, a "heedless and giddy lad," enjoyed a romantic adventure that would exert a mysterious grip on his imagination until his death.[53] In May 1858, while awaiting departure of a steamboat in New Orleans, he wandered over one night to another boat, the *John J. Roe,* one of whose officers he knew, William Youngblood. The ship had a piano and a big deck for dancing, and there Sam met fourteen-year-old Laura Wright of Warsaw, Missouri (not to be confused with Laura Hawkins of Hannibal), who had come downriver on the ship with her uncle Youngblood. The daughter of a rich Missouri judge, she was entrancing to Sam, who found her irresistible. In his frankly romantic retelling, he evoked the "enchanted vision" of "that comely child, that charming child . . . that unspoiled little maid, that fresh flower of the woods and the prairies." He limned an idealized girl "in the unfaded bloom of her youth, with her plaited tails dangling from her young head and her white summer frock puffing about in the wind."[54] Twenty years later, in a more circumspect mood, he described Laura, by then a teacher, to one of her pupils: "She was a very little girl, with a very large spirit, a long memory, a wise head, a great appetite for books, a good mental digestion, with grave ways, & inclined to introspection—an unusual girl."[55]

Sam Clemens—and then Mark Twain—found a special charm in beautiful young girls who trembled on the brink of womanhood, and Laura's appeal was instantaneous. "I was not four inches from the girl's elbow during our waking hours for the next three days."[56] At the end of this delirious encounter, they parted with a prophecy—"We shall meet again 30 years from now"—and Laura gave Sam a small gold ring as a gift.[57] Mark Twain would commemorate their parting date—May 6, 1858—as sacred for the rest of his days.

With his penchant for rewriting history, Mark Twain made it sound as if he had never met Laura again after this intoxicating meeting. Yet his correspondence makes clear that he swapped letters with Laura for a while and visited her at least once at her home in Warsaw. As they corresponded, some misunderstanding arose that led to hurt feelings, and both were too proud to hazard the first move toward a rapprochement. We know all this because in February 1861, Sam consulted a fortune teller in New Orleans named Madame Caprell, who read horoscopes. She got many things wrong, Sam believed, but described the contretemps with Laura with astonishing accuracy, claiming Mrs. Wright had sabotaged the relationship.

Afterward Sam wrote in detail to Orion and Mollie about the session: "But that about that girl's [mother] being 'cranky,' and playing the devil with me, *was* about the neatest thing she performed—for although I have never spoken of the matter, I happen to know that she spoke truth. The young lady has been beaten by the old one, though, through the romantic agency of intercepted letters, and the girl still thinks *I* was in fault—

and always will, I reckon, for I don't see how she'll ever find out the contrary . . . But drat the woman, she *did* tell the truth, and I won't deny it. But she said *I* would speak to Miss Laura first—and I'll stake my last shirt on it, she missed it there."[58] Sam had listened to Madame Caprell in silence for half an hour, transfixed by the "very startling things" and "wonderful guesses" she had made.[59] Three years later, he inquired of his mother and sister, "What has become of that girl of mine that got married? I mean Laura Wright"—now Laura Dake.[60] Not long after, he had a dream of meeting Laura when she was out driving in a carriage and they "said good bye and shook hands."[61] Still monitoring her doings in 1867, he wrote that one of the "old sweethearts I have been dreaming of so long has got five children now."[62]

The image of Laura Wright would never fade from Mark Twain's highly susceptible imagination, tantalizing him with an imperishable ideal of love. She would become the model for his future fascination with young girls who hovered on the borderline between girlhood and womanhood—chaste, pure, perfect—virginal girls on the eve of puberty. The whole relationship was as insubstantial as a dream, yet Mark Twain, an arch romantic, hung weighty memories on this slender wisp of reality. Laura would appear as a character in *The Gilded Age* and would reappear as his "dream-sweetheart" in the 1898 piece "My Platonic Sweetheart." As with his wife, Mark Twain romanticized and spiritualized his pursuit of a considerably younger female. In his rosy memories, Laura Wright would stay eternally young, never facing the tougher test of real human relationships, fraught with difficulties. Instead, she was allowed to float high above any conceivable reality in a gauzy sphere of untouched, ethereal perfection.

CHAPTER FIVE

"A Ragged and Dirty Bunch"

On April 9, 1859, after an impressively short two-year span of learning navigation, Samuel Clemens, at twenty-three, received his license as a steamboat pilot for journeys between St. Louis and New Orleans, a credential that catapulted him upward in the river world and for which his tutor, Captain Horace Bixby, was justly proud. "There never was a better boy," he declared. "He was bound to be great, whatever his course in life. I believe that he would have owned a line of steamboats had he kept to the river."[1] After the disapproving attitudes of Judge Clemens and Orion, Sam needed an older male figure who believed in him implicitly, and he had found that man in Horace Bixby. After his first run on the *Alfred T. Lacey,* Sam was assigned a pilot job on the *City of Memphis,* the largest boat operating on the river. Then, in October, he assumed the helm of the *A. B. Chambers,* winning general admiration. "He was not a great pilot, but he was a brave fellow," said first mate Grant Marsh. "He didn't know what fear was . . . When the steamboat went aground north of Cairo . . . Twain braved ice floes to lead a party scavenging for fuel."[2]

With his new financial security and a fair measure of status, Sam Clemens grew cocky, sprouting muttonchop whiskers and trading in his old garments for fancy new ones, including patent leather shoes, striped shirts, and white duck pants. Enjoying the role of big shot, he made a point of flashing large bills. In a bit of braggadocio, he told Orion about paying his pilot dues at the Western Boatmen's Benevolent Association, where he liked "to let the d–d rascals get a glimpse of a hundred dollar bill peeping out from amongst notes of smaller dimensions, whose faces I do *not* exhibit! You will despise this egotism, but I tell you there is a 'stern joy' in it."[3]

Even though Sam Clemens published little during his four-year stint on the river, he squandered nothing from a literary standpoint. He harvested the anecdotal riches of serving on more than a dozen boats and was so content that he foresaw a peaceful, never-ending life afloat. "Time drifted smoothly and prosperously on, and I supposed—and hoped—that I was going to follow the river the rest of my days, and die at the wheel when my mission was ended."[4]

Then the sudden outbreak of the Civil War shut traffic on the Mississippi and started the slow demise of the steamboat world Sam had cherished. The river that had witnessed so many joyous scenes was now stripped of color and brimmed with menacing black gunboats. Painfully ambivalent about the war, Sam Clemens reflected the manifold crosscurrents roiling Missouri. "It was hard for us to get our bearings," he admitted.[5] In general, he opposed secession, but that didn't mean he opposed slavery. In the 1860 presidential race, he had favored John Bell and the Constitutional Union Party, which was dedicated to preserving the Union and was neutral on slavery, and he would flip-flop on whether to side with the North or the South. When South Carolina seceded in December 1860, he and a copilot fell into a heated argument. "My pilotmate was a New Yorker. He was strong for the Union; so was I . . . A month later the secession atmosphere had considerably thickened on the Lower Mississippi, and I became a rebel; so did he."[6]

Sam Clemens happened to be in New Orleans on January 26, 1861, when Louisiana left the Union, and he later recorded this impression in his notebook: "Great rejoicing. Flags, Dixie, soldiers."[7] The next day he sent a note to a friend, his oldest surviving letter written to somebody outside his family. In a wild, anarchic style, sprinkled with humor, he showed an early skill at comic prose, but also an ability to shroud—and evade—grave subjects in a blizzard of jokes. There is scarcely a serious word about secession, just joshing about a pup named "Secession" and a hodgepodge of gossip about girls and trivia.[8] Sam sidestepped entirely the historic significance of the moment.

While steaming south on the Mississippi aboard the *Alonzo Child,* he first heard tidings at Vicksburg of the firing on Fort Sumter. His crew, captained by secessionist John De Haven, rejoiced, leaving no doubt of their Confederate leanings: "We hoisted stars & bars & played Dixie," Twain wrote.[9] A few days later, when the boat steamed into New Orleans, the Confederate flag fluttered from its jack staff, with Sam serving as one of its pilots. All romance was suddenly drained from the job, superseded by peril. As his niece Annie Moffett recalled of her uncle, "He was obsessed with the fear that he might be arrested by government agents and forced to act as a pilot on a government gunboat while a man stood by with a pistol ready to shoot him if he showed the least sign of a false move."[10] In traveling the river, Sam had passed by a string of secessionist states, disproportionately exposing him to the southern viewpoint.

At this stage of his life he was largely apolitical but abruptly found himself in a situation where he no longer enjoyed the luxury of straddling both sides. One pilot reckoned that of 128 pilots on the lower Mississippi, only five favored the Union, and they were threatened with being blackballed from future work if they served the North. The following year, when Jane Clemens tried to collect a $200 debt that Will Bowen owed to Sam, Bowen grumbled that "no secesh [i.e., secessionist] ever should have $1.00 of his money . . . I said Mr. B, Sam is no secesh." Jane reminded him that when they were on the *Alonzo Child* together "they quarreled and Sam let go the wheel to whip Will for talking secesh and made Will hush."[11]

Sam found himself on the last boat to slip through the Union blockade at Memphis, shutting the lower Mississippi to commercial traffic. The ship was shelled by batteries at Jefferson Barracks in St. Louis, shattering glass and shredding smokestacks on the voyage's last night. As Bixby observed of Sam, "He had tasted a bit of the difficulties of war; blockades were to be run, and hazard was to take the place of another charm the river had . . . His boat's smokestacks had bullet-holes in them—and the Civil War had only begun."[12] Sam Clemens swallowed hard, reflecting on the grim choices he faced. "I'm not very anxious to get up into a glass perch and be shot at by either side," he said. "I'll go home and reflect on the matter."[13] As a Confederate pilot, he would be exposed to ceaseless danger, but as a Union pilot, he would also face the double jeopardy of being suspected of southern sympathies. Describing her uncle's profound quandary, Annie Moffett observed that while he showed reverence for the Union and the American flag, "he was a Southerner, his friends were all Southern, his sympathies were with the South."[14] His river experiences had only deepened his ties to the South as he worked with predominantly southern pilots and plied the *lower* stretch of the Mississippi between St. Louis and New Orleans.

With Jane Clemens favoring secession and Orion strong for the Union, Annie noted Sam's "divided loyalty and the emotional strain he was under."[15] She said that when he came to St. Louis he was "almost afraid of leaving the house" and began to hide with a neighbor.[16] Barring nosy intruders, Jane Clemens issued "strict orders that if anyone called and asked for Mr. Clemens she was to be called."[17] Sam returned to Hannibal only to discover that federal troops occupied a town only recently bedecked with Confederate flags. At the wharf, he and two other pilots were swiftly approached by a Union lieutenant, taken under arrest, and brought to St. Louis. According to pilot Absalom C. Grimes, Union general John B. Gray attempted to coax them into serving as pilots on Union troop ships. When Gray got sidetracked by female visitors, the three pilots skedaddled out a side door and escaped to safety.

In terribly fractured Missouri, with families fiercely split over the war, the state contributed soldiers to both northern and southern armies. Mark Twain later evoked the violent, internecine dissension that engulfed Missouri, a border state riven "between Unionist and Confederate occupations, sudden maraudings and bush-whackings and raids."[18] The pro-southern governor, Claiborne Jackson, tried futilely to push through a bill of secession and flouted Washington's call for troops, telling Lincoln, "Not one man will Missouri furnish to carry on any such unholy crusade against her Southern sisters," and he interpreted the entry of Union troops as an "invasion."[19] Around the time Sam malingered in

"A RAGGED AND DIRTY BUNCH"

St. Louis, Captain Nathaniel Lyon and pro-Union troops swooped down on Camp Jackson, an encampment of pro-southern state militia established by the governor, who were poised to seize a huge cache of weapons at the federal arsenal. When Lyon publicly marched his captives through the streets, it provoked two days of riots, but the bloody encounter left the federal government in full control of the city.

To counter this foray, Governor Jackson passed a bill that transformed the old militia into the Missouri State Guard. It was not aligned with the Confederacy but was clearly designed to resist any federal incursion. It was headed by General Sterling Price and commanded in northeast Missouri by Thomas A. Harris, who had operated the Hannibal telegraph. One day a stranger under the assumed name of Smith arrived at the Moffett residence in St. Louis with a specific mission. "He had come," recalled Annie, "with the wild project of forming a company to join General Price. Uncle Sam, tired of his life of inaction and the role of semi-prisoner, joyously agreed to the plan."[20] Debarred from his river job and cooped up with his family, Sam may have seen no plausible alternative. Nothing in his behavior typed him as a rabid, fire-eating Confederate, although he was probably more enthusiastic than he later let on. It was likely Sam who printed a letter in the *Hannibal Messenger* that reported: "The boys are responding bravely to the call of the Governor" and were ready "to strike when the proper time comes."[21]

With Union forces patrolling Hannibal, Sam and other young men met secretly one night and formed a militia in response to Governor Jackson's call for fifty thousand troops to beat back Yankee invaders. For two memorable weeks, Sam would serve as a second lieutenant in a Missouri State outfit known as the Marion Rangers (also called the Ralls County Rangers) composed of his Hannibal compatriots. Talkative on almost every conceivable topic, Mark Twain withheld a full account of his experience until December 1885 when he knew he had dodged this touchy subject long enough and penned a semifictional article for the *Century Illustrated Monthly Magazine* called "The Private History of a Campaign That Failed."[22] Technically a member of a volunteer company, he had never served in the Confederacy, but he would admit numerous times to having been a "rebel" in the Missouri State Guard, whose Confederate tenor was transparent. Later on, after Missouri seceded, the Missouri State Guard was absorbed into the Confederate army.

In "The Private History," Twain minimized his weeks with the pro-Confederate militia by playing it mostly for laughs, sometimes reducing his service to a rollicking jaunt by harmless, overaged boys who knew nothing of combat. For years he would employ clowning to mask the gravity of the situation and lampoon himself as a laughable coward. He followed this strategy in private correspondence too, writing after the war to Confederate general M. Jeff Thompson: "I was a soldier in the rebel army in Missouri for two weeks once, we never won any victories to speak of. We never could get the enemy to stand still when we wanted to fight, & we were generally on the move when the enemy wanted to fight."[23] In another letter, he explained facetiously that he was "incapacitated by fatigue" through persistent retreating.[24]

"The Private History" starts as a boyish lark, with Twain contending that he was "grateful to have a change, new scenes, new occupations, a new interest. In my thoughts that was as far as I went."[25] In slapstick style, he describes the contingent of bumbling young men setting out from Hannibal on a dark night and heading toward Ralls County, ten miles away, where they swore allegiance to Missouri, their heads stuffed with noble legends of southern chivalry. According to one participant, the group had no "tents, arms or commissary stores," while Jane Clemens remembered a "ragged and dirty bunch."[26] The young men poach peaches and melons and curl up in corncribs at night. Twain seasons his story with funny bits about stubborn horses and mules. In later notes, he portrayed his youthful self thus: "Sam took mosquito blisters for a mortal disease. Used to sit on his horse in prairie on picket duty & cry & curse & go to sleep in the hot sun."[27] He suffered a troublesome saddle boil and sprained his ankle tumbling from a hayloft. In "The Private History," the playful romp is punctuated now and then by somber thoughts. When Union soldiers approach, the Marion Rangers crouch in a ravine on a rainy night and the author reflects: "The drenching we were getting was misery enough, but a deeper misery still was the reflection

"A RAGGED AND DIRTY BUNCH"

that the halter might end us before we were a day older. A death of this shameful sort had not occurred to us as being among the possibilities of war. It took the romance all out of the campaign."[28] After more episodes of "horse-play and school-boy hilarity," a Union soldier, dimly visible in the night, though not in uniform, appears in the forest.[29] Twain fires at the man and is horrified to see him sprawled dead in a puddle of blood. "The thought shot through me that I was a murderer; that I had killed a man—a man who had never done me any harm."[30]

It turned out that Sam was one of six people who fired simultaneously on the unarmed man, so the burden of guilt was equally shared. From its earlier, jocular tone, the reminiscence darkens into a searing indictment of war's cruelty. Sam can't banish thoughts of the death because "the taking of that unoffending life seemed such a wanton thing. And it seemed an epitome of war—the killing of strangers against whom you feel no personal animosity . . . My campaign was spoiled . . . I resolved to retire from this avocation of sham soldiership while I could have some remnant of my self-respect."[31]

However eloquent and heartfelt, the elegiac antiwar message concerned war in general, avoiding the critical question of what *this* war was all about: the preservation of the Union and, ultimately, slavery's extinction. In the end, "The Private History" is unsatisfying because it is devoid of any political or ideological content. Instead of rectifying Twain's twenty-four-year omission of what he did during the war, it left many critical questions dangling in the air—the sure sign of an unresolved conflict. The piece was Twain at his best and at his worst: one part sage, one part buffoon. It is also impossible to credit the story of the shot soldier. One of Sam's fellow soldiers, Absalom Grimes, said nobody was killed, only a horse, and that Mark Twain invented the human killing—a conclusion echoed by most Twain biographers.[32] Twain ends "The Private History" with a witticism: "I knew more about retreating than the man that invented retreating."[33]

Twain's misadventure with the Marion Rangers ends when the detachment receives word of a Union regiment bearing down on them. "So about half of our fifteen, including myself, mounted and left on the instant"; Twain wrote, "the others yielded to persuasion and staid—staid through the war."[34] To add spice to his tale, Twain claimed that the Union colonel in hot pursuit was Ulysses S. Grant, but the latter's thrust into Missouri against General Thomas Harris came somewhat later. Making light of his wartime experience, Mark Twain insisted that the company crumbled because they "ran out of Worcestershire sauce."[35] Its early dissolution enabled him to claim he had not deserted, but he was never quite sure of that. As he told a friend sixty years later, he was "troubled in my conscience a little, for I had enlisted, and was not clear as to my lawful right to disenlist."[36] His brief war tenure later left Mark Twain with an agonizing dilemma. He knew northerners would look suspiciously on his service on the Confederate side, while southerners would be no less contemptuous of his overly hasty desertion. Clearly Sam Clemens held glaringly ambivalent feelings about the war. He believed enough in secession to join a militia but opted out with a convenient speed that suggests something less than stern devotion to the southern cause. It is telling that Twain should have left such a welter of confusion about one of his life's most consequential decisions.

Luckily for Sam, Orion never wavered in his fealty to the Union or its war aims. While Sam mocked his brother's mutable views on politics, he conceded, with some overstatement, his consistency on one all-important issue: "Born and reared among slaves and slave-holders, he was yet an abolitionist from his boyhood to his death."[37] If Orion was a figure of fun, he was also high-minded. Of his absentminded brother, Sam said that he had "a grave mien and big earnest eyes" with "a precocious intellect, and a voracious appetite for books and study."[38] His switch from Whig to Republican had won plaudits from his St. Louis mentor, Judge Edward Bates. Bates had been a losing presidential contender against Lincoln, who then rewarded him with a cabinet appointment as attorney general. A former slaveholder who freed his slaves, Bates was an almost

"A RAGGED AND DIRTY BUNCH"

biblical-looking figure, with a full white beard, who helped to solidify Lincoln's support among moderate Republicans.

In January 1861, Orion traveled to St. Louis to solicit a government post from Bates and dragooned Sam into this lobbying campaign, asking him to send Bates a letter "recommending me for a clerkship . . . It will be a great advantage to me to get some such office, as I can then support myself and family, which will be a huge gratification, and probably be able to pay some debts, which will also be gratifying."[39] Once in office in March, Bates duly urged Secretary of State William Seward to name Orion as secretary of a territory. While Bates didn't submit a breathless endorsement of Orion and conceded he possessed only middling talents, he praised him as "honest & manly" and noted that he had braved "opposition amounting almost to persecution" for espousing Republican views in slaveholding territory.[40] The good news for Orion came through on March 27 when he was appointed secretary of the newly formed Nevada Territory—second in power only to the governor—with a yearly salary of $1,800. Sam, who envied his brother's newfound "distinction" and "financial splendor," was to accompany him.[41] Sam would thus be sprung, ironically, from the Civil War by Orion's solid Republican credentials and high-level contact in the Lincoln administration.

Stuck in political limbo after defecting from the Marion Rangers, Sam must have viewed Orion's appointment as a godsend and happily seized the chance to escape the moral quandary presented by the national conflict. Attorney General Bates had taken a tough, pitiless stand against secessionist partisans in Missouri, arguing that arrest alone was too lenient for them. "They should be *summarily shot by thousands*," he decided.[42] Sam Clemens would sneak out of Missouri under the auspices of an attorney general who might well have had him executed. Orion, bogged down in debt, needed to borrow money to make the Nevada trip, and Sam, still flush with cash from the river, struck a deal with him: if Orion excused his recent Confederate escapade, he would pay their joint passage overland. There also existed an expectation that Sam would serve as the private secretary to the new territorial secretary. He

AFLOAT

imagined that the war would last only three months and he would then resume his lovely idyll on the Mississippi. The detour, however, would prove more than temporary and would free Sam Clemens to redefine his personality far from the stifling constraints of Missouri and its slavery, starting his slow, halting, and never-quite-complete transformation into a northerner.

On July 18, Sam and his brother left St. Louis and set off on a marathon trip westward to the Nevada Territory. The conscientious Orion, noted Sam, toted along "six pounds of Unabridged Dictionary."[43] Although he didn't know it, Sam Clemens had made an irrevocable break from his past life in Missouri. Three days later, Union troops suffered a catastrophic rout at Bull Run, underscoring that the war would be no short-lived affair. As his steamboat, the *Sioux City*, traversed the Missouri River to St. Joseph, on the western edge of the state, Sam was giddily excited at the prospect of "the long strange journey" ahead and of the "curious new world" he would inhabit.[44] When the brothers arrived in St. Joseph, they booked passage on the overland stagecoach to Carson City, Nevada Territory, meaning they would ride behind large teams of horses and mules for eighteen days and nights. In his unforgettable, fictionalized chronicle of the trip, *Roughing It*, Mark Twain resurrected "the wild sense of freedom" as he headed west, wedged into a stagecoach alongside stacks of mail packed in with the passengers, a jolting, hell-for-leather ride "through sagebrush, over sand and alkali plains, wolves and Indians, starvation and smallpox—everything to make the journey interesting."[45]

As he describes his departure for Carson City, one feels all the footloose, carefree excitement of young Sam Clemens lighting out for the territory, shedding the burdens of his past and experiencing pristine feelings of joy. "It was a superb summer morning, and all the landscape was brilliant with sunshine. There was a freshness and breeziness, too, and an exhilarating sense of emancipation from all sorts of cares and responsibilities, that almost made us feel that the years we had spent in the close, hot city, toiling and slaving, had been wasted and thrown away."[46]

"A RAGGED AND DIRTY BUNCH"

He smoked his pipe with exquisite pleasure aboard a "great swinging and swaying" stagecoach, "drawn by six handsome horses."[47] Travel would always be a sovereign remedy for his troubles. Not surprisingly, he immortalized the Pony Express rider, who "was usually a little bit of a man, brim full of spirit and endurance . . . he must be always ready to leap into the saddle and be off like the wind!"[48]

Racing across country that was brand-new to him, Sam didn't distinguish himself by his tolerance for the new sights and sounds and he reserved special bile for Native Americans. In the wild country west of Salt Lake City, he wrote, "We came across the wretchedest type of mankind I have ever seen, . . . I refer to the Goshoot [sic] Indians. From what we could see and all we could learn, they are very considerably inferior to even the despised Digger Indians of California; inferior to all races of savages on our continent."[49] He described their poverty-stricken existence in virulently racist terms, an encounter, he asserted, that cured him of the "mellow moonshine of romance" about Indians.[50] Resorting to the most scurrilous language, he called the Goshoots "treacherous, filthy and repulsive."[51] Mark Twain showed no early enlightenment in his view of Native Americans nor any awareness of how white settlement had shaped their often lowly situation. With Blacks, he would be capable of considerable growth, but it would take much more time and experience for him to graduate to a higher level of awareness with Native communities.

As reported in *Roughing It*, Sam's first encounter with the Mormons in Salt Lake City brought forth equally unsparing reactions. He picked up a copy of the Mormon Bible and subjected it to a scathing critique—funny if unfair—that derided the tome as so sleepy and pretentious it constituted "chloroform in print. If Joseph Smith composed this book, the act was a miracle—keeping awake while he did it was, at any rate."[52] He drew laughs from a burlesque monologue in which he had the polygamist Brigham Young bemoan the bother of having to sleep with seventy-two wives. "It appeared to me that the whole seventy-two women snored at once. The roar was deafening . . . Take my word for it, ten or eleven wives is all you need—never go over it."[53] Mark Twain allowed that the Mormon code of morals was "unobjectionable," even as he grumbled that it was swiped from the New Testament without proper credit.[54]

On August 14, 1861, the overland stagecoach pulled into Carson City, the capital of the Nevada Territory, having survived endless stretches of desert splashed with sagebrush. A little the worse for wear, Sam stepped from the stagecoach "tired, discouraged, white with alkali dust" and not knowing a soul except Orion.[55] The sight that first greeted his eyes must have made him wonder whether the lengthy trip was worth the grueling effort. It was a strange town with a desert floor below and snowcapped peaks above. Boasting a population of a few thousand people, it featured a main street composed of small white frame stores and sidewalks that were loose wooden planks that wobbled underfoot. Instead of wallpaper, many houses were lined inside with flour sacks sewn together.

Appearances could be deceptive. Two years earlier, the discovery of the Comstock Lode had sparked a silver rush to the area on a scale unseen since the California gold rush a decade earlier, a frenzy that spawned many fortunes, including that of George Hearst, the father of William Randolph Hearst. No less fortuitous for a future novelist, this area rich in minerals was even richer in colorful figures who would populate his imagination. Two months later Sam wrote ecstatically to his mother: "Nevada Territory is fabulously rich in gold, silver, copper, lead, coal, iron, quicksilver, marble, granite, chalk, slate, plaster of Paris (gypsum), thieves, murderers, desperadoes, ladies, children, lawyers, Christians, gamblers, Indians, Chinamen, Spaniards, sharpers, cuyotes . . . preachers, poets and jackass rabbits." Fate had a way of depositing Sam Clemens amid the boisterous scenes he would most relish. "It is the dustiest country on the face of the earth," he concluded, "—but I rather like dust."[56] A proud mother, Jane Clemens saw to it that Sam's letter was published in the Keokuk *Gate City*.

CHAPTER SIX

"The Most Lovable Scamp"

Sam Clemens had gloried in his bad boy image, the rebel angel proud of his apostasy, the scourge of middlebrow morality, and in Nevada he found himself right in his element. He had a head full of curly auburn hair and penetrating eyes and soon added a mustache to his image. According to his first biographer, "He wore a rusty slouch hat, flannel shirt, [and] coarse trousers slopping half in and half out of the heavy cow-skin boots."[1] He had typically preferred the outsider role, operating beyond the pale of respectability, and now, a frontier denizen, he was surrounded by like-minded rogues. He would recall, with undisguised nostalgia, the notorious characters of those early days, an honor roll of "desperadoes, who made life a joy and the 'Slaughter-house' a precious possession: Sam Brown, Farmer Pete, Bill Mayfield, Six-fingered Jake, Jack Williams and the rest of the crimson discipleship . . . Those were the days!"[2] Years later, when he saw the Wild West show of Buffalo Bill Cody, he wrote him in an onrush of happy memories that "it brought vividly back the breezy, wild life of the great plains & the Rocky Mountains & stirred me like a war song. Down to its smallest details the show is genuine—cowboys, vaqueros, Indians, stage-coach, costumes & all."[3]

In *Roughing It,* Mark Twain portrayed a rough-and-tumble world where violence often ruled, decent citizens hobnobbed freely with criminals, and murder was commonplace. "After a murder, all that Rocky Mountain etiquette required of a spectator was, that he should help the gentleman bury his game—otherwise his churlishness would surely be remembered against him the first time he killed a man himself and needed a neighborly turn in interring him."[4] It was a place where a saloonkeeper or a blacksmith might be a notorious fugitive from justice, escaping his past with impunity. Sam never pretended that this world of outlaws represented a higher form of civilization, but he enjoyed socializing with disreputable characters. Gregarious and easygoing, he latched on to every conceivable type of personality—why he would corral so much of American life into his fiction. Unlike most writers, Sam Clemens had nothing solitary or contemplative in his nature. With transplants from many states and countries, Nevada had created a polyglot slang that would enrich his writing. As if by osmosis, he picked up scraps of dialect from everywhere, fusing them into a new idiom and making himself a master of vernacular speech. The new territory's lack of social barriers offered a welcoming environment for any newcomer.

With his omnivorous curiosity about people, Sam sought out depraved characters for closer inspection. In *Roughing It*, he would tell how he was intrigued by colorful legends about Jack Slade, a stagecoach agent in the Rocky Mountains, reputed to be a homicidal maniac. He wrote that Slade liked to postpone murderous vengeance against enemies "just as a school-boy saves up a cake, and made the pleasure go as far as it would by gloating over the anticipation."[5] Since rumor had it that Slade had killed twenty-six people, Twain allegedly sought him out on the ninth day of his journey west, but found a quiet, affable man, not a monster. When the coffee was running out, Slade offered to refill Sam's cup instead of his own, but Sam "politely declined. I was afraid he had not killed anybody that morning, and might be needing diversion."[6] It was all humorous invention: when Sam breakfasted with Slade during his stagecoach journey, he didn't yet know of his ghoulish reputation. Three years later, after another satisfying round of shooting sprees, Slade was hung by vigilantes in Montana.[7]

The brothers' first quarters in Carson City could not have been humbler. A landlady named Bridget O'Flannigan provided Orion with an office and bedroom on the ground floor, while Sam slept in a second-story bed—one of "fourteen white pine cot-bedsteads that stood in two

"THE MOST LOVABLE SCAMP"

long ranks in the one sole room of which the second story consisted."[8] Sam told of uproarious times there, including the night when a strong wind knocked over a shelf with glass bottles full of tarantulas, triggering a panic in the room. Sam clerked for Orion for a couple of months but was condemned to inaction. "I had nothing to do and no salary. I was private secretary to his majesty the Secretary and there was not yet writing enough for the two of us."[9]

Perhaps inevitably this young man who'd had fantasies of cornering the global coca trade was soon infected with a bad case of silver mania. Americans equated money with success, and Sam Clemens was never immune from this belief, his Nevada time reinforcing a get-rich-quick mentality instilled early by the Tennessee land saga. As he told Orion, "I shall never look upon Ma's face again, or Pamela's, or get married . . . until I am a rich man," and he was convinced he would land a fortune "as surely as Fate itself."[10] In Carson City, people babbled about their silver strikes, "prospecting parties" flocked to the hills daily, and novice miners emerged as instant millionaires. As Twain later reflected, "I would have been more or less than human if I had not gone mad like the rest . . . I succumbed and grew as frenzied as the craziest."[11]

As with steamboating, Sam dove headlong into this new world, expecting to "find masses of silver lying all about the ground."[12] For his first prospecting foray that September 1861, he traveled to Aurora, in mining-rich Esmeralda County, one hundred miles southeast of Carson City, and bought "feet"—mining shares—in a number of rocky ledges. After a brief stay, he returned to Carson City to clerk for Orion during the first legislative session. Then, in December, he and three companions loaded up a wagon with eighteen hundred pounds of supplies—picks, shovels, drills, and powder, along with fourteen packs of playing cards, two dogs, a cribbage board, and a copy of Charles Dickens's *Dombey and Son*—and rode 175 miles northeast, sometimes in pelting rain or snow, to the Humboldt Range. They often had to push the wagon because Sam's finicky horse Bunker balked at further movement. The horse was so "infernally lazy," Sam assured his mother, that he could have been "a blood relation of our family."[13] The road was thickly littered with the detritus of aborted mining ventures: "skeletons and carcasses of dead beasts of burden . . . and charred remains of wagons" as well as "chains, and bolts and screws."[14] In the evening, the four men gathered around a campfire in the desert stillness and found cheer in pipe smoking, song singing, and yarn spinning. Always a bard of nomadic life, Mark Twain would celebrate this open-air existence as "the very summit and culmination of earthly luxury."[15]

Arriving at Unionville, a settlement of stone and adobe houses, Sam and his companions threw up a log cabin that teetered beside a crevice. An amateur miner, Sam scoured the grounds for loose stones and returned excitedly with what turned out to be fool's gold. He discovered that serious mining—sinking shafts, drilling tunnels with iron drills and heavy sledgehammers—was backbreaking labor. "One week of this satisfied me," he said. "I resigned."[16] As he groused to his family, "Why, I have had my whiskers and moustaches so full of alkali dust that you'd have thought I worked in a starch factory and boarded in a flour barrel."[17] Nonetheless, he grew convinced that his mining investments would yield major results, even though his overactive mind sometimes cooled down. "Don't you know that I have never held in my hands a gold or silver bar that belonged to me?" he lamented to his mother and sister. "Don't you know that it's all talk and no cider so far? . . . By George, if I *just* had a thousand dollars *I'd* be all right!"[18]

Like many newcomers, Sam speculated in mining shares in Humboldt and Esmeralda Counties. Lacking sufficient capital, he tapped Orion for money, and they became partners in the Clemens Gold and Silver Mining Company. In a significant inversion of their former power relationship, Orion would provide the capital while Sam handled the business affairs, convinced—no doubt now through experience—that his older brother lacked "business talent enough to carry on a peanut stand." The result, he told his family, was that "if mines are to be bought or sold, or tunnels run or shafts sunk, parties have to come to me—and me only. I'm the 'firm,' you know."[19] Not only did Sam reserve to himself all business decisions, but he left Orion in the dark about any setbacks. He advised their partner Billy Clagett that Orion lacked the stomach to ride out failures and that he should always discuss things with his brother "in such a way that Orion cannot understand them." "I don't care a d—n for failures and disappointments, but they nearly kill him, you know."[20] Orion, of course, resented any money Sam squandered, reviving their old fraternal sparring.

The main locus of Sam's speculations centered in Aurora. When Sam and his associates went to test various claims in which they had invested, they had to brave wintry gusts in a cabin whose chinks let in icy air from the mountain slopes. Sam was so deflated by the mining results that he ordered Orion not to buy any more "ground, anywhere. The pick and the shovel are the only claims I have any confidence in now. My back is sore and my hands blistered with handling them to-day." Then, sounding more like *David Copperfield*'s Mr. Micawber, he added, "something must come, you know."[21] Like many Nevada prospectors, Sam Clemens was rich on paper, if broke in the real world. As he phrased it, he and his partners owned "not less than thirty thousand 'feet' apiece in the 'richest mines on earth,'" but "were in debt to the butcher" and "our credit was not good at the grocer's."[22]

Blinded by greed, Sam convinced himself that it was only a matter of time before he and Orion grew wealthy. Riches "*will* come," he assured his brother, "there is no *shadow* of a doubt."[23] As always, he was headstrong. "I have got the thing sifted down to a dead moral certainty," he said, stating flatly that the Monitor Ledge they owned would "contain our fortune. The ledge is 6 feet wide, and one needs no glass to see gold & silver in it."[24] This cocksure certainty about prospective riches would be his undoing. When their mining ventures faltered, Sam adopted a testy tone toward his older brother, one he would maintain for decades. "You have *promised* me that you would leave all mining matters, and everything involved in an outlay of money, in my hands," he scolded Orion. "Now it may be a matter of no consequence at all to *you*, to keep your word with me, but I assure you *I* look upon it in a very different light . . . Now Orion, I have given you a piece of my mind—you have it in full, and you deserved it."[25] Sam left no doubt who was boss—he was now the decisive, hard-charging brother—and he would henceforth lord it over

Orion, perhaps exacting revenge for his older brother's harsh treatment of him in their printing office days. Sam warned him that "when you stand between me and my fortune . . . you stand between me and *home*, friends, and all that I care for."[26]

At the nadir of his Nevada sojourn, Sam was reduced to working for a short period as a common laborer in a quartz mill, where he had to shovel silver tailings. It was gruesome, exhausting work in which the quartz was crushed, filtered, and rinsed in an effort to extract embedded shards of silver. Although Sam claimed that he had taken the job to learn the refining business for future use as a mining mogul, he lasted only a week in this filthy trade and regarded it as the most detestable work he had ever performed.

Despite his business frustrations, Sam loved the brash freedom of the West, its hedonistic permission to carouse and socialize, and one companion remembered how "he used to smoke pipes, and quaff lager and dress rather slouchily."[27] Surrounded by ruffians galore, he had an ideal setting to exercise his comic gifts. He had many boon companions, even if some back home worried about the wicked prankster from Hannibal. Pamela piously entreated him to "let the Spirit of God, which has been knocking at the door of your heart for years, now come in, and make you a new man in Christ Jesus."[28] Everyone in the family but Sam had embraced religion, and he seemed in no particular rush to remedy the omission.

Quite the bon vivant, effervescent and exuberant, Sam amused people at balls by dancing alone and crooning to himself, shutting his eyes in comic ecstasy, the court jester. "By the second set," friend Cal Higbie recalled, "all the ladies were falling over themselves to get him for a partner, and most of the crowd, too full of mirth to dance, were standing or sitting around dying with laughter."[29] Sam admitted to his sister-in-law, Mollie, that he might be sleeping with chambermaids. "I don't mind sleeping with female servants as long as I am a bachelor—by *no* means—but *after* I marry, that sort of thing will be 'played out.'" He also indicated that he intended to marry well or not at all and would postpone marriage "until I can afford to have servants enough to leave my wife in

"THE MOST LOVABLE SCAMP"

the position for which I designed her, viz.—as a *companion*. I don't want to sleep with a three-fold Being who is cook, chambermaid and washerwoman all in one."[30] The letter foreshadows the woman he would eventually marry: rich, genteel, and refined, and he may already have had a sixth sense that only marriage could cure his roaming nature and satisfy his social ambitions.

One underappreciated aspect of Mark Twain's career would be his sensitivity to nature and the magnificent word pictures he painted of it. Not long after arriving in Carson City, he and a friend, John Kinney, hiked to Lake Bigler—later known by its Indian name, Lake Tahoe— where they had staked out a timber claim, and they were smitten by their first glimpse of the water. "We plodded on, two or three hours longer, and at last the lake burst upon us—a noble sheet of blue water lifted six thousand three hundred feet above the level of the sea, and walled in by a rim of snow-clad mountain peaks that towered aloft full three thousand feet higher still!"[31] Clemens and Kinney fell under the spell of this untamed wilderness beauty, a version of the prelapsarian river paradise Tom and Huck would inhabit. Sealed off from the world, Sam and his companion spent days on a boat, drifting freely with the breeze, buoyed by lake water so crystalline "that the boat seemed floating in the air!" Mark Twain later gave the lake this hilarious endorsement: "Three months of camp life on Lake Tahoe would restore an Egyptian mummy to his pristine vigor, and give him an appetite like an alligator. I do not mean the oldest and driest mummies, of course, but the fresher ones."[32] Unfortunately, before leaving the lake, Sam accidentally set fire to the forest while attempting to cook dinner over a campfire, and he and Kinney went away looking "like *lava* men, covered as we were with ashes, and begrimed with smoke."[33] Much of their timber claim went up in flames.

The comic vitality that surged through Sam's letters home signals that he was flexing his powers as a writer—you can see him reveling in comic riffs—and Jane Clemens rushed them into print in the Keokuk *Gate City*. Though convinced he would be a rich capitalist by summer, he no longer expected to resume his piloting life because his pride was too injured by mining failures to return home. Hence, he searched for a new job of sturdy independence. "I have been a slave several times in my life," he told Pamela, "but I'll never be one again. I always intend to be so situated (*unless* I marry) that I can 'pull up stakes' and clear out whenever I feel like it."[34] He had begun sending satirical sketches to the *Territorial Enterprise* in Virginia City under the well-chosen name "Josh." He wrote for personal amusement and a desperate need for cash. With no clear literary calling, he "stumbled" into the writing profession, he said, "as a man falls over a precipice that he is not looking for."[35] To his everlasting amazement, he received a letter that summer from the affable Joseph T. Goodman, owner of the *Territorial Enterprise,* and William H. Barstow, its managing editor, offering him a job as a local editor for a weekly salary of $25. Not only did the sum seem princely—"a sinful and lavish waste of money"—but he needed work posthaste. "I do not doubt that if, at the time, I had been offered a salary to translate the Talmud from the original Hebrew, I would have accepted."[36] Aside from the Josh letters, the editors had two other pressing reasons for hiring Sam Clemens: the local editor, William Wright, who wrote under the pen name "Dan De Quille," was taking temporary leave for an eastern trip, and the editors may also have thought Sam would help win public printing contracts from Orion.

Before starting work on the *Territorial Enterprise,* Sam ventured one last attempt at mining in a leaky Aurora cabin. As he wrote with black humor, "Yesterday it rained—the first shower for five months . . . We went outside to keep from getting wet."[37] He and his partner Daniel Twing subsisted on hardtack and bean, and rooted around in garbage dumps to supplement their diet. During this bleak interval, they let empty food tins and champagne bottles pile up outside their cabin to foster the illusion of prosperity within.

When he began working for the paper in September, Sam Clemens operated on a much larger stage, for the *Enterprise* was the territory's foremost daily paper. The combined population of Virginia City and nearby Gold Hill had mushroomed from nothing before the mining craze to become Nevada's most populous city. Mark Twain left graphic descriptions of this town that sat astride the Comstock Lode. Sitting on the steep slope of Mount Davidson, the Virginia City hillside was honeycombed with shafts and tunnels. "Taken as a whole, the underground city had some thirty miles of streets and a population of five or six thousand."[38] Whenever miners touched off explosives, stores and houses shook from the impact. Working in an office where all the editors and printers seemed to pack revolvers, Sam knew when they were blasting quartz below. "Often we felt our chairs jar, and heard the faint boom of a blast down in the bowels of the earth under the office."[39]

The future author of *The Gilded Age* found himself at the white-hot center of silver euphoria. People traded worthless shares at blue-sky prices, and everybody believed his fortune was nigh. This was money madness in its purest form. Twain said "there was a glad, almost fierce, intensity in every eye, that told of the money-getting schemes that were seething in every brain and the high hope that held sway in every heart."[40] It was exactly the sort of free-wheeling, rip-roaring atmosphere that appealed to Sam Clemens's swaggering personality and subversive instincts. "There were military companies, fire companies, brass bands, banks, hotels, theatres, 'hurdy-gurdy houses,' wide-open gambling palaces, political pow-wows, civic processions, street fights, murders, inquests, riots, a whisky mill every fifteen steps."[41] In short, the perfect place for an aspiring writer to study human nature in its rawest form.

For the first time, Sam joined a community of writers with a rough western bravado, and he couldn't have found a more convivial crew, especially in thirty-three-year-old Dan De Quille and the twenty-four-year-old compositor Steve Gillis. There was as much drinking, swearing, and juvenile horseplay as he could possibly have desired. De Quille, who roomed with Sam at times, left interesting impressions of him, noting his "bushy brows," "curly pate," and half-shut eyes that sized up the world with a shrewd, appraising gaze.[42] He remembered Sam's chronic insomnia and nighttime prowling. Most of all, he recalled how Sam became a captive of his anger, the way things simmered inside him and refused to settle down. He "was nervously overstrung and always in danger of a neurotic upset or explosion . . . Things that wouldn't disquiet the average man would grate on him and set him wild, while just an ordinary annoyance hit with the force of an overpowering shock."[43]

Sam's first article appeared on October 1, 1862. Never having written on deadline and educating himself on the job, he panicked about filling his first two columns until he was blessed by a lucky occurrence: "a desperado killed a man in a saloon and joy returned once more. I never was so glad over any mere trifle before in my life."[44] Then a wagon train pulled into town, having survived hostile Native American territory, and Sam served up the story with lavishly macabre exaggeration: "I put this wagon through an Indian fight that to this day has no parallel in history. My two columns were filled. When I read them over in the morning I felt that I had found my occupation at last."[45] Mark Twain made light of the episode, but it helped to launch a career marked by embellishment and hyperbole that would frequently get him into scrapes, even as it delighted readers. Published in a spirit of entertainment as well as straight reportage, the *Territorial Enterprise* was an ideal home for someone with Sam's outsize powers of invention and casual relationship with facts.

From his teenage years, Sam was skilled in taunts and teasing, and this side of his personality meshed perfectly with the new job, which included trading barbs and engaging in mock feuds with rival journalists. Reporters in Virginia City were literary gladiators who amused readers by making blood sport of these vendettas. It was vaudeville in print, with reporters as clowns of the show. As he began to cover the Nevada legislature, he clashed, at least on paper, with Clement T. Rice of the *Virginia City Daily Union.* He coined a name for Rice, "The Unreliable," which he made stick by constant repetition, and Rice retaliated by branding Sam "The Reliable." It was mostly good-natured ribbing, with Sam advising the Unreliable in print on how to behave in church and other such matters, but the two men remained good friends. In time, this combative style of play would take a darker turn, albeit not with Rice.

Sam's fertile imagination was on full display that October when he published a report about the discovery of "The Petrified Man" in a desert cave near the Humboldt River. Dressed up in scientific jargon, the story described how a prehistoric man, dead three hundred years, was found petrified in rock, his body welded to limestone sediment. The tale was a hoax—"an unmitigated lie, made from whole cloth," Sam admitted—but it gained widespread credence and was reprinted by gullible California and Nevada papers, making it the author's first interstate story.[46] The outrageous farce was designed to ridicule Judge G. T. Sewall, who supposedly held an inquest of the Petrified Man. "The practical joke was a legal tender in Virginia [City]," noted a Twain biographer. Twain had turned his old Hannibal talent for mischief into a marketable skill.[47] The following year, Sam followed up with two equally preposterous hoaxes: "A Bloody Massacre Near Carson" and "The Great Landslide Case." Of these titillating, ghoulish stories, Twain explained that "the public needed matters of thrilling interest for breakfast. The seemingly tranquil *Enterprise* office was a ghastly factory of slaughter, mutilation and general destruction in those days."[48] It was the start of Mark Twain's persona as a man who spun wild yarns and minted tall tales.

Not everything the *Territorial Enterprise* did was risible, and the editorials composed by Joseph T. Goodman were widely read and influential. That November, he sent Sam back to Carson City to cover the Territorial Legislature. Sam resided with Orion, who had now been joined by his wife, Mollie, and their daughter, Jennie. In his new incarnation, Sam cut a foppish figure and was vain about his influence. As a journalist, he had a passport to people in power. "I was there every day in the legislature to distribute compliment and censure with evenly balanced justice and spread the same over half a page of the *Enterprise* every morning; consequently I was an influence."[49] After his Sunday letters from Carson City appeared, they tended to draw howls of derision from delegates the next day. Aided by information from Orion, Sam received an invaluable education in legislative back-scratching and maneuvers, their inner workings greased by bribery. It was telling that Sam's coverage also called attention to himself, making him a local celebrity. If he won plaudits, he also made many enemies. "I suppose he was the most lovable scamp and nuisance who ever blighted Nevada," said William M.

AFLOAT

Stewart, later known as the "silver senator" from Nevada, who alleged that Sam went around "stirring up trouble" and "did not care whether the things he wrote were true or not, just so he could write something."[50] Undoubtedly Sam qualified as a troublemaker, albeit one endowed with a rapier wit.

It was likely in early February 1863 that he published his first article under the byline "Mark Twain." Pen names were then in vogue among fellow journalists and particularly commonplace among the chief humorists of the day. Dan De Quille had left Nevada on December 27 for a prolonged leave, and Sam, in taking a pseudonym, may have been seeking continuity as his replacement. Sam liked that "Mark Twain" was short and melodious—a perfect spondee. On the surface, the origin of the moniker seems fairly simple: On the Mississippi River, the leadsman would sound the water's depth by lowering a weighted rope, and if he cried "mark twain," it meant two fathoms or twelve feet, considered a safe depth; hence, a pleasing sound. Twain maintained that he swiped the name from an old steamboat captain, Isaiah Sellers, who employed it in reporting on Mississippi River doings for the New Orleans *Picayune*. Although Sam had mocked his encyclopedic, pedantic comments, incurring Sellers's wrath, he claimed to have taken Sellers's pen name upon the captain's death. He regretted having made sport of an esteemed pilot, who "did me the honor to profoundly detest me from that day forth."[51]

Over the years, Twain grew testy whenever the pen name's derivation was questioned. "I have published this vital fact 3,600 times now. But no matter, it is good practice; it is about the only fact that I can tell the same way every time."[52] Twain scholars have pointed out glaring inconsistencies in Twain's story, including that Sellers didn't die until 1864 and that his newspaper columns never bore the Mark Twain byline. One Twain authority has suggested that he appropriated the name from a comic sketch titled "The North Star" in a January 1861 issue of *Vanity Fair*.[53] Still others have suggested that the true source of the pen name was a barroom practice of chalking up two marks—"mark twain"—for two drinks whenever Sam Clemens ran up a tab at a local saloon.[54]

"THE MOST LOVABLE SCAMP"

Whatever the truth, the nom de plume would come to wrap Sam Clemens like a tight cloak. Often he signed letters to intimate friends "Mark" and they addressed him as such. He always instructed dinner hosts to introduce him as Mark Twain and "not Clemens, for my private name embarrasses me when used in public."[55] He would even become the first author to claim his pen name as a trademark, suing pirated editions on that basis. Given the invective that he dished out to Nevada rivals, it was probably not a bad idea to shield himself with a made-up name. For twenty-seven-year-old Sam Clemens it was the ultimate act of reinvention, the start of an attempt to mythologize his life. Many commentators have noted the name's ingenuity, for it not only attached the author to the Mississippi River but reflected the striking dualities in his nature. As he later told Helen Keller, the name fit because he was "sometimes light and on the surface, and sometimes—" She completed the sentence: "Deep."[56]

After adopting his pen name, Mark Twain started to cultivate larger literary connections. In May 1863, he clambered aboard a stagecoach with none other than Clement T. Rice, the Unreliable himself, and crossed the Sierra Nevada en route to San Francisco. They stayed at the two best hotels in town, dining sumptuously and drowning themselves in champagne and claret. With the blessing of his Nevada employers, Twain met with the editor of the San Francisco *Morning Call* and walked away with a contract to send him letters from Virginia City, giving Twain a chance to write for a more literate audience than Nevada miners. He admitted that in covering mining stories, he planned to shake down companies for shares in exchange for touting their businesses, telling his mother and sister, "if I don't know how to levy black-mail on the mining companies,—who *does*, I should like to know."[57] Such extortion was, alas, all too common among reporters covering the Comstock Lode. Twain's time in San Francisco showed that his early literary successes had by no means quieted his lust for money. "I take an absorbing delight in the stock market," he informed his family. "I love to watch the prices go up. My time will come after a while."[58] When he departed San Francisco, he lamented that "it seems like going back to prison to go back to the snows & the deserts of Washoe, after living in this Paradise."[59]

AFLOAT

A controversial young man on the make, Twain attracted growing attention, albeit not always wanted or desirable. In October he scripted another hoax for the *Territorial Enterprise* titled "A Bloody Massacre Near Carson." It purported to tell how an investor cheated in a stock swindle had slaughtered his wife and children. This grisly tale was meant as a satire on financial shenanigans, but many Nevada and California papers that reprinted the story missed the point entirely. In the ensuing hubbub, said Dan De Quille, "Some papers demanded the immediate discharge of the author" by the *Enterprise* editors. Although Joseph T. Goodman stood by him, Twain was "so distressed that he could not sleep," De Quille recalled. "He tossed, tumbled and groaned aloud."[60] The young Twain gloried in the shock value of his writing, even if he was not always braced for the outrage it would generate.

With fortuitous timing, the young Artemus Ward, America's most-beloved humorist and a favorite of President Lincoln, visited Virginia City that December. Born Charles Farrar Browne, Ward gave Mark Twain a sense of the shape a humorist's career could take, uniting the roles of clown, entertainer, sage, and moralist. When Ward lectured at Maguire's Opera House, Twain reviewed him in the *Territorial Enterprise* and gave him his highest encomium by stating that any spectator who listened to Ward "without laughing either inwardly or outwardly must have done murder, or at least meditated it, at some time during his life."[61] His later descriptions of Ward's speaking style preview the poker-face style he himself would adopt. He lauded Ward's "inimitable way of pausing and hesitating, of gliding in a moment from seriousness to humor without appearing to be conscious of so doing . . . There was more in his pauses than his words."[62] Ward was only a year older than Twain, yet his profits that season totaled $30,000 to $40,000—a staggering sum that must surely have captivated Twain's imagination.

Around midnight on Christmas Eve, Ward, with flaming red hair, an aquiline nose, and a handlebar mustache, showed up at the *Territorial Enterprise* office and proposed to treat the editorial staff to an oyster

"THE MOST LOVABLE SCAMP"

supper. According to Joseph T. Goodman, during this uproariously funny dinner, Twain upstaged Ward, winning undisputed claim to the "King of Comedy" title. "It was on that occasion that Mark Twain fully demonstrated his right to rank above the world's acknowledged foremost humorist."[63] As dawn streaked the sky, Ward announced, "I feel like walking on the skies, but as I can't I'll walk on the roofs."[64] Ward, Twain, and De Quille then scrambled to the top of a building and raced across rooftops until the local police drew weapons, suspecting they were burglars. This famous literary odyssey ended with Twain sitting on a barrel in a local saloon and downing drinks with Ward.

A kindly, generous soul, Ward encouraged Twain to write for the New York *Sunday Mercury* and eased his path by sending a flattering letter about him to its editors. When the publication accepted two Twain sketches in mid-January 1864, it signaled a critical foothold for him on the Eastern Seaboard. Twain told his mother that while he couldn't "write regularly for the Mercury," he was mindful that it had "a more extended circulation than is afforded by a local daily paper."[65] Clearly Ward's visit served as a tonic to Twain's spirits and a spur to his ambition to think in national terms. In 1867 Ward would die of tuberculosis, just shy of his thirty-third birthday, leaving open a prime spot for Twain as America's premier humorist.

When he first arrived in Nevada, Twain had been decidedly junior to his older brother, but now as a rising personage in the territory, he was eclipsing Orion. "Everybody knows me," Twain boasted to his mother in August 1863, "& I fare like a prince wherever I go . . . And I am proud to say I am the most conceited ass in the territory."[66] He bragged of his power as a "wire-puller" in the legislature. "I passed every bill I worked for, & on a bet, I killed a bill by a three-fourths vote in the House after it had passed the Council unanimously. Oh, I tell you a reporter in the Legislature can swing more votes than any member of the body."[67] Since voters approved Nevada statehood in a plebiscite that September, with the first state elections scheduled for January 1864, Sam meant to get his older brother "some fat office" in the new government.[68]

This was hardly a foregone conclusion, the sojourn in Nevada having had differing effects on the brothers. Sam had soaked up experience and shown a worldly pizzazz, while Orion grew more dreamy and impractical. Mark Twain always viewed his brother as a well-meaning but hopeless bungler who dithered his way through life. The problem wasn't that Orion was stupid, for he was highly intelligent. Rather, he lacked common sense and could be headstrong with authority figures, while at other times he was so eager to please folks that he refused to stand his ground. Additionally, Orion suffered from some psychological ailment that clouded his mental faculties and often rendered him inert and depressed. As Twain wrote of a character based on his brother, he "read everything and digested nothing; he was a mine of misinformation and mental confusions."[69] Sam still chafed when Orion tried to usurp their father's place and keenly resented a letter from his brother chastising him for dissipated living. Sam seethed to his family that Orion would "learn after a while, perhaps, that I am not an infant, that I know the value of a good name as well as he does, and stop writing such childish nonsense to me."[70]

A photo of Orion shows a tall, handsome man with dark hair, a full beard, and shaggy eyebrows, but the telling feature is the eyes—large, staring eyes that betray fear or alarm and a hint of sadness. One can see nervous instability in the expression, a lifetime of disappointments, the variable moods. "You could break his heart with a word of disapproval; you could make him as happy as an angel with a word of approval," Twain noted.[71] Where the younger brother had an irrepressible force that lifted him from troubles, Orion seemed mired in dejection. "He moved through a cloud of gloom and depression all his days," Twain said.[72] For all of Orion's infuriating flaws, Mark Twain thought him "a sterling man," who was "beloved, all his life, in whatsoever community he lived."[73]

As territorial secretary, Orion worked directly under Governor James W. Nye, a former president of the Metropolitan Board of Police of New York City, who was, said one of Sam's friends, a "fat, vulgar, profane fellow whose colloquialisms were tainted with obscenity."[74] Orion had a demanding job, having to handle the finances and serve as acting governor during Nye's frequent absences. Without a capitol, Orion

"THE MOST LOVABLE SCAMP"

rented the second floor of a local hotel and divided it into chambers for the new legislature. He also had to arbitrate complex boundary disputes with California. Orion even had to design the territory's official seal: a miner hoisting a pick and waving an American flag. Although he didn't know it at the time, the job of territorial secretary would mark the pinnacle of Orion's career, even as he and Mollie grandly assumed the good times would persist. When they built and furnished an expensive house in Carson City, Twain blamed Mollie's social pretensions—"there was no other house in that sagebrush capital that could approach this property for style and cost."[75]

When President Lincoln declared Nevada a state on October 31, 1864, Orion aspired to be secretary of state. For this to happen, he needed to attend the Republican Party convention where nominations would be decided. In a typically quixotic move, Orion decided that "his presence there would be an unfair and improper influence," Twain recalled with exasperation, "and that if he was to be nominated the compliment must come to him as a free and unspotted gift."[76] A recent convert to teetotalism, Orion refused to frequent a saloon where critical politicking took place. "The paper next morning contained the list of chosen nominees," Twain remembered. "He had not received a vote. His rich income ceased when the State government came into power. He was without an occupation . . . He put up his sign as attorney at law, but he got no clients."[77] Compounding Orion's problems was that he and Mollie had lost their eight-year-old daughter, Jennie, to cerebrospinal meningitis in February 1864. Twain challenged the undertaker's excessive charges, launching a lifetime habit of disputing bills loudly and at length. By 1866 Orion and Mollie had left Nevada and returned impoverished to Iowa. They would never see their daughter's grave again, although they would, as a memorial, keep her empty chair in houses they subsequently occupied. To worsen matters for Orion's delicate self-esteem, just as his life commenced a long, depressing slide, his kid brother was about to stage a comet-like ascent in the American literary firmament.

CHAPTER SEVEN

"Heaven on the Half Shell"

Mark Twain would leave Nevada amid a blaze of controversy, and the cause can be traced to the very issues of race and the Civil War that he had sought to leave far behind. Although the Nevada Territory was dominated by the Union Party, there was still pervasive anti-Black sentiment and Orion was again denounced for his "Black Republican" politics.[1] With plenty of southern transplants in Virginia City, abolitionism was less popular locally than unionism. In March 1864, when Joseph T. Goodman decamped on a trip to the Sandwich Islands (as the Hawaiian Islands were then known), he asked Twain and Dan De Quille to take over the *Territorial Enterprise* in his absence. Still ducking the Civil War, Twain had already stipulated when he was hired "that I should never be expected to write editorials about politics or eastern news. I take no sort of interest in those matters."[2]

In his early days in Nevada, Sam Clemens still betrayed clear sympathy for the southern cause. When a mule named Paint-Brush, which he had ridden with the Marion Rangers, fell into Union hands, he exclaimed to his sister-in-law, "'Paint-Brush' in the hands of the enemy! God forgive me! this is the first time I have felt melancholy since I left the United States."[3] In February 1862, when northern general Samuel Curtis scored a major victory in Missouri by vigorously routing General Sterling Price and his mostly Missouri militia from the state into Arkansas, Sam, hopping mad, wrote to his friend Billy Clagett about Curtis's victory: "He has thrashed our Missourians like everything. But by the Lord, they didn't do it on the Sacred Soil, my boy. They had to chase 'em clear down into Arkansas before they could whip them. There's a consolation in *that*."[4] Shortly afterward, when he feuded with Judge G. T. Sewall, Sam commented sarcastically to Clagett, "I don't see why he should dislike *me*. He is a yankee,—and I naturaly [sic] love a yankee."[5] To Orion, Sam complained, "There *are* good men in the North, but they are d—d scarce."[6] Nevada governor James W. Nye had already disparaged Sam as "a damned Secessionist."[7]

Yet despite the racial slurs that still infested his notebook, Sam Clemens's time in the Nevada Territory had given him a chance for a slow disengagement from a southern identity. There may have been opportunism involved—he was writing in Unionist territory for a pro-Union paper—but a deeper evolution was at work. The Far West allowed him a convenient break from his Missouri upbringing, a chance to reimagine himself as a born-again Yankee. The most-dramatic rupture came in early July 1863 amid pivotal Union victories at Gettysburg and Vicksburg. As a violent electrical storm pounded Mount Davidson, black clouds blocked out everything but the American flag atop the mountain, which was illuminated by the setting sun. As Mark Twain wrote in the *Territorial Enterprise*, "It was the flag! . . . a mysterious messenger of good tidings . . . It was the nation's emblem transfigured by the departing rays of the sun . . . The superstition grew apace that this was a mystic courier come with great news from the war . . . Vicksburg fallen, and the Union armies victorious at Gettysburg." He concluded that "every man that had any respect for himself would have got drunk."[8] Twain showed no twinge of discomfort in expressing outright joy over the Union triumphs.

Twain's carefree Nevada life began to fall apart after he wrote an article about money raised for the United States Sanitary Commission, launched in 1861 to raise funds for medical care for sick and wounded Union soldiers. Pamela acted as a leader of the St. Louis branch, and the cause was also dear to Orion Clemens, who served as president of the Sanitary Commission of Ormsby County, while Mollie labored as its secretary. Western supporters had devised a fundraising gimmick of

"HEAVEN ON THE HALF SHELL"

auctioning off a fifty-pound sack of flour—it would be greeted in towns with bands and festive crowds—and cities competed proudly to top the highest bid. On May 17, 1864, Twain published an article suggesting that Carson City hadn't outbid nearby Dayton because of rumors that "the money raised at the Sanitary Fancy Dress Ball recently held in Carson... had been diverted from its legitimate course, and was to be sent to aid a Miscegenation Society somewhere in the East; and it was feared the proceeds of the sack might be similarly disposed of."[9] It was as tasteless and incendiary a jape as Mark Twain ever penned. A catalyst for controversy, he was still, at heart, an immature, smart-alecky young journalist, willing to wring cheap laughs from a harmful wisecrack, and he now paid dearly for this crisis of his own devising.

The term "miscegenation" had entered the political lexicon the previous year when Democratic Copperheads attempted to discredit Lincoln and the Republican Party by claiming they favored miscegenation—that is, racial mixing. Twain's introduction of this nasty innuendo offended the genteel ladies of Carson City, including Mollie Clemens, who oversaw the Sanitary Fancy Dress Ball, but it also typed him as a closet secessionist. The response to his article was ferocious, with the ladies dashing off a letter to *Enterprise* editors denouncing the "*tissue of falsehoods, made for malicious purposes,*" and insisting that all money raised thus far would go for the care of distressed Union soldiers.[10] Twain even faced duel challenges from outraged husbands of the ladies in question.

The author stood abashed. He tried to stammer out an explanation to Mollie, stating that when he wrote the piece he wasn't sober and that Dan De Quille had warned him "it would wound the feelings of the ladies of Carson."[11] He claimed, unconvincingly, that he had decided to shelve the piece, that he and Dan had then sauntered off to the theater, and that the next thing he knew the foreman had gone and printed the article in the *Enterprise*. Even as he confided that "the Sanitary expedition has been very disastrous to me," he resisted a printed retraction because he feared "the humiliation of publishing myself as a liar."[12]

With the crowd's angry roar still throbbing in his ears, Twain did issue a belated, if half-hearted, apology, saying, "We resemble the majority of our species in the respect that we are very apt to get entirely in the wrong, even when there is no seeming necessity for it; but to offset this vice, we claim one of the virtues of our species, which is that we are ready to repair such wrongs when we discover them."[13] Twain had already been hurt by his reputation as a literary brawler, with an opposing paper noting that "Sammy Clemens, or as he styles himself, Mark Twain," was fond of directing satirical fire at others but found it very tough to handle it when they reciprocated. "Merciless himself in perpetrating jokes on others, he winces like a cur with a flea in his ear when others retort."[14]

Twain inflamed the controversy further when he accused the *Virginia City Daily Union* of reneging on its donations for the flour sack, leading its publisher, James L. Laird, to denounce the *Enterprise* in turn. The exchanges between Twain and Laird became increasingly heated and brutal. Before it was over, Twain had blasted the rival publisher as a "putrid ... groveling, vulgar liar," an "ass," and a "craven carcass."[15] For his part, Laird tore into Twain as "an unmitigated liar, *a poltroon, and a puppy,*" charging him with "disregard for truth, decency and courtesy."[16] In high dudgeon, Twain issued duel challenges to Laird, who declined. "The more he did not want to fight," Twain later joked, "the bloodthirstier I became." In the end, Laird and his second offered an apology on the dueling ground and settled the conflict peacefully. Nevertheless, an 1861 Nevada law called for prison sentences for anyone involved in a duel, and rumor hinted that the governor might set an example and arrest the participants. When this news reached Twain, it forced him to flee to California, or so he said. Perhaps he mostly wished to escape ridicule and his sudden notoriety, his swashbuckling, outlaw style having finally caught up with him. Joseph T. Goodman urged him to resign his newspaper post and leave Nevada at once, which he did.

On May 29, 1864, Twain departed from Virginia City and headed by stagecoach to San Francisco, where, he told Orion, he expected to stay a month. A few days earlier, he had written to his brother in a defiant mood, still growling about the Sanitary Commission spouses who threatened duels. "However, if there is any chance of the husbands of those women challenging *me*, I don't want a straw put in the way of it. I'll wait for them a month, if necessary, & fight them with *any* weapon they choose."[17] The day before he left, when another irate husband pursued him, Twain remained unrepentant. Later he alleged that he left Nevada because he had grown restless, needed a change of scenery, and yearned to travel. As so often with Twain, his memories obfuscate events as much as clarify them. Whatever the true cause of his departure, he left a territory that, for all his atrocious judgment toward the end, had transformed him from callow youth into a seasoned newspaperman and afforded him "the most vigorous enjoyment of life I had ever experienced."[18] One Nevada paper thumbed its nose at his departure, saying, "Mark Twain's beard is full of dirt, and his face is black before the people of Washoe."[19]

When he had visited San Francisco the previous year with Clement T. Rice, he had returned to Nevada with reluctance. It was perhaps foreordained that he would now stay longer than a month, and this interlude would indeed stretch into a two-year period. Notwithstanding their limited cash, Twain and Steve Gillis checked into the swank Occidental Hotel, a hostelry that Twain crowned as "heaven on the half shell."[20] Of his time with Twain, Gillis observed: "Mark was the laziest man I ever knew in my life, physically. Mentally, he was the hardest worker I ever knew."[21] Indeed, Mark Twain had a brain that always buzzed with words, a whirring beehive of thoughts, jokes, and ideas.

Urgently needing money, Twain took a job as a local reporter for the San Francisco *Morning Call*, which boasted the largest circulation in the city. (He would also file weekly articles with the San Francisco *Golden Era*, a local literary journal.) The *Morning Call* editor George Barnes recalled how a "slim, awkward, hawk-eyed, tousle-haired Twain" slouched into his office one day. Beneath Twain's bravado, Barnes sensed a sad and lonely soul who had difficulty making friends. "The refugee from Nevada justice told a hard-luck story about being out of money and out of work in a strange city."[22] As a Nevada reporter, Twain had written in an ebullient style about whatever struck his fancy, whereas working for the *Morning Call* meant tamping down his creative flair and becoming a humdrum scribe. As he recalled in 1906, the daily schedule was "fearful drudgery, soulless drudgery, and almost destitute of interest" that started early in the police court and ended late in the theaters.[23]

The indolent Twain nursed multiple grudges against the paper, where he always felt rushed and hated the late hours. In the morning he attended police court, then spent afternoons making political rounds. At night he wrote theater reviews, visiting six houses. "We remained in each of those places for five minutes, got the merest passing glimpse of play and opera, and with that for a text we 'wrote up' those plays and operas, as the phrase goes, torturing our souls every night."[24] However arduous the routine, it sparked an interest in theater and supplied handy tips for public speaking. Of actor Fred Franks he wrote how he possessed "the first virtue of a comedian, which is to do humorous things with grave decorum and without seeming to know that they are funny."[25] Already busy as a master of ceremonies, Twain exhibited a certain thespian flair when he delivered a tribute to Major Edward C. Perry at Maguire's Opera House. Perry had raised a Union gunboat from the harbor bottom, and Twain praised him by reading aloud from a seven-foot-long parchment as the "entire audience was dissolved in tears of laughter," said a reporter.[26]

With a dawning sense of social justice at the *Morning Call,* Twain exposed the mistreatment of Chinese immigrants, especially by police abuse. One day he filed a strongly worded piece about "some hoodlums chasing and stoning a Chinaman who was heavily laden with the weekly wash of his Christian customers" as a policeman stood by, watching amusedly.[27] Twain was shocked when the article failed to appear the next day in what he considered an odious concession to Irish readers. He later mocked the paper's mission: "To lick the boots of the Irish & throw bold brave mud at the Chinamen."[28] Mark Twain was beginning to shed some of the bigoted provincialism of his youth. In *Roughing It,* he recorded blistering passages about how "the worst class of white men" made the Chinese suffer "fines for their petty thefts, imprisonment for their robberies, and death for their murders."[29] Not only did the white working class persecute Chinese immigrants, but "the policemen and politicians, likewise, for these are the dust-licking pimps and slaves of the scum, there as well as elsewhere in America."[30] Twain saw the Chinese immigrants as a peaceable, hardworking people, "a harmless race when white men either let them alone or treat them no worse than dogs."[31]

Always alert to official misdeeds, he wrote venomous articles for the *Territorial Enterprise* about Martin Burke, San Francisco's crooked police chief. Twain's discomfort with authority figures, first evinced as a Hannibal boy, now started to generalize into a larger critique of public figures. He was especially outraged by police laxity and corruption. One day he found a policeman snoozing on the job and turned it into a memorable incident. Grabbing an oversize cabbage leaf from a nearby vendor, he began to wave it lazily over the sleeping cop until a sizable crowd had gathered to laugh and watch the incident. News of Twain's stunt—street theater with a punchy political message—soon raced around the city.

While he felt trapped and demeaned by his *Morning Call* job, he knew he "couldn't get another berth if I resigned ... Therefore I swallowed my humiliation and stayed where I was."[32] Instead of taking his usual pride in his writing, "I took the pen and spread this muck out in words and phrases, and made it cover as much acreage as I could."[33] After his flush times in Nevada, the paper felt like a terribly poor fit for the easygoing Twain and he knew it, and by October he was fired. George Barnes broke the news in gentle, fatherly fashion, and while Twain understood the decision—"I neglected my duties and became about worthless as a reporter for a brisk newspaper"—the firing still stung him to the quick.[34] It was, he later claimed, the only time in his life that he was discharged, and the rejection bothered him for years.

Losing his job meant that Twain felt the insecurity of a freelance writer's life, devoid of any permanent paycheck, a brush with poverty that had a harrowing effect on him. "I became very adept at 'slinking.' I slunk from back street to back street, I slunk away from approaching faces that looked familiar, I slunk to meals ... I felt meaner, and lowlier and more despicable than the worms."[35] Whatever the hyperbole here, Twain was haunted by this early period of poverty, which reinforced his preoccupation with money, a leitmotif of his life. A *Morning Call* reporter published an item about "a melancholy-looking Arab, known as Marque Twain," who moved like a Bedouin from tent to tent. "His hat is an old one, and comes too far down over his eyes, and his clothes don't fit as if they were made for him."[36]

However low his spirits, Mark Twain managed to experience some rollicking times in San Francisco, writing to Jane and Pamela that after the Nevada snowbanks, "this superb climate agrees with me."[37] With prodding from his mother he joined the San Francisco Olympic Club, which featured a large gymnasium and classes in gymnastics, boxing, and fencing. One member testified that Twain's main exercise was "confined to studying up jokes to play on his fellow members."[38]

Twain and Steve Gillis were rowdy tenants who were usually laggards in paying rent and had to switch lodgings five times in four months. One disgruntled landlady said the two men smuggled beer into their room, and she also didn't care for the revolvers and bowie knives they kept lying around, or the women who waltzed in and out of their lair.[39] To make things worse, they had a vile habit of tossing empty beer bottles onto the tin roofs of Chinese residences below. Though he generated lots of noise himself, Twain was a light sleeper and driven mad by any sounds in the vicinity. According to his authorized biographer, he was awakened one morning by a howling dog and decided to get even with the creature. Steve Gillis awoke to find "his room-mate standing in the door that opened out into a back garden, holding a big revolver, his hand shaking with cold and excitement."[40]

Twain still had the option of resuming life as a Mississippi pilot, but he knew he would have to master anew the intricacies of a river that constantly reshaped itself. He had also become so accustomed to a bohemian life of odd hours—he could never fit into a conventional mold—that he didn't imagine he could return to the stern discipline of a river pilot. As he told Will Bowen, "I generally get up at eleven o'clock, because I am naturally lazy, as you well know . . . I am too lazy for 14-day trips—too fond of running all night & sleeping all day—too fond of sloshing around, talking with people." Nor did he think marriage would reform his wayward behavior. "Marry be d—d. I am too old to marry. I am nearly 31. I have got gray hairs in my head. Women appear to like me, but d—n them, they don't *love* me."[41] Women were fascinated by him—he was, after all, a charming rogue, a lovable scamp—but they may also have been wary of his mercurial personality and footloose existence.

As a writer, Twain craved respectability and gained a modicum of literary cachet writing for the *Golden Era*, a literary journal housed in the same building as the *Morning Call*. Now he started writing for an even classier publication, the *Californian*, which began publication in May 1864. Owned by Charles Henry Webb and employing a sophisticated format, it attracted the most-talented writers from the city's thriving literary community. Its chief ornament, main contributor, and sometime editor was Bret Harte, and Ambrose Bierce also appeared there. In late September, Twain reported home that he had dropped the *Golden Era*—"It wasn't high-toned enough"—and contracted to write weekly articles for the *Californian*, which "circulates among the highest class of the community, & is the best weekly literary paper in the United States."[42] Of special importance to Twain was that the publication "has an exalted reputation in the east."[43] One can see how Twain's social striving commingled with his literary ambitions as he sought to cultivate readers among people of better standing. His two-year association with the periodical would help elevate him to national prominence.

If a year younger than Twain, Bret Harte was already a literary star in San Francisco and held a cushy sinecure as secretary to the superintendent of the U.S. Mint, occupying an office one floor below the *Morning Call*. Harte's story was not unlike Twain's: In his teens he traveled west to California with his mother and stepfather and taught school in mining camps, where he learned to capture local manners and dialect. He then went to San Francisco, rising from typesetter to author at the *Golden Era*. Three weeks before sealing his deal with the *Californian*, Twain heaped printed compliments on Harte, who had just been named editor. "Some of the most exquisite productions which have appeared in its pages emanated from his pen and are worthy to take rank among even Dickens' best sketches."[44] The praise is noteworthy since Twain, in time, would emerge as a vitriolic critic of Bret Harte's work. In these early days, however, he was awed by the speed and facility with which prose flowed from his colleague's pen.

After being introduced by George Barnes, Twain would pop into Harte's office for chats, and they became close friends. Both were fluent talkers, and their friendship started with mutual fascination despite a pronounced status difference: Harte "was private secretary on the second floor and I a fading and perishing reporter on the third."[45] Harte would remember Twain's aquiline nose, curly hair, bushy eyebrows, and "an eye so eagle-like that a second lid would not have surprised me . . . His dress was careless, and his general manner one of supreme indifference to surroundings and circumstances."[46] A fastidious dresser, Harte, despite a face pitted by smallpox, was an exceedingly handsome man, with a handlebar mustache, flaring side whiskers, and luminous eyes. Friends found him graceful and witty, an adroit conversationalist. Twain would remember a "distinctly pretty" man with clothes so smart they "always exceeded the fashion by a shade or two," and an easy gait that bordered on affectation.[47] Whatever their later differences, Twain's early admiration for Harte is beyond dispute. "Though I am generally placed at the head of my breed of scribblers in this part of the country," Twain assured his family in January 1866, "the place properly belongs to Bret Hart [sic] . . . though he denies it, along with the rest. He wants me to club a lot of old sketches together with a lot of his, & publish a book together."[48]

What made Bret Harte eager to collaborate with Twain was the latter's unexpected success with a tale about a jumping frog. It would never have been written had not the small, combative Steve Gillis—"Steve weighed only ninety-five pounds but . . . with his fists he could whip anybody," Twain recalled—gotten into a barroom fight and fled to Virginia City ahead of possible prosecution. Since Twain had signed a $500 bail bond for him, Gillis feared his friend would now be required to pay it. To avert this fate, Twain and Steve's brother Jim traveled one hundred miles east of San Francisco to a place known as Jackass Hill, there to spend three months. Once home to a feverish gold-mining boom, the place had reverted to a sleepy backwater of pocket mines, where men panned for gold by hand.

"HEAVEN ON THE HALF SHELL"

A naturalist and literary scholar, Jim Gillis owned a rude log cabin on the crest of a hill in Tuolumne County, near Tuttletown, with an ample fireplace and library, where he and his brother Bill and a friend, Dick Stoker, dabbled in pocket mining. Mostly the three men savored the woodsy seclusion and quiet of the place. During the daytime, Mark Twain pitched in with pocket mining, rinsing pans for the men. With his nascent literary bent, he scribbled in a new notebook and stored up impressions. He made things sound pretty dismal and monotonous. "Rainy, stormy—Beans & dishwater for breakfast at the Frenchman's; dishwater & beans for dinner, & both articles warmed over for supper."[49] Were it not for books and billiards, Twain would likely have perished from sheer boredom. But one feature hugely redeemed his stay: in the evening, standing before the fire, hands clasped behind his back, Jim Gillis regaled them with superb anecdotes, and Twain admired his artistry.

In January 1865, the group switched over to Calaveras County for more pocket mining and found diversion in a run-down tavern at Angel's Camp (also spelled Angels Camp). Twain and Jim Gillis were especially enamored of a story told by a stout, bald old river pilot from Illinois named Ben Coon. Around January 25, 1865, as they huddled around a tavern stove, Coon, in his slow-witted way, told a strange tale about a man named Coleman who always bet on his jumping frog until a wily opponent secretly loaded the frog with shot to weigh it down. This simple story changed Mark Twain's life. He was struck by Coon's ponderous, humorless manner—the "spectacle of a man drifting serenely along through such a queer yarn without ever smiling was exquisitely absurd"—and the weird details.[50] He recorded in his notebook: "Coleman with his jumping frog—bet stranger $50—stranger had no frog, & C got him one—in the meantime stranger filled C's frog full of shot & he couldn't jump—the stranger's frog won."[51] Twain later memorialized Coon's telling as a "gleam of jollity shot across our dismal sojourn in the rain & mud of Angel's Camp."[52] He had a premonition about the power of the frog story, with its clash of style and substance, because he told his companions, "If I can write that story the way Ben Coon told it, that frog will jump around the world."[53]

In late February, back at the Occidental Hotel in San Francisco, Twain found a letter written in November by Artemus Ward, inviting him to submit a sketch for a new book of his. A disheartened Twain told Ward that he wished he had gotten the invitation sooner and mentioned the jumping-frog story. Ward insisted there was still time to include it, and he put him in direct touch with his New York publisher, George W. Carleton. Meanwhile, in local circles, Twain kept telling and perfecting the frog story. Oral and written storytelling would always be closely allied for him, one often evolving into the other. Bret Harte heard the frog tale from Twain's own lips. "He spoke in a slow, rather satirical drawl... He went on to tell one of those extravagant stories, and half unconsciously dropped into the lazy tone and manner of the original narrator."[54]

Twain wrote two drafts of the story that didn't quite mimic the tone-deaf hilarity of what he had heard. Then he realized an essential ingredient was missing: the dry, factual recitation by Ben Coon, oblivious of the tale's grotesque humor. The joke would be not only on the reader but on the obtuse narrator. Twain had stumbled upon a key device that would be integral to his style: deadpan humor, with a shrewd author hiding behind a doltish narrator. So in November he served up a third version that inserted a narrator named Simon Wheeler, a talkative but humorless rube, who told the story of one Jim Smiley and his jumping frog. In an ingenious touch, Twain named the frog "Dan'l Webster." He dashed off the story to Carleton, hoping it would appear in Ward's new book. In fact, when it arrived too late to be used, Carleton steered it to Henry Clapp, a friend of Walt Whitman's and the editor of the New York *Saturday Press*. On November 18, 1865, "Jim Smiley and His Jumping Frog"—the story's original name—appeared in that publication and immensely enhanced Twain's reputation as a humorist. A month later, Bret Harte published it in the *Californian* under the now more famous title of "The Celebrated Jumping Frog of Calaveras County." The story would be the centerpiece of Twain's first published book, a collection of sketches, published by Charles H. Webb in May 1867.

Twain was amazed to learn, belatedly, that his story had touched off a sensation. The New York correspondent for the *Alta California* declared the jumping frog had "set all New York in a roar . . . I have been asked fifty times about it & its author, & the papers are copying it far and near. It is voted the best thing of the day."[55] The story heralded a new voice and a pioneering style in American letters. Like Bret Harte, Mark Twain had taken the world of the Far West—the campfires, saloons, and mining camps, with their brawling, hard-drinking men—and portrayed them indelibly with comic exaggeration. He was slightly baffled by the success of the story, which he rated of only middling value. When he wrote to his mother and sister, he dismissed it altogether. "I don't know what to write—my life is so uneventful. I wish I was back there piloting up & down the river again. Verily, all is vanity and little worth—save piloting. To think that after writing many an article a man might be excused for thinking tolerably good, those New York people should single out a villainous backwoods sketch to compliment me on! . . . a squib which would never have been written but to please Artemus Ward, & then it reached New York too late to appear in his book."[56]

Even prior to the frog brouhaha, a New York article had ranked Mark Twain as "foremost among the merry gentlemen of the California press" and predicted he might "one day rank among the brightest of our wits."[57] Now, with his sudden fame, came a fresh nickname: "The Wild Humorist of the Pacific Slope."[58] Still, he had a sense of failure that he couldn't shake. Right before sending off his frog story, he was floored when Orion sent him a sermon he had written that showed unmistakable flashes of talent, and he urged his brother to renounce his desire to become a mediocre lawyer and become a gifted preacher. Sounding deflated, Twain pooh-poohed his own writing as a thing of small importance. "I *have* had a 'call' to [literature], of a lower order—i.e. humorous. It is nothing to be proud of, but it is my strongest suit."[59] Instead of writing true literature, he thought he was only titillating God's poor pitiful creatures. Only praise from impartial Eastern Seaboard critics gave him faith "that I really begin to believe there must be something in it."[60] Still darkening his spirit was his fretting about money. As he told Orion, "You are in trouble, & in debt—so am I. I am utterly miserable—so are you . . . If I do not get out of debt in 3 months—pistols or poison for one—exit *me.*"[61] This dread of poverty would never entirely desert him. After returning from Calaveras County, Twain was broke and survived only by working as a San Francisco correspondent for the *Territorial Enterprise* and contributing pieces to the *Californian* based on his sojourn in the pocket-mining country.

Despite the marvelous reception of the jumping frog, Twain's days in San Francisco may have reached their nadir when he feuded with Albert Evans, who wrote for the *Gold Hill Daily News*. On January 19, 1866, he alleged that Twain was "in the dock for being drunk over night." He said Twain had forced the police to drag him to the station house, where he stood "at the grating, cursing and indulging in obscene language." Twain broke down and told Judge Alfred Barstow that he couldn't pay the obligatory fine because he had "nothing in his pockets but a plug of tobacco and a broken jackknife."[62] The story gains credence from the fact that a shamefaced Twain admitted to his daughters many years later that he had once been jailed for drinking. It may have been around this time that he meditated suicide. "I put the pistol to my head," he recollected years later, "but wasn't man enough to pull the trigger. Many times I have been sorry I did not succeed but I was never ashamed of having tried."[63] Whatever fleeting glory his byline had brought, Twain still felt broke and desperately unsure of his future.

CHAPTER EIGHT

"Land of Indolence and Dreams"

During his time in San Francisco, Mark Twain wrote, the "vagabond instinct was strong upon me."[1] It always would be. The man who soaked up adventures seemed to have them at every turn. He always felt liberated by travel, when he could see new things, sample forbidden pleasures, explore taboo thoughts. In early 1866, he visited the offices of the Sacramento *Union*, hoping to wrangle an assignment to write some travel letters at an indeterminate location. "I had a sneaking notion that they would start me east," he told Will Bowen, but instead "they sent me to the Sandwich Islands."[2] The deal that Twain hatched would require him to file twenty to thirty letters, based on a monthlong stay, enabling him to "ransack the islands, the cataracts, and volcanoes completely."[3] The sugar industry had eyed the Sandwich Islands as a lucrative spot for closer trade relations or even outright annexation. Without any qualms, Mark Twain adopted this nationalist agenda, telling *Union* readers, "It is a matter of the utmost importance to the United States that her trade with these islands should be carefully fostered and augmented."[4] In an odd endorsement, he also admitted that annexation would bring such American blessings as "leather-headed juries, the insanity law, and the Tweed Ring."[5] Twain, with his all-devouring curiosity, would cobble together a comprehensive survey of the islands, studying them in the mode of a naturalist, anthropologist, and political scientist.

On March 7, 1866, he set sail for Honolulu aboard the steamer *Ajax*.

During his trip he would fume over Orion's failure to close a deal that he had orchestrated to sell the Tennessee land for $200,000 to a friend named Herman Camp, a speculator in Nevada mining stocks. Camp wanted to establish a wine-making colony on the land, staffed by European immigrants from grape-growing regions. Orion, on a temperance crusade, refused to countenance such a sale, insisting "he would not be a party to debauching the country with wine."[6] Twain was so disgusted by Orion squashing his deal that, awash with bitterness, he gave Mollie a severe tongue-lashing. "It is Orion's duty to attend to that land, & after shutting me out of my attempt to sell it (for which I shall never entirely forgive him,) if he lets it be sold for taxes, all his religion will not wipe out the sin. It is no use to quote Scripture to me, Mollie. I am in poverty & exile now because of Orion's religious scruples . . . I always feel bitter & malignant when I think of Ma & Pamela grieving at our absence & the land going to the dogs when I could have sold it & been at home now, instead of drifting about the outskirts of the world, battling for bread."[7] Twain was permanently fed up with the Tennessee land, that fatal mirage. "I don't want to be consulted at all about Tennessee," he told Orion five years later. "I don't want it even mentioned to me."[8]

On March 18, Mark Twain snatched his first unforgettable glimpse of the Sandwich Islands, arising "like a couple of vague whales lying in blue mist under the distant horizon."[9] As his ship streamed past Diamond Head, on Oahu, he beheld seawater of such clarity that it "shamed the pale heavens with the splendor of its brilliant blue."[10] Once ashore, he drifted about in a brown linen suit and native straw hat pulled low over his eyes, and he experienced instant enchantment—what blossomed into full-blown reverie—with a place he would anoint as "the only supremely delightful place on earth."[11] After the noisy bustle of Nevada and San Francisco, with their eternal striving for money, the islands breathed a pleasantly indolent air, with "no care-worn or eager, anxious faces in the land of happy contentment." In his notebook, he scrawled how in the islands there was "no rush—no worry—merchant goes down to store like a gentleman at 9—goes home at 4, & *thinks no more* of business till next day."[12] The blissful tone was reminiscent of two other experiences

"LAND OF INDOLENCE AND DREAMS"

safely beyond the trammels of society: piloting on the Mississippi and floating idly on Lake Bigler.

With his Victorian sensibility, Twain pondered this lush land of sensual fantasy where men wore no clothes or, as he phrased it more piquantly, wore "a smile, or a pair of spectacles—or any little thing like that."[13] He was bewitched by the slim-hipped women with their "rich dark brown" skin, who dressed in long, loose gowns and sometimes in nothing at all.[14] He couldn't quite figure out if they were "immoral" or "innocent & natural."[15] He noted two "strong characteristics" of the natives—horseback riding and fornicating women—the latter being an altogether novel concept for this prudish but leering spectator.[16] In *Roughing It,* he inserted a funny, voyeuristic passage about watching native women swimming naked. "At noon I observed a bevy of nude native young ladies bathing in the sea, and went and sat down on their clothes to keep them from being stolen. I begged them to come out, for the sea was rising and I was satisfied that they were running some risk."[17]

In the Sandwich Islands, the young correspondent did something novel for him: he began to analyze their history, structure, and political leadership. Although he favored American annexation of the islands and promoted the interests of sugar planters, he still wrote as if the natives were born innocent and only corrupted by foreign influences—a natural progression for a man who would celebrate childhood innocence and deplore society's stifling constraints. As he said in a later lecture, the Sandwich Islands, a century earlier, had a population of 400,000 and were happy and prosperous. "But then the white people came, and brought trade, and commerce, and education, and complicated diseases, and civilization, and other calamities, and as a consequence the poor natives began to die off with wonderful rapidity, so that forty or fifty years ago the 400,000 had become reduced to 200,000 . . . The nation is doomed. It will be extinct within fifty years, without a doubt."[18] This same pen would someday write of Huck Finn's refusal to be civilized.

Later on, Twain turned into a ferocious critic of Christian missionaries. While he now saw them wielding excessive influence in the islands, he also acknowledged that they had broken up the cabal of king and local chieftains and educated people so that they were "the most universally educated race of people outside of China." Most importantly, they had emancipated the downtrodden island woman, who had been expected to "do all the work, take all the cuffs, provide all the food, and content herself with what was left after her lord had finished his dinner . . . They liberated woman and made her the equal of man."[19] It was an early sign of Twain's future role as doughty defender of women's rights. Identifying with the natives and bewitched by their sexual freedom, he regretted that the missionaries had ended public hula-hula dancing and other frank expressions of sensuality practiced by a people who had before lived in blissful ignorance of both heaven and hell.

In his published writing, Twain dealt gently with the king, whereas he privately reviled him in his notebook, where he showed a chauvinistic feeling quite at odds with his anticolonial bent. "The King gets his loved and cherished compliments from the English & his revenues from the Americans—his gew-gaws & cheap adulation from the one & whatever of real worth & greatness his country possesses from the other—& with characteristic consistency he worships the men who have degraded his country & hates the strong & steadfast [American] hands that have lifted her up."[20]

By a remarkable coincidence, Twain spent time on the big island of Hawaii just as the active Kilauea volcano was in full eruption, and he witnessed vivid lava flows during a weeklong stay near the crater at Volcano House. "Occasionally the molten lava flowing under the superincumbent crust broke through—split a dazzling streak, from five hundred to a thousand feet long, like a sudden flash of lightning, and then acre after acre of the cold lava parted into fragments, turned up edgewise like cakes of ice when a great river breaks up, plunged downward and were swallowed in the crimson cauldron."[21]

At Volcano House, he met a stylish Englishman, Edward Howard, whom he introduced as Brown because he found it "easier to remember."[22] Howard would recall Twain as a bullheaded, conceited fellow who could never admit that he was wrong. Howard had insisted that they enlist a guide to take them to the brink of the boiling crater. Twain

"LAND OF INDOLENCE AND DREAMS"

"wouldn't hear of it, said the trail was so plainly worn on the rocks that we couldn't miss it, but before noon we were lost in the forest, following goat and cattle trails in every direction, riding around great cracks, some of which we nearly fell into." When night was upon the two lost travelers, Twain "pulled his saddle off his horse and made a pillow of it after scraping up some leaves, as if he were used to this sort of thing, and put his raincoat over him. Even then the man wanted to tell me a story, that he was reminded of, hungry as we were."[23]

In another lucky stroke, Twain strayed into the most sensational scoop yet in his journalistic career. In late June, he was bedridden with excruciating saddle boils from riding "the hardest mountain roads in the world" and holed up in his hotel room reading the poetry of Oliver Wendell Holmes.[24] Then came news of an extraordinary occurrence. On May 3, the clipper ship *Hornet* had burned in the Pacific Ocean, with fifteen survivors setting off in an open boat with just ten days' rations. Through miraculous endurance, the "lean and ghostly survivors" suddenly washed up on the Sandwich Islands, after drifting four thousand miles, and Twain recognized the journalistic riches that would flow to the correspondent who first filed their story.[25]

Even though he thirsted for fame, Twain was in no condition to capitalize on this journalistic coup had it not been for a stout, bewhiskered diplomat named Anson Burlingame who was en route to China to resume his post as U.S. minister. Burlingame, an unabashed imperialist, saw the Sandwich Islands as ripe for plucking by the United States—"He hungered for those rich islands," wrote Twain—but he took a fond interest in Twain and immediately fathomed the value of the *Hornet* story for his young friend.[26] As Twain recalled, "He came and put me on a stretcher and had me carried to the hospital where the shipwrecked men were, and I never needed to ask a question. He attended to all that himself, and I had nothing to do but make the notes."[27] Listening on his cot, Twain must have seemed in only marginally better shape than the emaciated crew of survivors.

However much he liked to joke about his laziness, Twain was now aroused to a furious burst of energy. With admirable tenacity, he skipped dinner and wrote all night, producing a detailed account of the *Hornet* survivors by nine the next morning. He then had a "strong hand" chuck the "fat envelope" containing the story onto a schooner setting sail for San Francisco.[28] It would be the first complete report to reach the outer world and "made the stir and was telegraphed to the New York papers," Twain wrote.[29] He got the Sacramento *Union* to pay ten times the going rate for his front-page story then scooped up more material when he returned from Hawaii with several *Hornet* survivors. By December 1866, he had published an article, "Forty-Three Days in an Open Boat," in *Harper's New Monthly Magazine,* his first appearance in a prestigious national organ. Heady stuff for a young writer, except that the periodical botched his byline as "Mark Swain" in its annual index.

On July 19, Twain stole his last glance of the Sandwich Islands. Their natural beauty, their relaxed atmosphere, the sensual charms of the young women—these would remain locked in his mind as lotus land, a blessed place free of strife. "It is Sunday land, the land of indolence and dreams, where the air is drowsy and lulls the spirit to repose and peace, and to forgetfulness of the labor and turmoil and weariness and anxiety of life."[30] For a man who found so many imperfections in the world, this place seemed free of them. Twenty-five years later, Twain could still tell a Sandwich Islands resident that his family had heard him "sigh for the Islands every year for twenty years, yet have never heard me sigh to return to any other place I had seen before."[31]

After this tropical bliss, Twain landed back in San Francisco with a heavy thud. In his notebook, he groused, "Home again. No—*not* home again—in prison again—and all the wild sense of freedom gone. The city seems so cramped, & so dreary with toil & care & business anxiety."[32] He hurried off his remaining Sandwich Islands letters and prepared the *Harper's* article for December but was otherwise adrift. Having attained a new plateau in his career, he didn't care to slip backward and resume writing for the *Territorial Enterprise.* Instead, aided by a friend, he came up with a fresh moneymaking scheme: he would hazard a public lecture on the Sandwich Islands, following a path already well trod by Artemus Ward. Bret Harte and other friends tried to dissuade him, saying nobody would show up, and that it might even damage his literary standing. Colonel John McComb of the *Alta California*, however, urged him to charge ahead. "Take the largest house in town," he advised, "and charge a dollar a ticket."[33]

It was an auspicious time to launch a side career as a lecturer. The early years after the Civil War saw a flowering of the lecture circuit as towns created lyceums or literary societies to meet the middle-class demand for such diversion. For a society of self-made citizens, the local lyceum was the perfect way to enrich one's stock of knowledge, have a good time, and enhance one's standing in the community. For speakers it was an easy way to promote causes, sell books, and earn good money. For Mark Twain, it was more lucrative than writing and entailed less work.

Plunking down fifty dollars on credit, he rented Maguire's Academy of Music in San Francisco for October 2, 1866. The posters he created exhibited his outrageous wit, trumpeting: "A SPLENDID ORCHESTRA is in town, but *has not* been engaged." "ALSO A DEN OF FEROCIOUS WILD BEASTS will be on exhibition in the next block." "MAGNIFICENT FIREWORKS were in contemplation for this occasion, but the idea has been abandoned." "A GRAND TORCHLIGHT PROCESSION may be expected; in fact, the public are privileged to expect whatever they please." Then came the line that would become his signature: "Doors open at 7 o'clock The trouble to begin at 8 o'clock."[34] For future lectures, he sometime varied the line to "The Orgies will commence at 8" or "The Insurrection will start at 8."[35] Gradually he learned to elevate the comic tease to an art form, even promising at one event to "DEVOUR A CHILD, in the presence of the audience, if some lady will kindly volunteer an infant for the occasion."[36]

Twain was petrified about appearing on a stage. After spending money on the house and promotion, he remained so jittery that he thought himself "the most distressed and frightened creature on the Pacific coast."[37] When the lecture sold out, it only advanced his stage fright, and he pretended that he would flee town and abscond with the proceeds. When he arrived two hours early at the empty theater on October 2, he tiptoed onto the stage, and his feverish mind transformed it into a hall of horrors, "gloomy and silent."[38] He had decided to paper the house, even recruiting a couple primed to laugh at his jokes on cue, and when curtain time came, he appeared in the "fierce glare of the lights" to wild applause and stamping feet.[39] For his first two minutes, he was simply paralyzed by fright. George E. Barnes said Twain saved the moment through an ingenious remark: "Ladies and gentlemen . . . this is the first time I have attempted to speak in public, and if I know myself as well when the lecture is over as I do now, it will be the last."[40] After that, with the audience in his palm, his fear vanished altogether and he delivered a ninety-minute memorized presentation on the Sandwich Islands that was so deftly performed as to appear spontaneous. He spoke with a slow, wry drawl and an almost pained expression that made the resulting laughter all the more thunderous. "I have never stammered, have never had any obstruction in my speech except slow delivery, and that obstruction perceptible to other people only; it does not seem slow to me," he later wrote.[41] Aside from humorous anecdotes, he also furnished such graphic descriptions of the Kilauea eruption that the grateful audience was transported to the faraway islands. Twain's descriptive powers would be no less consequential in establishing his reputation than his witty remarks.

There were some predictable gripes in the press: that his voice was too soft to be heard in the back or that his humor was too coarse for ladies. Mostly though, the lecture was praised for its humor, brilliance, and originality, and it proved a commercial success. Bret Harte saw a deeper significance, stating that with its "western character of ludicrous exaggeration and audacious statement," Twain had eclipsed Artemus Ward and now stood forth as "a new rising star in this western horizon."[42] The impact on Mark Twain's career cannot be overstated. He had felt his mastery over a crowd—an unforgettable sensation for a first-time speaker—and discovered his ability to project a theatrical persona that was a heightened version of himself. He wouldn't be a cloistered writer so much as a showman, a public personality, a professional crowd-pleaser. In short, a

"LAND OF INDOLENCE AND DREAMS"

celebrity. He now knew that his antic personality could resonate with a mass public, that he could endow his wicked ways with offhanded charm, as if they were just the confessions of a naughty boy fessing up to schoolyard peccadilloes. As he reminisced, "I launched out as a lecturer now, with great boldness. I had the field all to myself, for public lectures were almost an unknown commodity in the Pacific market."[43] Even as a boy in Hannibal, he was a born entertainer, and he was now converting those attention-grabbing skills into a giant career.

During the next month, he parlayed his San Francisco triumph into a lecture tour in towns in Nevada and California, even playing small places with names like Grass Valley, Red Dog, You Bet, and Gold Hill. In Nevada City, California, he perfected his use of advertising and promised that after the show he would "go out with any gentleman and take a drink . . . At a moment's warning he will depart out of town and leave his hotel bill unsettled."[44] In the mining town of Red Dog, where Twain appeared in a simple wooden schoolhouse, he coaxed a dusty miner, "slouching and awkward," to introduce him onstage.[45] Peering out at the audience, the miner said, "I don't know anything about this man [Twain]. At least I know only two things; one is, he hasn't been in the penitentiary, and the other is . . . *I don't know why.*"[46] Another time, when the curtain went up on Twain, he sat at the piano playing "I Had an Old Horse Whose Name Was Methuselah" and feigned surprise at seeing the audience. For all his success and growing fame in the West, Twain was nagged by a fear that would prey on him in future years: that he was a jester in motley, performing tricks for the masses, but not leaving them with anything substantial. A preacher manqué, he craved not just fame but distinction. After a lecture in Washoe City, Nevada, he told a companion, his voice choked with emotion, "but as a lecturer I am a fraud, ain't I, now?"[47] Indeed, after he played San Jose, California, a local critic balked at his earthy humor and comic excesses and advised him to "lop off . . . all of the buffoonery and not a little of the vulgarity."[48]

Although a prankster himself, Twain was victimized by a practical joke on this tour and he didn't appreciate it. After speaking in Gold Hill, Nevada, he and Dennis McCarthy, the former co-owner of the *Territorial*

Enterprise and his tour manager, were walking on a "lonesome, windswept road" when they were accosted by masked gunmen.[49] Twain gave them his coins and valuables, including a gold watch given to him as a gift, and he was furious at the loss, only to discover the next day that it was a cruel joke perpetrated by his Virginia City friends, with McCarthy in on the gag. Twain, who was not amused, fired McCarthy.

This ended, for the moment, Twain's involvement with Nevada and the West Coast. After a more than five-year absence, he wanted to reconnect with his family in the Midwest and also planned to file articles with the *Alta California* of San Francisco as a traveling correspondent. In mid-December 1866, he boarded the *America,* which would carry him down the West Coast to Nicaragua en route to New York. He was deeply touched by his farewell reception in San Francisco, telling his family proudly that he was "leaving more friends behind me than any newspaper man that ever sailed out of the Golden Gate."[50] Twain had a habit of collecting interesting people the way others collected postage stamps, and a prized possession would be the *America* skipper, Captain Ned Wakeman, a big, blustering man with an emphatic speaking style, who made you "cry and laugh at the same time," said Twain.[51] Steeped in the Bible, Wakeman concocted his own strange interpretation of many passages. What likely drew Twain to him was that he was a spellbinding storyteller who employed many literary devices Twain applied—burlesque, exaggeration, and bombast—liberally sprinkled with profanity. Ned Wakeman, in disguise, would surface in Mark Twain's stories whenever he needed a bluff seaman.

On December 28, when the ship arrived on the Nicaraguan coast, passengers learned of cholera cases on the isthmus they had to traverse. Soon after making it across and boarding the *San Francisco* to New York, Twain noted ominously in his journal: "Two cases of cholera reported in the steerage to-day."[52] The next ten days would be shadowed by so many mounting deaths that Twain felt inexpressible relief when the ship docked in New York on January 12.

The city had matured since his last visit, being much bigger and more crowded. He got an early glimpse into Gilded Age wealth as he saw "acre upon acre of costly buildings" that had gone up and "made five thousand men wealthy."[53] Staying first at the Metropolitan Hotel, he wrote nineteen letters for the *Alta California* in the coming months and tried to shop a book-length manuscript on the Sandwich Islands. Meanwhile, he devoured the sights "to test all the amusements of the metropolis," with his contradictions on full display.[54] He frequented risqué shows on the Bowery and remarked that "the scenery and the legs are everything."[55] At Plymouth Church in Brooklyn, he admired the hypnotic power that Henry Ward Beecher exercised over his congregants and clearly was sizing him up as a fellow practitioner. He went marching up and down the stage, Twain wrote, "sawing his arms in the air, hurling sarcasms this way & that, discharging rockets of poetry, exploding mines of eloquence."[56] Yet this same Twain who marveled at an abolitionist preacher still clung to retrograde notions of southern white gentility versus Black rapacity. "I have seen negroes sitting stuck up comfortably in a [street] car, and lovely young white ladies standing up before them, block after block, clinging to the leather supports that depended from the roof. And then I wanted a contraband [i.e., a runaway slave] for breakfast."[57] He visited the Century Association and other clubs, eager to ingratiate himself with the eastern literary elite, and befriended Edward House, a critic for the *New York Tribune*, with whom he would have a long and checkered friendship.

That Mark Twain had already traveled an unimaginable distance from his modest past grew clear when he journeyed to St. Louis in March and visited his mother and Pamela, now a widow with two children, and bore prodigal gifts from the Sandwich Islands and the West. When he delivered a lecture, he sang the praises of the local audience. They "snap up a joke before you can fairly get it out of your mouth."[58] In many ways, he reentered his childhood world, accompanying his mother and sister to prayer meetings and church gatherings. "I don't think I can stand it much longer," he said. "I never could bear to be respectable long at a stretch."[59] When he spoke in Keokuk, the local paper was agog at the transformation of its former resident. The "Mark Twain that is now, was S.L. Clemens, one of the cleverest and most popular of 'printer boys' in

Keokuk. He returns to us now, a famous man, and ... we trust that our citizens will honor him with a rousing house."[60] When he lectured in Hannibal, he drew "the largest and most delighted crowd ever gathered in a public hall" there.[61]

However resounding his Missouri reception, the trip also charted how much he had pulled away from his past—the painful inner conflict of many self-made people. At thirty-one, he had already been a pilot, a soldier, a miner, and a journalist, while his family still inhabited the narrow, provincial world he had outgrown. His childhood comrades now wore whiskers, and a few had "remained at their hearthstones prosperous and happy."[62] He felt elegiac about his lost boyhood, a theme that would recur frequently in his work. As he later concluded, "You shall never know the chill that comes upon me sometimes when I feel that long absence has made me a stranger in my own home."[63] The man who would dramatize his upbringing with such pungent humor and feeling would largely avoid the scenes of his boyhood and often evade his own family, even as he supported them financially.

After returning to New York in mid-April, he switched to the elegant Westminster Hotel, having arrived in time for the release to booksellers of *The Celebrated Jumping Frog of Calaveras County, and Other Sketches*. Reviews were friendly, with the *New York Herald* hailing "a little book full of good hard sense, wit pure, sparkling and sharp as a diamond ... and humor genial and inexhaustible."[64] According to Twain, James Russell Lowell commended it as "the finest piece of humorous writing ever produced in America."[65] Yet in the first example of his congenital grousing about publishers, Twain snarled to Bret Harte that the book was "handsome," but "full of damnable errors of grammar & deadly inconsistencies of spelling."[66] With modest sales, the book provided no major uplift to his career, and he pretended to be philosophic. "I don't believe it will ever pay anything worth a cent," he moaned to his mother. "I published it simply to advertise myself, and not with the hope of making anything out of it."[67] He inscribed a copy to her, tenderly calling her "The dearest Friend I ever/had, & the truest."[68] The book had a small print run and, hence, very modest sales, even though it sold out. Al-

"LAND OF INDOLENCE AND DREAMS"

though it was published by his friend Charles Henry Webb, Twain grew convinced that he had been defrauded in the accounting and would curse Webb's name for many years. He claimed that he never made a penny on the book, and there are no royalty statements to refute that.

On May 6, 1867, Mark Twain would deliver a lecture on the Sandwich Islands at the premier venue in New York: the Cooper Institute, where Abraham Lincoln had made his storied election speech in 1860, winning over eastern supporters. Twain longed to shed the stigma of being a provincial writer and had his eyes on a national audience. He claimed that his enthusiastic friend Frank Fuller, the former secretary of the Utah Territory, persuaded him to hire the Cooper Institute "under the impression that I was famous and could fill that house, and make a fortune."[69] Fuller's memory was exactly the reverse. He said Twain came to his Broadway office and declared, "Frank, I want to preach right here in New York, and it must be in the biggest hall to be found. I find it is the Cooper Institute, and that it costs $70 for one evening, and I have got just $7."[70]

When Fuller agreed to manage the event, Twain crafted a clever poster proclaiming that he would give a "Serio-Humorous Lecture" and promising "The Wisdom will begin to flow at 8."[71] He would also offer a topic dear to his heart: "How the natives dress, and, more particularly how they don't dress."[72] Unfortunately, ticket sales were slow, despite Twain's acclaim as the *Jumping Frog* author, and he blamed a competing troupe of Japanese jugglers, a speech by House Speaker Schuyler Colfax, and a Victor Hugo play starring a renowned actress. Unnerved by a disaster in the making, he announced to Fuller that "there'll be nobody in the Cooper Union that night but you and me. I am on the verge of suicide. I would commit suicide if I had the pluck and the outfit. You must paper the house, Fuller."[73] And paper the house he did, sending out last-minute notices to New York and Brooklyn schoolteachers to come and see the lecture for free. When Twain arrived at Cooper Institute that night, the streets were thronged with people and heavy traffic was stalled before the hall. "I did fill the house," Twain said years later, "but it was with three thousand dead-heads, sent for at the last moment, and nobody made any fortune."[74]

AFLOAT

Senator James Nye of Nevada was supposed to introduce him. When he failed to appear, Twain went onstage in his tuxedo and roamed around, glancing down into the orchestra pit as if searching for something. "There was to have been a piano here, and a senator to introduce me," he said. "I don't seem to discover them anywhere."[75] The packed house adored how he converted a mishap into this slapstick routine. From then on, Twain enjoyed total control over a rapt house. "I poured the Sandwich Islands out on those people, and they laughed and shouted to my entire content," he remembered. "For an hour and fifteen minutes I was in paradise."[76] In the *New York Tribune,* his new friend Edward H. House depicted how Twain's casual manner disarmed listeners and fostered immediate rapport. "He lounges comfortably around his platform, seldom referring to notes, and seeks to establish a sort of button-hole relationship with his audience at the earliest possible moment."[77] He dwelled on Twain's talent for exploiting pauses to give punch lines explosive effect. "But his style is his own, and needs to be seen to be understood."[78] Twain had long understood the importance of a New York triumph—"Make your mark in New York and you are a made man," he said—and he had now scaled that summit of success.[79]

CHAPTER NINE

"Grave of a Blood Relation"

The adulation aroused by Mark Twain's letters and lectures on the Sandwich Islands exposed the existence of a mass audience eager to hear about travel in exotic places. He spotted the chance for another such coup when he learned of a special excursion to Europe and the Holy Land, an early example of a tourist cruise, part of an incipient sightseeing boom after the Civil War. For Twain, fidgety, restless, and eager to see the world, five months at sea sounded like a godsend to settle his troubled soul and he foresaw a "jolly, sociable, homelike trip . . . for the next five or six months . . . a cheerful, careless voyage."[1] By mid-April, the *Alta California* agreed to pay $1,250 in passage money for its roving correspondent to join these pilgrims, and he, in return, agreed to file fifty letters, or about two per week. He would also contribute articles to the *New York Tribune* and even unsigned pieces to the rival *New York Herald*. With his usual wanderlust, Twain confessed that he was "wild with impatience to move—move—*Move!*"[2]

The cruise had originated with Henry Ward Beecher, who had meditated writing a life of Christ and hoped to enrich his tale by visiting sacred sites in Palestine. Forty members of his Plymouth Church in Brooklyn were to join him. Then rumors surfaced that Beecher wouldn't go—possibly because his pew-holders groused about his five-month absence and possibly because he needed time to finish his fictional work *Norwood*—and he and some forty faithful backed out. William Tecumseh Sherman was supposed to lend his august presence, then announced he needed to give priority to fighting Indian wars. It is worth flagging the interest of ex-Confederate Twain in touring with an eminent abolitionist preacher and a major Union general, marking a further stage in his evolution into an ersatz northerner.

The trip's impresario was Captain Charles C. Duncan, who had chartered the *Quaker City*—a 1,428-ton sidewheeler, built in Philadelphia, with a white oak hull—having converted this Civil War gunboat into a passenger ship outfitted with saloons, dining halls, and fifty-three berths (two passengers in each) suitable for the carriage trade he had hoped to attract. Twain touted it to his family as "a right stately-looking vessel."[3] It was not a foregone conclusion that a louche character like Twain would be accepted by the fussy applications committee. The first meeting on Wall Street between Twain, escorted by Edward H. House, and Captain Duncan is the stuff of legend, clouded by later animosity between the two men, so the story exists in several versions. Later on, Duncan described the encounter thus: "One of the first persons who made application for a berth in the Quaker City . . . was a tall, lanky, unkempt, unwashed individual, who seemed to be full of whiskey or something like it, and who filled my office with the fumes of bad liquor. He said he was a Baptist minister from San Francisco and desired to travel for his health. I knew him at once, it was Mark Twain, and I said, 'You don't look like a Baptist minister or smell like one either.'"[4]

It was always dangerous to joust in the public prints with Twain, who later fired back with deadly accuracy. "The captain says that when I came to engage passage in the Quaker City I 'seemed to be full of whiskey or something,' & filled his office with the 'fumes of bad whiskey.'" Twain noted that "for a ceaseless, tireless, forty-year public advocate of total abstinence the 'captain' is a mighty good judge of whiskey at second-hand." He said it was House who had introduced him as a Baptist minister. "But no matter, I should have done it myself if I had thought of it. Therefore I lift this crime from Mr. House's shoulders & transfer it to mine . . . why should I worry over the 'bad whiskey?' I was poor—*I* couldn't afford good whiskey. How could I know that the 'captain' was so particular about the quality of a man's liquor?" He ended by damning Duncan as a "canting hypocrite, filled to the chin with sham godliness."[5]

In the end, Duncan didn't cast Twain aside as a scoundrel of dubious honesty and accepted him as a cruise member, granting him cabin number 10, the posh stateroom slated for Sherman, which, Twain asserted, was "furnished like a palace."[6] Since Duncan was hunting for publicity, Twain's name soon popped up in the press as one of the celebrity pilgrims. Duncan had committed a colossal blunder, for he had introduced the most irreverent eye in America into a company of pious tourists who would furnish Twain with the comic fodder of his dreams.

On June 8, 1867, the *Quaker City* steamed away from its Wall Street dock in a pouring rain, carrying about seventy passengers, including many ministers, doctors, and military officers. Despite the inclement weather, Twain was heartened by the "cheering influence" of the sea. The "ceaseless buzz, and hurry, and bustle" of Manhattan had left him depressed, and being afloat was his supreme therapy.[7] He believed he had behaved shabbily toward his family on his Missouri trip and right before departing he wrote to them with regret. "My mind is stored full of unworthy conduct toward Orion and toward you all, and an accusing conscience gives me peace only in excitement and restless moving from place to place."[8] He acknowledged that his devil-may-care personality flimsily hid a tormented soul. "You observe that under a cheerful exterior I have got a spirit that is angry with me and gives me freely its contempt."[9] Easily bored and guilt-ridden, he possessed a metabolism that thrived on escapist adventures, and the *Quaker City* would provide that plentifully.

Other press correspondents had signed up for the cruise. "Everybody taking notes—cabin looks like a reporters congress," Twain grumbled in his notebook."[10] He would have to produce a fair quantity of prose as he would be cranking out articles for three publications. In writing about the Sandwich Islands, he had focused on the exotic locale, whereas on the *Quaker City* he would also home in on his fellow passengers—no less exotic specimens for his pen. With pilgrims drawn from many states, he could study his own country as he toured others and satirize both

AFLOAT

home and abroad. Twain found an ideal cabin mate in Dan Slote, the balding, rotund co-owner of a stationery manufacturing firm in New York. "I have got a splendid, immoral, tobacco-smoking, wine-drinking, godless room-mate who is as good & true & right-minded a man as ever lived."[11] Twain would come to revise that appraisal radically in the future, but for the moment he found Slote a welcome bulwark against all the philistine killjoys.

While he and Slote were contemporaries, Twain's attention was drawn to a young man of eighteen from Elmira, New York, one Charlie Langdon, the son of a coal and timber mogul. Charlie had been shipped off to Europe to woo him away from a romance that his parents thought ill-advised.[12] Bred in a respectable household, Charlie gravitated, a trifle guiltily, toward the carousing pair holed up in cabin number 10. "Mr. Clemens is just what he passes for a very funny man," he wrote from the ship. "His moral character is anything but good."[13] In his notebook, Twain jotted comments on Charlie, describing him as "pleasant, & well meaning, but fearfull [sic] green & as fearfully slow."[14] Charlie asked naive questions and was so inexperienced that he had gone to sea without a passport. Twain had no inkling that this callow adolescent was about to alter his life forever. In afteryears, Twain would bluntly portray Charlie as a rich young man who was excessively indulged by his mother, had never developed a bright mind, and ended up "conceited, arrogant, and overbearing."[15]

The ship was loaded with some pretentious fools, and Twain must have thanked his good fortune for this menagerie. Perhaps his favorite target was Bloodgood H. Cutter, a short, simpleminded farmer who cooked up poems for every occasion and distributed them on "printed slips of paper, with his portrait at the head," Twain noted. "These he will give to any man that comes along, whether he has anything against him or not."[16] Among Cutter's fatuous masterpieces were "The Good Ship Quaker City" and an "Ode to the Ocean." Cutter must have been an affliction to all the passengers, but for Twain, so allergic to banality, he appeared as a special torment. In his book about the cruise, he would christen Cutter the "Poet Lariat," and Twain never tired of jeering at

"GRAVE OF A BLOOD RELATION"

him. "His friends call him a lunatic—but it is pretty fulsome flattery; one cannot become a lunatic without first having brains."[17]

As the ship's resident reprobate, Twain was on full-time alert for religious hypocrisy. He had proudly informed his family that the passenger list included several "professional preachers," and he always proclaimed to enjoy their company.[18] Nevertheless, he developed a disdain for the sanctimonious passengers, "this picnic of patriarchs," with their nightly prayers, especially when they wanted to stop the ship in midvoyage to observe the Sabbath. Most passengers were forty to seventy years old and much too stodgy for Twain's tastes. "They never romped, they talked but little, they never sang, save in the nightly prayer-meeting. The pleasure ship was a synagogue, and the pleasure trip was a funeral excursion without a corpse."[19] Twain spent his leisure time with the Quaker City Nighthawks, whose smoking, drinking, and profanity rated as debauchery for their more staid shipmates. He was especially drawn to seventeen-year-old Emma Beach of Brooklyn, the daughter of a newspaper editor, who stood on the deck with him at night, gazing at the stars. Although Twain had a knack for shocking polite society, his underlying goodness could redeem him. William R. Denny, an ex–Confederate colonel from Virginia, criticized Twain as a "wicked fellow that will take the name of the Lord in vain," while granting him to be "liberal, kind and obliging, and if he were only a Christian would make his mark."[20]

Of course, even while flaunting his vices, Twain craved approval and wanted acceptance by genteel people, especially refined eastern women, who were far removed from the rambunctious western world he had known. He formed a fond attachment with a married lady named Mary Mason Fairbanks, thirty-nine years old, who wrote for the Cleveland *Herald,* a Republican paper co-owned by her husband. Writing in a stilted, flowery style, Fairbanks would publish twenty-seven letters about the cruise in the paper. A highly intelligent passenger, trapped in a stultifying marriage, she was a matronly woman with two stepchildren who needed an outlet for her well-stocked mind. She was "a Pegasus," Twain said, "harnessed with a dull brute of the field. Mated but not matched."[21]

Mary Mason Fairbanks would be a keen, sympathetic observer of

Mark Twain, whose odd slouch and drawl instantly beguiled her. "His drolleries and moderate movements rendered him conspicuous among the passengers, while from his table would come frequent peals of contagious laughter, in the midst of which his own serious and questioning face and air of injured innocence were thoroughly mirth-provoking."[22] She saw Twain's sensitive side beneath the buffoonery and uncouth behavior, especially when he told a fellow passenger, "I am like an old, burned-out crater; the fires of my life are all dead within me."[23] She noted how perceptive he was in judging character and how he exaggerated his foibles for comic effect to ward off critics. Mark Twain would spend a lifetime inviting women to reform him, with Fairbanks the first cast in this starring role. His relationship with her replicated that with his mother as he provoked a loving exasperation in an older woman who yearned to mother this wayward young man. He, in turn, wanted a woman to tame and domesticate him, and began referring to Mary Mason Fairbanks as "Mother," a nickname that stuck for the next thirty years.

In writing home about Mary Fairbanks, Twain described her maternal behavior toward him: "She was the most refined, intelligent, & cultivated lady in the ship, & altogether the kindest & best. She sewed my buttons on, kept my clothes in presentable trim, fed me on Egyptian jam, (when I behaved,) lectured me awfully on the quarter-deck on moonlit promenading evenings, & cured me of several bad habits."[24] Twain read aloud to her his letters for the *Alta California,* and she supplied cogent editorial advice. Like his future wife, she would reproach him for slang and vulgarity, and hoped he would aspire to "polite literature." She wanted him to be a moralist, not just a humorist. One afternoon a passenger saw Twain tearing up paper and flinging it into the sea, and asked why he threw away his writing. "Well," he replied, "Mrs. Fairbanks thinks it oughtn't to be printed, and, like as not, she is right."[25]

On June 21, the *Quaker City* reached the Azores, and Twain was soon mounted on a jackass, riding ten miles around the verdant hills and ravines of Horta, "with a troupe of barefooted noisy young patched & ragged devils" trailing him.[26] When the ship pushed on to Gibraltar, he seemed less than taken with the landmark, complaining that he was "clear

"GRAVE OF A BLOOD RELATION"

worn out with riding & climbing in & over & about this monstrous rock and its fortifications."[27] With a band of six shipmates, he crossed the strait to Morocco and waded into the bazaars of Tangier, reveling in scenes that surpassed in color anything he had ever envisioned. In his opinion, "the true spirit of it can never be found in any book save the Arabian Nights."[28] He stood transfixed, if slightly horrified, by the swirling activity and polyglot mix of "Africans, Moors, Arabs & Bedouins" from the desert. "This is the infernalest [sic] hive of infernally costumed barbarians I have ever come across yet."[29]

Before returning to the *Quaker City*, he stocked up on mementoes, including a red fez, dates, and tobacco pipes, and danced around the ship in Moorish garb. Meanwhile, in his notebook, he disgorged a farrago of slighting racial comments on the dark-skinned Arabs and Africans that he had seen and their supposedly ugly women. Full of racial denigration, puffed up with American pride, he brought a boatload of youthful prejudice to his observations, sparing nobody, including the five thousand Jews in Tangier. "Tell Moor Jews by noses," he wrote. "Tangier Jew won't touch fire on Saturday—steal though."[30] In *The Innocents Abroad*, the book he wrote about the *Quaker City* cruise, Twain would rhapsodize travel as the best way to broaden one's views. "Travel is fatal to prejudice, bigotry and narrow-mindedness, and many of our people need it sorely on these accounts."[31] Still, it would take Mark Twain time to conquer a wide variety of his own prejudices that were glaringly on display as he sprayed out satire wholesale during the trip.

In early July, Twain branched off from the cruise, boarded a train in Marseille, and set out for Paris. He wasn't the first American provincial smitten with the French countryside and from his train window admired "the presence of cleanliness, grace, taste in adorning and beautifying, even to the disposition of a tree or the turning of a hedge."[32] On July 6, he set eyes on Paris, his first European capital, and in an initial flush of enthusiasm, the city seemed faultless as he sat at an outdoor café with music in the air and sidewalks brimming with jaunty pedestrians. "It was a pleasure to eat where every thing [sic] was so tidy, the food so well cooked, the waiters so polite, and the coming and departing company so moustached [sic], so frisky, so affable, so fearfully and wonderfully Frenchy!"[33] (He may have been the first person in history with a kind word for Parisian waiters.) He was mightily impressed with how Napoleon III had rebuilt the city and was undisturbed that he had demolished much of medieval Paris in the process. Nevertheless, Mark Twain was an irascible personality and disillusionment soon set in. The barbers, the hoteliers, the crooked guides—he ended up believing that Paris swarmed with swindlers and even found the fabled Parisian women homely and in no way comparable to their American counterparts. "Thus topples to earth another idol of my infancy!"[34]

By mid-July, the *Quaker City* reached Genoa, its first stop in Italy. Like many travelers on the Grand Tour, Twain, having rejoined the cruise, regretted that he was rushing from seven in the morning to midnight every day. He was entranced by the Genoese women—"the most tastefully dressed & the most graceful"—and pleased by "this curious old city of palaces."[35] During two days there, his skeptical nature began to rebel against the myths glibly palmed off on gullible tourists. After he stood in "silent awe" before the supposed birthplace of Christopher Columbus, the guide admitted it was the birthplace of Columbus's grandmother. "When we demanded an explanation of his conduct he only shrugged his shoulders and answered in barbarous Italian."[36] Twain's incredulity was particularly aroused when shown the ashes of St. John in the Cathedral of San Lorenzo along with a chain that supposedly had held him in prison. He balked at these claims "partly because we could have broken that chain, and so could St. John, and partly because we had seen St. John's ashes before, in another Church. We could not bring ourselves to think St. John had two sets of ashes."[37] His exposure to such claims about holy relics would deepen his skepticism toward organized religion, and much of *The Innocents Abroad* would mock religious fraud and superstition. "We find a piece of the true cross in every old church we go into, and some of the nails that held it together. I would not like to be positive, but I think we have seen as much as a keg of these nails."[38]

After two days in Genoa, Twain took the train to Milan and again allowed free rein to his whimsical, if sometimes cruel, eye. "If you want

"GRAVE OF A BLOOD RELATION"

dwarfs—I mean, just a few dwarfs for a curiosity—go to Genoa. If you wish to buy them by the gross, for retail, go to Milan. There are plenty of dwarfs all over Italy, but it did seem to me that in Milan the crop was luxuriant."[39] Twain's humor was uncensored, voicing forbidden thoughts, many of them terribly hurtful, but we wouldn't have Mark Twain if he had been overly solicitous of people's feelings. He lived in an age when many more subjects were considered fair game for a satirist, and he could sometimes betray a mean spirit toward the helpless and disabled. Born with a curmudgeonly streak, he was unconstrained by modern issues of fairness or political correctness. He was a type of author hard to imagine today: a man born without an inner censor.

Prone to strong opinions, Twain delighted in bucking the crowd, and his motto could have been *"Épater les bourgeois."* At a time when Americans felt competitive with Europe, he enjoyed thumbing his nose at European culture and knocking their art down a peg or two. He liked to play the sophisticated rube who saw through foreign wiles, and his gibes at Old Masters became one of his trademarks. In Milan, when he visited Leonardo da Vinci's *Last Supper* and found a dozen artists painting copies, he wrote that he "could not help noticing how superior the copies were to the original."[40] Partly his grievance stemmed from the weathered condition of the mural painting, which struck him as a "mournful wreck" and a "perfect old nightmare of a picture," daubed on a "dilapidated wall" of the Church of Santa Maria delle Grazie.[41] He conceded, grudgingly, that the *Last Supper* might once have been a masterwork; in its current degraded state, however, "the spectator can not [sic] really tell, now, whether the disciples are Hebrews or Italians."[42] Traveling from one country to the next, he was also perplexed at how saints seemed to switch nationality in each new locality. "Can it be possible that the painters make John the Baptist a Spaniard in Madrid and an Irishman in Dublin?"[43]

In Venice, Twain vacillated between scorn and reverie. "In the treacherous sunlight we see Venice decayed, forlorn, poverty-stricken, and commerceless—forgotten and utterly insignificant. But in the moonlight, her fourteen centuries of greatness fling their glories about her, and once more she is the princeliest among the nations of the earth."[44] He fired new potshots at the Old Masters, grumbling that "when I had seen one of these martyrs I had seen them all. They all have a marked family resemblance to each other, they dress alike, in coarse monkish robes and sandals, they are all bald headed . . . and without exception they are gazing heavenward."[45] At the same time it grew clear that the past cast a potent spell over him, that he loved to daydream and escape into history. For all his anticlerical bent, he was transported by ancient churches. "We have stood in the dim religious light of these hoary sanctuaries, in the midst of long ranks of dusty monuments and effigies of the great dead of Venice," with a part of his being "walking among the phantoms of the tenth" century.[46] These comments preview the unalloyed joy with which he would later evoke Tudor and Arthurian England in his novels.

While in Venice, Twain hired a Black guide whose parents had been born into slavery in South Carolina and brought him to Venice as an infant. Twain was totally taken with this man—his mastery of four languages, his deep knowledge of art and Venetian history, his flawless dress, his beautiful manners. In describing him, he ended up making a bold statement about racial inequality in post–Civil War America. "Negroes are deemed as good as white people, in Venice, and so this man feels no desire to go back to his native land. His judgment is correct."[47]

As his Italian tour resumed in Florence, Twain was increasingly dismayed by the inexcusable gap in wealth between churches and their surrounding poverty. He passed by hordes of beggars clustered at the doors of magnificent cathedrals. "Now, where is the use," he wondered, "of allowing all those riches to lie idle, while half of that community hardly know, from day to day, how they are going to keep body and soul together?"[48] It grew clear that Twain's discomfort with the Old Masters arose partly from a belief that their work glorified tyrants who acted as their patrons. "Raphael pictures such infernal villains as Catherine and Marie de Medicis seated in heaven and conversing familiarly with the Virgin Mary and the angels . . . and yet my friends abuse me . . . because I fail sometimes to see the beauty that is in their productions."[49] Years

"GRAVE OF A BLOOD RELATION"

later, still blinded by rage toward Italian Renaissance art, he condemned the Sistine Chapel ceiling as "Michelangelo's nightmare," deriding its "ostensible human beings" as "repulsive monstrosities." Raphael fared little better and the people in his cartoons were castigated as "maniacs, even the dead ones."[50] Later, back in New York, Twain would pronounce his final epitaph on the Old Masters: "I am glad the old masters are all dead, and I only wish they had died sooner."[51]

Twain was back aboard the *Quaker City* on August 14 when it arrived at Athens, only to discover that it would be stuck in quarantine for twenty-four hours before sailing to Constantinople. To be denied a stop in Athens was intensely frustrating to Twain, who could view through a telescope "the grand ruins upon the Acropolis" and even "count the columns of the Parthenon."[52] Nothing spurred Mark Twain to action like a prohibition. In a stunt worthy of Tom Sawyer, he banded together with three other passengers and slipped ashore at eleven o'clock at night, "then straggled over the hills, serenaded by a hundred dogs, skirted the town under a clouded moon," and scrambled up to the Acropolis.[53] Twain fairly shivered with excitement as he stood "under the towering massive walls of the ancient citadel of Athens, walls that had loomed above the heads of better men than we, a thousand years before the son of God was born."[54] The rogue group made it back to the ship at 4:30 a.m. amid the first streaks of dawn.

The *Quaker City* steamed ahead to Constantinople, a city that at first appealed to Twain with a surface picturesqueness, only to repel him on closer inspection. Despite his brief stay, he unleashed a string of snap judgments about the city. "Mosques are plenty, churches are plenty, graveyards are plenty, but morals and whiskey are scarce."[55] Somehow, after two days, he knew perfectly well that "Greek, Turkish and Armenian morals consist only in attending church regularly on the appointed Sabbaths, and in breaking the ten commandments all the balance of the week"—a charge he would level at Americans as well.[56] At a Turkish bath, he imagined that he was going to fulfill his Orientalist fantasies of soft, sensual Eastern luxury. After the attendants brought him a narghile—a water pipe—he inhaled one puff and had smoke escaping from every pore. "The smoke had a vile taste, and the taste of a thousand infidel tongues that remained on that brass mouthpiece was viler still."[57] Things worsened when a masseur laid him on a raised platform and rubbed him with a "coarse mitten" and hot water. "I began to smell disagreeably. The more he polished the worse I smelt."[58]

After Constantinople, the pilgrim ship moved into the Black Sea and lingered at Sevastopol to tour ruins from the Crimean War, then made a memorable stop at the Ukrainian port of Odessa. Twain visited a beach where men and boys went naked while women wore "a single white thin garment." He admitted that he couldn't stop ogling these nubile females. "I never was so outraged in my life. At least a hundred times, in the seven hours I stayed there, I would just have got up and gone away from there disgusted, if I had had any place to go."[59] This hilarious comment—reminiscent of his reaction to Hawaiian ladies bathing nude—made it into his *Alta California* letter, but in deference to small-town American prudery, it was expunged from *The Innocents Abroad*.

On August 21, Twain wrote in his notebook that several gentlemen aboard had suggested a visit to the Emperor of Russia, Czar Alexander II, then spending the summer at his palace in nearby Yalta. This idea originated in a covert plan by *Quaker City* owners to try to sell their boat to the czar. Amazingly enough, the monarch agreed to receive the American visitors. By the standards of Russian czars, Alexander II was deemed relatively moderate, having abolished the system of serf labor. He had survived two assassination attempts, the second a month before the *Quaker City* visit. The scourge of a later czar, Twain was drafted to write a note to Alexander and composed a surprisingly flowery tribute. He didn't mind this, he told his family, "because I have no modesty & would as soon write an Emperor as to anybody else."[60] In his message, Twain zeroed in on the slavery issue. "One of the brightest pages that has graced the world's history . . . was recorded by your Majesty's hand when it loosed the bonds of twenty million serfs; & Americans can but esteem it a privilege to do honor to a ruler who has wrought so great a deed. The lesson that was taught us then, we have profited by, & are free in truth, to-day, even as we were before in name."[61]

"GRAVE OF A BLOOD RELATION"

On the appointed day, the passengers piled into carriages and rode to the palace to meet the emperor, expecting a fifteen-minute audience. Instead, they stayed for four hours, and Twain was astonished by the emperor's noble appearance and the simplicity and kindness of his family. "They all talk English & they were all very neatly but very plainly dressed," Twain wrote home. "You all dress a good deal finer than they were dressed. The Emperor & his family threw off all reserve & showed us all over the palace themselves."[62] This reaction set a pattern for Twain's future brushes with royalty: though stoutly antimonarchical in principle, he found royals congenial in the flesh and meeting them flattered his ego. The one embarrassing moment came when Daniel D. Leary, a *Quaker City* owner, buttonholed the emperor about coming to see the ship. As one observer recollected, Leary blocked the emperor's path and stood there "with his mouth wide open, showing his teeth, and putting his hand on his shoulder, urging him to come on board; three times was this repeated."[63]

That Mark Twain was famished for love grew clear when he fell for Russian girls not once but twice at Yalta. Improbably, he was all aflutter when he met the czar's daughter, a "weak, diffident school-girl . . . She was only a girl, and she looked like a thousand others I have seen, but never a girl provoked such a novel and peculiar interest in me before."[64] This sudden interest was consistent with his powerful, never-failing attraction to innocent teenage girls. Then he went to a ball and met a girl who absolutely hypnotized him. As he told *Alta California* readers, "I danced an astonishing sort of dance an hour long . . . with the most beautiful girl that ever lived, and we talked incessantly, and laughed exhaustingly, and neither one ever knew what the other was driving at."[65] This girl, too, possessed a strange staying power in his imagination, as he confided to his notebook. "That beautiful little devil I danced with at the ball in that impossible Russian dance, still runs in my head. Ah me!—if I had only known how to talk Russian!"[66]

Ripe for a love affair, Twain had reached age thirty-one without a long-term relationship and no real chemistry to speak of since his infatuation with the much younger Laura Wright. He was a wild man in every respect except sex. Then, one night in early September, while the *Quaker City* lay anchored in the Bay of Smyrna off the Turkish coast, he stepped into the stateroom of Charlie Langdon and was thunderstruck by a miniature ivory portrait, nestled in purple velvet, of his sister Olivia. She was twenty-one and had a round face, sweet and pure, with the innocent air of a child, albeit with obvious intelligence in her dark, steady eyes. With her small face and delicate features, she seemed a teenage girl on the eve of womanhood, an irresistible combination for Twain. Beneath his ribald mockery, Twain was a suppressed romantic who needed a spotless soul to worship, and he kept returning to Charlie's room to steal glimpses of the miniature, later claiming that "from that day to this [Olivia Langdon] has never been out of my mind."[67] A pardonable exaggeration, but not by much.

For the godly passengers on the *Quaker City,* the entire odyssey had been a preamble to the sacred destination of the Holy Land. This phase of the trip would offer Twain extraordinary opportunities for blasphemous laughs, and he seized them all. On September 11, he set off with seven others on a three-week journey on horseback from Beirut to Damascus to Nazareth, ending up at Lake Galilee before the ultimate prize, Jerusalem. The caravan consisted of tents and provisions, twenty-four mules and horses, and fourteen serving men. Almost immediately Twain quarreled with his companions, especially those demanding to rest on the Sabbath. However hard he tried to ease into a biblical mood, he had a tough time squaring the harsh, arid landscape with rosy illustrations from Sunday school. He jotted down screeds against Muslims they met—"I never hated a Chinaman as I hate these degraded Turks and Arabs"—but the Muslims, from his account, repaid the dislike. He especially detested the Bedouins, who reminded him of Native Americans: "they were infested with vermin, and the dirt had caked on them till it amounted to bark."[68] Clearly, the Holy Land had not purified Mark Twain's thinking.

On September 17, Twain recorded with a trace of heightened emotion: "This is the first place we have ever seen, whose pavements were

"GRAVE OF A BLOOD RELATION"

trodden by Jesus Christ."[69] Over the next two days, as Arabs stoned their camp and tried to stampede their horses, the pilgrims approached the Sea of Galilee, where Christ had performed miracles. At first blush, Twain thought the body of water paled in comparison with Lake Tahoe. To his dismay, an Arab boatman demanded an exorbitant eight dollars for a ride across, and his companions refused to pay, despite having come so far to see it. "Do you wonder now that Christ walked?" Twain asked in his notebook.[70] He experienced a similar letdown in Nazareth, with its "mud hovels" and "fantastic Arabs & dirty children," and moaned, "Imagine Christ's 30 years of life in the slow village of Nazareth."[71] Repeatedly Twain reverted to the theme that our imaginations paint much more vivid pictures of the Holy Land than the depressing reality can sustain. When he saw the River Jordan, it proved an anticlimax since he found it no wider than Broadway in New York City.

On September 22, he entered Jerusalem through the Damascus Gate and over the next two days strolled the familiar landmarks, including the Wailing Wall, Temple Mount, and Via Dolorosa. However much he satirized fellow passengers for vandalizing monuments, he himself stole precious bits of Solomon's Temple. He paused, in a moment of filial piety, to buy a King James Bible, which he inscribed to "Mrs. Jane Clemens—from her son—Mount Calvary, Sept 24, 1867."[72] Although sarcastic about many claims he heard in the Holy Land, he experienced deep awe at the Church of the Holy Sepulchre. "I climbed the stairway in the church . . . and looked upon the place where the true cross once stood, with a far more absorbing interest than I had ever felt in any earthly thing before."[73] Of course, being Mark Twain, he played even this church for laughs and did so at the discovery of Adam's supposed tomb. "How touching it was, here in a land of strangers . . . to discover the grave of a blood relation. True, a distant one, but still a relation . . . I leaned upon a pillar and burst into tears."[74] No less than Satan, Adam would always be a rich source of humor for him. "How lucky Adam was," he wrote. "He knew when he said a good thing that no one had ever said it before."[75]

Overall, the Holy Land failed to work its magic on Mark Twain, and he closed with a mordant punch line: "No Second Advent—Christ been here once—will never come again."[76] Not mincing words, he admitted to being glad to get away from Palestine's army of beggars and peddlers, not to mention the frauds and shams foisted on tourists. The trip had chipped away much of his remaining religious faith, and Charlie Langdon told his sister that Twain had shed the final vestiges of any "veneration he ever had for the Prophets & Men of Old"—a disillusionment she would someday have to contend with.[77]

After a side trip to the Dead Sea and Bethlehem, Twain was pleased to sail for Alexandria, Egypt. Along with Dan Slote and other passengers, he squeezed in a trip by train to Cairo, where he set out by donkey to Giza to contemplate the Great Pyramid and the Great Sphinx. All the while he kept scratching out prose for the home market, and Slote was astonished by his output. "Why, out in Egypt, where the fleas were so thick you couldn't breathe without swallowing a thousand, that man used to sit up and write, write, half the night."[78] Though Twain had contracted to write fifty-two letters for the *Alta California,* only a portion had been published when the *Quaker City* docked in Manhattan on November 19, 1867. Still, he had written in such a fresh, funny, blazingly honest voice, daring to skewer things sacred to others, that he had burnished a national reputation to a remarkable extent. With many newspapers having pirated his letters, he returned from the transatlantic trip a full-fledged celebrity. As Mother Fairbanks wrote with pride, "The Quaker City sailed out of New York harbor with no celebrities on board. She brought back the Great American Humorist."[79]

Mark Twain was not done with the *Quaker City* by a long shot, for his letters stirred up a flurry of controversy among his fellow passengers, leaving many wounded victims in their wake. He published an article in the *New York Herald* that poked wicked fun at the prayer meetings and psalm singing of the devout pilgrims. Though stung by what he wrote, Mother Fairbanks, a loyal soul, sought to rescue for the public a kinder, gentler Samuel Clemens: "I believe in his heart [he] reverences the sacred mission of prayer."[80] The unrepentant author, however, refused to retract his statements. "The Quakers are all howling, to-day, on account of the

"GRAVE OF A BLOOD RELATION"

article in the Herald," Twain grumpily reported home. "They can go to the devil, for all I care."[81] His sacrilege even provoked discomfort in his own sister, whom he needed to reassure that there would be "no scoffing at sacred things in my book or lectures."[82] In time, Twain would expand and refine his *Quaker City* letters into the book-length *The Innocents Abroad*, delighting legions of readers even as it infuriated religious folks of a more tender sensibility. If a major new presence on the literary scene had arrived, Mark Twain was by no means a comfortable one, but a burr under the saddle, someone willing to tangle with anyone, make enemies, and say aloud what other people only dared to think.

CHAPTER TEN

A Branch of Hell

From his tour of the Holy Land, Mark Twain went to the unholy land of Washington, D.C., having been proffered a job as the private secretary to Senator William Stewart of Nevada. Fate was kind enough to slip him into yet another rank, unweeded garden where he could thrive as a waspish journalist. Twain, as usual, had money in mind, believing he could convert his sinecure with Stewart into "one of the best paying berths in Washington," as he would also have time to freelance for New York and western papers.[1] Stewart was also amenable to his secretary devoting time to his *Quaker City* book. Because Orion had emerged as a fierce supporter of the Radical Republicans who ruled Congress, Twain hoped to wrest a job for him in the Patent Office or elsewhere in the federal government. "I will move Heaven & earth for Orion," he promised his family.[2] From having been Sam's boss in printing office days, Orion, on a fast downward slide, was now becoming something akin to his younger brother's helpless ward. From this point onward, he would be massively overshadowed by his brother's fame.

Twain had known William Stewart in Carson City when he was a lawyer richly paid by mining companies. A power in Washington corridors who served on the Senate Judiciary Committee, Stewart hoped to profit from Twain's renown and have him seed favorable mentions of him in his newspaper columns. His tale of Twain's arrival in D.C. was likely colored by subsequent disenchantment with the author. He was at his lodgings, he wrote, "when a very disreputable-looking person slouched into the room. He was arrayed in a seedy suit, which hung upon his lean frame in bunches with no style worth mentioning... and an evil-smelling cigar butt, very much frazzled, protruded from the corner of his mouth. He had a very sinister appearance."[3]

For a time, Twain roomed with Stewart and boarded at nearby Willard's Hotel, a tony watering hole for Washington power brokers, where he established himself with effortless speed. "Am pretty well known, now—intend to be better known," he informed his family during his first week in the capital. "Am hob-nobbing with these old Generals & Senators & other humbugs for no good purpose."[4] When Twain started smoking cigars in bed and feigning intoxication, the landlady found his habits intolerable and complained to Stewart, who summoned Twain for a scolding. "Clemens, if you don't stop annoying this little lady I'll give you a sound thrashing—I'll wait till that book's finished. I don't want to interfere with literature—I'll thrash you after it's finished."[5] Twain coolly blew smoke in his face. By mid-January, Twain had left his boardinghouse and, as in his peripatetic days in San Francisco, resided in five places during the next month. "Shabby furniture & shabby food—*that* is Washington—I mean to keep moving," he wrote home.[6] When he roomed near the Capitol, his landlord described his slovenly room as a "sight—books, papers and newspaper clippings by the bushel. He would not allow his room 'touched' and nothing to be disturbed."[7] His messy room seemed a symbol of his disorderly life, cavalier manner, and absentminded ways.

One Washington journalist confirmed that Twain camped out in his own private bedlam. He recalled "hundred[s] of pieces of torn manuscript which had been written and then rejected by the author. A dozen pipes were about the apartment—on the wash-stand, on the mantel, on the writing table, on the chairs... And there was... tobacco everywhere." Twain used to "strip down his suspenders... and walk back and forth in slippers in his little room and swear and smoke the whole day long. Of course, at times he would work, and when he did work it was like a steam engine at full head."[8]

From this hive of controlled chaos emerged disciplined writing for many papers, including the *New York Tribune* and the *Herald*. In a capital crawling with frauds, windbags, and rapacious lawmakers, Twain saved up ammunition he would discharge years later in *The Gilded Age*. As he wrote that January, "There are a lot of folks in Washington who need villifying [sic]."[9] In his notebook, he began filing away acerbic aphorisms about capital politics. "Whiskey is taken into the committee rooms in demijohns and carried out in demagogues."[10] He saw Capitol Hill as the refuge of small, selfish, cowardly souls, and Congress would remain on the business end of his best witticisms in future years, as when he observed that it constituted the only "distinctly native American criminal class."[11] Another time he said, "I think I can say, and say with pride, that we have some legislatures that bring higher prices than any in the world."[12] Then, still more memorably: "Reader, suppose you were an idiot. And suppose you were a member of Congress. But I repeat myself."[13]

At thirty-two, Twain hadn't thought about politics in any systematic way and his thinking flew off in many ideological directions. In his notebook, he put down thumbnail sketches of legislators and took a surprisingly friendly tone toward Union generals and Radical Republicans. Of Thaddeus Stevens he wrote—"*very* deep eyes, sunken unshaven cheeks, thin lips, long mouth, & strong, long, large, sharp nose . . . dark wavy hair Indian—club-footed.—ablest man."[14] He reserved kind words, too, for John Logan and his "splendid war record" and for "young, able & scholarly" James Garfield.[15] He left a piercing description of Benjamin Butler. "Butler is dismally & drearily homely, & when he smiles it is like the breaking up of a hard winter."[16] His praise for Stevens, an ardent abolitionist, and three prominent Union generals marked a striking shift in allegiance for a former Confederate. In a no less revealing manner, he described Congressman Charles A. Eldredge as a "leading and malignant copperhead"—"Copperhead" being a pejorative term used by Republicans to denote Democrats critical of Lincoln who were sympathetic to the South.[17] He even recorded a friendly encounter with Ulysses S. Grant, who still commanded the army, at a reception the general hosted. "Acquainted with Gen Grant—said I was glad to see him—he said I had the advantage of him."[18] He saw the bashful Grant as a martyr to the social protocols thrust upon him. "Poor, modest, bored, unhappy Grant stood smileless, anxious, alert . . . and nervously seized each hand as it came . . . He is not a large man; he is a particularly plain-looking man; his hair is straight and lustreless, his head is large, square in front and perpendicular in the rear."[19] Twain mused that he planned to waylay Grant "into a private room at Willard's & start his tongue with a whisky punch. He will tell everything he knows & twice as much that he supposes—he will be *glad* to do it."[20]

The evolution in Twain's political thinking can be traced in his shifting views toward the presidency of Andrew Johnson, whose coddling of southern white planters ran counter to the Radical Republicans' desire to empower emancipated Blacks in the South. Johnson had handed out wholesale pardons to former Confederates; obstructed Reconstruction legislation; gutted the Freedmen's Bureau designed to assist the once-enslaved; and allowed the Ku Klux Klan to murder Blacks in the South with impunity. Twain was slow to support Reconstruction. "The truth is," he wrote in January 1868, "that the more Congress reconstructs, the more the South goes to pieces."[21] As impeachment fervor took hold in Congress, Twain met Johnson at the White House and beheld a troubled man. The president "looked like a plain, simple, good-natured old farmer," and it was hard to conceive that this was the imperious tyrant. Twain was likely attracted to the embattled president as an underdog. "I never saw any man who looked as friendless and forsaken, and I never felt for any man so much."[22]

Nevertheless, Twain wrote electrifying articles about the "wild excitement" that seized the capital after Johnson fired Secretary of War Edwin Stanton, the darling of Radical Republicans, thus violating the Tenure of Office Act. In an article titled "The Grand Coup d'Etat," Twain left no doubt that he now sided with the Radicals, lambasting Johnson for his "open defiance of Congress—a kingly contempt for long settled forms and customs—a reckless disregard of law itself!" As irate citizens streamed through Washington's streets, Twain added: "Old citizens remembered no night like this in Washington since Lincoln was assassinated."[23]

A BRANCH OF HELL

Just how far Twain had journeyed from his political origins in a border state grew abundantly clear a year later when he wrote a newspaper piece, "The White House Funeral," that gave an imaginary version of Andrew Johnson's final speech to his cabinet. It was a savage burlesque that would have had Radical Republicans standing in applause, for it named the many sins they ascribed to the outgoing president. "My great deeds speak for themselves. I vetoed the Reconstruction acts; I vetoed the Freedmen's Bureau; I vetoed civil liberty; I vetoed Stanton; I vetoed everything & everybody that the malignant Northern hordes approved; I hugged traitors to my bosom; I pardoned them by regiments & brigades... I smiled upon the Ku-Klux, I delivered the Union men of the south & their belongings over to murder, robbery, & arson; I filled the Government offices all over this whole land with the vilest scum that could be scraped from the political gutters & the ranks of the Union haters."[24] This outspoken article never ran because editors at the *New York Tribune* killed it, probably due to a newspaper rumor that Johnson lay seriously ill in Tennessee.

Twain's stint in Washington lasted only a few months, and he shed no tears upon leaving. In a parting salvo he wrote, "I believe the Prince of Darkness could start a branch [of] hell in the District of Columbia (if he has not already done it), and carry it on unimpeached by the Congress of the United States."[25] Twain was gathering such a rapid following as a writer that he was besieged with lecture requests and eager to resume work on the *Quaker City* volume, which would propel him to a new peak of popularity.

Mark Twain had enjoyed a rootless existence with no fixed abode, a sign of inner turmoil. Given how sociable he was, it was a wonder that he had not yet married. For all his devil-may-care ways, he lacked confidence with women. Mother Fairbanks exhorted him to find a wife who would settle him down in a more regular life, leading Twain to respond, "I want a good wife—I want a couple of them if they are particularly good—but where is the wherewithal?"[26] Still haunted by fears of the poorhouse, he believed he lacked the steady income necessary to support a family.

On December 26, 1867, he traveled from Washington to New York to socialize with some boon companions from the *Quaker City*. The next day, he called on Charlie Langdon and his family at the St. Nicholas Hotel on Broadway, between Spring and Broome Streets. There he set eyes on the "sweet and timid and lovely young girl," Charlie's sister, Olivia, the same girl whose miniature portrait had hypnotized him aboard the ship.[27] At twenty-two, Livy Langdon embodied his female ideal, for "she was both girl and woman," he reminisced forty years later. "She remained both girl and woman to the last day of her life."[28] Pretty though not sturdy, she had a sharp intelligence, a fine character, and a fragile charm that doubtless heightened Twain's protective instincts. He immediately placed her high on a pedestal, seeing her as a rarefied creature with diaphanous wings. As he later told her, that first day she "seemed to my bewildered vision, a visiting *Spirit* from the upper air—a something to *worship,* reverently & at a distance—& *not* a creature of common human clay, to be profaned by the *love* of such as I."[29] Despite their ten-year age difference and Twain's budding fame, Livy possessed a quiet power over him and would give his life a calmer quality after his random wanderings.

It was an improbable match, to be sure. The sheltered daughter of extremely rich parents, Livy Langdon was as respectful of social proprieties as Twain was heedless. She wasn't the funniest person and could be tone-deaf to his humor. She would never dare to hurt another human being for the sake of a clever gibe. Yet something about this creative oddball, this brilliant, louche misfit, appealed to her. With his malodorous cigars and irreverent wisecracks, Twain must have been a lot to absorb, yet she wasn't frightened away by his intensity, whatever her unstated qualms. In later years, she told her longtime maid, Katy Leary, about her favorable response to Twain that day. "He didn't talk about the weather when he came in, like all the rest of the people, or something stupid like that, and she thought he was different from all the men she had ever seen—so brilliant and fascinating. She liked his being unusual and

A BRANCH OF HELL

bright."[30] Still, she would soon express a multitude of reservations before diving any deeper with this worldly, well-traveled man who had barged so abruptly into her life.

Although doubtless a bit bemused by Twain, Livy's parents liked him enough that they invited him along to a reading being given by Charles Dickens at Steinway Hall on New Year's Eve. It was Dickens's farewell tour in America, and throngs of readers flocked to the auditorium. At the lecture, without knowing it, Livy witnessed a historic moment. Mark Twain had been a toddler when Dickens enjoyed his first runaway success with *The Pickwick Papers*. Now the great novelist at the outset of his career scrutinized the great novelist at the close of his. It was there, Twain later said, that he held Livy's hand for the first time—a detail only a true romantic would never forget.[31] Twain also remembered how Dickens stood in a powerful spotlight, wearing a black velvet coat with a large red flower blossoming in his buttonhole. With considerable emotion, Dickens read and acted out the scene in *David Copperfield* in which James Steerforth perishes in a storm at sea.

Livy got a quick lesson in what a tough critic of other writers Mark Twain could be. He revealed a secret of his own lecture success when he said Dickens did not enunciate his syllables cleanly enough. In his *Alta California* review, he also faulted Dickens for purveying a false sentimentality that concealed, he thought, a coldness at its core. As he phrased it, "his pathos is only the beautiful pathos of his language—there is no heart, no feeling in it—it is glittering frostwork."[32] (In later life, Twain conceded that the audience had been swept away by feeling.) Two years hence he would write a piece satirizing the saccharine Cult of Dickens and its fervid acolytes. Dickens had made out handsomely on his lecture tour, booking $200,000 in fees, but Twain said his evening with Livy "made the fortune of my life—not in dollars, I am not thinking of dollars; it made the real fortune of my life in that it made the happiness of my life."[33]

The next day, New Year's Day, Twain saw Livy again on West 54th Street, at the home of some friends of the Langdons. It was the custom to make house calls on that day, and Twain claimed to have thirty-four on his list. Instead, he went straight to Livy and stayed the whole day with her and her dear friend Alice Hooker, a niece of Henry Ward Beecher. "We sent the old folks home early," he told his family, "with instructions not to send the carriage till midnight, & then I just staid [sic] there & deviled [sic] the life out of those girls."[34] By the time they parted, Twain had received a coveted invitation to visit the Langdons at their home in Elmira, in upstate New York, although he wouldn't manage to make the trek until August.

Hardly had the *Quaker City* docked than Elisha Bliss, Jr., of the American Publishing Company in Hartford, wrote to Twain and wooed him to produce a book about the cruise, possibly a compilation of his *Alta California* letters. Bliss had a massive bald, domed head offset by a mustache and muttonchop whiskers. He was a canny publisher with an eye on the main chance, and one author complained that he was "more difficult to open than an Egyptian tomb."[35] He assured Twain, "We are perhaps the oldest subscription house in the country, and have never failed to give a book an *immense* circulation . . . If you have any thought of writing a book . . . we should be pleased to see you, and will do so."[36] Subscription publishing, much in vogue after the Civil War as an alternative to bookstores, was conducted by legions of salesmen who went door-to-door, armed with fancy prospectuses for forthcoming titles, and took advance orders. Many remote rural areas lacked bookstores, and subscription houses filled the vacuum. Customers got to see sample pages and even select preferred bindings. What this prosaic method lacked in prestige—it was considered a lowly corner of the publishing world, shunned by high-toned writers—it made up for in profits since subscription books tended to sell at lofty retail prices. Twain became a convert to this lucrative style of publishing—he liked that subscription agents accosted farmers and small tradesmen in the heartland—and would be hooked on it long after its popularity had waned.

Jumping at the bait dangled by Bliss, Twain fired back a slew of pertinent questions, not the least of which concerned profit: "what amount of money I might possibly make out of it. The latter clause has a degree of importance for me which is almost beyond my own comprehension."[37] Twain was never a literary snob faking indifference to sales. In late January, he made his way to Hartford and met with Bliss, whom he described, in his later jaundiced view, as "a tall, lean, skinny, yellow, toothless, bald-headed, rat-eyed professional liar and scoundrel," with "the intense earnestness and eagerness of a circular-saw" when it came to money matters.[38] But this bitter view came with hindsight. Now he signed a contract with Bliss to publish his *Quaker City* book for a 5 percent royalty, leaving him giddy. As he told Will Bowen, "I have just come down from Hartford, Conn., where I have made a tip-top contract for a 600-page book, & I feel perfectly jolly. It is with the heaviest publishing house in America, & I get the best terms they have ever offered any man save one."[39] He mistakenly believed only Horace Greeley had secured better terms. A writer chronically dissatisfied, if not outright paranoid, toward publishers, Mark Twain was momentarily a happy man, having impressed upon Bliss the special place of money in his heart. "I wasn't going to touch a book unless there was *money* in it, & a good deal of it," he bragged to his family. "I told them so."[40]

Not only was Twain seduced by the contract, but by the air of comfort and prosperity he found in Hartford, home to many publishers, printers, bankers, insurers, and even arms manufacturers. However alien it might have seemed after the rowdy West, he was graciously hosted by John and Isabella Beecher Hooker, the parents of Livy's close friend Alice. "I have had a tip-top time here, for a few days," he reported home, praising eastern hospitality. "Puritans are mighty strait-laced, & they won't let me smoke in the parlor, but the Almighty don't make any better people."[41] Twain was aware that he made for a strange fit in these sedate precincts, where they frowned on chewing tobacco, drinking, and swearing. "It comes a little hard to lead such a sinless life," he admitted to Mother Fairbanks, "but then you know it won't be for long—I can let myself out when I get to Washington."[42]

Twain had scored a commercial breakthrough in Hartford that proved short-lived. He had already prepared the book's early chapters when he heard news from the West Coast that threw a shadow across his plans: the irate *Alta California* publishers owned his *Quaker City* letters and planned to publish them in paperback form just to spite Twain, having been blindsided by word of his Hartford book. Always careless with business details, Twain should have pinned down these literary rights before proceeding with Elisha Bliss, Jr. Howling with outrage, Twain told his brother, "That thieving *Alta* copyrighted the letters, and now shows no disposition to let me use them . . . now they want to publish my letters in book form."[43] Among other things, Twain knew his *Alta* letters were often rough and inelegant, and he dreaded their premature appearance between two covers. "If the *Alta*'s book were to come out with those wretched, slangy letters unrevised," he told Mother Fairbanks, "I should be utterly ruined."[44] Not losing any time, he resolved to sail to San Francisco and thrash out the matter in person. After arriving in early April, he haggled with *Alta* editors for a month before he informed Elisha Bliss, Jr., on May 5 that the reluctant editors had conferred their blessing on the Hartford volume. "I am steadily at work," he told Bliss, "& shall start East with the completed manuscript, about the middle of June."[45] The *Alta* editors agreed to drop their book plans. Henceforth, Twain would be a writer headquartered on the Eastern Seaboard and much less of a "western" writer than before.

While awaiting the final nod from the *Alta* publishers, Twain drummed up support for his forthcoming book with a *Quaker City* lecture tour as he revisited the same California and Nevada circuit he had trod for his Sandwich Islands engagements. He was now a celebrity who played to large, packed halls. This was a far more controversial tour, however, for his *Alta* letters had trespassed on some holy terrain and local ministers bristled. From the pulpit, one clergyman thundered against "this son of the devil, Mark Twain," while a Baptist preacher railed against "this person who visits the Holy Land and ridicules sacred scenes and things."[46] With some false bravado, Twain dismissed "the small-fry ministers who assail me."[47] One side of Twain gloried in being an apostate, cultivating a special rapport with the devil, but the censure of prominent clergymen surely dismayed him. He was in church for the Baptist preacher, and one newspaper reported that his remarks "caused many eyes to be turned toward Mr. Twain, who manifested considerable signs of uneasiness."[48] Twain handled the situation tactfully, approaching the preacher afterward and saying, "Sir, I never receive a good dressing-down which I deserve unless I thank the party for it. I am Mark Twain."[49]

His return to California had also enabled him to renew his friendship with Bret Harte. After Twain roughed out a complete draft of his book, working at a torrid pace, Harte supplied painstaking editorial advice for the *Quaker City* manuscript. Twain gave Harte credit for having "trimmed & trained & schooled me patiently until he changed me from an awkward utterer of coarse grotesquenesses to a writer of paragraphs & chapters that have found a certain favor."[50] Harte's edits were modest and sensible, shortening the text in places and toning down religious skepticism in others, but he didn't alter the book's essential character. A self-critical impulse was clearly at work in Twain, who knew he had to prune and polish his youthful journalistic writing to gain full favor as a national book author.

On July 6, he sailed from San Francisco aboard the steamship *Montana* and bid goodbye to the city forever. His life was a continual farewell to places he would enjoy revisiting in writing but not in person. By early August, he was back in Hartford to complete his manuscript while staying in the home of Elisha Bliss, Jr. This second visit only ratified his sense that Hartford was an ideal city, the most congenial place he had ever known: stately without being stuffy, aristocratic but not exclusive. "I never saw any place where morality and huckleberries flourished as they do here."[51] There might be poor people in Hartford, but Mark Twain could not spot them. He was transfixed by the imposing homes set back on wide lawns or enfolded in shady forests. "Everywhere the eye turns it is blessed with a vision of refreshing green," he wrote. "You do not know what beauty is if you have not been here."[52] It was noticeable how swiftly Mark Twain was scrapping his former world and adopting the Northeast as his new home.

The road to publication proved a bumpy one for *The Innocents*

Abroad. For all the aspersions Twain cast on him, Elisha Bliss, Jr., protected the book when skittish directors grew nervous about its "blasphemous" passages. Twain was constantly upset by delays in publication and protested to Bliss that his book had been postponed to make way for Albert D. Richardson's biography of Ulysses S. Grant and subsequent books. "These delays are too one-sided," he snapped at his new publisher. "Every one of them has had for its object the furthering of the Am. Pub. Co.'s interest, & to compass this, *my* interests have been entirely disregarded."[53] When Twain hinted at legal action to recoup his lost revenues, Bliss hit back hard. "If you want to say such things to me again, just come out plain & call me a d—d cheat & scoundrel—which will really it seems to me cover the whole ground & be a great deal more brief."[54]

In the end, Bliss did a magnificent job marketing the book, which made a huge splash when it appeared in late July 1869. This travelogue wasn't the work of a polite New England literary man sitting in a study; instead, it was rapidly sketched, seat-of-the-pants reportage from an observant wit. *The Innocents Abroad* had the freshness and exuberance of a prodigiously talented young writer embracing his newfound powers of satire and description. In this rambling narrative, Twain never let facts stand in the way or hesitated to embellish or invent material. With his magpie mind, he produced a rough, baggy monster, but one loaded with precious gems. As expected, some reviewers objected to its irreverence, even sacrilege, while most reviewers liked it and readers adored it. "Thirty tons of paper have been used in publishing my book *Innocents Abroad*," Twain boasted to his old piloting mentor Horace Bixby. "It has met with a greater sale than any book ever published except Uncle Tom's Cabin."[55] A pardonable exaggeration: Harriet Beecher Stowe's novel sold one hundred thousand copies in its first six months, compared to the *Innocents*' thirty-nine thousand.

Nevertheless, in its first year, the book sold an astounding sixty-nine thousand copies and became the rocket that lifted Mark Twain to literary stardom, guaranteeing that his pen name would be affixed to all future work. He dedicated the book thus: "To My Most Patient Reader and Most Charitable Critic, My Aged Mother, This Volume is Affectionately Inscribed."[56] He zealously promoted the work with his lecture on "The American Vandal Abroad." Even Twain had to admit that, in Bliss's capable hands, his book was selling "just like the Bible."[57] In many ways it proved a misfortune for Twain that this first complete book was the best-selling book of his lifetime, for it set a benchmark he could never match and that may partly account for his perennial dissatisfaction with publishers. He was like a gambler with a memory of an early killing that he could never quite duplicate, producing recurrent frustration.

Mark Twain was ruthlessly self-critical about his work, a perfectionist, and over time took a downbeat view of *The Innocents Abroad*, dismissing it as "apprentice-work."[58] Or, as he expressed it more poetically, "When the Lord finished the world, he pronounced it good. That is what I said about my first work, too . . . The fact is, there is a trifle too much water in both."[59] Twain's disdain for the book only intensified over time and Isabel Lyon, his later secretary, reported that "M.T. damned 'The Innocents Abroad' & said he wished he could buy up all the copies & plates & destroy them."[60]

Regrettably, the book began to bruise Twain's friendship with Bret Harte, who served up generous praise for it in the *Overland Monthly*. Calling Twain an "honest hater of all cant," he said, "Mr. Clemens deserves to rank foremost among Western humorists."[61] Yet Harte resented that Bliss's West Coast distributor refused to send him a free review copy, even after he had labored on Twain's manuscript, and when he relayed his keen displeasure to Twain, the latter bridled at the *"most daintily contemptuous & insulting letter."*[62] Twain blamed Harte for damaging their friendship "without any cause or provocation that I am aware of" and also slammed the West Coast distributor for his absurd stinginess about the review copy.[63]

Even as one literary friendship was being ruptured, another, much more lasting one, was being forged. In the universe of letters, the citadel of respectability was the *Atlantic Monthly*, and from its sanctum issued a long review of *The Innocents Abroad* that bestowed instant cachet on Mark Twain. Hailing the work's "delicious impudence," the anonymous reviewer opined: "It is no business of ours to fix his rank among the humorists California has given us, but we think he is, in an entirely different way from all the others, quite worthy of the company of the best."[64] The review stood out because the periodical seldom deigned to review plebeian books sold by subscription. Twain didn't take too seriously generous newspaper reviews. By contrast, he would come to consider William Dean Howells, the author of the anonymous review, the "critical Court of Last Resort in this country; from its decision there is no appeal."[65]

Eager to seek out the nameless reviewer, Twain, clad in a sealskin coat on a wintry day, mounted the steps at 124 Tremont Street in Boston and met chief editor James T. Fields in the cramped *Atlantic* office. Fields then introduced Twain to his thirty-two-year-old assistant editor, a well-groomed young man with dark hair parted in the middle, an ample mustache, and sad, yearning eyes. Before entering the literary world, Howells had written a campaign biography of Abraham Lincoln and served as the U.S. consul in Venice. He was a gentle, mild-mannered man who never swore and seemed rather prudish, as unflappable as Twain was irascible. Twain's housekeeper would remember the unaffected Howells as "short and stout and jolly."[66] Already the author of two books, he would publish novels of breathtaking subtlety that captured the tumultuous changes of the Gilded Age. His fiction was urbane, highbrow, and erudite—in many ways the antithesis of Twain's—and much closer to that of Henry James. Like Twain, Howells came from a small town, Hamilton, Ohio, then still considered part of the West, and again like Twain, he had graduated from the journalism world into that of belles lettres. He even had a steamboat connection, his uncles having been well-known riverboat captains.

The relationship between Twain and Howells would ripen into a selfless friendship, free of the acrimony that marred Twain's relations with other literary figures. Howells delighted in Twain's company and bubbled with almost boyish laughter in his presence. Twain fondly remembered how Howells "doubled himself up and laughed till his face was purple."[67] Howells had a modest ego, wasn't competitive with Twain, and was generously content to let his friend outshine him. As he wrote

Twain in 1882, "Sometimes I think we others shall be remembered merely as your friends and correspondents."[68] That Howells championed Twain's work was no trifling matter: he stayed at the *Atlantic Monthly* until 1881, soon graduated to chief editor, and had frequent opportunities to review Twain's work and promote his career. He gave Twain a critical foothold in the eastern literary establishment even as his vigorous, free-wheeling prose and demotic characters shook the foundations of that sedate bastion.

Twain reciprocated Howell's high regard for his writing. As a meticulous craftsman himself, Twain derived "continual delight and astonishment" from Howells's polished sentences and thought that when it came to felicitous phrasing he had no "peer in the English-writing world."[69] In fact, he rated Howells's opinion so highly that he would allow him to comment at length on his manuscripts before publication and resolutely heeded his advice. When the books then came out, Howells had no ethical qualms about reviewing them for the *Atlantic Monthly*.

To Howells we owe some of the most trenchant commentary on Twain. As a man strongly committed to social justice, he appreciated this tendency in his friend. "The part of him that was Western in his Southwestern origin Clemens kept to the end, but he was the most desouthernized Southerner I ever knew. No man more perfectly sensed and more entirely abhorred slavery, and no one has ever poured such scorn upon the second-hand, Walter Scotticized, pseudochivalry of the Southern Ideal. He held himself responsible for the wrong which the white race had done the black race in slavery."[70] Howells knew Twain's laughter but also the tragic depths stirring beneath it. "I warn the reader that if he leaves out of the account an indignant sense of right and wrong, a scorn of all affectation and pretense, an ardent hate of meanness and injustice, he will come indefinitely short of knowing Mark Twain."[71]

CHAPTER ELEVEN

"My Honored 'Sister'"

In late August 1868, Mark Twain arrived in Elmira, New York, situated in the Finger Lakes district of upstate New York, for his long-awaited reunion with Livy Langdon. A photo shows a young man with thick unruly hair, a handlebar mustache, and penetrating eyes that bespoke a personality of flaming intensity. With a completed manuscript and a book contract under his belt, he was no longer an impecunious author and could now contemplate marriage with a clear conscience. For quite some time he had felt too poor to make a proper match, whereas now he was bucked up by good fortune and a strong whiff of fame. When Charlie Langdon met him at the train station, Twain didn't look like promising marriage material. In fact, he looked downright seedy and disreputable "in a yellow duster and a very dirty, old straw hat."[1] Never a silky character, he brought a hint of the uncouth West to Elmira. Embarrassed by his appearance, Charlie asked him, "You've got some other clothes, haven't you?" then quietly slipped him into the three-story Langdon mansion, set on three acres in the heart of town, so he could change before being presented to his well-to-do family and impeccably dressed sister.[2]

Though unaccustomed to opulent surroundings, Twain adapted quickly to the luxurious home with its aristocratic French furniture. It may have represented everything he aspired to in the upper echelons of American society. He and Livy strolled the Langdon garden and greenhouse, and took carriage rides in the hills high above the Chemung River Valley. As he spouted his usual geyser of funny lines, they often flew straight over Livy's head, according to her cousin Hattie Lewis, who said Livy "could not see through a joke, or see anything to laugh at in the wittiest sayings unless explained in detail."[3] For Twain, it didn't matter: he sought a wife, not a responsive audience, and Livy struck him as perfection. He was also enchanted by the Langdons, telling his family, "This is the pleasantest family I ever knew."[4] Evidently he overstayed his welcome, which stretched to nearly two weeks, for Livy said her parents had begun to wish he would go. They must have wondered about this charming rascal who had whirled into their lives with such cyclonic force.

Before he left, Twain, with a sudden rush of emotion, proposed to Livy and was turned down cold. Livy said "she never could or would love me," although she left the door slightly ajar, saying he could write from time to time, as if she were his sister.[5] Undeterred, he pursued her with the most powerful weapon in his arsenal: words. He began sending her, almost daily, the first of two hundred courtship letters that were extravagant in their romantic rhetoric, their overheated tone suggesting just how famished he was for love. Addressing his first letter to "My Honored 'Sister,'" he thanked her for "the patience, the consideration & the unfailing kindness" her family had shown, terming his Elmira stay "the sole period of my life unmarred by a regret . . . For I do not regret that I have loved you, still love & shall always love you." Sticking to her ground rules, he promised to bear "simply the sacred love a brother bears to a sister." He wanted a woman who would teach him, train him, civilize him. "If you & mother Fairbanks will only scold & upbraid me now and then, I shall fight my way through the world, never fear."[6] In these letters, Twain dropped his array of funny poses, dispensed with sarcasm, and worshiped Livy as little less than an earthly saint.

In late September, Twain was back in Elmira for a brief visit, prolonging it by a clever ruse. As he and Charlie climbed into a carriage for the ride back to the train depot, the horse shied, jolting the seats loose and pitching the two men backward onto the ground. Charlie was badly cut; Twain, merely stunned. To Mother Fairbanks, he described how he milked the moment for everything it was worth. "I lay there about four or five minutes, completely insensible—& then the water the young la-

"MY HONORED 'SISTER'"

dies were pouring on my head brought me to."[7] To recuperate, the two young men were laid out in the Langdons' library, and Twain cherished this additional time in the household. After the visit, he "sinned" in a fit of "hot-blooded heedlessness" and proposed to Livy yet again, leading her to rebuke him for being too familiar. "I accept the rebuke," he said, "severe as it was, & surely I ought to thank you for the lesson it brings. For it has brought me back to my senses. I walk upon the ground again—not in the clouds."[8]

Among other things, Twain knew that with Livy he needed to establish his bona fides as an upright Christian, and he started devouring books of sermons so he could present a new, sanitized version of himself. This was the same man who had mocked the piety of *Quaker City* passengers, and he was fortunate that his scandalous *Innocents Abroad* had not yet appeared. He soon proudly announced that he had made a "splendid" new friend at a church social in Hartford, an amiable Congregational minister named Joseph H. Twichell. "I could hardly find words strong enough to tell how much I *do* think of that man," he told Livy. He had met Twichell's pretty, pregnant young wife, Harmony, and carried off the "choicest books in his library." Twichell had apologized for talking too much about religion, prompting the newly devout Twain to reassure Livy: "When religion, coming from your lips & his, shall be distasteful to me, I shall be a lost man indeed."[9] As he shed a sinner's garb and showily donned the lowly robes of religious devotion, he told Livy how he and Twichell had visited a local almshouse, where he aided the pastor to "preach & sing to the inmates."[10] Twichell even introduced Twain to a clutch of other ministers, who surprised him by saying that "certain trash" he had written had lit up their "gloomy days with a wholesome laugh."[11] When the Twichells urged him to marry, Twain brightened. "I am in love beyond all telling with the dearest and best girl in the whole world."[12]

That Twain was so persistent with Livy and so uninhibited in his ardor is remarkable when one recalls his habitual insecurity with women and the prudish Clemens household. "I am not demonstrative," he later admitted to Livy. "I am always hiding my feelings."[13] He was willing to swap his old life for a new one, turn himself inside out, and embrace things that he might have found alien before. Was he brazenly putting on an act? Was there systematic guile here? Thirty years later, he supplied the answer in an unpublished story, "Indiantown," about the courtship of a young couple. "Courtship lifts a young fellow far and away above his common earthly self . . . he puts on his halo and his heavenly warpaint and plays archangel as if he was born to it. He is working a deception, but is not aware of it. His girl marries the archangel. In the course of time he recognises [sic] that his wings and his halo have disappeared."[14]

In mid-November, Twain launched a lengthy lecture tour with "The American Vandal Abroad," yet he refused to relent in chasing Livy Langdon. Right before Thanksgiving, he returned to Elmira, and when he laid siege to her again, she finally capitulated. With tears in his eyes, he had cleverly played the Twichell card, telling Livy how magnificent Joe and Harmony were when Livy "jumped up and said she was *glad* and *proud* she loved me."[15] After what Twain called "twenty-four hours of persecution from me," Jervis and Olivia Lewis Langdon gave *conditional* consent to the match with this brilliant but unorthodox suitor.[16] Livy had extracted promises that Twain would cut back or abstain from alcohol, commit to clean living, and strive to become a decent Christian. Jervis Langdon promised him ten thousand dollars and a free trip to Europe with Livy if he would dispense with cigars and ale.

A jubilant Twain exulted to Mother Fairbanks that "if there were a church near here with a steeple high enough to make it an object I should go & jump over it."[17] He told Livy he knew the fallen world from firsthand experience—"its follies, its frauds & its vanities"—and that he sought to escape its misery in her arms.[18] He professed a simple, unquestioning faith in her, much like "the faith of a devotee in the idol he worships . . . I do love, love, *love* you, Livy!"[19] For Livy, her love of Sam Clemens was perhaps a plant of slower growth, though no less deeply rooted. She showed immense courage in her willingness to accept Sam Clemens with his welter of foibles and idiosyncrasies. As she informed her friend Alice Hooker, "a great satisfying love has slowly gradually worked its way into my heart—into my entire being."[20] Livy was true and sincere and, when she surrendered her heart, she committed it fully. With her dignity

"MY HONORED 'SISTER'"

and good sense, she was wise beyond her years, and Twain boasted to Twichell how her letters were loaded with "solid chunks of wisdom."[21]

Before yielding final consent, the wealthy Langdons wanted more than promises of moral reformation from Twain, who knew that no earlier suitor had been allowed to approach their well-guarded daughter. From close friends the Langdons had gotten an earful about Twain, with Anna Dickinson, the feminist and abolitionist, warning that he was a "vulgar boor . . . I heard of him all about the country at wine suppers, & late orgies,—dirty, smoking, drinking."[22] Twain had to combat upper-class condescension, a view that he was a low-class, unsavory ruffian. Charmed but also somewhat unnerved by Twain, Mrs. Langdon wrote to Mother Fairbanks and conceded that the author was "a man of genius," but she wanted her opinion of him "as a *man;* what the kind of man he *has been,*" and what kind he "is to become." Though well aware of Twain's newfound show of piety, Olivia Lewis Langdon was frankly suspicious. "Does this change, so desirably commenced make of an immoral man a moral one, as the *world* looks at men?"[23]

Understandably, the Langdons wanted to investigate his past life—to "prove that I had done nothing criminal or particularly shameful in the past," Twain told Twichell—and he knew that might spell trouble.[24] On December 29, Twain wrote a heartfelt letter to Jervis Langdon, admitting that his life on the Pacific Coast had not been irreproachable, but that he should be judged by the more relaxed standards of western society. "We go according to our lights. I was just what Charlie would have been, similarly circumstanced, & deprived of home influences."[25] It was a gentle reminder of class differences and that Twain had grown up with many disadvantages. To Mrs. Langdon he repudiated his past self as "a profane swearer; as a man of convivial ways & not averse to social drinking; as a man without a religion." All that lay behind him, he swore, and he could now claim to be a genuine Christian.[26]

In November, Jervis Langdon had asked for six character references, who were duly contacted. Even before these letters arrived, Twain anxiously supplied ten more. As the first batch came in, the results were pretty dismal. One San Francisco clergyman, Twain said, "came within an ace of breaking off my marriage by saying . . . that 'Clemens is a humbug . . . a man who has talent, no doubt, but will make a trivial and possibly a worse use of it.'" One California friend reported that Twain "got drunk oftener than was necessary, & that I was wild, & godless, idle, lecherous & a discontented & unsettled rover & they could not recommend any girl of high character & social position to marry me."[27] Things seemed to be skidding toward disaster for Twain as Jervis Langdon digested these unsettling assessments. "What kind of people are these?" he asked Twain. "Haven't you a friend in the world?" Abashed, Twain replied, "Apparently not." Then Langdon said something miraculous: "I'll be your friend myself. Take the girl, I know you better than they do."[28] On February 4, 1869, thirty-three-year-old Mark Twain and Livy Langdon, ten years his junior, were formally engaged with a plain gold ring, selected by Twain with Mother Fairbanks's approval, solemnizing the occasion. Twain's conquest of the Langdons was now complete, with Mrs. Langdon telling Mother Fairbanks that "I cannot tell you what a wealth we feel has been added to us."[29]

The author fairly shouted the good news to his family in St. Louis, hailing Livy as "the best girl in all the world, & the most sensible, & I am just as proud of her as I can be . . . if you know her twenty-four hours & then don't love her, you will accomplish what nobody else has ever succeeded in doing since she was born."[30] Even as he adopted a new eastern family, however, he felt estranged from his old western clan, his courtship having widened the distance that he felt from his past. As he confided to Mother Fairbanks, "There is something in my deep hatred of St. Louis that will hardly let me appear cheery even at my mother's own fireside."[31] In July, he had sent ahead his trunk to St. Louis for a family visit, then never showed up, leaving his mother, Jane Clemens, now sixty-six, deeply wounded. She bluntly scolded that she had seen him only once in six or seven years, and that seven years earlier "all the people I know could not have made me believe that one of my children would not think [it] worth while to come and see me. There is no excuse for a child not to go and see his old mother when it is in his power."[32] It was a heartbreaking and shockingly candid letter.

"MY HONORED 'SISTER'"

That Mark Twain studiously avoided his family speaks to a deep estrangement from them, even though he felt their unalterable love for him. They seemed frozen in their past lives, while he plunged ahead into a brighter future. To Livy he confided how a "chill" descended on him around his family, that he felt a stranger as he saw them "taking delight in things that are new to me, and which I do not comprehend or take an interest in... I turn me away with a dull, aching consciousness that long exile has lost me that haven of rest... that type and symbol of heaven, HOME—and then away down in my heart of hearts I yearn for the days that are gone and the phantoms of the olden time—for the faces that are vanished; for the voices that were music for my ear; for the restless feet that have gone out into the darkness, to return no more forever!"[33] Before too long, Twain would reach back and lovingly recreate that world and build an international reputation on the back of it. His future relations with his in-laws would be far smoother and more harmonious than those with his own family.

To fathom why the Langdons were so intent on shielding their daughter from harm, one must know something of Livy's childhood and trying adolescence. She expressed gratitude to her adoring parents for rearing her in a "free" and "generous" household.[34] Confirmed believers in women's education, the Langdons supported the founding of Elmira Female College in 1855; its successor, Elmira College, would be the first to grant degrees to women on a par with those for men. First a residential and then a day student, Livy had attended the Preparatory Department starting at age thirteen, studying French and German, and developing a taste for highbrow literature. Beyond voracious reading, she kept a commonplace book in which she recorded favorite sayings, including one from Thomas Carlyle that would someday come in handy: "Next to possessing genius one's self is the power of appreciating it in others."[35]

At sixteen, Livy slipped on the ice and was partially paralyzed. For two years, as Twain later narrated the story, she was completely bedridden, lying on her back in a darkened room. Over her bed her family rigged up a tackle, hoping she could grasp it and lift herself to a sitting position, but she lacked the strength to do so. Then a faith healer, Dr. James Rogers Newton, came to her bedside, lifted the shades, and threw open the window. He made some reassuring motions with his hands, uttered a prayer, and placed his arm behind Livy's shoulders. "Now we will sit up, my child," he ordered her gently. To her parents' amazement, Livy sat up. The next morning, Newton laid hands on her again, instructing her, "Now we will walk a few steps, my child."[36] Livy was indeed able to walk a few steps. From then on, said Twain, Livy could manage to walk a couple of hundred yards without resting, but only occasionally more.

Twain's storybook account woefully understates the severity of what had happened to Livy, as attested by her mother's diary. For once, the real story is much more dramatic than Twain's retelling. After her fall, Livy's parents sent her to the Elmira Water Cure, to a sanitarium in Washington, D.C., and to the Swedish Movement Cure in New York City. James Rogers Newton treated Livy over an extended period, joined by a family doctor, and her incapacity lasted much longer than two years. "This morning Livia breakfasted with the family," Mrs. Langdon wrote in her diary in February 1865. "The first she has done so in *three years*."[37] Nor did that end matters. A year later, in April 1866, Mrs. Langdon wrote, "Yesterday Livia got out of her chair, walked to the bureau and back and sat down again without help. It seems almost more than I can realise [sic] that my child can once more walk." She added that Livy had attended "family worship for the 1st time in 6 years."[38] So Livy's invalidism wasn't ancient history when she met Mark Twain in December 1867. Just as she daydreamed of weaning him from dissolute ways, Twain fantasized about nursing her back to health. While courting her, he visited some friends in Manhattan, the Wileys, and told them he was in love with a rich, beautiful girl. "She is quite an invalid . . . I can give that girl the purest, best love any man can ever give her. I can make her well and happy."[39] This was a risky hope, however chivalric, since Mark Twain's demanding lifestyle would subject the delicate Livy to physical and mental strains that would test her limited strength.

"MY HONORED 'SISTER'"

So what exactly ailed Livy Langdon? That she responded so quickly to Dr. Newton's ministrations suggests a psychosomatic source to her problem. Certainly the prolonged bed rest must have atrophied her muscles and made normal functioning difficult without a protracted bout of physical therapy. Several commentators have suggested that Livy suffered from a neurasthenia common to upper-class Victorian women who climbed into bed and never climbed out. Cynics have suggested it was all manipulative trickery on Livy's part, a way for her to wield power in a weakened state. Other commentators have noted that Livy's symptoms are consistent with tuberculosis of the spine—Pott's disease—which can destroy bones, cause spinal deformity, and lead to weakness and paraplegia. Whatever the underlying pathology, mental or physical, there's little doubt that Livy had an inner fire and grit that would make her more than a match for Mark Twain. Beneath the silk and lace, the petite, well-bred lady possessed a core of steel.

The other factor that must have made the Langdons leery of Twain was the vast size of their fortune: Livy was slated to become a minor heiress. Twain wasn't a fortune hunter, but neither was he exactly devoid of interest in money. Jervis Langdon enjoyed a golden touch in business. Friendly and open, he was a warmhearted man with a wide face, ample paunch, and side whiskers. Born in Oneida, New York, into an old New England family, Langdon had faltered early on as a storekeeper, grounding him in the hardships of ordinary people; his fortunes soared with the Civil War. He grew into a dominant figure in the coal fields of Pennsylvania, both as colliery owner and dealer, and his investments extended into timber and railroads as well. It was Langdon who would supply Cornelius and William K. Vanderbilt with coal to power their New York Central locomotives. He ran a gigantic operation that shipped more than two hundred thousand tons of coal by rail each year. About a third of Livy's inheritance was bound up with the family business. Had Twain toured the offices of J. Langdon & Company in Elmira, he would have encountered a Dickensian ambience of dark wooden walls, hung with oil portraits, and clerks perched on high stools.

Mark Twain's life was transformed by far more than the Langdons' largesse, for he was no less affected by their broad, philanthropic outlook. They ushered him into a tolerant atmosphere that stood a world apart from his blinkered Hannibal boyhood. The Langdons had endorsed numerous reform movements, including temperance and women's suffrage, but most especially racial justice. In their home they had entertained many storied abolitionists, from William Lloyd Garrison to Gerrit Smith, and they supported Black education in the South after the Civil War. As Twain remarked, Jervis Langdon "was an Abolitionist from the cradle, and worked openly and valiantly in that cause all through the days when to do such a thing was to ensure a man disgrace, insult, hatred and bodily peril."[40] Olivia Lewis Langdon, a smart and sociable woman, fully shared her husband's political leanings.

While residing in Millport, New York, the Langdons had assisted no less than Frederick Douglass after his flight from slavery. As Douglass would attest to Mrs. Langdon, "If I had never seen nor heard of Mr. Langdon since the days that you and himself made me welcome under your roof in Millport, I should never have forgotten either of you . . . I have carried the name of Jervis Langdon with me ever since."[41] According to Anna Dickinson, when Douglass lectured in Elmira in 1872, he paid a visit to Mrs. Langdon and grasped her hand, with "the tears so choking & blinding him, as to make him drop her hand & go out to the streets. 'Thirty years ago,' said he, 'when it was an invitation to the incendiary, your husband took me home, sick, nursed, & cared for, & tended me as a Mother."[42] By a nice coincidence, Twain ran into Douglass on a lecture tour in late 1869, and Livy must have cheered his reaction. "Had a talk with Fred Douglas, [sic] to-day, who seemed exceedingly glad to see me—& I certainly was glad to see *him,* for I do so admire his 'spunk.' . . . I would like to hear him make a speech. Has a grand face."[43]

Many runaways on the Underground Railroad passed through Elmira en route to Canada, and very few had done so "without receiving a benefit" from Jervis Langdon, claimed his preacher.[44] Many were also aided by a formerly enslaved man from Virginia, John W. Jones, who coordinated their passage through town and onto railway cars. Credited with saving eight hundred souls, Jones drew much of his financing from Jervis

"MY HONORED 'SISTER'"

Langdon. As their preacher confirmed of the Langdons, "The family horse and purse were at the service of fugitives from slavery."[45] That the Langdons retailed this history to Mark Twain is confirmed by a copy of a book originally owned by the Langdons—William Still's *The Underground Rail Road*, a compilation of "*Hardships, Hair-breadth Escapes and Death Struggles*," which told of perilous journeys north by the enslaved. On the book's flyleaf, Twain wrote a long account of how a Black man named Jones, a former slave who lived in Elmira (likely John W. Jones), had rescued his sister, Mrs. Luckett, and her three-year-old daughter from slavery in Richmond, spiriting them to Elmira. At the end, Twain commented: "This account given by Mother, who knew the several parties."[46] "Mother" was how he referred also to Olivia Lewis Langdon.

Back in 1846, the Langdons rebelled against the First Presbyterian Church in Elmira when it balked at taking a decisive stand against slavery. Facing strict ostracism, they and other congregants split off to form the Independent Congregational Church—later the Park Church—which took a brave, outspoken position on slavery: "That the using, holding, or trading in men as slaves is a sin in the sight of God . . . And that this church will admit no person into its pulpit or communion who is known to be guilty of same."[47] The crusading preacher who towered over the church was Thomas K. Beecher, and Livy adored him and his wife, Julia, her Sunday school teacher. A tall, handsome man with a finely chiseled nose and a full beard, Beecher was a half-brother of Henry Ward Beecher and Harriet Beecher Stowe, and no less charismatic. With rugged, populist sympathies, he practiced a robust brand of Christianity that emphasized good deeds on behalf of humble parishioners. He had regularly stopped by Livy's shaded room during her confinement years. Never too proud to perform menial tasks, he sported the clothes and cloth cap of a workman, enjoyed billiards, beer, and baseball with the townspeople, and expanded the church into a veritable social services agency. To appeal to the masses, he preached to giant crowds in the opera house and was shunned by some ministerial peers for this iconoclasm. He even dared to correspond with Charles Darwin when the naturalist still qualified as an arch devil for many churchmen. However radical and controversial he became, the Langdons steadfastly supported Thomas K. Beecher.

This was a weighty tradition for Twain to sustain, and he made a point of being there when the noted abolitionist Wendell Phillips dropped by the Langdon mansion in March. In the run-up to the wedding, Twain stayed on his best behavior and kept vowing to curb his vices, becoming a model citizen. He made sure his letters to Livy were coated with plenty of sugary religious sentiment. To please her, he struggled to recapture some particle of his boyhood religiosity. Praying nightly for his salvation, Livy sent him weekly summaries of Henry Ward Beecher sermons, to which he replied, presumably with a straight face, "I read them over & over again & try to profit by them."[48]

The couple stood on a sounder footing in discussing literature, and Livy helped to pore over page proofs of *The Innocents Abroad*, launching her new role as Twain's trusted editor, and he extended to her the "prerogative" to "scratch out all that don't suit her."[49] He gave her his marked-up copy of *The Autocrat of the Breakfast Table*, by Oliver Wendell Holmes, and their shared appreciation for the book was a salient feature of their courtship. Although Twain recommended *Don Quixote* to Livy, he then regretted, with his customary prudery toward women, not having bowdlerized the raunchy text. "Don Quixote is one of the most exquisite books that was ever written . . . but neither it nor Shakespeare are proper books for virgins to read until some hand has culled them of their grossness."[50] When he read *Gulliver's Travels*, he told Livy that he marveled at Jonathan Swift's "scathing satire" of the English government. "Poor Swift— under the placid surface of this simply-worded book flows the full tide of his venom—the turbid sea of his matchless hate." Still, he shrank from sending her the book. "If you would like to read it, though, I will mark it & tear it until it is fit for your eyes—for portions of it are very coarse & indelicate."[51] Twain succumbed to the Victorian stereotype of the overly protective husband, shielding his delicate wife from lewd thoughts.

It was unclear at first how Livy, with her cloistered life, would react to the tart opinions and outrageous humor that characterized Twain's work. "She thinks a humorist is something perfectly awful," he worried to

"MY HONORED 'SISTER'"

Mother Fairbanks. "I never put a joke in a letter to her without feeling a pang."[52] It took awhile for the ladylike Livy to get accustomed to his penchant for shocking statements. "I have been outraging her feelings again," he reported to his sister Pamela. "She is trying to cure me of making 'dreadful' speeches as she calls them."[53] The Langdon hothouse provided flowers for many town funerals, and Twain found the comic possibilities too juicy to resist. One day he announced to Livy, "I have been in the hot house and there is a perfect world of flowers in bloom—and we haven't a confounded corpse!"[54] Twain's humor, his acerbic way of looking at the world, would eventually rub off on Livy, at least a tiny bit, but she would also train her future husband to function more smoothly in polite society.

Raised in an emotionally arid household, Twain was overjoyed that Livy "poured out her prodigal affection in kisses and caresses . . . I was born *reserved* as to endearments of speech, and caresses, and hers broke upon me as the summer waves break upon Gibraltar," he observed later in life.[55] Even after marriage, he was shy and awkward about showing affection. "He would stand near Mother and surreptitiously take her hand," one of Twain's daughters later recalled. Then he would glance around to see if the children noticed and, if they did, "he gave a tiny toss of his head and a half-embarrassed little laugh."[56] Livy might well be "pure as the driven snow," as he told her, but he experienced a powerful physical attraction toward her. The oddly revealing thing is that he responded to her *child-like* physical qualities. One day before the wedding, Twain watched as she sewed lace by the window, staring raptly at her. "It is such a darling face, Livy!—and such a darling little girlish figure—and such a dainty baby-hand."[57] He repeatedly addressed her in letters as "My child."

The wedding was scheduled for February 2, 1870, in the Langdon mansion in Elmira. Aware of the extreme disparity in wealth between his family and the Langdons, Twain urged his folks in St. Louis to stay away from the ceremony. His reaction seems to disclose some unspoken embarrassment about their provincial world. "Livy says we *must* have you all at our marriage," he told them, "& I say we can't." He cited prohibitive costs and a long midwinter train trip, which would be "equivalent to murder & arson & everything else."[58] What grew clear, however, was that Twain, and perhaps his family as well, worried that they would look shabby beside the affluent Langdons. Sensitive to their plight, Livy wanted to ensure that the Clemens family did not feel shamed by their relative poverty. "*Don't* let your sister stay away from our wedding because she fancies her clothes are not fine enough," she warned Twain. "We want *her,* and her daughter here, we don't mind about their clothing."[59] In the end, Pamela and daughter, Annie, now seventeen, came to Elmira while Jane Lampton Clemens stayed behind. Livy worked to supply her absence with Mary Mason Fairbanks. "I *do* want you *very much* to come to our wedding—do not disappoint us—Mr. Clemens' own Mother cannot be here and I am sure that he should have his foster Mother here," she pleaded in an urgent missive.[60] Mother Fairbanks came even as Mother Clemens stayed away. It was symbolic of the way that Twain was swapping his biological family for a new surrogate family; although, in fairness, it should be noted that he would later be tremendously generous in supporting his relatives.

On the day of the wedding, a hundred guests, almost all drawn from Langdon social circles, gathered in their home in a ceremony presided over by Thomas K. Beecher and Joseph H. Twichell. It seemed an incredible tableau: the court jester from Hannibal, Missouri, marrying the elegant young heiress from upstate New York, decked out in long white gloves. It had been a long and circuitous road for Mark Twain to arrive at this moment, having cycled through periods as a pilot, miner, journalist, traveler, lecturer, and now best-selling author. Even though he and Livy had exchanged many letters about the simple, frugal life they planned to lead, it is hard to believe that Twain truly imagined that the Langdons would allow their rich, coddled daughter to revert to an existence of Arcadian simplicity. "I know very well that *she* can live on a small allowance," he conceded, "but I am not so sure about myself."[61] The family wealth and Livy's intelligent, affectionate nature would give Twain the sort of peaceful home life that he could not have achieved alone. His prolonged nomadic existence was now coming to an end: he had found the perfect wife and was about to exchange his old existence for an altogether new and more secure one.

CHAPTER TWELVE

Wedding Present

Livy had originally hoped that she and her new husband, in their marital bliss, would settle in Hartford, whose "good moral and religious atmosphere" would complete the desired reformation of her new partner.[1] It would also place her in the neighborhood of her dear friend Alice Hooker, recently married to John Day. Believing that "the best property in the world is a successful daily newspaper," Twain angled for part ownership of the *Hartford Courant* and would nurse a grievance at being rebuffed with "insultingly contemptuous indifference."[2] He also explored purchasing a stake in the *Cleveland Herald* after Mother Fairbanks and her husband sought to lure him with the post of political editor, a position he spurned by explaining, "I always did hate politics."[3] Well, not quite.

In the end, he acquired a one-third interest in the *Buffalo Express* for $25,000, with half the money advanced by Jervis Langdon. After clinching the deal in August 1869, Twain told the paper's readers "it would be immodest for me to suddenly and violently assume the associate editorship of the *Buffalo Express* without a single word of comfort or encouragement to the unoffending patrons of the paper." Perhaps with Livy in mind, he disavowed the use of slang and vulgarity and promised never to resort to "profanity except when discussing house rent and taxes." He also swore not to meddle in politics too much "because we have a political Editor who is already excellent and only needs to serve a term or two in the penitentiary to be perfect."[4] Notwithstanding his professed lack of interest in politics, he soon plunged headfirst into editorials for the reform-minded Republican newspaper—yet another step in his long march away from his Missouri past.

When Twain assumed his editorial duties in August 1869, he showed up at the *Buffalo Express* office exuding an air of brusque self-assurance. When his new colleagues invited him to take a chair, he shot back, "Well, if this is the editorial room of The Buffalo Express I think that I ought to have a seat, for I am the editor." He came ready to pounce on copy, and within five minutes, recalled a staff artist, he had "assumed the easy look of one entirely at home, pencil in hand and a clutch of paper before him, with an air of preoccupation, as of one intent on a task delayed."[5]

The newlyweds didn't relocate to Buffalo until right after the wedding, when Twain and his bride, along with a party of family and friends, boarded a private railroad car, courtesy of Jervis Langdon, and proceeded to their new home. One of Langdon's business associates, John D. F. Slee, had been deputized to search out a suitably modest boardinghouse for Sam and Livy. When the newlyweds arrived in Buffalo, they were provided with a sleigh that took them on a strangely roundabout route through the city before halting at a stately three-story brick mansion at 472 Delaware Street (later Delaware Avenue). Twain was sure a mistake had been made. "Oh, this won't do," he declared. "People who can afford to live in this sort of style won't take boarders."[6] After some momentary confusion, Twain rang the doorbell and found Jervis and Olivia Langdon, along with Pamela and Annie Moffett, awaiting him in the hallway. Tucked into a little box on a table was a deed to the house, plus a generous check from the Langdons. Privy to the surprise all along, Livy informed her husband that this was their new home—a statement that gave Twain an "intoxicating rush of pleasure."[7]

They entered a house lit by a brilliant blaze of gaslight. Twain wandered through the thirteen rooms in a daze of fascination, wonder, and disbelief. The drawing room was swathed in blue satin, the study upholstered in scarlet, all secretly arranged by Livy, who had fully stocked the pantry with food. The bedroom had a majestic bed with a blue satin canopy and matching curtains down the side. The expansive wedding present included an attached brick stable, complete with a horse and carriage, and a coachman, Patrick McAleer, decked out in blue livery; a cook, a maid, and a housekeeper rounded out the team of servants. Livy reassured her husband it wasn't a pipe dream. "Don't you understand, Youth," she said, employing her new nickname for him. "Don't you understand? It is ours, all ours—everything—a gift from father!"[8] Flustered and embarrassed, Twain did what he always did in such situations: he cracked a joke. "Mr. Langdon, whenever you are in Buffalo, if it's twice a year, come right here. Bring your bag and stay overnight if you want to. It sha'n't [sic] cost you a cent!"[9] He allowed himself a rare pun—he had a lifelong aversion to puns—and alluded to himself and Livy as the "Happy twain."[10]

Residing in this well-appointed palace, Twain, so recently an itinerant journalist, lived like a mogul and assumed the trappings of wealth without the slightest trace of guilt. Drifting about the house, uttering exclamations of delight, he enjoyed a sense of unreality. One morning he awoke, glanced at the drawing room, and sighed at what a "perfect *vision of loveliness*" it was.[11] The newlyweds supped in baronial splendor, attended by servants who addressed them as "Mr. Clemens" and "Mrs. Clemens." Afterward, they retired to the library, where Twain read poetry aloud to his wife. Of life in this "Aladdin's Palace," he assured a correspondent, he and Livy were as happy "as if we were roosting in the closing chapter of a popular novel."[12] This steep rise up the economic ladder was not entirely due to Jervis Langdon's benefactions, as Twain reminded Will Bowen. "My book gives me an income like a small lord, & my paper is a good profitable concern."[13] However he might think of Livy as a simple, saintly woman, she had grown up surrounded by luxury, and her parents were determined to keep it that way. In time this brand-new level of material comfort and its crushing overhead would have dire consequences for Mark Twain's life, but that day of reckoning still lay far in the future.

No less than her husband, Livy seemed agog at their good fortune. "Two weeks since we were married," she wrote her mother, "it all seems like a dream."[14] More than just a humorous man, her husband treated her with exemplary warmth and delicacy. "I wish that I could remember some of the funny things that Mr. Clemens says and does—and besides these funny things, he is so tender and considerate in every way."[15] The couple was off to an ideal start, yet they knew such perfection could not last. As Livy wrote home, "the clouds will come some time, but I pray that when they do I may be woman enough to meet them."[16] For Twain, the early days of marriage confirmed his excellent choice of wife. "She is the very most perfect gem of womankind that ever I saw in my life—& I will stand by that remark till I die."[17] In her joy, Livy became playful in a way that Twain had not witnessed before, and he told the Langdons she had become "so boisterous, so noisy, & so lawless in her cheery happiness that I, even I, am . . . forced to put on an irksome gravity & decorum in order to uphold the dignity of the house. She pulls & hauls me around, & claws my hair, & bites my fingers & laughs so that you might hear her across the street."[18] With Sam and Livy now settled in Buffalo, Jane Clemens and Pamela Moffett and her two children moved in April to the town of Fredonia, near Lake Erie, forty miles south. Jane came to Buffalo with the Moffetts that April, and even though Twain detected some signs of early dementia in his mother, it was a happy visit.

As co-owner of the *Buffalo Express,* Twain began by putting in long, if irregular, hours at the office, often starting early and lingering until ten or twelve at night. He recreated the same productive chaos that friends had once observed in his rooms. He would kick off his shoes, then slowly strip off his coat, tie, and collar. He churned out more than one hundred pieces—features, editorials, and brief items—during nineteen months at the paper. Some coworkers praised his easy charm and natural manner, while others described a mercurial personality who could be bountiful with his wit one moment, then take offense the next, his mood suddenly darkening. One employee complained that Twain "confined his humor to his writings . . . and was not given to wise cracking or the amusement of his associates."[19] As a boss, he showed scant patience for writers who failed to produce. "No man detested loafers more than Mr. Clemens, and assuredly no man could be more pitiless in his treatment of bores."[20] That Twain felt cramped by the paper was shown when he agreed to edit the humor department of the *Galaxy* magazine. As he explained to Mother Fairbanks, "I needed a *Magazine* wherein to shovel any fine-spun stuff that might accumulate in my head, & which isn't entirely suited to . . . *any* kind of newspaper."[21] And Twain was so seduced by the charm of his mansion, his love nest with Livy, that he began to slacken attendance at the *Express*, sometimes dropping by only once a week.

Twain mostly adhered to the Republican paper's editorial slant and delivered scorching pieces that lashed Democrats in the New York State legislature as hypocrites "whose religion is to war against all moral and material progress, and who never were known to divert to the erection of a school house moneys that would suffice to build a distillery."[22] Too free a spirit to toe any party line, he poured abuse on the corrupt machines running both parties.

In no area was he more contradictory than in his warring impulses about money. One Twain biographer has left this tough verdict: "It is hard to think of another writer so obsessed in his life and work by the lure, the rustle and chink and heft of money."[23] In 1869 Twain published an "Open Letter to Commodore Vanderbilt" in which he detailed stories of the magnate's cruelty and greed—stories designed to show "how unfortunate and how narrowing a thing it is for a man to have wealth who makes a god of it instead of a servant."[24] He was especially harsh about fawning flatterers of the rich who genuflected before their every platitude. Two years later he published a "Revised Catechism" of the rich that went as follows: "What is the chief end of man? A. To get rich. In what way? A. Dishonestly if we can; honestly if we must."[25]

At the same time, Mark Twain was now the son-in-law of Jervis Langdon and a beneficiary of his breathtaking munificence. This proved more than a theoretical problem, for the month before Twain bought into the *Buffalo Express*, protests had erupted in the city against rising coal prices charged by the Anthracite Coal Association. The local iron and coal monopoly was operated by none other than Jervis Langdon. No sooner had Twain occupied his editorial desk than the *Niagara Falls Gazette* leveled a blast at "the criminal rapacity of the forestaller of the market,

Mr. Langdon."[26] With Twain at the helm, the *Express* engineered a volte-face in its previous criticism of Langdon and said that what might seem like price-fixing in the coal market was merely the natural operation of market forces. The paper lauded Langdon's gift of fifty tons of coal to the Buffalo General Hospital and urged citizens to honor his charity. When Pennsylvania coal miners threatened to strike, the *Express* slashed at them as "mob terrorists" and identified them with the violent Molly Maguires.[27]

So close did Mark Twain grow to Jervis Langdon that he traveled to Washington on a lobbying mission for him. When Twain bumped into an old crony from his western newspaper days, the correspondent was taken aback by the spruce new Twain who now "dresses with good taste, never drinks or smokes. Such, alas! are some of the results of marriage."[28] Trading on Twain's fame with *The Innocents Abroad,* Senator William M. Stewart shepherded Twain to the White House on July 8, 1870, for a brief meeting with President Ulysses S. Grant. Twain worried that he would be flummoxed meeting the taciturn Grant, "but something occurred to make me change my deportment to calm & dignified self-possession," he told Livy. *"The General was fearfully embarrassed himself!"*[29] In a later version of the story, Twain claimed that he blurted out, "Mr. President, I am embar[r]assed—are you?"[30]

Where Twain's views evolved in a notably progressive direction was in racial matters, where the Langdons exerted a benign influence. Right after joining the *Buffalo Express,* Twain showed a radical shift in thinking with a short essay called "Only a Nigger" in which he condemned a Memphis, Tennessee, lynching of a Black man who had allegedly raped a white woman. Only after the lynching did the two real culprits confess to the crime and admit having framed the Black man by leaving his hat behind. Beyond denouncing the lynch mob, Twain wanted to expose the underlying barbarism of fine southern gentlemen who murdered Blacks on the side and rationalized their terrible crime. He wrote caustically: "There is no good reason why Southern gentlemen should worry themselves with useless regrets, so long as only an innocent 'nigger' is hanged, or roasted or knouted to death, now and then."[31]

WEDDING PRESENT

More evidence that Mark Twain was sloughing off his southern identity piled up. A few weeks later, he penned a sketch of Henry Ward Beecher that extolled him for persuading "communities to progress beyond the endorsing of slavery with their Bibles."[32] Then, in a piece titled "Life on the Isthmus," he took aim at two large targets braided together: racial injustice and police brutality. He narrated how "when 'Mr. Negro' did not move along quickly enough" to please a policeman, "he only persuaded him to go by jabbing the bayonet into the poor wretch's head with all his force, and then as the blood streamed over his face, striking him on the skull with the barrel of his musket."[33] A couple of years later Twain began to collect clippings related to Ku Klux Klan atrocities in the South.[34]

Nor was Twain's indignation less savage when it came to sadistic mistreatment of Chinese immigrants. Though he had signed with the *Galaxy* to contribute humorous pieces, he was already fashioning the role he later perfected as an all-purpose pundit on topical issues. Anti-Chinese sentiment was rampant in America, a prejudice that crested with the Chinese Exclusion Act of 1882. Twain latched on to a San Francisco story about a "well-dressed boy, on his way to Sunday-school," who was arrested for stoning Chinese residents.[35] Instead of indicting the boy, Twain indicted the society that had produced him. Whenever "any secret and mysterious crime" was committed, cruel members of that society would "go straightway and swing a Chinaman."[36] Twain clearly had in mind the analogous persecution of Blacks, for he echoed the wording of the *Dred Scott* decision: "It was in this way that the boy found out that a Chinaman had no rights that any man was bound to respect."[37] After the passage of the Fourteenth Amendment, which provided for "equal protection under the laws," Twain had issued a public mea culpa, admitting that the idea of citizenship for Blacks and Chinese was once "startling and disagreeable" to him, "but I suppose I can live through it now."[38] The one area where Twain still hadn't matured was in his racist scorn for Native Americans. In a *Galaxy* piece, "The Noble Red Man," he mocked the romantic view that the Indian was tall and muscular and moved with a regal mien. "He is little, and scrawny, and black, and dirty;

and, judged by even the most charitable of our canons of human excellence, is thoroughly pitiful and contemptible."[39]

Saddled with debt from his stake in the *Buffalo Express,* Twain had to resort again to the lecture circuit, and these protracted absences placed a terrible burden on Livy, who hated the enforced separations. "Didn't we have a good visit together?" she wrote after he returned home for a break. "I do hope that this will be the last season that it will be necessary for you to lecture, it is not the way for a husband and wife to live if they can possibly avoid it, is it? Seperation [*sic*] comes soon enough."[40]

Twain had bloomed as a star performer for the Boston Lyceum Bureau, a lecture agency recently established by the English-born James C. Redpath, a fearless abolitionist who had fought briefly alongside John Brown in Bleeding Kansas and written a favorable biography of him. "He had a small body of daring men under him," Twain said admiringly, "and they were constantly being hunted by the . . . pro-slavery Missourians, guerrillas, modern free lances."[41] The comment underscores how completely Twain had flipped sides on the Civil War and now identified with the radical wing of the antislavery cause. Redpath would represent other major humorists (Josh Billings, Petroleum V. Nasby), leading authors (Ralph Waldo Emerson, Henry David Thoreau), and fellow abolitionists (Wendell Phillips, Charles Sumner, Henry Ward Beecher). As Redpath booked speakers into lyceums across the country, he helped to professionalize the lecture business and turned his clients into national celebrities.

A Redpath season was long and arduous, usually amounting to 110 performances for the exhausted lecturer. Although Twain signed on for two extended tours, he was not happy with their demands. While regularly drawing one or two thousand people per speech, he suffered every indignity on the lecture circuit—"ten thousand petty annoyances & vexations"—including poorly ventilated trains, shoddy hotels, dimly lit halls, and stifling receptions at the hands of small-town bores.[42] "I am driven to death with travel, lecturing & entertainment committees," he groused to Elisha Bliss, Jr.[43] He especially resisted being booked into churches—not at any time his native milieu. "I never made a success of a lecture in a church yet," he explained to Redpath. "People are afraid to laugh in a church."[44] A humorist was a novelty for lyceum audiences who hoped for moral uplift, and Twain was often frazzled by the demanding schedule. He especially detested chambermaids who woke him early in the morning. "I wouldn't want any better fun than writing obituaries for chambermaids."[45] Periodically he would reach the end of his tether and say "I most cordially hate the lecture field."[46] Throughout his life, this supreme master of public speaking would swear that he was through with the stage only to renege on his pledge under money pressure.

For all his perpetual bellyaching, Twain was seldom less than scintillating in performance. Typically he would appear tense backstage only to saunter before the footlights with smooth aplomb, clad in evening wear. His shambling walk, his poker face, his mock solemnity, his odd gestures—all disarmed audiences and opened them up for the kill. He gave the impression of being absolutely at home, as if he had strolled into his parlor and was confiding in the audience. The drawling voice teased humorous meanings from even innocent words. As one reviewer noted, "His most ludicrous jokes were related with a serious air that imparted a fresh flavor to them."[47] In January 1870, during a speech in Utica, New York, he achieved an epiphany. In a daring experiment, he walked onstage and, standing motionless, said nothing. After a prolonged, anxious interval, the audience erupted in laughter and applause, and Twain felt the full force of his power over them. "An audience captured in that way *belongs* to the speaker, body and soul, for the rest of the evening," he boasted to Livy.[48] He specialized in lengthy pauses timed perfectly to precede explosive punch lines. "I used to play with the pause," he said, "as other children play with a toy."[49] No other American writer projected so vivid a personality when performing as Mark Twain.

No less than in his writing, Twain was a perfectionist who honed his craft and developed *"dead sure* tricks of the platform" that enabled him "to vanquish the audience."[50] His delivery seemed so effortless that audiences thought he was improvising when, in fact, he often minutely prepared and memorized lectures, whatever the witticisms tossed off spontaneously, and his memorization skills were prodigious. With

Redpath he would offer only one prepared lecture, although he always traveled with a second in case the first failed. He used a strange form of notes; instead of key words he would draw a series of pictures that reminded him where he stood in the text. Often he tested a speech in five or six small venues before springing it on big city audiences. His talks succeeded because he tried to educate, not simply entertain, believing laughter was worthless unless accompanied by a lesson. "*People can always talk well when they are talking what they feel,*" he explained to Livy. "This is the secret of eloquence—I wish you could hear my mother, sometimes."[51]

Twain had recurring problems that even his artistry found hard to combat. After one botched lecture in Illinois, he told Livy, the "idiot president" had introduced him too soon, so that people were still streaming in as he talked. "I grew so exasperated at last, that I shouted to the doorkeeper to close the doors & not open them again on *any* account."[52] The more intractable problem was the pompous welcoming committees that wore him out before lectures and self-promoting sponsors who gave him a "grossly flattering" but long-winded introduction that put audiences to sleep. "The introducer was almost always an ass, and his prepared speech a jumble of vulgar compliments and dreary efforts to be funny."[53] As he had done in Nevada with the dusty miner, Twain came up with ingenious ways to introduce himself. Sometimes he would appear at the side of the stage and apologize to the audience that Mark Twain's train was running hours late, and he wouldn't be able to speak there that night. Then, after the disappointed groans, he would say that Twain was being replaced instead by Mister Samuel Langhorne Clemens and, spinning around, he would indicate to the audience that he was that very man. This trick, of course, became impossible once his face grew instantly recognizable.

Aside from Twain's lecture tours, the marital gods granted the newlyweds three halcyon months after the wedding. Jervis Langdon had worried that his fragile daughter might "not be equal to what lies before her," but he needn't have worried: Livy was able to contain her husband's volcanic energy and ran the household with crisp efficiency.[54] She had a calming influence as she aimed to cool off his combative nature, softening his rough edges. As he proudly told Mrs. Langdon, "You know I have to walk mighty straight when she is around. She isn't very strong, but she can make *me* behave."[55] Deferring to Livy, Twain mostly refrained from tobacco and alcohol, allowing himself reprieves only on Sunday afternoons. He even accompanied his wife to a local Presbyterian church despite the "atrocious" singing of the congregation.[56] When he said something sacrilegious, she learned to contain herself, determined "that his home was going to be a place where he could say and do what he wanted."[57] In return, Twain doted on Livy with a sweet, rapturous tenderness.

There were minor annoyances to confront. When mice scurried around the mansion, Twain appealed to his sister-in-law Sue Crane to send a couple of cats. "We have not a cat on the place, & the mice will not patronize the little trap because it is cheap & small & uncomfortable, & not in keeping with the other furniture of the house."[58] He was also displeased with water cleaning the city performed on the street before their house. As he lectured the Buffalo Street Commissioners, in a letter published by his paper, "The manner in which Delaware Street is sprinkled . . . is simply ridiculous. A crippled infant with a garden-squirt could do it better."[59]

By spring, Livy was pregnant with their first child, but the couple's joy was soon abridged. Livy idolized her father, who had gone south to repair his health, only to lose thirty pounds on the trip. She was extremely upset in early April 1870 by reports that he was vomiting his meals and suffering extreme constipation. After Jervis Langdon returned to Elmira, Livy and her husband joined him there in early May. "Mr. Langdon has been dangerously ill for some days," Twain reported to his publisher, "& it is plain that he cannot travel a mile this year."[60] At first the family pretended that Jervis Langdon suffered from "nervous dyspepsia," though it was soon diagnosed as incurable stomach cancer.[61]

With blinds drawn in the somber household, Twain assumed two nursing shifts for his father-in-law, one from midnight to four in the morning, the other starting at noon. "I can still see myself sitting by that bed in the melancholy stillness of the sweltering night," he recalled, "mechanically waving a palm-leaf fan over the drawn white face of the patient" while fighting to stay awake.[62] The patient continued to deteriorate. "He has lost a good deal of flesh," Livy reported to her dear friend Alice Hooker Day, bemoaning how hard it was "to see Father so miserable, and of course the house is very much saddened by it."[63]

On August 6, 1870, Jervis Langdon died, a mere six months after the wedding. In the *Buffalo Express,* Twain mourned him as "a great and noble man" who had taken his accumulated gains and sowed them "broadcast for the good of the city, the church and the poor."[64] A shattered Livy was so oppressed by insomnia that her husband "gave her a narcotic every night" and made her take it.[65] "I often feel since Father left us, that he was my back bone, that what energy I had came from him, that he was the moving spring," Livy told Alice.[66] Jervis Langdon's death proved a financial windfall for the newlyweds, bumping them up into an even richer bracket. Livy got a quarter of her father's million-dollar estate, while her stepsister, Sue Crane, inherited Quarry Farm, the beautiful country house atop a hill outside Elmira. Beyond direct bequests, the Langdon coal partnership was expanded to incorporate Livy. Charlie Langdon was elevated to the presidency of the Clearfield Bituminous Coal Company, eventually the biggest coal producer in western Pennsylvania, with fifty-eight mines, and Mark Twain would become a substantial investor in the company's additional operations in central Pennsylvania.

For Twain and Livy, Jervis Langdon's death initiated a series of grave misfortunes that would only gather strength. Once they were back in Buffalo, an old Elmira schoolmate of Livy's, Emma Nye, decided to stay with the couple en route to a teaching position in Detroit. She was supposed to care for the grieving, pregnant Livy but instead contracted typhoid fever within a week of her arrival. Still struggling to recover from the death of Jervis Langdon, Sam and Livy were again thrust back into

WEDDING PRESENT

the anxious role of nurses. They even ceded their bedroom to Emma, who gave way to "phantoms of delirium," Twain wrote, and she died on September 29.[67] So harrowing was the deathwatch that Twain later cited these days as among "the blackest, the gloomiest, the most wretched of my long life."[68] Emma's illness and death proved such a devastating blow that Sam and Livy were forced to skip Charlie Langdon's wedding to Ida B. Clark in Elmira.

Amid such omnipresent sorrow, Livy nearly suffered a miscarriage in October, one that Twain attributed to a rapid ride to the train depot over uneven cobblestone streets. On November 7, a month ahead of schedule, a little boy, Langdon Clemens, was born, weighing just four and a half pounds and measuring sixteen inches. The baby had a smooth, open face, blue eyes, and a soft mop of glossy blond hair. Like his father, he was born with tenuous health, and Twain immediately despaired for his future. Being Mark Twain, however, he couldn't help but inject a note of levity into the situation and wrote to the Twichells in the baby's own voice. "At birth I only weighed 4½ pounds with my clothes on—& the clothes were the chief feature of the weight, too, I am obliged to confess."[69] Twain's mind was immediately clouded by terrible premonitions about his son. When a humor magazine asked to publish a caricature of him and Langdon, he asked them to omit the baby. "If I was sure it was going to live," he explained a week after his son's birth, "I wouldn't care, but its health is so precarious that I hardly dare utter a pleasantry about the little fellow lest he pass from us & leave it looking ghastly in print."[70] Mother and son remained sick into December, with Langdon "dangerously ill," while Livy, in many ways, relapsed into the invalid state of her adolescence.[71]

Just as she began to revive in February, she ran a high fever and "rose spots" popped out on her abdomen: she had contracted typhoid fever—the same disease that had killed Emma Nye—and nearly died. Typhoid is usually spread by contaminated food or water. Nursing Livy around the clock, with a house full of doctors and nurses, Twain scarcely wrote a page of *Roughing It*, his new book of sketches about his western adventures. "Sometimes I have hope for my wife . . . but most of the time it seems to me impossible that she can get well," he told his publisher. "I cannot go into particulars—the subject is too dreadful."[72] Merely to move from bed to chair was an effort for Livy, who had to be helped into sitz baths. "Livy is *very, very* slowly & slightly improving," Twain told Orion, "but it is not possible to say whether she is out of danger or not."[73] He seemed at his wits' end with loss of sleep. "I believe that if that baby goes on crying 3 more hours this way I will butt my frantic brains out & try to get some peace."[74] A worshipful husband, Twain exhausted himself caring for his wife. Finally, in March, with Livy feeling a bit better, he carted her off to Elmira, lying on a mattress, for an extended stay with her family. While there he hoped to clear his mind and work on his western manuscript.

By this point the young couple felt imprisoned in their Buffalo home and so debilitated by constant medical crises that the town had simply become unendurable. The fairytale house had been transmogrified into a house of horrors. That March, Twain informed his friend John Henry Riley, "I have come at last to loathe Buffalo so bitterly" that he had decided to advertise the house for sale and was willing to sell off his stake in the *Express* at a ten-thousand-dollar loss.[75] Wanting to start afresh, the Clemenses would move to Hartford, where Livy had wanted to reside initially. Twain had also grown disaffected with his newspaper—a "worthless sheet," he dubbed it—and seldom frequented the office.[76] "Eight months' sickness & death in one place is *enough*," he said emphatically.[77] He was in such an overwrought state that he moaned to Elisha Bliss, Jr., "You do not know what it is to be in a state of absolute frenzy—desperation. I had rather die twice over than repeat the last six months of my life."[78]

In the April issue of the *Galaxy*, Twain spilled out a morbid valedictory to his readers. "For the last eight months . . . I have had for my fellows and comrades, night and day, doctors and watchers of the sick! During these eight months death has taken two members of my home circle and malignantly threatened two others." Yet all the while he had been "under contract to furnish 'humorous' matter once a month for this magazine . . . I think that some of the 'humor' I have written during

WEDDING PRESENT

this period would have been injected into a funeral sermon without disturbing the solemnity of the occasion."[79] Twain feared that his decision to depart from Buffalo after so short a stay would leave behind a bitter residue among residents. When reviewing lecture sites with James Redpath, Twain instructed him, "Leave Buffalo *out*, altogether, & make some plausible excuse. I think they hate me there, for hating their town."[80]

During that summer in Elmira, Livy made halting progress and could walk only three or four steps while steadying herself with a chair. Twain must have wondered what life would be like with his semi-invalid wife. Though often bedridden, Livy remained "bright & cheerful," Twain said, and her tough spirit would allow her to ride out many infirmities.[81] The couple enjoyed intervals of peace and happiness with Langdon, even if they never lasted very long. By late August, Twain was confiding to Orion that "we have scarcely any hope of the baby's recovery" and claimed "overfeeding & surreptitious poisoning with laudanum & other sleeping potions is what the child is dying of."[82]

Langdon did, however, recover, and in October 1871 the Clemenses rented a lovely house in Hartford. "We are all well, our baby grows fat and hearty every day," Livy informed a friend in November when the baby celebrated his first birthday.[83] With Twain off lecturing, she sent him letters suffused with love for the child, if shot through with a poignant anxiety. "Oh Youth he is such a delight to me, I am so thankful for him—if anything happens to me you must love him *awfully*."[84] Now pregnant with their second child, Livy took special pains to avoid hazards and was terrified she might die in childbirth. The new parents were haunted by fears of mortality. Despite Twain being something of an absentee father, Langdon already recognized his face. "When we say where is papa," Livy wrote to him, "he looks right at your picture that stands on the bureau."[85]

Langdon had mysteriously recurrent health problems. More than Livy, Twain referred to his apparent developmental problems. To Mother Fairbanks he pointed out that Langdon failed to walk at sixteen months. Two months later, he told Hartford friends, "His teeth don't come—& neither does his language."[86] On March 19, 1872, at the Langdon residence in Elmira, Livy gave birth to their second baby, Olivia Susan, who would always be known as Susy (or Susie). For a fleeting instant, both children seemed relatively safe and healthy. Still, on May 15, Twain wrote a curious letter to Orion and Mollie that attempted to sound upbeat yet could not mask lurking problems with Langdon's health. "We find Langdon enjoying a heavy cough & the suffering & irritation consequent upon developing six teeth in nine days. He is as white as alabaster, and is weak; but he is pretty jolly about half the time. The new baby is as fat as butter, wholly free from infelicities of any kind. She weighed 4 1/4 pounds at birth—weighs about 9 now."[87]

What happened next with the Clemens clan has been the subject of much analysis. As the elderly Twain summed up the scene, he took Langdon out for a ride in an open carriage on a "raw, cold" May morning in Elmira, with the little boy well bundled up in furs. "But I soon dropped into a reverie and forgot all about my charge. The furs fell away and exposed his bare legs." By the time their coachman, Patrick McAleer, noticed this danger, Langdon "was almost frozen."[88] Nonetheless, after a few days Langdon was well enough to travel to Hartford. When Langdon died there on June 2, 1872, at only eighteen months old, Twain was convinced he had murdered the child and flagellated himself for the remainder of his days, as had happened with brother Henry. As he categorically told William Dean Howells about Langdon, "Yes, I killed him."[89] In fact, Langdon Clemens died of diphtheria, and Mark Twain was by no means to blame for that. Many years later, Sue Crane disputed Twain's version of events. "Yes, the drive was in Elmira, but we never thought of attributing Langdon's death to that drive, as I remember. It is true he took cold, but was so much better that the physician said he was perfectly able to take that journey. After he arrived in Hartford diphtheria developed. Mr. Clemens was often inclined to blame himself unjustly."[90] Still for Mark Twain there remained an emotional truth in his story that seemed to trump any literal interpretation: he had felt negligent with his son when he should have been most vigilant.

A new friend of the Clemenses in Hartford, Lilly Warner, said Livy was "almost heart-broken" by the death, triggering yet another health crisis for her, while Twain "was all tenderness but full of rejoicing for the baby—said he kept thinking it wasn't death for him but the beginning of life."[91] For Twain it proved an early lesson in an enduring theme: that human happiness was a snare, a fraud, and a delusion. After the bereaved parents made a death mask of Langdon's face, Livy wouldn't allow anybody to touch the green box that encased it. The outlook of the bride who had been so ecstatically happy two years earlier now darkened into extreme pessimism. "I feel so often as if my path is to be lined with graves," she wrote.[92] Langdon was buried in the family plot at Woodlawn Cemetery in Elmira, but Livy was too weak to travel from Hartford, and Twain stayed loyally by her side. Before proceeding to the cemetery, the child was laid out in the same parlor of the Langdon residence where his parents had joyously wed more than two years before. "We arrived in the sunlight," Sue Crane reported to Sam and Livy of the burial, "and with dear friends laid the pure beautiful sleeper near his grandfather just as the sun was going down."[93]

PART TWO

Floodtide

CHAPTER THIRTEEN

Church of the Holy Speculators

For two months during the summer of 1872, the Clemens family sought the restorative breezes of a seashore resort at Saybrook Point, Connecticut, on Long Island Sound. Livy still brooded over the loss of Langdon, telling Sue Crane, "Night before last I felt as if I must go and fix Langdon's grave as if it was all I could do and I longed to do that—He was so rarely beautiful, this house is full of children but there is none like him."[1] At the same time, an inborn resilience began to assert itself, and she increasingly diverted her thoughts to "little Susie" who "does grow in grace and sweetness every day."[2] The negligence for which Twain blamed himself in Langdon's death would lead to an extreme overprotectiveness toward his new daughter, a fear verging on panic at her slightest illness.

The Clemenses had launched a new chapter when they moved to Hartford on October 1, 1871, leasing a house from John and Isabella Beecher Hooker. It was through Isabella's relationship with her brother Thomas K. Beecher that Livy had grown so close to Alice Hooker Day, forging a link binding the Clemenses to Hartford. Ever since his first visit to the town in 1868, Twain had arisen as an unashamed booster. "I think this is the best built and the handsomest town I have ever seen," he told his readers.[3] The streets were straight and broad, flanked by handsome houses. Hartford was the antithesis of the western world he had now left behind. "I hear no swearing here," he observed with wonder, "I see no one chewing tobacco, I have found nobody drunk."[4] He couldn't believe the shortage of cigar stores and saloons.

The Clemenses had settled in a section of west Hartford known as Nook Farm, which was laid out by two abolitionists, John Hooker and Francis Gillette, who handpicked its residents. More than just a charming, leafy neighborhood, it was a cultivated community of like-minded people, forming an extended family. Like an exclusive rustic campus, scattered across hills and meadows, the elegant homes had no fences, and neighbors kept their doors unlocked, so people roamed freely across lawns and strayed into one another's homes. For someone of Twain's compulsive sociability, it was an idyllic setting.

A high-class enclave full of urbane, literate people, Nook Farm boasted esteemed writers, including Harriet Beecher Stowe and Charles Dudley Warner. There were prominent Yankees galore, such as former Connecticut governor Joseph Hawley, who had been a brevet major general of volunteers in the Civil War and co-owned the *Hartford Courant* with Warner, and former Connecticut senator Francis Gillette. Isabella Beecher Hooker, an ardent feminist, had labored tirelessly for women's suffrage rights. Back in the Sandwich Islands, the diplomat Anson Burlingame had given Twain advice that he never forgot and now applied: "Avoid inferiors. Seek your comradeships among your superiors in intellect and character; always *climb*."[5] And climb, climb, climb he did, now sealing his sudden eruption into the upper class.

Even as Mark Twain, as an author, rebelled against the eastern literary establishment, he became deeply embedded in its social structure. After the raucous Mississippi and western mining towns, he craved gentility and respectability. A solidly Republican neighborhood, Nook Farm would complete his exile from the small-town mores of Hannibal. As he wrote, "When I was a boy, in the back settlements of the Mississippi Valley . . . the 'Yankee' (citizen of the New England states) was hated with a splendid energy."[6] Now he was a full-fledged denizen of that Yankee world and talked of "splendid old New England."[7] After his roving years, he had finally found a foothold, a secure niche. Never again would he inhabit a place as congenial as Nook Farm, with its rich, toler-

CHURCH OF THE HOLY SPECULATORS

ant residents, aristocratic in their tastes but egalitarian in their social habits with neighbors. As Twain wrote a friend, "Fortunately a good deal of experience of men enabled me to choose my residence wisely. I live in the freest corner of the country. There are no social disabilities between me & my democratic personal friends. We break the bread & eat the salt of hospitality freely together & never dream of such a thing as offering impertinent interference in each other's political opinions."[8]

For Twain, a huge part of Hartford's attraction lay in the society of the genial, ebullient Joseph Twichell, the minister of the Asylum Hill Congregational Church—a liberal church that Twain memorably christened the "Church of the Holy Speculators" and that formed a keystone of the Nook Farm community.[9] Early in their friendship, Twain had promised Twichell that he and Livy "meant to live a useful, unostentatious & earnest religious life & that I should unite with the church as soon as I was settled."[10] Livy, still eager to adhere to the religious creed of her upbringing, queried her husband after moving to Hartford: "Do you pray for me Youth? oh we must be a prayerful family—pray for me as you used to do—I am not prayerful as of old but I believe my heart prays."[11] Already in Buffalo, Twain had begun to shelter heterodox beliefs, writing in an unpublished text that the Old Testament God was "irascible, vindictive, fierce and ever fickle," and expressing preference for a deistic God who ruled the universe through a "beneficent, exact, and changeless" machinery.[12] In Hartford, he escorted Livy to Asylum Hill services and remained active in church activities, but religious doubts weighed on him and sometimes slipped out indirectly. One of his daughters later recalled how embarrassed she was when her father teased Twichell: "Joe, that's a clever trick of yours to pound the pulpit extra hard when you haven't anything to say." Instead of feeling affronted, Twichell gave a hearty laugh. "Mark," he rejoined, "it was clever of you to discover it."[13]

Twichell had a résumé that fastened Twain ever more tightly to the Yankee world. Born in Southington, Connecticut, he had attended Yale, where he rowed in the Harvard-Yale regatta and was a member of Scroll and Key; he would sponsor Twain's honorary membership in that secret society. As a passionate foe of slavery, the young Twichell had revered the abolitionist Henry Ward Beecher as "a colossal figure" and his "hero-in-chief."[14] At the outbreak of the Civil War, Twichell was recruited as a Union chaplain, joining a New York regiment assembled by politician Dan Sickles, and he beheld a vast amount of carnage. At the battle of Gettysburg, where Sickles lost a leg, Twichell tended maimed soldiers in the rear. "The wounded were everywhere," he said, "and scenes of sickening horror were presented on every side."[15] With unremitting valor, he persisted in his wartime service, witnessing "heaps of rebel corpses" at the Bloody Angle at Spotsylvania and the massive Confederate surrender at Sailor's Creek in the war's waning days.[16] So fervently did Twichell identify with the Army of the Potomac that he delivered blessings and orations at their postwar reunions. After the war, he completed his theological studies at Andover Seminary in Massachusetts.

Twain hailed the Reverend Joseph Twichell as "that born prince of men."[17] From the pulpit, Twichell preached a cheerful, loving, muscular Christianity, devoid of the hellfire that Twain associated with his childhood, and people spontaneously confided in their pastor. "You have the touch that heals, not lacerates," Twain told him. "And you know the secret places of our hearts."[18] Tall, handsome, and outgoing, Twichell was a superb raconteur with a satirical bent, and Twain drank in his "booming yarns."[19] He was a clergyman after Twain's own heart: he liked to travel incognito so he could enjoy the bawdy comments of ordinary people. One of Twain's daughters later told him that Twichell reminded her "of you in his vivid, dramatic, moving, masterly way of painting an impressionist picture whenever he spoke," with similar tones of voice and gesture.[20] Steady conversation flowed between the two men, each storing up experiences, then eagerly conveying them to the other as they engaged in the easygoing banter that became a trademark of Mark Twain's male friendships.

Since Twichell was an athletic, outdoorsy type, much of his conversation with Twain took place on long, lively walks to a wooden tower on Talcott Mountain, five miles west of Hartford. These Saturday walks enabled Twichell to throw off his clerical reserve and indulge a boyish side. For Twain, the outings took on a retrospective glow. "There was a grove of hickory trees by the roadside, six miles out, and close by it was the only place in that whole region where the fringed gentian grow. On our return from the Tower we used to gather the gentians, then lie down on the grass upon the golden carpet of fallen hickory leaves."[21] So highly did the two men treasure these walks that they resolved to walk one hundred miles to Boston. After twenty-eight miles they decided to call it quits and took a train the remaining distance. They even went to baseball games together to watch the Hartford Dark Blues, and at one of the games a boy stole Twain's silk umbrella, leading him to place a comic ad in the *Hartford Courant* offering a five-dollar reward for the return of the purloined item. As for the young thief, "I do not want the boy (in an active state) but will pay two hundred dollars for his remains."[22]

Joseph and Harmony Twichell were well on their way to having nine children, a never-ending source of amusement for Twain. Someone once asked him how many children Twichell had and Twain replied, "I don't know. I haven't heard from him since morning."[23] On one holiday card, Twain slyly wished the Twichells a long, happy life and "eventually a sufficient family."[24] In time the large brood of children would place an enormous strain on Harmony Twichell's health and lead to financial stress as the couple sought to survive on a minister's paltry salary—distress the Clemenses would later seek to relieve.

However far he traveled from Hannibal, Mark Twain was never able to disentangle himself from the feckless Orion, whose career had peaked in Nevada then had slowly fallen apart. For a man who had handled the financial affairs of the Nevada Territory, it was a shocking case of downward mobility. After failing as a Keokuk lawyer, he struggled to survive as a newspaper proofreader. While Sam and Livy rose into a rarefied sphere of American life, Orion and Mollie sank into grinding misery. Meanwhile, Orion, a lovable but impractical eccentric, busied himself with a parade of far-fetched inventions, ranging from a flying machine to a paddlewheel boat that would cross the Atlantic in a day to an Anti-Sun-Stroke hat. He chased new projects the way a dog chases passing birds. As Twain put it, Orion was "always climbing a rainbow that has a pot of coin buried at the other end."[25] In dealing with his brother, Twain could be impossibly patronizing and overbearing one moment, then extremely generous the next.

In the fall of 1870, Twain had contacted Elisha Bliss, Jr., to see if he could find gainful employment for his older brother, who was now forty-five and hopelessly adrift. Failure was now so deeply ingrained in Orion that it seemed to trail him everywhere. "He will make a tip-top editor—a better than I, because he is full of talent & besides is perfectly faithful, honest, straightforward & reliable," Twain told his publisher. "There isn't money enough in America to get him to do a dishonest act—whereas I am different."[26] When Bliss hired Orion to edit a free circular, *The American Publisher*, Twain attempted to pump up Orion's courage, urging him not to "show any shadow of timidity or unsoldierly diffidence" before Bliss.[27] Orion didn't take his advice—he ended up as "Bliss's slave, his errand-boy, his door-mat," Twain concluded—and resented that Bliss didn't allow him sufficient editorial freedom.[28]

Bliss had hired Orion merely as a ploy to inveigle Twain into writing for his advertising circular, which the latter had no intention of doing, and also to prevent him from defecting to another publisher. Then Orion, in his blundering way, did something that infuriated his younger brother: swayed by Bliss, Orion badgered him to write for *The American Publisher*. He pleaded that he and Bliss would "hunt up any information you want, and do anything else you want done, if you will only write."[29] Twain, having just vowed to wash his hands of journalism, was livid that Orion had become a party to Bliss's pressure campaign. After a sleepless night of anger, Twain berated his brother in a blistering letter. "You talk as if I am *responsible* for your newspaper venture . . . As for being the high chief contributor & main card of the Publisher, I won't hear of it for a single moment. I'd rather break my pen & stop writing just where I am."[30] The episode ratified Twain's judgment that Orion was "as queer & heedless a bird as ever."[31]

CHURCH OF THE HOLY SPECULATORS

Then Orion, in his earnest, idealistic but bumbling way, accused Bliss of fraud in producing his brother's new western book, *Roughing It,* claiming the publishing house had secretly skimped on the quality of paper and bindings. As a result, Orion was either fired or resigned as editor of *The American Publisher* in March 1872. In writing to Orion, Twain acknowledged that he had acted from brotherly kindness and applauded "the virtue of the *motive*" underlying his action.[32] In private, however, he blasted his brother's self-destructive deed as "the act of a half-witted child" that "came almighty near *ruining* me."[33]

Afterward, Orion labored at a dead-end job at the *New York Tribune* and occupied a small attic room in lower Manhattan while Mollie went to live with Jane and Pamela in Fredonia. Later, Orion would complain of a "cloudy obscurity" that fogged his mind and "neutralized" his energy, while Mollie worried that "every thing he undertakes fails; and he lives the most dreadful life of *fear;* when he has a situation at *any* thing, he is in that everlasting state of fear fear FEAR."[34] Orion grew so obsessed with his inventions that Jane Clemens had to demand that he "make a solemn oath" not to "utter a single word about an invention of any kind."[35] She saw the inventions as a folly that distracted him from any serious business. For all his exasperation with his brother, Twain remained loyal and sent him $900 to make a down payment on a chicken farm in Keokuk. He thought Orion frittered away money on "pretentious flummery" and complained to his mother, "Nobody can dress as Mollie does & look like anything but a fool, on a chicken farm."[36] The farm, of course, never prospered, forcing Orion and Mollie to operate a boardinghouse. "If I ever become able," Twain told Jane and Pamela confidentially, "I mean to put Orion on a regular pension without revealing the fact that it is a pension."[37]

In July 1870, Twain had agreed to produce another six-hundred-page tome for Elisha Bliss, Jr. Twain had demanded half of all profits on the book beyond manufacturing costs, and Bliss insisted that a royalty of

7.5 percent would accomplish that. Twain was to recount his rollicking adventures out West, starting with the stagecoach trip he and Orion took to Nevada, through his mining and journalistic rambles, then winding up with his stints in San Francisco and the Sandwich Islands. From the outset, Twain encountered a major problem, confessing to Orion that "I remember next to *nothing*" about their overland trip and begging him to furnish names of people, scenes, or places they had passed.[38] To jog his memory, Twain also asked his brother to send him a scrapbook stuffed with his old *Territorial Enterprise* articles and the rest of his western output. But these would prove insufficient, and the book, as a result, would hover uneasily between genuine autobiography and pure invention, with a heavy stress on the latter.

Mark Twain was always tempted to improve a good tale and gave free rein to his imagination. With *The Innocents Abroad,* he had performed on-the-spot reportage and was tethered to reality by his *Alta California* letters. With *Roughing It,* he looked back fondly on a fast-disappearing frontier world: stagecoach drivers were already fading, supplanted by railroad conductors. Twain's story burst with outlandish characters and situations, which he captured with characteristic brio and a swaggering western style. Still insanely competitive with Bret Harte, he promised Orion that "I will 'top' Bret Harte again or bust."[39] He blotted out the Civil War and any other matters that might detract from the general air of hilarity. He hoped his record of "variegated vagabondizing" would "help the resting reader while away an idle hour [rather] than afflict him with metaphysics, or goad him with science."[40]

Early on in the writing, a hopeful Twain completed four chapters in one week and boasted to Elisha Bliss, Jr., that "the 'Innocents Abroad' will have to get up early to beat it . . . We shall sell 90,000 copies the first 12 months. I haven't even a shadow of a doubt of that."[41] Twain would always careen between such grandiosity and despair as he wrote. Having begun the book in Buffalo, he was stymied by the family misfortunes that gathered there. "I am not strong enough to fight against fate," he told Joseph T. Goodman. "I have been trying to write a funny book, with dead people and sickness everywhere."[42] His mood brightened as he went on, and two-thirds of the way through he boasted, "When I get it done I want to see the man who will begin to read it and not finish it."[43] Goodman told of arriving in Elmira and perusing *Roughing It* in manuscript. After the enormous success of *The Innocents Abroad,* Twain feared that he would not duplicate it with the new book and wanted Goodman's frank opinion. "I read along intently for an hour," Goodman recalled, "hardly noticing that Sam was beginning to fret and shift about uneasily. At last he could not stand it any longer, and in despair he jumped up exclaiming, 'Damn you, you have been reading that stuff for an hour and you have not cracked a smile yet.'"[44] In fact, Goodman was engrossed by the book, thinking it one of the best things Twain had ever written.

Twain was also hampered by the pledge made to Jervis Langdon to abstain from tobacco and alcohol, even though he suffered from writer's block without these crutches. "I must have a cigar to steady my nerves," he said. "I began to smoke, and I wrote my book; but then I couldn't sleep and I had to drink ale to go to sleep."[45] So Twain, strapped with a colossal level of creative angst, lapsed back into bad habits and never bothered with reform again. After the success of *The Innocents Abroad, Roughing It* was perhaps doomed to disappoint. Still, it sold a respectable seventy-three thousand copies in its first two years, slightly lagging behind the earlier work. As publication approached, Twain committed a major strategic error. Fearing the book would be "considered pretty poor stuff," he restricted review copies to two friendly critics, Howells and David Gray, which damaged sales once subscription copies were exhausted.[46] Twain admitted to having learned a costly lesson: that if one didn't "secure publicity . . . for a book the instant it is issued, no amount of hard work & faithful advertising can accomplish it later on."[47]

Twain wasn't averse to lobbying friendly parties for reviews. Far from it. To boost sales, he sent a copy of *Roughing It* to the *New York Tribune* and alerted his friend John Hay that he should ask Whitelaw Reid, its managing editor, if he could review it. Instead, Reid assigned it to George Ripley, their literary critic, who posted a favorable notice. Still, Twain expressed disgust. "The idea of setting such an oyster as that to prating about Humor!" he complained to Livy.[48] He began to nurse a grudge against Whitelaw Reid that would grow in time and fester into a vendetta.

Twain was always suspicious of publishers, and ever since Orion charged Bliss with cheating him, this suspicion had flamed into outright paranoia. Twain returned to his brother's claims against Bliss that he had cheapened the book's components to save money, thus cutting into *Roughing It*'s sales. He also believed that the 7.5 percent royalty did not, as Bliss claimed, equal half of the promised profits. The litigious Twain brought in a lawyer, Charles E. Perkins, and had him threaten to sue Bliss. When Perkins and an auditor pored through the books, however, they ended up endorsing Bliss's view that the royalty did, indeed, amount to half the profits. Twain not only dropped the lawsuit but invested $5,000 in the stock of the American Publishing Company, where he would serve as both a director and an author.

―・―

Right on the eve of the publication of *Roughing It,* in January 1872, Twain spoke about the book at Steinway Hall in New York to more than two thousand appreciative listeners, a crowd described by the press as "the most enormous audience ever collected at any lecture in New York . . . Peals of laughter followed every phrase."[49] Twain was fashioning a very modern sense of book publicity, with his book release timed to coincide with lectures, yet he still chafed at public speaking. After completing his second lecture tour for James Redpath, he swore to Mother Fairbanks that it was "the most detestable lecture tour that ever was" and that he refused to speak anymore unless he grew indebted again.[50] Nevertheless, prodigal with money, he would constantly be forced back onto the hated lecture circuit. In late August, he sailed to London for the first time, alone, planning to write a book about the country. By the time he reached the Irish coast, he missed Livy terribly. "I am standing high on the stern of the ship," he wrote her, "looking westward, with my hands to my mouth, trumpet fashion, yelling across the tossing waste of waves, 'I LOVE YOU, LIVY DARLING!!!!' "[51]

Twain was stunned by his triumphant London reception. Far from enjoying a quiet research trip, he was feted as a full-blown celebrity and found he was "by long odds the most widely known & popular American author among the English."[52] He was warmly received when he spoke at a London hall. Benefiting from a vogue for western American humor, he narrated scenes from *Roughing It* and was received as a fitting successor to Artemus Ward. In an astonishingly short span of time, he had established a major presence in England. When honored by the prestigious Whitefriars Club, the chairman claimed "his genius" was "recognized on both sides of the Atlantic," and he was toasted with lusty bonhomie. "Mr. Mark Twain responded after his peculiar fashion, amidst roars of laughter," noted a reporter, "of which the simple words convey but little idea, so much depended on the quaint and original manner of the speaker."[53] Twain made a witty speech in which he insisted that he had discovered the long-lost Scottish missionary Dr. David Livingstone, while the explorer Henry M. Stanley walked off with "all the credit."[54] Twain was bowled over by his flood of invitations, complaining to Livy, "Too much company—too much dining—too much sociability. (But I would rather live in England than America—which is treason.)"[55]

At moments Twain sounded giddy with the adulation. When invited to the annual Guildhall Dinner to install new Sheriffs and the Lord Mayor of London, Twain listened as a man read in respectful silence the names of the assembled guests. But then, he reported to Livy, "when he came to my name . . . there was such a storm of applause as you never heard . . . they could not go on with the list. I was . . . never stricken so speechless . . . for I had expected nothing of this kind—I did not know I was a lion."[56]

The three-month English sojourn proved pivotal for Twain, initiating his slow metamorphosis from an authentic American rustic, bred in the backwoods, into a cosmopolitan world traveler. He shed the wisecracking tone of *The Innocents Abroad* and showed an unexpected capacity for reverence. He adored England and planned on returning with Livy the following spring. Traveling with his future American publisher, James Osgood, he toured the Kenilworth ruins, Warwick Castle, Stratford-on-Avon, and Oxford University, and began to feel the pull of a picturesque past, a romantic tug that later flowered in *The Prince and the Pauper* and *A Connecticut Yankee in King Arthur's Court*. So bewitched was he by rural England that he said it was "too absolutely beautiful to be left out doors—ought to be under a glass case."[57] Twain's English infatuation was, in truth, a piece of puppy love: though he would never surrender his affection for the British, his views of England—its monarchy, aristocracy, and rigid class system—would come in for harsh criticism later on. For the moment, though, he was buoyed by this discovery of a new world that had so cordially embraced him.

It was already clear from Twain's habit of fictionalizing facts that he was tailor-made for a novelist's career. The shopworn tale of the genesis of his first novel, *The Gilded Age*, is that one evening circa December 1872 the Clemenses were conversing with their Nook Farm friends, Charles Dudley and Susan Warner, when the two men deplored the current state of fiction. Their two wives challenged them to team up and write a superior novel about contemporary society, and they accepted the dare. A colleague of Warner's on the *Hartford Courant* quoted Twain as saying of their joint enterprise: "We'll get together and write a story, chapter by chapter every morning, and we will so interweave our works that these wives of ours will not be able to say which part has been written by Mark Twain and which by Charles D. Warner; for once a week we will gather in my library and read the story to them as it has progressed under our pens."[58]

The standard story about the novel's origins leaves something to be desired. As early as March 1870, after dining in Washington with the crooked senator Samuel Clarke Pomeroy of Kansas, Twain had exclaimed to Livy, "Oh, I have gathered material enough for a whole book!"[59] A

CHURCH OF THE HOLY SPECULATORS

story about political corruption had probably simmered in his brain for a while, and the spate of scandals during late 1872 into early 1873—investigations into the Tweed Ring, bribery charges against Senator Pomeroy, and the Crédit Mobilier scandal in Congress—would only have hardened his determination to expose skullduggery. In later years, Twain complained that Warner pushed him into the collaboration, whereas the more likely version is what Twain told his last secretary, Isabel Lyon, that he himself had "suggested to Charlie Warner that they write a novel together. He did it because he had a fresh great reputation, and he had a fear that he must not stand alone."[60] That Twain agreed to this collaboration bespeaks an understandable insecurity about novel writing and perhaps a desire to ingratiate himself with the patrician world of Nook Farm, shedding the image of the wild westerner.

A graduate of Hamilton College and the University of Pennsylvania, with a varied background as a railroad surveyor, lawyer, and co-owner of the *Hartford Courant,* Charles Dudley Warner was known as a genial essayist, thoughtful, with a light, witty touch, as shown by his popular essay collection *My Summer in a Garden.* Ordinarily stingy with praise, Twain waxed ecstatic about these pieces, telling Twichell that their humor "transcends anything I have seen in print or heard from a stage this many a day."[61] Livy was drawn to Warner's charming gentility, whereas Twain may still have been silently fuming that Warner and Joseph Hawley had spurned his earlier offer to buy an interest in the *Hartford Courant.*

By yoking together two dissimilar writers, the collaboration was bound to be flawed. Still, the novel performed a vital service by providing a comprehensive critique of American society after the Civil War, capturing its glittering, meretricious aura so well that the period became known as the "Gilded Age." The war had shaken the country loose from its rural, small-town foundations. With peace, the growth of government, big business, and burgeoning cities spurred a wild carnival of greed. Twain was horrified by the rampant materialism (which he perhaps sensed in himself) and lamented the "incredible rottenness" and "moral ulcers" of America.[62] With spreading railroads, factories, banks, and mines, a new breed of robber baron bestrode the industrial landscape. "Jay Gould was the mightiest disaster which has ever befallen this country," he later declared. "The people had *desired* money before his day, but *he* taught them to fall down and worship it."[63] In *The Gilded Age,* the characters would all be besotted with business schemes, which teased them like perilous mirages.

Twain launched into the writing with a full head of steam. As Livy told her mother, "Mr. Clemens . . . is perfectly brim full of work, says he never worked with such perfect ease and happiness in his life."[64] As he drafted slightly more than half the chapters, his initial enthusiasm was soon tempered by a queasy awareness that his style and Warner's "refused to mix, & the book consisted of *two* novels—& remained so, incurably & vexatiously, spite of all we could do to make the contents blend."[65]

Twain wisely decided to write the chapters playing to his strong suit, seizing on memories of the Tennessee land that had taunted the Clemens clan with dreams of fabulous riches. In a thinly disguised retelling of the family saga, a Squire Hawkins (read: Judge Clemens) snaps up seventy-five thousand acres of barren, worthless land in eastern Tennessee and, in his stupid greed, rebuffs a $10,000 offer from an iron company. With his dying breath he tells his son Washington, an impractical dreamer (read: Orion Clemens), that the land will someday make him rich. Taking a dig at southern society, Twain noted that the daughters weren't allowed to work because they came from "a southern family, and of good blood."[66] The novel's central drama revolves around a corrupt scheme in which Washington Hawkins, Colonel Eschol Sellers, and a shady Senator Dilworthy (patterned on Senator Pomeroy) conspire to have the government buy the Tennessee land for a Black industrial university at absurdly inflated prices.

Of all the characters Twain ever created, Colonel Sellers defined an enduring archetype. He was based closely on James J. Lampton, a flamboyant cousin of Jane Clemens, a big-talking, incorrigible dreamer who "floated, all his days, in a tinted mist of magnificent dreams," said Twain.[67] Lampton delighted in telling the Clemens family how there were "millions" in the Tennessee land. In the novel, Colonel Sellers personifies a nation of bombastic salesmen who shy away from ordinary success as they pant after the jackpot. He is a lovable old humbug with the glib tongue of a charlatan who wraps everything in a gorgeous bubble of language. An affectionate fool, adored by wife and children, Sellers lives in a threadbare household that rebukes his fantasies of wealth. He fakes a lighted stove with a lit candle behind isinglass and forces guests to dine on turnips, assuring them that the turnips, "imported" from New Jersey, are "perfectly firm and juicy."[68] Sellers is a satire on the southern gentry, who must now resort to the hard sell and ruthless tactics they supposedly disdained in their antebellum glory. Twain was clearly fond of Sellers, telling Livy, "When I got to Seller's eye-water & his clock & his fireless stove & his turnip dinner, I could hardly read for laughing."[69] And it was all true, Twain insisted. "I ate the turnip dinner with him, years ago."[70]

Much of the novel was set in Washington, D.C., and Warner ceded many of those chapters to Twain, who portrayed the frenetic scramble for posts and patronage. In a brilliant satire of a new sharp-elbowed elite—the Aristocracy of the Parvenus—the central villain is Senator Abner Dilworthy. Sellers reserves his highest praise for the senator. "He's only been in Congress a few years, and he must be worth a million."[71] Dilworthy spouts cant about temperance and piety, talks to church groups and Sunday schools, and wraps himself in God and flag. He feigns interest in a government purchase of the Tennessee land "for the good of the colored races" and claims to . . . "never push a private interest if it is not justified and ennobled by some larger public good."[72] Previously, Twain had shown sympathy for Reconstruction, but in *The Gilded Age*, he seems to mock any concern for Black welfare as a hypocritical pretext for fleecing the government. The board and staff of the Knobs Industrial University for Blacks will be packed with congressional relatives. The whole fiasco collapses when Dilworthy is charged with bribery before the climactic vote.

With such a jaundiced view of Reconstruction, the novel has been criticized as a work of "reaction and despair," and there is merit in that argument.[73] One wonders whether Charles Dudley Warner was most to blame for this signal defect. In a later essay, "The Education of the Negro," Warner condemned Reconstruction as "an attempt to put the superior part of the community under the control of the inferior."[74] He suggested that Blacks only sought postwar education "as a sign of freedom" and because "it had formerly been the privilege of their masters."[75] He went so far as to aver that Blacks, in their enforced migration, had brought nothing to North America—"In Africa there has been no progress in organization, government, art. No negro tribe has ever invented a written language." For Warner, slavery had been needed to elevate benighted souls. "It is possible that the historians centuries hence . . . may reckon slavery and the forced transportation to the new world a necessary step in the training of the negro."[76] By the close of the essay, he bluntly saluted slavery for converting the enslaved "into an industrial being . . . Perhaps only force could do this, for it was a radical transformation."[77] Not surprisingly, he thought money spent on higher education for Blacks would be better employed to deal with "negro criminality."[78] Since such ferocious views find no echo in Mark Twain's other writings, it seems fair to assume that Warner had an overriding influence in shaping the plot twist about the Black university, although Twain was obviously a willing accomplice.

In ransacking his own life for the novel, Twain drew on the name of his childhood sweetheart from Hannibal, Laura Hawkins, for the seriously flawed heroine. She survives a steamboat explosion reminiscent of the one that killed his brother Henry. Despite being given the Laura Hawkins name, the character bears no resemblance to her sweet nature and is "willful, generous, forgiving, imperious, affectionate, improvident, bewitching."[79] After Laura is humiliated by the faithless young Colonel Selby, she avenges herself by luring, then rejecting, each new suitor so she can "calmly add his scalp to her string."[80] In the end, she murders Selby and is acquitted. It has been suggested that the true original of this heartless woman wasn't Laura Hawkins but Laura Wright, now married to Charles T. Dake, and that Twain was settling an old score based on his rejection.[81]

CHURCH OF THE HOLY SPECULATORS

In dividing up duties with Warner, Twain stipulated that "if there was any love making in the book I was not to be asked to do it."[82] Twain's inability to portray romance or mature women, despite his own highly romantic nature, would be a noticeable weakness in his fiction. He therefore must have found it the more dismaying when he discovered that Warner had plagiarized the description of Laura as a schoolgirl—a plagiarism, Twain told Livy, "that would have been detected in a moment."[83]

The American Publishing Company published *The Gilded Age* and paid a hefty 10 percent royalty. Although Twain sent out plenty of review copies, some notices were brutal, with the Chicago *Tribune* dismissing the book as "too inferior for recognition" and "a fraud to the reading public."[84] Reviving an old complaint, Twain thought Elisha Bliss, Jr., had used "wretched paper & vile engravings." As he told the author Thomas Bailey Aldrich, "You notice that the *Gilded Age* is rather a rubbishy looking book . . . Now I think seriously of *printing* my own next book & publishing it thro' this same subscription house."[85] Whatever the errors, the book sold fifty thousand copies in its first year. Twain always imagined he could publish his books much better than any publisher, a hypothesis he would maintain until he had a chance to test his theory in practice.

Twain reacted bitterly to the negative press reviews, especially from Whitelaw Reid's *New York Tribune*. He repeated the same error he had made before, trying to foist a friendly reviewer on Reid, this time his friend Edward House. Understandably, Reid took offense, saying that House had brought "a dishonorable proposal from Warner & me."[86] Twain was curiously blind to his lack of ethics here and could not comprehend Reid's principled objection. The editor was "a contemptible cur, & I want nothing more to do with him," he told Warner petulantly. "I don't want the Tribune to have the book at all. Please tell Bliss *not to send a copy there under any circumstances.*"[87]

In later years, Twain prevented his publishers from handing out any books he'd written before *The Gilded Age*, dismissing them as "hoary antiquities."[88] Yet his dislike of the book grew more intense with time, along with his memory of Charles Dudley Warner. As Isabel Lyon reported: "Mr. Clemens told me several times that he could not endure 'The Gilded Age,' nor the memory of anything connected with it. He had achieved an unnecessary dislike for C.D. Warner & all the Warners because of the enforced association. He said he had great difficulty in finishing the book & more than once had been ready to tear up all he had written."[89]

CHAPTER FOURTEEN

Mississippi Steamboat and a Cuckoo Clock

Twain's stay in England had whetted his appetite for more, and in May 1873, he sailed to England with Livy; little Susy and her nursemaid, Nellie; Livy's old Elmira friend Clara Spaulding; and Samuel C. Thompson, a secretary. Aside from wanting to bask in adoration—something never far from his mind—Twain needed to establish British copyright for *The Gilded Age* and also dash off pieces for the *New York Herald*. From the time they disembarked in Liverpool and boarded a train for London, Livy was taken with the English countryside, "the most charming that I ever could imagine . . . So many things that I had read were made plain to me as we rode along—the little thatched villages, the foot paths by the side of the road."[1]

Ensconced at the Langham Hotel, the Clemenses were swamped with invitations and met Anthony Trollope, Robert Browning, Herbert Spencer, Wilkie Collins, and dozens of other luminaries. So hectic was the social pace that Twain protested that "we seem to find no opportunity to see London sights. Tuesday we are to visit an English country gentleman & Friday dance at the Lord Mayor's."[2] Fleeing to Edinburgh for a rest, Livy required a physician and fell under the spell of John Brown, a charming, benevolent doctor and author. "We made the round of his professional visits with him in his carriage every day for six weeks," Twain recalled. "He always brought a basket of grapes and we brought books."[3]

FLOODTIDE

Back in London that fall, Twain drew large crowds for his lectures at the historic Hanover Square Rooms. He was now spending money at a furious rate—"I have already spent ten thousand dollars—& the end is not yet!" he groaned, and he needed to earn money from his platform artistry.[4] After returning with Livy and the rest of the party to America in early November, he turned around and sailed back to England, where he lectured nightly for three straight weeks. He had to cope with a fog that grew thick even by London standards, and one night, lost in a haze of blue smoke, he told his blurry audience, "Ladies & gentlemen, I *hear* you, & so I know that you are here—& *I* am here, too, notwithstanding I am not visible."[5]

Even as they were being toasted by the British elite, the Clemenses were building a house in Hartford and could not resist snapping up "little odds & ends for it," Twain wrote.[6] In January 1873, they bought the first of six parcels of adjoining land on Farmington Avenue, a broad thoroughfare adorned with fine residences. Despite the electric lights, the roadway ran through a Hartford area of almost bucolic charm. The house, perched atop a hill that sloped down to a meadow and running stream, offered excellent views of town and country. The Clemenses would live near Charles Dudley Warner and Harriet Beecher Stowe, forming a mini–writer's colony, with the Twichells not far away. Though the land, house, and stable would be registered in Livy's name alone, Twain warmed to his newfound status as country squire as he tramped the icy grounds. "Mr. Clemens seems to glory in his sense of possession," Livy told her sister; "he goes daily into the lot, has had several falls trying to lay off the land by sliding around on his feet."[7] To her mother, she noted a less attractive side effect of the land purchase on her husband. "Now that we have bought the lot he feels anxious to make all the money that he can"—a subtle pressure that would prey on him for years.[8] Twain admitted that "trying to support a family is a thing which compels one to look at all ventures with a mercenary eye."[9]

MISSISSIPPI STEAMBOAT AND A CUCKOO CLOCK

While pregnant with Susy, Livy had studied the interiors of Nook Farm friends and sketched out plans for the new house. She owned a copy of *Hints on Household Taste* by Charles L. Eastlake, the bible of the Aesthetic Movement, which reacted against the Industrial Age by emphasizing beautiful craftsmanship in everyday objects, lifting decorative arts to the level of fine art. Drawing inspiration from many historical periods, it favored an eclectic style with bold, ornamental patterns and exotic touches culled from Middle Eastern and Asian arts. However poor his eye for painting, Twain shared his wife's bottomless appetite for furnishings, and he could no more contain his itch to spend than he could stifle the flow of his humor.

Now that he was engaged for the first time in creating his own home, the bard of small-town life wished to live like a literary prince. To design the new house, the Clemenses drafted New York architect Edward Tuckerman Potter, the son of an Episcopalian bishop. Potter consulted closely with Livy, but Twain also expressed a desire for some flamboyant dash, stipulating that he wanted nothing like "the goods-box form of architecture, perfectly square" of other Hartford houses.[10] In response, Potter produced a three-story brick mansion of nineteen rooms—twenty-five, if one includes an adjoining staff wing—its woodwork influenced by the Stick style then popular in America. The High Victorian Gothic touches were reminiscent of churches Potter had built.

The resulting house was solemn and grand, playful and adventurous. On the outside it had striking patterns of black and vermilion bricks, with colored slate tiles on the roof. Instead of "good-box form," the exterior was enlivened by a veritable riot of turrets, balconies, chimneys, porches, gables, and nooks. One Twain biographer likened the house to "part steamboat, part medieval stronghold, and part cuckoo clock."[11] Instead of the front door facing Farmington Avenue, the servant and kitchen wing enjoyed that view. When asked why, Twain replied, "So the servants can see the circus go by without running out into the front yard."[12] This eccentric palace, with its bedlam of odd angles, fully reflected its owner. From the moment one stepped into the entrance hall, the grand home exuded the rich hush and glittering opulence of a Gilded

Age mansion, with marble floors, heavy wooden banisters, and an open three-story staircase.

Ever since he was a boy, Mark Twain had wished to be noticed, and this house was unquestionably conspicuous, with opinion sharply divided on its taste. Some newspapers had fun describing "Mark Twain's practical joke."[13] The *Hartford Daily Times* called it "one of the oddest buildings in the state ever designed for a dwelling, if not in the whole country."[14] An Elmira paper delivered this whimsical verdict: "It is a small brick-kiln gone crazy, the outside ginger breaded with woodwork, as a baker sugar-ornaments the top and side of a fruit loaf."[15] In Boston, the *Saturday Evening Gazette* mocked the "combination of Mark Twain and Queen Anne architecture," while admitting the house was "so peculiar and picturesque that tourists go to see it."[16] Of course, reporters solicited Twain's opinion as to a proper name for the house's style, which he gladly gave: "There are nineteen different styles in it and folks can take their pick . . . I guess we'll call it 'eclectic'—the word describes everything that can't be otherwise described."[17]

The interior contained 11,500 square feet, fourteen fireplaces, and five bathrooms, with many arresting features. It had a sumptuous dining room, with heavily carved wooden chairs and a sideboard decorated with Japanese tiles. The library, with velvet-covered armchairs, was the heart of the house, and its collection of several hundred volumes would swell to more than three thousand. The room had an enormous chimney piece of carved oak, topped by an intricate escutcheon in bold relief, with a quote from Ralph Waldo Emerson etched in brass: "The Ornament of a House Is the Friends Who Frequent It."[18] The library flowed into a glass-enclosed conservatory that brought the freshness of nature right into the house and provided the backdrop to many home theatricals and poetry readings.

At the top of the house was Twain's writing sanctum: the Billiard Room. This third-floor eyrie was relaxed and casual, and suited his temperament more than the somewhat self-important decor below. With a corner desk where he wrote and a billiard table smack in the middle, it offered the easy comfort of a fraternity house where Twain could be as untidy as he wanted. Not subject to Livy's elegant design, he would stuff manuscripts into pigeonholes and table drawers, and leave corncob pipes strewn everywhere. If he needed fresh air, he could step straight onto a balcony amid the treetops. When Mother Fairbanks asked him, in 1883, where he wrote, he answered, "In the billiard room, the most satisfactory study that ever was. Open fire, register, and plenty of light."[19] Enlisting the room as his personal clubhouse, he gathered friends there on Friday evenings for Scotch, billiards, and fraternal storytelling.

When the Clemens family moved into the Farmington Avenue house on September 19, 1874, it was still incomplete, which meant constant, hair-raising disruptions, and Twain left madcap descriptions of the scene. "The carpenters are here for time & eternity," he moaned. "I kill them when I get opportunities, but the builder goes & gets more." He was determined to banish the workers, "even if we have to import an epidemic to do it."[20] With his usual short temper, he felt frazzled having workmen on the first floor, while he and his family camped out on the second. "I have been bullyragged all day by the builder," he complained, "by his foreman, by the architect, by the tapestry devil who is to upholster the furniture, by the idiot who is putting down the carpets, by the scoundrel who is setting up the billiard-table . . . by the wildcat who is sodding the ground & . . . by a book *agent*, whose body is in the back yard & the coroner notified."[21] It wouldn't have been a Mark Twain project had he not conjured up a rogues' gallery of comic rascals.

Despite hefty bills, Twain experienced pride as the project neared completion. During the 1874 summer, as Livy joined her family in Elmira to escape building cares, he checked on the progress in Hartford. "You may look at the house or the grounds from any point of view you choose, & they are simply exquisite," he informed Livy. "It is a quiet, murmurous, enchanting *poem* done in the solid elements of nature."[22] For all his tooth-gnashing frustration during construction, the house held profound importance for Mark Twain, who had felt estranged from his own family and probably never imagined he would dwell amid such grandeur. The Nook Farm house gave his life a solidity that he had never enjoyed in his earlier vagabond days. As he told Livy, "It is a *home*—&

the word never had so much meaning before."[23] More happy memories would coalesce around this house than any other he occupied, and it would come to possess "a heart, and a soul, and eyes to see us with . . . We never came home from an absence that its face did not light up and speak out its eloquent welcome."[24] Possessing this abode inaugurated the happiest period of his life, and he crowed to a Scottish friend that "if there is one individual creature . . . who is more thoroughly and uniformly and unceasingly happy than I am I defy the world to produce him and prove him."[25]

The marriage to Livy Langdon had catapulted Mark Twain into a sphere of society in which well-to-do people inhabited spacious old homes, waited on by teams of servants. It was a union of opposites: he was a volatile figure of coruscating brilliance, of restless and irrepressible energy, whereas she was a gentle, delicate spirit. The high-strung Twain couldn't tolerate more than three or four hours of sleep per night. At meals, he would pace the floor between courses, discoursing at length, while Livy could scarcely stroll two hundred yards without resting. Yet it was Livy who ruled; Livy who took this glorious misfit and gave his home a veneer of normality; Livy who trained him in social graces, making him palatable to polite society. She civilized him, in the best sense of the word, and that took enormous courage. "Of course there couldn't ever be anybody who could train him so that he wouldn't drop a little back to his wildnesses, and his strengths," said Twichell. "But Mrs. Clemens did more than anyone else in the world could do."[26] Calling him "Youth" suggested her affectionate tolerance of his failings. She was like a mother who learned to control the moods, anger, and caprices of a marvelous child, and he repaid this care with infinite love. The Clemens children grew up with tales of how Mother had cleaned up Father's bachelor act, and they would speak of Father getting "dusted off" by Mother.[27]

One morning at Nook Farm, Twain stopped by the residence of Harriet Beecher Stowe, their next-door neighbor, and Livy was taken aback to discover that he had gone without a cravat. She insisted he return properly attired and apologize. Instead, Twain had a servant bear a cra-

MISSISSIPPI STEAMBOAT AND A CUCKOO CLOCK

vat on a platter to Stowe, with a note advising that he never made visits "in entirely full dress, lest the effect be too strong upon the person visited," and explaining that it was his custom "to send the cravat later, by a trustworthy hand, with a request that after sufficient & satisfying inspection it be returned to me—with a receipt."[28] An amusing note, but also Twain's way of showing he honored the strict etiquette dictated by Livy. She always feared that his withering sarcasms would antagonize people; he didn't realize how easily people were bruised by his sharp tongue. "He is very eccentric, disturbed by every noise, and it cannot be altogether easy to have care of such a man," observed an editor's wife, who studied the psychological dynamics between the fastidious wife and insouciant husband.[29] "He was always bringing the blood to his wife's face he said by his bad behavior . . . His whole life was one long apology. His wife had told him to see how well we behaved . . . and he knew he had everything to learn."[30] Mark Twain was often at war with somebody, forever threatening to sue or throw his adversaries in jail. When his dander was up, Livy trained him to draft an indignant letter and stuff it in the drawer until he had cooled off and could write a more sensible reply. Twain's files are chock-full of such apologetic letters that Livy prompted him to write the morning after he committed some dinner table gaffe.

Twain experienced no resentment about this education: he adored Livy and allowed her to remake him without protest—to a point. "I was a mighty rough, coarse, unpromising subject when Livy took charge of me four years ago," he told Dr. Brown, "and I may *still* be to the rest of the world, but not to her. She has made a very creditable job of me."[31] Yet Twichell was right that Twain secretly retained a hard untamed core. Twenty-five years later, in his unpublished story "Indiantown," he presented a couple, David and Susan Gridley, who are clearly inspired by him and Livy. Susan toils constantly to put "a shiny new outside" on David, and the world regards that as the real man. She keeps David's exterior "in such good repair that the general world did not even suspect that there was another Gridley and a solider one—a real one. But there it was: he was just a piece of honest kitchen furniture transferred to the drawing-room and glorified and masked from view in gorgeous cloth of gold."[32]

Early in his courtship of Livy, Twain's penchant for alcohol and cigars had troubled the Langdons, but his taste for profanities was no less problematic. "I swear all day," he explained to Orion, "but I do not lose my temper."[33] During their first ten years of marriage, when he was about to burst with frustration, he would flee outside from Livy's presence and give way to profanity in the open air. Swearing relieved his tension, and he was the undisputed master of colorful oaths. Once, when staying at a hotel, boiling water gushed into his bathtub, and he roared, "God-damn the God-damned son-of-a-bitch that invented that faucet! I hope he'll roast in hell for a million years!"[34] His swearing was almost a comic routine, sometimes not to be taken too seriously.

As a social planner, Livy reigned supreme in household matters. Where Twain was very disorganized, she had superlative executive skills. She had grown up surrounded by servants and knew how to superintend them with a firm but gentle hand. "She goes around with her bunch of housekeeper's keys . . . & is overbearing and perfectly happy," Twain marveled.[35] With people ducking in and out of one another's houses, the social demands of running a Nook Farm household were considerable. One Clemens daughter recalled how "Father and Mother were constantly preparing for lunch parties or dinner parties."[36] Their lavish soirees featured many courses, followed by wine, sherry, and cigars. Fussing over every detail, Livy showed her supreme proficiency in entertaining. One housekeeper, Catherine "Katy" Leary, recalled the ice cream: "No, never plain ordinary ice cream—we always had our ice cream put up in some wonderful shapes—like flowers or cherubs, little angels—all different kinds and different shapes and colors—oh, everything lovely!"[37] Exquisitely dressed, Livy strove for perfection in everything. At Christmastime, she and her children bundled up in furs, climbed into an open sleigh, and rode around the countryside, delivering baskets of food to the poor.

All this entertaining proved a heavy burden to bear for the fragile Livy. The holiday routine, however altruistic, was taxing, and Twain ranted about "that infernal Christmas-suicide."[38] Over the years, his letters would be full of concern for Livy's fatigue from overexertion. "I think my wife would be twice as strong as she is but for this wearing and wearying slavery of housekeeping," Twain remarked a few years later.[39] "Livy has been running down & getting weak, in consequence of overwork in re-arranging the house," he told his mother.[40] Once, alluding to his "reverent and quite conscious worship" of his wife, Twain explained how his love was strengthened by "the frailty of her body, which made us nurse her, & tend her, & watch over her & hover about her."[41] Nonetheless, Twain loved the social carousel over which Livy presided, even as she did all the work, and she had to warn him to curb his sociable impulses. "Don't be too . . . ready & cordial to invite people to visit you . . . when people come they generally come for twenty four hours."[42] Despite his concern for Livy's tenuous health, he didn't shield her from the excessive weight she had to endure, leading her to protest once, "The house has been full of company, and I have been 'whirled around.' . . . Sometimes it seems as if the simple sight of people would drive me *mad*."[43] When the couple had a second daughter, Clara, in June 1874, the demands of child-rearing were heaped upon Livy as well.

While Livy was no feminist firebrand, on one occasion she did issue an emotional outcry to her mother that reflects the mounting pressures she felt. "I told Mr. Clemens the other day, that in this day women must be everything[,] they must keep up with all the current literature, they must know about art, they must help in one or two benevolent societies— they must be perfect mothers—they must be perfect housekeepers & graceful gracious hostesses, they must know how to give perfect dinners, they must go and visit all the people in the town where they live, they must always be ready to receive their acquaintances—they must dress themselves & their children becomingly and above all they must make their houses '*charming*' & so on without end—then if they are not studying something their case is a hopeless one."[44] Whatever her dismay, Livy never stopped loving her maddening husband. "Youth darling," she once wrote to him, "I have nothing in particular to write you about except that I *idolize* you."[45]

Beyond housekeeping, Livy had to handle three sets of books, toting up the income from the Langdon coal mines and her husband's lecture fees and book royalties. She told him that she would much prefer to have him make less money on the lecture circuit if she had him more often at home, but they were already starting to run a very high overhead. She also stated that if, after three or four years, they discovered that they were living beyond their budget, "We will either board or live in a small cottage and keep one servant, will live near the horse cars so that I can get along without a horse and carriage—I *can not* and I WILL NOT think about your being away from me this way every year, it is not half living."[46] In fact, they were both big spenders—Livy by background, Twain by inclination—and would never settle for the frugal regimen Livy had fancifully envisioned in the event of hardship.

To help ease the responsibilities for Livy, the Clemenses assembled a team of domestic help of unswerving loyalty who formed an extended family. From their first day of marriage in Buffalo, they had employed their excellent coachman, Patrick McAleer. "He was Irish, young, slender, bright, quick as a cat, a master of his craft," noted Twain.[47] Patrick rode horseback with the Clemens children in the morning, then drove the carriage for Livy and her daughters in the afternoon. With talents that seemed magical to the little girls, he was recruited for special duties on Christmas Eve. "Patrick came down the chimney (apparently) disguised as St. Nicholas, and performed the part to the admiration of the little and the big alike," said Twain.[48]

In 1880 Katy Leary was hired as Livy's personal maid, also serving as seamstress, nursemaid, and nanny. She had a round, happy face, with bright black eyes and a ruddy complexion. A loquacious raconteur, Katy had a delicious Irish tang to her voice, and Twain valued her "heart of Irish warmth, quick Irish wit," and store of subtle humor.[49] She performed many unorthodox duties, including rubbing the master's head every morning. "He used to have a feeling that if his hair was massaged every day . . . he wouldn't ever get bald," Katy explained. "He had a horror of being bald-headed."[50] She also had the thankless task of cleaning up the Billiard Room, which left Twain cursing if she accidentally disturbed the wild clutter he had so artfully perpetrated. In caring for the

MISSISSIPPI STEAMBOAT AND A CUCKOO CLOCK

children, Katy was assisted by Rosina Hay, a high-spirited young woman from Germany who tutored the children in German.

Perhaps the most memorable member of the household was the Black butler, George Griffin, who came one day to wash windows and never left. Born into slavery in Maryland, he worked as a body servant to Union general Charles Devens, Jr., then drifted north to Hartford after the war, performing odd jobs. Twain effusively praised Griffin, and his affection for him was clear. "He was handsome, well built, shrewd, wise, polite, always good-natured, cheerful to gaiety, honest, religious, a cautious truth-speaker, devoted friend to the family, champion of its interests, a sort of idol to the children and a trial to Mrs. Clemens—not in all ways but in several."[51] A recently discovered photo of George shows a slim, confident young man with a sophisticated air and a commanding presence. George maintained peace in the kitchen and kept intrusive visitors at bay. At elegant dinner parties, he served the platters and didn't hesitate to laugh aloud if he heard something funny at the table. Although he had a young wife and may have been a deacon of the African Methodist Episcopal Zion Church, George was not a choirboy—which was just fine with Twain. George bet on everything from elections to horse races to prize fights, serving as a bookie for a fair portion of the Black community in Hartford. Susy would try to reform him, to no avail. When Livy periodically fired George, he would simply refuse to leave. "You couldn't get along without me, Mrs. Clemens," he would tell her, "& I ain't going to try to get along without you."[52]

However much he rejoiced in his mansion, Mark Twain found that with an active social life at Nook Farm he scarcely got any literary work accomplished. Almost all his serious writing was crammed into the three or four summer months that he and the family spent with their in-laws at the spacious hilltop farm just outside Elmira called Quarry Farm and nicknamed "Rest-&-be-Thankful."[53] Twain traveled like a plutocrat, taking a special sleeping car from Hoboken, New Jersey, so that Livy could lie down, if needed, and the children could spread out. The Clemenses, after spending their first summer at Quarry Farm in 1871, missed few summers for the next twenty years. For Twain the place was little short of perfection. "You have run about a good deal, Joe," he told Twichell, "but you have never seen any place that was so divine as the farm. Why don't you come here and take a foretaste of heaven?"[54]

Among the many enticements of Quarry Farm, high on the list for Twain was the company of Livy's adopted sister, Sue Crane, whose husband, Theodore, was a partner of Charlie Langdon's in the family coal business. She radiated a serene, beautiful spirit and often visited the poor of Elmira. With no children of her own, she counted as a second mother to the Clemens daughters; Twain's first daughter, Susy, was named after her. Twain expressed his adoration of Sue by dubbing her "Saint Susan," and she repaid the compliment by anointing him "Holy Samuel." Even in his last years, Twain would say of Sue Crane that "she is as pretty and winning and sweet as she was in those ancient times at her Quarry Farm, where she was an idol and the rest of us were the worshippers."[55] Before starting work in the morning, Twain had a routine of picking wildflowers with Sue, a devout Christian who often prepared bouquets for the local church. He liked to tease her about her religious beliefs, but she was more amused than miffed by his loving mischief.

A hundred yards up the hill from the farmhouse, reached by winding stone steps, Sue Crane created in 1874 a quaint study for Twain. Stunned when he first saw it, it was the stuff of any writer's fantasy: an enclosed octagonal gazebo with six windows that provided unobstructed views of the Chemung River Valley and faraway Pennsylvania hills. Meant to evoke the pilot house of a Mississippi River steamboat, the wooden structure was painted chocolate brown, trimmed with gingerbread, and always well supplied with pipes, tobacco, and cigars. The high altitude afforded stunning vistas of vivid sunsets emblazoned across the sky. As Twain told the Twichells, the study "sits perched in complete isolation on top of an elevation that commands leagues of valley & city & retreating ranges of distant blue hills. It is a cosy [sic] nest, with just room in it for a sofa & a table & three or four chairs—& when the storms sweep down the remote valley & the lightning flashes above the hills beyond, & the rain beats upon the roof over my head, imagine the luxury of it!"[56] On hot days, he flung open the study door and luxuriated in the gusting winds or thunderstorms whipping around him.

Each morning after breakfast, Twain trudged uphill to his study with a stack of papers tucked under his arm. "He often gave a little caper of delight as he left the house," recalled his daughter Clara, "and laughed one of his affectionate laughs."[57] Sometimes he wore the white linen suit that later became his trademark, and then worked uninterruptedly, puffing away at his cigar, until five in the afternoon. The rare visitor was asphyxiated with cigar smoke—he usually consumed fifteen cigars a day—while it seemed to act as a tonic on Twain's spirit. He tended to arrive at Quarry Farm with several unfinished manuscripts and might work on two or three during the summer. He was quick to catch fire on a book and equally quick to cool off. One huge advantage of life there was that in the evening he read aloud from his works-in-progress and benefited from commentary by Livy and the Cranes. In this literary atmosphere, Livy might also read aloud from a current book while family members loafed on sofas and lounged in hammocks. Twain further unwound with billiards, cards, and checkers.

In general, the Clemenses steered clear of parties at Quarry Farm and concentrated on family life. They started a tradition of planting stone water troughs on the road leading up to the house, inscribing names and birth dates of each new family member as she arrived: "Susie Clemens, 1872," "Clara L. Clemens, 1874," and in a few years, "Jean Clemens, 1880."[58] After the free-flowing social life of Nook Farm, Twain jealously guarded his privacy at Quarry Farm and conspired to bar most visitors, but didn't always succeed. "It never rains disagreeable people but it pours them," Twain wrote to Orion one day, telling how two women he hated had descended on the farm. "When I get a sight of either of these women I am 'done' for that day. When they both come in one evening I degenerate into pure lunacy."[59]

Ever since *The Innocents Abroad*, Livy had edited her husband's manuscripts, a process he referred to as "tooth-combing." A lifelong reader, she consumed authors from Emerson to George Eliot to Ibsen. As an editor, she performed a service for Twain not unlike what she did in social situations: she cleaned up his act, expunging vulgarity. As Twain phrased it, Livy "not only edited my works [but] edited me."[60] She sat on the porch at Quarry Farm, blue pencil at hand, and struck out profanities—much to the regret of her daughters. Twain would deliberately sneak into manuscripts remarks of a "felicitously atrocious character" for the pleasure of watching Livy spot and attack them.[61] Even when father and daughters favored some salty expression, Twain said, "we never stood on that because Madame was always in the majority, anyway."[62] Every Twain manuscript had to pass through Livy's editorial mill—he dubbed her his "Court of Last Resort"—and she often had a stack of manuscripts at her bedside.[63]

For all of Livy's innate sense of decorum, Twain believed she was a kindred soul and full-fledged literary partner. In bowing to her wishes, he thought nothing vital was lost and a certain readership might be gained. Livy and his daughters stood as perfect proxies for the mass audience he aspired to reach. He must have felt that Livy's countervailing force was useful, for he didn't seem to trust his own sense of when he went too far. We must recall that Twain engaged in a fair amount of self-censorship, especially when it came to sexual allusions. Even during their courtship, the puritanical Twain wanted to purge impurities from *Don Quixote* before Livy read it, and it was Twain who invited Mother Fairbanks to review *The Innocents Abroad* and pare away "offensive" language.

Livy's influence on Twain's career became controversial in the 1920s when the critic Van Wyck Brooks launched a searing attack on her, arguing that she had shackled his raw creativity. "From the moment of his marriage his artistic integrity, already compromised . . . had . . . been virtually destroyed . . . He had accepted his father-in-law's financial assistance; he had bought his post on the Buffalo *Express;* in return, he had pledged the freedom of his mind."[64] He cast Livy as "a young girl without experience, without imagination, who had never questioned anything, who had never been conscious of any will apart from that of her parents, her relatives, her friends."[65] To some extent, Livy sanitized the books by wiping out profanities, risqué jokes, and passing swipes at religion. In one manuscript she edited, she objected to her husband's use of "breech-clout" and "stench" and to characters' "retching and gagging and heaving" onboard a ship.[66] But she never altered the fundamental themes or storylines. Many things that she weeded out—grammatical errors, stylistic inconsistencies—any good copy editor would have flagged.

Livy helped her husband to overcome the hurdle of merely being a humorist as he outgrew that phase of his career. Twain once explained that after he'd written "some side-splitting story," she would spy deeper meanings obscured by his clowning. "You have a true lesson, a serious meaning to impart here," she would say. "Don't give way to your invincible temptation to destroy the good effect of your story by some extravagantly comic absurdity . . . Don't destroy your purpose with an ill-timed joke."[67] This was editorial criticism of a high order and went beyond merely bowdlerizing a book. Through the years, as Twain became more opinionated on certain topics, Livy would rightly restrain his dogmatism. He also respected her commercial judgment on contracts and which stories should go into which books as she became his literary agent as well as editor. Clara Clemens remembered her father saying that "whenever I have failed to follow the advice of Livy to change this or that sentence or eliminate a page, I have always come to regret it"—no small statement for an author so meticulous in his craftsmanship.[68]

Where Livy's influence was most troublesome lay in the stories Twain chose to tell. It wasn't so much that she squelched his exuberant humor as that she saw tender qualities in him that she wanted to see in print. Her sense of his potential as a writer sprang from her intimate knowledge of him as a husband. As Howells observed, "She wished him to be known not only for the wild and boundless humor that was in him, but for the beauty and tenderness and 'natural piety.'"[69] Livy would encourage him to broaden his output away from tales of Hannibal life and the West, and explore historical subjects such as *The Prince and the Pauper* and *Personal Recollections of Joan of Arc*—works that critics now find overly sentimental, lacking the zany edge, anarchic humor, and acute social commentary of his best works.

FLOODTIDE

That Mark Twain was evolving in a direction far beyond mere laughter was seen in his relationship at Quarry Farm with Mary Ann Cord, a Black woman who cooked for the Cranes and had been born into slavery. Photos show a woman of great strength and dignity, with hair parted in the middle, a firm mouth, and a slightly pugnacious gaze. Her determination is engraved in her furrowed brow. Twain described her as "turbaned, very tall, very broad, very fine every way."[70] Thanks to her remarkable vigor, Twain guessed she was sixty-two when she was actually seventy-six. From his early days in Hannibal, he had always prided himself on his knowledge of Blacks, but that complacency was shaken one summer twilight in June 1874 when he sat on the porch steps with Cord, who, as a servant, occupied a lower step. Twain had been misled by her cheerful demeanor and was blind (or so he claimed) to the tragic history staring him in the face.

He inquired of her: "How is it that you've lived sixty years and never had any trouble?" She sat there appalled by his naivete. "Misto C., is you in arnest?" she asked. Twain stammered out a confused reply. "Why, I thought—that is, I meant—why you *can't* have had any trouble. I've never heard you sigh, and never seen your eye when there wasn't a laugh in it."[71] In reply, she spilled out a woeful tale of how, in slavery, she had had a husband and seven children. When her Richmond mistress went broke around 1852, she sold her slaves at auction. Cord gave a harrowing description of standing high on an auction block, poked and prodded and chained, as her husband and children were abruptly torn away from her. She would only see one child again, her son Henry, who fled north via the Underground Railroad and became a barber in Elmira. (He was likely Twain's haircutter.) Never again did she see her husband and the six other children. She ended her grim tale with a blunt comment that must have shamed Twain. "Oh, no, Misto C.," she said sarcastically, "*I* ain't had no trouble. An' no *joy!*"[72]

Twain was struck by the story's visceral power and perhaps by his own ignorance as a well-meaning white man. He had always been fascinated by the eloquence that issued from deep emotion and praised Cord for "the best gift of strong and simple speech that I have known in any woman except my mother."[73] It perhaps suggested to him how the vernacular voice of an uneducated character could narrate an entire book. (The enslaved Jim's pain at his separation from his daughter in *Huckleberry Finn* would be linked in Twain's mind with Mary Ann Cord's story.)[74] Twain decided to transcribe Cord's monologue, verbatim, into an article titled "A True Story: Repeated Word for Word as I Heard It."[75] He knew this was a radical departure for him and sent it to William Dean Howells at the *Atlantic Monthly* with a suitably humble note: "I enclose also a 'True Story' which has no humor in it. You can pay as lightly as you choose for that, if you want it, for it is rather out of my line. I have not altered the old colored woman's story except to begin it at the beginning."[76] He also changed Cord's name to Aunt Rachel and tried to reproduce her speech phonetically with great accuracy.

When the *Atlantic* published the piece that November, paying handsomely for it, it marked Twain's first appearance there under his own byline. Although Howells deemed it one of the best short pieces he had ever published, it caused confusion among readers who expected something funny from Mark Twain's pen and found a deadly serious story instead. He had constantly worried about alienating faithful readers even as he sought to broaden his repertoire. "A True Story" pried open exciting new prospects. As the New York *Evening Post* wrote: "Mark Twain has never been a mere fun maker. In the midst of his most exaggeratedly humourous outbursts he has often grown serious for a moment . . . Occasionally, too, Mr. Clemens has written with scarcely any thought of making his readers smile, and with a distinct purpose to do a bit of genuine literary art work, as he did, for example, in the sketch of a negro woman's life story."[77]

A vehement Methodist, Mary Ann Cord often tangled in religious quarrels with the no less passionate John Lewis, a fierce Dunker-Baptist, and Twain enjoyed eavesdropping on their knockdown theological battles. About forty, Lewis had been born a free Black and labored hard with a slouch hat pulled low over his head as he raised pigs as a tenant farmer at Quarry Farm. "He is of mighty frame & muscle," said Twain, "stocky, stooping, ungainly, has a good manly face & a clear eye."[78] His wife, Mary, even nursed Clara Clemens for a couple of weeks.

Lewis ascended to heroic stature in the Clemens family in the summer of 1877 when he spied a runaway horse, carrying a wagon with Charlie Langdon's wife, Ida; his daughter Julia; and their nurse Nora, speeding down a steep road. With unbelievable courage, he stood in the horse's path and managed to grab its bit, yanking it to a halt. In gratitude, the Cranes canceled $400 in debt Lewis owed them. For the rest of his life, Lewis was showered with gifts, including $1,500 in cash, a costly gold Swiss watch, and a pension in old age. A marvelous 1903 photo shows Twain seated companionably beside Lewis, who has a full head of white hair, a white beard, and a rough-hewn cane resting between his legs. After the runaway incident, Lewis graciously said he was merely the instrument of "divine providence" and that the honors done him were "greater than the feat performed."[79] For Mark Twain, it was another classic example of eloquence fired by circumstance that rose "to the dignity of literature."[80]

CHAPTER FIFTEEN

Chartering a Comet to Mars

The Hartford years stimulated wide-ranging intellectual interests in Mark Twain, especially through his involvement with the Monday Evening Club. With membership restricted to no more than twenty men, the group met every other Monday from October through May and included many learned men of distinction—Governor Joseph Hawley; the theologian Horace Bushnell; the philologist James Hammond Trumbull; Calvin Stowe, the husband of Harriet Beecher Stowe; and Twain's friends and associates Twichell and Warner. The format provided that one member present an essay, followed by lively "gabble" and dinner. Between 1873 and 1887, Twain served up thirteen papers, a rate of about one per year. His essays were respectfully received, although his topics often verged on the unorthodox, including one on phrenology and another "On the Decay of the Art of Lying."[1]

Twain now wished to be taken seriously as a thinker, and as happened with his Mary Ann Cord story in the *Atlantic*, he encountered obstacles from people who wanted to pigeonhole him as a humorist. When he hazarded a critique of the jury system in the *New York Tribune*, he sparked a rebuttal from a writer who belittled him as a humorist who, along with "actors and clowns, make it a business to cater to our amusement in jest and burlesque."[2] The Monday Evening Club never condescended to Twain in this way, enabling him to employ it as a workshop for ideas, even controversial ones. In 1885 he recorded in his notebook: "Club Subject: The *insincerity* of man—all men are liars, partial or hiders of facts, half tellers of truths, shirks, moral sneaks."[3] When he read the club an early version of a later work, *What is Man?*, a dark book in which he alleged that men were merely automatons, shaped by circumstance and incapable of free will, the reaction was heated, leading everyone present, Twain recalled, "to scoff at it, jeer at it, revile it, and call it a lie; a thousand times a lie!"[4]

Under club rules, Livy was allowed to attend meetings when her husband spoke, although she couldn't speak herself, a situation that always applied to wives. Despite this clear sexual inequity, Twain delivered a thundering speech supporting female suffrage. "All that we require of a voter is that he shall be forked, wear pantaloons instead of petticoats, and bear a more or less humorous resemblance to the reported image of God . . . We brag of our universal, unrestricted suffrage; but we are shams after all, for we restrict when we come to the women."[5] Twain's views had advanced dramatically since 1867 when he wrote brash, cocky letters to the St. Louis *Democrat*, mocking female suffrage. With women voting, he had then snickered, there would be campaigns for state milliner and husbands serving as wet nurses for their children. He had ended with patronizing advice for women: "Content yourself with your little feminine trifles—your babies, your benevolent societies and your knitting—and let your natural bosses do the voting."[6]

By 1873, doubtless influenced by Livy, Twain had emerged as a militant voice for women's liberties. In an essay, "The Temperance Crusade and Woman's Rights," he showed immense sympathy for those women who camped outside rum shops and exhorted towns to shut them down. Betraying more than a trace of nativism, he wrote, "They find themselves voiceless in the making of laws and the election of officers to execute them. Born with brains, born in the country, educated, having large interests at stake, they find their tongues tied and their hands fettered, while every ignorant whisky-drinking foreign-born savage in the land may hold office." He admired the temperance women for "their heroism that boldly faces jeers, curses, ribald language, obloquy of every kind and degree."[7] Not only did he now favor female suffrage, he wanted a women's party. "Both the great parties have failed. I wish we might have a woman's party now . . . I feel persuaded that in extending the suffrage to women this country could lose absolutely nothing and might gain a great deal."[8]

For forty years, Twain stood forth as a staunch advocate of women's suffrage. In 1884, when their Nook Farm neighbor, Isabella Beecher Hooker, appealed to the Clemenses for money for the suffragist cause, they obliged. For Twain, Hooker was an "able and efficient" activist who deserved an honored place alongside Susan B. Anthony and Elizabeth Cady Stanton. "These brave women besieged the legislatures of the land . . . [and] achieved a revolution . . . They broke the chains of their sex and set it free."[9] In the 1890s, he expressed astonishment at how much the women's movement had achieved since the 1848 Seneca Falls Convention. "The women have accomplished a peaceful revolution, and a very beneficent one; and yet that has not convinced the average man that they are intelligent, and have courage and energy and perseverance and fortitude . . . perhaps nothing can ever make him realize that he is the average woman's inferior."[10] In his notebook, he wrote categorically that no civilization "can be perfect until exact equality between man & woman is included."[11]

After joining the Monday Evening Club, Twain assisted in creating, in 1877, another discussion club that met in his home: the Saturday Morning Club, modeled after a similar Boston club and composed of two dozen female members between the ages of sixteen and twenty. This was the first of three clubs Twain dreamed up in his lifetime marked by the same narcissistic structure: he would reign supreme as sole male member, surrounded by a bevy of adoring young females. As he told one woman, "I've been a member of it from the start; & I'm the only young girl of my sex that *is*. They waived sex, in my case, because they preferred solid wisdom to perfunctory technicalities. (Perfunctory is a pretty good word, though I am a little dim as to its meaning.)"[12] The club started with the essay model of the Monday Evening Club, then scrapped it in favor of frank, free-wheeling discussions. "To be able to talk with vigor and facility is worth heaps," Twain said, hoping to inspire young women to have the confidence to express their views.[13] He brought in an array of distinguished speakers, including William Dean Howells and Bret Harte. Not only did Twain address members on manifold topics—the life of Lord Macaulay, mental telepathy, temperance, and unionism—he stirred them with provocative views. On the subject of "What is Liberty?" he suggested 1865, not 1776, as the true date of liberty's birth, "For there was slavery before."[14] In a still more shocking mode, he characterized religious liberty as the "liberty to detach your mind from one form of slavery to chain it to another."[15] Amazingly enough, after swearing his club to secrecy, Twain read aloud *The Prince and the Pauper* in manuscript, half a dozen chapters at a time, several years before publication. "They profess to be very much fascinated with it," he reported to Mother Fairbanks; "so do Livy & Susie Warner."[16] In an extravagant gesture, Twain went to Tiffany & Company and ordered costly enamel pins for each club member. It should be said that the girls didn't "age out" of the club after turning twenty, and Twain would be on hand to celebrate the club's thirtieth anniversary in 1907, at which time he boasted that "to this day I am the only male member it has ever had."[17]

Twain exhibited a strong inclination to mentor young people, and he and Livy were instrumental in helping to launch the career of William Gillette, one of the renowned actor-playwrights of his generation, later known for his stage portrayal of Sherlock Holmes as well as impersonating Mark Twain. The Clemenses enjoyed a direct connection with Gillette, a Hartford native whose sister married George Warner, the brother of Charles Dudley. Gillette was also the son of former U.S. senator Francis Gillette, a Nook Farm founder. Sam and Livy advanced at least $3,000 to William Gillette for his dramatic education and worked to secure him a role in the Hartford production of *Colonel Sellers,* based on the popular *Gilded Age* character. Since many games and amateur theatricals were enacted in their living room, Twain later boasted that Gillette had "learned a part of his trade by acting in our charades."[18]

With special fervor, Twain promoted the Jubilee Singers of Fisk University, a school founded in Nashville at the close of the Civil War to educate Blacks, many born into slavery. The Jubilee Singers were started in 1871 to raise money for the school and to counter hideous caricatures of Blacks presented by minstrel shows then in vogue on the American stage. The school's choral director devised the notion of a concert tour that would present slave songs and spirituals in a way that made them accessible to white audiences. Twain first heard the Jubilee Singers in Hartford in 1872, possibly at Twichell's Asylum Hill Congregational Church, where they created a sensation. As the *Hartford Courant* reported, "It was like a revelation. One heard in those strange and plaintive melodies the sadness and the hope of a trusting and a really joyous race."[19]

The music touched deep chords in Twain, dredging up Hannibal memories dormant for many years. Eight of the group's eleven members had been born into slavery. For their London tour, he was asked to write an endorsement, which he gladly did. "I heard them sing once, & I would walk seven miles to hear them sing again. You will recognize that this is strong language for me to use, when you remember that I never was fond of pedestrianism." Then he reached back into his buried memories. "I was reared in the South, & my father owned slaves, & I do not know when anything has so moved me as the plaintive melodies of the Jubilee Singers. It was the first time for twenty-five or thirty years that I had heard such songs, or heard them sung in the genuine old way—& it is a way, I think, that white people cannot imitate—& never can . . . for one must have been a slave himself in order to feel what that life was & so convey the pathos of it in the music."[20]

When the Fisk Jubilee Singers came to Hartford in 1875, Twain contacted their musical director and expressly asked them to perform "John Brown's Body," which he had heard them sing in London, prompting "volcanic eruption of applause" from a "decorous, aristocratic English audience" hosted by Prime Minister William Gladstone.[21] This was quite a remarkable request: a former Confederate soldier was asking a Black choir, many once enslaved, to perform the moving song that was a tribute to a martyred abolitionist and, when turned into "The Battle Hymn of the Republic," became the song most closely associated with the Union cause. Twain's letter of request was read aloud prior to the performance.

FLOODTIDE

Twain's response to the Fisk singers charts his stunning growth in racial understanding since his marriage to Livy. He now stood forth as a proud champion of these Black performers and was perhaps surprised by the depth of his response. Throughout his life he insisted that no music surpassed in beauty and feeling the songs and spirituals that had arisen from slavery. Often, at social gatherings or at sad moments, he would rise and sing "Nobody Knows the Trouble I've Seen," or "Swing Low, Sweet Chariot." As he sang softly, he would sway with feeling, transported by the music's power. With one particular spiritual, he belted out at the end, in a loud, spirited voice, "Glory, Glory Hallelujah!"[22] Small wonder that when a magazine once requested that he name his favorite songs, five of the eighteen listed were Black spirituals. In Hartford, he was also quick to aid in raising money for the Black congregation at the Talcott Street Church.

In Hartford, Twain experienced the gravitational pull of another big-time showman fifty miles away in Bridgeport: Phineas T. Barnum. Barnum had the poetry and bluster of Colonel Sellers, but had parlayed them into a spectacular career. Like Twain in Nevada, Barnum specialized in hoaxes, promoting a 161-year-old woman as the childhood nurse of George Washington, and both men reveled in outlandish doings. Barnum's career ran the gamut of carnival amusements, from his American Museum of Curiosities, which opened in New York in 1842, to an itinerant circus that began touring in 1871 and was humbly billed by Barnum as "The Greatest Show on Earth."

Twain had already teamed up with Barnum in a ludicrous publicity stunt in the summer of 1874, when the public was riveted by Coggia's Comet, visible to the naked eye. Exploiting the brouhaha, Twain and Barnum offered a plan to "charter" the comet to anyone interested in a pleasure excursion to Mars, priced at a very affordable rate of $2 per 50 million miles. After Twain wrote the copy, Barnum was thrilled by the publicity, telling Twain, "Your *comet* article in the Herald last year wherein you had me for an *active* partner of course added much to my notoriety at home and abroad."[23] In 1874 Barnum displayed a no less urgent need for publicity when he planned to tour his Great Roman Hippodrome, which staged in an oval arena chariot races and other acts once seen in the Roman Colosseum. Pleading with Twain to plug the show in *Harper's Weekly,* Barnum listed the stupendous dimensions of his venture, performed under a giant tent, with 1,100 people, 750 horses, and enough camels, elephants, buffaloes, and ostriches to please even the most jaded animal lovers. Aware of Twain's fondness for the Far West, Barnum added: "I give a scene called INDIAN LIFE ON THE PLAINS wherein scores of Indians of various tribes appear with their squaws pappooses [sic] ponies and wigwams travelling as they do in the Indian territory."[24] Breathlessly admiring, Twain shot back, "But of all the amazing shows that ever were conceived of, I think this of yours must take the lead! . . . I mean to come to see the show,—but to me you are the biggest marvel connected with it, after all."[25] Amid all the ballyhoo, the extravaganza failed because audiences expected hordes of clowns, and Barnum had provided a meager few.

By this point in his career, Twain was besieged by never-ending letters from autograph hounds and strangers, begging for money or a book endorsement. For this reason, he was intrigued by the letters Barnum received from eccentric characters, peddling their services for his shows. For Twain, they were proof of human greed, mendacity, and low cunning. For several years, Barnum sent these begging letters to Twain, who planned to weave them someday into an article. He was staggered by the bountiful trove from Barnum and the oddball acts described. "It is an admirable lot of letters," he told Barnum. "Headless mice, four-legged hens, human-handed sacred bulls, 'professional' Gypsies . . . deformed human beings anxious to trade on their horrors, school-teachers [sic] who can't spell—it is a perfect feast of queer literature! Again I beseech you, don't burn a single specimen."[26] Barnum soon made a cameo appearance in Twain's story "The Stolen White Elephant," a spoof of detective fiction. As hapless but absurdly pretentious detectives stalk a missing white elephant, Barnum hatches a publicity deal to paste his circus poster on the renegade animal for a $7,000 fee.

It was ironic that Twain, a nonpareil satirist of schemers and hucksters, repeatedly fell prey to their wiles. In 1874 he was invited to sit on the board of the new Hartford Accident Insurance company—designed to compete with Travelers—and he made a substantial investment of $23,000 in the company, about a half million dollars in contemporary money. The firm's guiding spirit was John Percival Jones, a U.S. senator from Nevada and a silver millionaire from the Comstock Lode, regarded by Twain at first as a "big-hearted man with ninety-nine parts of him pure generosity."[27] Forever seduced by visions of becoming a tycoon, Twain allowed Jones to exploit his fame to promote the company's fortunes. Speaking at an insurance industry dinner that October, Twain said, "There is no nobler field for human effort than the insurance line of business—especially accident insurance . . . I look upon a cripple now with affectionate interest—there is a charm about a railroad collision that is unspeakable."[28]

Although Twain had been assured by Senator Jones that Hartford Accident Insurance was a foolproof investment and that he would make him whole for any loss, it proved the first of many business disasters to befall Twain. After eighteen months, the business "went to pieces and I was out of pocket twenty-three thousand dollars."[29] When Twain sought to recover his funds from Jones, he replied, through associates, that he was temporarily "straitened and would be glad if I would wait a while" for repayment. It took two or three years before Jones made complete restitution to Twain, who by that point excoriated him in his notebook as "lying thief US Senator Jno P Jones."[30] "He meant well," Twain added, "but he was a fool . . . whose proper place is [a] shyster in a Tombs court"—the Tombs being the dread prison in lower Manhattan.[31]

So entangled did Twain become with his investments that at times it was hard to tell whether he was a literary man with business sidelines or a businessman who dabbled in letters. Again and again, an inveterate speculator, he lapsed into money-mad schemes, helpless to break the habit. "I must speculate in something," he once admitted to Howells, "such being my nature."[32] He could never extirpate a rooted fear of poverty that had lingered from childhood. "There is never a month passes that I do not dream of being in reduced circumstances," he told his official biographer, "and obliged to go back to the river to earn a living."[33] Riches forever shimmered like a mirage at the edge of his consciousness. "The lack of money," he said, only half in jest, "is the root of all evil."[34] When it came to business dealings, he would submit to a glandular optimism and indulge in hyperbole worthy of Colonel Sellers. Henry Ward Beecher once told him, "You are one of the talented men of the age, but in matters of business I don't suppose you know more than enough to come in when it rains."[35] Livy didn't share her husband's investing manias and tolerated them as best she could. Twain's business record was so abysmal that the *Washington Post* once observed ruefully, "One good way to locate an unsafe investment is to find out whether Mark Twain has been permitted to get in on the ground floor."[36]

This was the heyday of inventors, a time that saw the development of an explosion of gadgets, ranging from telegraphs to electric lights, sewing machines to automobiles. Thomas Edison ranked as folk hero of the age, and Twain not only befriended Edison but would have his voice recorded on his wax cylinders and his movements captured by his motion picture camera. Like Edison, Twain wanted to accumulate patents, transform the world, and make a mint. "An inventor is a . . . true poet— and nothing . . . less than a high order of poet," Twain told his sister.[37] With his love of newfangled products, he was one of the first writers to adopt the typewriter. He marveled at the technological prowess of postwar America and said so with bumptious pride: "For we *do* live in an age compared to which all other ages are dull & eventless."[38]

If Twain seemed to have an infallible knack for losing investments, his record was no less unerring in walking away from winners. In spring 1877, he was invited to the *Hartford Courant*'s offices to witness operation of a new device called the telephone and claimed that Alexander Graham Bell offered him "a whole hatful" of stock for five hundred dollars. But after the insurance disaster with Senator Jones, "I was the burnt

FLOODTIDE

child, and I resisted all these temptations . . . I said I didn't want anything more to do with wildcat speculation."[39] The stock then soared from $110 to $995 by year's end. Twain soon had a telephone installed in his house and contended it was the first in a New England home. Nevertheless, Twain proved the customer from hell and complained loudly about the service, taking his gripes directly to Gardiner Hubbard, the president of Bell Telephone and the father-in-law of Alexander Graham Bell. "The Hartford telephone is the very worst on the face of the whole earth . . . they *charge* for night-service, in their cold calm way, just the same as if they had furnished it. And if you try to curse through the telephone, they shut you off. It is this ostentatious holiness that grovels me."[40]

Twain's sole paying investment came from an early brainstorm. In 1873 he had patented "Mark Twain's Self-Pasting Scrap Book" and ultimately sold about a hundred thousand copies in partnership with Dan Slote, his old pal from their *Quaker City* escapades. Preoccupied with his own celebrity, Twain was a fan of scrapbooks and hated the bother of glue and paste. Much like simple envelopes, his scrapbooks possessed adhesive strips that only needed to be moistened to retain clippings. Twain worked all the angles on his scrapbook, dreaming up thirty varieties, including the "Druggists Prescription Book," "Child's Scrap Book," and "The Masonic Scrap Book," produced with choice bindings from "Full Morocco" to "Full Russia, Rich Finish."[41] The firm dispatched salesmen to London and Paris, part of Twain's overarching ambition "to Scrap-Book the Eastern hemisphere," he told Mother Fairbanks. "It seems funny that an invention which cost me five minutes' thought, in a railway car one day, should in this little while be paying me an income as large as any salary I ever received on a newspaper."[42] Unfortunately, this early success misled Twain into thinking he had a certain flair for business, which he most decidedly did not.

In 1874 it was not apparent to Mark Twain, as it would be later on, that his most fertile stock of memory lay buried in the Mississippi mud of his boyhood. One day that October, Twain and Twichell were hiking through autumn woods when Twain harked back to his glory days standing in a pilot house on the river. "What a virgin subject to hurl into a magazine!" Twichell exclaimed. Strangely enough, Twain hadn't thought of it before.[43] The conversation marked a turning point. Twain contacted Howells at the *Atlantic*, who had pilots in his own Ohio family and could appreciate the bygone romance of the river, with the upshot that Twain would publish a series in the magazine from January through August 1875 titled "Old Times on the Mississippi." These seven articles tapped a fresh vein of recollection inside Twain and formed the kernel of his later book *Life on the Mississippi*. After the first installment, Howells complimented Twain: "The piece about the Mississippi is capital—it almost made the water in our ice-pitcher muddy as I read it."[44] The series only grew better. Twain had thrust open a portal to his past, and there on display were all the memories, splendidly untouched. His descriptions of Hannibal revealed a profoundly moving, new lyrical voice in Mark Twain. This was a starkly different narrator from the irreverent jokester of *The Innocents Abroad* or *Roughing It*, or the mordant cynic of *The Gilded Age*. Perhaps because he felt secure with Livy in Nook Farm, housed in their eccentric mansion, he could explore his past with tenderness and affection, and enjoy the perspective gained when a period of life has ended. Like many writers before him, Twain discovered that the past recaptured was often more poignant than the past actually lived.

For several years, his boyhood had streamed unbidden into his mind. In 1870 his old Hannibal friend Will Bowen sent him a letter that broke open the floodgates. "Your letter has stirred me to the bottom," Twain responded. "The fountains of my great deep are broken up & I have rained reminiscences for four & twenty hours. The old life has swept before me like a panorama; the old days have trooped by in their old glory, again; the old faces have looked out of the mists of the past; old footsteps have sounded in my listening ears; old hands have clasped mine, old voices have greeted me, & the songs I loved ages & ages ago have come wailing down the centuries!"[45] Twain had found the mother lode of experience—or perhaps it had found him. With hindsight, it seems inevitable that he would someday harvest this abundant crop of boyhood recollections.

The book that resulted from his rediscovery was *The Adventures of Tom Sawyer*, which was started as early as 1872 while he was vacationing on the Connecticut shore, and completed after Twain switched to the typewriter. A man spellbound by his own past, Twain worked from some well-worn anecdotes, smoothed by repetition, perhaps making composition easier. In the summer of 1874, he told his Scottish friend Dr. John Brown that he was so consumed by the new manuscript in his octagonal study at Quarry Farm that he cranked out fifty manuscript pages per day and was "dead to everything else . . . On hot days I spread the study wide open, anchor my papers down with brickbats & write in the midst of hurricanes, clothed in the same thin linen we make shirt bosoms of."[46] Twain wrote with such unfeigned longing for his past that he left no doubt as to the autobiographical wellspring of his novel. "I have always concealed it before," he said, somewhat facetiously, late in life, "but now I am *compelled* to confess that I am Tom Sawyer!"[47]

By the time he completed the book in July 1875, Twain had decided not to drag Tom Sawyer into adulthood and shatter the perfection of his boyhood world. For Twain, adult life was a disappointing anticlimax, and he didn't wish to inflict that torment on Tom. He thought that his one mistake might have been not writing the story in the first person—a regret that anticipates *Huckleberry Finn*, in which the chatty central character would narrate the story, submerging readers in his mind. While Twain considered *Tom Sawyer* a book *about* boys, he didn't necessarily think it a book *for* boys. "It is *not* a boy's book, at all," he informed Howells. "It will only be read by adults. It is only written for adults."[48] Howells, who thought it "the best boy story I ever read," begged to differ, saying, "I think you ought to treat it explicitly *as* a boy's story; Grown-ups will enjoy it just as much if you do."[49] After consulting with Livy, Twain discovered that she agreed with Howells. "Mrs. Clemens decides with you that the book should issue as a book for boys, pure & simple—& so do I," he wrote back to Howells. "It is surely the correct idea."[50] In the book's preface, he charmingly made the point that while the book was aimed primarily at boys and girls, he hoped it would "not be shunned by men and women on that account, for part of my plan has been to try to pleasantly remind adults of what they once were themselves."[51]

Mark Twain populated *Tom Sawyer* with numerous locales and figures from his childhood, drawn with sympathy and affection. A barely disguised Hannibal he renamed St. Petersburg; his childhood sweetheart Laura Hawkins was transformed into Becky Thatcher; Jane Lampton Clemens into Tom's Aunt Polly; his deceased brother Henry into Tom's half-brother Sid; and Judge Clemens into Judge Thatcher. Though they were based on fact, Twain created such distinctive characters that they would endure as American archetypes. He distilled Tom's character into the quintessence of American boyhood and made him a lovable renegade with a craving for mischief, all under the critical but forgiving eye of Aunt Polly. Tom is winning in his barefaced trickery as he gulls companions into whitewashing a fence for him while he "sat on a barrel in the shade close by, dangled his legs, munched his apple, and planned the slaughter of more innocents."[52] The visual clarity of the scene is worthy of a Winslow Homer painting of rustic boys at play on a summer day. Tom is an incurable fantasist, impatient with mundane realities and drunk with the moonshine of romantic adventure novels.

A cult of childhood purity sprang up in America after the Civil War carnage, exemplified by the work of Homer and Louisa May Alcott, and Twain joined in fostering radiant images of such innocence. Tom and his friends Huck Finn and Joe Harper crave freedom and take a raft to Jackson's Island in the Mississippi, an Edenic place where they eat bacon over an open fire and play at being pirates. Twain issues a memorable paean to their sense of freedom: "It seemed glorious sport to be feasting in that wild free way in the virgin forest of an unexplored and uninhabited island, far from the haunts of men, and they said they would never return to civilization."[53] When they do return, they are presumed dead and suddenly materialize in time to eavesdrop on their own church funeral.

For modern readers, the world of *Tom Sawyer* may flicker by in a golden haze of nostalgia, yet on closer examination, the foundations for

Twain's later, darker views can already be discerned. The seeds of alienation, almost unseen, were beginning to sprout. Tom, a boyish outlaw, is at war with small-town institutions and detests the sanctimonious little snobs, those Model Boys who behave perfectly in church and shine in Sunday school. Twain returns here to a favorite theme: that the good boys are phonies, and real virtue resides with the honest rebels. When Tom's cousin Mary drags him to Sunday school, it was "a place that Tom hated with his whole heart."[54] The severe church atmosphere stifles any feeling of boyhood exuberance, making children natural rebels against it. When a religious revival comes to town, Tom finds it a depressing affair that deadens joy. "Tom went about, hoping against hope for the sight of one blessed sinful face, but disappointment crossed him everywhere."[55]

The rest of Mark Twain's life would show that what he played for laughter in *Tom Sawyer* was no laughing matter for him. For all its charm, *Tom Sawyer* presents an inverted worldview in which middle-class moralists are hypocrites, and outcasts are people of true value. This outlook is embodied in the portrait of Tom's friend Huck Finn, the son of the town drunkard, an urchin who sleeps "on doorsteps in fine weather and in empty hogsheads in wet."[56] This devilish boy, a "juvenile pariah," secretly wins the allegiance of other children. "Huckleberry was cordially hated and dreaded by all the mothers of the town, because he was idle, and lawless, and vulgar, and bad—and because all their children admired him so, and delighted in his forbidden society, and wished they dared to be like him."[57] At the end, Huck casts off society's fetters when the Widow Douglas tries to domesticate him and he cannot long endure "the bars and shackles of civilization [that] shut him in and bound him hand and foot. He bravely bore his miseries three weeks, and then one day turned up missing."[58] Twain sees more morality in this outcast boy than in all the town's fine, upstanding citizens.

In the novel, Twain's sympathies don't extend to the Native American, Injun Joe, who is cast as the murderer exposed by Tom and painted in stereotypical fashion as savage, violent, and drunk. The character was based on an unoffending local man named Joe Douglass, an Osage or a Cherokee boy who had been brought to Hannibal and often turned up homeless. He always denied that he was the Injun Joe of the novel. Also bordering on caricature is the portrait of a Black boy named Jim, whom Tom tries to dupe into whitewashing the fence. Aside from this Black character, Twain presents a pretty sanitized view of race relations in Hannibal, scrubbed clean of slavery. There is a kindly and forgiving spirit to *Tom Sawyer*, but the author would soon return to his boyhood town and give it a colder, more searching scrutiny. He had only peeled away the top layer with *Tom Sawyer* and would go much deeper in later excavations.

For all its later fame, the novel didn't make the splash one might imagine. In the *Atlantic*, Howells was unstinting in his praise. "Mr. Clemens has taken the boy of the Southwest for the hero of his new book, and has presented him with a fidelity to circumstance which loses no charm by being realistic in the highest degree, and which gives incomparably the best picture of life in that region as yet known to fiction."[59] Unfortunately, Howells's review appeared in May 1876 and book publication was delayed until December, blunting its impact. Oddly enough, British reviewers were kinder than their American counterparts when the novel appeared there in June 1876. Moncure Conway, a clergyman and former abolitionist who was then Twain's British agent and arranged for Chatto & Windus to publish *Tom Sawyer*, believed Twain had attained a new plateau with the novel. "It is, as I think, the most notable work which Mark Twain has yet written, and will signally add to his reputation for a variety of powers."[60]

In an age of inadequate copyright protection, the publication of *Tom Sawyer* turned into a fiasco. The book first appeared in England, to secure copyright protection there, and didn't come out in the United States until December 8, 1876. Because of this delay, a large pirated edition was printed by Belford Brothers in Canada and sold briskly in the United States, robbing Twain of royalties and making him a militant, even a monomaniac, on the subject of copyright reform. "This piracy will cost me $10,000, & I will spend as much more to choke off these pirates," he promised, "if the thing can be done."[61] In the end, the American edition of *Tom Sawyer* sold a disappointing 23,638 copies in its first year, a figure far below the sale of Twain's previous volumes. The author, livid, wished the sale of pirated books to be "a penal offense, punishable by fine & imprisonment, like dealing in any other kind of stolen goods."[62] Four years later, he denounced the prevailing copyright law as "framed by an idiot, & passed by a Congress of muttonheads."[63]

Even though Twain was now a director and held stock in the American Publishing Company, he blamed Elisha Bliss, Jr., for the costly delay of *Tom Sawyer*. Even before publication, he sent Bliss a scorching letter in which he said his house was publishing way too many books to take adequate care of his own and advised him to slash his list by two-thirds and focus exclusively on *Tom Sawyer*. "I want it run by itself, if possible, & pushed like everything."[64] Bliss never formally replied to this rather breathtaking letter. Mark Twain's career now seemed prematurely in decline. Two weeks after the American publication, Twain wrote to Moncure Conway in a distraught mood. "It's a mistake, I am not writing any new book. Belford [Brothers] has taken the profits all out of 'Tom Sawyer.' We found our copyright law here to be nearly worthless, and if I can make a living out of plays, I shall never write another book."[65]

CHAPTER SIXTEEN

"Invertebrate Without a Country"

During the summer of 1876, at Elmira, Mark Twain covertly drafted a raunchy, pornographic sketch titled *Conversation as It Was by the Social Fireside, in the Time of the Tudors,* better known by its shorter title, *1601.* It would never appear under his name in his lifetime or be admitted into his collected works. Twain may have responded to the challenge of an editor who sighed, "O that we had a Rabelais—I judged I could furnish him one."[1] Or perhaps, after finishing *Tom Sawyer,* Twain wondered whatever happened to that naughty boy he once was and saw this sketch as his secret revolt against the propriety of northern life. This remarkable document proves that Twain's reticence about sex was not because he failed to think about it, but because he lacked the opportunity to express it. However much he hungered for the freedom of a Rabelais, he suppressed such salacious impulses throughout his career. In private, he decried the hypocrisy of the puritanical censors of Walt Whitman's poetry who also honored ribald passages in Rabelais, Swift, Shakespeare, and Balzac.

The immediate stimulus for *1601* was that Twain was researching *The Prince and the Pauper* and steeping himself in old English books, including *The Diary of Samuel Pepys,* in order to master archaic English. As he did so, he was struck by "the frank indelicacies of speech permissible among ladies and gentlemen of that ancient time."[2] *1601* originally had an audience of one: Joseph Twichell, whom Twain wanted to divert with the bawdy speech of Elizabethan England. Every word of it was coarse and vulgar and would have been edited out of existence by Livy.

The twenty-three-hundred-word manuscript was supposedly taken from the diary of a stodgy old cupbearer to Queen Elizabeth I. The scene is set at her court with Francis Bacon, Sir Walter Raleigh, Ben Jonson, Francis Beaumont, and William Shakespeare in attendance, as well as invented figures such as the Duchess of Bilgewater. The sketch begins with Queen Elizabeth commenting on a vast, stinking fart and quizzing those present to root out the culprit. Sir Walter Raleigh finally rises up and confesses, but he is ashamed that his burst was so weak that he lets loose an even more powerful blast. When Shakespeare tells the group that Montaigne claimed widows in Perigord wore headdresses shaped like "wilted" members, the Queen laughingly says, "Widows in England doe wear prickes too, but 'twixt ye thyghs, & not wilted neither, till coition hath done that office for them."[3] When Lady Helen, all of fifteen, reveals that she sprouted pubic hair two years earlier, the Queen teases Beaumont by asking if he doesn't have a "small birde" that "stirs at hearing tel of soe sweete a neste?"[4] Shakespeare reads a selection from *Henry IV* only to have the cupbearer say such stuff puts him to sleep. The sketch showcases Twain's linguistic ingenuity in weaving together highborn noble talk with base tavern chatter.

So often pornography reflects purely male desire. Here, by contrast, Twain is frank that women share the same level of libido as men and possibly more. In fact, the women are as coarse and lusty as the men. This may tell us something about Twain's sex life with Livy and that she had a sexual appetite no less hearty than his own. On their walks to the tower on Talcott Mountain, Twain and Twichell would stop by the roadway to read aloud from *1601* and "laugh ourselves lame and sore."[5] The sketch made Twain roar with laughter—a rare thing. "I don't often write anything that I laugh at myself," he told his notebook, "but I can hardly think of that thing without laughing."[6]

The piece had a curious afterlife. Twain would show it privately to a privileged few, requesting that they keep no copy and return the original. *1601* gradually found a select circle of fans, starting with John Hay,

"INVERTEBRATE WITHOUT A COUNTRY"

Lincoln's former private secretary, who called it a "most exquisite bit of old English morality," and he had four unbound copies privately printed.[7] Twain's friend Dean Sage produced another dozen copies. In 1882 Twain discreetly visited West Point and entrusted Lieutenant Charles Erskine Scott Wood to print an edition of fifty copies. According to Twain, Wood was "an able & artistic amateur printer" and the perfect man for the job.[8] Using Old English–style type and large sheets, Wood ran off deckle-edged vellum copies at the West Point Academy Press. It was a risky thing for Twain to do since *1601* might be made public at some point and embarrass him. "I shall get into trouble with it yet before I die," he told Wood.[9] Though *1601*'s authorship was often a mystery and the work never surfaced widely in public, it developed a quiet cult following. Nevertheless, over the years all copies vanished, and in 1905 Twain lamented to a friend that "frequent & diligent search has failed to turn one up."[10]

After the dispiriting sales of *Tom Sawyer*, Twain had vowed that he would renounce novels and devote himself to plays. A career writing for theater was then more lucrative, and Twain scored a hit with a five-act play based on *The Gilded Age* that was ultimately named after its central character, *Colonel Sellers*. He sold the rights to the actor John T. Raymond, who had established his reputation with *Our American Cousin*, the play Lincoln attended the night that he was assassinated, and the role of Colonel Sellers was to be his foremost stage triumph. "I don't think much of it, as a drama," Twain said of the play, and critics agreed that it was often disorganized and incoherent, merely a setting for Colonel Sellers.[11] In September 1874, when Twain addressed an opening-night audience, he mingled humor with humility. "I hope you will overlook the faults in this play because I have never written a play before . . . and maybe I won't offend again. I wanted to have some fine situations and spectacular effects in this piece, but I was interfered with. I wanted to have a volcano in a state of eruption . . . but the manager wouldn't hear of it; he said there wasn't any volcano in Missouri—as if *I* am responsible for Missouri's poverty."[12]

For the lead part, Twain had initially hoped to entice Edwin Booth, the illustrious tragedian, then settled for Raymond as "the superior money-maker. He had the masses with him—and I was pressed for funds."[13] He faulted Raymond for presenting an overly broad caricature of Colonel Sellers, missing the poetry and pathos of "a fine old Southern gentleman."[14] Twain, never an easy partner to work with, ended up reviling Raymond as "empty and selfish and vulgar and ignorant and silly, and there was a vacancy in him where his heart should have been."[15] Nonetheless, the show toured for a decade and proved extremely profitable for Twain. It earned him $100,000 in royalties during the first three years alone, and since its plot revolved around the Tennessee land, Twain quipped that he had made "just about a dollar an acre."[16]

Despite doubts about Bret Harte's character and past strains in their relationship, Mark Twain remained a huge admirer of the author of "The Luck of Roaring Camp" and "The Outcasts of Poker Flat." When he reviewed Harte's *Poems* for the *Buffalo Express,* he didn't mince words: "The true genius of Bret Harte is found in his vividly dramatic California sketches."[17] Twain, who was forever competitive with Harte, asked a friend in 1871, "Do you know who is the most celebrated man in America to-day—the man whose name is on every single tongue from one end of the continent to the other? It is Bret Harte. And the poem called the 'Heathen Chinee' did it for him."[18] Harte had written a verse drama about a Chinese immigrant named Ah Sin, a parody of Algernon Charles Swinburne, and published this doggerel at the last moment because of a shortage of copy at the *Overland Monthly.* It ignited a national sensation. While Twain praised Harte's writing, he also sneered at his slick clothes and affected, high-toned manners, and had grown increasingly critical of Harte's handling of dialect, which he found stilted and unconvincing. For Twain, his own precise delineation of dialect was a major source of pride.

Harte felt the rivalry no less acutely than Twain, and he watched with envy as Twain grew steadily in wealth and celebrity. "You ought to be very happy with that sweet wife of yours and I suppose you are," he wrote to Twain when Susy was born. "It is not every man that can cap a hard, thorny, restless youth with so graceful a crown."[19] By 1874, as his writing career began to dry up, Harte turned to the lecture circuit to support his wife and children. Heavily in debt, he began giving off an air of desperation. When he decided to write his first novel, *Gabriel Conroy*, Twain encouraged him to publish with the American Publishing Company, and for an extended period Harte subsisted off advances from Elisha Bliss, Jr. With creditors closing in on him, Harte constantly badgered Bliss for money and blamed Twain for not protecting him. When his novel was published, it met with poor sales and reviews, making crystal-clear that Mark Twain had vaulted far ahead of Harte.

In the fall of 1876, Harte journeyed to Hartford, hoping to collaborate with Twain on a comic melodrama, *Ah Sin*, which plucked the Chinese laundryman from Harte's poem and a later play and set him in a mining camp in Calaveras County, California, where he would hornswoggle the miners to solve a murder mystery. Twain's windfall profits from *Colonel Sellers* and his awareness of its defects may have made him amenable to working with Harte. Both he and Harte constructed separate plots, then merged the two. Later on, Twain attempted to distance himself from the botched result: "Bret wrote it while I played billiards, but of course I had to go over it to get the dialect right."[20] Yet his contemporaneous letters tell a different tale. "My plot is built—finished it yesterday—six days' work, 8 or 9 hours a day, & has nearly killed me," he complained to Howells at the time.[21]

Aside from the play's defects, Twain was mortally offended by Harte's behavior during his two stays at his Hartford house that fall. He was aghast when Harte criticized Livy and the home she had created—sacred topics for Twain. At the end of Harte's first stay, Twain warned him to "spare Mrs. Clemens . . . you have made sarcastic remarks about the furniture of the bedroom, and about the table-ware, and about the servants, and about the carriage and the sleigh, and the coachman's livery—in fact about every detail of the house and half of its occupants."[22] It also bothered Twain that during Harte's second stay, he stayed up all night, writing and drinking and forcing George Griffin to replenish him with fresh bottles of whiskey.

Recriminations flew back and forth between the two men. When Harte asked Twain for yet another loan, Twain offered Harte a deal instead: he would pay him $25 a week, along with room and board, if he returned to Hartford and cowrote another play. On March 1, 1877, Harte retaliated with a long, heated letter that charged Twain with trying to degrade him to the status of an indentured playwright. For good measure, he harshly blamed Twain for the failure of *Gabriel Conroy*. "Either Bliss must confess that he runs his concern solely in *your* interest . . . or else he is a fool."[23] On the back of the ninth and concluding page of this diatribe, Twain scrawled, "I have read two pages of this ineffable idiotcy—it is all I can stand of it."[24] The letter effectively ended their relationship, and the two men never saw each other again.

When *Ah Sin* opened in Washington, D.C., in May 1877, with Charles T. Parsloe playing the Chinese laundryman, Twain was laid low by a bronchitis attack. At the final curtain, Parsloe read aloud a telegram from Twain: "I am on the sick-list, and therefore cannot come to Washington; but I have prepared two speeches—one to deliver in event of failure of the play, and the other if successful. Please tell me which I shall send. May be better to put it to vote."[25] The audience cheered, declaring the play a success, but this may only have endorsed Twain's beguiling note. Twain and Harte had managed to steer clear of each other during rehearsals. The play ran for less than a week apiece in Washington and Baltimore, although Augustin Daly decided to produce it in New York.

In July, Twain spent two weeks in Manhattan trying to wrestle the play into a more manageable form. As he phrased it, he was "licking that dreadful play of Ah Sin into shape & rehearsing it 4 hours a day with the

"INVERTEBRATE WITHOUT A COUNTRY"

actors."[26] Motivated by anger with Harte, he sought to purge the play of his cowriter's influence and boasted that he "left hardly a foot-print of Harte in it anywhere."[27] His extra work yielded scant results, and the play had a short, money-losing run after opening on July 31. Twain told Howells bluntly that the show was a "most abject & incurable failure!"[28] "We didn't trim & polish it at all—& we shall live to repent it, too," Twain had already grumbled to his mother before the opening. "It was not my fault; it was wholly that of that natural liar, swindler, bilk, & literary thief, Bret Harte, son of an Albany Jew-pedlar."[29]

Harte skipped the New York opening, but fearful that he might not, Livy prepared her hotheaded husband: "Be as civil as you can to Mr. Hart [sic] if he should come about."[30] A day later she wrote to him again, warning him against reprisals and his own vengeful nature. As always, she sounded the calm voice of reason. "Youth I want to caution you about one thing, don't say harsh things about Mr. Harte, don't talk against Mr. Harte to people, it is so much better that you be reticent about him, don't let anybody trap you into talking freely of him—We are so desperately happy, our paths lie in such pleasant places, and he is so miserable, we can easily afford to be magnanimous toward him."[31]

Twain could not admit that *Ah Sin* was a mutual failure, so he heaped all the blame on Harte. To Howells, he poured out his wrath at Harte's "deliberate thefts & plagiarisms, and my own unconscious ones. I don't believe Harte ever had an idea that he came by honestly. He is the most abandoned thief that defiles the earth."[32] Twain could be generous and loving with friends until they disappointed him and abused his generosity; then he would lash out with ungovernable vengeance. With his volatile temperament, his hurts did not heal normally and his anger did not abate.

In 1878, upon learning that Harte sought a consular post from President Rutherford B. Hayes, Twain grew apoplectic. "Harte is a liar, a thief, a swindler, a snob, a sot, a sponge, a coward . . . he is brim full of treachery," he told Howells.[33] Finding no accusation too extreme, he said Harte "had cheated his publishers out of money . . . I told the publishers that they ought to have him put in prison."[34] Twain now meditated extreme revenge upon Harte. He asked Howells, whose wife was related to Hayes, if he could intercede with Hayes to block any Harte appointment. "Wherever [Harte] goes his wake is tumultuous with swindled grocers, & with defrauded innocents who have loaned him money."[35] Somehow the two scathing letters Twain wrote to Howells about Harte ended up in the hands of the president, who solicited Howells's advice, noting he had heard "sinister things about [Harte] from Mark Twain."[36] Howells crafted an artfully ambiguous reply, confirming Harte's "notorious" history of borrowing and drinking, but concluding, "From what I hear he is really making an effort to reform."[37] In the end, Harte succeeded in getting an appointment from Hayes as U.S. consul in Crefeld, Germany.

Twain would spend the rest of his life cursing Bret Harte. He never stopped admiring at least *some* of his writing and credited one book of Harte's sketches for their "evidences of genius."[38] Yet he was fully capable of becoming a prisoner of his hatreds and no statute of limitations ever curtailed his vendettas. Three years before Twain died, he flayed Harte bitterly as "a man without a country; no, not man—man is too strong a term: he was an invertebrate without a country. He hadn't any more passion for his country than an oyster has for its bed; in fact not so much, and I apologize to the oyster."[39]

Distressed by his squabble with Harte, Twain fled to Bermuda, telling Sue Crane, "I am going off on a sea voyage . . . It is to get the world & the devil out of my head so that I can start fresh at the farm early in June."[40] When he set sail with Twichell in May 1877, he claimed it was his first trip ever undertaken "for pure recreation," but copious observations made in his notebook foreshadowed that it would soon result in an *Atlantic Monthly* series, "Some Rambling Notes of an Idle Excursion."[41] Twain was enchanted by this island realm, frozen in time, spared "the triple curse of railways, telegraphs & newspapers."[42] He was pleased by the spotless white houses, carved from coral blocks and whitewashed, and the sea gleaming with blue and green shades. Most of all, he mar-

"INVERTEBRATE WITHOUT A COUNTRY"

veled at the harmonious interracial society. "Mighty well dressed people of both sexes & colors & all ages . . . Fine colored complexions & handsome faces & easy carriage."[43] When he attended church, he was startled to find a congregation evenly split between Blacks and whites—a racial mixture startling to American eyes. It was exactly the restorative trip he needed after the Bret Harte debacle—"not a heartache in it," he told Twichell, "not a twinge of conscience."[44]

In truth, with the lackluster sales of *Tom Sawyer* and the blowup over *Ah Sin,* it was a troubled time for Mark Twain, and in his dejected state, he would publish only one book between September 1877 and March 1880. He and Livy relied heavily on Langdon coal income that was hurt by the economic slump that started in 1873. For years coal barons had conspired to keep prices high—an arrangement Twain had condoned in the *Buffalo Express*—and this collusion ended in the summer of 1876. "This recent bust-up in the coal trade hits *us* pretty hard," Twain told a friend that September. "My wife's whole fortune is in coal, & so her income utterly ceases for the next five or six months to come."[45] With the profligate spending on their house and a relentless social calendar, Twain felt monetary stress, which proved a constant distraction from his writing.

In March 1878, he wrote to his mother that his current mode of life seemed simply unsustainable. "Life has come to be a very serious matter with me. I have a badgered, harassed feeling, a good part of my time. It comes mainly of business responsibilities & annoyances, & the persecution of kindly letters from well-meaning strangers . . . There are other things, also, that help to consume my time & defeat my projects. Well, the consequence is, I cannot write a book at home. This cuts my income down. Therefore, I have about made up my mind to take my tribe & fly to some little corner of Europe & budge no more until I shall have completed one of the half dozen books that lie begun, up stairs."[46] He fantasized about tracking down a German village where nobody knew his name and he could work daily incognito without interruption. He planned to shut down the Hartford house for two or three years—it turned out to be sixteen months—and furlough the staff, except for the coachman, Patrick McAleer, and his family. It was a momentous change just a few years after he and Livy had completed their dream home.

Also contributing to Twain's desire for escape was a traumatic episode in a Boston hotel on the evening of December 17, 1877, when Twain had the signal honor of addressing sixty distinguished figures at the seventieth-birthday dinner for John Greenleaf Whittier, the Quaker poet and abolitionist. Here were assembled the eastern mandarins who had lorded it over American letters. Howells introduced Twain in superlative terms as a "humorist who never makes you blush to have enjoyed his joke, whose fun is never at the cost of anything honestly high or good."[47] Misreading his audience, Twain concocted a burlesque tale of visiting a solitary old miner who told of a visit the previous evening by three tramps named Henry Wadsworth Longfellow, Ralph Waldo Emerson, and Oliver Wendell Holmes—all gray eminences seated at the dinner. The miner described how these ruffians bombarded him with quotations from their writings before they stole his boots. Where Twain had expected laughter, a queasy silence gripped the room. From the outset, said Howells, "the amazing mistake, the bewildering blunder, the cruel catastrophe was upon us."[48] Nobody felt the grave misstep more than the speaker himself, who told Howells, "I must have been insane when I wrote that speech & saw . . . no disrespect toward those men whom I reverenced so much."[49]

Awash with guilt—Twain wanted to please these eastern worthies, even as his writing subverted their canons of literary propriety—he sent the three men identical letters of remorse, begging forgiveness. "I did it as innocently as I ever did anything . . . But when I perceived what it was that I had done, I felt as real a sorrow . . . as if I had done it with a guilty intent . . . As to my wife's distress, it is not to be measured; for she is of finer stuff than I; & yours were sacred names to her."[50] Since Emerson already suffered from dementia, his daughter replied that he had not heard the speech. The other two men graciously strove to set Twain's mind at rest. "I do not believe that anybody was much hurt," Longfellow assured him. "Certainly I was not, and Holmes tells me that he was not. So I think you may dismiss the matter from your mind, without further remorse." Holmes indeed proved equally forgiving. "It never occurred to me for a moment to take offense, or to feel wounded by your playful use of my name."[51] Twain soon came to revise his view of the speech, telling Mother Fairbanks that while the speech was in "ill taste," it was still a good one, "above my average, considerably."[52] Nevertheless, he was so mortified by the episode that he informed Howells, "I feel that my misfortune has injured me all over the country; therefore it will be best that I retire from before the public at present."[53] It was yet another factor contributing to his decision to close shop and flee to Europe.

By late March 1878, the pictures had come down at Farmington Avenue and the carpets rolled up and placed in storage, leaving the house "empty, desolate & filled with echoes," wrote Twain.[54] On April 11, the Clemens family sailed for Hamburg, Germany, aboard the SS *Holsatia*, and the harried author immediately felt freed from his many Hartford cares. Susy was now six and Clara almost four, and they traveled with their nursemaid, Rosina Hay. Rounding out the group was Livy's old friend Clara Spaulding, known to the children as "Aunt Clara." After a week in the "*very* beautiful city of Hamburg," Twain became a complete convert to German culture. "What a paradise this land is!" he wrote to Howells. "What clean clothes, what good faces, what tranquil contentment, what prosperity, what genuine freedom, what superb government!"[55]

From Hamburg the party proceeded to Heidelberg, in southwest Germany, where they stayed at the Schloss Hotel and delighted in their glass-enclosed balconies overlooking the Rhine plain. Twain found a suitable workspace right across the Neckar River. For the first time in months, he experienced a sensation of tranquility and repose and was able to resume writing on a regular schedule. Livy, too, felt peace descend, telling her sister, "Sue it is the most lovely place that any one ever saw."[56] Twain was eager for his daughters to be well versed in the excruciatingly difficult language. For three hours every morning, Rosina spoke German exclusively to Susy and Clara and made them answer in kind. In his notebook, Twain coined witticisms about his tooth-gnashing tussles with German, a tongue that drove him into mad ecstasies of comic fury.

He hated having to decline words and was aghast at the length of portmanteaus: "Some of the words are so long that they have a perspective."[57] All the adults in the household slaved over German and were being driven slowly insane. As Twain wrote, "Clara Spaulding is working herself to death with her German" and having "dreams of enormous serpents" who glare at her "with red-hot eyes & inquire about the Genitive Case & the declensions of the Definite Article."[58]

Beyond the impossible German language, Twain had other pet peeves in Germany, starting with the national passion for opera. He cynically believed that most Americans only pretended to like opera, whereas the German affection seemed genuine, if mystifying. When he attended a sold-out performance of *Lohengrin,* he allowed that he enjoyed the bridal song and some choruses, but that was as far as he would go. "The banging and slamming and booming and crashing were something beyond belief. The racking and pitiless pain of it remains stored up in my memory alongside the memory of the time that I had my teeth fixed."[59] He had gone to operas for fourteen years and enjoyed arias from *Il Trovatore* and other familiar works. By contrast, the "intense but incoherent noise" of *Lohengrin* reminded him "of the time the orphan asylum burned down."[60] Leaving the opera house with a headache, he had many future scores to settle with Richard Wagner.

Though the whole rationale of the European trip was to save money, there were immediate signs that the Clemenses, incurable spendthrifts, would slip back into their prodigal old ways. In June, Twain notified Howells of a startling change in mood: "*We've quit feeling poor!*" He and Livy had sat down and totaled up their income and decided they could afford "to live in Hartford on a generous scale," even though Twain fretted that "the communists & the asinine government" might take away their funds.[61] In the meantime, they had decided to stop worrying about money, a fateful attitude that left them captives of their huge, costly house.

On August 1, the Clemens party met up with Joseph Twichell in the Black Forest resort of Baden-Baden. Twain had conceived the idea that he and Twichell would spend five and a half weeks wandering through Germany and Switzerland, a ramble he would then write up in the vol-

"INVERTEBRATE WITHOUT A COUNTRY"

ume *A Tramp Abroad*. Much of the time they would hike, though they would employ other modes of conveyance, from donkey carts to trains. On the eve of their trip, Twain had been afflicted with rheumatism and imagined the Baden-Baden hot springs had cured it. "I left my rheumatism in Baden-Baden," he said. "Baden-Baden is welcome to it."[62] In fact, he would be hobbled intermittently as he and Twichell strode through the Black Forest and took a boat ride up the Neckar River to Heilbronn before forging ahead to Switzerland.

Hiking for seven hours in the Gemmi Pass, Twain enjoyed an idyllic day: he tied a paper bag to his lapel and collected wildflowers as they strolled. His dreamy state of mind was disrupted by two nights spent in Leukerbad, where his morning sleep was disturbed by crying babies and caged hotel birds, not to mention "stupid" yodeling.[63] In his notebook, he bade the town good riddance. "Avalanche destroyed the whole town 50 yrs [*sic*] ago & killed 120 people. A semi-centennial avalanche would clean the town & do good."[64] In the next town, St. Niklaus, Twain, always crazed by noise, was maddened by church bells clanging near his hotel. "I hope an earthquake will topple a mountain on it," he wrote.[65]

For all his gripes about the towns, nobody responded more powerfully to the majesty of the Swiss Alps than Mark Twain, and he wrote many lyrical descriptions of the mountains, which held him in a strange, mystical thrall. "Neither pictures, paintings nor the imagination can give one any idea of the glittering splendor of the snow with the sun on it— the dazzling, intense whiteness of it."[66] He stood mesmerized by the Matterhorn, noting that its "tall sharp peak very well represents a volcano, with his vast wreaths of white cloud circling about his summit & floating away from it in rolling & tumbling volumes."[67]

In *A Tramp Abroad*, Twichell would show up as "Harris," Twain's hapless sidekick and comic foil. The pastor rejoiced in Twain's company, was immensely proud of their friendship, and characterized their traipse together as "my Golden Vacation."[68] Twain gave him a chance to escape stuffy Hartford society and church orthodoxy, and enshrine himself in American letters. Nonetheless, the trip had its share of bumpy moments. Somewhat reluctantly, Twain prayed with Twichell in their room every night. He was reading *Romola* by George Eliot, a novel examining Christian faith in Renaissance Florence, which led to a religious discussion that forced Twain to come clean about his doubts. "Joe, I'm going to make a confession. I don't believe in your religion at all. I've been living a lie straight along whenever I pretended to. For a moment, sometimes, I have been almost a believer, but it immediately drifts away from me again. I don't believe one word of your Bible was inspired by God any more than any other book." It wasn't that Twain lacked all spiritual feeling, but he found no expression for it in currently organized religions. "The problem of life and death and eternity and the true conception of God is a bigger thing than is contained in that book."[69]

After they parted in Geneva, Twain brooded that he had been unfair to Twichell and sent him an apology for "the times when I misbehaved toward you & hurt you"—perhaps an allusion to the religious talk. He paid tribute to the "charming hours of the journeys" and said Twichell's companionship ranked second only to Livy's in his heart. To retire any lingering hurt, Livy (who may well have encouraged the note) even appended a message that they both missed Twichell "*desperately*," telling him: you have left us with "a stronger affection for you than when you came to us."[70] Twichell, a magnanimous soul, reassured Twain that he had committed no offense. "There's nobody that I want to travel with henceforth but you."[71]

Twain had a perpetually impatient spirit, so it is not surprising that many of his works deal with travel and motion. Only to a limited degree could Livy share in the active, mountain life he enjoyed in the Alps. When they went to Chamonix, they traveled together in a two-horse carriage, and when they arrived, Livy "ascended part of a mountain in a chair borne by men, & then walked to an ice-cavern in the great glacier below the Grandes [sic] Mulets, & back again."[72] It was the last such outing for Livy, for the next stage of their European travels took them by rail from Geneva to Venice. As he contemplated their Italian stay, Twain was transported back to the flippant cynicism of *The Innocents Abroad*, recording in his notebook: "Italy the home of art & swindling; home of religion & moral rottenness."[73]

"INVERTEBRATE WITHOUT A COUNTRY"

Notwithstanding this sour note of anticipation, Twain pronounced Turin "the finest city I have ever seen."[74] In Milan, he toured the picture gallery, which allowed him to resume his tirades against the Old Masters. "There are artists in Arkansas today who would not have had to paint signs for a living if they had had the luck to live in the time of the old masters."[75] The Clemens family finally relaxed for several weeks in Venice, where Susy and Clara became fast friends with their gondolier. As Livy told her mother, "It is so fascinating, so thoroughly charming—I sit now before a window that opens on to a little piazza; where I can look right on to the Grand Canal . . . We have the morning sun in our rooms and the weather for three days has been perfect."[76]

With its maze of beautiful shops, Venice easily defeated the Clemenses' vow to economize. Loading up on expensive objects for the Hartford house, Twain listed in his notebook purchases for brass plates, mirrors, tapestry, oil paintings, Venetian glass, brass bowls, an incense burner, and a music box.[77] In a much-beloved purchase, he and Livy bought an old carved walnut bed with four removable cherubs atop the twisted corner columns, which would enable the Clemens girls to play with them. So enamored were Sam and Livy of this bedstead that they would sleep backward, facing the headboard. In the end, their shopping spree swelled to a colossal proportion: during sixteen months in Europe, Livy posted $5,000 in home furnishings in her ledger, or about $158,000 in contemporary currency. All this loot would require twelve trunks and twenty-two freight boxes for the homeward journey. It should be noted that Livy's mother subsidized many purchases, or the European vacation would scarcely have produced any economies at all.

When the Clemens party moved on to Rome, Twain carped at both the art and Roman Catholicism, deprecating the Eternal City as "a great fair of shams, humbugs, & frauds."[78] Despite his dogmatic reiteration of antireligious views and contempt for the Old Masters, Livy didn't buckle in the face of the onslaught. As Twain reported from Rome, "Livy & Clara [Spaulding] are having a royal time worshiping the old Masters, & I as good a time gritting my ineffectual teeth over them."[79] Livy would be no less independent in her literary opinions.

From mid-November to late February, the Clemens party settled into Munich, enabling Twain to commence a prolific period of work on his travelogue. At first, Munich came as something of a shock—"a damp, dark, muddy place"—after radiant Italian sunshine.[80] Before long, however, the family enjoyed their lodgings and the eternal German lessons. In fact, Twain found the place so satisfying that he didn't mind "even the dirt, now that we are used to it & don't mind seeing it caked around."[81] After squandering a fortune in Italy, Sam and Livy were horrified at how much they had spent. In a contrite letter, Livy wrote to her mother: "We are feeling very poverty stricken just now we have spent so much in Italy—I don't know as we have done right, but it is such a temptation when things seem so reasonable and you get such a good premium on your letter of credit. Venice was the place where we spent the most money on the furniture that I wrote you about—Charlie writes that the coal business is so bad—and it does cost so much to travel, but now we are living very economically much more so than we could do at home."[82]

By the time the family left for Paris in late February 1879, Susy and Clara could speak German "glibly and prettily," so all their suffering had paid off.[83] The Parisian stay was made miserable by cold, rainy weather. "Paris the cold, Paris the drizzly, Paris the rainy, Paris the Damnable," Twain later wrote.[84] He was plagued by rheumatism and Livy by neck and spinal pains, and their letters home abound with constant references to colds. "The children have French colds which can't be told from German ones by people ignorant of the language," Twain reported. "Rosa has a horrible cold. Clara Spaulding has the twin to it. She studies hard & has got into the new language so deeply now that the French can't understand her French & we can't understand her English."[85] A social highlight of the Parisian sojourn was that Twain got to know the Russian novelist Ivan Turgenev, whom he revered as "great in literature & equally great in brave & self-sacrificing patriotism."[86] Occasionally Twain went off to socialize with the Stomach Club at the studio of sculptor Augustus Saint-Gaudens. At one such dinner, Twain held forth in a speech memorably titled "Some Thoughts on the Science of Onanism."[87]

Despite his own ribaldry, Twain grew obsessed with French immorality and wrote acidly in his notebook that French literature was "confined to the two great branches ... of modern Fr[ench] thought—Science & adultery."[88] He piled up a heap of aphorisms on this theme. "French are the connecting link between man & the monkey." "A Frenchman's home is where another man's wife is."[89] This was harsh stuff, even by Twain's acerbic standards. Strangely enough, he found no beauty in the French language, sneering at it as "a mess of trivial sounds" and pitying Livy and Clara for studying it.[90] His derision of the French seems directly related to his prudery and undisguised fear of mature female sexuality. While in Paris, he jotted down an extended commentary on Titian's nude portrait of Venus, which shocked, horrified, and titillated him. He blasted it as "grossly obscene ... wholly sensual ... the Goddess of the Beastly ... She inflames & disgusts at the same moment ... Young girls can be defiled by looking at V ..."[91] On the trip, Twain had become worldly and well traveled but only sporadically cosmopolitan in spirit.

Before leaving Paris, Livy wrote regretfully to her mother about the stupendous lifestyle that she and her husband had enjoyed. She was always shopping for lace or silver spoons or glassware, and now promised to reform. "Of course we shall give up decorating the house, and shall only buy what we really need ... I wish that we were living less expensively at home as well as here—when times seem hard I always regret that we have such an expensive establishment." She admitted that she and Sam were far too attached to material things. "I wonder why we feel depressed at the prospect of not having money ... We dread changing our manner of life and how very foolish and weak minded that is in people as young as we are."[92] Of her patent love of beautiful objects, she said, "I often reproach myself for liking them so well."[93]

In July, the Clemens party raced through Brussels, Antwerp, Rotterdam, Amsterdam, and The Hague before winding up their trip with a monthlong stay in England, which would be marked by several notable meetings. Twain took a steamer up to Grasmere in the Lake District to spend time with Charles Darwin, who often kept Twain's books on his bedside table to help him sleep at night. "I am glad to have seen that mighty man," wrote Twain, who had read *The Descent of Man*.[94] His curmudgeonly views of painting erupted again when he encountered the large, vivid canvases of J. M. W. Turner. "Galleries of pictures where there is much splendid conflagrations of color have the effect of nauseating the spectator. Turner soon makes one sick at the stomach—it is partly intense admiration & partly the color."[95] It is remarkable that an author responsible for so many innovations in the literary field would be completely shut off to such experimentation in painting.

Whereas Twain had been deliriously happy in England when he first went there, criticism began creeping into his view of the place. He found the people "kind & likeable," but criticized their newspapers as "snobbish" and "pretentious."[96] He noticed that while Americans praised everything English, that warmth was not reciprocated. "English individuals like & respect American individuals; but the English nation despises America & the Americans."[97] In a competitive spirit, he listed in his notebook superior American inventions, from the sewing machine to the telephone, and insisted that nobody wrote a "finer & purer English" than William Dean Howells, Nathaniel Hawthorne, and Oliver Wendell Holmes.[98] Of course, Twain himself would personify the break away from British literature toward a purely homegrown variety.

By the time the Clemenses left Liverpool for New York aboard the SS *Gallia* on August 23, 1879, they were ravenous for everything American: hot biscuits, fried chicken, and cornbread, not to mention fast trains, well-heated homes, and good plumbing. It took a European stay to awaken this latent chauvinism. When the boat docked in New York on September 2, the Clemenses had to steer all their purchases through customs, and Twain took advantage of the delay to sit for an interview with the *Hartford Courant*. "He looks older than when he went to Germany," the reporter said of Twain, now forty-three, "and his hair has turned quite gray."[99] Twain said he was halfway through writing *A Tramp Abroad*, "but I've got to go through the last half and throw whole rafts of it away."[100] The Clemens family hastened to the spot where Twain was always most productive: Quarry Farm.

In his religious discussion with Twichell, the trip may have been pivotal for Twain, but perhaps no less so for Livy. In the early days of mar-

"INVERTEBRATE WITHOUT A COUNTRY"

riage, they had gone to church together—"Oh yes, I go. It 'most kills me, but I go," Twain told Howells—whereas, over time, it would just be Livy and her daughters.[101] While in Germany, Livy had chastised herself for not being more religious, confiding to her sister, "I am not striving these days . . . I want to be good but I don't try hard."[102] Then, during the fall of 1879 at Quarry Farm, while striding fields with Sue Crane, Livy unburdened herself still further, saying she no longer believed in the orthodox biblical God, who watched over every human soul. She had been influenced by her husband, to be sure, but also by the myriad cultures they had observed on their travels. As Twain's authorized biographer described her evolving view: "Her God had become a larger God: the greater mind which exerts its care of the individual through immutable laws of time and change and environment."[103] If Twain felt guilt-ridden about robbing Livy of religious consolation, he certainly compensated with the deep love he showed for her. When she turned thirty-four that November, he conceded that the pace of time seemed to quicken, a sure sign of growing old, yet, "what we lose of youth, we make up in love, so the account is squared, & to nobody's disadvantage."[104]

A Tramp Abroad was published by the American Publishing Company on March 13, 1880. It was a witty, if uneven, performance, padded with digressions and gossip and written, Twain asserted, "by one loafer for a brother loafer to read."[105] As usual, his mind proved inventive in creating characters and situations no less than in transcribing actual events. Still, the book sold sixty-two thousand copies during its first year, nearly equal to *The Innocents Abroad* and far eclipsing the weak sales of *Tom Sawyer*. As he was compiling the book, Twain harbored a poor opinion of it and, slightly embarrassed, sent review copies only to Howells and one other journalist. Now he expressed "stupefying surprise" at the sales figures and thought that maybe the reading public knew something he didn't.[106] If sales reached a hundred thousand copies, he declared in mild triumph, "I will throw prejudice aside & sit down & read it myself."[107]

CHAPTER SEVENTEEN

Toast to the Babies

When he was younger, Mark Twain had disclaimed any interest in politics, but with his rising fame as a writer, he engaged more and more with the wider society. "Upon most current events he had strong opinions," recalled Howells, "and he uttered them strongly."[1] Like most Nook Farm residents, he voted Republican but regarded the rampant corruption of the Gilded Age as a bipartisan affair that threatened to corrode American democracy. In October 1875, he published an unsigned article in the *Atlantic Monthly*, "The Curious Republic of Gondour," which supported widespread suffrage, women included, while advocating a system of weighted voting in which those with education and property would wield disproportionate power. Having supped with eastern financiers, he expressed an elitist fear that the "bottom layer of society"—the "ignorant and non-taxpaying classes"— would exercise undue influence.[2] He seemed blind to the abuses wealth could bring, or at least hoped the educated class would bring them under control. These were views that he would radically revise over the years.

In the 1876 presidential race, Twain, with some trepidation, endorsed the Republican Rutherford B. Hayes in his contest against the Democratic Samuel J. Tilden. Allied with the Hayes campaign, having written an official biography for him, Howells recruited Twain to join the cause. "There is not another man in this country," he told Twain, "who could help him as much as you."[3] Twain identified with the Liberal Republican wing of the party, which endorsed civil service reform, but had soured on Reconstruction. Hayes promised to withdraw federal troops from the South—troops that had protected persecuted Blacks against white supremacist violence—and Twain expressed no evident dismay about that position.

On October 1, after marching in a torchlight parade, Twain delivered his maiden political address at a Hayes rally in Hartford, where he applied his trademark humor to winning over the crowd. As a member of the "literary tribe," he admitted that he had not participated in an election before and inveighed against the spoils system, emphasizing his support for Hayes's embrace of civil service reform. "We even require a plumber to know something about his business," he told the laughing crowd, "so that he shall at least know which side of a pipe is the inside."[4] He favored distributing government jobs on the basis of "worth and capacity" rather than how much "party dirty work the candidate has done."[5] The next day, an approving *New York Times* publicized the speech with a banner headline, "MARK TWAIN IN POLITICS."[6] Twain held such a dim opinion of Tilden that he suggested the Hayes people issue a book with pages the size of a postage stamp titled "What Mr. Tilden Has Done for His Country."[7] At first, Twain was elated when Hayes won, but in the bitterly contested election, he later came to believe that Tilden lost only because of a "cold-blooded swindle."[8] Nevertheless, once Hayes was in office, Twain was happy to have him there and thought he achieved "real & substantial greatness."[9] The president, for his part, told a mutual friend that Twain's books were "one of his chief instruments of relaxation and refreshment."[10]

Despite his chronic fear that outspoken views might undermine his popularity, Twain could never muzzle his opinions. However conservative Hayes might be on Reconstruction, he was still a Republican, and the party remained anathema in the South. After the Hayes rally, Twain received a bitter letter from a distant relative, the former Virginia congressman Sherrard Clemens, who lectured him that "the Republicans of the North . . . had swept away the old aristocracy of the South with fire and sword," and that it ill behooved Twain, "an aristocrat by blood, to train with that kind of swine." He asked Twain if he had forgotten that he was a Lampton.[11] Just how firmly Twain had switched allegiance from South to North was revealed when a Tilden club in Jersey City approached him for advice about a flag-raising. "In view of Mr. Tilden's Civil War record," he replied, "my advice is not to raise the flag."[12] Tilden had voted against Lincoln, was slow to favor the application of force to stop secession, and in 1864 supported for president George B. McClellan, who wanted to sue for peace without ending slavery. It was quite telling that Twain, having served in a Confederate militia, now chastised northerners who had offered such lukewarm support for the war.

The figure whose friendship would exemplify Twain's status as an honorary northerner was the victorious general of the Union army: Ulysses S. Grant. The development of their relationship was an improbable one, for Twain had counted as a scathing critic of corruption inside the Grant administration. During the Hayes-Tilden contest, he gave a newspaper interview in which he scolded President Grant for being blind to the culprits around him and slow to punish them. "I want a man who isn't near sighted," he said. "I want a man who will not go on seeing angels from heaven in such buzzards . . . I want to see a man in the chief chair who can not only tell a buzzard when he sees it but will promptly wring its neck."[13]

Then Twain received an invitation to be a guest at a banquet honoring Grant at a Chicago reunion of the Army of the Tennessee. With Grant just back from a postpresidential around-the-world tour, many illustrious Union generals would flock to his side. "General Grant's progress across the continent," Twain observed, "is of the marvelous nature of the returning Napoleon's progress from Grenoble to Paris."[14] At first, Twain balked at the Chicago invitation before warming to the notion of being the sole Confederate soldier to participate. He had been asked to deliver a toast to Woman at the banquet and instead came up with an inspired substitute: the Babies. As he explained to the reunion organizer, "the Babies have never yet had the slightest mention at a banquet, since Adam invented them."[15]

When he arrived in Chicago in November 1879, the city was bedecked with bunting and placards for the Grant celebration. Staying at the Palmer

House, he was flabbergasted to discover his own central place in the festivities. A temporary structure, festooned with flags and covered with a canopy, had been erected before the hotel so that Grant could emerge from a second-story drawing room and survey streets packed with cheering throngs. To his amazement, Twain was one of seventeen people allowed to stand on the reviewing platform with Grant.

The Chicago mayor brought Grant over to meet Twain, and the ex-president, with his legendary memory, still remembered their awkward encounter at the executive mansion. Teasing Twain, he said, "I am not embarrassed—are you?"[16] Twain was stunned by his exact recall. "But I'll step back, General. I don't want to interrupt your speech." To which Grant facetiously replied, "But I'm not going to make any . . . I'll get you to make it for me."[17] It was a dreamlike moment: Mark Twain, reared in a slaveholding town, stood hobnobbing on the reviewing stand with Union generals such as William Tecumseh Sherman and John A. Logan. Meanwhile, down below, riding at the head of the procession, General Philip H. Sheridan passed by to delighted roars from the crowd "in his military cloak & his plumed chapeau, sitting as erect & rigid as a statue on his immense black horse—by far the most martial figure I ever saw," Twain reported excitedly to Livy.[18]

At Haverly's Theatre, Twain sat up on the stage with about thirty people as the hall resounded with blaring music and waves of applause from the assembled veterans. As he told Livy, "I think I never sat elbow-to-elbow with so many historic names before. Grant, Sherman, Sheridan, Schofield, Pope, Logan, Auger, & so on."[19] He was riveted by the oratory, but what most amazed him was the unflinching, immovable figure of Grant, who sat with legs crossed, listening to the crescendo of tributes. As Twain wrote, "Gen. Sherman stepped to him, laid his hand affectionately on his shoulder, bent respectfully down & whispered in his ear. Then Grant got up & bowed, & the storm of applause swelled into a hurricane. He sat down, took about the same position & froze to it till by & by there was another of those deafening & protracted roars, when Sherman made him get up & bow again."[20]

Twain now knew his mission for the Palmer House banquet the next

TOAST TO THE BABIES

evening: to use laughter to shake Grant from his statue-like immobility. Dinner organizers had saved Twain's toast to "The Babies" until the end, which meant his turn didn't come until two in the morning, when he climbed atop a dinner table as the fifteenth and final speaker. He contrasted the Grant who scored heroic victories at Fort Donelson and Vicksburg with Grant as a puling infant in the nursery and wondered how that cradled infant had found a way to stick his big toe in his mouth. Then Twain delivered his magnificent punch line: "And if the child is but a prophecy of the man, there are mighty few who will doubt that he *succeeded*."[21]

The line brought down the house in a pandemonium of laughter—including Grant's. "And do you know, Gen. Grant sat through fourteen speeches like a graven image, but I fetched him!," a delirious Twain told Livy in the early hours. "I broke him up, utterly! He told me he laughed till the tears came & every bone in his body ached."[22] For two and a half hours, Twain was mobbed by hundreds of well-wishers. The entire leadership of the Union army sought him out to pump his hand. "Lord bless you, my boy," General Sherman said, "I don't know how you do it—it's a secret that's beyond me—but it was great—give me your hand again."[23] Calling it "a grand night, a historical night," Twain dashed off impressions to Livy at dawn in maybe the most intoxicating letter he ever wrote. For Twain, the dinner must have ranked as some final defection from his southern heritage. To Howells, he described the Chicago scene when "a bullet-shredded old battle flag" was displayed to the veterans, who began belting out "Marching Through Georgia." "Well, you should have heard the thousand voices lift that chorus & seen the tears stream down. If I live a hundred years I shan't ever forget these things."[24] It was hard to believe that Twain had fought briefly for the other side and would become the speaker of choice for many Union army reunions.

In the 1880 presidential race, Twain favored the successful Republican candidate, James A. Garfield, a brigadier general in the war, who "suits me thoroughly & exactly," and he was actually glad that the party spurned Grant's bid to win a third term.[25] If Twain was lukewarm about Grant's political prospects, the general remained a towering presence to him for his wartime feats. When Grant visited Hartford that October to promote Garfield, Twain strung flags all around his home balcony. Designated as an official greeter, he celebrated Grant at a rally of five thousand people in Bushnell Park that included two thousand Union army veterans, and he celebrated Grant with gusto. "Your country *loves* you—your country's *proud* of you—your country is *grateful* to you . . . Your country stands ready from this day forth to testify her measureless love . . . in every conceivable—*inexpensive* way."[26] With Grant it had been a sore point that he had received no pecuniary reward for his wartime service and he "nearly laughed his entire head off" at Twain's pointed remark, according to eyewitnesses.[27] If the South had derided Grant as a brutal butcher, he now stood forth as a hero, pure and simple, for Mark Twain.

On November 2, after Garfield's victory, Twain addressed thousands of joyous supporters at the opera house and delivered an ironic speech titled the "Funeral Oration Over the Grave of the Democratic Party." In mock-sepulchral tones, he uttered, "The aged and stricken Democratic party is dying." Then he pictured the party as a dying actor. "In the South he played 'The Assassin of Freedom,' and mouthed the sacred shibboleths of liberty with cruel and bloody lips."[28] Now an accomplished political speaker, Twain enjoyed the zest of campaigning. "We had a gorgeous time of it here in the Opera House till midnight," he told a friend the next day. "This town is feeling pretty good to-day."[29]

Twain solicited only a single favor from president-elect Garfield: that he retain Frederick Douglass as U.S. Marshal for the District of Columbia. "I offer this petition with peculiar pleasure & strong desire," he wrote, "because I so honor this man's high blemishless character, & so admire his brave long crusade for the liberties & elevation of his race. He is a personal friend of mine, but that is nothing to the point—his history would move me to say these things, without that."[30] After Charles Langdon sent him a copy of this letter, Douglass thanked Twain for the "kind and characteristic note," which would "put the President elect in a good humour in any case, and that is very important."[31] Unfortunately, Garfield failed to heed Twain's advice and demoted Douglass to the position of Recorder of Deeds for Washington. Garfield's presidency was short-lived after he was shot by a deranged office-seeker, Charles J. Guiteau. The prolonged period when the president lay dying left Twain "apprehensive & gloomy-spirited," and he thought it inappropriate to publish any humorous articles.[32] "This house, like all others in the land," he wrote, "became a house of mourning."[33]

It is important to note that for all the progress Twain made in his racial awareness, he never achieved perfection and should not be regarded as a paragon. Racial epithets could still pop up in his letters with dismaying frequency. He, of all people, should have known better, but, despite his growth, he could never escape *all* the reflexes with which he had grown up. While in London in 1873, he was startled by the sight of an interracial couple and its casual acceptance. In his notebook he recorded his shock that "today in Regent's Park saw a pretty, modest looking English girl, hanging on the arm of a darkey, conversing. Both quiet, honest looking air. Never taking any notice. Never seeming to see anything improper or unusual about it."[34] So visionary in many other ways, Twain still found it hard to comprehend a future of interracial romance.

The return to Hartford had been exhausting for Livy since the pictures had to be restored to the walls and the carpets rolled back on the floor, and Twain had to whisk her off to Elmira to recuperate in January 1880. Livy was already pregnant with their third child. The daughter born that July was named Jane Lampton Clemens, to honor Twain's mother; she was always referred to as "Jean." The Clemenses, having returned to the United States full of noble vows about living within their means, could not mend their self-indulgent habits. Even in Paris, Livy had told her mother that "I do hate to settle our house without decorating it—the white walls are not pleasant and it seems as if now when it is all torn up was such a good time to finish the inside."[35]

FLOODTIDE

By March 1881, the Clemenses had embarked on another gargantuan spending binge, acquiring a greenhouse and one hundred more feet of adjoining land. They began to dismantle the kitchen to build a bigger one, and in June tore down the reception room to expand the front hall. Masons and bricklayers swarmed through the house as plumbers installed modern conveniences. "When I was done," Twain noted drolly, "I had three hundred dollars in the bank which the plumber didn't know anything about."[36] Sam and Livy were only warming up: designers would come in to decorate the walls and ceiling for the entire first floor. Once again they had to clear away the furnishings to make way for them—Twain described Livy as "head over heels in ... ordering & superintending the snaking-up of carpets, storing of pictures etc"—and then the Clemenses evacuated the house for the summer.[37] By that point they had spent, Twain estimated, "a generous pile of money."[38]

He and Livy had no intention of scrimping on the redesign of the house, and in October signed a contract with the prestigious new firm of Louis C. Tiffany, Associated Artists. Twain had admired their work for the Seventh Regiment Armory in Manhattan, soon followed by the refurbishing of the White House staterooms for President Chester Arthur. The firm was headed by Louis Comfort Tiffany, best known for his stained-glass windows and lamps, but no less important was Candace Thurber Wheeler, an expert in textile design. She would launch the first all-female interior design company and develop into a dear friend of the Clemenses. The interior work produced for the Farmington Avenue house proved stunning: gold and blue wall stenciling and ceilings decked in glittering patterns, conjuring up a fantasy world of Moorish opulence. The profusion of ornamental elements was never gaudy, but eye-catching and harmonious.

In October, when the Clemens family returned to the house, it was shrouded with scaffolding and colonized by mechanics and decorators, forcing the family to live "like a gang of tramps on the second floor," said Twain.[39] Though driven mad by hammering, he deemed the finished product a masterwork. "How ugly, tasteless, repulsive, are all the domestic interiors I have ever seen in Europe compared with the perfect taste of this ground floor, with its delicious dream of harmonious color, and its all-pervading spirit of peace and serenity and deep contentments."[40] In this sumptuous setting, Twain could feed hordes of guests at his table. The staff of six full-time servants, plus part-time maids and secretaries, and governesses and nurses for the children, meant a crushing overhead for any writer to carry. The economic pressure to maintain this luxurious existence would strengthen Twain's hankering after colossal wealth, spurring his speculative instincts. At odd moments he acknowledged the psychological toll of this domestic extravagance. "A life of don't-care-a-damn in a boarding house is what I have asked for in many a secret prayer."[41]

For all his adoration of Livy, Twain had preserved, sealed in some secret compartment of his mind, the memory of his early romance with Laura Wright. That relationship was unexpectedly rekindled in March 1880 when Twain received what seemed like a routine letter from a twelve-year-old Dallas schoolboy, David Watt Bowser, who signed his letter "Wattie." As a school exercise he had been assigned to select some great figure and pose a smart question to him, and he inquired whether Twain would like to live boyhood over under certain conditions. Then he said something that must have instantly seized Twain's attention: "O! I forgot to tell you that our principal used to know you when you were a little boy and she was a little girl, but expects you have forgotten her, it was so long ago."[42] Wattie was doubtless surprised when the famous author favored him with a long, charming response, saying he would want to be a pilot on a "big dignified freight boat" that was never in a hurry.[43] He gave a sentimental evocation of the Mississippi River on a summer twilight that was clearly meant for Laura's eyes alone. He also gave Wattie advice on writing, telling him not to "let fluff & flowers & verbosity creep in."[44] Then came more lines clearly directed at Laura: "No indeed, I have not forgotten your principal at all . . . Another flight backward like this, & I shall begin to realize that I am cheating the cemetery."[45]

Twain refused to let the correspondence with Wattie drop, exploiting him as his intermediary with Laura. When Wattie wrote later in the year that he had won a gold medal for his paper, Twain requested that the boy "remember me kindly to your teacher."[46] The following year, when Wattie sent Twain a photo, some pictures, and even a frog, it grew clear that Twain was desperately trying to string out their correspondence, even taking things a step further with an invitation to visit him. "When you come east I shall be very glad if you will come & see me, wherever I may be—Elmira, N.Y., most likely—we spend our summers on a farm near there."[47] The romance with Laura Wright (Dake) obviously still haunted Twain's imagination, a memory not effaced by his years of happy marriage to Livy. On May 26, 1885, he commemorated in his notebook the date he had parted from Laura. "This date, 1858, parted from L, who said, 'We shall meet again 30 years from now.'"[48] It is curious that, even in the privacy of his notebook, he felt compelled to camouflage her identity from prying eyes. They would not meet on that thirtieth anniversary or, for that matter, ever again.

Since at least 1876, Twain had tinkered with a novel about a prince and a pauper who accidentally swap identities in sixteenth-century England. At Quarry Farm, he had read a novel by Charlotte M. Yonge in which an aristocrat assumed the guise of a blind beggar. Twain took the concept and then doubled the fun by having a ragamuffin simultaneously take on princely trappings. His hero would be Tom Canty of Offal Court, who trades places with young Edward Tudor, the son of Henry VIII and later the boy king Edward VI. As he sketched out the story's kernel in his notebook: "Edward VI & a little pauper exchange places by accident a day or so before Henry VIII's death. The prince wanders in rags & hardships & the pauper suffers the (to him) horrible miseries of princedom, up to the moment of crowning, in Westminster Abbey, when the proof is brought & the mistake rectified."[49] Twain had long been struck by how nurture, not nature, governs human destinies and how many sceptered dolts sat on European thrones. As he browsed in Old English chronicles, he told Susy and Clara about the nobility and made them "shiver by his twilight tales of suffering under the cruelties of English law," as Twain later said.[50] He dashed off the story with such glee that in a matter of months he had completed a third of it before he broke away for his trip to Europe and *A Tramp Abroad.*

After several visits to England, Twain had an abiding affection for the place, albeit tempered by mounting ambivalence. In 1879 a reporter asked why he had not yet written a book about England. "I couldn't get any fun out of England," he explained. "It is too grave a country . . . When I was there I couldn't seem to think of anything but deep problems of government, taxes, free trade, finance . . . One is bound to respect England . . . but she is not a good text for hilarious literature."[51] *The Prince and the Pauper* proved his elegant solution to the problem. It was a critique of the severity of British law, set safely in a storybook past. By situating his action in a remote century, Twain could offer a radical portrait of a society riddled with corruption as the young prince witnesses firsthand the injustices that prevail in his land.

Where he had cursed his way through *A Tramp Abroad,* the new book charged him with a sense of rollicking delight. As he told Howells, "If I knew it would never sell a copy my jubilant delight in writing it would not suffer any diminution."[52] He scoured *The Diary of Samuel Pepys* and Shakespeare's history plays and Sir Walter Scott's novels to familiarize himself with archaic vocabulary. His pleasure was enhanced by unusual support from his wife and daughters, who believed the tale represented a finer style of literature than its coarse, humorous predecessors. Each night he would read the manuscript aloud and bask in their unaccustomed approval. "I have even fascinated Mrs. Clemens with this yarn for youth," he told Howells. "My stuff generally gets considerable damning with faint praise out of her, but this time it is all the other way."[53] Susy, whose opinion increasingly mattered to him, would call it "unquestionably the best book he had ever written . . . full of lovely charming ideas, and oh the language! It is *perfect.*"[54] It wasn't just that Twain was trying to please his family: he wanted to please himself. "I like this tale better than Tom Sawyer," he wrote, "because I haven't put any fun in it . . . You know a body always enjoys seeing himself attempting something out of his line."[55]

Twain craved the recognition accorded serious writers and jumped at this chance to expand his repertoire into historical fiction. After he finished a draft of the book in September 1880, he worried that his name on the cover would mislead readers into expecting a work rife with humor, and he considered publishing it anonymously. Howells, in dissent, sent Twain a canny letter that he shouldn't worry about "some marauding ass" who might misunderstand the book. He understood that Twain's work always had a serious agenda lurking beneath the wit. Of the new work, he insisted, "It is a book such as *I* would expect from you, knowing what a bottom of fury there is to your fun."[56] Twain responded with elation. "My Dear Howells—I was prodigiously delighted with what you said about the book—so, on the whole, I've concluded to publish intrepidly, instead of concealing the authorship."[57]

For devoted Twain readers, *The Prince and the Pauper* didn't sound like Twain. There wasn't the mischievous smirk on the author's face nor the sarcastic asides, and he didn't turn the novel into a comedy sprinkled with sly jokes. But unlike much of Twain's writing, the book is tightly constructed and devoid of the rambling, episodic feel that often mars his work. One senses the author's sheer joy as he projects himself into the past, luxuriating in its quaint language and gorgeous pageantry. Twain's reformist impulse is paramount in his portrait of a benighted age of superstition and injustice. A poor woman is hanged for stealing cloth from a weaver and another killed for poaching a deer in the king's park. The prince, confined to a prison, learns firsthand of his kingdom's draconian laws. After being treated gently by two Baptist women, he is aghast to discover they will be scourged for their religious beliefs and burned at the stake, and he pledges: "That which I have seen . . . will never go out from my memory, but will abide there."[58]

The book is veined with quiet humor in demonstrating that Tom Canty, by becoming a prince, is not transported to a kingdom of delights. Rather, he becomes a captive of the stale, tedious court ceremonies that make the simplest things—like rising in the morning—unimaginable chores. A dozen courtiers have to pass him each item of clothing until Tom wants to scream. The world of Offal Court shows Twain operating in a Dickensian mode. Tom has a cruel, brutish father and a predatory hag of a grandmother, but the women are otherwise pure and virginal. As in a Dickens novel, the story brims with both kindly and menacing figures, especially the Quixote-like Miles Hendon, who befriends and protects the little prince. In many ways, *The Prince and the Pauper* has a quietly subversive spirit similar to *Tom Sawyer*, because Tom Canty rebels against adult responsibilities, feels trapped by court formalities, and longs for the poor boy's freedom of the streets. Twain shows that ordinary people have a native vigor and intelligence often lacking in their supposed betters. The book ends with a celebration of life's simple pleasures as Tom, released from royal duties, beds down for the night with a calf in a barn as the narrator assures us that "he was warm, he was sheltered; in a word, he was happy."[59] He would have been right at home with Huck Finn.

Right around the time Twain finished a draft of the book, his longtime publisher, Elisha Bliss, Jr., died of heart disease. Convinced he had suffered "ten years of swindlings" at Bliss's hands, Twain did not mourn the loss and began secretly shifting his business to a new publisher.[60] He worked out a novel arrangement with his friend James R. Osgood of Boston under which they swapped the usual publisher and author roles— a swap worthy of *The Prince and the Pauper*. Twain would finance the new book's publication and pay Osgood a 7.5 percent royalty for selling it. Osgood was a cordial, conscientious publisher, and Twain spoke fondly of the "bald-headed but chaste & godly Osgood."[61] Unfortunately, he was a mediocre businessman and a novice in the subscription publishing Twain preferred. Twain bristled with nonstop instructions, warning Osgood of the laziness of the modern canvasser who "sublets to an idiot, on a percentage, & sits at home in aristocratic indolence."[62] Twain was shifting into a self-publishing mode and eventually became a publisher outright, a move driven by his need for money, but also by a certain hubris that he was smarter than any publisher—a belief that would cost him dearly one day.

Twain could be an insanely litigious man—dissatisfaction was perhaps the keynote of his nature—and decided to launch a lawsuit against the American Publishing Company, charging them with paying more for paper and bindings than needed. He hoped to use the lawsuit as a way to coerce them into handing over to him the copyrights for his books they had published. He directed his lawyer, Charles Perkins, to investigate the books of American Publishing and was astounded to discover that his paranoia had greatly exaggerated the amount of supposed cheating. "Look here," he told his new business manager, Charles L. Webster, "the Am Pub Co. swindled me out of only *$2,000?* I thought it was *five*. It can't be worth while to sue for $2,000, can it? If we gain it will it pay lawyer's fees?" Eventually Twain stopped paying fees to Perkins.

The sales history of *The Prince and the Pauper* wasn't auspicious for the Twain-Osgood partnership. Self-publishing meant a huge outlay of money for Twain, and despite his considerable anxiety about the venture, he was slow to perceive the hazards involved. "I find myself a fine success, as a publisher," he boasted, much too soon, right after the American publication.[63] Although he and Osgood started with a first printing of twenty-five thousand, nearly five thousand would still be unsold two years later—a sharp fall-off from his previous publication history.

Twain had long been harried by pirated Canadian editions of his books. To forestall this, he traveled to Canada for two weeks in late November 1881 and tried futilely to secure a Canadian copyright for *The Prince and the Pauper,* published on December 1 by Chatto & Windus in England. Though he hoped his presence in Canada at the time of British publication would give his book protection, two pirated editions later appeared. With time on his hands, Twain sauntered around Montreal and was appalled by the religiosity at every turn. "This is the first time I was ever in a city where you couldn't throw a brick without breaking a church window."[64] In Quebec City, he trudged around the snowy Plains of Abraham, a visit spoiled by his ancient shabby hotel. "The hotel is infernal," he told Livy. "You couldn't endure these beds. Everything in the hotel is of the date of Champlain, or even of Cartier, & thoroughly worn out."[65] On the warpath against cheats, Twain would lobby for changes in American copyright laws and favor imprisonment, not just fines, for offenders, arguing that "the crime is a peculiarly vile & dirty one & ought not to be raised to the dignity of a finable offense."[66] He insisted that literary property be regarded as "sacred as whisky."[67]

While reviews of *The Prince and the Pauper* were mostly friendly and Howells liked it "immensely," it caused some of the confusion Twain had anticipated.[68] When he got a batch of London reviews, to his surprise they were "profoundly complimentary; even the 'London Times' stoops to flatter."[69] Nonetheless, the *Pall Mall Gazette* pummeled him mercilessly. "The author, a noted representative of American humor, has essayed to achieve a serious book. The consequences are at once disastrous and amazing."[70] In addition to his adoring family, Twain's book had other passionate admirers at Nook Farm. Harriet Beecher Stowe, his next-door neighbor, was suffering from early dementia and often wandered around the property picking flowers. One day she ran into Twain, took his hands, and blurted out, "I am reading your Prince & Pauper for the *fourth* time, & I *know* it's the best book for young people ever written!"[71] Former president Rutherford B. Hayes reported to Twain that his entire household was taken with the work. "The child in his eighth year and the child in his sixtieth, and all between them in age and of both sexes were equally hearty in their applause and delight."[72]

Still, some voices that Twain respected claimed he had betrayed his talent and that the book lacked everything that had distinguished his earlier writing. For years he had twinges of regret that he had not published the book anonymously. His old editor from the *Territorial Enterprise*, Joseph T. Goodman, sent him a blunt appraisal. "'The Prince and the Pauper' is the first of your works in which I have ever been disappointed. Aside from the clear-cut English and an occasional bit of elegant description or quiet humor, there is no evidences [*sic*] of your handiwork in this volume. It might have been written by anybody else— by a far less masterly hand, in fact . . . I have such a high opinion of your abilities that I can't bear to see them misdirected or exerted at a disadvantage."[73] But Twain, a protean talent, had the courage to explore many sides of his nature, however mixed the results. Nothing would ever surpass his inspired writing about his Mississippi youth. Still, he spent more time reading history and biography than novels, and it would have been surprising had he not yearned periodically to follow his fancy into faraway places and long-forgotten times. He was, after all, the original version of that famous time traveler, Tom Sawyer.

CHAPTER EIGHTEEN

"Inspired Bugger of a Machine"

Even as Mark Twain's mind produced a torrent of fresh writing, darting off in multiple directions, his imagination poured forth a cornucopia of would-be inventions—what he termed "the invention of useful trifles."[1] Occasionally his fancies flourished in the marketplace, as with the Self-Pasting Scrap Book, but more often than not they languished. He dreamed up an idea for a bed clamp that would prevent children from kicking off their blankets; a vest that would require no suspenders; a shirt that would have collar and cuffs pre-attached (then a novelty); a memorandum book that opened to the last page written; and a "perpetual-calendar watch-charm which gives the day of the week & the day of the month."[2] He invested in two devices patented by H. C. Bowers—one to desalinate water, the other to improve steam generators for tugboats—but Bowers vanished before the devices were done. He latched on to an idea that anticipated microfilm when he sought to reduce large maps to "fly-specks" and have users view them through a microscope.[3] In a visionary flash, he conceived of something akin to modern television: "Portraits and pictures *transferred by light* accompany everything."[4] As a believer in extrasensory perception, he envisioned a day when "people *will* be able to call each other up from any part of the world and talk by mental telegraph—and not merely by impression, the impression will be articulated into *words*."[5]

As a businessman, Twain knew he operated beyond the bounds of his well-known talents. His problem was never one of an absence of long-range vision, in which he excelled, but one of short-term execution. His later financial angel on Wall Street, Henry H. Rogers, aptly summed up Twain's dilemma: "Clemens has a very remarkable business head for large things, but absolutely none for small. He has an eagle-vision for wide business horizons, but he can't take in the details that lie between and it frets him to try."[6] Twain's repeated failure to bridge that divide and the large sums his setbacks cost him never throttled his speculative urges. No less compulsive when gambling in the stock market, by spring 1882 he owned more than 150,000 shares in twenty-three companies, often buying in the riskiest manner: on margin. As with any gambler, missteps only led him to plunge back in again to redeem his losses.

Twain had assigned scrapbook sales to Dan Slote, his former *Quaker City* roommate, whom he had idealized as "the noblest man on earth."[7] Although Slote, Woodman & Co. drew robust profits from the scrapbook, Twain was always suspicious of his business partners and grew convinced that Slote had bilked him and that he should have made "3 times as much" in profits.[8] With hindsight, he claimed that Slote "took advantage of my utter confidence in his honesty to cheat me . . . and also knew I was ass enough to believe him."[9] One day in July 1878, Slote asked him for a $5,000 loan at 7 percent interest, and Twain agreed, unaware of problems with his partner's firm. Then Slote's establishment "failed inside of three days—and at the end of two or three years I got back two thousand dollars of the money."[10] What makes Twain's story puzzling is that he allowed Slote's bankrupt company to continue marketing his scrapbook, and even more remarkable, the two men soon embarked on a still more momentous business venture.

In early 1880, Slote sold to Twain a new patented process for engraving on a sheet of steel coated with clay. The user drew on the clay surface, creating a mold to make plates for printing. The clay mineral was called kaolin, and, hence, the trade name for the process was Kaolatype. Twain later said that Slote concealed the small fact that the process had not actually been invented, much less developed and perfected. Quick to blow up slender ideas to gigantic proportions, Twain thought the method

"INSPIRED BUGGER OF A MACHINE"

could be applied to molding brass dies for stamping book covers. In his best Colonel Sellers mode, he trumpeted exorbitant claims for Kaolatype, assuring Orion that it "will utterly annihilate & sweep out of existence one of the minor industries of civilization, & take its place—an industry which has existed for 300 years."[11] To develop the process, Twain formed the Kaolatype Engraving Company, with himself as president and Dan Slote as treasurer. With shares pegged at $25, Twain took four-fifths of the $25,000 in stock and agreed to subsidize the company with liberal loans. It was one thing for Twain, a book writer, to invest in established companies, run by professional businessmen, and quite another to act as financier of a start-up with a large, open-ended money commitment.

For the Kaolatype process to engrave book covers, certain technical milestones had to be achieved. Many in the industry derided the idea of molding brass stamps for bookbinders, and Slote suggested that they employ metallurgist Charles Sneider, a young German who had supposedly "invented" Kaolatype. Not only did Twain pay Sneider monthly, but he set him up with a headquarters and a workshop on Fulton Street in Manhattan. At one point, Sneider brought "six specimens of moulded brass stamps" so Twain would keep up his payments. As Sneider labored on Twain's payroll, the author daydreamed about new applications for this method, including wallpaper and calico printing and embossing leather. A sucker for grifters, he even wanted to ornament his Hartford home with Kaolatype and "sheathe our library walls & ceilings with elegant brass plates."[12]

Growing uneasy about the steady money drain, Twain made an appointment to visit Sneider's Fulton Street headquarters, which, inconveniently, burned down the night before. When he set up a second appointment at his workshop, that, too, went up in flames before he arrived. Losing faith in his partners, Twain recruited the twenty-nine-year-old Charles Webster, who lived in Fredonia, New York, and had married Pamela's daughter, Annie. With a background in real estate and insurance, Webster had enough business expertise to ferret out wrongdoing at

Kaolatype. In March 1881, Twain wrote forthrightly to Dan Slote, saying his business concerns were now interfering with his writing. At this point, he blamed Sneider, not Slote. "I feel pretty sore & humiliated when I think over the history of the past few months. The book I was at work on & intended to rush through in two months time is standing still. One can't write a book unless he can banish perplexities, & put his whole mind on it."[13] He had just bought the extra land for his Hartford house and had begun to renovate the interior, and now found himself in an agonizing financial bind.

Poring over Kaolatype's sloppy books, Charles Webster presented himself as Twain's white knight and personal auditor, promising him, "You are not being cheated & stolen from while I am here watching."[14] By late April, Twain instructed him to make a final payment to Sneider and gave Webster sweeping authority over the company. "No money . . . is to be paid out in any circumstances without your distinct authority."[15] He loaded Webster with titles—vice president, treasurer, and manager—as the young man began to evolve into Twain's general business manager, even selling the final remnants of the hated Tennessee land.

On May 6, a disillusioned Twain instructed Webster that he had decided "to arrest Sneider on a charge of obtaining money under false pretenses," with Dan Slote paying half the expenses of the lawsuit.[16] In his naivete, Twain still imagined that Slote was ignorant of Sneider's machinations instead of possibly being complicit in them in some way. On May 18, Webster dropped a bombshell on Twain: "The bubble has burst. Sneider has confessed to Slote . . . that the whole thing was a swindle from the beginning, and that he went into it for the purpose of getting your money . . . Now you see beyond a single doubt that that thing was a wicked fraud deliberately planned and as deliberately carried out to rob you."[17] That he was so brazenly duped must have been a blow to Twain's pride—and bank account. Only reluctantly did he conclude that Slote had stolen from him "during at least seven years . . . I came very near sending him to the penitentiary."[18] Webster found a backlog of unpaid Kaolatype bills, evidently withheld to conceal from Twain the burgeoning operating costs.

"INSPIRED BUGGER OF A MACHINE"

With his trust in Slote betrayed, Twain was out for blood. Once cheated, he flew into an uncontrollable rage and demanded that Slote give up all his stock and repay every dollar. Webster recommended that Twain close the Kaolatype business, but still afloat in a fantasy world, Twain couldn't cut loose from his error. He was like a losing gambler who could not walk away from the roulette wheel. "You wish to know when I shall 'close up?' When the business pays me $5,000 a year clear profit. Not before. The brass alone shall pay me more than that, before I am done with it."[19] Twain regarded his nephew-in-law, Charley, as a miracle worker who had flushed out Slote's villainy. From personal vanity as much as anything, Twain attempted to induce James Osgood and Chatto & Windus to use his brass stamps for the covers of *The Prince and the Pauper;* the innovative process was, in fact, employed on the binding of the novel's first American edition. Charles Webster moved Annie and their children from Fredonia to Manhattan and worked late into the night on Kaolatype. With Twain a hard-driving boss, the beleaguered Webster found it hard to keep up with his unremitting demands.

When Dan Slote died in February 1882, Twain told Mother Fairbanks that if he had "died thirteen months earlier, I should have been at the funeral, and squandered many tears; but as it is, I did not go and saved my tears." He no longer had any illusions about Slote's innocence. "We found he had swindled me freshly and recently, and in order to do it, had leagued himself with a common blackguard and loafer."[20] Fairbanks urged Twain, for his own good, to drop the posthumous legal vendetta against Slote, pointing out that "the hundreds of friends who buried Dan Slote with honor . . . will all espouse his cause now, and resent his defamation—and thus become your enemies."[21] Like Livy, Fairbanks knew Twain could be damaged by his temper when he submitted to vindictive rage. He didn't respond to the letter, although he did refrain from further public assaults on Slote. Charles Webster continued to stir up Twain's animosity and found evidence of wrongdoing dating back to Slote's early handling of the scrapbook. Twain did not sell his Kaolatype interests until 1886 and by then he had poured $50,000 ($1.7 million in present-day money) down the drain of this luckless venture. A superior photographic engraving process would supersede Kaolatype, consigning it to the rubbish bin of printing history.

Unfortunately, the Kaolatype debacle wasn't an isolated event in Mark Twain's life. Like many in the Gilded Age, he had a weakness for newfangled contraptions and believed devoutly in the American cult of mechanical progress. Easily inflamed by the lure of riches and never content with small, incremental gains, he could not shelve his dream of becoming a tycoon and landing a whopping return. Now accustomed to ample living, he constantly searched for a windfall that would spring him from the demands of writing and lecturing, and offer him a leisurely, well-upholstered life. He had the worst possible temperament for business. He was a chronic worrier but didn't worry enough about the things that mattered. With his extraordinary imagination, he readily magnified the commercial potential of any invention, losing any realistic sense of its true worth. Twain's life, like his art, would be thickly peopled with con artists and swindlers who sized up his weakness for a clever sales pitch.

One day in 1880, Dwight Buell, a Hartford jeweler, called at the Farmington Avenue house and was ushered into Twain's billiard room. He came with a business proposition: he wanted Twain to buy stock in a new typesetting machine being developed at the Colt Patent Fire-Arms Manufacturing Company. Twain, having set type by hand himself, was dubious that any machine could duplicate that time-honored, labor-intensive process. When he visited the factory, he was startled to see a machine doing the work of four manual compositors and was dazzled by its speed and productivity. The wizard behind this contraption was an inventor from Rochester, New York, James W. Paige, who had received his first patent on the machine six years earlier.

Wedged into the compact form of this small man was every trait Twain admired and loathed. As he recalled, Paige was a "little bright-eyed, alert, smartly dressed inventor" and "a most extraordinary com-

"INSPIRED BUGGER OF A MACHINE"

pound of business thrift and commercial insanity." He was Colonel Sellers sprung to life, a man whose "imagination runs utterly away with him. He is a poet; a most great and genuine poet, whose sublime creations are written in steel."[22] Twain said Paige could persuade a fish to leave the water and take a stroll with him.[23] With his gifted tongue, he knew just how to sneak past Twain's rational defenses.

The machine, with its thousands of moving parts, was fiendishly complex. Paige could not construct such a machine himself and supervised draftsmen and workmen at the factory. He structured his deals so as to load all financial risks onto investors while keeping much of the financial rewards for himself, and his deal with Twain gave him every incentive to fritter away money without penalties. He also kept patents in his own name and refused to invest in the machine. A decade later, Twain was clear-sighted about the folly of this setup. "I quite understand that I am confessing myself a fool; but that is no matter, the reader would find it out anyway, as I go along."[24]

Undeterred by his experience with Kaolatype, Twain joined Hartford City attorney William Hamersley as an early stockholder in the Paige Compositor. He leaped into the project with abandon, investing an initial $5,000. In briefing Charles Webster, Twain disclosed that they would need $300,000 to develop the typesetter, saying breezily that "it seems to me that it is a thing which might be arranged in New York without much difficulty." He added the astounding statement that such a would-be investor could clear $2 million on the contract in just four or five years—a profit of almost 700 percent.[25]

For Twain, the machine had already attained the summit of perfection, and writing to newsman John Russell Young, he wallowed in hyperbole. "I never saw such an inspired bugger of a machine. Anybody can set type with it; nobody can get it out of order . . . A man who owns a newspaper can't look at this creature unmoved."[26] Twain hatched extravagant assumptions that it would sell in countless numbers and swallow up the newspaper world. As he assured Webster, "I reckon it will take about a hundred thousand machines to supply the world, & I judge the world has got to buy them—it can't well be helped."[27] In his notebook, he listed other indisputable advantages: "The typesetter does not get drunk. He does not join the printer's union."[28] Twain was now off and running with a full-blown monomania, and his initial $5,000 investment would slowly grow to a stupendous $300,000 (about $10 million in today's money).

There were legitimate reasons for excitement. The foreman of the *New York Herald* composing room, after inspecting the Paige typesetter, stated that he would recommend its purchase by the paper. Experts who went over it pronounced it a marvel. But Charles Webster, despite his youth, injected a cautionary note and reminded Twain that "you know how difficult it is to start a new thing, so it would not do for us to be too sanguine as a thousand things might yet happen."[29] Webster zeroed in on one simple, practical factor that would decide the machine's fate: its reliability. He had shown it to one publisher, who said "he should like to see it work a week," a concern echoed by other publishers who "all say so and of course it would be for our interest to have it too."[30] To his credit, Webster preferred to walk away from the *development* of an unfinished machine, with its attendant uncertainty, and wait to invest in a *perfected* machine that they could bring to market.

Twain ignored plenty of additional warning signals. On December 24, 1881, the law firm of Alexander & Green submitted a report on the typesetter after having it examined by experts. "The result of the examination is that we discovered the Machine as now exhibited is not what it was represented to you to be namely a Machine complete in all its details and parts and prepared to stand any reasonable test to be applied to it by experts or practical Printers."[31] Paige refused to subject the machine to durability tests, such as thirty straight days of work on a daily newspaper. No less unsettling was a report relayed by Webster that a publisher told him that typesetting machines "were spattered all over the country thick as weeds."[32] Webster thought they should investigate competing patents before spending more money on Paige's machine. But Paige, a fast talker, swore at one 1883 meeting that "he knew the machine to be now flawless."[33]

"INSPIRED BUGGER OF A MACHINE"

The typesetter would dominate the minds of the entire Clemens family, and even the housekeeper and maid Katy Leary grew amazed at the castles in the air created by her boss. "He was expecting such wonderful things from it. Why, he thought he could buy all New York. He was asking how much it would take to buy all the railroads in New York, and all the newspapers, too—buy everything in New York on account of that typesetting machine. He thought he'd make millions and own the world, because he had such faith in it. That was Mr. Clemens' way."[34]

With a mind always humming with ideas, Twain figured out ways to make education more appealing for his three daughters. During the summer of 1883 at Quarry Farm, their governess was trying, without success, to drum into their heads the names and dates of the thirty-seven English kings, from William the Conqueror in 1066 to the present. Twain came up with an ingenious alternative to brute memorization: he would "make them SEE the reigns with their eyes."[35] A long carriage road wound up the hill to the farm. One day, Twain knocked off work early and went forth armed with a basket of little pegs. Using the rule of one foot per historical year, he drove in at the start and end of each reign a three-foot-high white pine stake with the name and date of the king crowned that year. At a glance, the children could survey the entire sweep of British history, an interest aroused of late by Queen Victoria's reign having surpassed those of Henry VIII and Elizabeth I. As Twain explained to Orion and the family, "You can look out over the grounds and see the little pegs from the front door . . . It gives the children a realizing sense of the length or brevity of a reign."[36]

No sooner had Twain come up with this educational concept than it got mixed up with his money madness. Lying in bed one night, he realized that his concept could be translated into an indoor game played on a cribbage board. Within days he had instructed Charles Webster to go ahead and take out patents on the idea. Such commercial fantasies seemed to germinate like fiction plots in Twain's imagination. At first his board game would have English kings, then he expanded the concept to include kings of other nations and leading statesmen and famous battles. Twain "sweated blood" as he extracted dates and facts from encyclopedias and enlisted Orion and his nephew Samuel Moffett to assist with research.[37] Even as he labored over *Huckleberry Finn,* Twain worked out the board game in minute detail, including the size of pinholes representing various dates. "The board should be so thick that the pin will go down about a quarter of an inch—as we decided last night," he advised Webster. "However, we better have experiment-boards of various thickness made, so that we can determine the matter with exactness."[38] The forbidding-looking board, unfortunately, had all the allure of a railway schedule, even as Twain remained sure "There's bushels of dividends in those games."[39]

The history game occasioned a serious, unexpected breach in the friendship between Twain and Twichell. On July 20, 1883, Twain sent a full description of his board game to Twichell, who forwarded it, without permission, to Charles Clark of the *Hartford Courant,* who published it on July 24. Other newspapers ran the story as well, and Twain was scandalized by the exposure of his top-secret invention, grumbling to Howells: Twichell "not only made me feel ridiculous but he broke up & ruined a fine large plan of mine."[40]

Twain rushed off an "immeasurably bitter" letter to Twichell, who took a full month to reply.[41] And when he did reply, he didn't offer an apology so much as a defiant defense of what he had done. "You have made a great fuss about my letting Charley print that little extract from your letter; and abused me brutally for it . . . But since the deed was done I'm entirely impenitent on the subject. It was a good sin that I committed. The extract has gone and is going the rounds, as I wanted it to, and knew it would." In sending Twain the published article, he commented, "Just run your eye over it and see how nicely it reads, and what a creditable and amiable M.T. it is, who shines forth in it."[42] Twichell didn't understand that Twain considered the history game a lucrative idea and intended to make a small fortune from it. Twain sent Twichell's misguided reply to his family in Missouri along with a blunt warning: "I send this to beg that at least *you* folks will avoid this damned fool's example."⁴³ It is mystifying why Twichell violated Twain's confidence in such a blatant manner, and not surprising that Twain never answered his letter. The incident didn't destroy their friendship, though it dented the trust Twain reposed in his friend. The history game was patented in 1885 and marketed by Twain in 1891 as "Mark Twain's Memory-Builder: A Game for Acquiring and Retaining All Sorts of Facts and Dates."⁴⁴ The public found it too dull and complex to kindle any interest. In hindsight, Twain said ruefully of his most recent disappointment, "I am sorry I put my *name* to the Game. I wish I hadn't."⁴⁵

As part of their affluent Hartford existence, Sam and Livy emerged as cultural benefactors, a move grounded in good impulses, though further proof of their free-spending ways. In a giddy leap, Sam went from artist to a patron of artists. The transformation started in fairy-tale fashion one day when a pretty young blonde woman—"she seemed scarcely more than a child," said Twain's authorized biographer—showed up at Farmington Avenue and asked for Twain.⁴⁶ She spun a bewitching tale of how her husband, Karl Gerhardt, worked as a machinist at Pratt & Whitney, but his true vocation was as a sculptor, and she dearly wished Twain to see one of his clay statues. Hattie Gerhardt was eighteen, and she unfolded her tale so "bravely, & most winningly simply," Twain said, that he consented.⁴⁷ The Gerhardt home proved a humble affair, a second-story apartment in a small wooden house. Hattie showed Twain a nude Karl had sculpted of her—"a graceful girlish creature . . . nude to the waist, & holding up a single garment with one hand"—and Twain savored the craftsmanship and model alike. He was clearly thrilled by the sweet aplomb with which Hattie introduced her sculpted naked body. "Well, sir, it was perfectly charming," Twain told Howells, "this girl's innocence & purity."⁴⁸ When Karl arrived for dinner, Twain was no less taken with him—"a slender young fellow with a marvelous head & a noble eye."[49] The next day, when Livy and Clara viewed the statue, they came away similarly impressed by the Gerhardts.

Twain and Charles Dudley Warner sent an illustrious sculptor, John Quincy Adams Ward, to appraise Gerhardt's work, and he was bowled over by pieces "full of crudities," but "full of genius, too."[50] It was a dramatic endorsement for a twenty-eight-year-old sculptor who had thus far avoided lessons. "Hartford must send him to Paris for two years"; Ward declared, "then, if the promise holds good, keep him there three more."[51] When Livy heard this, she was stirred to a statement of aristocratic munificence. "Youth," she told her husband, "we won't wait for Hartford to do it. It would take too long. Let us send the Gerhardts to Paris ourselves, and say nothing about it to any one else."[52]

The Clemenses tendered a breathtaking offer: they would pay for the Gerhardts to spend five years in Paris, while Karl studied at the École des Beaux-Arts, fortified by recommendations from Ward and Augustus Saint-Gaudens, and with an introductory letter from Twain. Saint-Gaudens met with Gerhardt and "posted him thoroughly in regard to the studios and how to go about doing things generally for his studies in Paris."[53] Twain sent the couple off in style, with all financial arrangements made in advance. Treating them royally, he urged them to travel to Paris by first-class rail after they arrived in Le Havre. The Clemenses had developed a sentimental attachment to the young couple, perceiving no flaws in them. As Livy wrote, "Every time we see them we are more in love with them, they seem like story book people."[54] The affection was reciprocated. The day they sailed from New York, Hattie wrote to the Clemenses: "I love you—I love you—I love you, I love you. And, well all I can say is we will make you very, very proud of us."[55] In a fatherly mode, Twain entreated them to write often "& thus keep the bridge strong & firm between your hearts and ours."[56]

In a burst of energy, Karl started laboring ten hours a day in Paris, and Twain had to caution him not to overexert himself. The teenage Hattie was the more active correspondent, likely knowing that Twain was an easy touch for a pretty young face. She teased him with flirta-

"INSPIRED BUGGER OF A MACHINE"

tious missives, and it was impossible to tell whether she was being perfectly sincere or utterly manipulative. "I wonder & wish so very often if you do love us just a little bit—even aside from the talent and do you know I do not like to have you fond of anyone else but me and truly, I often get quite jealous thinking that perhaps you do a great deal."[57] As so often with teenage girls, Twain idealized Hattie as beautiful and pure, alluding to her as a "child." As he told Howells, "If I had that child's artless way of saying the moving thing, I would quit humor & write on the higher plane . . . She is always sure to get in a sentence or two that makes me think the Creator intended her for a writer."[58]

The Clemenses were ideal patrons, generous and undemanding, even as the Gerhardts stepped up their requests for money. Pretty soon, Sam and Livy were paying for private sculpture lessons for Karl and drawing lessons for Hattie, who also entertained artistic ambitions. The young couple must have seen the Clemenses as rich folks of unlimited means, while Twain indulged the fantasy that he was a grandee who could sponsor young struggling artists. At first, he praised the Gerhardts as smart and frugal, but then it seemed to him that they were overspending. By September 1882, Twain grew so uneasy about the rising costs that he informed them they were outpacing their five-year budget and would have to settle for three years instead. Around this time, the Clemenses learned that Hattie was pregnant; she gave birth in March to a girl named Olivia, after Livy. The idyllic relationship between the two couples had already begun to fade a bit.

Pretty soon, Twain was riding herd on the couple's spending, asking them to set down budgets with precise estimates for rent, washing, concierge, restaurants, coal, and lessons. He reminded the Gerhardts that they were assisting several people and "must go carefully, & know beforehand what the sum required for each is going to be for the year."[59] It was clear that Twain was starting to nurse a quiet resentment against Karl Gerhardt that would only fester in time. When he asked Howells to visit the young couple in Paris, Howells reported that he was touched by the "virtuous poverty" of the Gerhardt home with "a stove in the middle of the room . . . and a curtained corner where I suppose the Gerhardts slept . . . You are those poor little people's god—I don't know but they'd like me to write you with the large G."[60] Aware that the Clemens money would soon run out, Karl scouted public commissions in the United States and learned of a proposed equestrian statue for Paul Revere. If he entered a model, he asked Twain, "may I have the assurance that you will use your influence."[61]

Happily, Karl's sculpture was starting to attract attention in Paris, and his medallion portrait of Twain was accepted at the 1883 Paris Salon. A pleased Twain told the couple in August 1883 that they were "the only investment we have made in the three years that has really paid."[62] He urged them to spend another year in the "inspiring life-giving *art atmosphere*" of Paris. "I imagine that it must be as dreary for an artist to live in America as it would be for a humorist to live in England."[63] As with William Gillette, the Clemenses structured their support of the Gerhardts as a loan that could be repaid, if and when Karl was in a position to do so. Twain supplied him with good, practical suggestions, advising him to pursue commissions for soldier monuments and portrait busts, but the sculptor grew dismayed as his return to America approached in July 1884 and he was not hauling down commissions.

To an extent, the Gerhardts may have abused Twain's generosity, but the basic problem was that Twain wanted to act the magnanimous donor without being in a secure enough financial position to sustain it. In May 1884, he sat down and wrote the Gerhardts a letter that candidly expressed the parlous state of his finances and his incessant anxiety about money. This was a self-created problem from reckless investments and profligate spending. "I'm afraid we shan't see you in Europe; we've abandoned the idea of going over. We *want* to go, but we can't well afford it. We have made but few investments in the last few years which have not turned out badly. Our losses during the past three years have been prodigious. Three or four more of such years would make it necessary for us to move out of our house & hunt for cheaper quarters."[64] There was always a sense of Sam and Livy wavering on the edge of a financial cliff and foreseeing the day when they might fall over.

The Clemenses performed another meritorious service for a worthy artist in promoting the career of Charles Ethan Porter, a painter adept at landscape and still-life canvases. A Black artist born into a poor, working-class Hartford family, he was, unlike Karl Gerhardt, well trained and educated, having studied painting at the Wesleyan Academy in Wilbraham, Massachusetts—its chapel was a stop on the Underground Railroad—and the National Academy of Design in New York, where he may have been the first Black student. He perhaps came to Twain's attention when the *Hartford Daily Times* printed an article headlined "A New Painter A Colored Man."[65] Two years later, Porter received a major boost when Hudson River artist Frederic Edwin Church stopped by Porter's Hartford studio and declared that he had "no superior as a colorist, in the United States."[66] Yet Porter faced severe career handicaps, including the unfair stigma that still life was associated with female painters, and his skin color made his work a hard sell with critics and collectors.

The Clemenses first knew Porter when Livy sat on the board of the Hartford Society of Decorative Arts, and Porter exhibited in its inaugural show in April 1880. With American artists flocking to Europe, Porter decided to join the tide, auctioning off a hundred paintings in his studio in April 1881 to fund two years abroad. When he left for Paris, he bore a letter from Mark Twain to Karl Gerhardt, requesting that the sculptor share with Porter the list of people Twain had provided. The letter hinted at the high hurdles Porter had to scale. "Without money or moneyed friends he has fought his way steadily to a good & substantial place in the esteem of the people here, by sheer force of talent & patient diligence in the study & practice of his art."[67] Living near the Gerhardts on the Left Bank, Porter studied at a popular art school and repaired to the countryside south of Paris so he could paint *en plein air*. He wrote a humble, high-minded letter to Twain, thanking him for "the interest you have shown in my welfare" and expressing hope that Twain would watch him "rise from the now seeming beginning to a place among men."[68] Though he mentioned in April 1883 that his money was running out, he didn't solicit Twain for funds, nor could the author have afforded to bankroll another artist after the ballooning expenses with the Gerhardts.

Both Twain and Porter knew the artist's career had immense significance for other Black artists. Porter wrote to Twain of *"the colored people—my people*—as a race I am interested in, and my success will only add to others who have already shown wherein they are capable the same as other men."[69] With his money ebbing away, he asked Twain for help in lining up commissions. This placed Twain in what he termed "a bothersome position" because he had heard from a source that "Porter had gone to the dogs or was on his way there."[70]

Although there's no evidence that Twain assisted Porter with jobs, he made to the Gerhardts a remarkable statement on white guilt for Black shortcomings, stating "that on every sin which a colored man commits, the just white man must make a considerable discount, because of the colored man's antecedents. The heirs of slavery cannot with any sort of justice be required to be as clear and straight and upright as the heirs of ancient freedom. And besides, whenever a colored man commits an unright action, upon his head is the guilt of only about one tenth of it, and upon your heads and mine and the rest of the white race lie fairly and justly the other nine tenths of the guilt."[71] One can fault Twain for implying that Blacks can't be held to the same standard of moral conduct as whites, but his vision of white responsibility for slavery's crippling legacy is patent and quite unusual for the time. Charles Ethan Porter lived until 1923, producing a body of beautiful paintings and watercolors, and his works still frequently appear at auctions, fetching handsome prices. One of his peony paintings would grace the Clemens dining room in Hartford.

CHAPTER NINETEEN

"Hallelujah Jennings"

For Mark Twain, the halcyon days with his children came in the 1880s, when Susy and Clara were in their early teens and Jean was a small, adorable creature. It was then that the three daughters felt the full force of his charm, before the onset of adulthood when they grew more independent and not quite as entranced with their moody, strong-willed father. At this early time, he was a magical being with an antic disposition, who was tender and doting and could enter into their imaginative worlds. Whether sitting with his daughters on his lap or crawling on the floor, he was always ready to clown and amuse them, or sit down at the piano and belt out a tune. He skated and biked with them while Livy applauded from a window. When Susy and Clara were small, he would get down on all fours and play an elephant, the girls riding his back, toting guns and hunting game, with George Griffin often pretending to be a lion or a tiger. With an almost madcap glee in dramatizing clues, Twain joined in their games of charades. The airy household spirit was reflected in a story Susy recorded of her father sitting with them and blowing soap bubbles. Twain filled his bubbles with cigar smoke so that "as the light shone on them, they took very beautiful opaline colors. Papa would hold them and then let us catch them in our hand and they felt delightful to the touch, the mixture of the smoke and water had a singularly pleasant effect."[1] Although Twain didn't realize it, his happiness would prove as fleeting and insubstantial as those soap bubbles.

He added imaginative touches even to commonplace occurrences.

While in New York for the *Ah Sin* opening in 1877, he bought two dolls with two bathtubs for Susy and Clara, then invented droll stories of why the dolls required constant baths. "Susie dear, *Your* doll is named Hallelujah Jennings. She early suffered a stroke of some sort, & since that day all efforts of the best physicians have failed to take the stiffening out of her legs. They say incessant bathing is the only thing that can give her eventual relief."[2] As for Clara, her doll, Hosannah Maria, was "in quite delicate health . . . She was out driving & got rained on, & caught a very severe cold . . . They say constant & complicated bathing will fetch her."[3] These comments, however amusing and charming, were also full of black humor and disturbing content, perhaps unsuited for small children. One notes that the tale of Hosannah Maria seems to conjure up Langdon Clemens, who had been out driving unprotected in the cold before he took ill and died.

Attracting neighborhood children, the Clemens household was the scene of amateur plays that frequently revolved around British history, especially Queen Elizabeth and Mary, Queen of Scots. According to Twain, the diminutive Jean executed a single grim function. "She sat at a little table about a foot high and drafted death-warrants for these queens to sign."[4] Susy and Clara wrapped themselves in Livy's gowns, "for nothing charmed these monarchs like having four or five feet of gown dragging on the floor behind . . . It was grand to see the queens stride back and forth and reproach each other in three- or four-syllable words dripping with blood."[5] As the girls got older, these home theatricals became more elaborate and evolved into major social events for the Clemenses and their circle of intimates. It should be noted that Twain made a successful debut on the Hartford stage in 1876, playing a comically obtuse Dutch farmer named Peter Spyk in *The Loan of a Lover*. Echoing press notices, one theatergoer found it "amazing to see what a man of genius can do besides what is usually considered his legitimate sphere."[6] Twain improvised lines that had the audience convulsed with laughter—as always, he aimed to monopolize the limelight—while throwing his fellow actors off stride.

In bedtime stories for his daughters, Twain gave free rein to his imagination. He invited them to select a magazine picture, then wove a narrative around it. Once they handed him an illustration from *Scribner's Monthly* that simply outlined a human form, and for six straight nights he concocted far-fetched escapades for this ghostly figure. "I wore that poor outline devil's romantic-possibilities entirely out before I got done with him. I drowned him, I hanged him, I pitted him against giants and genii, I adventured him all through fairy-land, I made him the sport of fiery dragons of the air and the pitiless monsters of field and flood, I fed him to the cannibals."[7] His daughters never allowed him to repeat himself, demanding fresh renditions at each session. On the walls of the Hartford house hung pictures of a girl nicknamed "Emmeline" and another of a cat, and Twain, on demand, would furnish fresh plots for them. When he was on the road, he sent his daughters letters brimming with delightful nonsense. "I saw a cat yesterday, with 4 legs—& yet it was only a yellow cat, & rather small, too, for its size. They were not *all* fore legs—several of them were hind legs; indeed almost a majority of them were."[8]

With blazing intensity to his thoughts, Twain's energy could spray out unexpectedly in all directions. A mercurial man, he was subject to rapidly changing opinions. "My father could shift from one stand to its opposite with equal élan," recalled Clara. "Sometimes he poured out condemnation and praise on the same person in the same moment, which might confuse a listener."[9] He knew his feelings were mutable and he "sometimes cursed the flexibility of his moods which vaulted from extreme to extreme."[10] At times, his daughters found his temper amusing, even lovable, tagging him the "spitting gray kitten" because he kept a soft, fuzzy side even when his fur was ruffled. "My father's face used to snarl up like a tiger's when he found a button missing from his shirt," Clara said, "or that he had been making an appointment from a watch that had stopped."[11]

At other times, his behavior could be more hurtful. Later on, Jean would smart when her father, before strangers, reproached her for using slang or corrected her grammatical errors. She also faulted him for being headstrong in his views. "For, although he is very good and generous, when he has an idea in his head, it's like melting marble with a piece of ice to make him change his mind!!"[12] For all of Twain's magical properties, it could be trying for his daughters to reside with such an explosive genius. One day in December 1886, when Susy was fourteen, Clara twelve, and Jean six, Twain sent Howells a letter about a "thunder-stroke" that had befallen him, a "sudden & awful disaster: I found that all their lives my children have been afraid of me! have stood all their days in uneasy dread of my sharp tongue & uncertain temper. The accusing instances stretch back to their babyhood, & are burnt into their memories: & I never suspected, & the fact was never guessed by *anybody* until yesterday."[13] The revelation bespoke a strange poverty of self-awareness in Twain. Given his rough style and brusque opinions, it should have come as no shock that his daughters feared his moods. Often exasperated by his temperamental side, Livy and the girls labored to reform him, but he was a headstrong personality and not easily changed.

With her children, Livy radiated an unalloyed love that bound them tightly to her, a balm needed as an antidote to her husband's unpredictability. She was even in her temper and reliable in her promises, commanding instant obedience from her daughters. Her husband said she adhered to a simple formula: "'Do this'—and it had to be done. It was kindly and gently spoken, but it admitted of no deflection from the exact performance. She is a perfect mother, if ever there was one."[14] Livy was quick to commend the children but not to flatter them, lest they become vain about their beauty or intelligence. The girls confided in her and placed implicit trust in her goodness. They so gravitated to her warmth that they didn't mind getting sick so that they could cuddle up in bed with her.

The parents were determined to have well-educated daughters. Twain exposed them to poetry, drama, foreign languages, and singing, and left the bulk of the teaching to Livy, who, along with their governess Lilly Foote, homeschooled the children until they went to Hartford High School at fourteen or fifteen. Livy contrived ingenious ways to enrich learning. "Yesterday the children and I decorated the school room with wild flowers, grasses and ferns for today's examination," she wrote in her diary. "We made the room exceedingly pretty."[15] Livy and Lilly Foote instructed their young charges in American history, Latin, ancient history, English poetry, geography, and arithmetic. Special emphasis was placed on learning German, with Twain boasting to his mother that "the children speak German as well as they do English."[16]

Livy was capable of giving straightforward lessons in ethics, something that might have been difficult for her husband. In 1882 he gave a humorous speech titled "Advice to Youth," filled with suggestions that flew in the face of convention. "Always obey your parents, when they are present. This is the best policy in the long run, because if you don't, they will make you." "If a person offends you, and you are in doubt as to whether it was intentional or not, do not resort to extreme measures; simply watch your chance and hit him with a brick."[17] Of course, this could be chalked up as humor, but there was always subtle truth lurking inside Twain's witticisms. Livy provided her daughters with a clear moral compass, whereas Twain's views skewed toward the skeptical, if not the subversive.

Though the Clemenses believed in corporal punishment, it fell to Livy to administer it. Twain thought her exemplary in the fair-minded way she meted it out, saying the children "knew that she never punished in revenge, but in love, and that the infliction wrung her mother-heart, and was a sore task for her."[18] In July 1885, Twain was so infuriated by a *Christian Union* article about training children that he broke his rule of never mentioning Livy in print so that he could describe her method of punishing children. First, she led the misbehaving child to a private place and "reasoned with him and loved him out of his wrong mood." Only if the child resisted was a whipping delivered. "The child never goes from the scene of punishment until it has been loved back into happy-heartedness and a joyful spirit."[19] A private person averse to publicity, Livy was horrified to be drawn into the public controversy that her husband's letter provoked.

While Twain loved all three daughters, there was no doubting his special fondness for Susy, the eldest, whom he found full of gumption and poetry, fire and intelligence. Her letters ran "a good deal to italics & double adjectives," said Twain, an expression of her overflowing emotional nature.[20] The father-daughter adoration was mutual. They would stroll up and down the library at home, their arms around each other's waists, locked deep in conversation. When asked at age ten to list great figures in history, Susy included her father right alongside Columbus and Lord Tennyson. When she was thirteen, her father discovered that she was secretly compiling a biography of him, which he found "the dearest compliment I could imagine, and the most gratifying."[21] As she began recording his sayings, Twain remembers trying a little too hard to sound memorable at breakfast, and Susy "observed to her mother privately, a little later, that papa was doing that for the biography."[22] Susy always implored her father to be more than a mere humorist and show his philosophical side. However admiring, she was a clear-eyed observer of him. "When we are all alone at home, nine times out of ten," she wrote, "he talks about some very earnest subject . . . he seems to enjoy reasoning out things, no matter what; in a great many such directions, he has greater abillity [sic] than in the gifts which have made him famous."[23] Susy's biography would stand as a sacred text for Mark Twain, who had already initiated a counter project, "A Record of the Small Foolishnesses," in which he preserved precocious things said by Susy and Clara.

As with her father, people never knew what would pop from Susy's mouth, and she was almost as quotable as he was. "Papa," she asked, "how will brother Langdon know us, in heaven?—it is so long that he has been there; and he was such a little fellow."[24] She had her father's off-kilter way of viewing things and his originality of expression, and liked musing on abstruse theological matters. When not allowed one night to stay up late to see fireworks in Elmira, she sighed, "I wish I could sit up all night, as God does."[25] In a line that could have been composed by her father, she offered this prayer: "I pray that there may be a God & a Heaven—or something better."[26] When her parents noticed, at one point, that she had stopped praying, she explained matter-of-factly: "When I want anything, I just leave it to Him—He understands."[27] As Livy and Clara Spaulding commented on the queer ways of Europeans, Susy interjected, "Well, mamma, don't you reckon we seem queer to *them*?"[28]

She was a poet and a dreamer with a probing mind, and there was an

"HALLELUJAH JENNINGS"

intensity to her that portended future trouble. As Twain noted, when "her spirit was at rest," she "was reflective, dreamy, spiritual."[29] But she was highly emotional and prone to depression, and in sketching her, he often depicted himself. "Her approval was passionate, her disapproval the same, and both were prompt. Her affections were strong, and toward some her love was of the nature of worship"—a worship first directed at Livy.[30] Well into her teens she was bedeviled by bad dreams, especially a recurring nightmare of being devoured by a bear. The morning after such a dream, she protested, "But mamma, the trouble is, that I am never the *bear*, but always the PERSON." Twain keenly relished her offbeat perspective. "It would not have occurred to me that there might be an advantage, even in a dream, in occasionally being the eater, instead of the party eaten, but I easily perceived that her point was well taken."[31]

Both Susy and Clara were sensitive and high-strung, inheriting their father's quick wit and linguistic proficiency. If Susy was poetic, inhabiting a world of enchantment, Clara was efficient and alert—a "sturdy, independent, orderly, practical, persistent, plucky" child, said her father.[32] Or, as he wrote another time: Susy's thoughts ran to "the heavenly & the supernatural; but Bay's mind ['Bay' was one nickname for Clara] is essentially worldly."[33] A young daredevil with a tomboy streak, Clara injured herself in falls but was forever ready to brave the next physical challenge. "I could fall under horses, burning cribs, descending ceilings, and emerge with nothing worse than fresh injuries to my nervous system."[34] Her remarkable survival skills prompted Twain to remark, "I don't believe God cares much about meeting her."[35] Short and pretty, with a full head of black hair, she had such a sharp mind and clever tongue that her father nicknamed her "the sassmill," and the two liked exchanging banter.[36] (Clara's many nicknames also included "Ben" and "Black Spider.") Where Susy revered her father, Clara felt overshadowed and competitive with him, although that dynamic only surfaced clearly later on.

In general, Twain identified pluck and fortitude as Clara's salient traits. When traveling in Europe, where Susy shrank timidly from large crowds or new lodgings, "Bay always marched far in the lead and alone, and tramped up the steps and invaded those hotels with an air of a proprietor taking possession."[37] This unconquerable sense of military command could be misleading, as darker currents swirled beneath the surface. Like her father, Clara was prone to sleepwalking well into her teens. From age five to twelve, she was tormented by a repeated nightmare in which "an old woman in a hideous blue, green and red plaid dress" haunted her. At first the woman floated in a boat beneath a hotel ceiling, then recurred in various guises, sometimes spying on her through a window. For Clara, these appearances often coincided with premonitions of imminent deaths, and she could accurately pinpoint the victim. Even when the hideous lady vanished from her dreams, she remained subdued by lingering fits of depression, especially when her nurse would say good night and close the bedroom door behind her.

Clara displayed a hearty appetite for the arts, and there was scarcely one she didn't sample. An avid theatergoer—"there is nothing almost that I enjoy as much," she proclaimed—she regularly saw Shakespeare as an adolescent and was enthralled by performances of Ellen Terry and Henry Irving.[38] Her bedroom wall was plastered with photos of admired actresses, and she could mimic people with such deadly accuracy that Livy confided to her husband, "You should have been here today to see Clara imitate you telling them stories and eating at the same time. It was just as funny as it could be. She bit a piece of bread exactly as you bite it. She said: 'I don't know what it is but Papa always seem[s] to be having a quarrel with his piece of bread to make it let go.'"[39] Clara studied piano and violin, and exhibited an admiration for musical talent that approached idolatry. After hearing the young Polish Jewish concert pianist Moriz Rosenthal, she could not contain her enraptured response. "It was supernatural, superb, marvellous . . . If I had been a man, I should have risen & *shouted shrieked* Rosenthal! oh! Rosenthal!"[40]

Susy and Clara were born two years apart, then six years passed before Livy gave birth to Jean. Perhaps it was the novelty of another baby after the lapse of years that made Twain uproariously merry as he dandled her. "Jean is as fat as a watermelon," he informed his sister, "& just as sweet & good, & often just as wet."[41] On another occasion, he termed

"HALLELUJAH JENNINGS"

the baby "as fat & gross as a goose" being plumped for pâté de foie gras.[42] Mostly Twain beheld a resemblance between the happy, robust baby and her grandmother, although he admitted she was "like me when the devil is in her."[43] In a photo of Jean at age three, she has thick, dark hair parted in the middle, with a sweet round face and a snub nose, but the enormous eyes arrest the viewer's attention—so dark, sad, and mournful, as if prematurely intuiting a vision of her future life.

Jean was distinguished by her fondness for animals, and her doting father catered to this obsession. When he overheard her praying and upbraiding God for his failure to deliver a goat as requested, he vowed to remedy the omission. "Livy," he declared, "if there is a goat in Hartford that prayer is going to be answered"—and it materialized a day or two later.[44] He knew that Jean, distracted by animals, wasn't as attentive to her studies as her older sisters. "Jean thinks she is studying, too," he reported to his sister from Elmira, "but I don't know what it is unless it is the horses. She spends the day under their heels in the stalls."[45] Even when Jean was four, Twain recorded an affecting vignette of being with her in the Quarry Farm barn where the animals held her in a hypnotic trance. "She goes out to the barn with one of us every evening toward 6 o'clock, to look at the cows—which she adores—no weaker word can express her feeling for them. She sits rapt and contented while David milks the three, making a remark now and then—always about the cows. The time passes slow and drearily for her attendant, but not for her—she could stand a week of it . . . The other evening, after contemplating them a long time, as they stood in the muddy muck chewing the cud, she said with deep and reverent appreciation—'Ain't this a sweet little garden!'"[46] Twain whimsically predicted that she would end up "a horse jockey & live in the stable."[47] This adoration for animals adumbrated her later involvement with the Society for the Prevention of Cruelty to Animals and other humane groups. Her abhorrence of suffering also made her far more outraged than her father about the discriminatory treatment of Native Americans.

Mark Twain feared Jean wasn't quite as bright as the two older girls—"Jean has a good head, but she is as dull at learning as I was," he wrote when she was six—but this produced tenderness, not dismay.[48] Where Jean excelled unquestionably was in foreign languages, as she evinced the superb linguist's gift of projecting herself into the culture and character of a language. Even when Jean was four, her father marveled at how one "could hear the music of the German tongue as discoursed by Jean Clemens when she gets into an angelic fury & finds the English language inadequate."[49] Whenever he read to her in German, Jean would pounce on his slightest errors in pronunciation—she was fussy about how things were done—and she ended up fluent in German, French, and Italian. Starting in childhood, Jean possessed an exacting sense of right and wrong, a judgmental streak that persisted well into adulthood. Once when she was convalescing from an illness, Livy asked her husband to go into the nursery and read to Jean for a while. He picked up the first book that came to hand—*Huckleberry Finn*. Although Twain seldom laughed at his own writing, on this occasion he allowed himself to chuckle aloud, and Jean pointedly rebuked him. "Grenouille," she said—using the French word for "frog," the children's nickname for him—"you shouldn't laugh at what you write—it sounds too proud." "Oh Jean dear," Twain apologized, "I can't help it; it's so damn funny."[50] Not exactly indifferent to her father's writing, Jean was far less swayed by his status as a major writer than Susy and Clara were, perhaps because they were older and already more involved in reacting to his manuscripts.

Ever since Langdon's death, the Clemens household had been thrown into high alert by illness among the children, sickness being commonplace at Farmington Avenue. "The entire family is sick, without an exception," Twain told the Gerhardts in March 1882.[51] He himself struggled with rheumatism and lumbago, conditions that dogged him for years. Then, in June 1882, sixty-seven children packed the Clemens household to celebrate Clara's eighth birthday, and Jean, not yet two, contracted scarlet fever. A ghastly, sometimes fatal disease that afflicted children, it provoked special dread in families since it resulted from a streptococcal infection that resisted treatment. Though the Clemenses sequestered Susy and Clara from Jean, Susy came down with a fever so fierce that it

"HALLELUJAH JENNINGS"

made her delirious, even though it proved *not* to be scarlet fever. When Twain joined the fray with a slight fever, he injected a note of levity into a household that resembled a busy hospital wing: "I myself was stretched on the bed with three diseases at once, & all of them fatal. But I never did care for fatal diseases if I could only have privacy & room to express myself concerning them."[52] With Sam and Livy carefully nursing Jean, the house remained in strict quarantine, its front door barred to visitors. Finally, by mid-July, when Jean recovered, the Clemens family packed up their trunks and left by special railroad car for their annual summer retreat in Elmira. By fall, the rash of family illnesses had subsided. "Every body here is well but myself," Twain assured his mother, "and in my case some doctors think it is malaria, and some think it is laziness. I am taking medicine for both."[53]

This healthy interlude was brief, and by January the Hartford house was ravaged by another wave of virulent illness. Twain was leveled by "a rattling attack of rheumatism" that proved the least of his concerns, for Livy was seriously depleted by nursing and worry. "Mrs. C. is killed with unceasing headaches, a heavy cold in the head, & constant watching with the sick children."[54] Through winter and well into spring, she suffered a series of alarming ailments, including diphtheria and quinsy (throat inflammation), which rendered sleep and speech difficult. Fragile since adolescence, a semi-invalid, she now lost all appetite and seemed to wither away. "Mrs. Clemens is just about *without* strength—that is the amount of it; she will not be on her feet for goodness knows how long," Twain told his publisher; "she is fallen away to skin and bone."[55] He echoed his description of her condition to the Gerhardts: "She has wasted away to nothing; she has no more flesh on her than a basket; is all bones, and has no strength at all."[56] Livy could only rise up and walk with his assistance, and his descriptions of her haggard state make for heartrending reading. "I could shave with her shoulder blades"; he told Mother Fairbanks, "she has no more flesh than one of those old-fashioned hoop skirts. I am sure I never have seen so emaciated a person."[57] Livy may have suffered from atrial fibrillation—Twain mentioned that her pulse ran from 130 to 150 for two days—which perhaps portended more serious heart trouble later on.[58] Upset enough that he refrained from writing, Twain appointed himself chief nurse for his bedridden wife. By summer, Twain was able to transport her to Elmira, where she began to regain flesh and slowly rebuild her health, though she was tortured by severe back pain racing down her spine.

That autumn, as Livy gradually rebounded, Twain reflected on the massive domestic pressures that tended to overwhelm her. She supervised the girls in their home studies and managed the household through quiet diplomacy, attentive to the most trifling details. Meticulous in how she wanted things accomplished, she found it hard to delegate tasks to a housekeeper. The Hartford house was enormous, the social schedule grueling, and the demands of being the doyenne of this extravagant setting for Mark Twain's entertainments exceeded Livy's limited physical capacity. "House keeping is such an awful burden upon Mrs. Clemens, that I believe she will break down under it unless I can get her out of it for a year or two," he bemoaned to a friend. "If I could only get a thoroughly competent *housekeeper!*—one who would run this concern softly & smoothly . . . Mrs. Clemens won't listen a moment to the suggestion of a housekeeper, & yet she won't quit this treadmill & board. If some true friend only would set this house on fire!"[59]

CHAPTER TWENTY

Twins of Genius

In 1875 William Dean Howells had published in the *Atlantic Monthly* the series of articles "Old Times on the Mississippi," in which Mark Twain evoked the dreamy spell the Mississippi River had cast on him. For all his colorful exploits, nothing in Twain's life had ever quite matched the romance of his days as an apprentice pilot, which condensed all the freshness and vigor of his youth. Those bright days offered the promise of a happy life that would be difficult to fulfill, leaving him, ultimately, feeling bitter and cheated. In early 1882, as he contemplated a book that would expand upon the magazine series, he longed to resurrect those lost days. "The prospective pleasure of writing that book grows with the moments; & already I foresee that in the building of it I am going to find a delight comparable to going to heaven," he predicted to a friend.[1]

The first portion of *Life on the Mississippi* would present a lightly edited version of the *Atlantic* series, enriched with additional material on his days as a cub and licensed pilot. Twain consulted a batch of books that gave local histories of the river towns. The remainder would be based on his return trip to the river in April 1882, his first in twenty years, an event related at the opening of this narrative. For all his fond memories of his salad days, Twain couldn't mask the anti-southern, pro-northern tilt of his book. He faulted southern whites for being "as far from emancipation as ever" and for imposing a uniformly Democratic vote in the region.[2] Sounding a familiar refrain, he criticized the region for the "maudlin Middle-Age romanticism" foisted on it by Sir Walter

Scott novels.[3] Not all his observations were harsh criticisms: he also praised a Boston-based cotton-growing syndicate working to liberate southern Blacks from sharecropper bondage by paying them real wages and providing opportunities to purchase small farms. For the first time, Twain visited Civil War battlefields and was appalled at the butchery of Black Union soldiers perpetrated by Confederates at Fort Pillow, Tennessee, branding it the worst massacre in U.S. history.[4]

From the outset of the trip to New Orleans, Twain was mobbed as a celebrity. "Livy darling," he wrote home, "we are in the midst of a whirlpool of hospitality—breakfasts, dinners, lunches, cock-fights, Sunday schools, mule-races, lake-excursions, social gatherings, & all sorts of things."[5] When exhausted from the weeklong festivities, Twain boarded the *Baton Rouge,* a steamboat piloted by his former mentor, Horace Bixby, for the trip to St. Louis. He signed into the Southern Hotel in St. Louis under the name "John W. Fletcher," and the clerk immediately said, "Show Mr. Clemens to Number 165."[6] He managed to sneak in a Hannibal stay that was heavily freighted with melancholy. "That world which I knew in its blossomy youth is old & bowed . . . its soft cheeks are leathery & wrinkled, the fire is gone out in its eyes, & the spring from its step. It will be dust & ashes when I come again."[7]

As a pilot, Twain had plied the lower Mississippi between St. Louis and New Orleans. His 1882 trip gave him the chance to explore the river as far north as Minneapolis, and the South suffered decidedly in the comparison. "From St. Louis northward there are all the enlivening signs of the presence of active, energetic, intelligent, prosperous, practical nineteenth-century populations. The people don't dream; they work."[8] In 1886, when Twain visited his mother in Keokuk, he expanded this critique in a newspaper interview, saying the southern shoreline that preoccupied him as a young pilot now seemed boring. "Neither in this country nor in any other have I seen such interesting scenery as that along the Upper Mississippi . . . The river below St. Louis has been described time and again, and it is the least interesting part. One can sit on the pilothouse for a few hours and watch the low shores, the ungainly trees and the democratic buzzards, and then one might as well go to bed."[9] It was a startling volte-face for an author so associated with that stretch of river, which he had elevated to mythic proportions. Partly this was a matter of seeing the South through more adult, cosmopolitan eyes; partly it was the decline of steamboat culture, lost to train traffic; and partly it was the sad evaporation of boyhood magic. He concluded, "I had lost something which could never be restored to me while I lived. All the grace, the beauty, the poetry, had gone out of the majestic river!"[10]

During the trip, Twain contracted malaria and returned to a Hartford household still harried by illness. Usually Quarry Farm administered a summer fillip to his spirits, but as he wrestled with the new manuscript, Livy said she had never seen him labor with such difficulty. As he toiled in his octagonal study, she reported, he was drained of energy and "so often comes down at night, with his head so sore & tired that he cannot bear to have the simplest question asked him, or be compelled to talk at all so our evenings are mostly spent in playing Cribbage."[11] Twain confirmed the extreme effort expended in writing the book. "Never was a book written under such heavy circumstances," he told Twichell. "I am full of malaria, my brain is stuffy & cloudy nearly all the time. Some days I have been five hours writing two note-paper pages."[12] He toyed with several titles, mulling over "Abroad on the Great River" and "Abroad on the Mississippi" before settling on the classic, magisterial *Life on the Mississippi*.[13]

When he returned to Hartford in late October, the manuscript still fell thirty thousand words short of completion, and he put in marathon stints to finish it. For the first time, he employed help to type drafts of the copy, a man named H. M. Clarke. Livy worked hard on the book and wouldn't let any manuscript go to the publisher until she had "read it & possibly damned it," Twain said.[14] Aside from medical difficulties, one suspects Twain was disturbed by his river trip and struggled to reconcile his old-fashioned nostalgia with more jarring recent impressions that had intruded on sacred space. Winding up the book in January, he told Charles Webster flatly, "I will not interest myself in *anything* connected with this wretched God-damned book."[15]

By this point in his career, Twain had sold a half million volumes in the United States, a superb record for six books, but he remained on the warpath against publishers and was always ready to believe he was being fleeced. When it came to publishing, his natural suspicion of human nature only intensified. More than ever, he was convinced that the American Publishing Company of Hartford had been swindling him for a good ten years. "I have lost considerably by all this nonsense," he told Orion, "sixty thousand dollars I should say."[16]

When he traded the American Publishing Company for his genial Boston friend James R. Osgood, who accompanied him on the Mississippi trip, he was very pleased. Osgood had a stable of top-drawer authors, had published the first books of Henry James and Sarah Orne Jewett, and had just issued Walt Whitman's controversial *Leaves of Grass*. Twain recommended Osgood warmly to a fellow author. "He is a fine man every way; he knows his business; & it is less bother to publish a book with him than a pamphlet with another man."[17] He credited Osgood with selling his "occasional magazine rubbish at figures which make me blush."[18]

With the hypercritical Twain, such good humor was bound to vanish. As with *The Prince and the Pauper,* he experimented again with self-publishing, relegating Osgood to the role of manufacturer while he paid for the publication of *Life on the Mississippi.* Not having reckoned on large up-front costs, he grumbled, "It cost me fifty-six thousand dollars before the first copy issued from the press."[19] Disgruntled, he had Charley Webster take over dealing with Osgood.[20] As he steeped Charley in the mysteries of subscription publishing, he began to groom him as his personal publisher, shoving Osgood aside. "I am sending Webster to talk with you," Twain warned Osgood in October 1882. "I would like him to take pretty full charge of the matter of running the book, if this will disadvantage you in no way."[21] Webster became the New York agent for Osgood's subscription department, signaling his promotion as Twain's actual publisher. "Charley," Twain notified him, "if there are any instructions to be given" to the book's canvassers, "you may give them."[22] Soon the words "General Agent for Mark Twain's Books" popped up on Webster's letterhead.[23] Already plotting to start his own publishing house, Twain confidentially advised Webster to start assembling "a corp of canvassers to use on our own books, later."[24]

Though he proposed leaving publishing decisions to Webster and Osgood on the Mississippi book, Twain lacked the self-control to put this pledge into practice. He resembled the bullheaded coach who always wishes to rush onto the field and throw the ball himself. He foresaw stupendous sales for the new book—a hundred thousand copies in the first twelve months—as he schooled Osgood in the subscription business. "*The orders that come in after the ISSUE of a subscription book don't amount to a damn*—just write that up amongst your moral maxims; for it is truer than nearly anything in the Bible."[25] Pretty soon, Osgood had to endure a steady stream of exasperated suggestions and criticisms that came flying in from his star author.

When *Life on the Mississippi* appeared, it bore a handsome brown cover, brightly embellished in black and gilt, with a pilot steering a boat on its spine. Though some reviewers squawked that Twain had recycled his articles from the *Atlantic Monthly*, he also collected many fine notices. The *Hartford Courant* quickly anointed the book "one of his best and most entertaining works, and likely to be one of his most successful."[26] It expanded Twain's range to encompass works beyond the humorous, marking a new phase of maturity. "Notwithstanding its lively spirit of fun," the New Orleans *Times-Democrat* weighed in, "the volume is a more serious creation by far than *The Innocents Abroad;* and in some respects seems to us the most solid book that Mark Twain has written."[27] In London, Thomas Hardy, who read the book at once, told a private gathering, "Why don't people understand that Mark Twain is not merely a great humorist? He is a remarkable fellow in a very different way."[28] Joseph T. Goodman, who had regretted Twain's detour into British history with *The Prince and the Pauper*, hailed his reversion to his finest form. "The revival of boyish emotions is one of your strongest suits."[29] Despite his hand-wringing during its composition, Twain spoke so positively about the book that Howells had the impression that Twain thought it his best book.

The commercial reception was a far different matter. The huge burst of sales never materialized, and subscription agents booked only thirty-two thousand orders instead of the hundred thousand that Twain projected. As sales flattened, many printed copies remained unbound or were dumped on bookstores. Twain heaped the blame on Osgood, swore that he had cost him $50,000, and all but vowed that his next book, *Huckleberry Finn*, would be published by him and Webster alone. Conceding that Osgood had lovely traits as a person, Twain found him a hopeless publisher. In December 1883, in a spirit of mounting fury, he wrote a blistering letter to Osgood that said his book would have succeeded had Osgood only listened to him. "The Prince & Pauper & the Mississippi are the only books of mine which have ever failed. The first failure was not unbearable—but this second one is so nearly so that it is not a calming subject for me to talk upon . . . there were things about the publishing of *my* books which you did not understand. You understand them now, but it is I who have paid the costs of the apprenticeship."[30]

To disappoint Mark Twain was to become the butt of his most caustic humor. After his business relationship with Osgood ended, Twain told Howells, "The bare suggestion of scarlet fever in the family makes me shudder; I believe I would almost rather have Osgood publish a book for me."[31] He also joked grimly that if Osgood "were given the copyright on the Bible, his gang are stupid enough to publish it in such a way as to lose money on it."[32] By May 1885, with considerable schadenfreude, Twain learned that Osgood's firm had fallen into receivership.

What Twain could never quite admit was that the two books whose sales had disappointed him so sorely were largely published by himself. Most amazing of all, he began to hold up the American Publishing Company—his long-running bête noire—as his new standard of excellence. "Bliss never issued an octavo for me with less than 43,000 subscribers," he pointed out to Webster.[33] When a writer asked him to recommend a publishing house, Twain referred him to the American Publishing Company. "They swindled me out of huge sums of money in the old days, but they do know how to push a book; and besides, I think they are honest people now . . . there was only one thief in the concern, and he is shoveling brimstone now."[34]

TWINS OF GENIUS

During his 1882 stay in New Orleans, Mark Twain befriended another renegade southern writer who was far more outspoken in condemning southern racism: George Washington Cable, who had served in the Confederate cavalry and wrote for the New Orleans *Picayune* after the war. Twain thought him one of the few southern writers to avoid the flowery style of Sir Walter Scott, capturing the authentic Creole dialect of New Orleans. Twain extolled him as "the South's finest literary genius" and the "only master in the writing of French dialects that the country has produced," and he loved to listen as Cable crooned Creole tunes in a melodious tenor voice.[35] By the time they met, Cable had established his bona fides as a peerless chronicler of New Orleans life with a story collection, *Old Creole Days* (1879), and his first novel, *The Grandissimes* (1880). After reading one of the books, Twain, deeply affected, told Cable that "the charm of it, & the pain of it, & the deep music of it are still pulsing through me."[36]

With a crusading spirit not yet apparent in Twain, Cable had employed his *Picayune* columns to declare war against corrupt officials and the filthy streets in New Orleans. A devout Presbyterian who headed the church's mission school, he worked on behalf of the city's poor. As secretary of the Prisons and Asylums Aid Association, he also protested the shocking abuse of prisoners leased to private contractors. His boldest forays dealt with racial justice as he staunchly supported the city's integrated schools and excoriated a mob that forcibly ousted Black pupils from an all-female high school. The displeasure felt toward Cable by the city's conservative elite, spurred by these articles, would only gather strength in coming years.

Still bursting with energy, prone to wild mood swings, Twain seemed open to collaborations with other writers. He and Howells coauthored a new play, *Colonel Sellers as a Scientist,* that failed to galvanize any interest despite its distinguished auspices. Howells believed Twain had "life enough in him for ten generations, but his moods are now all colossal, and they seem to be mostly in the direction of co-operative literature."[37]

Twain was eager to form a road show with other writers to break the solitary monotony of the lecture circuit. For this "menagerie," as he dubbed it, he envisioned a team that would include Howells, Cable, Thomas Bailey Aldrich, and Joel Chandler Harris, author of the Uncle Remus stories, all grandly traveling in a private railroad car, with Twain as impresario. Howells and Aldrich didn't cotton to the idea, and Harris being morbidly shy onstage left Cable as the lone potential partner.

Though Cable had natural stage talent, he was still a fledgling speaker, and Twain wanted to test his skills in a modest setting. In November 1882, he invited him to Hartford and then to a raucous dinner in Boston, rounds of socializing that heightened Twain's sense of Cable's platform potential. "Cable has been here, creating worshipers on all hands," he informed Howells. "He is a marvelous talker on a deep subject."[38] Twain began to coach Cable and gave him lecture tips: "When an audience do not complain, it is a compliment; & when they *do* it is a compliment, too, if unaccompanied by violence."[39] Twain decided to book Cable into Unity Hall, a smallish auditorium in Hartford, so that he could experiment with a lecture on "Creole Women," provoke newspaper interest, and build a northern audience. It would also be an audition for the two-man tour Twain had begun to project.

As the date approached for Cable's appearance, April 4, 1883, Twain plugged his protégé in the *Hartford Courant* as a "gifted southerner" and summoned up a picture of "well-known Bostonians & New Yorkers" flocking to the lecture.[40] When Cable arrived in town, he visited the Clemens household, which was again beset with illness. According to Cable, Twain growled that Livy had "a pulse that ran up to 150 in the shade!" while Twain "strode up & down the room holding his headachy forehead & brandishing his arms." When Cable made the mistake of departing from the house without an overcoat, Twain rushed out in alarm. "The air is full of a soft, warm glow," Cable assured him. "Soft, warm glow!" Twain retorted. "It's full of the devil!—the devil of pneumonia." Twain insisted that Cable don one of his own overcoats.[41]

On April 4, having staked his prestige on Cable, Twain papered the house with literary celebrities. To brisk applause he introduced Cable before an overflow crowd. Slight, boyish, weighing a little more than one hundred pounds, with black hair and eyes, Cable was seized with stage fright and could scarcely proceed until Twain passed him one of his books and told him to read. The *Hartford Courant* critic thought the evening went swimmingly. "In the dialogues, especially in the Creole dialect, which is so musical on his lips, he held his audience almost breathless under the spell he wove so quietly and without apparent effort."[42] Appraising the evening with a critical eye, Twain wondered whether Cable had spoken loudly enough and faulted his selections from his fiction. When Twain booked him for his Saturday Morning Club of young ladies, Cable changed reading matter and scored a "splendid triumph," Twain reported, and Cable agreed that the audience sat "completely enraptured."[43] This performance wiped away any residual doubts that Twain held about the man's ability, and Cable left Hartford on April 7 convinced that a new chapter of his career had opened.

To improve his performance, Cable hired a well-known elocutionist. Later on, Twain reflected that this training detracted from Cable's natural charms and made him "merely theatrical and artificial," but at the time he was mightily pleased with improvements wrought by the coach.[44] When Cable stayed with Twain in November, he told Howells that Cable was "training under an expert, & he's just a rattling reader now—the best amateur I ever heard; & with 2 seasons of *public* practice, I guess he'll be the best professional reader alive."[45] Whatever pride Twain experienced in raising Cable to professional standards, he may also have experienced the first twinges of rivalry with a man who could approach his own platform artistry.

In late January, Cable stayed at the Clemens home during a lecture tour and came down with mumps, which he managed to communicate to the three Twain daughters. Twain hired a private nurse to care for Cable and blamed his illness on his refusal to wear an overcoat, attributing this to his southern heritage. Although Twain knew Cable would be sidelined from lectures, he continued to orchestrate his career and approached Francis E. Bliss (the son of the now deceased Elisha Jr.) of the American Publishing Company about a possible book deal for him.

"By the middle of next lecture season," he prophesied, "Mr. Cable's name will be a household word in this country. He has in his hands a couple of literary bonanzas which I think ought to be published in no way but by subscription."[46]

After Cable was confined to bed for two weeks, Twain was able to dismiss the hired nurse. "I seem to have made great way in the hearts of these dear good people," Cable told his wife. "Clemens, specially, seems to warm to me more & more."[47] In reality, Twain was developing a more jaundiced view of Cable and privately began to mock the "fuss" his guest had made over "his little pains." Twain had suppressed smirks during Cable's convalescence. "Lord, if I dared to laugh as I *want* to laugh—but Mrs. Clemens would kill me," he told a friend.[48] Twain's annoyance only grew when Cable left the house—and left his three daughters grappling with mumps. Susy's stoic response made Cable seem like a weakling in comparison, and Twain ridiculed him for having "shed whole barrels of noiseless tears."[49] In writing to thank Twain for his kindness, Cable made light of the whole affair. "If I can pick up any other mild contagion about the country anywhere," he wrote, "I'll bring it to your house, you seem so pleased to have me give your babies the mumps."[50] Fiercely protective of his children's health, Twain must have found this a tasteless witticism.

Cable redeemed himself with a celebrated April Fool's joke. He had heard Twain rail at autograph hounds who besieged him with requests but failed to send self-addressed stamped envelopes. He therefore contacted dozens of Twain's friends and asked them to send him autograph requests, all timed to arrive on April 1, with no self-addressed envelopes. A host of celebrities, including Ellen Terry, Henry Irving, John Hay, Oliver Wendell Holmes, and Henry Ward Beecher, swung into action, and an enormous stack of mail piled up at the Clemens doorstep on April Fool's Day. The first two or three letters fooled an irate Twain, who was about to have George Griffin throw them away. "Youth dear," Livy warned him, perhaps in on the joke, "there might be some there that you'd regret not sending your autograph to."[51] Twain's face must have widened into a smile as the practical joke sank in. "He did me a valuable favor," a pleased Twain said of Cable's jest. "It will be long before I part with those autographs."[52]

Twain had vowed several times to quit the lecture platform and had stayed away for many years. What finally persuaded him to embark on an extended tour with Cable was the heavy drain on his finances from his risky business ventures. "It has been the roughest twelve-month I can remember, for losses, ill luck, and botched business," he told Howells, noting that a joint tour would mitigate the "dreary work" of traveling alone.[53] Inspired by Dickens's American tour, the new vogue for reading aloud from one's books instead of lecturing also made the idea more palatable since Twain could read from the forthcoming *Huck Finn*. As his lecture agent, he chose Major James B. Pond, who had purchased the Redpath Lyceum Bureau in Boston and established his own agency in New York City. An ex-abolitionist, member of the Underground Railroad, and Union army officer, Pond had broken into the business when managing Ann Eliza Young, the twenty-seventh wife of Brigham Young, who could speak with some authority about the trials of polygamy. On Pond's roster was also Charles Sumner, Arthur Conan Doyle, and Henry Ward Beecher, and the agent had mounted a vigorous campaign to haul in Twain.

The "Twins of Genius" tour, as Pond christened it years later, would be an ambitious, four-month odyssey that started in early November and ended in late February, taking Twain and Cable to eighty cities. In mapping out the scheme, Twain crowned Pond "boss & head-ringmaster" of the "menagerie," drawing 10 percent of the profits.[54] "Pond must make the journeys as short & easy as circumstances will allow; for I am old & shaky, & a breakdown would be expensive." Twain insisted they begin in small towns where he and Cable could weed out weak material before playing big metropolitan halls. He whimsically added that if the gentle Cable "should become unmanageable & go to thrashing people, I should not want to have to pay his daily police court expenses."[55] For all his jocularity, Twain was the undisputed boss and paid Cable $450 a week plus expenses. He demanded a two-hour limit to each program so that the audience would "go away hungry, not surfeited."[56] Never bashful,

Twain insisted that he get the lion's share of stage time and end each evening. Since one of his pet peeves was paper programs that crackled or functioned as fans, he insisted that Pond print them on small, stiff cards instead. Twain scrupulously planned the evenings, each to have two alternating appearances by him and Cable.

Though Twain would come to mock Cable's piety, there was no question about the latter's extraordinary courage in denouncing racial discrimination as so-called Redeemer governments restored white supremacy in the South, dismantling the biracial gains of Reconstruction. On September 11, 1884, Cable delivered a speech, "The Freedman's Case in Equity," that became a *Century Magazine* article in January and aroused the holy wrath of white southerners. Identifying himself as an "ex-Confederate soldier" and the "son and grandson of slave-holders," Cable pleaded with fellow southerners to shed racist "sentiments."[57] In impassioned language, he challenged whites to take full responsibility for racial oppression. "The African slave was brought here by cruel force, and with everybody's consent except his own . . . There rests, therefore, a moral responsibility on the whole nation never to lose sight of the results of African-American slavery until they cease to work mischief and injustice."[58] He regretted Supreme Court decisions that nullified Reconstruction legislation and lamented northern weariness over racial issues. The South still maintained "a purely arbitrary superiority of all whites over all blacks," demoting Blacks to "an alien, menial, and dangerous class."[59] Cable concluded by insisting that the country could not "afford to tolerate . . . a class of people less than citizens" and that Blacks should become full-fledged citizens who showed no special deference toward whites. The white southern reaction was ferocious, with critics arguing that Cable had advocated social equality between the races and even miscegenation. Twain would not have dared to publish such a jeremiad, lest he alienate southern readers. On the other hand, he spent four months, in a widely publicized tour, sharing the stage nightly with a courageous writer who had now become notorious in the white South, and he warmly supported his crusade for racial equity.

A small but telling difference between the two men emerged when

Twain asked Cable to comment on his proposed lecture selections from *Huck Finn*. Twain was tempted to dramatize a section in which Huck concludes that you "can't learn a nigger to argue." Cable, while approving the choice of passage, balked at Twain's title for fear the word "nigger" appearing in programs and newspapers, out of context, might needlessly hurt people. Twain evidently conceded Cable's point, and the section was retitled "How come a Frenchman doan' talk like a man?"[60]

Since Twain had long been absent from the lecture stage, when the tour opened at the New Haven, Connecticut, Opera House on November 5, it qualified as a cultural event, with a large, tony audience. That day, Twain sent greetings to Chatto & Windus, his London publisher. "I take to the platform to-night, after an eight or ten years' absence from it. This trip's my *last*—forever & ever."[61] (A couple of weeks later, he admitted to an interviewer that "lecturers and burglars never reform" when promising to quit the trade.[62]) Cable declared the opening night an "emphatic success" and his comments would be more upbeat than Twain's throughout the tour.[63] Livy accompanied the two men to Springfield, Massachusetts, for their performance, then left them on their own. Twain desperately missed Livy as soon as they parted "in the forever accursed town of Springfield—the only town where we have suffered a defeat."[64]

Suddenly basking in the huge fame Twain enjoyed in the North, Cable was exhilarated by the large, enthusiastic crowds. He had only recently emerged from obscurity into national celebrity, and the tour was heady stuff for him. Twain's humor, joined to the pathos of Cable's Creole songs and readings, made for an unbeatable evening. "You will be proud when I tell you that Mark & I seem to divide the honors as nearly even as two men well could," Cable wrote to his wife, Lucy, from Providence, Rhode Island. "Mark seems greatly pleased with my work, as I am with his. As I came off the platform yesterday afternoon followed by a tremendous clatter of applause & he met me in the door as he was going to take my vacated place he exclaimed "superb! superb!"[65] When they played the Music Hall in Boston, they enjoyed a rambunctious crowd. "We had a great time last night," Cable reported home. "Twenty-two hundred people applauding, laughing & encoring in Music Hall."[66]

Curiously enough, the Boston *Daily Advertiser* regarded the tour as a prime example of North-South reconciliation, with Cable the southern gentleman and Twain the Connecticut resident; the boy from Hannibal was now firmly typed as a Yankee. Other observers construed them as two renegade southerners touring the North. As the hard-driving maestro of the tour, Twain went on the rampage against Major Pond after a poor Boston turnout and he hectored him to resort to the hard sell. "Louder advertising is absolutely necessary. We *must* have, in *every* town & city, one or two or half a dozen vast red posters with the single lines, 'MARK TWAIN-CABLE' . . . And we must have men to patrol the streets with bill-boards on their backs."[67] This may have been the first use ever of sandwich men to promote a literary event.

In the tour's early stages, Twain and Cable seemed a harmonious pair, deriving joy from each other's success. "Mark is on the platform, there goes a roar of applause!" Cable wrote backstage to his wife from Philadelphia. "We have a superb audience . . . & we are beating ourselves . . . There goes another round of applause. The laughter is almost continual & even my milder humor is interrupted with laughter and applause."[68] Twain believed that their contrasting styles—he rousing the audience, Cable soothing them—enabled them to hold the audience's attention for two hours. For Cable, the tour's high point came at a Congregational Church in Washington, D.C., when he strode offstage to discover President Chester Arthur waiting in his dressing room to congratulate him. Then, adding to his amazement, Frederick Douglass entered and greeted him and the president. "They met as acquaintances," Cable told his wife. "Think of it! A runaway slave!"[69]

With neatly combed hair and spade-shaped beard, Cable onstage was a precise and dignified presence, dapper and elegant. By contrast, Twain would shuffle onstage in a swallow-tailed evening coat, hair tousled, eyebrows bristling, his manner anything but elegant. When Twain appeared onstage, one person observed, his eyes shrewdly searched the audience "as a lawyer scans his jury in a death trial."[70] "He came forward with a lazy air," noted a Baltimore critic. "It was as much as he seemed able to do to drag one foot after another . . . As he walks, he stoops

TWINS OF GENIUS

slightly. He never smiles. When he says anything that creates laughter, he simply pauses, throws his head a little on one side and peers sleepily out of the corner of his eye."[71] It was the strategy of the canny old fox, shambling onstage, playing coyly with the audience, then pouncing with his wit. A gifted thespian, Twain learned to deliver his anecdotes colloquially, without notes, rather than reading extracts from *Huck Finn* or *A Tramp Abroad*. In so doing, he transformed himself from reader to actor and never carried a book onstage again.

Twain hated lecture tours because of the oppressive train trips and the long waits for evening performances to begin. He also suffered nagging guilt that he was a mere entertainer who failed to give listeners serious food for thought. One night in Toronto, after Twain received a particularly ecstatic response, Cable found him "in an absolutely wretched condition of mental depression, groaning and sighing" as they drove back to the hotel. When Cable asked what could justify such a mood after his triumph, Twain harrumphed, "Such a triumph? A triumph of the moment; but those people are going home to their beds, glad to get there, and they will wake up in the morning ashamed of having laughed at my nonsense."[72]

Certain tensions started to brew between the two men, especially given Twain's paranoid suspicion that Cable was lengthening his readings at his expense. "His name draws a sixteenth part of the house," Twain badgered Major Pond, "& he invariably does two-thirds of the reading . . . his constant disposition is to *lengthen* his pieces—he never shortens one."[73] Once Twain got irritated with someone, he kept scratching that itch. Years later, he still groused that "Cable always stole 2/3 of the platform-time when we were together—& with *his* platform-talent he was able to fatigue a corpse."[74] Ever the peacemaker, Livy intervened with her husband: "Don't allow yourself to get awry with Mr. Cable; he is good and your friend and it is an advantage to you to have him."[75]

A man with a taste for sacrilege, Twain had limited patience for religious rigidity, while Cable was a devout Presbyterian who honored the Sabbath. At the start of their tour, Twain was lounging in bed and reading one night when Cable came in and read aloud a chapter from the Bible.

Twain tolerated this behavior for another night or two, then announced, "See here, Cable, we'll have to cut this part of the program out. You can read the Bible as much as you please so long as you don't read it to me."[76] Twain's short fuse burned ever brighter when Cable refused to travel on the Sabbath because he wanted to rise early and attend local churches and Sunday schools, a factor that would throw off their tour schedule.[77]

In early December, when Twain and Cable were in Albany, they were invited to pay a call on Governor Grover Cleveland, now president-elect of the United States. Twain had broken ranks with fellow Republicans to vote for the Democratic Cleveland, likely prompting the invitation. Exceedingly affable, Cleveland apologized that he couldn't come to their lecture that evening because he had to host the state's presidential electors at a banquet. In his naturally casual style, Twain unthinkingly sat on the edge of the executive desk, only to discover he had accidentally pressed four electric bells, promptly summoning four pages. By the time he repeated the story for his *Autobiography* in 1906, he had quadrupled the number to "sixteen bell-buttons on the corner of the table"—a fine instance of his tendency to exaggerate any story.[78]

A few days later, as Twain and Cable browsed in a Rochester bookstore, Cable bought his fellow author a copy of *Le Morte d'Arthur* by Sir Thomas Malory, predicting "you will never lay it down until you have read it from cover to cover."[79] It was a lyrical fifteenth-century rendering of King Arthur, Queen Guinevere, and the Knights of the Round Table. Within two days, Twain had devoured the book and "vivid pink spots" appeared on his cheeks that signaled to Cable intense creative chemistry at work—the initial inspiration, in fact, for *A Connecticut Yankee in King Arthur's Court*. Later admitting the seminal role of the work in his novel, he conceded to Cable, "Yes; you are its godfather."[80] The two men were so charmed by the book's antique prose that they bandied about invented phrases in the manner of Malory, with Twain telling Livy that "we have all used the quaint language of the book in the cars & hotels."[81]

By mid-December, Twain felt fit and robust, and ate three square meals a day—a novelty for him. In late December, he added a new reading from *Huck Finn*, which he thought "the biggest card in my whole repertoire," and served up helpings from the book at every opportunity.[82] He now boasted to Livy of the "terrific days of travel! . . . We prance out onto the platform half asleep, now-a-days, but it isn't any matter, we could do our work & do it well, too, if we *were* asleep . . . We have rattling good times on the platform."[83] His giddy joy fit a pattern: he would dread lectures and groan about their misery in advance only to be energized by the boisterous crowds and glory in his power to command their laughter. Livy collaborated on program selections and scoured his books for fresh passages to deliver. Cable had no idea that a disaffected Twain was telling Major Pond that he wished he could make a $200 severance payment to Cable and drop him from the tour altogether. He said that "but for Mrs. Clemens's restraining hand," he would simply refuse to read with Cable again.[84]

For Twain, one appeal of life on the road was reverting to the disarray of bachelor life instead of the exquisite order enforced by Livy in Hartford. When a reporter for the *Rochester Herald* arrived at Twain's hotel room, he described a scene reminiscent of earlier days: "The room was in an alarming state of disorder. Articles of clothing, books, letters and various other things were scattered about in the most promiscuous fashion. The humorist's capacious valise, which lay open upon a center table, looked as though it had been struck by a cyclone."[85] Twain was patenting an enduring style of performing interviews in bed. The reporter said that Twain lay in an embroidered bathrobe, "his head propped up with two pillows and a bolster," while he was "vigorously pulling smoke from a well-burnt cob pipe."[86] Twain was increasingly adept at projecting a graphic image of himself that would be burned into the public consciousness until it became his trademark. Never a stranger to self-promotion, he had already licensed the use of his image for sales of tobacco, cigars, and cigarettes.

As they ventured into Kentucky, the Twins of Genius rediscovered the pleasures of southern audiences and their ready wit. Twain reported to his wife how "they laugh themselves all to pieces. They catch a point before you can get it out."[87] On the tour, Twain felt reclaimed as a prodigal son of the South and declared his appreciation for its culture, telling

Livy that "none but a Southern audience can bring out the very best that is in a man on the platform. There is an atmosphere of *affection* for you, pervading the house that you seldom feel . . . in a northern audience."[88] Of course the South had molded his humor, and audiences felt a special kinship with his brand of fun. Twain also had reminders of less endearing sides of the region. Traveling on a train from Indianapolis, he observed the following: "A small country boy . . . discussed a negro woman in her easy hearing-distance, to his 17-year-old sister: 'Mighty good clothes for a nigger, *hain't* they? I never see a nigger dressed so fine before." Twain commented to Livy: "She *was* thoroughly well & tastefully dressed, & had more brains & breeding than 7 generations of that boy's family will be able to show."[89]

The southern detour provided a test case of how Cable would fare as his *Century Magazine* article on "The Freedman's Case in Equity" stirred national debate. When he addressed the Press Club in Louisville, Kentucky, on the "negro question," he noticed how southern whites glanced at each other in silence, afraid to voice an opinion. "Freedom of speech has yet to come to us of the South," he concluded, yet he deemed it a sign of progress that he could speak "with perfect freedom and gave no offense."[90] Having achieved heroic status among southern Blacks, Cable visited a "Colored High School" and was touched when students sang a lovely psalm in his honor. Back at the hotel, he received a delegation of Black citizens who thanked him for his essay. "You would have not got off with dry eyes had you been there," he told his wife. "One said, 'Good-bye, my hero of heroes.' I thought of the great dead—Lloyd Garrison, Wendell Phillips & the rest and felt ashamed to let them give such praise to me."[91] Subject to vicious criticism back home, Cable would decide to leave New Orleans—"I shall not from choice bring up my daughters in that state of society"—and ended up relocating his family to Northampton, Massachusetts.[92]

However much Twain sniped at Cable for his religious observances and stinginess—he charged the tour for his dirty laundry—he applauded his courage on race. "Yes, Cable has his littlenesses, like Napoleon," he told Livy, "but I tell you he is a brave soul & a *great man*."[93] If he persisted in his struggle for the Black population, "his greatness will come to be recognized—& it will be a greatness of a kind & size that will overshadow his merits as a novelist & make them small by contrast."[94] Livy was delighted to hear about Cable's crusade for racial justice. "I seem to be *with* you when I get such full letters from you & I assure you it is a *tremendous* comfort."[95]

Twain instructed Pond to book them into both Hannibal and Keokuk, where his mother and Orion lived, and he insisted that when he spoke in his hometown, all his proceeds should go to a local charity. Although he had visited Hannibal on his research trip almost three years earlier, nothing quite prepared him for the flood of emotion that enveloped him. "This visit to Hannibal—you can never imagine the infinite great deeps of pathos that have rolled their tides over me," he told Livy. "I shall never see another such day. I have carried my heart in my mouth for twenty-four hours."[96] He felt the heartbreak when he was approached by a boyhood friend, Tom Nash, who had fallen into the icy Mississippi while skating nearly forty years before, rendering him deaf. Nash shyly handed him a letter, then walked away.

There were other "great deeps" that Twain plumbed. When he visited his eighty-one-year-old mother in Keokuk—she braved a snowstorm to hear him lecture—he feared it might be the last time he saw her, a fear heightened by her early signs of dementia and the great geographic distance that separated them. If still spry, she was very deaf and had to use an ear trumpet to hear her son, who now had curly gray hair and a mustache. Flush with emotion, he sent Livy a tribute to his mother, whom he found "her old beautiful self; a nature of pure gold—one of the purest & finest & highest this land has produced. The unconsciously pathetic is her talent—& how richly she is endowed with it—& how naturally eloquent she is when it is to the fore! What books she could have written—& now the world has lost them."[97] The passage makes clear that Twain traced the source of his own literary talents to his mother.

Twain was rejuvenated by the tour, scoring one rousing success after another, with up to six performances per week. He told Livy how he arrived in Davenport, Iowa, feeling "old & seedy and wretched from travling [sic] all night & getting no sleep," but then he gulped down some black coffee, walked out onstage, and received spirited calls for encores. "When I am in such trim as I was last night," he told Livy, "I would rather be on the platform than anywhere in the world."[98] From Chicago, where he had the audience shaking with laughter, he exulted, "we hit them again last night, & hit them hard."[99] The one thing he could not endure was prolonged separation from Livy for four months and the constant waves of loneliness. On February 1, the eve of their anniversary, he wrote to her, "I love you, my darling, & I am not forgetting that tomorrow is the great day, our most prized & memorable day."[100] Livy had already written: "Fifteen years married sixteen years engaged. And I do love you a scrap even now. I don't much fancy having you away on our anniversaries . . . Good bye Youth, *I love you with my whole heart.*"[101] Twain urged Susy to write to him two or three times a week to spare the fragile Livy the onus of daily correspondence.

Twain almost never missed a day writing to his wife, but he skipped one in mid-February when he spoke in London, Ontario, before an audience that included 151 young women from Hellmuth Ladies' College. His peculiar behavior previewed a fascination with young women that became pronounced in later years. After the lecture, he bounded down from the stage and pursued female students as they left. In a charming if slightly manipulative way, he told the young women that he was a lonely stranger and coaxed an invitation from the female principal to toboggan at the college the next day. Twain and Cable, with their tight schedule, had no time to lose for tobogganing, but they went anyway.

Arriving by sleigh, with the temperature twelve below zero, the authors found a hilltop campus carpeted in deep snow. After they signed seventy-four autographs for the young women, they then boarded toboggans that could accommodate large groups. "You sit in the midst of a row of girls on a long broad board with its front end curled up," Twain described, "& away you go, like lightning."[102] Twain sent Livy a fairly subdued description that emphasized fatigue as well as excitement. Writing to his wife, Cable presented a very different picture of a euphoric Twain riding heavily bundled in furs with young women on the toboggan. "I saw him in a pretty sleigh behind a tandem team whisking through the distant gate of the grounds and those seventy girls waving and hurrahing and he swinging his hat and tossing kisses right and left; and the scene repeated again as he swept around the slope of a hill & came in sight again a few hundred yards farther on."[103] Twain had long been a stickler for catching trains on time—he had, after all, blamed Cable's refusal to travel on the Sabbath for disrupting their tour schedule—yet he and Cable now ended up missing a train by a few minutes.

During the tour's final weeks, Twain's tensions with Cable worsened as he found his partner's cheapness unbearable. For three and a half months, Cable had sponged stationery from hotels and now borrowed Twain's writing pad and used up the remaining sheets. Twain's anger boiled over. "His body is small," he told Livy, "but it is much too large for his soul. He is the pitifulest human louse I have ever known."[104] Onstage Twain engaged in an unspoken rivalry with his fellow performer. "It is Cable's fault that I have done inferior reading all this time," he declared privately. "He has hogged so much of the platform-time that I have always felt obliged to hurry along at lightning speed . . . but now I take my own time, & give 25 minutes to pieces which formerly occupied but 15."[105] If Cable noted a mystifying change in Twain, he had no notion just how miffed Twain felt, and his letters blindly sang his colleague's praises. When the four-month tour ended on February 28, 1885, Twain outwardly honored Cable, whose "gifts of mind are greater & higher than I had suspected," but his refusal to travel on the Sabbath still rankled. "He has taught me to abhor & detest the Sabbath-day," Twain informed Howells.[106] Twain wondered whether the tour had indeed been worth the strain. "I ought to have staid [sic] at home & written another book," he complained to Charley Webster. "It pays better than the platform."[107] In fact, the extended tour, with its 103 stage appearances, had netted Twain a handsome $16,000 and provided invaluable publicity for the publication of *Huck Finn*.

Twain's true feelings about Cable spilled into the press in May when the Boston *Herald* ran an article that featured Twain's major gripes and could only have originated with Twain himself. The article described difficulties with Cable's Sabbath observance and, according to Major Pond, his stinginess in charging to the tour "so highly luxurious a thing as champagne and so lowly a one as the blacking of his boots."[108] When the story surfaced, Cable wrote to Twain to deny he had ever intimated anything unpleasant about Twain. "If you care to know it, I esteem you more highly since our winter's experience than I ever did before & should deeply regret if scandal mongers were to make an estrangement between us."[109] Twain likewise assured Cable that he was not distressed by the "slanders of a professional newspaper liar."[110] In later years, the two men would say laudatory things about each other, but they seldom met or even communicated, and there was never a sequel to their celebrated speaking tour.

Awaiting Twain at the end of the tour lay a special surprise: Livy and the girls, having decided to stage an amateur theatrical in his honor, had selected *The Prince and the Pauper*. Livy assembled the script and directed it, Susy played the Prince, and Clara was Lady Jane Grey, and a half dozen neighborhood children participated, rehearsing for several weeks before Twain's return. In the drawing room, chairs were set up for dozens of guests, with a stage erected at the end of the library, the conservatory serving as a backdrop. The Gerhardts, now back from Paris, painted scenes and made costumes. A neighbor slated to play Miles Hendon got sick at the last minute, and Twain stepped into the role with scant preparation. When he could not remember lines, he simply made them up. "Papa acted his part beautifully," Susy wrote, "and he added to the scene by making it a good deal longer. He was inexpressibly funny, with his great slouch hat, and gait! oh such a gait!"[111] The line drawing the biggest laugh from the excited crowd came when Susy said, "Fathers be alike, mayhap; mine hath not a doll's temper."[112] Twain pronounced the show "one of the prettiest private theatrical performances I have ever seen," and Livy was thrilled to recapture a rich family life after the four-month hiatus.[113] "Youth darling," she told him. "Life is not so interesting with you away . . . My wish now is that we might live yet together twenty or twenty five years and never one night be seperated [sic]."[114]

CHAPTER TWENTY-ONE

"A Sound Heart & a Deformed Conscience"

Mark Twain had long been an author with vehement opinions about the optimal way to publish books, so it was not too much of a leap for him to inaugurate his own publishing house. He had dismissed his first publisher, Elisha Bliss, Jr., of the American Publishing Company, as "a most repulsive creature . . . It is my belief that Bliss never did an honest thing in his life, when he had a chance to do a dishonest one."[1] As for James R. Osgood, he concluded that he was "the loveliest man in the world," but "the most incapable publisher."[2] With this bottomless bile for his previous publishers, Twain chose to launch his own firm of Charles L. Webster and Company in May 1884.

At the time, his speculative losses had mushroomed, with his poor bets on stocks bought on margin having grown perilous. In early 1883, he had purchased two hundred shares on margin of Oregon & Transcontinental Company, a railroad with plans to build a trunk line from the Great Lakes to the Pacific. He scooped up $15,000 worth of stock at $75 per share, then watched it shoot up to $98. When it plummeted to $40, Twain was fooled into thinking it a bargain and added another hundred shares. In May 1884, when he started his new publishing house, he had to liquidate his entire position for $12 a share—a catastrophic fiasco.

Impressed by Charles Webster's energetic handling of the Kaolatype business, Twain had groomed him as his all-purpose business manager. As he instructed his young nephew, "You are my businessman . . . I *won't* talk business—I will perish first. I hate the very idea of business, in all its forms."[3] Though he made such statements, they were belied by his constant meddling with Webster. Twain was an exacting boss, and he and Livy converted Webster into a trusted factotum. When Livy needed dining room chairs, she told Webster, "I want to know if you will go about in the old shops and see what you can find in the way of some nice old chairs for me."[4] Twain dispatched Webster to Tiffany to buy a fancy watch for Livy. A man for all seasons, Webster had to find someone to fix the furnace in the Hartford house. When the Clemens family went to Elmira, he attended to their private railroad car. "Provide a comfortable chair for Livy, Charley—she doesn't like the sleeping-car seats," Twain told him.[5] Against his better business judgment, Charley pursued Twain's brainstorm of marketing a clamp that would prevent infants from kicking off bedclothes. Ditto for the perpetual calendar. He was forced to follow up on Twain's myriad ideas for board games about history and other subjects. Charley even had to search out a star actor for *Colonel Sellers as a Scientist*.

The immediate purpose of Charles L. Webster and Company was to publish *Huckleberry Finn* and other works by Mark Twain. Webster became the firm's business manager and nominal head, with its headquarters near Union Square in lower Manhattan. In March 1885, Charley signed a formal contract making him a partner. Since Twain supplied two-thirds of the working capital, he would get roughly that percentage of profits on his books. Charley was to receive a $2,500 annual salary and one-third of all profits up to $20,000; after that, he was entitled to 10 percent of profits, with Twain gaining 90 percent. Given later developments, two clauses in Twain's agreement with Webster should be flagged. Twain had to approve any expenses surpassing $1,000, and Webster wasn't allowed to sign book contracts without Twain's consent.

Even from afar, in Hartford, Twain was a demanding boss who could never decide whether Webster sent him too much or too little information. Already, in September 1884, when Webster alerted him to pirated editions of his books, Twain protested: "Try to remember that I fly off

"A SOUND HEART & A DEFORMED CONSCIENCE"

the handle altogether too easily, and that you want to think twice before you send me irritating news."[6] Another time he admonished him: "It is not my function to help arrive at conclusions in business matters. The thing should not be submitted to me except in a complete & determined form," his function being "solely to *approve* or *disapprove*."[7] In seeming contradiction of these directives, Twain had once reprimanded his nephew, "Now what I have felt the want of, in you . . . is, *reports*, REPORTS, man! I haven't doubted your diligence or your capacity."[8]

Copyright violations remained a sore point with Twain, and in December 1884, he spotted a catalog of the bookseller Estes & Lauriat that advertised *Huck Finn* at reduced rates before it was even available. Apoplectic, Twain warned Webster that "if we have no chance at them in law, tell me at once & I will publish them as thieves and swindlers."[9] He composed a perfervid letter that blasted the bookseller and threatened a lawsuit.[10] As always, Livy had to cool off her husband's hot temper and oppose his lawsuit, lest he commit an injustice. "Youth dear," she began in a chastising letter that frankly informed her husband that his letter "makes me feel sick to read . . . How I wish that you were less ready to fight, and more ready to see other peoples [*sic*] side of things . . . If you write, write civilly."[11] It was much too late for civility. Twain's lawyer had already filed for an injunction against the bookseller, and he remained unrepentant in the press: "It is interfering with my legitimate business, and is a piece of impudence sure to damage me."[12] In the end, a federal judge denied the injunction he sought.

Charles L. Webster and Company would specialize in subscription publishing. "When a book *will* sell by subscription," Twain had advised one author, "it will sell two or three times as many copies as it would in the trade; and the profit is bulkier because the retail price is greater."[13] Because subscription salesmen sold books through fancy prospectuses, they favored large, ponderous books, profusely illustrated with engravings and with ornate bindings that plumped up the price. For this reason, Twain studiously monitored cover designs and illustrations for all books published by Charles L. Webster and Company.

FLOODTIDE

As early as summer 1876, at his hilltop gazebo at Quarry Farm, Twain had drafted several hundred pages of *Adventures of Huckleberry Finn*, roughly half of a book intended as a sequel to the newly published *Tom Sawyer*. At the time, Twain showed no awareness that he had struck a vein of pure gold. "I like it only tolerably well, as far as I have got," he told Howells, "and may possibly pigeon-hole or burn the MS when it is done."[14] As so often with Twain, his creative process was messy, dynamic, and prolonged. With *Huck Finn*, he didn't tackle the manuscript again until 1880 and didn't finish it until 1883. When he resumed it in Elmira in June 1883, he rode a swelling wave of energy, telling the Gerhardts that he was "grinding out manuscript by the acre."[15] Instead of working his customary fixed hours at the gazebo, he didn't stop in the late afternoon and went on writing until voices down below summoned him to supper at twilight. He even skipped his usual days off, working six or seven days without a break. As if a new compartment sprang open in his brain, he was astonished at his productivity as he churned out up to four thousand words a day. "I haven't had such booming working-days for many years," he told Orion and Mollie. "This summer it is no more trouble to me to write than it is to lie."[16] This child of his imagination already held a special place in his heart, and he was fiercely protective of it. "And *I* shall *like it*, whether anybody else does or not," he warned Howells.[17] With uncommon speed the new baby burst into the world, and on September 1, Twain alerted his British publisher, Andrew Chatto, that he had completed *Huck Finn*.

As he wrote the book, it was clear to Twain that the unfinished business of his literary life revolved around the consequences of slavery. If *Tom Sawyer* offered a sunlit view of antebellum Hannibal, in *Huck Finn* Twain delved into the shadows. As he dredged up memories anew, he now perceived a town embroiled in slavery. People who had seemed wholesome and innocent in *Tom Sawyer* now conspired in a monstrous system of inequality. When Jim and Huck flee the town, it isn't for a brief holiday on a nearby island, as in *Tom Sawyer*, but a wholesale flight for freedom down the river, mingling the daring of young fugitives with a landscape teeming with vignettes of southern depravity. In revising the book, Twain shifted the slavery subplot to the center of the narrative. He now gazed back at his boyhood with critical northern eyes while still allowing himself considerable affection for Huck, Jim, and Tom and the mores of southern boys, but especially for the terrified runaway, Jim.

Having escaped from boyhood poverty into well-bred Hartford gentry, Twain turned his attention to lowly people and showed sympathy for them. He presented an inverted social order in which the meek and downtrodden can be superior to their supposed betters. His protagonist is the town's social outcast, Huck Finn, the son of the local drunkard, trapped at the bottom of the social scale. He was modeled on Twain's boyhood friend Tom Blankenship, who was "ignorant, unwashed, insufficiently fed; but he had as good a heart as ever any boy had."[18] Twain found nobility in Tom's rejection of the supposedly respectable townsfolk. Frowned upon by polite society, this barefoot ragamuffin had been admired by Sam Clemens as truly independent in his vagrant life. He also inhabited a world blessedly free of homework, Sunday school, and clean clothes. Of the Blankenship clan of poor whites, Twain later summarized them: "The parents paupers and drunkards; the girls charged with prostitution—not proven. Tom, a kindly young heathen. Bence, a fisherman. These children were never sent to school or church. Played out and disappeared."[19] It was Tom's brother Benson (Bence) who had helped to conceal and feed for weeks the fugitive slave who had been hiding on an island off the Illinois shore and who was later found murdered and brutally mutilated—an episode that clearly helped to inspire *Huck Finn*.

From his mother Twain had learned how the plainspoken language of ordinary people can rise to the level of eloquence and he prided himself on his command of vernacular and his ability to render regional dialects precisely. "A nation's language is a very large matter," he wrote. "It is not simply a manner of speech obtaining among the educated handful; the manner obtaining among the vast uneducated multitude must be considered also."[20] With *Huck Finn,* he gave voice to the buried portion of the population, the commoners unheard and unseen in the polite, East Coast precincts of Hartford and Boston. He would revolutionize the American novel by scrapping the omniscient, third-person narrator and allowing the unlettered Huck to tell the tale in his own voice, showing how expressive colloquial language could be. In the novel, Twain seems to be eavesdropping on Huck's thoughts, not inventing them. He had used this first-person device in stories but never in a novel. The steady flow of Huck's chatter would mirror the steady flow of the raft coursing down the Mississippi River.

Often blind to the humor of what he is saying, Huck employs the dry, deadpan style that Twain had perfected onstage of never smiling when he said something funny. The audience sees the joke; Huck doesn't. Twain wanted his stage voice to have the subtlety and nuance of his writing voice, and his writing voice to have the freshness and immediacy of his lecture voice. In *Huck Finn,* we hear Huck talking in the idiom of the heartland, in a voice so pure and natural that it grows artful. As Twain later said, "when the heart speaks it has no use for the conventions . . . and the result is *literature* and not to be called by any less dignified name."[21]

As shown in his reminiscence of Mary Ann Cord for the *Atlantic Monthly,* Twain was fascinated by the speech patterns of Black people and envied how George Washington Cable and Joel Chandler Harris captured their voices phonetically. "It is marvelous the way you & Cable spell the negro & creole dialects," Twain told Harris.[22] So keen was Twain's ear for Black speech that the scholar Shelley Fisher Fishkin has argued that Twain may even have based Huck's distinctive rhythms on a Black boy he called Sociable Jimmy whom he encountered in Paris, Illinois, in late December 1871. "Both boys are naive and open, engaging and bright . . . They free-associate with remarkable energy and verve."[23] Twain himself said of Jimmy that he was "the most artless, sociable, and exhaustless talker I ever came across."[24]

If Twain traced the source of Huck's character to his boyhood friend Tom Blankenship, he molded several figures into his composite portrait of the enslaved fugitive, Jim, including Uncle Daniel, whose ghost yarns at the Quarleses' farm made young Sam Clemens shiver with delight;

"A SOUND HEART & A DEFORMED CONSCIENCE"

John Lewis, who rescued the runaway carriage at Quarry Farm; and George Griffin, the inimitable butler and font of wisdom in the Hartford household. In the "Notice" at the outset of *Huck Finn,* Twain famously warns: "Persons attempting to find a motive in this narrative will be prosecuted; persons attempting to find a moral in it will be banished; persons attempting to find a plot in it will be shot." The reader is given a hint of this molding device in the Notice's attribution: "By Order of the Author / Per G.G., Chief of Ordnance."[25] "G.G." was Twain's humorous tribute to George Griffin, who had just chased away a burglar with a pistol.

In *Huck Finn,* Twain wanted to show how slavery could warp an entire community, down to Huck and his father, at the bottom of the social heap. The most innocent child could be corrupted with ghastly doctrines. In the end, Huck's natural impulses prove superior to the wicked doctrines internalized from the grown-ups. Or, as Twain would indelibly phrase it, the moral of his story would be to show how "a sound heart & a deformed conscience come into collision & conscience suffers defeat."[26] Twain often spoke of abolitionists as despised figures in his upbringing, yet when Huck meets Jim hiding on Jackson's Island, he promises to keep it a secret. "People would call me a low-down Abolitionist and despise me for keeping mum—but that don't make no difference. I ain't a-going to tell, and I ain't a-going back there, anyways."[27] In escaping on the raft down the Mississippi River with Jim, Huck risks permanent ostracism from white society.

Huck, all of fourteen, and Jim, an enslaved man of middle age, might seem like an incongruous pairing, but Twain saw them bound together by a "community of misfortune. Huck is the child of neglect & acquainted with cold, hunger, privation, humiliation, & with the unearned aversion of the upper crust of the community," he explained.[28] Twain served up an unforgettable portrait of Pap Finn, a brutal drunk who beats his son, rants against the government, and spouts white supremacist ideology as he rages against a free mulatto Black from Ohio who dares to be a professor and wear fine clothes, cursing him as "a prowling, thieving, infernal, white-shirted free nigger."[29] Small wonder that W. H. Auden called Pap Finn "a greater and more horrible monster than almost any I can think of in fiction."[30] Pap is one of many figures in the novel who illustrate how slavery cruelly disfigures the ruling whites no less than the subjugated Blacks.

With Pap as his sole parent, Huck is saturated with all the bigotry of his environment. Twain establishes this unforgettably when Huck tells Aunt Sally Phelps about a steamboat accident in which the boat "blowed out a cylinder-head." Phelps replies, "Good gracious! anybody hurt?" "No'm. Killed a nigger." "Well, it's lucky; because sometimes people do get hurt."[31] Black lives are coolly reduced to collateral damage in the accident. The Widow Douglas and Miss Watson work to "sivilize" Huck with clean clothes and regular prayers, but their conception of morality seems tragicomically limited amid the horrors of a slaveholding town. Later in the novel, Huck will reject a Christianity that condones slavery, but already at the outset he renounces any heaven he has to share with the likes of Miss Watson. "Well, I couldn't see no advantage in going where she was going, so I made up my mind I wouldn't try for it."[32]

As Huck and Jim set off on the raft, they float downriver at night and hide onshore by day. Only the river, magically alive with mystery and existing beyond the bounds of society, offers a wild taste of freedom. "It's lovely to live on a raft," Huck tells us. "We had the sky up there, all speckled with stars, and we used to lay on our backs and look up at them, and discuss about whether they was made or only just happened."[33] Huck and Jim plan to ditch their raft at Cairo, Illinois, where they will take a steamboat up the Ohio River and find sanctuary in the free states.

Jim represents all the benevolent feelings—compassion, affection, honesty, and dignity—that Huck missed in his relationship with Pap Finn. As Jim mourns his missing wife and two children, Huck realizes, contrary to what he has been taught, that Jim is a sensitive man and an ideal father. "I do believe he cared just as much for his people as white folks does for theirn. It don't seem natural, but I reckon it's so."[34] Huck receives heartrending glimpses of Jim's suffering at being separated from his family. "When I waked up just at daybreak, he was setting there with his head

"A SOUND HEART & A DEFORMED CONSCIENCE"

down betwixt his knees, moaning and mourning to himself."[35] Movingly, Jim tells Huck about discovering his daughter's deafness. "Oh, Huck, I bust out a-cryin', en grab her up in my arms."[36]

At a time when southern whites demanded absolute deference from Blacks, Jim protests, strongly and eloquently, when Huck plays a mean trick on him, leading an ashamed Huck to repent. "It was fifteen minutes before I could work myself up to go and humble myself to a nigger but I done it, and I warn't ever sorry for it afterwards, neither."[37] Such a scene of white apology to a Black man would have been inconceivable in Twain's boyhood. In his sympathetic, if often quite limited, depiction of Jim, one cannot help but feel Twain's deep affection for Uncle Daniel, Mary Ann Cord, John Lewis, and George Griffin. Whatever the shortcomings of Twain's presentation of Jim, the Black man emerges as the morally superior figure in the story, surrounded by an appalling menagerie of whites who cheat, scheme, lie, and kill. As the South drifted into the grip of Jim Crow segregation, Huck and Jim embody an elusive vision of a biracial society.

Twain published *Huck Finn* at a time when Lost Cause apologists in the South argued that antebellum slaves had been happy until stirred up by northern agitators. Jim's flight and heartbreak boldly give the lie to that. Lost Cause theorists also advanced a vision of the superior culture of southern planters, endowed with aristocratic graces, versus the cold materialism of the northern barbarians. To present a countervision of the South, Twain deliberately has Huck and Jim miss the crucial turnoff at Cairo, Illinois, forcing them to plunge ever deeper into slave territory. Instead of southern refinement, Twain presents a squalid backwoods world awash in swindlers and hucksters, such as the Duke and the King, who present mangled scenes from Shakespeare in a one-horse town. Huck notes: "All the streets and lanes was just mud; they warn't nothing else *but* mud—mud as black as tar and nigh about a foot deep in some places, and two or three inches deep in *all* the places."[38] He describes loafers sitting outside main street stores, whittling wood, chewing tobacco, and sponging off each other as wild drunks roar through town.

In dramatizing the insane feud between the Grangerford and

Shepherdson families, Twain took dead aim at the honor culture that ruled the Old South and showed it taking the form of violent vendettas. Buck Grangerford coaches Huck on the meaning of a feud: "Well," says Buck, "a feud is this way. A man has a quarrel with another man, and kills him; then that other man's brother kills *him;* then the other brothers, on both sides, goes for one another; then the *cousins* chip in—and by-and-by everybody's killed off, and there ain't no more feud."[39] Twain also mocks the ubiquitous gun culture when Huck describes the two warring families arriving at church. "The men took their guns along, so did Buck, and kept them between their knees or stood them handy against the wall. The Shepherdsons done the same."[40] Feeling trapped amid these lunatic white folks, Huck and Jim yearn to return to the freedom of the river, their true state of nature.

Twain had not directly criticized Klan violence and related white supremacist mayhem that engulfed the South after the Civil War. But in *Huck Finn,* he spotlights a central feature of that violence: the lynch mob. When a mob comes to lynch Colonel Sherburn, who has just murdered a man, he bravely stares them down and lectures them on the psychology of such mobs. "The average man don't like trouble and danger... But if only *half* a man... shouts 'Lynch him, lynch him!' you're afraid to back down—afraid you'll be found out to be what you are—*cowards*—and so you raise a yell."[41] While Twain doesn't couch this clash in racial terms—this is a white man confronting a white mob—contemporary readers would have associated this with racial assaults in Dixie. When Twain later wrote an essay, "The United States of Lyncherdom," directly addressing racial lynching, he dwelled on the same component stressed by Colonel Sherburn—cowardice—strengthening the suspicion that he expected readers to make the racial connection in *Huck Finn.*

The final section of the novel is the least successful (Ernest Hemingway even suggested that readers skip it altogether). Tom Sawyer appears with news that Miss Watson has died and freed Jim in her will, but he fails to inform Huck and Jim of this. Jim is chained to a bed in a cabin on the Phelpses' farm where Tom elaborates a number of silly games by which Jim can escape to freedom—an escape he calls an "evasion." On the river,

"A SOUND HEART & A DEFORMED CONSCIENCE"

Jim has attained a nobility and a dignity that are then squandered for cheap laughs in the "evasion" chapters, where Twain lapses back into the hijinks and boyhood foolery of Tom Sawyer. A number of scholars have argued that the seemingly tasteless gags of the later chapters mask a serious point: that Twain was commenting on the collapse of Reconstruction and the pain it visited on supposedly free Blacks, as the white South reinstated the status quo ante with sharecropping, lynching, prison chain gangs, and other indignities, while banishing Blacks from the ballot box. At the end of *Huck Finn*, as Jim gains a tenuous freedom, Huck opts to jettison his southern upbringing and start afresh elsewhere. "But I reckon I got to light out for the Territory ahead of the rest, because Aunt Sally she's going to adopt me and sivilize me and I can't stand it. I been there before."[42] One wonders whether there is a touch of autobiography here since Twain had quit the South in 1861 when he lit out for the Nevada Territory along with Orion.

It has been the paradoxical fate of *Huck Finn* that Mark Twain's most searing indictment of racism has itself been accused of racism. Much of the criticism has arisen from the use of a single, ugly word: the N-word appears about two hundred times in the narrative. Of course, it is Huck, not Twain, who applies this notorious epithet to Jim. Huck's incessant, pathological repetition of the word deepens the reader's sense of the pervasive racism of the society in which he was reared. We know Twain took immense pains to reproduce accurately the many dialects in the book, especially Huck's. He was trying to show how deeply racism had seeped into the thoughts of this outcast white boy, who discovers Jim's full humanity during their journey. As Hilton Als has written: "Huck, the paradigm of the American boy, doesn't know what manhood is until he learns to trust and love a nigger, and the nigger in himself, the part of him that lies outside the status quo, that runs toward a dream of America, in love with a freedom just out of reach."[43]

The controversy over the N-word in *Huck Finn* presents an almost insuperable problem for educators. The word cannot be expunged from the book without robbing it of the authentic voice that is so key to its artistry, yet it can be a painful experience for any child, Black or white, to suffer the word's repetition so many times. For that reason, starting after World War II, the NAACP and other civil rights organizations denounced the "racial slurs" and "belittling racial designations," leading many school boards to ban the book.[44] There have even been suggestions that it should be sanitized of the N-word altogether and reissued without it, although the cure might be worse than the disease. It may be a book better reserved for higher education or else studied in conjunction with other contemporary works about slavery and abolitionism. Mark Twain himself never displayed concern over the word, and it doesn't help his historical reputation that he sometimes used it in his private correspondence when he should have known better. George Washington Cable's displeasure with Twain's use of the N-word in a *Huck Finn* selection during their lecture tour shows that, at least for some whites, the term already had strongly pejorative connotations.

Black writers have long divided over Twain's handling of Jim. Langston Hughes recognized that his story was embedded in an ongoing critique of the Old South that had spawned slavery. He said Twain's book "punctured some of the pretenses of the romantic Old South. The character of Jim in *Huckleberry Finn* . . . is considered to be one of the best portraits in American fiction of an unlettered slave clinging to the hope of freedom."[45] With a photo of Twain over his desk, Ralph Ellison wrote that "the spoken idiom of American negroes [was] absorbed by the creators of our great nineteenth-century literature even when the majority of blacks were still enslaved. Mark Twain celebrated it in the prose of *Huckleberry Finn*."[46] At the same time, Ellison recognized Twain's racial blind spots and saw Jim as marred by stereotypes drawn from minstrel shows. "Writing at a time when the blackfaced minstrel was still popular . . . Twain fitted Jim into the outlines of the minstrel tradition, and it was from behind this stereotype mask that we see Jim's dignity and human capacity—and Twain's complexity—emerge."[47]

Other Black writers have been far more merciless toward *Huck Finn*, perhaps none more so than Julius Lester, who thought the book "demeans blacks and insults history." He deplored Jim as a reassuring fantasy intended to soothe white readers. "It is a picture of the only kind of black that whites have ever truly liked—faithful, tending sick whites, not speaking, not causing trouble, and totally passive." Lester was an outright supporter of efforts to expunge the book from school curricula. "I am grateful that among the many indignities inflicted on me in childhood I escaped *Huckleberry Finn*. As a black parent, however, I sympathize with those who want the book banned, or at least removed from required reading lists in schools."[48]

In 2024 Percival Everett published an excellent, poignant retelling of *Huck Finn* titled *James,* in which Jim narrates the story and protects Huck, instead of the other way around. He presents a rich, multi-dimensional portrait of Jim/James on a par with what Twain did for Huck. Everett suggests that the slave patter and superstition that define Jim in Twain's novel were merely ways that enslaved people learned to dupe and manipulate white people to protect their own lives. When talking to other Blacks, Jim switches to standard English, thus exposing the slave patter and pose of naivete as deliberate minstrel affectations adopted by the enslaved for self-preservation. Everett has been a staunch defender of *Huck Finn* despite its flawed presentation of Jim. "Anyone who wants to ban *Huck Finn*," he has said, "hasn't read it."[49]

It would have been surprising had a white author in the 1880s delineated with perfect accuracy the experience of an enslaved person. Twain was simply not equipped to do that. Even in the case of Mary Ann Cord, Twain had guessed wrongly about her experiences during slavery until she opened her mouth and straightened him out. Still, it is hard to imagine any other major white author in that era projecting himself so powerfully into the experiences of a Black man running away from bondage. Twain had cast off much of the prejudicial dogma that permeated his youth, even if unacknowledged remnants lingered. And he did so at a time when white liberals in the North had largely washed their hands of racial problems, resigning southern Blacks to the fierce retaliation of the white Redeemer governments that dismantled Reconstruction. *Huck Finn* reminded white audiences of the persistence of racial inequality and strife—something they may have wanted to forget—and corrected the mythology of the Lost Cause. It testified to the harmful, lingering effects of slavery in American society.

———◆———

No sooner had Twain finished the book than he doffed the author hat and put on the publisher cap, having decided to make *Huck Finn* the first title published by Charles L. Webster and Company. Seldom has an author been so deeply involved in marketing his books. He urged Webster to take *Huck Finn, Tom Sawyer,* and *The Prince and the Pauper* and package them together in a discount deal. Relying on the subscription model, he wanted his new house to book forty thousand orders for *Huck Finn* by December and set it up as a holiday book. To reach that goal, he dangled prizes before the top-selling agents. As usual, the proofreading process drove him to distraction, and he told Howells of his "cursings, both loud and deep" and how the distortions he found were "of a nature that make a man swear his teeth loose."[50] For Webster, Twain refined the insult: "Charley, your proof-reader is an idiot; and not only an idiot, but blind; and not only blind, but partly dead."[51]

While Livy has been accused of bowdlerizing Twain's books, she felt kindly toward "dear old Huck," and her editorial interventions were minor, such as getting Twain to drop the word "stark" before "naked."[52] She and Susy never felt as comfortable with the earthy *Huck* as with Twain's politer literature, such as *The Prince and the Pauper* and later *Joan of Arc.* It was Richard Watson Gilder, editor of the *Century Illustrated Monthly Magazine,* who cleaned up what he saw as coarseness in the novel, when he serialized it that winter along with *The Bostonians* by Henry James. Often the prudery emanated from Twain himself, as when he ordered the removal of one illustration: "the lecherous old rascal kissing the girl at the campmeeting [sic]."[53] Many critics have noted that even though Huck is around fourteen, his mind is devoid of sexual thoughts or fantasies. The book did carry one unintentional obscenity: a raunchy engraver tampered with an illustration, endowing Uncle Silas Phelps

"A SOUND HEART & A DEFORMED CONSCIENCE"

with an erect penis. Two hundred fifty copies escaped the publishing house before the vandalism was belatedly discovered; with thousands of copies remaining, the mischievous picture had to be snipped out by hand, a laborious process that postponed publication until February and cost Twain profitable Christmas sales.

With the official publication of *Huck Finn* on February 18, 1885, the book quickly surpassed the gold standard of forty thousand copies set by Twain. A century later it would reach an estimated twenty million copies in fifty languages. "Your news is splendid," a buoyant Twain told Charley in mid-March. "*Huck* certainly is a success."[54] After three months, Webster handed him a check for $54,500, persuading him "that as a publisher I was not altogether a failure."[55] By September, sales had jumped to sixty thousand copies. It was a liberating moment for Twain, who had escaped, for once, the talons of other publishers, vindicating his decision to self-publish. Since none of his books had ever sold this rapidly, he feasted on every morsel of good news. "Every time you sell a thousand Huck's," he instructed Webster, "let me know."[56] Only in England did sales prove disappointing, which Twain attributed to British difficulty in understanding the tapestry of American dialects he had so skillfully woven. The discomfort may have gone deeper. In creating *Huck Finn*, Twain had made his boldest break yet from the Anglophile tradition of American letters and staked a claim for an American language as ample as the British tongue. "There is no such thing as the Queen's English," he later wrote in his notebook. "The property has passed into the hands of a joint stock Company, & we own the bulk of the shares."[57]

As with *Tom Sawyer*, Twain wrote about young boys in *Huck Finn*, albeit with an adult audience in mind. "If the boys read it & like it, perhaps that is testimony that my boys are real, not artificial. If they are real to the grown-ups, that is *proof*."[58] Twain had turned fifty and the past seemed brighter to him with the years. As he said of his daughters, "They have youth—the only thing that was worth giving to the race."[59] Once youth ended, he believed life degenerated into a cruel sham. "I should greatly like to re-live my youth," he once stated, "& then get drowned."[60] Although he wrote sequels in which Tom and Huck would reappear, they never matured into adults, as if Twain could not bear to imagine them stripped of their youthful appeal. He admitted to a puzzling lack of "interest in handling the men & experiences of later times," leaving that field wide open to such writers as Edith Wharton, Henry James, Theodore Dreiser, Thomas Hardy, and Joseph Conrad.[61] With *Huck Finn,* Twain had exhausted much of the fertile literary terrain of his youth and believed he had written himself out—one reason why he turned his principal attention to publishing.

Such was Twain's tender regard for *Huck* that he branded it his favorite book. (A decade later he often named *Joan of Arc* as his favorite child.) With a soft spot for Huck, Twain was stung by the savagery of some reviews. The Boston *Evening Traveler* denounced the book as "singularly flat, stale, and unprofitable," while the *New York World* mocked Huck as a "wretchedly low, vulgar, sneaking and lying Southern country boy."[62] The two reviews that galled Twain the most appeared in the Springfield *Republican,* which called the book "trashy and vicious," and the Boston *Transcript,* which labeled it "the veriest of trash."[63] Twain responded to these notices in a manner that harked back to his freewheeling Nevada days, when he traded insults freely with rival editors. In future editions of *Huck Finn,* he planned to insert a "prefatory remark" that would identify the editors of the two newspapers as Twain's uncles and the originals from which he had drawn Huck. "In character, language, clothing, education, instinct, & origin, he is the painstakingly drawn photograph & counterpart of these two gentlemen as they were in the time of their boyhood, forty years ago."[64] This was a classic author's revenge fantasy, and Livy again saved him from vengeful impulses. As Twain informed Webster, "Livy forbids the 'Prefatory Remark'—therefore, put it in the fire."[65] In the privacy of his notebook, however, he ranted against the *World* for deploring his book as "a mass of rubbish" and listed pages of tabloid trash it printed.

Those reviewers who recognized the book's extreme originality didn't stint on praise, seeing it as a welcome return to Twain's most fruitful style. "Mark Twain may be called the Edison of our literature," asserted the San Francisco *Chronicle.* "There is no limit to his inventive genius."[66]

"A SOUND HEART & A DEFORMED CONSCIENCE"

The most insightful response came in the London *Saturday Review* from Brander Matthews, who acknowledged the supreme artistry that Twain brought to Huck's first-person narration, free of authorial intrusion. "We see everything through his eyes—and they are his eyes, and not a pair of Mark Twain's spectacles. And the comments on what he sees are his comments—the comments of an ignorant, superstitious, sharp, healthy boy, brought up as Huck Finn has been brought up . . . one of the most artistic things is the sober self-restraint with which Mr. Clemens lets Huck Finn set down, without any comment at all, scenes which would have afforded the ordinary writer matter for endless moral and political and sociological disquisition."[67]

Even at the time, Twain's fellow writers expressed appreciation for the book. His friend Robert Louis Stevenson, who read it four times, said it contained "many excellent things; above all, the whole story of a healthy boy's dealing with his conscience, incredibly well done."[68] Not until the twentieth century was the novel granted a seminal place in American letters, with H. L. Mencken describing *Huck* as "a truly stupendous piece of work, perhaps the greatest novel ever written in English," and christening Twain as "the true father of our national literature, the first genuinely American artist of the blood royal."[69] Perhaps the most influential appraisal came from Ernest Hemingway, who observed succinctly that "all modern American literature comes from one book by Mark Twain called *Huckleberry Finn*."[70]

At the time, moral censors savaged the book and rushed to defend the nation's youth from its contagion. "If Mr. Clemens cannot think of something better to tell our pure-minded lads and lasses," Louisa May Alcott supposedly warned, "he had best stop writing for them."[71] The book dealt with many topics banned in well-bred homes and was denounced as coarse, vulgar, irreverent, and ribald. In short, a dangerous book to leave lying around the house. The extent of the outrage grew clear when the Concord Public Library of Massachusetts decided to ban it as "the veriest trash" and was even upset by Huck's "systematic use of bad grammar."[72] In other words, they were outraged by what made the book groundbreaking—that it had created literature of a very high order by using the authentic language of poor, disadvantaged people. There was also religious discomfort with Huck having decided he would rather go to hell than betray Jim back into slavery. Many editorial writers across the country amplified the message issued by the moral overlords of Concord.

Far from being disturbed, Twain professed to glory in the Concord news as a sure way to sell another twenty-five thousand copies and boasted to Webster that the library had "given us a rattling tip-top puff which will go into every paper in the country."[73] To his sister, he thundered that "those idiots in Concord are not a court of last resort, & I am not disturbed by their moral gymnastics. No other book of mine has sold so many copies within 2 months after issue as this one has done."[74]

Yet Twain was often most thin-skinned when he feigned indifference, and to a fellow writer, he referred to Huck as "that abused child of mine who has had so much unfair mud flung at him."[75] Unloading his big guns, he sent a withering letter to an eminent Concord citizen about the library having "excommunicated" his book, thereby doubling its sales. "This generous action of theirs must necessarily benefit me in one or two additional ways. For instance, it will deter other libraries from buying the book; & you are doubtless aware that one book in a public library prevents the sale of a sure ten & a possible hundred of its mates. And secondly it will cause the purchaser of the book to read it, out of curiosity, instead of merely intending to do so after the usual way of the world & library committees; & then they will discover, to my great advantage & their own indignant disappointment, that there is nothing objectionable in the book, after all."[76] That this sarcasm was something of a pose is confirmed by a letter Twain wrote in 1902, when told that the Sunday school library of a Baptist church in Elizabeth, New Jersey, owned a complete set of his books. Expressing pleasure, Twain wrote that the news "squares an old account, heals an old sore, banishes an old grievance: the turning of Huck Finn out of the Concord (Mass) circulating library 17 years ago."[77] *Huck Finn* would never be quite free of moralistic critics, and before Twain died, it would also be banished by libraries in Denver, Omaha, and Brooklyn.

CHAPTER TWENTY-TWO

Pure Mugwump

After campaigning for Rutherford B. Hayes in the 1876 and James Garfield in the 1880 presidential races, Mark Twain seemed, at least outwardly, to have become a stalwart of the Republican Party, the political creed of his Nook Farm neighbors. But, an iconoclast to the core, he was not cut out for strict party allegiance, telling a reporter between those two elections: "I am neither a Republican nor a Democrat—for any length of time. Vacillation is my particular forte."[1] He identified with the Liberal Republican wing of the party, which detested political bosses, favored civil service reform and free trade, and endorsed clean government. These Republicans stressed morality rather than ideology in political matters and clung to the belief that character was the foremost criterion for public office, not a candidate's partisan agenda.

Twain's dalliance with the Republican Party ended abruptly on June 6, 1884, when he was playing billiards in his Hartford home with some Republican chums, and George Griffin entered and relayed the shocking news from Chicago that James G. Blaine of Maine had been nominated as the party's candidate for president. "The butts of the billiard cues came down on the floor with a bump," Twain recalled, "and for a while the players were dumb."[2] Twain had loathed Blaine for his shady dealings with railroads when he was Speaker of the House and was especially incensed at his advocacy of the Chinese Exclusion Act. Always indignant about anti-Chinese discrimination, Twain had spurned the bill as "a proposal to return from the nineteenth to the eleventh century, and convert to the use of a modern free republic something in the likeness of a medieval edict against the Jews."[3]

Even though the *Hartford Courant* had pilloried Blaine for two years, the Republican paper unashamedly reversed course and promoted his candidacy, leaving Twain aghast. The paper had painted Blaine, he said, as "black, and blacker, and blacker still, for a series of years . . . But within thirty days after the nomination that paper had him all painted up white again."[4] Twain was staggered that upright Republican friends prostituted themselves for such an unsavory candidate. "*Isn't* human nature the most consummate sham and lie that was ever invented?" Twain asked Howells. "Isn't man a creature to be ashamed of in pretty much all his aspects? Is he really fit for anything but to be stood up on the street corner as a convenience for dogs?"[5]

The 1884 presidential race would be the most significant event in shaping Twain's future political outlook. Profoundly disenchanted with Hartford Republicans, many of them close friends and neighbors, he defected to a group of disgruntled Republicans known as the Mugwumps, who dared to support Democrat Grover Cleveland for president. Twain was joined, quite courageously, by the Reverend Joseph Twichell, who had to face the wrath of many churchgoers. Although the term "Mugwump," derived from an Algonquin word for "great chief," was first used to tar the group, these mavericks soon embraced it, and Twain proudly identified himself henceforth as a Mugwump—"pure from the marrow out," as Susy recorded him saying.[6] At a time of bitter partisanship, it was no small thing to bolt a party, but Twain stuck to his position despite local ostracism. In certain quarters of Hartford society, criticism of him would linger for many years because of his supposed political heresy.

Twain was perplexed by friends who supported Blaine, especially Howells. "Somehow I can't seem to rest quiet under the idea of your voting for Blaine," he told him. "I believe you said something about the country & the party. Certainly allegiance to these is well; but as certainly a man's *first* duty is to his own conscience & honor—the party &

the country come second to that, & never first."⁷ On October 20, Twain presided over a Mugwump rally in Hartford, introducing its chief speaker, Carl Schurz. In his own talk, Twain scoffed at the notion that he had deserted the Republican Party. "I easily perceive that the Republican party has deserted us, and deserted itself; but I am not able to see that *we* have deserted anything or anybody. As for me, I have not deserted the Republican code of principles."⁸ The *Hartford Courant* made a point of not covering Twain's speech, even though the paper had slavishly followed his doings. The Mugwump defection helped to install Grover Cleveland, a reform-minded Democrat, as the new president. "I think the country spewed up the filthy Blaine yesterday," Twain wrote his London publisher the day after the election. "At least such is our hope & belief this morning."⁹ Twain never regretted voting for Cleveland, nor did he relinquish his view that he was one of the great living American statesmen. The white South hailed the election of a Democratic president, although racial issues didn't seem to inform Twain's views of the contest. While Cleveland endorsed civil rights for Blacks, he opposed a critical voting rights bill.

With the Mugwumps, Twain found his natural spot on the ideological spectrum. Their positions fit his quirky, feisty spirit and enabled him to fire freely at both sides of the political aisle. He came to see Mugwumps as the supreme prophets and change-makers in history: "Washington, Garrison, Galileo, Luther, Christ. Loyalty to petrified opinions never yet broke a chain or freed a human soul in this world—and never will," he told the Monday Evening Club.¹⁰ More and more he found party orthodoxy a frightening force that made people blindly follow ideas, however wrongheaded. "If you could work the multiplication table into a democratic platform the republicans w[oul]d vote it down at the election," he wrote.¹¹ While most people fancied that they originated their political ideas, Twain argued that they were usually shopworn relics, borrowed from stale party organs. "Men think they think upon great political questions, and they do; but they think with their party, not independently."¹²

FLOODTIDE

Coincidentally, just as Twain abandoned the Republican Party in 1884, the most prominent Republican swam directly into his field of vision: Ulysses S. Grant. Twain's opinion of Grant had changed radically over the years. Back in 1869, writing under the pen name "Slocum," Twain had mocked the war hero as an overrated mediocrity. "I know Grant thoroughly . . . and he is the greatest farce that ever was thrust upon a people . . . I tell you, sir, Grant is nothing more than a bundle of petty spites, jealousies and resentments."[13] When Grant became president, the widespread corruption in his cabinet filled Twain with such dismay that he flirted briefly with living in England for a while. "He is so unhappy and discontented with our government that he says he is not conscious of the least emotion of patriotism in himself," recounted Annie Fields, wife of the *Atlantic Monthly* editor James T. Fields, of an April 1876 conversation with Twain. "He is overwhelmed with shame and confusion and wishes he were not an American."[14] When Rutherford B. Hayes succeeded Grant as president, Twain confided to Howells: "Well, it's a long time since we've had anybody to feel proud of & have confidence in."[15]

However much Twain criticized President Grant, he still remained a lofty figure to him for his wartime feats, levitating above party politics. In 1880, when Grant lost a third bid to grab the Republican nomination, Twain was content to see him lose to Garfield. "The Presidency can't add anything to Grant," he told Howells. "It is ephemeral; he is eternal."[16] Beyond Grant's prowess as a military commander, Twain honored him for his lenient behavior toward Robert E. Lee at Appomattox Court House. "I did not admire him so much for winning the war as for *ending* the war," Twain explained to a friend. "Peace—happiness—brotherhood—that is what we want in this world."[17] Thus the affection Twain showed when he addressed the Grant banquet in Chicago in 1879 was genuine, and the adulatory speech he gave for Grant in Hartford the following year underscored how far Twain had traveled from his southern roots. "By years of colossal labor and colossal achievement," Twain hailed Grant before the crowd, "you at last beat down a gigantic rebellion and saved your country from destruction."[18] Here Twain negated a central tenet of the Lost Cause school of southern historians: that the Civil War was a war of northern aggression. Instead, Twain aligned himself with the prevailing northern view that secession had marked an illegal rebellion and that Ulysses S. Grant was heroic in stamping it out.

In the early 1880s, Grant resided in New York, lending his name and prestige to an investment firm known as Grant and Ward, housed at 2 Wall Street. Twain lunched with the former president several times to ask for favors, and each time came away impressed by the courteous, patient way Grant handled his requests. There was something unpretentious about the hero that vastly appealed to Twain, who urged him in 1881 to write his memoirs. He knew that Grant, despite his taciturn image, was a fluent storyteller, who "spun out a lot of secret national history that would make a stunning chapter."[19] Grant demurred, fearing it would seem vain for him to pen his story, and he also worried that he lacked the requisite literary skills. Twain, of course, had not yet turned publisher, but he imagined that Grant, thanks to his brilliant young partner Ferdinand Ward, was a millionaire in no need of supplementary income.

Although Twain had largely ducked Civil War service, sitting out the conflict in Nevada and San Francisco, he thought it an auspicious moment to revisit the war. "Clemens was entirely satisfied with the result of the Civil War, and he was eager to have its facts and meanings brought out at once in history," Howells wrote. "He ridiculed the notion, held by many, that 'it was not yet time' to philosophize the events of the great struggle; that we must 'wait till the passions had cooled,' and 'the clouds of strife had cleared away.'"[20] The *Century Magazine* had launched a landmark series called "Battles and Leaders of the Civil War." Grant had contributed three articles, at $500 per article, and arrived at an understanding that the magazine's parent company would publish his memoirs. His earlier reticence about doing so had vanished for two dramatic reasons: His personal fortune had been wiped out by the shocking revelation that Ferdinand Ward had run a giant Ponzi scheme, leaving Grant almost penniless. Around the same time, Grant learned he was suffering from cancer of the throat and tongue, and feared that he would die and leave his wife, Julia, destitute.

In November 1884, after Twain and Cable spoke at Chickering Hall in New York, Twain learned from *Century* editor Richard Watson Gilder of Grant's intention to publish his memoirs with them. With a sure sense of the mass audience for such a book, Twain rushed over to Grant's town house on East 66th Street the next day and found Grant and his son Fred poring over the *Century* contract. He was appalled to discover that *Century* editors had offered him a stingy 10 percent royalty. "Strike out the ten per cent and put twenty per cent in its place," Twain said. "Better still, put seventy-five per cent of the net return in its place."[21] When Grant responded that the *Century* would never consent, Twain assured him there was "not a reputable publisher in America who would not be very glad to pay" that.[22] Twain also thought the $500 per article paid to Grant by the *Century* was a "monumental insult" and should have been at least $10,000 since Grant's popular articles had beefed up their circulation.[23] Grant, the soul of honesty, had not yet signed the *Century* contract yet felt duty bound to stick with them since he was already negotiating with the editors. The moment proved a turning point, not just for Grant, but for Twain. He had never planned to convert Charles L. Webster and Company into an all-purpose publisher—it was set up to publish his work alone—but here beckoned an irresistible chance to nab a bestseller.

On the spot, Twain gave Grant a primer in publishing, laughing at the *Century* contract as absurdly cheap. He pointed out that they evidently expected to sell a mere five or ten thousand copies, whereas he thought the memoir should sell at least a quarter million, possibly double that number. Twain had first planned to direct Grant to the American Publishing Company and "enrich that den of reptiles."[24] Instead, Twain issued a startling offer: "General, I am publishing my own book [*Huck Finn*], and by the time yours is ready it is quite possible that I shall have the best equipped subscription establishment in the country. If you will place your book with my firm . . . I will pay you twenty per cent of the list price, or, if you prefer, I will give you seventy per cent of the net returns."[25] It was a move of breathtaking daring, coupled with a fair bit of chutzpah, given Grant's advanced talks with the *Century*. In a still more extravagant gesture—Twain loved playing the tycoon—he offered to write a $50,000 check to Grant on the spot as an advance for a two-volume memoir.

Shaken by the encounter, Grant consulted with his old friend George W. Childs of the Philadelphia *Public Ledger,* who registered his opinion that Charles L. Webster and Company could publish the book as profitably as Twain claimed. Yet it still bothered Grant's conscience that he had entered into negotiations with the *Century*. He thought it was they who had suggested the idea for the memoir and likely considered them deserving to publish it, when, in fact, Twain had already done so three years earlier. As Twain recalled, "He thought it placed him in the attitude of a robber—robber of a publisher. I said that if he regarded that as a crime it was because his education had been neglected. I said it was not a crime, and was always rewarded in heaven with two halos."[26] As Grant pondered the Charles L. Webster and Company offer, Twain, the short-lived Confederate militiaman, tried to round up another renowned Union general and publish his memoirs: Philip H. Sheridan. "I beg to introduce to you Mr. C.L. Webster, who may not succeed with the conspiracy which he has in mind, but I very much hope he *will*," Twain wrote the bantam general, perhaps hoping a Sheridan contract would sway Grant.[27] It was now clear that Twain was thinking of his new publishing firm in far more ambitious terms than before, even as the commercial success of *Huck Finn* might have pushed him in a more literary direction. Once Grant's contract was signed, Twain would temporarily halt his own career as a writer and lecturer to become a publisher.

As Twain went off barnstorming with Cable, Charley Webster sustained the Grant relationship and regularly dropped by his house, telling Twain in mid-February that he expected to score a major killing on the book. "There's big money for us both in that book and on the terms indicated in my note to the General we can make it pay *big*. I know it is a good deal of an undertaking but we can carry it through and make a clean sweep."[28] "Your news is splendid," replied Twain, saying that robust sales of *Huck Finn* "sets my fears about at rest as regards the General's book. It *insures* a sudden sale of 250,000 copies of the first volume."[29] It now looked as if he would have two best-selling books on his hands to initiate his publishing venture, and his mind reeled with visions of sudden riches.

On February 26, 1885, Twain went to Grant's home, aiming to clinch the deal that would give Grant 70 percent of the profits for his memoirs. From newspaper reports, Twain had gathered that Grant's medical condition was improving, but he was "astonished to see how thin & weak he looked."[30] When Twain mentioned to Grant the hopeful newspaper commentary, Grant smiled wistfully and said, "Yes,—if it had only been true."[31] Grant announced that he had decided to publish with Charles L. Webster and Company, but, being a gentleman, wanted to write first to his *Century* editor, Roswell Smith, and "tell him I have so decided. I think this is due him."[32] Whatever jubilation Twain felt was tempered when Grant's son Fred stopped him on his way out "and stunned me by telling me confidentially that the physicians were trying to keep his father's real condition from him, but that in fact they considered him to be under sentence of death and that he would not be likely to live more than a fortnight or three weeks longer."[33] Grant had already written the first volume of his *Memoirs* and much of the second, so he was not exactly starting from scratch. Nevertheless, the news from Grant's son must have made it seem doubtful that Grant would ever survive to finish the manuscript.

With Grant's contract in hand, Twain had catapulted Charles L. Webster and Company almost overnight into a major publishing operation. By May 1, orders for the two-volume memoir had reached sixty thousand sets. Webster moved the firm into new quarters, a full fancy floor in a building overlooking Union Square. Later on, Twain would fault Webster for extravagance, but he did not block the move. On the contrary, he grew starry-eyed at how young Charley was handling the Grant commission, telling Orion that Grant "conceived a liking for [Charley] & confidence in him. Charley has tackled the vastest book-enterprise the world has ever seen, with a calm cool head & a capable hand, & is carrying it along in a serene unhalting fashion which is fine to see."[34] By autumn, Grant's *Memoirs* had twenty presses at work night and day along with seven large binderies to fill the order. Webster monopolized so much of the printing capacity in New York that competing publishers had to manufacture their books in distant cities. Webster took delight in conjuring up the project's unprecedented scale, stating that the paper used for Grant's *Memoirs* "would make a ribbon . . . one inch wide which would stretch seven and one third . . . times around the world."[35]

Webster boasted that the firm he headed was now "the finest subscription publishing office in the world," and the heart of the operation consisted of a team of sixteen general sales agents and ten thousand canvassers going door-to-door booking orders.[36] Twain and Webster assembled a thirty-seven-page manual full of advice for salesmen touting Grant's *Memoirs,* including such cynical advice as "Avoid men in groups as you would poison" and "One of the strongest arguments that can be used to get a man's order is by telling him of his influence."[37] Twain also told Webster to hire as many Union army veterans as possible and have them sport their Grand Army badges as they canvassed for the general's book. They were told to avoid "the Bull Run voice" and to "keep pouring *hot shot*" until prospective customers submitted.

On March 3, 1885, the *New York Times* posted a small item announcing that Twain's firm had signed up Grant's memoirs, and it didn't touch off any immediate controversy with the *Century* people. In fact, a couple of weeks later, the *Century* editor Robert Underwood Johnson wrote to Twain to solicit a contribution for its Civil War series, saying the magazine was eager to enlist "yourself among the eminent rebels."[38] Although Twain agreed, he deferred writing it until summer, and in December the *Century* published his tragicomic account of his two-week Civil War service, "The Private History of a Campaign That Failed." Here and elsewhere, Twain played the war for comedy, satirizing his own cowardice, and Johnson reinforced this approach. "Don't fail to bring out clearly," he told Twain, "that you were the only Confederate that Grant really feared."[39] But on occasion, Twain gave voice to a darker vision of what had happened. In a letter several years later, he said he "was hunted like a rat the whole time" and that "death-on-the-pale-horse-with-hell-following-after" was "a raw soldier's first fortnight in the field . . . which . . . is the most tremendous fortnight and the vividest he is ever going to see."[40]

Twain was enraged in July when the *Boston Herald* alleged that he had stooped to unscrupulous methods to lure Grant from the *Century* people, leading the general to break an "understanding" with them. In Twain's mind, the *Century* had behaved shabbily in offering Grant an insultingly low royalty. It bothered him, too, that Grant's integrity was being impeached, and Twain reacted with a vigorous rebuttal. He was never a turn-the-other-cheek author. "I seem to be fast getting the reputation in the newspapers, of being a pushing, pitiless, underhanded sharper—but I don't quite deserve it. General Grant was *considering* the *Century*'s offer for his book—that is all; there was no 'understanding.'" He noted that he had offered Grant terms that would double his profits and that Grant had "the wisdom to decline the Century offer."[41] The *Century* editor William W. Ellsworth later commented, "There never was any feeling in our office against Mark Twain for taking away the Grant book. He continued to write for The Century and . . . was on the best of terms with every one about the place."[42]

Twain got to know Grant well at a time of excruciating pain for the general, when it tortured him to swallow food or drink water. He was amazed at how mildly Grant discussed Ferdinand Ward, who had impoverished him: "*he never uttered a phrase concerning Ward which an outraged adult might not have uttered concerning an offending child.*"[43] Twain felt deeply for Grant's financial plight and grew angry on his behalf. "As for myself I was inwardly boiling all the time: I was scalping Ward, flaying him alive, breaking him on the wheel, pounding him to jelly, and cursing him with all the profanity known to the one language that I am acquainted with."[44]

Convinced though he was that Grant's memoirs would be the best-selling book in American history, Twain knew the cancer was incurable, and many times in March and April Grant's death seemed imminent. To finish the book, Twain realized, would be "a colossal task for a dying man."[45] Church bells across the nation were poised to toll sixty-three times (Grant's age) the moment he died. To assist with the writing, Twain hired for Grant a stenographer named Noble E. Dawson, and Grant managed to switch successfully to dictation, his words pouring out with remarkable speed and clarity. For his part, Twain was uncharacteristically speechless when Grant dictated ten thousand words in a single sitting. "In two days General Grant has dictated 50 pages of foolscap, & thus the Wilderness [campaign] & Appomattox stand for all time in his own words," Twain reported.[46] He regarded Grant with reverence and admired his lean style, yet he never ventured to compliment him. Then a member of Grant's household confided that Grant was disappointed that Twain had never offered an opinion of his writing. "I was as much surprised as Columbus's cook would have been to learn that Columbus wanted his opinion as to how Columbus was doing his navigation."[47] For all his fame, Grant was still a first-time author needing encouragement, and Twain told him that he placed his memoirs on the same lofty plateau as *Caesar's Commentaries*. "I learned afterward that General Grant was pleased with this verdict. It shows that he was just a man, just a human being, just an author."[48]

To edit the memoir, Grant had enlisted his old military secretary from the war, General Adam Badeau, who probably leaked a story to the *New York World* in early May that claimed that he was the ghostwriter of the book. Grant had always prided himself on his writing skills—he had written all his wartime orders and presidential speeches—and he grew furious at the insinuation. The litigious Twain urged Fred Grant to institute a libel suit with "damages placed at nothing less than $250,000 or $300,000; no apologies accepted from the World, & no compromise permitted for anything but a sum of money that will cripple—yes, *disable*—that paper financially."[49] After Grant dictated an eloquent letter denying Badeau's allegations, Twain ensured it got wide circulation in the New York press. Suddenly, all mention of Badeau's charges stopped, leading Twain to retract his idea of a libel suit, which would only give the *New York World*—"that daily issue of unmedicated closet-paper"— free publicity.[50] Despite rumors naming Twain as the book's secret author, in truth he strictly limited his editorial interventions to grammar and punctuation.

As Grant raced to finish his book before he died, the mood was often somber, yet he and Twain found lighthearted moments of camaraderie. In late May, Grant read Twain's wartime reminiscence, "The Private History of a Campaign That Failed," and both were surprised to discover that their early wartime campaigns in Missouri had nearly coincided. In August 1861, Grant had pounced on an empty Confederate camp near Florida, Missouri (where Twain was born), and Twain's own militia had occupied that same spot a month or two earlier. (Twain claimed, wrongly, that they had missed each other by a day or two.) Twain told Grant that "I did not know that this was the future General Grant, or I would have turned & attacked him. I supposed it was just some ordinary Colonel of no particular consequence, & so I let him go."[51] The two men laughed over the strange coincidence. "It is curious & dreadful," Twain admitted in his notebook, "to sit up this way & talk cheerful nonsense to Gen. Grant & he under sentence of death with that cancer."[52] Surely Grant found some temporary relief from pain in Twain's therapeutic humor.

Ever since Karl Gerhardt had returned from Paris, Twain had searched for ways to forward his career, albeit not without some frustration. He advised Karl to seek employment in the workshop of Augustus Saint-Gaudens or John Quincy Adams Ward, which would provide training and steady income, but the sculptor reacted like a prima donna: "*I am willing and glad to start in a small way, but I must be independent or it's the end of my career . . . don't make me be a second fiddle that would kill me.*"[53] It was the first sign of a conceited, headstrong streak that would be Gerhardt's undoing. For weeks, Gerhardt labored over a bust of

PURE MUGWUMP

Twain at Quarry Farm that proved an excellent likeness. Still playing Pygmalion, Twain told Major Pond that he wished to commission Gerhardt to make medallions of him and George Washington Cable for their lecture tour. "I want the things to be made by *Gerhardt*—it will advertise him."[54] Twain also got Gerhardt a coveted commission to sculpt Henry Ward Beecher.

Yet even as he generously landed premier clients for Gerhardt, Twain had an intuition their relationship would end badly, telling his notebook in German: "The principal feature of Gerhardt's character is thanklessness. Don't forget this statement."[55] With Twain's assistance, Gerhardt sought a prestigious commission to sculpt a statue of the Connecticut patriot Nathan Hale for the state capitol in Hartford, the decision to be made by a committee. After Twain returned from his travels with Cable, he was shocked that Gerhardt hadn't accomplished a shred of remunerative work. "Gerhardt had waited four long months on that committee . . . and I was thoroughly provoked. I told him that he ought to have had more pride than to permit me to support him and his family during all that time with no assistance from his idle hands . . . that he ought to have been shoveling snow, sawing wood, all these four months, and that the revelation that he had been so engaged would have been a credit to him in anybody's eyes."[56] This started a slow-motion deterioration in their relationship. No longer were the Gerhardts seen as pure, idealistic souls.

By far the biggest favor Twain conferred on Gerhardt was slipping him into the inner circle of the dying Grant. Fond of a small bust of Grant that Gerhardt had crafted from a photograph, Twain took the sculptor along to Grant's house on March 20, 1885, and persuaded the family to allow him to study the general and refine his bust. Julia Grant ushered him in to meet her husband, who lay back in his easy chair, a scarf wrapped around the cancerous tumor bulging from his neck. Grant responded favorably and invited Gerhardt to bring in his clay and set up a worktable while he dozed for an hour. When Grant was awake, his expression hid his pain, but when his face relaxed in sleep, it creased his features, allowing Gerhardt to capture the sad, downcast Grant rather than Grant in his prime. Twain possessed an ulterior motive, hoping to use a photograph of the bust as a frontispiece for Grant's *Personal Memoirs*. Twain considered Gerhardt's terra-cotta bust "the best likeness of the General ever made, in clay, oil or any other way," and it promised to acquire great commercial value as the last such work made while Grant was alive.[57] Twain also knew that a quarter of the royalties from the Grant bust would be paid to him by Gerhardt in repayment for the generous loan he had extended to finance his Paris stay.

Gerhardt was intent upon securing rights to create the death mask of General Grant, even when faced with a competing claim by sculptor James Wilson Alexander MacDonald. Twain balked at lobbying the Grant family, explaining in his notebook that "I could not bring myself to be a party to the request, there is something so dreadful about it."[58] Nevertheless, Gerhardt persisted and got the necessary permission from Fred Grant, a fact that suited Twain, who realized a "mask must be made when the General dies, & it is so much better that Gerhardt who is honest & whom the family know, should do it than some tricky stranger."[59]

On June 16, a frail, shrunken Grant shuffled from his Manhattan town house and took a train from Grand Central Terminal up to Saratoga, New York, his doctors having convinced him that the pine-scented air atop Mount McGregor would act as a tonic to his health. By this point, Grant had essentially finished the second volume but still had pencil revisions to make, and he invited Twain to join him upstate in late June. As the cancer burrowed deeper into Grant's throat and tongue, he was reduced to scribbling terse messages on paper strips, and Twain was stirred by his stoic fortitude. "He made no braver fight in the field than he made on his death-bed."[60] Grant had undertaken the memoir to guarantee his wife's financial security, and he now inquired anxiously as to whether the proceeds would protect her. Luckily, Twain could tell him that canvassers had already taken orders for more than 100,000 two-volume sets and that the final amount would be at least double that. Grant wrote down his extreme pleasure at this news.

In these final months, Twain had grown to adore Grant and regarded their relationship as one of the highlights of his life. He felt tenderness and awe as he watched Grant dying with such dignity. On July 1, Twain wrote to Livy that "the General is as placid, serene, & self-possessed as ever, & his eye has the same old humorous twinkle in it, & his frequent smile is still the smile of pleasantness & peace. Manifestly, dying is nothing to a really great & brave man."[61] Twain's last glimpse was of the general sitting with his shawl around his shoulders, pencil and paper at his side. On July 18, 1885, Charley Webster went up to Mount McGregor to collect the completed manuscript, and Grant died five days later. Twain had not the slightest doubt that Grant, with his matchless willpower, had forced himself to stay alive to complete the project and save his family. "He would have died three months ago, if his book had been completed," Twain told Livy. "I am satisfied of that."[62] For all his cynicism, Twain found in Grant an irreproachable character, a man of exemplary simplicity, kindness, and modesty. A decade later he called him "the greatest man I have ever had the privilege of knowing personally. And I have not known a man with a kinder nature or a purer character."[63]

As bells rang and flags flew at half-staff, the nation began to prepare for the spectacular pageantry of Grant's funeral, befitting his status as the foremost living American. Twain already had teams of printers and binders hustling around the clock, and the *New York Sun* could not resist jabbing at him with a cynical piece titled "Mark Twain's Big Speculation." "The man heavily enriched by Grant's death is Mark Twain . . . The shrewd humorist had to risk his entire fortune in the enterprise."[64] Since the article implied that Twain and Charley Webster would split profits evenly with Julia Grant from the book, the two men published a letter in the *New York Times,* affirming that Julia Grant would "receive nearly three-fourths of the profits arising from the sale of the book, and upon some sales even more."[65]

When a competition arose among several cities to house Grant's tomb, Twain leaped into the controversy with a strongly worded plea for New York. "But as long as American civilization lasts New York will last . . . Twenty centuries from now New York will still be New York, still a vast city, & the most notable object in it will still be the tomb & monument of Gen. Grant."[66] In the end, the Grant family chose Riverside Park in

Manhattan, overlooking the Hudson River, as the site, partly because the city promised Julia she could lie buried beside her husband and partly because a New York site would make it easier for her to visit her husband's resting place. It was not often that Twain regretted a decision, but he soon believed his involvement in the controversy was unseemly; coming from Grant's publisher, it might strike some as a crass advertisement for the book. "It is very seldom that I have an uncomfortable sensation; it is still more seldom that I apply for one. When a man deliberately offends other folk, he invites sorrow; when he deliberately offends himself, he insures it."[67]

On August 8, Twain kept a solemn vigil for five hours as he watched Grant's funeral procession from a window of Webster and Company at 14th Street and Union Square. The general's coffin was mounted beneath a catafalque pulled by twenty-four black horses, and tens of thousands of veterans marched in the great procession. The town was draped in black, with huge photos of Grant posted in store windows against black backdrops. Porticos, capitals, columns—everything was cloaked in black fabric. At the Fifth Avenue Hotel, Twain sat over whiskey and cigars with General William Tecumseh Sherman and pondered Grant's personality, with Sherman declaring of Grant's military genius, "Never anything like it before."[68] During the day, Twain also chatted with Grant's other outstanding wartime deputy, General Philip Sheridan.

The emotional occasion confirmed Twain's improbable metamorphosis from southern militiaman to confidant of Union generals. When asked, a few days later, to address a gathering of Union veterans, he replied, "I am very proud to have you tell me the boys out there consider me 'one of them'; & some day I shall hope to break bread with them again," but he was now "overwhelmed with engagements & business for months to come."[69] Twain's heroes were now northern heroes; he never published a Confederate general. The only one he even considered was James Longstreet, who had become anathema in the South from his support for Reconstruction.[70] In later years, Twain remarked, "Thousands of geniuses live and die undiscovered . . . But for the Civil War, Lincoln and Grant and Sherman and Sheridan would not have been discovered, nor have risen into notice."[71] The list is telling. Twain thought Lincoln's Gettysburg Address had no peer in the English language other than *Morte d'Arthur*, and he recorded this harsh comment in his notebook: "Advantage to Jeff Davis if he'd never been born."[72] Sherman had long been the bugbear of the South, but when he lay dying in 1891, Twain told him that "I, like all the rest of this nation, grieve to think that the kindest heart & the most noble spirit that exist to-day are about to be taken away from us."[73] Sherman died the next day.

Sales of *Personal Memoirs of U. S. Grant* amply vindicated the pledges Twain had made to the general. In the end, it sold three hundred thousand copies of the two-volume set, netting Julia Grant a whopping $450,000. When Twain handed her the first check for $200,000, it counted as the biggest royalty check in history. After the book's appearance in December, Twain stopped by the Grant residence and found a jubilant Julia Grant hugging "three of the new books affectionately . . . She was in a happy mood, & very proud of the handsome appearance of the book & the unimpeachable excellence of the paper, print, & binding."[74] The book's critical reception matched the hyperbole Twain had lavished on its inimitable style. "The general verdict upon General Grant's Memoirs," announced the *New York Evening Post*, "is that the book at once takes its place among the great histories of the world."[75] That judicious critic, William Dean Howells, chimed in: "I think he [Grant] is one of the most natural—that is, *best*—writers I ever read. The book merits its enormous success, simply as literature."[76]

The publication was a staggering logistical feat, and Twain spent months in Manhattan, riding herd on the seven binderies cranking out copies. With a touch of paranoia, he urged Webster to keep Grant's proofs locked in his safe at night, lest "thieves & bribers" steal them.[77] However certain he felt about the book's success, he had to deal with the enormous financial strain. "I need every penny I can raise," he told his mother in June, predicting accurately that he would have to borrow $100,000 to bring the book to fruition.[78] He was taking giant risks that he could not well afford since the Grant book entailed crushing outlays of money. "Since last March, you know," he told Howells in October, "I am carrying a mighty load, solitary & alone ... From now till the first of January every dollar is as valuable to me as it could be to a famishing tramp."[79]

By January 1, 1886, with sales brisk, Twain was out of debt and hugely relieved, but the phenomenal success of the Grant memoirs ended up having a detrimental impact on his career. It convinced him that he had a magnificent head for publishing when he was likely the beneficiary of an extreme case of beginner's luck. Money pouring in from the book led him to turn his back on his own literary talents and concentrate on his mediocre business skills instead. After *Huck Finn,* Twain didn't perpetrate another volume on the reading public for four and a half years. His experience with the Grant tome should have alerted him to the danger of his furnishing all the capital and shouldering any losses for Charles L. Webster and Company. In retrospect, Twain cursed Grant's *Memoirs* as "That terrible book! which made money for everybody concerned but me."[80] This was not really true: in his notebook for spring 1887, he listed his profits on the *Memoirs* at $93,481 (or about $3 million in present-day money).[81] Twain also blamed the book for inflating Webster's vanity to dangerous proportions. "Webster was in his glory ... He loved to descant upon the wonders of the book."[82] This critical perspective, it should be noted, only came with hindsight: at the time, Twain thought Charley had pulled off a publishing miracle with the Grant book, and he raised his partner's salary and share of the profits.

Thanks to Twain, the dying Grant had proved a bonanza to Karl Gerhardt, who had insinuated himself into the good graces of the Grant clan. In Grant's final weeks at McGregor, Twain was upset by criticism that Gerhardt was ghoulishly standing by and waiting to do the death mask; he urged him to pack up and leave at once. "The General sick all these months, the family distressed, worried ... don't you see, it is a most easy thing for you to become a burden & one too many."[83] Twain's queasy suspicion that there was something pushy about Gerhardt proved

PURE MUGWUMP

correct. On October 25, 1885, the *New York Times* ran a piece that made a shocking charge of greed against the sculptor. "The death mask which was allowed to be taken from Gen. Grant with such undue haste by the young sculptor, Karl Gerhardt, is held by him as his private property"— an allegation Gerhardt himself confirmed. The report concluded that "the mask belongs to the Grant family, not to Mr. Gerhardt."[84]

Twain sided with Gerhardt's critics and believed the sculptor should yield the mask unconditionally to the Grants; Julia Grant would then have the option of giving him exclusive rights to the mask for a limited time. Despite the incalculable debt he owed to Twain and the Grants, Karl Gerhardt was adamant that he wouldn't hand over the mask to the family unless he were paid $17,000. Crestfallen, Twain told Charley Webster that he was "full of solicitude & shan't feel easy & comfortable till it is settled to Mrs. Grant's satisfaction."[85] To avoid scandal and a lawsuit that would not only hurt the Grant family at a time of mourning but also slash sales of the *Memoirs,* Twain proposed to forgive $17,000 in debt that Gerhardt owed him for his Paris education if Gerhardt delivered the death mask to the family. Twain was angling to get a contract for Julia Grant's letters and probably regarded the lost $17,000 as a business expense. On December 21, Gerhardt seems to have agreed to this deal, although he had furtively made a copy of Grant's death mask for his own future use.

For years, Karl Gerhardt continued to attempt to cash in on the Twain connection, seeking his help with commissions and even a permanent job at Charles L. Webster and Company. At one point, he asked if Twain wanted to build a factory for his Paige typesetter on some land he owned in Hartford. With Karl and Hattie Gerhardt a chronic drain on his time and money, Twain distanced himself from the couple. Hattie died in 1897—the "victim of a rusty nail," said Karl—but by then Twain had mostly lost touch with them.[86] Karl sank ever lower in the artistic universe and ended up as a tailor in Shreveport, Louisiana.

With the Gerhardts, Twain had again shown a tendency to be excessively trusting and generous only to end up feeling betrayed. Ingratitude was to form a recurrent theme in his writing. He even wrote a work titled "About Magnanimous Incident Literature," whose theme was that no good deed goes unpunished. In it, Twain told tales of virtue rewarded, then gave them a different, more realistic slant, showing how the recipients of kindness became greedy and tyrannical instead of grateful. In *Pudd'nhead Wilson,* Twain included the following aphorism: "If you pick up a starving dog and make him prosperous, he will not bite you. This is the principal difference between a dog and a man."[87]

Mark Twain stands in Nikola Tesla's laboratory as a high-tension current passes through him and lights an incandescent lamp. Tesla is faintly visible on the far left.

Jane Lampton Clemens as an elderly woman. Her vivacity, spunk, and eloquence had a lasting influence on her son.

Sam Clemens, just turning fifteen, proudly poses as a printer's devil in Hannibal, Missouri, November 29, 1850.

MARK TWAIN'S SIBLINGS

Orion: An odd, endearing but quixotic character, he forever labored in the shadow of his younger brother.

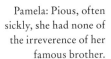

Pamela: Pious, often sickly, she had none of the irreverence of her famous brother.

Henry: The adored younger brother whose death in a steamboat explosion on the Mississippi fed lifelong pangs of guilt in Mark Twain.

This photo of Livy Clemens, taken in 1872–73, shows the beauty and purity that so powerfully attracted Mark Twain when they married in 1870.

Jervis Langdon and Olivia Lewis Langdon, Livy's parents, not only brought immense wealth into Twain's life, but a philanthropic spirit and a profound sense of racial justice.

Sam, Livy, and their three daughters pose on the veranda of the Hartford house in 1884 during an idyllic time for the family.

This picture of Susy was taken in Florence, Italy, in 1892, soon after her tumultuous year at Bryn Mawr College.

TWAIN AND THE BLACK COMMUNITY

Mary Ann Cord, the formidable cook at Quarry Farm whose story Twain narrated in the *Atlantic Monthly*.

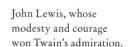

John Lewis, whose modesty and courage won Twain's admiration.

George Griffin, the longtime Black butler in Hartford, in a recently discovered photo of him. Smart, elegant, and enterprising, he was a notable figure in the local Black community.

MARK TWAIN'S COMPANIONS

Mark Twain at Stormfield with novelist and critic William Dean Howells, whose unfailing support helped to secure Twain's literary reputation.

Joseph H. Twichell, the hearty and worldly Hartford pastor who was likely his dearest friend.

Henry H. Rogers, the shrewd Standard Oil mogul who saved Twain from imminent financial ruin.

Mark Twain and George Washington Cable in 1884, when they shared top billing in a lecture series later dubbed the 'Twins of Genius" tour.

Twain in 1874 in his octagonal writing study at Quarry Farm, where he wrote much of his best fiction during the long summers spent there.

CHAPTER TWENTY-THREE

Reparation Due to Every Black Man

Right on the eve of publishing Grant's *Memoirs*, Livy celebrated her fortieth and Sam his fiftieth birthday. The year 1885 represented a pinnacle of happiness for Twain, who had attained peak success as an author with *Huck Finn*, as a publisher with the Grant memoir, and as a lecturer with the extended George Washington Cable tour. All the while he was blessed with a marriage of mutual adoration. When Twain was on the road, Livy always missed him and sent him loving letters: "Youth darling I long for you uncommonly tonight . . . you are sweet and good and I do delight in you."[1] She recognized his shortcomings but made allowances. "You are sometimes bad," she teased him, "but then life is much more interesting when you are here."[2] The couple enjoyed a halcyon period with their three bright, beautiful, and affectionate daughters. On February 2, 1885, their fifteenth wedding anniversary, Twain told Livy how he loved her dearly when they married, but even "more dearly now."[3]

By this point, Twain, as a writer, had mostly emptied the larder of his past—the "half-forgotten Paradise" of his Hannibal boyhood, the steamboat idyll on the Mississippi, the western mining towns.[4] In the future, he would need to unearth new sources of inspiration and would struggle to find equally productive terrain. For all his present joy, he bore a heavy load of nostalgia for his glorious early days. That summer he went twice to see the Wild West show of William F. "Buffalo Bill" Cody and sent the impresario his congratulations. When he read Howells's novel *Indian*

Summer, he said it made the reader feel "so old & so forlorn; & gives him gracious glimpses of his lost youth that fill him with a measureless regret, & build up in him a cloudy sense of his having been a prince, once, in some enchanted far-off land, & of being an exile now, & desolate—& Lord, no chance to ever get back there again!"[5]

The pangs of disappointment clashed incongruously with the gracious, civilized life Twain enjoyed with his family. When Livy turned forty, she came down to breakfast to find a selection of lovely gifts from her family: a shapely copper vase from her husband, a blotter adorned in sepia watercolor from Susy, a tiny Japanese matchbox from Clara, and a little steel device from Jean to protect her sleeves. When Twain turned fifty, the *Critic* ran a stunning string of laudatory essays and, at Livy's request, a poem by Oliver Wendell Holmes. Charles Dudley Warner averred that few had done as much as Mark Twain "for the entertainment and good fellowship of the world," while Joel Chandler Harris claimed he had "earned the right to grow old and mellow. He has put his youth in his books, and there it is perennial."[6] Yet for Twain these literary honors, however much appreciated, could never compare with the recollected joy of those golden summers vouchsafed to a barefoot boy in a Missouri backwater.

Despite his severe disappointment in Karl Gerhardt, Twain plunged into another act of creative philanthropy that proved far more consequential. In fall 1885, he went to New Haven to address the Kent Club, a debating society at Yale Law School, and was greeted at the train station by the club's president, a young Black man named Warner T. McGuinn. McGuinn had attended Lincoln University, a historically Black college in Pennsylvania, and had supported himself by checking hats at a Rhode Island casino during the summer. Before entering Yale, he had studied law in Washington with Richard Greener, the first Black graduate of Harvard. Once at Yale, he boarded with the college's Black carpenter and held down a host of part-time jobs to survive. On Christmas morning 1885, he received an invitation to dine with Dean Francis Wayland but was forced to decline because he did not possess a proper suit.

It soon became apparent that McGuinn had won the admiration of a

REPARATION DUE TO EVERY BLACK MAN

very special benefactor. On Christmas Eve, with his Grant profits on the horizon, Twain wrote to Wayland to inquire about McGuinn. "Do you know him? And is he worthy? I do not believe I would very cheerfully help a white student who would ask a benevolence of a stranger, but I do not feel so about the other color. We have ground the manhood out of them, & the shame is ours, not theirs; & we should pay for it. If this young man lives as economically as it is the duty & should be the pride of one to do who is straitened, I would like to know what the cost is, so that I may send 6, 12, or 24 months' board, as the size of the bill may determine."[7]

This generous offer provides a window into Twain's racial attitudes quite unlike his satirical writings, which can be subjected to varied interpretations. When Wayland responded promptly on Christmas Day, he offered encouragement: "I think the colored youth is a promising case & deserving of help from someone . . . I am glad you are interested in this matter & thank you for writing to me."[8] Five days later, Wayland rendered a still more generous assessment: "McGuinn is very studious, & well behaved, above the middle of a very good class & very anxious to succeed. I think him & so do other members of the faculty a very deserving man . . . I have loaned him books out of my own law library & we have given him indefinite extension as to tuition."[9] The financial aid Twain promised would free McGuinn to concentrate solely on his studies, and Twain would end up covering his entire board for his remaining year and a half at the law school. Twain had devised his own form of racial reparations. As Howells noted, "He held himself responsible for the wrong which the white race had done the black race in slavery, and he explained, in paying the way of a negro student through Yale, that he was doing it as his part of the reparation due from every white to every black man."[10] Not many white Americans—especially those who grew up amid slavery—would have acknowledged white guilt so forthrightly, much less expressed the need to make amends. With Twain it was not just talk but backed up by good deeds.

Warner McGuinn thrived on the scholarship money Twain advanced. When Dean Wayland renewed the money request in October 1886, he gave it his emphatic endorsement, saying that McGuinn "was last year by his examination considerably above the average of his class." He deemed McGuinn, "on the whole, the most promising colored youth we have ever had"—he was only the fourth Black student in the law school's history—and before he graduated he had won a distinguished oratory award.[11] Twain was so pleased that he was fully prepared to underwrite the expenses of a second Black student, Charles W. Johnson, who did not end up attending Yale Law School.

For McGuinn, his legal education prepared him for a career of spectacular and lasting accomplishment. He edited a Black newspaper in Kansas City, Kansas, before moving to Baltimore, where he argued cases for women's suffrage and won a landmark ruling against the city's segregated housing. In addition to establishing a branch of the NAACP and serving on the city council, he befriended and counseled a young lawyer in an adjoining office named Thurgood Marshall, who would argue *Brown v. Board of Education* before the Supreme Court in 1954 and ascend as the high court's first African American justice. "He was one of the greatest lawyers who ever lived," Marshall said of McGuinn after his death. "If he had been white, he'd have been a judge."[12]

The McGuinn aid wasn't the first time Twain had subsidized a Black student. In August 1882, he had communicated with Lincoln University and offered to provide scholarship money to a worthy student. An agent of the school, the Reverend J. Chester, informed Twain that the faculty had selected A. W. Jones of Wilson, North Carolina, who would enter as a freshman that fall. Four years later, after Jones graduated near the top of his class and decided to become a preacher, Chester contacted Twain in the hope of securing further aid for his postgraduate theological studies. For Twain, with his complicated feelings toward clergy, this was a bridge too far to cross. "Of course I made no *stipulation* that would hamper my student in the slightest degree in choosing a profession—I would rather starve a man than curtail his liberty in any way. No, I merely hoped he would make choice of some useful occupation; he has disappointed me, & I feel no further interest in him."[13] Twain apparently believed Chester had misled him about Jones's professional objectives,

REPARATION DUE TO EVERY BLACK MAN

and in his notebook, he unleashed scathing epithets, deriding him as a "humbug," a "clerical fraud," and a "bilk."[14]

Twain's indignation toward slavery only intensified through the years. In 1886 he threw his prestige behind an effort to give Prudence Crandall Philleo, whom Twain dubbed the "Connecticut anti-slavery heroine of 53 years ago," an annuity of $400.[15] For having dared to educate Black females, she had been terrorized by mobs and forced to shutter her school. "It is a matter of great surprise to me," she wrote to Twain gratefully, "that any one could be so kind to an old woman like me."[16] When America celebrated the centennial of the Constitution's ratification in 1888, Twain scrawled tartly in the margin of a book: "Human liberty—for white people—may fairly be said to be one hundred years old this year."[17] That same year, he was quoted in the *New Princeton Review* as stating that "we used to own our brother human beings, and used to buy them and sell them, lash them, thrash them, break their piteous hearts—and we ought to be ashamed of ourselves."[18] The more Twain contemplated slavery, the more he wondered at the deep-seated human capacity for sadistic behavior. In the late 1880s, he recorded this pessimistic insight: "There are in Conn[ecticut], at this moment & in all countries, children & disagreeable relatives chained in cellars, all sores, welts, worms & vermin . . . 2 recent cases in our state. This is to suggest that the thing in man which makes him cruel to a slave is in him permanently & will not be rooted out for a million years."[19]

During these years, Twain showed dramatic progress in his hitherto benighted views of Native Americans. In a speech to the New England Society of Philadelphia in December 1881, he shocked the audience by condemning the Pilgrims for annihilating the American Indian. "Your ancestors skinned him alive."[20] The shift was also made plain in a notebook entry of May 1882, when he wrote that the federal government had spent $2 million to kill two hundred Indians. Twain's blunt response: "You could have given them a college education for that."[21] Still more striking was his response to a New Mexico newspaper article announcing that Grant County would offer a $250 reward "to any citizen of said county for each and every hostile renegade Apache killed by such citizen, on presentation to said board of the scalp of such Indian."[22] Twain expressed his horror in an impassioned letter to President Grover Cleveland. "What can be said of a people that will tolerate the publication of such an atrocious reward for murder and outrage! . . . Because there have been terrible outrages perpetrated on settlers by a handful of renegade Apaches, a notice is issued which makes the civil authorities parties to the murder of every Indian who may fall a victim to the cupidity of reckless cowboys or outlaw frontiersmen."[23] Since Twain quoted a speech by Francis Wayland of Yale Law School, who had denounced a massacre of 125 Apaches, it seems likely that the dean had instigated Twain's forceful letter.

Now that Twain had shifted his focus to publishing, he could never make up his mind about how much time he cared to devote to business. He demanded weekly reports from Charley Webster and prodded him to compile a list of things to track, telling him to "stick it on the wall where you can see it when you go to bed & when you get up."[24] Beyond publishing, Webster had to attend to assorted inventions Twain had contrived, such as the clamp for children's beds. "Even $2 is much too low for the bed-clamp," Twain advised Webster. "If I go into it eventually, it must be at $2.25 for small size, and $3 for the large."[25] It is amazing that an author of Twain's stature got bogged down in such petty minutiae of business.

Nevertheless, the contradictory Twain kept telling Webster, as if scolding a wayward child, not to bother him with business matters. "You are there to take care of my business, not make business for *me* to take care of . . . I want no business that I must look personally after."[26] At other times, encouraged by his wife, Twain assumed a more caring manner. "Livy told me the other day that she wished to warn you against overwork . . . overwork killed Mr. Langdon, & it can kill you."[27] There was no recognition that Twain himself was heaping excessive work on

Charley, who had to chase down furniture for Livy and measure bureau drawers. For all his fits of pique, Twain voiced admiration for his nephew's hard work and acumen, telling Annie Webster that her husband "has had a most tremendous season of hard work & watching . . . but he has come through it with a superb record; & with all its array of business-inventions, ingenuities & triumphs, he has not made a single business misstep, that I am aware of."[28] When Twain wooed William Tecumseh Sherman to write a book, he told the general that "good generalship is as necessary in the publishing field as in the military field; & Webster has shown much the best generalship I have ever seen in the former—both in the handling of my last book & now General Grant's."[29]

The contract that Webster negotiated with Twain in March 1885 had restricted the profits the latter could withdraw from the firm. When $100,000 was needed to cover the costs of printing Grant's *Memoirs*, Twain resented that he alone had to borrow the money and bear a solitary load. "Charley is legally correct when he says that *you* are bound to furnish all the capital," the lawyer Daniel Whitford informed Twain.[30] A novice in business, Twain was beginning to comprehend the perils of subscription publishing. As he later grumbled, "The money-borrowing . . . made bad blood for this reason. I went home & borrowed it, and gave notice of the fact [to Webster], & got some impudence in return. I sent a rude telegram. It brought me a brutal letter—the letter of a hog."[31]

Twain would blame Webster for poor book selections, but Twain himself always hovered as the tutelary spirit of the publishing house, bringing many projects to Charley, and he enjoyed veto power over new books. Many choices reflected Twain's interests and personal connections. That November, Twain received a manuscript from his old friend Rollin M. Daggett, once minister to the Sandwich Islands, who sought a publisher for a book he had written with the islands' king about the folklore of the common people. Twain would publish it only if the king were listed as coauthor. "I said we preferred to keep up our standard, & be known in the world as a house that publishes only for Kings & full Generals."[32] The king duly appeared on the cover as sole author—"his

Hawaiian Majesty Kalakaua"—with Daggett demoted to editor, but the sales anticipated by Twain never materialized.[33] The book proved an "absolute and flat failure," despite every device employed to boost its success.[34]

In his new role as a best-selling publisher, Twain was seldom content with modest gains and displayed, as so often in business ventures, more than a touch of greed. With his speculative instincts, he didn't want small, steady profits so much as spectacular killings. The subscription method forced him to specialize in celebrity publishing instead of smaller works of literary merit, and he showed no interest in scouting out new talent or promoting fellow authors. Subscription sales locked him into a costly form of publishing that would force him and his thinly capitalized firm to shoulder a heavy financial burden. In December 1885, Twain learned that Charles A. Dana of the *New York Sun* was acting as agent for an authorized biography of Pope Leo XIII, written by Father Bernard O'Reilly. At once, Twain was dazzled by the prospect of heavenly dollars raining down on him. It seemed an inspired idea. "It's a clear 100,000," he assured Webster, adding that it was "a book which we *must* have. With the priesthood to help, Dana's book is immense."[35] Despite his dim view of the Catholic Church, Twain hurried Webster off to see Dana, and they secured the rights to the Pope's life story for $100,000.

Much as with the Paige typesetter, Twain's imagination ran riot as he pictured the giant sales of the book to the Catholic faithful. "He had no words in which to paint the magnificence of the project, or to forecast its colossal success," Howells recalled. "It would have a currency bounded only by the number of Catholics in Christendom."[36] Twain foresaw a book sold in many languages and countries, its sales straddling the globe. That he had caught a whale the size of the Pope flabbergasted some in the press corps, with the *Boston Herald* opining that the publishing coup "surpasses the most audacious travesty of Mark Twain's books. As a stroke of 'business,' it is probably supreme in its way."[37] With his tendency to substitute wild fantasies for realistic commercial projections, Twain grew convinced that sales of the Pope's life would eclipse those of Grant's *Personal Memoirs*. He was traveling with Twichell on May 5,

1886, when he received word of the contract being officially signed. "The issue of this book will be the greatest event in the way of book publishing that ever occurred," Twichell wrote in his diary, doubtless echoing Twain's remarks, "and it seems certain, M.T. will make a vast amount of money by it."[38] Twain felt positively enraptured and liberated from money worries. Livy had postponed buying an expensive sofa until the deal was closed. "You can order 1000 such sofas now, if you want to—the future bank account will foot the bill & never miss it," Twain told her. "The Pope's book is ours & we'll sell a fleet load of copies. I love you, sweetheart, deeply, fondly, & always."[39]

In June, Charley and Annie Webster were scheduled to travel to Rome for a private audience with the Pope to iron out the publication details. With a flair for showmanship worthy of P. T. Barnum, Twain decided to have Charley hand the Pope a special presentation copy of Grant's *Memoirs*. The idea blossomed in Twain's mind until it became the kernel of a publicity strategy. The copy would be bound in solid gold and weigh a couple of pounds and be designed by Tiffany. It would then be placed in Tiffany's window so "all New York & all strangers visiting New York would flock to see it; the illustrated papers would make pictures of it & descriptions of it would appear in all languages & in all the newspapers in the world—& Webster & Co would score another point in the way of originality & enterprise."[40] In the end, Charley had to settle for a humbler version of Grant's book, but Twain's elaborate scheme showed how his novelistic flair was being transferred to the world of salesmanship.

In July, Charley and Annie Webster arrived at the Vatican in high style, in a carriage escorted by a plumed footman. Charley sent Twain a meticulous account of the meeting, describing how a silver-haired pope, in a long white cassock, sat on a "large gilt throne chair, upholstered in red plush... Upon a finger of his right hand was a gold ring with an emerald setting nearly an inch in diameter... We advanced and, kneeling at his feet, kissed the seal upon his ring."[41] During a thirty-minute audience, Charley was impressed by the goodwill in the Pope's smiling countenance. He found a shrewd, worldly prelate who showed intense interest in Grant's business failure and final hours, and was astonished that

Charles L. Webster and Company had already booked one hundred thousand orders of his memoirs. With a surer feel for the marketplace than Twain, the Pope interjected modestly "that my Life should have such a sale seems impossible."[42]

With image-making in mind, Twain approved Charley's posh approach to the Vatican. "You did well to go to Rome, & you did wisely to spend money freely," he told him, and he planned to sneak mentions of the audience into the American press.[43] The Pope had been favorably taken with Charley, later anointing him a Knight of the Order of Pius, and he also blessed a rosary that became a prized possession in the Clemens family, which was temporarily seized by rosary madness. Twain confessed to Charley that he would have felt tongue-tied and uncomfortable had he met the Pontiff himself. "But I should like to swap courtesies with the cardinals & archbishops first rate. They are nearer my size."[44]

Whenever he worked himself up into a Colonel Sellers state of euphoria, Twain was getting ready for a major fall—"That book is going to *go*, sure," he told Webster—and that happened with the Pope's life, which didn't approach sales of 100,000 copies despite simultaneous publication in six languages.[45] For Twain, it was a bumpy ride back to planet Earth. In Howells's view, Twain hadn't stopped to consider how many Catholics could read or how many might wish to read about the Pope's life. "The failure was incredible to Clemens; his sanguine soul was utterly confounded, and soon a silence fell upon it where it had been so exuberantly jubilant."[46] It was the first of several major book failures that would eventually snowball into disaster.

Aside from his papal foray, Twain converted his publishing company into an unofficial clubhouse for Union army generals. Not only would he publish works by Sherman, Sheridan, and Samuel W. Crawford, but he would also negotiate contracts with the widows of George Armstrong Custer, George B. McClellan, and Winfield Scott Hancock for volumes about their late husbands. Since he now published only a few books each year, he seemed to be doing little else besides Civil War accounts, the Pope's life being the clear exception. Twain found himself in an odd position. With Webster & Company now booked solid for several years, he fretted that he wouldn't be able to publish his own books with the house. As he confessed to Howells, "It wouldn't do to go outside of my own shop—people would say I didn't believe in my own shop."[47] Though the marketplace was soon glutted with Civil War memoirs, Webster remained sanguine about the publishing firm's future. "I think it is the best subscription publishing office in the world," he told Twain, "as it ought to be."[48]

With his combative bent, Twain spluttered with rage when he learned in June 1886 that John Wanamaker, the owner of a Philadelphia department store, was selling Grant's *Memoirs* below cost to advertise his own wares. Since Wanamaker was a devout Presbyterian who superintended a large Sunday school, Twain pummeled him as a hypocrite, instructing Webster to "go for Wannamaker [sic]—otherwise I will go down there & rise up in his Sunday School & give him hell, in front of his whole 3000 pupils."[49] And Twain was just getting started. In a fire-breathing letter, he lambasted that "Sunday school-slobbering sneak-thief John Wannemaker, [sic] now of Philadelphia, presently of hell."[50] He told Frederick J. Hall, a new assistant to Webster, to contact the law firm of Alexander & Green about a possible lawsuit, and "if they approve, let the attack begin."[51]

Twain's lawyers sought an injunction from a U.S. circuit judge in Philadelphia that would prevent John Wanamaker and Company from selling the *Memoirs* on the grounds that it was a subscription book being sold as a trade book. Twain grew alarmed as other large retailers imitated Wanamaker's trespass. "Macy has Grant books for sale cheap," Twain told Hall, as if mapping out a military campaign. "We must assault him, next."[52] Twain attended the Philadelphia trial, but the judge ruled against him. To worsen matters, Wanamaker alleged that Twain had fallen asleep in court. To get even with the retail mogul, Twain meditated placing malicious squibs about Wanamaker in the *New York Sun*. Far from fearing reprisals from Wanamaker, Twain told Hall, "I would like Wanamaker to sue me for libel in New York if agreeable to him."[53] But the feud seemed to go no further.

FLOODTIDE

At least on the surface, Twain embraced his new role as publisher with panache, leavened with his usual humor. "In my combined character of publisher and author," he told one trade dinner, "I receive a great many manuscripts from people who say they want a candid opinion whether that is good literature or not. That is all a lie; what they want is a compliment."[54] He spread the word that he was now a prosperous publisher, a gentleman of means, who had the luxury to retire from most writing. When a Boston publication asked him in May 1886 if he would write for magazines that year, he swatted away the idea. "No sum of money however flattering could induce me to swerve from a resolution I have made to enjoy a solid old-fashioned loaf this summer . . . Besides there is more money in being a publisher. At any rate that is my experience and if I perform any more literary work in future it will be only to 'keep my hand in.'"[55] Ambrose Bierce, who saw Twain as being corrupted by money, contended that the author turned publisher had traded in the role of "Mark the Jester" for "Mark the Money-worm."[56]

In 1886 Twain's publishing house was still in a relatively comfortable position and, thanks to the Grant bonanza, worth $500,000. In late April, Frederick J. Hall became a junior partner and would receive one-twentieth of the firm's net profits. Most significantly, Hall was "to have the entire active management and control" of the firm in Webster's absence.[57] In its plush new headquarters, Webster & Company's overhead had only grown steeper. The cardinal weakness of the capital structure, however, was that Twain alone carried the financial burden and in a bank failure would "get worse hurt by an accident than my brother partners."[58] By the year's end, he buckled under the weight of the forthcoming papal book just as he had in the run-up to Grant's publication. He told a friend in December that for the next twelve months he would have "to sail just as close to the wind, financially, as I possibly can, & look sharp & see that no penny is placed where I cannot put my hand on it at once when it is needed. We have one book in preparation which will require every

REPARATION DUE TO EVERY BLACK MAN

cent I have in the world, & possibly more."[59] Once again, he stood in a precarious position, and he knew it.

In early January 1887, Webster brought in another project with jackpot potential: the autobiography of Henry Ward Beecher, the famous abolitionist preacher, albeit a man stigmatized by a sex scandal with a female member of his Brooklyn congregation. "I do not love Beecher any more than you do," Webster told Twain, "but I love his money just as well, and I am certain that that book would sell."[60] Twain again hatched pie-in-the-sky projections, saying that if Beecher "leaves in just enough piousness, it will sell (hoping it may be 2 volumes) 200,000 of vol 1, & 125,000 of vol 2: profit $350,000."[61] After a contract was signed, Beecher died of a stroke on March 8, and Webster & Company had to settle for a banal biography written by his family. Twain was chagrined at the missed opportunity but vexed all the more so when he considered the money already spent on paper and supplies. "That is a clear loss of $100,000 to the firm, & possibly more."[62] In signing up aging luminaries, Webster & Company engaged in the ghoulish business of hoping their authors would last long enough to eke out a book, then try to capitalize on their posthumous fame.

Following hard on the Beecher fiasco was the discovery in March 1887 that the firm's bookkeeper, Frank Scott, had embezzled $25,000. Scott was subsequently sentenced to six years of hard labor at Sing Sing prison. (Magnanimously, Twain and Webster later got the governor to commute that sentence to half the time.) Twain felt bitter that Webster had not bothered to investigate Scott's résumé adequately. "It was easy to trace him from employment to employment," Twain wrote. "In fact you could trace him from one employment to the next by the stolen money which he had dripped along the road."[63] Scott had first been suspected in August or September 1886, but Webster, following the advice of lawyers, waited to confront him. In Twain's indignant view, the lawyers had advised Webster "to keep a thief's hand in my pocket."[64] He thought Charley had enjoyed the chance to play detective and catch the culprit in the act.

A clash that had long simmered between Twain and Webster now boiled over, and Twain issued a demand that expressed a complete loss of trust in Webster: "A desk in the office for my agent, and free access to the books, balance-sheets, and every detail of the business... When I put up $50,000, it will be in a new concern entitled S L Clemens & Co.—that or 'The Mark Twain Pub. Co.'"[65] That Twain wished to strip Webster's name from the marquee and replace it with his own while planting his own representative there was rightly interpreted by Webster as a hostile act. "I cannot deal with my partner in business through the intervention of an agent... no business can succeed where partners deal with each other at arms length."[66] Webster suggested that Twain come to New York so that he could show him how well the business was being managed. When Twain did, they arrived at an amicable agreement, at least temporarily. "Everything is on the pleasantest possible basis, now, & is going to stay so," Twain wrote to Charley. "I blame myself for not looking in on you oftener in the past—that would have prevented all trouble."[67] He promised to reform, though he was still troubled by the ballooning expenses and minimal profits.

Aside from the Grant memoir, the most astute literary judgment Twain made as a publisher proved to be, from a business standpoint, a calamity. The *Library of American Literature* was an anthology stuffed with more than seventeen hundred selections from five hundred authors, published in eleven volumes. This banquet of American prose spanned everything from Frederick Douglass speeches to Anna Dickinson lectures to Black spirituals. Although it contained three excerpts from Twain's own work, all editorial decisions were made by Edmund Clarence Stedman, a New York literary poet and critic, and Ellen Mackay Hutchinson, who covered literature for the *New York Tribune*. Initially, Twain was less than enthusiastic about the project—"I think well of the Stedman book," he told Webster, "but I can't somehow bring myself to think *very* well of it"—but he failed to exercise his prerogative and veto it.[68]

Soon enough, Twain struck a plaintive note about the projected expense. "What has that Lib of Lit cost, thus far?" he asked in his notebook. "How much *more* will it cost?"[69] The problem was not lagging sales, but the tricky economics of subscription publishing for a small, thinly capitalized house. The lengthy series had to be printed long before the house received revenues from readers. Compounding the problem was that customers were invited to pay on a slow installment plan, while printers had to be paid speedily. Customers would also get the entire eleven-volume set with the first payment, while Webster & Company had to wait a year to collect full payment. What this meant was that the faster the anthology sold, the steeper the financial hole dug by the publisher. To cover costs, the firm began borrowing heavily and bank loans piled up. As Twain later noted, the *Library of American Literature* "secured the lingering suicide of Charles L. Webster and Company."[70]

Bad business decisions worsened the feud smoldering between Twain and Webster. Twain believed Webster had grown arrogant from the Grant success and created the swank office on Union Square to feed his vanity. As he put it, Webster "was young, he was human, he naturally mistook this transient notoriety for fame, and by consequence he had to get his hat enlarged."[71] Twain's brawl with Webster would form yet another chapter in his bitter, bruising history with business associates.

By early 1887, Charley suffered from a debilitating neuralgia that may have been tic douloureux. One side of Twain sympathized with a medical affliction that caused crippling headaches, and he invited Charley to Hartford for a day or two of rest. "A moment's rest from work is good medicine for neuralgia," Twain advised in a paternal manner.[72] By the summer of 1887, however, the depth of the problem grew clear when a doctor pronounced Charley in "great danger" and said he needed a year's rest.[73] "I had no idea that Charley's case was so serious," Twain told his sister. "I knew it was bad, & persistent, but I was not aware of the full size of the matter."[74] Owing to his condition, Charley grew more irritable and temperamental, and spent much of that summer away from the office, recuperating at the beach in Far Rockaway, Queens.

While publicly professing his retirement from writing, Twain had embarked on *A Connecticut Yankee in King Arthur's Court*. Still, his mind was so clouded by incessant worry about his publishing house that it interfered with his work. He told Webster that the fun he had at first experienced with the new book had now "slumped into funereal seriousness, & this will not do . . . I work seven hours a day, & am in such a taut-strung & excitable condition that everything that *can* worry me, does it; & I get up & spend from 1 o'clock till 3 a.m. pretty regularly every night, thinking—not pleasantly."[75] With his fitful sleep and ragged nerves, Twain had premonitions of doom about his publishing business. Ironically, he was damaging his own talent so that he could publish a stable of lesser writers.

Because Twain hesitated to confront the ailing Webster directly, he filled up his notebook with a slew of charges against him, accusing him of publishing too many books simultaneously; paying rent in four places; increasing salaries without profits; and using chaotic office methods. He wrote as if he were dressing down Charley with mockery: "*You* got the G. [Grant] book! *You* told him it would sell 300,000 sets! . . . You, a mere apprentice,—with the trade half learned, proposed to strike for a full third of the profits, did you?"[76] And then came this damning conclusion, written in German, as if he feared to express it in English. "A superb *business* ruined in *two years and a sixty thousand dollar debt created.*"[77]

Webster believed that his health had been broken by his exhausting effort in selling the Grant book and the wild business schemes Twain made him pursue. Pretty adept at sarcasm himself, he said he hoped Twain wouldn't ask his successor to neglect the book business "to revive that 'patent baby clamp' business, to prevent lively infants from kicking off the bed clothes and catching cold."[78] Webster had been forced to contend with a development that threatened the financial stability of the firm: Twain was dealing with a parallel disaster, the Paige typesetter, now siphoning off $3,000 a month from his bank account. Twain stumbled under its weight, always hoping the machine was near completion and "then the strain will let up and we can breathe freely once more."[79] Webster feared Twain's capital withdrawals to underwrite the typesetter would place the publishing house in jeopardy, and he negotiated an agreement by which Twain promised to keep $75,000 in capital in Webster & Company, a requirement his primary partner resented.

REPARATION DUE TO EVERY BLACK MAN

By late December 1887, it was evident that Twain's relationship with his nephew had been ruptured beyond redemption. "Webster ill and about ready to resign," Twain wrote.[80] Despite his departure, Twain would blame the young man for the firm's future woes, and his bitterness in business situations could be endless. He argued that Webster had already been "a lunatic" two years earlier.[81] He accused him of having abused a new German drug, phenacetine, prescribed for his neuralgia. "It stupefied him and he went about as one in a dream."[82] To the end of his life he poured scorn on his nephew's memory and demonized him as if he had been guilty of criminal duplicity. "Webster was a limitless liar . . . he was treacherous. Envy was a disease with him. He was as base a character as the century can furnish."[83] When Webster died on April 26, 1891, at thirty-nine years old, a newspaper obituary attributed the death to "an attack of grip, which led to peritonitis and hemorrhage."[84] There is no certainty about the cause of death; scholarly conjecture has run the gamut from bowel inflammation to pancreatic cancer to suicide. Twain, pleading rheumatism, didn't attend the funeral. He accepted no blame for Webster & Company's troubles and made Charley Webster the scapegoat for all future problems of his publishing house.

With the Paige typesetter, Twain had a lush imagination for the machine's potential and an impoverished imagination for its shortcomings. For four years, the machine had absorbed "all my love, & interest, & spare time."[85] As early as April 1885, he had insisted that it was "in lucrative shape at last" and stood ready "to submit itself to any test an expert chooses to apply."[86] It was a refrain he would sing often in coming years as he spent an exorbitant amount of time in daydreams, calculating hypothetical customers for the typesetter. Within three years, he was certain the company would rent out a thousand machines and record $2.5 million in profit. The nub of the problem was that Twain, a former printer's devil, fancied himself an expert here, which gave him unshakable confidence in his most elaborate fantasies. "I know all about composition"; he boasted, "& so I know that a paper that once uses this machine in its now perfect shape, will always use it."[87] The only person he managed to convince was himself.

Sure the end was near—it always seemed near—Twain made large, open-ended commitments to complete the machine's development. In November 1885, when he wrote a $3,500 check, he told Webster to "make a particular entry of it to remember the circumstances by, for it finishes the type-setter business in a very satisfactory fashion."[88] In fact, years of grinding development lay ahead. In January 1886, when Twain, Paige, and William Hamersley gathered in Twain's billiard room in Hartford to chart the future, Paige pledged his solemn word that "'every expense connected with making the model machine *cannot* reach $30,000—can't possibly go *over* it.' This includes every possible cost of wages, drawings, building the machine, taking out *all* the patents, &c," Twain recorded.[89] Twain agreed to fund future development for half ownership of the compositor. Unfortunately, it was a beautiful but fiendishly complex machine that weighed five thousand pounds and had eighteen thousand parts. At his core Paige was a wild dreamer, a manic perfectionist, and ignorant of business realities.

Fixated on future profits, Twain was blind to the stiff competition posed by a young German inventor in Brooklyn, Ottmar Mergenthaler, who created a machine with a keyboard inspired by the typewriter. Twain received fair warning of the progress of the Mergenthaler Linotype machine. In January 1886, when William M. Laffan of the *New York Sun* traveled to inspect the machine in use at the *Baltimore Sun*, he warned Twain, "I saw the Baltimore machine set type . . . I incline to the belief that every daily in [New York] will set up by that machine inside of twelve months."[90] True to Laffan's prediction, on July 3, 1886, the *New York Tribune* printed part of that day's issue with Mergenthaler machinery. Though not as sophisticated as the Paige model, it was a reliable workhorse, giving publishers needed confidence it would not break down. Mergenthaler also had the priceless advantage of first entry in a new field, even as Paige dithered and tinkered. "Business sanity would have said, put it on the market as it was, secure the field, and add improvements later," Twain recalled. "Paige's business insanity said, add the improvements first, and risk losing the field."[91] Paige devoted four years to making refinements as Twain poured money into this bottomless hole. When a friend warned him of the danger, he brushed it aside: "I can get a thousand men worth a million apiece to go in with me if I can get a perfect machine."[92] While conceding that the Mergenthaler was an ingenious machine, he added that so was "a racehorse; but he can't run no competition with a railroad."[93] In fact, the truth was the reverse: the Paige machine was the racehorse; Mergenthaler was the railroad.

While he carped mercilessly at the competition, Twain was guilty of hubris and blindness toward his own machine. By the end of 1887, his typesetter payments had already ballooned to $50,000, or $20,000 more than Paige had promised, with no end in sight. And this happened as he struggled with the shrinking finances of Charles L. Webster and Company. For someone in Twain's position, it would have been oppressive enough to bear the responsibility of one money-draining operation. To carry both at once would eventually overwhelm him. He was a drowning man, gasping for air. During the summer of 1887, he reported to his Hartford business agent, Franklin G. Whitmore, "I got no sleep last night . . . I ought to have known, long ago, that when Paige thinks a thing will cost $100, *that* is proof that it will cost $1000."[94]

CHAPTER TWENTY-FOUR

"No Pockets in the Armor"

Notwithstanding the tribulations of his business investments, Mark Twain always managed to sneak in some fun and entertainment. In April 1885, he took along Susy for a speech that he delivered at Vassar on Founder's Day. The thirteen-year-old Susy was still stuck in the hero-worship phase with her father, whom she had never heard read in public before. "When he came out onto the stage I remember the people [b]ehind me exclaimed 'oh how queer he is!' 'isn't he funny?' I thought papa was very funny although I did not think him queer . . . and I enjoyed the [reading] inexpressibly much."[1]

Twain would excel at private readings to all-female audiences, and at Livy's behest they formed a Browning Society that met weekly in their library on the ground floor of the Hartford house. No poet sustained Twain's interest quite as much as Robert Browning, whom he had met in London in the early 1870s. With his dense, abstruse style, Browning might have seemed an odd choice for Twain, but both writers employed, to scintillating effect, dramatic monologues in which the first-person narrator reveals far more than he or she realizes.

For each session of the new society, Twain prepared thirty or forty pages of verse to read aloud and even marked in his book the syllables to stress. Instead of presenting dry analyses, he wanted the poems to speak for themselves, and his readings were so clear and fervent that the opaque poetry grew lucid. He joked that he could "read Browning so Browning himself can understand. It sounds like stretching, but it's the cold truth."[2]

Three dozen women turned up for these Wednesday readings, and it was a sought-after invitation in Hartford society. Grace King, the Clemenses' writer friend from New Orleans, watched Twain wrest ideas embedded in the verse. "His slow, deliberate speech and full voice gave each sentence its quota of sound, and sense followed naturally and easily. He understood Browning as did no one else I ever heard."[3]

Sam and Livy were a vivacious couple who enjoyed the company of writers, artists, and intellectuals. They spent part of the summer of 1885 at the Onteora Club in the Catskill Mountains, near Tannersville, visiting Candace Wheeler, the pioneering designer who had fashioned tapestry and fabrics for their residence. She and her brother had created a mountaintop artists' summer colony, meant to be rustic but conducive to serious conversation. It was animated by a spirit not unlike Nook Farm, a sophisticated, well-to-do community of people prominent in the arts and letters. Twain immediately arose as a star attraction, and following his usual habit, he paced and pontificated while other guests sat at the luncheon table. "As he generally wore slippers on these peregrinations, the family dog used to follow his footsteps, trying to get a bite at the loose heels of them," Candace Wheeler recalled. "He was entirely unconscious of this, being occupied in arguing some position or telling a story which illustrated it."[4] Every morning before lunch, Twain stopped by the cottage of a neighbor who was losing her eyesight, and people gathered to eavesdrop as he read aloud to the woman.

Two summers later, the Clemenses and Grace King stayed at Olana, the Moorish fantasy of a mansion perched atop a mountain in Hudson, New York, that was home to Frederic E. Church, the eminent painter of the Hudson River School. Since Church was devout, he led his guests in prayers and Bible readings after breakfast. To offset this piety, Twain performed a hilarious imitation of a sermon he had heard when he was in New Orleans with George Washington Cable. "He is the greatest circus I was ever at," Grace King wrote her sister. "One can soon discover, however, that under his great shock of grey hair lies a very profound vigorous intellect. He is not at all refined,—wore slippers all the time at the Church's and smokes a pipe," and he gorged like a field hand at the dinner table.⁵ She gave an excellent description of Livy as "very prim and precise but an unaffected little woman[,] the very essence of refinement."⁶ For dinner, Livy dressed exquisitely and expensively, with Grace noting her "picturesque tunic of white crepe with a satin stripe on it . . . over a heavy ended white silk—trimmed with pearl passementerie."⁷ Twain, after having a thoroughly jolly time at Olana, declared the stay "an ideal holiday, in a Garden of Eden without the Garden of Eden's unprotection from weather."⁸

Over the years, Twain wrote frequently to his family back home and sent them money with only intermittent face-to-face contact. In June 1886, he mapped out a journey that would take his Hartford clan to Keokuk, Iowa, so the children could spend time with Jane Clemens, Orion and Mollie, and Pamela Moffett. Twain, who hated rail journeys and never shed his special joy in water travel, figured out a route that would take them there by the Great Lakes and the Mississippi River. "On a lake or river boat one is as thoroughly cut off from letters and papers and the tax collector as though he were amid sea," he wrote.⁹ Once in Keokuk, the family endured four or five days of "hell-sweltering weather," but still had an enjoyable time.¹⁰ In a follow-up letter, Twain entertained his eighty-three-year-old mother with a comic riff on Keokuk heat. "I remember that I burnt a hole in my shirt, there, with some ice cream that fell on it; & Miss Jenkins told me they never used a stove, but cooked their meals on a marble-topped table in the drawing-room, just with the natural heat . . . I was told by the Bishop of Keokuk that he did not allow crying at funerals, because it scalded the furniture."¹¹

Since Twain's visit coincided with the Fourth of July holiday, he and Orion were dragooned into participating in the festive ceremonies. With Twain garbed in a white suit and tall hat, the two brothers rode down Main Street in a carriage bedecked with bunting and ribbons, and dismounted at Rand Park, with its panoramic views of the Mississippi River that Mark Twain had immortalized. First, Orion rose to deliver the Declaration of Independence "in a clear and distinct manner."¹² In his speech, instead of trotting out the Founding Fathers, Twain offered a paean to American ingenuity: "In the address to-day, I have not heard much mention made of the prog[r]ess of these last few years—of the telegraph, telephone, phonograph, and other great inventions ... I say 'Better this decade than the 900 years of Methuselah.' There is more done in one year now than Methuselah ever saw in all his life."[13] It was an appropriate speech for a man staking his fortune on a revolutionary typesetter, and he sounded a theme soon to resonate in *Connecticut Yankee*. Never again would Sam and Orion Clemens share a stage together.

The trip occurred as Twain still basked in the limelight of publishing *Huck Finn* and Grant's *Memoirs*, and he seemed in a mood of overflowing generosity. He offered financial support to Pamela; thanked her for sheltering him in his early, callow days on the river; said he was "in debt to her for a thousand affectionate kindnesses & services besides"; and admitted to being a brother "of a fractious disposition & difficult to get along with, but nevertheless ... not ungrateful."[14] Orion and Mollie, understandably proud of Sam's presence, strung their home with lanterns and hosted four hundred guests at a reception for the famous author. Jane Clemens presided with motherly pride in the front parlor, surrounded by her children and grandchildren.

It is hard to escape the impression that Orion was stricken with severe psychiatric troubles. His problems had gone way beyond being doomed to mediocrity. Six months after his brother's visit, Orion swallowed a bottle of ammonia water, imagining it was cough medicine. When he screamed, Mollie rushed to his side and found him "white as death," his jaw hanging slack. When she asked what he had done, he gasped, "Oh my God, I have taken poison."[15] Somehow he survived, spitting up blood and suffering scalding burns on his tongue and in his throat. Mollie, deeply shaken, told Sam and Livy that she was mystified and frightened by the episode, since Orion's cough medicine stood "on our bureau behind the door and he took this bottle off our wash stand," adding, "I don't know how or why."[16] Orion, scarcely able to speak, gave way to gruesome groans. A loyal brother, he worried only about the time he lost helping Sam with his board game about British kings. "I am grievously disappointed for I wholly lost yesterday, and may lose all this week from your work."[17] Surely moved by this display of fraternal love and the pathos of Orion's almost canine eagerness to please him, Sam urged him to take it easy. "Vary your day with anything that will afford relaxation for the mind. The kings have waited 800 years—we'll not let them rush us now."[18]

The Clemens clan continued spending the bulk of their summers in Elmira. When Livy contemplated a trip to England in early 1887, Twain, chained to the Paige typesetter, was obliged to veto it. "I can't go to England without my machine"; he told a correspondent, "one doesn't go abroad & leave his soul & entrails behind."[19] The paterfamilias, when not writing at Quarry Farm, was game for novel experiences. Though not athletic, he was enlisted that June as home-plate umpire for a baseball game and quickly established his jester style when the first pitch sailed eleven feet wide of the plate. According to the Boston *Daily Globe*, Twain called it a strike and laid down eccentric rules, many designed to speed up the slow-moving game. "Any ball is a strike that passes within eight feet of the plate on either side of it. To wait for good balls causes delay and public dissatisfaction, and is not going to be allowed on this occasion. The batsman will strike at everything that comes whether he can reach it or not . . . The batsman is denied all professional affectations; he must stand up straight and attend strictly to business."[20] By the end of the game, Twain had promulgated a motley set of regulations that included that "the pitcher must not wipe the ball on his pants; neither must he keep inspecting it and squirming and twisting it and trying to rub the skin off it with his hands. He must not keep the public waiting while he makes allusory [sic] feints at reputable parties on first and second base."[21] A decade later, speaking at a baseball dinner at Delmonico's in New York, Twain pronounced baseball "the outward and visible expression of the drive, and push, and rush and struggle of the raging, tearing, booming nineteenth century!"[22]

Perhaps Twain's most unique speaking foray came when he addressed 850 convicts at the Elmira Reformatory. Twain admired superintendent Zebulon Brockway for his enlightened ideas on prison reform, including providing recreation for the men. Twain saw Brockway's kindness reflected in his benevolent face. "He has associated with criminals all his life, and look at what it's done for him. If I had associated with criminals I might have such a face, too, but I've always been associated with Christians."[23] This inversion of conventional morality was Twain's comic specialty. In his reformatory speech, he read a selection from *Huck Finn* and poked fun at the awful German language, and his talk proved a huge success. His verdict: "Afterwards, they always say that for a splendid audience give them a houseful of convicts; it's the best audience in the world."[24] With his curiosity about human nature, Twain always rose to the challenge of addressing unconventional audiences. "Once I talked to the inmates of an insane asylum, in Hartford," he said. "I have talked to idiots a thousand times, but only once to the insane."[25]

Writing a story based on Arthurian legend had percolated in Twain's mind ever since George Washington Cable recommended *Le Morte d'Arthur*, whose lyrical purity of language appealed to his ear and reminded him of the "quaint and pretty phrases" Tennyson employed in the *Idylls of the King*.[26] As shown by his passion for history and biography, the distant past exerted a potent hold over him. Even as a boy, he had been enchanted by the adventures of Robin Hood. "Sherwood forest & its matchless society—rascals, no doubt, but the most darling sweet rascals that ever made crime graceful in this world."[27] Clearly, he saw Robin Hood and his comrades as early forerunners of Tom Sawyer and his lovable gang malingering on the outskirts of society.

The seed for *A Connecticut Yankee in King Arthur's Court* sprouted in a dream Twain recorded in his notebook of suddenly being transported to King Arthur's Court, equipped with his present-day personality. This suggested a simple comic conceit of introducing a modern slant on the early Middle Ages, deflating medieval chivalry by dramatizing its practical defects. "Dream of being a knight errant in armor in the middle ages. Have the notions & habits of thought of the present day mixed with the necessities of that. No pockets in the armor. No way to manage certain requirements of nature. Can't scratch. Cold in the head—can't

"NO POCKETS IN THE ARMOR"

blow—can't get at handkerchief, can't use iron sleeve. Iron gets red hot in the sun—leaks in the rain, gets white with frost & freezes me solid in winter. Suffer from lice & fleas. Make disagreeable clatter when I enter church. Can't dress or undress myself. Always getting struck by lightning. Fall down, can't get up. See Morte DArthur [sic]."[28] In short, the novel's strategy would be to "dump the nineteenth century down into the sixth century and observe the consequences."[29]

By February 1886, Twain read to his approving wife and daughters the novel's opening section, but he was now so sidetracked by his publishing ventures and the finicky typesetter that the book would take several years to complete. In November, having written only two or three chapters, he made light of the delay, as if he were now a gentleman of leisure, writing only for his pleasure. As he told Mother Fairbanks: "I expect to write three chapters a year for thirty years; then the book will be done. I am writing it for posterity only; my posterity; my great grandchildren. It is to be my holiday amusement for six days every summer the rest of my life. Of course I do not expect to publish it; nor indeed any other book"—except his autobiography.[30]

After a sluggish start, Twain's imagination caught fire at Quarry Farm in July 1887 when he confessed that he was "headover [sic] heels in a book & am writing without rest or stop—steam at high pressure."[31] In a tribute to his creative ferment, he even swept aside talk of the Paige contracts and put in seven-hour writing days. "Tell Paige to go ahead," he informed an intermediary. "When this spurt of mine breaks—which I hope won't be soon—I'll come down to earthly business again."[32] As he wrote, the urgent need for money to feed the maw of the insatiable typesetter preoccupied him. When he read through the existing manuscript that summer, he was puffed up with pride, having "found out that I am making an uncommonly bully book—& am swelled up accordingly."[33] Ironically, he had no special need to rush because Webster & Company was glutted with titles and appeared to have no room for another big subscription book, even his own, until 1889.

By thrusting a nineteenth-century American named Hank Morgan into sixth-century England, *Connecticut Yankee* presented a rich, sprawling work with a comprehensive critique of society, past and present. It would have a much more cynical edge than the storybook charm of *The Prince and the Pauper*. There had been a trend in England to romanticize Arthurian legends, whether in Tennyson's poetry or the posed photos of Julia Margaret Cameron or the medieval aesthetic of the Pre-Raphaelite painters. Twain would strip away this veneer and expose the seamy underside of medieval life. He did not reveal solely the plight of downtrodden peasants, but unmasked the royal and ecclesiastical powers who oppressed them, and he was no less interested in scoring points against church and state in the modern world.

It was a particularly contradictory moment for Twain. Having married a rich woman, and with his publishing venture and the Paige typesetter consuming his time, he was doing everything possible to join the plutocrats. Yet the flame of political radicalism flickered ever more brightly inside him. Periodically, he read *The French Revolution* by Thomas Carlyle, which helped him to measure his own political development. Upon rereading it in August 1887, smack amid the creation of *Connecticut Yankee,* he realized how radical he had become, life having made him "a Sansculotte!—And not a pale, characterless Sansculotte, but a Marat," bloodily attacking political and religious privilege. The sansculottes were the radical poor of France, who, unlike the aristocracy, didn't wear knee breeches. In his notebook, Twain spouted increasingly splenetic views about European nobility and royalty, whom he styled the "criminal classes."[34] In one scorching passage, he wrote: "Let us take the present male sovereigns of the earth—and strip them naked. Mix them with 500 naked mechanics, and then march the whole around a circus ring, charging suitable admission, of course,—and desire the audience to pick out the sovereigns. They couldn't. You would have to paint them blue."[35] He blamed a servile European press for glorifying monarchs and credited an irreverent American press with laughing "a thousand cruel & infamous shams & superstitions into the grave . . . Irreverence is the champion of liberty, & its only sure defence."[36]

Eager to finish his book, Twain considered dictating it into an Edison phonograph, but the company experienced delays in its release and Twain

"NO POCKETS IN THE ARMOR"

canceled his order. When he returned to Hartford from Elmira in late September 1888, he planned to complete the manuscript in a month, then had to reckon with constant interruptions in his Hartford home; he decided to hole up in Twichell's house by day. The Twichells were having construction work done, and a frazzled Twain had to cope "with the noise of the children and an army of carpenters . . . It's like a boiler factory for racket, and in nailing a wooden ceiling on to the room under me the hammering tickles my feet amazingly sometimes and jars my table a good deal, but I never am conscious of the racket at all."[37]

By the time the book was ready for Livy's critical appraisal the following summer, she had been sidelined by pinkeye. As Twain told his sister, "There was nothing left of Livy but semi-blindness & headache."[38] He entreated Howells to scrutinize the book, explaining that Livy was "afraid I have left coarsenesses which ought to be rooted out, & blasts of opinion which are so strongly worded as to repel instead of persuade."[39] This last concern signaled something new for Livy—worry about the sheer ferocity of her husband's views, a fear that his more strident politics might alienate readers. Not surprisingly, Howells adored the book and assured Twain it contained "masses of virgin truth never touched in print before!"[40] "It's my swan-song, my retirement from literature permanently," Twain told him, "and I wish to pass to the cemetery unclodded."[41] A month later, he added: "Well, my book is written—let it go. But if it were only to write over again there wouldn't be so many things left out. They burn in me; & . . . they can't ever be said. And besides, they would require a library—& a pen warmed-up in hell."[42] That final phrase—"a pen warmed-up in hell"—expressed the wrath boiling inside Twain and the multitude of opinions knocking about in his brain. During the next twenty years, he would air those views, often at elaborate length and at some risk to his popularity as a humorist. With *Connecticut Yankee,* the wall between his public persona and deeply held private views began to crumble.

As it had been four and a half years since Twain published his last book, Fred Hall was extremely nervous about how to handle it, this being the first time he had marketed a Twain book. He went so far as to try, futilely, to persuade Twain to publish *Connecticut Yankee* as a trade book, not by subscription. For illustrations, Twain recruited the talented Dan Beard, whose socialist leanings made him sympathetic to the book's viewpoint, and Beard delighted the author by using the face of Jay Gould for the image of a slave driver.

Knowing that he would be charged with lèse-majesté in England, Twain took pains to assuage the fears of Andrew Chatto, his London publisher, insisting that "Mrs. Clemens has read it & made me strike out many passages and soften others; I have read chapters of it in public several times where Englishmen were present, & have profited by their suggestions."[43] But the erstwhile Anglophile then issued a stern warning. He had nursed grievances against the British ever since the poet and critic Matthew Arnold had criticized Grant's *Memoirs* and American journalism. In his notebook, he had labeled England "The arrogant nation."[44] Now he lectured Chatto: "*We* are spoken of, (by *Englishmen!*) as a thin-skinned people. It is you that are thin skinned. An Englishman may write with the most brutal frankness about any man or any institution among us, & we re-publish him without dreaming of altering a line or a word. But England cannot stand that kind of a book, written about herself."[45] He warned Chatto that he would not alter a single word for the British edition, although Chatto published the book under the more respectful title of *A Yankee at the Court of King Arthur.*

It is noteworthy that Twain chose "Yankee" for his title—a hated term in his Hannibal boyhood and further proof of his northern identification. At the outset of the novel, he situates Hank Morgan, the Yankee, in his own neighborhood. "Born and reared in Hartford," Hank supervises men at the Colt Arms-Factory until a workman knocks him out with a crowbar one day, and he wakes up sitting under an oak tree in a beautiful landscape.[46] When Hank sees a rider in a helmet and iron armor on horseback, he thinks him an escapee from a circus and imagines the hilltop town in the distance to be Bridgeport (home of P. T. Barnum), when, in fact, it is Camelot, and he has been transported back to King Arthur's Court in the

"NO POCKETS IN THE ARMOR"

sixth century. Hank, an arrogant American, plans to boss the Camelot locals since he has a head start of thirteen hundred years of knowledge. He sees the vaunted knights as overgrown boys and Merlin as the biggest blowhard and charlatan of them all. With the wizard, Twain mocks superstitions that held the medieval world in thrall. As Merlin drones on, the whole court dozes off from sheer boredom, and Twain presents the knights as pathological liars who inflate their tales of prowess.

At one point, true to Twain's seminal dream, Hank is tortured by his suit of armor as he rides to liberate captive princesses from a distant castle. "When I trotted, I rattled like a crate of dishes ... and moreover I couldn't seem to stand that shield slatting and banging ... And you had to be always changing hands, and passing your spear over to the other foot, it got so irksome for one hand to hold it long at a time."[47] Encased in metal, he can't figure out how to blow his nose or eat food, and when flies enter his helmet, they torment him.

Hank saves himself from execution by pretending to banish a solar eclipse and drives a hard Yankee bargain for his action, becoming second in command to the king. Still, he misses the small conveniences of the modern world. "There was no gas, there were no candles ... There were no books, pens, paper, or ink; and no glass in the openings they believed to be windows."[48] When Hank blows up Merlin's castle with a lightning rod, unmasking the court magician as a fraud, Twain shows modern science rendering the old-time magic ridiculous. Hank pities the common people who bow before all-powerful institutions, "as if they had any more occasion to love and honor king and Church and noble than a slave has to love and honor the lash."[49] Twain takes dead aim at *contemporary* England, not just Arthur's Court, with Hank denouncing "the seventh-rate people that have always figured as its aristocracies."[50] As Twain settles into a full-throated diatribe, the reader begins to fathom that this is not a quaint book, but a very angry one. "The most of King Arthur's British nation were slaves, pure and simple, and bore that name, and wore the iron collar on their necks ... The truth was, the nation as a body was in the world for one object, and one only: to grovel before king and Church and noble."[51]

In his new position, Hank seeks to introduce American modernity into Camelot. Arguing for a republic, he is accused of fomenting revolution among the passive masses, leading to some of Twain's most radically egalitarian passages. "So to speak, I was become a stockholder in a corporation where nine hundred and ninety-four of the members furnished all the money and did all the work," Hank muses, "and the other six elected themselves a permanent board of direction and took all the dividends. It seemed to me that what the nine hundred and ninety-four dupes needed was a new deal."[52] (President Franklin Roosevelt may—or may not—have adopted his New Deal slogan from Twain's novel, an issue that has been hotly disputed.)

Fresh from reading Carlyle, Twain was so fiery and bloody-minded that Hank justifies the Reign of Terror during the French Revolution, claiming that it had "inflicted death upon ten thousand persons" versus the "hundred millions" killed by nobility during the previous thousand years.[53] Hank is thought a lunatic by the people of Camelot, allowing Twain to comment on his own lonely plight as a person harboring dangerously unpopular truths and forced to keep them buttoned up inside himself. As Hank says, "As I was the only person in the kingdom afflicted with such impious and criminal opinions, I recognized that it would be good wisdom to keep quiet about this matter, too, if I did not wish to be suddenly shunned and forsaken by everybody as a madman."[54]

We learn more about Twain's views on slavery when Hank comes upon a procession of manacled slaves. He gives a hair-raising description of a master mercilessly flogging a woman, a scene influenced by his reading of Charles Ball's slave chronicle, *Fifty Years in Chains*. "He snatched the child from her, and then made the men slaves who were chained before and behind her throw her on the ground and hold her there and expose her body; and then he laid on with his lash like a madman till her back was flayed, she shrieking and struggling the while, piteously... All our pilgrims looked on and commented—on the expert way in which the whip was handled."[55] An aristocracy, he notes, is nothing more than "a band of slaveholders," motivated by "the possessor's old and inbred custom of regarding himself as a superior being."[56]

"NO POCKETS IN THE ARMOR"

In a reprise of *The Prince and the Pauper*, the Yankee aids the king in traveling incognito, putting a bowl over his head and cutting his hair until he resembles a commoner. When the two men are captured and sold into slavery, nobody recognizes the king. "Dear, dear, it only shows that there is nothing diviner about a king than there is about a tramp after all," Hank reflects.[57] When a storm strikes their slave coffle and two men and three women die, he notes: "Our master was nearly beside himself . . . and he was more brutal to us than ever, after that, for many days together, he was so enraged over his loss."[58]

After Hank and the king are rescued by Sir Launcelot and knights on bicycles, Hank defeats Sir Sagramour le Desirous in a tournament by throwing a lasso around him and yanking him from his horse. After doing the same with Launcelot, Hank prematurely declares that "knight-errantry is dead."[59] The story takes a bloody turn as he shoots down knights who challenge him. "The day was mine . . . The march of civilization was begun."[60] As he takes charge of the country, Hank introduces features of nineteenth-century society—schools and newspapers, phonographs and typewriters, factories and mills—and champions a republic with universal suffrage for men and some women. In this new Camelot, however, knights are converted into sharp businessmen and become members of a Stock Board with Sir Launcelot as president and chief stock market operator. "Sir Launcelot was a bear, and he had put up a corner in one of the new lines, and was just getting ready to squeeze the shorts to-day; but what of that?"[61]

Hank Morgan's mechanical improvements end when a feud between King Arthur and Sir Launcelot generates a civil war and Hank's dream of a republic falters. He realizes that his attempt at modernity has failed and the credulous people, still prey to superstition, fall back under the sway of a single Church and side anew with the nobles. With the king gone, Hank faces an onslaught from knights of the Church and blows up their approaching army, which becomes "a whirling tempest of rags and fragments."[62] In this strangely violent fantasy, Hank, the modern reformer, has become a mass murderer of twenty-five thousand knights in his aborted attempt to create a republic. He had hoped to liberate the masses from backward ways, but the finale suggests the difficulty, if not futility, of reform. What starts as a paean to Yankee ingenuity ends with a darker vision of invention run amok.

Twain could have written a lovely, droll book about a Connecticut Yankee awakening in a picturesque Camelot. Instead, he wrote a book bulging with controversial asides and provocative opinions. Though one of Twain's funniest books, it feels bloated and undisciplined, and is marred by his exploiting his story as a soapbox to sound off on contemporary issues. Too often the author is readily visible behind the transparent mask of Hank Morgan. The more Twain fancied himself a political philosopher, the more he felt stifled by fiction's limitations and wished to express himself directly, yet it was fiction that gave him license to tear off the gag that muzzled him on many topics. The further back in time he went, the greater his freedom to skewer the contemporary world.

In private, Twain's views had grown more militant. In his notebook, he averred that in a constitutional monarchy "a royal family of Chimpanzees would answer every purpose, be worshiped as abjectly by the nation, & be cheaper."[63] He told a correspondent, "In a few years from now we shall have nothing but played-out kings and dukes on the police, and driving the horse-cars, and whitewashing fences, and in fact overcrowding all the avenues of unskilled labor."[64] Howells noticed that the contradictory Twain found it easier to criticize society than to propose workable alternatives and was "a theoretical socialist and a practical aristocrat."[65] Twain acknowledged the criticism. "I am a democrat only on principle, not by instinct—nobody is *that*."[66]

While Twain hated Communism, he was sympathetic to unions and hailed the workingman as "the rightful sovereign of this world."[67] He had a paradoxical belief that organized labor would benefit from labor-saving machinery, a point he made in promoting the Paige typesetter, which he said would end up employing more people than it displaced. Increasingly drawn to quixotic movements, he befriended Edward Bellamy and endorsed his Utopian socialist novel *Looking Backward,* touting it as "the latest and best of all the Bibles," and also supported Henry George

"NO POCKETS IN THE ARMOR"

and his campaign for a single tax on land to be employed for an expansion of public works.[68]

By the time of *Connecticut Yankee*, Twain had become an unabashed American patriot, proudly democratic and dismayed by compatriots who fawned over European aristocrats. "Merit alone should be the only thing that should give a man a title to eminence," he told a British reporter.[69] More and more he was bothered by British condescension and maintained the superiority of American culture and politics. "We Americans worship the almighty dollars!" he scoffed. "Well, it is a worthier god than Heredity Privilege."[70] Speaking in a shrilly radical voice, he blasted the English character as "a curious admixture of cur & lion" and noted that an Englishman was "a person who does things because they have been done before," while an American was "a person who does things because they *haven't* been done before."[71] For Twain, the Civil War and the abolition of slavery had eliminated the major blot on America's escutcheon, and in 1890 he asserted that "there is today but one real civilization in the world, and it is not yet thirty years old. We made the trip and hoisted its flag when we disposed of our slavery."[72]

After *Connecticut Yankee* was issued in December 1889, its sales proved sluggish, with only thirty-two thousand copies sold in the United States after a year. Because Twain believed "the publisher who sells less than 50,000 copies of a book for me has merely injured me," the numbers sorely disappointed him. After he sent copies to friendly reviewers, the Hartford *Times* weighed in with a favorable notice that lauded the book's robust humor while also crediting the "sober and genuine purpose" behind its underlying politics.[73] Twain's friend Sylvester Baxter of the Boston *Sunday Herald* likewise appreciated the book's "abundant fun" and approved its attack on "aristocratic privileges and royal prerogatives that yet linger in the world."[74] The most perceptive review came from Howells in the *Atlantic Monthly*, who saw Twain peeping from behind the curtain in a book that contained "more of his personality than in anything else he has done. Here he is to the full the humorist, as we know him; but he is very much more, and his strong, indignant, often infuriate [sic] hate of injustice, and his love of equality, burn hot through the manifold adventures and experiences of the tale."[75] Howells knew Twain well enough to see his hot-blooded politics breaking through the carapace of his narrative.

Though American reviews were mixed, enough were friendly to show that Twain could move beyond his image as a beloved humorist and that the public was prepared to accept his incisive political views if wrapped in satire. In contrast, the book endured a savage drubbing in England. If Twain had hoped to teach the English a political lesson, he was sadly disabused, with the London *Daily Telegraph* branding the book a "vulgar travesty" and asking, "Under which King will the American serve ... Will they own allegiance to KING ARTHUR or JAY GOULD?"[76]

Wounded by this critical reception, Twain mailed an anguished letter to English critic Andrew Lang, complaining that some critics judge "all books by one standard—the cultivated class-standard."[77] In his pain, Twain issued an explicit credo for his art. Proud and unapologetic, he said that he had worked to create a new democratic literature for ordinary people. "I have never tried in even one single instance, to help cultivate the cultivated classes ... I never had any ambition in that direction, but always hunted for bigger game—the masses ... I never cared what became of the cultured classes; they could go to the theatre and the opera." Twain ended his letter with a poignant plea: "Help me, Mr. Lang; no voice can reach further than yours in a case of this kind, or carry greater weight of authority."[78]

The letter yielded results. Lang published a glowing piece titled "The Art of Mark Twain" in the *Illustrated London News*. He ducked the issue of the *Connecticut Yankee*, which he claimed he had not read, and focused instead on *Huck Finn*, which he christened "the great American novel." "I can never forget ... the exquisite pleasure with which I read *Huckleberry Finn* for the first time, years ago."[79] But Lang could not undo the damage done by the hostile reviews of *Connecticut Yankee*, and for several years Mark Twain's books carried an ineradicable stigma in England.

CHAPTER TWENTY-FIVE

"The Deriding of Shams"

Long before publishing *Connecticut Yankee,* Mark Twain had exhibited a delicate ego about being a humorist, partly because the tag didn't do justice to the sheer breadth of his writing and partly because of the low prestige assigned to such writing. Humorists didn't collect honors accorded to high-class scribes. For that reason, Twain, who never went to college, was elated when Yale College (assisted by alumnus Joe Twichell) bestowed on him the honorary degree of Master of Arts in June 1888. "To be made a master of arts by your venerable college is an event of large size to me, & a distinction which gratifies me quite as much as if I deserved it," Twain told Yale president Timothy Dwight. Matthew Arnold had "rather sharply rebuked the guild of American 'funny men' in his latest literary delivery, & therefore your honorable recognition of us is peculiarly forcible & timely."[1] Instead of disclaiming the humorist label, Twain hastened to enhance its meaning. The humorist's mission was "the deriding of shams, the exposure of pretentious falsities, the laughing of stupid superstitions out of existence; & that whoso is engaged in this sort of warfare is the natural enemy of royalties, nobilities, privileges & all kindred swindles, & the natural friend of human rights & human liberties."[2] He confessed to more than a touch of pride in being a recipient of the award. "I am the only literary animal in my particular sub-species who has ever been given a degree by any College in any age of the world, as far as I know."[3]

Early in his career, in his freewheeling western days, Twain had enjoyed hobnobbing with humorists such as Artemus Ward; later on, the small cadre of writers he befriended tended to be elegant stylists who appreciated his work. Twain and the entire Clemens family rejoiced in the fiction of Robert Louis Stevenson, especially *Kidnapped* and *Treasure Island*. They had "bathed in them, last summer, & refreshed our spirits," Twain told Stevenson, who returned the compliment by confessing that he had read *Huck Finn* four times and was "quite ready to begin again tomorrow."[4] Stevenson's father had guffawed so uproariously while reading *Roughing It* that he had declared, "It cannot be safe for a man at my time of life to laugh so much."[5] During the winter of 1887–88, Stevenson was treated for tuberculosis at Saranac Lake in upstate New York, even as he smoked four packs of cigarettes a day. At the end of his stay, he met Twain in New York, and the two men spent five hours together, some of that time sharing a bench in Washington Square Park. Before he died in 1894, at the age of forty-four, Stevenson fondly evoked "that very pleasant afternoon we spent together in Washington Square among the nursemaids like a couple of characters out of a story by Henry James."[6]

One of Twain's most consequential literary friendships started in August 1889 when a twenty-three-year-old reporter named Rudyard Kipling made a fourteen-thousand-mile pilgrimage from India to track down his hero in Elmira. Writing for the Allahabad *Pioneer,* he had covered British soldiers in northern India and studied the dynamics of colonial life there. Upon arriving in America, he took a steamboat ride on the Columbia River in the Pacific Northwest and viewed the whole experience through the prism of *Huck Finn* and *Life on the Mississippi*. Once installed in a "frowzy" hotel in Elmira, Kipling made his way to Quarry Farm, where he encountered Susy sketching in a wooden shed, and she informed him that her father could be found at the downtown Langdon home. Ordinarily, Twain would have rebuffed this sudden interloper with the spectacles and handlebar mustache, but his attention was arrested by a single trait: his marvelous talk, which, Twain argued, could "be likened to a footprint, so strong and definite was the impression it left behind."[7] Of course, the precise selection of words was Mark Twain's own forte, and he must have spotted in young Kipling a kindred soul.

At the ivy-clad Langdon mansion, Kipling found Twain lounging in

"THE DERIDING OF SHAMS"

a "huge chair" in a dark drawing room and recorded a vivid impression of a man with "a mane of grizzled hair, a brown mustache covering a mouth as delicate as a woman's, a strong, square hand shaking mine, and the slowest calmest, levellest voice in all the world."[8] Despite his gray hair, there was a youthful sparkle in Twain's eyes and he had a light-footed manner. Puffing on a meerschaum pipe with one leg thrown over the chair's arm and his right hand stroking his chin, Twain corresponded to the image Kipling had carried of him from India. "Blessed is the man," he wrote, "who finds no disillusion when he is brought face to face with a revered writer."[9] Twain was irreverent toward his own fiction in a way that startled the young man, who asked whether there would be a sequel to *Tom Sawyer,* with the protagonist advanced to adulthood. Twain said he had mulled over two options. "In one I would make him rise to great honor and go to Congress, and in the other I should hang him. Then the friends and enemies of the book could take their choice."[10] Taken aback, Kipling protested that Tom "isn't your property any more. He belongs to us"—which elicited a warm, hearty laugh from Twain.[11]

During their two-hour talk, Twain dispensed enough aphorisms to delight his new acolyte. "Your conscience is a nuisance," he told Kipling. "A conscience is like a child. If you pet it and play with it and let it have everything that it wants, it becomes spoiled and intrudes on all your amusements and most of your griefs . . . I think I have reduced mine to order."[12] Twain likely shocked Kipling when he said that he never read novels, "except when the popular persecution forces me to—when people plague me to know what I think of the last book that every one is reading."[13] He expressed a decided preference for facts and statistics, whether the topic be radishes or mathematics. "Get your facts first," he advised Kipling, and "then you can distort 'em as much as you please."[14] It was evident that Twain had turned on the full spigot of his charm for this young man who had so powerfully impressed him; despite his obscurity, Twain treated him as a peer. "That is a most unusual man," Twain observed afterward. "He knows almost everything that is worth knowing, and what he doesn't know, I know. We had a very good time."[15] Susy saved Kipling's calling card, with its exotic Allahabad address and flattering words about her father, as a cherished souvenir. A year later, Kipling began to earn an international reputation with his stories and poems.

Kipling never abandoned his hero worship of Mark Twain. "I love to think of the great and God-like Clemens," he told an American publisher. "He is the biggest man you have on your side of the water by a damn sight, and don't you forget it."[16] Many years later, Kipling anointed Twain "the largest man of his time."[17] Twain reciprocated this effusive admiration. "I am not a lover of all poetry," he declared, "but there is something in Kipling that appeals to me," and he derived special pleasure from reading aloud his melodious verse.[18] He admired the prose no less, especially *Kim* and the *Jungle* books. "They never grow pale to me; they keep their color; they are always fresh."[19] When Kipling later suffered medical problems, Twain told a friend, "I am so sorry for the bitter time he is having, but glad he has been spared to a world which he made a hundred thousand times richer than it was when he entered it."[20] Through the years, Twain's political views would be diametrically opposed to those of Kipling, whom Twain called "the militant spokesman of the Anglo-Saxon races."[21] Twain became as bitter a foe of imperialism as Kipling was its tenacious defender. Nonetheless, Twain was beguiled by Kipling's style and never ceased to thrill to his words. "Kipling's name, and Kipling's words always stir me now, stir me more than do any other living man's."[22]

The bloodiest literary feud that erupted in Mark Twain's career was with the critic-playwright Edward H. "Ned" House, and it made the contretemps with Bret Harte seem tame in comparison. In the aftermath of their quarrel, Twain denied that he and House had been old friends, but their relationship dated back to Twain's early bohemian days in New York when they hung out at Pfaff's Restaurant and Lager Beer Saloon on Broadway with Walt Whitman and Artemus Ward. Tall, handsome, and engaging, House himself was a quick-witted man who could trade barbs with Twain. As prestigious drama critic for the *New York Tribune*, he had posted an encouraging notice of Twain's 1867 lecture at the Cooper Institute.[23] "The mantle of the lamented Artemus Ward seems to have fallen on the shoulders of Mark Twain, and worthily does he wear it," House concluded in his influential review.[24] The journalist had made his mark reporting on the abolitionist movement, helping turn John Brown into a legendary figure. He also had a hand in shaping a play by Irish writer Dion Boucicault called *Arrah-na-Pogue*, though that was later hotly contested by Twain. When Twain signed up for the *Quaker City* cruise, it was House who accompanied him to see Captain Charles C. Duncan and introduced him as a Baptist preacher. House even read *The Gilded Age* in manuscript, supplying pertinent suggestions.

House would inevitably be associated with Japan, where he taught English literature at the Imperial University of Tokyo and became the first regular American newspaper correspondent in the country. He fervently admired Japanese culture. "To lead my own countrymen to a just appreciation of this pleasant land . . . has been my self-assigned task for many years," he wrote.[25] He ended up as editor of the English-language Tokyo *Times,* something of a house organ for the Japanese government.

Ned House had two sides to his nature: he could be gracious and hospitable, but he was also hypersensitive, quick to find fault with editors, and fretful about money, especially after his career tumbled into decline in the 1880s. Mark Twain, who had long credited his graceful prose, would experience both the force of his charm and the sharp lash of his tongue. The most unusual feature of House's personal life was his decision to adopt a young Japanese woman named Aoki Koto, who had entered into a wretched marriage that ended in divorce after a year. Such was the shame attached to divorced women in Japan that Koto contemplated suicide, prompting House to adopt her "to lessen the griefs of a suffering girl" and "to save her from subsequent humiliation."[26] A firm proponent of education for women, House had established an innovative school for girls from humble backgrounds and was well positioned to help Koto, with whom he would have a stormy relationship.

In 1880 House returned to the United States, riddled with debt and gout so searing it felt like "rivets of red hot iron" strapped to his ankles.[27]

FLOODTIDE

Twain urged House and twenty-one-year-old Koto to stay with the Clemenses in Hartford, which they did in February 1882. During that stay, House pored over *The Prince and the Pauper* and later claimed he performed some editing. "He may really and honestly have thought that was so," Twain was to say, "for at intervals his gout so tortured him that he drank laudanum in startling quantities, and that sort of a beverage probably assists the imagination."[28] This cynical view only came in retrospect. At the time, the Clemens family adored the petite, artistic Koto, with her picturesque Japanese costumes. After they left, Twain informed House they all longed "for one more glimpse of the dearest little Koto that's in the world."[29] So thoroughly did Twain revive his friendship with House that he lobbied Grant and President-elect Garfield for a diplomatic post for him in Japan. In inviting House and Koto to Hartford for a January visit, Twain had pleaded with them to stay until mid-April. "We want as much of you as we can get."[30] It was rare for Twain to implore people to come for a full week, much less several months, and he later falsified the nature of their relationship, making House sound like a distant acquaintance. The truth was that House and Koto had become much like family, with Koto's photo displayed on the mantelpiece in Hartford.

After House returned to Japan, he was felled by a stroke in 1883 that confined him to a wheelchair. A government pension retired his worst money fears, but he needed to keep writing to support himself. Twain later denigrated House's theatrical credentials, overlooking his past invitations to have them collaborate on stage projects. "Howells & I have written a play together," he wrote to House in January 1884. "I wish *you* were here to write plays with. Why the devil *did* you go away out there?"[31] Twain contended that he had been duped into thinking House coauthored *Arrah-na-Pogue,* when he had merely contributed a few lines. The following month, Twain decided to apply for a copyright for a play based on *The Prince and the Pauper,* with House not yet involved. Twain still addressed House with deep affection, ending one May 1885 letter by saying, "Goodbye! and the Lord love you & Koto."[32]

By the time House returned to New York in May 1886, his mood had

"THE DERIDING OF SHAMS"

darkened considerably due to his agonizing incapacity. That summer, editor Whitelaw Reid visited him and was appalled by his ghastly condition. "His knee-joints were kept bent so long by gout that they have solidified," he told John Hay. "It has been years since he has stood on his feet and he can never hope to move about, even on crutches. It comes the nearest to a living death of any case I have ever seen, and is most pitiful."[33]

To make things still more macabre, House's landlord on West 32nd Street began to threaten him, so House procured a pistol to protect himself. In this ghoulish situation, Twain offered House asylum in Hartford, claiming afterward it was from pity, not friendship. "The reason we invited him to come to us for a month was because his letters indicated that he & Koto were being brutally treated by their landlord & were afraid of bodily assault. I wished he was in hell, but we *had* to offer him an asylum. He & Koto & their servant were here 5 or 6 weeks. Within the first 10 days he grossly insulted me in the library, & I told him that if he were not disabled I would throw him into the street. I made preparations to have him carted out, but he wrote & sent me a long & outspoken apology, & Mrs. Clemens required me to accept it."[34] Nonetheless, contemporary letters demonstrate that House still felt close enough to Twain that he wished to transfer his property to him, so he could care for Koto in the event of his death. Twain rebuffed the idea, claiming that Livy thought "I might most seriously harm Koto's interests through my indolence, forgetfulness, impatience of everything like business-detail, & she can't allow it or think of it."[35] Meanwhile, the Clemens family remained enchanted with Koto, Twain rhapsodizing her as "the dearest & loveliest spirit that lives in this earth."[36]

The heart of the controversy set to blaze into open warfare between Twain and House centered on conversations that took place in late 1886 when Twain proposed that his friend dramatize *The Prince and the Pauper*. On December 17, Twain wrote to House that "I can't dramatize it. The reason I say this is because I *did* dramatize it, & made a bad botch of it. But *you* could do it ... The work might afford you good amusement when the pains mercifully retire at times."[37] In return, Twain offered House one-half or two-thirds of the play's proceeds. Twain had Charley

Webster dispatch two copies of the book to House and also sent him the crude work he had performed on the play. On December 24, House announced to Twain that he was "well pleased to undertake a dramatization" and could start work "in a day or two."[38] No formal contract existed between the two men, and their subsequent legal dispute would hinge on whether their letters of December 17 and 24 could be regarded as binding. Flying in the face of certifiable facts, Twain said House had never accepted his offer to turn the book into a drama. "He did not discard the proposition, but there was nothing in his letter [of December 24] that can be construed into an acceptance."[39] On another occasion, Twain stated categorically that House "was indifferent and declined."[40]

Twain and House had wildly divergent recollections of what happened next, neither side being wholly convincing. House maintained that the following spring he wrote to Twain at least eight times, discussing the play and possible casting. In May he stayed at the Clemens household for six weeks, where he finished the first act and read several hundred lines to Twain, who said approvingly, "that's a play" and "I see that on the stage."[41] In the House version of events, he plugged along at the manuscript, telling Twain on August 29: "This morning I had the satisfaction of seeing the whole five acts completed . . . with the exception of the closing scene of Act I."[42] House told Twain that he had finished the play, but by then Twain had seemed to lose interest.

With his selective memory, Mark Twain had a mind geared to invention, not retaining facts, and he offered a competing vision of what had happened: In his view, he had received only three letters from House in the spring, none alluding to the play. During the Hartford visit, House had outlined a "skeleton of the first act," which covered only two or three pages and "contained hardly more than fifteen lines of dialogue."[43] Twain spurned the idea that he had approved this still shadowy act and insisted that he and House had no further communication about the play. Of House's contention that he verbally told him of the play's completion in September 1887, Twain dismissed this as "pure laudanum."[44] "So far as I knew or know," Twain was to testify in court, "the play was

"THE DERIDING OF SHAMS"

never completed."[45] Though House spent many months afterward in Hartford and saw Twain often, the two never seemed to talk about *The Prince and the Pauper* again. It was, Twain said derisively, "eighteen months of petrified absence of interest in this dramatization" by House.[46]

There the matter rested until December 4, 1888, when Abby Sage Richardson approached Twain with a request to dramatize the novel, extolling it as "one of the most beautiful stories . . . I had ever read."[47] An actress, writer, and editor, Richardson had enjoyed a racy personal life straight out of a stage melodrama. Twenty years earlier, her ex-husband had shot her lover, Albert D. Richardson, in the *New York Tribune* offices. Best known for books and articles on the Civil War, Richardson had written a biography of Ulysses S. Grant. Abby married Richardson as he lay dying, in a ceremony performed by Henry Ward Beecher. Twain granted Abby Sage Richardson the right to dramatize *The Prince and the Pauper,* and they proceeded swiftly to sign a contract on January 3, 1889. Richardson was eager to cast seven-year-old Elsie Leslie, then starring in *Little Lord Fauntleroy,* as the lead performer, playing both the prince and the pauper, with Daniel Frohman producing. Perhaps having gotten wind of House's earlier involvement, Richardson inquired of Twain, "Does this contract prevent any other person from attempting dramatization of the book while I am doing the work[?]"[48]

Twain was so innocent of any evil intention toward House that he actually urged Abby Sage Richardson to consult with him, which she declined. It never dawned on him that House might react with frenzied wrath upon learning of the contract. "I gather the idea from your letter that you would have undertaken the dramatization of that book," Twain told House on February 26. "Well, that would have been joyful news to me about the middle of December, when I gladly took the first offer that came and made a contract. I remembered that you started once to map out the framework for me to fill in, and I suggested to this lady that possibly you would collaborate with her, but she thought she could do the work alone. However, I never thought of such a thing as your being willing to undertake the dramatization itself—I mean the whole thing."[49]

These two grown-up men had both behaved in a mystifying manner. Why had Twain not checked with House before choosing a replacement, even though they had no formal contract? And why had House stayed silent for more than a year about a play he allegedly finished and wished to see produced? That House hastened to secure a copyright from the Library of Congress for his manuscript on February 15, 1889—only after learning of the Abby Sage Richardson deal—suggests either guilt or duplicity on his part. "The manuscript has many longhand alterations," one scholar has observed, "as if it might have been hastily thrown together to bolster a claim."[50] It seems likely House overstated the matter when he implied that he had brought the play to polished completion.

On March 19, Twain sent House an exemplary letter, stating that if a wrong had been committed, he wanted to see proof and make amends. Twain was often scattered and absent-minded and may honestly have forgotten his promises to House. "There is no time to lose," he wrote to House. "If I have heedlessly, ignorantly, forgetfully, gone & made a contract which I had no right to make, it is a serious thing & I must move in the matter without loss of time. Send me the evidence at once; & send me copy of any & all writings, notes, letters, that throw the light upon the thing."[51] Instead, House initiated a protracted, acrimonious lawsuit against Twain to stop the Richardson play, and all communication between the former friends ceased. Twain may have been right that no conventional contract existed. But, as his brother Orion alerted him, a judge would likely construe the exchanged letters of December 17 and 24, 1886, as constituting a legal agreement. Adamant in his position, Twain signed a new contract with Abby Sage Richardson on May 13 that gave her half the royalties and required her to finish the play by October 1, submitting it to Twain and Frohman for their approval, with Frohman given exclusive production rights for five years.

Despite looming legal obstacles, *The Prince and the Pauper* opened in Philadelphia on Christmas Day 1889 and on Broadway on January 20. As so often with Twain and pretty young girls, he doted on Elsie Leslie, who had blond curls and brown eyes, and was a frequent guest at the Clemens home. Twain and the actor William Gillette embroidered a pair of slippers

"THE DERIDING OF SHAMS"

for Elsie, which Twain sweetened with an ardent note. "Take the slippers and wear them next your heart, Elsie dear; for every stitch in them is a testimony of the affection which two of your loyalest friends bear you . . . will you please explain that I embroidered this slipper without any instruction in Art, and *all* for love of you?"[52] It was a strangely excessive, if seemingly harmless, romancing of a young girl. When he presented Elsie with an inscribed copy of *A Connecticut Yankee*, he included verses addressed to her: "I'll be your friend, your thrall, your knave / I'll be your elder brother / I'll be for love, your very slave / Or anything you'druther."[53] Again, the resort to mock-romantic language seemed peculiar.

On opening night, Twain appeared before the curtain at the close, holding Elsie's hand. He sang her praises to the audience, saying her Prince had ruled by "the divine right of an inborn supremacy in art."[54] Twain spoke so long that one reporter noted that Elsie "glanced from time to time inquiringly up at Mark Twain's lips as if wondering when he would stop talking."[55] It had been a mostly exhilarating evening for the Clemens family, with nine-year-old Jean seeing her first play and clapping in imitation every time her parents did. Onstage, Twain paid homage to Abby Sage Richardson. "To write a book one must have great learning, high moral qualities . . . But to make a play requires genius . . . And therefore the honor of this curtain call belongs not to me but to Mrs. Abby Sage Richardson."[56] After Twain escorted Elsie offstage, he returned with Richardson, who bowed in "a pert bonnet of gray silk and from above a gala gown of maroon satin," said a reporter.[57]

Elsie Leslie came in for some criticism, ladled out in gentle fashion, as befit a child actor. The *Times* acknowledged her precocious aplomb. "She has already learned how to receive bouquets over the footlights, and a great many were handed to her last night." This didn't soften the stinging verdict that came next. "Elsie Leslie is not yet an actress, and 'The Prince and the Pauper' is not yet a good play. Elsie may become an actress in time."[58] Indeed, critics singled out for praise passages that retained Twain's original dialogue and suspected that Richardson had mostly bypassed the book. The night of the performance, the Clemenses, caught up in audience enthusiasm, didn't notice the play's glaring flaws. Twain confessed that he "was bewitched by Elsie's acting, & carried out of myself by the pretty stage-pictures & the rich color of the dresses."[59]

Once the opening-night luster had faded, however, Twain minced no words with Daniel Frohman. Despite his graceful tribute to Richardson, he was actually seething about the play she had produced and expressed frank disgust at the "infinite repulsiveness of the piece."[60] He branded it "the worst perversion of a story" that he had ever seen, arguing that Richardson had taken names and storylines from his book while dropping his characters, dialogue, scenes, and conversations. "Is this mess of idiotic rubbish & vapid twaddle a 'dramatization' of the book? It resembles it about as a riot in a sailor boarding-house resembles a Sunday-school."[61] Instead of Twain's fresh, delicate language, Richardson had disgorged a mass of turgid writing. She had failed to seek his contractual approval for changes, and he was hurt that his work had been disfigured. Rabidly protective of her husband's writing, Livy thought the play utterly failed to match up to the standards of the book. "Such inferior English is put into the mouths of the actors in many places," she complained to Grace King.[62]

Twain now fought a two-front war: one against Richardson, the other against House. Nine days before the New York opening, House sought an injunction against the Richardson play, asserting that Twain had given him exclusive rights to the story, and this began seven weeks of hearings. "It has not worried Mr. Clemens as much as I was afraid it would," Livy told Grace King of the legal standoff. "I think it has not greatly fretted him because he felt so free of guilt in the matter. Then he is not sorry, as Mr. House has taken the initiative, to cut away from that tiresome friendship or semblance of friendship."[63]

As the acrimony between the two writers spilled into the press, it grew into one of Twain's most widely publicized donnybrooks. Controversy now seemed an inescapable part of his career, litigation his perennial state. House snickered at his highly convenient memory and "habitual readiness to avail himself of the labor of others."[64] He may have had a point when he scolded Twain's tendency to embellish things, his inability to remember "anything whatever with literal accuracy."[65] He needled Twain by saying "the distinguished humorist is happier in the manufac-

"THE DERIDING OF SHAMS"

ture of modern fictions than in the application of ancient fables."[66] Even Judge Joseph Daly wondered at Twain's remarkable forgetfulness, observing the short time span between his discussions with House about the play and his contract with Mrs. Richardson—certainly "not so great as to efface" from Twain's mind his earlier dealings with House.[67] House was also insistent that he first suggested having a single child actor play both leading roles. Because of his infirmity and straitened finances, the press naturally sympathized with the ailing House. As the *Times* summed it up, "Briefly it is a story of an alleged injustice done to an author and playwright in straitened circumstances because of physical infirmity by a very wealthy author and publisher."[68]

For Twain, it was yet another case of his fondness and trust for a friend giving way to implacable rage, as if he could never maintain a middle ground with people. He complained to his lawyer, Daniel Whitford, that House had stuffed his affidavit with lies and concocted a fake diary for 1886–87 to show meetings that never occurred. He wondered why, if House had truly finished the play, he never demanded an official contract. Livy was wrong that the fracas with House didn't worry her husband, for he found House's behavior an unconscionable betrayal of their friendship. As he told Howells, "I want to get far, very far away from plays, just now, for any mention of the stage brings House to my mind & turns my stomach. What a gigantic liar that man is!—& what an inconceivable hound."[69]

On March 8, 1890, House won the legal battle, gaining a temporary injunction against performance of the Richardson play. As Orion had warned, Judge Daly held that Twain's correspondence with House had the standing of "a contract definite and certain."[70] He said House's carefully documented assertions were more persuasive than Twain's persistently vague memory. Although Frohman wrested from House permission to continue performing the play, he had to share a portion of the royalties with House and couldn't transfer any money to Twain himself, who was outraged that he made not a penny. "I *must* have some rights somewhere," he protested to his lawyer, "& I wish to know what they are."[71] That September, House staged his own version of the play in Brooklyn before his action was blocked by the busy Judge Daly.

FLOODTIDE

The saga of Twain's battle royale with Edward H. House didn't result from malice or mendacity on Twain's part so much as from his breezy, careless way with facts and heedlessness dealing with an old friend. Once again he had shown no head for business. Neither man covered himself in glory in this ugly dispute. Twain should have notified House before hiring Abby Sage Richardson, and House should have honored the extraordinary hospitality the Clemenses had shown him in Hartford. Twain never betrayed any remorse for his actions and continued to belittle House as "that lowest down of all polecats & liars."[72] What maddened him most was less money lost than reputational damage. "I *do* seriously hate to see my character made the so easy prey of a rancid adventurer like that scoundrel. I'm not going to law again with a man who is willing to tell lies & swear to them."[73]

As was the case with Bret Harte, Twain could muster phenomenal energy in a feud, which stirred up his pugnacious nature. In private, he released a flood of recriminations against House. As usual, words were his catharsis, his therapy, his preferred form of revenge. In a lengthy screed titled "Concerning the Scoundrel Edward H. House," he portrayed House as "a man who does overmuch crying, for a grown person, and doubtless he will go on dripping his tears on me through the press, although he knows that no one likes to be wet and disagreeable. I seem to have proved quite a 'find' for House. A year or two ago he used to complain that he could get very little of his literature accepted and published. He is finding out, now, that if he will write fictions about notorious people, their names will service [sic] as kite, and lift the tail aloft into print, signature and all."[74] Twain never discarded a sense of injustice in the matter. In 1894 he sued Daniel Frohman for money he believed that he was still owed from the play. Unlike what occurred with House, the two friends remained on civilized terms as the legal process unfolded. "While the suit was in progress," Frohman recalled, "Mr. Clemens and I played our nightly games of pool at The Players with unruffled amity."[75] In the end, Twain received no share of royalties from a play based on the coinage of his own brain.

CHAPTER TWENTY-SIX

Death and Delusion

By February 1888, Twain had induced Charley Webster to exit from the publishing firm that bore his name. The author's animus toward his nephew never waned, but he hoped to turn a fresh page with Fred Hall, who had replaced Webster and acquired his share of the business.[1] "You and I," Twain told Hall in a burst of premature optimism, "will never have any trouble."[2] He found Hall hardworking and well-meaning, though he later concluded he was "wholly incompetent for the place."[3] It was yet another relationship destined for disappointment with the hypercritical Twain.

The main problem for Hall was that irrevocable decisions had already been made that would plague him for years. Twain had bet heavily on Civil War literature, which had paid handsome dividends with Grant's *Memoirs*, but then, as one general after another rushed to cash in on the boom, public fatigue set in. Having known Phil Sheridan for many years, Twain visited him at the War Department with Charley Webster, and they persuaded him to overcome his reluctance to publish a memoir. Once again, Webster & Company raced to obtain a completed autobiography before its author had departed this earthly scene, which Sheridan did on August 5, 1888. With the book headed for publication, Hall toured midwestern cities and reported back gloomily to Twain: "There is one thing this trip has convinced me of viz: *war literature of any kind and no matter by whom written is played out*. We have got to hustle

FLOODTIDE

everlastingly to get rid of 75,000 sets of Sheridan."[4] Twain was again realizing the truth that in publishing timing was everything.

With Sheridan's book, Twain experienced his first twinge of panic with his publishing firm as it slipped into a dangerous dependency on bank loans. On July 14, he received notice from Webster & Company's bookkeeper that cash reserves had sunk to a perilous new low: less than $1,500. Stunned by this revelation, Twain scribbled on the statement: "Observe this. 2½ years ago . . . Webster insisted on keeping $100,000 in bank right along, to 'keep us strong.' And then he went to work and wasted it, squandered it in every idiotic way he could think of. Behold the result. We need $30,000 to build General Sheridan's 100,000-copy edition, and we've got $1500!"[5] Twain had no choice but to borrow heavily from the Mount Morris Bank.

That fall the firm's slide only accelerated, and on October 23, its bookkeeper informed Twain of a $16,500 loss in six months. No less startling was that the firm's indebtedness to Twain had mushroomed to almost $73,000. Under an arrangement signed with Webster, Twain had agreed to provide up to $75,000 in capital and now grew alarmed as that limit was approached with no end in sight. He knew he stared at a doomsday scenario. "Can I be held for debts made beyond the capital?" he wondered in his notebook. "I will buy out or sell out. Since the spring of '86 the thing has gone straight downhill toward sure destruction. It must be brought to an end Feb. 1 at all hazards. This is final."[6] Like Tom Sawyer, he found himself watching his own funeral. By year's end, Twain had clamped stringent new limits on what could be published. "We can't take any more books for a long time yet," he told one author. "We are over-crowded, & must wait till we work the list down."[7]

Like Webster, Hall was handicapped by the eleven-volume *Library of American Literature*, whose costs outpaced anything a small firm like Webster & Company could handle. At first, Hall made hopeful noises about its potential sales. "I think this book is going to pan out big eventually, as the results attained so far have come without any particular pushing," he assured Twain.[8] The operative word was "eventually." Customers would pay $3 for the first monthly installment of a $33 set, even though the firm had to pay at once $13 in manufacturing and shipping costs and $12 to agents. "The faster installments came in," Hall admitted, "the faster our capital shrank."[9] Delinquent payments piled up. The *LAL* series proved such a financial albatross that Twain thought of putting it up for sale. Series editor Edmund C. Stedman chided Twain for being shortsighted and said *LAL* was "the most valuable & *substantial* property the firm possesses" with "no limit to the profit from it. Thus far, we have scarcely *scratched* the end of the buying elephant's nose."[10] Twain knew, however, that every penny of profit was being siphoned off by this costly series. The whole subscription model, with its high overhead of sales agents, was also threatened by the spread of bookstores. To his credit, Fred Hall tilted the firm's emphasis toward trade books, and by 1890, aside from *LAL,* these sales would make up three-quarters of its business.

Dogged by his hatred of Charley Webster, Twain was at first inclined to exaggerate Hall's prowess. "The substitution of brains for guesswork was accomplished when you took Webster's place . . . We are not sailing a pirate ship any longer; we have discarded the pirate ways . . . along with the pirate himself."[11] The two men worked out a modus operandi in which Hall would make decisions and only inform Twain of them afterward. As expenses mounted with the typesetter, Twain had hoped his publishing venture might subsidize the Paige machine. That looked like a forlorn wish in May 1889 when Twain's request for $1,000 brought this pessimistic response from Hall: "As you know the dull season is upon us . . . so I think it would be well for you . . . not to count on getting any money from us until Fall, as it might embarrass us somewhat."[12] The reliance on loans from the Mount Morris Bank cast a pall over the firm's activities.

In business situations, Twain grew easily depressed. He now carried the cumulative weight of Webster & Company, the Paige typesetter, and the House lawsuit, and instead of blaming himself, he vented his fury upon the departed Charley Webster. As he told Orion, "I have never hated any creature with a hundred thousandth fraction of the hatred which I bear that human louse, Webster."[13] Even when writing to

FLOODTIDE

Pamela—Charley's mother-in-law—Twain found it impossible to censor his rage. "My feeling against Webster—who is not a man, but a hog—is so bitter that I could not even endure the idea of addressing a letter whose mere envelop could pass under the defilement of his eye. I love Annie, & deeply honor her; but as for—well, I will drop that subject."[14] As Howells noted of Twain's intemperance, "If a trust of his own was betrayed—Clemens was ruthlessly, implacably resentful."[15] His mood swings had become more volatile than ever.

As Twain's payments for the Paige typesetter soared to $3,000 monthly, he and his family became captives of the monstrous machine that soaked up all their cash. Twain's letters are replete with references to his family economizing and the shadow cast by austerity. One day, when Marie, the governess, wanted to buy black shoe polish for the children, eight-year-old Jean piped up, "Why, Marie, you mustn't *ask* for things now. The machine isn't done."[16] As he gambled with his family's future, Twain had to postpone trips and sell stock as he dug into his personal savings and whittled down Livy's vanishing fortune. She had come to share his fantasies of untold wealth when the machine was perfected. "How strange it will seem to have unlimited means," she told her sister, "to be able to do whatever you want to do, to give what you want to give without counting the cost."[17] With her inherited wealth, she should not have needed a second fortune, but seemed prepared to make the financial sacrifices required by the typesetter. "She is scouring around all the time after economical Christmas presents—presents unobtrusively capable & clever in the expression of love & a low financial condition," Twain told his mother-in-law.[18] Only Jane Clemens in Keokuk, endowed with midwestern common sense, posed the inescapable question: "Suppose the machine should fail?"[19]

Hostage to the contraption, Twain fretted as the competing Mergenthaler machine surged ahead and was adopted by the *New York Tribune*.

DEATH AND DELUSION

He made feverish calculations as to how much money newspapers would save by installing Paige's creation, noting that the *New York World* "had 185 compositors at work. It would take 37 machines to supply their place."[20] Twain refused to recognize that economic triumphs don't necessarily come to the most technically advanced inventions so much as to reliable products that arrive early at an affordable price. The Mergenthaler machine was simple, sturdy, and dependable, and much less fragile than its Paige rival. Meanwhile, Twain had missed out on a much bigger bonanza. In May 1888, Nikola Tesla received a patent for an alternating current motor, which he sold to George Westinghouse for $1 million. Four years earlier, Paige had come up with a similar idea for alternating current, recalled Twain, "but we lacked the apparatus . . . I would furnish nothing more because I was burdened . . . with vast expenses on the Paige type-setting machine."[21]

Although he had projected a completion date of April 1, 1888, for the compositor, that date, like so many others, flitted by without resolution as Twain began to realize that the machine was a cruel mirage that kept receding into the distance. After further setbacks, he wrote in August: "I wonder if the machine *is* really going to be finished some time or other, after all."[22] Then, near despair, he sent Livy the following greeting on December 31, 1888: "Happy New Year! The machine is finished, & this is the first work done on it."[23]

On January 5, Twain described to Orion the first successful operation of the Paige typesetter. If he had reported on the Second Coming, he could not have produced more delirious prose. "At 12:20 this afternoon a line of movable types was spaced and justified by machinery, for the first time in the history of the world! And I was there to see." So historic did the occasion seem to him that he recorded the exact hour and minute when this blessing was bestowed upon humanity. "All the other wonderful inventions of the human brain sink pretty nearly into commonplace contrasted with this awful mechanical miracle. Telephones, telegraphs, locomotives, cotton gins, sewing machines . . . all mere toys, simplicities! The Paige Compositor marches alone and far in the lead of human inventions."[24] He declared that "the most amazing and extraordinary invention ever born of the brain of man stands completed and perfect. Livy is down stairs [sic] celebrating."[25]

Two days later, using the new keyboard, Twain set the first proper name: "*William Shakspeare*," which he misspelled. Still unable to restrain his jubilation, he wrote to one London printer, "This is by far and away the most marvelous invention ever contrived by man."[26] In fact, Twain's troubles were just beginning, for the type kept breaking down, and Paige had to dismantle the machine and start repairs anew. Though Twain had begun to invite newspaper editors to witness the marvel, the imperfections forced delays in showing it to potential customers. Instead of restraining his euphoria, as he awaited a new July 15 completion deadline, he added up the number of American publications that would supposedly buy the machine. "We had 4,000 papers & periodicals in 1860; we had 8,000 in 1873, 16,000 in 1886; we should have 32,000 in 1899, without the Paige; with it we shall have—what? 40,000? or will it be 50,000?"[27] As with the Pope's book and the putative number of Catholics in the world, Twain indulged in wishful thinking on an elaborate scale as he wildly hyped the Paige and depreciated the Mergenthaler machine. Of other typesetters, Twain jeered that "they are bound straight for the junk-shop; every one of them."[28]

When Paige missed the July 15 deadline, it proved a costly postponement for Twain, who had secured a pledge from Charlie Langdon to buy a stake in the company if the machine was finished by the end of August. Scheduled to sail for Europe September 3 for a yearlong stay, Charlie stuck to his guns and departed with no investment. As Twain explained to an associate, he "says he has talked with me every summer for three years & that I have always been mistaken when the machine was going to be finished, & once more I was mistaken; that I promised another finish for Aug. 12, & another for Sept. 1 & failed twice more." Twain hoped to offer Charlie a higher royalty rate "for time is short & the corner I am in is distressingly tight."[29] This last line speaks to the extreme pressure the typesetter exerted on him.

In late September, Twain's anxiety was somewhat assuaged when he

DEATH AND DELUSION

negotiated with Paige a deal by which he would receive a $500 royalty on each machine sold. He then turned around and sold shares in those royalties to family and friends, relieving some financial distress. By this point, Twain had poured $100,000 into the machine's development ($3.4 million in today's dollars), with no end in sight. His hubris about the machine only grew, often bordering on complete intoxication. In October he boasted to Joseph T. Goodman that one Paige machine could perform the work of eight human compositors. "This fact sends all other typesetting machines a thousand miles to the rear, and the best of them will never be heard of again after we publicly exhibit in New York . . . We own the whole field—every inch of it—and nothing can dislodge us."[30] Twain's peerless imagination placed his mind beyond doubt, and his promotion of the Paige typesetter could sound like pure moonshine. "In construction," he told Goodman, "it is as elaborate and complex as that machine which it ranks *next* to, by every right—Man—and in performance it is as simple and sure."[31] He assigned Goodman to pursue as an investor his rich chum from Nevada, Senator John P. Jones, the silver mogul, with Goodman getting a 10 percent commission. Without a single finished machine on hand, Twain's florid imagination conjured up sales of fifteen thousand machines over a fifteen-year period.

Some warning voices went unheeded. Twain's friend Dean Sage inspected the machine in Hartford and perceived that the author was in way over his head. In exchange for rights to the Paige machine, Twain planned to disburse $2 million for a typesetter factory. Instead, Sage suggested that he subcontract the first few hundred to machine shops before making such an outsize commitment. "You have either got a great bonanza or nothing, & until you have a good number of the machines actually turning out successfully the work they are expected to do this is a question . . . To tell the truth I feel anxious about *you*—as I understand it, *you* are the man who will have to furnish the capital, so large in amount that a failure in the business might sweep away all you have, or seriously embarrass you."[32] These wise, loving words came from a true and knowledgeable friend, and unfortunately they proved prophetic.

Twain had come to share Paige's manic perfectionism, and both men wanted to produce a faultless machine with all the kinks ironed out in advance. In late November, Twain and Paige again examined the machine and found it wanting. "When we took the machine apart the other day," Twain wrote, "it was perfect enough to satisfy everybody in the world except two people—the inventor & me . . . But if it *doesn't* satisfy us, the perfecting will go on. It shall not go out of the shop with even the triflingest defect in it."[33] At the same time, he predicted that "the 15th of January we expect her to be perfecter than a watch."[34] All the while, Mergenthaler was stealing a march on Paige.

Amid the worries associated with Twain's business ventures, his family endured a welter of illnesses. During the winter of 1887–88, Livy suffered from the throat inflammation known as quinsy and in the spring added diphtheria to her troubles. Though afflicted with "a most infernal cold" himself, Twain noted his wife's symptoms with a novelist's clinical eye. "Her throat is excessively sore & painful," he informed Sue Crane, "& her tongue looks rutted & ragged, like a country road in muddy weather; & it has a great whitey-yellow flake in the middle of it."[35] Although Livy recovered, Twain archly observed, "The more I see of diphtheria the less I think of it as a spring recreation."[36] Despite the financial strain, Sam and Livy never shed their love for each other, and hardship bound them closer together. When Livy turned forty-three, he sent her a tender birthday message: "Livy darling, I am grateful—gratefuller [*sic*] than ever before—that you were born, & that your love is mine & our two lives woven & welded together."[37] In his ever more turbulent life, he needed the bedrock of her support.

Twain had hoped the usual summer escape to Quarry Farm would rejuvenate his family, but in September 1888, his brother-in-law Theodore Crane suffered a stroke that paralyzed him on one side. A man largely devoid of drive or ambition, he had served as chief clerk and then partner of the Langdon family coal firm. With his recovery complicated by long-standing diabetes, the whole family maintained an anxious bed-

DEATH AND DELUSION

side vigil, fearing he would die. As Crane slowly mended, he spent much time at the Twain house in Hartford that winter. The Clemenses became social hermits, preoccupied with his illness, while Livy and Sue Crane sank into deep dejection. At times Theodore seemed to rally, only to lapse back into pain and morbid depression. Twain worried about the emotional toll this ordeal took on his wife and sister-in-law. In early March, he told Sue that it "broke [his] heart to see Theodore this morning, he looked so exhausted, so depressed, so indifferent to life."[38] The Reverend Thomas K. Beecher was summoned to dissuade the patient from suicidal urges. By mid-June, the Clemenses stood by for the final deathwatch. "Mr. Crane can hardly last many days"; Twain wrote his sister, "he is very weak, & begs pitifully for release."[39] When Theodore Crane got his final release on July 3, 1889, Sue Crane was shattered by the loss.

There had not been a death in the family since Jervis Langdon, and it profoundly affected Mark Twain, already blue from business misadventures. He had left Livy and their daughters in Elmira while he returned alone to Hartford, where the solitude haunted him. Susy was now seventeen, old enough that he could write to her privately with adult concerns. "This is a very dark and silent cavern, now—this house. The thick foliage and lowered curtains make deep twilight; the little piano is gone and the big one locked up." He groped to define the melancholy that had seized him, labeling it an amalgam of "revery, and dreariness, and lonesomeness, and repentance."[40] To Livy he wrote a hopeful letter about the afterlife, one likely designed more to soothe her than to express his true beliefs. "I don't *know* anything about the hereafter, but I am not afraid of it. The further I get away from the superstitions in which I was born & mistrained, the more the idea of a hereafter commends itself to me & the more I am persuaded I shall find things comfortable when I get there."[41]

However much Twain boasted of his mother's spunk in old age, there was pardonable exaggeration in the portrait. A bespectacled old woman, partial to lace caps and lavender ribbons, Jane Lampton Clemens resided with Orion and Mollie in a simple brick house in Keokuk. Although Twain seldom visited, he generously sent monthly checks to all three. "If there is anything that can be done to your room or stove or furniture to make you more comfortable," Twain urged his mother, "have it done & let me pay the bill."[42] As early as 1882, his niece, Annie, hinted gently to him that Jane "does such queer things and takes such funny notions."[43] A year later it grew clear that she had succumbed to early dementia and was sometimes delusional. "It is as pathetic as it can be, the way Ma's infirmities affect her," Twain told Mollie. "May I never be old with ruined faculties!"[44] Jane sometimes had hilarious hallucinations, as when she imagined Orion pursuing Mollie's lover with a pistol, fantasies that attested to the literary imagination Twain had long attributed to her.

The power of Jane Clemens's imagination and the pathos of her life were vividly on display in fall 1885 when she traveled to the Tri-State Old Settler's Association reunion. She hoped to track down her old flame, Dr. Richard Barrett, who, she believed, had jilted her as a young woman. But Barrett had died in 1860, and Jane may have only imagined that she saw his name listed on a reunion program. She thought she had narrowly missed seeing him at the hotel. Whatever the case, the episode unlocked a story that she had kept hidden for more than sixty years: "When I was eighteen a young medical student named Barrett lived in Columbia (Kentucky) eighteen miles away and he used to ride over to see me . . . I loved him with my whole heart and I knew that he felt the same towards me, though no words had been spoken." When there was a party in a neighboring town, Barrett wrote to Jane's uncle "asking him to drive me over in his buggy and let him (Barrett) drive me back, so that he might have that opportunity to propose. My uncle should have done as he was asked . . . but instead he read me the letter and then, of course, I could not go, and did not. He (Barrett) left the country presently and I, to stop the clacking tongues and to show him that *I* did not care, *married* in a pet."[45] Had it not been for this errant uncle, Mark Twain would never have existed, and he was overwhelmed upon hearing the tale. "Think of her carrying that pathetic burden in her old heart sixty-four years," he told Howells, "and no human being ever suspecting it!"[46]

In her last years, Jane retreated deeper into the twilight of dementia.

DEATH AND DELUSION

She no longer remembered living in Hannibal, the town her son made famous, and resided again in the Kentucky of her youth, socializing with dead friends. She imagined Pamela had been stolen from her at age five by Indians. One night she wouldn't go to sleep because she was sure Sam was there and would occupy her bed. Even though she lived with Orion, she sometimes forgot who he was and mistook him for her uncle. "She wanted to know the other day if I was Orion, and who were my brothers?" Orion notified Sam. "She remembered that Sam was Mark Twain, but thought there were more brothers."[47] Perhaps she vaguely remembered Henry. One day, when Orion read to her a loving letter Sam had written about her recovery, she was unmoved by the sentiment. "Tell him I want the horses and carriage he promised me," she instructed Orion. "He never can pay me for all the trouble he was. He was the worst child I had—hollered and squalled day and night—and wouldn't let the nurse nor me, either, rest."[48] Of course, Jane was senile by this time, and Twain may have savored the black comedy.

In January 1888, when his mother had a stroke, Twain reacted with infinite pity, telling Orion, "Poor Ma, life pursues her relentlessly; & she has not deserved it. It is a pity that one so old should be assailed with pain; when the faculties fail, it is but fair that the senses should, too."[49] After a second stroke in August 1890, Jane Lampton Clemens deteriorated swiftly and died on October 27, 1890, at age eighty-seven. She was buried in Mount Olivet Cemetery in Hannibal between John Marshall and Henry Clemens. Twain returned to his hometown for the funeral and was relieved to see the "serenity & peace" expressed in her face instead of the "worn & hunted look" that she had shown for many years.[50]

In this season of death, the final blow fell on Olivia Lewis Langdon, who had played Lady Bountiful in the Clemens household. She was always a strong, benevolent presence, stationed in her accustomed rocking chair in Hartford, a generous woman who celebrated her birthday by handing out gifts to her children and grandchildren. She had doled out numberless presents to Sam and Livy, who had invariably responded with gratitude. "Oh Mother," Livy wrote, "you are too good to send us *so much money*. It is too much—you are too good to us." Or another time: "I think you are the very best Mother in the world how could you offer that thousand dollars!"[51] Twain wrote with identical feeling, if extra wit: "Mother, dear, thank you ever so much for my end of that check; I shall buy me something nice & warm with it—whisky, or something like that."[52]

As Twain struggled with Webster & Company bills in early November 1890, Mrs. Langdon loaned $10,000 to Livy, who turned around and loaned it to the publishing house. Two weeks later, when a telegram arrived in Hartford saying that Mrs. Langdon was dying, Sam and Livy quickly made their way to Elmira, leaving Clara and Jean at home. For a time, they were both posted by Mrs. Langdon's bedside, reassured by telegrams from Katy Leary in Hartford that the children were well. In spite of this, Livy succumbed to a premonition of something amiss at home. "You must take the next train to Hartford"; she told her husband, "something is wrong there."[53] Livy's hunch was vindicated: Twain found ten-year-old Jean running a dangerously high fever.

Twain felt sharp pangs of guilt about leaving Livy alone, but he knew Jean's well-being was at stake. "I have fed so full on sorrows, these last weeks that I seem to have become hardened to them—benumbed," he told Howells.[54] More sorrows soon came. On November 28, 1890, Mrs. Langdon died at eighty while Twain was stranded in Hartford. "Livy darling," he wrote to her, "my heart goes out to you, & I wish I could comfort you & stay & support you now when you so need it in the first intolerable stress of your grief." He could offer only qualified encouragement about Jean. "She is a pale, weak little thing, & just as brave & good & dear as she can be."[55] Although Susy and Clara joined their mother in Elmira for the funeral, Twain stayed behind to care for Jean. Mrs. Langdon was buried in Woodlawn Cemetery between her husband, Jervis, and Sam and Livy's baby son, Langdon. Undoubtedly it was Twain's guilty memory of Langdon's fate that made him feel especially protective toward Jean.

Twain would refer to the "double blow" that death had dealt out to the family, first with his mother and now, a month later, with his mother-in-law.[56] That winter he would drastically curtail his social activities and try to be as cheerful and supportive as possible with his wife, who felt lost and dispirited, as she had after her father's death years earlier. "I feel so much older since mother was taken away," Livy told Grace E. King. "When you are no ones [sic] child when no one will pet you as your mother had always done, when you are the oldest generation of your family, then you begin to feel that you are growing old. My mother was eighty and I try to realize that I had a long lovely life with her—yet I am very lonely for her."[57] The death of Mrs. Langdon would rob the Clemenses of a critical source of financial and emotional sustenance just as grave threats loomed in the near future.

CHAPTER TWENTY-SEVEN

"One of the Vanderbilt Gang"

Beyond the death of family members, Mark Twain was now constantly oppressed by monetary worries and felt trapped by the high overhead of his luxurious life in a gigantic Hartford house. "I wish there was some way to change our manner of living," he had confessed to Mrs. Langdon before she died, "but that seems next to impossible unless we sell our house."[1] For the summer of 1890 he had projected a family excursion, but as expenses preyed on him, Livy sought to console him. "Youth don't let the thought of Europe worry you *one bit* because we will give that all up. I want to see you happy *much* more than I want any thing else even the children's lessons. Oh darling it goes to my very heart to see you worried. I don't believe you ought to feel quite as you do, things are not yet quite as desperate as they appear to you... Youth sweet, I have only one word to say & that is that I love you with all my heart."[2]

The plight of Twain's publishing firm looked precarious, and it irked him that he had to keep royalties from his books sequestered there to subsidize other authors. The capital demanded by publishing the *Library of American Literature* grew so onerous that he was ready to ditch the project altogether, and he and Fred Hall plotted to sell a one-third interest to other publishers. By year's end, Twain was so morose about business that he sent Fred Hall this holiday greeting: "Merry Xmas to you!—and I wish to God I could have one myself before I die."[3] Although Webster & Company had managed to turn a profit for the year, its debt had crept steadily upward, rising from $13,000 to $36,000 in twelve months.

Still stuck on Civil War publishing, the firm issued a revised edition of the memoirs of General William Tecumseh Sherman, who, like Grant and Sheridan, finished it right before he died on February 14, 1891. Twain hoped to milk the death for everything it was worth. "What is the very *quickest* you can issue it?" he inquired of Hall. "Its market is best for the next 30 days, I think; then nearly as good for 30 more; then comes the fading quickly out."[4] With his stable of major Union generals now complete, his publishing house planned a "Great War Library," with books by or about Grant, Sherman, Sheridan, McClellan, Crawford, Hancock, and Custer, all distinguished by a uniform look and format.

In a sure sign of desperation, Twain returned to the idea of selling his board games, including "Mark Twain's Memory-Builder" and "Mark Twain's Face and Date Game." Hall sounded out one or two toy stores, which responded with lukewarm enthusiasm. When the games failed to catch on, Twain cringed that his name had been associated with them. All the while, Webster & Company's debt mounted to unsustainable levels. In spring 1891, Hall borrowed $15,000 from friends and asked Twain to raise another $30,000. Twain felt so strapped for cash that he even cut back on his monthly allowance to Orion. He believed his publishing firm would resume dividends by January 1892. In the interim, he had to write in order to make some money. "I am at work again—on a book," he told Joseph T. Goodman in April. "Not with a great deal of spirit, but with enough—yes, plenty." He felt pressed to earn $50,000 with his pen to float the firm until January, all because of the calamitous *Library of American Literature*. "This additional capital is needed for the same book," Twain added, "because its prosperity is growing so great & exacting."[5] The success of *LAL* threatened to sink the firm. Twain accurately diagnosed the slow-motion crisis, saying, "We are trying to do too large a business on too small cash capital."[6]

"ONE OF THE VANDERBILT GANG"

With the Paige typesetter, Twain was also besieged with cash demands, and he scoured the landscape nervously for a crop of fresh investors. Among those enlisted were Sir Henry Irving, the illustrious Shakespearean actor, and Bram Stoker, the author of *Dracula*. The main fundraising target continued to be Senator John Jones of Nevada, and Joseph Goodman traveled to Washington to corner him with a sales pitch. While Jones agreed to go to Hartford to view the machine, he feared it was "an unknown thing in an unknown line."[7] In April 1890, Twain lured Jones and a group of potential investors to Hartford, softening them up with a dinner beforehand to get them in a jolly mood—the prelude to disaster. As Katy Leary recalled: "And they had champagne, too, and after they eat up everything, they went to Pratt & Whitney's factory to see the machine. And what do you think? If that darned old thing didn't break down right when those men were just looking at it! It broke right in front of their faces! The old thing busted itself and went to pieces . . . It almost killed Mr. Clemens."[8] The investor group departed in disgust, to Twain's everlasting dismay.

Though still certain the Paige compositor would make him one of the world's richest individuals, Twain knew his bank account was fast dwindling. To Goodman, he sighed, "I am one of the wealthiest grandees in America—one of the Vanderbilt gang, in fact—& yet if you asked me to lend you a couple of dollars I should have to ask you to take my note instead."[9] On March 31, 1890, he informed Goodman that he had reached a financial breaking point. "But I am in as close a place to-day as ever I was; $3,000 due for the last month's machine-expenses, & the purse empty . . . I have talked with the madam, & here is the result. I will go down to the factory & notify Paige that I will scrape together $6,000 to meet March & April expenses, & will retire on the 30th of April & return the assignment to him if in the meantime I have not found financial relief."[10] Twain won a timely, though difficult, reprieve when William J. Hamersley extended a three-month loan to him, but he kept delaying payment, forcing Twain to beg abjectly for him to honor his pledge.

Around this time, Paige announced, yet again, the machine's long-awaited completion. What should have been a joyous moment devolved into a fresh ordeal for Twain. Years earlier, Pratt & Whitney had estimated that each machine would cost $1,500 to manufacture; now Twain learned that $6,000 was closer to the mark. He had committed an amateurish business error: he had squandered all his money creating the machine without setting aside funds for its manufacture and distribution. From the outset, he had not been wealthy enough to fund an open-ended start-up, and he certainly didn't have the wherewithal to carry it to completion. His failure was not one of vision, but of basic business math. As he reviewed his harrowing history with Paige, he remembered how years earlier, when he had already spent $30,000, he was assured that it would take $10,000 to finish the machine. Since then, he had sunk another $100,000 into the typesetter's yawning money pit.

For all his severe disenchantment with Paige, the machine still hypnotized Twain, like a failed love affair he couldn't bear to renounce. With his obsessive mind, hunches would harden into certitudes, and he was sure the Paige typesetter would triumph in the end. Even as he bemoaned its cost, he told Goodman, in a state of sheer bedazzlement: "I have been sitting by the machine for 2½ hours, this afternoon, & my admiration of it towers higher than ever. There is no sort of mistake about it, it is the Big Bonanza . . . This machine is totally without a rival."[11] His mind spun exorbitant fantasies of a $150 million worldwide market that would double or triple during the life of his patents. The machine was a monomania he seemed powerless to stop.

Unrelenting in pursuit of Senator Jones, Twain prodded him and John W. Mackay, another Comstock Lode millionaire, to come to Hartford. This time the typesetter performed well, and they begrudgingly offered to invest a piddling $5,000 apiece, or $30,000 as a group. For Twain, who had heaped big expectations on these two moguls, it was a lacerating experience. What he desperately needed was a huge investment to build the typesetter factory, and he hadn't even come close. In early August, with the fervor of a high-pressure salesman, he wrote to Jones and conjured up a phalanx of businessmen "who own big printing

"ONE OF THE VANDERBILT GANG"

offices" across the country and maintained that "when the time comes to invite them to inspect the 'Paige Compositor' they will become its champion to a man."[12] Later that month, Twain spent an anxious week in Washington lobbying Jones and followed up with a letter that slammed the Mergenthaler machine as "capricious & unreliable," claiming it would prove "wholly unendurable in a daily newspaper office."[13] With the Paige machine susceptible to constant breakdowns, this was a tough argument to make.

As Twain drastically slashed payments for the typesetter, Paige began all-day-and-night tests on the machine, designed to simulate newspaper conditions. There was urgency to this since the *New York Herald* was considering a trial installation of the Mergenthaler machine. When the *New York World* signed up another rival, the Rogers Typograph, for its Sunday edition, Twain set to work to discredit it. "If we can't set up & correct that amount in one-sixth of the time, we'll go hang ourselves," he told Goodman with the bravado he adopted when belittling competitors. The Rogers machine, he declared, "has nothing but certain death before it."[14] Although Twain calculated that the Paige was faster and cheaper than competing models, he never paused to wonder why these other machines were being adopted by major newspapers and his was not.

Twain now executed his most foolhardy move. In August he hatched a deal with Paige by which the inventor sold him all rights to the typesetter for $250,000, payable within six months. Should Twain default on that payment, the rights would revert to Paige, with Twain limited to a $500 royalty for each machine sold. The whole deal hinged on Senator Jones forming a stock company within a six-month period to produce the typesetter. A fickle investor, Jones had agreed to this action during Twain's visit to Washington, but also said he didn't want to approach potential investors until December or January. "Thinks he will have no trouble raising the money then," Twain assured Orion and Mollie. "Well, we must wait & see. So I am feeling reasonably comfortable."[15] One person grievously uncomfortable with the deal was Twain's Hartford business agent, Franklin G. Whitmore, who warned him that he had been "deceived with promises" before and stood unprotected by the contract.[16]

In early December, Paige, for the sixth time in a year, pronounced the typesetter "finished" only to discover that the all-important "period" was malfunctioning. He and a mechanic promised Twain that repairs would require one day. "Well, the best part of 2 weeks went by," Twain fumed in his notebook. "I dropped in (last Monday noon) & they were still tinkering. Still tinkering, but just *one hour*, now, would see the machine at work, blemishless, & never stop again for a generation: the hoary old song that has been sung to weariness in my ears by these frauds & liars! Four days & a half elapsed, & still that 'one hour's' work was still going on, & another hour's work still to be done."[17] The triple repetition of "still" testified to Twain's seething frustration as he reenacted the dreary old psychodrama with Paige. He now felt venomous toward the inventor, his admiration having curdled into hatred. "Paige and I always meet on effusively affectionate terms; and yet he knows perfectly well that if I had his nuts in a steel-trap I would shut out all human succor and watch that trap till he died."[18]

Twain still counted on Senator Jones to rescue him before the six-month option deadline. Much like Paige, the senator was a big, blustery talker, and when he met with Joe Goodman in California in December, he said he wouldn't bother with trifling investors but "was going straight to Westinghouse, Carnegie, Morton, Jay Gould, etc., any one of whom … could organize the company without difficulty."[19] The typesetter company, he swore, would be his first order of business back in Washington. When Twain visited him in the capital, the senator was sidetracked by silver legislation and deigned to give Twain only a few minutes of his time. Jones's ardor about the typesetter had cooled, and he said the capitalists he knew didn't like to speculate on new technologies. All the while, the clock ticked away on Twain's six-month option. Two days prior to its expiration, Jones informed Twain that "within the time named it is impossible to accomplish anything, and that even with time, so far as my investigations had gone, the difficulties seem almost insurmountable."[20] To rub it in, he mentioned that a fellow senator had invested in Mergenthaler Linotype. Incensed by this last-minute betrayal, Twain denounced Jones as a "penny-worshipping humbug & shuffler," and swore he never

"ONE OF THE VANDERBILT GANG"

wished to see the damn machine again and would pay no more bills for it.[21] He drafted a furious letter to Jones, which he never sent. "For a whole year you have breathed the word of promise to my ear to break it to my hope at last. It is stupefying. It is unbelievable."[22]

Jones's betrayal again left Twain at Paige's mercy. All he would now have were royalties on future sales. For a time, it looked as if a publisher named Marshall H. Mallory would buy Twain's royalty share for $250,000, but that deal also fell through. What vexed Twain more than anything was that he was running through his wife's inheritance, the cornerstone of their opulent Hartford existence. "I spent a hundred and seventy thousand dollars" on the machine, he recalled. "More than two-thirds of it came out of Mrs. Clemens's pocket."[23] (That would be $5.9 million in today's money, with $3.9 million siphoned from Livy's fortune—a scandalous amount.)

Unfortunately, the typesetter crisis coincided with the Webster & Company troubles and the failure of the Mallory sale, robbing Twain of his final chance of adding capital to his publishing firm. When he broke the bad news to Frederick J. Hall, he said, "You will now have to modify your installment system to meet the emergency of a constipated purse; for if you should need to borrow any more money I would not know how or where to raise it."[24] Twain was financially played out in both his business ventures and had to contemplate writing new books and articles merely to survive. The investments that he had hoped would emancipate him forever from writing drove him instead into even deeper dependence on his pen.

Even as Twain struggled to keep his businesses afloat, his close-knit family life in Hartford began to falter, and the trouble stemmed from an unlikely source: his beloved eldest daughter, Susy. Twain loved the purity of teenage girls but found it hard to adjust as they grew into adulthood, and Susy, to his surprise, would rapidly cross over from sheltered teenager to daring young woman. She had developed into a pretty adolescent with a round face, full lips, thick wavy hair, and deep, soulful eyes. Passionate and high-strung, shy and moody, she had an artistic nature that found expression in the home theatricals she staged. She had already written a fanciful play called *The Love Chase* and was a seasoned performer. She had her father's gift for language and his searching nature. "I dread to have to say I am so old!" she told Sue Crane when she turned eighteen. "And nothing done and such unsettled notions of things. Why, I should be a well-poised woman instead of a rattle-brained girl."[25] She was always hard on herself, felt a giant void in her life, and worried too soon about ending up an old maid. She continued to prize the profundity of her father's writing and protested when *Connecticut Yankee* reviews emphasized "the humor and grotesque situations" and "entirely overlooked and left unmentioned the earnest purpose, and philosophy of the tale."[26]

Like her sisters, Susy had been schooled at home, and Twain queried several educators for advice on what preparation she needed to enter college. Livy grew anxious as the day approached when her daughters would leave their cloistered life and step forth into the world alone. "I feel very unsettled about what I shall do with them," she had written her mother, "nothing in the way of a school seems to be exactly what I want."[27] Livy knew her daughters had been sequestered in their Hartford cocoon and needed to break out, but her "mother's pride" was injured when a friend remarked that her girls had been overly protected.[28] The Clemenses hired a tutor to bring Susy up to college level in French and geometry, and when she was accepted at Bryn Mawr in June 1890, she was overjoyed. Neither Sam nor Livy could conquer the fear of being separated from their eldest daughter. "We look forward with a good deal of dread to the prospect of having Susy away from us next Winter," Livy confided to Grace King.[29] Given later events, Twain would conveniently forget that he had been a big supporter of Bryn Mawr, touting it as "by long odds the best female college in the world."[30]

En route to taking Susy to Bryn Mawr, Sam and Livy stayed with her at the Murray Hill Hotel in Manhattan and bought her a handsome set of Shakespeare volumes she came to treasure. When they arrived at the college outside Philadelphia, Susy was assigned to Radnor Hall, then

"ONE OF THE VANDERBILT GANG"

under construction, and for two weeks she stayed with her parents at the Summit Grove Inn. The situation seemed rife with symbolism, with Susy stranded between the home life she feared to depart and the new life she reluctantly embraced. This interregnum had lasted a week when Twain informed the college authorities that, much as he would like to spend freshman year with Susy, he needed to return to work and did not care to leave his daughter in a hotel. With that, the college found a proper dorm room for Susy, which was followed by a tearful farewell scene when Susy saw her father off at the train station. "Our train was moving away," Twain wrote, "& [Susy] was drifting collegeward afoot, her figure blurred & dim in the rain & fog, & she was crying."[31] The separation was no less painful for her parents, Twain describing the first week apart as "about the longest week the almanac" had ever furnished to his family.[32]

Although Susy claimed to be content, she sent her grandmother a poignant lament, naming Bryn Mawr as "an ideal place, but oh! it *does* not, *can* not compare with home!"[33] Twain could not bear the separation either. About three weeks after the bleary-eyed train station farewell, he was back at Bryn Mawr, this time with Clara, for a three-day visit with Susy. Since their evening arrival coincided with a college dance, Twain lustily joined in the fun. "I danced two Virginia reels & another dance, & looked on & talked the rest of the time," Twain told Livy. "It was very jolly & pleasant, & everybody asked after & was disappointed when I said you hadn't come."[34] It seemed Twain would never be able to let go of his eldest daughter. Susy's classmate Evangeline Andrews found Susy "a frail, attractive, charming young girl" but realized "how strong was the tie between her and her father, how much they minded being separated, and also how eager Mrs. Clemens was that Olivia should be happy in a new environment."[35] A month after arriving at Bryn Mawr, Susy still felt homesick, and Livy feared her return to Hartford for Thanksgiving would exacerbate this ache. Though an excellent student, Susy was accustomed to being homeschooled and was easily shaken when it came to taking tests.

Then something surprising happened: Susy's mood began to improve—amazingly. As if announcing a new identity, she began to introduce herself as Olivia, her real first name, an early sign of independence that must have rattled her father. "Susy seems by her letters to be well," Livy informed Mrs. Langdon, "and the last one was not as homesick as the other ones have been."[36]

As Livy and Sue Crane stood vigil by the dying Mrs. Langdon, Livy seemed stunned that Susy, usually so attentive to her needs, did not write at this traumatic moment. "I have not had one line from Susy since all this trouble began."[37] In fact, Susy had befriended a sophomore named Louise Brownell, who was to head the student government, and began to grapple with powerful homoerotic desires for her new friend. Their letters would take on an unmistakably romantic tone, then full-blown love, but it was hard to say whether their passionate relationship was sexually consummated. We do know they would kiss and embrace each other tightly, but we have few details beyond that.

The first American article on lesbianism appeared in 1883 and only referred to transvestites and poor women. Carol Smith-Rosenberg has noted that at the time, college women who engaged in sex with each other would be classified as "masturbators," while young men doing the same thing were labeled homosexual. Susy's behavior toward Louise may have fit a pattern described by Havelock Ellis in 1895: "A school girl or young woman forms an ardent attachment for another girl, probably somewhat older than herself, often a school fellow, sometimes her school mistress, upon whom she will lavish an astonishing amount of affection and devotion . . . The girl who expends this wealth of devotion is surcharged with emotion but she is often unconscious or ignorant of the sexual impulses and she seeks for no form of sexual satisfaction."[38] Of course, Susy and Louise may have engaged in overt sexual behavior. Susy was exceedingly emotional and not given to halfway measures. As erotic attachments between students became more commonplace at women's colleges, the schools began to institute restrictive dorm practices, including bans on students spending the night with each other.

In January 1891, Susy, with a fine soprano voice, played the role of Phyllis in a student production of Gilbert and Sullivan's comic opera *Iolanthe*. Her role helped to establish her as a personage on campus. Livy went to Bryn Mawr to help with costumes—men were barred from student productions—and to give her daughter some distance from her father, telling Evangeline Walker that Twain would have seized upon any excuse, including bringing her laundry, to visit his daughter. Despite Susy's complaints about poor food and late hours, she suddenly wanted to stay at the college three or four years instead of the two that she had originally planned. Where Twain had once feared that Susy would never overcome her homesickness, he now feared the opposite: that she was too much attached to the school. In February he told Howells that Livy "has been in Philadelphia a week at the Continental Hotel with Susy (who, to my regret is beginning to love Bryn Mawr) & I've had to stay here [in Hartford] alone."[39]

Soon afterward, James E. Rhoads, Bryn Mawr's president, issued an invitation for Twain to speak on campus on a topic of his choice. Six years earlier, Susy had proudly accompanied her father when he spoke at Vassar College. Even then she had dreaded "The Golden Arm" ghost story that made people jump with fright at the end. Learned as a boy from Uncle Daniel at the Quarleses' farm, Twain delighted in telling this scary story in which a man digs up his wife's body to obtain her golden arm. If Twain found it a showstopper, Susy loathed it as profoundly unsettling. She wanted her father to be a sage, not a mere funny man. As soon as Twain accepted Bryn Mawr's offer, she experienced a keen premonition of trouble ahead and "became very restless and nervous," said Evangeline Andrews, fearing the selections her father would choose. She had outgrown her uncritical adoration of him and worried that he would tell a tale unsuitable for "the sophisticated group at Bryn Mawr College."[40] She and the invitation committee traded letters with Twain and agreed upon an acceptable program. On the day of the speech, Evangeline went with Susy to the train station to greet Twain. "The moment we met him at the station and had exchanged greetings Olivia clung to his hand saying repeatedly as we walked from the Bryn Mawr Station to the College: 'Father, *promise* me that you will not tell the "Ghost Story."' He laughed and patting her hand said 'I have written you that I would not tell the "Ghost Story!" Let's forget about it.'"[41]

FLOODTIDE

Twain drew a packed house, and Susy sat on the main aisle beside Evangeline, who noticed that Susy's hand grew damp and "she was shaking like a leaf." As Twain approached the end of his talk and the room darkened, he paced the platform, pretending to ponder his next selection. Susy whispered urgently to Evangeline: "He's going to tell the 'Ghost Story'—I *know* he's going to tell the 'Ghost Story.' And he's going to say 'Boo' at the end and make them all jump."[42] Evangeline tried to reassure her, but Susy's intuition was unerring: contrary to his promise and his knowledge of how this story would upset her, Twain plunged into the ghost story with unbridled gusto. Mortified, Susy slipped from her seat, fled up the aisle, and burst into an empty classroom across the hall. "In she went and flung herself down and with her head on a desk wept aloud!" recalled Evangeline. "She was heartbroken!"[43] Finally, as Twain exited the hall to a thunderous ovation, he rushed into the classroom and clasped his daughter. "'But Father,' she moaned, 'you promised, you promised!' 'Oh my Dear,' he wailed, 'I tried to think of something else and my mind refused to focus. All I could hear was your voice saying: "Please don't tell the *Ghost Story,* Father—*Promise* not to tell the Ghost Story"—and I could think of *nothing* else. Oh, my Dear, my Dear, how could I!'"[44]

What to make of this strange and disturbing tale? Twain was the most spontaneous of speakers, and it is hard to fathom that, after twenty-five years on the lecture platform, he could not think of anything else to say. Had he resented her offering him advice? Did he feel that as she matured she had become embarrassed by his humor and he bristled at that? Or did he think her fears excessive and that she would settle down and enjoy the ghost story once she saw how it pleased her classmates? We will never know. We only know that Susy felt humiliated by the father on whom she had so long doted.

A month later, Susy Clemens left Bryn Mawr College forever. Sam and Livy settled on the narrative that she left school because she was homesick and her health was damaged at school. "Bryn Mawr began it," Twain asserted. "It was there that her health was undermined."[45] He later regretted sending her "to that deadly college."[46] Probably echoing Sam and

| 438 |

"ONE OF THE VANDERBILT GANG"

Livy, their family friend Grace King deemed Susy too fragile to withstand the rigors of college and that "a very short time proved the utter impossibility of hard study for Susy."[47] It seems at least as likely that the Clemenses got wind of the relationship between Susy and Louise Brownell and felt the need to break it up, especially since Louise had suggested to Susy that they room together the following year. As Twain said, "We had to take her away from Bryn Mawr College to her deep and lasting grief. She was never in really promising health again."[48]

When Livy went to retrieve Susy that April, Louise was off in New York City tending to her sick mother. "It breaks my heart to find you are in trouble and gone," Susy wrote to her. "I feel that I ought not to intrude upon you, but you are so constantly in my thoughts that I must send you my deep, deep love and sympathy . . . I write in Mama's room and she wishes to send her loving sympathy."[49] The letter confirms that Livy enjoyed cordial relations with Louise, whatever she suspected about the secret romance. That same day, doubtless holed up in the privacy of her room, Susy sent Louise a far more intimate letter in which she longed "to see you with my whole heart, because I love you so with my whole heart. Often at night I feel myself touching your dear soft cheek."[50] Twain's total silence about Susy and Louise Brownell speaks eloquently of his discomfort with this taboo issue. It would have been hard enough if Susy had fallen in love with a young man, but it would have been unbearable to be replaced in her affection by a young woman. For a straitlaced Victorian father, this unconventional relationship would have been extremely difficult to accept or even to comprehend. He and Livy chose not to look too deeply at their daughter's relationship with Louise—or not to look at all.

The other reason the Clemenses needed to yank Susy from Bryn Mawr was that they had come to an abrupt but momentous decision: after seventeen years, they would shut up their Hartford house in June, sell their horses, and head off to Europe for an extended stay. After years of posh living, they had to return to fiscal sanity, and Twain envisioned a "hermit life in a French village for one or two years."[51] It would be a genteel form of economizing, since they would bring along housekeeper Katy Leary. Still, the separation from longtime employees—the coachman Patrick McAleer and the butler George Griffin—was agonizing; these people had formed their extended family. Only the gardener, John O'Neill, was retained for the upkeep of the grounds. When Livy informed the domestic staff of the decision to leave, she held out hope that the family would soon return, though everyone knew this was likely wishful thinking.

This hard decision had resulted from Twain's self-inflicted wounds. He was being driven into exile, not by banishment, but by his own financial improvidence. Having married a rich woman and with a lucrative stream of publishing royalties, he could have devoted himself to a placid life of writing books and giving lectures. Instead, he had started a publishing house and financed a typesetter before he had the expertise or requisite fortune to bring them to completion. Both had depleted his bank account, making maintenance of the Hartford house prohibitively expensive. Now he had to curtail expenses and cancel everything, from club dues to periodical subscriptions.

The family didn't fathom at first what a watershed moment this was or that they would remain European castaways for nine years. What they did know was that the curtain was descending on a very grand way of life that they could no longer afford. In late May, after a farewell dinner in Hartford, Livy wrote wistfully, "I am so truly fond of my home and I love so tenderly my Hartford friends that I cannot bear to think of leaving them."[52] For her, people's homes were inseparable from their existence, making this break excruciating. "There is nothing that I am fonder of than getting pictures in my mind of the homes of people and carrying about with me the sense of them in their homes."[53]

A medical agenda also lay behind the European sojourn. Livy now suffered from the early stages of heart disease as well as rheumatism. Doctors urged her to try the European baths, and Twain had in mind a "little-visited nook up in the hills back of the Rhine somewhere."[54] No

"ONE OF THE VANDERBILT GANG"

less important for the frail Livy, the move to Europe would spare her the heavy duties of overseeing a spacious house with a crowded social calendar of dinners and receptions.

For his part, Twain was coping with rheumatism that crept up his right arm and nearly disabled him, a condition so debilitating that he tried dictating a new book on phonograph-recording cylinders. "I filled four dozen cylinders in two sittings," he concluded wearily, "then found I could have said about as much with the pen and said it a deal better. Then I resigned."[55] One wonders whether there was a psychosomatic dimension to this crippling disorder in his writing arm, the somatic emblem of a stalled writing career. At times, he was completely bedridden with rheumatism, telling a friend drily, "There is less recreation about it than you would think."[56] He, too, hoped to find a medicinal spring to cure him.

Despite his reputation as a travel writer, Mark Twain had come to detest travel. He guessed they would be gone six or eight months, but he knew that was pure conjecture. "I don't know how long we shall be in Europe," he admitted to Howells. "I have a vote but I don't cast it . . . Travel has no longer any charm for me. I have seen all the foreign countries I want to see except heaven and hell, & I have only a vague curiosity as concerns one of those."[57]

The change in continents happened with bewildering suddenness. Just two years earlier, Livy had written to her friend Alice Hooker Day: "Mr. Clemens and I are fully convinced that we are the two happiest people in all the earth."[58] The Clemens family now knew that something precious and irretrievable was being lost, that they were passing from the beauty of a known and familiar world, full of friends and memories, into a cloudy future. Their house had been a sentient being, a repository of their spirits, and now it was being emptied of furniture, books, and carpets, all packed up and shipped off to a warehouse. Years later, Clara expressed the foreboding she felt in leaving Hartford. "We adored our home and friends. We had to leave so much treasured beauty behind that we could not look forward with any pleasure to life abroad. We all regarded this break in a hitherto smooth flow of harmonious existence as something resembling a tragedy . . . Instinctively, we felt that life would never be more vivid or bright than it had been during these years of childhood. We passed from room to room with leaden hearts, looked back and lingered—lingered. An inner voice whispered we should never return, and we never did."[59] Perhaps fittingly, Livy was the last to leave the house, though she must have been pleased that it would be rented to Alice Hooker Day and her husband, John.

On June 6, 1891, the Clemens family, freighted with twenty-five pieces of luggage, including bed and table linen, sailed for Europe aboard the *Gascogne*. They had no idea how deep and lasting their departure would be, or how disconnected they would become from their Hartford past. They would land in Le Havre before proceeding to Paris and points south. That America's most famous writer was leaving for a protracted European stay rated a story in the press, and Twain painted a rosy, misleading portrait for the Boston *Journal Supplement:* "The children will have their tutors; Mrs. Clemens will enjoy the luxury of a complete rest from housekeeping and kindred evils, while I want nothing but my pipe and my pen. I have no special literary plans in mind, but shall probably do a little something . . . We are going to live in quiet fashion, somewhere away from everybody, where no one knows us, and enjoy each other's company."[60]

PART THREE

Rapids

CHAPTER TWENTY-EIGHT

"Paradise of the Rheumatics"

After installing Susy and Clara at a boarding school in Geneva, the rest of the Clemens party settled into Aix-les-Bains, a French thermal resort famous for its sulfur springs. Still hobbled by rheumatism in his right arm, Twain promised a copious stream of letters to his daughters if only he could figure out how to write left-handed. As a tony spa, Aix-les-Bains seemed an odd place to start economizing since it boasted "a rabble of nobilities, big and little . . . and often a king or two," Twain noted.[1] He delighted in the town's steep, narrow streets, market squares, vistas of distant mountains, and open-air concerts in the evening. Livy thought their rooms in a *pension* possessed all the charm of a barn, but Jean was pleased by the ground-floor rooms overlooking a rose-filled garden and arbor. Strictly as a voyeur—he had no money left to squander—Twain dropped by the fashionable casino, its patrons "clothed richly and speaking all the languages," but found little appeal in gambling blatantly stacked for the house. "Constantly money and chips are flung upon the table, and the game seems to consist in the croupier's reaching for these things with a flexible sculling oar, and raking them home. It appeared to be a rational enough game for him, and if I could have borrowed his oar I would have stayed, but I didn't see where the entertainment of the others came in."[2]

Twain christened Aix "the Paradise of the Rheumatics," and its central feature was its thermal baths, operated by the French government. "The bathhouse is a huge and massive pile of white marble masonry, and looks more like a temple than anything else," he observed.³ Clients underwent a rigorous sequence of showers and baths and were also supposed to drink sulfur-laden water secured from a local druggist. In a later article, Twain claimed that he informed the pharmacists he preferred to "wait till they could get some that was fresh, but they said it always smelled that way." They bragged that their water contained thirty-two times as much sulfur as the baths. "It is true," Twain said, "but in my opinion that water comes from a cemetery, and not a fresh cemetery, either."⁴ After he soaked his rheumatic arm for five weeks, the pain ebbed away. Unfortunately, the therapeutic effect wore off pretty quickly, and he soon returned to grousing that "every pen-stroke gives me the lockjaw."⁵

As a writer, Twain felt idle and useless. With an urgent need to earn money, he had committed to write six European letters, at a thousand dollars apiece, for the McClure Syndicate and the *New York Sun*, only to be stymied by the crippling arm pain. "My!" he told one magazine editor. "I could write reams & volumes I'm so hungry to get hold of a pen, & the place, & the air are so inspiring, but my arm won't let me."⁶ According to Jean, her father consulted daily with a doctor who told him that if he kept writing his rheumatism would persist. "The very deaf doctor didn't know who papa was," Jean recorded in her diary, but when his wife told him, "he stood there for five or ten minutes with his mouth wide open."⁷

Taking a break from their spa treatments, the Clemens party opted for a full program of Wagner operas at the Bayreuth Festival. Even though Wagner had died, the Wagner cult still flourished, and tourists overran the town each summer. Of course, Twain had been exposed to opera before, and the results were not pretty. Nothing aroused his wit more than a good, healthy grudge, and opera topped the list. In 1866, in San Francisco, he had reviewed *Martha* by Friedrich von Flotow and bristled at "the greasy, mushy Italian accents," while still "applauding every two minutes and a quarter, as is customary and proper."⁸ He was just sharpening his knife for the kill. In 1878, in Baden-Baden, he blasted to smithereens the entire art form. "To me an opera is the very climax & cap-stone of the absurd, the fantastic[,] the unjustifiable. I hate the very name of opera—partly because of the nights of suffering I have endured in its

"PARADISE OF THE RHEUMATICS"

presence, & partly because I want to love it and can't."[9] These last words were significant, expressing the yearning of a small-town boy to appreciate high culture and his miserable failure to achieve it. He came to believe that people preferred cheap, popular tunes and only pretended to love opera. It was actually humorist Bill Nye, not Mark Twain, who said that "Wagner's music is better than it sounds," though Twain could gladly have claimed authorship.[10]

The Clemenses were a highly musical clan—Susy studied voice, Clara skipped college to continue her piano studies, Jean faithfully practiced her violin—and they set aside ten days to absorb the complete Bayreuth experience. They headed to the opera daily with Twain loading up beforehand on corned beef and cabbage. "Then, he said, he could stand anything—even Wagner operas," recalled Katy Leary.[11] This immersion in opera yielded one of Twain's funniest screeds against the composer, "At the Shrine of St. Wagner." Of *Parsifal*, he wrote, "the first act of the three occupied two hours, and I enjoyed that in spite of the singing."[12] (In truth, he enjoyed *Parsifal* and was dismayed when critics dismissed its "wailing" and "screeching."[13]) After seeing *Tristan und Isolde,* he was baffled by weeping theatergoers. "Sometimes I feel like the one sane person in the community of the mad; sometimes I feel like the one blind man where all others see; the one groping savage in the college of the learned."[14] No matter how hard he tried to appreciate Wagner—and try he did—he always left with the same tooth-gnashing frustration. Finally, he decided to have mercy on himself and read in the hotel while Livy and his daughters sat through the Ring Cycle. Susy and Clara filtered out their father's scorn for Wagner, and their Bayreuth stay left them more determined than ever to pursue musical careers.

In opera, Twain knew he had a juicy target and returned to Wagner for periodic refreshment. "I think opera is spoiled by attempting to combine instrumental and vocal effects," he later told an interviewer.[15] Perhaps his most savage attack came when he professed that he greatly enjoyed "the first act of everything which Wagner created, but the effect on me has always been so powerful that one act was quite sufficient; whenever I have witnessed two acts I have gone away physically exhausted; and whenever I have ventured an entire opera the result has been the next thing to suicide."[16] Nevertheless, reports of Twain hating Wagner can be exaggerated, for he was transported by a few operas, doubtless to his embarrassment. "Certainly nothing in the world is so solemn & impressive, & so divinely beautiful as Tannhäuser," he would write. "It ought to be used as a religious service."[17] In his early days, he had exhibited the same philistine resistance to classical music, then overcame that to treasure Beethoven symphonies, Chopin nocturnes, and Schubert impromptus.

The next watering hole in the Clemens family quest was the spa town of Marienbad, now in the western Czech Republic. Clara was enchanted by it, taking poetic strolls through pine-scented woods and along a promenade frequented by handsome young officers. "What a world of romance lay in those braided coats and plumed helmets!" she remembered.[18] Less enamored of officers, Susy confessed to Louise Brownell that she felt "lonely and uninterested."[19] With an undertow always tugging her back to Hartford, Livy found it difficult to enter unreservedly into the spirit of the place. "These lands over here are desperately interesting and charming," she told Grace E. King, "yet I must confess to waves of homesickness, when I should like to see my friends and sit down in our library beside an open wood fire, instead of a stove, for a visit with them."[20]

By this point, Twain was able to start writing his stories on Aix and Bayreuth and added a third to the portfolio: "Marienbad—A Health Factory." He found the town cold and rainy—"a most strange place to get rid of disease"—and had huge fun mocking the hypochondriacal hordes who gravitated to its springs.[21] The ailing people who came to Marienbad wanted to blather on endlessly about their ailments and seek out other people with the same condition to commiserate. Twain discovered that "dyspeptics are the worst. They are at it all day and all night, and all along. They have more symptoms than all the others put together." As he grew familiar with the place, he could identify a specific malady at twenty paces. "Wherever you see two or a dozen people of ordinary bulk talking together, you know they are talking about their livers."[22] Twain shared the general hypochondria, especially after a Marienbad doctor examined him and "said with quite unnecessary frankness that he could not *prove* that I hadn't a heart, but that if I had one it would be an advantage to trade it for a potato."[23]

From his boyhood days, Twain had regarded water travel as the sovereign remedy for all ills, the ideal way to loaf and read and daydream. The indolent pleasure of coasting on water was an urge he could never resist. Thus it was not altogether unexpected that with his harried business life and an aching arm he chose in mid-September to deposit his family in Ouchy, Switzerland, while he ventured a boat trip down the Rhône River that might offer "lazy repose, with opportunity to smoke, read, doze, talk, accumulate comfort, get fat," and, most important, "avoid the world and its concerns."[24] Aided by a boatman and his former courier Joseph Verey, Twain would drift for ten days in a flat-bottomed boat, hooded by a sun screen, starting from Chatillon on Lake Bourget and ending up at Avignon and Arles. He scratched out notes all the while, hoping to cash in on the adventure, a writing project that yielded the posthumous essay "Down the Rhône."

After just three hours on the river, Twain settled into a state of perfect bliss. "It is unimaginably still and reposeful and cool and soft and breezy," he wrote to Livy, while sliding along at eight miles an hour. "No rowing or work of any kind to do—we merely float with the current—we glide noiseless and swift."[25] He was reunited with a simplicity that he had sorely missed in business and spent a night in a peasant's house, "occupied by the family and a lot of cows and calves."[26] Peace descended on his troubled spirit. "This morning I breakfasted on the shore in the open air with two sociable dogs and a cat. Clean cloth, napkin and table furniture, white sugar, a vast hunk of excellent butter, good bread, first class coffee with pure milk, fried fish just caught."[27] The courier and the boatman did the work while Twain lazily reclined and watched the world drift by. Joseph Verey even dressed Twain and laid out his toiletries on the washstand. "Thank goodness I can once more write with my rheumatic arm, but that is all," he told Charles Dudley Warner. "I can't dress myself & the arm is painful & just next to useless."[28]

Ordinarily Twain would have stopped to explore the quaint, ancient towns they passed, but floating along was too dreamily delicious a sensation to stop, and the world flickered by at a safe distance. He needed to escape into pure relaxation. If apart from Livy, she constantly passed through his thoughts, and he sent her daily updates. "I love you, love you, *love* you, my sweetheart," he wrote.[29] The next day he climbed a mountain at Valence and wandered through a ruined castle, then ended by telling her, "I do assure you that I love you & miss you all the time."[30] Rising at seven a.m. every day and in bed by nine p.m., he was purified by the routine and carried back to his youth. "If I ever take such a trip again," he reported to Livy from Avignon, "I will have myself called at the first tinge of dawn & get to sea as soon after as possible. The early dawn on the water—nothing can be finer, as I know by my old Mississip[p]i experience. I did so long for you & Sue yesterday morning—the most superb sunrise!"[31] By the time he gave up his raft at Arles, he had recaptured the thing he most missed, the sense of pure freedom and escape. "In fact, there's *nothing* that's so lovely," he told Twichell. "But it's all over."[32]

Even as he rushed off tender missives to Livy, Twain could never have imagined that his eldest daughter was sending no less ardent notes to Louise Brownell, who had returned to Bryn Mawr. "I think of you these days, the first of college," Susy wrote. "If I could only look in on you! We would sleep together tonight—and I would allow you opportunities for those refreshing little naps you always indulged in when we passed a night together." A few days later, she resumed on the same romantic note: "My darling I do love you so and I feel so separated from you. If you were here I would kiss you *hard* on that little place that tastes so good just on the right side of your nose." At the end of the month, she still pined for Louise. "I love you night and day with all my might. You are so sweet, dear, so lovely lovely! Goodby [sic] my darling, Your Olivia." She ended with a heartbreaking plea. "Oh, Louise if I could only see you! I am so afraid—DON'T FORGET ME!"[33] Susy panicked at the thought that, with their prolonged separation, Louise might drift away from her forever.

"PARADISE OF THE RHEUMATICS"

By October, the Clemens party had moved on to Berlin, where they planned to spend the winter and subsist economically. Livy and Sue Crane went ahead to scout out an apartment and, to save money, dispatched Katy Leary back to Elmira. Livy could not manage stairs and needed a ground-floor apartment, which they found at 7 Körnerstrasse in a working-class district. Clara slammed it as "a cheap apartment in a disagreeable quarter of the city"—it had a warehouse on the same street— and the sharp comedown in status after Aix and Marienbad was psychologically jolting for the family, who recoiled from the new quarters.[34] For all its fleeting charms, the boat trip down the Rhône had worsened Twain's rheumatism, and he was tortured by "unappeasable pain" and an arm "howling in the night."[35] He exhausted himself translating a beloved German children's book, *Der Struwwelpeter* (*Slovenly Peter*), hoping to have it published by Webster & Company, but Fred Hall shot down the possibility of an American publication timed for Christmas. (Twain's translation would not appear for another forty-four years.) He sank into such a dejected state that when he addressed an audience of 250 Americans in late November, they projected a dated portrait of him on a screen, and he lamented this "sorrowful reminder" that fifteen years earlier he didn't have a single gray hair.[36]

If at first disappointed by Berlin, the Clemens clan soon came to relish it. Twain viewed the city as a model of modernity, an efficient, newly remade metropolis with wide, straight streets illuminated at night by "double ranks of brilliant lights stretching far down into the night on every hand . . . and between the interminable double procession of street lamps one has the swarming and darting cab lamps," he wrote.[37] He was gratified by the clean, orderly urban culture and widespread literacy, with newspaper kiosks scattered through the city. He also valued Berlin's cultural attractions, its august place in the arts and sciences, and came to know the historian Theodor Mommsen and the diplomat and author Rudolf Lindau. In fact, because Mommsen had an unruly shock of white hair that jutted out in twin wings, Twain was mistaken for him twice in the street. "We have the same hair," he conceded, "but on examination it was found the brains were different."[38] For Twain, with his immense respect for historians, Mommsen was "a giant myth, a world-shadowing specter, not a reality," and he couldn't believe it when he sat near Mommsen at a beer festival amid a thousand German students.[39]

Livy attended lectures on German literature and studied German even as her husband, in his notebook, marched ahead with his pitiless mockery of the language. "I don't believe there is anything in the whole earth that you can't learn in Berlin except the German language. It is a desperate language. *They* think it is the language of concen*tration*. They hitch a cattle-train of words together and vestibule it, & because there isn't a break in it from one end to the other they think that is concentration . . . I wrote a chapter on this language 13 years ago & tried my level best to improve it & simplify it for these people . . . It hurts me to know that that chapter is not in any of their text books & they don't use it in the University."[40]

On the last day of December, the Clemenses switched addresses to the fancier Hotel Royal on Unter den Linden, giving them "six chambers & one dining room & one parlor," lifting the family's mood.[41] Though the hotel was a more suitable abode for a famous author, it again seemed an unlikely place to save money. This fashionable spot afforded the family a front-row seat to watch the kaiser speed by in an open carriage or young noblemen trot swiftly past with white-plumed footmen perched behind them. Reports of Twain's presence spread throughout the city, and when he ate in the hotel dining room, he sat there like a waxwork on display as curiosity seekers crept ever closer to the table. Clara thought her father "utterly unconscious" of these voyeurs, but he never minded the spotlight and fed off the public attention. A much-loved figure in Germany, he was soon courted by notables from the political and academic worlds, a renown that posed problems for Livy, who had been forewarned by doctors to curtail her social whirl to one night out per week, and she craved more rest and quiet than bustling Berlin could afford. With Clara and Susy now invited to court balls, Livy was distressed that she was not healthy enough to exercise the needed maternal supervision of her growing daughters.

In early January, Sam and Livy escaped to the Harz Mountains, where

"PARADISE OF THE RHEUMATICS"

they stayed for eight days with a pastor and his family in a tiny village favored by several members of the nobility. However much he raged against aristocrats on paper, Twain again swelled with pride in their company and was flattered by their attention. When he dined with Fürst Otto zu Stolberg-Wernigerode and his son, Twain was, if not ecstatic, extremely pleased by their company. "He is a very handsome man, and the proudest unroyal prince in Germany, and the richest," he wrote. "He brought several carriage-loads of young princesses with him."[42] He proudly noted that he and Livy were the only people below the princely rank at the dinner, except for a doctor and his wife. Sensitive to slights inflicted by the powerful, Twain recorded the Fürst's cutting condescension when "the doctor's wife put out her hand & the Fürst let on that he didn't see it. Poor thing, instead of taking warning, she raised her hand *higher*, imagining he hadn't seen it. He *ignored* it. It was tragic. She had a cry that night."[43] Despite such odious behavior, Twain ended by noting what "a pleasant and sociable time" he and Livy had had, and they stayed until midnight.[44]

That Twain's health had been grievously undermined by the strain of Webster & Company and the Paige typesetter grew evident in January when he gave a lecture in a packed hall that he branded as "hot as the Hereafter."[45] Afterward, he milled about at a late-night ball thrown by General Maximilian von Versen, who had married his distant cousin, Alice Clemens, and then felt frozen when driving home at two a.m. Weakened by exhaustion, he woke up the next morning with lung congestion that deepened into pneumonia, a siege that lasted more than a month. He would always insist that the episode caused lasting damage to his right lung.

Confined to bed for thirty-four days, Twain diverted himself with reading and struggled to translate parliamentary debates from the newspaper. "By reading keep in a state of excited ignorance," he noted, "like a blind man in a house afire."[46] He was buoyed by an invitation from the kaiser, inviting him to a ceremonial event. When he had to decline, the kaiser replied that he would like to dine with him at Frau von Versen's once he felt better. Eleven-year-old Jean was dazzled by the imperial summons. "I wish I could be in Papa's clothes," she commented, "but it wouldn't be any use, I reckon the Emperor wouldn't reconnize [sic] me."⁴⁷ With rheumatism spreading to his right foot, it was now Sam's turn, not Livy's, to be ordered by doctors to travel south to a warmer climate, and he despaired of resuming full-time writing. "I do not expect to be able to write any literature this year," he told Fred Hall. "The moment I take up a pen my rheumatism returns."⁴⁸

Once Twain recuperated from pneumonia, the kaiser made good on his pledge and invited Twain to dine with him at the von Versen residence on February 20. "In that day," Twain predicted, "the Imperial lion and the Democratic lamb shall sit down together, and a little General shall feed them."⁴⁹ When the imperial card arrived, it was passed around for inspection, and Jean was again awestruck by this royal artifact. "Why papa, if it keeps going on like this, pretty soon there won't be anybody left for you to get acquainted with but God."⁵⁰

When the evening came for the dinner, Jean stood gazing down the von Versen stairway from an upper floor as the kaiser strode majestically up the stairs, and she couldn't believe how handsome he was. By regal standards it was an intimate dinner: fourteen guests, mostly from military ranks. Twain sat immediately to the right of the emperor, who astounded him with his excellent English and thorough familiarity with his writings, pronouncing *Life on the Mississippi* his most important work. At one point, the emperor expressed praise for the generous military pensions in the United States, and Twain bumbled his way into a faux pas by arguing that it "had little by little degenerated into a wider and wider and more and more offensive system of vote purchasing."⁵¹ This was more candor than the kaiser could stand, and according to Twain, he pointedly ignored him for the rest of the dinner and during beer and cigars afterward. Twain was always flustered when it came to etiquette and court rules, which must have made him feel like a rude schoolboy straight from the boondocks.

During his time in Berlin, Twain wrestled with contradictory feelings toward the kaiser. He knew the grandiloquent emperor exhibited considerable amour propre. "If he had occasion to refer to his Maker," Twain once said, "he would speak of Him as the junior member of the firm of

"PARADISE OF THE RHEUMATICS"

which he, the Kaiser, is senior partner."[52] While Twain gloried in attention from royalty and the homage paid to his talent, it was a tumultuous period in German politics, with much controversy engulfing the emperor, especially after he made an inflammatory speech in Parliament in which he said that "grumblers," dissatisfied with the government, should shake sand from their slippers and exit the country. An angry mob ringed the palace in response, shouting revolutionary slogans. These "crowds of the proletariat," as Twain labeled them, swarmed up and down Unter den Linden, "but the emperor rode out as usual, and after him I saw the whole force of royal carriages following—apparently all the royal women and all the children have turned out to show that they are not afraid."[53] In these notebook comments, Twain did not condemn the protesters, but neither did he cheer them on. If he had an instinctive sympathy for the underdog, he had a no less instinctive tendency to socialize with the wealthy and high-born who acknowledged his achievements.

With Twain ambulatory again, he and Livy left the children behind and departed on February 29 for what they hoped would be a restorative stay in Menton, on the French Riviera, near the Italian border, Twain vowing that "I'm going to have a long holiday from writing now."[54] He jested darkly that he had been "reluctant to pay my railway fare in advance, because I did not believe I was going to finish the trip."[55] If the Clemenses had pictured a warm, charming sojourn amid Menton's lemon, tangerine, and orange groves, they instead had to deal with a penetrating cold that left them huddled around a wood fire in their hotel room. Twain's medical troubles, including an intractable cough from the damaged lung, followed him from Berlin, and Livy wrote to Alice Hooker Day of a disturbing day when he "lay and slept almost in a comatose state, he seemed so unnatural that it was frightful."[56] Before leaving Hartford, Livy had consulted two prominent physicians about her heart troubles, and they predicted she might live two years, if she took good care of herself. Now she was full of foreboding. "I say to Mr. Clemens sometimes 'think of the horror of dying over here among these new people.' I want to be with my own people or my own old friends when I go out of this world."[57] Pleased by elegant people, Livy was depressed by the plain, countrified dress and gauche manners of English guests at the hotel—perhaps another symptom of her homesickness. As Twain gradually felt strengthened by their stay, he was still "not content; for I cannot touch a pen without disabling my right shoulder."[58] In the end, Menton did end up being a happy and restful interlude for Sam and Livy.

The enforced separation from their children meant Sam and Livy were lingering in Menton when Susy turned twenty. Twain didn't parcel out praise lightly when it came to writing, but he was singularly impressed by Susy's literary abilities and took advantage of her birthday to tell her so. "Susy dear, I have been delighted to note your easy facility with your pen and proud to note also your literary superiorities of one kind and another—clearness of statement, directness, felicity of expression, photographic ability in setting forth an incident—style—good style—no barnacles on it in the way of unnecessary retarding words . . . You should write a letter every day, long or short, and so ought I but I don't."[59]

To please Sue Crane, Sam and Livy sneaked in a trip to various Italian cities. Twain proved, as usual, a grumpy traveler, and after being told that the Hotel Grande Bretagne and Arno in Florence was the best in town, he begged to differ. "It is a vast confusion of halls and sleeping-holes, a huge congerie of rats' nests, furnished with rubbish, probably bought at pauper auctions."[60] When the family pushed on to Rome, Susy sounded like her father in her commentary on Italians. "There is no brilliancy and intellectual vivacity in their faces," she complained to Louise, "but only beastliness and dirt."[61] While in Rome, the Clemens party toured the studios of several American artists, including Harriet Hosmer, a neoclassical sculptor who pioneered in art and in her romantic relationships with other women; the sculptor Richard Greenough; and the symbolist painter Elihu Vedder. The busy touring schedule took a toll on the delicate Livy. "Mamma has been ill again for a few days," Susy told Louise, "and Rome is too exciting for her by far."[62] Travel was now too strenuous for Livy, yet she allowed herself to be swept along on this ambitious tour, a situation that must have made her hanker for Hartford's quiet.

By June, Livy could finally rest as they settled into Bad Nauheim. A famous resort north of Frankfurt renowned for its salt springs—Twain

"PARADISE OF THE RHEUMATICS"

nicknamed it "Bath No-harm"—it represented another stop in the restless search for health by the Clemenses.[63] To their relief, the bath doctors reversed the pessimistic diagnosis of the Hartford doctors and pronounced Livy's heart condition "curable, & *easily* curable," Twain told Clara, clearly hoodwinked by a specimen of local self-promotion. "They say these baths will do it, & that these are the only baths in the world that can."[64] Twain was not the first spouse swayed by the happy talk of doctors who said the right thing. As he told Orion excitedly: "The bath physicians say positively that Livy has no heart disease, but has only weakness of the heart-muscles & will soon be sound & well again. That was worth going to Europe to find out."[65] Despite this sanguine verdict, the doctors wanted to shield Livy from visits even by close friends and family, lest they upset her—she needed a year of "absolute seclusion from human society," as Twain termed it.[66] The mild diagnosis and severe treatment didn't quite fit. In spite of Panglossian words from the doctors, Livy's daily routine delivered tangible benefits: she took baths at eleven a.m., followed by light gymnastics, and a long afternoon rest. "Lately I have had none of that tired confused feeling in the head that for a year or two I have had so much of," she told her husband, who had taken a five-week business trip back to the United States.[67]

Twain returned to Bad Nauheim in time for a memorable dinner encounter. The Clemens family grew distracted by an author in the room whose celebrity rivaled even that of Mark Twain: Oscar Wilde, there taking the waters with Alfred Douglas, his young lover and the partner in his scandalous downfall. "He was remarkably dressed and highly vivacious in manner and speech," recollected Clara. "It was not difficult to recognize Oscar Wilde. He and Father became aware of each other at almost the same moment and rose to exchange greetings, although as far as I know they had never met before."[68] The moment stood engraved on Susy's memory. "Oscar Wild[e] was over here the other day in a suit of soft brown with a pale pink flowered vest, a blue necktie and some strange picturesque white flower in his button hole," she told Louise.[69] We have no idea what witticisms the two men exchanged, but we do know how much Wilde revered Twain. In fact, George Bernard Shaw believed

"Oscar Wilde got much of his humour, especially his fondness for exaggeration, from Mark Twain."[70] Five years earlier Wilde had published a sparkling review of a Twain article titled "English as She Is Taught."[71]

The other notable figure crossing Twain's path that summer was the Prince of Wales, later King Edward VII, a chance encounter that occurred when Twain and the visiting Joseph Twichell took a side trip to Bad Homburg "to watch the crowd of invalids take the waters at the springs," Twain said.[72] He happened to bump into the British ambassador Sir Edward Malet, who asked whether he might like to meet the prince. Once again, Twain expanded happily in the presence of royalty, lauding the prince in his notebook as "one of the heartiest & pleasantest Englishmen I have ever seen, absolutely un-English in his quickness in detecting carefully concealed humor."[73] Twain dined with the prince, escorted him on a mile-long promenade, and was pleased by his easy-flowing conversation. Watching these two stroll along, Joseph Twichell was struck by their comical incongruity: "the prince solid, erect, stepping with a firm, soldier-like tread; Mark waving along in that shambling gait of his, in full tide of talk, brandishing, as an instrument of gesture, an umbrella of the most scandalous description."[74]

As the Clemenses' stay in Bad Nauheim approached its end, their departure was thwarted by a deadly cholera outbreak in Hamburg. Twain gritted his teeth over a paucity of accurate information issuing from the German press. "When the Last Day comes it will note the destruction of the world in a three-line paragraph and turn over and go to sleep again," he wrote.[75] He planned to take Clara to Berlin, where she would resume music lessons, when he read of two or three cholera deaths there. He and Livy, who had decided to rent a villa in Florence for the fall and winter, were now blocked by quarantines and fear that the cholera might spread there. Stranded in Bad Nauheim in early September, Twain regretted that "we are now under the double expense, indefinitely—the house & servants in Florence & our keep here in the hotel."[76] The Florentine villa, with a full staff, coachman, and horses, would count as yet another Twain extravagance.

Money continued to preoccupy Mark Twain since his royalties and profits had to be reinvested in capital-short Webster & Company. Nonetheless, he believed Fred Hall had rescued "a business that was in ruins," and he was heartened by a midsummer report that gave at least a temporary reprieve from worries.[77] "We are charmed with the handsome summer business which you report—may you continue to boom!" Twain cheered Hall before pressing him for more money. "You speak of $500 left over. Suppose you send me a draft on London for it."[78]

As they prepared to leave Bad Nauheim in September, Twain touted the progress Livy had made and boasted that he had "grown ruggedly healthy" and was writing books again.[79] For Livy, the improvement proved short-lived, for as they prepared to leave Bad Nauheim, her skin grew red and swollen with erysipelas and she experienced tormenting headaches. She may also have suffered from hyperthyroidism, or Graves' disease, which can lead to weight loss, goiters, irregular heartbeats, and various eye problems, including painful, bulging eyes. With such a variety of dreaded symptoms, Livy brooded on her own mortality. "One feels at this time," she told Grace King, "that one holds life and health by a very slender thread."[80] When the family was finally able to travel to Florence, the trip turned into a hellish ordeal for Livy. "She is tortured with headaches which never cease," Twain wrote, "therefore railroading comes mighty hard."[81] The family was forced to halt the trip for four days in Frankfurt solely to deal with what Susy called "a strange and sudden illness of Mamma's."[82] With her medical problems, Livy was unsuited for these endless tourist rambles, and her nostalgia for peaceful Hartford days only grew.

For Susy, it was a particularly lonely and disturbing time. She had suffered a triple disruption to her life: she had been wrenched away from Bryn Mawr and Louise; had lost the house she grew up in with its affluent lifestyle; and had to deal with a once happy but now badly damaged family, with two aging, ailing parents. With Louise as her constant mental companion, she sent her poignant letters of palpable longing. "Hundreds of times a day I say 'there!' Louise would admire this or laugh at that and so on, but you are not here & I *cannot* talk to you. It is dreadful & grows more so every day."[83] She felt cruelly the transatlantic distance from Louise, who was still at Bryn Mawr, and worried that they would never be reunited, that the temporary breach would lengthen and harden into permanence. Susy wrote to her: "I begin to have a kind of dreadful fear that it will be long long, longer than we had at all thought at first; before we go home."[84] Wherever the Clemens family traveled, no matter how picturesque the spot, Susy was haunted by Louise's eternal image. "I throw my arms around you and kiss you over and over again," she assured her from Venice. "I hope you are happy and not depressed. I love you with all my heart and more every day."[85] For Susy Clemens, love was an all-out proposition. The intense love she had once focused exclusively on her family had now found a new but distant object.

Of the three daughters, Clara was most insistent on having an independent life and an identity apart from her parents. Long passionate about music, she had studied piano in New York with an elderly pupil of Franz Liszt and Clara Schumann, and Livy noticed how "faithful and industrious" she was as she practiced four to five hours daily.[86] Coming from a family of high-strung, creative people, Clara approached the piano with considerable tension, fearful of not matching up to the necessary high standards. Sam and Livy allowed Clara to reside in Berlin, rather than have her join them in Florence, so that she could study with the brilliant pianist and teacher Moritz Moszkowski. Where Susy could seem frail and withdrawn, Clara was more outgoing and worldly. Instead of being pleased by the social entree that she enjoyed as a member of the Clemens family, she chafed at being known as "the daughter of Mark Twain," as she wrote glumly to her mother from Berlin. "I do hate society today & people & the world. I wish one could get into a little hole where there wasn't even a *worm* to recognize one; people do make it so embarrassing for you. I am so tired of having Papa & his books praised because I never do anything but sit & smile & wish I was at home."[87] Clara would contend with severely conflicted feelings toward her father, an inner rage that vied with love for him. What made the conflict so much harder to resolve was that, when necessary, she would be happy to trade on his fame, which would form no small part of whatever professional success she managed to have in the music world.

CHAPTER TWENTY-NINE

"A Lady Above Reproach"

Mark Twain's rheumatism had struck at the most inopportune moment, just as he felt a desperate need to earn money from writing. In February 1891, still hoping to salvage his option on the Paige typesetter, he had decided, with cold-blooded calculation, to earn $75,000 from his pen in three months. He rallied enough to dive into a new novel, written at headlong speed, called *The American Claimant*. In his haste to make money, he had pulled out a play that he and Howells had written years earlier based on Colonel Sellers and a distant relation on his mother's side, Jesse M. Leathers, who had absurdly claimed the legal right, as a Lampton, to the earldom of Durham. From time to time, Leathers had pestered Twain with nuisance letters, seeking to drag him into this futile family quest. Like Colonel Sellers, "the Earl" was a pathetic gasbag who lived in a dreamworld of his own devising. "He was a Kentuckian," Twain recalled, "and a well meaning man; but he had no money, and no time to earn any; for all his time was taken up in trying to get me, and others of the tribe, to furnish him a capital to fight his claim through the House of Lords . . . And so he dreamed his life away, always in poverty."[1]

Both amused and appalled by this escapade, Twain tried to prod Howells into running a magazine piece by Leathers. As with Colonel Sellers (based on James Lampton) and Ned Wakeman, Twain was eager to pounce when ready-made characters came his way. "Now here is my little game," he told Howells. "I won't have this tramp under my roof, nor on my hands; yet at the same time he is a perfectly stunning literary bonanza, & must be dug up & put on the market."[2] Believing that the drivel Leathers wrote didn't turn up often, Twain was shocked when Howells declined to publish it. "Howells don't seem to have no taste," he protested to James R. Osgood. "The Earl's literary excrement charmed me like Fanny Hill. I just wallowed in it... You are as dainty and effeminate as Howells; so I know perfectly well that you will simply urinate on the Earl's MS and send it back to him without other comment."[3]

In the end, Twain and Howells teamed up on a play that was finally titled *The American Claimant,* its lead character combining elements of both Colonel Sellers and Jesse Leathers. Howells dropped out before the play had a brief but disastrous run in 1887. The theater was a bewildering riddle that Twain could never solve, and the play drew merciless reviews. The *New York Times* greeted it with a snide notice, dripping with disdain. "'The American Claimant... is as much like a play as a school exhibition dialogue... [Mark Twain] is an original humorist, beyond dispute, but he is not a dramatist. 'The American Claimant' has neither plot nor action."[4]

By the time Twain embarked on the novel in 1891, he was still bothered by rheumatism in his arm and again experimented with dictating into phonographic cylinders. When he found the machine "as grave & unsmiling as the devil," he scrapped it and wrote longhand.[5] Working at maximum intensity, he placed intolerable pressure on himself, wanting Webster & Company to start the subscription canvas by September 1. Oddly enough, given its later critical reception, he thought the book would "simply howl with fun. I wake up in the night laughing at its ridiculous situations."[6] Twain raced through the manuscript, finishing in seventy-one days. Samuel S. McClure paid $12,000 for the serial rights, with the first installment set to appear in January 1892, and Webster & Company then produced the hardcover. The publishing house tried hard to tap into the popular love of Colonel Sellers, as if he were a franchise Twain could trot out at will. "The most widely known character in American fiction," one advertisement trumpeted, "Col. Mulberry Sellers is again introduced to readers in an original and delightful romance, replete with Mark Twain's whimsical humor."[7]

The American Claimant opens with one of Twain's funniest prefatory notes. "No weather will be found in this book . . . This weather will be found over in the back part of the book, out of the way. *See Appendix.*"[8] In the novel, Twain mocks the pretensions of our allegedly democratic culture, which is supposed to frown on royalty. Mulberry Sellers, with his outrageous claim to the earldom of Rossmore, grovels before British nobility. He is a con man but not a malevolent one, since he believes in his crackpot theories even as he tries to palm them off on others. Mrs. Sellers describes him as "the same old scheming, generous, good-hearted, moonshiny, hopeful, no-account failure he always was."[9]

In England, the real Earl of Rossmore (sounding much like Twain snubbing Jesse Leathers) tells his son, Lord Berkeley, that the American claimant has made his life "a purgatory for ten years with his tiresome letters, his wordy reasonings, his acres of tedious evidence."[10] The son, with an idealized view of America as an egalitarian paradise, decides to go there and courts Mulberry's daughter, Sally Sellers, under the pseudonym Howard Tracy. Twain puts the young couple through excruciating complications before Berkeley finally discloses his true identity as a viscount and the young couple marry. Twain deals here in stereotypes, not individuals, and Howard Tracy and Sally Sellers act like generic young stage lovers. One can see the novel's genesis as a stage play since characters emote in theatrical fashion and don't have the private, mysterious inner life of genuine fiction.

The American Claimant is a book of ideas, a philosophical debate tricked out as fiction, lacking heart or soul. Twain continues the exploration of identity that he started with *The Prince and the Pauper,* stripping Lord Berkeley of his title and inherited privilege, and seeing how he fares in the rough-and-tumble of a democratic culture. Twain shifts from mocking British aristocracy to skewering America's egalitarian pretensions. With the young lord holding a saccharine view of America as a land "where all men are equal and all have an equal chance," Twain tests whether the country lives up to its founding ideals.[11] As Lord Berkeley seeks to find his first job as a clerk, he discovers that "he stood no chance whatever. There, competency was no recommendation; political backing, without competency, was worth six of it."[12] Hunting for work, searching for a classless society, he discovers an America honeycombed with hidden class distinctions, making it the story of a disillusioned idealist. *The American Claimant* did not sell well, and one Twain scholar would later revile it as "the most jumbled piece he ever published."[13]

When Twain needed money, he wasn't reluctant to recycle characters from previous books and cash in on their commercial value. He pictured, but never wrote, a sequel to *Tom Sawyer* and *Huck Finn* in which both boys age—badly. As he wrote in his notebook, "Huck comes back, 60 years old, from nobody knows where—& crazy. Thinks he is a boy again, & scans always every face for Tom & Becky &c. Tom comes, at last, 60 from wandering the world & tends Huck, & together they talk the old times; both are desolate, life has been a failure, all that was lovable, all that was beautiful is under the mould. They die together."[14] Thanks to his terrible business mishaps and financial concerns, Twain's worldview had only darkened, and boyhood seemed even more of a lost paradise, followed by repeated hardship.

During the Bad Nauheim summer, Twain rounded up his old characters in a more cheerful story, informing Fred Hall that "I have started Huck Finn and Tom Sawyer (still 15 years old) & their friend the free slave Jim around the world in a stray *balloon,* with Huck as narrator . . . I have written 12,000 words of this narrative, and find that the humor flows as easily as the adventures and surprises."[15] The book was called *Tom Sawyer Abroad,* and Twain knew he was banging out a potboiler, hoping Hall would sell the opening sections for a magazine serial. "If the first numbers should prove popular, I could go on & furnish additional parts without delay, if desired."[16]

Twain's heart wasn't in the writing, and his fine sense of comedy degenerated into slapstick and farce. After his experience with Paige, he ridiculed the mad, vain inventor of the balloon that carries Huck, Tom, and Jim over the Sahara Desert and the Egyptian pyramids, and insists that it is propelled by a secret power known only to him. "A new power, and a thousand times the strongest in the earth. Steam's foolishness to it . . . Why, there's power aboard to last five years, and food for three months." Of his critics, he scoffs, "They are fools, what do they know about it?"[17] Tom is swept up in the inventor's ecstasy while Jim and Huck yearn to be free of this madman and his creation. Jim loses the nobility and dignity he possessed in *Huck Finn* and is reduced to a purely racist caricature. As one critic has noted, "Throughout the story Jim responds in the manner expected of a sideshow darky who finds himself up in the air with two venturesome white boys. He groans, faints, pouts and prays."[18]

Of course, with Twain's genius, even his worst productions were enlivened by some witty stuff, and there is piquant, Swiftian humor on display in *Tom Sawyer Abroad*, published in 1894. As Huck, Jim, and Tom float over the Sahara, they watch lions devouring dead lions down below. Huck comments: "It was strange and unnatural to see lion eat lion, and we thought maybe they warn't kin. But Jim said that didn't make no difference. He said a hog was fond of her own children, and so was a spider, and he reckoned maybe a lion was pretty near as unprincipled though maybe not quite. He thought likely a lion wouldn't eat his own father, if he knowed which was him, but reckoned he would eat his brother-in-law if he was uncommon hungry, and eat his mother-in-law any time."[19] This was pure vaudeville, the stuff of stand-up comedy. Twain also gave comic expression to his conviction of there being fewer saints than sinners in the world. Tom invokes his uncle Abner, a Presbyterian preacher, who notes the shortage of saints by saying that "heaven was the Rhode Island of the Hereafter."[20]

While passing through Florence in May 1892, Sam and Livy were so enthralled by the beauty of the Tuscan hills and the history surrounding them that they decided to rent for the winter Villa Viviani, set on a hillside near the village of Settignano, northeast of Florence. The house had two stories, two hundred years of history, and ancient foundations. "It is a plain, square building, like a box, and is painted light green and has green window-shutters," Twain wrote. Beyond a garden blooming with lemon trees, magnolias, and masonry walls overrun with roses, "the vineyards and olive groves of the estate slant away toward the valley."[21] The house even had a family chapel with altar paintings and seating for ten or twelve people, a room that was wasted on Twain.

For Twain, the villa's supreme feature was its remote view of Florence, "pink & gray & brown, with the ruddy, huge dome of the cathedral dominating its center like a captive balloon." With his eye for natural beauty, he sat transfixed in the evening as twilight settled over the city. "To see the sun sink down, drowned in his pink & purple & golden floods, & overwhelm Florence with tides of color that make all the sharp lines dim & faint & turn the solid city into a city of dreams, is a sight to stir the coldest nature & make a sympathetic one drunk with ecstasy."[22] He rated this view "the fairest picture on our planet" and never retracted his opinion.[23] His historical sense was entranced by the villa's dark oil portraits of Florentine senators and judges with their possible literary associations. "One of them is dated 1305—he could have known Dante, you see," he wrote. "Another is dated 1343—he could have known Boccaccio and spent his afternoons in Fiesole listening to the Decameron tales. Another is dated 1463—he could have met Columbus."[24] The Mark Twain who read history and biography and wrote historical fiction sprang vividly to life in the Villa Viviani atmosphere.

Livy hoped to convert the villa into a "pleasant and cozy" place for visiting family and friends, but cozy it was not: it was a sumptuous affair with twenty-eight rooms and a cavernous salon, forty feet high, big enough to swallow five divans. "All the rest of the house was built around it," wrote Grace King. "There were long suites of bedrooms and endless corridors connecting them."[25] The high ceilings and tall windows flooded the interior with sunlight. The villa had a housekeeper, a cook, and a butler; Livy retained a German girl to attend her; and Susy had a French governess to teach her the language and chaperone her to town. Meanwhile, Twain hired a four-wheeled carriage, with horses and a coachman, to cart his family around. He and Livy were simply addicted to luxury, and the trip again added to money worries instead of subtracting from them. When Livy gave Susy a gift on her twenty-first birthday, it was "the most exquisite little pearl necklace with a clasp of sapphires set in diamonds."[26] "We are getting slowly settled here—*very* slowly," Twain wrote Fred Hall. "It will be as expensive as living in hotels—besides the extra cost of getting *started*."[27]

No sooner had Twain reached Florence than he had his head shaved bald. Susy blushed and screamed with fright when she saw him, while Clara thought his head was "clipped like a billiard ball."[28] That summer, he had complained of losing hair "by the hatful," likely a stress-induced form of alopecia that he now hoped to halt by cutting all his hair.[29] His family, horrified, beseeched him to avoid social contacts and retreat like a hermit till his hair returned. His impulsive move, if it upset his family, yielded a comic gem, a droll riff on baldness. "No matter how closely I shut myself away from drafts it seems to be always breezy up there. But the main difficulty is the flies. They like it up there better than anywhere else; on account of the view, I suppose. It seems to me that I have never seen any flies before that were shod like these. These appear to have talons. Wherever they put their foot down they grab. They walk over my head all the time, and cause me infinite torture. It is their park, their club, their summer resort. They have garden parties there, and conventions, and all sorts of dissipation."[30]

Installed in a downstairs apartment to avoid stairs, Livy at first seemed rejuvenated by Florence, recapturing the rosy health she had enjoyed at Bad Nauheim. It seemed a superlative time of peace and beauty. She would join the family for tea on the open terrace and watch the sun setting over the hills west of Florence. Not needing direction, the self-sufficient domestic staff performed household tasks that had proved so burdensome to Livy in Hartford. "There is no housekeeping to do," Twain noted with satisfaction, "no plans to make, no marketing to superintend—all these things do themselves, apparently."[31] These days were so restorative that Twain thought Livy might wish to extend their residence an extra year, but her health problems were now chronic, and by November she was debilitated by dysentery. "Mamma is still ailing along, & it is just heart-breaking to see her," Twain advised Clara, then studying piano in Berlin. "She is patient & uncomplaining—just as always—but she is very weak & all wasted away."[32] Sue Crane disclosed to a friend that Livy had to "live in seclusion, & be free from all extra care and all excitement," and said her heart condition necessitated this.[33] As soon as they arrived in Florence, Livy was seen by an American doctor, William Wilberforce Baldwin, who treated many prominent Americans in Italy, including J. P. Morgan, Henry James, William Dean Howells, and Edith Wharton. At some point during their time in Florence, Livy suffered such acute attacks of pain that Twain asked Susy to request a laudanum prescription from the doctor.

While Susy struggled with her taboo feelings for Louise, Livy, in hiring a French governess to escort her, fell back on Victorian proprieties and attempted to mold her as a proper young lady. She felt nervous about leaving Susy alone when she wasn't healthy enough to accompany her into society. Susy continued to love Louise, albeit with an underlying insecurity. She always wanted more letters and devoured them when they arrived. "That you love me I am glad every day of my life," Susy wrote to Louise, "and *proud* oh *very* proud but I never get over feeling surprise that you do."[34] She confessed to being desperately lonely and unsure of her place in the world. At night, she said, the villa gave off an eerie, ghostly air as she ascended the stairs with a candle and heard her footsteps echoing in the gloom. With her mother often resting on the sofa and her father writing, Susy was left alone with her sewing and reading, and was unsettled by a new irritant: her father's temper. "I have to go down to breakfast now," she told Clara, "and I don't enjoy this one bit, altho Papa hasn't *stormed* yet. Still I feel constrained and he pierces me thru with his eye as if he were determined to see whether I am embarrased [sic] or not."[35] Often bored, she complained of being "*heartily* tired of *books,* and *sewing* all day . . . and the long long lonely evenings when we read AGAIN by way of a CHANGE."[36]

In November, Susy grew somewhat less lugubrious when she found a new purpose in life. She took her first singing lesson with Luigi Vannuccini, a famous instructor of bel canto opera who had befriended Rossini. "Vanuccini [sic] is a fat genial kindly old gentleman that I liked very much," she informed Clara. "He seemed pleased with my voice said it was very sweet, very high, and very true."[37] Susy began attending operas and recitals more frequently as she worked on her voice. Of the beauty of her vocal instrument, nobody doubted; what she needed was more strength and volume. Her father, a definite admirer, discerned a marked improvement. "You will be charmed by Susy's singing," Twain told Clara. "She has made very great & rapid improvement, & it is a genuine pleasure to hear her."[38] He saw a striking change in her mood as she fashioned a new identity in singing. "Susy is in good health & good spirits," he told a friend, "& is becoming a lark, under the training of a capable singing-master."[39] Unfortunately, in her melancholy frame of mind, she depreciated her own talents. As Livy told a friend, "Her father and I feel that she is making good progress, but she does not feel that her voice amounts to anything."[40]

Unsure of her future with Louise, Susy opened herself up to relations with men and attended a couple of Florentine balls. She confessed to Clara that she had become "smitten" with a Count de Calry, whom she met at various teas, and was stung by his "marked discourtesy" in not asking her to dance at one ball. "He *is* a fascinating man altogether the most fascinating person I have met in Europe but I cannot understand his performances."[41] Clara zeroed in on something unspoken in Susy's letter. "Isn't this Count a married man that you're smitten with? You poor thing: It must be hard!"[42] Susy seemed to have a penchant for latching on to unavailable people and taboo relationships. Chafing at "family discipline" imposed by her parents, she wasn't bothered by the idea of having an affair with the married count.[43] "Oh, yes de Calry is a married man!" Susy confessed to Clara. "My goodness yes married to the homeliest woman in existence, a rich American. I am afraid he does not love her, poor thing, but she worships him."[44] Susy despaired of having a normal life as she sought an outlet for her pent-up emotions. She attempted to communicate to Clara the count's mysterious charm. "His hands are beautiful and he uses them constantly in quick magnetic gestures. He looks at you with a strange sort of distant caressingness and often gets very near you."[45]

Livy was taken with the count herself and kept inviting him to tea, seemingly oblivious that her eldest daughter was infatuated with this married man. "Count de Calry," Livy would say, "I hope you will come out here Wednesdays whenever you feel inclined," to which the count would bow and say, "Thank you for the privilege."[46] But when the count came what he said was always unpredictable. Slowly a resentful tone crept into Susy's commentary about him. As she told Clara, "He's too much of an egotist to fall in love with *anyone* . . . Besides I have seen him with his wife and he apparently loves her . . . Mamma thinks as I do that he is a rather ill bred spoiled capricious man who doesn't take the trouble of being polite except when he wants to."[47] Even while pretending to be over the count, Susy had more of a crush on him than she cared to admit. When he shook her hand coldly at a tea, Susy said, "I being tired and nervous and not very well, *changed color!!!* I could have *committed suicide* afterward."[48] When the count later stopped to inquire about her father, Susy spurned him, turned her back, and marched away. Her disappointment cut deep, and a month later she said Florence "has somehow become associated in my mind with de Calry's abominable rudeness. It leaves a bad taste in my mouth and I can't help it."[49]

Bereft of Hartford friends and repeatedly felled by illness, Livy clung to her daughters. At least until Susy went to Bryn Mawr, the Clemenses had been a tightly knit family, accustomed to being constantly together. Soon after arriving at Villa Viviani, Livy was pained by Clara's absence in Berlin. "My own darling," she wrote her. "I did not know that we should miss you so terribly! If I had known I do not know that I should have found the courage to let you go. The house is empty, *empty*, EMPTY and it is very hard for Susy and me to settle ourselves to doing anything."[50] She could not bear an absence of eight or nine months. While she had permitted Clara to study piano in Berlin, she wrote her guilt-inducing letters about its emotional toll on the family. Most of all, she feared Clara might achieve independence from them. "Don't get weaned from us," Livy pleaded, "and feel that you are happy without us but always have a little longing in your heart to be with your own family."[51]

When the whole family was in Berlin, Clara had felt suffocated by her father's giant presence in social settings, where she was relegated to being "Mark Twain's daughter." "At social gatherings graced by his presence, my existence was on the level of a footstool—always an unnecessary object in a crowded room. Father, fresh from bed, would completely flood the place with his talk."[52] She also found him excessively protective whenever men showed the slightest interest in her. One night in Marienbad, while Livy and Susy were in Berlin to scout out lodgings, she had gone to a military ball with her father and met an officer who called the next morning wearing "a sky-blue coat . . . and a white plume waved from his helmet." Twain received him as coldly as possible and grew perturbed when he popped up at nearby tables at meals. His fury began to mount. "He decided to proceed radically," Clara recalled years later. "I was to be locked up and Katie was to bring me my meals. At first I thought it was a joke . . . Surely I could not be incarcerated like a damsel of the Middle Ages. Yet that was just what happened." Clara dreaded her mother's return, thinking she would reproach her behavior. Instead, when Livy returned, "she burst with peals of laughter till her cheeks were bathed in tears. That was the most victorious moment of my life. On that occasion Father had been filled with the spirit of strict conventions which struck Mother as highly ludicrous."[53]

In Berlin, Clara had enjoyed a far more emancipated life than her sisters as she studied with Moritz Moszkowski. "*Hasn't Moskowski [sic] turned affectionate YET,*" Susy teased her. "Come *answer honestly.*"[54] As it happened, Moszkowski had gotten overly aggressive with Clara and she quit lessons with him. Through Frau von Versen, Clara, now eighteen, was invited to many balls, and her behavior at one provoked a scandal—at least at Villa Viviani. Clara had wandered into a room where she found herself inadvertently alone with forty male officers. Apparently, she did not exit as quickly as etiquette dictated, and her father sent her a reproachful letter. "Was there occasion to add yourself to the list of

American girls who bring their country into disrepute? Didn't it occur to you that there was but one course for you to pursue—leave that room the moment you found yourself the only representative of your sex in it? . . . If you would not have yourself and us talked about, there is but one course for you—to make yourself acquainted at the earliest moment, with the nicest shades of what is allowable by German custom."[55] Twain added that Clara should be "a lady above reproach—a lady always, modest and never loud, never hoydenish—a lady recognizable as such at a glance, everywhere, indoors and out."[56]

It is hard to believe that an author who scoffed at so many ridiculous social conventions should pressure his daughter to be such a model of propriety. Twain was tethered to a traditional view of women, even as social mores changed with the rise of the so-called New Woman, who demanded a more independent life and her own means of support. Sam and Livy prodded Susy to write a letter to Clara that, at first glance, seemed designed to soften her father's criticism. "You mustn't misunderstand papa's letter or think he's *severe* or *angry* or anything of the sort."[57] Then the letter broadened her father's critique to include Livy and even Susy herself in the attack. "Mamma wants you to write me or her some explanation . . . of how it came about, and then as she feels sure that it was entirely improper and will be talked about all over Berlin she thinks perhaps you had better take papa's letter to Frau von Versen . . . so that she can see that *you* were innocent and meant no harm, and also that papa and mamma have brought you up in the right way . . . I am as perplexed as Mamma and Papa. I cannot understand how you got into such a position!!!"[58]

What is striking in both letters is the not-so-subtle suggestion that Sam and Livy were worried about their own reputation, not just Clara's, and were afraid people might ostracize them or impugn their parental ability. Mary B. Willard, who ran Clara's boarding school for American girls, reassured her parents about her respectable behavior in Berlin. "She never goes out unattended, to any place of amusement, or on any trivial errand . . . I hope I have been able to relieve you of natural anxiety."[59] But Livy refused to let the matter drop, telling Clara that "it is not that we do not trust you for the future, but your description made us very anxious and we wanted to put you on your guard. I felt that if you had gotten a little free from being away from my checking influence that all you needed was to be reminded."[60] Separated by distance, Livy felt her power over Clara slipping away, especially since Clara was sure of herself and far more flirtatious and ambitious than her sisters. Livy could not accept that her middle daughter was entering adulthood and spreading her wings. Slowly, Clara was being weaned away from America and accustomed to European ways, a fact that her mother found hard to swallow. Susy had to coach Clara: "Enthuse just as much as you *want* to about Berlin in your letters to *me* but not *quite* so much in your letters to Mamma."[61]

Jean, now twelve, had an ease with foreign languages that set her apart, and Twain applauded her rapid progress at the villa. "When she talks German it is a German talking—manner & all; when she talks French she is French—gestures, shrugs & all, & she is entirely at home in both tongues. She is getting a good start in Italian & will make it her property presently."[62] Lithe and athletic, Jean loved the outdoors and went walking with Susy in the early morning, gathering wild violets. Because of her age, being uprooted from Hartford had perhaps been hardest on her. Celebrating Christmas at the villa, she insisted on having a tree and continuing a family tradition of making lace stockings since that "would seem like home," and her voice broke as she said that.[63] Having grown so needy, Livy was irate when Clara failed to join the family for the holidays. "I cannot bear to have you so far away from me and such a big piece of your life that I am not sharing it," she wrote with unwonted bluntness. "It is the first Christmas in 18 years that you have not been with me and I do not like it at all."[64]

For the fifty-seven-year-old Twain, Villa Viviani represented his last spell of relative serenity before business calamity broke over his head. Every day, he joined family and friends for tea on the terrace and drank in the spectacular sunsets. He showed his old flashes of gaiety, naming the resident cat Michelangelo Buonarroti Botticelli. Delighted with his high spirits, the visiting Grace King recalled many evenings of "pure fun" when Susy "would parody scenes from Wagner's operas and Mr. Clemens would give an imitation of a ballet dancer, posturing, throwing kisses and making grimaces, while Susy played a waltz on the piano."[65] At other times, Twain read aloud selections from Browning, as in Hartford, or sometimes Tennyson. He found the setting so restful and the winter weather so bracing that he had stupendous bursts of energy, managing to produce "a ton of manuscript in the last few months." Working on two novels, he finished *Pudd'nhead Wilson* and began *Joan of Arc*. Seldom given to expressions of outright contentment, he fairly burst with joy. "I've never enjoyed being alive more than I enjoy it now."[66] Americans visiting Florence found their way to Villa Viviani and delighted in the host's inimitable whimsy. William James called Twain "a fine, soft-fibred [sic] little fellow with the perversest twang and drawl, but very human and good. I should think one might grow very fond of him, and wish he'd come and live in Cambridge."[67]

It was Livy who felt premonitions of some dark fatality hovering in the air. "If you speak of next year," she noted in her journal, "the Devil laughs."[68] She was bedeviled by symptoms that presaged worse conditions ahead. "Mrs. Clemens is constantly awakened in the night by excessive dryness of the mouth & lips," Twain warned Dr. Baldwin.[69] Livy dwelled on her mortality, a fear intensified by stabbing pangs of homesickness. She never surrendered her faith that they would return home and resume their dear old life in Hartford. But she monitored family finances closely and was acutely aware that Jervis Langdon & Company had failed to sell a vital coal mine put up for sale. She laid out for Clara what this meant: "So we are not going to receive any money from J.L. & Co. at present therefore there is no present prospect of our feeling flush with money."[70] With such worries hanging over his head, Mark Twain set sail for America on March 22, 1893, to take care of some overdue business.

CHAPTER THIRTY

"Boss Machine of the World"

As he managed Charles L. Webster and Company, Fred Hall had continued to send Twain contradictory messages, forwarding plans for cutting expenses and publishing fewer books even as he boasted of the brisk business he was doing. Twain was still sufficiently fond of Hall that he invited him to spend a full month at Villa Viviani. As late as December 1892, Twain praised a "handsome" statement that Hall had sent him. "It looks as if [we're] about out of the woods at last," he wrote.[1] Later on, Twain would blame Hall for freely borrowing money while he was in Europe, but he admitted to having signed off on some of these loans. He would accuse Hall of "borrowing on notes endorsed by me and renewed from time to time. These notes used to come to me in Italy for renewals. *I endorsed them without examining them*, and sent them back. At last I found that additions had been made to the borrowings, without my knowledge or consent."[2] (Italics added.) It is astonishing that Twain, with his finances in such ruinous straits, was so negligent in a vital business matter.

The publishing house was still smothered by the expense of the multivolume *Library of American Literature,* and Twain, in daydreams born of desperation, pleaded with Hall to track down Andrew Carnegie and borrow money to defray the costs of a thousand sets per month. Beyond Carnegie's money, Twain sought the cachet of an association with a rich, prestigious capitalist. In his eager search for company saviors, he even sent Hall a letter of introduction to Carnegie. By this point, the firm owed Twain nearly $80,000, much of that Livy's money. After she chided her husband for taking a critical tone with Hall, he wrote to Hall sheepishly, "Mrs. Clemens is deeply distressed for she thinks I have been blaming you or finding fault with you about something. You have done magnificently with the business, and we *must* raise the money somehow, to enable you to reap the reward of all that labor."[3]

After Twain left Florence, Livy took her daughters to Venice, where she tore open a parcel of papers meant for her husband and was shocked by the contents. "The items that were marked made me *sick*, SICK. They were slurs at you," she told her husband, wanting to know if there was any truth to these irate charges.[4] They emanated from Rollin Daggett, who had published a book on Hawaii with Twain and alleged that he never received a penny of profit even though the first printing sold out. He further claimed that despite keen interest in Hawaii, Twain would "neither sell the plates nor get out another edition, that you are [a] good hater—a bitter, jealous man &c &c." Livy's reaction: "It makes me so desperately unhappy I could lie down and cry my eyes out when there is any word said against you."[5] What is so remarkable about Livy's letter was that she didn't reflexively defend her husband but credited these scurrilous accusations, warning him to "be careful in your dealings with people with the magazines and all that you do do not drive too close a trade with them. Be generous my darling even if we are poor as church mice."[6] That Livy thought them as "poor as church mice," even as they occupied a twenty-eight-room villa staffed by a full team of servants, says much about the rarefied world of her upbringing. Afraid of having been too critical with her husband, she followed up with a conciliatory note, explaining that "I want people to never do anything but praise you . . . You are my pet and you ought to be everybody elses [sic]."[7]

Soon after arriving in New York in April, Twain accepted a dinner invitation from Andrew Carnegie. "To me it has the look of a conspiracy," the author quipped, "& I have always hankered for a chance to conspire against something or somebody."[8] He took advantage of the dinner to lobby Carnegie to invest in his publishing firm, or the typesetter, or both. Presumably being facetious, Twain counseled his host not to put

"BOSS MACHINE OF THE WORLD"

all his eggs in one basket. "That's a mistake," said Carnegie shrewdly, "put all your eggs into one basket—and watch that basket."[9] Though he failed to walk away with any funds, Twain sent Carnegie a charming thank-you note. "Notwithstanding all that conspiring last night I slept the dreamless sleep of the average assassin the night before he is hanged. There is no soporific like crime."[10]

A few days later, Twain met with James Paige and was seduced anew by a blizzard of fake numbers and bogus visions thrown up by the inventor. Paige had assembled a group of investors, the Connecticut Company, who would supposedly start a factory in July to build the typesetters. He sketched out a glorious future in which they would build ten typesetters by year's end and five or six monthly after that. Soon they would construct and rent ten thousand machines, blanketing the newspaper universe. As usual, Paige was blowing fairy dust in Twain's face and convinced him that no other machine could possibly equal his typesetter. In his notebook, a credulous Twain noted the machine's new claims for efficiency and asserted, "Competition is impossible."[11]

To view the latest iteration of this mechanical wonder, Twain dragged Fred Hall to Chicago, where they also hoped to tour the World's Columbian Exposition in celebration of the four-hundredth anniversary of Columbus's landing in the Caribbean and featuring the legendary "White City." Checking into the Great Northern Hotel, Twain promptly came down with a cold so dreadful that he was trapped in bed for eleven days and never glimpsed the fair. His confinement gave him a chance to read *Cranford* by Elizabeth Gaskell. "I never could read it before," he told Livy, "but this time I blasted my determined way through the obstructing granite, slate & clay walls, not giving up till I reached the vein—since then I have been taking out pay ore right along."[12]

While recuperating, Twain was visited by sixty-seven-year-old Orion, and Fred Hall commented on the odd relationship between the brothers. In Hall's view, Orion had "no sense of humor, and was the simplest, best natured, most impractical and delightfully naive man I ever met."[13] In short, he was the antithesis of his brother. Twain often treated his brother with testy impatience, and Hall noted Orion's passive acceptance of this patronizing treatment. "The way in which he received Mr. S.L. Clemens' remarks about himself, and biting sarcasms, was at once pitiful and amusing."[14] Too defeated to fight back, Orion absorbed the satiric blows in more or less good humor, as if expecting little better from life.

As Twain lay in bed, Paige came and poured out a sob story about his difficulties, then moved right in for the kill. "When his European patent affairs are settled," noted Twain, "he is going to put me in for a handsome royalty on every European machine. We parted immensely good friends." Twain knew Paige had the royal gab of a flimflam man, but he remained in thrall to his golden tongue. "When he is present I always believe him—I cannot help it. When he is gone away all the belief evaporates," Twain wrote. "He is a most daring and majestic liar."[15] By the time Twain left Chicago, the spell of Paige's charm had begun to wear off. His illness had monopolized his time in America and left him feeling tired and wretched, as if the entire trip had been wasted. In New York, his health sputtered again, making one suspect that he had experienced a physical breakdown from cumulative stress.

While still under the influence of Paige's sales pitch, Twain wrote letters to Livy giddy with hope. Her response shows how much she enjoyed spending money and how much she shared her husband's dream of untold wealth from the typesetter. She said his letters "made me just about wild with pleasurable excitement. It does not seem credible that we are really again to have money to *spend* . . . Well I tell you I think I will jump around and spend money just for fun, and give a little away if we really get some . . . Are n't [sic] you glad that we did not sell any royalties[?] Always I have wanted them kept . . . It is astonishing to think that perhaps there is not yet a very long time for us to keep up this economy."[16] Relieved of financial worry, she poured out expressions of love for her husband. "Youth dear if you could be in my room . . . when I am there alone you would hear 'I love him to death' 'I just worship him' 'He is the dearest old pet in the world,' and similar expressions."[17]

Livy's wild enthusiasm was premature. On May 13, 1893, Twain sailed back to Genoa aboard the *Kaiser Wilhelm II*. Nine days earlier a panicky sell-off on the New York Stock Exchange led to the collapse of three brokerage firms, beginning a steep contraction that would culminate in a massive depression. Before it was over, fifteen thousand commercial firms would go bust along with six hundred banks and seventy railroads—a turn of events that would shatter Mark Twain's life. On the voyage home, he felt debilitated by the strain of business. "I am older by ten years than when I left New York," he told his notebook.[18] He knew his publishing firm subsisted on large loans from the Mount Morris Bank, which might abruptly dry up in any economic downturn. Back at Villa Viviani, he wrote Fred Hall in a bleak spirit. "I am terribly tired of business. I am by nature and disposition unfitted for it and I want to get out of it."[19] He reminded Hall that the firm now owed him and Livy somewhere between $170,000 and $175,000, and he wished to sell his two-thirds interest to another publishing house for $200,000 in notes paying 6 percent interest. He closed on a pathetic note: "Get me out of business! And I will be yours forever gratefully S.L. Clemens."[20] Twain made lists of Webster & Company's bank borrowings, which had now ballooned to $200,000. Some loans he remembered; others not at all. He was an amateur publisher swimming in statistics and pleaded with Fred Hall for assistance, saying he was "ignorant of business and not able to learn a single detail of it."[21] Twain had gone from fancying himself a budding tycoon to confronting the reality that he had been bluffing himself and others all along and that he didn't know the slightest thing about business. Gone was the old pose of worldly assurance that he had regularly flaunted before Charley Webster and Fred Hall.

Having trimmed Webster & Company's staff to skeletal levels, Hall had to inform Twain that he was lost in a fantasy world. He disputed that the firm owed the Clemenses upwards of $175,000, stating the true figure was much lower. Amid the panic, he also thought it preposterous for Twain to "sell your interest for anything like the amount of money you have invested in it nor could you find a purchaser at that price or any other price just at present."[22] Twain, who had moved to Munich so Livy could consult a heart specialist, sent Hall a scaled-down version of what he would accept for his share of the firm, saying he would waive principal if the buyer paid interest for five years. He also proposed selling the

Library of American Literature, that fatal error, to another house. Hall had already suspended sales of the series. Twain wanted to wash his hands of Webster & Company entirely, telling Hall that "I am not made for business; the worry of it makes me old, & robs life of its zest."[23] Livy chimed in as well. "I think Mr. Clemens is right in feeling that he should get out of business, that he is not fitted for it; it worries him too much."[24] Livy told Hall not to send them more money, that they would try for a few weeks to live off income from her brother. This was wishful thinking. On July 3, Charlie Langdon apprised his sister, "We have in hand now the hardest times & greatest stringency in money that this Country has ever seen," and he worried that the Langdon family firm might actually go bankrupt.[25]

That month, as the Clemenses experimented with yet another health resort, this time in Bavaria, Sam and Livy stared into a financial abyss. Stranded with shrinking funds, marooned in a foreign land, they felt powerless to do anything. "It is my ingenious scheme to protect the family against the almshouse for one more year—and after that . . . well, goodness knows!" Twain told Hall. "I have never felt so desperate in my life—and [with] good reason, for I haven't got a penny to my name, and Mrs. Clemens hasn't enough laid up with Langdon to keep us two months. It makes me quake to think that . . . even my royalties might be siezed [sic] before we got the Mount Morris bill paid . . . we sincerely wish we could relieve you, but it's all black with us and we don't know any helpful thing to say or do."[26] It is amazing to think that Sam and Livy, with their opulent lifestyle, could only fall back on a two-month cushion of savings. Twain rebuffed all attempts to send him details about Webster & Company's business, telling Franklin G. Whitmore, "Don't send me any more letters that relate to the publishing business . . . even though they come from the Apostles. They are in Mr. Hall's line & have never been in mine."[27] He wrote this even though an embittered Twain later blamed Hall for taking on debt without his knowledge.

Even as he moaned about his unsuitability for business, Twain concocted a fresh brainstorm in late July: once Hall sold off the *LAL,* they would launch an inexpensive magazine. Twain had worked out all the

"BOSS MACHINE OF THE WORLD"

numbers—price per issue, size of the first print run—and was ready to roll with publication as soon as *LAL* was gone. "With our hands free and some capital to spare," he told Hall, "we could make it hum."[28] Even with bankruptcy imminent, he wrote with a blithe assurance rendered ludicrous by events.

As the Mount Morris Bank, Webster & Company's main lender, recorded heavy losses from the failure of business clients, it refused to renew some loans coming due from Webster & Company. The firm was only rescued when Charlie Langdon took over two notes of $3,000 each and agreed to endorse another $15,000 in notes, if the bank renewed them. Despite this reprieve, Twain was petrified that he would forfeit his last source of income: his book royalties. "What I am mainly hoping for, is to save my royalties," he told Hall. "If they come into danger I hope you will cable me, so that I can come over & try to save them, for if they go I am a beggar."[29] He pleaded with Hall to sell the magazine serial rights for *Pudd'nhead Wilson*. "Do your best for me, for I do not sleep, these nights, for visions of the poor-house . . . Everything does look so blue, so dismally blue!"[30]

Such was Twain's despair that he badgered Hall for news that the Paige typesetter was completed, as if one disastrous business might bail out another. "I hope the machine will be finished this month," Twain wrote ruefully, "but it took me four years & cost me $100,000 to finish the other machine *after* it was apparently entirely complete & setting type like a house-afire."[31] In sober moments, Twain realized that the typesetter's success was a receding mirage that had fooled him many times before. "The bloody machine offered but a doubtful outlook and will still offer nothing much better for a long time to come," he admitted to Hall. "That is unquestionably the boss machine of the world but is the toughest one on prophets, when it is in an incomplete state, that has ever seen the light."[32]

By late August, Twain had planted his family in Franzensbad, a Bohemian health spa, and sailed back to the United States to deal with the horrendous business crisis. He was accompanied by Clara, whose persistent cough, doctors hoped, would profit from a sea voyage. The trip was another blow to family unity as the Clemenses dealt with extreme adversity. From Munich, Jean informed Clara that she had run through the park bawling "My sis-te-r has gone—to Amerika and—I miss her so—badly that I can scarcely—live!! . . . Susy and mamma are both in a rather tearful condition."[33] Upon arriving in New York, Twain sent Clara off to Elmira while he stayed with his physician, Clarence Rice, on East 19th Street before settling into cheap lodgings at The Players Club in Gramercy Park. He stayed in a quiet top-floor room with an electric light over the pillow, once occupied by the actors Edwin Booth and Lawrence Barrett. Being in New York gave Twain a far more graphic picture of the country's dire economic state. "The whole United States stopped work two or three weeks ago, the machine along with the rest," he told Livy. "I shall stay right here until this business cyclone abates."[34]

Hustling to earn money, Twain sold a short story, "The Esquimau Maiden's Romance," to *Cosmopolitan,* and serial rights to *Pudd'nhead Wilson* to the *Century Magazine.* Judging from his letters, his mood seemed to cheer up a bit as he waxed poetic about the ripe, luscious fruit stalls of Manhattan, which made European stands seem poor in comparison. "I bit into a peach & the juice squirted across the street and drowned a dog," he told Livy.[35] But he wrestled with a strong head cold and a violent cough so racking that he had to down a "whole bottle of whisky" to sleep.[36] As he raced around town, trying frantically to scrounge up money for Webster & Company, he found credit markets frozen and capital unavailable at any price. He swallowed his pride, rushed up to Hartford, and tried to borrow from old friends, to no avail—a bruising experience. He appealed to Sue Crane, who came up with $5,000. "The billows of hell have been rolling over me," he told Livy.[37] The economic collapse had also halted work on the Paige machine. "The type-setter is standing dead still," he reported. "Neither here nor in Chicago can they raise any money to finish the machine with, thus far."[38]

Then something miraculous happened to Mark Twain: a deus ex machina arrived in the form of a Standard Oil mogul named Henry Huttleston Rogers. With a scary deadline looming for Twain—$8,000 in notes from the Mount Morris Bank were due on Monday, September 18—

"BOSS MACHINE OF THE WORLD"

Clarence Rice suggested that he meet a business friend who admired his writing. (Actually, Twain had encountered Rogers aboard a yacht two years earlier.) On Friday evening, September 15, Twain met the tycoon at the Murray Hill Hotel, and Rogers expressed reverence for the author. "I heard you lecture a long time ago on the Sandwich Islands... When I came away I realized that Mark Twain was a great man, and I have read everything of yours since that I could get hold of."[39] Before the evening ended, Rogers agreed to extend an $8,000 loan to Webster & Company, collateralized by the firm's assets, and Hall picked up the check at Standard Oil headquarters the next morning. With a touch of wonder, Twain notified Clara: "The best new acquaintance I've ever seen has helped us over Monday's bridge."[40] Twain had gotten just what he needed: a smart, wealthy benefactor with plenty of cash and business savvy to spare. Twain, having aspired to be a tycoon, had now met the genuine article. In dealing with Twain's business crises, Rogers would offer not only limitless money, but supreme confidence and a shoulder to lean on, and he did so, Twain informed Livy, "without putting upon me... any sense that I was the recipient of a charity."[41]

A tall, handsome man with a gray mustache, Rogers, age fifty-three, moved with an unhurried sense of command that bespoke the depth of his power and the size of his bank account. He wore a black derby, well-tailored suits, and a diamond stickpin in his cravat; he typified Gilded Age excess. He was the president of six of the twenty companies that comprised Standard Oil and presided over a vast industrial empire from his eleventh-floor suite at 26 Broadway, controlling substantial stakes in an array of firms, including steel, coal, copper, gas, and insurance. Among his many exploits, he had formed Consolidated Gas (later Con Edison) and Amalgamated Copper, and joined with Edward H. Harriman in forging the Union Pacific Railroad. For his daring, often ruthless forays on Wall Street, Rogers had won the moniker of "Hell Hound Rogers." "We are not in business for our health," he instructed a government panel, "but are out for the dollars."[42] Often prosecuted for his business maneuvers, he was so agile at wriggling free that the *Wall Street Journal* dubbed him "the Artful Dodger."[43] His personal fortune may have approached that of J. P. Morgan himself. In his everlasting gratitude to Rogers, Twain exempted him from the brickbats he usually flung at financial pirates. "He's a pirate all right," Twain admitted, "but he owns up to it and enjoys being a pirate. That's the reason I like him."[44]

If Mark Twain embodied the American paradox of being both an enemy of greed and a captive of it, Henry H. Rogers was no less a walking contradiction. For all his buccaneering image, he had immense warmth and charm and, like Twain, loved to clown and banter. When it came to repartee, he seemed almost as quick-witted as the humorist himself. Openhanded in philanthropy, he lavished money on his hometown of Fairhaven, Massachusetts, endowing schools, a library, a town hall, a church, and a park. Twain especially admired the calm serenity with which Rogers carried out his responsibilities, never showing haste or conveying the impression that he expected repayment for his generosity. Twain responded to the man, not the résumé. Even Ida Tarbell, who wrote the famous exposé of Standard Oil, felt obliged to pay tribute to Rogers, calling him "as fine a pirate as ever flew his flag in Wall Street."[45]

The most onerous weight that Charles L. Webster and Company bore was the *Library of American Literature*. In more candid moments, Twain accepted at least partial responsibility for the fatal decision to take on this millstone. As he told Livy, "The whole trouble comes of Mr. Hall's unspeakable stupidity (& mine) in not seeing 3 years ago, that we were not strong enough to carry L.A.L. A child should have seen it. He should have been trying to get us rid of that burden a good 3 years ago."[46] Henry Rogers arranged for his son-in-law, William Evarts Benjamin, a subscription publisher, to take *LAL* off Twain's hands at a fire-sale price of $50,000. This bittersweet victory didn't begin to cope with the $200,000 Webster & Company owed to a clamorous host of bankers, printers, and binders. For the first time, Twain began to contemplate a global lecture tour that would clear away his debts. He felt lonely, missed his family, and agonized over the transatlantic separation, telling Livy, "I'm doing my best, dear heart—& you are my stay & my courage. Without you I should be nothing."[47]

With his incomparable wit, Twain did what he could to buck up the

"BOSS MACHINE OF THE WORLD"

morale of his daughters. He headed off to Huyler's candy shop to secure sweets for Clara, "but gave it up," he told her whimsically. "There were fifteen thousand women in there & I could not get near the counter. Besides, I was the only man, & I was afraid of them."[48] Twain's overwhelming concern was for Livy, who now prepared to spend the winter in Paris with Susy and Jean. "I hate going to Paris with no money to spend," she told her husband. "To feel that we cannot go to the Opera or theater or do any of the things we should like to do, yet on account of Susy's lessons I feel that we must go if we can possibly afford it . . . Poverty is hard!"[49] Caring for Livy had become a crusade for Twain, and he recruited Susy in that effort, even though she had been listless. "It is necessary to [Livy's] health that she be kept free from money-anxieties," he wrote to Susy from The Players Club. "We must all look sharp to that. We must never let her be low-spirited for one moment if we can help it. She is my only anxiety; I have no other."[50] This was a remarkable statement from a man with three daughters whose lives were deeply affected by his business crisis.

Henry Rogers proved a true financial angel. After spending three weeks in exhaustive study of the Paige typesetter, he concluded that it was worth pursuing and promised to raise the funds to resume work on it, which would allow Twain's royalties to regain their value. "In the meantime," he told Twain, "*you stop walking the floor. Go off to the country & try to be gay. You may have to go to walking again, but don't begin till I tell you my scheme has failed.*"[51] Twain imagined Standard Oil might take a stake in the typesetter, a fantasy that never materialized. Rogers's enthusiasm for the machine rekindled Twain's faith, and he assured Susy his royalties would make them millionaires in twelve months.[52]

Though Twain didn't want to oppress a busy man like Rogers with so much work, the magnate reacted with exquisite grace. "It rests me to experiment with the affairs of a friend when I am tired of my own," he said soothingly to Twain. "You enjoy yourself. Let me work at the puzzle a little."[53] Twain was flabbergasted at such kindness from a stranger. When a friend suggested that he publish *Wealth Against Commonwealth* by Henry Demarest Lloyd, the first major indictment of Standard Oil,

Twain angrily rejected the book, telling Livy that "the only man *I* care for in the world; the only man I would give a *damn* for; the only man who is lavishing his sweat & blood to save me & mine from starvation & shame, is a Standard Oil fiend."[54]

Now that Rogers gave him permission to enjoy life for a while, Twain was feted by many Manhattan organizations. A longtime member of the Lotos Club, he was honored by a crowded dinner at its elegant new clubhouse on Fifth Avenue. "I am glad to see a club in these palatial quarters," he remarked in his speech. "I knew it twenty years ago when it was in a stable, and later when it was in a respectable house, but nothing so fine as this."[55] He also attended a dinner at The Players Club for a group of old-timers from his Pacific Coast days, and his reactions betray his nostalgia for their early exploits, set against the dark complexity of the present. As he described the occasion to Livy: "The talk was of the days when we went gypsying a long time ago—thirty years. Indeed it was a talk of the dead . . . All the friendly robbers are gone. These old fools last night laughed till they cried over the particulars of that old forgotten crime."[56]

By far the most poignant encounter Twain had in New York was with George Griffin, the Black butler who had served the Clemens family loyally for seventeen years. He now had a wife and a four-month-old daughter, and was employed as second headwaiter at the Union League Club. As resourceful as ever, he had developed a lucrative sideline lending money to other Black waiters as well as white club members squeezed by the panic. A sprucely dressed Griffin called on Twain just as he was on his way to the *Century Magazine*. On the spur of the moment, Twain did something remarkable, given the interracial strictures of the day. "I took him along & introduced him to the editors . . . which seemed to puzzle them a good deal," Twain told Livy. "I showed him a number of engravings . . . for 'Tom Sawyer Abroad' & asked for his opinion of them—& that puzzled those editors again. Then when the art-editor asked me to cross Union Square & take a drink, & I invited George to come along & help, that was another surprise. I knew George would decline, at the bar, which of course he did."[57]

In another version of this story, Twain added a revealing comment on the visit to the *Century* offices: "The array of clerks in the great counting-room glanced up with curiosity—*a 'white man' & a negro walking together was a new spectacle to them.* The glances embarrassed George, but not me, for the companionship was proper; in *some ways he was my equal, in some others my superior.*"[58] Mark Twain was far from a perfect human being on racial matters and continued periodically to slip the N-word into letters, but that meeting with George Griffin counts as an extraordinary moment. For the first time, Twain stepped briefly outside the employer relationship with a Black man, shed white privilege, and treated him as a peer. "He is about as remarkable a character as I know," Twain told Livy. "I must put him in my next book."[59] When, four years later, George Griffin died of heart disease, Clara Clemens wrote that "it seemed as if we had lost a member of the family."[60]

CHAPTER THIRTY-ONE

"Too Much of a Human Being"

While Twain worked to salvage his sinking businesses, he and Livy had to deal with the intractable sadness of their eldest daughter. Susy had been pulled from Bryn Mawr, then forced to care for an invalid mother. Where Clara had broken free of this stifling situation, Susy had not. She was still hopelessly in love with Louise and her ardor showed no sign of abating. Susy's inner life was stormy, passionate, and melodramatic; Louise seemed more self-contained and enigmatic. Their separation, with its extraordinary pain for Susy, was beginning to resemble a permanent state of affairs. "I love you so very much and I *do* hope we shall meet soon," Susy told Louise on the eve of leaving Florence, "but the prospect doesn't look near to me, somehow."[1] While her father and Clara had grown accustomed to Europe, Susy never quite shed her dream of returning to their old Hartford life. "America looks further & further away recedes & recedes till I am ready to *scream*," she wrote.[2]

Aware of Susy's sadness, if mystified by it, her parents decided to adapt their plans to her desire to pursue a singing career in Paris. Susy traveled there alone with her French governess, a grueling rail journey of twenty-seven and a half hours from Florence; Twain growled that it was a trip "of inconvenience, discomfort & irritation at $40 apiece."[3] Once in Paris, Susy took a dozen lessons with Mathilde Marchesi, a famous vocal coach who ran her own school and was associated with the bel canto repertoire. Marchesi found Susy's voice pleasing and thought she showed promise, but was shocked that Susy was so pale and emaciated. Before giving her further instruction, she insisted that Susy take a break to rebuild her strength. As Twain wrote, the voice coach demanded a strict regimen: taking the mineral springs at Franzensbad in Bohemia, followed by sea bathing, all the while "eating certain specified hearty food & great abundance of it & never using her voice except to talk with—then return in October & *if* she was then no longer a bloodless weakling but a person with a body robust & capable of *supporting* a singing voice, the lessons would be continued, but not otherwise. This teacher being a monarch... is privileged to command, & must be obeyed. Therefore Susy eats—for the first time in her life."[4]

Susy found the Franzensbad spa a pretty desolate place—especially after Twain left for the United States on a prolonged absence—and her old ennui soon returned. Shy, nervous, and insecure, she seemed in the grip of agoraphobia. She had always been fussy about people, with her father's hypercritical nature, but this withdrawal was more crippling. "I can't explain the unspeakable *cowardice* that has taken possession of me lately about every conceivable person and thing," Susy complained to Clara. "I would rather be locked up in a box *alone* for the rest of my life than gather up courage to go out into the world and enjoy myself."[5] The melancholy afflicting Susy was all the more unfortunate in that she had a rare gift of expression and a penetrating power to analyze literature. While in Franzensbad, she read Victor Hugo's *Les Misérables* and gave this trenchant reaction to Louise: "Ah me once you detect his literary tricks and affectations... it really is a most painful revelation and awakening and leaves one truly sad. He *is* tremendous and profoundly stirring and unique but with it so *pompous* and self-conscious. Absorbed as he may be in his subject I think one can be sure he is doubly absorbed in himself and the effect he is producing... He is always reaching off far from the purpose and trend of the story to make some theatrical effect which has no bearing upon it."[6] Reading this incisive commentary makes one feel a bit sorry for Susy, who was forced to depart from Bryn Mawr before she had fully developed her critical skills.

By autumn, Livy, Susy, and Jean were installed at the Hôtel Impérial

"TOO MUCH OF A HUMAN BEING"

in Paris, and a somber mood pervaded the household. To spare her husband additional worry, Livy saved all her complaints about noise, thin walls, and poor food for Grace King. A perceptible grayness entered Livy's Parisian letters. Forced to crimp in never-ending economies, with her husband still dangling on the brink of bankruptcy, Livy found it hard to strike a joyful note, and her physical limitations made it impossible for her to gad about town.

At first, Susy was heartened by lessons with Madame Marchesi's daughter, who assured her that her voice, properly trained, could fill a large hall. Then, after two lessons, Susy's voice began to fade. Tormented by insomnia, she would awake after a sleepless night to find that she had lost her voice. She was obliged to narrow her range to simple vocal exercises and feared that she might have to discontinue her lessons altogether. "I am frightened to death for fear this will last, in fact I am entirely broken-hearted," she confided to Clara. "Cold douches, eating, walking, sleeping, *nothing* helps . . . If my breath doesn't return to me it will be a wasted winter. Isn't it *dreadful?*"[7] Dejected, Susy had to suspend lessons for two months. Livy took her to a new doctor, who diagnosed her as anemic and recommended gymnastics to develop her chest. Very attuned to Susy's moods, Livy grew downcast right along with her daughter. "It has been very pitiful to see her look so miserable," Livy told Twain, "and sometimes it has been hard to keep cheerful with her so downhearted."[8] Louise Brownell was now studying at Oxford, and with Livy's blessing, Susy went to England to visit her, Livy explaining that "we thought the little change might be of benefit to her."[9] Again, it isn't clear whether Livy understood the romantic nature of her daughter's attachment to another young woman or suspected anything beyond an exceedingly intimate friendship.

With Twain passing through a fad for Mind Cure he advised Livy to "find that Christian Scientist for Susy."[10] He would later have reason to regret Susy's attraction to this particular form of therapy. Strongly suspicious of traditional medicine, he had a natural predilection for nostrums and elixirs. Brought low in New York by a persistent cold and cough, he consulted a "mind curist" on Madison Avenue named Dr. Whipple. "He sat with his face to the wall & I walked the floor for 1/2 an hour . . . Don't know if *he* is the reason, but I haven't coughed since," Twain wrote.[11] It never seemed to dawn on him that his constant smoking might be the cause of his recurrent bronchitis. He consulted with William James of Harvard, who proclaimed that "mind cure and hypnotism are exactly identical" and suggested that Livy track down the successor to Jean-Martin Charcot, the leading French neurologist, who had recently died.[12] Charcot had exerted a profound influence on Sigmund Freud, helping to switch his focus to hysteria, hypnosis, and other psychological issues. "The very source, the very *centre,* of hypnotism is *Paris,*" Twain excitedly told his wife. "Dr. Charcot's pupils and disciples are right there and ready to your hand."[13] An enthusiast by nature, Twain, once he had latched on to an idea, could not let it go.

In later years, Mark Twain would publish a famous diatribe against Mary Baker Eddy, the founder of Christian Science and saintly among her followers, but Livy was the one who voiced early misgivings. When Alice Hooker Day sent her a magazine article about Mrs. Eddy, Livy recoiled at the ostentatious wealth displayed. "The advertising so freely of the pictures of her summer home, the big picture to be exhibited in Chicago, the small pictures to be sold at $1.50 a piece give one such an unpleasant feeling of trying to make an honest penny, bring forward so very unfortunately the commercial. I cannot understand how people who have a grand idea, who feel that they have a beautiful new religion to teach can so basely mar it."[14]

Livy placed thirteen-year-old Jean in a school, this being the first time that, as a child of homeschooling, she was subject to academic discipline. If Livy was depressed by Susy's troubles, she was uplifted by Jean's innocence. "She is the dearest, sweetest, helpfullest [sic] child in the world," Livy told her husband.[15] Sporadically homesick, Jean developed a passion that would last a lifetime: the prevention of cruelty to animals. Every time Livy and Jean got into a carriage, they had to order the driver not to whip the horse, so "naturally we take some pretty long, slow drives in consequence," Livy noted wryly.[16] However meritorious her views, Jean issued rigid judgments and informed her mother that when they went out together, they should choose "the worst looking old horses," since handsome ones were well taken care of. "In that way," Jean announced, "we could protect the old bony horses."[17]

Meanwhile, Mark Twain struggled with guilt that his enforced presence in New York meant Livy had to face Susy's difficulties alone. He told Rogers that his daughter's problems made him doubly eager to escape his financial quagmire and rejoin his family. In this helpless state, he pumped Livy full of advice and made windy pronouncements of the good things he would do for Susy when he was set free. "Now the minute I can get my matters here in safe shape & rake in some money for your use," he told Livy, "I mean to rush over & get Susy & fetch her to Hartford & board her with Lilly Warner, & let her have mind cure from the same person who cured Lilly Foote."[18] Many of their letters revolved around the quandary that Susy refused to eat and found food revolting, and one wonders whether she was dealing with anorexia at a time when it was only recently recognized. Her teacher at the Marchesi school worried about her "voluntary self-starvation."[19] Twain was eager to sail for France and pitch in with his family. As he told Pamela, "I have left Livy to fight her way long enough among strangers, in indifferent health & with a sick daughter on her hands. Susy's health—but she hasn't any; it has all wasted away."[20] Though loving and well-meaning, Twain was incorrigibly naive in dealing with Susy's problems and didn't realize how firmly rooted they were. To a complex problem he offered simplistic solutions: If Susy only ate when hungry and went to bed when sleepy, everything would be fine. "In three days she will be better; keep it up & she will soon be well and hearty."[21]

At first, Henry Rogers was enlisted to stave off bankruptcy at Webster & Company, but his involvement with Twain's finances expanded that December as he sought to negotiate a new contract with the typesetter investors. Their plan was to create a new, restructured company that would leave them as principal owners, with Rogers supplying the working capital. Twain enjoyed the masterly way Rogers supervised this business situation, saying it was "better than a circus" to watch the tycoon in action.[22] "He takes his steps swiftly," Twain told Livy, "yet no step is bungled or has to be taken over again."[23] Poised and polished, Rogers was as much an artist in his realm as Twain was in his, and he hammered at investors until he got them to sell out for twenty cents on the dollar. Twain explained to Livy that despite his heartbreak at their being apart, he had to stay in the United States to avert disaster. "I've got to stick right where I am till I find out whether we are rich or whether the poorest person we are acquainted with in anybody's kitchen is better off than we are. I stand on the land-end of a spring-board, with the family clustered on the other end, if I take away my foot."[24]

To sell the new structure to Paige, Twain and Rogers took the Pennsylvania Railroad to Chicago, traveling in the posh private car of the railroad president. It contained sofas that turned into beds at night, cushioned cane armchairs, and a "darling back porch" that enabled the two men to sit outside and watch the scenery flashing by. When they got to Chicago, Paige was desperately short of cash, which Rogers was prepared to supply *if* he came to terms. To apply maximum pressure, Rogers stalled, and Twain took deep satisfaction watching the inventor squirm, gloating that "every day now, adds to his gray hairs, & spoils his sleep. I am full of pity & compassion for him, & it is sincere. If he were drowning I would throw him an anvil."[25] After years of being manipulated by Paige, Twain was bent on revenge. In the end, Paige refused a lucrative deal that would have given him a million dollars, or one-fifth of the stock, if he yielded control to Rogers and Twain. Stymied once again by his nemesis, Twain snorted that he had not gone out "to negotiate with a man, but with a louse."[26]

Then, on January 15, 1894, a telegram arrived saying that Paige had agreed to the proposed terms. In his notebook, a jubilant Twain recorded the epochal moment: "This is a great date in my history . . . Yesterday we were paupers, with but 3 months' rations of cash left & $160,000 in debt, my wife & I, but this telegram makes us wealthy."[27] He calculated that his typesetter royalties were now worth $330,000. Returning to The

"TOO MUCH OF A HUMAN BEING"

Players Club, he was overwhelmed by his joyous release from worry. "I walked the floor for half and [sic] hour in a storm of excitement. You see, the intense strain of three months & a half of daily & nightly work & thought & hope & fear had been suddenly taken away."[28] During this premature celebration, he dashed off a cablegram to Paris with instructions that it be slipped under Livy's breakfast plate on February 2, the date of their anniversary: "Wedding-news. *Our ship is safe in port.* I sail the moment Rogers can spare me."[29] Livy cabled back: "We rejoice with you & congratulate you on your well-earned success."[30]

Flush with victory, Twain dined with Dr. Oliver Wendell Holmes and novelist Sarah Orne Jewett, and happily reported to Livy, "I told [Holmes] you & I used the Autocrat [of the Breakfast-Table] as a courting book & marked it all through, & that you keep it in the sacred green box with the love letters, & it pleased him."[31] When Twain attended a boxing match to watch the reigning world heavyweight champion, James J. Corbett, architect Stanford White took him to the fighter's dressing room. As he admired the perfectly muscled body of the boxer, Twain warned him, "You have whipped Mitchell, and maybe you will whip Jackson in June—but you are not done, then. You will have to tackle me."[32] Amid his myriad business concerns, Twain enjoyed a frenzied social life, as if he could not bear a quiet evening of solitude, and he told Clara how a society friend had conferred on him the nickname the "Belle of New York."[33]

Twain imagined he would soon be free of business cares and could devote himself exclusively to writing. "Farewell—a long farewell—to *business*! I will *never* touch it again! I will live in literature, I will wallow in it, revel in it, I will swim in ink!"[34] In more realistic moments, he recognized that it would take months of rest to be in a position to write again. He delighted in huddling with Rogers and mocking the moves of their thwarted business opponents so that this tragic period was also "a comedy—and certainly the killingest one, the darlingest one and the most fascinating one that ever was."[35]

Now that he and Rogers had taken charge of the typesetter and work on its manufacture resumed, Twain maneuvered to sell shares to *Dracula* author Bram Stoker and promptly reverted to bumptious salesmanship, assuring him the shares would double in price in six months. "It is the strongest company that—well, there couldn't be a stronger company, I guess. It has the best businessman [i.e., Rogers] among the millionaires of America at its back, & he has chosen its President, its board of directors, its executive committee & the Chief Engineer of the factory himself."[36] Not only was Twain trading on Rogers's name, but he confided to Livy that he nourished a secret hope that he would hook the Standard Oil chieftains as investors. "I mean to ask Mr. Rogers to let me sell some stock to the other big Standard Oilers"—John D. Rockefeller and John D. Archbold.[37] It wasn't clear that Rogers would allow such a move, and Twain admitted the tycoon was "very cautious & conservative, & loath to have people put money into a thing on his recommendation."[38] Twain did end up wooing two Standard Oil executives to invest in the Paige machine, with Rogers's approval.

By now, Twain wished to be completely disengaged from Webster & Company. If Rogers had already averted one crisis at the publishing house, he didn't entirely grasp its parlous state until Twain broached the subject one night after billiards. "I did hate to burden his good heart and over-worked head with it," Twain told Livy, "but he took hold with avidity & said it was no burden to work for his friends, but a pleasure."[39] This was stunning generosity from Rogers, whose wife had just had a savage heart attack. However fond he was of Twain, he must have wondered when the endless requests would cease. Once he learned the true state of Webster & Company's finances, Rogers recommended that Twain wind up the house and transfer his own books to the folks at the *Century*. Such a sale, Twain knew, would entail heavy losses: "But that is no matter if it will only get me free of debt to the banks & the manufacturers."[40]

Inwardly, Twain seethed against the deceased Charles Webster and Fred Hall, and regretted having ever started Charles L. Webster and Company. "It was insanely managed from the day it got the Grant book till now," he told Pamela. "*Privately*, I will confide to you that I am trying to wind up that hated concern."[41] With the outlook so bleak, Twain

"TOO MUCH OF A HUMAN BEING"

estimated that Webster & Company had, at most, $60,000 in assets, while it owed banks and printers $83,000. No less important: the firm owed Twain the $110,000 he had poured into it and the $60,000 Livy had lent it. "But I am going to get out at *whatever* loss," Twain promised his sister before taking a parting shot at her former son-in-law. "Webster—however, the blatherskite is dead, let him [rot] in peace."[42] The word "rot," crossed out, was still legible. Twain consigned Fred Hall to the lowest circle of hell along with Webster, claiming to Rogers that Hall "deceived me and got my name on $15,000 of new Mt. Morris notes, allowing [me] to believe I was endorsing the old ones."[43]

Fred Hall would mount a vigorous defense against Twain's allegation that he alone was responsible for the ruinous borrowing. Refusing to be made a scapegoat, he bluntly denied that Twain was ignorant of such borrowing. As he later told Twain's authorized biographer, "You have probably noticed he [i.e., Twain] states he did not know that these obligations existed. As all notes, both for discount and renewal, were endorsed by him; as statements were rendered him, and as the company's financial condition was a constant topic of conversation and correspondence, this mental attitude can only be explained by Mr. Clemens's ignorance of commercial matters and extreme impatience of business details."[44] Indeed, Twain's correspondence with Hall provides abundant proof that he kept warning Hall not to send him so much information. There was nothing sly or underhanded about Hall's borrowing. Twain would cite two $15,000 bank loans made in 1892 as "the cause of our ruin," yet he endorsed both, and two years elapsed before he made an issue of it.[45] In endorsing the second $15,000 loan, he said he thought he was merely renewing the first, but the loans had been made close in time to float the *Library of American Literature*, making it hard to understand how he confused them.

To repay Rogers's extraordinary generosity, Twain agreed to speak on February 22, 1894, at the dedication of a new town hall in Fairhaven, Massachusetts, an imposing French Gothic building that was a gift from Rogers to his hometown. The two men traveled to Massachusetts in fine plutocratic style, in a private railroad car well stocked with champagne.

Twain's speech was hilarious as he noted that the ceremony took place on the birthday of "George Washington, the Father of Those Who Cannot lie. The family has dwindled a good deal. But I am left yet . . . the sole remnant of that old noble stock, it makes me feel sad, sad, and, oh, so lonesome."[46] He contended that from early youth he had been guided by Washington's example. "The first time I ever stole a watermelon in my life—I think it was the first time—it was the thought of Washington that moved me to make restitution."[47]

By March 7, Twain had made enough headway in his business affairs that he was able to sail for France, ending the longest separation that he had endured from Livy. Before departing, he gave Rogers a power of attorney to handle business in his absence. Right before he left, he composed a beautiful letter of gratitude to him. "I am not able to put into words . . . how grateful I am to you. In truth there are no words that could do that. You have saved me & my family from ruin and humiliation. You have been to me the best friend that ever a man had, & yet you have never by any word made me feel the weight of this deep obligation."[48]

While Twain was at sea, Rogers navigated a critical step for the future salvation of the Clemenses. He transferred Twain's copyrights and royalties, his shares in the Paige compositor, and the Hartford house into Livy's name, shielding these assets from seizure by creditors in case of bankruptcy, thus safeguarding the couple's financial future. The ethics and legality of this move have been called into serious question as it gave Livy preferred status over other creditors.[49] Livy herself, the soul of honor, confessed to queasy feelings about the cozy arrangement. "I have so much greater horror of Webster & Co. failing because you have put your property into my hands," she told her husband. "I hate and feel as if I could not bear what the newspapers will say . . . Do be careful, I care too much for the speech of people and you do not care enough."[50] Rogers believed that Livy, as the firm's largest creditor, was entitled to special treatment, and Twain bridled at any insinuation of impropriety. "Nobody finds the slightest fault with my paying you with all my property," he told Livy. "There is nothing shady or improper about it. We make no concealment of it."[51]

"TOO MUCH OF A HUMAN BEING"

Despite the storm clouds about to burst over Webster & Company, Twain spent a delightful three weeks with his family at the Hôtel Brighton in Paris, a small hostelry opposite the Tuileries Garden. Finding Livy better than expected and Susy with improved appetite, he hoped to bring them along when he sailed back to New York on April 7. Yet Livy's doctors balked because she had responded well to a new electric treatment, and they feared she might lose ground on an ocean crossing. She consented to her husband returning to America alone if he stayed only three weeks and returned on May 7. Neither suspected the gigantic crisis awaiting Twain upon his return to New York.

On the afternoon of April 16, 1894, Henry H. Rogers appeared at The Players Club and delivered dreadful news to Twain. After an abrupt change of leaders at the Mount Morris Bank, it was demanding payment on two $5,000 notes coming due. This was the scenario that had long haunted Twain. He now faced a choice between raising a massive amount of money on the spot or entering into voluntary bankruptcy. Twain knew Livy would blanch at the latter option: she retained a patrician belief that bankruptcy meant failure and dishonor and would smear the family with an ineradicable stain. "Mr. Clemens," Rogers told him, "assure her from me that there is not even a tinge of disgrace in making this assignment. By doing it you will relieve yourself of a fearful load of dread, and in time will be able to pay everything and stand clear before the world. If you don't do it you will probably never be free from debt, and it will kill you and Mrs. Clemens both."[52] On April 18, Charles L. Webster and Company went bankrupt, shutting its doors forever, having just published its final book, *Tom Sawyer Abroad*. Besides banks and printers, the firm owed money to the families of Ulysses S. Grant and Phil Sheridan, and to the widow of George Armstrong Custer. At first Twain thought the lawyer Bainbridge Colby, the new receiver, might resume operations on a more "stringent basis" without Hall's "stupid and extravagant management," but that never happened.[53] The $10,000 in notes coming due comprised a small fraction of the $100,000 the firm owed to creditors, not to mention the $60,000 owed to Livy.

Bankruptcy freed Twain from the crushing weight he had borne—he felt liberated, indeed lighthearted—even though he knew Livy would be miserable, and he lost no opportunity to console her. "*Except* when I think of you, dear heart—then I am not blithe; for I seem to see you grieving and ashamed, & dreading to look people in the face . . . This is temporary defeat, but not dishonor—& we will march again."[54] He accurately forecast her response to bankruptcy—"poor Livy—it will nearly kill her"—although he never plumbed the depth of her despair.[55] With her sense of shame and scandal, her mood bordered on the suicidal. "I have a perfect *horror* and heart-sickness over it," she told Sue Crane. "I cannot get away from the feeling that business failure means disgrace . . . I have grown old very fast during this last year. I have wrinkled. Much of the time I want to lie down and cry . . . I do not make things go very well, and I feel that my life is an absolute and irretrievable failure. Perhaps I am thankless, but I so often feel that I should like to give it up and die."[56] She simply couldn't bear the stigma of bankruptcy. "Oh it is hard that Webster & Co. could not have been closed up with no stain on its good name," she told her husband. "I hate it so."[57] This crisis brought out true nobility in Livy, who wished to hand over the Hartford house, including land and furniture, to the creditors, a move squarely vetoed by her husband and Rogers.

On April 18, the New York newspapers, with blaring headlines, trumpeted the news of Twain's bankruptcy, and the *Brooklyn Eagle* detected the irony at work: Twain, having lectured readers on the perils of greed, had now succumbed himself. "It is another case of a shrewd and bright observer of things missing a moral which he could readily have taught to other people."[58] Twain tried bravely to put the best construction on things and told Livy he was devoid of any shame, experiencing only "an immense sense of relief." Instead, he took out his frustration on Fred Hall, who, he claimed, could "hardly keep from crying" when he signed the assignment. "In all my days I have never seen so dull a fool."[59] As with Charles Webster, Hall had been handpicked to run the firm by Twain, who never questioned his judgment in hiring and superintending him. Henry Rogers took charge of dealing with creditors. It was decided

"TOO MUCH OF A HUMAN BEING"

that Twain would pay fifty cents on the dollar and he and Livy felt honor-bound to pay off the other fifty cents. Schooled by his wife, Twain went around saying that "honor is a harder master than the law. It cannot compromise for less than a hundred cents on the dollar."[60] Feeling high-minded, he likened himself to the bankrupt Sir Walter Scott, who had taken six years to satisfy creditors.[61]

In May, Twain sailed to Paris, having wearily crisscrossed the ocean for three years to ward off the very disaster that had just overtaken him. He diverted himself by writing a scathing article about the factual absurdities in James Fenimore Cooper's novel *The Deerslayer*, which he hooted at as "the most idiotic book I ever saw."[62] In a defiant mood, he told Rogers that he was ready to take down many of the most popular American and English novelists of the past two generations. Instead of being angry with himself, he turned his anger against another writer. An economical writer himself, he found Cooper's prose stiff, bloated, and turgid. After quoting a long passage from *The Deerslayer*, he edited it down for the reader, stripping it of excess verbiage. His verdict: "Number of words, 320; necessary ones, 220; wasted by the generous spendthrift, 100."[63] Twain never cared to muzzle his views of other authors, which could be unsparing. "Cooper hadn't any more invention than a horse, and I don't mean a high-class horse, either; I mean a clothes-horse."[64] He signed the essay "Mark Twain, M.A. Professor of Belles Lettres in the Veterinary College of Arizona."[65]

Twain joined Livy at the Hôtel Brighton in Paris. Between their exorbitant living standards and his compulsive speculations, he had destroyed most of her inheritance. "Thank you for being glad that I have a separate fortune," Livy undeceived Alice Hooker Day, "but unfortunately a good deal of my money has gone too. I will not write more about it except to say the two most important things, that there was nothing dishonorable about the failure, and that the debts will all be paid."[66] Livy, a good wife, never blamed her husband for the terrible wreckage he had caused.

Although Webster & Company's problems were past repair, Twain remained convinced that he would be bailed out by the Paige typesetter, that graveyard of so many hopeless dreams. "The new machine will be finished in June," he announced to his brother. "We already know it will work like an angel. Mr. Rogers's doubts are all gone—he believes the machine's great future is secure."[67] If Rogers was a financial wizard, he was no more prophetic about the machine than the famous author. A born salesman, with a glandular optimism, Twain referred to the typesetter stock as "the best stock in the United States, & should not be lightly fooled away."[68] He persuaded himself that compositors at New York newspapers were privately snapping up this stock and even borrowing money to double down on their bets.

Before returning to America, Twain, on doctors' orders, took Livy and his daughters to the small town of La Bourboule, in central France, a place with lovely scenery and bracing air. Staying in cramped rooms in a fashionable hotel, the Clemens family frequented the spa for its bath and waters. The wan, discontented Susy, not Livy, was now the main cause of concern. While Twain found the air invigorating, it did nothing to rouse Susy, who had a "sore throat and fever and a stiff neck and a little cough" and "looked so very miserable," said Livy.[69]

With extreme misgivings, Sam and Livy allowed Clara to take a cold-water cure in the Canton of Uri in Switzerland, where she followed a healthy routine of swimming, hiking, and climbing. She savored the time apart from her parents. Unable to let go of her twenty-year-old daughter, Livy regretted having given permission for this side trip. "*I do not at all like it,*" she told Alice Hooker Day. "I am never satisfied except when we are all together. I have told Clara that this is the last time I shall ever consent to it."[70] Sam and Livy were shocked to discover that Clara wasn't living with a peasant family, as imagined, but had checked into a private hotel. As had happened with Clara in Berlin, her parents dreaded the long shadow of scandal. "Mamma prefers that if you are not perfectly private on that balcony & not under fire of curious eyes, you had better take all your meals in your room," Twain ordered Clara. "I think you had better take this suggestion as a requirement—so keep on the safe side & out of range of foreign criticism & remark."[71] Once again, Twain feared gossip might hurt Clara and reflect on her parents. When Livy learned of Clara hiking alone, she hastily put her foot down. "*Now my pet I want you to hire a woman or a girl and have her come to you in the morning and see whether you are going to want her that day . . . When you write tell me that you have secured some one to go with you; and take your walks regularly.*"[72]

When Twain returned to America in July to attend to the typesetter, he made revisions to his Joan of Arc book aboard the ship. Once in New York, he spent time at Rogers's office at 26 Broadway, where he would stretch out on the sofa behind the mogul's desk and watch him coolly transact business. From the Standard Oil offices, Twain sent a bittersweet note to Livy for Jean's fourteenth birthday. "Give the child my deep strong love—I am bankrupt & haven't any other present. But we are rich, although we haven't any money, & by & by we will make up to the children all the lacking presents."[73] Eager to start selling his shares in the typesetter, Twain was convinced by Rogers to wait until the machine was tested at the Chicago *Herald*, after which people would line up in droves. Rogers, who had been mostly clear-eyed about Webster & Company, was now sucked into the typesetter maelstrom along with Twain.

After Twain boasted to Livy about clever retorts Rogers gave to Webster & Company creditors, she wrote him a letter of rebuke. She was more concerned with reputation than with saving money, and perhaps feared her husband had been seduced by the wiles of Hell Hound Rogers. "You say Mr. Rogers has said some caustic and telling things to the creditors . . . I should think it was the creditors place to say caustic things to us. My darling I cannot have any thing done in my name that I should not approve. I feel that we owe those creditors not only the money but our most sincere apologies that we are not able to pay their bills when they fall due. When these bills are all paid, as they of course will be, I do not want the creditors to feel that we have in any way acted sharply or unjustly or ungenerously with them. I want them to realize & know, that we had their interest at heart, more, much more than we had our own."[74] One senses Livy's acute distress at being given preferential treatment versus the other creditors. She was implicated in everything happening at these meetings where Twain was always instructed, for legal reasons, to say "Mrs. Clemens's book," "Mrs. Clemens's copyrights," and "Mrs. Clemens's type-setter stock" to keep these assets safely beyond the creditors' reach.[75]

Aware of how much Livy needed him, Twain was tormented by indecision as to how long he should linger in New York and confessed his dilemma to her. "All day I am tortured by a conscience which howls & tugs & pulls & upbraids & reproaches—an infernal conscience which is twins—the one twin pulling one of my arms & saying 'Come-sail!'—the other one tugging at the other arm & saying 'Stay where you are & settle your business matters!'"[76] Twain admitted to Orion that, despite all attempts at economy, his family expenses still came to $1,700 a month (or $62,000 in today's money)—a considerable sum for a man buffeted by bankruptcy.[77] He longed to bring his family back to America, but the cost of resuming their former life remained prohibitive. As Susy remarked simply, "We cannot now afford to live in Hartford."[78]

For August, the Clemenses had rented a chalet in Étretat in Normandy, set back from the coast with its chalk cliffs and with a sea view from their windows. The house in the fishing village came equipped with a cook and a maid. "Yes we feel the grind of straitened circumstances," Livy told Grace King, feeling virtuously parsimonious, "but without doubt it is good for us all and wholesome for the young people."[79] When Twain sailed for France in mid-August, a reporter for the *New York Sun* spotted him on deck, "a languid man with fluffy gray hair," and Twain treated him to a comic monologue that reflected his brooding about money. "I am going over to see my wife and family at Étretat, where they are supporting a couple of doctors. You see, over there when a doctor gets hold of a patient he keeps him. They generally take you to a small place and keep you there. Then they pass you along to a friend in another place, and they keep you moving like the Wandering Jew. My wife has been doing this for three years. I don't dare to have even a headache after I land on the other side."[80]

The Étretat stay was a peaceful interval for Twain, who mocked the

"TOO MUCH OF A HUMAN BEING"

house as so small that "the family can't find room to sleep without hanging their legs out of the windows."[81] Still, it was tranquil and secluded, an ideal spot to write, and for once the family seemed in a buoyant mood, with Livy feeling better after her electro-therapy in Paris and Susy stimulated by the coastal air. "I have become *hopeful* and *industrious* and am interested in life," Susy told Clara, attributing her contentment to the fact that she was now writing fiction seriously and planned to pursue literature or singing in the future. "I take a cold sponge bath and do gymnastics every morning and am leading an altogether virtuous and exemplary life inspired by your example."[82] She rebelled at the notion of ending up "a silly society girl" and wanted to do something productive with her life.[83]

Susy's sudden plans for an independent life were probably her way of coping with the loss of Louise Brownell, who shocked her in late July with news that she was returning to the United States—without seeing Susy again. On July 29, 1894, Susy sent a long, overwrought reply, throbbing with pain. "I was all unforewarned & it made my heart stand still. I would not, *could* not dream this would happen and that I should lose you now *now* at the moment of having you again, after all these years of waiting. IT IS IMPOSSIBLE. I CANNOT BELIEVE IT. IT CANNOT BE TRUE."[84] She abjectly pleaded with Louise to visit her in France one last time and noted that her family's financial predicament made a return to Hartford unlikely. "This being apart *breaks* my heart . . . It is a *nightmare* . . . Promise me that you will not go away and put the water between us without letting me see you." She signed the note "Yours for ever & ever."[85]

Louise never came to say goodbye. One senses that her love for Susy had cooled or perhaps she had met someone else or was frightened by the sheer intensity of Susy's feelings. Maybe she had simply opted to live a more traditional life. The difference in their situations was instructive. Susy had led a stultifying life in Europe, forced into a prolonged adolescence with her parents, while Louise had been allowed to flourish intellectually. She would do graduate work at Bryn Mawr and by 1897 would be named warden of Sage College, the women's division of Cornell University, where she taught English literature. While there she met a chemist and hybridist named Arthur Percy Saunders and, at age thirty, married him in 1900. The couple would have four children, the second of whom was named Olivia—in honor of Susy.

Like wife and daughter, Twain felt revived by Étretat, where he would "stand out on a porch & pour buckets of sea water over himself."[86] "This place is a kind of paradise," Twain told Rogers, "it is beautiful, and still, and infinitely restful."[87] He could devote undivided attention to his Joan of Arc book, and Livy and Susy, as in-house editors, blessed it with their most enthusiastic approval. In a month he wrote thirty-five thousand words and crowed that "only 300 have been condemned by Mrs. Clemens and short of 3,000 destroyed by myself."[88] After he and Livy decided to spend the winter in Paris, they stopped off en route in Rouen, where Twain roamed the town that had witnessed Joan's burning at the stake as a heretic.

While Twain busily scribbled away in Étretat, the Chicago *Herald* launched its sixty-day trial of the Paige typesetter. As soon as he received a page from the newspaper set on the machine, he was ecstatic. "It affects me like Columbus sighting land," he told Rogers, bragging that "Some day the Mergenthaler people will come and want to hitch teams with us."[89] So convinced was he of the machine's superiority that he thought there would be no real competitors. Before long, however, the Paige machine began to show serious defects. Type began to break, and Paige had to be summoned to fix the problem. The machine was too complicated, too delicate, too unreliable, for everyday use at a newspaper.

When Twain in Paris received a report delineating breakdowns in the first sixteen days of the test run, he simply refused to accept the devastating evidence. "When the machine is in proper working order," he lectured Rogers, "*it cannot make a mistake.*"[90] The italics testify to the magnitude of his unconquerable delusion. Rogers had sent his son-in-law to Chicago to get a firsthand report on the typesetter and, based on this, began to think the machine a practical failure. "Certainly it was a marvelous invention," Rogers later reflected. "It was the nearest approach to a human being in the wonderful things it could do of any machine I have ever known. But that was just the trouble; it was too much of a human

"TOO MUCH OF A HUMAN BEING"

being and not enough of a machine. It had all the complications of the human mechanism, all the liability of getting out of repair, and it could not be replaced with the ease and immediateness of the human being."[91] Twain never understood the trade-off between technical perfection and business reliability, and that, in the end, dependability trumped mechanical sophistication.

As the abysmal reports filtered in from Chicago, Twain warned himself that "your fine ten-year-old dream will blow away like a mist and you will land in the poor-house for sure."[92] In desperation, he devised an unscrupulous scheme by which Rogers would delay his public withdrawal from the failed Paige company while they secretly scooped up depressed shares of their Mergenthaler rival. When Twain's withdrawal would then be announced, Paige would be forced to sell his patents to Mergenthaler at distress-sale prices and "that will boom the Merg. Stock, for their machine will then be cock of the walk, and *permanently*, without possibility of rivalry."[93] Such scandalous trading on inside information was not then illegal, but it certainly was unsavory, and an incredible comedown for Twain after years of disparaging the Mergenthaler machine.

Right before Christmas, Twain received from Rogers definitive news that the typesetter had flunked its Chicago test. Even the legerdemain of Henry Rogers had not saved things. "It hit me like a thunderclap," Twain replied to Rogers. "It knocked every rag of sense out of my head, and I went flying here and there and yonder, not knowing what I was doing."[94] He was in a distraught state, although Livy managed to calm him down by bedtime. Then he woke up the next morning, his mind brimming with fresh schemes on how to salvage the typesetter, including substituting brass type, discarding half the keyboard, and so on and so forth. "Don't say I'm wild," he told Rogers. "For really I'm sane again this morning."[95] Nothing could shatter the idée fixe he had cultivated over more than a decade. Determined to deal with this crisis in person, he rushed off to a steamship office and booked a ticket on the boat train to Le Havre, then returned to his apartment and scribbled six pages of notes on how to rescue the typesetter. All his life he had felt lucky, having been pulled from the water nine times as a boy in Hannibal. "And so I have felt entirely certain that that machine would turn up trumps eventually. It disappointed me lots of times, but I couldn't shake off the confidence of a life-time in my luck."[96]

Gradually Mark Twain acknowledged his abrupt reversal of fortune and the truth of what had happened. The end of the typesetter saga tore to shreds the last hope that the Clemens family would return to the Hartford house and resume their former lives. "We can never live in it again," Twain confided to Rogers, "though it would break the family's hearts if they could believe it."[97] The royalties for the Paige typesetter that Twain had prized now became worthless as the Mergenthaler Linotype Company emerged as the dominant operator in the market. The two surviving Paige machines would end up as dusty museum pieces, curiosities for Twain afficionados. Years earlier, Twain had anointed James W. Paige as "a poet, a most great and genuine poet, whose sublime creations are written in steel. He is the Shakespeare of mechanical invention."[98] In the aftermath of the typesetter's demise, he labeled Paige "a natural liar and thief" and said the machine stood as "a monument of human ingenuity and stupidity—the ingenuity was Paige's, the stupidity was mine."[99] Twain evinced an inexhaustible bitterness. When an author asked for a blurb for books he had written on inventors and patents, Twain shot back: "Dear Sir,—I have, as you say, been interested in patents and patentees. If your books tell how to exterminate inventors send me nine editions. Send them by Express. Very truly yours, S.L. Clemens."[100]

CHAPTER THIRTY-TWO

"Paris the Damnable"

Even in the throes of turmoil with his business ventures, Mark Twain somehow managed to produce a brilliantly derisory and, for him, quite novel piece of literary criticism titled "In Defense of Harriet Shelley," published in three installments in the *North American Review* in 1894. In a blistering, sixteen-thousand-word essay, Twain took issue with the way that Harriet Shelley, the young wife deserted by Percy Bysshe Shelley, had been treated in a biography of the poet by Edward Dowden. In standing up for wronged womanhood, Twain again showed the chivalric, Victorian side of his personality. As would happen with Joan of Arc, he was seized with protective sympathy for a pure teenage girl who he felt had been badly abused. In classic Twain fashion, his imagination was fired by indignation over a perceived injustice.

It was likely Susy, who found Harriet "a gracious and pathetic figure," who touched off her father's interest in this subject.[1] We know she read a biography of Shelley in early 1893. Indeed, Twain starts out his "Defense" by expressing shock that the Dowden biography "is accepted in the girls' colleges of America and its view taught in their literary classes."[2] He found its prose prissily affected and branded the author a dolt. "This is perhaps the strangest book that has seen the light since Frankenstein... It is strangely nearsighted, cross-eyed, and purblind. Sometimes when a mastodon walks across the field of its vision it takes it for a rat; at other times it does not see it at all."[3]

Twain was less infuriated by the book's style than by its thesis, which

RAPIDS

blamed the innocent Harriet Westbrook, not the poet, for his desertion of her. Shelley, age nineteen, and Harriet, sixteen, married and had a child a year later. Twain dubs her the "girl wife," hovering on the verge of adulthood, a type that always mesmerized him. When Shelley turns his attention to a Mrs. Boinville and her married daughter Cornelia, Twain gloriously mocks the notion that Shelley was sentimentally studying Italian poetry with Cornelia. As Shelley abandons his young bride, Twain charges that Dowden's readers never hear Harriet's view of the betrayal. "She must have opinions about such things," Twain protests, "she cannot be indifferent . . . but we get only the other side, they keep her silent always."[4] Gently glossing over Shelley's infidelity, Dowden turns Harriet into a scapegoat for her husband's treachery.

Twain probes the shame and resentment Harriet must have known. After a brief attempt at reconciliation with Harriet, Shelley fell in love with sixteen-year-old Mary Wollstonecraft Godwin and made love to her half-sister Claire, eliciting Twain's tart comment: "To the end of his days he liked to be in love with two women at once."[5] He spews bile at Mary's father, the philosopher William Godwin. "Godwin was not without self-appreciation; indeed it may be conjectured that from his point of view the last syllable of his name was surplusage."[6] After Shelley ran off with both Mary Godwin and Claire, a pregnant Harriet drowned herself. Unlike Dowden, who exonerates Shelley, Twain rides to Harriet's defense, holding the poet responsible for her death. By the end of the essay, Twain is in high dudgeon, as if protecting his own slandered daughter. "How any man in his right mind could bring himself to defile the grave of a shamefully abused and defenseless girl with these baseless fabrications, this manufactured filth, is inconceivable."[7] Nothing kindled Twain's wrath so much as violated female innocence.

The most inspirational friendship Mark Twain formed with a young woman came with Helen Keller, who contracted an illness at nineteen months that left her deaf and blind. At age six, she was rescued from her isolation by a teacher, Anne Sullivan, who introduced language into her life. Twain first encountered Helen on a Sunday afternoon in March 1895 at the home of the critic Laurence Hutton, who invited Twain, Rog-

"PARIS THE DAMNABLE"

ers, and other well-heeled guests to meet her. One visitor remembered how Twain, after his first glimpse of fourteen-year-old Helen, would "impetuously dash the tears from his eyes as he looked into her sweet face."[8] As guests were introduced, Anne Sullivan spelled out their names by tapping Helen's hand with telegraphic speed. As Twain related funny tales to the gathering, Helen erupted in "cackles, chuckles, and care-free bursts of laughter," he said. Sullivan asked Helen what Mr. Clemens was distinguished for. "For his humor," she said. Twain softly added, "And for his wisdom." Before Sullivan could translate, Helen chimed in, "And for his wisdom."[9] When Twain had to leave, he passed by Helen and patted her head lightly. "Oh, it's Mr. Clemens," she exclaimed immediately. "Perhaps someone can explain this miracle," Twain was to remark, "but I have never been able to do it."[10] Twain cherished this "wonderful creature who sees without eyes, hears without ears, and speaks with dumb lips."[11] He developed a profound affection for Helen, devoid of any tincture of pity or condescension. "Seen once, the moving and eloquent play of emotion in her face is forever unforgettable."[12]

Helen left perceptive impressions of Twain. She approved his pen name for having "a funny & quaint sound that goes well with his amusing writings, & its nautical significance suggests the deep & beautiful things he has written."[13] She expertly intuited his personality from reading his hands and wrote of Twain's being "full of whimsies and the drollest humor."[14] Endowed with a sixth sense, she was no less insightful in interpreting his voice when she pressed her fingers to his lips. "His voice was truly wonderful," she said. "To my touch, it was deep, resonant. He had the power of modulating it so as to suggest the most delicate shades of meaning."[15] For Helen, Twain possessed a quick understanding of her situation, as if he could project himself into her mind. "He knew with keen and sure intuition many things about me; how it felt to be blind and not to be able to keep up with the swift ones—things that others learned slowly or not at all. He never embarrassed me by saying how terrible it is not to see, or how dull life must be, lived always in the dark. He wove about my dark walls romance and adventure which made me feel happy and important."[16] So deeply did Twain affect Helen that, aside from

RAPIDS

Anne Sullivan and Alexander Graham Bell, she contended that nobody else had aroused in her such a "feeling of mingled tenderness and awe."[17] She also believed that nobody else had such a fine-grained appreciation of Anne Sullivan's "brilliancy, penetration, wisdom, character and the fine literary competences of her pen."[18]

In 1896 John Spaulding, a Boston sugar magnate, died, depriving Helen of a benefactor and creating an urgent need for a successor. Partly through Twain's good offices, Henry Rogers volunteered to be her financial angel and foot the bill for her education at Radcliffe College, where she graduated with honors in 1904 and went on to a career as a writer and a lecturer. Twain never ceased to honor her attainments. "To-day Helen Keller is one of the best educated women in the world," he later said. "She is a college graduate, and is a competent scholar in Greek, Latin, German, French, and mathematics; she is familiar with the literature of those languages, and not many persons can write so ably, so gracefully, and so eloquently as she."[19] Like Twain, Helen would betray a radical political bent and work on behalf of women's suffrage and workers' rights. In later years, Twain assisted Helen at fundraisers for the blind. At one such gathering, he read aloud a letter from Helen of such surpassing eloquence that he said that "no fellow to it had ever issued from any girl's lips since Joan of Arc, that immortal child of seventeen, stood alone and friendless in her chains."[20]

A no less notable friendship sprang up between Twain and Nikola Tesla, the Serbian American inventor, who possessed a special affinity for Twain ever since he made a "miraculous recovery" from a youthful illness while reading his books.[21] Tesla's supreme breakthrough came when he sold patents to George Westinghouse for alternating current devices, which would form the basis of public power distribution in America. As mentioned earlier, in the late 1880s, James W. Paige had developed sketches for an alternating current motor, and Twain turned for advice to Tesla, who faulted its design as dated.[22] We don't know whether Twain

"PARIS THE DAMNABLE"

and Tesla met then, but by 1894 the two enjoyed regular contact. Using phosphorescent light, Tesla had developed a new photographic method and wanted to craft photos of Twain and other celebrities for the *Century Magazine,* displaying his technology to advantage. With his flair for publicity, Twain wasn't averse to lending his celebrity to the project, as one showman exploited another. Twain must have known the mass appeal of such photos, burnishing his own image as a technological wizard. The resulting pictures glittered with a spark of surreal magic: in one, Twain stares down at a glowing sphere cupped in his hands, while a ghostly Tesla peers from the left-hand corner.

Twain experienced another Tesla invention of more dubious benefit. The inventor had experimented with a small mechanical oscillator attached to the bottom of a platform. When he stepped on the platform during its operation, he noticed that his body shook with pleasing vibrations and was convinced that this would have therapeutic effects on bodily organs. One day, when visiting Tesla's laboratory, Twain was invited to sample the vibrating platform, assured it would aid his stamina and vitality. He was also warned that if he stayed on too long, the machine could produce a laxative effect. After Twain had stood on the platform awhile, Tesla discreetly nudged him to dismount. "Not by a jugfull," Twain retorted. "I am enjoying myself." Deaf to repeated warnings, he then stiffened with sudden alarm. "Quick, Tesla! Where is it?" Instantly, Tesla pointed Twain to a corner bathroom.[23] Afterward, he returned for shorter, safer stints, and Tesla claimed that they had had remarkable medicinal benefits for Twain. "He came to the laboratory in the worst shape suffering from a variety of distressing and dangerous ailments but in less than two months he regained his old vigor and ability of enjoying life to the fullest extent."

By the summer of 1892, Twain had labored excitedly over a "howling farce" that he christened *Those Extraordinary Twins.*[24] Always fascinated by Siamese twins, emblematic of the contradictions of human nature,

Twain had encountered a photo of Italian twins connected at the chest, with two heads and four arms and one pair of legs. In his story, he named the twins Luigi and Angelo Capello, and he dropped them into the town of Dawson's Landing on the Mississippi River. He imagined Luigi as wicked, Angelo as righteous. "They were a troublesome pair in every way," Twain wrote. "If they did any work for you, they charged for two; but at the boarding house they ate and slept for two and only paid for one. In the trains they wouldn't pay for two, because they only occupied one seat. The same at the theatre."[25]

That fall, at Villa Viviani, seeking a financial savior for Webster & Company, Twain felt under extreme pressure to produce a commercially viable novel. Spurred by money anxiety, his productivity was so astonishing—six thousand words one day, five thousand the next—that he registered these feats in his notebook.[26] It took him time to spot a flagrant flaw in his story: he would have to punish the righteous twin for the sins of the wicked one. Never shrinking from a radical rewrite, Twain converted the tale from a farce into a tragedy. He would pull the Capello twins apart and demote them in the story, while promoting a minor character, David Wilson, a young lawyer whose nickname became the novel's title—*Pudd'nhead Wilson*. Wilson's hobby would be the brand-new technique of identifying individuals by fingerprints, and this would supply a key plot twist.

The gist of the tale involved an enslaved mulatto mother named Roxana (or Roxy) who decides to swap her baby, Chambers, with an almost identical rich white baby, Tom Driscoll, born the same day to the slave master Percy Driscoll, thus giving her son a better chance in life. The plot hinges on a changeling swap reminiscent of *The Prince and the Pauper*: the high-born child will be brought up as a slave and the enslaved child reared as an aristocrat. In dramatizing this, Twain strikes a blow at the notion of white racial superiority and Black inferiority, revealing the arbitrary power of social status over genetic inheritance. At the core of the novel is a powerful antislavery theme: Roxy's horror at the misery her son would endure in slavery and her desire to redeem him from such a fate.

"PARIS THE DAMNABLE"

Why did the rollicking farce of Siamese twins metamorphose into a dark tragedy of race relations in the antebellum South? It is hard to imagine that newspaper headlines didn't exert a significant pull. In June 1892, a New Orleans man named Homer Plessy, who was one-eighth Black and looked white, bought a first-class ticket, boarded the East Louisiana Railroad, and sat in the "Whites Only" car. A detective forcibly removed and jailed him. When the case rose to the Supreme Court, it produced the infamous *Plessy v. Ferguson* ruling of 1896, which endorsed segregation as providing "separate but equal" accommodations for Blacks and whites. In *Pudd'nhead Wilson,* the enslaved Roxana looks white while her one-sixteenth Black blood condemns her to slavery. The theme was especially topical since slavery had produced many mulatto children, some of whom passed for white yet were classified as Black and discriminated against under America's racially biased laws.

In the 1890s, so-called Redeemer governments in the South, composed of white Democrats, stripped away Reconstruction's gains and imposed draconian segregation through Jim Crow laws; this enforced racial separation soon spread to every form of public life. The trend was accompanied by an epidemic of lynchings—1892 witnessed three times as many lynchings as any year in the previous decade—with more than one hundred Black men lynched annually in the South, typically on bogus charges of raping or defiling white women. All the while, Blacks entered professions in record numbers, with twenty-one thousand teachers, fifteen thousand preachers, nearly two thousand doctors, three hundred journalists, and seven hundred lawyers practicing by 1900, showing that Blacks were fully capable of holding any job in society.[27]

In *Pudd'nhead Wilson,* his last major novel, Twain returns to the antebellum South of his boyhood, which allows him greater leeway to delve into racially taboo subjects. He evokes a quaint small town on the Mississippi, Dawson's Landing, lodged in the heartland and seemingly populated by kind, decent people, only to show how, blighted by slavery, pervasive cruelty lurked beneath the surface. In introducing the fair-complexioned Roxy, Twain notes the absurdity that she is one-sixteenth Black and enslaved on that basis, and by the same logic, her child,

RAPIDS

Chambers, who has "blue eyes and flaxen curls" and is one-thirty-second Black, is doomed to slavery.

In one of the book's most powerful scenes, Roxy is crazed by the thought that her enslaved child could be sold down the river. She even contemplates drowning herself and her child to spare him this fate. Instead, she dresses Chambers in Tom's rich gown and Tom in her enslaved baby's tow-linen shirt, and recognizes that a switch will succeed. In time, "Tom" becomes master to "Chambers" and bullies and abuses him, with Twain showing the cruelty that accompanies the master's role. As a teenager, "Chambers" is subjected to every conceivable indignity by his young master. During the winter, he had "to drag a sled up the hill for Tom, warmly clad to ride down on; but he never got a ride himself . . . He was Tom's patient target when Tom wanted to do some snowballing, but the target couldn't fire back."[28]

Twain shows how completely the master role defines "Tom's" behavior toward his mother, Roxy, as well, who has not yet revealed to him his true identity. "She saw her darling cease from being her son . . . all that was left was master—master, pure and simple, and it was not a gentle mastership, either. She saw herself sink from the sublime height of motherhood to the somber depths of unmodified slavery . . . She was merely his chattel, now, his convenience, his dog."[29] Roxy, with more than a touch of Mary Ann Cord in her depiction, is one of the few full-bodied, mature women in Twain's fiction, and her drop of Black blood makes her more dynamic than the straitlaced white women in his writings.

Reflecting the growing abstract turn in his thoughts, Twain introduces each chapter with an aphorism from *Pudd'nhead Wilson's Calendar*, a device that allows him to editorialize on many topics. "TRAINING is everything," he writes, making explicit his nurture-over-nature argument. "The peach was once a bitter almond; cauliflower is nothing but cabbage with a college education."[30] Elaborating on this, he produces epigrams about the force of habit that imprisons us. "HABIT is habit, and not to be flung out of the window by any man, but coaxed downstairs a step at a time."[31] The *Calendar* enables Twain to sneak in subversive, irreverent themes, as when he writes, "*October 12, the Discovery.* It

"PARIS THE DAMNABLE"

was wonderful to find America, but it would have been more wonderful to miss it."[32] In all, Twain created thirty-five sayings that helped to popularize the book, adding a new dimension to his public persona. Through these aphorisms, he took the tradition of uplifting maxims minted by Benjamin Franklin and gave them a hilariously cynical twist. As a result, he became the most quotable of writers, providing sayings for nearly every occasion. When the *Century Magazine* serialized the book, it also published *Puddn'head Wilson's Calendar,* with aphorisms plucked from the book. With the demise of Webster & Company, the novel was published on November 28, 1894, by the American Publishing Company—Twain's ironic return to his roots as a book writer.

Pudd'nhead Wilson turns into a detective story that climaxes in a dramatic courthouse scene. The swap of the two babies is belatedly discovered in a murder trial in which the young, freckled easterner, David Wilson, uses the novel fingerprinting technique—"virgin ground," Twain boasted, "absolutely *fresh,* and mighty curious and interesting to everybody"—to identify the culprit.[33] "Tom" is exposed as the enslaved Chambers and a murderer and is seized by his creditors and sold down the river. The real Tom, meanwhile, has been seared by slavery.

Like *Huck Finn, Pudd'nhead Wilson* has been seen as an enlightened work on race relations, but has had its quota of detractors. For one thing, it employs the N-word seventy-five times—not nearly as much as *Huck Finn,* but more than enough to create discomfort. Some scholars have objected that the Black child who is brought up as the white master becomes brutal and domineering, while the white child brought up as enslaved is meek and compassionate. As one scholar argues, "Twain seems to be stressing that the one drop of Black blood in [Tom's] veins was responsible for his failure as a human being."[34] More than likely, Twain was illustrating his deterministic view that we are all creatures of roles assigned to us by society. Another scholar has pointed out that the "book doesn't make the argument that a black child raised as a white will be as good as a white; it argues that a black raised as a white will be as bad as a white."[35] Roxana has been criticized as neither convincingly Black nor white—"the victim of Mark Twain's own color confusion," says one scholar—though for most readers she is the tale's most compelling character.[36] The one certainty is that the novel shows how slavery has warped and deformed everyone in this supposedly innocent town.

That Twain never believed that "one drop" of Black blood tainted a person was evident in his reaction to the Johnson Whittaker case a decade earlier. Born into slavery in South Carolina, Whittaker was the only Black cadet at West Point when he was savagely beaten in the early morning hours by three white students. Instead of his assailants being charged, Whittaker, a mulatto, was expelled from the academy. Press accounts accused him of faking the attack and teemed with vile statements that one could expect nothing less from a Black man. William Dean Howells recalled Twain's outrage at the notion that if Whittaker were one-sixteenth Black, it must have been the drop of Black blood that undid him. "The man was fifteen parts white, but 'Oh yes,'" Clemens said with bitter irony, "it was the one part black that undid him. It made him a 'nigger' and incapable of being a gentleman. It was to blame for the whole thing."[37] The man who said that could never have imagined that Chambers's misbehavior as "Tom" resulted from his one drop of Black blood. The entire point of *Pudd'nhead Wilson* is that our social status, not our biological identity, makes us who we are, and that masters grow brutal with the unchecked power they wield over oppressed human beings. In later life, Johnson Whittaker served as a high school principal in Oklahoma City, where one of his pupils was Ralph Ellison. Speaking of slavery's legacy, Ellison praised Twain for having comprehended "the moral situation of the United States and the contrast between our ideals and our activities."[38]

At the time of publication, reviewers found many of *Pudd'nhead Wilson*'s characters bland and unconvincing (except for Roxy), and the plot loaded with melodramatic contrivances. The white South construed the novel as a vigorous critique of slavery. Writing in the *Southern Magazine*, the daughter of a Tennessee plantation owner slammed the book as "tremendously stupid" and a "malicious and misleading" slander of southern slaveholders.[39] This opinion was echoed in the Richmond *Dispatch*, which argued that "the author has tried to be fair to the slave-

"PARIS THE DAMNABLE"

holders of the South, we believe, but has not done them justice."[40] The book has had its share of modern admirers, who have applauded its potent indictment of slavery. Toni Morrison cited the novel as an instance of how "Mark Twain talked about racial ideology in the most powerful, eloquent, and instructive way I have ever read... What is exciting about American literature is that business of how writers say things under, beneath and around their stories. Think of *Pudd'nhead Wilson* and all these inversions of what race is, how sometimes nobody can tell, or the thrill of discovery?"[41]

As Twain began his winter stay in Paris in November 1894, he faced a reversal of the typical state of affairs that ruled his family: Livy was looking well, and Susy was "well again, & fatting up," while he was leveled by gout in both ankles and estimated that medical problems cost him two months of work. Depleted by agonizing joint illness, he slept from midnight till three every afternoon. "Then followed 5 or 6 hours wherein the gout was the only presence present, Mrs. Twain and I counting for nothing at all."[42] He experimented with one treatment after another, including electrotherapy, with no lasting success. As usual, Twain was able to exorcise his rage against doctors by subjecting them to his astringent wit. "The first physician forbade red wine but allowed whisky; the second forbade whiskey but allowed red wine... by consulting six doctors I achieved permission to drink anything I wanted to—except water. The trouble with less thoughtful people is, that they stop with one doctor."[43]

After the economic calamity back home, Sam and Livy had slimmed their household to three servants: a cook, a manservant, and a chambermaid. They had initiated their Paris sojourn at the Hôtel Brighton on the Rue de Rivoli, but Twain griped about all the hotels squeezed among the shops that sheltered under the arcade. "I never know whether I am going to get caught in a jewelry shop with a pest of a salesman at my elbow," he complained, "or be allowed to walk peacefully into the hotel."[44] After a brief stay, the Clemenses transferred to a town house owned by their rich journalist friend Marcus "Brick" Pomeroy, at 160 Rue de l'Université, on the Left Bank, near the Quai d'Orsay. Because it was furnished by an American, Twain praised the house at first, finding it large and lovely and "not a museum of infernal colors, tasteless 'decorations,' & odious furniture."[45] Within three weeks, however, he soured on this new abode and made it sound like a claustrophobic prison, grumbling to Rogers about "this little private house, with two stories, eight staircases, no end of cells and passages, and *little or no room*. It was built by an idiot, I think. There is but one bedroom on our floor. All other bedrooms are far away, and one couldn't make anybody hear if one were in trouble."[46] Livy found it odd that a house hung with tapestries and other costly articles didn't contain such basics as tea and coffee cups.

After her heartbreaking disappointment with Louise Brownell, Susy seemed to rebound in Paris. Her voice coaches hoped that as she built up her health and amplified her volume, she might attain the dramatic force of a Wagnerian soprano. As she began to write, her father encouraged her to submit stories to magazines. He knew that she had prodigious powers of speech and treasured the novel statements that popped from her mouth. "Sometimes in those days of swift development in Paris, her speech was rocket-like. I seemed to *see* it go up—& up—& up, a climbing—of fire, & finally burst in the zenith & rain colored fire all around." In retrospect, he regretted that he had not been more openly expressive in supporting her. "But I came of an undemonstrative race."[47]

Livy regained strength enough to throw dinner parties once or twice a week. After twenty-five years of marriage, Twain was still gauche enough to require constant etiquette lessons from his wife. The moment guests left, she would explain "the various things which I had been doing which should have been left undone, and she was able to say, 'I have told you over and over again, yet you do these same things every time, just as if I never had warned you.'" The children stayed up late to experience the joy of overhearing these lectures. "Nothing charmed them, nothing delighted them, nothing satisfied their souls like seeing me under the torture."[48] Twain had worked out a system of social signals with Livy so that she could, on the spot, correct his boorish behavior during a dinner. If Livy mentioned a blue card, it meant, "Let the lady on your right have a reprieve." A red card meant: "Oh, are you going to sit there all the evening and never say anything? Do wake up and talk."[49]

Twain had long expressed a low opinion of Parisian weather. "Paris the cold, Paris the drizzly, Paris the rainy, Paris the Damnable."[50] Now he had to cope with a cold, rainy winter that allowed him plenty of time to read.[51] One book that made a huge impression was *A Dictionary of Miracles* by Ebenezer Cobham Brewer. Brewer narrated the story of young Richard Mainy, who back in 1602 had confessed to feigning trances and faking visions of seeing Christ accompanied by angels or the Virgin Mary. As a boy, Twain had fooled a crowd of gullible townspeople when he pretended to be hypnotized. His marginal comments about Mainy have an autobiographical ring, as if he had found an early forerunner. "He was a merry, high-spirited boy, and partly from curiosity & partly from love of enterprise, he pretended to be possessed, and allowed the priests to take him in hand. Finding the part he played made him an object of notoriety, he increased his eccentricities, and drew crowds to see him."[52] A similar amalgam of vanity, insecurity, and attention-seeking had led the young Sam Clemens to cultivate outrageous behavior in Hannibal and beyond.

While in Paris, Twain toured many French Revolution landmarks and again read Thomas Carlyle on the period. The French had never particularly warmed to Mark Twain, who reciprocated their displeasure. After wading through three volumes of Saint-Simon's memoir of the court of Louis XIV, he reviled the courtiers as so many "gilded lice."[53] The letters of Madame de Sévigné he mocked for not even having "the common French merit of being indecent."[54] He found Talleyrand's witticisms vastly overrated, preferring those of his pal Thomas Bailey Aldrich. "Talk about wit, why, Tom Bailey Aldrich has said 1,500 if not 15,000 things as brilliant as the things Talleyrand said and which are labeled 'French wit.'"[55]

Much as with the Old Masters, Twain made a specialty of disparaging the French, an abhorrence that mostly arose from their relaxed sexual mores. Once Twain got on a hobbyhorse he refused to dismount, and this one he rode particularly hard. "Money cannot do everything. It failed to find the man who could explain how the French lost their tails."[56] "The Race consists of human beings & French."[57] "'Tis a wise Frenchman that knows his own father."[58] "An isolated & helpless young girl is perfectly safe from insult by a Frenchman, if he is dead."[59] "The <French> Parisians, the adulterous nation."[60] "Write a 'French' novel—37 cases of adultery, & they all live happy to the end."[61] These mordant observations may say more about Twain's own prudery than about supposed French immorality.

Perhaps the funniest thing Twain wrote about Paris was his droll description of a French elevator. "It held two persons, and traveled at such a slow gait that a spectator could not tell which way it was going. If the passengers were going to the sixth floor, they took along something to eat; and at night, bedding. Old people did not use it; except such as were on their way to the good place, anyhow. Often people that had been lost for days were found in those lifts, jogging along, jogging along, frequently still alive. The French took great pride in their ostensible lift, and called it by a grand name—*ascenseur*."[62]

Twain's stay in Paris provided only a brief reprieve from his troubled financial prospects. By January 1895, he was brooding over heavy payments to Webster & Company creditors that would fall due by year's end and started saving money by curtailing expenses at his Hartford house. "I want *repairs* on the house reduced at once to $15 a month," he instructed Franklin G. Whitmore, "even if the roof [should] fall in."[63] The house he had long adored now weighed on him as an unholy burden. "We've *got* to rent that house," he told Whitmore, "or sell it or burn it."[64] Before sending the letter, he struck out "sell it or burn it." Once the house was rented, he began to reflect more seriously on the frugal existence that Webster & Company's bankruptcy would foist upon his family, telling Rogers, "The thing for me to do is to begin to teach myself to endure a way of life which I was familiar with during the first half of my life but whose sordidness and hatefulness and humiliation long ago faded out of my memory and feeling."[65] Never before had he expressed so clearly his hatred of poverty and how it had scarred his early years. He knew he was sliding down a slippery pole, one that he had laboriously climbed in his career. By his computation, he and Livy could no longer afford to live in the United States, especially New York, their expensive city of choice, and they considered Paris or Vienna a cheaper alternative.

The Clemenses could not renounce their dream of re-creating the status quo ante in Hartford. Alice Hooker Day and her family were slated to rent the house from March to September, and the Clemens family hoped to occupy it after that. Livy kept running numbers—"acres of figures," said Twain—and thought that with fewer servants and no horses they might be able to eke out an existence there.[66] In a throwback to the past, the family even planned to spend the summer in Elmira. Twain returned to the United States first, sailing in late February with a twofold mission: to find a publisher for the *Personal Recollections of Joan of Arc* and possibly to introduce a uniform edition of his work that would generate fresh income. He would also launch discussions with Major James Pond about a global lecture tour to wipe away his debts.

After arriving in New York, Twain traveled to Hartford but feared returning to the old house, even though Katy Leary had restored many furnishings to their former place. In the end, he made an emotionally fraught visit to the residence, which contained the ghosts of his happy past life, the essence of a world he had fumbled and frittered away. As he wrote to Livy: "But as soon as I entered this front door I was siezed [sic] with a furious desire to have us all in this house again & right away, & never go outside the grounds any more forever—certainly never again to Europe."[67] As he glided about the house, he felt awed by its beautiful colors, its perfect taste and harmony. "You did it all, & it speaks of you & praises you eloquently and unceasingly. It is the loveliest home that ever was . . . Katy had every rug & picture & ornament & chair exactly where they had always belonged, the place was bewitchingly bright & splendid homelike & natural, & it seemed as if I had burst awake out of

RAPIDS

a hellish dream, & had never been away, & that you would come drifting down out of those dainty upper regions with the little children tagging after you."[68] It was an unbearable moment for Mark Twain as the whole beauty of their past life rushed back in his train of memories. But they were now just memories, never to return. The past was always a powerful intoxicant for him, and he assured Livy that all of Hartford clamored for her return, "for I have spread it around that you are coming to America in May. Words cannot describe how worshipfully & enthusiastically you are loved in this town . . . I have made up my mind to one thing: if we go around the world we will move into our house when we get back."[69] It was a brave but forlorn vow by a man who could not admit that his past life had now ended.

CHAPTER THIRTY-THREE

"'Colossal' Is a Tame Word for Him"

For all his unfailing mastery of the form, Twain dreaded his return to the lecture circuit and the specter of a global tour squashed his creative spirit. Sailing back to Paris in April, he made a stab at writing at sea, without success. "Every attempt has failed—a struggle every day, and retreat and defeat at nightfall," he confessed to Rogers.[1] When he returned to Rue de l'Université, he suffered from a mind too tired, too clogged with worry, to function. "It comes of depression of spirits, I think, caused by the impending horror of the platform."[2] While still in Paris, he signed a contract that charted an ambitious six-to-nine-month tour that would take him to the Sandwich Islands, New Zealand, Australia, Ceylon (today Sri Lanka), India, and South Africa, as well as to the United States and possibly England. He simply hated having to "turn out in my lazy old age and go in the platform again," but he urgently needed cash to keep creditors at bay, and writing would take too long to generate that.[3] To further his misery, he was again handicapped by gout and unable to put weight on his right foot.

Back in Elmira in May, he finalized with Major James B. Pond plans for the tour, which would commence in Cleveland on July 15, stop in twenty-one cities, then wind up in Vancouver before moving on to the Sandwich Islands. They opted for a northern route across North America, fearing Livy couldn't stand the heat of a southern circuit. Aside from working on *Joan of Arc*, Twain prepared three readings for the engagements, hoping to sample them with various audiences. Privately he said he needed one daughter along to serve as Livy's maid and couldn't afford to invite all three daughters. "Livy and Clara go with me around the world," he notified Orion, "but Susie refuses because she hates the sea, & Jean refuses because she can't spare the time from school."[4] Aside from a phobic fear of ships burning at sea, Susy may also have wanted to stay available for Louise, whom she would meet twice during her father's absence. Her reluctance to join the tour would have momentous consequences.

Just as Twain geared up for his trip at Quarry Farm, he was laid low in late May by a fresh problem: a carbuncle, "big as a turkey's egg," sprouted on his left thigh even as gout still tormented his right leg.[5] These pus-filled boils make victims feel miserable. He was treated daily by a family physician, Theron Wales. To hear Twain tell it, the carbuncle ache was mild compared to the tedious twaddle of the doctor, who "loved to hear himself talk, and was a spirit-rotting bore. With all his boasted experience he knew nothing about carbuncles that was not known by our old ex-slave cook, Aunty Cord."[6] Twain seldom met a doctor he didn't think gouged him financially, and Dr. Wales joined that luckless fraternity. "That Elmira leech knew that I had fallen heir to a heavy debt . . . but that did not move him to spare me when he had a chance to afflict me with social calls and charge pirate-rates for them."[7] Twain monitored his carbuncle's progress with a morbid curiosity, especially when it "sloughed out a big hunk of decayed protoplasm like a Baltimore oyster . . . & left a corresponding raw cavity in my leg."[8] To his immense frustration, the wound responded sluggishly to lancing and draining—"slower than chilled molasses," in Twain's phrase—and he feared he would need to be carried on a stretcher to his first Cleveland lecture.[9]

While Twain plotted his trip, he couldn't rid himself of the legal repercussions of his bankruptcy, and on June 25 was served with a subpoena for $5,000 owed to Thomas Russell & Son for binding books for Webster & Company. The firm suspected Twain had secreted assets elsewhere. He had to appear in New York on July 5 and grew furious that while other creditors remained charitable when faced with his goodwill, this printer had turned vindictive. If he defied the subpoena, Twain feared "a bad advertisement for my lecture-trip," with newspapers saying "I have dodged the courts and fled the country."[10] Right on the eve of his tour, still plagued by the carbuncle, Twain traveled to Wall Street for his examination, escorted by a male nurse. Major Pond remembered the gruesome event: "I declare that never have I witnessed a more pathetic spectacle than this sick man, facing what seemed to be a merciless court and a still more heartless creditor, who owed more of his business success to his victim than to any other source."[11] Twain was about as fond of lawyers as he was of doctors, and he never forgave his attorneys for permitting this questioning. "It is incredible," he protested to Rogers, "the worry and anger that that Russell business has cost me since the day my idiot lawyers allowed me to be dragged to New York by a court which had no more authority over me than the Mikado of Japan."[12] Returning to Elmira, he found Livy distraught because news of the examination had leaked into the press, and she feared creditors might try to attach proceeds of the Cleveland lecture. "I said we would immediately compromise with Russell or pay him in full," Twain informed Rogers. "Maybe I might be able to endure further annoyance, but [Livy] has reached her limit and is entitled to a release."[13]

Before setting off on his world tour, Twain tested out his material at the Randall's Island House of Refuge before an audience of seven hundred young delinquents who sat there unimpressed. "Oh, but wasn't it a comical defeat . . . Delivering a grown-folks' lecture to a sucking-bottle nursery!" Twain bemoaned.[14] According to the *New York Sun*, when Twain then spoke extemporaneously to slightly older boys at the Elmira Reformatory, he fared much better "and the boys were in a roar . . . from the time they found—that it wasn't against the rules to smile until the speaker sat down."[15] The reformatory newspaper expressed this gleeful response more strongly when it said "many in the audience were on the verge of apoplexy."[16]

When Sam, Livy, and Clara departed for the world tour on July 14, 1895, it marked an emotional separation from Susy that was to last a year. When George Warner had seen her in May, he reported that Susy was "thin, seems easily flushed and speaks huskily. She says a year at the farm will be good for her."[17] Katy Leary confirmed that Madame Marchesi had advised Susy "to go on a farm for a year and drink lots of milk, live outdoors . . . to get her chest stronger" and "she'd have more volume to sing with."[18] As the train pulled away from the Elmira station at half-past ten on July 14, Twain wrote, "Susy stood on the platform in the blaze of the electric light waving her goodbyes to us as the train glided away, her mother throwing back kisses & watching her through her tears."[19] The emotional moment would remain engraved in Twain's memory. "She was brimming with life and the joy of it," he said.[20]

The tour's impresario was Major James B. Pond, the ex-abolitionist editor and Union major during the Civil War. He was a garrulous man, a big talker whose stock in trade was grandiosity. As Twain observed: "Pond never deals in small adjectives—'colossal' is a tame word for him."[21] A cheerful companion and ready raconteur, he was good company for the Clemens family on the trip across North America. Twain enjoyed sharpening his wit by teasing Pond, who became a favorite butt of his satire. Like many Twain friends, Pond would have been shocked by Twain's snarling private appraisal of him. "Pond is not an interesting liar; it is the only fault he has . . . Pond is also a fool. I have seldom seen so complete & compact a one. But he is a most kindly & pleasant one, & I would not trade his society for that of the average wise man."[22] For his part, Pond noted that Twain, beneath his crusty facade, could be warm and tenderhearted, though he spotted his vengeful streak. "Injure him," he once said, "and he is merciless, especially if you betray his confidence."[23]

When the party arrived at the Stillman Hotel in Cleveland, Pond said Twain looked "nervous and weak," feared he wouldn't be able to stand up onstage, and worried that a creditor would materialize from thin air. Aside from Livy's ministrations, Twain was heartened when the press flocked to interview him and he could settle into some well-worn comic routines. For his inaugural lecture at the Music Hall, conditions were challenging. The hall was packed with twenty-six hundred people who sweltered in ninety-degree heat. Twain had to follow a concert, and when he spoke, a barking terrier nearly drove him mad. Meanwhile, a

"'COLOSSAL' IS A TAME WORD FOR HIM"

contingent of newsboys seated behind him engaged in noisy horseplay. What made it all worthwhile was the huge outpouring of affection from audience members, who knew of Twain's financial plight, and he felt immersed in their infectious warmth. "As he hobbled upon the stage," Pond wrote, "there was a grand ovation of cheers and applause which continued for some time. Then he began to speak, and before he could finish a sentence the applause broke out again. So it went on for over an hour on a mid-July night."[24] Twain's prolonged tussles with Webster & Company and the typesetter having distanced him from his readers, he now felt their love return in enhanced form.

During the tour, Twain varied his repertoire for each performance. On the first night he fell back on some old favorites. Standing conventional morality on its head, he impressed upon the audience the importance of committing a crime. "Make it permanent; impress it so that you may never commit the same crime again . . . then you will see yourself what the logical result of that will be—that you get interested in committing crimes."[25] He told his shopworn tale of stealing a watermelon from a farmer and only repenting when he discovered it was green. He restored the watermelon to the farmer and made him give him a ripe one instead. "Ever since that day to this I never stole another one—like that."[26] He regaled them with the vignette of Jim Smiley and his jumping frog, "Dan'l" Webster, loaded with shot by a stranger, and transported them back to his Hannibal boyhood. "When a schoolboy it often fell to my lot to come across a rainy day—one of those days which schoolboys all over the world regard as too rainy to go to school, and just rainy enough to go fishing."[27] He ended the program on a graceful note. "I thank you very cordially for the indulgence with which you have listened to my scheme for revolutionizing the morals of the globe as I go round."[28]

As the party took a steamer across Lake Erie to Michigan, Twain's celebrity trailed him at every turn. As Pond noted, "Wherever 'Mark' sits or stands on the deck of the steamer, in the smoking room, dining room, or cabin, he is the magnet, and people strain their necks to see him and to catch every word he utters."[29] Twain, as usual, felt emancipated by water travel and sunny, balmy weather. "I have seen no boat in Europe that wasn't a garbage-barge by comparison," he told his notebook.[30] It was an auspicious start to the tour, which had already acquired the air of a triumphal procession. As his boat approached Port Huron, passengers on other craft waved flags and fluttered handkerchiefs amid salutes of cannon fire. Twain had a charisma and renown more often associated with politicians and star actors than authors. He had become part of the common property of the country's culture. "I don't believe that there is another man in America that attracts the people as he does," marveled Major Pond.[31] When they steamed into Detroit, a reporter gave this sketch of the lionized visitor: "A man past the middle age of life, with bushy gray hair that fell well down upon his coat collar, a moustache of the same color, that was inclined to bristle, and a clear, ruddy complexion."[32]

After checking into the Grand Hotel there, Mackinac seemed such a ghost town that Twain and Pond didn't know whether they should bother to show up at the local hall. At 8:30 p.m., Pond was about to tell the janitor to close up the place when a trickle of people arrived that soon turned into a riptide, and by nine, Pond was rapidly taking dollar bills at the door. Twain went onstage and Pond later said, "I don't believe an audience ever had a better time of an hour and a half. 'Mark' was simply immense."[33] When Twain and Pond traveled to Petoskey, Michigan, their train plowed through thick smoke on all sides, blown downwind by forest fires. Twain suffered terribly from his carbuncle, which he had to dress twice daily, and one reporter thought he resembled a "bushy-headed careless looking, little wizen-faced man . . . taken along to look after the baggage."[34] In spite of the smoke, 750 people squeezed into a hall that typically seated 500. Animated by a "constant ripple of laughter," Twain entertained the crowd for seventy minutes until applause and shouts of "Go on, go on" induced him to stay and tell one last story.[35]

After landing late in Duluth, Minnesota, Twain hurried off the boat, addressed a huge, perspiring crowd of 1,250 people—it was 100 degrees in the shade—and hopped on a train bound for Minneapolis ninety minutes later. The remaining portion of the tour would be by rail to the Pacific Coast. Before he appeared at the Metropolitan Opera House in St. Paul, six reporters clustered around Twain as he sat up in his hotel

"'COLOSSAL' IS A TAME WORD FOR HIM"

bed and diverted them with stories for two hours. Accompanied by a gaggle of newsmen, he seemed to warm to the press, which recorded his every utterance. The bed interview became his trademark, although in this case the recumbent position was necessitated by his carbuncle. Major Pond often functioned as his straight man, not always to his pleasure. When the hearty Pond told reporters, "I was in Minneapolis when there were no saloons here," Twain shot back, "Well, you didn't stay long," and listeners roared with merriment.[36] Livy had warned her husband that audiences could become sated with laughter, and that night he mixed in tales of Jim and Huck fleeing slavery on the raft, Pond noting the new strategy of "blending pathos with humor."[37] That pathos had been the key ingredient supplied by George Washington Cable, and the new medley of moods enabled Twain to perform alone and satisfy audiences eager for a well-rounded dramatic experience. He attempted to embed nuggets of wisdom into each story he told.

Traveling with the Clemenses, Major Pond studied how Livy softened her husband's behavior. In Minneapolis, a Mr. Chute sent flowers to the ladies in the party, and Livy reciprocated by inviting him to dinner. "Mark was not very attentive" to his visitor, Pond wrote, "and after dinner Mrs. Clemens reminded him of his seeming impoliteness, whereupon Mark wrote Mr. Chute a letter of thanks, regret and praise, such as few people ever received from that source. Mr. Chute proudly showed it to me and said he would rather have that letter than $1,000 profit on the lecture."[38] Livy still had to train her hapless husband in the social graces.

The stop in Minneapolis–St. Paul was followed by a six-hundred-mile train trip to Winnipeg, Manitoba. After years of business worry, Twain enjoyed the glimpses of tranquil farmland through his window. "Seas and seas of wheat . . . I know of nothing more delightful & enthusing than this lovely green vast level, with its remote islands of timber showing a darker green here & there & yonder," he observed in his notebook.[39] In Winnipeg, after the lecture, Twain was feted at the Manitoba Club but retired by midnight because he knew the lengthy train trip had taxed Livy. Back at the hotel, he found Clara seated at a piano in the parlor as young men from the club sang along with her for an hour.

As the tour charted a path across North Dakota and Montana, Twain was reunited with reminders of long-forgotten landscapes. The journey updated his picture of the country, a sense of just how fast modernity was overtaking the small-town America of his youth. Arriving at the Great Falls of the upper Missouri River, he noted "the crystal-clear atmosphere & deceptive distances; first time I have seen it in a generation... This town is webbed overhead with electric lights & trolley wires."[40] One morning, the party was roused at 4:30 a.m. to make a 5:40 train, and Twain gnashed his teeth when the train was forty-five minutes late. "'Mark' complained and grumbled; he persisted that I had contracted with him to *travel* and not to wait about railway stations at five o'clock in the mornings for late trains that never arrived," Pond recorded. "He insisted on traveling, so he got aboard the baggage truck and I *traveled* him up and down the platform, while Clara made a snapshot as evidence that I was keeping to the letter of my contract."[41]

When the party reached Butte, in western Montana, Twain reconnected with old mining veterans from the Comstock Lode, who carried him off to a champagne celebration after his lecture. At Helena, he met another round of boon companions from Virginia City days. His most moving encounter in Butte came when he was asked to review a contingent of Black troops. Early in the Civil War, Union commanders had questioned whether Blacks would make good soldiers—an impression quickly answered when they began to fight valiantly—and Twain found them in superb condition. He strolled down the center row of their barracks, with the troops standing at the foot of their beds, and he captured in his notebook their pride, dignity, and patriotism. "Splendid big negro soldiers; obedient, don't desert, don't get drunk; proud of their vocation, finest and pleasantest soldiers—and Pond says great in battle... They all have the look and bearing of gentlemen." As the all-Black band struck up martial tunes, soldiers strutted by, trooping colors, while an embarrassed Twain committed the double faux pas of forgetting to doff his cap and throw away his cigar. "Goodwill," he concluded of the Black soldiers. "They take a pride in it. *I* think the negro has found his vocation at last."[42]

By the time the tour reached Washington State, Twain was recuperating from his carbuncle and was more ambulatory than previously. For someone who had grown up in the antebellum Midwest, the modern western cities, thrown up after the war, were simply a revelation. In Spokane, Twain and Pond toured the city on foot, awestruck. "Mark and I walked about this remarkable city, with its asphalt streets, electric lights, nine story telegraph poles, and commercial blocks that would do credit to any Eastern city. Buildings nine stories high, with the nine top stories empty."[43] Twain had spent so many years in Hartford and Europe that the trip acquainted him anew with his own country. Regardless of how impressed he was with the development, he still harbored retrograde opinions and expressed dismissive reactions to Native Americans: "See squaws prowling about back doors & windows begging & foraging—a nuisance once familiar to me."[44]

Although the captivating Livy joined them on the tour, Major Pond seemed more taken with Clara, designating her "the most beautiful girl I ever saw" and a great pianist. One night after dinner, she sat down at a grand piano, played a Chopin nocturne, and held a roomful of hotel guests spellbound. "Never did I witness a more beautiful sight than this sweet brunett [sic] unconsciously holding a large audience of charmed listeners," Pond wrote. "Her mother saw and heard her and if it was not one of the supreme moments of her life, then I have guessed wrong."[45]

The next day, the tour party climbed aboard the Great Northern Railroad as it cut a zigzagging route through the Rocky Mountains, with Twain riding up on the engine, "greatly to the delight of the engineer," said Pond.[46] Twain had one of his brightest triumphs in Portland, Oregon, where, by the time he arrived, the Marquam Grand Opera House had posted a sign, "Standing Room Only." In reviewing Twain's appearances, many reporters paused to assess his career as someone who had transcended the status of a funny man to capture deeper truths about the American experience. A critic for the Portland *Oregonian* noted that Mark Twain was as well known to young people as he was to their elders, and drew both fashionable and simple people. "To have accomplished this, there must have been more to his work than simply humor. This humor must have been true to life rather than an exaggeration to

RAPIDS

provoke mirth. In many cases, it is a question whether his mirth is not rather pathos, and the two are so delightfully blended that it is not hard to conceive why Mark Twain stands where he does today."[47] Pond said Twain was particularly pleased by this assessment, which acknowledged his new lecture strategy.

Upon arriving in Seattle, Twain was again greeted by a "Standing Room Only" sign, and his hoarse voice didn't detract from his performance. What had grown clear as he crossed the continent was just how beloved he was, the Mark Twain phenomenon having only burgeoned during his absence abroad. "I find I have twenty-five friends in America where I thought I had only one," he told nephew Samuel E. Moffett.[48] He was mobbed in the street by people wanting to shake his hand and wish him well. At his time of need, they hoped to repay all the pleasure he had given them over the years. The reaction to his lectures solidified his reputation as the greatest platform artist of his age, and people felt lucky to view him in the flesh, to hear the twang of his drawl and witness the shambling walk, see the glint in his eye. "To tell the story of such a lecture is like trying to narrate a laugh," said the Seattle *Post-Intelligencer*. "Those who heard it enjoyed it, and those who did not cannot conceive of it."[49] Twain, having started the lecture in a sickly, depressed state, now felt robust. "Lecturing is gymnastics," Twain told Moffett, "chest-expander, medicine, mind-healer, blues-destroyer, all in one. I am twice as well as I was when I started out; I have gained nine pounds in twenty-eight days, and expect to weigh six hundred before January. I haven't had a blue day in all the twenty-eight."[50] In fact, even as Twain wrote, Major Pond reported that he had a cold that had only worsened.

Through the good offices and judicious editing of Samuel E. Moffett, the San Francisco *Examiner* published on August 17 an "interview" in which Twain explained his bankruptcy and determination to pay his debts in full since a man of honor cannot "compromise for less than one hundred cents on the dollar."[51] He had been angered by a newspaper article that suggested he undertook the tour simply to enrich himself. In the "interview," Twain defended himself from any imputation of sharp practice in transferring to Livy the copyrights of his books and pointed out that her claim as a creditor "nearly equaled the claims of all others combined." He also explained the necessity that led him to the arduous tour. "I do not enjoy the hard travel and broken rest inseparable from lecturing, and if it had not been for the imperious moral necessity of paying these debts . . . I should never have taken to the road at my time of life . . . In my preliminary run through the smaller cities on the northern route I have found a reception the cordiality of which has touched my heart and made me feel how small a thing money is in comparison with friendship." He promised that if he could pay off his debts in four years, by age sixty-four, "I can make a fresh and unencumbered start in life."[52]

The tour ended in Vancouver, where Twain's raw voice turned so raspy that he landed in bed; when he gave a postponed lecture, it was "by whispering, mainly."[53] Twain often boasted of perfect health, yet he was chronically sick. "He smokes constantly . . . Physicians say it will eventually kill him," observed Major Pond, who noted that Twain had laid in a cache of three thousand cheroots for the Pacific crossing.[54] Atmospheric conditions didn't help matters in British Columbia. Although Vancouver was encircled by beautiful scenery, "We can't see it," said Pond. "Smoke, smoke, everywhere, and no relief. My eyes are sore from it."[55] Twain agreed, more colorfully, "The smoke is so dense . . . that you can't see a cathedral at 800 yards."[56]

Due to the delayed departure of the ship slated to take them westward, Pond sneaked in a final lecture in Victoria on August 20. The Governor-General and Lady Aberdeen attended and Twain was conducted to their private box at the end. Despite his medical problems, Twain had kept up a rugged pace on the road: he had delivered 24 lectures in 22 cities and yet the tour, which would cover 53,000 miles, was just starting. He had already spied a new carbuncle, which he didn't yet deem a "strong threat," but he had "laid in materials for a war upon it."[57] The North American tour had sapped his strength, and when they went for a final walk together, Pond found Twain "tired and feeble . . . He was nervous, and weak, and disappointed."[58]

Surprisingly enough, Livy had been buoyed by the cross-country travel and seemed refreshed. When Major Pond snapped a photo of her in a railway carriage, there was a warm glow in her eyes and a kindly, unaffected happiness in her face. She had been an invaluable aid to her husband, helping him to gauge the success of various stories by audience responses. Clara reported her pleasant surprise to Susy that their mother looked "chipper and bright . . . She has borne this travelling so *excellently* that I am not afraid of the future."[59] With her family about to embark across the Pacific, Susy, in Elmira, told Clara of her renewed pangs of loneliness, how unbearable she found the separation. "Your sailing away seems like another terrible parting and good bye almost worse than the first for we shall be such an eternity without news of you, and that will be hard."[60] She was oppressed by guilty feelings that she had let her family down. Whether that was because of Louise Brownell or her eating disorder or the infatuation with the married Count de Calry, it is impossible to say. "I am often deeply cast down with the thought of how I have failed to be what I should have been to you all . . . I love you all and *could not* have wanted more to be a 'nice child.'"[61] She wished for one more chance to try again.

After Vancouver, Pond and his wife returned east and visited Elmira to show Susy pictures from the tour. It proved heartrending for her to see them. "Ah me," she wrote Clara, "was I not a fool to stay here instead of going with you? How happy and adventurous and chic you do look in these pictures! . . . There will be no extricating and separating me from you again. *We* are such a congenial family. It seems to me no one ever understands us as we understand each other. We *do* belong together. When I think of you and Mamma and Papa your superior charms and attractions make me look upon other mortals with contempt and a profound indifference."[62] At twenty-three, Susy still felt on the threshold of life, as if she had not yet begun to experience it fully. Life was always something happening somewhere else to some other people.

On August 23, 1895, Major Pond and his wife partook of a last collation with the Clemens family onboard the RMS *Warrimoo* before it set off across the Pacific. The first glimpse of the ship convinced the Clem-

"'COLOSSAL' IS A TAME WORD FOR HIM"

ens trio that it didn't rise to their usual standards. "Mrs. Clemens is disappointed in the ship," Pond wrote. "The whole thing looks discouraging, and our hearts are almost broken for the poor woman. She tells me she is going to brave it through, for she must do it. It is for her children."[63] As so often before, Livy steeled herself to support her husband and to pay off the creditors at home. The trip brought out a stoic toughness beneath her fragility. Whenever Twain got grouchy, Livy's "gentle and smooth manner" overcame obstacles and made "everything lovely," Pond remarked.[64] She held the antidote to every situation, the balm that alleviated each hurt. She was, Pond concluded, "the most noble example of woman I have ever had the honor to know."[65] To cheer up the family, Pond snapped a final photo of Twain smoking a pipe alongside Livy and Clara as they leaned against a deck rail above a sign that warned: "NOTICE: ALL STOWAWAYS WILL BE PROSECUTED AT HONOLULU, AND RETURNED TO THIS PORT.—BY ORDER." After taking this comical picture, the Ponds retreated to the dock and waved sadly to the departing Clemens family until they had disappeared from sight.

CHAPTER THIRTY-FOUR

"Clown of the Sea"

It was a relief for Sam and Livy and Clara to leave behind the forest smoke for ocean breezes and a shining blue sea. They ate decently, though not healthily, aboard the *Warrimoo* and were upset mostly by "an over-supply of cockroaches."[1] Twain was finally able to read and smoke his store of cheroots, and play hearts with the family. Clara recalled her father's childlike "capacity for getting angry over cards." When he lost, he would fling his cards on the table and say in disgust, "I don't care a rap about beating, but I can't stand the sight of such cards. They make me boil—only a saint on ice could keep cool."[2] He played shuffleboard with a boyish, competitive zest and beamed with pride when he won a tournament. The lecture hall stress slowly drained away, at least by day, for at night it surged anew into his unconscious. "Recurrent Dream," he wrote. "Mine is appearing before lecture-audience in my shirt-tail. A most disagreeable dream."[3] His sleeping thoughts may attest that he was not as supremely confident as he appeared onstage or that he feared something carefully hidden might be disclosed.

Twain eagerly anticipated his brief stopover and lecture in the Sandwich Islands, a place that had never relaxed its romantic hold over his imagination. Seven days out from Vancouver, Diamond Head came into view and Twain approached "a Paradise which I had been longing all those years to see again."[4] When the boat dropped anchor off Honolulu, a small craft pulled alongside to announce that passengers couldn't disembark because of cholera on the island; the harbor was shut to visiting ships. Staring at his old Shangri-La, sequestered in quarantine, he could only summon distant memories. "The silky mountains were clothed in soft, rich splendors of melting color, and some of the cliffs were veiled in slanting mists... It was just as I had seen it long before, with nothing of its beauty lost, nothing of its charm wanting."[5] His recollections came deep-dyed with nostalgia. "In my time it was a beautiful little town made up of snow-white wooden cottages deliciously smothered in tropical vines and flowers and trees and shrubs."[6] As he contemplated Oahu from afar, he reflected, "If I might I would go ashore and never leave."[7] When Twain sailed away without going ashore—he was also upset by the lost lecture fees—he was saddened to think that he might never set eyes on the Sandwich Islands again.

As the ship moved south toward Sydney, Australia, the weather grew so infernally hot that even the decorous Livy could not bear to sleep belowdecks, grabbed her pillows, and slept on hard wooden benches in the ladies' salon. Clara complained that her cabin swarmed with cockroaches, setting her nerves on edge. "There was no article of furniture so large that I couldn't make a cockroach out of it, & their familiarity went beyond all bounds!"[8] Twain focused on a sea full of wonders and grew fascinated by schools of porpoises that shone "like luminous sea serpents" at night and schools of flying fish that looked "like a flight of silver-fruit-knives."[9] He delighted in a lunar eclipse. "At total it was like a rich rosy cloud with a tumbled surface framed in the moon & projecting *from* it. It resembled a Saucer of strawberry ice."[10]

To outward appearances, Twain seemed buoyant, though Livy knew surfaces could deceive, and as they approached the equator, she reported to Sue Crane that beneath a contented demeanor her husband had "a steady, unceasing feeling that he is never going to be able to pay his debts."[11] Despite his doubts, Livy was far more sanguine. As they progressed on the tour, Twain kept forwarding to Henry Rogers his lecture payments for creditors. Small wonder that he felt so beleaguered. Luckily, he could find humor in almost anything and joked about the unfair neglect the equator endured in the middle of the ocean. "Yet it was wisdom to put it here," he observed drily, "for if it had been run through Europe all the kings would have tried to grab it."[12]

In mid-September, the *Warrimoo* docked in Sydney, where Twain would speak four times in nine days. The Clemenses felt an instant fondness for Australia, with Sam rhapsodizing the beauty of Sydney Harbour and the clear, dry, bracing air, while Livy found poetry in the landscape's muted colors—"like music in a minor key"—and was enchanted by the "soft ethereal blueness of the sky."[13]

The Australian press, never having seen a live performance by him before, left many sketches of Twain's showmanship. Despite trepidation about his reception, once he stepped onstage people cheered and flapped their handkerchiefs, and he saw with relief a sea of "guffawing heads, of swaying bodies and shoulders."[14] One reviewer noted that during the lecture Twain scarcely budged from a single spot while the audience erupted with laughter. "His characteristic attitude is to stand quite still, with the right arm across the abdomen and the left resting on it and supporting his chin. In this way he talks on for nearly two hours; and, while the audience is laughing uproariously, he never by any chance relapses into a smile."[15] He captivated his listeners with wit and language alone, and didn't embellish talks with artificial gestures, coming across as a folksy old gentleman, chatting heart-to-heart with his down-home audience, sometimes with hands plunged into his trouser pockets. "The eyes, arched with bushy brows . . . flash out now and then from their deep sockets with a genial, kindly, pathetic look . . . He talks in short sentences, with a peculiar smack of the lips at the end of each."[16] Beloved by the throngs who arrived to hear him, Twain proclaimed, "I am almost in love with the platform again."[17]

The press was no less charmed by his wife and daughter, and one Sydney reporter developed an instant crush on Clara, "a beautiful girl, perhaps twenty years of age, with a face like a New England Madonna."[18] Reporters gushed over Livy's grace and charm, and how she rescued her husband from his worst verbal gaffes. In one interview, he was sounding off about his feud with a French author when he began to blurt out, "I hope one day to meet him in—"[19] The reporter noted how Livy placed a ladylike hand over his mouth before he could finish the sentence, and she asked the reporter to omit the offensive remark. She hovered over him protectively and made sure he conserved his energy if interviews lasted too long. With Twain still battling carbuncles, Livy had to dress them once or twice a day. She and Clara—his busy handlers—also packed bags, wrote letters, returned visits, and critiqued his lectures.

Twain got the full celebrity treatment in Australia and reveled unashamedly in the spotlight. When he arrived by rail in Melbourne, he was greeted by two hundred people at the train station and pronounced it "a stately city architecturally as well as in magnitude," full of grand, spacious houses.[20] He was horrified when a second carbuncle popped up on his left calf, stranding him at the hotel. "I have greater respect for it than for any other possession I have in the world," he noted. "I take more care of it than I do of the family."[21] A Dr. Fitzgerald treated this second carbuncle, freezing it and lancing it, and also gave Twain an "opium hypodermic," which may explain why he then extolled medicine and surgery as "the loftiest of all human vocations."[22] Only on the lecture stage, distracted by audience laughter, did he feel free of incessant pain.

Owing to the carbuncles, a debilitated Twain had to cancel a few Melbourne appearances before departing for Adelaide on a seventeen-hour train ride. If his social contacts were restricted by pain, Twain found the Australians a bluff, hearty people, more like Americans than the British, and he felt very much at home. With his eclectic curiosity about the customs of a country, he toured an agricultural college outside Horsham, where he was delighted to watch pupils shearing sheep. "The fleece when spread out is as big as a bed quilt . . . The sheep are shorn dirty—buyer prefers it—& the shorn sheep looks as white as snow."[23] Two weeks later, he visited Melbourne's wool exchange and registered the sheer bedlam arising from the trading pit. "Bidders like barking dogs—Babel-racket—gesticulation—nobody calm but the President. Everybody yelps, yaps, barks, at once, & the Pres[iden]t decides which barked first—no appeal."[24]

When Twain spoke in Horsham, Livy thought he had never addressed

"CLOWN OF THE SEA"

a more responsive audience. In this tiny country town, people traveled vast distances to attend, and they lined the side aisles of the packed hall and sat on the stage. When the program began, Livy couldn't believe the spirited response, telling Susy it was a "most jolly house to talk to, they made me laugh most heartily, much more at them than at Papa's talk, as that really was not all new to me." She sat beside a young man who lapsed into such hysterical laughter that he "began to pound his sides as if troubled with stitches in them and turning to me said, 'Well if it is all as funny as this I shall die.'" She couldn't believe the "constant unceasing adulation" of her husband and the "most appreciative words about him."[25] Afterward, Twain reclined on a hotel sofa and entertained reporters under the watchful gaze of Carlyle G. Smythe, who, along with his father, now managed the tour. These interviews usually unfolded amid a thick haze of tobacco smoke that would have choked a horse. "Mark Twain is an inveterate smoker," remarked one reporter of his oral fixations, "and when he relinquishes his cigar it is to transfer his attention to a pipe."[26]

If Twain devoted nothing but kind words to the people, climate, lakes, and gardens in Australia, he cast a stern gaze on the hotel accommodations and let loose a fire-breathing blast in the town of Bendigo. "Originally an idiot went through here & decided that in country hotels . . . the clothes should be placed so high as to make a step-ladder necessary. Just as in America some idiot decided that the mirrors should be so low as to require every middle-sized man to stoop."[27] Impressed by the country's lovely railroad stations, he nonetheless found the train system a mad maze of inefficiency—"slow trains, no drinking water, no sanitary arrangements, every conceivable inconvenience, an utterly idiotic & insane system—the jackass system."[28] Twain also lacked patience with the canary birds caged in Australian hotels. "To me a canary's 'music' is but the equivalent of scratching a nail on a window-pane. I wonder what sort of disease it is that enables a person to enjoy the canary."[29]

While touring Tasmania, Twain dug deeper into Australian history and began to formulate a tragic view of colonial history, a new emphasis for him. As his boat sailed between Tasmania and its neighboring islands, he pondered the fate of Aboriginal people who had been expelled by white settlers and from their island refuges "used to gaze at their beloved land & cry; & die of heart-break."[30] He visited the Tasmanian Museum and Art Gallery, paying special attention to the Tasmanian Room with its Aboriginal artifacts. In *Following the Equator,* the travelogue he published about his tour, he returned to the story of the native population of Tasmania and the corrupting effect of colonialism. After years of employing violence to subjugate them, the white government tried to "civilize" them, to their everlasting detriment. "The Natives were not used to clothes, and houses, and regular hours, and church, and school, and Sunday-school, and work, and the other misplaced persecutions of civilization, and they pined for their lost home and their wild free life. Too late they repented that they had traded that heaven for this hell."[31] It was Tom Sawyer's story, or Huck Finn's, transposed to a foreign climate and elevated to a political plane.

As the Clemens party moved on to New Zealand, Twain's notebooks abounded with testimonials to brilliant blue skies, green pastures, and herds of sheep. The magnificent landscape struck him as a cross between "the fiords of Norway and the scenery of Alaska."[32] It therefore seems strange that his view of the natural world darkened as he reflected on the dog-eat-dog nature of existence, insisting that "there is nothing kindly, nothing beneficent, nothing friendly in Nature toward any creature, except by capricious fits and starts; and that Nature's attitude toward all life is profoundly vicious, treacherous and malignant."[33] Even as he worked audiences into a storm of merriment, he faulted himself for ducking hard truths and accused himself of pandering and cowardice. "It is the strangest thing that the world is not full of books that scoff at the pitiful world, and the useless universe and violent, contemptible human race—books that laugh at the whole paltry scheme and deride it... Why don't *I* write such a book? Because I have a family. There is no other reason."[34] In time he would indeed write such a book.

Where the purpose of his trip was to talk, make money, and retire debt, it set his mind working on a broad range of subjects. A born autodidact, he could sound, in turn, like an amateur anthropologist, natural-

"CLOWN OF THE SEA"

ist, ethnologist, historian, and cultural critic. This man who never went to college was a perennial student who gorged himself on a steady diet of facts. A reporter spoke truly when he said Twain "can talk, to any extent, on almost any subject that may be started in his presence."[35] In his notebook, he gathered sweeping reflections on colonialism, patriotism, the American character, and Christian missionaries and unburdened himself on many controversial topics. "We easily perceive that the peoples furtherest [sic] from civilization are the ones where equality between man and woman are further apart—and we consider this one of the signs of savagery," he wrote while in New Zealand. "But we are so stupid that we can't see that we thus plainly admit that no civilization can be perfect until exact equality between man and woman is included."[36]

Twain was enamored of Christchurch, a town he found clean, orderly, and civilized. "It is a settled old community, with all the serenities, the graces, the conveniences, and the comforts of the ideal home-life."[37] It was a social time for the Clemens party, who were swamped with invitations for teas and receptions, and besieged with thirty-eight gifts from well-wishers, including flowers, candies, photographs, and a stuffed platypus, which Twain adored. The one thing marring their New Zealand stay was that the country could only be toured by small coastal steamers. After a few days in Christchurch, they had a nightmarish voyage aboard a ship called the *Flora*, which Twain branded a "floating pigstye," with accommodations more suitable for cattle than for people.[38] Because the ship was overbooked, travelers slept in passageways, on deck chairs, and curled up on tables. Stuck in a room with two strange women, Livy and Clara had to keep shaking cockroaches from their clothes. As for Twain, "I had a cattle-stall in the main stable—a cavern fitted up with a long double file of two-storied bunks" that "smelt like a kennel."[39] When he disembarked at Wellington, he prayed "with all my heart" that the ship "would sink at the dock."[40]

The crowds he drew were large and enthusiastic—a thousand per night in Auckland—but he was now threatened with the advent of a third carbuncle, this time in his armpit. By the time he reached Napier, he had to rest in his hotel bed for several days. The carbuncles were a curse that he

RAPIDS

couldn't shake and that left him feeling extremely dejected. Writing to Sue Crane, Livy also sounded blue. "Oh dear me! I wonder if we ever shall get our debts all paid, and live once more in our own house. To-day it seems to me as if we never should."[41] She was about to turn fifty, her husband sixty, and their future was still murky with uncertainty.

Later on, Twain confessed that when he departed on this tour, he was a "red-hot imperialist" who "wanted the American eagle to go screaming into the Pacific."[42] It was a moment when European imperial powers were carving up the globe. Since his trip covered British colonies, he had frequent opportunities to reflect on colonialism and stoutly believed that, if they had to be ruled by someone, Australia and India couldn't have found a better overlord than the British. But his views were changing, and his encounters with the Maori, an indigenous people in New Zealand, buttressed his nascent critique of imperialism. One day he visited a monument that commemorated twenty Maori who had died fighting alongside white colonizers against their own people. They were honored for defending "law & order against fanaticism & barbarism." Twain was appalled at the praise of Maori who had betrayed their own community to aid white settlers. "This is the most comical monument in the whole earth," he protested. "Try to imagine the humorless deeps of stupidity of the idiot who composed that inscription—& the dulness of the people who don't see the satire."[43] For Twain, the true message of the monument should have been, "Desert your flag, slay your people, burn their homes, shame your nationality—we honor such."[44]

Twain visited a dimly lit Maori council house full of beautiful carvings and also toured an exhibition of Maori artifacts in Christchurch. When a Dr. Hotchkin showed him his collection of Maori art, with pictures of past native chiefs, Twain wrote: "There is nothing of the savage in the faces; nothing could be finer than these men's features . . . nothing nobler than their aspect."[45] One can begin to see how Twain's sympathy for the underdog, so apparent in his writings on enslaved Americans, was now being generalized to repressed people elsewhere. All the while, he continued to mingle with well-to-do white people. Before leaving Australia, the Clemenses stayed in a swank home in the Melbourne sub-

"CLOWN OF THE SEA"

urbs. "I think it is one of the most superb ones that I was ever in . . . The hall is about twice the size of ours," Livy told her sister before making a telling comment about her husband. "Mr. Clemens is naturally perfectly happy entirely in his element. He was born for just this kind of luxury, I think."[46] It was, of course, that taste for luxury that had landed them in bankruptcy and made this trip necessary.

Steaming north into equatorial waters en route to Ceylon, the Clemens party traveled in grand style aboard the P&O steamer *Oceana,* an elegantly appointed ship where passengers dressed for dinner. Twain described the high-class scene: "Beautiful dresses, low necks, vivid colors, with the broad shield of the other sex's shirt-bosom, interspersed officer in uniform at the head of each table, electric light, richly decorated dining saloon."[47] Nonetheless, in torrid heat, the staterooms turned into ovens, and Clara had to sleep in a hatchway. Although Twain came down with yet another cold, he found time to rework his three speeches. As always aboard a ship, he enjoyed its tranquility and seclusion from the outside world despite a persistent cough and irritated throat. He studied wildlife that visited the ship, including a bald red vulture known as the jackass bird. "The very look of a professional assassin, and yet a bird which does no murder."[48] From the ship's railing, he watched porpoises sporting below in the Indian Ocean. "The porpoise is the clown of the sea—evidently does his wild antics for pure fun; there is no sordid profit in it."[49]

Amid the ship's calm atmosphere, Twain hazarded an experiment and renounced profanity—something Livy had long coveted. Then one morning he was in the bathroom when the ship lurched and shattered a tumbler he held, whereupon "I released my voice. Mrs. C. behind me in the door: 'Don't reform any more, it is not an improvement.'"[50] The story shows that Livy had a dry sense of humor, especially when teasing her adored but cantankerous husband.

Upon arriving in Colombo, the capital of Ceylon, Sam and Livy marveled at the rich profusion of colors and vegetation. For Twain the town satisfied his storybook conception of Asian splendor, and he hailed it as "most sumptuously tropical, as to character of foliage and opulence of it."[51] Livy echoed his enthusiasm, calling Colombo "the most fascinating, picturesque place" she had ever seen."[52] After checking into the Bristol Hotel, they explored the city and were entranced by the sensual beauty of the mostly barefoot residents. "The freedom and grace of these dark people, with their bronze like skins is an unceasing delight to the eye," Livy wrote home.[53] For her husband, too, it was a paradise marred only by the work of Christian missionaries. As he toured a market square, he stood dazzled by the "most amazing varieties of nakedness & color . . . Ingredients, a shining black body nine tenths naked & one of bright colored rags & you have the perfection of dress—grace, comeliness, convenience, comfort, beauty."[54] Only when he spotted a dozen Ceylonese girls dressed in the prim costumes of a missionary school did he find an "offensive discord."[55] His reaction reflected an evolving view of how colonial powers corrupted the purity of native cultures, and it wiped away any residual belief that he retained about the superiority of white people. The encounter of East and West only served to intensify his distaste for aspects of his own culture and civilization.

Twain, never blind to poverty, reacted with sympathy to the human suffering he saw. For the first time in his life, he drove in a two-wheeled rickshaw, pulled by a thin man whose plight moved him. "After the half-hour there is no more pleasure for you; your attention is all on the man, just as it would be on a tired horse, and necessarily your sympathy is there too."[56] Clara recalled her father stating that "he was disturbed by the feeling that it was wicked for one man to be drawing another, even though he got paid for it."[57]

Unable to lecture in Colombo due to a cold, Twain booked passage for Bombay aboard an aging wreck of a vessel, the *Rosetta*. "This is a poor old ship," he concluded, "and ought to be insured and sunk."[58] For the three-day voyage, Twain with his cold remained in his broiling cabin, while Livy and Clara enjoyed sleeping on mattresses on deck. It was a weird inversion of the usual family situation: Twain was chroni-

"CLOWN OF THE SEA"

cally sick while Livy, the supposed invalid, was doing fine despite occasional hardships.

No sooner did the Clemenses arrive at Watson's Hotel in Bombay (today Mumbai) than Twain contracted yet another cold—likely his chronic bronchitis from smoking. "Been shut up all the time with this infernal cough," he ranted in his notebook. "It does not improve. I wish I was in hell."[59] The hotel summoned a doctor, who diagnosed a fever and bronchial cough, and prescribed a host of useless medicines. As usual, Twain thought he was being royally bilked by a venal physician. "He charged me double price per visitation because I was not a resident. I paid half the bill."[60] For the next six weeks, Twain said he had to "bark" at audiences before "the cough expired by statute of limitation."[61]

Because of his ailment, Twain postponed his initial lecture for several days. Always a light, easily irritated sleeper, he had to endure an infernal racket that started at five each morning—"equal to a riot, an insurrection, for noise."[62] While Livy and Clara roamed the city, Twain's first impressions of Bombay were limited to what he glimpsed from his window, including a "juggler in his turban," standing under a shade tree "with his snakes and his magic."[63] The most revealing moment came inside the hotel when an Indian employee got down on his knees to clean a glazed door to the balcony. His boss, a "burly German," chided his work and gave him "a brisk cuff on the jaw and *then* told him where the defect was ... The native took it with meekness, saying nothing, and not showing in his face or manner any resentment." Unexpectedly, Twain experienced a powerful flashback to his Missouri boyhood and the brutality inflicted upon Blacks. "I had not seen the like of this for fifty years" and had forgotten "that this was the *usual* way of explaining one's desires to a slave. I was able to remember that the method seemed right and natural to me in those days ... but I was also able to remember that those unresented cuffings made me sorry for the victim and ashamed for the punisher."[64] Following this train of thought, he remembered how his father, "a sternly just and upright man," had "cuffed our harmless slave boy, Lewis, for trifling little blunders and awkwardnesses."[65] Twain was reminded anew of the power of memory to vanquish time, thrusting him back to his "Missourian village, on the other side of the globe, vividly seeing again these forgotten pictures of fifty years ago."[66] The episode highlighted Twain's growing awareness that the methods of slaveholders in America and imperial colonists abroad were based on a similar power dynamic, informed by the same unexamined racial prejudices.

Finally liberated from his hotel room, Twain was beguiled by the romance of Bombay. "*Bombay!* A bewitching place, a bewildering place, an enchanting place—the Arabian Nights come again!"[67] He was hypnotized by the spectacle of streets brimming with people, and he lost himself in the booths of a great bazaar with its "sea of rich-colored turbans and draperies."[68] At the train station, he stared agog at the swirling, turbulent masses of "rainbow-costumed natives" swept along in the rush.[69] Although he devoted overheated passages to India, he also realized that his views were tinged by storybook images that he had carried since boyhood.[70] Soon enough, when his prose cooled off, he dwelled on the colossal poverty. With India "everything is on a giant scale—even her poverty; no other country can show anything to compare with it."[71]

Twain repeatedly commented on the beautiful skin color of the people. One day he was invited to meet a turbaned delegation of Jains, drawn from many sections of the country, leading him to comment on the inferiority of white complexions. "It is not an unbearably unpleasant complexion when it keeps to itself, but when it comes into competition with masses of brown and black the fact is betrayed that it is endurable only because we are used to it. Nearly all black and brown skins are beautiful, but a beautiful white skin is rare." It was remarkable how Twain surrendered any notion of white Anglo-Saxon or European superiority and discovered so much to appreciate in races thought to be inferior. "Where dark complexions are massed they make the whites look bleached-out, unwholesome, and sometimes frankly ghastly. I could notice that as a boy, down South in the slavery days before the war."[72]

Still struggling with his cough, Twain had to postpone a luncheon invitation from the governor of Bombay. By contrast, Livy, usually so frail, was a whirlwind of energy, telling Sue Crane that Bombay was "the *most* fascinating place I have seen . . . Social life and sightseeing *all* the

"CLOWN OF THE SEA"

time—breakfasts, lunches, teas, dinners, balls."[73] For Twain's initial lecture, all of Bombay's upper-echelon citizens packed the Novelty Theatre and greeted his stories with "round after round of loud, prolonged and enthusiastic applause."[74] Speaking in a palace a week later, Twain noted that the Maharani listened behind a screen while outside the window "three long gray apes capered across the road" as well as a "train of laden camels."[75]

With his anthropological curiosity, Twain visited a Parsee funeral site known as the Towers of Silence. Only people bearing corpses could enter this consecrated ground, where vultures perched on tower rims, awaiting their prey. Once the bearers left the dead bodies behind, Twain wrote, "the ring of vultures rose, flapping their wings, and swooped down into the Tower to devour the body. Nothing was left of it but a clean-picked skeleton when they flocked out again a few minutes afterward." After a month of exposure to the elements, the parched skeletons were tossed down a well. Far from being horrified, Twain endorsed this ghoulish process and found it sanitary, "a perfect system for the protection of the living from the contagion derivable from the dead," and he commented approvingly on cremation at home for similar reasons.[76] There was a humility to Twain's approach on the tour. If seen as the archetypal American, he was not there to proselytize for his own culture, but to imbibe lessons from others.

As the tour moved on to Allahabad in Uttar Pradesh, Twain experienced both extremes of Indian society. After staying with an eastern prince, he thanked his host by saying "the grace & beauty & dignity of it realized to us the pictures which we had long ago fathered from books of travel & oriental tales."[77] At the same time, he retained a keen eye for downtrodden Indians. He saw a "parched land sown thick with mud villages in all stages of crumbling decay. It is a sorrowful land—a land of unimaginable poverty & hardship."[78] His appetite for Indian experience was omnivorous. When the group left for Benares, he said in his notebook: "Thought this would all become commonplace in a week: 3 weeks of it have only enhanced its fascinations."[79]

The limits of Twain's tolerance grew clear in the holy city of Benares (today Varanasi), where the Hindu faithful bathed in the Ganges. He and his family took several boat trips along the river, shaded by an awning as they observed shrines and temples lining the shores. It was here that Twain's cynicism toward Indian religion as a profitable racket for some began to emerge. He saw priests on the Ganges preying on the pilgrims who poured in. "A good stand is worth a world of money. The holy proprietor of it sits under his grand spectacular umbrella and blesses people all his life, and collects his commission, and grows fat and rich."[80] Of the holy river water that supposedly purified souls, Twain found only pollution, rank and revolting. Of one temple he wrote: "You pass in by a stone image of the monkey god, Hanuman, and there, among the ruined courtyards, you will find a shallow pool of stagnant sewage. It smells like the best limburger cheese, and is filthy with the washings of rotting lepers."[81] At another place he noted, "the foul gush from a sewer was making the water turbid and murky all around, and there was a random corpse slopping around in it that had floated down from up country."[82]

After Benares and another cold, Twain was confined to his hotel in Calcutta (now Kolkata), where he tried to "starve out" the cold by not eating—a pet theory of his. Livy and Clara continued to floor him with their perpetual energy as they went "gadding around and dissipating socially."[83] When Twain recuperated and investigated Calcutta, he was the guest of honor at a private dinner thrown by the lieutenant-governor of Bengal. However contradictory it seemed with his mounting anti-imperialist views, Twain was full of enthusiasm for the British Empire at this time. Interviewed by a Calcutta newspaper, the *Englishman*, he burst forth with bombastic statements about the benefits Britain bestowed on India, "whether the Hindus or Mohamedans like it or not."[84] Nor was that all: he thought the British had a right to rule around the world. "It is my belief that in the development of the world the strongest race will by and by become paramount—the strongest physically and intellectually. Now if we look round upon the nations we find that the English [race] seems to possess both these qualifications. It has spread all over the earth. It is vigorous, prolific, and enterprising. Above all it is composed of merciful people, the best kind of people for colonizing the

"CLOWN OF THE SEA"

globe."[85] This idealized view of the British Empire, of course, clashed with numerous satirical things Twain had written about the British monarchy and aristocracy.

His attitude also ran counter to the cruelty of the class system he observed and the docility inculcated into servants. He noted that employers never bothered to make provision for servants eating or sleeping. "The servant lies by your door nights, on the stone floor," Twain noted.[86] Livy was also indignant at their inhumane treatment. "When you walk onto a porch . . . you are likely to stumble over a servant that is rolled up like a cocoon by your door."[87] Twain monitored his two servants with a mixture of affection and exasperation, especially when they helped with his three packed lectures in Calcutta. "Barney is slow & not sure, Mausie is quick & not sure. Barney was to put a glass of water on my stage-table. He seemed to understand perfectly after I had explained (behind the scenes) four times & pointed to the stage. What he finally did was to put a vast empty glass on the stage & a full one behind the scenes."[88]

Curiously enough, in an interview with a Calcutta newspaper, Twain had a kind word for Native Americans—a group for whom he had rarely shown much tolerance. The interviewer asked why Indians in Canada had peaceful relations with their government, while American Indians had "continual rows" with theirs. Twain laid the blame squarely on the white man. "In the States we shut them off into a reservation, which we frequently encroached upon." Bloodshed had resulted between Indians and settlers. "If an Indian kills a white man he is sure to lose his life, but if a white man kills a red skin he never suffers according to law."[89]

In India, Twain was genuinely fond of the locals, whom he found a gentle and fascinating, if often baffling, people. When his family traveled to Darjeeling, in the Himalayan foothills, he stared in amazement from the train window at hundreds of closely crowded villages, shaded by palms and bamboo, a seemingly interminable tide of humanity. In his notebook, he printed in capital letters, "INDIA THE MARVELOUS" and added, "Ah, *this* is India. Tropical, beautiful & just *alive* with villages!"[90] Clara had never seen her father submit to such youthful enthusiasm. The Clemenses sped across the muddy landscape in comfort, the railway company having put the directors' car, equipped with easy chairs and sofas, at their disposal. As they sat down for tea and cake, two servants stood at attention behind them.

When they ascended a steep mountain to Darjeeling, the trip took seven or eight hours, but they were surrounded by wonders as they wound among cliffs and chasms, with Twain exclaiming, "What a world of variegated vegetation!—and ribbony roads squirming and snaking, cream-yellow over the rounded hills below."[91] Once on Darjeeling's high plateau, Livy yielded to dreamy thoughts, writing to her youngest daughter: "Jean Darling: Look on the map, and try to realize that we who belong to you are away up here in the Himalayas . . . I cannot myself feel that it can be true."[92] She noted with disbelief her unwonted energy: they rose at six each morning and went to bed at midnight, yet she scarcely needed naps. In Darjeeling, Twain spoke at a club frequented by British officers and colonial administrators, but spent the rest of his time sitting at the hotel window, smoking his pipe and watching the sun sparkle on snow-clad mountains.

In Agra, the Clemenses enjoyed ideal conditions for viewing the Taj Mahal. When they arrived before midnight, there was a full moon soon obscured by a total lunar eclipse—"an attention," Twain quipped, "not before offered to a stranger since the Taj was built."[93] In fact, Twain found the Taj a disappointment, the victim of the sort of hyperbole that he had ridiculed in *The Innocents Abroad*. The problem was not that he didn't find it beautiful; it was simply that nothing could match his preconceived image. "My Taj had been built by excitable literary people; it was solidly lodged in my head, and I could not blast it out."[94]

More moving than his reaction to the Taj was his description of the firing of his servant Mousa, who suffered from an incurable drinking problem. When Twain told him that his services would end at seven o'clock that evening, "He laid his fingers against his forehead as usual, made the usual inclination, gently said—'Wair good' (very good) just as he always does when receiving an order and that was all. Turned and went about his errand. In his noiseless bare feet—it was pathetic. Was it Indian fatalism which accepts without murmur whatever the two million gods send, or had he had this experience so often that it no longer affects him?"[95] It was typical of Twain's contradictory nature that even as he enjoyed elite company, he could still identify with the predicament of the poor and dispossessed.

At Jaipur, Twain found himself sick yet again and at the mercy of another cursed doctor. "He made me cancel a week's engagements and shut myself in my room and rest. Said he would not be responsible for the consequences if I didn't."[96] Twain had a mysterious tingling sensation in his left hand and arm that alarmed his family. Because of his medical problems, he delivered only a fraction of the lectures scheduled for India, and locals warned him not to linger as the deadly summer months approached. As a result, the Clemenses decided to leave India at the end of March, and fearful for her husband's health, Livy insisted that he end the tour in South Africa altogether.

In Jaipur, Livy had an experience that made her realize how exotic she was to the locals. She visited a museum that allowed only women to visit before noon and found the place "packed full of these brilliantly dressed ladies. The only trouble was that I was as great a curiosity to them as they were to me. They crowded about me and chattered & examined me, & followed me about. I would get behind cases & get into other rooms to try to get away, but always without success."[97]

Touring Lahore, the capital of the Punjab, Twain had a chance to mount an elephant owned by the lieutenant-governor—"a fine elephant, affable, gentlemanly, educated," he said—and steer it through the teeming streets of the city.[98] He loved watching children and horses leap out of the way as he barreled along atop the huge animal. "I am used to being afraid of collisions when I ride or drive, but when one is on top of an elephant that feeling is absent . . . I could easily learn to prefer an elephant to any other vehicle, partly because of that immunity from collisions, and partly because of the fine view one has from up there, and partly because one can look in at the windows and see what is going on privately among the family."[99]

While in Rawalpindi, Twain entered into conversation with a British general that showed his compliments about the British Empire may have been mostly for public consumption. The general told him that half the hospital beds in India were filled with young British soldiers with venereal disease. Twain was simply astounded that authorities had allowed this situation to flourish. "By all accounts," he fumed in his notebook, "England is the home of pious cant; & cant of a most harmful sort." He couldn't believe that the British didn't ensure that clean women, "subject to rigid inspection," were available to soldiers to satisfy their natural passion.[100] (Of course, British soldiers could have dated Indian women, but that would have been considered racially taboo.) Unwilling to entertain honest conversations about sex, British officialdom left soldiers to their own devices, with disastrous results. "Then these 70,000 men go home & marry fresh young English girls & transmit a heritage of disease to their children & grandchildren."[101] It was a rare occasion where Twain spoke frankly about sex and venereal disease, and may explain why he had not been more sexually adventurous as a young man in those riotous western towns.

When he had traveled down the Hooghly River to Calcutta, Twain had another blinding flashback to his boyhood. On the six-hour journey, he found the broad river, with its low, wooded banks, almost indistinguishable from the Mississippi. Only the "cocoa trees & mud villages" brought him back to Indian reality. But the resemblance went beyond similar geography, for the power structure displayed was disturbingly similar. There would be a great white-columned European house, reminiscent of the dwellings of Mississippi and Louisiana planters, while a "thatched group of native houses" conjured up "the negro quarter familiar to me near 40 y[ear]s ago—& so for 6 hours this has been the sugar coast & the Missi[ss]ippi.[102] For all his favorable view of the British Empire, this unjust world was bottomed on a racial hierarchy that Twain knew all too well.

In late March, the Clemens family sailed from Calcutta on the SS *Wardha,* and Twain luxuriated in four peaceful weeks at sea as they moved west toward Mauritius and South Africa. "There is nothing like this serenity," he said, "this comfort, this peace, this deep contentment, to be found anywhere on land."[103] He was Huck again adrift on the raft.

"CLOWN OF THE SEA"

He had time to dip into esoteric subjects, poring over Sir John Lubbock's book on the habits of ants. He found that the ship, with its deck games and knots of chatting people, called to mind "a big summer hotel."[104] His wife and daughter were much less charmed, with Livy bothered by the hot, dry winds that bit into her face, and Clara again revolted by cockroaches "large as mice & more familiar."[105] In consequence, Livy and Clara slept on deck every night.

In this interval of leisure, Twain occupied his mind with many topics that would dominate his final years. After hearing a shipboard sermon, a dose of the old-time religion, he trained his critical faculties on Christianity and mocked the notion of Christ sacrificing His life for humanity. "If Christ was God, then the crucifixion is without dignity. It is merely ridiculous, for to endure several hours' pain is nothing heroic in God, in any case."[106] He pointed out that "every girl takes a risk superior to that when she marries & subjects herself to the probable pains of childbirth indefinitely repeated."[107]

Both Livy and Clara believed that turning sixty had hurled Twain into a state of depression, especially since he didn't believe he would ever regain the old Hartford life or any sense of freedom about money. Feeling a dark undercurrent of doubt, Livy was no less despondent about the future, telling Sue Crane that she didn't expect to reclaim the Farmington Avenue house for a long time. "You know I have a pretty good courage, but sometimes it comes over me like an overwhelming wave, that it is to be bitterness and disappointment to the end."[108] She had a poignant dream that summed up her mingled sense of longing and foreboding about returning to Hartford. "I dreamed the other night of going to Hartford," she told Alice Hooker Day, "and taking a room in a boarding house in Farmington Avenue."[109] The one lasting thing that Sam and Livy possessed seemed to be their three smart, beautiful daughters. For that reason, Livy was deeply shaken to learn that her friend Harriet E. Whitmore had lost a child. From the SS *Wardha* she wrote in condolence: "How entirely unaccountable it all is! Why, Why—we must constantly ask—are we allowed to love and rear these children and then have to sit by helpless when they are taken away from us."[110]

CHAPTER THIRTY-FIVE

"Circumnavigation of This Great Globe"

As they steamed west toward South Africa, the Clemens party was relieved to be fast approaching the final leg of their tour. "We feel now the back of our journey is broken," Livy wrote home, "and that we are starting toward home at least toward England which will be so much nearer home."[1] When they landed at Durban, on the Indian Ocean, Livy was disappointed to find no letter from Susy, which gave her a vague premonition of something amiss.

During their first night at a Durban hotel, Twain, as usual, was driven to distraction by early morning noise, this time from "crowing roosters" that "heartlessly serenaded" them.[2] The man who made audiences laugh around the world again sank into a funk, said Livy, convinced "we must all our lives live in poverty . . . The platform he likes for the two hours that he is on it, but all the rest of the time it grinds him, and he says he is ashamed of what he is doing."[3] This same worry had oppressed Twain in his early days on the lecture circuit, when he feared he was a mere vaudevillian, dispensing jokes rather than solid wisdom.

As in India, Twain was startled that the presence of so many familiar Black faces transported him back to his upbringing. "Some of the blacks have the long horse-heads & the very long chins of the negroes of our Southern States—round faces, flat noses, good-natured, & easy laughers."[4] As he watched Black couples strolling along, their faces and dress made it easy to "imagine myself in Texas."[5] There was, as always, a palpable warmth when Twain spoke of Blacks, and he was sharply aware of the inequities visited on them. "Natives must not be out after the curfew bell without a pass," he noted. "In Natal there are ten blacks to one white."[6]

Speaking to capacity crowds in Durban, Twain retailed his usual repertoire of stories, except that he now added a fresh target to his satirical lineup: doctors. "They always cure the disease they are dealing with—and leave you with another," he told the audience.[7] After several speeches, Twain left Livy and Clara in Durban—he wanted to spare them a lengthy train journey—and headed west to Pietermaritzburg along with lecture agent Carlyle G. Smythe, who had developed into a great family favorite. Clara labeled him "a most attractive companion" who had catered to their needs on tour and made sure everything ran smoothly.[8]

Despite their extended separation, Sam and Livy maintained close contact by mail, with Livy prodding him that "Youth Darling . . . you must continue to miss me & to think that you do not get on as well without me as you do with."[9] She plied him with advice on lectures and told him to make sure they were long enough so audiences felt "they have had the worth of their money."[10] Sam reciprocated her tenderness. "It is pretty lonesome without you, dear heart; I miss you all the time. By & by we'll be together again."[11] Absentminded by nature, he admitted that, bereft of Livy's secretarial skills, he was prone to commit social blunders. "I think I have engaged myself to lunch with 2 different crowds at 1 o'clock today. This would not have happened if you had been there."[12]

The next stop on Twain's tour was the gold-bearing region of the Rand, where he faced a demanding schedule: seven lectures in Johannesburg and three in Pretoria. Twain was overwhelmed with interview requests at his Johannesburg hotel, and on his first morning there, he entertained reporters while propped up by pillows in bed. He got more publicity than he could possibly have wanted, for he had arrived at a fraught moment in South African politics. On December 29, 1895, Leander Starr Jameson had led a group of six hundred volunteers and British South Africa Police on a raid into the Transvaal. Cecil Rhodes, prime minister of the Cape Colony and Britain's foremost imperialist in Africa, had worked to instigate the incursion with the aim of toppling the Boer government of President Paul Kruger. Boers promptly captured the raiders, who were turned over to Britain for punishment, and Kruger's government jailed Johannesburg citizens who had sympathized with them.

With scant understanding of the convoluted politics of the conflict, Twain, straight from India and at the height of his pro-British sympathies, naturally sided with the raiders and gave them the friendly appellation of Reformers. He likened them to American revolutionaries fighting at Lexington and Concord. He met with a Missouri friend, Natalie Harris Hammond, who had married John Hays Hammond, an American mining engineer who had supervised British gold-mining interests in South Africa and was arrested after the raid. Escorted by Mrs. Hammond, Twain decided to visit the fifty political prisoners.

"A Boer guard was at my elbow all the time," Twain wrote, but "was courteous and polite."[13] John Hays Hammond stepped forward to grasp his hand, saying, "Mr. Clemens, I'm certainly glad to see you again. How did you ever find your way into this God-forsaken hole?" "Getting into jail is easy," Twain responded. "I thought the difficulties arose when it came to getting out."[14] Hammond introduced the prisoners to Twain, who addressed them in a sun-struck courtyard where he sat in his white linen suit on a dry-goods box. He delivered a droll chat that if funny in another context proved tone-deaf in this one. Twain summarized the gist in his notebook: "Explained to the prisoners why they were better off in jail than they would be anywhere else; that they would eventually have gotten into jail anyhow, for one thing or another, no doubt; that if they got out they would get in again; that it would be better all around if they remained quietly where they were and made the best of it; that after a few months they would prefer the jail and its luxurious indolence to the sordid struggle for bread outside; and that I would do everything I could, short of bribery, to get the government to double their jails terms."[15] He pointed out that John Bunyan might never have written *Pilgrim's Progress* nor Cervantes *Don Quixote* had it not been for satisfying stretches in prison.

It was typical Twain tomfoolery, and his intentions were benign: he wanted to entertain and cheer up imprisoned men. Nevertheless, he had woefully miscalculated their mood—one prisoner had just slit his throat in despair—and misread the incendiary political moment. After he left the prison, a reporter inquired if the prisoners were badly treated, and Twain said he didn't think so. "As a matter of fact," he volunteered, "a great many of these gentlemen have fared far worse in the hotels and mining-camps of the West."[16] Seizing on this flippant comment, a Boer editorial insisted on more stringent treatment of the prisoners, and President Kruger responded with punitive measures, abruptly slashing their rations. "The privations, already severe enough, were considerably augmented by [Twain's] remark," said John Hays Hammond, "and it required some three or four days' search on the part of some of our friends . . . to get hold of Mark Twain and have him go and explain to Kruger that it was all a joke."[17]

Twain was prevailed upon to meet with Paul Kruger, a rugged old man who smoked a long pipe and wore a silk hat. "He was exactly as I had fancied him," said Twain. "He treated me very graciously, and I had a long talk with him."[18] Despite Kruger's "bad cold & a very husky voice," the two men chatted constructively, and Twain explained that his comments about prison conditions were meant to be humorous. By early June, virtually all the prisoners would be fined and released. By then Twain had begun to concede privately to Livy that the "leading Reformers were accessories" to the illegal raid.[19] A year later, in London, Twain wrote approvingly of a parliamentary committee that condemned the raid. "It was a shabby and trivial episode," Twain concluded, "and all the heroics have vanished out of it."[20]

While in Pretoria, on a Sunday, Twain recorded vignettes of life among the religious Boers, evoking the "deep Sunday stillness," which he characterized as "the Puritan Sabbath of two centuries ago come back to the earth again."[21] He believed the Boers had stolen land from the Black population and mocked their self-righteous show of superiority over them, including their prohibition on "native" marriages, rendering their offspring illegitimate. "And yet the Boers are *so* pious! The natives hate the Boers—& well they may."[22] So familiar were the Black faces

"CIRCUMNAVIGATION OF THIS GREAT GLOBE"

from his boyhood that it seemed strange to Twain that he couldn't converse with them in English. "The voices, too, of the African women, were familiar to me—sweet and musical, just like those of the slave women of my early days."[23] He added that "I followed a couple of them a mile to listen to the music of their speech & the happy ripple of their laugh."[24] It should be said that Twain depicted the Blacks with a fair number of racist clichés and pejorative language. They were good-natured, cheerful, and friendly, but also dirty and indolent. Still, he had far more affection for them than for their white overseers, calling the Boer "a white savage, who is dirty; houses himself like a cow; is indolent, worships a fetich [sic]; is grim, serious, solemn, and is always diligently fitting himself for heaven, probably suspecting that they couldn't stand him in the other place."[25]

In defending the British role in South Africa, Twain resorted to absurdly tortured reasoning. He thought that Great Britain, as the superior civilization, was destined to exert hegemony over the Black population at the same time that he deplored the brutal methods Cecil Rhodes and "his gang" adopted to attain this. "They are chartered to rob and slay, and they lawfully do it, but not in a compassionate and Christian spirit. They rob the Mashonas and the Matabeles of a portion of their territories in the hallowed old style of 'purchase' for a song, and then they force a quarrel and take the rest by the strong hand."[26] It was not clear what for Twain a "humane" version of this process would have looked like or why a country that practiced such rapacity deserved to rule over the native population being plundered.

Whatever horror he expressed about the political situation in southern Africa, Twain was thoroughly enchanted by the climate and landscape. Of the elevated, treeless plateau of the veldt, he said that clothed in "its sober winter garb" it was "as beautiful as Paradise."[27] He left wonderful descriptions of the rolling land, "its pale brown deepening by delicately graduated shades to rich orange and finally to purple and crimson where it washed against the wooded hills and naked red crags at the base of the sky."[28] He seemed no less intoxicated as he toured the Orange Free State and found it "ecstasy, to breathe the divine air," while passing through a landscape "made of dream-stuff & flushed with colors faint & rich."[29] He was so invigorated by the climate that he felt refreshed on the lecture stage despite the long distances to get there.

After arriving in Cape Colony, Twain informed Livy that he thought he could get the job of U.S. consul at Johannesburg for a year. "I might make a fortune, I might not. But a Consul there must have mighty good chances."[30] Livy didn't care to prolong their exile from home and sent back a succinct refusal: "No, Colonel."[31] Stuck in Port Elizabeth, Livy found separation from her husband unbearable and prayed it would be the last time. On June 17, they were reunited in the Eastern Cape, and Livy hoped that, within a month, they would be back in England with Susy and Jean. Even after the globe-trotting tour, she still felt bowed beneath the weight of the sizable debt. "Of course Mr. Clemens feels that he must make all the money that he can, for we *long* so to be out of the bondage of debt," she told Sue Crane. "It seems as if we should have to work a long, *very* long time yet before we should be free. Forty or fifty thousand dollars is a very large sum to try to earn."[32] She knew Langdon Coal was swimming in debt and she might be liable for any losses. Far from feeling triumphant, Twain, in a fatalistic mood, thought himself cursed and doomed. "I don't think it is of any use for me to struggle against my ill luck any longer," he confessed to Rogers. "If I had the family in a comfortable poorhouse I would kill myself."[33]

Stung by life's injustices, Twain set down some of his most bitter ruminations on the Judeo-Christian God, who he thought enforced a selfish bargain in which He asked for worship in exchange for conferring benefits. Of his ideal God, he wrote: "He would not stoop to *ask* for any man's compliments, praises, flatteries; and He would be far above *exacting* them . . . He would not be a merchant, a trader. He would not buy these things. He would not sell, or offer to sell, temporary benefits or the joys of eternity for the product called worship."[34] He wanted a God motivated by Love and giving freely of that love, not one imposing Original Sin upon humanity or terrifying visions of hell.

Twain couldn't resist an invitation to inspect the original Kimberley diamond mine, housed in a crater "roomy enough to admit the Roman Coliseum," as well as the vast De Beers works that processed eight thousand carloads of earth daily to extract three pounds of diamonds.[35] He met with African workers who stayed in the De Beers compound for three-month stints and, for security reasons, couldn't leave during that time. "They are a jolly and good-natured lot, and accommodating," Twain wrote breezily in *Following the Equator*. "They performed a war-dance for us, which was the wildest exhibition I have ever seen."[36] However, he noted the sad irony of impoverished workers handling such large fortunes. "Young girls were doing the sorting—a nice, clean, dainty, and probably distressing employment. Every day ducal incomes sift and sparkle through the fingers of those young girls; yet they go to bed at night as poor as they were when they got up in the morning."[37] In the privacy of his notebook, Twain took a much darker view of the whole operation and recorded shockingly racist things that white managers told him. One English railroad magnate said, "We claim the right to deal with our servants" (slaves) "as we think expedient."[38] The manager of a large mine was no less brutal: "We don't *call* our blacks slaves, but that is what they *are,* & that is what we mean they shall remain."[39] Of Cecil Rhodes, Twain noted that while many people thought he should have been hanged thirty years ago, he found this "an over-severe judgment; but if you make it twenty-nine & a half, I am with you."[40]

The tour ended in July with four speeches in Cape Town, and at the final one on July 13, Twain struck an appropriate note of laughter by pointing out the remarkable parallel that he had started the tour in Elmira on July 13, 1895, by addressing seven hundred men who made their mark in the world—just like his audience tonight. "There is one little point I must not forget to mention," he added, "which is that my first audience was—in a penitentiary. But there the comparison ends. For while those men are expiating their crimes, the gentlemen in front of me have not even commenced to repent of theirs."[41]

On July 15, accompanied by Livy and Clara, Twain sailed to England aboard the *Norman* after a yearlong tour that he had managed to

RAPIDS

complete despite harrowing pain. "I was never very well," he told Major Pond, "from the first night in Cleveland to the last one in Cape Town... I did a good deal of talking when I ought to have been in bed."[42] As for retiring the Webster & Company debt, the tour had been, at best, a partial success. Twain had nursed daydreams of clearing $100,000 from his lectures, freeing him from $40,000 in debt, but his constant ailments had meant many canceled appearances, reducing his take to between $20,000 and $30,000. Then, in October, Miss Harrison, the formidable secretary of Henry Rogers, sent him a distressing financial statement. "I find now," he wrote to Rogers, "that my debt was nearer $70,000 than $40,000. In which case I need not dream of paying it. I never could manage it."[43] The heroic rhetoric of the lecture tour was deflated in an instant.

On the *Norman*, Twain reveled in his respite from the lecture stage. "Father luxuriated in cigars and books all the way from Africa to England," Clara recalled, "and we thought of nothing but the pleasure of seeing Susy and Jean again. They were to be brought to London by the faithful maid, Katie, early in August."[44] Livy notified Sue Crane that she should be ready to start Susy and Jean on their transatlantic journey the second week of August, by which point they would be settled in England. When the ship slipped into the pier at Southampton, Twain reflected that he had departed from that very pier fifteen months earlier. "It seemed a fine and large thing to have accomplished—the circumnavigation of this great globe in that little time, and I was privately proud of it. For a moment."[45]

Back in his early days as a printer's devil in Hannibal, young Sam Clemens had reportedly snatched a stray page of a biography of Joan of Arc, kicking about in a windy street. As it happened, the passage in question appealed to his chivalric instincts and lifelong fixation on chaste teenage girls on the eve of adulthood. It described the virginal Joan imprisoned in Rouen, where two English captors stole her clothes and taunted her,

"CIRCUMNAVIGATION OF THIS GREAT GLOBE"

while she defended herself with dignity. The chance finding was the catalyst for Twain's lifelong, voracious passion for Joan, French history, and history in general. Sometime in the early 1880s, he began reading the official transcript of the "Trials and Rehabilitation of Joan of Arc," which he lauded as the "most thrilling historical document he had ever read."[46] Before it was first published in the 1840s, Joan had been relegated to the realm of romance, not history. For a dozen years, Twain pored sedulously over so many books about Joan, both in French and English, that he became an amateur authority on the subject, scouring musty bookshops and library shelves. He told of "piles of dusty reference books" that he amassed and the "chaos of letters, manuscripts, notebooks" that surrounded him as he wrote.[47] As Clara remembered, "For years, around the dinner table he talked and talked about the character and feats of Joan, until it became a family joke that 'Papa loves two women—Mamma in the present, and Joan retrospectively.'"[48] Twain also loved writing about the Middle Ages, where he could record the antique rhetoric and quaint manners of the time.

For Livy and her daughters, Twain's novel on Joan of Arc would embody the "fine" literature that they had longed for Father to write, a way to live down his reputation as a mere humorist. It even had a female protagonist. Amid the Webster & Company and Paige typesetter debacles, Susy's depression, and European exile, Joan bound the family in an inspirational circle. "Papa is progressing finely with his Joan of Arc which promises to be his loveliest book," Susy told Clara in February 1892. "Perhaps even more sweet and beautiful than the *Prince and the Pauper*. The character of Joan is pure and perfect to a miraculous degree. Hearing the M.S. read aloud is an uplifting and revealing hour to us all."[49] Twain would even credit Susy with having been a partial inspiration for the central character. With *Joan*, Livy and her daughters could share wholeheartedly in Father's writing. When he read aloud from it, Susy would jump up and say, "Wait, wait till I get a handkerchief."[50] During these readings, according to Grace King, Livy's "great eyes shone with emotion and admiration."[51] Surrounded by such rapt listeners, Twain was not likely to question his idealized portrait of the Maid of Orleans.

As shown in the "Golden Arm" episode at Bryn Mawr, Susy had grown militant in her belief that her father should move beyond the coarse, rustic humor of Mark Twain. "How I hate that name!" she said in fall 1892, while her father wrote *Joan of Arc* at Villa Viviani. "I should like never to hear it again! . . . He should not be known by it! He should show himself the great writer that he is, not merely a funny man."[52] In writing about Joan, Twain, too, wished to overcome the confining image of a humorist. The problem was that in trying to tamp down his own unruly, rambunctious side, Twain would suppress what was most singular about his work.

At times, Twain professed that the book was a labor of love and pretended that he didn't care about sales, yet he could hardly afford such aristocratic indifference to money and was, in reality, preoccupied with potential sales. Early on, Howells told him that the book's success could equal that of *Ben-Hur*. "He says the presses that print Ben Hur are not idle any day in the year," Twain relayed to Livy. "I believe the sale long ago rivaled that of Uncle Tom's Cabin."[53] The book's commercial prospects expanded in his mind until he fancied a potential bestseller in the making. "All the signs of the times show that a year hence Joan of Arc will be *the* commanding conspicuous figure in the current literatures of the world," he insisted to Livy.[54]

In discussing the novel's serialization with J. Henry Harper, the editor of *Harper's Magazine*, Twain said he wished to disguise his authorship, lest readers expect laughter and feel betrayed. He feared "it would be defrauding my public to have my name associated with it in serial form."[55] In many ways, he explained, he had become a captive of his image, so that when he rose to deliver an after-dinner speech, "the guests are all on the verge of laughter before I begin."[56] This became a growing problem as he wished to deal with serious subjects that engrossed his attention and lay outside the well-known orbit of his earlier writings. He regretted that from the outset of his career he had not established two pen names: one for humorous writing, another for graver work. It was agreed that the magazine serialization and even the subsequent book by Harper & Brothers would not bear his name on the title page. He worked out an arrangement for an improved royalty if his nom de plume were later attached to the work. In the meantime, the imposture would be maintained that the book was "freely translated out of the ancient French" by "Jean François Alden."[57]

That Twain had a powerful connection with Joan is transparent in his prose. Susy said he shed tears whenever he read Joan's words, and he was more than a little in love with this young woman who fulfilled his fantasy of female purity. Shapely and pretty, she was an adolescent girl raised to a higher power, a virgin poised on the delicate line separating girlhood from womanhood. With *Joan,* Twain set aside his worldly cynicism and wrote in worshipful terms, making no attempt to debunk her saintly nature. His searing skepticism about religion vanished as he venerated a young woman guided by voices and visions from God. To some extent, he tried to salvage his religious skepticism by vilifying the "English-French priests" who burned Joan at the stake and by fulminating against the contemporary Catholic Church for seeking to confer on Joan "a tinsel saintship—a girl who was *born* a saint & never was anything else till she died."[58]

Twain stood in awe of Joan's battlefield prowess and uncanny ability to parry questions from her learned inquisitors at trial. "Only one human being has lived in this world whose merits are beyond the reach of over-praise—Joan of Arc," he wrote. "When we praise other heroes, there are limits beyond which we cannot go & not strain the truth, but with her it is not so. She was finer than any words can convey; she was nobler than the noblest words can set forth; she was greater than any standard of greatness that can be framed in speech."[59] In the margins of a source book, he wrote, *"A child of 17, commander-in-chief of an army. There is no similar instance in history. Napoleon & Caesar were young, but they were not children."*[60] Notwithstanding his cynicism about the French, he admitted they had spawned two "prodigies . . . Napoleon and Joan of Arc,—that wonderful man and that sublime girl who dwarf all the rest of the human race."[61]

After twelve years of sketchy, intermittent research, Twain devoted two years to writing the *Personal Recollections of Joan of Arc* and tackled it with rare dedication. "I have never done any work before that cost so much thinking and weighing and measuring and planning and cramming, or so much cautious and painstaking execution," he told a friend.[62] He made six false starts that Livy shot down with silent reproach. But once he found the right form, he said, it was "a book which writes itself, a tale which tells itself."[63] The final portion of the book, however, proved exhausting as he sat down to narrate Joan's trial with eleven French and English sources at his side. He poured so much energy into the book that when he had to burn Joan at the stake on January 29, 1895, it left him in a state of physical exhaustion. For their twenty-fifth wedding anniversary, Twain inscribed a copy of *Joan of Arc* to Livy "in grateful recognition / of her twenty-five years of valued / service as my literary / advisor & editor."[64]

When the first serial installment appeared in *Harper's* in April 1895, some literary detectives lost no time identifying Mark Twain as the author. Although lacking his signature mischief, it was seasoned with enough wry asides to give the game away. As the *Hartford Courant* declared on April 11, "It is now known for a fact that Mr. Clemens is the author."[65] Nevertheless, Twain kept readers guessing about the author's identity, perhaps because such publicity sparked sales. When a reporter asked at the start of his North American tour whether he had written *Joan*, Twain replied blithely that "I never deny the authorship of anything good. I am always willing to adopt any literary orphan that is looking for a father, but I want to wait until I'm sure that nobody else is going to claim it."[66] On August 17, 1895, Twain wrote to J. Henry Harper and lifted the seal of secrecy on his authorship, arguing that it would help sell tickets for his around-the-world tour. Then Livy, showing her commercial influence, overrode the decision. Twain wrote to Harper again, telling him to continue to publish *Joan* anonymously, saying that Livy didn't wish to hamper his freedom of action. It was not until January 1896 that it was known for certain that Twain was the author, and his name subsequently appeared on the book published that year.

With his exalted view of Joan, Twain had neither the impartiality of the historian nor the detached sympathy of a novelist. A smooth read,

"CIRCUMNAVIGATION OF THIS GREAT GLOBE"

written with clarity, zest, and an almost childlike sense of wonder, the book has, alas, not aged well. It has a mildly pleasing flavor instead of the biting, piquant wit associated with Mark Twain. "In *Joan of Arc*," wrote Major Pond, "I see Mrs. Clemens as much as 'Mark Twain.'"[67] Twain identified it more with Susy, writing that "she took as personal an interest in that book as if she had written it herself, not merely inspired a part of it."[68] Alone among Twain's books, it contains nothing subversive or irreverent. It is narrated by the Sieur Louis de Conte, a friend and colleague of Joan, who exalts her as a "sublime personality" free of "self-seeking, self-interest, personal ambition."[69] Of course, this defied Twain's firm conviction that we are all motivated solely by self-interest. Joan was the antithesis of the selfish human beings Twain had spent a lifetime mocking. Where his usual satirical victims blustered with fake courage, Joan was genuinely brave and fearless. Even though *Joan of Arc* is largely forgotten today, Twain took inordinate pride in his research and always listed it among his favorite books—often as *the* favorite book. Not long before he died, he wrote: "I like the Joan of Arc best of all my books: and it *is* the best, I know it perfectly well. And besides, it furnished me seven times the pleasure afforded me by any of the others."[70] This retrospective judgment was surely colored by certain family misfortunes that followed hard on the heels of *Joan's* publication.

CHAPTER THIRTY-SIX

"The Only Sad Voyage"

L ivy had retained an amorphous hope that by autumn 1896 the family would be able to return to America and resume their former existence in the Hartford house. She had a lifetime of memories stored up there and refused to relinquish them. "I want to say a word about the renting of our house," she told Franklin G. Whitmore, their business agent, on the eve of the global tour. "There are so many things in that house that father and mother gave me and that I can never replace, so I am entirely unwilling to risk their being handled by careless servants or used by unloving hands."[1] A return to Hartford, however, remained well out of reach: the tour had only partially winnowed down the Clemenses' debt load, and they decided to stay in England for a few months after docking at Southampton.

After a year spent entertaining audiences, Twain sorely needed rest. "Why, there *isn't* any slavery that is so exacting and so infernal," he complained to Rogers of platform work. "I hope I have trodden it for the last time; that bread-and-butter stress will never crowd me onto it again."[2] His dream was to locate a hideaway in a small village outside London where he could complete his travel book about the tour. As a stopgap measure, he and Livy rented a house in Guildford while she hunted winter quarters in London. Their highest priority was to reincorporate Susy and Jean back into their lives and mend their broken family. They saw themselves on the eve of a blissful reunion after a yearlong separation and were especially eager to see Susy, whose compromised health concerned them. "Susy is in pretty good shape, but not robust—she's never that; the rest of us *are* robust," Twain reported to Mother Fairbanks prior to his world tour.[3]

While missing her family, Susy had stayed behind to develop her bodily strength and cultivate her operatic voice, and attempted to enjoy their trip vicariously through their letters. A young woman full of yearning, trailed by a sense of failure, her letters often sounded a wistful note. She told Clara things were pleasant but uneventful in Elmira. "The other night . . . there was a ball at the Reynolds where I did my usual duty as wall-flower."[4] Like many people in distress, Susy sought a panacea, some rule of behavior to give new direction to her life. As she wrote to Clara, "I have become determined to get hold of a philosophy that will if possible straighten me out morally, mentally, and physically and make me less of a burden to myself and others. I am tired *tired* of all my *sins* . . . this discord, this restlessness, making every undertaking impossible and spoiling and frittering away my life."[5]

Twain had long urged his daughter to adopt a program of Mind Cure, which, like Christian Science, stressed the spirit's power to overcome maladies. In fact, the leading exponent of Mental Science (also known as the New Thought), Phineas Parkhurst Quimby, had treated Mary Baker Eddy, who then adapted his principles into Christian Science. Susy turned to Mental Science in earnest after encountering her old governess, who had become an adherent of the movement. From India, Twain applauded Susy's embrace of this approach. "I am perfectly certain that [my] exasperating colds & the carbuncles came from a diseased mind, & that your mental science could drive them way . . . I have no language to say how glad & grateful I am that you are a convert to that rational & noble philosophy. Stick to it; don't let anybody talk you out of it."[6] Twain's emphasis on Mental Science unfortunately made Susy reluctant to consult conventional doctors.

Nor was Livy slow to endorse her new enthusiasm. "I am truly thankful that you are getting interested in Mental Science," she wrote from New Zealand. Before her parents left for the world tour, Susy had evidently quarreled with Livy, voicing things that she later regretted. As

"THE ONLY SAD VOYAGE"

ever, Livy was quick to forgive. "You dear sweet darling little child in your self reproachings you seem to entirely forget that we had many, many, many happy beautiful hours together, beautiful hours that I remember with such infinate [sic] pleasure . . . So my darling child do not repine for the things that you did that were wrong. I feel that when we come together again we shall feel alike that we never shall want to be separated."[7] This strong desire to transcend old disagreements must have deepened Livy's eagerness to see her eldest daughter and to lay to rest any lingering disquiet still floating in the air.

When she spent three weeks in New York in December 1895, Susy's experimentation with Mental Science passed an all-important test. At first she was "*absolutely* disgusted with everything," she told Clara, until she applied "mental science" with a vengeance. Then she enjoyed a wild social success "without the help or presence of that mighty power the grey grenouille"—the "Gray Frog," her nickname for her father. Like Clara, Susy felt the need to flee from his lengthy shadow. Far from being shy and timid, in New York she became a "full fledged lover of society, at least of N.Y. Society . . . Yes, the life there *can* be ideal, the sort of life that 'Mark Twain' could attract to him . . . the three weeks I was there I met nothing but literary people or musicians or artists and the atmosphere was *alive* in a wonderful *large* way."[8] In passing, she mentioned having seen Louise Brownell, but only casually, as if she were finally moving beyond that love affair. Susy's stay in New York and the chance to mingle with a sophisticated, artistic set pried open new vistas for her, suggesting she *was* capable of a happy, independent life. It may say something about the excessive hold family life had over her that she experienced such an epiphany only in the absence of her parents.

Though she found her old friends a trifle dull after New York's bracing society, Susy, along with Katy Leary, returned to Hartford in the summer of 1896. While spending nights with Charles Dudley Warner and his wife, she went back to the Farmington Avenue house during the day, where she read, played piano, and developed her voice. Her singing improved so dramatically that neighbors gathered outside to eavesdrop on her practice. When Major Pond dropped by the house, he confirmed to Twain that Susy had arrived at some new sphere of happiness. "She seems quite happy where she is. She says it seems very much like home to her, and she wished you would come back. The place is beautiful, but there is a terrible atmosphere of lonesomeness there."[9] A discordant note emerged from Katy Leary, who thought Susy had fallen under the sway of a spiritualist who came to the house and passed her hand over Susy's throat to strengthen it. Katy smelled trouble. "That woman's crazy and the worst kind of a Spiritualist," she warned Susy. "Yes, maybe," Susy replied, "but she's a good healer." "There's nothing to her," Katy persisted. "She's a pirate, a regular pirate! Don't you go near her again."[10]

Susy's longing to see her family remained as intense as ever, and she ached to join them. "Goodbye and oh, I hope we can all come *safely* together never to part again!" she told Clara.[11] "To leave Elmira and all its bores to rejoin *you*, brilliant, experienced, adorable people, to whom I belong and to rejoin you in Europe!!! Oh, quell [sic] bonheur! *can* it ever come true?"[12] Sometimes she seemed to have a foreboding that she might never see her family again. "I shall be so *glad* when we are all together again, *if we ever are*," she wrote to Clara.[13]

Then, in early August, Susy had begun to roam about in a nervous, restless state, and her health started to decline. On August 14, 1896, Sam and Livy received an upsetting cablegram that Susy was ill in Hartford. They didn't know how to interpret this ambiguous news, but Livy, despite a sprained ankle, and Clara acted swiftly on their intuitions and decided to sail for America the next day. Twain promised, if the cablegrams did not improve, he would follow a few days later. There was one sure tip-off that something serious was afoot. As Twain informed a friend, "We can't get an answer to our cablegrams! We began telegraphing at 11 this morning & now at 11 p.m. we still have no answer & cannot imagine what the trouble is."[14] Until midnight he hung about the local post office, hoping for a message that never arrived. The next day he accompanied his wife and daughter to Southampton, where they received a cable saying that Susy's recovery would be slow but certain. "This was a great relief to me," recalled Twain, "but not to my wife. She was frightened."[15] As it turned out, Livy's maternal instincts proved far more accurate than

"THE ONLY SAD VOYAGE"

Twain's complacent, dilatory attitude toward the threat looming across the ocean.

The next day at noon, Livy and Clara departed aboard the *Paris* from Southampton on a voyage disturbed by fearful musings. Twain wrote a letter to his wife that expressed a pessimism inexplicably at odds with his behavior. "You & Clara are making the only sad voyage of all the round-the-world trip. I am not demonstrative; I am always hiding my feelings; but my heart was wrung yesterday. I could not tell you how deeply I loved you nor how grieved I was for you nor how I pitied you in this awful trouble that my mistakes have brought upon you. You forgive me, I know, but I shall never forgive myself while the life is in me. If you find our poor little Susy in the state I seem to foresee, your dear head will be grayer when I see it next. [Be good & get well, Susy dear, don't break your mother's heart.]"[16] This self-flagellation went on. "Livy darling, you are . . . the highest & finest & loveliest character I have ever known; & I was never worthy of you. You should have been the prize of a better man—a man up nearer to your own level."[17] Twain was consumed by such dread about Susy that it makes one wonder—and Twain himself would have cause to wonder—why he had not rushed with his wife and daughter to America.

Amid sultry Hartford weather, Susy had begun to run a fever and grow delirious, just as she prepared to leave for England. Because of her newfound faith in Mental Science, abetted by a Nook Farm friend who was a Christian Scientist, she resisted pleas to summon a conventional doctor and preferred a spiritualist. We will never know whether the delay cost Susy Clemens her life. It turned out she had bacterial meningitis—infection of the membranes surrounding the brain and spinal cord, brought on by bacteria. When Katy Leary finally brought in the family physician, Dr. Porter, he at first diagnosed Susy as simply run-down and overworked, and advised moving her into the Farmington Avenue house. Then he abruptly switched his diagnosis to spinal meningitis. A viral-induced meningitis can be mild and heal on its own, but one caused by bacteria can be fatal, with no cure then available. "She was very sick and she wouldn't take a bit of medicine from anybody but me," Katy Leary recalled. "She wouldn't let the nurses touch her or come near her, so I sat by her night and day."[18]

When Joe Twichell, vacationing in the Adirondacks, learned of Susy's illness, he raced back to Hartford, and as soon as he arrived, his son recalled, "Susie had her first attack of violent insanity. I remember my father saying he had to hold her by sheer force on a bed for an hour until help could be summoned from the Insane Retreat."[19] Twain knew that Twichell had sat by Susy and comforted her, but it is not clear whether he ever knew of this mad, convulsive behavior. Jean Clemens believed her sister had suffered irreparable brain damage and regretted her reluctance to enlist qualified medical help. "We *said* Susy was sick, but we *knew* she was insane," she told Sam Moffett, her cousin. "Mental science, spiritualism, together with her own desire for going away did their work. Poor Susy was too frail to support her brain."[20]

As her condition spiraled downward, Susy shuffled about the house in a delirious state. When she glanced out at traffic on Farmington Avenue, she intoned, "Up go the trolley cars for Mark Twain's daughter. Down go the trolley cars for Mark Twain's daughter."[21] Every day, to cheer her up, the gardener piled roses by her bedside. Even in her delirium, her identity as Twain's daughter remained constant, Twain later wrote: "When out of her head, she said many things that showed she was proud of being my daughter."[22] Finding in the closet a gown Livy had worn, Susy clutched it, kissed it, then broke into tears, imagining the garment incarnated her mother. She erupted into outbursts in French. Verbal to the end, Susy covered forty-seven sheets of paper with scribbled sentences in which she hallucinated about a nineteenth-century European mezzo-soprano, Maria Malibran, who had died at twenty-eight after being thrown from a horse. In these ravings, one can see Susy dealing with the guilty, sinful feelings she had confessed to Clara. "Let her [Madame Malibran] say . . . that darkness is not bad but good not monstrous but beautiful that I stand as high in my destiny as she stands in hers. She is a queen of God's light but I am a queen of his darkness."[23] Toward the end of her medical ordeal, with her brain lining swelling, Susy went blind and said to Charles Langdon, who stood by her, "I am blind, Uncle Charlie & you are blind."[24] Her feverish hands groped for Katy Leary's face, stroking it fondly. Then she breathed the word "Mamma" and lapsed into a coma for two days before dying at age twenty-four on the evening of August 18.[25] At her side when she expired were Jean Clemens, Katy Leary, Sue Crane, and Charlie Langdon.

Mark Twain was standing in the Guildford dining room, expecting hopeful news, when he read the cablegram that changed his life—"Susy was peacefully released to-day"—and he was trapped alone with his guilty, inconsolable grief.[26] Just on the eve of a happy reunion with his daughter, his world had been shattered in an instant. "It is one of the mysteries of our nature that a man, all unprepared, can receive a thunderstroke like that and live," he said.[27] At that moment, Livy and Clara, afloat in the mid-Atlantic, were unaware of the dreadful fatality that awaited them. On their penultimate day, they consoled themselves by thinking, "Tomorrow we shall hug that darling girl and start to nurse her back to health!"[28] When their ship arrived in New York, Dr. Clarence Rice, Joseph Twichell, and other friends boarded a tugboat and headed out to the *Paris* in quarantine to convey the horrid tidings. Twichell branded it "one of the most distressing duties I ever had to perform."[29] They decided to break the news first to Clara, who might then tell Livy gently. But before the ship had landed, the captain showed Clara a newspaper with the headline that Mark Twain's daughter had died of spinal meningitis. In shock, Clara went to her mother's stateroom, but before she could say a word, Livy could read the anguish on Clara's face and cried out, with a deathly pallor, "I don't believe it."[30] "The mother was prostrated and swooned when the news was conveyed to her," the *New York Times* reported.[31] Sue Crane described Livy's face as "the most grief stricken . . . I ever looked upon."[32]

Dressed by Katy Leary, Susy's body was transported to Elmira for burial. When Livy and Clara arrived by train, Susy was there to greet them—"not waving her welcome in the glare of the lights as she had waved her farewell to us thirteen months before, but lying white and fair in her coffin, in the house where she was born," Twain wrote.[33] Jean would long remember her mother's "agony when she came home and found my sister dead."[34] Livy spent every waking moment beside her daughter's corpse and still managed to find time to comfort others. "Clara," she said, "you look so ill, can't you rest a little while?" Or to Sue Crane: "Sue dear, don't worry about me. I shall find strength to bear it some way."[35] Susy was buried at Woodlawn Cemetery in Elmira, her headstone inscribed with words adapted from a poem by Robert Richardson: "Warm summer sun / Shine kindly here, / Warm southern wind / Blow softly here," and ended "Good night, dear heart, / Good night, good night."[36] For a young woman so enamored of poetry, it seemed an appropriate send-off from her disconsolate parents.

There is some evidence that Louise Brownell was banned from the funeral proceedings, because on September 16, her Bryn Mawr classmate Elizabeth Ware Winsor sought to console her: "Some day Mrs. Clemens will send for you and you will be given a little of that touch with Olivia's family you were so cruelly robbed of."[37] The sentence suggests that Livy had excluded Louise, though there would be future contacts of a much more moving nature between Louise and Twain.

Because of the time required for a transatlantic crossing, Twain missed the funeral and was condemned to soldier on alone as best he could. The day after Susy's death, it drizzled all day in Guildford, and the dark, somber atmosphere matched his mood. He searched for a scrap of correspondence from Susy but could find none and worked himself into a rage. "I wish she had written something to me—but I did not deserve it," he told Livy, who was then at sea. "You did, but I did not. You always wrote her, over burdened with labors as you were—you the most faithful, the most loyal wife, mother, friend in the earth—but I neglected her as I neglect everybody in my selfishness. Everybody but you."[38] With pardonable exaggeration, he said, "I loved Susy, loved her dearly; but I did not know how deeply before." As he searched for some solace, he lacerated himself with the bitterest self-accusations. "She died in our own house—not in another's; died where every little thing was familiar & beloved; died where she had spent all her life till my crimes made her a pauper & an exile."[39] Hour after hour Twain played billiards, he explained, "to keep from going mad with grief & with resentful thinking."[40]

"THE ONLY SAD VOYAGE"

Tortured by the notion that he had neglected his beloved daughter, Twain pored over her notebooks and got to know Susy in a manner that had eluded him while she was alive. Though he had chided her for not writing and exercising her literary gifts, he now found that she had left extensive notes for future projects. "Apparently her proposed industries: Acting, singing, teaching singing; guitar, language, translation, writing."[41] To Livy, Twain contrasted the escapist manner in which he reacted to his brother Henry's death with the excruciating turmoil he felt with Susy. "In Henry's case I would not allow myself to think of my loss, lest the burden be too heavy to bear; but in poor Susy's case I have no disposition or desire to put it out of my mind—I seem to want to think of it all the time."[42] He described his vicious mood swings as his emotions lurched "to fury, & I [vomit blasphemies] rage until I get a sort of relief."[43] If Susy were back again, he knew he would be as neglectful as before. "My selfishness and indolence would resume their power and I should be no better father to her."[44] Angry, depressed, at his nadir he spied no redeeming features in this sublunary world. "It is an odious world, a horrible world—it is HELL."[45]

For many days after absorbing the news of Susy's death, Twain was enraged not to hear from Sue Crane, Jean, Katy, or Joe Twichell, the only message he received being a condolence note from his publisher, Harper & Brothers. Was this a rebuke? Indignantly Twain wrote that he refused to "believe that there are any human beings in the world, friends or foes, civilized or savage, who would close their lips *there*, & leave me these many, many days eating my heart out with longings for the tidings that never come."[46] Whether their silence resulted from being numb with grief or distracted with funeral arrangements, or because they blamed Twain for not having accompanied Livy and Clara on the voyage home, it is impossible to know.

For the Clemens family, it would be exceedingly difficult to regain any semblance of normal life, and the best they could manage was a ghastly simulacrum. "And now what can we do?" Twain wondered. "Where can we go & hide ourselves till we earn release? For what have we further to do with the world?"[47] He and Livy fled from the Guildford house, blackened with awful memories, and repaired to London "to hide from men for a time, & let the wounds heal."[48] Twain's mood was foul, his wit positively ghoulish, as he took refuge in despairing reflections. "This Infernal Human Race," he told Twichell, "I wish I had it in the Ark again—with an auger."[49] He assured Orion and Mollie that they were all "fairly well; & not apparently near to death—which is regrettable."[50] After his fleeting period of reform, he now gave way to the old profanities that had so long bothered Livy.

They found a furnished flat in Chelsea, in a brick building at No. 23 Tedworth Square, where they had a cook, maids, and a man to perform odd jobs. An inconsolable couple, trapped in grief, Sam and Livy enacted elaborate Victorian rituals of mourning. For years they would refuse to celebrate birthdays and holidays, including Thanksgiving and Christmas, as if holidays without Susy were mere obscenities. When Twain gave friends his address, he swore them to secrecy so his family might maintain a hermit existence. "We keep in hiding," he wrote, "because we are four broken hearts, and I do not go out and my wife and daughters never see anybody—they cannot bear it yet."[51] Barricaded in his solitude, with curtains drawn, Twain succeeded in keeping the press at bay for three weeks before his whereabouts became known.

In the immediate aftermath of Susy's demise, Twain heaped blame on himself for the yearlong separation made necessary by his bankruptcy. Livy was also merciless toward herself, saying Susy "was not a child that we should ever have left."[52] As time passed, the Clemens family redirected their anger toward those entrusted with Susy's care. Without naming culprits, Livy complained to Grace King that Susy was "badly managed" in her absence.[53] The closest she came to criticizing the Warners outright was an oblique reference to the "undesirable Hartford atmosphere" Susy experienced.[54] Clara was balder in her denunciations, telling Alice Hooker Day, "Susy you know was simply killed by mental science & spiritualism, without the least exaggeration. A murder it was,

"THE ONLY SAD VOYAGE"

a demented cold-blooded unforgivable murder!"[55] Of course, her parents had encouraged Susy's attachment to Mental Science, which Twain had extolled as that "rational & noble philosophy."

At first, Twain exempted Mental Science from his indictment of Susy's treatment and was scathing toward the doctors, whom he blamed for doing both too much and too little, and claimed that once they diagnosed Susy with meningitis, they gave up on her. "It was assassination through ignorance." On the other hand, had doctors acted to save her, "they could only have done damage, which is their main trade . . . It is my conviction that outside of certain rather restricted limitations they are all quacks without an exception."[56] He later told his secretary Isabel Lyon that as he barnstormed around the world, Susy had become interested in Mental Science and "refused to see a doctor & then it was too late. Mr. Clemens referred to this more than once & with great bitterness."[57] He implicitly blamed the Warners, who had offered Susy their hospitality. "The hard part to bear," he told Henry Rogers, "is the knowledge that if she had been with wise and thoughtful friends those last six months instead of"—here he struck out the word "fools"—"she would be as well to-day as she was when we left her."[58] Twain had unshakable faith that Susy "would not have died if we had been there."[59] He called up his ancient loathing for Charley Webster, whom he blasted as "the primal cause of Susy's death & my ruin . . . I am not able to think of him without cursing him . . . I have no such bitterness against Hall; he was merely a baby, & an incurable & unteachable fool . . . He has many excellent and likeable qualities; Webster had none. He was all dog. And he put me where I am, & Susy where she is."[60] This was a heavy charge to lay at Charley Webster's feet. Twain continued to eschew personal responsibility for Webster & Company's failure, preferring to scapegoat his deceased partner.

Twain could not stop punishing himself over his behavior toward Susy. He never forgave himself for not being with her when she died or seeing her in her coffin. He compared her to a bank treasure whose value he had not recognized until it vanished in the night, telling Twichell, "The bank is broken, my fortune is gone, I am a pauper."[61] He indulged in lofty evaluations of Susy's talents and retreated into a romanticized view of her life. She had been a prodigy, an incomparable intellect, who would have produced great books. She had an operatic voice "eloquent with feeling" and of "unexampled power and volume."[62] After studying Susy's writings, he concluded that "I know better, now, the treasure that was mine than I knew it when I had it . . . I see now—as Livy always saw—that she had greatness in her; & that she herself was dimly conscious of it. And now she is *dead*—& I can never tell her."[63]

Susy's death deprived him of a chance to reclaim the peculiar intimacy that they had enjoyed when, as a teenager, she had written his biography and worshiped her heroic father. Always he had hoped she would complete that biography. In his memory, Twain erased the uneasy years that preceded Susy's death when she had been, not the magical adolescent, but the troubled young woman, wan and listless. "Susy died at the right time, the fortunate time of life; the happy age—twenty-four years. At twenty-four, such a girl has seen the best of life."[64] This summary sadly misrepresents the woman who was tormented by her thwarted desire for Louise Brownell and felt herself a sorry burden to her family. When Twain undertook a searching review of her history, he found his own behavior wanting. He remembered the Paris stay when she had swiftly developed. "And I *felt* like saying, 'You marvelous child!'—but never said it; to my sorrow I remember it now."[65] He castigated himself for not getting published a play she wrote. "If I could call up a single instance where I laid aside my own projects & desires & put myself to real inconvenience to procure a pleasure for her," he told Livy, "I would forget all things else to remember that."[66] Brought low by sadness, he tried to compose a memorial to Susy and failed. Clara believed that he never got over Susy's death or his remorse that his business failures had led to the world tour that separated him from a dying daughter.

No less than Sam, Livy was distraught after Susy's death. She sat secluded in the Tedworth Square flat, refusing to see visitors and vowing never to enter the Hartford house again. "Now my world is dark," she told Alice Hooker Day. "I cannot find Susy & I cannot find the light."[67] She, too, blamed the Warners for letting Susy succumb to the "terrific evil influence" of Spiritualism instead of calling for her own sister and brother, "Susy's natural and wise protectors."[68] For Livy, Susy was special, inimitable, irreplaceable. When William Dean Howells and his wife sent a letter of condolence, citing their loss of a daughter, Livy thought, "What do *they* know? They have not lost a Susy Clemens."[69] She told her friend Alice that the letters Susy had written to her were "much more like a lover's letters than like a daughter's," and Twain confirmed that Susy and Livy conversed more like sweethearts than simply mother and daughter.[70]

On November 27, Twain sent fifty-first birthday greetings to Livy of a notably somber hue. "This is the blackest birthday you have ever seen: may you never see its mate, dear heart."[71] By way of consolation, he noted that they still had two precious daughters. For Clara, Susy had been "my other half," and she felt the loss no less traumatically than her parents.[72] What happened to Susy would make Sam and Livy cling to Clara more possessively as she sought to branch out into a career in music. The much younger Jean had never been a close confidante of Susy and confessed that she had reacted abnormally to her sister's death, with a curious absence of feeling. In later years, she berated herself for failing to "appreciate the beauty of the character of one now gone" and blamed the medical problems encroaching on her own life.[73] She had the true Clemens trait of self-condemnation as she addressed her departed sister in her diary. "Oh Susy—do show yourself in some sure, certain way to some of us! Do you forgive me my brutalities? Do let me know in some way, dear Susy."[74]

CHAPTER THIRTY-SEVEN

"A Book Written in Blood & Tears"

Even as he agonized over Susy's death, Mark Twain realized that he had to resume his writing career and further pare down the stack of debt that he believed had cost Susy her life. On October 24, he recorded in his notebook that he had finished the first chapter of "Around the World," a chronicle of his world tour.[1] Saddled with the demanding schedule of his lectures, Twain hadn't been able to do the fresh, direct reportage that had enlivened *The Innocents Abroad*—Livy had boasted "we have not loitered *one* day for sight-seeing"—and he wrote his new book largely from other books written about lands he had visited.[2] *Following the Equator*, as it was finally titled, is not exactly an account of the lecture tour, and Twain doesn't dramatize his appearances or even mention his wife, daughter, or agents. Rather, it is a travelogue inspired by his trip, with a running commentary on the people, customs, and history of places visited. Twain writes as if he were a curious tourist composing a guidebook for other curious tourists, and he doesn't allow his own celebrity to intrude for a second.

For six months, Twain labored day and night with his writing, taking shelter from his sorrow in "a book written in blood & tears under the shadow of our irremediable disaster—a book whose outside aspect had to be cheerful, but whose secret substance was made all of bitterness & rebellion."[3] Aside from the occasional dinner with Bram Stoker or Henry M. Stanley, Twain was indifferent to anything beyond the book. Its creation was a conscious flight from Susy's death, which perhaps lent a darker shading to his memories. "I wrote my last travel-book in hell," he would tell Howells, "but I let on, the best I could, that it was an excursion through heaven . . . How I did loathe that journey around the world!—except the sea-part & India."[4] Perhaps no book Twain wrote cost him so much pain and anguish. "I would rather be hanged, drawn and quartered than write it again."[5]

Like all his travel books, *Following the Equator* was a baggy monster, loose and episodic, and so dense with facts that it feels encyclopedic in places. It needed Livy's editorial hand. She strove to give the book a genteel veneer and objected to words deemed indelicate. Of the word "breech-clout" in the manuscript, she reproached him: "It's a word that you love and I abominate." Twain protested: "You are steadily weakening the English tongue, Livy." The word "stench" did not meet her high standards of propriety. "You have used that pretty often," she pointed out, to which he replied, "But can't I get it in *any*where? You've knocked it out every time."[6] Livy got him to reduce it to three uses. Sometimes she made factual corrections, as when she informed her husband his "green rubies" must have been emeralds. They had a fascinating exchange when Twain told of the Indian servant getting a "brisk cuff on the jaw" and how this reminded him of an incident in Hannibal when a master killed his slave simply for irritating him. "Surely public feeling would be *strong* against the slaveholder," Livy objected. Twain set her straight: "*No* ma'm—it *wasn't*."[7] He also wrote of how the Indian incident had triggered a sudden memory of his father's violence against an enslaved boy. "I hate to have your father pictured as lashing a slave boy," Livy said. "It's out," Twain rejoined, "and my father is 'whitewashed.'"[8]

One conspicuous feature of the book was its decidedly anti-imperialist tone, as if Twain felt less gagged after Susy's death. The trip had prompted a meditation on "civilization" and how murderous it could be beneath its technical advances. Reflecting on a native population reduced by 80 percent during the first twenty years of British rule in Australia, he was brutally frank: "It is robbery, humiliation, and slow, slow murder, through poverty and the white man's whisky . . . There are many humorous things in the world; among them the white man's notion that he is

"A BOOK WRITTEN IN BLOOD & TEARS"

less savage than the other savages."[9] He disputed the "low-rate intellectual reputation" of Aboriginal peoples, which he chalked up to "race-aversion."[10] He decried violence inflicted on the dingo, the wild Australian dog, for merely raiding herds of sheep. "He has been sentenced to extermination, and the sentence will be carried out . . . The world was made for man—the white man."[11] His outrage at colonial exploitation clearly owed something to parallels that he saw in America's history with slavery. "In many countries we have taken the savage's land from him, and made him our slave, and lashed him every day, and broken his pride, and made death his only friend, and overworked him till he dropped in his tracks; and this we do not care for, because custom has inured us to it." [12] In an essay titled "Man's Place in the Animal World," Twain came to this cheerless conclusion: "Man is the only Slave. And he is the only animal who enslaves."[13]

Perhaps Susy's death also made Twain more fervent in his advocacy of women's rights. While discussing women having the vote in New Zealand, he paid tribute to the American feminist movement after the 1848 Seneca Falls Convention. "The prophets [of doom] have been prophesying ever since the woman's rights movement began in 1848—and in forty-seven years they have never scored a hit. Men ought to begin to feel a sort of respect for their mothers and wives and sisters by this time . . . In forty-seven years [women] have swept an imposingly large number of unfair laws from the statute books of America. In that brief time these serfs have set themselves free—essentially." Twain presents this peaceful revolution as proof of the intelligence, courage, and perseverance of women. "It takes much to convince the average man of anything; and perhaps nothing can ever make him realize that he is the average woman's inferior."[14] As the husband of a smart wife and with smart, talented daughters, Twain occupied an excellent vantage point to appreciate the merits of women.

By now Twain had carved out a special niche for himself as a fount of aphorisms. In *Pudd'nhead Wilson*, he began each chapter with a fresh saying and continued this practice in *Following the Equator*, labeling these epigraphs *Pudd'nhead Wilson's New Calendar*. Some of them alluded (unacknowledged) to Susy's death. "Pity is for the living, envy is for the dead."[15] His contempt for doctors emerged when he said "the only way to keep your health is to eat what you don't want, drink what you don't like, and do what you'd druther not."[16] His cynicism about politics flared anew: "It is by the goodness of God that in our country we have those three unspeakable precious things: freedom of speech, freedom of conscience, and the prudence never to practice either of them."[17] He trumpeted a favorite theme on the staying power of lies: "The principal difference between a cat and a lie is that the cat has only nine lives."[18] And he produced one of his most lasting aphorisms by defining a "Classic": "A book which people praise and don't read."[19] Never averse to the hard sell, Twain pushed a moneymaking scheme to take sixty of his wittiest maxims and have his publisher peddle them on postcards.

When the book was finished, Twain, grateful to Henry H. Rogers, inscribed a copy to his son. "THIS BOOK is affectionately inscribed to my young friend HARRY ROGERS with recognition of what he is, and apprehension of what he may become unless he form himself a little more closely upon the model of THE AUTHOR."[20] Some reviews of the book detected that Twain was not fully engaged in his material. One review in London, where it appeared as *More Tramps Abroad*, complained about "wads of padding" and found the writing often "merely labored and contrived."[21] For other reviewers, the book confirmed how inadequate the "humorist" title was for Mark Twain and what a penetrating thinker he was. As the Boston *Daily Globe* observed, "He is, in fact, a man of the strongest intellectual power and will compare favorably with the brightest minds of the age."[22] Writing in *Harper's Monthly*, Twain's friend Laurence Hutton accurately diagnosed why the book produced less delight than his earlier travel volumes: "The cause is easily found in the loss of Susan Clemens just as the world tour came to an end."[23] Sales of the book were pretty lackluster, with only twenty thousand copies sold in the first three months, well below Twain's usual benchmark.

In November 1896, *Harper's Monthly* had also published, in a single volume, *Tom Sawyer, Detective* and *Tom Sawyer Abroad*. In *Tom Sawyer, Detective*, written in a matter of weeks, Twain cranked out a potboiler intended to capitalize on the vogue for detective fiction created by Sherlock Holmes. Tom, Huck, and the old crowd still milled about in Twain's brain, and he never seemed to worry about cheapening these famous characters by recycling them into third-rate fiction. As Tom figures out a murder case and exonerates a decent, innocent man, he is plucky and resourceful, while Huck is slow and plodding. The problem with the story is that it consists only of plot—action and dialogue—and never endows the characters with any trace of interior lives. Twain reduces himself to a raconteur telling a tall tale as he keeps the reader dangling in a primitive state of suspense. He misses the essence of detective fiction, that slow accretion of tantalizing details about the potential culprit that enables readers to test their wits against the famous detective. While writing the story, Twain professed delight, but he may have revised his opinion later on. "What a curious thing a 'detective' story is," he wrote. "And was there ever one that the author needn't be ashamed of, except 'The Murders in the Rue Morgue'?"[24]

Throughout the fall of 1896 at 23 Tedworth Square, Susy remained an unseen but inescapable presence. When Twain wrote letters, the stationery bore a black mourning border, and he ordered up a dozen photos of her from an old carte de visite. He came up with a new maxim that signified his state of mind: "The best way to cheer yourself up is to try to cheer somebody else up."[25] When Thanksgiving came, the holiday wasn't celebrated as it was the anniversary of Susy's mounting her first play in the Hartford house on that day seven years earlier. For the Clemenses, Christmas had customarily been a bountiful season of gifts. Now the holiday was devoid of jollity and not even mentioned by name. "It was in our minds," admitted Twain, "but we said nothing."[26] With few exceptions, the family neither visited nor received friends.

Clara occupied a precarious spot since she had to care for her mother, who felt adrift after editing *Following the Equator*, while dealing with her father's titanic moods. "It was a long time before anyone laughed in

RAPIDS

our household, after the shock of Susy's death," she wrote. "Father's passionate nature expressed itself in thunderous outbursts of bitterness shading into rugged grief. He walked the floor with quick steps and there was no drawl in his speech now."[27] Often, observing Livy's heartbreak, Twain felt powerless to dispel the gloom that clung to her as she avoided people and shed her habitual interest in reading. "She sits solitary; & all the day . . . wonders how it all happened, why," Twain wrote. "We others were always busy with our affairs, but Susy was her comrade," and Livy could not get accustomed to her daughter's absence.[28] Plaintively Livy told Grace King that Susy was "my joy & pride. Life is so dull, the poetry seems gone out of it . . . I long to be with Susy."[29] In his notebook, Twain outlined a tale in which a mother in heaven keeps an anxious eye out for her long-lost daughter. When she can't find her in heaven, she turns her attention to hell instead. "Musing, she hears a shriek, and her daughter sweeps by. There is an instant of recognition by both—the mother springs in, perceiving there is no happiness in heaven for her any longer."[30]

A markedly superstitious man, Twain began to suspect that a jinx had settled over his entire family. "Since bad luck struck us it is risky for people to have to do with us. Our third cook's sweetheart was healthy— he is rushing for the grave, now. Emily, one of the maids, has lost the sight of one eye, & the other is in danger. Wallace carried up coal & blacked the boots 2 months—has suddenly gone to the hospital—pleurisy & a bad case. We began to allow ourselves to see a good deal of our friends the Bigelows—straightway their baby sickened & died. Next, Wilson got his skull fractured. Visited him today, at the hospital. Returning my cab ran over a little boy."[31]

Perhaps responding to his remorse over Susy's death, Twain adopted an overly aggressive posture in protecting Clara and Jean. One day his daughters went to the Lyceum Theatre and sought to buy two cheap seats for four shillings; for some reason, this drew an insulting response from the box office clerk. Flying into a rage, Twain wrote to Bram Stoker, the business manager of the theater. "My object in writing this note, is, to say to you that the large blonde man with spectacles who was selling seats in your box office this afternoon ... insulted my two daughters by his brutal & surly behavior, & I wish to ask you if it is your intention to discharge him, & if it is your purpose, to do it at once."[32] Not content with a mere firing, Twain asked for the man's name so he might "make future use of him in print" and denounce him as a "mangy cur" and "a hog."[33] The episode evinced Twain's extreme need to mete out punishment to anyone who threatened his daughters—a belated compensation for Susy's death.

Those daughters had to battle against the increasingly saturnine worldview he spouted as they walked by the Thames or strolled through Regent's Park. "It was on such days that Father created the habit of vituperating the human race," Clara recalled. "What started in formless criticism grew into a sinister doctrine. There was no hope for the human race because no appreciable improvement was possible in any individual ... Walking through the streets and parks of London we crucified and resurrected people of all nations and times."[34]

When Twain wasn't sounding like the Grim Reaper, he showed a passionate interest in walks about London, a place he found endearingly eccentric, a great city composed of a patchwork of cozy neighborhoods. "I believe that London is the pleasantest and most satisfying village in the world," he wrote.[35] He was charmed by its slow pace, its low-key friendliness. At the same time, he faulted the British for "unconscious arrogance ... adultery in high places; incompetent cooks."[36] In exploring the city, he was affected by the plight of the poor, never losing sight of those in need. "I wish the Lord would disguise himself in citizen's clothing & make personal examination of the sufferings of the poor in London. He would be moved, & would do something for them Himself."[37] Twain engaged in his own brand of philanthropy, explaining why he gave a shilling to a drunk. "He was drunk enough for me, but not drunk enough for himself. I relieved him ... It was but a little thing I did—for me; yet it was such a large thing for him."[38]

One striking feature of Twain's London wanderings was his Victorian shock at the sexual freedom of young people. Coming home on the Underground one night, he was appalled by "a young fellow & his girl" who "hugged & kissed straight along quite unembarrassed by our presence... In Am[erica], not even a drunken man would have shown so little shame."[39] This outrageous misbehavior went unchecked. Another day he wrote: "More hugging & kissing by boys & girls & young men & maids in the streets at night & parks by day! & no chaffing them by anybody." He watched one teenage couple, locked in an open embrace, circulate a dozen times around a garden—and nobody complained! "They ought to have done the blushing, but I presently found they could not be depended upon & had to do it myself."[40]

That Twain bore his own cargo of repressed libido was disclosed by a carnal dream that he had in London that winter, perhaps stimulated by the uninhibited young couples whom he observed. The dream is so startling, so loaded with symbolism, that it is worth quoting in full:

> I was suddenly in the presence of a negro wench who was sitting in grassy open country, with her left arm resting on the arm of one of those long park-sofas that are made of broad slats with cracks between, and a curve-over back. She was very vivid to me—round black face, shiny black eyes, thick lips, very white regular teeth showing through her smile. She was about 22, and plump—not fleshy, not fat, merely rounded and plump; and good-natured and not at all bad-looking. She had but one garment on—a coarse tow-linen shirt that reached from her neck to her ankles without break. She sold me a pie; a mushy apple pie—hot. She was eating one herself with a tin teaspoon. She made a disgusting proposition to me. Although it was disgusting it did not surprise me—for I was young (I was never old in a dream yet) and it seemed quite natural that it should come from her. It was disgusting, but I did not say so; I merely made a chaffing remark, brushing aside the matter—a little jeeringly—and this embarrassed her and she made an awkward pretence that I had misunderstood her. I made a sarcastic remark about this pretence, and asked for a spoon to eat my pie with. She had but the one, and she took it out of her mouth, in a quite matter-of-course way, and offered it to me. My stomach rose—there everything vanished... My, how vivid it all

was! Even to the texture of her shirt, its dull white color, and pale brown tint of a stain on the shoulder of it.[41]

In conveying his overwhelming arousal by the young Black woman and utter revulsion at the same time, the dream captures Twain's clumsy ambivalence about his own sexuality. It also suggests that he saw a sensuality, a sexual freedom, in Black people that he found both alluring and disturbing. He wanted it, feared it, even as he tried to cloak his inner desire beneath sarcastic asides. The "pale brown tint of a stain" at the end of the dream hints at a consummation he could not frankly avow.

By early 1897, the first five volumes of the Uniform Edition of Twain's works had begun to appear, bolstered by a flattering review by William Dean Howells in *Harper's Weekly*. Writing to Howells to thank him, Twain confessed that he was now indifferent to everything but work and said he would not break from the grip of grief until Livy bounced back. "She was always so quick to recover herself before, but now there is no rebound, and we are dead people who go through the motions of life."[42] He noted that "Jean's spirits are good, Clara's are rising. They have youth, the only thing that was worth giving to the race."[43] When Sam and Livy reached their twenty-seventh wedding anniversary in February, nothing was done to mark the occasion and no gifts were exchanged. Bereavement had quenched Twain's desire to lecture as he concentrated solely on writing books, which he hoped would provide a future income stream for his family. The debt that still trailed him from the Webster & Company bankruptcy was a dark cloud that always lowered in the sky. "Let us begin on those debts," he told Rogers. "I cannot bear the weight any longer. It totally unfits me for work."[44]

Twain's secluded London life spawned a host of rumors, as he discovered when Twichell sent him an enormous clipping from the American press claiming that he was scraping by in penury in London, abandoned by his family. Twain wrote furiously in his notebook, "This would enrage

& disgust me if it came from a dog, or a cow, or an elephant or any other of the higher animals, but it comes from a man, & much allowance must be made for Man."[45] Twain had felt safe in London, where he thought the British press respected his privacy, but this article reminded him that he was still public property. Twain had a distant cousin living in London, Dr. James Ross Clemens, who read of his supposed poverty and sent a letter proffering financial assistance, leading to a friendship. When Dr. Clemens met Twain, his first impression erased any fears of Twain's financial hardship. "Entering his bedroom long past the hour of noon I found him in bed, luxuriously propped up on pillows and busily skimming through a crowd of books he had intrenched himself among."[46]

In early June occurred a case of mistaken identity that ended up producing Twain's most indelible quote. After Dr. Clemens suffered a serious illness, rumors sprang up in America that Samuel L. Clemens was dying in poverty in London. The mistake arose because Twain had visited "Dr. Jim" daily in the hospital. The New York *Journal* dispatched a reporter to Twain's doorstep in Tedworth Square, armed with two sets of instructions: "If Mark Twain dying in poverty, in London, send 500 words." But also: "If Mark Twain has died in poverty, send 1000 words."[47] Upon hearing the rumor, Twain was both amused and annoyed, and furnished the reporter with a statement to cable back to New York: "James Ross Clemens, a cousin, was seriously ill here two or three weeks ago, but is well now. The report of my illness grew out of his illness, the report of my death was an exaggeration. I have not been ill."[48] The message, garbled in transmission, appeared in its now famous version: "Reports of my death are grossly exaggerated."[49] Twain seemed to make a specialty of premature death jokes. Years earlier Livy had received a condolence note from a friend when reports surfaced that Mark Twain had died in Australia. The figure in question was a perennial Mark Twain impersonator. "Being dead I might be excused from writing letters," Twain told the friend, "but I am not that kind of a corpse."[50]

Press disruptions continued to flare up, albeit with a somewhat different slant. On June 12, Frank Marshall White of the New York *Journal* showed Twain an article from the *New York Herald* that announced

"A BOOK WRITTEN IN BLOOD & TEARS"

Twain's "Mental and Physical Collapse" and claimed he was "almost penniless . . . Friends—say his physical condition is brought about by a broken heart."[51] The paper declared that a fund was being opened to provide monetary relief to the author. One might have expected Twain to blanch at such a story, but, instead, he seemed unaccountably pleased. "You can say in reply that if it is true, it is pleasanter news than I have been accustomed to receive for some time past. I was expecting a monument by and by, but if my friends wish to pay my debts I will do without the monument."[52]

Twain was much more complicit than he let on, for the next day, in its Sunday paper, the *Herald* ran a full-page interview with him, promoting the relief fund. "Of course I am dying," Twain began. "But I do not know that I am doing it faster than anybody else. As for dying in poverty, I had just as soon die in poverty here in London as anywhere."[53] Of course, Twain subsisted in considerable comfort in Tedworth Square, attended by a team of servants, but the *Herald* reporter omitted mention of this and said of Twain: "His air . . . seemed dreadfully like that of a man trying to keep his head above water and not succeeding too well."[54] The newspaper revealed that it was kicking off a subscription fund for Mark Twain with a thousand-dollar donation from its own coffers and invited others to do the same to show "the feeling of esteem, gratitude and sympathy which we all feel for one who made life lighter with laughter."[55] Andrew Carnegie matched the *Herald* donation dollar for dollar.

Back home, Twain's intimate friends reacted with shock to the fund, fearing it would degrade Mark Twain into a pitiful object of public charity. The publisher Frank Bliss rushed off an urgent message: "Herald Fund hurting you/will you cable us disapproval."[56] Henry Rogers was no less adamant in disapprobation. "All friends think Herald movement mistake/withdraw graciously/Langdon approves this Rogers."[57] In reply, Twain explained to Rogers the surprising genesis of the relief fund, how a friend had broached the idea three months earlier, he had approved it, and it was now too late to back out. He hadn't mentioned it to Livy since she would have forbidden the project. Then came Twain's most startling admission: he didn't *want* to drop the relief fund. "The project may end in a humiliating failure, and show me that I am not very popular, after all; but no matter, I am used to humiliations these years, and they do not come so hard now as once they did."[58] That Twain would countenance such a fund shows that the long struggle to throw off the yoke of debt had stripped him of his pride and dignity. It was telling that he hadn't consulted Livy and Rogers, his two best confidants, who would have objected. Instead, he sounded like a beaten-down man who no longer cared what people thought and just wanted to be rid of the goddamn heap of debt, no matter how base the method.

As a woman of impeccable dignity and honor, Livy would not tolerate being the object of charity and forced Twain to withdraw from the scheme. On June 19, he drafted a letter to James Gordon Bennett, the proprietor of the *New York Herald,* and asked him to close up the fund and return the money to donors. "I have grown so tired of being in debt," he asserted, "that often I think I would part with my skin and teeth to get out," but his family had convinced him that he should not pocket other people's money.[59] Twain told Rogers that he had bowed out in deference to Livy, but, as far as he was concerned, "there was nothing discreditable to me about it, whether it failed or succeeded . . . If I were younger I should be in an awful state of mind, now, but I am old and played-out and pretty nearly callous; and distresses do not distress me as much as they ought."[60] Among other things, Twain had been dismayed by the embarrassingly small amount—less than $3,000—collected by the fund, an insult to his vanity. To counter this, he resorted to a patent piece of trickery, requesting that Rogers—"if your conscience will let you"—should "collect $40,000 privately for me from yourself, then pay it back to yourself, and have somebody tell the press it was collected [from the public] but that by Mrs. Clemens's desire I asked that it be returned to the givers and that it was done."[61] Rogers wanted no part of this shady transaction.

Before leaving London, Twain accepted a whopping fee from the Hearst Newspaper Syndicate to cover the Diamond Jubilee celebration for Queen Victoria, who had reigned for sixty years, then the longest stretch in British history. Frank Marshall White secured for Twain,

"A BOOK WRITTEN IN BLOOD & TEARS"

Clara, and Jean places on the reviewing stand outside the Hotel Cecil on the Strand, where Twain drew more attention than all the dignitaries assembled there. As the procession passed, Twain jotted notes on a pad propped on his knees and warned reporters not to interview him. "You mustn't ask me to talk," he told them. "We reporters mustn't quote one another."[62]

Twain rated the procession the most thrilling that ever passed through London's thoroughfares. For all his habitual denunciations of the British aristocracy, he still harbored a streak of Anglophilia that emerged in his published article, a real puff piece for the British Empire. The queen's reign had been a time of wonders and marvels, he argued, with English liberty, newspapers, and medical science all expanded. He put the spotlight on women's advances in her reign. "She has seen woman freed from the oppression of many burdensome and unjust laws . . . in some regions rights accorded to her which lifted her near to political equality with man."[63] The workday for all had been shortened and trade unions had flourished, and he delivered a paean to the nonstop expansion of the British Empire. "Great Britain has added to her real estate an average of 165 miles of territory per day for the past sixty years."[64] It was hard to believe that this was the same writer who had cataloged the evils of imperialism in *Following the Equator*. The grand finale of Twain's reportage was the queen's passage in "a landau driven by eight cream-colored horses, most lavishly upholstered in gold stuffs." In prose worthy of a palace publicist, he wrote: "The Queen Empress was come . . . It was realizable that she was the procession herself; that all the rest of it was mere embroidery; that in her the public saw the British Empire itself. She was a symbol, an allegory of England's grandeur and the might of the British name."[65] On this occasion, Katy Leary might have served as a better witness to history than Mark Twain. "Queen Victoria looked pretty old and feeble," she remembered. "[She] sat there like a little mummy in the back of her carriage."[66]

CHAPTER THIRTY-EIGHT

"Letters to Satan"

Toward the close of Twain's London stay, in 1897, the irrepressible Major Pond attempted to lure him back to America by proposing a lucrative lecture tour that would pay him $50,000 plus all expenses for 125 performances that fall and winter. Twain was tempted to say yes, believing he could retire his debt once and for all, but Livy scotched the notion, convinced another tour would ruin his health. Instead, they decided to spend the summer in Switzerland, followed by a fall and winter sojourn in Vienna, where Clara could resume her piano studies.

The Clemens party ended up in the scenic town of Weggis, Switzerland, situated on the northern shore of Lake Lucerne, south of Zurich. They stayed at Villa Bühlegg, which offered spectacular views of the glassy lake and snow-topped peak of Mount Pilatus, a mountain whose changing aspect mesmerized Twain. Like an impressionist painter, Twain closely studied the shifting patterns of light and shadow on the mountain, dazzled by perpetual surprises and penning one word portrait after another. The Clemens party also had access to bikes, rowboats, and chairs scattered about the villa grounds, offering shade and privacy for reading, conversation, and daydreaming. As Twain assured Rogers, "I believe this place . . . is the loveliest in the world, and the most satisfactory . . . And Sunday in heaven is noisy compared to this quietness."[1] He found the Swiss a stolid bunch—"if they know how to smile . . . they keep that secret to themselves"—though courteous and good-hearted.[2]

RAPIDS

For his writing, Twain rented a room at Villa Tannen, a quarter-mile away, where he enjoyed the interplay of lake and sky as he worked. He had a small, quaint room, barely big enough for a writing table, two chairs, and a sofa. The beauty of the place shed a beneficent peace on his turbulent spirit. Sue Crane, who had joined the party, found Twain "looking well, and seeming quite himself. He is cheerful & full of work, and never more gentle & lovely. It is a joy to see him, & hear him talk." At the same time, she found Livy and Clara thin and pale, and "often very sad, but they both seem to me less sad than when we first saw them in London."[3]

The thought of Susy was never far distant from the thoughts of the Clemens family. In spurning Major Pond's offer, Twain explained, "It would not be right for me to lecture at this time; I owe Susy's memory that grace."[4] He and Livy read Tennyson's elegiac poem "In Memoriam" and were comforted by its healing grace. With apprehension they approached August 18, the first anniversary of Susy's death, a date that "trailed its black shadow" over their Weggis stay.[5] "There will never be an August day, perhaps, in which I shall be sane," Twain concluded. "It is our terrible month."[6] Livy still could not accept that Susy was gone forever. "It is impossible to believe that she will not come," she confided to a friend. "Constantly she visits me in my dreams and I feel that if I were to go to the Hartford house or to Elmira, I should certainly find her. Friends say that time softens trouble . . . I hope it may be so, I have not found it yet."[7]

On August 18, Livy did something strange and uncharacteristic. Instead of spending the solemn day with her husband, she opted to be alone with her memories. That morning she took a bag, boarded a steamer, and went off to an unspecified town on the lake, where she booked a room at an inn and reread Susy's letters. No one dared to ask her destination. Was Livy silently punishing her husband for not crossing the Atlantic when news of Susy's illness came? Or for the crushing debts that had forced them to make the global tour and abandon Susy? Or was there a zone of privacy with Susy that she refused to share? "It was evening when she returned," wrote Twain's authorized biographer, "and her husband, lonely and anxious, was waiting for her at the landing."[8] Livy said that when she returned to the villa, she found on the chair in her room a memorial poem about Susy that her husband had composed.

Twain had spent the day seated beneath some trees, writing the tribute. It evoked an idyllic valley, shut off from the world, where a temple stood inhabited by a spirit made of pure light. Only the "adoring priests" who worshiped there knew the "power and depth" of that spirit and feared the profound loss if "it should fade and fail and come no more." When that disaster happens, the townsfolk forget the Light, but the adoring priests—that is, the Clemens family—do not, and pray for its return. In his grief, Twain had turned Susy into a saint worthy of worship. He mailed out the poem to friends on a mourning card, trimmed in black, and it was published that fall in *Harper's Monthly*.

For Mark Twain, the universe now stood steeped in darkness, and he detected misery lurking in every corner. He wrote a piece, "In My Bitterness," in which he delved into Susy's death, placing the blame on a malevolent deity who enjoyed taunting mortals by giving them gifts then snatching them away. In his radical alienation from organized religion, Twain criticized the God of the Bible as an often frightening figure. "He never does a kindness. When He seems to do one, it is a trap which He is setting . . . No, He gives you riches, merely as a trap; it is to quadruple the bitterness of the poverty which He has planned for you. He gives you a healthy body and you are tricked into thanking Him for it; some day, when He has rotted it with disease and made it a hell of pains, you will know why He did it."[9] Perhaps Livy fled his company on August 18 because she needed solace and could not bear the pessimistic lessons he had drawn from Susy's death. When she first met him, she had been a woman of simple, conventional faith and now she had to deal with his resolute denial of the basic comforts of religion. Earlier that summer, he had said flatly, "If Christ were here now, there is one thing he would *not* be—a Christian."[10]

It was not only the death of his eldest daughter that blasted Twain's vision that summer, for a terrible crisis now unfolded with his youngest daughter. Jean turned seventeen that July, and to all outward appearances she looked like a tall, healthy girl who enjoyed boating, biking, and brushing up on her French and German. In 1896, she had her first convulsion—likely a grand mal seizure—and her parents grew terrified that she had epilepsy. A doctor prescribed a daily medication that seemed to work and said that if Jean could avoid another seizure for a year, she might be cured. *"Might"*—it was a word freighted with much anguish. Then, at Weggis, after a fifteen-month remission, Jean suffered two seizures and "nearly destroyed our hope," Twain wrote.[11] The family now saw the epilepsy diagnosis as irrevocable. For five years, Twain had also noticed a mysterious personality change in Jean that he later attributed to her epilepsy. From being a warm, sweet child, she had grown moody and withdrawn, prone to harsh judgments about people and subject to fits of temper. Sam and Livy had already experienced so much heartache with Susy, had exhausted so many emotional resources, that it left them depleted when they had to deal with yet another major crisis.

However somber his family life, Twain never shed his stamina for work, and the worse things got, the more he submerged himself in writing. After the August 18 anniversary, he put in nine-hour days, seven days a week, mapping out four new books and generating a staggering twenty-eight hundred words daily. Coincidentally or not, Susy's death opened up a new range of nontraditional female characters in his fiction, including plucky tomboys, cross-dressers, and androgynous figures, a corrective to the many traditional females, pure and innocent, who had populated his work.

Exactly two weeks before the anniversary of the death, Twain began a story titled "Hellfire Hotchkiss" that suggests that he may have been thinking of Susy and her relationship with Louise Brownell. It also reflects his obsession with a certain type of lithe, spirited teenage girl. In the story, a boy named Oscar "Thug" Carpenter nearly drowns when the ice on the river cracks beneath him, and a girl named Rachel—aka "Hellfire Hotchkiss"—arrives to fish him out. "Now arose the ringing sound of flying hoofs, and a trim and fair young girl, bareheaded and riding horseback and astride, went thundering by on a great black horse."[12] Oscar is yet another character based on Orion, a noble fool who constantly switches churches, while Rachel is benevolent and quick-witted. With these two characters, Twain swapped the usual gender roles. One person calls Hellfire Hotchkiss the only genuine male in town, and Thug the only genuine female. In his portrait of Hellfire, Twain borrowed a bit from Susy in her sudden, mutable moods, but Susy was fragile and not at all like the athletic Hellfire. The more likely model for Rachel was a woman named Lilly Hitchcock, whom Twain had known in San Francisco in 1864, who smoked cigars, cross-dressed, and played poker.

At school, Hellfire Hotchkiss rebels against other girls and their dolls and gravitates to the more rugged pursuits of the boys. She is also fearless, and when she encounters a young man named Shad Stover beating up a stranger, she fights him off with her baseball bat, saving the victim. When the boys then accept her, she learns to swim, skate, fish, boat, hunt, trap, box, and break horses. Twain clearly exhibits a keen appreciation for Rachel adopting these "masculine" traits and living the life of a boy, but he scorns Oscar for his so-called feminine traits. He musters no sympathy for figures like Orion, while clearly excited by the colorfully androgynous Rachel.

One day, when Rachel is a teenager, her aunt Betsy comes to warn her that the town is gossiping about her. "There is one kind of gossip that this town has never dealt in before, in the fifty-two years that I've lived in it—and has never had any occasion to."[13] Aunt Betsy urges the girl to mend her ways—and fast. Though the word "lesbian" is never mentioned, it seems to overshadow the conversation; it may also be that Rachel was accused of being the town tramp with the boys. Whatever the case, Rachel pledges to reform and give up doing "ungirlish things except when it is a duty and I ought to do them."[14] But she lodges a protest at the conventional roles society has foisted on her and Thug. "Thug Carpenter is out of his sphere, I am out of mine. Neither of us can arrive at any success in life, we shall always be hampered and fretted and kept back by our misplaced sexes, and in the end defeated by them . . . I am sorry for him, and yet I do not see that he is any more entitled to pity than I am."[15] Twain never finished this extended story, perhaps because it embroiled him in moral quandaries he wasn't prepared to face as a

Victorian man. He gloried in portraying emancipated female adolescents even though he didn't know how to handle them as adults.

While in Weggis, Twain completed a remarkable document titled "Villagers of 1840–3," a compilation of more than one hundred thumbnail sketches of characters from his Hannibal youth. He had often written about his boyhood with sentimental affection. In the unpublished "Villagers," he writes in a far more waspish vein, venting his true opinions of the townspeople and why he had distanced himself from them. He strips away the Tom Sawyer sugarcoating and uncovers a scene of surpassing horror. "Villagers" is an eye-opening compendium of disappointed lives and further proof for Twain that fate was malevolent. It shows that had he dared to try, he had enough material for two dozen tragic novels and might have rivaled anything from the pen of Thomas Hardy or Edith Wharton. He felt nostalgia for his own boyhood in Hannibal, not for the town as a whole. In fact, the backwater now seemed cursed with misfortune. In the aftermath of a calamity in his own life, he revisited his past to unveil the darker truths that lay buried in his earlier fictional accounts of Hannibal.

In "Villagers," Twain employs invented names, but the sketches are transparently based on real people. The Clemens family appears as the Carpenters: Jane Clemens becomes Joanna Carpenter, Orion becomes Oscar Carpenter, and so on. Perhaps the most common theme is that highly romantic courtships are followed by abysmal marriages as husbands abuse or abandon once-loved wives. Life chews up people and destroys them. Here is the capsule summary of Mary Moss:

> Mary, very sweet and pretty at 16 and 17. Wanted to marry George Robards. Lawyer Lakenan, the rising stranger, held to be the better match by the parents, who were looking higher than commerce. They made her engage herself to L.L. made her study hard a year to fit herself to be his intellectual company; then married her, shut her up, the docile and heart-hurt young beauty, and continued her education rigorously. When he was ready to trot her out in society 2 years later and exhibit her, she had become wedded to her seclusion and her melan-

choly broodings, and begged to be left alone. He compelled her—that is, commanded. She obeyed. Her first exit was her last. The sleigh was overturned, her thigh was broken; it was badly set. She got well with a terrible limp, and forever after stayed in the house and produced children. Saw no company, not even the mates of her girlhood.[16]

Perhaps Twain wanted to illustrate his thesis that life lifted people's hopes only to violate them cruelly. It also vindicated his sense that youth was the only worthwhile period and that it was all downhill after that. For Lavinia Honeyman, he writes:

she captured "celebrated" circus-rider—envied for the unexampled brilliancy of the match—but he got into the penitentiary at Jefferson City and the romance was spoiled.[17]

For Letitia Honeyman:

School. Married a showy stranger. Turned out to be a thief and swindler. She and her baby waited while he served a long term. At the end of it her youth was gone, and her cheery ways.[18]

With Jim Quarles, Twain presents yet another dissolute husband:

Tinner. Set up in business by his father—$3,000—a fortune, then. Popular young beau—dancer—flutist—serenader—envied—a great catch. Married a child of 14. Two babies the result. Father highly disapproved the marriage. Dissipation—often drunk. Neglected the business—and the child-wife and babies. Left them and went to California. The little family went to Jim's father. Jim became a drunken loafer in California, and so died.[19]

In his current frame of mind, Twain saw far more evil than good in the universe and toyed with a manuscript called "Letters to Satan," in which Satan's deputy reports to him about the fertile territory on Earth. Satan is described as a person "who for untold centuries has maintained the imposing position of spiritual head of 4/5 of the human race, and political head of the whole of it," possessing "executive abilities of the highest order."[20] The deputy strives to induce Satan to visit Earth, where he would be treated as a superstar. "You would have a vast welcome in Paris, London, New York, Chicago, Washington, and the other capitals of the world; if you would go on the lecture platform you could charge what you pleased."[21] With imperialism on Twain's mind, the satanic deputy takes a swipe at Cecil Rhodes's growing influence in South Africa. "I doubted if it was needful to grease Mr. Cecil Rhodes's palm any further, for I think he would serve you just for the love of it."[22]

Amid these gloomy reflections there came a happy reminder of Black life in America when the Fisk Jubilee Singers performed in Weggis. The a cappella group was touring to raise money for Fisk University in Nashville, and Twain again responded to their songs of joy and lamentation, which had sometimes contained coded messages for the enslaved. As early as 1873 Twain had written a publicity blurb honoring the Jubilee Singers as authentic voices of the Black experience and scoffed at comparisons with fake minstrel shows: "I think these gentlemen & ladies make eloquent music . . . they reproduce the true melody of the plantations, & are the only persons I ever heard accomplish this on the public platform. The so-called 'negro minstrels' simply mis-represent the thing; I do not think they ever saw a plantation or ever heard a slave sing."[23]

When the Jubilee Singers performed in Weggis at a local beer hall that August, Twain's love for the group and its music flamed anew. At first, he observed, the German and Swiss patrons chattered over their beer mugs and seemed indifferent to the sextet preparing at the far end of the room. "The Singers got up & stood—the talking & glass-jingling went on. Then rose & swelled out above those common earthly sounds one of those rich chords the secret of whose make only the Jubilees possess, & a spell fell upon that house. It was fine to see the faces light up with the pleased wonder & surprise of it."[24] For Twain, "their music made all other vocal music cheap."[25] In the end, he bestowed on this music his highest encomium as "the perfectest flower of the ages." Stirred to his core,

Twain said that the singing was "utterly beautiful . . . and it moves me infinitely more than any other music can."[26]

The next day in his notebook he wrote that the six singers were "diviner, even, than in their early days, 26 years ago. They came up to the house this morning & sang to us. They are as fine people as I am acquainted with in any country."[27] Their private performance for Twain expressed the depth of their affection for him. He had a chance to get acquainted with the six singers—three born into slavery, the other three children of the enslaved—and found them as endearing as their music. "How charming they were—in spirit, manner, language, pronunciation, enunciation, grammar, phrasing, matter, carriage, clothes—in every detail that goes to make the real lady and gentleman, and welcome guest."[28]

On September 19, 1897, the Clemens family bid farewell to Weggis and worked their way east via rail toward Vienna, stopping en route at Lucerne, Zurich, Innsbruck, and Salzburg. Vienna was the destination of choice so that Clara could continue her piano studies there. In the wake of Susy's death, Sam and Livy found it difficult to deny their daughters' desires. Twain felt refreshed by his Weggis dalliance and the temporary relief from worldly cares. "I have seen a newspaper only 3 times in 10 weeks," he boasted. "I do not know what has been happening in the world, and do not seem any the worse for it."[29] He felt more confident about his ability to repay the remnant of his debt, ahead of schedule, and be spared the fatigue of the lecture platform.

Upon reaching Vienna, the Clemenses poked their heads into eight hotels before settling on the luxurious Hotel Metropole, an emblem of Old World splendor and a favorite haunt of the aristocratic class. The hostelry gained special cachet from the presence that winter of the emperor's sister. The Clemenses occupied a palatial suite—seven rooms with tall ceilings, including a music room for Clara and a study for Twain—with views of the nearby Danube Canal and the distant new Ferris wheel, shining in the Prater park. Of the spacious hotel, Twain observed: "The bathroom on our floor was 50 yards distant, and as I was often tired and they didn't allow bicycles in the hall, I didn't take any baths that year."[30] Despite the summer interlude in Weggis, Sam and Livy immediately succumbed to fresh medical ailments, Sam laid up with gout—what he dubbed "toothache in the toe"—and Livy stricken with painful rheumatism that kept her bedridden for several days.[31]

Twain was instantly recognized in the hotel and soon received a coveted invitation from Princess Pauline von Metternich to visit her parlor. She thrust out her hand in a "hearty grasp" and greeted her famous visitor: "I am very, very glad to meet you and know you, Mr. Clemens—I have read your books and am familiar with them and they have given me great enjoyment." The princess had read *Joan of Arc* three times and was still upset at Joan's treatment by the clerics. "Poor child," she said, "but for the priests it would not have happened; but whenever *they* meddle, harm must come to somebody." "Particularly when they and politics join teams and meddle *together*," retorted Twain, who was astonished when the princess seconded his view with gusto.[32] It was the start of a social whirl for Twain that would stand in stark contrast to his London seclusion the previous winter, when the sting of Susy's death was still fresh.

Even before his arrival, the Viennese press heralded the news that Mark Twain planned to spend many months in their city. No other American author enjoyed such renown in Austria—*A Tramp Abroad* had been a special favorite in central Europe—and readers quickly emptied bookstores of his titles. Reporters, photographers, and autograph hounds descended on the Hotel Metropole, eager to glimpse Twain. Since attention acted as a tonic to his spirit, he was happy to appease this feverish curiosity and gave a collective interview to a flock of reporters as he smoked a pipe in his hotel bed. When Livy objected that one reporter might be embarrassed to find him in bed, he shot back, "Why, if you think so, Livy, we could have the other bed made up for him."[33] He was no less readily accessible to ordinary Viennese as he loitered on a nearby bridge over the Danube, or sat in Johann Strauss's private box at a concert, or was ogled by strangers on the Ringstrasse.

"LETTERS TO SATAN"

Twain befriended two of the town's most illustrious journalists. One was Eduard Pötzl, the hugely popular satirist for the *Neues Wiener Tagblatt*. Witty and colorful, he had quizzically arched brows, penetrating eyes, an upturned mustache, and a salt-and-pepper Van Dyke beard. A decade earlier, he and nine other writers for his newspaper, most of them Jewish, had been beaten by anti-Semitic nationalist thugs who denounced their "shameful Jewish rag."[34] This gifted storyteller was Twain's cicerone as he explored Vienna, and he dined frequently with the Clemenses. The other writer who latched on to Twain was Siegmund Schlesinger, who came from an assimilated Jewish family and had worked as a theater critic. Schlesinger proposed to Twain that they collaborate on two comedies, with Twain responsible for plots and characters and Schlesinger supplying German dialogue. Neither project ever came to fruition.

Twain was deluged with invitations from diplomats, writers, and society figures, and embraced these social opportunities. As he burst from his mourning shell and became a bon vivant in Vienna—his calendar hadn't been this crowded in years—Livy stuck to the safety of the hotel, though she graciously received callers at five p.m. Twain attempted to induce her to join him in his forays, but she couldn't shake the presence of Susy, and he often had to settle for Clara as his escort. Though Twain socialized without her, his bond with Livy remained solid during their long stay in Vienna. When they learned that Dr. James Clemens was getting married, Livy sent a congratulatory note to the bride. "I believe you have done, or are about to do, wisely. I have found that marrying a Clemens the very best and happiest thing that I ever did."[35]

On the rare occasions when Sam and Livy ventured out together, sharp-eyed observers spotted that the two had survived recent trauma. When they went to tea with Madame Laszowska—the Scottish-born Jane Emily Gerard—their hostess could still discern the shadow cast by Susy's death. "Mark Twain himself is older looking than I had expected and strikes one at first as an excessively serious almost solemn person—I don't think I have seen him smile and only a curious sort of twinkle in his wonderfully expressive eyes betrays the real man at times—He was here yesterday to afternoon tea and talked almost incessantly for an hour and a half on every possible subject—Mrs. Clemens is also very intelligent and charming in manner but looks delicate—They are all still in deep mourning and have evidently not yet recovered from the loss of an eldest daughter."[36]

One factor that perhaps kept Livy close to home was Jean's worsening condition. Twain suspected that her epilepsy had resulted from a bad blow to her head when she fell at age eight or nine, although she had also fallen "head first off a high porch" when she was one.[37] In 1892, while staying at Bad Tölz in Bavaria, Twain had first noticed the mysterious alteration in his youngest daughter. From a sweet, outgoing child, she had metamorphosed into someone "often gloomy; prone to uncharitable judgments . . . From that time forth she was a mystery, and remained one for four years, until she fell in a fit at school one day and a physician was called who discovered that she was epileptic and said she had long been possessed by this hideous disease."[38] At first, when Jean grew difficult, Twain suspected that her "real" nature was emerging. In retrospect, he perceived that epilepsy had blotted out her true nature, substituting a more difficult one.

Jean suffered her first grand mal seizure in February 1896 while staying at Quarry Farm during her father's world tour. She came under the care of Dr. M. Allen Starr, a New York physician and professor of neurology at Columbia University, a leading expert in neurological diseases. He prescribed daily doses of bromide—an effective sedative in low doses but with potentially lethal effects in higher ones—as well as exercise, a diet of fruits and vegetables, and plenty of water. "There is nothing to do in an attack but to keep her quiet, loosen her dress, put a spoon between her teeth, and cool cloths to her head," Dr. Starr counseled Sue Crane, then caring for Jean. "The attack is not harmful or dangerous, tho' disagreeable to see."[39] That a second daughter had come down with a major illness during his world tour could only have multiplied Twain's already massive guilt about his forced absence.

Outwardly, Jean led a normal, if restricted, life in Vienna, developing a love of wood carving and learning Polish. But after she suffered two seizures in Weggis, her parents had grown more anxious and alarmed. Around the time the Clemenses arrived in Vienna, Jean suffered an epileptic seizure that Twain recorded as the sixth she had experienced. There was clearly a disturbing progression in the disease, now erupting with growing frequency. From Dr. Starr, Twain had gotten a referral to Professor Heinrich Obersteiner, a colleague of Sigmund Freud and an expert in pediatric neurology, who had helped to train Dr. Starr. Twain was a man well schooled in humane lies, and he informed Obersteiner that knowledge of her actual condition had been withheld from Jean— not surprising given the enormous stigma then attached to the disease. "She does not know what her difficulty is, but thinks herself subject to merely ordinary attacks of fainting; & we prefer to keep her in ignorance regarding their true character. Can we bring her to see you?"[40]

Dr. Obersteiner explained to the Clemenses that his young patients sometimes outgrew the disease, but he knew of no authentic cures. Under his management, Jean avoided attacks for three months. Then, on January 2, 1898, she was racked by a grand mal seizure, and Dr. Obersteiner upped her bromide doses to two daily, with three to six doses for emergencies. He warned the Clemenses that the medication could be poisonous, and "we were careful to obey," Twain said.[41] He and Livy kept a close record both of Jean's grand mal seizures—the outright convulsions— and of the fits of absentmindedness known as petit mal seizures. In January 1898, Jean's epilepsy grew so severe that Twain set down this grim toll: "Jan. 2. 1898, two convulsions, with interval of consciousness between. *Interval of 7 days.* Jan. 25, bad. Four convulsions, with intervals of consciousness between." While the grand mal seizures were more frightening, the prolonged petit mal seizures were also severely debilitating. "March 20, bad; absent-minded; *Interval of 8 days.* March 28, bad all day; gave 6 powders."[42] Over an eighteen-month period, from January 1898 to July 1899, Jean Clemens swallowed 648 doses of a drug that was intermittently effective but could be toxic in large quantities.

Still reeling from Susy's death, Sam and Livy now faced the gruesome task of monitoring their youngest daughter's illness day and night. The need to administer the bromide made them constantly watchful of her slightest symptoms. Of the brief episodes of lost awareness during petit mal seizures, Twain wrote: "The signs of coming trouble were easily detectable: a sudden extinction of expression in the face as if a light had been blown out; speech ceased, perhaps in the middle of a sentence; vacant fumbling with the fingers, as if searching for something. This might continue half a minute; then the light would come back, the fumbling cease, and the sentence be taken up where it had broken off. If these absences occurred at considerable intervals apart, nothing was done, but a strict watch was kept; but if they came at brief and shortening intervals, and amounted to half a dozen within an hour, an extra bromide powder was administered."[43] After these episodes, the patient was often unaware that anything had happened. Kept on tenterhooks as they braced for the next episode, the Clemens family had to act as both doctors and nurses. It was "like watching a house that was forever catching fire, & promised to burn down if you ever closed an eye," Twain said, an image that suggested how worn out by anxiety he and Livy were.[44]

Of course, the grand mal seizures were far more harrowing for Jean than for her family. They always started with her screaming and could last several minutes, accompanied by spasmodic movements of arms and legs and shrieking sounds. Sometimes patients experience foaming at the mouth and even involuntary bladder or bowel movements. Breathing can momentarily stop and the skin can turn bluish. Unlike petit mal seizures, a grand mal leaves the patient feeling confused and exhausted, often bruised and depressed. There is reason to believe that Twain found these major seizures so unbearable to watch that he left it to others to deal with them. In 1902 he told Henry Rogers that he had just seen Jean have a grand mal seizure, adding, "I have seen it only three times before, in all these five fiendish years."[45] Clara, a witness to everything, recalled that "it was not easy to see the life of a lovely young girl blighted by so devastating an illness and still less so because my sister was heroically uncomplaining."[46]

While Twain attended social events in Vienna with Clara, he always left Jean behind, probably fearing she might have an attack in public—

something that would be embarrassing or even dangerous to Jean and would broadcast her secret to the world. So Jean and Livy stayed behind at the Hotel Metropole. Aware that Jean might harm herself if left alone, her parents became extremely protective and restricted her social life, stunting her emotional growth and trapping her in a protracted adolescence. During the summer of 1898, which the Clemenses spent in the suburb of Kaltenleutgeben, the Countess Wydenbruck-Esterházy assigned her thirteen-year-old daughter, Clementine, to stay with Jean, play with her, and keep an eye on her, although she didn't know the exact nature of her illness. The girl found Jean trying at times. As an elderly woman, Clementine remembered "Mr. Clemens's great tenderness" toward Jean and "his many acts and expressions of gratitude to my mother and me."[47] To repay her kindness, Twain gave three readings for the countess.

While Jean certainly suffered most from her disease, it was a crushing blow to her parents, who were already weakened by bankruptcy and bereavement. Livy tried to be brave and hopeful. "Sometimes I feel courage that [Jean] will overcome her difficulty," she wrote to her brother in April 1898, "but I do not always feel it."[48] Jean's absentminded spells could leave her in a listless, almost comatose state. After one bad day, Livy wrote to Sue Crane: "She had no falling time but it seemed as if she were almost the same as unconscious all day long. Sometimes I am deeply discouraged about her. Then sometimes she goes for several days without a sign or symptom of absentmindedness. Poor dear little Jean, what an intolerably hard world it seems most of the time & to the great majority of people."[49] In addition to worrying about Jean, Twain fretted about the intolerable toll this stress took on his fragile wife. Jean's "disease, and its accompanying awful convulsions, wore out her gentle mother's strength with grief and watching and anxiety."[50] Twain was no less drained by this incessant care, later recalling that "we were always dreading that some frightful accident would happen to her that would stretch her mutilated upon her bed for the rest of her life—or, worse—that her mind would become affected."[51] Of course, the specter of Susy's last days was never far from their minds.

CHAPTER THIRTY-NINE

"Stirring Times in Austria"

Not long after he arrived in Vienna, Twain received an invitation that gave him a choice opportunity to revile a favorite target: the infernal German language. No newcomer to this territory, he had contributed an appendix on "The Awful German Language" to *A Tramp Abroad*. He had a sneaking fondness for a tongue so turgid you can "travel all day in one sentence without changing cars."[1] Even in *A Connecticut Yankee* he took swipes at the language: "Whenever the literary German dives into a sentence, that is the last you are going to see of him till he emerges on the other side of his Atlantic with his verb in his mouth."[2] He spent wearisome years trying to master the language. He had a fair German vocabulary locked in his brain and sometimes even hazarded conversation. According to one Viennese who met him, he spoke passable German "with an American accent and underscores his speech with emphatic gestures."[3]

One morning, two young men in evening dress came to the Hotel Metropole and invited him to make remarks on the German language at a banquet of the Concordia Press Club. Only once before had the club deigned to ask a foreigner to speak—Henrik Ibsen, six years earlier. Twain elected to title his speech "*Die Schrecken der deutschen Sprache*"— "The Horrors of the German Language," as he translated it.[4] The local press, softening its tone, reported it as "The Difficulties of the German Language." For the event an enormous hall was decked with red-white-and-blue bunting and a large portrait of Twain floated above the motto "e pluribus unum." It seemed as if every luminary in Vienna packed the banquet room and scarcely a distinguished name in literary or cultural circles was absent. Among the eminent throng sat Gustav Mahler, the opera director and composer, and Theodor Herzl, visionary of the Zionist movement.

Amid a boisterous, beer hall atmosphere, Twain delighted the audience by speaking in German, explaining that while he spoke German poorly, he had been told he wrote it "like an angel." Of course, he added, he only knew that secondhand since he had never dealt with angels. He had practical suggestions to reform the language's lengthy sentences by forbidding no more than thirteen subjects in one sentence. Of the German habit of placing the verb at the end of the sentence, he proposed pulling it "so far forward that one may discover it without a telescope."[5] Twain, a gracious speaker, concluded to rousing cheers. "I'm a foreigner but here among you in Vienna's hospitable atmosphere, I have completely forgotten it."[6] There was an undercurrent of discontent with Twain's speech since he had satirized the German language at a delicate moment in the Austro-Hungarian Empire: in administering Bohemia and Moravia, there was a plan to give the Czech language parity with the German, a move that angered German nationalists. As Twain would soon learn, Vienna was roiled with political passions. "The atmosphere is brimful of political electricity," he wrote. "All conversation is political . . . every man is a battery . . . and gives out blue sparks when you set him going on the common topic."[7]

On October 15, Twain appeared in the press box at a meeting of the Vienna City Council, held at the ornate town hall, and watched a rowdy session defined by two incendiary issues: the large Czech presence in the city and the paucity of Jews appointed to municipal judgeships. Twain glimpsed the dynamic but demagogic new mayor, Dr. Karl Lueger, who had embarked on a program of urban renewal to modernize utilities, public housing, and transportation in the old imperial city. With his populist charisma, Lueger had no scruples about exploiting anti-Semitism to rally his working-class base, and Adolf Hitler would laud him as "the last great German to be born in the ranks of the people" and "a states-

"STIRRING TIMES IN AUSTRIA"

man greater than all the so-called diplomats of the time."[8] At the session, Twain found it hard to pass himself off as just another journalist, and his presence was covered as an event in its own right.

This was a warm-up for the contentious parliamentary debates Twain attended on October 28 and 29. The arrangement that held Austria and Hungary together, the *Ausgleich,* had to be renewed by year's end, or the two nations would revert to separate entities. Government opponents in the Austrian legislature threatened to stall *Ausgleich* renewal to block the hated language bill. When this bill was introduced by the prime minister, Count Kasimir Badeni, in the Reichsrat, the federal Parliament, German nationalists were furious that German-speaking judges and bureaucrats in Bohemia and Moravia would have to learn Czech. During the stormy session, Twain heard Dr. Otto Lecher, a Moravian socialist, deliver an all-night, twelve-hour tirade in which he pleaded for Czech civil servants to have the right to speak their own language. German nationalists greeted his marathon speech with insults, catcalls, and table banging, plus a medley of horns, drums, and bells. Twain dubbed the twelve-hour oration "the longest flow of unbroken talk that ever came out of one mouth since the world began."[9] Upon returning to the Hotel Metropole, he babbled about the extraordinary spectacle. "Just think of it!" he told his family. "That man not only had material in his head to keep him talking for twelve hours, but he delivered this material in picturesque, literary language. And consider the physical side of it! What it would be to stand for twelve hours!"[10]

Political tension in the Austrian capital exploded in another parliamentary session on November 24, with Twain again present to witness the mayhem. He scribbled notes even as legislators stole glances at him. "There was hammering with fists, chokings, threatenings with chairs, a wound made with a penknife. A knife was drawn on the President, Abrahamovich."[11] Twain was back the next day when, anticipating trouble, conservative deputy Count Franz Falkenhayn introduced a measure that gave the presiding officer power "to use whatever force he thought necessary to maintain order," including summoning the police.[12] This triggered an indignant response from alarmed Socialists. The following day, when they elbowed aside the presiding officer and seized the podium, Twain described the entrance of a helmeted battalion of policemen, marching double file into the chamber. "To-day, 1.30, saw the great dramatic incident in the House when 60 policemen marched in & cleared the Presidium of 10 Social Democrats by violence. 4 were imprisoned on the premises."[13] As offending legislators were roughly dragged away, Twain found it scandalous to see "a free parliament profaned by an invasion of brute force."[14] In Austria, he decided, it was hard to distinguish parliamentary debate from artillery practice. There were false reports that Twain was caught up in the scuffle and hustled from the chamber, which amused him greatly. "The cable said a Czech hit me over the head in the Reichsrath, but it suppressed what I did to the Czech. There are orphans in that family now."[15]

Twain, having witnessed this historic moment, wondered whether parliamentary government or even the monarchy would survive this upheaval. His forecast proved accurate: the emperor cashiered Badeni as prime minister, dissolved Parliament, and allowed the government to act by decree. In the words of one historian, "From this moment the Habsburg realm was doomed."[16] Within twenty years, the monarchy would collapse as World War I and its aftermath overthrew royal houses across Europe.

In March 1898, Twain published an article, "Stirring Times in Austria," in *Harper's New Monthly Magazine*, detailing the pandemonium he had witnessed. It was an admirable attempt by Twain to do something he had never done before: penetrate the language and customs of a foreign political culture, even if he spilled more ink on insults and profanities than analysis. "The Badeni government came down with a crash; there was a popular outbreak or two in Vienna; there were three or four days of furious rioting in Prague, followed by the establishing there of martial law; the Jews and Germans were harried and plundered, and their houses destroyed; in other Bohemian towns there was rioting . . . and in all cases the Jew had to roast no matter which side he was on."[17] Twain, who never skirted controversy, was outspoken in denouncing the anti-Semitism rampant in Austria. The Jew haters pounced upon Twain,

"STIRRING TIMES IN AUSTRIA"

even claiming, because his first name was Samuel, that he was Jewish. When Twain was quoted as saying "There is not a single Austrian who has made a name for himself that would be known around the entire globe," the anti-Semitic press cast it aside as "another Jewish lie."[18]

Throughout his life, Mark Twain issued compliments about the Jews, remarkable for a man often churlish in his outlook. This friendly feeling may have stemmed from his mother, who always liked to stop by synagogues as well as churches. As a boy, Twain had experienced an uneasy fascination with Jewish boys in his school. "To my fancy they were clothed invisibly in the damp and cobwebby mould of antiquity."[19] As early as 1870, he protested that the Crusaders, before their Holy Land exploits, had engaged in "wholesale butcheries and burnings of Jewish women and children."[20] In 1879 he wrote in his notebook: "Samson was a Jew—therefore not a fool. The Jews have the best average brain of any people in the world . . . They are peculiarly & conspicuously the world's intellectual aristocracy."[21] Twain told Joseph Twichell that the difference between the average Christian and Jewish brain "is about the difference between a tadpole's brain & an Archbishop's. It's a marvelous race—by long odds the most marvelous that the world has produced, I suppose."[22] In her biography of her father, Susy Clemens recorded Twain's reaction when asked why he never ridiculed Jews. He replied that "the Jews had always seemed to him, a race much to be respected; also they had suffered much, and had been greatly persecuted; so to ridicul[e] or make fun of them, seemed to be like attacking a man that was already down."[23] When Twain elaborated, he asserted that he had "never felt a disposition to satirize the Jews" because Jews never begged or engaged in manual labor and lived exclusively by their minds.[24]

Despite his evident warmth toward Jews, Twain had an awkward way of correcting one stereotype while stumbling into another. In *Life on the Mississippi*, he published an unfortunate passage about Jewish vendors preying on Black sharecroppers, so that "at the end of the season, the negro's share belongs to the Israelite, the negro is in debt besides."[25] To worsen matters, the accompanying illustration showed a stereotypical Jewish vendor with sideburns and a prominent hooked nose, while the Blacks were thick-lipped and laughing. Twain's frequent association of Jews with business cleverness could border on anti-Semitic caricature. He even saw the Old Testament God as a deity with "a good business head. He always stopped talking shop . . . & came right down to business whenever there was matter concerning shekels on hand."[26] Touring the Vienna stock exchange, he saluted enterprising Jewish brokers. "They are the smartest of the lot here . . . I say it again; the Jews are the greatest people let loose."[27] Whatever his shortcomings, Twain always meant well toward the Jews and was quick to take a stand in their defense. When invited to become a member of an anti-Semitic supper group called the Twilight Club, he vetoed the idea and wrote in his notebook: "Accept no courtesies of the Twilight Club; it thinks itself better than Jews."[28]

The heated anti-Semitism coursing through Viennese politics profoundly affected a Jewish writer named Theodor Herzl, who came to believe that the only answer to Jewish hatred in Europe would be establishing a Jewish homeland. Twain had briefly met the future father of Zionism at a Paris reception in 1894 when Herzl covered the Dreyfus affair for the *Neue Freie Presse*. In January 1898, when Herzl attended the premiere in Vienna of his play *Das neue Ghetto* (*The New Ghetto*), both Twain and Sigmund Freud formed part of the audience. (Freud later referred to Twain as "our old friend," and their friendship may have dated from this theater opening.[29]) Herzl's play dramatized an assimilated Austrian Jew who discovers that while Jews had escaped the physical ghetto, they were still penned in by social and psychological walls thrown up by the Gentile community. Twain, powerfully taken with this play, began to translate it in April and only dropped it because it would not sell well in New York. In his curiously divided mind, Twain opposed the creation of a Jewish state in Palestine, worrying what a "concentration of the cunningest brains in the world" would produce.

Few issues stoked Twain's righteous indignation more than the Dreyfus case. As one scholar observed, "References to the Dreyfus affair permeate almost everything Mark Twain wrote in Vienna."[30] In December 1894, Captain Alfred Dreyfus, a French army officer and a Jew, was wrongfully found guilty of treason and sentenced to Devil's Island in a proceeding that smacked of anti-Semitism. For years, the controversy would provoke outraged protests against the injustice done to Dreyfus, and Twain was a stalwart supporter of his innocence. "I remember Mother saying that Father was among the first few who were incensed at the unfair trial given Captain Dreyfus when he was dismissed from the Army and banished to a lonely island," Clara recalled.[31] Twain's writings on Joan of Arc had left a residue of anger against the French legal system, and the Dreyfus case inflamed his rooted prejudice against the French. As he wrote, "O Dreyfus! In his case the nation lost its head entirely . . . As for magnanimity, generosity, charity, manliness . . . They seem to be absent from that race."[32]

The Dreyfus case took an unexpected turn when evidence appeared that fingered French army officer Ferdinand W. Esterhazy as the real culprit. The anti-Semitic press blew up in protest against reopening the case. After Esterhazy was acquitted, Émile Zola wrote his famous letter "*J'Accuse . . . !*" in *L'Aurore,* berating the French government for having framed Dreyfus. A decade earlier, Twain had condemned Zola's novels as lewd and immoral, saying they poured from "Zola's sewer."[33] But after "*J'Accuse . . . !,*" Zola leaped to the top of his list of heroic French figures, and he drafted a tribute to Zola that appeared in the *New York Herald:* "It is a grand figure—Zola—standing there all alone fighting his splendid fight to save the remains of the honor of France . . . Ecclesiastical and military courts made up of cowards, hypocrites & time-servers can be bred at the rate of a million a year & have material left over; but it takes five centuries to breed a Joan of Arc & a Zola."[34] Just how passionate Twain was about Zola became clear to novelist Owen Wister when the French writer's name came up. "Mark Twain was striding up and down again, whirling on me once in a while, scowling fiercely at me, his blue eyes burning beneath the scowl, and the mound of hair all of a piece with the electric total of the man . . . Zola was the subject, he was wholly serious, very concentrated."[35]

Twain stuck to his guns on the Dreyfus case, even if he courted controversy. When he appeared at a pacifist meeting of the Austrian Friends of Peace, which had registered support for Zola, an anti-Semitic paper sneered at "the unavoidable Mark Twain, who seems to have no idea of how he is being mishandled by the Jews in Vienna."[36] Back in November 1897, Twain had been so appalled by anti-Semitic screeds against Dreyfus that he suggested that his British publisher, Chatto & Windus, publish a collection of them along with his own barbed reactions. "Together they ought to make a showy exhibition of the French backside. A book of those windy French editorials ought to be luxurious reading-matter now, & be a selling book."[37] As usual, Twain commingled idealism with greed, persuaded the book could sell two million copies. Chatto countered that the English had scant interest in the case and spurned the idea. When Zola then riveted press attention with "*J'Accuse . . . !*," Twain believed a huge commercial opportunity had been frittered away, scolding Chatto, "I'm trying hard not to cry over the spilt milk, but I *am* crying over it just the same; for I knew, at the time, that we were wasting the opportunity of the century, & of course I know it all the better now."[38]

With the fate of the Jews an inescapable topic in Vienna, anti-Semites charged them with nefarious control of banks, newspapers, and businesses. An influx of Jews in the late nineteenth century had fomented a backlash from those who resented their economic competition. Moving in a milieu rich with Jewish writers, artists, and intellectuals, Twain was naturally drawn to this debate. In July 1898, responding to libels printed against him in the anti-Semitic press, where he was pilloried as "*der Jude Mark Twain*"—the Jew Mark Twain—he wrote an article, "Concerning the Jews," that was published in *Harper's Magazine*.[39] Immensely proud of the piece, he told Henry Rogers that it was "my gem of the ocean . . . I really believe that I am the only man in the world who is equipped to write upon the subject without prejudice . . . If I have any leaning it is toward the Jew, not the Christian."[40]

In the piece, Twain depicted himself as a man singularly free of prejudice: "All that I care to know is that a man is a human being—that is enough for me; he can't be any worse. I have no special regard for Satan;

but I can at least claim that I have no prejudice against him. It may even be that I lean a little his way, on account of his not having a fair show."[41] Turning to the Jews, Twain enumerated their virtues: they were hardworking, didn't engage in murder or violent crimes, and enjoyed a close-knit family life. Then he turned to discreditable charges leveled against the Jew: "He has a reputation for various small forms of cheating, and for practising oppressive usury, and for burning himself out to get the insurance."[42] Twain didn't endorse these views but he did list them. He repeated the story of Jewish storekeepers exploiting sharecroppers in the South, leaving them indebted. "Before long, the whites detested the Jew, and it is doubtful if the negro loved him."[43] Pretty soon he had perpetuated stereotypes of bloodsucking Jewish businessmen, cheating people through sharp practices. He denied that anti-Semitism arose from Christians blaming Jews for the Crucifixion. Instead, he traced it to the inability of Christians to compete successfully with the Jew, who is "a money-getter."[44] He said the Jew made the pursuit of wealth "the end and aim of his life," while failing to acknowledge that the vast majority of Jews in history, owing to discrimination, were impoverished.[45] Despite constant attacks on Jews in Vienna, Twain naively imagined that they were now safe from persecution. He saw Jews as doomed to be "strangers—foreigners . . . and that will probably keep the race prejudices against you alive."[46]

For a man who prided himself on his absence of prejudice, Twain had produced an incredible farrago of myths and half-truths combined with some enlightened thinking. He was trying to make the case that Jews had provoked criticism because of their business success, which he admired, but he was blind to the damaging stereotypes he had perpetuated. In another context, he made the more levelheaded statement: "Envy of Jewish talents and brains has moved the Gentiles to behave like wild beasts toward a people in some respects their superior."[47] When the essay was published in the United States, the Jewish community, while acknowledging Twain's good intentions, faulted him for insinuating that Jews had an "unpatriotic disinclination to stand by the flag as a soldier—like the Christian Quaker."[48] Rabbi M. S. Levy, in "A Rabbi's Reply to

Mark Twain," cited the large number of brave, patriotic Jews who had fought in America's wars. The most vigorous riposte came from Simon Wolf, a prominent lawyer in the Jewish community, who sent Twain a copy of his book *The American Jew as Patriot, Soldier and Citizen*, listing the names of thousands of Jewish soldiers and the wars they had fought in. Acknowledging his error, a contrite Twain agreed to correct the false impression that he had conveyed and did so in 1904 in a "Postscript: The Jew as a Soldier." He would never stop fighting to protect Jews, and much of his later criticism of Czar Nicholas II arose from outrage over "the daily slaughter of the helpless Jews that that infamous [Russian] Government has been carrying on daily for two years."[49]

After Susy's death, Sam and Livy refused to be separated from their two remaining daughters and catered to Clara's musical wishes despite ambivalent feelings about her career. Always well turned out, Clara was attractive, dark-haired, and petite, with eyes that sparkled like her father's, and one newspaper depicted her as "dainty and pretty as a cameo."[50] She also suffered from depression, insomnia, and uncertain health. Katy Leary said a stream of "elegant military men" flocked to the Hotel Metropole to join Clara for music and tea, and she enjoyed gleaming evenings of waltz music and dancing.[51] Like her father, she was a restless, temperamental soul, with a driving creative urge that would, at various times, seek an outlet in piano playing, singing, and writing, but she never prospered to the extent she desired, her ambition always exceeding her talent. With Susy's death and Jean's epilepsy, Clara was the "normal" child, supposed to lend emotional sustenance to her parents. "When Clara is away from me for a day the sense of loneliness is so great," wrote Livy, "that it makes me hope that it will be many a long day before any one succeeds in persuading her to leave home."[52] With her strong-willed personality, Clara would thrash against the bars of her family cage, torn between career and family loyalty. When she turned twenty-four in June 1898, no reference was made to her birthday out of deference to Susy.

The lodestar for every aspiring pianist in Vienna, if not Europe, was the brilliant Polish pedagogue Theodor Leschetizky, a stellar pianist in his own right. A hearty, bearded man of sixty-seven with energy to spare, he had hobnobbed with Anton Bruckner, Johann Strauss the Younger, and Johannes Brahms, and his tutelage helped launch the careers of Ignacy Jan Paderewski and Artur Schnabel. As soon as the Clemenses had unpacked at the Hotel Metropole, they rushed over to Leschetizky so Clara could audition for him. Everyone knew that he was an exacting, indeed a terrifying teacher, and Clara was so unnerved by his presence that she "stammered through" an interview in German before stumbling through a piano piece.[53] A man with multiple wives and mistresses, Leschetizky had a reputation as a notorious lecher who seduced his students, and Clara's charms may not have been lost on him when he accepted her as a student.

To become a Leschetizky student was to enter into his rarefied social circle. Twain and Clara were soon invited to a glittering soiree at Ritter von Dutschka's, where twenty people dined and listened to "Leschy," as Twain called him, who delivered a "marvelous performance" at the keyboard.[54] On January 19, 1898, Sam and Livy drove out to Leschy's home to attend a piano class. The maestro's teaching style was to have two pianos in a room crowded with friends, family, students, and musical personalities. First the student played a piece—looking "ill with terror," Clara remembered—as the bearish Leschy marched about the room before sitting down and demonstrating on his piano how it should have been played.[55] Sometimes, in a fit of pique, he would tear up sheet music that the pupil was playing. "Beautiful as the pupils' work had been," acknowledged Twain, "the superior splendor of the master's touch was immediately recognizable. He gave one young lady a devastating dressing down—poured out wrath, criticism, sarcasm and humor upon her in a flood for 10—no, as much as 12 minutes. He is a most capable & felicitous talker—was born for an orator, I think. What life, energy, fire, in a man past 70! And how he does play! He is easily the greatest pianist in the world."[56] That Twain admired Leschy's piano prowess isn't surprising. That he was so bowled over by him as a talker testifies to the teacher's stupendous personality. At a subsequent dinner, it was Leschy, not Twain, who held the group spellbound, serving up three hours of lively anecdotes about his participation in the 1848 revolution, and "his battle pictures were magnificently worded," Twain wrote.[57] It was unquestionably a novel experience for Twain to yield the spotlight to another speaker.

Clara practiced piano three to four hours each day, and "between her work & her society-intercourse she gets some sleep now & then, but not much," Twain noted.[58] She claimed that Leschy treated her beautifully—he nicknamed her "Night" because of her partiality for black clothes—but then she had to perform at one of his high-pressure salon recitals. In this environment, she had a sense of total inadequacy. As she sat down to play a Mendelssohn piano concerto, her mind was invaded by anxious thoughts. "Everyone has better hands than mine; miserable dwarf things! And of course those vultures know every note of this concerto."[59] As Clara performed, Leschy sat at his second piano, playing the accompaniment, and he "entered with such thundering chords, that I was frightened to a complete standstill. My hands dropped from the keys and I stared at him. This drew uproarious laughter from the audience and my remaining wits took flight."[60] Clara's hands were so small that as she moved through the concerto, people continued to laugh. Afterward she escaped to a small reception room where she was comforted by an extraordinary young Jewish pianist from Russia, Ossip Gabrilowitsch, Leschy's star pupil. "You must not mind those people," he told Clara. "They like to laugh. It was just the size of your hands. You played the slow movement beautifully. I'll show you some exercises for stretching the fingers."[61] Gabrilowitsch was hardly the only young man in Vienna bewitched by Clara. "Boys," Leschy told one gathering, "it seems to me that you are all suffering from the same trouble—'Delirium Clemens.'"[62] Before these hordes of admiring young men, Twain stood vigilant guard over Clara.

A few years younger than Clara, Gabrilowitsch was a twenty-year-

"STIRRING TIMES IN AUSTRIA"

old prodigy who had started piano studies at age five and attracted Anton Rubinstein as a mentor, who declared him destined to be a great musician. By sixteen, he had graduated from the St. Petersburg Conservatory with honors and was already making public appearances by the time Clara met him. He was pale and thin with a sheaf of wavy hair that swept up majestically from a high forehead. The composer Charles Ives once said Ossip "looked the way musicians are supposed to look in novels, from his long hair to his habit of screwing up one's eye while he was talking."[63] Ossip was poetic, imaginative, and charming, which appealed mightily to Clara's idealism, but in his fire, sensitivity, and passion, she recognized similarities to her father. His humor, his wordplay, his talent for mimicry—all were reminiscent of Father. Clara feared Ossip had an autocratic streak and suffered from "Russian melancholy."[64] It would take years before these two intense personalities would merge their lives. With her fiercely independent streak, Clara was reluctant to wed, while Gabrilowitsch's demanding professional schedule meant incessant travel around the world. Their long, stormy relationship would recapitulate Clara's conflicted relationship with her father. Avis Bliven Charbonnel, who also studied with Leschetizky, recalled of Clara and Ossip: "They fell in love and would have married except for Mr. Clemens's objection... At one time I heard Gabrilowitsch say, 'I will wait. If I can't marry Clara, I'll never marry.'"[65] They would be twice engaged and twice it would be broken off—"both times to Mrs. Clemens' great regret," Twain said.[66] If Twain opposed the marriage, it wasn't from any dislike of Ossip, for he liked him as a person, admired him as an intellect, and adored him as a performer, but probably Twain's extreme protectiveness informed his caution.

By October 1898, Clara came to a difficult decision to abandon the piano; her small hands boded ill for a career. It may also be that the sensitive Clara knew she lacked the temperament to endure sustained practice and punishing criticism. She had also discovered that she might be better matched with a singing career. She had an Italian friend, Alice Barbi, who had heard her sing that summer, was pleased by her voice, and steered her to a teacher named Marianne Brandt. Clara's contralto voice, if not big enough for opera, was well suited to *Lieder*. Clara soon grew tired of Brandt's methods and dismissed her, saying she "knew nothing about voice production."[67] Insecure and temperamental, Clara ran through a series of voice coaches. From the outset, she was plagued by vocal problems that forced frequent rest cures, setting a pattern that would recur throughout her singing career.

Exhibiting a mixture of emotions about Clara's plans, Livy told a friend that she and her husband were "both glad & sorry" about her decision to switch to vocal training.[68] They believed that it would be less taxing and possibly more remunerative than piano, but they hated to see her throw overboard all the hard training with Leschetizky. "Clara has worked at the piano so long & faithfully & seemed so nearly to have reached her goal . . . that we felt many pangs in seeing her give it up."[69] Sam and Livy had also nursed hopes that once Clara wound up her training with Leschetizky in spring 1899, they could end their long European exile. "Then we shall go home & shall be deeply content to burn the trunks & stay there," Twain told a friend.

Twain's immersion in the rich musical culture of Vienna elevated him to a new level of sophistication in his appreciation of classical music. In many ways, the city gave him the musical education that he had sorely missed. In the future, he would display much more familiarity with classical works and no longer have to concentrate so hard to enjoy them. At the Court Opera (now the State Opera), where Gustav Mahler was the director, Twain saw works by Wagner, Bizet, Mozart, Verdi, and Beethoven. When attending a concert in the great hall of the *Musikverein*, Twain was invited to join "the Waltz King" of Vienna himself, Johann Strauss, Jr., in his private box. The two men became friends, and when Strauss died after Twain had left Vienna for London, he wrote to the widow: "When I talked & smoked with him in your house only twelve days ago, he seemed in all ways his old natural self—alert, quick, brilliant in speech, and wearing all the graces of his indestructible youth; & now—why it seems impossible that he is gone!"[70]

CHAPTER FORTY

"The European Edison"

Even as Mark Twain captivated Viennese society, he was abruptly thrust back into his checkered family past when his brother Orion died on December 11, 1897. Orion had been a kindly man, doomed to mediocrity and susceptible to quixotic gestures and mental instability. Because his brother's story had struck him as a cautionary tale, Twain had modeled many characters on him and that July had projected another Huck Finn book in which Orion would appear as Tom Sawyer's uncle, "full of political & religious changes, lawyer & editor."[1] Eleven days before his death, Orion wrote to congratulate his brother on retiring his debt and suggested using him as a "fool character" in his fiction—a sad touch of humility so characteristic of the man.[2]

To the end, Orion aspired to his own literary achievements in a lifelong game of sibling rivalry that he was destined to lose. He had been hard at work on a biography of Judas of Galilee and an Essene sect known as the Society of the Dead Sea. One cold December morning, he had descended to the kitchen to light a fire, then sat down to record some notes. According to one version, Mollie found him dead, his head sunk low, both arms hanging at his side. Twain, perhaps improving on the pathos, had Orion holding a pencil "resting against the paper in the middle of an unfinished word"—symbolic of his incomplete life.[3] Twain responded to Mollie's news with purehearted concern. "We all grieve for you, our sympathy goes out to you from experienced hearts, and with it our love . . . [Orion] was good—all good, and sound; there was nothing bad in him, nothing base, nor any unkindness."[4] Twain omitted any mention of the failures, heartache, and screwball projects that had gone nowhere and advised his Hartford business agent to go on subsidizing Mollie to the tune of fifty dollars per month.

Those who knew Orion echoed Twain's bittersweet reflections upon him. "Our memory of him," wrote Twichell, "is of a gentle and amiable spirit—remarkably disposed to the things of good will. May he rest in peace."[5] After the many misfortunes of his brother's wayward life, Twain believed his death had been swift and merciful. Though he could sound cold-blooded about his brother, the death had an impact on him, coming so soon after Susy's. "Clara and I had started into society," he told Rogers, "and were dining and lunching and going to operas, and were getting at times cheerful once more; but we are all once more under a cloud, through the death of my brother, and have resumed our former seclusion."[6]

By the summer of 1897, Twain saw his mountain of debt dwindling ahead of schedule, thanks to book royalties and savvy speculations executed by Henry Rogers. He didn't care to advertise an end to the debt drama, however, explaining to Rogers that for his current book the subscription "canvassers will want to use my load of debt as a persuader, and make people buy the book to get me out. By George it's a shabby business."[7] Enough debt lingered on the books that it impaired his writing that fall, and he claimed that he started and flung aside twenty projects in disgust. By December, Webster & Company's creditors were truly repaid and showered the Clemenses with effusive notes of gratitude. "I appreciate Mr. Clemens's manliness no less than his incomparable humor," said one creditor, while another rejoiced, "We have read of examples of such sterling integrity but this is the first time where a similar thing has occurred to us in our business experience."[8] "For the first time in my life," Twain joked to Rogers, "I am getting more pleasure out of paying money than pulling it in."[9] Livy, meanwhile, reaped "millions of delight out of it."[10] Feeling vindicated in her decision to press for full repayment of the debt, Livy read the thankful letters from creditors over and over again, telling her husband this was "the only really happy day

"THE EUROPEAN EDISON"

she has had since Susy died"—a testament to her unimpeachably honest nature.[11] *Following the Equator* had gotten off to a quick sale, and by the end of January 1898, the long-indebted Twain enjoyed a surplus in his bank account. Instead of the five-year repayment period he had initially projected, he had wiped out the debt in four. Newspapers weighed in with a flurry of cheering editorials that played up the historical analogy with Sir Walter Scott, who had labored for years to pay off his debt after his publishing firm went bust.

Now free of his worst nightmare, Twain told Howells that "the dread of leaving the children in difficult circumstances" had passed and he could "sleep as well as any one."[12] As the mental oppression that hampered his work vanished, he was giddy with delight and bursting with fresh energy as he crowed to Rogers, "Work is become a pleasure again—it is not labor, any longer. I am into it up to my ears, these last 3 or 4 weeks—and all *dramatic*."[13]

One might imagine that his ghastly experiences with Paige and Webster would have cured Twain forever of investing mania, yet one would be wrong. One of the things that bothered him most about the debt saga was the public perception that he was an incompetent businessman. When a reporter for the *New York World* asked how it felt to be out of debt, he gave a revealing reply: "What I hate as much as anything is to have the public regard me as unwise in business. I consider that the contrary was proved by the way I published General Grant's book in 1885, which could not have been done by a bad businessman."[14] Despite everything that had happened to him in business, he couldn't resist the fatally alluring fantasy that he was cut out to be a tycoon. And just two months after he eliminated the ruinous debt that had so gravely injured his family, he attempted to dash straight into a new speculative arena.

This rash venture started on March 15 when Livy had tea at the Hotel Metropole with a British correspondent named Amelia S. Levetus, who let slip that nobody had yet grabbed the American patent rights to a new machine designed by a young inventor named Jan Szczepanik, a former schoolteacher from rural Galicia with black hair and piercing eyes. Still in his twenties, he was already celebrated in the Viennese press for his inventions. His device, called the Raster, would print patterns on tapestries, carpets, and other textiles in a manner that supposedly surpassed the current industry standard, the Jacquard loom. Needless to say, Twain had no knowledge of this industry and acted purely on impulse. Quickly forgetting the sorrowful tale of the previous years, he wrote to Levetus: "I am sorry I didn't hear that talk about the wonderful invention, for I would like to have the opportunity to raise the capital & introduce it in America. I am acquainted with a lot of enterprising New York millionaires, & I should have as little trouble as anyone in quickly & advantageously placing such a thing. Is it too late? Will you ask (for) me?"[15] Levetus arranged for Szczepanik and his banker, Ludwig Kleinberg, to meet with Twain at the Clemens quarters at the Hotel Metropole at nine the next evening.

All that day, Twain immersed himself in statistics related to the industry at the British and American consulates, giving himself a crash course and drawing up eleven pages of questions for his meeting. He fancied that in a day he could graduate into an instant authority on the business. When his guests arrived that night, "I was ready for business, & rich with my new learning. My extraordinary familiarity with the subject paralyzed the banker for a while, for he was merely expecting to find a humorist, not a commercial cyclopedia—but he recovered presently."[16] It never dawned on Twain that his guests were either being polite or manipulating him with such barefaced flattery. After talking till midnight and meeting again the next day, they agreed upon a price of $1.5 million for the American patents, with Twain to receive a 12 percent commission for each tranche of the purchase price he raised. He would have two months to secure the deal. Once again, Twain's overactive mind had cooked up a cockeyed business scheme, as if he had never heard the name of James W. Paige.

The whole deal was predicated on selling the rights to Henry H. Rogers, with Twain planning to retain a substantial 10 percent portion of the eventual stock for himself, and he hurriedly mailed off the option proposal to New York. "I've landed a big fish to-day," Twain told Rogers in the brash, boastful style that he adopted in business situations. "He is

"THE EUROPEAN EDISON"

a costly one, but he is worth the money—worth it because America has *got* to buy him whether she wants to or not."[17] He explained that he had tracked down statistics on two thousand textile factories and the capital employed plus the number of designers and their wages. Szczepanik's invention, he alleged, would save these businesses $18 million, and "we can hog $3,000,000 of the $18,000,000 saved."[18] The over-the-top rhetoric and grandiose thinking were reminiscent of Twain's typesetter days, when he conjured up gigantic profit numbers and took them seriously.

Twain was presumptuous enough to tell Rogers what to do next: he should run up and visit a New York or New England mill, then come over and examine the machine, then return home and create a five- or ten-million-dollar company "and take my fish off my hands, and give me one-tenth of that Company's stock, fully paid up, for my share . . . Then the whole Jacquard industry in America will be in the hands of that Company. And people will call it a Trust . . . But you must not be troubled by that, such things cannot be helped . . . And *I* think the Standard Oil should take the *whole* of it . . . If you can't come, send Archbold"—John D. Rockefeller's successor at the world's largest oil company.[19] This was one of the most astonishing letters Twain ever wrote, not only because he traded on his friendship with Rogers, treating him as an errand boy, but because he so brazenly tried to exploit his connection with Standard Oil—something that he had never done quite this blatantly before. He made no mention that Kleinberg had agreed to pay him a 12 percent commission for completing the sale, though presumably this was in the option agreement he mailed to Rogers. Still, Twain would be shamelessly double-dipping, taking a hefty fee from both Kleinberg *and* Rogers for doing the deal. In a case of magical thinking, Twain imagined that with a few rapid strokes they would become the robber barons of the textile-printing industry, enjoying a total monopoly—something that didn't bother him in the least. As he played the buccaneer, he never seemed to fear that Rogers might be appalled at his proposal coming so soon after he had labored for years to extricate him from his hefty debt load.

So convinced was Twain that he had hit the jackpot that he rebuffed an inquiry from a William Wood, an agent for an American carpet manufacturer, who came seeking rights to the Raster. "I was afraid he would offer me half a million dollars for it," Twain confessed in his notebook. "I should have been obliged to take it. But I was born with the speculative instinct and I did not want that temptation put in my way."[20] So when Wood broached the subject, Twain deflected it, and it would qualify as yet another of his costly business blunders.

Awaiting Rogers's verdict, Twain let his imagination soar to new heights of fantasy. No longer content with an American monopoly for this new technique, he now wanted to take over the entire world market. When he found out that Kleinberg was engaged in negotiating Raster rights in Italy, France, and the Netherlands, he boldly intervened and "asked Mr. Kleinberg to stop them, & postpone them indefinitely. I placed before him a scheme for concentrating the patents for all the world in the grip of a single giant company. The world has a capital of $1,500,000,000 invested in the industry affected by this invention—an invention able to reduce one of its very important expenses 90 per cent."[21] A week earlier, he had known nothing about this business; now he was ready to reorganize it globally on a brand-new basis. He dabbled in the same lunatic accounting that had beguiled him with Paige. He thought he was avoiding the pitfalls into which he had stumbled with the typesetter, when he was not. "Szczepanik is not a Paige, but a gentleman," he said, and added of his banker: "Mr. Kleinberg is a gentleman, too, yet is *not* a Clemens—that is to say, he is not an Ass."[22]

Clearly, Twain had a sense of humor about himself, and when he posted another letter to Rogers, he began it by stating: "I feel like Col. Sellers."[23] He then laid out his plan for world domination, as if he were a magnate on a par with Rogers. "So far as I know, no great world-patent has ever yet been placed in the grip of a single corporation. This is a good time to begin."[24] He invoked a vision of a worldwide monopoly that would have chilled the heart of any trustbuster. "Competition would be at an end in the Jacquard business, on this planet. Price-cutting would end. Fluctuations in values would cease. The business would be the safest and surest in the world . . . When the patents died the Company would be so powerful that it could still keep the whole business in its hands and strangle competition."[25] John D. Rockefeller and J. P. Morgan had met their match.

Much as with Paige, Twain fell under the spell of Jan Szczepanik and ended up in lengthy, beer-laden talks with him that lasted until midnight. He persuaded himself that the young man was "the European Edison" and rushed off an article about him for the *Century Magazine* titled "The Austrian Edison Keeping School Again."[26] Meanwhile, Henry Rogers undertook a sober, methodical study of the Raster's American prospects. Of course, Twain had never spoken to anybody in America who actually used the Jacquard loom. Rogers contacted William Whitman, a large investor in Arlington Mills in Boston, and showed him a pamphlet describing the Austrian invention. "I do not feel that it would be of any value to us in our mills," Whitman replied, "and the number of Jacquard looms in use in America is so limited that I am of the opinion that there is no field for the exploration of a company to develop the invention here."[27] Twain, it seems, had built his speculative castle on quicksand. When Rogers forwarded this deflating report to him, Twain conceded that Whitman's facts were "worth a good deal more than foggy guesses out of a census-report 18 years old" and that it was best to shelve the project.[28]

One would have thought that having been bamboozled by Kleinberg, Twain would give business a rest. But in the same letter to Rogers in which he lowered the flag on the Raster, Twain broached another brainstorm from Kleinberg: a method of making blankets and other cloth from peat fiber mixed with cotton or wool. Twain had already turned himself into an expert salesman for this project too. "I want a holiday, and am going to England with a project to market this thing there—shall start ten or twelve days hence, with cloth samples and statistics of cost etc."[29] Once again, he gave Henry Rogers a lecture on business. "I know you are doubtful about patents, and it is natural. Still the whole vast modern civilization is built up, course by course, upon patents."[30] It is very hard to picture Mark Twain peddling cloth and toting his samples to London. Kleinberg must have dangled another lucrative commission to get him to submit to this degradation. The idea was that Twain would go to England and set up a factory to manufacture peat wool for sale to weavers. Soon he walked away from the project when it turned out that the chemicals needed to treat peat wool proved much more expensive than anticipated.

The speculative fever never ceased with Twain. The next year, he tried to sell his friend John Hay, now secretary of state, on a plan to have the post office issue postal checks that would be similar to prepaid money orders. One could buy a postal check, mail it, and the recipient could cash it at a local post office. "If it were a new & particularly comprehensive way of killing Christians I know the War Department would buy the idea," Twain teased Jay, "but I know that governments have sometimes bought ideas of purely commercial value."[31] Twain sought to impress upon the secretary his own modest share of the swag. "I merely want a royalty for a while—no lump sum. I only want the government to issue & sell a thing which is as simple as a post-card & pay me a royalty of *one percent* on the sales *for twelve years*."[32] A proposal for a postal check, though introduced in Congress, was never enacted.

Mark Twain could serve as both a social critic of something and an exemplar of the very thing he criticized, especially when it came to money. His bitter struggles in business had left him with a dim view of humanity. Around the time he paid off his last creditor, he observed that "the foundation-stone of the [human] race is shabbiness & selfishness. There are those who believe the race is to be damned; I am of those [who] believe it is not worth that attention."[33] His notebook shows he already revolved in his mind a story that would dramatize how lust for money could shatter an entire town. He knew the world's failings because he knew himself. "Buried treasure in a Missouri village—supposed by worn figures to be $980. Corrupts the village, causes quarrels and murder, and when found at last is $9.80."[34] From this kernel germinated his brilliant story "The Man That Corrupted Hadleyburg," a cynical allegory of an

"THE EUROPEAN EDISON"

entire town swept and ravaged by greed. Here small-town America has lost the rosy charm of the early Hannibal stories as nineteen godly citizens are duped into submitting false claims for the sake of gold. Twain strips away any air of innocence from these bumpkins, who are puffed up with tawdry dreams of riches. At the first whiff of temptation, the most extravagantly greedy fantasies gush from their brains—something Twain had experienced in his own life.

Twain begins his story thus: "Hadleyburg was the most honest and upright town in all the region round about."[35] The town soon sheds this reputation when it offends a passing stranger, who seeks revenge by depositing a sack of gold with the wife of the bank cashier, ostensibly to repay the kindness of a person who aided him. The passing stranger doesn't leave the name of the deserving recipient. "This is an honest town, an incorruptible town," he announces, "and I know I can trust it without fear."[36] To get the money, the recipient must only reveal the advice given by the stranger. Nineteen couples contend they're in line for the money and hatch wild fantasies about spending it. Twain shows how prospective riches break down the sanctimony of even the most self-righteous people. "In some cases light-headed people did not stop with planning to spend, they really spent—on credit. They bought land, mortgages, farms, speculative stocks, fine clothes, horses, and various other things."[37] When local residents gather at a hall to discover the fate of the sack of gold, squabbles break out among the many citizens claiming the right to it. But the bag is full of gilded lead disks, and the whole thing is a cruel hoax.

Both in life and in fiction, Twain was always interested in the theme of revenge, and the passing stranger, in a letter read to the gathering, has enacted the ultimate revenge fantasy: "I wanted to damage every man in the place, and every woman—and not in their bodies or in their estate, but in their vanity—the place where feeble and foolish people are most vulnerable. So I disguised myself and came back and studied you. You were easy game. You had an old and lofty reputation for honesty, and naturally you were proud of it . . . I knew how to proceed."[38] Twain concludes with a mordant observation about Hadleyburg: "It is an honest town once more, and the man will have to rise early that catches it napping again."[39]

Twain took justifiable pride in this extraordinary tale with its unsparing verdict that every man has his price. He had engineered a major change in his literary image, and critics applauded the development. Increasingly Twain was a man possessed by a bleak message. "Mark Twain, censor and critic, is rapidly taking the place of Mark Twain-fun-maker," observed one reviewer. Another concurred: "Mark's Twain's humor has grown more quiet with the passing of the years, but more subtle as well, more philosophical, with a substratum of wisdom that gives a higher value."[40] As his authorized biographer, Albert Bigelow Paine, wrote, "'The Man That Corrupted Hadleyburg' is one of the mightiest sermons against self-righteousness ever preached . . . It is Mark Twain's greatest short story . . . he was no longer essentially a story-teller. He had become more than ever a moralist and a sage."[41] For Twain, the story was a liberating act, expressing his true feelings without compromise, and he was pleased when *Harper's Monthly* decided to publish it, noting "it had a sort of profane touch in the tail of it."[42]

In November 1902, Twain received a letter from a young Danish fan who admired the story and wondered why Twain hadn't written more in that vein. In reply, he explained that he had always longed to write in this freer style but had erected "a wall across my Nile . . . damming my feelings and opinions behind it, and trying to caulk the leaks." His motive had been fear of inflicting pain on Livy, his in-house editor. "I have put this restraint upon myself and kept it there all these years to keep from breaking my wife's heart."[43] He was correct in thinking that his progressively more deterministic worldview upset her. Occasionally, as with "The Man That Corrupted Hadleyburg," he would devise ways to present this vision in fictional form, but increasingly he turned to nonfiction as a more direct route for elaborating his heated thoughts.

The most compact form he found to adumbrate his philosophy was the aphorism, and he continued to dream up scores of them. They perfectly suited his temperament and love of pithy expression. He turned the aphorism into an ideal blend of the philosopher's maxim, à la Rochefoucauld, and the comic one-liners of a stand-up comedian. He carefully polished and reworked these sayings in his notebook until they had just the right epigrammatic power and ironic twists at the end.

Some of his Viennese aphorisms presented the sly, genial style that he had patented in stage performances going back decades. "Good friends, good books and a sleepy conscience: this is the ideal life."[44] He still reveled in sayings in which he gloried in his laziness. "Never put off till tomorrow what can be done day after to-morrow just as well."[45] Nothing pleased him more than shocking stolid citizens by standing bourgeois morality on its head. "There is a Moral Sense, and there is an Immoral Sense. The Moral Sense teaches us what morality is and how to avoid it; the Immoral Sense teaches us what immorality is and how to enjoy it."[46] There was a naughty spirit in such sayings that harked back to the mischievous boy in Hannibal, but there was also a psychological system expressing how people were motivated solely by self-interest and feigned altruism. "Good breeding consists in concealing how much we think of ourselves," he wrote, "and how little we think of the other person."[47]

During his Viennese period, Twain's adages more and more shifted from pure laugh lines to sardonic reflections on the human condition, some so freighted with dark meanings as to stop us cold in our tracks. On the eve of his arrival in Vienna, he wrote: "Unfortunately none of us can see far ahead; prophecy is not for us. Hence the paucity of suicides."[48] A year later, his faith in life had scarcely brightened: "The suicide seems to me the only sane person," he wrote.[49] Nor did religious belief offer any consolation; playing on the line from Robert Burns, he wrote: "God's inhumanity to man makes countless thousands mourn."[50] His cynicism toward Christianity progressed: "There has been only one Christian. They caught Him and crucified Him early."[51] He even questioned the motivations of those devoted to God: "No man that ever lived has done a thing to please God—primarily. It was done to please himself, *then* God next."[52] He noted the mutability of public opinion, whether in religious or political matters: "The altar-cloth of one era is the door-mat of the next."[53] "The radical of one century is the conservative of the next."[54]

Despite the deeply personal nature of these sayings, Twain had no qualms about commercializing them to the utmost. When the publisher Frank Bliss hoped to market a calendar adorned with his maxims, Twain balked at the idea because lowly calendars lost their value after a year. Instead, he advocated "a delicately tinted *postcard*, with *one* maxim at the top of the side that is to be written on, *that* will be new . . . & the sale needn't stop at the end of the year." He then plunged into excruciatingly detailed suggestions about every facet of this prospective trade, as if he were again a working publisher. "You could make them for a tenth of a cent apiece & furnish them to the trade at 2 or 3 cents apiece in packages of 500 at ten or twelve dollars & let the trade retail them singly at 5 cents apiece or 3 or 4 cents when several were bought—say 10. The package of 500 should be in set of 10."[55] It was yet another example of his constant craving for business success. It was hard to believe that the man who could forge such ingenious sayings should be so attracted to the mundane task of selling them by the bushel.

CHAPTER FORTY-ONE

Dream Self

During his European exile, Mark Twain, the most American of authors, had grown worldly and cosmopolitan, and his Viennese sojourn sped up this process. "You cannot live a couple of years in Vienna," he wrote, "without becoming pretty thoroughly saturated with the fascination of both the people and the city."[1] His stay coincided with unprecedented cultural ferment: the daring experimentation of Gustav Klimt in art, Gustav Mahler in music, Arthur Schnitzler in theater. Even as these artists delved into the kingdom of dreams and sexual passion, the unconscious and the irrational, Sigmund Freud, a member of the university faculty of medicine, worked on his opus *The Interpretation of Dreams*, which was published in 1900 and began to lift the veil on the submerged portion of the human mind.

Such an atmosphere was bound to rub off on Twain, who had been preoccupied with dreams at least since his prophetic dream about his brother Henry's death. He trusted that we contained two selves, a waking self and a dream self, bundled together in one body. Dreams didn't just represent fleeting escapes from reality, but separate worlds of equal weight and importance. He engaged in musings on our dual nature and how the dream self, free of social inhibitions, could traffic in taboo emotions. Twain disputed Stevenson's portrayal of Jekyll and Hyde as split personalities with a fluid interchange between the two. By contrast, he believed the spiritualized self could detach itself from the conscious mind and "go wandering off upon affairs of its own."[2] Pondering his "dream self," Twain commented: "I go to unnamable places, I do unprintable things; & every vision, every sensation . . . is *real*."[3] In the last dozen years of his life, his consuming interest in the entire phantasmagoria of the human mind grew apace.

Throughout his life, Twain recorded his dreams in some detail. Back in 1887, a Professor Loisette, an expert on the subject, had tutored him on how to retrieve memories from "the dark cellar" of memory and preserve them.[4] Twain's dreams provide a window on his inner turmoil, betraying the psychic stress he lugged through life. Though he seemed superbly confident onstage, he had dreams in which he appeared before the audience with no subject to discuss, nor notes to jog his memory. Other dreams disclosed forbidden, hedonistic feelings, like one in which he caught a "beautiful, slender, silver-white fish 14 inches long, & thought what a fine meal it would make—I was very hungry. Then came a feeling of disappointment & sorrow; it was *Sunday*, & I could not take the fish home, for it would deeply grieve Livy to know that I had been fishing on the Sabbath."[5] Twain had always joked about his Civil War cowardice, but his dreams dramatized the reality of those fears. Periodically he dreamed of being a soldier in the thick of battle who realized he should "get back a little—about three miles."[6] His dream self would crawl under a wagon only to be blown up by shells.

What most astonished Twain about dreams was not simply that he could whiz around the planet in a fraction of a second. Rather, it was that his slumbering self bore prodigious talents that he lacked in waking life. For instance, he had always struggled to form pictures of people's faces, "but my dream-self can do all this with the accuracy & vividness of a camera. Waking, I cannot create in my mind a picture of a room & furniture which I have not recently seen or have never seen, but my dream self can do this, to the minutest detail."[7]

Twain's dream stories mirror his life's vicissitudes, especially the spectacular bankruptcy that upended his harmonious Hartford life. They are all parables of loss and wreckage. At Weggis, he had worked on a thinly autobiographical tale, "Which Was the Dream?," which tells of a General X who went to West Point, won battlefield distinction, and be-

DREAM SELF

came a U.S. senator. He has two daughters, and one of them, Bessie, is closely patterned on Susy. "She is not clay. She is a spirit... She is all life, and soap-bubbles, and rainbows and fireworks."[8] The general's wife provides a no less direct portrait of Livy and her beautiful trait of not meddling with a sore point of his at an "inopportune time."[9] The wife, born to wealth, is careful with money, while the foolish general has blindly insisted on building an extravagant house and "talked her out of her reluctance and gained my point."[10] When the house burns down, it proves to be uninsured, ruining the family. The naive general is also fleeced by his trusted aide, Jeff Sedgewick, in a manner reminiscent of Ulysses S. Grant and the swindler Ferdinand Ward—or perhaps Twain and Webster—and lies buried beneath a mound of debt. In this incomplete story, the beautiful past recedes forever, becoming as insubstantial as a dream.

One summer night in Austria, Twain dreamed "of a whaling cruise in a drop of water" and embarked upon a Swiftian narrative, known as "The Great Dark," which he hoped would improve upon "Which Was the Dream?"[11] Another sad psychodrama about his life, it narrated the story of a once happy family torn apart by disaster. It starts with Henry, the father, and his two daughters examining a microscope slide of stale water from a puddle. To their astonishment, they view monstrous sea creatures plowing across the drop. "An ocean in a drop of water—and unknown, uncharted, unexplored by man!" declares Henry.[12] Lapsing into a dream, he finds himself and his family aboard a ship inside the water drop amid a "howling storm at sea" where he is supervised by a Superintendent of Dreams.[13] Like Jonathan Swift, Twain was mesmerized by minutely small and grotesquely large things, and the relative nature of size—what he labeled "a dispute between a microscope and a telescope."[14] The tiny drop of water, a nightmarish place, spans six thousand miles steeped in perpetual night.

These stories of lost beings in turbulent, sunless seas reflect Twain's dazed instability after the serenity of his Hartford years. At one point, when Henry alludes to being trapped in a dream, the Superintendent retorts: "The dream? *Are you quite sure it is a dream?* ... You have spent your whole life in this ship. And this is *real* life. Your other life was the dream!"[15] In this exchange, one sees Twain's constant anxiety that his fallen state after bankruptcy, not the high-rolling days beforehand, constituted the true baseline of his life. Where their fallen state had once seemed shocking to the Clemenses, it now arose as their normal condition. After spending ten days on the boat, Henry reflects that "by comparison the life I had lived before them seemed distant, indistinct, slipping away and fading out in a far perspective."[16] He clings to the notion that this new life is a dream, while his clear-eyed wife, Alice, regards their *past* life as the dream. "Alice, haven't we ever had a home?" he asks. "Don't you remember one?" "Why, yes—three," she replies evenly. "That is, dream-homes, not real ones. I have never regarded them as realities."[17] Her perspective embodies Twain's ultimate nightmare: not only to surrender past happiness, but to have it crumble away in half-forgotten dreams.

Twain had long prided himself on his personal rapport with Satan, a world-class renegade who allowed him to express a growing contempt for bourgeois morality. "Yes, sir, there *is* a Devil," he wrote, "but you must not speak disrespectfully of him, for he is an uncle of mine."[18] Vienna unleashed these darker imaginings, and no sooner had Twain checked into the Hotel Metropole than he began scribbling an unpublished work, "Conversations with Satan," which started thus: "It was being whispered around that Satan was in Vienna incognito, and the thought came into my mind that it would be a great happiness to me if I could have the privilege of interviewing him."[19] Gazing down from his hotel room to the plaza below, the narrator watches Satan materialize amid theatrical pyrotechnics of thunder and lightning. Instead of being endowed with stereotypical horns and tail, the devil is an elegant, shapely man, scrupulously dressed as an Anglican Bishop, with courtly manners. No newcomer to the narrator, Satan is "an old friend of mine, and also one of my most ardent and grateful admirers." Twain suggests that the American territory is already well worked by the Devil. When the narrator inquires if Satan is familiar with the place, he replies, "Well—no. I have not been there lately. I am not needed there."[20] This scene led

Twain to explore the subject further as he launched into an unfinished novel, "The Chronicle of Young Satan," which would occupy him sporadically for several years. It would form part of a fascinating group of manuscripts known as *The Mysterious Stranger* that he would tinker with over the next decade.

During the summer of 1898, in the Vienna suburb of Kaltenleutgeben, Twain began to articulate his own "Bible" in a work he later recast as a Socratic dialogue between an older and younger man titled *What is Man?* Much like the Deists, he summoned up a cold, mechanistic world in which God creates a vast, sublime universe, then steps back from his creation. While God brings forth beautiful forms and immutable laws of nature, he is heedless of the petty dealings of human beings, so many invisible microbes in the larger scheme of things. "The book of Nature tells us distinctly that God cares not one rap for us; not for any living creature . . . It may be mere indifference."[21] The human mind cannot originate anything new, but only regurgitate things absorbed from its environment. In the end, people are motivated solely by self-interest, their desire to please themselves and win the esteem of others. Altruism was a shabby delusion, a mere cover story for selfishness. Twain had tested these ideas on his Monday Evening Club in Hartford a quarter-century earlier, and they had warned him that "if this insane doctrine of mine were accepted . . . life would no longer be worth living."[22]

Twain felt liberated as he put these thoughts on paper—he referred to it as "a luxury! an intellectual drunk"—even though, fearing retribution from readers and press, he shrank from publishing such views. Livy had watched her husband being drawn down shadowy byways before and simply couldn't abide such dogmatic opinions. Twain told Howells that Livy "loathes, & shudders over" his so-called Bible and "will not listen to the last half nor allow man to print any part of it."[23] In his notebook, he admitted that he could not afford to publish such controversial views. "I have no pluck to publish it, the outside influences (my wife, the risk of destroying my reputation & my family's bread) being dead against it & stronger than my desire to print."[24] Depressed after his bankruptcy, Susy's death, and Jean's epilepsy, he found little to lighten his mood.

RAPIDS

When he read the morning papers, he gagged on the world's pageant of depravity, baseness, and hypocrisy. As he told Howells, "We all belong to the nasty stinking little human race, & of course it is not nice for God's beloved vermin to scoff at each other."[25] A month later, he sputtered: "Damn these human beings; if I had invented them I would go hide my head in a bag."[26] Twain never related his grimly reductive philosophy to his own grief-stricken state of mind, a form of self-awareness that seemed to elude him.

Perhaps as an antidote to such gloom, Twain had recurrent wish-fulfillment dreams about meetings with a bewitching young woman, a strange history that he recorded in the summer of 1898 in "My Platonic Sweetheart." The obvious basis for this dream figure was Laura Wright, the teenage girl whom he had met in New Orleans in 1858, an encounter that had haunted him ever since. In the dream's first iteration, Twain is seventeen, the girl fifteen, when they meet on a rustic wooden bridge in the Missouri countryside. In real encounters with women, Twain was shy and awkward, but in the dream everything runs smoothly. "I put my arm around her waist and drew her close to me, for I loved her; and although I did not know her, my behavior seemed to me quite natural and right . . . She showed no surprise, no distress, no displeasure, but put an arm around my waist and turned up her face to mine with a happy welcome in it, and when I bent down to kiss her she received the kiss as if she was expecting it."[27] This was a magical world free of many taboos against which Twain had long rebelled. Superficially, it was a sexy dream, yet really quite chaste. It was neither the love of brother and sister nor of sweethearts, but hovering in some middle ground. The dream suggests that for Twain, the highest love transcends sexuality—in other words, it is an idealized asexual love. George and Alice, as they call each other, come upon a quaint log house with a fireplace and roast turkey dinner on the table. Everything is perfect until Alice stands up, passes through the door, and disappears. When George goes out to find her, he emerges into a cemetery, "a city of innumerable tombs and monuments," and is distraught as he vainly rushes about, trying to find her.[28]

In the dream's next installment, years later, the boy and girl remain

DREAM SELF

seventeen and fifteen respectively. This encounter takes place in a twilit magnolia forest near Natchez, Mississippi, an enchanted place with fragrant blossoms. "I was sitting on the grass, absorbed in thinking, when an arm was laid around my neck, and there was Alice sitting by my side and looking into my face. A deep and satisfied happiness and an unwordable [sic] gratitude rose in me, but with it there was no feeling of surprise; and there was no sense of a time-lapse. We dropped in the tranquilest way into affectionate caressings and pettings, and chatted along without a reference to the separation."[29] They now refer to each other as Jack and Helen. Although the girl has black hair, not gold as before, and dark-brown eyes instead of blue, she is demonstrably the same girl. Everything about the dream suggests unreal innocence, puppy love. Helen takes off her summer hat and says to Jack, "It was in the way; now you can kiss me better."[30]

The saccharine, storybook scene has a chilling sequel. Jack and Helen enter a large plantation house, and Helen's parents are there. Jack knows them, although they have never met before. Then the light dims on this rosy picture, the place is plunged into blackness, and Jack finds himself crossing a frozen lake with empty arms. He is shaken by a wave of grief as he awakens in a San Francisco newspaper office in 1864. The dream is suddenly suffused with a fear of death and loss and unutterable grief for the vanished beauties of childhood. Twain, growing older, knows he will never attain such happiness again.

When the Platonic Sweetheart next appears, Twain finds himself on a stage at the San Francisco Opera House. Bathed in bright lights, he forgets what he is supposed to talk about. The heartless audience pelts him with "insulting cries, whistlings, hootings and cat-calls" and he sits crestfallen onstage, head bowed, as the audience empties out. "Soon that familiar dream-voice spoke my name, and swept all my troubles away."[31] The pair, now called Robert and Agnes, are transported to a beautiful, flower-laden gorge in Hawaii on the island of Maui. Again, the romantic scenery is pierced by sudden death. An old wrinkled native man shoots an arrow into the sky that disappears for a moment, then it plunges down into Agnes, who clutches Robert and says, "Hold me to your heart—I am afraid to die . . . It is growing dark—I cannot see you. Don't leave me—where are you? You are not gone?"[32] Soon he finds himself holding mere clay in his arms, the spirit having fled her body.

After Agnes dies, the scene shifts to a snowy Bond Street in New York. Robert falls drowsily into a dream that spirits him off to Athens. "He passes the Parthenon and climbs a grassy hill toward a palatial mansion built of red terra-cotta and supported by fluted Corinthian columns. He passed into the house and Agnes was there."[33] Agnes, now in Greek costume, has been fully restored to life, and there is a calm, happy, matter-of-fact acceptance to their reunion. They are still seventeen and fifteen. While they talk, some ancient Greeks, including Socrates, enter the room. Agnes and Athens then vanish in an instant, and the dreamer is whisked back, alone, to his room in New York. The aching loss of youth and loved ones are both wrapped up in these parables.

Though Twain dipped into books on dreams, including William James's *The Principles of Psychology* and Georg Christoph Lichtenberg's dream writings, he exhibited no interest in the symbolic meaning of dreams—what they say about the psyche constructing them. At the close of his platonic sweetheart essay, he harks back to a premodern theory: of dreams being realer than waking life. Of the recurring girl, he says: "To me she is a real person, not a fiction, and her sweet and innocent society has been one of the prettiest and pleasantest experiences of my life."[34] Of her agonizing death on Maui, he writes: "That was a terrible thing to me at the time. It was preternaturally vivid; and the pain and the grief and the misery of it to me transcended many sufferings that I have known in waking life."[35] That Twain paid such painstaking attention to his dreams shows his interest in the mind's interior life. Yet he reveals no introspective curiosity as to why this fantasy exerted an inflexible hold on his imagination. His dreams speak to an inability to deal with women as they mature beyond adolescence—a fact that accounts for a major weakness of his fiction, where he often stuck to conventional portraits of virginal young women. Alice/Helen/Agnes are trapped in an eternal, haloed adolescence, and Twain doesn't seem to realize that this recurring fantasy is an emotional trap for him, expressing his stunted growth in un-

DREAM SELF

derstanding women. He was in thrall to an imaginary female who was not allowed to grow old. His platonic sweetheart dreams also betray discomfort with raw, visceral sexuality as opposed to chaste petting. He voices no frustration at the lack of sexual consummation and seems to delight in the safety and security it confers.

Twain tinkered with details of these dreams, and may have improved them, as if he were composing a story. Still, that makes them no less valuable as a commentary on his romantic views. When he finished "My Platonic Sweetheart," he jubilantly pronounced it "thundering good," and shipped it off to the editor at *Cosmopolitan*. After other magazines rejected it, Twain wrote to Richard Watson Gilder of the *Century* in November that "if you haven't already rejected it, reject it *now*. I wouldn't have it printed for $3,000. I liked it when I sent it, but that was because it was *recent* and I hadn't had a chance to give it a cold examination."[36] One wonders what Livy thought of her husband's fixation on this phantom woman who had seized possession of his mind. She seems to have spiked the story. On October 10, Twain wrote to Edward Bok, the editor of the *Ladies' Home Journal*, that Livy had "'retired the 'Platonic Sweetheart.' It was a good idea, & I said I would."[37] The piece would only appear posthumously in *Harper's Magazine*, two years after Twain's death.

Even as Twain pondered the mysteries of the mind, he and his family frequented health resorts in Austria that were numerous enough to satisfy the most hardened hypochondriacs. "The empire is made up of health resorts; it distributes health to the whole world," Twain wrote. "Its waters are all medicinal."[38] For five months, in spring and summer of 1898, the Clemens family repaired to the health resort at Kaltenleutgeben, nestled in wooded hills near Vienna. This tony enclave attracted hordes of Austrian aristocrats, its medical rigors enlivened by an active social life, and Countess Misa Wydenbruck-Esterházy made sure the Clemenses were well received in high-ranking circles. Renting the furnished Villa Paulhof, a capacious place with eight rooms, Twain hoped the town's famous water cure would heal Livy's rheumatism and low spirits. Its hardy regimen demanded cold plunges and calisthenics every morning. Livy was suffering from heart trouble, and Twain later reflected that Kaltenleutgeben "was the only treatment in nine years that made a good showing."[39] The town seemed to rejuvenate his writing—it had been years since Livy saw him "write with so much pleasure and energy as he has done during this last summer"—and he also enjoyed hiking on rare occasions when the rain let up.[40] He was shaking off the somberness from Susy's death and slowly rejoining the human race.

While Sam and Livy were no longer paupers and lived in privileged style, they still chafed at their vagabond life and yearned to return to America. Nor could Twain return home alone for an extended stay. "The family will not allow me to leave them," he explained to Henry Rogers that summer. "We cannot divide the family after our disastrous experience."[41] They had become hostages to Clara's musical training in Vienna, which they didn't care to interrupt. Twain, awash in guilt, was still atoning for the global tour and Susy's death apart from him. "Well, I robbed the family to feed my speculations, and so I am willing to accommodate myself to their preferences."[42] Twain made no mention of Jean, her epilepsy still a dark secret to the outside world. He hoped Clara's musical training would wind up the following spring, and they could bring down the curtain on their European exile. As he told Thomas Bailey Aldrich, "I like Europe—I like it very much indeed—but I am two or three thousand years old sometimes, & don't like so much padding around."[43] His dream stories preached a contrary moral: that once happy families were detached from their past life by extreme misfortune, they could never find their way back.

When the Clemenses returned to Vienna, they changed hotels, moving into the ritzy new Hotel Krantz. Twain had been self-conscious about welcoming titled visitors to the "rusty and rather shabby Metropole" and preferred the chic environs of the Krantz.[44] On a summer outing to Vienna, Livy had wandered into the hotel lobby and was taken aback to spot a large oil painting of her husband on the wall—the best she had ever seen. "We don't know who made it or when," Twain told

DREAM SELF

Rogers, "but we recognize that it is a hotel that has taste."[45] Never missing the main chance, Twain parlayed his celebrity into a significant hotel discount and booked an extravagant suite of fourth-floor rooms. "We have a dining room, a parlor, a music-parlor, a study, and 4 bedrooms—and there are bathrooms attached to 3 of the bedrooms," he informed Rogers.[46] If Twain shamelessly haggled for a discount, the hotel no less shamelessly extracted publicity from his presence, running an ad in the *New York Tribune* that announced: "HOTEL KRANTZ / 'Newest and Most Modern in the City'/ First Class Family House / The Home of Mark Twain."[47] In these new quarters, Twain would entertain such an unending stream of guests that he labeled himself the "self-appointed ambassador-at-large of the United States of America—without salary."[48] Twain knew that in New York these quarters would cost twice as much, introducing doubt as to whether he could afford to return to the United States without a precipitous drop in living standards. Still, he made inquiries, through friends, about the prices of New York hotels and residences.

An early visitor to the Krantz was Ossip Gabrilowitsch, the brilliant young Russian pianist who had entered into a romance with Clara. He came on an urgent mission. As soon as he and Clara were alone, he blurted out: "You and I are not of the same race. I descend from the Jewish people." Clara saw Ossip through a philo-Semitic lens inherited from her father. "The quiet nobility of his honesty impressed me, and I immediately thought of my father. Since childhood I had heard him rail at the crass stupidity and barbarity of race prejudice. Oftenest, of course, he ridiculed the persecution of Jews, a member of whose race the entire world daily worships."[49]

Thanks to the Spanish-American War and its aftermath, 1898 was a consequential year in Mark Twain's political maturation. By nature an antiwar activist, he had been wooed earlier in the year by the pacifist Austrian Friends of Peace. Despite practical differences with them, Twain assured their leader that "armaments were not created chiefly for the protection of the nations but for their enslavement."[50] Two days earlier, the American battleship *Maine* had blown up in Havana Harbor, killing more than 260 sailors and igniting war with Spain. When the United States sided with the Cuban insurgents against their Spanish colonial overlords, the Austro-Hungarian Empire, predictably, rallied to the Spanish royalist side. Despite his pacifist credentials, Twain at first thought his fellow Americans were fighting a just war against a colonial oppressor. In late April, after President McKinley asked Congress to declare war, Livy sent a jittery note to her brother, Charlie. While she confessed ignorance of Cuban history and wished that America had pushed harder for peaceful change, she accurately forecast the dilemma for American residents in Austria: "It will be almost like being in the enemy's country to be here and I know we shall soon find ourselves hated."[51]

At first, Twain was sure he was contesting imperialism and siding with the virtuous colonial underdog in the conflict. "Old as I am, I want to go to war myself," he told Major Pond with jingoistic fervor. "And I should do it, too, if it were not for the danger."[52] In early May, he exulted when Commodore George Dewey sailed into Manila Bay and destroyed the Spanish fleet—an event that alerted the world to the breadth of U.S. naval power. Twain believed that the United States lacked territorial ambitions and was motivated by a high-minded ideal to aid Cuban rebels, and he rhapsodized the conflict as a "most righteous war."[53] The Austrians dismissed such talk as a transparent excuse for greed, so much claptrap masking American expansionism. At a dinner party thrown by Livy, Leschetizky made this argument vociferously, regarding the United States as a rapacious world power like any other.

In Vienna, Twain seemed a lonely voice for the war, griping to his London publisher, "I come across no end of people who simply can *not* see the Cuban situation as America sees it—people who cannot believe that any conduct can justify one nation in interfering with the domestic affairs of another."[54] Even his wife and daughter differed with him on the issue. As usual, Twain worked himself into a noble rage and indited a stinging piece that blasted European powers aligned with Spain, singling out France for rough treatment. "Are our shabby and pusillanimous ways outraging the fastidious people who have sent an innocent man (Dreyfus) to a living hell, taken to their embraces the slimy guilty

DREAM SELF

one, and submitted to a thousand indignities Émile Zola—the manliest man in France?"[55] He flayed hypocritical Spaniards, who had driven "all the Jews out of Spain in a day . . . roasted heretics by the thousands . . . in her public squares . . . her Holy Inquisition imported hell into the earth."[56] Twain grew ever more vehement in endorsing the war, and when Twichell's son enlisted in the army, he sent a lusty cheer across the ocean. "It is a worthy thing to fight for one's own freedom; it is another sight finer to fight for another man's. And I think this is the first time it has been done."[57] He still had no inkling how the Spanish-American War would transform American foreign policy, and by June was saying that America's conduct in freeing Cuba had shown the Viennese he was right and they were wrong.

Twain celebrated victory prematurely. The turning point came when President McKinley signed a joint resolution to annex Twain's beloved Hawaiian Islands to the United States. The terrible, self-reinforcing logic of imperialism began to surface as the United States argued that with Dewey's victory at Manila Bay, the United States needed a coaling station in the Pacific. William Dean Howells, a steadfast foe of imperialism, spotted the fatal backsliding and sent Twain a seething letter in early August that "our war for humanity" had been degraded "into a war for coaling stations."[58] Far from freeing Cuba, the United States extended a protectorate over it, as a taste for acquisition proved addictive to American palates unaccustomed to such conquest.

The scales fell from Twain's eyes on August 12 when the United States signed an armistice confirming that the country had supplanted Spain as colonial landlord in the Caribbean and the Pacific, acquiring for the first time an overseas empire stretching from Puerto Rico to the Philippines to Guam. No less than Twain, the Filipinos and their revolutionary leader, Emilio Aguinaldo, were shocked that instead of supporting their new republic, the United States had arbitrarily imposed its rule. The United States negotiated a peace settlement with Spain in Paris that pointedly excluded Filipino participation, dooming the hopes of Aguinaldo and his followers. In the coming years, Mark Twain's diatribes against American rule in the Philippines would possess a sharp edge of disillusionment because he had once believed so fervently in the cause. He would never forgive the betrayal of the high ideals he had espoused. "When the United States sent word to Spain that the Cuban atrocities must end she occupied the highest moral position ever taken by a nation since the Almighty made the earth," he later said regretfully. "But when she snatched the Philippines she stained the flag."[59]

CHAPTER FORTY-TWO

"A Hundred Capering Clowns"

Such was Twain's spreading renown in the Austro-Hungarian Empire that he and his family were invited to Budapest for a week in March 1899 to celebrate the jubilee of Hungarian press emancipation, when the Magyars had first been allowed to publish papers in their own language. Only recently Twain had sworn he would never lecture again, but with his fickle nature, he had broken this vow many times before. "Nothing has saved me from being a harlot but my sex," he confessed to a friend.[1] Twain, his wife, and two daughters boarded a private railroad car, placed at their disposal by the Hungarian railways, which whisked them to Budapest in a luxurious manner. A cheering crowd welcomed them at the train station. Like Vienna, Budapest boasted many modern conveniences, including electrified streetcars and a subway system, and despite a heavy snowfall when they arrived, the family pressed on with sightseeing ahead of Twain's big speech. When they were ushered into the visitors' gallery of the new parliament building, all debate halted as legislators looked up and acknowledged the celebrated family.

A glorified member of the press, Twain was the subject of constant news coverage and frequently squawked about its excesses. He prepared a carefully wrought speech in which he exhorted journalists to aspire to the loftiest standards of press freedom—"liberty without licence; liberty with dignity; liberty to lash wrong-doing, but not the license to imitate it."[2] At the event, his mind abruptly scrubbed the speech from memory when he rose to speak, and he treated journalists to extemporaneous commentary, including some old chestnuts, such as "The Stolen Watermelon." "I think I will never embarrass myself with a set speech again," Twain promised Twichell. "My memory is old & rickety & cannot stand the strain... It was a great night, & I heard all the great men in the Government talk."[3] The speech sent the audience into a frenzy of enthusiasm.

On their last day, the Clemens family was invited to a tea, accompanied by music, at which Clara and Jean were taught the steps of Magyar dances. Where Jean was proper and ladylike, one reporter captured Clara's more daring nature by saying she was "much more naughty and much more lively"—as Sam and Livy had learned to their regret.[4] Among the guests was a Hungarian feminist author, Clementina Katona Abranyi, who left an interesting description of Twain as "sensitive, reflective and introverted," noted his "erudition," and complimented his enlightened views on the status of women.

Throughout their Viennese stay, Sam and Livy had been courted by royalty, often to their astonishment. After one of his readings, they were introduced to Her Royal Highness Countess Bardi, the daughter of the king of Portugal, and her sister, the Archduchess Maria Theresa, the mother of the heir-apparent of the Habsburg throne. The following morning, abiding by protocol, they scurried to the palace to inscribe their names in the visitors' book at the porter's lodge. Then there intervened a moment of dreamlike confusion, reminiscent of Twain's recent writings: They were told that they were expected and escorted upstairs. Astonished and sure some error had been made, they waited for the mystery to be solved. Livy was in a panic, lest they had sinned against etiquette, and Sam was amused by what he figured was a delicious mix-up. As they mounted the stairs with trepidation, they dreaded exposure and humiliation. Then the countess and the archduchess duly appeared with their children and spent "a charming twenty minutes" with their American visitors.[5] It turned out that the Clemenses' invitation had arrived belatedly at their residence, and they were actually expected an hour and a half later. Twain was fully aware that his constant flirtation with royalty violated every political principle that he supposedly held dear—and it bothered him not a whit. Aware of court rules, Sam and Livy did their best, as commoners, "to waddle out backward like a couple of old ducks" at the end, said Clara.[6]

On June 26, 1898, Twain, shaded by a balcony awning, watched twenty-five thousand marchers parade down the Parkring to honor the fiftieth anniversary of Emperor Franz Joseph I's reign. Stirred with boyish delight, Twain devoured the spectacle of costumes from many centuries. It would not have surprised readers of *The Prince and the Pauper* and *A Connecticut Yankee* that he savored the spears, breastplates, chainmail armor, and plumed helmets. With his penchant for storied realms, Twain was merely a graying version of Tom Sawyer. He chronicled the swashbuckling men-at-arms with their richly caparisoned steeds and the many vivid figures tossed in for comic relief—"a hundred capering clowns in thunder-and-lightning dress, or a band of silken pages out of ancient times, plumed and capped and daggered, dainty as rainbows, and mincing along in flesh-colored tights."[7]

No imperial subjects could have been more distraught than Sam and Livy when the Empress Elisabeth, wife of Franz Joseph, was assassinated by an anarchist in Geneva on September 10, 1898. They were still in Kaltenleutgeben when Countess Wydenbruck-Esterházy, who was a friend of the empress, came rushing in with the news. "'Oh such terrible, terrible news, our Empress is murdered,'" Livy recalled her saying. "She looked so white & was so breathless that I thought she would faint. I gave her some brandy to steady her a little."[8] For Twain, it was a sudden brush with world history, as if Antony had shown up and said, "Caesar is butchered—the head of the world is fallen!"[9] The royal death brought out his sense of the exalted purity of women; he dropped all cynical asides about monarchs and converted the dead empress into a sublime being. "She was so blameless, the Empress; and so beautiful, in mind and heart, in person and spirit; whether with a crown upon her head or without it and nameless, a grace to the human race, and almost a justification of its creation . . . In her character was every quality that in woman invites and engages respect, esteem, affection, and homage."[10]

Twain returned to Vienna for the funeral, striding through deserted streets draped in black, with pictures of the dead empress posted in many shop windows. He had not seen anything like it since Grant's death. From windows at the Hotel Krantz, Twain observed the funeral procession that terminated at the small Capuchin church across the square, which housed the imperial crypt for the Habsburg dynasty. In an unpublished piece, "The Memorable Assassination," he noted the historical frequency of regicide while empresses were rarely murdered, and that fact multiplied his horror at the event. He contrasted the hideous perpetrator of the crime—"a mangy, offensive, empty, unwashed, vulgar, gross, mephitic, timid, sneaking human polecat"—with the blessed creature murdered, "the world's accepted ideal of Glory and Might and Splendor and Sacredness!"[11] Empress Elisabeth joined the ranks of idealized women in Twain's life—Laura Wright, Joan of Arc, Susy Clemens, the Platonic Sweetheart, and, of course, Livy Clemens. Twain professed to be a stranger to religious feeling, yet he might have been describing the Virgin Mary, as if some mystical side in his nature found a substitute in these secular women.

As sunlight glinted from the helmets of the soldiers massed below, Twain was again smitten with the nobility. As they came robed and hatted in the ancient costumes of their kingdoms and principalities, they surpassed in splendor anything that he had seen in the theater, at the opera, or within picture books. "Gold, silver, jewels, silks, satins, velvet; they were all there in brilliant and beautiful confusion."[12] At the finale "the sumptuous great hearse approaches, drawn at a walk by eight black horses plumed with black bunches of nodding ostrich feathers; the coffin is borne into the church, the doors are closed."[13] In his notebook, Twain felt obliged to tone down his rhetoric, return to planet Earth, and reconcile his cynical view of royalty with the effusive prose that he had just disgorged. "Essentially, nobilities are foolishnesses, but if I were a citizen where they prevail I would do my best to get a title, for the consideration it furnishes—that is what we want. In Republics we strive for it with the surest means we have—money."[14] Suddenly, he reduced nobility to a racket for personal advancement.

As if snapping awake from a trance, Twain engaged that fall in a crusade for peace and disarmament, telling a packed hall of pacifists that the Spanish-American War had "cost much in money and human suffering on both sides and had achieved nothing that could not have been done without a war."[15] When Czar Nicholas II issued a call for reducing armaments, Twain saw an opening for both advocacy and humor, his special blend. When William T. Stead, the editor of the *Review of Reviews* in London, asked for his opinion, he began his published reply thus: "The Tsar is ready to disarm. I am ready to disarm. Collect the others; it should not be much of a task now."[16] Cynical about human motivation, Twain believed that disarmament could be achieved only by compulsion, not persuasion. With lethal whimsy, he informed the newspapers that he had "discovered a method for suddenly withdrawing all the oxygen from the atmosphere and thus destroying the entire human race in four minutes."[17] If Emperor Franz Joseph or another sovereign threatened to unleash this doomsday weapon unless the world disarmed, countries would renounce their arms within minutes. Twain pursued this murderous fantasy with his old friend and secretary of state John Hay, warning that he was "expecting to touch the button and abolish the race this afternoon, as an experiment, but must postpone it & think further, for I do not know what to do with my family."[18] In the end, Twain despaired of serious progress on disarmament. With human nature immutable, all protest movements struck him as futile in the end. As he told a correspondent, the "human race is still on deck & hasn't lost its character. It is never serious about anything. I mean, anything that is worth being serious about."[19]

By the end of 1898, the Clemens finances stood in better shape than they had for many years, with $200,000 in annual income from book royalties and another $107,000 in the bank. Just before Christmas, Twain learned that Rogers had earned a windfall for him by scooping up shares of Federal Steel, a new steel combination in which he was involved. This news made the holidays bright for the family and led them into a round of suppers, parties, and private theatricals. "We are resembling the long-vanished Clemenses of 10 years ago," Twain told Rogers. "God knows what we should be resembling if it had not been for you."[20] A series of miraculous gains in the stock market—Brooklyn Gas, American Smelting, Amalgamated Copper—continued to fall from the sky, leaving Twain starry-eyed. It never bothered him that he was investing alongside management in many trades with Rogers—what would be branded insider trading today—he merely rejoiced that Rogers was happy to cut him in on the take. "For a week, now, the Vienna papers have been excited over the great Copper combine," Twain wrote to Rogers, "and sometimes they say you are the president of it, other times they call you vice-president . . . and I am very glad of that, for you know how to make a copper hen lay a golden egg."[21] Evidently Rogers had promised Twain an allotment of stock when the trust issued shares.

In this upbeat mood, the family meditated their next move after Vienna. For the past year, Clara's musical studies had detained them in Austria and guided their decisions on where to live, but another, even larger factor began to emerge in their internal calculations, one that still entailed profound secrecy: Jean's epilepsy. "If it weren't for my sister we should probably remain one more winter in Vienna," Clara told a relative, "but there must sometime come an end to our wanderings."[22] Twain began to contemplate a quiet country village, perhaps one in England, as the next stop on their itinerary. Clara planned to study singing with Blanche Marchesi in London that summer, which helped to steer them in that direction.

Before the family left Vienna for good in May, Emperor Franz Joseph indicated that he would be delighted to meet Twain. On May 25, 1899, the author went to the palace in a horse-drawn carriage, and following protocol, arrived in striped pants and swallow-tailed coat. He had expected to form part of a group and was stunned to discover that he was booked for a fifteen- or twenty-minute private tête-à-tête with His Majesty. "I perceived a special kind of courtesy in this not for my humble self but much more for the country I belong to, and a goodwill gesture toward the literary circles of my nation."[23] Twain had taken pains to

"A HUNDRED CAPERING CLOWNS"

memorize a German sentence of eighteen words—short, he noted, by German standards—but it evaporated in the monarch's presence. The sixty-nine-year-old Franz Joseph, with his bald head, huge muttonchop whiskers, and field marshal uniform, set Twain at ease by warmly squeezing his hand and telling him how much he admired his writings. Twain sang the praises of Vienna and may have told the emperor about his disarmament plan to withdraw oxygen from the atmosphere. They proved a companionable pair, the emperor and commoner, and Twain said only kind things about the ruler. "Necessarily, he must have a great deal of good, plain, attractive human nature in him, or he could not have unbent in the easy manner which I have described. You and I could not unbend if we were emperors."[24]

The day after the audience, when the Clemens family departed from Vienna at the train station, they were astounded by the huge outpouring of affection, their two-year stay having yielded many friends who showered them with flowers and presents. It was an emotional send-off with hugs and kisses—even Twain stood tearful—and Livy counted twenty-seven sobbing friends on the platform as they pulled out. "My sister and I did not hide our feelings," said Clara, "but wept frankly with all the tragedy of youthful suffering."[25] Twain issued a statement bound to please the Viennese. "One quickly becomes accustomed to Vienna, feels contented here, and never completely departs."[26] But with his complex and contradictory nature, this didn't disclose everything Twain felt about Vienna, and once in London, he added to an American correspondent that "Vienna is the most politically corrupt nest on the face of the earth."[27]

The Clemens family still toyed with returning to the United States, even to the Hartford house, a decision heavily laden with emotional freight and financial calculation. As Twain had written in January, "A Hartford with no Susy Clemens in it . . . It is not the city of Hartford, it is the city of Heartbreak."[28] Still, he regretted that many friends back home were aging and dying off without his presence. "It has become a funeral procession, & if I want to get a good place in it I must apply soon."[29] Such was America's gravitational pull that Twain, in March, had his friend Laurence Hutton scout rooms at an inn in Princeton, New Jersey, which would afford needed distance from Hartford. While New York City was the family's ideal destination, prices there remained prohibitively high. Two weeks before leaving Vienna, Sam and Livy ruled out a return home on money grounds. "It is a pity we can't go home now," he told Rogers. "We are all pretty home-sick."[30] So the footloose family, weighed down by eight trunks of luggage, was condemned to wander the earth for another season. By early June, they had checked into the Prince of Wales Hotel at Kensington, in London. No sooner had they arrived than Clara came down with a catarrh and sinus infection, and under doctor's orders, the family removed to the coastal town of Broadstairs, in east Kent, for a week before returning to London.

After his two years in Vienna, the English embraced Twain, who basked in Anglo-Saxon goodwill and catered to the prevailing sentiment, telling a London reporter, "It has always been a dream of mine, this closer relationship between England and America."[31] He speedily became the toast of London clubs, and within a week of arriving was made only the fourth honorary member of the Savage Club. On June 9, he was in superlative form at its award dinner, telling the assembled that he hadn't visited the club in twenty-seven years. "I was six feet four then—now five feet 8½ and daily diminishing in altitude . . . In those days you could have carried Kipling around in his lunch-basket—now he fills the world."[32] The dinner chair had assigned him to the ranks of great authors. "I was sorry to hear my name mentioned as one of the great authors, because they have a sad habit of dying off. Chaucer is dead, Spenser is dead, so is Milton, so is Shakespeare, and I am not feeling very well myself."[33] Earlier in the year, Kipling had nearly died from lung congestion in a New York hotel, and news reports elicited sympathy in the Anglo-Saxon universe. At the Authors Club dinner on June 12, Twain cited this episode and allowed himself a rare pun: "Since England and America may be joined together in Kipling, may they not be

"A HUNDRED CAPERING CLOWNS"

severed in 'Twain.'"[34] Four days later, at the Whitefriars Club dinner, Twain acknowledged the presence of U.S. senator Chauncey Depew and American ambassador Joseph H. Choate. "I think we have spent our lives in serving our country," he remarked, "and we never serve it to greater advantage than when we get out of it."[35] Twain had reestablished his London presence by deftly playing to Anglo-American opinion. A naturally gregarious creature, he thrived on socializing, which didn't wear him down, but seemed to energize him.

A major, unspoken reason behind the London move was that Jean had failed to respond to the advice of medical sages in Vienna. For fourteen months, from January 1898 to March 1899, Sam and Livy had recorded her frequent petit mal seizures and infrequent but infinitely more terrifying grand mal convulsions as well as the bromide doses (up to six per day) dispensed in response. Sometimes her seizures struck twice a day. Of this sad vigil, Twain remembered, "There was nothing for us to do but go on watching and dosing, and wait for the end. But to continue the dreary and disheartening record could afford neither profit nor comfort."[36] One can imagine how Twain, at this period, developed the view that God, if He existed, had cursed humanity with endless maladies. Jean Clemens wasn't the only family member with intractable medical complaints. Clara had constant colds and vocal problems; Livy was bedeviled by back pain, rheumatism, and heart trouble; and Twain suffered from rheumatism, gout, a hernia, hemorrhoids, and chronic bronchitis. The family was a veritable hospital ward of maladies.

A turning point came in London that June when Twain's friend Poultney Bigelow, an American author, stopped by the Prince of Wales Hotel. Though rumored to be dying of dysentery contracted in the Philippines, Bigelow was not the emaciated figure Twain had expected, but a hale, sprightly man, "blooming with health," and Twain marveled at his unexpected recovery.[37] Bigelow attributed his swift recuperation to an osteopath named Jonas Henrik Kellgren, who practiced his Swedish Movement Cure at offices in Belgravia and at a sanitarium in Sanna, Sweden. After his dispiriting experience with bromides for Jean, Twain's ears must have perked up when he heard that Kellgren scorned traditional medicine, frowned on medication, and specialized in bodily manipulation. With Jean having made no progress in three years, Twain was ready to try anything that even remotely promised relief.

When he visited Kellgren, the doctor told him that if Jean had "nonhereditary" epilepsy, he might be able to cure her—a word Twain hadn't heard before. Kellgren had supposedly performed wonders in such cases. (Livy only belatedly found out that she had a relative who had suffered from epilepsy.)[38] Like many parents grappling with a chronically sick child, Twain entertained fantasies not just of treating, but of eliminating the awful disease. To be on the safe side, he underwent Kellgren's treatment himself—massage with the flat of the hand—before subjecting his family to this new method. Pleased, he booked passage by ship to Sanna for July 7, and when notifying friends, studiously avoided mention of Jean's epilepsy, making it sound like a wholesome medical outing for the entire family. (Clara would come later.) When the *New York Times* reported on the trip, it said Twain would "take the Swedish cure"—a cover story surely planted by the author himself.[39]

The sanitarium stood in a solitary clearing on a lake in Sweden, a place that Clara found "dull and gray."[40] At first, her father bristled at the simple, rustic setting, which he disparaged as "Hell . . . Sanna Branch."[41] He was pestered by flies, deplored rooms "the size of a tiger's cage," hated reading at night by tallow candles, and loathed the outhouses in the absence of indoor bathrooms. Then he began to be impressed by Kellgren's capable staff and noticed how their energetic manipulation of his limbs "freshens me up & makes me feel fine & gay all day," he told a friend. "I have never taken any exercise, & I never shall; but I find that exercise *is* good, provided someone else takes it for me."[42] When it came to health fads, Twain could sign on with wild enthusiasm; shrewd and sarcastic about many things, he could discard all skepticism, as in business ventures. "Every day, in 15 minutes it takes all the old age out of you & sends you forth feeling like a bottle of champagne that's just been uncorked."[43] After initial skepticism, Twain became a die-hard convert to osteopathy, something of a cultist, who

"A HUNDRED CAPERING CLOWNS"

would not listen to contrary medical opinions. "To ask a doctor's opinion of osteopathy," he declared, "is equivalent to going to Satan for information about Christianity."[44] A desperate father looking for a panacea, he stood ready to invest miraculous powers in any healer at odds with the medical establishment. As Twain said of Kellgren: "In fact an acute attack of any breed of disease disappears under his hands like enchantment."[45]

Since Twain was a walking encyclopedia of ailments, Kellgren had many chances to demonstrate his technique on him. Twain reveled in the vigorous treatment that shook up his system, boosted his pulse, and brought him alive. "With their hands they plow me up and down and all over, from crown to sole, apparently leaving no muscle and no nerve unvisited, but waking up and shaking up all my machinery."[46] For six years, Twain had worn a truss to treat a hernia he had gotten from bronchial coughing, and Kellgren made short work of it. "Take it off—throw it away," he told Twain, explaining that muscles were a natural truss that atrophied with artificial aids; the Kellgren method would invigorate those muscles, making any truss superfluous.[47] Kellgren's manipulations banished rheumatic tingling in Twain's wrist, a pricking sensation that traveled down his left arm, and bronchial coughs that typically lingered for weeks but now vanished in days; it even cured his "itching piles" after three sessions.[48]

Far more consequential was Jean's dramatic progress. After two years of taking one to three bromide doses daily, Kellgren acted to flush the toxic medicine from her system and made her stop taking them altogether. So petrified was Livy as they initiated this experiment that she secretly smuggled two bromides to Jean. Within a week, however, Jean's bouts of absentmindedness plummeted from fifteen or twenty to two. Kellgren was honest enough to warn that bad attacks would still come, and a terrible one unfolded on July 20. "Jean fell in a spasm striking her head on the slop jar," Twain wrote in his notebook. "A bad convulsion; she lay as if dead—face purple & no light in the eyes."[49] After Kellgren revived her, he boldly proclaimed that she would have to ride out these seizures while refraining from bromides. Five days later, Sam and Livy watched their youngest daughter endure two grand mal seizures in a single, dreadful day. "Jean had a convulsion in bed at noon—fortunately the Director had just entered the room. It was tolerably severe. He relieved her." At five p.m. Jean had the second seizure while sitting on the porch with her parents. "We were not able to carry her in—so laid her on the floor & did what we could . . . By & by it passed . . . we got her to bed."[50] One can only imagine the helplessness that Sam and Livy experienced as they watched Jean suffering these frightful episodes. For the moment, Kellgren remained a strong, confident presence, reassuring the anxious Livy: "It's all right. Keep your grip."[51]

Even as they waited for the seizures to subside, the Clemenses noticed a stunning change in Jean's behavior after Kellgren's treatment and being cleansed of the bromides that had dulled her mind. Seven years earlier they had witnessed an unaccountable change in her personality, from a sweet, loving child to a difficult and obstinate one. Yet little more than three weeks after arriving at Sanna, there were flashes of Jean's old personality. As Twain wrote, "She has ceased from being moody, irritable, wilful, capricious and determined to have her own way in spite of argument and opposition . . . She came here hostile to this treatment and with her mind convinced that she would never come to respect it nor get any benefit from it. This flag was hauled down as much as a fortnight ago . . . this is the first flag she has voluntarily lowered in two years."[52] The Jean of old had been unexpectedly, blessedly, restored to her parents.

True to Kellgren's prediction, the major seizures began to decline and largely stopped for more than a month. Sam and Livy, after years of despair, suddenly had reason to hope for improvement, if not a cure. Though small episodes of absentmindedness happened regularly, and Twain still observed "that ominous trick of the hands—a searching with her fingers for something in her dress or the bed clothes—as if for a pin, for instance—sliding the fingers along and feeling carefully"—these occurrences grew less frequent and less severe. Jean, formerly an active, cheerful, outdoor personality, began going on picnics in the woods, playing tennis and croquet, performing native dances in Swedish costumes, and studying the local language. No longer did the Clemenses need to maintain nocturnal vigils for her, and they slept more soundly. Kellgren frankly admitted that the convulsions hadn't passed but would recur at wider intervals. This tallied with Sam and Livy's own assessment, with Sam writing on August 20: "It is 21 days since the last attack—a long stretch of peace and comfort."[53]

With each passing week, Twain grew into a more vocal booster of the Swedish Movement Cure, which he lauded with the undying faith of a proselyte. "The patients tell such wonderful things that you half believe you have wandered into an asylum of Christian Science idiots."[54] He avidly heeded their stories and saw wonders everywhere, telling of one patient who hadn't walked for six years, but now "he hobbles around . . . without a cane, & has been doing it a week."[55] Now that Twain had gotten religion about Kellgren, he wanted him to work on every family member. "Tomorrow Clara will arrive to go into training," he told Poultney Bigelow in late July.[56] As had happened with Susy, Clara's voice coach in London, Madame Marchesi, thought she had to build up her bodily strength before embarking on a singing career. Kellgren would now have the entire family under his care, and with the Clemenses there was never any shortage of symptoms. "This family always carried a drug-store around, & were always calling doctors & taking medicines—often with pretty poor results," said Twain, who knew Kellgren's staff would be kept very busy delivering their ministrations.[57]

CHAPTER FORTY-THREE

"The Bastard Human Race"

The problem with Kellgren's treatment wasn't that it failed to bestow benefits—Jean, weaned from bromides, had again blossomed into a hopeful, energetic young woman—but that Twain had heaped such outsize expectations on the outcome. In early September, he rushed off a necessary correction to Henry Rogers. "I thought it was held that Jean could be cured in six months, but [Livy] says no, it was to be six months *possibly*, but it might take 9 and even 12. It puts off America a good while, and makes me tired to think of it."[1] Wishes with Twain tended to strengthen into certainties with timetables often compressed. Operating on a questionable premise, he now planned to have Jean continue her Kellgren treatments in London until her epilepsy was cured, and he canceled earlier plans to spend the autumn at the Princeton Inn.

Never a tepid convert to any cause, Twain blithely assumed the Kellgren treatment was a cure-all for almost any conceivable illness. "These people cure a deadly *acute* malady with splendid swiftness & certainty—scarlet fever, diphtheria, lung-fever, bronchitis, peritonitis, broken bones, bad wounds, shoulders out of joint &c—without medicines, anaesthetics, or antiseptics," he explained to nephew Samuel E. Moffett.[2] He stated categorically that Susy should never have died and that "Kellgren would have cured her without any difficulty."[3] At first, Twain had found Sanna a bleak, dreary northern outpost, but he ended up enchanted by the place, dazzled by its skies and sunsets. He told Laurence Hutton it was like "leaving heaven. I've *never* spent such a delicious summer."[4]

On September 27, the Clemens family packed up and left for London, where they planned to spend the winter and spring while Jean resumed her routine with Kellgren. Their first residence was at Queen Anne's Mansions, a new apartment complex overlooking St. James's Park that boasted London's tallest residential building, its height and complexity affording comic fodder for Twain: "It was said that in the course of time many persons had got lost in that place and were never found again, and this was true; for I often met their remains hunting around for their apartments and moaning."[5] They finally settled on a costly residence at 30 Wellington Court, in Knightsbridge, placing Jean within striking distance of Kellgren's practice on Eaton Square. In the aftermath of Susy's death, it was Clara's musical education and Jean's epilepsy that determined where their guilt-ridden father resided.

Twain kept a low profile in London and requested that close friends lie and say he was elsewhere, allowing him to work in seclusion. He and Livy shied away from throwing dinner parties and opted for the more economical alternative of inviting people for afternoon tea. "We wished it were something more substantial," he apologized to one person, "but we can't ask a Christian to eat the dinners they provide here; it would be suicide on the Christian's part & assassination on ours."[6] He gave way to money worries as tax and insurance payments for his Hartford house seemed to pose an intolerable financial burden. "I wish the house would burn down," he told Franklin G. Whitmore. "See that the insurance is kept up; & don't give the alarm if it catches fire."[7] Twain allowed Whitmore to entertain bids for the house, which he seems to have done on the sly. "The place is a profitless drain & a dead expense, & *I* could be tempted, though I can't answer for the family."[8] Whitmore faced the unenviable task of requesting urgent house payments from Twain and got precious little thanks for his service. "How I *do* wish that man was in hell," Twain told Howells. "Even the briefest line from that idiot puts me in a rage."[9]

Once committed to spending the winter in London, Twain came in for a rude awakening. He had imagined that Dr. Kellgren was a lonely genius who had single-handedly devised his therapeutic method. Then he wrote to Pamela, praising the Swedish Movement Cure, and was flabbergasted by her reply: for two months, she had enjoyed a remarkably similar course of treatment from a Dr. Steele in Buffalo. This method, known as osteopathy in America, had been practiced there for twenty-five years. Perhaps embarrassed that osteopathy existed in his own backyard, needlessly keeping him in Europe, Twain refused to admit that American doctors could have made their own discoveries. "I find that America has borrowed or stolen Kellgren's system," he wrote, "& is booming it, & *legalized* it in 8 States!"[10] Twain went so far as to argue that Kellgren had beamed his method to American practitioners by Mental Telepathy. In short order, Twain located three osteopaths in Manhattan, which would permit the Clemens family to return home the following year.

Such had been Twain's extreme idolatry of Dr. Kellgren that it was only a matter of time before disenchantment set in. By December, with no end in sight for Jean's cure, Livy began losing faith, despite the general improvement in her daughter's health. When she herself developed influenza and bronchitis in December and repaired to Kellgren for treatment, the experience was "nearly unendurable for violence," wrote Twain, and "has made her sore & lame, & filled her mind with black thoughts & antagonisms toward the system."[11] To worsen matters, Dr. Kellgren had accomplished little with Clara's chest problems. He had promised too much, and Twain had taken seriously his inflated promises. He complained to Sue Crane: "These people *have* cured this disease—we know this—or we should not meddle with it any longer; but we can't find out when Jean's cure is to begin, nor how many months or years it will take, for these idiots keep no records of their cases . . . I believe it is the most stupidly administered institution that exists in the earth."[12] Consequently, when making inquiries about American osteopaths, Sam and Livy tried to glean specific information about their success with epileptic patients.

With the prospect of a spring or summer return to America just ahead, the homesick family vacillated over whether to return to the Hartford house. The gorgeous place was now populated by ghosts and exercised an enduring influence on them. For Livy, it was frightful to contemplate being there without Susy, but no less horrid to imagine the dear house passing into strangers' hands. She chided herself for her attachment to material things, the way "every chair & book & corner of the house" exerted power over her mind.[13] Other factors intruded, including whether she could manage the house on a reduced income and whether her compromised health would constrain her ability to supervise it. She knew "the great care of that big place" was "sort of a care that I have been more or less free from for several years."[14] Frankly ambivalent, Clara balked at selling the house even though she felt "a great repulsion at the thought of going back," said Livy.[15] Jean, wedded to returning to the house, grew tearful whenever talk arose of selling it. "Jean is so steadily and unwaveringly attached to the place," Livy told Grace King, "that I feel as if I must take her back to it. I don't know whether she could endure it if we sold the place."[16] Of course, Twain, the one paying the bills, now regarded the house as a vast money pit that he was eager to unload.

Twain's arrival in London had nearly coincided with the start of the Second Boer War, pitting the British against two Boer republics for control of southern Africa. Even before it began, Twain could smell the "stench of gunpowder" and hear the "thunder of guns."[17] This bloody conflict, marked by high casualties and British concentration camps, provoked conflicted feelings in him. On the day war broke out, he privately wrote a piece saying it was "murder, & England committed it by the hand of [Joseph] Chamberlain & the Cabinet, the lackeys of Cecil Rhodes & his Forty Thieves, the South Africa Company."[18] Although he wrote this screed for anonymous publication in the London *Times*, he knew it would be explosive and stashed it in his drawer instead. During his stop in South Africa on the global tour, he had written in his notebook that the Boer was a "white savage," who was dirty and indolent and a tough taskmaster of Black workers.[19] Nonetheless, he instinctively sympathized with the Boers as underdogs, even though he knew Great Britain was an important U.S. ally and essential bulwark against Russia and Germany. He had many British friends who lost family members during the war—he described dinner parties as "Lodges of Sorrow"—and remembered that murky winter as a season of fog and mud, mourning and darkness.[20]

Shadowed by the war, Twain dissembled his true feelings about the culprit. Clara recalled that when it broke out, her father's "sympathies were not with the English and he found it best to accept no more invitations, except to the houses of those with whom he was on intimate terms."[21] It was similar to his lonely plight in Vienna when Austrians sided with the Spanish during the Cuban war. Occasionally Twain discussed the Boer War with British friends, but only when they introduced the topic. "Then I say 'My head is with the Briton, but my heart & such rags of morals as I have are with the Boer—now we will talk, unembarrassed & without prejudice.'"[22] The war deepened Twain's cynicism about war in general, especially when he heard the British mouth "smug pieties" and show contempt for Boer piety. "I notice that God is on both sides in this war . . . everybody here thinks He is playing the game for this side, and for this side only."[23] This astute observation, before long, would flower into Twain's famous "War Prayer." The war also made Twain wonder at God's judgment in creating the human race with its appalling appetite for carnage.

The pervasive grief in London must have reawakened memories of Susy's loss, for on May 17, 1900, Livy visited an English psychic named Mrs. Thompson to make contact with her dead daughter. Four years hadn't dampened her grief. Throughout his life, Twain had been a superstitious man who patronized psychics and palm readers and placed stock in their findings. Long intrigued by psychic phenomena, he became an exponent of what he dubbed Mental Telegraphy—the mind's ability to flash silent messages through the air to another person. Often he claimed to know the contents of a letter before it arrived and went so far as to assert that one didn't need to mail a letter but merely write it to get a response. Repeatedly he was struck by the many remarkable times when he and Livy had identical thoughts. In his notebook in 1882, he wrote: "The things which pass through my mind when I lie awake in the morning are pretty sure to be the topics introduced by others at breakfast or dinner, that day or the next."[24]

Two years later, Twain accepted membership in the Society for Psychical Research and published an article on "Mental Telegraphy" in the December 1891 issue of *Harper's Magazine*. In 1894, after going bankrupt, he had consulted a twenty-six-year-old palmist named Cheiro and was amazed at his conclusions. After studying Twain's thumb, Cheiro pronounced him a person who "hasn't much art in placating offended people or in making himself pleasant & agreeable to people toward whom he feels dislike or indifference"—a verdict to which Twain pleaded guilty.[25] The palmist also predicted that Twain would become enormously rich in 1903 and that his fame would someday be greater than ever—forecasts that came to pass.

In May 1900, when Livy met Mrs. Thompson at the Society for Psychical Research at 87 Sloane Street, she brought along one of Susy's brooches. The folks at the society took great pains to avoid giving Mrs. Thompson any clues about her client. They didn't provide Livy's name or allow her to speak, lest her accent give her away; in fact, Livy was only escorted into the room when Mrs. Thompson was already worked into a trance. Afterward, Frederic W. H. Myers, the society's founder, gave Livy a transcript of the session in which Mrs. Thompson said, "This is some one who died in America . . . She was interested in literary matters & in the writers of books . . . She was disturbed about some one who was ill—a relation—like a father. He was ill also had worries & troubles— I don't know exactly what—This lady was rather tall & thin . . . She is happy because people collected money & wanted to give it to some one for a present—in the winter-time."[26] Although this mostly sounds like Susy, Twain wasn't entirely gullible and doubted that the living could communicate with the dead. A year later, he told a correspondent that he and Livy had consulted two mediums whom Myers "considered quite wonderful, but they were quite transparent frauds. Mrs. Clemens corrects me: *One* of those women was a fraud, the other not a fraud, but only an innocent, well-meaning, driveling vacancy."[27] Clara remembered her parents visiting a famous palmist in London, separately and under assumed names. Livy returned heartbroken after the palmist predicted that she would be a widow within a year. "Father hastened to the same place and returned laughing. He had been told he would be a widower within the year."[28]

The chance of an imminent return to the United States and the complex financial calculations that attended it heightened Mark Twain's concern with money, a topic never distant from his thoughts. The likelihood that the family would wind up in expensive New York City, where Jean could consult with local osteopaths, lent special urgency to monetary matters. As shown by his abortive venture with Jan Szczepanik, nothing could quench Twain's thirst for speculation, not even bankruptcy. His newest investing mania arose from a problem that had bedeviled him for years— indigestion—which once led him to pen a verse that "Indigestion hath the power / to mar the soul's serenest hour."[29] While in Vienna in 1897, he had sampled a health food product known as Vienna Albumen, derived from skim milk and later marketed under the trade name Plasmon. To Henry Rogers, Twain insisted that this miracle substance had cured him of a "fiendish dyspepsia of 8 years standing."[30] Soon Plasmon became Twain's newest nostrum as he turned into both a consumer and a crusader for it, and foisted it on his wife and daughters. Eight times daily he swallowed this tasteless, odorless additive with cold milk, or washed down the dry powder with water, or dipped it into his coffee, hot chocolate, or soup.

When the Plasmon merchants created a London-based syndicate, Twain plumped down an astounding $25,000 (roughly $936,000 in today's money)—"all the cash I could spare," he said—and signed on to its board of directors.[31] Livy had recently received a windfall from J. Langdon & Company Coal, and Twain thought, "It was about time for me to look around and buy something."³² Soon he issued outlandish statements about Plasmon's supposed benefits, contending that a "pound of powder contains the nutriment of 16 pounds of the best beef."³³ Not only would Plasmon aid people with indigestion, it would, quite simply, solve the problem of world hunger. As he advised fellow investor John Y. W. MacAlister, the company should "deliver in Calcutta or Bombay, carriage free, 2,500,000 pounds of Plasmon per month," thus ending famine there and ensuring a bonanza of worldwide publicity for their product.³⁴

As with the Paige typesetter, Twain turned into a glad-handing salesman and evangelized for his panacea at every turn. "I was down at the House of Commons last night," he told MacAlister, "talking Plasmon to the membership."³⁵ Unlike the Paige typesetter, Plasmon earned profits, paid bankable dividends, and led Twain to boast to Rogers that the business was "as good as railroading."³⁶ Soon he hatched schemes to found an American affiliate where he planned to rope in Henry Rogers, Sir Thomas J. Lipton (of Lipton tea fame), and Andrew Carnegie. When the London syndicate sold American rights to Henry A. Butters, Twain told Rogers to keep an eye on him and have Standard Oil buy the Plasmon company, if possible.

Twain's religious zeal for Plasmon was probably a reaction to the medical situation that made him feel powerless: Jean's epilepsy. So much of his life now revolved around her treatment that on February 5, 1900, he sent a note marked "Private" to Rogers that confessed, for the first time, the true reason why his family lingered in London—"the reason being one which a family conceals from even its friends as long as it can, let alone the world."³⁷ That Twain stalled so long in telling Rogers about Jean's epilepsy makes a potent statement about the stigma attached to the disease. Only Sue Crane had been privy to the secret. Until Jean showed signs of definite improvement, Sam and Livy were reluctant to pull her away from Kellgren, and they needed absolute confidence in American osteopaths before taking her home.

Twain plunged into the literature about American osteopathy and was heartened by its similarity to Kellgren's work, as well as the claim that it could cure four in ten cases of epilepsy—a grossly irresponsible assertion for an incurable disease. Twain began to correspond with Andrew Taylor Still, the founder of osteopathic medicine, but immediately began to quarrel with him and cast aspersions on the "indifference, unfaithfulness, incapacity, discourtesy, & chronic fatigue" of his secretary.[38] On the other hand, he was persuaded that American osteopathy was at least as good as Kellgren's method and arguably even better. Having located an osteopath named Dr. George J. Helmer on Madison Avenue in Manhattan, Twain disclosed Jean's epilepsy to Samuel Moffett, now an editor in New York, and dispatched him to see Helmer and *"pump him dry;* then pour out the result upon me without stint."[39] Desperate for reliable information, Twain even asked Moffett to bring along a shorthand expert to record the conversation in detail. Meanwhile, he continued to spread the Kellgren gospel, got Henry Morton Stanley to consult him, and recommended him to William James, then suffering from heart disease, saying he was sure Kellgren "can mend your disorder."[40]

By late April, stymied by Jean's lack of progress, Twain stewed in a foul swamp of pessimistic reflections on the "bastard human race" and wondered why God, after inventing it, "chose to make each individual of it a nest of disgusting & unnecessary diseases, a tub of rotten offal."[41] In early May, he and Livy braced for a second summer in Sanna when Kellgren grandly announced that "Jean has turned the corner & will get well."[42] This would prove another overblown hope, but when Samuel Moffett sent an approving letter about Dr. George Helmer and Helmer himself sent an encouraging note to Twain, he felt rescued from the thrall of European doctors and relief in the prospect of returning home. "When we elect to go home, now," he told Moffett, "we can go with confidence."[43]

By mid-May, Twain stood amazed at Jean's improvement—"she is quite another person—the change is very marked. To-morrow it will be 4 weeks since she had a convulsion."[44] Buoyed by these gains, Kellgren lobbied for more time with Jean, and overcoming their eagerness to be back home, Sam and Livy acceded to his request. "Kellgren has never doubted that he could achieve a perfect cure," Twain told Moffett. "We believe he will do it. Fairness to him requires us to give him an extension of time; therefore it is not now our purpose to sail for home until October."[45] Once again, Kellgren grossly oversold his competence, and Twain set himself up for another grievous disappointment. As he told Mollie Clemens: "At intervals there will be minor crises yet, but that is no matter—the corner is turned, the back of the thing is broken."[46] Convinced he would be back home in October, the exiled author alerted the American press to the end of his long odyssey, telling the *New York World*, "I have postponed sailing for home until October . . . I am going home for good this time."[47]

Instead of going to Sweden, the Clemenses searched for a furnished house on the outskirts of London, a rustic spot from which Jean could commute into London three times weekly for Kellgren's treatments, and Clara could go for singing lessons. Even as they looked, Twain reported that Jean had "drifted into one of her bad times this morning."[48] He found the secluded, pastoral spot he wanted, a place called Dollis Hill House, where William Gladstone had once been a guest, in the north London suburbs. When the Clemens family arrived in early July, Twain carped at the commodious brick house as "certainly the dirtiest dwelling-house in Europe—perhaps in the universe."[49] The mercurial Twain was always prone to shifting opinions, and he came to regard the house as "nearer to being a paradise than any other home I ever occupied."[50] Surrounded by woods, it had a spacious lawn, a lily pond, and plenty of sheep. In this sedate country atmosphere, Jean and Clara would recline in hammocks stretched between trees or read on the lawn. It had been a long time since such peace and bliss had fallen upon the family. The plan was that Dr. Helmer would come to England in August to examine Jean; if he had any doubts about effecting a cure, then Sam and Livy would stay in England and keep Jean under Kellgren's care.

Despite the easy pace at Dollis Hill, the Clemens family remained a hotbed of medical symptoms. Jean, who turned twenty that summer, continued to have seizures. Twain was hobbled by gout and spent much of his day in his nightshirt, working on "The Chronicle of Young Satan." With her heart trouble, Livy stuck close to home. "Even when she is

"THE BASTARD HUMAN RACE"

well," Twain wrote, "she finds a two-hour summer-journey by rail a heavy tax upon her vitality."[51] When the anniversary of Susy's death rolled around in August, the full horror of it again descended upon the family, who received no visitors that day. As Twain told Twichell, "It is five years & a month that I saw her alive for the last time—throwing kisses at us from the railway platform when we started West around the world. Sometimes it is a century, sometimes it was yesterday."[52]

By mid-September, the Clemenses were packing their bags and preparing for the long journey back to America. They experienced a twinge of regret at departing from a restful home that they had grown to cherish. It is unclear whether Dr. Helmer had come to England and offered encouragement about Jean or whether Sam and Livy had lost faith in Kellgren. Their decision to move to New York, not Hartford, was settled by Helmer's presence in Manhattan, although emotional concerns clearly mattered. "New York was selected for our future abiding-place," recalled Clara, "as none of us felt able to face the old Hartford home without Susy."[53]

Before sailing for New York, the family lodged in London hotels, giving Twain the opportunity, in a letter, to record a comic jewel about the town's so-called Family Hotels. "They are a London specialty. God has not permitted them to exist elsewhere . . . The once spacious rooms are split up into coops which afford as much discomfort as can be had anywhere out of jail for any money. All the modern inconveniences are furnished, and some that have been obsolete for a century. The prices are astonishingly high for what you get. The bedrooms are hospitals for incurable furniture . . . The rooms are as interesting as the Tower of London, but older I think. Older and dearer. The lift was a gift of William the Conqueror. Some of the beds are prehistoric. They represent geological periods. Mine is the oldest."[54] He blamed his lumbago on that stiff bed, England's parting gift to him.

On October 6, the Clemens family boarded the *Minnehaha*, bound for New York, ending a nine-year stay. This quintessential American author had now spent a considerable portion of his life abroad, and his time in Europe would total eleven years by his death. Despite his small-town

RAPIDS

roots, he had evolved into one of America's most cosmopolitan citizens, at home in several countries and languages. The *Minnehaha* was a new and spacious ship and the transatlantic crossing was smooth. Not surprisingly, Twain devoted time aboard the boat to proselytizing for his favorite new health product: Plasmon. After one passenger endured a drinking spree, preventing his stomach from holding down food, Twain alerted him to the perfect antidote. "Day before yesterday the surgeon plasmonised [*sic*] him, & now he is all right; is up & around & takes his meals," he wrote to MacAlister. Nor was the hungover passenger the only person introduced to the derivative. "We took our maid out of bed & out of her seasickness with a single dose of plasmon; since then she takes plasmon daily & has had no return."[55] Twain was ready to preach the virtues of Plasmon to anyone with an ailment and surely scoured the ship for seasick souls.

PART FOUR

Whirlpool

CHAPTER FORTY-FOUR

"The Ancient Mariner"

When the *Minnehaha* docked at West Houston Street in New York on October 15, 1900, a squadron of reporters awaited Mark Twain, the first sign of the triumphal reception he would receive. Treasury Secretary Lyman J. Gage conferred the freedom of the port upon him, which meant he was whisked straight through customs. His extended absence and the well-known saga of his global tour to pay off debt had endeared him to the American public; it was a strange fate for someone so profligate in his spending to now be lionized as an exemplar of bourgeois morality. Amid scattered applause and welcoming cries, the *Herald* reporter noted the "smile of good-natured fun on [Twain's] lips . . . as he came down the gangplank."[1] The *World* reporter rattled off his familiar features—bushy hair, twinkling eyes, languid drawl—and was startled by the renewed spring in his step. "He looked as young as he did twenty years ago, and younger than he did when he shook American dust off his feet in 1891."[2] Whatever his criticisms of America through the years, Twain's love of his native country was palpable. "If I ever get ashore," he had told a friend, "I am going to break both of my legs so I can't get away again."[3]

For years, Twain had routinely ducked reporters because of debt or illness or a simple desire to shield his privacy. Now he showed his expertise in press relations as he gloried in the attention. Even before he sailed he had orchestrated his reception by granting an interview to the *World* to run on the eve of his arrival, signaling he was coming home, with guns blazing. After years of worry about touchy political topics, he let loose a volley of opinions that were bound to stir up controversy, especially his trumpet blasts against American imperialism. Of the occupation of the Philippines, he stated: "I have tried hard, and yet I cannot for the life of me comprehend how we got into that mess . . . I thought we should act as their protector—not to get them under our heel . . . But now—why, we have got into a mess, a quagmire from which each fresh step renders the difficulty of extrication immensely greater."[4] If Twain embraced his sudden popularity, he refused to make concessions to public opinion by hedging his forthright stands.

In a signal that he had landed on home soil for good, Twain regaled the huddled reporters with a brilliant impromptu performance, declaring that when he paid off all his debt, he "felt like the Ancient Mariner when the dead albatross fell into the sea. I became a new man."[5] He dispensed handy aphorisms: "I never told the truth that I was not suspected of lying, and never told a lie that I was not believed."[6] In travels through Europe, he preferred Vienna "with the poor old Reichsrat . . . It was one of the biggest jokes I have ever seen, and I enjoyed it immensely."[7]

What reporters hungered for most was Twain's witty political punditry. He had already floated the humorous notion that he planned to run for president on the Plutocratic ticket against President William McKinley. Now he admitted he might vote for McKinley, could not support his Democratic opponent, William Jennings Bryan, and stuck to his doughty old Mugwump independence. He reserved his most-forceful salvoes for U.S. foreign policy and explained the evolution of his thinking in Europe. When he sailed off on his worldwide tour, he confessed to having been "a red-hot imperialist," even hoping the American eagle would spread its wings over the Philippines, only to discover that "we do not intend to free but to subjugate the people of the Philippines. We have gone there to conquer, not to redeem."[8] This was strong stuff. A beloved author, Twain could have returned quietly to America after a long absence. Instead, he had never been so fiery and feisty and ready to topple sacred idols.

Twain informed reporters that his family would reside at the Earling-

"THE ANCIENT MARINER"

ton Hotel on West 27th Street, spend the winter in New York, then transfer back to Hartford in the spring. Then, five days after returning home, Twain was summoned to Hartford by the sudden death of Charles Dudley Warner, his coauthor on *The Gilded Age,* who had died of a heart attack. Because Livy was too weak to attend the funeral and feared the emotional strain, Twain went alone with Clara. Their reunion with Nook Farm neighbors brought back to Twain a floodtide of memories of nights spent debating essays with the learned Monday Evening Club. Twain remembered "all those men as they were in those days talking upon all subjects and regulating the affairs of this planet . . . the Monday Club is [now] assembling in the cemetery."[9] Along with Clara, he stepped warily into the house that had been the scene of so much happiness, now associated with such misery. Afterward he confided to a friend that he had realized "if we ever enter the house again to live, our hearts will break. I am not sure that we shall ever be strong enough to endure that strain."[10] Beyond the poignant banishment from the past, the Hartford visit confirmed that Susy's death was a wound that would never heal. "Clara was in a terrible state when she got back," Jean wrote in her diary. "She says she wept almost without stopping from the time she arrived in Hartford till the time she left."[11]

As the Clemenses searched for a furnished Manhattan apartment for the winter, they balked at the lofty prices and had to pass on a place on Washington Square that they simply couldn't afford. For all the sorrow of the Hartford funeral, Twain seemed rejuvenated by being back in America, where he was the cynosure of all eyes. "He looks like a fighting cock," Livy wrote.[12] Howells also noticed how unexpectedly spry his old friend was. "Younger and jollier than I have seen him in ten years," he remarked to Thomas Bailey Aldrich. "He says it's all Plasmon, a new German food-drug he's been taking, but I think it's partly prosperity."[13]

Shortly the Clemenses found a house at 14 West 10th Street, which they occupied on November 1, 1900. Whatever financial constraints they faced in New York, they still lived richly by normal standards and would enjoy the services of a cook, two maids, and a butler. The four-story brick residence was a large, rambling old house—"large & bright &

sunny," wrote Livy—and her husband was so eager to occupy it that he didn't wait to sign the lease before moving in, much to the chagrin of Frank Doubleday, who had referred them to the house.[14] Never an easy tenant, Twain was soon griping about everything from the furnace to the windows to the oven. Prodded by his family, he also complained to a neighbor about raucous boys who gathered on their front steps. In a graceful note of protest, he admitted that "I am weak & faithless where boys are concerned, & I can't help secretly approving pretty bad & noisy ones," but he emphasized that he was acting at Livy's behest.[15]

Twain's instant celebrity in New York followed him to West 10th Street, which "was always full of people just walking by to see where Mark Twain lived, 'cause he was very famous then and all his books was read by everybody," recalled Katy Leary.[16] Clara had the same recollection of unending hubbub around her father's door. "One could never begin to describe in words the atmosphere of adulation that swept across his threshold. Every day was like some great festive occasion."[17] As Twain resumed his former madcap life as a bon vivant, popping up everywhere as a toastmaster, he was inundated with invitations and declined as many as seven banquets per day. Enlisting Livy's help, he once had to answer thirty-eight letters in a single day, a process he found exhausting.

As various clubs vied to honor him, Twain chose his old haunt, the Lotos Club, as the first venue for his official homecoming talk. The banquet was loaded with luminaries—Henry Rogers, Senator Chauncey Depew, William Dean Howells, Booker T. Washington—but when it started, the hopelessly absentminded Twain was nowhere to be seen, so a messenger was dispatched to West 10th Street. "I am sorry," Twain told him at the door, "but I had forgotten this was Saturday; I thought it was Friday; I'll go right upstairs and dress. It won't take me fifteen minutes."[18] When Twain arrived belatedly, St. Clair McKelway introduced him with the perfect remark: "Sinners love him, and saints are content to wait for him," and the audience greeted the honoree with long, lusty cheers.[19]

Twain immediately poked fun at the presence of former Speaker of the House "Czar" Thomas B. Reed. "They tell me that since I have been away Reed has deserted politics and is now leading a creditable life. He has reformed, and God prosper him."[20] He reminisced about the bankruptcy that drove him abroad and thanked the ninety-five of his ninety-six creditors who behaved honorably. Then he undertook a review—half facetious, half serious—of political events that had unfolded in his absence and noted that former New York governor Teddy Roosevelt had been catapulted to the vice presidency by his "Rough Rider" exploits in Cuba. "Why, I would have been a Rough Rider myself if I had known that this political Klondike was going to open up, and I would have been a Rough Rider if I could have gone to war in an automobile—but not on a horse!"[21] He didn't soft-peddle his critical views on the Philippine occupation and said he would never understand how the United States had betrayed its original "righteous purpose" to free the Filipinos. More than ever a gadfly, Twain ventured into territory that he would once have deemed verboten as he cast a scathing eye on American patriotism. He no longer felt the need to censor himself on many topics as the inner man increasingly emerged. He ended his talk with heartfelt reflections on what it meant to him to "come back from my exile young again, fresh and alive, and ready to begin life once more."[22] As he basked in the adoration, he felt reborn, having thrown off the terrible weight of the decade abroad.

Such was Twain's razor-sharp sense of justice and short temper that he undertook quixotic crusades to punish individual malefactors around town. One night a cab brought Katy Leary from Grand Central Terminal to West 10th Street, and Twain believed the driver charged an extortionate $7 instead of $1, the proper amount. Twain made the payment but only after delivering a tongue-lashing to the driver and demanding his cab number. Twain then complained to David Roche, the mayor's marshal, and when he marched up to see him and confront the cabman, he attracted twenty reporters to the hearing. The *New York Times* described the scene: "Mark Twain looked with a cold, steely eye from under his bushy brows at the official. Marshal Roche seemed to shiver as if a sudden arctic draught had been wafted into the room. It became apparent at once that Mr. Clemens would have no joking at his expense."[23] Twain confronted the red-faced driver and got him to admit his overcharge. To his credit, he was less interested in a vendetta than in making a larger point about citizenship. "Here is a man who is a perfectly natural product of an infamous system . . . He is not the criminal here. The criminal is the citizen of New York and the absence of patriotism."[24] When the driver lost his license, Twain paid him for his lost time and asked a judge to reinstate him. Twain could be gruff, but also forgiving, a duality characteristic of the man.

Thrust back into New York's social whirl, Twain was something of a flâneur who enjoyed strolling the city streets or riding on the upper level of an omnibus. The city had been so transformed in his absence that he surveyed it with a sense of wonder as he gazed up at new skyscrapers. By day, he found them ugly monuments, but "at night, seen from the river, when the great walls of masonry are all a-sparkle, the city is fairy-like. It is more beautiful than any other city since the days of the Arabian nights."[25] Of course, skyscrapers relied upon efficient American elevators, leading Twain to ridicule, by way of comparison, one of his favorite targets—"the cigar boxes of Europe called 'lifts.' . . . In Europe, when a man starts to the sixth floor on a lift he often photographs his family so he may recognize them when he gets back."[26] Twain likewise found the street lighting and cable and trolley cars of New York far superior to their London counterparts and celebrated the city's heterogeneous population, many foreign-born. Curiously enough, Twain felt no impulse to transmute this roaring, bustling metropolis into fiction. The contemporary urban world was scarcely reflected in his fiction even as writers such as Stephen Crane and Theodore Dreiser captured its momentous upheavals.

The move to New York was predicated on the hope that Jean could transition seamlessly to the osteopathic treatments of Dr. Helmer at Madison Avenue and 31st Street. She kept a diary during this period, affording vivid glimpses of her physical and psychological state. She appreciated the soft, scattered couches at 14 West 10th Street that presented safe places to tumble during seizures. She reported regularly to Dr. Helmer, who gave her vigorous muscular stimulation that she often found quite painful. "Dr. Helmer as usual nearly pulled me to pieces," she wrote after a session, "and he seemed to think my bones were wonderfully solid and hard to move."[27] She suffered daily fits of "absentmindedness"—that is, petit mal seizures—often starting when she swallowed an oatmeal breakfast and recurring throughout the day. These sudden lapses might occur amid a conversation, or a tea party, or while watching a play, and she would awaken unaware of what had happened. She also gave way to "fainting turns"—grand mal seizures—sometimes two per day, harrowing experiences that drained her and left her feeling "unstrung and tired out when I wakened," with Katy Leary assisting her as she rode out these traumatic events.[28] Clearly Dr. Helmer's methods produced no miraculous breakthroughs, and he lowered the Clemenses' expectations by saying that in treating diseases, "when they had gotten to the root of the evil that it would seem to be getting worse."[29]

For a long time the family had concealed Jean's epilepsy diagnosis from Jean herself, and now at age twenty, she was left with an empty feeling after learning her diagnosis, and a pessimism about her future prospects. She dreaded that the disease would ward off potential suitors and even make marriage impossible. "Is it going to be my miserable lot never to really love and be loved?" she wondered in her diary. "That would be too dreadful & would offer another very fair reason for suicide," even if Dr. Helmer cured her epilepsy.[30] This was a powerful statement of her depression, of her feeling not just unloved, but unlovable. "It is dreadful though to feel as I so often do," she sighed another day. "To have no real friends, no talent of any kind, no love, no home . . . and no health or more truly an abominable health. If I could only have a real love, a real talent & a decent sort of health."[31] She envied Clara with her talents and boyfriends, while she had to stick close to home in an endless adolescence. When she had her heart set on attending a ball that fall, she was mortified when Dr. Helmer said that she could dance for only an hour, then needed to leave and go to sleep. In retrospect, she realized, her "horrid illness" had left emotional dead spots in her life that had prevented her from grieving properly when Susy died.[32]

In her misery, Jean was hypersensitive to any perceived missteps from her parents. She described a cozy visit with Joe Twichell in which she sat on her heels to be near him, only to find that her feet went to sleep. When she stood "to rouse them I stamped them somewhat; that annoyed Mamma who told me to go to my room if I wanted to stamp. I continued for a moment & then stopped. Before I had quite stopped she turned & glared at me which made me simply boil. I am not an infant and don't choose to be treated like one, certainly not before people. After the visitors had left I said good-night to Papa & later to Clara but not at all to Mamma & then came to bed where I read for some time."[33] Although Jean admitted the next morning that her behavior might have been trying, the episode illustrated the strong clash of wills between the genteel Livy and the firm-willed personality that epilepsy had produced in her daughter. By contrast, Jean referred affectionately to her gouty father as the "Poor little lame man."[34] To lighten his workload and give Jean useful work, Twain had her learn the typewriter and experimented with dictating to her. But the unpredictable nature of her illness created tension for the entire family, who felt themselves sitting on the rim of a volcano that could blow up at anytime.

Dr. Helmer must have been startled to find himself soon treating the entire Clemens clan. They were a dream family for any practitioner looking for steady work. Even though it was hard to spot signs of progress, Jean liked Dr. Helmer immensely and felt "no end of confidence in him."[35] Pretty soon Livy saw him twice weekly as he identified a raft of problems with her—a malfunctioning liver, a large goiter, misplaced collar bones, and a faulty tear duct. Lest she feel left out, Clara was treated by Dr. Helmer for a sore throat. Twain was always extolling Helmer's virtues—"No physician could do that wonderful thing," he exulted after a cold was cured in one meeting—but he had such a lengthy litany of maladies that it was hard to figure out why Twain reposed such faith in him.[36]

By February, despite severe gout attacks, Twain was sufficiently passionate about osteopathy that he testified for an hour before a committee of the New York State Assembly, then considering a bill to license osteo-

"THE ANCIENT MARINER"

paths; in 1896, Vermont had become the first state to do so. The New York County Medical Society sent five physicians, big guns of the profession, to testify against the bill and mock its most famous apostle. One of them, Dr. Frank Van Fleet, conceded that "Mark Twain is a very funny man. He writes humorous books . . . But no one ever takes Mark Twain seriously."[37] Dr. Robert T. Morris also used Twain's reputation as a funny man to discredit him. "Mark Twain may come to you with jokes, but we are here dealing with life and death. It is a part of the game which these people play to get noted men to indorse [sic] their practice."[38]

It was a fool's errand to try to ruffle Mark Twain with mockery, since he was a past master of the art. One medical foe criticized him on the grounds that his knowledge of osteopathy arose from experience in Sweden. "That is true," he noted. "About a year and a half ago in London I met Mr. Kellgren, who I believe is the most noted practitioner of this kind abroad. He calls himself Mr. because he has not acquired the privilege of giving a certificate when a patient dies on his hands."[39] Heretofore, Twain archly noted, there had been two schools of medicine in America: "The regular physicians and the grandmothers. Now all I ask is the same liberty you give to the grandmother. The grandmother has been practicing without a license as far as the memory of any one of us goes back."[40] In closing, Twain mentioned the unmentionable subject: that regular physicians were bent on maintaining a high-priced cartel. "The physicians think they are moved by regard for the best interests of the public. Isn't there a little touch of self-interest back of it all?"[41] Twain performed a brave act in testifying against a well-heeled lobby, and the *New York Times* pilloried him as "a defender of quacks" who was "assuming the role of a public enemy."[42] As in his outspoken remarks on American imperialism, Twain was showing a new crusading spirit and willingness to risk his reputation as America's premier humorist.

It is easy to see why Jean would have been envious of the highstrung Clara, who, despite her own medical problems, was bright, quickwitted, and ambitious. Jean often felt like a pariah, the black sheep of the family, when social invitations flooded in for her sister and she was conspicuously snubbed. An emancipated young woman, Clara didn't wish to sacrifice her music career to marriage, dreaded having babies, and didn't think she could love only one man—modern notions that shocked love-starved Jean, who had to watch her sister enjoy the attention of surplus men. It is also easy to see why Clara wished to escape the darkness of her family after Susy's death—she'd been much closer to her than Jean had been—and wanted some distance from Jean's intractable epilepsy. By the time Clara returned with her family to New York, she had a love affair going with a Swede named Swalenberg, leading Jean to reflect sadly that by the time Clara was her age, twenty, "five or six men had shown signs of great affection or friendship for her even if they hadn't said it in so many words."[43]

That Clara truly didn't care to be tied down by one man became apparent that November when Ossip Gabrilowitsch suddenly materialized in New York for his American debut, performing Tchaikovsky's Piano Concerto No. 1 at Carnegie Hall under the baton of Walter Damrosch. He set aside a large box at the hall for Clara and her family. During rapturous applause, they sent an enormous wreath to the stage with gold lettering that read "Welcome to America, from the Clemenses."[44] Ossip played four solo pieces in all, and after his Liszt selection, "the house simply went mad," said Jean. "They positively stormed! Howled, & stamped and [the] applause was like a tornado."[45] Several times, Ossip looked up and bowed toward the Clemens box, and he came as their guest for dinner the next night. When he had a chance to hear Clara sing, he thought she had improved markedly and gave her an impromptu lesson on the spot.

Outwardly her parents supported Clara's singing, though they wondered whether her health could support it and were quietly troubled by the uncertain outlook for any performing artist. Clara placed extreme emphasis on succeeding without assistance from her father's name, but it was an unrealistic expectation, as became clear that fall when an announcement for her first American recital appeared in the *Concert Goer.* As soon as it appeared, Clara's manager was swamped with inquiries from newspaper reporters who clamored for her photograph. As Jean observed, "The cause of all the rumpus & excitement is the fact that her

"THE ANCIENT MARINER"

being Mark Twain's daughter has in some way leaked out & was in the Concert Goer too. Clara didn't want it to become known and Papa was very highly amused at the idea that she thought it could be kept secret; he will be more amused than ever now when he knows it's out already."[46] For years there would be an unresolved conflict between Clara's resistance to succeeding on the strength of her father's fame and Twain's vanity at being pleased by this attention.

When Clara made her professional debut as a singer in Washington in January, Livy rallied her strength and attended the event. Clara was fighting off a bad cold and had to visit a doctor twice before taking the stage. The first reviews were charitable and not exactly glowing. While Clara "was evidently undergoing the sufferings of a newcomer to the stage yesterday," the *Washington Times* noted, "after her first numbers, her singing was in every way delightful."[47] Whether due to his crippling gout or as a mark of disapproval, her father stayed at home, although he did maneuver to get Clara plugged in the press. Nor did he show up for her second recital in Hartford, where she got a "wonderful reception."[48] According to Livy, Clara was "just out of bed after bronchitis," forcing her to cancel her remaining recitals that winter, a pattern to be repeated in her career.[49] Livy was deeply torn as to whether, from motherly love, she should encourage her daughter or express instead her honest dismay about her chosen career. "We do not oppose her," Livy told Grace King, "for of course that is not best, but we are very sorry indeed that she wants this public life."[50] It puzzled Livy that whereas she herself was so shy and private, Clara craved the limelight and already displayed her father's fondness for attention.

CHAPTER FORTY-FIVE

The Anti-Doughnut Party

On December 12, 1900, at the close of an autumn packed with so many appearances that Mark Twain seemed almost ubiquitous in Manhattan, he introduced Winston Churchill at a lecture on the Boer War at the Waldorf-Astoria. Though only twenty-six, Churchill was soon to take his (unpaid) seat in the British Parliament and had come to America to shore up his finances through a lecture tour arranged by Major Pond. Churchill had been catapulted to instant celebrity when as a war correspondent in southern Africa, he escaped from a Boer prison and made his way, amid omnipresent danger and hairbreadth escapes, to British lines. Churchill was an unashamed British imperialist, and his talk drew dissent from some committee members hosting the event. While Twain admired his talents—he later referred to "that soaring and brilliant young statesman, Winston Churchill"—he was then flaunting his anti-imperialist credentials and was bound to differ with Churchill over the Boer War.[1] The prospective clash of views guaranteed that the Waldorf ballroom would be jammed with twelve hundred people.

It was a tricky, indeed a perilous, spot for Twain, who had to honor Churchill as a courageous young man while deploring British policy in South Africa, but he tread this tightrope nimbly. He credited Churchill with having made a record "which would be a proud one for a man twice his age. By his father he is English, by his mother he is American—to my mind the blend which makes the perfect man."[2] Twain candidly admitted that "Mr. Churchill and I do not agree on the righteousness of the South African war, but that is of no consequence. There is no place where people all think alike—well, there is heaven; there they do, but let us hope it won't be so always."[3] It was a graceful way of acknowledging their disagreement, and Twain was no less diplomatic in saying "England sinned in getting into a war in South Africa which she could have avoided without loss of credit or dignity—just as I think we have sinned in crowding ourselves into a war in the Philippines on the same terms."[4] The United States and Britain, having been kin in blood, were now "kin in sin, the harmony is complete, the blend is perfect, like Mr. Churchill himself, whom I now have the honor to present to you."[5] It was an adroit performance as Twain equated British and American imperialist behavior without adopting a holier-than-thou position on the Boer War. The episode illuminated why he was in such demand as a speaker: he had a way of being utterly frank while intermingling his opinions with diverting asides that endeared him even to opponents.

After an anxious start to his maiden speech in America, Churchill gave a riveting account of his escape in South Africa and ended by saying that Twain had given his lecture "an importance and a dignity which it could not have otherwise obtained."[6] Once the lecture was over, Twain autographed a complete set of his works for Churchill, writing in the first volume, "To do good is noble; to teach others to do good is nobler, and no trouble."[7] For Churchill, it was an unforgettable encounter, a pleasure that far outweighed their political disagreement. "I was thrilled by this famous companion of my youth. He was now very old and snow-white, and combined with a noble air a most delightful style of conversation. Of course we argued about the war. After some interchanges I found myself beaten back to the citadel, 'My country right or wrong.' 'Ah,' said the old gentleman, 'when the poor country is fighting for its life, I agree. But this was not your case.'"[8] In the future, Churchill would join the International Mark Twain Society, receiving its Gold Medal during World War II.

On August 13, 1895, Twain paused on his around-the-world tour to take this photo with, from left, nephew Samuel Moffett, Livy, Clara, an unidentified older woman, and Martha Pond, wife of Twain's lecture agent. Twain is dressed in white tie for a speech at the Seattle Opera House.

Twain standing before his boyhood home in Hannibal in May 1902. The house, he said, was much smaller than he remembered it. "I suppose if I should come back here ten years from now it would be the size of a bird-house."

Twain posing in the Oxford robe that he treasured. He considered the honorary degree from the university the highest accolade of his career.

From the moment he landed at Tilbury, en route to Oxford, Twain was besieged by reporters eager for witty quotes.

Twain clowning during a theatrical performance at Onteora Park with daughter Susy in the summer of 1890. Twain was an excellent actor and mimic.

Mark Twain in bed, photographed by biographer Albert B. Paine in 1906. A master of projecting a memorable image, Twain often met with reporters while propped up with pillows in his bed.

Mark Twain socializing in Bermuda with Woodrow Wilson (standing far right), then president of Princeton University, and other friends.

Twain with Helen Keller at Stormfield. It was Twain who christened Helen's teacher, Anne Sullivan, the "Miracle Worker," a label used for film and stage dramatizations of her relationship with Helen.

Clara Clemens, Twain's middle daughter, could never conquer her ambivalence toward her father. As she pursued her musical career, she wasn't reluctant to trade on his name.

Ossip Gabrilowitsch, Clara's husband, a superb concert pianist and later director of the Detroit Symphony Orchestra.

TWAIN AND THE ANGELFISH

Twain playing billiards with Louise Paine and Dorothy Harvey in June 1908.

Twain seated with the same two girls. Far from hiding his relationships with the angelfish, Twain flaunted them in many photos.

In a gentle, forgiving mood, Jean Clemens at Stormfield with her father in 1909, after her long exile from home had ended.

In this holiday photo, Twain appears with Isabel Lyon and Ralph Ashcroft. He would later decide that his "pets" had betrayed his trust and bilked him.

Right after her mother died in Italy, Jean Clemens took this solemn photo of Livy at her final rest after years of suffering from heart trouble.

This 1901 photo captures the melancholy and pessimism that seized Mark Twain in his final years.

THE ANTI-DOUGHNUT PARTY

By the time Mark Twain returned to America after years abroad, he had graduated from being merely famous to a relatively new category of "celebrity," his name and face instantly recognizable, his personality transformed into a trademark. He understood the secret of modern celebrity—that "*conspicuousness* is the only thing necessary in a person to command our interest and, in a larger or smaller sense, our worship."[9] His persona was a product he never stopped perfecting. Twain had become the archetypal American, even though he remained a very private man behind the shifting masks he so adeptly presented to the public. Perhaps surprisingly, he had soared to the zenith of his fame long after his fiction career had largely ceased. Of the enduring appeal of his novels, he once remarked, "High & fine literature is wine, & mine is only water. But everybody likes water."[10] He had also won popularity among a new generation that knew him more for his adages, topical quotes, and anomalous views than for his Hannibal characters.

Twain, who thrived in the spotlight, delighted in strolls down Fifth Avenue. On Sundays he timed his walks so as to pass churches just as congregants spilled onto the sidewalk, and he would be mobbed by admirers. Always friendly and accessible, he enjoyed "loafing along & gossiping" with strangers he encountered.[11] "I like being the center of attraction," he confessed. "It's very pleasing, and no trouble!"[12] When he entered public places, whether theaters or restaurants, people greeted him with applause. He was the city's court jester and reporters dogged him everywhere. When he sat in the reviewing stand for a parade to honor the local police department and journalists asked why he dressed in black, he patiently explained that he didn't care to be spotted by the officers. "I've always liked the police, but I suppose that's because they've always seemed to take such a deep, abiding interest in all that I do."[13]

Twain's emergence as author-celebrity can't be understood apart from the rise of mass media in America. Huge newspaper chains assembled by Joseph Pulitzer, William Randolph Hearst, and other media barons created a need for all-purpose pundits who could manufacture instant opinions on any subject, and Twain, with his wide-ranging knowledge, possessed that incomparable gift. The entourage of journalists who followed him knew that they could always count on him for something funny, quotable, and pertinent. He was "The Quotable Mark Twain" long before books with that title appeared. "It always puzzled me," Clara said, "how Mark Twain could manage to have an opinion on every incident, accident, invention, or disease in the world."[14] Twain obsessively cultivated his image in the press—"Always remember that in America there is nothing so important to a person in the public's eye as the Press," he observed—and left nothing to chance as he lobbied editors for favorable mentions and reviews, with his doings vividly chronicled.[15] "Mark's spectacular personality is just now very busy all over the world," Thomas Bailey Aldrich told Howells. "I doubt if there is another man on earth whose name is more familiar."[16]

Twain expressed a contradictory attitude toward the hundreds of interviews he granted. He liked to project the image of a comical, eccentric sage who held court with reporters in his ornate bed, supported by pillows and sporting a nightshirt. Yet he thought reporters missed the art and nuance of his speech, rendering it flat on the printed page, and he found errors galore. "I have often been quoted but never, unless I have written out the interview myself, have I been quoted accurately."[17] He groused that "the poorest article I ever wrote and destroyed was better worth reading than any interview with me that ever was published."[18] That Twain was so fearful of being misquoted often gave a confrontational edge to his interviews, however leavened with humor. He also believed that he should be paid for his opinions and resented sharing them with reporters free of charge.

Twain knew that the double-edged nature of fame made him a convenient target for critics and publicity seekers. He experienced both the joys and terrors of having his every syllable quoted. As a rule, he professed indifference to heckles thrown in his direction. He once told Mother Fairbanks not to bother with "slander printed in an obscure and characterless paper" and gave his comical philosophy in the matter: "It is my inflexible rule to be satisfied & content with anything & everything a newspaper may say about me so long as it confines itself to statements that are not true. I have never seen an opinion of me in print which was as low down as my private opinion of myself."[19] In truth, he was deeply hurt by insinuations reported against him, and a petulant tone crept into his private ruminations about the press. In his notebook for October 1902, he wrote: "Journalism: an anonymous conspiracy against private character & public morals conducted for gain. Journalist: a tiny creature without name or authority who hides behind a blanket sheet & squeaks, & some of the awed people think it is the thunder & the others think it is God."[20] One lesson he learned, from hard experience, was that it was often better to ignore libelous statements than futilely seek to refute them. As he put it, "Few slanders can stand the wear of silence."

Whatever his personal frustrations Twain never lost sight of the sovereign importance of the press in a democracy. Back in 1888, he had written an unpublished piece, "The American Press," that was a riposte to Matthew Arnold, who had faulted the American press for lacking respect for authority. He mocked the British press for servility toward the Crown and for regarding its chief responsibility as keeping "the public eye fixed in loving and awful reverence upon the throne, as a sacred thing."[21] By contrast, the American press professed no such reverence for kings, nobility, or an established church. "For its mission—overlooked by Mr. Arnold—is to stand guard over a nation's liberties, not its humbugs and shams . . . to my mind a discriminating irreverence is the creator and protector of human liberty."[22] This almost reads as a credo of Twain's own satirical writings, his belief that the corrupt and powerful can withstand anything but well-aimed mockery. As he said, "The devil's aversion to holy water is a light matter compared with a despot's dread of a newspaper that laughs."[23]

One liability of Twain's renown was that he was constantly bombarded with letters—what he called early on "the persecution of kindly letters from well-meaning strangers."[24] The choice was simple: he could either be silent and rude or answer letters and steal precious hours from writing. "Correspondence is the despair of my life," he warned his sister. "Suppose you had to have 15 teeth pulled every day; & every time you lost 3 days."[25] Partly the problem was that Twain was incapable of writing short, banal replies and demanded original prose from himself. He reserved special scorn for those who solicited autographs along with special requests. When a fan sent him a polite request for an autograph with the plea—"Will you kindly preface your 'auto' with a 'sentiment' of some kind?"—Twain scribbled, "From some low-bred & unrefined son of a bitch in Pennsylvania."[26] He did not reply to the letter. Despite his irritation, Twain was quite solicitous about sending out autographs and would scrawl his name many times on a large sheet of paper and have an assistant snip them out and send them to people as needed. Letters flooded in from around the globe, and Livy maintained a special file of those that reached him without any specific address. One sent to "Mark Twain, God knows where" arrived in his mailbox, as did another directed to "Mark Twain. Somewhere, (Try Satan.)"

Among the bushels of letters crossing his threshold, the ones that he detested the most came from would-be authors soliciting book blurbs or asking his honest opinion of their writing when they were merely fishing for compliments. Often these requests came with long, effusive letters, flowery in their tributes to Mark Twain and how much he had influenced them, offering praise and incense in exchange for coveted quotes. Twain bristled at what he considered moral blackmail and fell back on the old dodges, telling the writer how he promised himself "at an early date" the pleasure of reading his book.[27] Meanwhile, he sat and fumed. "It is not right for a stranger to send me his book himself . . . I have not earned this treatment, I have not done him any harm."[28] As he often did, Twain subjected everyday behavior to merciless dissection, stripping away the facade of human interactions to disclose the selfish core of motivations.[29] No matter how flattering the letters from aspiring authors, Twain descried self-interest at work. "As I have remarked before about one thousand times the coat of arms of the human race ought to consist of a man with an ax on his shoulder proceeding toward a grindstone, or . . . several members of the human race holding out the hat to one another; for we are all beggars, each in his own way."[30] Such was Twain's worldwide reputation that he had to deal with an impersonator

THE ANTI-DOUGHNUT PARTY

in Australia as early as 1881, when he had not yet visited the country. A year later, Twain learned of another person mimicking him in Belfast and fooling people, and he asked his British publisher to expose him. Some of these bogus Mark Twains borrowed money and vanished, while others sought to cash in on the lecture circuit. "Man swindled audience with pretended lecture here last night, claiming to be you," came a message from New Orleans.[31] Twain had become such a certified character that the temptation to mimic him had become irresistible for many people.

As for product endorsements, Twain had no qualms about capitalizing on his fame—yet another way that he anticipated the celebrity culture of modern times. Not long after he published *Tom Sawyer*, cigars were marketed with his name and likeness, and the exhortation "Smoke the Popular Mark Twain Cigars Sold Everywhere."[32] When he consented to the use of his name to promote a new style of collar in 1883, he explained that "I think it is time the name should be connected with something useful—it has been confined to the aesthetic & ornamental long enough."[33] Twain's *Innocents Abroad* spurred Parker Brothers to issue a board game titled "The Amusing Game of Innocence Abroad."[34] Twain never seemed to worry that such product tie-ins might detract from his literary image. Such was his extreme comfort with product promotion that he even got involved in marketing campaigns. After lending his name to a new pipe, Twain suggested the advertising copy: "It is the cleanest of all pipes; and after you get it properly charred & broken in, you will find it the sweetest."[35] Twain was no less eager to supply the Paul E. Wirt Fountain Pen Company with a testimonial they could promote everywhere. "With a single Wirt Pen I have earned the family's living for many years. With two, I could have grown rich."[36] Beyond earning money for Twain, these product endorsements made his name and image pervasive and gave the reading public a pleasing sense of knowing the author intimately.

Twain's attention to detail reflected the same zealous involvement that he craved when it came to publishing his books, where he wanted to dictate everything down to the cover art, paper, and bindings. Long tantalized by the idea of publishing a deluxe uniform edition of all his works, he even planned at first to market it by himself, monopolizing the profits and supervising every aspect. Frank Bliss of the American Publishing Company urged Henry Rogers to dissuade Twain from this unfortunate notion. "In the first place I do not believe that he would succeed in selling very many sets from personal efforts. He might easily place a few, but I imagine that he would find it very distasteful when he had to settle down to asking people to buy the book."[37] Twain succeeded in striking a deal by which Harper & Brothers would handle his new trade books, while Bliss would take care of subscription books and the Uniform Edition. This last would feature a critical introduction by Brander Matthews of Columbia University, a name that would add cachet to the twenty-three-volume set. Though Twain had long enjoyed a complicated relationship with the Bliss family, he was pleased as Frank set about work on the new edition "with an energy which reminds me of his sainted father, who is now in hell," Twain wrote to Howells.[38]

While publication of *The Writings of Mark Twain* signified the capstone of Twain's career, it did not mean its completion. "I'm not expected to write any more for publication," he wrote in June 1899, explaining that he had hoped to quit some time ago but kept the pot boiling from financial woes. "The man is entitled to a holiday for the rest of his life who has written for twenty-five years."[39] Yet Twain immediately backtracked, admitting he would actually write two more books, one that would never be published, the other not for a hundred years. In fact, Twain would never stop writing—his mind was too active, his imagination too rich, his opinions too pronounced—and he would leave behind a host of unfinished fictional manuscripts, many dreamlike in structure, dark and tragic in their drift. At the same time, the pace of his nonfiction would quicken as the fiction slackened. Now seeking a more direct impact on public opinion, his preferred form would be the polemic, produced on short notice and targeted at a specific controversial issue.

If Twain was hard on Frank Bliss, he saved some cynicism for his other publisher, Harper & Brothers. "They are a tough lot," he wrote in December 1899, "with their shabby one-sided contracts, & I wish I had kept out of their shop."[40] He was sure the firm was pushing everybody else's Christmas books but his own. Despite his customary paranoia

THE ANTI-DOUGHNUT PARTY

about publishers, he gave Harper exclusive rights to publish both his magazine work and books. According to publisher George Harvey, no other author had ever received more than ten cents a word, and Twain ultimately reaped thirty cents a word for everything he wrote. Eventually Harper would buy out Twain's contract from the American Publishing Company, consolidating his work under one roof. The Harper contract would prove lucrative for Twain, relieving him of long-standing financial worries—he would be guaranteed $25,000 annually—but he was wont to grumble that "I was a Harper slave & couldn't get free."[41] In his notebook, he blustered: "A publisher is by nature so low & vile that . . . from the bottom of my heart I wish all publishers were in hell. / And particularly: / Elisha Bliss (already there)."[42] In his contradictory way, Twain expressed jubilation when he signed the Harper contract on October 22, 1903, an event that validated the prediction of Cheiro the palmist that he would grow enormously rich that year. "The contract signed that day concentrates all my books in Harper's hands and now at last they are valuable; in fact they are a fortune."[43] Twain was right: for the rest of his life he would bank a handsome income in royalties from previously published work. His days of grating financial anxiety had ended.

Ever since he developed Mugwump tendencies back in 1884, Mark Twain had largely refrained from direct political involvement even as he poured forth political commentary. With appalled fascination, he had followed municipal corruption in New York as far back as 1871, when he published a denunciation of Boss Tweed and his associates in Tammany Hall for looting the public treasury. Sporadically he signed up with good government groups, but in the end, he always pulled back in the belief that reform was a lost cause. As he told Samuel Moffett, "I find myself agreeing with Ambrose Bierce that there is no good government at all & none possible . . . the fault must be in the human race. Once more we are forced to admit that it was a mistake & a misfortune that Noah & his gang were not drowned."[44] More and more he saw the average citizen locked into party dogma, not wanting "to know the other side—he wants arguments & statistics for his own side & nothing more."[45]

Once back in New York, Twain found a town rank with corruption as boss Richard Croker ruled over Tammany Hall, the colorful name for the Democratic machine. On January 4, 1901, Twain gave a talk at the City Club Dinner on "The Causes of Our Present Municipal Corruption." In the best Mugwump tradition, he asserted that good people in the city far outnumbered shady politicians and could best exert their will by voting for "the best men for the offices, no matter what party they belong to, and which will solve all your political problems."[46] He described how in his adolescence, he supposedly belonged to a third party branded the "Anti-Doughnut Party" by its enemies. Its members swore never to be bribed with doughnuts, the coin of the realm in local politics. Instead of nominating their own candidates, the Anti-Doughnut people chose impartially the best people put forward by the two main parties, with character overriding ideology.

Twain fared well in his speech until he waded into remarks on the two recent presidential candidates—William Jennings Bryan and President William McKinley. Because of the Democratic Bryan's populist, free-silver monetary policy, Twain said that he had not been able to vote for the man. Then came the line about McKinley that would damn him: "I know enough about the Philippines to have a strong aversion to sending our bright boys out there to fight with a disgraced musket under a polluted flag, so I didn't vote for the other fellow."[47] The audience sat stunned. Twain was followed to the podium by his friend St. Clair McKelway, who defended President McKinley in ringing tones: "I believe that our gallant Army is fighting behind no dishonored muskets and under no polluted, but under a glorious flag."[48] The entire audience jumped to their feet and applauded, while Twain sat coolly defiant, fiddling with his cigar. He had unfurled his own banner of resistance. For many admirers this was a new Twain, breathing fire and willing to disconcert his audience, no longer fearful of sacrificing his image as America's favorite humorist. With his return from Europe, Twain was willing to court a new level of

THE ANTI-DOUGHNUT PARTY

controversy. Perhaps some of this came from lingering bitterness from his bankruptcy or the residual darkness from Susy's death and Jean's epilepsy. Maybe some of it came from the fact that most of his writing career now lay behind him, making him less vulnerable to bad publicity.

Newspaper editorials thundered against Twain's City Club position, then a minority stance in the country. There were some voices raised in his defense, including that of Moncure Conway, his friend and sometime literary agent in England, who noted that Twain had always employed humor "to feather a serious arrow" and that his comments were echoed by leading intellectuals, including William Dean Howells and Charles Norton.[49] Whether his statement was premeditated or not, Twain was in no mood to back down. He was telling the public what it didn't want to hear and knew the consequences as he exposed a raw anger that had always lurked at the heart of his satire. To a supporter, he wrote: "I am glad you regard the round of cursing I have got from one end of the country to the other on that speech's account, as a valuable compliment to me; I certainly regard it in that light itself."[50] It didn't help Twain when President McKinley was assassinated by an anarchist in Buffalo that September and was succeeded by Theodore Roosevelt.

In October, Twain took a giant stride forward in his new activism when he flung himself into campaigning for Seth Low, the president of Columbia University, now running for mayor of New York City on a Fusion ticket backed by the Citizens Union and the Republican Party against Tammany Hall stalwart Edward M. Shepard. Never had Twain thrown himself into a race in such an outspoken, public manner, and he talked about the contest as if it were little short of Armageddon. "As between living in N.Y. under Tammany & in hell under Satan, I know of no choice."[51] He was prepared to do anything to help elect Low, except to deliver campaign speeches. "I dread a speech because if I do prepare one I never can remember it when the time comes for me to deliver it."[52] Of course, he seasoned his remarks to reporters with a healthy sprinkling of humor: "The report that the enemy has tried to buy me off by offering a life interest in the profits of the Police Department is a base canard."[53] He also described his successful effort to persuade one policeman to vote for Seth Low: "I convinced him that there was no authentic record of any Tammany man ever having gone to heaven."[54]

Despite his pledge to refrain from speeches, Twain bent this rule when he joined a reformist group called the Order of Acorns, speaking at their Waldorf-Astoria dinner on October 17. Tammany chieftain Richard Croker had derided the group as "The Popcorns" and Twain unloaded a fusillade of accusations against him, likening him to Warren Hastings, the head of the East India Company in the eighteenth century, who had been accused by Edmund Burke of corruption, and he blamed Tammany Hall for a plethora of municipal ills. "We all realize that Tammany's fundamental principle is monopoly—monopoly of office; monopoly of the public feed trough; monopoly of the blackmail derivable from protected gambling hells, protected prostitution houses, protected professional seducers of country girls for the New York prostitution market."[55] After his speech was printed in *Harper's Weekly*, the Acorns circulated hundreds of thousands of copies in pamphlet form.

At noon on October 29, Twain appeared at a rally with Seth Low and Joseph Johnson, Jr., the president of the Acorns, and a happy pandemonium broke out among the two thousand assembled supporters when they caught sight of the author. "As Mark Twain and Seth Low stepped upon the platform," said the *Times*, "the yell that arose was deafening, and it was many minutes before Mr. Johnson, assisted by the humorist, could restore order."[56] In his talk, Twain explained that against the advice of doctors, he had risen from his sickbed to be there and blamed his poor health on a Tammany banana he unwisely devoured. "The first nibble of it is white and pure, but all the rest of it is rotten and will contaminate . . . New York has eaten the Tammany banana, and needs a doctor. I think I can introduce you to a competent one in Dr. Seth Low."[57] After this touch of comedy, Twain launched into a heated denunciation of Tammany Hall and described young girls waylaid into houses of ill repute to the point that New York "has far exceeded Sodom and Gomorrah."[58] As ever, the theme of protecting spotless young girls resonated in his mind.

THE ANTI-DOUGHNUT PARTY

For local papers, Twain provided irresistible copy, and he was happy to cater to their journalistic needs. When a feud sprang up between the Low campaign and the Tammany forces, who had plastered posters along the walls of the rapid transit tunnel, Twain marched down to the Citizens Union office and told Captain Arthur F. Crosby, the deputy attorney general of the city, "Give me a brush and a pot of paste." Crosby, perplexed, asked why. "I want to cover up those Tammany posters along the tunnel. The tunnel does not belong to Tammany, but to the people, and Tammany does not represent the people."[59] Perhaps because of Twain's threat, the Tammany posters came down overnight, and Twain had no need to wield his brush, but the incident showed his very modern flair for public relations stunts.

On Election Day, Seth Low sailed to victory by thirty-three thousand votes, and Twain wasn't shy about claiming that he and the Acorns had accomplished it. It was a qualified sense of triumph, though, as he observed, "the amazing thing to me is, that *any* vote was cast for Tam[many]." Still, the good government folks had "removed the chains from the limbs of every man in N.Y."[60] Twain joined the victory celebration at Acorns headquarters, which was garlanded with brooms to symbolize the clean sweep of crooks from the city. Twain and the Acorns leaders spearheaded a parade of five thousand people who surged up to 42nd Street, then headed south again and paused before the Metropolitan Opera House, where Richard Croker was burned in effigy as the crowd belted out "The Battle Cry of Freedom." In a mock eulogy of Tammany, Twain proclaimed that the "old gang" had been defeated, with pulpit and press allied against them. "Tammany is dead, and it is no use to quarrel with a corpse."[61] Though Low's victory was a marvelous example of the independent Mugwump spirit Twain had longed to harness, the mayor served only a single term and was defeated for reelection in 1903. He had delivered on campaign promises to introduce civil service reform, reduce police graft, and improve education, but, as Twain suspected, people had trouble sticking to their ideals and knuckled under to authority, allowing the forces of greed to reassert their control over the city.

CHAPTER FORTY-SIX

"The United States of Lyncherdom"

With unceasing demands on his time, combined with his unstinting sociability, Mark Twain required periodic retreats from society and found a lovely sanctuary in the Adirondacks on Lower Saranac Lake during the summer of 1901. For four months he leased a lake cottage that was sheathed in rough bark and tucked away in a pine forest above the town of Ampersand. He christened it "The Lair," telling his rental contact, "Lairs do generally contain dangerous animals, but I bring tame ones to this one."[1] So eventful had his recent life been that when he described the place as "reposeful as a cemetery," he meant it as high praise.[2] The family led a very outdoor life, with swimming and boating and meals on the porch, while Twain would retreat to a nearby tent with a plank floor for his private writing haven, laboring at least four hours daily. Among the stories he produced was "A Double Barrelled Detective Story," a spoof of Sherlock Holmes, whom he found pompous and sentimental, deploring his "cheap and ineffectual ingenuities."[3] The only newspaper that penetrated the Lair was the weekly issue of the *Adirondack Enterprise*. For Twain, the place was a rustic paradise marred only by some sultry weather and persistent mosquitoes. For the most part, the family enjoyed huddling under blankets during the cool, crisp nights.

Even as he honed his image as a populist hero, Twain favored the society of grandees, and in early August boarded Henry Rogers's luxurious new yacht, the *Kanawha*, for a two-week cruise. The ship, crafted to

Gilded Age proportions, measured 227 feet and was capable of a top speed of 22 knots, making it, said the *New York Times*, "easily the superior of J. Pierpont Morgan's Corsair."[4] Steaming up the East Coast, it stopped at Fairhaven, Massachusetts, where Rogers dedicated a new church that he had donated to his hometown. After that, the all-male company luxuriated in long days of badinage, poker, drinking, and horseplay, stopping at various ports in Maine and Nova Scotia. On these cruises, Twain functioned as lighthearted master of ceremonies, feeding the uproarious high spirits, then regaled Livy with the stories. After the former House Speaker Thomas B. Reed joined the cruise, Twain taunted him good-humoredly about people who wanted him "to explain votes of the olden time or give back the money." If more honest people were aboard the ship, Twain alleged, "the yacht would be welcome everywhere instead of being quarantined by the police in all the ports."[5]

Even amid this merriment, Twain grew somber as the fifth anniversary of Susy's death approached on August 18. In his most self-flagellating manner, he wrote to Livy and recalled how her "mother-instinct" had immediately warned her of danger with Susy while he had dallied in England until the "awful cablegram found me unprepared, & struck with force unmitigated. I wish I could be with you these days; I know what you are suffering, & although I could do nothing to relieve your pains by words, neighborhood & sympathy would be a help for both of us."[6] Aside from this harrowing remembrance, Twain claimed the cruise refreshed his spirit, reinvigorated his body, and was as pleasing as any he had ever taken.

For Twain, being back in the United States meant a return to racial issues that had preoccupied the country since Reconstruction, and his responses were often muddled and inconsistent. On February 11, 1901, he officiated at a crowded gala at Carnegie Hall that celebrated Abraham Lincoln's birthday and raised money for the Lincoln Memorial University in Tennessee. The orator for the occasion was another former Con-

"THE UNITED STATES OF LYNCHERDOM"

federate, Colonel Henry Watterson, who had served as a staff officer for Nathan Bedford Forrest (the first Grand Wizard of the Ku Klux Klan), Leonidas Polk, and John Bell Hood. The hall was thronged with both blue and gray generals, as well as Andrew Carnegie and J. Pierpont Morgan. It was a type of ceremony that had grown commonplace in the decades after the Civil War, pageants of ersatz reconciliation, with former divisions dissolved in a bath of sentimental, uplifting rhetoric. The bravery of both sides was equally applauded while the root cause of the conflict, slavery, lay buried beneath a heavy dose of platitudes.

Twain introduced Henry Watterson as a fine son of the South: "Always honest, always noble, always loyal to his confessions, right or wrong, he is not afraid to speak them out."[7] Watterson had, in fact, opposed Reconstruction and advocated southern home rule. Twain noted the irony that two former Confederates had been chosen "for the honorable privilege of coming here and bowing our heads in reverence and love to that honorable soul whom, forty years ago, we tried with all our hearts and all our strength to defeat and suppress—Abraham Lincoln. But are not the blue and the gray one today? By these signs we may answer here, 'Yes.'"[8] Then Twain turned to his own past, coming from a slave-owning family and serving as a second lieutenant in the Confederate service. "We of the South were not ashamed of the part we took. We believed in those days we were fighting for the right—and it was a noble fight, for we were fighting for our sweethearts, our homes, and our lives. Today we no longer regret the result, today we are glad that it came out as it did, but we of the South are not ashamed that we made an endeavor; we did our bravest best against despairing odds, for the cause which was precious to us and which our consciences approved."[9]

Twain was now able to acknowledge, in a public and unqualified manner, Lincoln's greatness as an American, second only to George Washington. Introducing "The Battle Hymn of the Republic," he touted it as "the most beautiful and the most sublime battle hymn the world has ever known."[10] And for once he frankly admitted that he had fought for the Confederacy instead of ducking the issue and making his service seem risible. Aside from that, his message echoed the worst apologetics of the

Lost Cause theorists who refused to concede that the war was fought over slavery and justified secession as a high-flown moral crusade to protect home and hearth. Twain didn't mention slavery a single time, but drew a false moral equivalence between North and South, arguing that both were involved in causes sacred to them, even though the right cause—the northern—won. After decades spent backing away from his southern origins, Twain proudly identified with the South, viewing the Confederacy as a gallant, romantic undertaking. Courageous of late on so many political issues, he failed this serious test. Of course, in fairness to Twain, the theme of the Lincoln gathering was North-South reconciliation, and he may have simply followed instructions from the organizers. The speech didn't sound like anything else he ever said.

What most refuted the Lost Cause case was the proliferation of Jim Crow segregation in southern states and the prevalence of lynching, which perpetuated the terror of slavery and Klan violence. Lynch mobs were condoned by politicians and police, who sometimes joined in, and local press accounts glorified bloodthirsty crowds who supposedly gave victims what they deserved. Thousands of Blacks lost their lives in cases that weren't prosecuted. The full scope of lynching was documented by a remarkable young Black journalist named Ida B. Wells, who scoured the country and, at grave personal risk, compiled the first comprehensive record. After she published her first shocking exposé, Frederick Douglass told her, "If American conscience were only half alive . . . a scream of horror, shame, and indignation would rise to Heaven wherever your pamphlet shall be read."[11]

We know that in conversation Twain denounced lynching in no uncertain terms. One day Ossip Gabrilowitsch inquired whether Twain thought, "as most Southerners do, that lynching negroes is a necessity as protection for the white people?" The elder's response was adamant: "I don't think murder is right under any circumstances, and when a hundred men kill one trembling, terrified rag of humanity, I think those men are guilty of fantastic cowardice—*shameful* cowardice."[12] He was a student of mob psychology, which he had discussed in Vienna with the psychiatrist Richard von Krafft-Ebing, telling him that "men in a crowd

"THE UNITED STATES OF LYNCHERDOM"

do not act as they would as individuals. In a crowd they don't think for themselves, but become impregnated by the contagious sentiment uppermost in the minds of all who happen to be en masse."[13] From personal experience he knew how lies could blanket and smother a society, and remembered the "universal stillness that reigned" in Hannibal's white community about slavery's horrors.[14]

As Twain condemned America's imperial adventure in the Philippines, he saw striking parallels to the treatment of southern Blacks, with racism at the bottom of both situations. Twain became a champion of Emilio Aguinaldo, the Philippine leader who led the rebellion against the U.S. occupation and later became the first president of an independent Philippine republic. When Aguinaldo was exiled to Hong Kong, Twain commented sardonically, "They keep the young Alabama 'nigger' moving, he gets plenty of exercise. Do not wince at the word. I note that many of our people out there use it to describe the Filipino."[15] When charges arose that the Philippine army abused its prisoners, Twain shot back that "they are not worse than were our Christian Ku-Klux gangs of a former time, nor than our church-going negro-burners of to-day."[16] This was one of Twain's most explicit references to white persecution of Blacks after the Civil War, first with the Klan during Reconstruction, then with the rise of Jim Crow and Black lynching. When he wrote an unpublished piece about imperialism called "The Stupendous Procession," he felt the need to reword the Declaration of Independence: "All *white men* are created free and equal."[17]

Twain knew that lynchings around Hannibal cropped up at the rate of one or two a year, and he experienced an urgent need to write about them. Should he do so, he would be treading on risky turf, especially with southern readers. During the Saranac Lake summer, his interest was stoked when the *Century Magazine* sent him a batch of clippings about courageous southern sheriffs who dared to defy lynch mobs. He was aroused to further indignation by horrendous events in Pierce City, Missouri, when three Black men were lynched and many more chased into the woods. A week later, likely fired up by this event, Twain contacted Frank Bliss: "The thing I am full of, now, is a large subscription book to be called 'History of Lynching in America'; 'Rise & Progress of Lynching'—or some such title."[18] He thought there might have been three thousand lynchings in all, and he wanted, as a first step, to dispatch a researcher to the Hartford or Boston library to compile clippings to supply him with detailed case studies. In particular, he sought more information about two incidents remembered from childhood, one being the 1837 death in Alton, Illinois, of the young abolitionist editor Elijah Lovejoy, murdered by a white, proslavery mob. Twain harbored high hopes for his projected book, thinking it would "rouse-up the sheriffs to put down the mobs & end the lynchings," which were "growing in number, & spreading northwards."[19]

Almost immediately, Twain began to balk at doing the book, "for I shouldn't have even half a friend left, down there, after it issued from the press."[20] He had already composed an essay with the electrifying title "The United States of Lyncherdom," one etched with such "vitriol" that it would "make a splendid stir—in fact I know it."[21] It was an incendiary essay that wouldn't be allowed to make a stir until it was posthumously published in 1923, and then only in a bowdlerized version. Though Twain had based his career on fearless truths, garbed in the cloak of humor, a book on lynching proved a step too far. The essay he wrote is a curious melding of apologetics and fierce denunciation of lynching, showing how profoundly ambivalent he was about writing it.

"The United States of Lyncherdom" opens on a disappointing note, with Twain defending his home state of Missouri against any insinuation that its people support lynching, which he sees as confined to a very small number. He doesn't start by denouncing racism, but by defending the white South. Then comes an extended discussion that only ten people in a lynch mob actually enjoy the spectacle; the rest fear ostracism and are only coerced into attending by their neighbors. His main grievance seems to be that justice can be brought against Black criminals by taking them to court instead of dragging them out and hanging them. It reads like a tiresome rationalization by a defensive southern white.

Then Twain suggests, mockingly, that Chinese missionaries ought to

"THE UNITED STATES OF LYNCHERDOM"

be brought in to stem the problem, and he quotes a telegram from Texas showing the true sadistic nature of lynching. The townsfolk in question didn't just want to fry a Black man in a hot fire, they wanted to *prolong* his agony, so they paused and brought in coal oil to make the torture more exquisite and long-lasting. This telegram punches a needed hole in the essay. Twain belatedly warms to his theme and conjures up a horrifying vision of a million Christians standing and watching the lynching of 203 Blacks during the preceding year and a half. The essay jeers at the false piety of southern white Christians who have banded together to burn Blacks. The Texas telegram rips away the cover story that whites aren't enjoying the spectacle, when, as we know from photographs, there was usually a palpable glee and cruel sense of triumph in the grinning white faces. By the end, one can see why Twain never published the essay: the first part would have infuriated northern admirers, with its reflexive defense of southern whites, while the finale would have outraged southern whites by conjuring up the spectacle of a million of them turning out to roast a Black man for pleasure.

In early September, the assassination of President William McKinley by anarchist Leon Czolgosz prompted Twain to dwell again on the contagious nature of violence, the way an atrocity can ferment in the brains of unstable people and set off copycat acts; the McKinley shooting, he predicted, would lead to another "ruler-tragedy" within six months. The same applied, he asserted, to the rash of lynch mobs afflicting the country. "Every lynching-account unsettles the brains of another set of excitable white men, & lights another pyre—115 lynchings last year, 102 inside of 8 months this year; in ten years this will be *habit*, on these terms," he wrote to Twichell.[22] At the end of the day, when it came to lynching, Twain was a captive of his fame, afraid to voice his true detestation of the practice. Around 1901 he had written an unpublished piece, "Corn-Pone Opinions," in which he talked about people muzzling their innermost opinions for fear of offending the majority. "I suppose that in more cases than we should like to admit, we have two sets of opinions: one private, the other public; one secret and sincere, the other corn-pone, and more or less tainted."[23] By suppressing his unvarnished views on lynching, Twain missed a major opportunity to foster a national debate and retreated into self-protective silence.

Whatever his inhibitions about lynching, Twain vented increasingly radical utterances about American foreign policy. After the United States occupied the Philippines and fought to suppress the independence movement spearheaded by Emilio Aguinaldo—which Twain considered a rank betrayal of American promises of freedom to the local population—his angry words punctured the self-congratulatory rhetoric. In unctuous tones, President McKinley had described America's mission as "benevolent assimilation" and "the bestowal of the blessings of good and stable government upon the people of the Philippine Islands under the free flag of the United States."[24] Twain was having none of this claptrap. "Apparently we are not proposing to set the Filipinos free & give their islands to them," he wrote glumly to Twichell. "If these things are so, the war out there has no interest for me."[25] With jingoistic fervor, the United States had now emerged as an expansionist power, bringing Cuba, Puerto Rico, Guam, and the Philippines under its umbrella. Mark Twain had embarked on a broad-gauged critique of imperialism, whether undertaken by Germany, Russia, England, or America.

More and more he doubted the ability of the American public to exercise independent judgment and believed that most people parroted what they heard from politicians and the press. Questioning what constituted true patriotism, he grew enraged by the expression "Our country, right *or* wrong!" In his notebook, he commented: "We have thrown away the most valuable asset we had:—the individual's right to oppose both flag & country when he . . . believed them to be in the wrong. We have thrown it away; & with it, all that was really respectable about that grotesque and laughable word, Patriotism."[26] In an unpublished essay, "As Regards Patriotism," he discussed the culture's frightening power to brainwash or bully people into their political beliefs and "debase angels to men and

"THE UNITED STATES OF LYNCHERDOM"

lift men to angelship. And it can do any one of these miracles in a year—even in six months."[27]

Ever since, as a young journalist, Twain had written feelingly about abused Chinese immigrants in San Francisco, he had shown a special interest in Chinese affairs. As usual, his views could be patently contradictory, and in his Lotos Club speech of November 1900, he warned of a "Yellow Terror" that was "looming vast and ominous on the distant horizon."[28] At the same time, he followed with sympathy the Chinese nationalist movement known as the Boxers, who agitated against the influence of European powers and their missionaries. Two weeks after his Yellow Terror speech, he executed an extraordinary volte-face in his position. "The Boxer is a patriot," he told an audience, and added the shocking statement "I am a Boxer myself."[29] This was a perilous admission at a time when the American public was reading stories about Boxers attacking churches and murdering foreign missionaries. When an international force arrived in China to repress the uprising, Twain sided with the Chinese. "They have been villainously dealt with by the sceptered thieves of Europe," he told Twichell, "& I hope they will drive all the foreigners out & keep them out for good."[30]

The issue of missionaries in China was an explosive one for the author to dabble in. Back in July 1900, Twain had drafted a hot-blooded letter that the *Times* of London had refused to print, in which he scoffed at the notion of missionaries as noble people, engaged in uplifting work. "Wherever the missionary goes he not only proclaims that his religion is the best one, but that it is a true one while his hearer's religion is a false one."[31] For Twain, the missionary was a tool of the colonial enterprise, luring children from the faith of their parents and making them view local cultures as inferior. He blamed the trouble in China on the presence of missionaries and their desire to corral the Chinese into their "Concert of Christian Birds of Prey."[32]

Imperialist violence in China, South Africa, and the Philippines sparked a rage in Twain that spilled from him with ever great frequency. When the Red Cross Society asked him to dash off a greeting from the nineteenth to the twentieth century, he obliged, on December 30, 1900, in lines that throbbed with savage indignation: "I bring you the stately nation named Christendom, returning, bedraggled, besmirched, and dishonored, from pirate raids in Kiao-Chou, Manchuria, South Africa, and the Philippines, with her soul full of meanness, her pocket full of boodle, and her mouth full of pious hypocrisies. Give her soap and towel, but hide the looking-glass."[33] Twain's lines circulated widely as the New England Anti-Imperialist League printed them on cards and sent them around the country, and the author was soon made an honorary vice president of the organization.

As happened with his crusade against Tammany Hall, Twain graduated from merely voicing opinions to more formal involvement. He had clearly decided, on many subjects, to tear off the muzzle that had muted his views and risk a cold rebuff from his compatriots. In early January 1901, he wrote a strongly worded essay, dark and harsh in tone, that not only attacked American imperialism but also missionaries in China. Prepared to suffer for such candor, he bristled when Twichell advised him to moderate his views. "I'm not expecting anything but kicks for scoffing... but if Livy will let me I will have my say . . . You are a public guide & teacher, Joe, & are under a heavy responsibility to men, young & old; if you teach your people—as you teach me—to hide their opinions when they believe their flag is being abused & dishonored, lest the utterance do them & a publisher a damage, how do you answer for it to your conscience?"[34] Gone were the gentle disagreements of yesteryear between Twain and Twichell.

Clara said Livy signed off on the article, as did Howells, who advised the author to hang himself, Twain noted, "to save the public the trouble, because when the story appeared in print they would surely hang me."[35] Another version of events comes from publisher William Webster Ellsworth, who said Livy could typically prevent Twain from publishing something he had written. "It is said that only once did she fail, and that was when Mark Twain attacked the missionaries. She begged him with tears in her eyes not to publish the manuscript, but he would do it."[36] Writing a friend after publication, Livy said, resignedly, that her hus-

"THE UNITED STATES OF LYNCHERDOM"

band could not "have done otherwise than he has done because his convictions were so very strong."[37]

When "To the Person Sitting in Darkness" ran in the *North American Review* in February 1901, it unleashed exactly the furor Howells had foreseen. The title made a satirical allusion to Matthew 4:16—"The people who sat in darkness have seen a great light."[38] The immediate occasion for the piece was a statement by the Reverend Dr. William Scott Ament of the American Board of Commissioners for Foreign Missions, who had traveled to China to collect an indemnity for the murder of missionaries and damage done to Christian property by Boxer militants. A news report claimed Ament had demanded fines amounting to thirteen times the actual damages, and Twain was aghast that a missionary organization should be involved in extracting such an extortionate payment. In his essay, Twain aired many of his current grievances against imperialism. He reviewed the history of U.S. involvement in the Philippines, describing how the local independence movement had helped Admiral George Dewey defeat the Spanish occupiers and expected freedom in return. Instead, the United States had betrayed them—had "petted them, lied to them—officially proclaiming that our land and naval forces came to give them their freedom and displace the bad Spanish Government—fooled them, used them."[39] Instead of the American flag fluttering proudly abroad, Twain said, it was "just our usual flag, with the white stripes painted black and the stars replaced by the skull and cross-bones."[40]

The essay dissected the sanctimonious ideology used by imperial powers, who dressed up their depredations in highly moralistic language. Twain took jabs at what he dubbed the Blessings-of-Civilization Trust, which claimed they could not do "an unright thing, an unfair thing, an ungenerous thing, an unclean thing."[41] It was a full-bore attack on Christian missionaries who made a living from "our Brother who Sits in Darkness" and ends up paying for the Gospel "with his blood and tears and land and liberty."[42] Twain cited the excessive reparations demanded in China by the Reverend Dr. Ament.

It was as fiery a harangue as ever flowed from Mark Twain's pen, and his authorized biographer contended that he "never wrote anything more scorching, more penetrating in its sarcasm, more fearful in its revelation of injustice and hypocrisy."[43] As soon as the article appeared, it created the predictable sensation, and heaps of mail tumbled in at Twain's door as he became the center of a swirling national controversy. Livy confided to Grace King that "many of our friends do not approve [his position], on the other hand very many do & he receives more letters of approval than of disapproval—in fact ten to one I should think."[44] She said sadly that some "dear friends are silent so we feel their disapproval."[45] "Cutting, abusive letters and newspaper attacks flooded our home," Clara recalled, "and it was pathetic to see the effect they had on Mother."[46]

The Anti-Imperialist League of New York rushed out copies in pamphlet form, although it dropped the section about missionaries, and Twain was held up in the press corps as the country's leading new voice against imperialism. Andrew Carnegie waded in—"there's a new Gospel of Saint Mark in the *North American* which I like better than anything I've read for many a day"—and he volunteered to invest a thousand dollars so that "many thousands of the holy little missals" could be distributed by the Anti-Imperialist League.[47] Many readers appreciated Twain's courage in publishing the essay right after his long European exile, and he enjoyed a newfound popularity in certain quarters. "I hail you as the *Voltaire* of America," a nonprofit executive wrote to him. "It is a noble distinction. God bless you, & weary not in well-doing—in this noblest, sublimest of crusades."[48] An American veteran who had witnessed firsthand American military action on the island of Luzon corroborated Twain's belief that "the Americans who crossed the Pacific 'to liberate' remained there to enslave . . . I congratulate you on your overwhelming truthful exposition of the great crime." On the envelope, a gratified Twain recorded his seal of approval: from "a soldier/first rate."[49]

Twain knew he was a "moralist in disguise" and got into trouble when he delved into political questions.[50] No longer content to wrap his views in fables or fictions, he resorted to direct, biting prose. He now went after things—religion and politics, faith and patriotism—where citizens

"THE UNITED STATES OF LYNCHERDOM"

felt virtuous and didn't care to hear contrary perspectives. The *New York Times* castigated Twain for "discarding the grin of the funny man for the sour visage of the austere moralist," and vice president–elect Theodore Roosevelt labeled Twain a "prize idiot."[51] Critical letters arriving at Twain's residence must have been wounding to read. "None have enjoyed your writings more than I," wrote an anonymous New Jersey woman, "or laughed more heartily . . . But you have looted pure and noble Christian character . . . You join those hooting at your Savior on the cross."[52] Another anonymous critic denounced him for sacrilege, saying he was losing his literary powers, "and you clearly evidence the fact when for material you turn the Holy Scripture into ridicule." It was signed "A Once Great admirer."[53]

Having spent a lifetime building a readership, it could not have been easy for Twain to sacrifice loyal fans, but there's no sense that he regretted his decision, and when he responded to critics, he did so with vigor and asperity. "I have been reading the *North American*," a Boston schoolteacher wrote to him, "and I am filled with shame and remorse that I have dreamed of asking you to come to Boston to talk to the teachers." On the envelope, Twain wrote sarcastically, "Now, I suppose I offended that young lady by having an opinion of my own, instead of waiting and copying her."[54] This wasn't a man having second thoughts and there was no turning back now. This was a new version of Mark Twain: emphatic, divisive, and polarizing. According to Howells, Twain was lusty in battle, and even as he took "hard knocks from the blackguards and hypocrites," he was "making hosts of friends, too."[55] Twain seemed to feel freer as many taboo feelings were finally articulated, and he was willing to withstand the heat. "I have done very little work," he told a friend, having gotten into "hot water with the clergy and other goody-goody people, but I am enjoying it more than I have ever enjoyed hot water before."[56]

The missionaries fought back against his onslaught. Twain got embroiled in fresh controversy when Judson Smith of the American Board of Commissioners claimed that the Reverend Ament had not secured punitive damages from the Chinese thirteen times the actual damages; the true figure, he alleged, was one-third above the actual damages, and he blamed a single faulty newspaper report. The original dispatch was written as "1/3," but when the report was transmitted, the slash was accidentally dropped, and "1/3" became "13." "So collapses—and convulsively—Mark Twain's sensational and ugly bombardment of a missionary whose character and services should have exempted him from such an assault."[57] Smith said the reparations demand perfectly accorded with Chinese practice. In reply, Twain acknowledged the mistaken news report, but otherwise reacted with hearty contempt: "It is observable that . . . you are quite satisfied with Mr. Ament's fashion of despoiling the innocent to square the damages created by the guilty—& why? Because it is in accordance with *Chinese* law custom! . . . For broad humor, the situation puts opera bouffe to shame."[58]

Far from dodging fights with missionaries, an unrepentant Twain headed back into the fray in April when he published in the *North American Review* a piece titled "To My Missionary Critics." He reviewed the controversy with Judson Smith and the mistaken newspaper cable, allowed that missionaries meant well, but still characterized their reparations as extortion. "We all know that Dr. Ament did not bring suspected persons into a duly organized court and try them by just and fair Christian and civilized methods, but proclaimed his 'conditions,' and collected damages from the innocent and the guilty alike, without any court proceedings."[59]

For many years, Mark Twain would tirelessly publish articles, make speeches, grant interviews, and sign petitions calling for Philippine independence and an end to American atrocities there. He believed that the country's new overseas empire was simply incompatible with its democratic ideals. This would be no less part of his legacy than his creation of Tom and Becky, Jim and Huck. Just how acutely he felt the injustice of America's presence in the Philippines is beautifully captured in an account written by Helen Keller, who described a visit to her Princeton friend Laurence Hutton:

> One evening, in the library [Mark Twain] lectured to a distinguished company—Woodrow Wilson was present—on the situation in the

"THE UNITED STATES OF LYNCHERDOM"

Philippines. We listened breathlessly. He described how six hundred Moros—men, women, and children—had taken refuge in an extinct crater bowl near Jolo, where they were caught in a trap and executed by the Americans. A few days afterwards, the Americans captured Aguinaldo by disguising their military marauders in the uniform of the enemy and pretending to be friends of Aguinaldo's officers. Upon these military exploits Mr. Clemens poured out a volume of invective and ridicule. Only those who heard him can know his deep fervor and the potency of his flaming words . . . He thought he was a cynic, but his cynicism did not make him indifferent to the sight of cruelty, unkindness, meanness, or pretentiousness. He would often say, "Helen, the world is full of unseeing eyes—vacant, staring, soulless eyes." He would work himself into a frenzy over dull acquiescence in any evil that could be remedied.[60]

CHAPTER FORTY-SEVEN

"Magnificent Panorama of the Mississippi"

By October 1, 1901, the Clemens family had leased a roomy, furnished house on the old Appleton estate in the tony enclave of Riverdale in the Bronx, continuing their wayward existence. They still owned the Hartford house since Livy was unable to sever the bond that tied her to the place, even as memories of Susy hindered her from returning there. With panoramic vistas of the Hudson River and the Palisades, and stately trees on its ample grounds—one chestnut tree was so elaborate that a tea party could be held on a platform in its spreading branches—the Riverdale house had seclusion and suburban quiet. It also bore a suitable literary and artistic pedigree: William Henry Appleton had been the American publisher of Charles Darwin and had leased the villa one summer to Teddy Roosevelt's family when the future president was a boy. It was later incorporated into a larger property owned by a J. P. Morgan partner, George W. Perkins, and it would be known to posterity as Wave Hill and count among its many illustrious occupants Arturo Toscanini.

When the Clemenses first inspected the fieldstone Victorian mansion, they dithered as to whether it was the right spot until they "arrived in a dining-room that was 60 feet long, 30 feet wide, and had two great fireplaces in it, that settled it," recalled Twain.[1] The venue put them within striking distance of Manhattan—it was twenty-five minutes by train to

Grand Central—allowing Clara to commute twice weekly for singing lessons and Jean to maintain her osteopathic treatments. Livy fretted about the size and expense of the mansion, but they had never lived economically before, and the sense of enforced austerity from the 1890s was dissipating. In addition to her worsening heart troubles, Livy was plagued by gout, and would find it hard to enjoy the property's charms. "Mother's illness had taken deeper root and she was confined to her bedroom," Clara recalls. "From her windows she could watch the changing lights reflected from the sky in the wide river and there were beautiful ice and snowstorms that winter."[2]

Twain's occupancy coincided with a spate of burglaries in the neighborhood, and reporters duly showed up to hear his comic slant on the situation, summed up in the headline "Mark Twain Will Warmly Greet Robbers."[3] In several interviews, he made the point that burglars, too, were entitled to make a decent living and that their victims were duty bound to cooperate. "Now if the burglars will only let me know when they intend to grace my new home with their presence," he pledged, "I will see that they have a full assortment of good wine on the ice and a full cupboard. I will also tie my dog so that he will not disturb them."[4]

Soon after moving to Riverdale, Twain was tipped off by Twichell that he would receive an honorary doctorate at Yale University for its bicentennial commemoration. The honor would come to him, Twichell said, despite the fact that a majority of the Yale Corporation members didn't "agree with the views on important questions which you have lately promulgated in speech and in writing"—a comment underscoring how controversial Twain had become.[5] He would later express surprise at being made a Doctor of Literature "because I was not competent to doctor anybody's literature but my own, and couldn't even keep my own in a healthy condition without my wife's help."[6] Decked out in hood and gown, Twain took a two-hour tour of the campus and received a hero's welcome from the students. As he related to Livy: "In the campus a great crowd of students thundered the Yale cry, closing with M-a-r-k T-w-a-i-n—Mark *Twain!* & I took off my hat & bowed."[7]

Aside from Howells, one other honoree was President Theodore

"MAGNIFICENT PANORAMA OF THE MISSISSIPPI"

Roosevelt, the country's foremost imperialist, who looked askance at Twain and said he should be skinned alive. Earlier in the month, Roosevelt had performed an unprecedented act when he invited Booker T. Washington to dine at the White House, an overture to a Black man that did not sit well with the white South. "The President asked me if I thought he was right in inviting Booker Washington to lunch at the White House. I judged by his tone that he was worried and troubled and sorry about that showy adventure." One would have guessed that Twain would have approved this courageous act, but not so. "I said it was a private citizen's privilege to invite whom he pleased to his table . . . but that in a case where it was not required by duty, it might be best to let it alone, since the act would give offence to so many people when no profit to the country was to be gained by offending them."[8] Another strange lapse of judgment from a man who had paid for the education of a Black law student at the same university that now honored him, and it again showed his fear of antagonizing the South on race.

From the time he settled into Riverdale, Twain had to deal with the continuing crisis of Jean's epilepsy as his excessive faith in osteopathy ran up against the reality of her incurable disease. "Jean is bad again," Twain told Rogers that winter. "It is a continuous distress—without a break these 5 years."[9] The comment is telling, for the five-year period included time with Kellgren, which had seemed to herald a breakthrough. Such was the dread of an unescorted Jean suffering an attack that the Clemenses insisted she have a companion when she went into the city. In January, Sam, Livy, and Jean took the train to a snowy Elmira, hoping for a spell of tranquility, but the trip upstate, on a bright and beautiful day, was overshadowed by Jean's inescapable malady. To Clara, who had stayed behind in Riverdale, Twain wrote that "Jean was bad all day long, & until the middle of dinner this evening. She lay in the stateroom on the train all the journey, & was persistently absent. The day's anxiety—not the journey—is what has made your mother so tired."[10] Worry about

WHIRLPOOL

Jean was a constant drain on Livy's health when she could scarcely afford it. A role reversal was taking place as Livy turned increasingly to Clara, her remaining healthy child, for protection. "My darling I feel as if I could not bear you ill," she wrote to Clara before the Elmira trip, "& how shall I get on without you for so many days."[11] She thanked Clara for appreciating more "the point of view and the burdens of older people than is usual with the dear young ones."[12]

The Clemens family had entered a precarious time in which Livy needed a soothing, restful environment—Twain said she was "threatened with a nervous break down" in early 1902—but he had entered into the most dogmatic, opinionated phase of his career, kindling controversy at every turn.[13] He expressed his radical views on politics and religion and his mechanistic view of human behavior with such abrasive force that he could be a combustible presence. In March 1902, a young writer named Marie Van Vorst, a friend of Jean's, stayed at the Riverdale house and said something that provoked Twain to draft a testy letter to her. When she read it, Livy was heartsick and wearily composed the following note to him:

> *Youth darling, have you forgotten your promise to me? You said that I was constantly in your mind and that you knew what I would like and you would not publish what I disapprove. Did you think I would approve the letter to Marie van Vorst?*
>
> *I am absolutely wretched to-day on account of your state of mind—your state of intellect—why don't you let the better side of you work? Your pressent [sic] attitude will do more harm than good. You go too far, much too far in all you say, and if you write in the same way as you have in this letter people forget the cause for it and remember only the hateful manner in which it was said. Do darling change your mental attitude, try to chang [sic] it. The trouble is you don't want to. When you asked me to try Mental Science I tried it and I keep trying it. Where is the mind that wrote the Prince & P. Jeanne d'Arc, The Yankee, &c. &c. Bring it back! You can if you*

"MAGNIFICENT PANORAMA OF THE MISSISSIPPI"

will—if you wish to. Think of the side I know; the sweet, dear, tender side—that I love so.

Why not show this more to the world. Does it help the world to always rail at it? There is great and noble Work being done. Why not sometimes recognize that? You always dwell on the evil until those who live beside you are crushed to the earth and you seem almost like a monomaniac. Oh I love you so and wish you would listen and take heed.[14]

This was a loving but brutally frank letter to her husband, the most sweeping criticism that Livy ever sent him. She implied that he was belligerent and intolerant, was acting like a madman, and had descended into a darkness that had become intolerable to those around him. In this cri de coeur, she yearned for him to return to his earlier self, and her references to *The Prince and the Pauper, Joan of Arc,* and *A Connecticut Yankee* chart the distance that he had traveled from those days when he could write in a more charming, sentimental vein. She still cherished the "sweet, dear, tender side" of his personality, but the weight of his philosophic gloom, overheated language, and depressed personality were difficult to take at a moment when she needed some lightness and buoyancy in her life.

Perhaps to give Livy breathing room, Twain went off that March for an extended Caribbean cruise with Henry Rogers aboard the *Kanawha*. The party traveled much of the way to Florida by train, giving Twain glimpses of a South still languishing in poverty. "Livy darling," he wrote, "it is hours & hours of flat country, with thin forest standing knee-deep & melancholy in swamps; but little cultivation; at wide intervals . . . miserable cabins . . . a dreary & unpeopled & poverty-stricken piece of the earth."[15] It was a startling contrast when they arrived in Palm Beach and checked into the Royal Poinciana Hotel, built by Henry Flagler of Standard Oil and boasting corridors so long that bellhops were forced to deliver messages by bicycle. Seated at a round table for dinner, Twain told Livy, "there were 150 similar round tables in *our part* of the dining room, & more than 200 glimpsable in the other part of it . . . The hotel corridors afford fine perspectives—in fact about three times that of St. Peters at Rome, where the people furthest away look like children."[16]

Proudly likening the *Kanawha* to the grand pirate ship of a buccaneer, Twain drew up a farcical log that appointed Rogers "Commodore" of the expedition, former House Speaker Thomas B. Reed as "Czar," Dr. Clarence Rice as "Surgeon," Colonel Augustus G. Paine as "(partially) Reformed Pirate," Wallace T. Foote as "Unreformed Congressman," and "S.L. Clemens, Chaplain."[17] Princeton professor Laurence Hutton was the only passenger to escape a ludicrous title. As the assembled buccaneers played poker and swapped banter, the *Kanawha* took them to Cuba and Jamaica. Touring Havana, which he dismissed as "this cheap-built, ill-paved, & ratty old town," Twain was reminded of his early, idealistic support of the Spanish-American War and hopes for Cuban independence versus the sordid American presence he now saw, with the American flag "waving its sarcasms to the breeze everywhere."[18] The *Kanawha* anchored near the remains of the famous ship whose explosion had unleashed the dogs of war. As Twain told Livy, "Dearheart, [sic] we are anchored fifty yards from the wretched & tangled & battered bunch of rusty iron which stands for the 'Maine' & looks like a brobdingnagian tarantula in his death-squirm."[19]

With Jean sidelined by her ailments, Twain, too, came to rely on Clara to care for Livy, but she was a weak reed to lean upon. Now twenty-seven, Clara was torn between extreme devotion to her parents and a desire to strike out on her own and forge an independent identity. In April, she managed to coax her reluctant parents into allowing her to go to Paris with a chaperone for a few months, advancing several reasons: to take voice lessons, to study French and German, and to see Ossip Gabrilowitsch. Guilt-ridden, Clara said, "when the time approached for leaving my mother, who was never very strong, I had a sense of sin on my consciousness. It even amounted to a premonition that something terrible would happen if I left her."[20] Ossip reassured her—"Such thoughts are childish"—and she enjoyed her Parisian interlude until August, but no extant letters passed between mother and daughter, and

"MAGNIFICENT PANORAMA OF THE MISSISSIPPI"

Livy grumbled to a friend, "We shall all be very thankful when it is over & she says she shall never do it again."[21] The relationship between Clara and Ossip grew steadily, and they were engaged at some point during 1902–3, but then Clara despaired that they were "pulling against an invincible current. My mother was very ill and needed my daily attendance. It was madness to think of leaving her."[22] Clara suspected that Livy's congestive heart failure was deteriorating into a new phase: in bed at night she had to sit up to breathe.

Even before his *Kanawha* cruise, Twain had tramped around Tarrytown in Westchester County searching for a permanent home. "Examined 12 county seats from garret to cellar," he complained, "and it ended my usefulness, and my strength."[23] Despite her limited energy, Livy pursued the search while he was off on the yacht, and by the time he returned, she had purchased for $45,000 a stone mansion in Tarrytown, set on nineteen acres overlooking the Hudson. The move put the Clemens family in a tenuous spot because the deal hinged on their selling the Hartford house for $75,000. "For the Lord Jesus H. Christ's sake," Twain muttered to Franklin G. Whitmore, "*sell or rent that God damned house.*"[24] He advised Rogers to cash in his shares in Union Pacific and U.S. Steel and warned that he might have to borrow from him as well. During the next six months, the offering price in Hartford skidded, and the residence would evetually sell for $28,000—a small fraction of the money the Clemenses sank into it. As for the Tarrytown house, they would rent it for a while, then sell it without ever having occupied the property.

In mid-April, Twain was notified of an honor that struck a deep chord inside him: an honorary degree from the University of Missouri. Usually he belittled such honors, but this one felt intimate and mandatory. "I think when an institution, especially in a man's native State, offers to confer a decoration on him it is equivalent to a royal invitation . . . He ought to go if he has to go in a hearse."[25] For the most part, he had exhausted the stock of boyhood characters that had furnished the raw materials for his early success. Now those same characters—Tom, Jim, Huck, et al.—came flooding back into his imagination, only this time reunited

WHIRLPOOL

fifty years later; the mood was elegiac, both dreamlike and nightmarish. In his notebook, he sketched out a story in which the boys search for the "Cold Spring" but "they can't find it—all railway tracks. No levee & no steamboats."[26] The railroad had banished these landmarks, so their past flitted by irretrievably. The next day, Twain wrote to his old pal William R. Gillis and urged him along with Steve and Jim Gillis to attend the degree ceremony in Columbia, Missouri, "otherwise we shall not meet again on this side of the grave—& certainly not on the other side."[27] Though Livy yearned to join him, she knew the journey would tax her waning strength, telling a Clemens relative, "I was greatly tempted to go and make the visit to you and see the other cousins . . . Don't let him [Sam] stay long for I find life very lonely when he is away."[28]

When Twain arrived at the Planters Hotel in St. Louis in May, he had to deal with reporters and hundreds of well-wishers who flocked to see him—"Everything he said or did was spontaneous and humorous and kept the group constantly in a ripple of smiles," a reporter noted—and he mixed homespun wisdom with his wisecracks.[29] "Our inclination," he drawled, slouching in an armchair, "is to win the approval of others by thinking as they think and doing as they do."[30] As Twain entertained his audience, a spry, gray-bearded man stood beside him: Captain Horace Bixby, his old tutor from the *Paul Jones* in 1857, who had baptized him in the mysterious ways of the river. Twain asked his age. "Why, I am 62," said Bixby. "Lord, man, you were 62 it seems to me when I first met you in 1857," Twain retorted.[31] As his mind wandered back to those days, a touch of nostalgia infused his words. "I've been all over this small world—in India, Australia, Africa, way up in Iceland, down in South America, but do you know there never was such an old river as the Mississippi?"[32] However worldly he had become, he still felt the force of his formative years with a never-failing poignancy.

When Twain decided, on a sudden whim, to travel the hundred miles north to Hannibal, the cradle of his career, he must have known it would be his last visit to those boyhood scenes. As he checked in at the Windsor Hotel, the desk clerk eagerly announced, "Mr. Clemens, I was born close to your birthplace at Florida, and have been in the house where you

"MAGNIFICENT PANORAMA OF THE MISSISSIPPI"

were born, often." "I was not born often—only once," Twain replied drily, "but I'm glad to see you, all the same."[33] Once word got out that Twain had checked in, swarms of pedestrians and carriages ringed the hotel while the author rested inside.

The next day, with a crowd in tow, Twain, dressed in a light gray suit, toured the town in a stroll suffused with strong emotion. He lingered long enough in front of his old wooden home with the famous whitewashed fence for a photographer to snap his picture. "It all seems so small to me," he said. "I suppose if I should come back here ten years from now it would be the size of a bird-house."[34] Then Helen Garth, the widow of his old friend John H. Garth, drove him to Mount Olivet Cemetery, where he paid his respects to John Marshall, Jane Lampton, and Henry and Orion Clemens. Twain estimated that in Hannibal he encountered twenty people from his past, but that number was now dwarfed by the honor roll of the departed. Of his cemetery visit, he said, "Almost every tombstone recorded a forgotten name that had been familiar and pleasant to my ear when I was a boy there fifty years before."[35]

That afternoon, he appeared at Decoration Day ceremonies at the Presbyterian church and was greeted with such sustained applause that this sinner had to collect his emotions before he could speak in a voice that didn't crack with sentiment. Fighting back sobs, Twain said, "I am overcome by the something more than friendship which has entered into my reception—an evidence of true affection."[36] That evening he personally handed out diplomas at the high school graduation, tossing off quips with each. "Take one," he would say. "Pick out a good one. Don't take two, but be sure you get a good one."[37] He apologized for not having accepted an invitation from the high school a year earlier, blaming his laziness. "I acquired it in Hannibal; I acquired many things here; and among others, laziness, which is now complicated with old age."[38] He also told of the unimaginative schooling of his youth, with its rote learning and forced recitations of trite poems, and he must have wondered how this backwater had spawned an original like him. Sitting in the audience was Laura Hawkins Frazer, his first sweetheart, now a short woman with the round, plump face of a grandmother. That evening, Twain dined with her, attired in evening clothes, and the next day visited the Home for the Friendless shelter that she ran. Twenty-five women from Hannibal claimed to be the original for Becky Thatcher, and Laura thought she likely claimed the honor, though she never knew for sure. And what of Tom Blankenship, the model for Huck Finn? Twain heard that he had turned respectable and become a justice of the peace "in a remote village in Montana."[39]

Right near Twain's boyhood home rose Holliday's Hill—Cardiff Hill in his fiction—and he and his friend John Briggs mounted the steep path to obtain the best possible glimpse of the place lodged at the heart of his memories: the river that embodied his notions of freedom. They "looked out again over that magnificent panorama of the Mississippi River, sweeping along league after league, a level green paradise on one side, and retreating capes and promontories as far as you could see on the other, fading away in the soft, rich lights of the remote distance. I recognized then that I was seeing now the most enchanting river view the planet could furnish. I never knew it when I was a boy; it took an educated eye that had traveled over the globe to know and appreciate it."[40] As Twain suspected, it proved his last visit to Hannibal, and it churned up an overpowering rush of memories, showing how the place had formed the foundation for everything that followed in his life. There was so much old joy and newfound sorrow locked up inside him that he constantly trembled on the edge of tears. After he left town, the *Hannibal Courier-Post* ran a front-page interview in which Twain reflected, "My visit has been a most enjoyable one, and I do not recall a single instance when I ever had a better time."[41]

Before moving on to the University of Missouri, Twain retraced his steps to St. Louis, where an old harbor boat had been rechristened the *Mark Twain* in his honor. As he stepped aboard the ship, with the band striking up "Swanee River" and the governor and mayor in attendance, a reporter noticed that Twain "lifted his Panama, as if in salutation to the river, which once was his pride."[42] As he piloted the boat, he knew this would be his last, fleeting chance to helm a craft on the broad, muddy river, and a reporter captured the moment well: "Standing in the pilothouse far above the crowd on the decks, the river breezes caressed his frosty hair, the great wheel moved obediently to his master hand, while the kind, blue eyes of the celebrated humorist were lifted dreamily up the current."[43] When Twain finished his half-hour stint at the wheel, the harbor exploded in a medley of bells and whistles and blasts of salutation, and he raised his hat in homage to the crews honoring him on the water.

On the emotional train trip to Columbia, Missouri, welcoming committees greeted him with flowers at each station. At the University of Missouri ceremony, Twain, robed in his Yale gown, was flanked by James Wilson, the secretary of agriculture, and Ethan Allen Hitchcock, the secretary of the interior. But Twain rated as the main attraction—literary stardom superseded earthly power—and he was last to receive the honorary degree. For once, he stood speechless, awkward and uncertain, fumbling as to what to say, until the audience rose in unison, and after a solemn interval of silence, began to belt out the word "M-i-s-s-o-u-r-i," one letter at a time, followed by raucous applause and calls for a speech from their beloved homegrown luminary.

Twain obliged with vintage stuff, the patter that he had mastered over many years, narrating funny tales about stealing peaches as a boy. "I believe that I can honestly say that I have never stolen as much as a ton of peaches."[44] He was so profoundly bowled over by the emotions welling up inside him that, for once, he passed beyond the point of witticisms. He was still brimming with the Hannibal visit and the worn faces that he couldn't erase from his mind. "I looked in the faces of women—faces clothed in wrinkles and whose heads were as gray as mine—faces which when I last saw them were beautiful with the peach bloom of early youth—now on their heads the frosts of age, and in their faces wrinkles and the weatherbeaten look, not that which comes from exposure to bad weather. I experienced emotions that I had never expected, and did not know were in me. I was profoundly moved and saddened to think that this was the last time, perhaps, that I would ever behold those kind old faces and dear old scenes of childhood."[45] Far from being spent, Twain was so invigorated by his eleven bittersweet days in Missouri that he assured a friend, "I would not trade those days for any others I have seen in a quarter of a century."[46]

CHAPTER FORTY-EIGHT

"Spirit of a Steam Engine"

Although he didn't know it when he returned from Missouri, Mark Twain's life was about to embark on a downhill slide from which it would never quite recover. In June he rented a furnished house on forty acres in York Harbor, in southeast Maine, not too far from the Howells residence at Kittery Point, and Henry H. Rogers was kind enough to dispatch the *Kanawha* to Riverdale to whisk the family there. Despite cloudless skies, the family was blindsided by a harrowing seizure that Jean suffered en route. As Twain wrote: "It is 3.30 now, & a brilliant day, but we have missed the most of it through having to stay below & watch Jean, who . . . is under threats to-day."[1] The burden of Jean's illness fell heavily on Livy. Whether from fear or upset, Twain tended to absent himself from Jean's worst episodes—and Livy didn't sleep for two nights as she anxiously tended her daughter.

Once ensconced in Maine along the York River, in a house named "The Pines" after the forest that enveloped it, Twain hoped Livy would relinquish her cares and submit to a thorough rest, something that clashed with her responsible nature. "She had the spirit of a steam engine," said Twain regretfully, "in a frame of flesh."[2] Not long after they arrived, Jean was racked by a violent grand mal seizure, an episode that tore Livy apart, and for once her husband was an eyewitness. In "five fiendish years," Twain told Rogers, it was only the fourth time he had beheld this. "It comes near to killing Mrs. Clemens every time, and there is not much left of her for a day or two afterward. Every three weeks it comes. It will break her down yet."³

The cumulative stress of Jean's malady aggravated Livy's medical decline, shattering her composure. Her heart disease and Jean's epilepsy made for a fatal combination. When she went riding in a carriage, Livy was now assailed by unreasoning fears. "Anything approaching swift motion terrified her," Twain recalled. "She was afraid of descending grades, even such slight ones as to be indeterminable and imperceptible in the summer twilights. She would implore the coachman not only to walk his horses down those low and imperceptible hills, but she watched him with fear and distress, and if the horses stepped out of a walk for only a moment she would seize me on one side and the carriage on the other, in an ecstasy of fright. This was the condition of things all through July."⁴ She began to experience heart palpitations and found it difficult at night to maintain "a recumbent position as the heart is so greatly disturbed," she wrote.⁵ It grew so difficult for her to breathe when lying down that night after night she sat upright in bed for seven hours, often needing oxygen or brandy to settle her nerves and restore her breathing. These were classic symptoms of congestive heart failure.

With a sick wife and daughter on his hands, the frazzled Twain somehow managed to work most days, held enjoyable conversations on the veranda with Howells, and even entered into the cultural spirit of the old town. On the 250th anniversary of its local government in early August, he delivered a speech that shoveled in some humor about a confusing postal system that had to contend with York Cliffs, York Beach, York Harbor, York Village, and York Corner. "In fact," he said, "one cannot throw a brickbat across a thirty-seven acre lot without danger of disabling a postmaster."⁶ Ever the faithful wife, Livy showed up for her husband's appearances, quite against his wishes, and paid the price for her steadfast love. "She was over-exerting herself, overtaxing her strength, and she began to show it."⁷

Then came a black day in August that would be forever engraved on Twain's memory. At seven that morning, he was startled awake by a sudden cry. "I saw Mrs. Clemens standing on the opposite side of the room,

"SPIRIT OF A STEAM ENGINE"

leaning against the wall for support, and panting. She said 'I am dying.'"[8] She feared she would die from suffocation—an attack possibly exacerbated by asthma—and her husband shared that fear. He summoned a Dr. Lambert, a New York physician staying nearby, who diagnosed the problem, wrongly, as a nervous breakdown and prescribed three things that would rule the remainder of Livy's life: "absolute rest, seclusion, and careful nursing."[9] It was common medical practice at the time to sequester patients from disturbing influences, and the temperamental Twain was identified as a major cause. Livy would never bounce back to true health and went from being a normal person, running the household, to a bedridden patient and a heavy burden on her loving family. Luckily, Clara returned from Europe the next day, and Sue Crane came from Elmira to take charge of a chaotic situation. "My mother had suffered a serious heart attack," Clara recalled, "and the day I reached York Harbor the doctors gave no hope of her recovery."[10]

Perhaps from an excess of guilt at having deserted her mother for months, Clara turned into an assertive, even imperious presence in caring for her, hiring and firing nurses without first consulting her father. Of her executive abilities, Twain boasted to Rogers, "Clara does all the generalship . . . and is doing it like an expert—same as her mother."[11] In her eternal conflict between family and career, Clara knew which way to jump now. "My mother or my art? The *sacrifices* will be made for the former."[12] Livy deemed Sue Crane her most "valuable comforter," and Twain recognized that she fit the bill better than he. "We mean well, but we make a poor job of it; & I suffer mortification & premature damnation by consequence of my share in it."[13] This last line shows how Twain blamed himself for exacerbating Livy's decline. In one lacerating notebook entry, he elaborated: "Our dear prisoner is where she is through overwork—day and night devoted to the children & me. We did not know how to value it. We know now."[14]

At first Twain formed part of a circle of rotating caregivers, hovering over Livy until a doctor came from Boston and decreed that one nurse—and one nurse alone—should stay with her, banishing Twain as too intense a presence. Even Howells could understand why Livy "should have found some compensation, when kept to her room by sickness, in the reflection that now she should not hear so much about 'the damned human race.'"[15] Twain resorted to sleeping at the nearby house of Millard Sewall, a local fisherman, where he went to write. On August 18—as if he needed further sadness in his life—he composed yet another poem, "In Memory of Olivia Susan Clemens," to honor the sixth anniversary of her death. Three of the four people in his life had now become sources of exquisite pain. The one bright spot in this hellish summer was that Jean unexpectedly prospered at York Harbor, and her seizures vanished for several months—"the longest interval," Twain noted, "in four years."[16]

Though by nature a hopeful personality, Livy turned pessimistic about her chances and repeatedly blamed herself for buying the Tarrytown house before their Hartford home was sold. Twain knew she had endured a life-changing event and feared that she would expire at York Harbor. She was now kept in a sheltered environment and shielded from faint noises and even letters from dear friends, lest they inadvertently raise her pulse. It was a feat in late August when, wan and emaciated, she sat upright in a chair for ten minutes. Twain still clung to his messianic faith in Plasmon. He insisted that Livy digest Plasmon and milk when she couldn't keep down solid foods, but the results were frightful: "belchings of gas constantly, an hour & more on a stretch."[17] A man wedded to his nostrums, Twain brought up Dr. Helmer from New York to administer osteopathic treatments. However well-meaning Helmer was, his methods produced cruel side effects, with even Twain admitting in his notebook that "a severe treatment left Livy sore and lame and she slept but little, the night."[18] Twain could not relinquish the fantasy that some alternate therapy would magically restore his wife's health. "I wish I could have had old Kellgren here from Sweden when Mrs. Clemens was taken, the 12th of August," he informed Howells. "With his two hands he is worth fifty osteopaths and fifty million doctors. He would have had the madam on her feet and as sound as a nut in three days."[19] This was wishful thinking on a rather grand scale.

The doctors needed to manage Twain and his settled animus toward conventional medicine even as they treated Livy. He was riding his

"SPIRIT OF A STEAM ENGINE"

hobbyhorses to Livy's detriment and confessed to being alone in his belief that Helmer had helped her. The doctors tried to convey to him that Livy had entered a terminal phase of life, from which there might be temporary reprieves, but no real recovery. On September 23, Livy survived such an abysmal heart attack that her husband thought "the end was very close at hand," but somehow she weathered it and declared, "*I intend to get well.*"[20] Much of the time, though, she was nervous and querulous, trying to cope with one short-lived nurse after another.

By the end of September, Twain computed that Livy had been bedridden for seven weeks and "near to death three times," but he still hoped she would rally if they could only get her back to Riverdale.[21] Despite Rogers's offer of his yacht to return Livy to New York, Twain concluded that she couldn't endure a sea voyage and made extensive arrangements on October 10 to transport her by train in a specially designed "invalid car." All the while, he was kept at a safe distance from his wife. "It is a long time since I have seen the patient," he told Rogers, "but the reports are pretty fair."[22] On October 15, as Twain held his breath, Livy was lifted into a stationary bed on the train, one that unfortunately responded to "every jump and jerk and whirl of the train" as it made its nine-and-a-half-hour journey southward.[23] Once at home, a husky English butler hoisted her up the stairs and into her bedroom at the Riverdale house. Unable to let go of the York Harbor experience, Twain accused one of Livy's doctors, Wilson L. Hawkes, of charging exorbitant rates. He let loose a blistering letter that accused the doctor of "robbery" and demanded a refund, or else he would sue and expose him in print. "I shall expect you to return $96 to me at your early convenience—& I shall have then paid you for as many as 20 entirely unnecessary visits—visits which you well knew to be unnecessary."[24]

Shortly after returning to Riverdale, Twain hired a thirty-eight-year-old woman named Isabel Van Kleek Lyon to assist him with social correspondence that Livy had ably handled. Isabel would usher in a new chapter in his crowded life, though this was not apparent at the time. She came warmly recommended by Harriet Whitmore, and Livy was duly grateful. "I should have been greatly distressed if she had slipped away from me after what you said about her."[25] When Isabel arrived, she was candid with Twain about her shortcomings as a secretary, telling him, "I can't possibly use a typewriter and I don't know shorthand." He soon set her mind at rest. "Well I wouldn't have one of those goddam machines in the house and I couldn't read it if you did write shorthand."[26] Instead, Isabel would write letters longhand, and Jean would type them before mailing them.

Isabel Lyon came from a literate, well-heeled family that had been shadowed by a series of misfortunes. Her father, a Columbia College professor and an author of Greek and Latin textbooks, died when she was nineteen, followed soon after by her uncle's death, trapping her unexpectedly in a world of domestic service to support herself and her mother. Things only worsened when her sole brother, who drank and gambled, died of a morphine overdose, likely a suicide. Isabel's plight resembled that of a pretty young woman in an Edith Wharton novel: she was single, vulnerable, stuck in a perilous spot, schooled to function in a genteel world but now forced to survive in a harsh market environment. Bookish and educated, she functioned nicely as governess for two well-off families, first the Whitmores at Nook Farm, then the clan of the art critic Charles Edmund Dana in Philadelphia. Twice during her stint with the Whitmores, Isabel had passing meetings with Twain—once when she delivered a package to his door and another time during a whist game at the Whitmores', when she dazzled him with her daring moves. Upon being invited by the hosts for a rematch, Twain rejoined: "I'll come if I can play with the little governess."[27]

For someone with Mark Twain's eye for the ladies, Isabel offered warmth and charm and dark, alluring eyes that were full of curiosity and intelligence, coupled with a youthful mien. She was "slender, petite, comely, 38 years old by the almanac, & 17 in ways & carriage & dress," said Twain.[28] She was capable and efficient in a way that pleased Twain, and she had an easy rapport with the daughters, especially Clara, whom

"SPIRIT OF A STEAM ENGINE"

she found "a sweet morsel of a woman, alluring beyond words."[29] Isabel helped to alleviate the gloom of Livy's confinement. Thanking Mrs. Whitmore for the referral, Clara said of Isabel, "She not only is sweet and attractive, entirely lacking any disagreeable qualities, but she is also a pleasure for she has a cheerful manner and way which are particularly welcome in a house at a time of illness & consequent depression."[30] Isabel knew she had formed a dreamlike match with the Clemens family. She liked to read, was supremely aware of Twain's literary status, and appreciated the famous friends who called on him. "*I must tell you how much I like, no—love the duties here, now that Mr. Clemens uses me how and when he will,*" she told Franklin G. Whitmore.[31] For Isabel, the victim of downward social mobility, who desperately hoped to re-create her former status in the world, the new job offered the miraculous possibility of ascending again into a special realm and escaping the extreme insecurity of her lowly status. Having found this niche, she worked hard to ingratiate herself with the man who made it possible.

Most of Isabel's dealings were with Twain, who liked to roost in the vast downstairs hall with its Hudson River view. On November 24, she told Franklin G. Whitmore that Twain hadn't seen his wife *in two months*.[32] Only twice in Riverdale did Isabel set eyes on Livy and was captivated by her beauty and mysterious personality. She praised Livy's thin hands, lovely smile, and gracious manner. "I saw [Livy] twice in Riverdale, frail & very lovely, in flowing black silk garments & soft white lace shawls or scarfs. She didn't try to be a picture out of the lovely Italian School. She *was* the picture and she was many pictures in her quaint frocks made of rare stuffs & with her glorious dark eyes that said everything to you, or said nothing."[33] Smitten with Livy, Isabel found it easy to understand why Twain worshiped her. "Oh she is sweet beyond words. Instantly putting one at ease—as the greatest souls ever do by their simplicity."[34]

Although Isabel didn't board with the Clemenses, she was vouchsafed glimpses into the internal family dynamics. One morning, in early January, Twain shuffled into Isabel's presence clad only in "night shirt, Jaeger blanket dressing gown, bare legs & black felt slippers." Isabel didn't mind this shocking informality, but Clara suddenly appeared and firmly ordered her father to march upstairs and dress himself properly. When Twain balked, Clara insisted, and she got him to go upstairs. Some minutes later, Twain called down to Isabel from the landing: "Is Clara gone?" When warned that Clara was still hanging about, he lamented, "Then I'll go back to bed."[35] Far from feeling uncomfortable with Twain's indiscreet behavior, Isabel found the vignette delightful, and it previewed the way she would glide, by silent, imperceptible steps, into the most-private recesses of his world.

Bereft of Livy's company, Twain felt lonely and unsettled by the "stillness & solitude" of the sickroom that had settled over the Riverdale house.[36] Two or three times a day he would discreetly slip notes—kind, loving, humorous—under Livy's door, and she would brighten at these messages. With his gift for compressing affection in a nutshell, he brought the sights and sounds of the outside world into her cloistered bedroom, telling her one morning that "it is a soft and pensive foggy morning, Livy darling, and the naked tree branches are tear-beaded, and Nature has the look of trying to keep from breaking down and sobbing, poor old thing. Good morning, dear heart, I love you dearly."[37] Or one evening: "Livy dear, your daughter Clara is looking powerful sweet and trim and pretty tonight, and I haven't heard her in finer voice . . . Goodnight, my darling, I love you heaps more than I can tell."[38] Livy answered with penciled notes that grew shorter as her strength ebbed. Even though Twain's bedroom stood next door, separated only by a bathroom, he was kept in the dark about her condition. In November, when he believed Livy was gaining ground, he overheard a conversation between Clara and the doctor that made him realize, with a start, that she had experienced three terrible nights in a row. Jean said she had suffered two heart attacks that rivaled the worst episodes at York Harbor. "She was only a shadow when I saw her last, a month ago," Twain informed Franklin G. Whitmore, "& could hardly raise herself in bed; Clara reveals to me that she is still frailer now, & weaker."[39] The house was full of people with badly frayed nerves. Outwardly, Clara managed things smoothly, hiring and discharging staff as needed, and sharing nursing duties for her mother, yet Twain intuited, correctly, that under the surface her "anxieties are telling on her."[40] Jean, too, worried that her sister wavered "on the verge of a serious illness . . . caused by nervousness and anxiety."[41] In a family that specialized in extreme guilt, Clara was certain her trip to Paris in defiance of her mother had led to her woes. She told her friend Dorothea Gilder that though "my absence could not have caused my mother's illness I am certain it hastened it . . . Besides if she should not get well now I shall always have reminded myself that the last days of her life I gave her tears instead of smiles, which is enough in itself to drive one mad with remorse."[42]

Like her father, Jean was excluded from Livy's presence and busied herself on the third floor with wood carving or by roaming outdoors, often moving in a sphere apart from her lonesome, dazed father. As in York Harbor, she remained free from seizures, the longest such interval in five years. When she had a seizure on November 21, it was the first in four months. It is clear that Twain blamed Livy's collapse on the awful burden of caring for Jean. "It is those 5 years that put Livy where she is," he told Twichell, a recurring theme that complicated his emotions toward his youngest daughter.[43]

Given the gravity of the situation, Twain curbed his social life that fall and turned down most invitations until Colonel George Harvey of Harper & Brothers offered to host a banquet for his sixty-seventh birthday at the Metropolitan Club in Manhattan. It was a luxurious setting—J. Pierpont Morgan had told the architect Stanford White to "build a club fit for a gentleman! Damn the expense"—and guests at the dinner received leather folders containing a caricature of Twain, a self-portrait sketch.[44] For Morgan himself, who had bailed out Harper & Brothers a few years before, Twain inserted a special note: "For financial advice apply without diffidence to Mark Twain."[45] In addition to Twichell and

Howells, the audience was studded with illustrious figures, including ex-Speaker Thomas B. Reed and Senator Chauncey Depew, while Twain sat beside his old friend, Secretary of State John Hay.

It was after midnight when Twain rose to speak and made jokes about the various luminaries present. Then he shed his pose of irony and spoke straight from the heart, paying tribute to Livy. "Now, there is one invisible guest here. A part of me is present; the larger part, the better part, is yonder at her home; that is my wife, and she has a good many personal friends here." Despite her medical issues, "I think it quite appropriate that I should speak of her. I knew her for the first time just in the same year that I first knew John Hay and Tom Reed and Mr. Twichell—thirty-six years ago—and she has been the best friend I have ever had, and that is saying a good deal; she has reared me—she and Twichell together—and what I am I owe to them."[46] Everyone present recognized the special nature of the statement and gathered around Twain afterward to tell him so. Back in Riverdale, he wrote a note to Livy, describing the bursts of applause throughout the evening, "but it was the last name & the last praise (yours) uttered that night that brought the *mighty* burst." He closed tenderly by saying, "I'm a-loving you with all my might, Youth."[47]

With mortality on his mind, however mingled with comic mischief, Twain had published an open letter in the November 15 issue of *Harper's Weekly,* inviting readers to enter a contest in which they would imagine him dead and draft his obituary. He explained that he hoped "to acquire, by courtesy of the Press, access to my standing obituaries, with the privilege . . . of editing not their Facts, but their Verdicts. This, not for present profit . . . but as a favorable influence usable on the Other Side, where there are some who are not friendly to me."[48] Twain promised he would select the finest obituary, one "calculated to inspire regret," with the winner receiving "a Portrait of me done entirely by myself in pen and ink without previous instruction. The ink warranted to be the kind used by the very best artists."[49] It was characteristic of Twain, at such a lugubrious moment, to take his despondency and transmute it into sparkling humor.

Twain stuck to the doctors' program of keeping Livy sequestered in a

"SPIRIT OF A STEAM ENGINE"

worry-free environment and curtailed his political activities so as not to upset her. When the Anti-Imperialist League asked him to speak out about people being tortured through the "water cure" used by American forces in the Philippines, he refused, citing the need "to keep from breaking my wife's heart, whose contentment I value above the salvation of the human race."[50] When Speaker Thomas B. Reed died, Twain spared Livy the news—the first of many deaths she never knew about. The sequestration strategy encountered a major obstacle in December when Jean fell on the ice, followed by two epileptic attacks. One day, after a long frolic in the snow, she developed a chill, then ran a high fever and rapid pulse that progressed into a dangerous bout of double pneumonia. Around this time, Isabel Lyon wrote that she received a "blackmail letter" concerning Jean, which she said "froze my heart."[51] One suspects that somebody had discovered Jean's epilepsy—a dark secret to the outside world—and was threatening to extract payments to keep it hidden. We know no further details of this incident.

Although Jean had been kept apart from her mother since summer, Livy remained curious about her activities and pumped Clara for the latest news, and Clara had to deliver a steady patter of lies about her younger sister, knowing that her mother's heart couldn't withstand bad news about Jean's health. Usually shrewd in ferreting out deceit, Livy never knew that in another section of the house doctors and nurses bustled in and out taking care of Jean. "During all this time her mother never suspected that anything was wrong," Twain recalled. "She questioned Clara every day concerning Jean's health, spirits, clothes, employments and amusements, and how she was enjoying herself; and Clara furnished the information right along, in minute detail—every word of it false."[52]

As the lies multiplied, the charades became more elaborate. To buoy Livy's spirits, Clara invented parties and matinees that Jean attended, or winter sports that she engaged in even as she "knew that Jean might be dying at that moment," said Twain.[53] At one point, Jean was shipped off for several weeks to recuperate at Old Point Comfort, Virginia, while Clara kept up an uninterrupted narrative about the high times she was enjoying in Riverdale. A pretty fair liar himself, Twain was impressed by

Clara's artistry in stringing Livy along and eagerly awaited each new installment. "Father gave a cunning little chuckle at each invention of mine and would ejaculate: 'You are learning the art of lying pretty rapidly, you little blatherskite.'"[54]

Livy had been promised time with her husband after Christmas, but he now had to stall since a visit would elicit a wish from Livy to see Jean as well. On December 30, for the first time in three months, Twain spent three minutes and fifty seconds with his "radiant" wife—"A splendid 5 minutes!" Twain crowed.[55] The scene was both heartbreaking and ridiculous: a nurse stood there with a watch, timing his visit. He was hurried into her presence for four minutes on New Year's Eve. These visits, however fleeting, were an indescribable luxury for the couple. As long as Livy avoided another attack, Twain was promised five-minute daily visits that lengthened to fifteen minutes by mid-January, but fearful that he would blurt out too much, doctors muzzled the greatest talker in America.

Of course, Livy ached to see him and even longed to hear him pottering about in the adjoining bathroom–dressing room. One day she wrote to him: "Youth my own precious Darling. I feel so frightfully banished. Couldn't you write in my boudoir? Then I could hear you clear your throat and it would be such joy to feel you near. I miss you sadly, sadly. Your note in the morning gave me support for the day, the one at night, peace for the night. With the deepest love of my heart, Your Livy."[56] When the experiment was made, the nurse feared that Sam and Livy might be tempted to talk through the door, and Twain's writing materials were removed. After Livy had a setback in late January, Twain's visits were again suspended, although they were allowed a rapturous five minutes together on February 2, their thirty-third anniversary. Even amid illness, the spark of their romance was never extinguished, and Twain wrote Livy of "a love which has grown . . . and is worth more each year than it was the year before."[57]

One of many bizarre features of this period was that Twain published a story in the December *Harper's Magazine* that eerily foreshadowed the situation his family now experienced. In York Harbor, Howells had told him the tale of a mother who had died in a cottage "happy in the belief that her daughter was well, & not suspecting that she had been buried from the house a few days before," as Twain told Twichell.[58] As soon as Twain heard the story, "I put it on paper at once while it was fresh in my mind, & its pathos still straining at my heartstrings."[59] The mother in his story, dying from typhoid, had no idea that her teenage daughter had also contracted the disease and was dying, too. Two spinsterish, maiden aunts wrestle with the morality of lying to her and finally come to share Twain's belief that there exist holy lies that spare people from further suffering.

The emotional toll of Susy's death and Livy's and Jean's persistent ailments produced in Twain a potent need for escape, which expressed itself in peculiar fashion: an inordinate fascination with young girls and women who wrote him fan letters. He was simply starved for affection. It started with an exchange of letters with a Muriel M. Pears, whom he alluded to as his "Scotch lassie in the Highlands." As with the Platonic Sweetheart he had written about, he conjured up a (mostly unreal) fantasy about Muriel based entirely on her letters. Even though she wrote to him in a high-spirited style, flowery and childish, Twain praised her as "the best letter-writer now alive, I think."[60] As he told (an undoubtedly mystified) Howells, "I have never seen her, but she is just a dear—just an explosion, an effervescence, an uncorked bottle of champagne that pours out youth & sparkle & grace of speech & spirit, & the worship from the lips we love—& all in a torrent! What a breeze she is! & how young she makes an old body feel. She has enslaved this household, one & all."[61] Clara wrote to Muriel, too, so there was nothing secretive about this correspondence, at least in the beginning.

Then, in February 1902, Twain added another young woman to his epistolary harem, this time a young Frenchwoman, Hélène Picard, age twenty-nine, to whom he wrote in a tone of undisguised intimacy after a single letter. "Dear Miss Helene—If you let me call you so, considering that my head is white and that I have grown-up daughters. Your beautiful letter has given me such deep pleasure! I will make bold to claim you for a friend and lock you up with the rest of my riches; for I am a miser who counts his spoil every day and hoards it secretly and adds to it when he can."[62] He invited her to become a member of his new, secret, exclusive club that would be composed of one young woman per country; they wouldn't know the names of other members, and Twain would be the sole male member, as in the old Saturday Morning Club. It was his way of tightly binding these young women to him, as if afraid they might slip from his grasp. He named the group the Juggernaut Club and had Jean type up its constitution and bylaws. When she expressed curiosity about its purpose, he rebuffed her. "There are much cheaper typewriters than you are, my dear, and if you try to pry into the sacred mysteries of this Club one of your prosperities will perish sure."[63] That he was so defensive about the club shows he knew something was fishy about the private impulse he indulged. We know of at least five members of the club, which included "a Mohammedan girl as Member for Bengal," "a Princess of a royal house," and Twain's niece.[64]

Obviously, Twain didn't need to concoct this zany club, for any fan would gladly have corresponded with him. Instead, motivated by some hidden impulse, he deeply flattered the girls, made them feel special, and laid them under a sense of obligation to him. Since the young women didn't correspond with each other or even know one another's identities, the club was all about him. He was committing himself to a time-consuming correspondence with total strangers and didn't hesitate to pour out his personal sorrows to them, telling Muriel Pears about the "disastrous two months . . . freighted with fears & anxieties" that Livy had passed at York Harbor.[65] As he endured separation from his wife in mid-December, he confided to Hélène Picard: "There isn't going to be any merry Christmas here, because Mrs. Clemens is still a prisoner in the bed she has occupied now more than four months, but I hope you will have one anyway. I kiss your hand."[66] This last line, with its loony chivalry, tells how lonely and desolate Twain was, how much he missed romance in his life, and how his mind cranked out compensatory fantasies to cushion his profound misery.

CHAPTER FORTY-NINE

Divine Healing

With his deep-seated scorn for conventional medicine, Mark Twain had long been enamored of so-called Mental Science, a belief that positive thinking could conquer many diseases where traditional doctors failed. With Susy he had pushed her down that path only to wonder guiltily whether she might have survived her meningitis had she consulted a medical doctor sooner. From India, he had written to her, with an acolyte's fervor, about the power of Mental Science: "Of all earthly fortune it is the best, & most enriches the possessor."[1] Heeding her father's words, Susy stuck to Mental Science and may have paid the price.

The epitome of the mind-over-matter movement came with the sensational advent of Mary Baker Eddy and her Christian Science religion. Her 1875 book, *Science and Health,* preached a doctrine of "divine healing" by which people could cure themselves of illness through belief in Christ. A patient's failure to recover was blamed on insufficient prayer and lack of faith in Christian Science. Eddy built both a branch of religion and a business empire that made her a rich, powerful, and quite reclusive magnate.

Despite his respect for faith healing, Twain was always on the prowl for charlatans and believed that he had nabbed one in Eddy. He sharpened his blade against her in a *Cosmopolitan* article in 1899, followed by vitriolic pieces in the *North American Review* in early 1903. Even though Twain believed the mind had curative powers—"I feel quite certain that

Christian Science heals many physical and mental ills; but I also feel just as certain that it could call itself by any other name and do the same work"—Eddy was too juicy a subject to resist.[2] He mocked the stilted prose of *Science and Health,* questioned whether Eddy had solely authored its various editions, and sneered at her New Testament interpretations. She was portrayed as a megalomaniac with an organizational genius that stifled critical thinking. He hated that her followers, with her blessing, elevated her into a second Christ, telling Isabel Lyon that Eddy was "the world's supreme faker, who had stolen her creed & enriched herself by a suffering humanity's credulity." He scoffed at comparisons with Christ. "Think of the contrast. Christ came riding into Jerusalem on a confiscated jackass, whereas Mother Eddy travels around in a 90 horsepower 'mobile.'"[3]

Despite her movement's phenomenal growth—her book sold a half million copies by the time Twain grew interested—he vastly exaggerated its long-term prospects, telling Twichell, "Somehow I continue to feel sure of that cult's colossal future . . . I regard it as the Standard Oil of the future."[4] He believed that Christian Science was "destined to make the most formidable show that any new religion has made in the world since the birth and spread of Mohammedanism, and that within a century from now it may stand second to Rome only, in numbers and power in Christendom."[5] With thousands of members and seven hundred churches, Christian Science inspired enough fear at Harper & Brothers that the publisher declined to publish Twain's book on the subject in 1903. Not until 1907 did they collect his magazine articles into a book titled *Christian Science.*

While at Riverdale, Twain completed an unpublished satire of Christian Science with the title "The Secret History of Eddypus, the World-Empire." The narrator looked back on the world a thousand years hence after Christian Science had monopolized everything. Christianity had been abolished in favor of Eddymania; Christmas was renamed Eddymas; and Heaven bore the new title Eddyville. With Christian Science having absorbed the Roman papacy, all popes were now dressed in female garb and called Her Divine Grace Pope Mary Baker Eddy, followed

DIVINE HEALING

by the number of her reign. Twain excoriated Eddy with the same zest that he always displayed for prime targets. "I take a strong and indestructible interest in Mrs. Eddy," he allowed. "But this is merely because she is picturesque and unusual. I take the same interest in Satan."[6] There was an obsessive quality to Twain's writings on Mary Baker Eddy, with his bottomless capacity for anger again grasping a target and not letting go. If he overstated the future of Christian Science, he did foresee the marriage of politics and religion in the twentieth century and the faddish power of cults to brainwash people.

———◆———

Through the winter seclusion of 1902–03, the Riverdale house remained a high-class hospital in disguise, with Twain allowed to see his wife twice a day for twenty minutes with briefer and less frequent visits for Jean; otherwise Clara, Katy Leary, doctors, and trained nurses enjoyed exclusive access to the patient. Aside from sporadic sightings of Howells or Rogers, Twain was mostly alone and seldom set eyes on his daughters during the day. He was at loose ends as he grappled with a biblical plague of ailments, including his own rheumatism, gout, a cold, bronchial attacks, and an ulcerated tooth, and both Jean and Clara came down with measles that spring, Clara having black measles, a severe form in which dark eruptions cause bleeding under the skin. Was there ever a family so cursed and badgered by illness as the Clemenses?

By April, Livy, now bedridden for eight months, made modest enough gains that doctors promised she could leave the house by summer and urged her to go somewhere in Europe where a milder climate might heal her. They asserted, contrary to all available evidence, that she could make a complete recovery from her illness, even though she could barely stand up alone and had trouble talking. Twain put it accurately when he noted that Livy "hasn't had anything but lies for 8 months. A fact would give her a relapse."[7] Clara busily contacted friends about renting a villa in Florence, Italy, where they had once dwelled so happily.

With the Hartford house still unsold and expenses soaring, Twain reverted to a full-blown panic one night as he contemplated his financial plight. "During that night I was back again where I was in the black days when I was buried under a mountain of debt," he stated to a friend, and he summoned his daughters the next morning. "Our outgo has increased in the past 8 months," he informed them, "until our expenses are now 125 per cent greater than our income."[8] His math was faulty and the situation not quite so desperate as he depicted, but it showed how scarred he had been by bankruptcy and how much he still feared the poorhouse. "It is quite within the possibilities that two or three nights like that night of mine would drive a man to suicide . . . I cannot get that night out of my head, it was so vivid, so real, so ghastly."[9]

By May, Livy could sit on the terrace and was cheered by happy memories of Florence and the thought of returning there. She got to know Isabel Lyon, who read to her by the hour. By June, a touch of normality had returned to Riverdale along with warmer weather, and Isabel and Jean grabbed opera glasses and went bird-watching together, identifying warblers, thrushes, and hummingbirds. It was declared safe to transport Livy to Quarry Farm for the summer—a blessed return to tradition—where she would remain under the watchful eye of Sue Crane.

It proved an elaborate production to get Livy to Elmira in early June. First, she had to be carried to the Riverdale dock, where she was set down in a launch that took her to Henry Rogers's yacht, anchored in the river. While the air on the water refreshed her, the railroad car specially outfitted for her was "suffocating & awful," Twain complained, choking with heat and dust and leaving Livy depleted the next day.[10] Despite chestnut trees blooming at the farm and the usual serene river view from the porch, Livy was "melancholy & homesick" before she regained some strength and was wheeled about the property by a nurse, Margaret Sherry.

The old Quarry Farm routine was less comforting than Livy had anticipated, in part because Clara had remained behind with tonsil trouble and also because it exposed the distance between past happiness and current travail. As she sat on the familiar porch, with birds winging overhead, she bared her thoughts in a letter to Clara. "I must confess however to a great feeling of pathos & sadness. Everything here is so full of the

DIVINE HEALING

past—the cherry tree, the air the odors the sounds of summer evry [sic] thing is so suggestive of a time long ago, that one feels overwhelmed with a cloud of sorrow. At night it seems almost unendurable."[11] Livy began sleeping part-time on the porch, hoping to still her insomnia. Twain strove to resume his former habits at Quarry Farm, tramping up to his old octagonal study and writing a sentimental story called *A Dog's Tale* that was likely the last product of his pen written in that cozy den. In October, his dread of debt was relieved when he signed the contract with Harper & Brothers that gave them exclusive rights to publish his work and ensured him an ample income of at least $25,000 annually—$897,000 in today's money. Financial security had finally arrived, but at a moment of great medical insecurity.

Livy now broached the subject of death more openly. When Twain was absent on business in New York, she wrote, "I don't expect to die today, as I felt that I might on Tuesday."[12] Twain had long believed in consoling lies and saw the need to comfort Livy by feigning a conversion in his religious beliefs. From New York, he said, "Dear, dear sweetheart, I have been thinking & examining, & searching & analyzing, for many days, & am vexed to find that I more believe in the immortality of the soul than misbelieve in it. Is this inborn, instinctive, & ineradicable, indestructible? Perhaps so."[13] He ended by saying, "Livy darling, I love you dearly & worship you."[14] Whether she credited the truth of this conversion or not—Howells said it was a heroic lie and Livy penetrated the ruse—she sounded heartened by his message. "How much of immortality you have in your dear blessed self . . . Darling with all my heart—I love you."[15]

It seems strange that Livy should have been so eager to make the lengthy voyage to Italy—she could scarcely walk halfway across the room—but she retained such fond memories of Villa Viviani and her husband writing *Joan of Arc* there that she was game to risk a transatlantic crossing. To please her, Twain rented a villa near Fiesole for a year, hoping the salubrious climate would help her. A year later, with the benefit of hindsight, he realized that taking Livy on such a journey was "invented by insanity! And it is piteous to remember how eager she was to go, poor child. She so longed for health; it was returning to her by leaps & bounds—I wished she had changed her mind & said 'Let us turn back.'"[16] Perhaps thinking that he might never return to America, Twain placed flowers on Susy's grave and intoned "Good Night, Dear Heart, Good Night."[17]

On October 24, 1903, Sam and Livy, their two daughters, Katy Leary, and Margaret Sherry boarded the *Princess Irene* for the two-week voyage to Genoa. (Isabel Lyon and her mother would soon follow.) Henry Rogers did his best to give them a festive send-off, festooning their cabins with fruit and flowers, but the family felt worn out, and Twain was in a foul mood from the unbearable tension. The fourteen days at sea proved nightmarish for Livy due to "savages" who "kept her awake night and day . . . I want no more contact with ladies and gentlemen and other s[ons] of bitches," Twain wrote.[18] He indulged in vengeful fantasies against loud American boors who tortured Livy with thoughtless talk below her port window. "These chattering, cackling squaws & monkeys will all be in hell in a hundred years. There is something pleasant in the thought."[19] Twain, a constant protective presence for Livy, warned acquaintances not to speak with her when she sat on deck and reprimanded those who disobeyed.

Despite months of inquiries, only on the eve of sailing did Twain learn the name of the place they were renting, Villa di Quarto. "Take it altogether," Willard Fiske, a retired Cornell professor, told him, "I know of no place in Florence where you can be so thoroughly comfortable as at Quarto."[20] It was a hasty, last-minute decision, thrust upon Twain by circumstance, and he would have many opportunities to regret it. When the Clemens party disembarked in Genoa, a reporter noted how prolonged illness had aged Livy, with her face "dry and severe under the large spectacles which bestride her thin nose."[21] The final leg of the journey—a six- to seven-hour train ride to Florence—presented yet another trial for her to endure.

A few miles outside Florence, Villa di Quarto was magnificent in scale, with sixty rooms, rose gardens, a vineyard, and rows of olive trees. With a faded grandeur redolent of old Florentine nobility, it was staffed

DIVINE HEALING

with seven servants, ranging from a cook and a coachman to a butler and an upstairs maid. Its central salon was so large that five sofas sat below a painted vault ceiling, and its outsize dimensions and slippery floor made Twain dub it the "skating rink." He found much of the interior pretentious, a colossal waste of space, and thought the endless corridors lent the house a chilly, impersonal feel. In the past it had been owned by a string of royal families, and for Katy Leary, at least, it seemed romantic. "Every window was open during the night, and the smell of the roses and the scented laurel . . . and the orange blossoms—and all those mingling in together while the nightingales was singing. Oh, it was perfectly beautiful!"[22]

The surface charm was deceptive, for presiding malevolently over the scene was its owner, the American-born Countess Raybaudi-Massiglia, who began to harass the Clemens family with petty, mean-spirited actions. She made them spend two nights in a Florence hotel before they were allowed to occupy a villa that she hadn't bothered to heat beforehand. When Twain selected for Livy a room hung with silken tapestry, the countess vetoed this on the grounds that it violated the terms of the lease. "She was correct in her position," said Twain, who took an instant dislike to her. "The lease showed that this reptile with the filthy soul had protected her house and her body against physical contamination by inserting in the lease a clause prohibiting the lessee from introducing into that particular bedroom any person suffering from an illness of any kind."[23] With the countess's husband away on diplomatic service, she had to occupy the stable house and resented the presence of her paying guests. No less than Twain, Isabel Lyon abhorred the countess with "her painted hair, her great coarse voice, her slit-like vicious eyes, her dirty clothes, and her terrible manners."[24]

The countess found endless ways to torment her guests; Livy's sickness brought out no compassion in her, only a punitive attitude. At first Livy was able to sit on the terrace, with its stunning views of the Duomo and Campanile in Florence, for an hour daily. Then she suffered the inevitable attack, the frantic gasping for breath, and Twain discovered that the telephone wires had been mysteriously cut. When a Florentine doctor and his assistant belatedly arrived, Twain learned that the countess had locked the outer gates at six each evening without informing him. There wasn't even a bell to alert the Clemenses to visitors, and Clara saw her father fly into a titanic rage. "By the thunder of Zeus," he said, "I swear I'll take your mother back to America tomorrow. That's a sane country, with sane people in it."[25] The countess had a rabid donkey that tore into Isabel Lyon so viciously that she was bedridden for days. Twain tried futilely to scout out another villa: there was no taking his invalid wife back across the ocean to America. His misery was now total: for the moment, he and his daughters had no choice but to endure the hellish tricks perpetrated by the Countess Massiglia. In despair, Twain coined a new name for the villa: Calamity House.[26]

The countess's next act of mischief was to shut off the villa's water, making it impossible to flush the toilets. "The stench was persistent, and dangerous to health," said Twain. "The windows had to be kept open, no matter what the weather was like."[27] To his horror, he discovered that the house sewage drained into cesspools that stood almost directly beneath the room where Livy hoped to recuperate. Out of his wits with anger and worry, Twain had water hauled to the house from a nearby spring. "I've seen enough," Twain exclaimed to Clara. "The doctors at home never should have advised this trip. An idiotic idea to start with. I always thought so. Look at what your mother has to endure in this place. It's criminal to subject her to such things."[28]

Nothing went as planned, and even the weather refused to cooperate. Instead of the mellow, sun-ripened warmth envisioned by American doctors, the Clemenses endured heavy fog and steady rain that mirrored their downcast mood. Soon Livy had to be isolated from her family again, and Twain slipped back into his old Riverdale regimen of sliding notes under her door. To some extent, he took refuge in work, dictating letters to Isabel Lyon or jotting thoughts in his notebook as he meandered about. He savored the vision of Florence in the distance and sometimes accompanied Clara and Jean into the city, visiting art galleries or joking with street urchins. Given Livy's situation, Twain's mood was somber, and he seemed more short-tempered than usual with his daughters. One day, sitting in a Florentine tearoom, he grew upset when some Italian officers began to ogle Clara and her large hat adorned with grapes and other artificial fruits. Perhaps he felt Clara was being flirtatious or was unduly encouraging their attention. Whatever the case, back at Villa di Quarto, he hotly grabbed a pair of scissors and snipped off every bit of fruit from the provocative hat.[29] Clara was now twenty-nine, had a career, and longed to be a liberated woman, yet her father had great difficulty in accepting her maturity.

While at the villa, Isabel Lyon turned forty, and with scant opportunities to meet eligible men, her unmarried status surely preoccupied her. She showed a tendency to entertain romantic fantasies about men who crossed her path and grew fond of a local priest, Raffaello Stiattesi, who officiated at "the sweet little chapel on the hill," as Jean termed it.[30] Isabel began to tutor the priest in English in exchange for Italian lessons. "Yes, he is very lovely and is showing us a new world," she said, writing worshipfully of "his beautiful face, his lovely buoyancy of manner, and his great sweetness of soul."[31] In her journal, her amorous feelings grew clear: "The priest is tall, dark, high forehead, good features and a lovely deep voice."[32] Although nothing came of the liaison, despite romantic twilight meetings, it revealed how much Isabel pined for a relationship with a smart, soulful man.

While Isabel spent little time with the secluded Livy, she passed many absorbing hours with Twain because, aside from writing magazine articles, he had hit upon a new method of dictating his autobiography, suggested by Livy, and it brought him immoderate joy. In a small room facing the terrace garden, he would pace and talk and reminisce freely, casting aside chronology and taking up topics as they sprang to mind, including memories of John Hay, Robert Louis Stevenson, Thomas Bailey Aldrich, and Henry H. Rogers. This new method captured his voice in all its freshness and "makes my labor amusement—mere amusement, play, pastime, and wholly effortless."[33] After years on the lecture platform, Twain was able to speak in perfectly formed paragraphs, elegantly phrased. Isabel proved the ideal amanuensis because she didn't just record his words, but responded with delight and appreciation.

Albeit unawares, Isabel Lyon was stepping gradually into the editorial role Livy had held down for several decades. She was enthralled by Twain, and he by necessity was deprived of Livy's company. How could he not respond to Isabel's charm? She progressed swiftly from being Twain's secretary to his best friend and companion. That January, she thanked Harriet Whitmore, who had referred her to the Clemens family: "Perhaps you may be interested to know how very entirely Mr. Clemens absorbs all my time—every minute of it—even my evenings. I attend to an infinite number of Things for him, and when he is lonely and restless we play cards—play cards? Why I play with him all day Sunday even. He is delicious; this morning he had a run of very bad luck and biting his cigar hard he said 'Christ couldn't Take Tricks with the kind of cards you give me.' Oh darling Mrs. Whitmore you have given me all this joy, and Truly I am the wealthiest woman ever."[34] Twain didn't set personal or professional boundaries with Isabel, and his intermingling of work and socializing with a lonely, single, attractive woman created a situation fraught with future trouble.

After many years of extreme intimacy, Twain could share only a portion of his life with Livy, who still had to be screened from distressing information. He withheld news of the death of Orion's wife, Mollie, in Keokuk as well as the loss of an old friend, explorer Henry Morton Stanley. Aside from chronic heart trouble, Livy coped with a host of other ailments, including tonsilitis, gout, and rheumatism. She never succumbed to self-pity or despair, and sometimes imagined she would recover her former life. Despite the plague of problems at Villa di Quarto, she even planned, on good days, a trip to Egypt in the fall.

Relations with Countess Massiglia only deteriorated. She wouldn't rein in her dog, whose barking prevented Livy from sleeping. She refused to tie up the aggressive donkey that had terrified the high-strung Isabel. Twain and the countess quarreled over installing a telephone that would allow him to summon a doctor quickly in a medical emergency. In private, he unpacked his full arsenal of insults against the countess: "She is easily the most fiendish character I have ever encountered in any walk of life."[35] "I was losing my belief in hell until I got acquainted with the

DIVINE HEALING

Countess Massiglia."[36] "I was not dealing with a human being but with a reptile."[37] He meditated a lawsuit against "the American bitch."[38] Having perfected the art of revenge, Twain never tired of attacks on such a supremely deserving target.

On February 2, 1904, Twain marked their thirty-fourth wedding anniversary by sending an affectionate note to Livy. The next day, Clara snapped and yielded to a temper tantrum that startled the entire household with its pure savagery. As she described it to a friend the day after, she suddenly "began to scream & curse & knocked down the furniture." Everyone came running in, and with her father present, "I said I hated him hated my mother hoped they would all die & if they didn't succeed soon I would kill them, well on & on for more than an hour, I don't know all I said but mother hearing the noise & being told that I was overwrought got a heart attack and as you can imagine today I can hardly meet anyone's eyes."[39] Clara, already spending half her days in bed, admitted to a fit of temporary insanity and still felt resentful of her family after the outburst.

What are we to make of this extraordinary episode, so long unknown? (The letter wasn't published until the year 2000.) For two years, Clara had assumed enormous responsibility for her mother and had to deal with her father's sadness (and strictness) and her sister's illness. She must have felt like a prisoner of this protracted crisis, with her career and private life held hostage. Her rising level of stress finally overflowed the banks of her self-control. As Clara expressed it, "It all comes of controlling controlling controlling one's self 'till one just bursts at last in despair."[40] She cited her mother's illness, the doctors' discouraging prognosis, and her father's proposed lawsuit against the countess. Awash in guilt, she believed she didn't "belong in good society anymore."[41] Every time Clara tried to assert her existence apart from her parents, she felt punished.

In his embattled mood, Twain supported no fewer than three lawsuits against the countess—two civil, one criminal—and was gearing up for more. Instead of focusing on Livy, he fixated his rage against her tormenter. Every day he scoured the area for another villa and was prepared to move Livy as soon as she could withstand the change. He fired two Florentine doctors, partly because his wife had made no progress for two months—she had regressed since Riverdale—and partly because they prescribed bromides, a drug that had produced unfortunate side effects with Jean. The strain of this miserable time was palpable in Twain's appearance and manner. When he performed a reading for the British Relief Fund in Florence—he gave a funny speech about Italian grammar and how "even the regular verbs were irregular"—the *Italian Gazette* detected the sadness bottled up inside him.[42] "The great humorist looked as full of vitality as ever though it was plain that he was labouring under a stress of emotion, and at times he nervously tore the paper he was holding in his hands. At the end of his talk, with a break in his voice, he bade his hearers good night, and everyone admired his generous courage when it was known that he had left Mrs. Clemens at home seriously ill."[43]

On the evening of February 22, Livy's medical condition lurched toward a climax that looked as if it might prove fatal. As Twain recorded, "At midnight Livy's pulse went to 192, & there was a collapse. Great alarm. Subcutaneous injection of brandy saved her."[44] Even though the crisis passed, her pulse fluctuated between 115 and 140. The next medical casualty in Calamity House was Twain himself, who lay bedridden with a hacking cough—his old friend bronchitis—for the first half of March. Doctors suggested that he curtail his smoking habit, but he fended off this advice with his usual defensive witticisms and always kept a cigar stuck in his mouth. When Yale professor William Lyon Phelps came to visit for an hour, Twain "smoked three cigars; there was a constant twitching in his right cheek and his right eye seemed inflamed."[45]

On the first day of spring, Twain delivered this grim summary to Thomas Bailey Aldrich: "It is a year & seven months that [Livy] is a prisoner, & in pain & despondency."[46] He later wrote with deep feeling of the lonely nights Livy passed sitting up in bed, a taper burning nearby and Katy dozing at her side. "She so dreaded death, poor timid little prisoner; for it promised to be by strangulation. Five times in 4 months she went through that choking horror for an hour or more, & came out of it white, haggard, exhausted, & quivering with fright.[47] He knew that, if Livy lingered on like this, it was not a life worth living. Compounding the pain for Twain was that he blamed himself for Livy's condition, having questioned so bluntly her religious faith. "I do love you so, my darling," he wrote to her, "and it so grieves me to remember that I am the cause of your being where you are. I WISH—I WISH—but it is too late. I drove you to sorrow and heart-break just to hear myself talk. If I ever do it again when you get well I hope the punishment will fall upon me the guilty, not upon you the innocent."[48]

In April, Clara gave her first concert in Florence, and the *Italian Gazette* gave her a cordial review: "Miss Clemens possesses a very sympathetic contralto voice of considerable extension and of a remarkably sweet and touching quality."[49] Twain, in the audience, rated Clara's performance a triumph and quipped, "now my daughter is the famous member of the family."[50] When Clara came home that evening, Livy summoned her at midnight, eager to hear news of her concert. But the next night Livy suffered a severe attack and sat gasping for air while Clara sat with her for an hour, with Twain and Jean listening at the door.

On April 20, Livy weathered a paroxysm of such frightening intensity that Twain and Jean were banned from her room altogether, and Clara was permitted to spend only one hour daily with her. It must have devastated Jean to be continually tagged as a disturbing presence when her sister was not, a constant reminder of the deleterious impact of her epilepsy on her mother's health. Twain described for a friend Livy's complete isolation: "No letters nor papers enter there any more & the madam is not strong enough to hold up a book or magazine. We have saved her, by a close shave; starvation, visiting & excitement were killing her; she neither ate nor slept; she does not weigh as much as a cat; she would not have lasted a fortnight."[51] Twain professed to retain vague hope for Livy's recovery, but he knew she was suffering stupendous blows that left her sadly diminished.

In a familiar pattern, Twain hired a heart specialist named G. W. Kirch and then grew convinced he was gouging him—"It is robbery . . . The man is a hog"—but he knew it would be dangerous to switch doctors.[52] He and Clara rented a new villa for the summer as a way to boost Livy's courage, but it was something of a charade, for she was too weak to move. In a sign of sharpening pain, Livy received morphine injections, though her illness could still produce miraculous moments of relief, as when Katy Leary came flying excitedly into Twain's presence on May 11: "Mr. Clemens, Mrs. Clemens is really & truly *better!*"[53] The Livy of old—"bright and young and pretty"—was momentarily restored, and she was wheeled into the sunshine on the terrace, an indescribable release after being cooped up. Twain knew this reprieve wouldn't last long and that the "fiendish malady will play new treacheries upon her."[54]

Soon afterward, Twain invited Dr. William Wilberforce Baldwin to come from Rome to examine Livy. In preparing Baldwin for the visit, Twain fell back on his old belief, so often practiced in Riverdale, that there are sacred lies needed to sustain hope in the patient. "I hope that you will come with your mind & conscience all prepared to commit a lofty & righteous deception—if need be—to save Mrs. Clemens's life."[55] At a time when Livy was having weekly attacks, Baldwin gave Livy "comfort & courage," and his visit bolstered the mood of the entire family.[56]

By now, Livy dreaded that she was dying and could not reconcile herself to it, as Twain disclosed to Howells. "It was too pitiful . . . to see the haunting fear in her eyes, fixed wistfully upon mine & hear her say, as pleading for denial & heartening, 'You don't think I am going to die, do you? Oh, I don't want to die.'"[57] With the sturdy Katy Leary, Livy faced the prospect of death more frankly than with her family. When she heard owls hooting outside her room one night, she remarked, with a sense of foreboding: "Do you hear those owls, Katy? I know that's a sign of death." This opened a frank discussion between the two women, with Livy saying, "Katy, I don't think I can live much longer." She instructed Katy on what dress she wanted to wear when she died. "A flowing lavender satin dress, beautifully trimmed with lace."[58]

CHAPTER FIFTY

The Dread Cavalcade of Death

Because of bankruptcy and Livy's illness, the Clemens family had gone from a happy life, firmly rooted in Hartford, to many years of exile. At fifty-eight, Livy keenly longed for some permanent residence, and on June 5, 1904, Twain proudly informed her that he had found a villa to purchase that would delight her. "Her eyes danced with pleasure," he said, "for she longed for a home of her own."[1] So bright and hopeful was the moment that he allowed himself to linger longer than his fifteen-minute medical limit. When she kissed him, she asked, "You will come back?" and he promised to return to say good night, sealing this moment by blowing her a kiss from the door.[2] During this interlude, Livy had shown, he thought, "the most perfect expression of her love for me within my whole knowledge of her."[3] With an ebullience missing since Susy's death, Twain sat down at the piano and thumped out two of his favorite Black spirituals: "Swing Low, Sweet Chariot" and "My Lord He Calls Me." Livy, when she caught the distant strains, was cheered. "He is singing a good-night carol to me," she said.[4]

Katy Leary was comforting her, propping her up and fanning her face, when Livy, chatting and smiling, suddenly slumped over on her shoulder. Death came in a peaceful instant at 9:15 p.m. When her heart failed, she died "just as a tired child falls asleep," Twain later wrote.[5] Katy ran to alert the family. Twain rushed in, took his dead wife in his arms, and said her name repeatedly. At first he was unaware what had occurred—why did she not respond?—then he understood and spread her body back on the pillows. "How beautiful she is—how young and sweet—and look, she's smiling!" Twain said. Death had smoothed the creases from her face. "Oh, he cried all that time," remembered Katy, "and Clara and Jean, they put their arms around their father's neck and they cried, the three of them, as though their hearts would break."[6] Within two hours, Twain started to commit his grief to paper, the first chapter of an extended outpouring. "She was my life, and she is gone; she was my riches, and I am a pauper . . . She was the most beautiful spirit, and the highest and the noblest I have known."[7] All night, Twain would tiptoe downstairs, pull back the sheet, and plant a kiss on Livy's brow. By the time embalmers showed up the next day, Twain thought her face had fully reverted to her sweet, girlish self of thirty years before. Jean snapped pictures of her dead mother dressed in white—haunting photos of Livy's round face resting on the pillow under an elaborate, wrought-iron bedstead. That night, Twain paced beside the coffin.

With his legendary capacity for guilt, Twain lost no time laying down a litany of charges against himself. He tortured himself with the knowledge that he wasn't with Livy at the instant of her death and expressed "remorse for things done & said in these 34 years of married life that hurt Livy's heart."[8] He angrily blamed fate and the medical establishment for her "22 months of unjust and unearned suffering."[9] Livy had been the linchpin binding her family together, and without her, her husband and two daughters felt adrift. Jean passed a sleepless night and quickly gave way to her first grand mal seizure in more than a year. Clara, having wrestled with complex feelings toward her parents, simply fell apart. First she lay crying beneath her mother's casket, then retreated to her room and lay down on her bed, where she remained barricaded in catatonic silence for four days.

Aside from making plans to return home with Livy's remains on a German steamer sailing from Naples in two weeks, the Clemens family was paralyzed by indecision. As Twain explained pathetically, "Our life is wrecked; we have no plans for the future; she always made the plans, none of us was capable."[10] He discovered how much harder it was to lose a close partner than to die oneself. He worried most about Clara, who

THE DREAD CAVALCADE OF DEATH

remained numb, either staying in bed or drifting about like a sleepwalker. Twain told Howells that he feared she was on the edge of collapse. "It would break Livy's heart to see Clara."[11] What Clara was actually feeling was quite hidden from view and only a couple of friends back home knew the shocking truth. "It is nearly two weeks since [Mother] died," Clara wrote, "& I seem to grow happier as the days pass . . . The family seems quite cheerful about me but I am beginning to wonder if I shall ever know what happened."[12] As condolence letters poured in, Clara puzzled over her abnormal response. "Friends write me beautiful words of sympathy & here I sit feeling *nothing* . . . I can hardly remember my mother's face."[13] Perhaps grief had induced a state of shock in Clara, or she may have felt freed from the weight of caring for her mother. Until the family left Villa di Quarto on June 20, Clara stuck to her room as a fortress from her family, or maybe from her own emotions.

With Livy having overseen his world, Twain didn't know where to turn, telling Charlie Langdon that he had become "a man without a country." It maddened him that Susy and Livy had been rudely snatched away from him, ratifying his pessimistic worldview. "Ah, this odious swindle, human life," he swore when Jean had an epileptic attack as they were about to leave Villa di Quarto.[14] No longer did he have Livy to govern his temper, curb his vengeful impulses, and keep him on an even keel. Instead, he would sublimate his sadness into unbridled anger.

Twain was hell-bent on making the Countess Massiglia pay dearly for the hurt she had inflicted on his family. Hiring a lawyer named Traverso to bring a lawsuit against her, he would play out the case for two years and gloat over the torment he caused her. Isabel Lyon recorded this reaction in November 1905 when he got a progress report from Traverso. "All the misery that Mr. Clemens ever hoped the Countess would get out of this suit she has got, for she has spent a lot of money . . . and long ago Count Massiglia went to Signor Traverso begging him to ask Mr. Clemens to drop the suit, for it was killing his wife & life at the villa was made impossible for them, for every hand was against them & life had become a Hell. Mr. Clemens listened to Traverso's story with a keen

| 769 |

satisfaction, for the Countess has garnered what she sowed."[15] Livy would have fathomed her husband's bitterness, but would have moderated his rage and barred him from carrying his reprisals too far. She had always rescued him from the wilder and darker impulses of his nature.

Twain also fought a running battle with Dr. Kirch, whom he felt had fleeced him, and balked at paying his second bill. He had only kept him on, he argued, because it would have been dangerous for Livy to change doctors. "Dr. Kirch is a mere robber, & I told him so, & invited him to sue for his lacking 2200 francs. It is not likely that he will expose his case in a court, but I will find a way to make him unhappy."[16] Working himself into self-righteous rage, Twain insisted that "a gouge is never unimportant to me; if it were but 3 francs I would spend several hundred in a court of law before I would pay it . . . A *court* must settle whether this is a gouge or not."[17] However warranted his feuds with Countess Massiglia and Dr. Kirch, Twain himself paid a heavy emotional price, as the legal battles kept alive in his mind the bleak days of Livy dying at Villa di Quarto.

On June 28, Twain and his daughters departed from Naples aboard the *Prinz Oskar*, and throughout this "melancholy voyage," he was achingly aware of his wife's body down below, sealed in a leaden case inside an oak coffin.[18] He brooded in his journal: "In these 34 years we have made many voyages together, Livy dear—& now we are our making our last. You down below & lonely, I above with the crowd & lonely."[19] Throughout his life, he had suffered a strange inability to reproduce faces in his mind and now reflected, "It is a curious infirmity—and now at last I realize that it is a calamity."[20] Despite splendid weather and bright blue seas, Clara remained incommunicado in her cabin. A photo shows her dressed all in black, with a black hat and black veil covering her face. A family shadowed by memories, they all stayed in their cabins on the Fourth of July, brought low by thoughts of happier holidays.

When the ship arrived in New York on July 12, the family sped through customs, thanks to a special order from President Theodore Roosevelt and his cabinet. The Clemens trio looked ghastly as they trooped from the ship, strongly marked by misfortune, like survivors of a shipwreck. Among those receiving them was Twain's nephew, Jervis Langdon, who wrote: "Uncle Sam, Clara & Jean very dear, but—pitiful, pitiful."[21] In past years, Twain had made reporters gathered at the dock roar with laughter. How different things were now. "As Mr. Clemens left the ship his step was faltering he seemed much more feeble than when he left here last Fall," the *New York Times* reported. "He wore mourning, and the usual spirit of good-fellowship which he shows was missing. To the reporters he said that he knew nothing and preferred to be left alone in his sorrow."[22] After a night in a Manhattan hotel, the Clemens party, along with Joe Twichell, journeyed up to Elmira by private railway car.

A small private funeral was held in the parlor of the Langdon home where Livy had grown up. It was presided over by Twichell, who, thirty-four years earlier, had officiated at Sam and Livy's wedding on the very spot where the coffin now stood. On this warm summer day, towns-people thronged the surrounding yard, silently paying their respects. At the cemetery, Twain vowed never again to stand by a grave and watch a loved one disappear into the earth. After having been contained for weeks, Clara submitted to a violent convulsion of grief. "When it was all over," said Katy Leary, "Miss Clara gave a great cry and threw up her hands and her father caught her in his arms and held her. Her cry, it went through everybody. It hit everybody's heart. He didn't say a word. He just held her until the carriage came along and he put her in it, with Jean. Mr. Clemens was just like a dead person. It was all over and our lives was just broken in two."[23]

In the weeks following, sporting a black mourning band on his left arm, Twain could not let go of the sensation that he had failed Livy, who had never ceased to love him no matter how much he hurt her. After the funeral, he needed to unburden himself to Sue Crane. "Never a day passed that she did not say, with emphasis & enthusiasm, 'I love you so. I just worship you.'" He couldn't believe he had earned such uncondi-tional love, even though "what little good was in me I gave to her to the utmost—full measure, the last grain & the last ounce—& poor as it was, it was my very best, & far beyond anything I could have given to any other person that ever lived." As he surveyed his life with Livy, Twain was very tough on his own behavior. "I try not to think of the hurts I gave her, but oh, there were so many, so many!"[24]

The dread cavalcade of death continued on August 31 when Twain's sister, Pamela Moffett, died at seventy-six in a sanitarium in Greenwich, Connecticut. With some exaggeration, he said she had been "sixty years an invalid."[25] Twain had regarded her as a benign hypochondriac, who experimented with new diseases "as fast as they came out, and always enjoyed the newest one more than any that went before."[26] At the same time, with no trace of irony, he esteemed her as a woman of pure character and "a most kindly and gentle disposition."[27]

Perhaps the most moving condolence letter Twain received came from a "Mrs. A.P. Saunders" in Clinton, New York. This was the married name of Louise Brownell Saunders, who wrote to inform Twain of something that startled and pleased him. A month before Livy died, Louise had named her second daughter Olivia Saunders. Of course, Olivia was the name Susy had used at Bryn Mawr, and since it was also Livy's real name, it must have seemed to Twain to confer a double honor on his family. Whatever discomfort he may have felt about Louise's relationship with Susy—and we don't know that for sure—he sent her a beautiful reply, radiant with warmth: "Dear Mrs. Saunders: I am grateful to have those hallowed names thus consecrated, and in reverence I bow my white head before them in their new place. How long they stood for the grace and beauty and joy of life—and now, how they stand for measureless pain and loss! We are come upon evil days: may they be few! Affectionately S.L. Clemens."[28]

This didn't end their correspondence. Two years later, Twain published reminiscences of Susy and Livy in the *North American Review* and evidently tapped a high tide of feeling in Louise, who wrote appreciatively to Twain after the anniversary of Susy's death. He replied: "Your moving letter has reached me—& my heart—& finds a grateful welcome. It is a deep pleasure to me to know that you think I am writing worthily of Susy & her mother—that beautiful & inspiring & pathetic theme. So rare they were! I think they left not many of their lofty rank in the world when they quitted it. I wish, with you, that Livy could have

THE DREAD CAVALCADE OF DEATH

known that your child was to bear Susy's name & keep her dear memory green in your heart. I thank you, *thank* you, for your letter. With my love—S.L. Clemens."[29] We don't know whether Twain understood the romantic depth of Susy's relationship with Louise, but in these two letters he clearly honored Louise as a profound living link with Susy and belatedly blessed their union with his own special brand of eloquence. Decades later, Olivia Saunders was to marry the novelist and film critic James Agee.

Had Livy known the nearness of death, Twain said, "she would have told us where to go and what to do," but the end came suddenly, forcing the Clemenses to engage in planning that had long been Livy's domain.[30] It dawned on Twain that they should take a summer house in the Berkshire Mountains, in western Massachusetts, in the town of Tyringham, next door to *Century* editor Richard Watson Gilder and his family. Gilder offered them a cottage on his spread, Four Brooks Farm, and Clara and Jean consented, glad to be near intimate friends. After he arrived, Twain was morose and didn't care to socialize with people. When a kindly farmer offered to drive him to Stockbridge, he said bluntly, "My friend, I don't want to hurt your feelings, but, to tell you the truth, I'd just as soon go to hell as go to Stockbridge!"[31] Richard Watson Gilder attempted to buoy the spirits of his famously crotchety friend. "Mark, in our cottage next door," he told a friend, "is most grim and unhappy, but full of life and abounding in scorn of a mismanaged universe. Imagine Rabelais and Voltaire rolled into one discoursing . . . of a fiendish and ingenious Providence."[32]

The most obvious casualty of Livy's death was Clara, who arrived in such an overwrought state—"pale, weak, exhausted," said Isabel— that Gilder's son Rodman had to carry her into the house and deposit her in an upstairs bed.[33] Given her fragile condition, Isabel asked Rodman to spend the night. Dazed after her mother's death, Clara was now incapacitated and didn't rise from bed for four days. With her nerves badly shot, she couldn't stand the smallest house noises or country sounds of cowbells. Six days after arriving, accompanied by Katy Leary, she departed for New York to place herself under the care of Dr. Angenette Parry, an obstetrician who had studied medicine in Vienna. For Clara, Dr. Parry recommended treatment eerily similar to Livy's: seclusion, inactivity, and insulation from anything disturbing. Within a few days, Clara was able to send her father a reassuring note from Dr. Parry's sanitarium on East 69th Street.

Though not outwardly apparent, Jean was in a tenuous mental state, less because she missed her mother than from fear of what the future held for her as a woman with epilepsy. Since Livy had warned her that she must never marry, she felt condemned to an insufferably loveless life. "Am I never to know what love means because I am an epileptic and shouldn't marry if I had the chance?" she wrote in her diary on the *Prinz Oskar*. "I seem never to be attractive to men. Will I have to go on indefinitely leading this empty, cheerless life without aim or real interest?"[34]

Jean had been the most athletic member of the Clemens family, a skilled rider, but her father feared she might suffer an attack on horseback. Livy had bought her daughters saddle horses in Florence that were shipped home. On July 31, while Clara was in New York, Jean and Rodman Gilder rode these two horses on a moonlight jaunt when Jean's frightened horse collided with an oncoming trolley, killing the animal and throwing Jean to the ground, where she lay bleeding and unconscious. Rodman bore her to a doctor, her face awash with blood from shattered window glass, and Twain recorded the damage in his notebook: "Face, nose, side, back contused; tendon of left ankle broken."[35] To Rogers, Twain expanded on her plight, saying she had endured "4 wounds on her back and neck, one at the base of her skull, and 5 on her forehead, eyes, nose, and mouth."[36] For weeks a crippled Jean, her leg in plaster of paris, hobbled about on crutches, while a depressed, fatalistic Twain viewed the whole affair as "simply another stroke of a relentless God."[37] Twain got Jean to give up horseback riding for a time, but with so few pleasures in her life, she rebelled and resumed her riding.

When the accident was picked up by the press, Twain raced to contact

THE DREAD CAVALCADE OF DEATH

Dr. Parry and urged her to prevent Clara from reading any newspapers. He set out for New York the next day, planning to break the news gently to his daughter in person. Then Twain, in his well-meaning but impetuous manner, bungled the task and immediately thrust a newspaper into Clara's hands with the lines: "It is hoped that Mark Twain's youngest daughter, Jean, may live. Her horse fell on her and crushed her." Clara stared at the paper, stupefied: "I read and reread the sentence, unable to feel anything but a sharp pain in my head . . . Then slowly Father began to tell the story in his most feeling and dramatically impressive way. It would have been interesting to know what kind of wheels were revolving in his mind, when his actions were so at variance with his intentions."[38] It was exactly the shock to Clara's system that Twain had sought to avert.

Alarmed by her father's message, Clara hurried back to Massachusetts to visit her sister—Twain stayed behind in Manhattan—though it's doubtful her stay helped Jean. It simply threw an extra burden of care on Isabel Lyon, who already functioned as much more than Twain's secretary. With Livy's death, her duties had started to shade over into nursing and, dare one say, *mothering*. Whatever repose Clara had begun to experience under Dr. Parry's care was lost, as Isabel recorded in her meticulous journal. She started to dub Clara "Santa" or "Santissima," an affectionate nickname, though sometimes applied ironically. Now she reported: "Santissima saw a lot of people today—too many. Tonight she was hysterical and alarmed me much." The next day Clara remained equally agitated. "Today Santissima stayed in her bed all day. She had dinner with me down stairs. Last night I stayed with her until 3 o'clock."[39] It was probably no coincidence that as soon as her father returned, Clara dashed back to New York, likely still fuming about how he had burst into her room with the scary news.

Before leaving Tyringham, Jean struck up a relationship with an older married farmer who tried to convert it into a romantic affair. In her loneliness, she may have raised expectations with the farmer that she was not prepared to meet. The man evidently kept disturbing her with letters; she was afraid to rebuff him outright lest he spread false stories, and she kept him at bay with anodyne replies, finally telling him that she was terminating their correspondence "on account of my health."[40] The clandestine liaison went nowhere and seemed to have caused her intense shame.

Twain's time in Tyringham, a place of rural peace, held no therapeutic benefits for him. "It is dreamy & reposeful here," he admitted to Charlie Langdon, "but it does not heal the heartbreak."[41] That August, he searched for a quiet house to rent in New York, having opted to rejoin society. He had been inhabiting another planet, and the move would thrust him back into the hurly-burly of Manhattan social life. He signed a three-year lease for a roomy town house at 21 Fifth Avenue, at the corner of East 9th Street, with occupancy starting in December after extensive repairs. In September, Clara entered the sanitarium of Dr. Edward Quintard, in Norfolk, Connecticut, where the extreme "rest cure" prohibited books, letters, and visitors—"a horrid solitude with grief and memory for company," said Twain.[42] This led him to decide, in selecting a new house, that "Clara is going to need the quietest kind of quiet for many months to come, I think. She is not perceptibly better or stronger than she was when she arrived on this side. Katy says she is thinner than her mother was."[43] In October, when Clara was given a three-week reprieve to redecorate 21 Fifth Avenue, she exerted herself too much and had to return to the care of Dr. Parry on East 69th Street, where she was largely cut off from family. For a year, she was forbidden to have any communication with her father. Her treatment now recapitulated that assigned to Livy, with Twain again stigmatized as an upsetting presence. Commenting on her "strict captivity," Twain explained that Clara would have "no company but a cat & a trained nurse, & no visitor but the specialist."[44] Twain feared he had intruded on Livy's peace and didn't care to do the same with Clara. This time he would strictly heed instructions.

About to embark on her term of "captivity," Clara sent her father a tender, loving farewell note. For all the complications of their relationship, Clara was funny and quick-witted, and had more of a secret rap-

THE DREAD CAVALCADE OF DEATH

port with her father than Jean. Now she wrote: "Dearest little Marcus: I feel like sending you one more fluttering goodbye before the bars are bolted . . . I want to make you realize that you will daily be in my thought this long winter and that I shall be hoping all the time that nothing will go wrong with you in the smallest ways . . . Au revoir Marcus dear. My deep love to you with a warm hug . . . Your loving Saphead."[45]

In late August Twain stopped by the seaside home of Colonel George Harvey in Deal, New Jersey, and spent time with Henry James, another guest there. Though neither writer was a special fan of the other's work, they had a cordial stay and enjoyed each other's company. "The weather, the air, the light etc. are delicious, and poor dear old Mark Twain beguiles the session on the deep piazza," James wrote.[46] After this literary encounter, Twain went off on the *Kanawha* with Henry Rogers to dedicate a church that he had built in Fairhaven, Massachusetts.

Everyone who visited 21 Fifth Avenue noticed that with its Gothic flourishes above doors and windows, there was an ecclesiastic grandeur about the four-story town house, which had been designed by James Renwick, Jr., the architect of St. Patrick's Cathedral, nearby Grace Church, and the Smithsonian Institution Building. Twain liked places flooded with natural light, but despite the tall windows overlooking Fifth Avenue, the house lay steeped in shadows. "Livy would have thought of that," he moaned. "Livy always thought of everything."[47] He holed up at the Grosvenor Hotel as Katy Leary unpacked belongings from the old Hartford house—stuff hidden from family view for many years—and she wept as she gazed upon the old furniture, so rich in associations. "I had forgotten it was so beautiful," she said, "and it brought Mrs. Clemens right back to me—in that old time when she was so young and lovely."[48]

When Twain and Jean moved into the house in late November, there lingered a fatal ambiguity about Isabel Lyon's position. Was she an employee or a family member, or did she occupy some intermediate position? Arriving amid Livy's illness, Isabel never held a clearly demarcated status. Clara was insistent that Isabel should live elsewhere, but Twain disagreed and sided with Isabel: she would stay.[49] With Livy and Susy dead and Clara off in a sanitarium, a vacuum yawned open in Mark Twain's domestic life, and Isabel stepped into it ably, serving as a surrogate wife in all but name. Livy had been sickly for so long, whereas Isabel was a resourceful and versatile younger woman with boundless energy. She played cards with Twain, took dictation, and arranged his scattered library. She picked up his secretarial duties, answering the vast number of queries he received, with an uncanny ability to mimic his written voice. When Twain received an irritating letter from one woman and instructed Isabel to "Tell her in a Christlike way to go to Hell," she knew the exact language in which to couch the reply.[50]

Twain didn't wish to be bothered by mundane cares, and Isabel happily took over one household duty after another. "I can talk to her about anything I please," Twain said to Howells. "But when she darns my socks and looks after me then I know she's a woman."[51] When Twain's foot hurt with gout, she pumped the foot pedals of his new Aeolian Orchestrelle, a large, dark, ornate structure, eight feet tall, that was a sort of player reed organ with sixty installed classical pieces. While Isabel played, he sat rapt with pleasure and asked repeatedly for certain pieces associated with the dead: Handel's "Largo" (Livy) and Mascagni's "Intermezzo" (Susy). After years of straining to appreciate classical music, he now bathed in its beauty, and the Orchestrelle became his preferred form of consolation.

Problems abounded with Isabel as a substitute for Livy. Where Livy had showered her husband with unalloyed love, she was also clear-eyed about his shortcomings and never hesitated to correct them. Isabel gave Twain the hero worship of a younger, newer woman. She was smitten with his genius, would begin calling him "The King," and lovingly recorded in her journal the original phrases and humorous anecdotes that flowed from his lips. She was increasingly attentive to his every need, as she boasted to Harriet Whitmore: "I have very little to do with Jean—never go out with her anymore; you see Mr. Clemens wants his secretary on deck—and where he can have her services when he needs them."[52]

Without realizing what he was doing, Twain allowed Isabel, who was bright and capable, to graduate from secretarial functions to a more ma-

THE DREAD CAVALCADE OF DEATH

ternal role in financial matters and medical advice. The problem was that she lacked the authority of a mother, or even of a stepmother, occupying a gray area where she could be perceived as an upstart or usurper by Clara and Jean. In dealing with Twain's daughters, Isabel always stood on shaky ground and could seem to presume too much in making decisions. Twain had saddled her with these responsibilities and she accepted them. Isabel's role was especially tricky when it came to dealing with Jean's epilepsy: Twain should never have delegated this responsibility to a nonfamily member. Maybe he thought, after Livy's death, that caring for Jean was inherently "woman's work"; or maybe he was exhausted from years of struggle with this awful problem; or maybe he just didn't want to see any more seizures.

As Isabel's job description steadily expanded to de facto mistress (minus the romance) and head of the household, it never seemed to occur to Twain to raise her salary—a paltry $50 per month. She was desperately eager to keep this job, which placed her next to one of the world's foremost writers, and, hesitant to complain, she mostly suffered in silence. High-strung and turbulent, Isabel endured terrible headaches and depression that only worsened as more responsibilities were piled on her. The self-centered Twain was oblivious to these problems. None of this dimmed Isabel's dreamy, idealized view of Twain. She wrote in her journal of the "solemn joy of living in the same house with Mr. Clemens who grows ever sweeter with the white white years."[53] When it came to her boss, she slipped into a tone of schoolgirl rapture. "All the days are so full of dear duties down stairs that I never have a moment to be in my own pretty room . . . All my days are hallowed by Mr. Clemens's wonderful presence . . . It is something beyond words."[54] That winter, he succumbed to terrible bronchitis—he still smoked forty times per day, Isabel noted—and painful gout made him weak and unsteady on his feet. He missed Livy and needed a constant audience as he lounged in his nightshirt. To her other duties, Isabel gladly added that of nursemaid and companion.

As Twain went through the winter pestered by bronchitis, he blamed his medical ills on his landlord, James A. Renwick. From the time the

Clemens family moved in, they all complained about the horrid racket made by the radiators, which kept them awake at night and didn't even produce much heat. Katy Leary remembered Twain saying that "he was going to *sue* that landlord for all the days he'd had to stay in bed and couldn't work."[55] Isabel Lyon's records confirm that the litigious Twain was prepared to drag Renwick into court. As she notified Twain's lawyer: "Mr. Clemens directs me to ask if it would not be well to declare war by suing for damages incurred by the severe bronchitis that Mr. Clemens had in the last winter, and by his being obliged to stay in his bed for many weeks owing to that illness."[56] Renwick at last got the message and installed brand-new radiators the following summer.

CHAPTER FIFTY-ONE

"The War Prayer"

During the early winter days of 1904–05, Mark Twain read, smoked, and wrote upstairs in the old bed that he and Livy had bought in Venice twenty-five years earlier. He was clearly depressed and "lives much in the past," wrote Isabel, "speaking constantly of those who are gone."[1] The state of his mood was defined by the dirges, funeral marches, and other doleful tunes he asked Isabel to pump out on the Orchestrelle. When Andrew Carnegie came to visit, Twain seized his hand and murmured softly, "A ruined home, a ruined home."[2]

Gradually, Twain threw off his indolent air in late January and began to come downstairs and dress normally. He also began writing a series of robust polemical screeds, a continuation of the activist streak that began with his return to the United States, interrupted by Livy's lengthy illness. In most lives there comes a mellowing, a lovely autumnal calm that overtakes even the stormiest personalities. In Twain's case, it was exactly the reverse: his emotions intensified, his indignation at injustice flared ever more hotly, his rage became almost rabid. Perhaps with his wife and eldest daughter dead and the bulk of his books behind him, he wondered why he needed to fret about his popularity any longer. He had always written political satire but now returned with a vengeance to his new medium of choice, satirical polemics, freighted with powerful political messages. He no longer had Livy's delicate restraining hand.

The first target arousing his critical ire was a political atrocity committed by Czar Nicholas II when he fired on striking Russian workers in

St. Petersburg on January 22, 1905. When Isabel tapped on his door one morning, she found her employer in a small tempest of fury, "pacing with a clipping in his hand reporting some cruelties perpetrated by . . . the Czar's Government upon his subjects."[3] Eight days later, when Twain appeared at teatime, she noticed a sheaf of papers in his hand—a satirical monologue in which he allowed the czar to indict himself for his own misdeeds. When Nicholas gazes at his naked body after his morning bath, he notes how unimpressive a monarch he is, devoid of regal garments. "I had never heard him read any of his writings before, and he is at his best then," said Isabel. "Today he was wonderful. Thrilled with the tremendous interest of the naked Czar's soliloquy. His voice shook with emotion."[4] Not only was this an outlet for strong emotions percolating inside Twain, but it allowed Isabel to grow into the role of listener and commentator formerly occupied by Livy. A few days later, Twain read her his revision, confirming her place as his new in-house editor and sounding board.

The misery of the Russian people had disturbed Twain dating back to the reactionary rule of Alexander III. While on vacation in the summer of 1890, he had, boiling mad, written an unmailed letter to the editor of *Free Russia,* expressing impatience with the mild dissent of liberal opposition parties. Quite simply, he wanted the czar assassinated. "Of course I know that the properest way to demolish the Russian throne would be by revolution. But it is not possible to get up a revolution there; so the only thing left to do, apparently, is to keep the throne vacant by dynamite until a day when candidates shall decline with thanks. Then organize the Republic."[5] Clearly, Twain had come a long way since his fawning tribute to Alexander II on the *Quaker City* voyage. Twain had always worried that if he expressed his true political views, he would alienate regular readers. Nevertheless, when he published "The Czar's Soliloquy" in the *North American Review* in March 1905, some faithful followers approved, one writing that he had always suspected, between the lines of Twain's writing, "a something that makes for liberty. He feels it, he understands it, he promotes it."[6]

Twain's Russia interest was inflamed by the Russo-Japanese War that

"THE WAR PRAYER"

year when the world stood amazed that an Asian power could mount a successful challenge to European might. Twain didn't pretend to be an impartial observer. "I wish somebody would assassinate the Russian Family," he told Twichell. "So does every sane person in the world—but who has the grit to say so? Nobody."[7] Russia's defeat led to spontaneous demonstrations at home as disillusioned soldiers returned to shortages and disorder, and "Nicholas the Bloody" attempted to stifle dissent by force plus modest reforms. The world cheered when Teddy Roosevelt brokered a peace between Russia and Japan in the Treaty of Portsmouth, but Twain wanted the war to persist until the czarist regime was dismantled. As he told the Boston *Globe,* "I think that this was a holy war in the best & noblest sense of that abused term, & that no war was ever charged with a higher mission . . . that mission is now defeated and Russia's chains re-riveted, this time to stay . . . this peace is entitled to rank as the most conspicuous disaster in political history."[8] When a major Catholic prelate eulogized TR as an "angel of peace to the world," Twain grunted contemptuously.[9] TR had "postponed the Russian nation's imminent liberation from its age-long chains indefinitely—probably for centuries."[10]

One strand of Twain's animosity toward the czar stemmed from indignation over the treatment of Russian Jewry, a special target of violence that year. In December, Twain teamed up with Sarah Bernhardt, the incomparable French actress then touring America, for a fundraiser to aid Russian Jews. While Twain was beguiled by the actress in person, he was less than transfixed by her stage work. When he joined Jean and Isabel for a *Phèdre* performance, Isabel was much more impressed than her boss. "Mr. Clemens was pretty well bored but we were in a box so he could walk around outside when the confinement was too oppressive."[11] At a benefit matinee for the Jewish sufferers in Russia, Bernhardt starred in a one-act play for an audience replete with New York Jewish royalty, including the Guggenheims, the Lehmans, and the Schiffs. When Twain came out at the end, he paid tribute to Bernhardt's "speech flowing in that lucid Gallic tongue" and her beautiful, fiery personality.[12] In his way he showed that he could seduce an audience as well as she could. "Madame Bernhardt is so marvelously young. Why, she is the youngest person I ever saw, except myself—for I always feel young when I come in the presence of young people. She and I are two of the youngest people alive."[13]

With his high-profile support for Russian radicals, Twain served as a magnet for those activists seeking to boost their American support. They knew that he didn't shrink from sanguinary solutions to Russian oppression. When Nikolai Chaykovsky, the founder of the Socialist Revolutionary Party, visited New York in March 1906 to raise money for weapons to fight the czar, he envisioned Twain chairing a mass meeting. He didn't know how to reach him until Charlotte Teller, a beautiful young socialist writer, steered him to 21 Fifth Avenue. Twain cooled off the fervor of the grizzled revolutionary and explained how William McKinley, Teddy Roosevelt, and Jay Gould had destroyed the ideals of the American public. Twain declined the offer to chair Chaykovsky's rally—he pleaded a prior commitment to a meeting for the blind—but sent a message to be read aloud: "Government by falsified promises, by lies, by treacheries, and by the butcher-knife for the aggrandizement of a single family of drones and its idle and vicious kin has been borne quite long enough in Russia."[14] Although Twain knew people might think him bloody-minded, he reminded them that the American Revolution was fought "with guns and the swords . . . Revolutions are achieved by blood & carnage alone."[15]

The next emissary for aid to Russian revolutionaries scarcely needed introduction to literate Americans. Maxim Gorky was celebrated for his play *The Lower Depths,* from 1902, and for his more recent arrest in 1905 for revolutionary activities. When he docked in Hoboken, New Jersey, he was greeted by thousands of Russian immigrants and was soon honored at a white-tie dinner hosted by Twain and other writers. What started out as a promising fundraising tour was soon entangled in a press rivalry between William Randolph Hearst's *New York American* and Joseph Pulitzer's *New York World.* After Hearst published a front-page puff piece on Gorky, the *World* countered with a shocking headline: "Gorky Brings Actress Here as Mme. Gorky."[16] The actress in question, Maria Andreyeva, of the Moscow Art Theatre, was presented to the

"THE WAR PRAYER"

public as Gorky's mistress, posing as his wife. That Gorky had been separated from his wife for years got lost in the unfavorable coverage, and Gorky and Andreyeva were asked to vacate a succession of New York hotels. America was a puritanical society and Twain a man of Victorian propriety. Instead of flying to the defense of a slandered writer, Twain bowed to the prevailing criticism. "Gorky made an awful mistake," he told the press, stating that he should have respected American customs. "He might as well have come over here in his shirttail."[17] Twain wasn't a revolutionary about sexual mores. When an embittered Gorky sneered at New York as a "monstrous metropolis," Twain retorted: "He hits the public in the face with his hat & then holds it out for contributions."[18]

The next cause to engage Twain's passion involved the horrid depredations of King Leopold II of Belgium against twenty million Africans in the "Congo Free State" (today the Democratic Republic of the Congo) who were subject to his brutal rule. Leopold sent Christian missionaries to his colony and preened as a "philanthropic" monarch, while millions died extracting rubber and ivory for him in what amounted to slave labor. The most hideous aspect of his plunder was that rubber companies amputated the hands of Africans failing to harvest their quota of rubber. The plight of Leopold's African victims was first exposed by a Black writer, George Washington Williams, who met with Leopold and traveled to his African domain, but the main worldwide protest movement came a decade later, and was organized by Edmund Dene Morel, a tireless orator, and his Congo Reform Association. Morel was especially keen to enlist the United States in his moral crusade because it had supposedly been the first country to recognize the Congo.

In September 1904, Morel arrived in America to organize the American Congo Reform Association and lobby in Washington. After he sent Twain a packet of literature, Twain invited him to stop by 21 Fifth Avenue: "All days are alike to me in these black days of my bereavement—I do not go anywhere."[19] Twain and Morel had a spirited exchange. "I can see him now," recalled Morel, "pacing up and down his bedroom in uncontrollable indignation, breaking out ever and again with his favourite exclamation, 'By George!'; or with some rapid, searching question."[20] The visit paid dividends: Mark Twain was recruited as one of the new organization's vice presidents along with Booker T. Washington. On at least two occasions, Twain journeyed to the nation's capital to press the Congo issue—he lunched with Teddy Roosevelt and met with State Department officials—and Booker T. Washington was awed by his inexhaustible energy. "I think I have never known him to be so stirred up on any one question as he was on that of the cruel treatment of the natives in the Congo Free State . . . he never seemed to tire of talking on the subject."[21] For Washington, Twain's activism formed part of a broader indictment of racial exploitation at home and abroad, so that his efforts on behalf of "the black natives of the Congo" also "exhibited his sympathy and interest in the masses of the negro people."[22]

Having sharpened his satire with the czar's sermon and doubtless influenced by Browning's dramatic monologues, Twain hazarded another mordant soliloquy, this time with King Leopold boasting about his Congo atrocities. He tested it out in a private reading to Isabel, Jean, and the visiting Sue Crane, who sat there riveted. "Breathless we sat, & were weak with emotion when he finished the bald truthful statements that rolled from Leopold's vicious lips," Isabel recorded in February 1905. "Horribly, too horribly picturesque it is . . . but I suppose it would be too strong a diet for people & governments."[23] "King Leopold's Soliloquy" was indeed too strong for Frederick Duneka at Harper & Brothers. Twain claimed that the Catholic Duneka feared to criticize a Catholic monarch, and he even imagined that Leopold had "bought up the Harper silence along with that of hundreds of other papers."[24] Twain circumvented the publishing industry and in September 1905 issued his tirade in pamphlet form, its proceeds directed to the Congo Reform Association. "I shall feel sweeter inside after I have spewed out my opinion of Leopold," he stated.[25] The fifty-page book incorporated shocking photos of African children with hands lopped off by Leopold's henchmen. At his own expense, Twain sent copies to more than a hundred people, many of them clergymen.

In "King Leopold's Soliloquy," no laughter lurks in the background to soften Leopold's words. Twain's disgust is served up raw as he presents a vivid caricature of a human monster trying to minimize his spectacular crimes. He focuses much of his satire on Leopold's enraged responses to "slanders" in the press. "Grant them true, what of it? They are slanders all the same, when uttered against a king."[26] Leopold hypocritically clutches his crucifix and claims that he has brought Christianity to the people he butchers. While he clothes himself in religion, the garment scarcely conceals his sins. Twain builds up his case against Leopold by having him quote from tracts exposing the malevolence of his regime. One comes from an American missionary who states that the U.S. government would never have recognized the Congo scheme had it known that "having put down African slavery in our own country at great cost of blood and money, it was *establishing a worse form of slavery right in Africa*."[27] Before the advent of the Kodak camera, Leopold grouses, he was "looked up to as the benefactor of a down-trodden and friendless people. Then all of a sudden came the crash! That is to say, the incorruptible *kodak*—and all the harmony went to hell!"[28]

As an activist, Twain enjoyed an immense advantage in commanding press attention, and he leveled a powerful salvo of criticism against Leopold. In November 1905, during an interview to celebrate his seventieth birthday, he yielded to an astonishing outburst. "Here sits a King in luxury and debauchery, placidly ordering thousands of innocent human creatures driven to death, tortured, crippled, massacred in order that his foul revenues may be increased!"[29] Twain emerged as a true citizen of the world, noting how the steamship and electric cable had made "the whole world one neighborhood" and that it was every person's duty "to prevent murder, no matter who is the murderer or how far away he seeks to commit his sordid crime."[30] Twain was especially appalled by the amputations. "I have seen photographs of the natives with their hands cut off because they did not bring in the required amount of rubber . . . to cut off their hands and leave them helpless to die in misery—that is not forgivable."[31] Thank God for the camera, Twain observed, which had certified "the charge of wholesale murder" against Leopold.[32]

In a fiery, noble mood, Twain flitted from one cause to the next. He would lend his name and energies to a crusade for a time, but he wasn't an organizational creature by nature. In January 1906, he notified the Congo activists that while he wished them well, he was now calling it quits. "I have retired from the Congo . . . My instincts & interests are merely literary, they rise no higher; & I scatter from one interest to another, lingering nowhere. I am not a bee, I am a lightning-bug."[33] Twain explained that he had operated under an error, believing the United States signed the 1884 Berlin Act that validated Leopold's claim on the Congo. The State Department, in searching its records, had discovered that this was not the case. Twain thought this weakened America's moral authority against Leopold and damaged the cause of Congo reformers. He was also upset that they had led him into printing this embarrassing error in his pamphlet.

As his activist streak started to wane, Twain began insisting on an ironclad rule for limiting his involvement. "When asked for the use of my name in a good cause," he explained, "I always say yes, but on the condition that I shall not be called upon at any time to *do* anything. And so I am a sleeping official on many a list."[34] Highly aware of his own mortality, he would "soon be needed in Heaven or elsewhere; wherefore I must confine myself strictly to my own work henceforth."[35] Twain lacked the visceral optimism of a bona fide activist, having too poor an opinion of human nature to proselytize too much. People, he thought, were cowards who shunned the ugly truth whenever possible. In August 1908, Congo reformers achieved a notable victory when the Belgian government took the Congo Free State, long the personal domain of King Leopold II, and reconstituted it as the Belgian Congo. By this time, Twain had pushed on in other directions.

Where Twain's portrait of the czar and Leopold were somewhat weakened by a dogmatic petulance, as if he couldn't contain his anger, far more artful was his 1905 antiwar piece titled "The War Prayer." For many years, he had dwelled on the perils of extreme patriotism—how it blinded countries to their own vices and the virtues of others. "Talking of patriotism, what humbug it is; it is a word that always commemorates a robbery," he wrote in 1896. "Patriotism is being carried to insane excess. I know men who do not love God because he is a foreigner."[36] Chauvin-

"THE WAR PRAYER"

ism, he thought, bred war and undermined Christian professions of the "brotherhood of man." Despite his longtime strictures on monarchy and the notion that "The King can do no wrong," he feared America had adopted a no less servile formula: "Our country, right or wrong!" In America, he regretted, "free speech is confined to the dead" and the majority were typically wrong. "Whenever you find that you are on the side of the majority, it is time to reform—(or pause and reflect)."[37]

In "The War Prayer," Twain imagines a country seized by war fever, invoking "the God of Battles" to protect its soldiers.[38] Amid such patriotic mania, a pale, aged stranger, "clothed in a robe that reached to his feet . . . his white hair descending in a frothy cataract to his shoulders," strolls down the center aisle during a church service. The minister has been imploring God to grant victory to their country when the stranger intones, "I come from the Throne—bearing a message from Almighty God!"[39] He points out that the prayers being read contain spoken and unspoken parts. The spoken part prays for victory, but its unspoken corollary is horrifying: "O Lord our God, help us to tear their soldiers to bloody shreds with our shells; help us to cover their smiling fields with the pale forms of their patriot dead; help us to drown the thunder of the guns with the shrieks of their wounded, writhing in pain; help us to lay waste their humble homes with a hurricane of fire; help us to wring the hearts of their unoffending widows with unavailing grief; help us to turn them out roofless with their little children to wander unfriended the wastes of their desolated land in rags and hunger and thirst."[40] The congregation sits speechless, startled by this sudden, unwelcome outburst, and Twain concludes: "It was believed afterward that the man was a lunatic, because there was no sense in what he said."[41]

Compact in expression, hard-hitting in its force, "The War Prayer" was Mark Twain at his most eloquent and impassioned. He told his friend Dan Beard, the illustrator, that when he read the piece to Jean, she advised against publishing anything so controversial. "Still you are going to publish it, are you not?" asked Beard as Twain paced in dressing gown and slippers. "No, I have told the whole truth in that, and only dead men can tell the truth in this world. It can be published after I am dead."[42]

Twain sought to get *Harper's Bazaar* to print it, maybe hoping its humane perspective would appeal to women, but the magazine turned it down cold as "not quite suited to a woman's magazine."[43] In the end, "The War Prayer" was published posthumously.

For Twain, the man who embodied many of the worst excesses of American politics was Theodore Roosevelt. He had once been invited to lunch with Roosevelt and was exhausted by the Rough Rider's bombastic self-promotion. "He dragged San Juan Hill in three or four times, in spite of all attempts of the judicious to abolish the subject and introduce an interesting one in its place. I think [Roosevelt] is clearly insane in several ways, and insanest upon war and its supreme glories."[44] In 1904 Twain favored his friend John Hay, the secretary of state, in the presidential race, but TR became the Republican candidate. Twain saw TR as so power-hungry that he actually feared that if he lost the office, "he will take it anyhow."[45] He was especially outraged by Roosevelt's high-handed methods in pushing through the Panama Canal and engineering what he considered the theft of the Philippines. While TR was widely admired (outside the business community) for standing up to trusts, Twain thought he was all bluff, a showman feigning political courage. Twain was still a Mugwump, a permanent apostate from the Republican Party, and when Joe Twichell signed a letter supporting Roosevelt, Twain sent him a scathing rebuke unrestrained by their decades-long friendship. "Oh, dear! get *out* of that sewer—party-politics—dear Joe. At least with your mouth."[46]

Twain felt the full force of TR's charm, the warmth and energy that surged through him when they shook hands. After lunching at the White House, he told Isabel Lyon, "You can't help liking him for he is a magnetic creature, and he shows his teeth in his forceful smile, just as much as ever, and . . . says that he is 'De-lighted' to see you, just as the caricaturists have it on record."[47] Still, Twain judged him the worst president ever—"the most formidable disaster that has befallen the country since

"THE WAR PRAYER"

the Civil War"—an unprincipled politician willing to do anything to sustain his popularity.[48] The nation, he thought, had been bewitched into hero worship by an overrated man. "Mr. Roosevelt is the Tom Sawyer of the political world of the twentieth century . . . always hunting for a chance to show off; in his frenzied imagination the Great Republic is a vast Barnum circus with him for a clown and the whole world for audience."[49] Such craving for attention was a charge often directed against Twain himself, which may have sensitized him to that failing in TR.

Part of Twain's displeasure with Roosevelt involved his handling of race relations. Many northern liberals had applauded him when he invited Booker T. Washington to lunch at the White House—"a man worth a hundred Roosevelts," declared Twain, "a man whose shoe-latchets Mr. Roosevelt is not worthy to untie."[50] That produced a southern backlash that was not to TR's liking. According to Twain, his subsequent desire to placate the white South explained TR's shabby behavior in dealing with controversial events in Brownsville, Texas, on the Mexican border. After the War Department sent a Black regiment to the town, a racial confrontation broke out with white townspeople in 1906, leading to the death of a white civilian. In a shocking reprisal, Roosevelt discharged the entire regiment of 167 Black soldiers, destroying their careers and stripping them of pay and pensions, all without a military trial. As Twain protested of the president, "He convicted the entire command himself, without evidence and without excuse, and dismissed them from the army, adding those malignant and cowardly words, 'without honor.'"[51] Not until 1972 did the army reinvestigate and find the Black soldiers innocent of all charges.

One other action by Roosevelt is worth mentioning, for it revealed Twain's startling evolution in his formerly retrograde attitude toward Native Americans. When Roosevelt declared Thanksgiving Day on November 30, 1905, Twain's seventieth birthday, it prompted the author to examine the whole mythic aura surrounding the holiday. Instead of the typical sentimental story of white settlers sitting down harmoniously with Indians, Twain said acerbically that white New Englanders were thankful that "they had succeeded in exterminating their neighbors, the

Indians, during the previous twelve months instead of getting exterminated by their neighbors the Indians." As time passed, "it was perceived that the exterminating had ceased to be mutual and was all on the white man's side, consequently on the Lord's side, consequently it was proper to thank the Lord for it . . . The original reason for a Thanksgiving Day has long ago ceased to exist—the Indians have long ago been comprehensively and satisfactorily exterminated and the account closed with Heaven, with the thanks due."[52] Twain had shown praiseworthy sensitivity toward the Black population, both in life and fiction, but when it came to Native Americans, he had deplored them as dirty and shiftless, showing no awareness of the harm done to them by white settlers. Clearly, in his final years, Twain had come to see them much more sympathetically and with a historical perspective that had been conspicuously absent.

CHAPTER FIFTY-TWO

"An Artist in Morals and Ink"

Whether he realized it or not, in admitting Isabel Lyon into his household, Twain had cobbled together a new family, albeit an inherently unstable one. As he recalled, Isabel "lived with us & . . . was to all intents & purposes a member of the family. She sat at table & in the drawing-room when there was company & when there wasn't; our intimates became her intimates; they visited her & she visited them; of her own motion & by her own desire she became housekeeper."[1] In short, Isabel occupied the gigantic hole blown open in Twain's life by Livy's death, serving as secretary, hostess, and social director, all rolled into one.

For Isabel, the interlude at 21 Fifth Avenue was an inimitably happy one—in fact, little short of ecstasy: she breathed the same air, shared the same life, with one of the world's most remarkable men. "Never never on sea or shore of spiritual or terrestrial being could there be a man to equal Mr. Clemens," she wrote.[2] When a Mrs. Judd visited, she showered compliments on Isabel and praised Twain, "who stands as my complete master," Isabel confessed. "She said that I will not need a heaven when I die for I have it here."[3] Some superstitious voice whispered that she would eventually pay a fearful price for this dreamlike contentment. "Some day the penalty for such perfect living will come."[4]

A healthy younger woman, in her early forties, Isabel freshened up Twain's life and wiped away the sickroom atmosphere of recent years. He groomed her to do things Livy had done. "More than once he cautioned me not to allow him to do or say anything that could cause criticism. He was a child, & his moods & opinions could be influenced by the last person expressing himself forcefully."[5] Like Livy, she learned to cope with his "titanic rages, which could be quickly—tactfully dissolved into peaceful moods."[6] Where Livy's impulse had been to muzzle Twain's more extreme opinions, Isabel wished to release them. "More than once I said to SLC 'Why don't you let yourself go & write as you really feel?' He said it was too late!"[7]

Their relationship never took a romantic turn. Even in the privacy of her journals, Isabel referred to him as "Mr. Clemens" or "The King," and he referred to her as "Miss Lyon" or just plain "Lyon." Nevertheless, Isabel was an attractive younger woman, with a flirtatious side, and her living arrangement didn't permit a private life beyond her job. A bohemian in disguise, she had a daring, subversive streak. When she found out that Twain's friend Poultney Bigelow was having an adulterous affair, she wondered, "Why don't I condemn the man or woman who loved outside of his or her marriage bond? Most unmarried women of my age do condemn."[8] Isabel dwelled on men who remarried. "I've known of several men who have married several times," she wrote in her journal. "They couldn't live without the companionship & sympathy of a woman."[9]

During this rose-colored period, Isabel's adoration of the King spilled over to Clara, whom she puffed up in such overheated prose that it almost sounded as if she had a crush on her. "Oh, Santissima—you who make a shrine of any house you inhabit—you who are a gift to every one who falls under your sweet thrall—Oh Santissima."[10] It was similar to the extravagant language she employed about the King.

Of course, Clara was stuck in a sanitarium and barred from seeing her family, leaving few opportunities to clash with Isabel. Her breakdown had been so total that not until February 1905 was she allowed to sit up and read—she then asked for Plato, Byron, and *The Iliad*—and was permitted brief walks. When Clara had an urgent appendectomy that May, an anxious Twain was allowed to visit her and, according to Isabel, "found her plump & Oh so pretty."[11] Visiting restrictions were briefly lifted for Clara, who saw her father daily as she recovered, and she told

"AN ARTIST IN MORALS AND INK"

him of the comforts she had discovered in religion. When she reverted to her rest cure sequestration, Twain promised that he would not shake her newfound faith: "I hope I shall be spared the crime of violating its sanctities and impairing its solaces and comforts as I did in your mother's case—almost the only crime of my life which causes me bitterness now. (I must not dwell upon this subject.)"[12] The appendectomy presented yet another hurdle to her singing when a throat specialist told her she couldn't sing a note for four months, forming part of a pattern of vocal setbacks that would undercut her career.

For the summer of 1905, Twain sought to escape 21 Fifth Avenue and find rustic peace in a community of collegial souls. "This family is not rightly constructed for city life," he stated, and found exactly the right spot in Dublin, New Hampshire, in the state's southwest corner, a green, hilly region with houses tucked deep in the woods.[13] He knew two artists who summered there, Abbott Thayer and George de Forest Brush—"Any place that is good for an artist in paint is good for an artist in morals and ink," he observed—and he had always gravitated to artist colonies. The town brimmed with eminent figures, including Thomas Wentworth Higginson, the author and friend of Emily Dickinson; Raphael Pumpelly, the head of the U.S. Geological Survey in New England; and Interior Secretary Ethan Allen Hitchcock.[14] These were well-to-do people who shied away from the vulgar nouveaux riches in Gilded Age watering holes such as Newport and Saratoga Springs, preferring a more sedate, cultivated crowd.

In March, Jean and Katy hunted houses in Dublin and found a superb place, Lone Tree Hill, owned by the Boston writer Henry Copley Greene. A prime piece of real estate, it sat high on a hill with wide-angle views of Mount Monadnock as it rose above a deep, plunging valley. The vista encompassed large swatches of New Hampshire and Vermont, and was loaded with literary lore. Thoreau had tramped up Monadnock on a walking trip, while he and Emerson had both composed poems inspired by the mountain. Like a landscape painter, Twain enjoyed writing word portraits of the shimmering panorama—"the billowy sweep of remote great ranges . . . soft and blue and unworldly to the horizon fifty miles away."[15] It was an ideal spot for Twain, who could choose to be sociable or solitary. He liked the extreme privacy of houses shrouded by woods with easy access on fine roads to other houses.

Isabel and Jean relocated there in early May—Twain lingered behind to deal with Clara's appendectomy—and Isabel wrote poetically of the view of distant hills and the exquisite objects in the house. A figure from the Hartford days, the coachman, Patrick McAleer, was imported to work around the house. Bathed in sunlight, Jean and Isabel went out picking violets together. At this juncture, the two were constant companions, with no sense of discomfort on either side. They hiked together; read aloud to each other. "Dear Child that she is, such a complex nature & yet so entirely simple . . . there is a power in that young nature," Isabel said.[16]

We have Jean's diary from that summer and know the complete measure of her sadness. After she had a seizure, she could perceive her father's difficulty in handling it. "Unfortunately he saw that I wasn't well & got terribly upset about it. He calmed down later."[17] It was her mother who had taken upon herself the burden of her condition, and Jean now mourned her loss. In early June, on the eve of the anniversary of Livy's death, she asked Isabel to play Chopin's funeral march on the Orchestrelle, brought up from the city, unleashing a storm of emotion inside her. "The Chopin always brings back that last awful night so clearly and then, those few days when I was permitted to sit quietly on the sofa by the window & read or study, while poor, patient, suffering little Mother tried to rest, eternally propped up in a sitting posture, with her tired little back almost raw, through Miss Sherry's carelessness. What a blessing that she was released!" Jean knew that she had luckily been spared the nursing duties, which fell on Clara, but she had lost precious time with her mother. "I never knew her; & I might have! Fortunate and at the same time most unfortunate spider!"—Jean's nickname for her older sister.[18] Livy's death had seemed more sudden to Jean because she had been kept so distant.

"AN ARTIST IN MORALS AND INK"

A subdued Twain spent the death anniversary working, doubtless fearing his own emotions. He had always sentimentalized his past, but now, when glimpsing it through the prism of a doleful present, he was overcome by an even more extreme nostalgia. When an old companion invited him to Reno, Nevada, to reminisce about the good old days, Twain, in reply, rattled off an affectionate list of Nevada desperadoes, members of what he called the "crimson discipleship . . . Those were the days!—those old ones. They will come no more. Youth will come no more. They were so full to the brim with the wine of life; there have been no others like them. It chokes me up to think of them."[19] Who can blame Twain for such sentiment? He could now count a dead son, a dead daughter, a dead wife, a daughter in a sanitarium, and an epileptic daughter at home. The wonder is that he didn't drop dead from sheer sadness. Mark Twain had given the world laughter and now had gotten only misery in return.

Twain could never let go of Livy, who enjoyed the one sure form of immortality: she survived in dreams that were intensely expressive. While in Dublin, Twain dreamed of Livy dressed all in black and "sitting up in my bed (here) at my right & looking as young & sweet as she used to do when she was in health." Livy asked for his sister's name and he scribbled "Pamela" on a pad. "The conviction flamed through me that our lamented disaster was a dream, & this a reality. I said, 'How blessed it is . . . it was all a dream, only a dream!' She only smiled & did not ask what dream I meant, which surprised me. She leaned her head against mine & I kept saying, 'I was perfectly sure it was a dream; I never would have believed it wasn't.' "[20] This loving dream exerted such hallucinatory power over his mind that, upon awaking, he didn't know if he had indeed been dreaming, confirming his deeply held conviction that the dream world could be no less substantial than the waking world.

As the Dublin summer passed, Clara seemed to rally in her rest cure in Norfolk, Connecticut, under the supervision of Dr. Edward Quintard, and slept normally for the first time in a year. Able to sing and play the piano again, she projected a concert tour that winter; the doctors even granted her a July visit from her father and sister. At the same time, Twain knew how entrenched her depression was and how tentative was her recovery. At one point, when the flow of Clara's letters dried up, Twain commented to Muriel M. Pears: "It is one of those intervals that come in nervous prostration when a whole year's progress vanishes in a week & the patient work must all be done over again."[21] For all her adoration of Clara, Isabel descried a "tragic something hanging near" her that would drop its full load of darkness on her someday.[22]

Only Isabel was privy to the secrets of both Clemens daughters. On the surface, Jean seemed to have a comparatively happy summer. She brushed up on her French, German, and Italian, and hiked and birdwatched to her heart's content, while also typing for her father and driving him to suppers. "Jean is in fine strength," an upbeat Twain reported, and "does a deal of wholesome driving & horsebacking."[23] She applied herself to her woodworking hobby with discipline and passion. She found a new circle of friends, the children of Abbott Thayer and George de Forest Brush, who were nearly a decade younger, perhaps reflecting her feeling that she had sacrificed her youth to epilepsy and that many women her age—twenty-five—were already married.

Behind the scenes, Isabel witnessed Jean's many seizures and had to monitor their frequency and severity—the melancholy service Livy once performed. "Jean wasn't well today," Isabel wrote in a typical journal entry. "She went . . . to her study but came back weary & dazed."[24] Or: "Jean not well—3 attacks. One at 11:30–1:20—& 5:30 very droopy all day."[25] Isabel was not the ideal person to assume this solemn responsibility. She was herself high-strung, suffered from headaches, and was full of phobias. When a squirrel ran across the roof of her room one night, she awakened "with a terrible clatter of fear in my brain" and couldn't get back to sleep.[26] A flutter of moth wings could set her heart racing with fear.

Bereft of Clara, Twain leaned enormously on Isabel, telling his daughter, "*I think a very great deal of Miss Lyon.*"[27] In handling his correspondence, Isabel enjoyed perfect pitch. Despite his total reliance on her, Isabel still had to skimp to make ends meet and made 172 pincushions that summer to supplement her income. Perhaps aware that Isabel was underpaid, Twain devised a plan that might earn her some money: she would one day publish his "Letters" along with Jean and Clara, gathering his extensive correspondence with Twichell, Howells, and others. Psychologically speaking, this was a major step, for it certified Isabel's status as a family member on a par with Twain's two daughters. By fall, Twain had dropped Jean from the plan and would have Clara oversee the project, with Isabel performing the bulk of the legwork.

In the Hartford days, before bankruptcy struck, Twain had produced much of his best writing during summer vacations at Quarry Farm. Now, at Dublin, he felt as if he had recaptured some of that same old spirit. In five weeks' time he cranked out thirty-one thousand words of a new book, *Three Thousand Years Among the Microbes,* and stood amazed at his output. "I am ashamed to say what an intolerable pile of manuscript I ground out."[28] Isabel noted the sparkle in his eyes, the new vitality animating his step. "The flush of a girl in his cheeks, and oh the lustre of his hair. It is too terribly perishably beautiful."[29] As she listened to him read aloud from his manuscripts in the evening, her rapture over this privileged intimacy only grew.

The book idea had germinated since 1883, when Twain confided to his notebook, "I think we are only the microscopic trichina concealed in the blood of some vast creature's veins and it is that vast creature whom God concerns Himself about and not us."[30] Now he devised the autobiography of a man who, through experimental error, is transformed into a cholera germ named Huck that inhabits a bald old tramp named Blitzkowski. It is another story of a man torn loose from his past, which seems so distant, next to present misery, that it takes on the aura of a dream. Twain pretends that the narrative had been written by a microbe seven thousand years earlier and "Translated from the Original Microbic By Mark Twain."[31] The conceit was a Swiftian one: that the body of the tramp appeared to the microbe a wondrous world of vast mountains and oceans, rivers and lakes. It was another way of spotlighting the vanity of the human race, which took on a cosmic self-importance it didn't deserve.

The manuscript is full of marvelous set pieces: how the cholera germ narrator "loved all the germ-world—the Bacilli, the Bacteria, the Microbes . . . I was the germiest of the germy,"[32] and how the tramp's body contained "upwards of a thousand republics in our planet, and as many as thirty-thousand monarchies."[33] The microbes are Lilliputians, and the humans, by comparison, Brobdingnagians. When the microbial narrator informs two of his fellows, Lemuel Gulliver and Louis XIV, that the Earth contains 1.5 billion human beings, "There was [a] general explosion of laughter, of course, and Lem Gulliver said—'Why, my land, it doesn't even amount to a family—I've got more blood-kin than that, myself!'"[34] Huck evokes the incredible size of a human being by describing how "his mere umbrella would spread from your North Pole far and away below your Equator, and hide two-thirds of your wee Planet entirely from sight!"[35] The microbes think this is wild invention.

Oddly enough, even though Twain said that he had not enjoyed writing a book so much in twenty years, he never finished it after five weeks of nonstop effort, punctuated by one day of rest: June 5, the anniversary of Livy's death. The strange thing is not that he stopped, but that he never resumed it after such frenzied composition; the manuscript wouldn't be fully published until 1967. Isabel had thrilled to the nightly installments—"Oh he is such a marvel, such a marvel"—and in short order was turning herself into an expert on his work, reading first *The Gilded Age*, then *The Innocents Abroad*. After a lifetime of exposure to their father, Clara and Jean had grown inured to his writings and his ways, while Isabel experienced the reverence of a newcomer. She closely observed Twain's manner and recorded his tics with an acolyte's attentive eye. When Twain wrote something amusing, she said, he would "knock out the ashes of his pipe with Sharp quick taps," whereas when he wrote something contemplative, he would "knock out the pipe ashes in slow deliberate dreamlike fashion."[36]

That summer, Twain produced a lovely tribute to Livy in an unexpected form: a diary supposedly authored by Eve. As far back as 1893, Twain had tinkered with versions of a diary written by Adam, our "celebrity ancestor," and published extracts from it in *Harper's Monthly Magazine* in April 1901.[37] When he published *Extracts from Adam's Diary* in book form in 1904, he facetiously claimed they were "translated from the original MS," embellished "with photographic reproductions of the original Diary carved on stone."[38] In part, the story served as a vehicle for Twain to take sly swipes at religion, as when Adam observes irreverently of God's creating the week: "I believe I see what the week is for; it is to give time to rest up from the weariness of Sunday."[39] The expulsion from the Garden of Eden is uproariously funny. When Eve begins to converse with the snake, Adam reflects, "I am glad, because the snake talks, and this enables me to get a rest." When Eve brings him forbidden apples, he cannot resist; "I was obliged to eat them, I was so hungry. It was against my principles, but I find that principles have no real force except when one is well fed." When they are expelled from the Garden, Adam strikes a poignant note that anticipates *Eve's Diary:* "I find [Eve] is a good deal of a companion. I see I should be lonesome and depressed without her, now that I have lost my property."[40] The conclusion pays homage to womankind—and implicitly to Livy—when Adam declares, "It is better to live outside the Garden with [Eve] than inside it without her."[41]

When it came to writing the much more affecting *Eve's Diary,* Twain revised portions of Adam's diary, then alternated portions with Eve's narrative, giving her an unspoken "text" to address. He completed the writing in six days in July 1905, with Isabel cheering him on. "The 'Eve's diary' is beautiful. Mr. Clemens has made her such a lovable creature & so innocent & so human."[42] Twain informed Clara that "Miss Lyon says she reminds her of you all the time."[43] In fact, Twain condensed traits of *all* the Clemens women into Eve, especially Livy. In his portrait of Eve's fidelity to the flawed Adam, he gracefully compliments his late wife, who had stuck by him loyally despite his highly fallible nature, while Eve's delight in the animal kingdom is reminiscent of his daughters, who adored all creatures, domestic and wild.

The portrait of Eve that emerges in *Eve's Diary* is an idealized one of womanhood as soft, beautiful, and gentle, while men are rough and aggressive. Eve would happily put stars in her hair, while Adam is earthbound and blind to natural beauty. Eve loves to be with Adam and hear him talk, but he banishes her into the rain—"it was my first sorrow"—and he comes across as a comical dolt who only wants to build things and gorge himself on melons and grapes.[44] When the narration switches to Adam's voice and he describes Eve's beauty, Twain gives us the archetypal girl-woman that tantalized him his entire life. Eve has an athletic young body and is "lithe, slender, trim, rounded, shapely, nimble, graceful."[45] Twain has affectionate fun with Eve's indiscriminate love of animals—so much like that of Jean's—as when Eve wants to welcome home a brontosaurus. "She believed it could be tamed by kind treatment and would be a good pet; I said a pet twenty-one feet high and eighty-four feet long would be no proper thing to have about the place."[46] As she rides on the backs of tigers, leopards, and elephants, Eve enjoys a carefree harmony with the animal kingdom.

With Eve, Mark Twain re-creates the sensations of childhood, when everything seems magically fresh, and Eve shows the innocent logic of a child. At first, she lives in a state of grace, imagining that the purpose of life is "to search out the secrets of this wonderful world and be happy and thank the Giver of it all for devising it."[47] Her love for Adam seems sufficient recompense for losing paradise. No proto-feminist, she exhibits a powerful, unconditional love for Adam. Whatever Adam's behavior, Eve says, "I would work for him, and slave over him, and pray for him and watch by his bedside until I died."[48] She deems her basic nature and Adam's to be inborn and immutable, and prays that she will die before Adam because life would be unendurable without him. At Eve's grave, Adam has the last word, paying tribute to her in an eloquent summation of Twain's own adoration for Livy: "Wheresoever she was, *there* was Eden."[49] Lest there be any doubt about the matter, Twain later wrote to Twichell, "Wherever Livy was, that was my country."[50] The vision of love presented in *Eve's Diary*—of woman enduring love for her chosen man, no matter the consequences—is exactly the one that Twain articulated to Sue Crane right after Livy's death. "Yes, she did love me; & nothing that I did, no hurt that I inflicted upon her, no tears that I caused those dear eyes to shed, could break it down, or even chill it. It always rose again, it always burned again, as warm & bright as ever."[51]

Twain finished *Eve's Diary* with an exhilarating flourish, striding up and down the porch of the Dublin house and gazing at the hills and the sky. "Eve's diary is finished," he told Isabel. "I've been waiting for her to speak, but she doesn't say anything more." Twain shipped off the Adam and Eve diaries to Frederick A. Duneka at Harper & Brothers, hoping the two would be published together in book form, something that never came to fruition. In December, *Eve's Diary* came out in the Christmas issue of *Harper's Magazine* before appearing in book form.

Isabel also held a very traditional view of men and women. When Twain spoke at the Dublin Lake Club, clad all in white, Isabel, transported, wrote that "the flame of life burns so strongly in men with their brain forces, & their magnetism, & so I was uplifted & borne away up over all the others, and just didn't care about anything, only to see how people appreciated" Twain.[52] Isabel later insisted that she had never loved Twain, but such dizzying passages in her journals and her exalted sense of him as a superior being make it hard to believe that. More than anything, the lonely Twain needed an audience, and Isabel—curious, smart, bookish—was perfect for the job, treasuring his musings, reveries, and even his tirades. In a remarkably short span, he had come to rely on her literary judgment, although she was too gushing in her admiration for his work and lacked Livy's critical knowledge of him as a writer.

During that productive summer of 1905, Twain devoted time to his last unfinished novel, *No. 44, The Mysterious Stranger*. No piece by Twain possesses a more complicated history or exists in more versions than this enigmatic fable, which he nearly completed that July, having burned much of the earlier versions. *No. 44* traces its origins back to 1897, when Twain first dabbled in a novel titled *The Chronicle of Young Satan*, set in eighteenth-century Austria. That version reflected his comic fancy that he enjoyed a special relationship with Satan.

By July 1905, Twain had revamped and completed most of *No. 44*,

The Mysterious Stranger, which remained unfinished and was only published posthumously. There would eventually be four unfinished stories based on the *Mysterious Stranger* theme. The dreamlike tale was now set in an Austrian village in 1490. A mysterious, penniless boy of sixteen or seventeen appears, introduces himself as No. 44, and sets to work in a print shop, with the story narrated by the obtuse, gullible August Feldner. The town of Eseldorf—"Assville" in German—is a medieval version of Hannibal, a paradise for boys, but steeped in religious orthodoxy. In a searing portrait of religious intolerance, the town is terrorized by Father Adolf, a religious zealot. August Feldner and No. 44 are printer apprentices, although the Church considers the printing press dangerous since it can foster independent thinking. Like Huck Finn, No. 44 is an outcast, dirty and ragged, but pure at heart and possessed of supernatural powers, including the ability to read people's minds and communicate with Feldner via mental telepathy.

When No. 44 is bullied by other printers, he bears his torment with Christ-like humility. Twain condemns the conformity of the townspeople, who are too cowardly to protest cruelty or show sympathy for the magical boy. While Feldner tries to rescue No. 44 with Christianity, there is more true religion in this heathen boy than in the overtly religious townspeople. Twain seems to be saying that if a Christ-like figure appeared in the world, he would be shunned by people professing to be Christians. No. 44 dies, then comes back from the dead. If he has risen Christ-like, Twain gives him a personality of boyish delight, not solemnity. He is also a messenger from the future because he knows about America's creation. He becomes the mouthpiece for many of Twain's pet theories, lecturing August Feldner on how he is composed of two selves, a Workaday-Self and a Dream-Self. He also speaks for Twain when he says, "I have known the [human] race a long time, and out of my heart I can say that I have always felt more sorry for it than ashamed of it."[53] In his farewell scene with Feldner, No. 44 asserts that life is nothing but a dream. "Strange, indeed, that you should not have suspected that your universe and its contents were only dreams, visions, fictions!"[54] For all its fascinating metaphysical speculations and flights of fancy, *No. 44,*

"AN ARTIST IN MORALS AND INK"

The Mysterious Stranger ultimately sags beneath the weight of Twain's grievances, obsessions, and dogmatic opinions.

Toward the end of that Dublin summer, Twain wrote a short story, "A Horse's Tale," that showed his regard for animal welfare, a sensitivity shared with his daughters. When riding with him in carriages, people noticed that Twain bristled if a horse was whipped or driven hard. And he was second to none as a cat lover. By 1899 he had become a crusader for animal rights and a supporter of the Anti-Vivisection Society in London, his passion unmistakable. Of animals used for scientific experiments, he wrote: "They have been boiled, baked, scalded, burnt with turpentine, frozen, cauterized; they have been partly drowned and brought back to consciousness to have the process repeated; they have been cut open and mangled in every part of the body and have been kept alive in a mutilated state for experiments lasting days or weeks."[55] In 1903, to gratify Jean, he published "A Dog's Tale" in *Harper's Magazine*, which was then published in pamphlet form by the London Anti-Vivisection Society. It told the sentimental tale of a loyal dog who saved her family's baby from a fire only to have her puppy killed in a scientific experiment.

While in Dublin, Twain received an appeal from the actress Minnie Maddern Fiske, who had enjoyed "A Dog's Tale" and pleaded with him to write a similar story to aid her campaign to stop violence inflicted on horses at Spanish bullfights. Twain embraced the idea, hoping his story would stimulate reform among young Spaniards. The star of "A Horse's Tale" is a saddle horse named Soldier Boy, who has served Buffalo Bill and the U.S. Cavalry, and is full of vanity, charms, and foibles. "My mother was . . . of the best blood of Kentucky, the bluest Blue-grass aristocracy . . . My father was a bronco."[56] Soldier Boy is attached to Fort Paxton, where General Alison, the commandant, is caring for his nine-year-old orphaned niece Cathy, who has come from Spain and worships animals. She has exactly Susy's temperament—passions that flare up and fade out quickly—and falls in love with Soldier Boy. Perhaps no less significantly, Cathy shows an androgynous streak, mingling traditional male and female traits: she loves dolls and "girl-plays," but also drums and fifes and soldiering on the frontier.[57] "A Horse's Tale" ends with

Cathy back in Spain, where she attends a bullfight and recognizes Soldier Boy as a broken-down nag in the ring. As she watches in horror, "the bull had ripped him open and his bowels were dragging upon the ground and the bull was charging his swarm of pests again."[58] In a flash, the heroic Cathy swoops down on the ring, where Soldier Boy is dying, and before she knows it, the bull has gored her to death as well. At first Twain didn't fully fathom his motivation in depicting her, but later explained, "The heroine is my daughter, Susy, whom we lost. It was not intentional—it was a good while before I found it out."[59] When the story ran in *Harper's Magazine* in August and September 1906, Twain urged the magazine to reproduce Susy's portrait as an illustration.

Not surprisingly, the darkness of his later years continued to swamp Twain's fiction, baffling many readers who still associated him with charming boyhood romps. After the story appeared in *Harper's*, a Connecticut woman named Lillian R. Beardsley wrote and beseeched him not to "write any more such heart-breaking stories." If she had known what would happen to Soldier Boy, she said, she would never have read the story. "You used to write so differently. The note of pathos, of tragedy, of helpless pain creeps in, now and more insistent. I fancy life must have taken on its more somber colours for you, and what you feel is reflected in what you write. You belong to all of us—we of America—and we all love you and are proud of you, but you make our hearts ache sometimes."[60] Twain replied that sometimes he needed to wring people's hearts to get them to think, but he, too, must have reflected on the trying circumstances of his life, now refracted through the darker lens of his writing.

CHAPTER FIFTY-THREE

"The Swindle of Life"

Despite the healthy Dublin environment, the Clemens family was still badgered by the nemesis of ill health. After his Norfolk visit, Twain had hoped Clara could resume her vocal training in earnest, but the following month she needed a sinus operation that debilitated her. She could, however, return to 21 Fifth Avenue. Struggling with gout, Twain looked white and pasty as he strove to revive himself with a diet of thin gruel and Plasmon. "If I drink coffee it gives me dispepsia" [sic], he protested to Rogers; "if I drink wine it gives me the gout; if I go to church it gives me dysentery."[1] Before leaving Dublin, Jean suffered two epileptic attacks in September and another two in October, with Isabel characterizing the one on October 20 as "unusually long and severe . . . Her malady seems to be increasing in violence."[2]

Before leaving New Hampshire that October, Twain delighted in the warm and brilliant autumn landscape displayed outside his window, "a bewildering intoxication of color—why, it is a joy to be alive! There is no place like Dublin."[3] What detracted from the moment's perfection was the tragic aura gathering around Jean. As her attacks intensified, her opinions of people became harsher, something noticed by both Twain and Isabel. "Some youngsters here for dinner & a romp," Isabel reported. "Jean in a turmoil & a nest of tempers because those young guests didn't assemble in invited sequence."[4] Jean's judgmental streak had strengthened since the advent of her epilepsy in the 1890s, and Twain tried to figure out how to correct it. "Miss Lyon & I are persuading her to look out for and *report* the *attractive* points of the people she meets, & ignore the others," Twain confided to Clara. "She can learn to be uncensorious."[5] Jean's faultfinding with human beings stood in sharp contrast to her genuine affection for the animals she encountered in the woods on her rides and hikes.

Clara and Katy Leary arrived back at 21 Fifth Avenue in October, followed by Twain, Isabel, and Jean in November. Jean had clashed with an Italian servant named Ugo, prompting Twain to issue an unusual directive to Clara: "Clara dear, assume full & *sole* authority in the house. Require that all complaints be brought to you—none to any one else. Allow no one but yourself to scold or correct a servant. All of this is for Jean's sake, & to keep her out of trouble—particularly with Ugo."[6] This message, though meant to forestall problems with Jean, not Isabel, raised an awkward question left maddeningly unresolved after Livy's death: Who exactly ran the household and had final say?

If upset by Jean's behavior, Twain was a loving parent who struggled to make proper allowances for his daughter. He wrote tenderly about her, telling Clara how he tried "to keep constantly in mind that she is heavily afflicted by that unearned, undeserved & hellish disease, & is not strictly responsible for her disposition & her acts when she is under its influence (if there is ever a time when she is really free from its influence—which is doubtful)."[7] In desperation, Jean pinned her hopes on a surgical procedure that might relieve her symptoms. Meanwhile, she nursed many regrets: that she had never mourned properly for Susy; that she had never really known her mother; that Clara had grown cold and distant; that her father was easily dismayed by her illness; and, most of all, that she felt unwanted by men despite her classic beauty and what her father labeled her "finely chiseled statuesque face."[8]

On the night of November 1, 1905, Clara greeted Isabel and Jean when they returned to 21 Fifth Avenue. "In a minute her sweet black figure appeared in the doorway," noted Isabel upon seeing Clara. "I had not seen her for more than a year."[9] That month, with the entire Clemens clan reunited for the first extended period since Livy's death, it was not clear how the household would function without Livy's beneficent pres-

"THE SWINDLE OF LIFE"

ence. Jean's epilepsy introduced a volatile element that nobody could control, and Twain and Isabel felt overwhelmed by it. By default, the task of dealing with it fell to Isabel, who had no training as a nurse, much less as a surrogate mother. And she had taken on these extra duties without any commensurate raise in pay.

For years, Twain and Livy had adapted their lives to Jean's illness, going to Sweden then to London so she could continue her treatment. He thought Jean's disease and its "awful convulsions" had worn out "her gentle mother's strength with grief and watching and anxiety, and caused her death, poor Livy!"[10] Perhaps with such memories in mind, Twain abdicated paternal responsibility for Jean and delegated it to Isabel, even though it formed no part of her official duties and wasn't something a hired secretary should have had to do. Complicating matters was that Isabel didn't enjoy easy relations with Jean, as she did with Clara. For Isabel, Jean's erratic moods and violent seizures spoiled the otherwise idyllic existence she enjoyed with Twain.

In November, Isabel's journals recorded a rising trend of seizures for Jean, including three in one day on November 20. Then, in December, Clara, seemingly restored to normal health, suffered a serious relapse and was bedridden, forcing her to cancel singing engagements. "Santissima is very very far from well," Isabel observed.[11] Both sisters now existed in fragile states, and the new radiators installed in the house after Twain's complaints the previous winter produced such fearful clanging that Jean and Clara had to sleep in their sitting rooms away from the noise. For his part, Twain did not adjust well to the frenetic Manhattan social life after Dublin's woodsy quiet. Always dreading that Jean might have an attack, he didn't invite her along on his social engagements, and she, of course, noticed her glaring exclusion.

For Isabel, the dream job had acquired a nightmarish edge. With all this angst bottled up in the Clemens household, Isabel spent a tearful forty-second birthday with her mother in mid-December. She was expected to be a strong pillar in the household, but she was becoming as emotionally frail as the others. "My brain is so brittle these days," she wrote. "I feel it could snap so easily."[12] Even as she suffered intense pressure—her journals are littered with cryptic asides about her precarious mental state—she became more involved in intimate family matters. She must have been highly flattered when Twain took her to the bank and gave her access to his safety deposit box, then lifted her spirits with a Christmas Day bonus deposited on her breakfast tray—things that would have tightened Twain's grip on her loyalty. But this job was testing her strength in ways she could not possibly have foreseen.

The day after Christmas it grew evident that Jean's condition was lurching toward an unavoidable crisis: she was sick all day without the usual closure of a climactic seizure. A week later, she endured another infernal day: three seizures stretching from late morning to early evening, with stress and anxiety likely exacerbating her condition. As she was torn apart by illness, Isabel watched with sympathy, but also alarm. "Jean is not well," she wrote. "Not only has her malady increased, but her whole physical condition is at a low ebb, and the child calls for great waves of love from those of us who care."[13] Having seen Jean as moody and willful, Isabel now saw her fiery spirit briefly fade away. "In these last few days a sadness has settled over her, a gentleness that is pitiful, and you long for the masterful young creature whose powerful moods spread consternation, but always back of the moods there are an individuality, a frankness of a very high order."[14]

Jean knew she was "wretchedly ill," and in her misery could lash out at people. On January 11, she wrote a revealing letter to her Dublin friend Nancy D. Brush, whose artist father had stopped by 21 Fifth Avenue but missed seeing Jean. Disappointed at having missed him, Jean wrote Nancy: "I sat right down and wrote what to him may have sounded like a rude, or possibly even an impertinent letter. It was not meant in such a way, of course . . . However, I know that I am pretty violent at times when I feel strongly and I did feel very strongly when I was writing that letter, so it may not have sounded as it was intended to sound. Your father's answer seemed to me a trifle chilly, which distressed me."[15]

Jean's unsettled state sent out signals of a deteriorating situation that warranted urgent medical intervention. Two days after writing to Nancy, Jean acted oddly while her father was reading aloud a manuscript. As

"THE SWINDLE OF LIFE"

Isabel wrote: "But oh, a disturbing element stopped it. (A mood of Jean's.)"[16] A week later there followed a seizure so gruesome that Jean fell and badly burned her arm, face, and back on a radiator. Eager to improve Jean's mood when illustrations for "The Horse's Tale" arrived two days later, including pictures of Soldier Boy, Twain shuffled rapidly down the hall in slippers and dressing gown, but he and Isabel found Jean "only half aware."[17]

Then, on January 27, 1906, an episode occurred that had profound and lasting ramifications for the Clemens family. As Isabel described it: "This was a tragic day. I came in from a shopping expedition for Jean and others and when I went into her room for tea, she told me that a terrible thing had happened. In a burst of unreasoning rage she struck Katie [Leary] a terrible blow in the face . . . She described the wave of passion that swept over her as being that of an insane person . . . she had wanted to kill Katie."[18] Many years later, Isabel claimed there had been an earlier episode, on November 26, when Jean had been violent with Katy after suffering two seizures. In her journal, next to the second attack, Isabel had written "Katie," underlining the name twice. She added a line that confirmed that something traumatic had ensued. "I've been on my couch all day—weak-illish—some breath of life is gone."[19] Isabel later claimed that she had been warned by the family physician, Dr. Edward Quintard, "never to let Jean get between her and the door, and never to close the door."[20]

Some scholars have argued that Isabel, decades later, tampered with her diary to make Jean's behavior seem more murderous. They point to the fact that Katy Leary never mentioned these two incidents and continued caring for Jean. But the timing of the attacks, after a stretch of increasingly erratic behavior by Jean, seems far from implausible. The day after the January 27 attack, Jean had another pair of seizures. That Sue Crane rushed down from Elmira while Isabel went off to consult Dr. Quintard strengthens the case for something terribly disturbing afoot.

One scholar, Laura Skandera Trombley, has offered a hypothesis to explain Jean's behavior: that she suffered from a condition known as postictal psychosis, which can follow grand mal seizures. First, the patient is listless and confused, followed by an "interval of apparent normality," before the patient succumbs to a psychotic state that can include "confusion, visual and auditory hallucinations, and paranoid ideation." It is impossible to imagine that Jean attacked Katy Leary with cold-blooded malice, but her recent seizures may have led to fleeting, abnormal behavior. Another possibility is that Katy Leary, with no professional training, simply mishandled Jean after a seizure. A contemporary epilepsy expert, Dr. Orrin Devinsky, has noted that "the false association between epilepsy and aggressive behavior is one of the most damaging stigmas cast on people with epilepsy."[21] At the same time he advises caregivers in a recent book that "after the seizure is over, do not try to restrain the person. He or she may be confused and disoriented. Restraint may provoke agitation and a violent reaction."[22] The Clemens household was trying to care for Jean without proper supervision at a time when there were no antiseizure medications, and doctors' knowledge about epilepsy was limited.

An overlooked letter written by Jean to Nancy Brush gives insight into her frame of mind on January 27. After being badly burned on January 22, she said, she "had to stay in bed for ten days because I couldn't wear any clothes on my burned arm . . . I felt almost worse because I was so weak and unable to study, see any friends or do much of anything but sit in my room and read and feel most deadly melancholy."[23] It doesn't sound as if Jean could have done much damage with a burned arm, but the letter confirms that she had slumped into an abysmal depression. She also mentioned to Nancy how hard the doctors' prohibition of vigorous exercise was for her. "You know I am the kind of person who always wants to do a great deal, consequently when I was obliged to do *nothing* at all because my health could not be improved, the natural result was a feeling of anger and at times a desire to cry."[24] The days of enforced inactivity after being burned would only have amplified her anger.

In later years, Isabel related many stories about Jean's violent temper. "There were times when Jean's savageries [or savageness] disturbed . . . even terrified her father, just as her fine linguistic abilities & her ability to express herself charmed him."[25] She said that Jean's epileptic attacks

"THE SWINDLE OF LIFE"

"left her in savage moods, or in depressions . . . when her mind was trying to find itself again."[26] On another occasion, Isabel recalled Twain lying on the couch when Jean began to stroke him. "The shaking grew into a pulling & then a savage pounding of his chest. Mr. Clemens said gently, 'Now, Jean, I think that's enough. It ceases to be a mark of affection.' Later he said the look in Jean's eye was not comforting."[27] Jean herself knew that she had a sharp temper and referred to it in letters. To take but one example: In 1908 she was sharing a house in Gloucester, Massachusetts, with two sisters named Cowles and found their company insufferable. She said she had to "keep an iron grip on myself, or I should fly off the handle at almost any moment."[28] A month later, she said of the sisters: "I am boiling with helpless rage & if I could get at them, would probably strangle those Cowles monsters."[29] This is not to deny Jean's warmth, compassion, and kind heart, but only to say that her disease caused distortions in her personality. What is certain is that Isabel, only five feet tall, feared Jean and was unnerved by her moods as she cared for her.

Not until February 2, when Twain returned from a trip to Washington, did Isabel sit down and brief him on what had happened with Jean and Katy and her subsequent talk with Dr. Quintard. "The dreadfulness of it all swept over him as I knew it would and with that fiercest of all his looks in his face he blazed out against the swindle of life and the treachery of a God that can create disease and misery and crime . . . that men would be ashamed to create." He stared up at a wall portrait of little Jean, who had been an adorable child, with "angry, pitiful, helpless tears there—tears over the swindle of *her* life. Dr. Quintard is going to change her treatment, and they are going to give up Dr. Starr."[30]

On February 5, Isabel and Jean consulted a new doctor, Frederick Peterson, a distinguished specialist on epilepsy. That Twain assigned Isabel to escort Jean instead of going himself proved a decision of immense significance. Isabel was neither Jean's parent nor guardian, just an overworked secretary. Perhaps Twain felt, as a matter of self-protection, that he needed to keep some distance or he would be sucked into the maelstrom of Jean's illness. As Isabel noted, he "keeps away from anything that wrings his heart. He has too many speeches to make, too many people to see in these days & he must remain cheerful."³¹

Placing Isabel in charge was a decision that shaped the rest of Jean's life. Clara, still bedridden, was too consumed by her problems to offer much help. There was no one else to assume the caretaker role other than Isabel, who might have feared Twain's adverse reaction if she ruled out this dreaded task. By performing it, she inserted herself inextricably into the Clemenses' family life, taking on a motherly—indeed, a wifely—position for which she was poorly equipped.

As the first professor of psychiatry at Columbia University and the former head of the New York Neurological Society, Dr. Peterson at forty-seven was tall and handsome, and he seemed a superb choice of doctor. At a time when people with epilepsy were cruelly stigmatized, he had overseen the Craig Colony for Epileptics, near Rochester, New York, a residential facility founded to treat patients with dignity and allow them to lead rewarding lives. He had other credentials that would have endeared him to Twain: he was a published poet and an authority on Chinese poetry and art. Although epileptics had been victimized by a bogus mythology of being criminally insane, Dr. Peterson published a book in 1911, *Nervous and Mental Diseases,* in which he acknowledged that "acute mental disturbances" could follow epileptic seizures and that the patients "as a rule, have no knowledge of such acts." He added that "sudden wild, maniacal outbursts, in which the patient may be destructive and dangerous to others, are encountered, and these may terminate suddenly or be protracted for several days."³²

Dr. Peterson reacted cautiously to Isabel's visit, saying he would take on Jean's case only if he felt that he could benefit her. When he did so and gave Jean a tonic and some pills, her relief was wondrous. "The very next morning I felt like a different person!" she told Nancy Brush. "Well and strong and so full of life and high spirits that I wanted to whistle and dance the entire time."³³ Jean's life, alas, was always full of high hopes and subsequent disappointments. She went off to a resort in Lakewood, New Jersey, only to undergo a return of her seizures, including three on

"THE SWINDLE OF LIFE"

March 25, and Isabel found her ill and "quite pale" when she returned home.[34]

It is very hard for us to project ourselves into the pain and suffering of Jean Clemens. Her disease affected her memory and mental clarity and made her very self-conscious in company. One morning in May, she cited as a "remarkable" occurrence that she hadn't vomited after breakfast—her everyday experience. "Nobody not having my disease would be able to appreciate what it means to me to waken on a bright, beautiful morning and realize as soon as I am awake that my head is clear."[35] Conversely, the days of petit mal seizures would be dreadful beyond description. "I was wretchedly ill all day long," she wrote in July. "Of course there were short moments in between the absent-minded turns, when I was clear-headed, but they were very short and often, all during the entire day, the turns were very long. After supper I was desperately tired and exhausted, so much so . . . that I preferred not to see Father."[36]

CHAPTER FIFTY-FOUR

Pier 70

On November 30, 1905, Mark Twain turned seventy, and Colonel Harvey of Harper & Brothers threw a huge bash for him at Delmonico's, the opulent clubhouse for Gilded Age magnates. This was no minor-league affair: a forty-piece orchestra from the Metropolitan Opera House regaled 172 guests who sat amid gilt mirrors and potted palms for five hours of hearty toasts and tributes. Many snickered at the ceremony as a barefaced attempt by Harvey to promote his publishing empire, but Twain didn't seem to mind, telling Isabel that he "could live longer on one good compliment than most men could on a dozen square meals," and the evening delivered a much-needed fillip to his drooping spirit.[1] Newspapers noted that he had graduated from the ranks of a mere humorist to become "America's greatest student of human nature and common life."[2]

Twain was bowled over by the birthday tributes that poured in from British authors, including Arthur Conan Doyle, J. M. Barrie, G. K. Chesterton, Thomas Hardy, and Rudyard Kipling, who all wired congratulations. Helen Keller inquired: "And you are seventy years old? Or is the report exaggerated, like that of your death?"[3] At the dinner, William Dean Howells and George Washington Cable anointed Twain as the King. Among the guests were Willa Cather, Dorothy Canfield, and Emily Post. Also in attendance was Charles W. Chesnutt, the first Black writer to publish a short story in the *Atlantic Monthly*, who would keep a plaster bust of Twain in his library. In fact, every guest took home a foot-high bust of the author as a souvenir.

When Twain rose to speak, he had not shed his old touch, returning to his birth in 1835: "I hadn't any hair, I hadn't any teeth, I hadn't any clothes, I had to go to my first banquet just like that." Nobody had dared to compliment this infant. "Their opinions were all just green with prejudice, and I feel those opinions to this day . . . That was my cradle song, and this is my swan song, I suppose."[4] He noted that, at seventy, people always ask your secret of longevity, and you "explain the process and dwell on the particulars with senile rapture."[5] He attributed his lengthy life to exemplary health habits. "I have made it a rule never to smoke more than one cigar at a time . . . it has always been my rule never to smoke when asleep, and never to refrain when awake."[6] Twain ended with a poetic image of arriving at Pier 70, where you board "your waiting ship with a reconciled spirit, and lay your course toward the sinking sun with a contented heart."[7] This finale was both a crowd-pleaser and a tearjerker, and those present testified that all eyes glistened with emotion.

At a time of deep sadness at home, Twain was rejuvenated by this outpouring of love. On this seventieth birthday, Isabel declared, he was "only a young & beautiful 50."[8] Katy Leary, recalling how Twain ran up three steps at a time, said, "Nobody could believe Mr. Clemens was seventy years old . . . He didn't look or act old, and he never was, either."[9] On the day of the banquet, Clara, after seeing her father's quick movements and spontaneous laugh, thought, "Father is younger now than I have ever felt."[10] These household accolades were echoed in a newspaper description of Twain's youthful appearance. "His erect, supple, well-knit figure and springy step would be creditable to a man of forty. The clear, healthy pink and white of his complexion are unmarred by wrinkles. His hazel eyes are as keen and searching as ever."[11]

In baring his health secrets, Twain never mentioned Plasmon, the skim milk supplement that he had promoted as a panacea, a business venture that had ended with disappointment, rage, and lawsuits. At the outset, he had tried to waylay Henry Rogers, John D. Rockefeller, and Andrew Carnegie into backing American Plasmon and had projected booming sales that would sweep across America. In 1902 Twain had subscribed to $25,000 worth of shares from the company chief, Henry A. Butters. By the following year, he grew convinced that the company was "crooked, and has private schemes which will not bear the light."[12] It was the same sad farce Twain had experienced in other business ventures: he dreamed of riches only to discover that his partners were knaves or fools cheating him at every turn.

The general manager of American Plasmon, Howard E. Wright, had departed from the company in 1903 amid allegations of dishonesty and stock fraud. While in Florence, Twain retained a lawyer to redeem his investment from Henry Butters, a total of $32,500. "As soon as I get back," he warned, "we will pull Butters into Court, & I guess we can jail him. We will try, anyhow. And I will add [to] that libel, & see if he has grit enough to prosecute me."[13] Twain knew how to nurse a grudge and even took revenge against Butters in his fiction. When he wrote "Three Thousand Years Among the Microbes," he employed Butters's name for a "bucket-shop dysentery germ," and included a horse thief named Hank Butters in "A Horse's Tale."[14] As he waged his legal battle, Twain was assisted by the company secretary Ralph Ashcroft, a Liverpool native and son of an English minister, whom he esteemed as "truthful, honorable, careful, & as a bright & good business man & *very* efficient manager."[15] After many lawsuits and internecine battles, Twain heaped curses on Henry Butters as "easily the meanest white man, and the most degraded in spirit and contemptible in character I have ever known."[16] Aside from his investments with Rogers, Twain seldom entered into speculations that didn't end up in bitterness. As he sheepishly admitted to Rogers, American Plasmon was "one of those investments of mine that I am ashamed of, and would like to forget."[17]

For posterity, Mark Twain would be pictured as the man in the white suit, but he did not adopt this signature attire until 1906. He had always exhibited a special distaste for black, and when Livy donned a mourning dress after Jane Clemens died, he made her take it off. "Well, Livy, it was very sweet of you," he said, but "I never want to see you in black clothes."[18] At the opera, he envied women in their "delicate fabrics" and "beautiful colors," and was depressed by the sight of the men, somber as crows in black garb. "I would like to dress in a loose and flowing costume made all of silks and velvets, resplendent with all the stunning dyes of the rainbow, and so would every sane man I have ever known."[19] He memorably stated that men's dark suits accumulated so much dirt "you could plant seeds in them and raise a crop."[20] Though he had dressed in white linen during Quarry Farm summers, he knew he would offend propriety by wearing that color at winter gatherings in New York.

In her journal, Isabel recorded Twain's momentous change of heart in October 1906. "The King is filled with the idea of defying conventionalities & wearing his suitable white clothes all winter, so he has bidden me order 5 new suits from his tailor."[21] Katy Leary said he came to own fourteen white suits—one for each day of the week, with another seven at the cleaners. (He retained a gray suit or two for the road.) To flout tradition, he also sported green, pink, and lavender socks. What to make of this late-life conversion? It may have been his way of expelling the darkness that enfolded him after Susy's and Livy's deaths. It also advertised a clamoring for attention, a characteristic that can be traced back to his boyhood. He also believed it made a symbolic statement that he was "clean in a dirty world; absolutely the only cleanly-clothed human being in all Christendom north of the Tropics."[22] What he stressed most about the white clothing was that he had reached an age where he no longer truckled to conventional wisdom and didn't give a damn what people thought. He nicknamed his white outfit "my don'tcareadamsuit."[23]

The white suit, whether in serge or linen and slightly baggy at the ankles, became his trademark and yet another way that he gave birth to celebrity culture as an instantly recognizable personality. Nothing pleased him more than to strut down Fifth Avenue, all in white, and enjoy the gaze of spectators, who spotted him with pleasure. "I go out very frequently and exhibit my clothes," he explained to Clara. "Howells has dubbed me the 'Whited Sepulchre.' Yes, dear child, I'm a 'recognized immortal genius' and a most dissipated one too."[24] It wasn't long before people expected to see Twain with a mane of white hair and matching white suit, and they felt cheated if he showed up in dark clothes.

Twain knew that a significant component of his mythmaking would be to leave a record of his life for future generations. Already he had promised publication of his letters to Clara and Isabel, but what about his biography? Though an avid reader of history and memoirs, he had an enduring suspicion of the genre. "Biographies are but the clothes and buttons of a man—the biography of the man himself cannot be written."[25] Wanting to preserve his choicest anecdotes for his autobiography, he fended off a multitude of would-be biographers who descended on him. As early as 1887, he had forewarned Orion, "I hate all public mention of my private history, anyways. It is none of the public's business."[26] Still, it was only a matter of time before a biographer swooped down on his life, and that happened with a persistent pest named Will Clemens (no relation). "A man's history is *his own property* until the grave extinguishes his ownership in it," the famous Clemens lectured the obscure one and darkly hinted at legal peril if the man persevered with his project.[27] In private, an irate Twain expended satirical energy on Will Clemens, deriding him as "that singular tapeworm who seems to feed solely upon other people's intestines."[28] He had a lawyer keep an alert eye out for any Will Clemens publications. "Watch for advertisements of these books . . . He is a mere maggot who tries to feed on people while they are still alive."[29] Will Clemens was published by Bobbs-Merrill in Indianapolis, which Twain insisted on misspelling as the Bowen Merrill Company.[30]

Twain must have known he could keep a biography at bay for only so long. He basked in publicity, stirring up public curiosity even as he sought to rebuff it. He thought William Dean Howells would be the ideal biographer, but he declined the project. One possibility was a writer named Albert Bigelow Paine, who had first seen Twain sitting on a couch at The Players Club in December 1901. "I have no idea how long I stood there watching him. He had been my literary idol from childhood."[31] Five months later, he saw Twain at a reception and conversed with Livy and "felt the gentleness and beauty of her spirit."[32] Then, in 1904, Paine published *Thomas Nast: His Period and His Pictures,* a biography of the political cartoonist. Nast was well-known to Twain—he had tried to recruit him for a joint lecture tour in 1867. Twain granted Paine permission to quote letters that he had written to Nast. The next contact between the two men came at the Delmonico's dinner for Twain's seventieth birthday. Bedazzled by the celebration, Paine talked briefly with Twain and thanked him for the use of his letters to Nast. Then, seizing the opportunity, he sent him a copy of the biography, inscribed "with love and gratitude."[33] He had fantasized about doing Twain's biography but had little inkling of the machinery that he had now set in motion.

On January 3, 1906, Paine sat nearly opposite Twain at a Players Club dinner where Twain was being feted. Paine had learned from David Munro, an editor of the *North American Review,* that his Nast biography sat on Twain's bedside table and that Twain had pronounced it "damn good."[34] At the dinner, Paine sat beside the writer Charles Harvey Genung; when Paine commented on how spry Twain was at seventy, Genung urged him, "You are the man to do his biography."[35] These two remarks simmered in Paine's brain and led him to ask Twain boldly if he could stop by 21 Fifth Avenue to see him. When he did, Paine found Twain reclining in his massive oak bed, ready to hold court. At that meeting, in short order, Paine proposed himself as Twain's biographer, to which Twain retorted, "When would you like to begin?"[36] Paine had landed a very big fish—indeed, the Moby Dick of the literary world—with breathtaking speed. "It had all the atmosphere of a dream," Paine conceded.[37]

Paine had come to the world of biography by a circuitous route. As a boy in the Midwest, he had listened enraptured at eight as his parents read aloud nightly from the newly published *Innocents Abroad.* Starting out as a photographer in St. Louis at nineteen, he then moved to Fort Scott, Kansas, where he expanded into the photographic supply business. (He would continue to dabble in photography and snap candid photos of Twain.) His artistic ambitions led him to study guitar and art, memorize reams of poetry, and mail off short stories to eastern magazines. After

Harper's Weekly accepted a piece in 1895, he, his wife, and daughters moved to New York, where he joined the editorial staff of *St. Nicholas* magazine and produced literature for children and adults. The Thomas Nast biography elevated his standing in the literary firmament, and the Twain assignment would represent another giant step upward, one that he would jealously guard from potential intruders.

Twain had been experimenting again with dictating letters into recording cylinders, but Isabel found "something infinitely sad" about the voice reproduced, and the trial run was ended.[38] Paine suggested an excellent alternative: he would prompt Twain with questions about his life while a professional stenographer set down a verbatim transcript. Twain loved the idea. He was enchanted by his own voice and with good reason: he could speak in beautifully formed sentences, inflected with fine humor and just the right tang of irony. The interview sessions would serve a double purpose for Twain: not only would Paine have exclusive material for his biography, but the transcripts would provide the basics for Twain's own autobiography, which would take the form of an extended monologue. Twain jumped at Paine's suggestion and offered him an office to work in and access to a "trunkful or two" of manuscripts and letters—biographer's gold. "Whatever you need will be brought to you," said Twain. "We can have the dictation here in the morning, and you can put in the rest of the day to suit yourself. You can have a key and come and go as you please."[39] This arrangement betrayed remarkable trust in Paine, especially for a newly minted septuagenarian who had spent years erecting tall barricades against biographical interlopers.

On January 9, 1906, the first of 242 dictation sessions took place—half a million words would pour forth in all—when Paine arrived with Josephine Hobby, an experienced stenographer. Twain sat up in bed in his nightshirt, surrounded by smoking paraphernalia. According to Isabel, who had a front-row seat, Twain's cheeks flushed with color and his eyes sparkled as he narrated his early mining adventures in Nevada. "It's the greatest treat in the world to sit in the brown easy chair and watch that master of mine talk," wrote Isabel. "He was magical this morning."[40] The challenge for Paine, as for all future Twain biographers, was that

Twain was peerless at bending the truth. He had never been a stickler for details and he wasn't going to start now. The trick for Paine would be to strip away the embroidery and probe to the bottom of things. When Paine confronted him with contradictory facts, Twain would blink with incomprehension. "When I was younger I could remember anything, whether it happened or not," he said, "but I am getting old, and soon I shall remember only the latter."[41]

Paine was a conscientious biographer, and Isabel was hugely pleased as he took Twain's disorderly mass of papers and brought order to that "great chaos."[42] That August, Paine signed a contract for the authorized biography with Harper & Brothers on terms approved by Twain, who specified that it shouldn't interfere with the publication of his letters by Clara and Isabel. Paine's wife, Dora, would transcribe more than two thousand letters gathered from friends while Paine traveled to Hannibal and the western states, as well as to Europe and the Mideast, to interview Twain cronies and family members. Twain had no qualms about having a bowdlerized life. When he found out that Sam Moffett had provided Paine with old letters, he was upset and halted it. "I don't like to have those privacies exposed in such a way to even my biographer," he explained to Howells.[43] While regarding Twain as a great writer, Paine saw his subject clearly as "the supreme expression of the human being, with every human strength—and weakness."[44] He left many perceptive impressions of Twain's mercurial nature. "His likes and dislikes are erratic, quickly formed, and like railroad time-tables, 'subject to change without notice.'"[45] One day people would be in favor with Twain, inexplicably out the next.

Unfortunately, Paine committed the cardinal sin of any biographer: his relationship with Twain began to metamorphose from professional detachment to unstinting friendship. He described his close relationship to Twain thus: "It was my wish only to serve him; it was a privilege and an honor to give him happiness."[46] In December 1906, to the dismay of his wife and daughters, Paine moved into the Clemens residence and spent endless hours playing billiards with Twain. When his biography reached 1906, it would often sound like a rambling reminiscence of his own time with Twain. Paine studiously avoided the family intrigue swirling around his subject and saw himself as a sentry, guarding the Twain fortress from literary vandals. "I have no desire to parade the things [about Twain] he would wish forgotten." His aim, instead, was to "build a personality so impregnable" that Twain would "remain known as we know him, loved and honored through all time."[47] In the beginning, Isabel Lyon was his co-conspirator in the worshipful cult of Mark Twain, writing two weeks after the first dictation, "This morning Mr. Paine said such a beautiful thing about Mr. Clemens. Oh, he's the *King*—he's the *King* and it's so glorious to know he is crowned."[48] In time, Paine and Lyon would clash over access to Twain's letters as well as more personal matters.

———•———

For decades, Twain had meditated about an autobiography and struggled with the conundrum of how to be true to his heterodox views yet keep faith with loyal readers. As early as 1876, he had announced at a luncheon that he would someday write a searingly honest account of himself for posterity; Livy had laughed and responded that she would vet it for disagreeable content. Twain rebuffed her, saying, "*You* are not to edit it—it is to appear as it is written with the whole tale told as truly as I can tell it."[49] At intervals of three or four years, he would make a stab at dictating an autobiography, only to scrap it shortly thereafter. When Rudyard Kipling interviewed him in 1889 in Elmira, Twain scoffed that anyone could lay down the unvarnished facts in a memoir. "But in genuine autobiography, I believe it is impossible for a man to tell the truth about himself or to avoid impressing the reader with the truth about himself."[50] He told of urging an honest friend to compose an autobiography and "in every single detail of his life that I knew about he turned out, on paper, a formidable liar."[51]

By the turn of the century, Twain was convinced that nobody could tell the truth about himself, that even Samuel Pepys felt contemporaries peeking over his shoulder. As a result, he shifted emphasis from his own escapades to a "portrait gallery of contemporaries with whom he has come into personal contact."[52] He added a new wrinkle: that such a work would be published one hundred years after his death, so he need not fear "hurting [the subject's] feelings or those of his sons or grandsons."[53] Capitalizing on Twain's idea, Colonel George Harvey of Harper & Brothers proposed that Twain assemble a memoir to be published a hundred years hence, and Twain agreed to "grind out chapters" by dictating to Jean and then publishing magazine excerpts along the way.[54] No formal contract was then signed. Before the arrival of Paine and Hobby, Twain had dictated autobiography to Isabel Lyon, but she took down his words longhand, cramping his style. With Paine, Twain had an informed interlocutor, and with Hobby an efficient recorder.

Twain believed fervently that he had stumbled upon a new form of autobiography governed by the principle of free association (long before James Joyce's *Ulysses*). Inspired by a newspaper article that he had read or a story he had heard, his mind would jump freely from one subject to the next, so he would never be imprisoned by strict logic or linear chronology. He believed, as did Carl Jung, in a shadow self, the repressed side of a person. Twain wanted to get at that turbulent, unspoken life of the mind. He sought the mass of "any person that was hidden—it and its volcanic fires that toss and boil, and never rest, night nor day."[55] The central premise was that Twain would be spontaneous and uncensored, but he never lived up to his own expectations. It was already deeply ingrained in him to shape his image, and he was working with an authorized biographer who would deliver his preferred narrative. There was a patent conflict between his plan to tell the unexpurgated truth and his hopes for a carefully sanitized biography. He also had an instinctive tendency to improve any story. There was the further obstacle that Miss Hobby was rather prudish, and he found himself censoring certain passages in consequence. In the end, however, the real problem was that we can't speak the truth to other people because we can't speak the truth to ourselves.[56]

Conversation had long been Twain's most congenial form of expression. Having perfected the art of public speaking, he turned his autobiography into a tour de force of verbal dexterity. On every page, he displayed his verbal riches, his incomparable control of the English tongue, and the vast stores of information in his capacious mind, with humor embedded in almost everything. "What a dewy and breezy and woodsy freshness it has," an elated Twain told Howells.[57] For an hour or two each morning, clad in a silk dressing gown, he held forth from his Venetian bedstead—the closest the King came to a throne—while at other times he smoked and paced the floor, speaking in his slow, measured way. His spontaneous brilliance, Paine learned, was a bit of an illusion: he found memoranda Twain had written beforehand as he prepared for certain topics. Still, everyone who watched the waterfall of words agreed that it was something to behold, even Clara. "There was something supernatural in his ability to pour out thoughts that flowed in finished phrases . . . the gestures he naturally used to emphasize his speech, and the poses that belonged to his personality, turned such hours into dramatic experiences."

Paine quickly fathomed that Twain's anecdotes were so encrusted with invented details that they "bore only an atmospheric relation to history."[58] Yet for those willing to sift through his unreliable memories, the dictations included moving accounts of events that had affected him: the deaths of Henry and Langdon, Susy and Livy. Paine soon perceived that Twain was a man tortured by guilt. "More than once after such dictations he reproached himself bitterly for the misfortunes of his house . . . he blamed himself for the lack of those things which might have made Susy's childhood still more bright." Of Susy's biography of him, Twain said, "Oh, I wish I had paid more attention to that little girl's work. If I had only encouraged her now and then, what it would have meant to her." The remorse grew more severe when it came to Livy: "I always told her that if she died first, the rest of my life would be made up of self-reproaches for the tears I had made her shed . . . I have known few meaner men than I am . . . I doubt if any member of my family except my wife ever suspected how much of that feature there was in me."[59] The dictating sessions may have proven therapeutic, granting Twain a chance to air profound sorrows.

A paramount objective of the autobiography was for Twain to express thoughts on politics and religion that lay outside the mainstream of American society, and here he proved a veritable Vesuvius of gushing opinions. In late June 1906, he uttered an extended monologue about the God he believed in, the God of a universe so limitless that all "the other gods whose myriads infest the feeble imaginations of men are as a swarm of gnats scattered and lost in the infinitudes of the empty sky."[60] Twain's God is neither just nor unjust, kind nor unkind. He doesn't listen to prayers because he is remote, oblivious of trivial human concerns, indifferent to squabbles here on earth.

Then, quite illogically, Twain switched from this indifferent God to a blithely malicious one who inflicts perpetual pain upon earthly creatures. "In the case of each creature, big or little, He made it an unchanging law that that creature should suffer wanton and unnecessary pains and miseries every day of its life." He bemoaned the "contriving of elaborate tortures" for even the planet's meanest inhabitants.[61] In the end, the God he proposed seemed "a malignant master," who took no interest in earthly beings other "than to torture them, slay them, and get out of this pastime such entertainment as it may afford."[62] Twain thought the existence of heaven highly unlikely and hell almost certain. As for human beings, Twain viewed them as vain and deluded, mere automatons in a hellish universe, who dressed up their sorry plight with pretty pictures. He also had scores to settle with Charley Webster and a dozen others, whom he "flayed and mangled and mutilated . . . beyond the dreams of avarice."[63] Aware of having uttered "fearful things," Twain told Howells that his "heirs & assigns" would be "burnt alive" if his thoughts were printed before the hundred-year embargo expired.[64] Twain could never have said these things, even for a future audience, while Livy was alive, for she would have found his reflections too disturbing.

Twain possessed an ulterior motive in undertaking the autobiography. Always a militant on copyright extension, he had a brainstorm that whenever one of his works was approaching the end of its forty-year limit, he would introduce into it twenty thousand words from the autobiography, thus making a new book and extending its copyright. He also stood to make good money by selling excerpts. In August 1906, Colonel

PIER 70

Harvey persuaded Twain to publish sections in a newly revamped *North American Review,* and they ran from September 1906 through December 1907. Not surprisingly, in twenty-five short extracts, Harvey presented a cleaned-up version of Mark Twain without his vinegary comments on Christianity or American imperialism in the Philippines. The Twain he fashioned was tender and sentimental, reminiscing about Livy and Susy, or recollecting boyish antics in Hannibal, or triumphing over adversity. In other words, he resurrected the Mark Twain beloved by readers. But true to Twain's vision, the complete, unexpurgated version didn't start to appear until 2010, one hundred years after his death—exactly as planned.

CHAPTER FIFTY-FIVE

Angelfish

The death of Livy Clemens brought to the surface latent tendencies in her husband that, if not exactly concealed before, had been sublimated into more socially acceptable forms, and one was his attraction to teenage girls. As early as 1866 he had written, "Young girls innocent & natural—*I* love 'em same as others love infants."[1] In later years, he wrote, "Nothing else in the world is ever so beautiful as a beautiful schoolgirl."[2] He had been enamored of the teenage Laura Hawkins and Laura Wright, and when he met Livy was aroused by her girlish appearance—she seemed on the verge of womanhood—telling her, "It is such a darling face, Livy!—and such a darling little girlish figure—and such a dainty baby-hand."[3] Nobody in Hartford found anything odd when he started his Saturday Morning Club of teenage girls, and he boasted that of its many members, he was "the only male one they have ever admitted."[4] There were other iterations of this fascination with young women, including the somewhat older Juggernaut Club, where he again served as sole male member.

On the afternoon of December 26, 1905, Twain's attraction to teenage girls entered a startling new phase when he and Isabel attended a Carnegie Hall recital. Afterward he chatted with a fifteen-year-old girl, Gertrude Natkin, who recognized him and was eager to talk. Twain gratified her wish and spoke to her sweetly. The next day, Gertrude sent a note of thanks. "I am the little girl who loves you."[5] From 21 Fifth Avenue, Twain promptly replied, striking a mock-romantic tone, as if engaging in old-fashioned courtship. "It was very sweet of you, dear, to let me shake hands with you, that day; & mind, don't you forget to remember that you are to be just as sweet & dear *next* time, and shake *again*, you charming child. This from your oldest & latest conquest—SL Clemens."[6] However playful, there was a seductive tone at work here, a pseudo-chivalric voice suddenly leaping from his pen, and Gertrude adopted a lighthearted, flirtatious tone to match his own.

Twain wrote to her six times a month, for three months, discarding any inhibitions about expressing affection toward a teenage girl who was a complete stranger. "Aren't you the dearest child there is?" he told her in February. "I am perfectly sure of it. I was never surer of anything in my life . . . Indeed, yes, you are a dear, sweet, honest, unspoiled, adorable little maid, & I would trade you for a housefull [sic] of those gray-heads whom I have loved so long & so well."[7] Their relationship developed with absurd speed, a crazy version of love at first sight. Perhaps part of the fantasy for Twain was redoing his adolescence, only this time with the wit and confidence of fame and age. He sent his "winsome witch" romantic, rhymed couplets for Valentine's Day.[8] When he spoke at the Majestic Theater on March 4, he arranged seats for Gertrude and her parents, and Isabel noted how deeply he cared about her presence. His chief concern was "that Gertrude was there, 'that darling child.' We went in the stage door & for a very long time Gertrude didn't arrive. Mr. Clemens's look of disappointment made me heartsick and feebly I tried to find the child in that vast crowd."[9] Gertrude was "his dream grandchild," Twain said. "I shouldn't want a sweeter one, & there couldn't be a dearer one."[10]

Two weeks later, when Twain came down with a cold, Gertrude sent flowers and Twain responded with profuse gratitude. "*Aren't* you dear! Aren't you the dearest child there is? To think to send me those lovely flowers, you sweet little Marjorie. [His nickname for her, after the child writer Marjorie Fleming.] Marjorie! don't get any older—I can't have it. Stay always just as you are—youth is the golden time."[11] Twain gave away the game here: the girls weren't allowed to age and had to exist in a perpetual childhood, the Neverland of Peter Pan. Around this time, Twain befriended actress Maude Adams, and when he saw her playing Peter in

ANGELFISH

November 1905, he found the play enchanting. "It breaks all the rules of real life drama," he told reporters, "but preserves intact all the rules of fairyland, and the result is altogether contenting to the spirit."[12] The next month, when Gertrude turned sixteen, Twain told her: "So you are 16 to-day you dear little rascal! Oh, come, this won't do—you mustn't move along so fast . . . *Sixteen!* Ah, what has become of my little girl?" He was afraid to send her a kiss now, he declared, because it would come "within an ace of being improper!"[13] After all his overheated blather about how dear and perfect she was, Twain started writing to Gertrude less and less often, then cut her off abruptly. When she sent him birthday greetings, he replied coldly, "The same to you and good health and happiness SLC."[14] Clearly, growing old was the greatest crime for Twain, who never stopped to think how upsetting this about-face must have been for poor Gertrude.

As a speaker, Twain was making the rounds of female colleges and openly rejoiced in the company of the students. He knew how to present himself as a lovable old codger. When he spoke at Barnard College, he told Paine, "Girls are charming creatures. I shall have to be twice seventy years old before I change my mind as to that."[15] The day after his Barnard talk, while Isabel tended Jean, he went off for a ride with three Barnard students. Clearly Twain found nothing dark or shameful about these liaisons, admitting, "I have the college-girl habit."[16] He was deliriously happy when he addressed a Vassar benefit and mingled with five hundred college girls, almost all "young and lovely, untouched by care, unfaded by age."[17] The next day, the *World* ran a story, "Mark Twain Was Wreathed in Girls," and quoted his announcement that henceforth in his lectures, "I shall only talk to audiences of college girls. I have labored for the public good for many years, and now I am going to talk for my own contentment."[18] Gertrude Natkin was the first of at least a dozen girls whom Twain would soon honor as "angelfish" in his Aquarium Club—his club of handpicked platonic sweethearts, a passionate endeavor that would become all-consuming. If Twain thrashed himself with guilt about many things, he never had regrets about the angelfish. Far from being ashamed, he was positively proud of this development and posed with the girls for the press. People regarded this not as the sinister hobby of a lecherous old pedophile, but as the charming eccentricity of a sentimental old widower. In a more innocent age, the public found the behavior quaint and endearing.

Why this strange obsession that so defined his final years? Twain had an innocuous, warmhearted explanation: that he woke up one morning with grandfatherly feelings and no outlet for them until the angelfish appeared. As he said, "I had reached the grandfather stage of life without grandchildren, so I began to adopt some."[19] Or as he wrote in 1908: "I am 73 & grandchildless; & so one might expect the whole left hand compartment of my heart to be empty & cavernous & desolate; but it isn't because I fill it up with schoolgirls."[20] On one level, he was nostalgically trying to reclaim the lost childhood of his daughters before the terrible misfortunes befell them, when he was still the magical paterfamilias, telling yarns and playing games with them. He wanted to re-create that feeling of a lively household bustling with happy children. While in Riverdale, he and Livy had already mourned the loss of their daughters as little girls. "We were always having vague dream-glimpses of them as they had used to be in the long-vanished years—glimpses of them playing and romping, with short frocks on, and spindle legs, and hair-tails down their backs."[21]

Twain now suffered from extreme loneliness and the angelfish filled the large void left by Livy's death, giving him a chance to create a happy new family. As he remarked to Albert Bigelow Paine, "There is no appreciation of my books that is so precious to me as appreciation from my children. Theirs is the praise we want, and the praise we are least likely to get."[22] Twain had an insatiable need for unconditional love and got it from the angelfish, not from his own daughters. Susy had engaged in a forbidden love affair and was dead; Jean was often angry and depressed from illness; and Clara, when not recuperating in a sanitarium, was caught up in her career or figuring out ways to avoid her father. Several angelfish reminded Twain of Susy, and he could now correct mistakes that he had made with her. Most of all, the girls provided him with simple love and admiration, while his adult daughters viewed him more critically. For a bitter, lonely old man, the angelfish represented an escape into a brighter world of youth.

Twain's idealized view of teenage girls was clearly linked to his idealized vision of adolescence, so clearly visible in his early fiction. His pessimistic outlook late in life found its mirror image in a gilded vision of young people untouched by misfortune. The more morose he became, the more he believed that only the young were capable of true happiness. "For the romance of life is the only part of it that is overwhelmingly valuable, & romance dies with youth," he wrote. "After that, life is a drudge, & indeed a sham."[23] The angelfish offered Twain the opportunity to disappear back into his vanished youth, to stop time, to blot out all the disappointments of adult life. Always besotted with youth, Twain never lost touch with his sense of childhood wonder and searched to recover that with these young girls. After Livy's death, he needed the purity of these girls who were honest, unspoiled, and still free of life's taint. As one friend noted, Twain found in them "a restful solace—a refuge from all worldly conceits and masks and even from the grandeurs of his own imagination."[24] He almost never detected imperfections in his angelfish and laid aside his usual carping tone.

Twain has not escaped charges of pedophilia from modern critics. "The circumstantial evidence is substantial and almost incontrovertible," writes one Twain biographer, "that he was a latent pedophile obsessed with prepubescent lasses."[25] Another Twain scholar agrees that Twain "and his protective circle transformed his pedophilia into a culture-approved, circumspect affection for children."[26] In fairness, it should be noted that Twain was never accused of any groping or predatory behavior by the girls, who were always chaperoned by a mother or grandmother, and with Isabel always present. The girls never reported forbidden sexual overtures from Twain. They played billiards and hearts and engaged in innocent pastimes. Albert Bigelow Paine's daughter Louise was among the angelfish. Where Lewis Carroll drew pictures of his young girlfriends naked and collected nude photos of them, Twain's behavior was always chaste. The angelfish came from well-to-do families, attended private schools, and respected propriety. That he "graduated" them from the

Aquarium Club when they reached sixteen suggests that he feared some potential impropriety as the girls grew older.

A puritanical man, Twain never stood accused of being a womanizer, and no trace of sexual scandal tainted his career. If anything, he showed arrested development when it came to sexuality. In his fiction, he seldom dealt with mature women—a major shortcoming in his oeuvre—and he admitted to Isabel that he never wrote a successful play because he couldn't handle "the love element . . . He never knew what to do with the woman."[27] Such a man was perhaps more comfortable with the idealized, presexual world of children. Many of his friends delighted in Twain's obsession, including his adult female friends.

Yet there *were* many seriously disturbing oddities about the situation. Twain claimed that he wanted to feel like a grandfather, but why then no boys, only girls, in his club? This was the man who had delivered the most memorable depictions of boyhood in American letters, yet he scarcely evinced any interest in associating with boys in later years. When a friend sent Twain photos of his two children—the boy about ten, the girl about eight—Isabel recorded Twain's response. "What a handsome boy. I don't care much for boys but I should like to borrow that little girl."[28] Marion Schuyler Allen, the mother of an angelfish, recounted a similar impression of Twain. "He used to pretend that only girls were interesting, that boys ought not to exist until they were men."[29] Twain knew he amused the girls and exerted a special power over them. In his loneliness, he craved their attention and demanded all their time, constantly pressing them to visit for days at a time. In general, the girls adored him and were very flattered by his attention. He encouraged one of them, Dorothy Quick, to become a writer, and she later published a glowing memoir, *Enchantment: A Little Girl's Friendship with Mark Twain*.[30] As she wrote, "Mark Twain brought more into the life of this little girl than anyone could guess . . . For the time we knew him we lived in a rarefied atmosphere in which all things of life seemed to assume their true and proper proportions."[31]

Between 1905 and 1910, about three hundred letters passed between Twain and his angelfish. Twain had grown-up conversations with these

ANGELFISH

girls and made them feel that he was their intimate friend, disclosing his private affairs. At the same time, one senses in his letters that the girls were curiously interchangeable. Starting with Gertrude Natkin, he applied exactly the same terms of endearment—"you dear child," "you little rascal," "you little witch," and so on—so that the letters all have the same cloying, affectionate ring. However much he liked the girls as individuals, he made them sound like pleasant objects or commodities, his personal marionettes. "I collect pets: young girls—girls from ten to sixteen years old; girls who are pretty and sweet and naive and innocent— dear young creatures to whom life is a perfect joy and to whom it has brought no wounds, no bitterness, and few tears. My collection consists of gems of the first water."[32]

A major question is how Clara and Jean reacted to their father suddenly having this newly adopted family of teenage girls. They were not openly hostile so much as puzzled and disdainful of this weird turn of events. They must have interpreted the angelfish as a form of rejection, a tacit criticism that they had paid insufficient attention to their father and were being supplanted by these strange new girls in their own home. It perhaps suggested to them that Twain had preferred them when they were young and innocent, much less so as they matured into womanhood. Twain would devote more time and send more letters to his Aquarium Club than to his own daughters.

For later public consumption, Clara chose to give a benign gloss to her father's fondness for the angelfish. "He liked to go driving or paying calls with some little child as companion and this feeling increased as he grew older. In fact, in the last years of his life the youthful side of his nature lay uppermost, partly because he found this the best way to crowd out melancholy thoughts."[33] In private, however, Clara worried that her father's fascination with teenage girls signified something darker. When Twain's friend Elizabeth Wallace wrote a book about his late-life stays in Bermuda, she received a warning from Albert Bigelow Paine. "I should avoid any 'affectionate' photographs with young girls. Clara feels pretty strongly about that."[34] And when Marion Schuyler Allen planned in a memoir of Twain to use a photo of him with his arm around her angelfish

WHIRLPOOL

daughter Helen, an agitated Clara sent a strongly worded request that this picture be deleted. So at least one person close to Twain suspected a disturbing undercurrent to his behavior with these young girls.

Isabel Lyon was, in many ways, the doyenne of the Aquarium Club, undoubtedly a reassuring presence for mothers who might have been concerned about their daughters. In fact, Isabel would sometimes fetch the girls and bring them to Twain's home if their mothers were unavailable. The angelfish could only have heightened her own feelings of jealousy and insecurity. After all, she had already reached an age when women, at that time, were supposedly doomed to be old maids. If Isabel professed to be charmed by the Aquarium, she had one entry in her journal that hints at a frisson of sexual excitement when Twain first spotted his girls. "Off he goes with a flash when he sees a new pair of slim legs appear; & if the little girl wears butterfly bows of ribbon on the back of her head then his delirium is complete."[35]

Even as the angelfish phenomenon got underway, Twain was drawn to a young playwright, novelist, and socialist activist named Charlotte Teller, who had just turned thirty—quite ancient by Twain's new standards. Charlotte hailed from a prominent Colorado family, had graduated from the University of Chicago, was already divorced, and was writing a novel called *The Cage*. When she shepherded a Russian revolutionary to Twain's door, he learned two things that piqued his interest: she had written the play *Joan d'Arc* and lived a few doors down at 3 Fifth Avenue. Twain asked her to come back and read the Joan play aloud to him the next day, and he was so taken with her ability to plot an intricate drama—something that had always stymied him—that he declared there is "greatness in you, Charlotte,—more of it than you suspect, I think. You are going to surpass your utmost anticipations."[36]

Pretty soon, to the dismay of an envious Isabel Lyon, the woman Twain dubbed "dear lady Charlotte" was paying him daily visits.[37] This relationship was a rarity in Twain's days as a widower—he was

ANGELFISH

wooing a mature woman of considerable intellect. His letters to her sometimes had the rhapsodic quality of the angelfish correspondence—"Charlotte dear, you have come through handsomely, you remarkable creature!"—but this was a substantial friendship, rich in political discussion and literary shop talk. In a tribute to Charlotte's talent, when she completed a play on Mirabeau, Twain read it aloud to judge its quality, and he and Isabel reacted with "sustained enthusiasm."[38] Though usually parsimonious with praise and not in the habit of mentoring young writers, Twain extolled the play extravagantly. "Mirabeau is greatly portrayed; you have missed no detail of his rich & varied nature, he stands forth clear, winning, worshipful, a majestic & benignant colossus."[39] He rendered a major service for Charlotte in helping to place *The Cage* with a publisher.

In her relationship with Twain, Charlotte encountered two insurmountable roadblocks—Clara and Isabel. Perhaps fearing that Charlotte had designs on Twain, Isabel "watered her wine,"[40] according to Clara. Isabel claimed that the young woman's friendship was disturbing the King and fretted in her journal, "He is often animated by a devastating something in these days—a something destroying his peace of mind." She added in pencil: "Charlotte Teller."[41] One notices that Twain's correspondence with Charlotte was always about her writing and that she never seemed to reciprocate his curiosity. He constantly attempted to cheer her and buck up her confidence. Usually his great subject was himself, but not with Charlotte. It is hard to escape the impression that he felt unusually insecure as he strained to impress her.

Then, on October 22, 1906, Isabel startled Twain with the news that scurrilous gossip circulated at The Players Club about his relationship with Charlotte. Twain summoned Charlotte, told her about the rumor, and was so alarmed by the potential for scandal that he asked if she would consider moving away from 3 Fifth Avenue. Charlotte flatly refused, reminded Twain that he was old enough to be her grandfather, and demanded to know the source of the story. After some hesitation, Isabel revealed what she knew—"I gave what I dared."[42] Charlotte was so angry that she contacted her publisher and asked him to drop the foreword

WHIRLPOOL

Twain had written for *The Cage*. It is noteworthy that when it came to grown-up sexuality, Twain was extremely sensitive to gossip and public opinion, and was willing to bow to the stodgiest conventions—something apparent in the Gorky affair. After this episode, Twain's correspondence with Charlotte pretty much dried up, although it was not, as will be seen, the end of the rumormongering.

Twain's romantic attachment to the fourteen-year-old Laura Wright (later Dake), the girl who entranced him in New Orleans in 1858, never dimmed in his memory. The alluring vision still beckoned. Unlike his adoration of his Hannibal sweetheart, Laura Hawkins (the original of Becky Thatcher), the liaison with Laura Wright was brief and dreamlike, hazy and quasi-mystical, and perhaps more durable for that reason. Laura was more an idea than an actual person permitted to grow into womanhood. She was the first Platonic Sweetheart, the prototype for the teenage girls who enthralled his imagination.

Even as a happily married man, he continued to commemorate that early relationship. He wrote about Laura in the sentimental language that he spilled so copiously on the angelfish. In January 1906, when old friends invited him to their golden wedding anniversary, Twain told of how their letter conjured up "Laura Wright, that unspoiled little maid, that fresh flower of the woods and the prairies! Forty-eight years ago!"[43] On May 26, 1906, Twain picked up the *New York Times,* saw the date, and announced to Isabel, "This is one of my anniversaries—48 years ago I said good bye to my little sweetheart. He told me then how he had said that he wouldn't see her for years . . . & she had given him a little gold ring, & then he went away."[44] Before Livy came along, Twain confessed to Isabel, he had experienced only two romances: Laura Hawkins and Laura Wright.

Then, on July 27, 1906, the distant past erupted with volcanic force when a letter arrived from Laura Wright Dake. Notwithstanding the lapse of many years, Twain recognized the handwriting at once, and he said it "shook me to the foundations."[45] Laura, now a widow at sixty-two, was a schoolteacher in San Diego, with a disabled son to support. "Here's a romance for you!," Twain blurted out to Sue Crane, then told her about his long-ago romance with Laura. "She is poor, is a widow, in debt, & is in desperate need of a thousand dollars. I sent it."[46] This was a huge outlay—$35,000 in today's money—for someone not seen for forty-eight years. It was pretty cheeky of the "innocent" Laura to request such a fantastic sum from Twain after so much time had passed. She coyly framed it as a request for him to ask his friend Andrew Carnegie for the money, but she must have suspected Twain would indulge her.

Three days later, in his autobiographical dictation, Twain, profoundly moved, transported Paine back to 1858, evoking a "slip of a girl . . . a frank and simple and winsome child who had never been away from home in her life before, and had brought with her to these distant regions the freshness and the fragrance of her own prairies."[47] His rose-colored descriptions sounded plucked from a Currier & Ives print. "That comely child, that charming child was Laura M. Wright, and I could see her with perfect distinctness in the unfaded bloom of her youth, with her plaited tails dangling from her young head and her white summer frock puffing about in the wind of that ancient Mississippi time."[48] These images of a girl in pigtails were curiously chaste, devoid of any erotic charge. That such an innocent creature was now old and suffering hardship kindled Twain's furious sense of injustice. "It is an awful world—it is a fiendish world . . . What had that girl done, what crime had she committed, that she must be punished with poverty and drudgery in her old age?"[49] When Twain sent a final letter to Laura in February 1907, he didn't bother to write it himself, but assigned it to Isabel after he dictated some witticisms for her to employ. Clearly, he didn't want the cold reality of the aging, widowed Laura to undermine the potent spell of his long-held fantasy of the "comely child."

CHAPTER FIFTY-SIX

A Fan and a Halo

By early 1906, with the reformist zeal having ebbed again in Twain's life, he wanted to be carefree and enjoy himself after so many troubled years. The political requests for help still piled up in his mailbox, and his sympathies were often stirred, but he began to say no more often, even though "it costs me a pang to do it."[1] When an invitation arrived to address the Minnesota Society of Colonial Wars, he instructed Isabel: "Miss Lyon, tell him NO—I wouldn't make such a journey to see the Resurrection."[2] When the Anti-Imperialist League tried to enlist him anew in the struggle of the Philippine people, he scribbled on the letter: "The woes of the wronged & the unfortunate poison my life and make it so undesirable that pretty often I wish I were 90 instead of 70."[3]

The most important event in which Twain participated was a fundraiser at Carnegie Hall for the silver jubilee of the Tuskegee Institute in Alabama, whose principal was Booker T. Washington. The author of *Up from Slavery*, a leading figure in the African American community, Washington was born into slavery and supported his education by working as a janitor before becoming the head of the Tuskegee school. By the lights of a later generation he was a conservative figure, favoring incremental change and accepting the "separate but equal" doctrine in education. Some Black leaders, notably Ida B. Wells and W. E. B. Du Bois, faulted his emphasis on industrial education for Blacks as a mistaken concession to the white power structure. Washington had worked closely with Twain in protesting King Leopold's atrocities in the Congo.

WHIRLPOOL

At Carnegie Hall, Twain drew thunderous applause from a fashionable crowd that counted members from the Rockefeller, Rogers, Huntington, Warburg, and Schiff families. Introduced by Joseph Choate, Twain noted that "Mr. Choate has been careful not to pay me any compliments. It wasn't because he didn't want to—he just couldn't think of any."[4] He paid tribute to Tuskegee for grounding its students in a thorough system of Christian morals, then returned to a theme that had informed his work as a Mugwump: that people tended to shed their morals when it came to politics. "During 363 days in the year the American citizen is true to his Christian private morals . . . then in the other two days of the year he leaves his Christian private morals at home, and carries his Christian public morals to the tax office and the polls and does the best he can to damage and undo his whole year's faithful and righteous work."[5]

Rich folks in the audience surely squirmed as he railed against their penchant for tax evasion. "I know all those people," he joked. "I have friendly, social, and criminal relations with the whole lot of them."[6] Mixing humor with outrage, he described how he became a tax cheat upon learning that millionaires paid only a third of what he did. He had therefore fallen in the esteem of tax collectors, "and I should have fallen in my own, except that I had already struck bottom, and there wasn't any place to fall to."[7] Twain applauded Washington's work at Tuskegee in providing Black students with an education and instructing them in "thirty-seven useful trades."[8] Whatever the limitations of his vision, Twain clearly possessed enormous goodwill toward the Black community, whether paying for Warner McGuinn's education at Yale Law School or supporting the Fisk Jubilee Singers. It is hard to think of another white author of his era who felt so warmly toward Blacks or cared more about their plight.

Though he masked it with comedy, Twain's mind dwelled insistently on mortality, and he told an editor, "In a little while—ah, such a little while—you will be borrowing a fan and I a halo."[9] With Clara and Jean distracted by their problems, Isabel rode the subway with Twain, escorted him to the barber, and continued to perform wifely duties. She also received his most rueful reflections. He would sit ensconced in a large green armchair as Isabel tapped out tunes on the Orchestrelle. "Oh, his soul is so lonely," she sighed. "Days are when it is *so* terrible."[10] Somebody else might have felt trapped by Twain's dark moods and antireligious diatribes, but Isabel rewarded him with uncritical adoration. "I don't want any Earthly Things outside of this house," she wrote.[11] It is hard to believe that she didn't harbor hopes of marrying Twain, despite the age difference, as she pumped him up to godlike proportions in her journal. "What a glorious creature he is! It is his greatness—his genius—his magnetism—his strong humanness—and his great sweet soul."[12] Twain seemed blind to the fact that he was dealing with a lonely, love-starved woman and might be fostering expectations that he could not fulfill.

Like Livy before her, Isabel came to see the hardship of living with this mad genius with his grim view of existence. One day, Twain sounded off at length about the flaws of the damned human race, and Isabel felt helpless against the onslaught of his pitiless logic. "After a talk like the ones he gives me I grope all the rest of the day with my soul spirit weak with the terrible mental weeping that is with me, & then when every one is sleeping the real tears come . . . My soul is not moored to anything. I can't keep it up where it ought to be—& so I cry & cry."[13] Isabel was prone to depression, and Twain's philosophic rants set up disturbing reverberations that she simply could not control. She was thrown into turmoil after reading Edith Wharton's *The House of Mirth*, with its haunting portrait of a desperately isolated woman without money seeking to secure a firm niche in a male-dominated world.

The instability of Clara's life compounded Isabel's insecurity. That winter, Clara drifted in and out of the Norfolk sanitarium, and between visits tried to advance her singing career. Her physical and mental state handicapped her musical development. When she sang for some friends at home, Isabel reached a mixed verdict. "Some of her notes were very, very beautiful, but she has the beginning of another cold & so she was a little nervous."[14] When she auditioned for Loudon Charlton to be her manager, he judged that she was "not yet ready for public appearances, not yet ripe."[15] Afterward Clara couldn't sleep and crept up to Isabel's room for consolation, staying till two in the morning. Isabel had become Clara's confidante and assumed the maternal role of salving her hurt feelings. There was unseen peril in this situation as Isabel was an employee, not her mother, and went on shopping expeditions and performed other domestic services for Clara.

In his most wretched days of grief, Twain mocked 21 Fifth Avenue as "The Valley of the Shadow"—he found it a sunless, dreary place—and he dreamed of residence in a rural hideaway. Recently Albert Paine had bought land in Redding, Connecticut, and suggested that Twain buy a seventy-five-acre parcel there of bucolic land with an old farmhouse on it. With a strange impulsiveness, Twain forked over a $100 down payment. At the very least it would be a decent investment and maybe the site of a future residence. On the spot, Isabel also hatched a private dream: she would occupy a farmhouse there that would become her permanent home, ending years of wandering. "Life is such a tiny bubble that why we reach out for material things I don't know; but we do it and that old beamed farmhouse on top of the hill held out its arms to me."[16] Such a rustic residence would simultaneously give her a home and embed her inextricably in Twain's affairs.

Twain had been so taken with Dublin, New Hampshire, the previous summer that he signed on for a second. With the former house already booked, he had to settle for Mountain View Farm, a home owned by the Upton family, which sat in a more secluded, woody spot on the eastern slope of Monadnock. As Isabel Lyon prepared to vacate 21 Fifth Avenue, she toiled under such stress that she was gripped by fugitive feelings of terror and an abiding sense of calamity. When she couldn't sleep, she drowned herself with powerful bromides and resorted to alcohol. "When Santa started for Gilders tonight I told her I'd go for whiskey—but there was not whiskey to quiet me—Foolish for me to think it would—it doesn't."[17] So as the household braced for their Dublin summer retreat, a combustible situation had developed: Twain, Clara, Jean, and Isabel were all grappling with the demons of depression.

By far the most formidable challenge facing Isabel was Jean's epilepsy,

A FAN AND A HALO

which got worse on the eve of their departure. On her first day in Dublin, May 1, despite six preventative pills, Jean felt absentminded and had long petit mal attacks, although her head then cleared and she went out hiking. A handsome young friend from the previous summer came calling, Gerome "Gerry" Brush, the eighteen-year-old son of the painter George de Forest Brush. Gerry was a precocious teenager who acted, drew, and wrote plays, and though Jean was twenty-six, she developed a schoolgirl crush on the young man—"as sweet, gentle, courteous and attractive boy as I ever hope to see"—that would last the entire summer.[18] When she paid a return visit to the Brushes two days later, Jean grew terrified when she could not find the familiar route. "If I ever went anywhere often," she told her diary, "it certainly was to the Brushes' & the idea of not being able to find it!!!"[19] It was not the first time epilepsy had blunted her memory. Jean balked at telling Gerry and the Brush family about her epilepsy, lest they fear having her around children.

In the coming days, Jean was bedeviled by absentminded fits that left her tired and disoriented. Her head was cloudy almost every day, and she often retched at breakfast from a single slice of toast. On May 10, she had an attack at breakfast, then another two hours later, "and this time I fell off the bed and onto my face on the floor. I struck my cheek bone and made it sore but without bruising."[20] As her attacks grew more frequent, it became clear that she was a danger to herself and needed professional care. This was no job for Anna Sterritt, her maid, or Isabel Lyon, and it must have terrified them to witness Jean's attacks. After having another grand mal seizure on June 7, Jean wrote, "Anna said she had never seen me so violent before and that it had been difficult to keep me on the bed. The bed isn't very large and they have decided to rent a larger one for me . . . so that there will be less danger of my falling off the bed."[21] The attack left Jean with aching eyes, and "rather limp and lifeless from the experience."[22]

Still in New York, Twain grew alarmed over Jean's plight, and when she went to the dentist, he insisted that Anna accompany her. "Consequently," Jean wrote, "to my utter fury, I found when I came down this morning, that Miss Lyon had ordered a carriage . . . & that Anna was going with me . . . I don't see any necessity for having a maid in the next room when you're at the dentist's . . . I was as 'mad as a hatter' when I started, but of course that wore off in time."[23] This awful situation had no satisfactory solution: Twain naturally wanted to protect his daughter, while she didn't care to be reduced to childlike dependency. When he arrived at Dublin in mid-May, he found Jean still in bed at five in the afternoon and unable to rise to greet him.

Prior to leaving for New Hampshire, Twain was nagged by bronchitis and suffered a collapse after his speaking engagements amid "the rage & turmoil of New York."[24] Once he arrived in Dublin, he found that the house, set deep in the woods, calmed his ruffled spirit, but that proved not to be long-lasting, and he soon came to regret the place's "perfectly heartbreaking solitude."[25] Always clever at nicknames, Twain labeled the Upton house "The Lodge of Sorrow" and, sardonically, "The House of Mirth."

Twain had brought along Albert Paine and Josephine Hobby to resume work on the autobiography. Dressed in white flannel, shod in comfortable Moroccan slippers, Twain paced the long veranda, spouting memories, invigorated by the fresh country air and magnificent mountain views. Sometimes he dropped into a rocker, a pansy sprouting from his buttonhole, as he roved over the scenes of his past life. In the afternoon, Twain read manuscripts aloud to Isabel, then literature in the evening—Emerson's poem "Monadnoc," *The Rubaiyat, Julius Caesar,* and Kipling's *The Jungle Book*. His melodious voice made Isabel quiver with bliss. "There never was anyone to read so beautifully before & to charm you so & hurt you so."[26] Twain had movers lug the bulky Orchestrelle up to Dublin so he could enjoy nightly installments of Schubert, Beethoven, and Chopin. As usual, he was surrounded by an array of mischievous cats with colorful nicknames, this time a trio—one named Sackcloth and two look-alikes named Ashes.

Conspicuously missing was Clara, who remained sequestered in Norfolk, battling depression. "I am at present trying to bail out of a sinking boat," she told Isabel, "with a weapon the size of a thimble."[27] She still had a special rapport with Isabel, her principal source of family gossip, and was amazed that Isabel found her father's presence so comforting. Clearly for her it was not. With Isabel in a tense supervisory role with Jean and enduring intermittent hostility, it was much easier for her to communicate with Clara. While Clara sent Jean imaginative presents and long letters, Jean picked up an underlying coldness in her older sister. "I am afraid we have grown apart," she reflected in her diary. "I know that she cannot understand or sympathize with my curious nature and while my love for her has not diminished, I cannot help feeling that lack of sympathy in her."[28] Finding the Upton house gloomy and isolated, Jean created a studio up the hill where she immersed herself in wood carving, hoping to earn some money. Paine saw a young woman veiled in melancholy. "She dressed always in white, and she was tall and pale and classically beautiful, and she was often silent, like a spirit."[29] Another time he said that Jean possessed "the tragic beauty of a young queen doomed to the block."[30]

During this terrible Dublin summer, it grew evident how shattered the Clemens clan was and how much turmoil was stored up in the small household. Minor tiffs blew up into major rows. Jean's disease made her irritable, and Twain's mood swings were no less marked. "His moods have been quite at variance with his former self," wrote Isabel. "He is none the less great, but he is living in a world apart."[31] One day, Jean went to see her father while he was having breakfast and "was very curtly told that I shouldn't go into his room while he was breakfasting." Jean stormed out in a huff, saying, "I had been told that that was a good time, but since it wasn't, I shouldn't go in at all any more."[32] Either feeling guilty about his reaction or to punish Jean, Twain failed to appear for lunch or supper. Isabel noted that "Jean was insolent to her father," making the punishment theory more likely.[33] Twain was sweet to Jean when she went to say good night, but that disappeared the next day. "Father was horrid to me tonight and I hadn't done anything to warrant his saying what he did."[34] For Jean, her father was the moody, difficult one; for her father and Isabel, it was the reverse. All the while, Isabel was harassed by feelings of impending calamity and "nervous terrors," and she found solace in long walks in the woods with Albert Paine.[35]

WHIRLPOOL

Twain's quarrels with Jean and discomfort at the Upton house spilled over into his professional life. Having long been suspicious of publishers, he now feuded with Frederick Duneka at Harper, who had suppressed for a while his *Christian Science* book. Duneka then issued a new edition of *Mark Twain's Library of Humor,* even though it had no resemblance to his 1888 original. Calling Duneka "slippery beyond imagination," Twain assured Isabel that all publishers were "scamps, but Mr. Duneka is more fool than knave."[36] To Henry Rogers, he expanded on this, saying Duneka's conduct marked him as "being not merely a thief, but a particularly low-down sneak-thief. I desire his scalp."[37]

Twain enjoyed the daily two-hour dictation of his autobiography, releasing feelings cooped up for years. He made grandiose claims for his stream-of-consciousness method, alleging its originality would rank with "the steam engine, the printing press and the electric telegraph."[38] The process, he contended, had broadened his sympathy for ordinary people. "I can take their heart affairs into my heart as I never could before."[39] Yet his temper frayed when it came to Miss Hobby, a conventional woman who made minute errors and seemed shocked by Twain's scandalous opinions, such as his contempt for the Immaculate Conception. To Isabel, he jeered at her as "that devilish woman! I'd like to take her out & have her scalped and gutted!"[40]

On June 26, spurred by the unutterable sadness of Jean's condition, Twain left Dublin and fled to Boston and New York, and enjoyed boyish pastimes aboard Rogers's pleasure craft. Jean was left to languish in her misery. She continued to dote on Gerry Brush but was self-conscious about her memory lapses. "I wonder if he regards me as [a] terribly lacking specimen & is bored to death by being obliged to be with me?"[41] With her encyclopedic knowledge of woodland trees, birds, flowers, and fauna, Jean had already turned into a crusader for animal rights, protesting cruelty to horses and the butchering of egrets to produce feathers for ladies' hats. She would have made a fine naturalist or an animal trainer, but nobody sought to turn her passion into a useful trade. She fell back on wood carving and drifted at loose ends, unable to attract a husband or engage in remunerative work. Blind to Jean's virtues, Isabel said "she found escape in her games & associations with juveniles 8 or 10 years younger—and in small tyrannies over female servants."[42]

Increasingly, Jean and Isabel were locked in a deadly trap. Twain could not do without Isabel, and Isabel found it hard to put up with Jean. If Isabel found Jean insolent, Jean was no less impatient with Isabel's "nervous, snappy moods."[43] After her father left Dublin, Jean wrote to him about "an atrocious evening" she had passed with Isabel. "We couldn't seem to talk pleasantly." Isabel always expressed glorified views of Clara without realizing how much this depressed Jean. "When Miss Lyon talked as only she can of Clara's marvelous grace, subtlety, and wonderful powers . . . it almost unvariably irritates me & last night it did more than ever."[44] Isabel left much to be desired as a psychologist. "Clara is heaven & earth," Jean fumed, "but I never get sufficiently used to her gushings for them not to bore, and as a rule, even annoy me."[45] Since Twain had lapsed into a dejected state, he could not rise above the tensions between Isabel and Jean and arbitrate a truce between them.

During the summer of 1906, Twain published privately a work that stood as a testament to his despair. *What is Man?* was a gloomy and rigidly deterministic work that summed up the desolation of his later years. He thought society forced us to mouth comforting lies, platitudes, and pieties. We all had bills to pay, families to support, reputations to uphold. In this work, he thought he bravely said what we knew to be true but hadn't dared to voice: that the mind is a machine, that we mistake instinct for original thought, that free will is a farce, that our lives are predetermined by outside forces, and that all acts are selfishly motivated. That Twain's own career seemed a supreme refutation of this mechanistic thesis is one of many paradoxes of his life. The most original character in American history credited himself with no originality at all. Perhaps the solution to the mystery lies in the fact that he felt himself a prisoner of his own nature and powerless to change his ways, however flawed or disturbing.

The onetime bard of boyish hopefulness had dabbled with these dangerous ideas since 1883, when he delivered a talk to the Monday Evening Club titled "What Is Happiness?" It laid out a theory that previewed the later work: that people were mere machines, lacking free will or originality, incapable of selfless actions. He followed up with an unpublished essay, "The Character of Man," in which he wrote: "There are certain sweet-smelling sugar-coated lies current in the world which all politic men have apparently tacitly conspired to support and perpetuate"—notably, independence of thought, opinion, and action. He began *What is Man?* in Vienna in 1898, and its dogmatic certitude provoked controversy within his family. "Fortunately, his heart was fully as strong as his head," Clara recalled. "It could blaze with genuine emotion while his mind held to a logically formed idea. Had it not been for this fact, we should have been greatly depressed by his theories."[46] The early drafts of *What is Man?* pushed Livy to the limits of her tolerance, with Twain admitting to Howells that "Mrs. Clemens loathes, and shudders over, and will not listen to the last half nor allow me to print any part of it."[47] Jean hated the manuscript so much that she refused to type it up.

Livy's displeasure with what Twain called his "gospel" continued to simmer. In 1901 Twain informed Twichell that Livy wouldn't allow him to publish it "because it would destroy me. But I hope to see it in print before I die . . . I've often tried to read it to Livy, but she won't have it; it drives her mad & makes her melancholy. The truth always has that effect on people."[48] That Twain clung so tenaciously to the project is mystifying given how much it distressed his ailing wife. After Livy died, Isabel remembered Twain "pacing the long sombre drawing-room" in Florence and voicing "his grief for having caused her perpetual distress by his 'Gospel.' Moaning, he said, 'I took Livy's religion away from her, & gave her nothing—worse than nothing—in return.'"[49]

Still in the throes of hero worship and with a large appetite for heterodox views, Isabel Lyon adored *What is Man?* when Twain first read it aloud to her in Dublin. She had been afraid to hear it "because my only knowledge of it was through Jean who hates it," but she found it "full of wonderful thoughts—beautiful thoughts, terrible truths."[50] Her effusive admiration must have been seductive for Twain and made her feel even more essential to his happiness. In May 1906, Twain got Frank Doubleday to read his "Gospel," and he arranged a deal to publish 250 copies through the De Vinne Press, withholding Twain's name and entering the copyright under the name of "J. W. Bothwell." The book was passed around secretly, and Twain was disappointed by all the negative reactions. It attracted so little interest that he was sorry he had published it.

Twain's ideas were not so shockingly new as he had supposed and had been anticipated by the likes of Nietzsche, Ibsen, and Shaw. When Isabel gave Twain a copy of *Thus Spake Zarathustra,* he grumbled, "Oh damn Nietzsche! He couldn't write a lucid sentence to save his soul."[51] Isabel, however, noted strong parallels in their beliefs and quoted "telling passages" to Twain "for Nietzsche is too much like himself."[52] Twain claimed that he didn't need to read Nietzsche or any other philosopher, for he had "gone to the fountain-head for information—that is to say, to the human race. Every man is in his own person the whole human race, with not a detail lacking."[53]

What is Man? takes the form of a Socratic dialogue between an Old Man, who believes we are imprisoned by our temperament and environment, and a Young Man, who contests him. When the Old Man denies the possibility of original creation, the Young Man counters with Shakespeare's characters. "Shakespeare created nothing," the Old Man insists. "He correctly observed, and he marvelously painted. He exactly portrayed people whom *God* had created."[54] The Old Man makes a radically egalitarian argument that the well-born don't succeed on their own merits, nor the poor fail on their defects; both are products of their environment. He denies that altruistic actions exist: when we do a generous deed, we are motivated by a secret vanity to feel good about ourselves. In the end, Twain was saying that we are all monsters of ego, and one begins to wonder if he was not preoccupied by this theme because he saw it operating so powerfully in himself. At the end, the Old Man delivers a harangue against unthinking patriotism, which he sees merely as a form of national vanity. Even though *What is Man?* is written as a Socratic dialogue, there is no real give-and-take between the two men. The Old Man

WHIRLPOOL

is a monomaniac—there's no arguing with him—and this introduces a certain deadness into the book. The reader feels trapped with a closed-minded author seized by an intellectual obsession. At this point in his life, Twain lacked the ability to step back and examine his views skeptically, and nobody in his inner circle of family and friends stood ready to challenge him.

CHAPTER FIFTY-SEVEN

Wuthering Heights

During the summer of 1905, Mark Twain had fled New York City to Dublin, whereas in the summer of 1906, he fled *from* the New Hampshire town. He had tacked on a new nickname to the Upton house: "Wuthering Heights," a lament echoed by Isabel, who said, "Even the good, good servants find it very depressing."[1] Twain left without giving any return date. In Manhattan he hung out with Rogers at his Standard Oil offices or confronted his publisher at Harper—"Mr. Duneka is frying in the fire which he prepared for himself, & is a very humble & suffering sinner"—then spent cool, breezy evenings with the Rogers family aboard their yacht before they all sailed up to Fairhaven.[2] Socializing with them was hearty and cordial, free of the tensions that cramped Twain's life at home. Such were his family conflicts that he felt obliged to report to Howells in July a singular comment made by Clara: "That miracle has happened again which happened months ago, one of my children has complimented her father."[3] Without Livy's softening influence, the beloved father of earlier years could seem an embittered, dyspeptic old man.

By leaving Jean and Isabel alone, Twain removed any remaining buffer between the two women, creating a combustible situation. Jean had to endure multiple sources of misery. Because of her disease, she was forced to ride by carriage and noted with exasperation that "it isn't enough to have this fiendish disease, but . . . riding has to be declared the most injurious occupation for me."[4] Isabel's superior air made Jean feel like a dunce.

As she put it, "When Miss Lyon is about I am always more painfully conscious of my ignorance and stupidities."[5] Surrounded by sparkling intellects, Jean could not trust her memory anymore. One morning she found young Gerry Brush and "the Lioness," as she now called Isabel, having breakfast and talking about Shakespeare and Bacon, "and most of it was away over my poor head."[6] Her love for young Gerry grew obsessive, and when she learned that he and his family planned to spend two years in Italy, she foresaw that, by the time they returned, she would be twenty-eight years old and a "stolid old maid."[7] Hanging over everything was her dread of never marrying or even knowing love. In a major step, Jean disclosed to Gerry and her Dublin friends the true nature of her illness—a rare admission on her part.

Because Isabel harbored similar fears about her own marital prospects, she was hardly the ideal companion for Jean, who needed to address her as "Miss Lyon." With her nervous tension, headaches, and insomnia, Isabel increasingly leaned on Albert Paine for companionship, while her position vis-à-vis Jean remained ambiguous. As Jean noted accurately, "She is not my governess, and has no right whatsoever to dictate to me in the way she does."[8] But if Isabel wasn't Jean's governess, then what exactly was she, and what role was she to have in Jean's life? Twain left this critical relationship undefined. Jean found Isabel bossy and overprotective as she insisted that Jean be chaperoned on every social outing, a posture perhaps befitting a dutiful mother, but not her father's secretary.

That July, Jean and Isabel had a peculiar quarrel when Jean playfully added some words to a note Isabel was writing to Twain. Annoyed, Isabel said she would now have to rewrite the entire letter. "In joke I gave her a light tap on her left cheek," said Jean. "She flared somewhat so I gave her another, not in the least in anger, on the right cheek. At that she lost her balance completely, tore the paper across the centre & said she wouldn't stand such treatment . . . and so I advised her to go & cry about it. She was half crying already."[9] Neither woman comes off well here: Jean seems cruel and imperious, while Isabel comes across as hypersensitive.

WUTHERING HEIGHTS

Both Jean and Isabel hoped that Clara would visit, but Twain decided that the railway trips would be too taxing, and Jean's disappointed reaction was telling. "I suppose it is best for her," she wrote. "Our disgusting family always has something the matter with its health."[10] Meanwhile, Isabel had to stand guard and impose restrictions on Jean's movements, while also studying her for telltale signs of imminent petit mal attacks—an arduous nursemaid assignment. To take but one sad entry from Isabel's journal that July: "Jean, 10:45, violent. 6:40, long, violent. Petit mall [sic] all day."[11] Isabel now wrote first-person letters for Twain to which he merely appended his signature. In this job she had ascended to Mount Olympus, but her status at this lofty altitude was purchased at a sometimes intolerable cost. When Twain was in Dublin, dictating to Paine and Miss Hobby, she found the place a scene of charming domesticity; when he was gone, she was burdened with frightful loneliness.

When her father returned for her birthday in late July, Jean seemed jubilant. "So the dear little man is coming home after all. I am wildly thankful."[12] She found him rosy-cheeked and cheerful, clearly replenished by his absence. When he came to her study with $25 for her birthday, they discussed the possible move to Redding, Connecticut. He would use his $30,000 profit from selling excerpts from his autobiography to build a house there, employing Howells's son John as the architect. Convinced that her health would improve with country life, Jean expressed enthusiasm, though she regretted leaving her coterie of Dublin friends, the only stable companions she'd had in her adult life, an attachment strengthened by her profound affection for Gerry Brush. Isabel, too, erected an edifice of hope on the Redding move. After talking with Paine, she wrote, "If I am good—very good—I am to have a Strip of land in Redding to build me there a little house. AB [Albert Bigelow] will let me use the strip from his own property. Oh I must be good—monotonously good."[13] Before the month was over, Isabel, Clara, and John Howells traveled to Redding and surveyed with approval the proposed site for Twain's house.

Staying in Dublin for the first half of August, Twain engaged in brilliant clowning when playing charades with Jean, Isabel, and a clutch of local friends. However much she welcomed her father's return, Jean chafed under the restrictions he imposed on her. He hesitated to allow her to go to a dance because he feared overexertion. It bothered Jean when he opposed her climbing a mountain alone with a young man—an objection based on propriety, not health. In her diary, she protested that "Clara has gone wherever she wished to with her friends, such as John, etc. & they were young gentlemen, too, & not boys . . . I should hate to have a fight with Father & yet I am no child but older than mother was when she had two children!"[14] Jean was crushed to discover that Gerry Brush's true love was a young woman named Anna Cabot. Even as she lectured herself not to be jealous, she was emotionally devastated and unable to stop thinking compulsively about Gerry.

Twain now disliked Dublin intensely, and his impulse was to fly from family problems. He had developed a fascination with Henry Rogers's daughter-in-law, Mary Benjamin Rogers, who was twenty-six, pretty and elegant, an accomplished painter, and skilled at wordplay. Twain exchanged flirtatious letters with her, writing from Dublin: "You are a very dear partner in crime, and if you have missed me half as much as I have missed you, I am very well satisfied—& pretty vain, too, besides."[15] As with the angelfish, Twain wrote in a pseudo-romantic idiom, calling Mary "sweet pal, sweetest of pals" and ending one letter: "I miss you—dear me, yes! Affectionately, your uncle Mark."[16] Suddenly, Twain decamped for Fairhaven on August 17, with Isabel noting that he would have "pretty Mrs. Harry Rogers and the yacht and he is so glad to have the holiday."[17]

Resorting to a second childhood, Twain had a craving to play all the time, especially with attractive young girls and women. Jean understood that he was lonely, but she was lonely, too, and she sent him a plaintive note "asking him to come home soon & not stay eternally playing billiards."[18] After ten days, he returned thoroughly revivified by his trip, according to Isabel, and was "gay & jolly & darling; & full of his yachting trip to Bar Harbor, and Mrs. Harry & the joy of living. Sly, he was; & like a boy fresh from his wild oats."[19] In a rocking chair on the veranda, he sat for a sequence of seven photos designed to show "the progress of a moral purpose through the mind of the human race's Oldest Friend."[20]

While Twain was off on his skylarking holiday, Jean had grown despondent about her condition. "Of late," she wrote, "I have had no reasons for hoping to escape the regular routine of the attacks."[21] Right after Twain returned, she suffered another hellish day and was "deadly sick" with vomiting after breakfast. When she felt a bit better, she took a bath and went to chat with him. "I wasn't wise, then, because I spoke of my bad memory as being caused by the disease and it made me feel desperately unhappy, so that I couldn't entirely restrain my tears and that upset Father ever so much."[22] Before the day was over, she had two more attacks and a grand mal seizure later the same week. The vignette of Jean crying with her father encapsulates the pain of the whole situation. Jean couldn't cope with this intolerable disease and neither could he. It was a nightmare for both of them, making Twain's retreat into childish escapades more understandable. With her self-confidence badly eroded, Jean despaired: "I am beginning to believe myself very stupid and utterly incompetent of judging books or plays."[23]

By September, Clara was ready to resume her singing career, and her father cheered her on with encouraging notes. After years of dedicated work, interrupted by periodic breakdowns, she was set to perform in Norfolk, Connecticut, on September 22, accompanied by her voice coach, Isidore Luckstone. She retained her old unresolved ambivalence about her father's influence on her career. "Clara dreads to have me present," Twain told Mary Benjamin Rogers, "but she hasn't asked me not to come, in so many words."[24] Ultimately Clara consented to his presence. When he suggested that he lead her onstage, she balked. "You'll get all the welcome & I none."[25] Clara feared that with her father's exhibitionist tendencies, he would make a speech and monopolize the house. To Twain's delight, Clara changed her mind and allowed him to appear after the finale. "Mariechen, it's butter from the butterless! & very gratifying," Twain told Mary Benjamin Rogers. "Next, there'll be butter from Jean."[26] When the concert was done, Clara took three curtain calls before leading her father onstage, where her worst fears were soon realized. "I didn't make a speech," Twain recalled, "but only talked. I talked fifteen or twenty minutes."[27] He spoke of his stage fright during his platform debut in San Francisco in 1866. "I want to thank you for your appreciation of [Clara's] singing," he concluded, "which is, by-the-way, hereditary."[28] In Twain's telling, Clara congratulated him warmly on a felicitous talk, but she declined requests to pose with him afterward for photographs, saying she wanted to stand or fall on her own merits.

In the end, the small-town recital was reviewed in major organs solely because Clara was Mark Twain's daughter. The *New York Sun* covered it under the heading "Twain's First Appearance," with the subhead "At His Daughter's Singing Debut He Tells How Stage Fright Once Gripped Him." Clara was not mentioned until the final paragraph, where the reviewer carped that she "displayed some nervousness" in her first number, then "acquitted herself with coolness and effect" as she sang *Lieder* by Grieg, Schubert, and Haydn.[29] A *Town & Country* critic praised the beauty of her person and contralto voice while griping that "she has things still to accomplish . . . such as a better control of her voice."[30] Despite earlier misgivings about Clara's career, Twain now brimmed with pride in her talent, informing Jean that her sister's debut was "a clean straight triumph."[31] Of Clara's sterling qualities as a singer and a person, Twain confessed to Howells, "Others knew it before, but I have always been busy with other matters"—a recurring theme of self-recrimination concerning his daughters.[32] Clara had projected this concert as the start of a tour that would stretch into Hartford and Providence. Before she could complete it, however, her worried doctors suspended it and ordered her back to the sanitarium for two months. Whatever her musical talents, a high-pressure stage career for someone with Clara's chronic vocal problems and vulnerable psyche made little sense—hope always outstripped performance—but it was the all-important identity she needed to strike a pose of independence from her father.

WUTHERING HEIGHTS

Back in Dublin, things were careening rapidly toward a crisis. Without the King around, Isabel found her loneliness intolerable, and she smoked, drank, and swallowed toxic bromides to sleep. When Twain left again in mid-September, she saw him off in a manner worthy of a wife. "I got up to see the King off this morning at 5:45 & as I tied his necktie & flicked some shaving lather from his waistcoat & helped him into his overcoat," he told her a little anecdote.[33] Nothing happened sexually between them, but Twain allowed Isabel to cross boundaries that should have been respected. She was a highly emotional and increasingly unstable woman whose exact relationship to Twain was never adequately defined, leaving her in a psychological limbo.

It also grew clear that the situation with Jean's illness had become unsustainable. Her diary descriptions make for heartrending reading. On September 16, she took a "taste of toast" for breakfast, then at once "began to retch & after I had drunk two cups of coffee[,] I threw up every-thing although I was lying flat on my back." Not long afterward, she had another attack that left her "weak & exhausted, which must mean that the attack was rather hard."[34] Shut up together as they were in this solitary country house, Isabel's mental health was now inseparable from Jean's. "The seriousness of Jean's disease is increasing," Isabel wrote, "and I am very anxious about her."[35] After Jean endured yet another attack on September 23, Isabel wrote in her journal, "I went to pieces & stayed in a dark room all day—suffering."[36] With Twain constantly away, Isabel was understandably overcome with fear and anxiety. She was not a trained nurse. When Twain got wind of her mental state, he wrote, "Miss Lyon is suffering a severe nervous collapse."[37] Isabel should never have been left alone in this situation.

Finally, on September 27, Jean and Isabel sat down to discuss a practical solution to the crisis. "I talked sanitarium a good deal this morning with Miss Lyon," Jean wrote. "It seemed that she has already spoken of it to Father & that he agreed to it absolutely, provided it was considered at all desirable. Lioness believes that I may be able to have Anna with me in the kind of place I would go to. That would make it ever so much less lonely. I am really very anxious to have the matter discussed with Dr. Hunt, because I am beginning to feel that it is the one & only thing to try."[38] At this point, there was no villainous plot on Isabel's part to ship Jean off to a sanitarium, which arose as a mutual decision. The situation had simply gone beyond Isabel's ability to handle. What is noticeable again is how Twain abdicated responsibility and dumped it all on Isabel, who was progressively more afraid of Jean. After Jean had two attacks in one day, Isabel wrote: "She subconsciously feels my weakness & all her venomous points are to the fore."[39] Another day she told her diary: "In Jean's present condition it isn't safe for me to be alone with her—She could easily lapse into the violence the doctors fear may come in time."[40] When Gerry came for a walk alone with Jean—something expressly forbidden by Twain—Isabel blew up and lectured him, in Jean's words, "that when Father was away she was in supreme control over everything here & that she forbad him to go out walking with me before luncheon."[41]

When Twain returned in early October, Jean expressed relief. "It is *beautiful* to have him back again and he doesn't seem unglad to be back. But I suppose that as soon as the cold weather really begins he'll want to run away again, and to stay that time."[42] That same day, Twain admitted to Thomas Bailey Aldrich: "I have worked pretty steadily for 65 years, & I don't care what I do with the 2 or 3 that remain to me so that I get pleasure out of them."[43] This was his rationale for his escapist behavior, from yachting and billiards to card playing and angelfish: he had earned the right to a rest from life's travails, his recompense for years of hard work. But he also acknowledged abandoning Jean at a critical moment. "The truth is, I had no business to leave here, & I must not do it again; for Jean's health is very bad this last fortnight, & I must stay by her henceforth, for no authority but mine can control her when she is ill—& she is always ill, poor child, these latter months."[44] It was an important concession, even if he didn't always make good on his pledge in coming years. "Jean is strong, hearty, & very sweet & demonstrably affectionate," he told Clara. "But it is pretty plain that she has to have at her elbow an indisputable authority. And so I realize that I must stop junketing & stay at my post & not try to delegate its duties & large responsibilities to another."[45] This was more grown-up language than Twain had used on the subject in some time, and he canceled plans for a spring trip to the South of France. Unbeknownst to his family, he was experiencing chest pain and shortness of breath that portended future trouble.

For Isabel, Twain's return was the deus ex machina that saved her sinking spirits. "The King has come back—now all things will be right, for I have . . . dropped my responsibility—ordinarily I can carry it, but not when it has sucked out all my strength . . . But the joy of having him back. I almost cry with happiness & with relief."[46] There was often excessive melodrama in Isabel's gushing praise of Twain in her journal. Even she admitted, "These pages are full of repetitious adoration of the King; but that's how they should be, for each day brings its wave of recognition of his greatness & my spirit sings & claps its silent hands over the wonder & the beauty of him. He is the saint & the shrine before the saint—the God behind it all."[47]

Isabel's nerves, after caring for Jean, were so shattered and her insomnia so crippling that her doctor recommended a rest cure. Twain, recognizing her condition, said she was "still feeble & has to go carefully & not over-exert herself."[48] He was now surrounded by three women—Jean, Isabel, and Clara—flirting with nervous breakdowns. For all his contrition, Twain failed to confront the essential problem between Jean and Isabel: that Isabel had no authority to order Jean around. When Jean invited a young man over for tea, she defied Isabel's "heated advice" and complained in her diary, "I am no baby & I don't consider that she has any right whatsoever to give me injunctions as to my behavior toward my friends."[49] When Jean told a Dublin friend about her illness, Isabel berated her and said people would gossip, then committed the extreme indiscretion of telling that friend about Jean's sanitarium stay. "If ever anyone can be absolutely & utterly infuriating, it is Lioness," Jean wrote.[50] Though driven to near collapse by taking care of Jean, Isabel didn't elect to step away from that responsibility, writing that "Jean is unmanageable & I must have his authority over her."[51]

It is amazing that Twain didn't intervene to separate the two women and restrict Isabel to secretarial duties alone. Their antipathy had become mutually destructive, and Twain allowed a dangerous situation to fester. He could write tenderly about Jean and lash himself into a rage about her unjust illness, but he could also be curiously obtuse about her. At first, he feared that she had taken up wood carving solely to earn money. "But it isn't that," he told Clara. "Jean mourns because she is the only member of the family who has no calling, & is accomplishing nothing in the world."[52] This somehow came as a revelation to him. When Jean wrote an article about a London statue dedicated to a dog tortured by vivisection, she asked him to read it, and he was complimentary. "He actually said he liked it and thought it was very good! If that wasn't a glorious compliment for a poor creature like me."[53] Twain had failed to shore up Jean's confidence or address the absence of love in her life—an absence so acute that she said she would probably fall in love with and marry any man who showed her the slightest attention.

Dr. Peterson, having pioneered residential communities for people with epilepsy, now recommended that Jean go to a private sanitarium in Katonah, in Westchester County, just north of New York City, which would enable Jean to have visitors. Twain approved the plan—"There's been a cloud-lift today," he told Mary Rogers, "and I've got to jubilate with somebody or expire with satisfaction"—and Jean consented, though not without some last-minute jitters.[54] She would be separated from her family, but she hoped to rebuild her health and be back in Dublin the following summer. When she departed the town in mid-October and Gerry Brush failed to show up to say goodbye, she wept inconsolably.

Back at 21 Fifth Avenue, Jean consulted the young, bespectacled Dr. Frederick Hunt, who would supervise her stay at Katonah, and she was shocked to discover that Isabel had given him the impression that she wanted to sleep in the same room with Anna. "Considering how I loathe having anyone in the room with me that really seemed laughable," Jean wrote. "Dr. Hunt doesn't care at all about having anyone sleep with me."[55] Once again, Isabel had inserted herself into intimate family matters. Dr. Hunt feared that Jean might be lonely at first at Katonah and urged her to give the place a chance, and Jean agreed, "That is my main desire."[56] When Jean and Isabel visited Hillbourne Farms in Katonah, it seemed a promising place for her rehabilitation. Sprawled across forty acres of woods and meadows, the residence emphasized exercise and featured a piano, bowling alleys, tennis and squash courts, even a carpentry shop where Jean could pursue her wood carving. The main house stood on a hilltop, and Jean thought the elevation would be good for her health. Best of all, Jean hoped to have visitors since the express train from Manhattan took only one hour. She tried to sound brave and hopeful despite her extreme trepidation.

When Clara, in a delicate state, learned that Jean was going into a sanitarium, it cast her into a three-day, bedridden depression. Jean wrote a remarkable comment that contrasted how she and Clara viewed their father. Jean could feel hurt and abandoned by his absences, but she still felt pure love for him. Not so with Clara, she thought. "I can't help feeling that Clara's love for Father is not what it should be. She shows a good deal of irritation and even that she is hurt, by his many little ways that are exasperating until one gets used to them. I know just how they affect her, as I have been all through it, but I do believe that I have passed that undesirable stage of not being truly devoted to him. Of course Father's rude and ungentlemanly ways often make me angry and I don't in the least refrain from criticizing those things, but with all that I am most fond of him."[57] Where Jean could never get enough of her father's presence, Clara contrived ways to slip away from him.

Twain, noticing this tendency in Clara, felt miffed by her sense of entitlement and the money she demanded for her musical tours. "Clara has been in here to shake her engagements in my face," he told Emilie Rogers, "and prove to me that her time is already worth a thousand dollars a month." Clara searched for excuses to flee to Europe. When she told her father that Leschetizky was dying and she couldn't miss the funeral, Twain responded with a tart comeback. "I am persuading her that she would feel very funny if she attended his & missed mine. I guess that that settled it & she won't go; for naturally she wouldn't miss mine for anything."[58] A rather cynical gibe about his daughter. Leschetizky managed to put off his death for another nine years.

WHIRLPOOL

On October 24, 1906, Jean left 21 Fifth Avenue, bid a tearful farewell to her family, and traveled to Katonah with Isabel and Anna. "It was desperately hard to leave Father and Clara in order to come out to a totally strange place. I tried my hardest not to cry before them, but as the time of departure began to approach I found it growing more and more difficult to restrain myself, especially when Clara began to cry, too, then it was really hopeless. Poor little Father seemed to feel badly, too, and the whole business was perfectly *horrible* to me."[59]

No sooner was Jean in the sanitarium than Twain's mind reverted to his own personal pleasures. As Isabel wrote two weeks earlier, "He wants his playmates and his intellectual associations—mostly the playmates I think though."[60] The day before Jean went to Katonah, a fourteen-year-old English girl named Dorothy Butes wrote to Twain, applauding his books, and he invited her to visit; she arrived with her mother on October 30. Bright and witty, Dorothy would become an angelfish and official member of the Aquarium Club. That same week, a restive Twain responded with zest to a proposal by his friend Leigh Hunt to travel on the Nile with him all winter. Then he came down with a cold and decided to abandon "the Egyptian trip," Isabel wrote, "for he knows that instead of spending the winter in Egyptian sunshine, he'd spend most of it in an Egyptian cemetery."[61] It is astonishing that Twain would have contemplated such a trip right after his anxious daughter had entered a sanitarium.

Whereas Twain had been barred from Clara's presence during her rest cure, Jean prayed that her father would visit frequently. Two days after Jean arrived in Katonah, Clara came and brought her sister some carnations and told her about the proposed Egyptian trip. Jean reflected that "it certainly seems hard on Clara, to be entirely deserted in this way."[62] Clara seemed happy at the prospect of her father's absence and thought it would be good for his writing, while Jean wasn't pleased. According to Isabel, Clara returned from Katonah "much depressed over the place & the great pathos of the situation."[63] Twain was supposed to visit Jean two days later, then postponed the trip because of cold, inclement weather.

WUTHERING HEIGHTS

Almost a week after Jean arrived at the sanitarium, she mused in her diary, "I wonder if Father is at all likely to come out?"[64] Without Livy's love and wisdom, her selflessness and common sense, the Clemens family had been blown apart and couldn't restore any reasonable facsimile of the life they had known before.

PART FIVE

Shipwreck

CHAPTER FIFTY-EIGHT

Man in the White Clothes

There were aspects of the regimen at Hillbourne Farms that pleased Jean, especially the emphasis on brisk outdoor activity, including skiing and tobogganing when it snowed, but she bridled at other rules, especially the severe dietary restrictions. She wasn't allowed to walk alone with male patients or go on the road outside the compound by herself and blamed Clara's intervention with the doctors—"the meddlesome little wretch!"[1] Clara was struggling to resume her concert tour, and Twain said Dr. Quintard was "loading her up with medicine as a preparation."[2] Fatigued with gout and a hacking cough—his familiar bronchitis—Twain sent sweet notes to Jean, but when he went up to see her, he found the place "a pathetic exile and captivity; I must have a country home for her."[3] Evidently with Jean in mind, he made a final resolution to build the Redding house, with John Howells commissioned as the architect.

Whatever Jean's frustration with naps, cold showers, and other institutional remedies, the resident doctor, Edward A. Sharp, was preventing her attacks. "I telephoned to town this morning & had a talk with Father," Jean wrote in mid-November. "The dear man was overjoyed by Dr. Sharp's success in warding off my attack."[4] The celebration was premature: six days later, Jean was stricken with severe vomiting and diarrhea. Still censorious with people—such episodes didn't exactly sweeten her mood—she snapped at Anna and reduced her to tears. "I am much too easily irritated, & even if I am ill, I have no reason for speaking as I

SHIPWRECK

so often have to Anna, or any other person, for that matter & I must control myself in some way."[5]

For a long time, Clara had been absent from her family in Norfolk, Connecticut, but now that she had returned to 21 Fifth Avenue, she sparred with Isabel over who was to run the household. Her father had given Clara "full and sole authority" to "scold or correct a servant," and on November 8 she ordered Isabel to fire the cook. "Mary the good little cook went away today," Isabel noted.[6] Many years later, Isabel claimed that Clara found her crying over this dismissal and said angrily, "After this I'll do my own dirty work." With memories likely colored by later events, Isabel also said Katy Leary had warned her about Clara. "In time she'll do the same to you & worse. She hates you and don't you forget it."[7] For all her psychological frailty, Clara had a strong and willful nature. When Twain told her that he was the "boss in this house," she retorted, "Oh no, you're not. You're merely owner. I'm the captain—the commander-in-chief."[8] If Isabel thought Jean's departure would make life much easier for her, she was sorely disabused. She was now bedridden for a week, and Twain had to whittle down alone the gathering pile of unanswered mail. Finally, doctors decided that Isabel should go to Hartford for a rest, which lasted more than two weeks. Even apart from Twain, Isabel could not suppress her worshipful thoughts about him and wrote of her "heart torn into sobbing shreds by my homesickness for the King."[9] She had become emotionally dependent upon Twain in a way that far surpassed the bounds of any ordinary job.

With Jean in Katonah and Isabel in Hartford, Clara was ordered by Dr. Quintard to take a short rest cure at a Westchester sanitarium not far from Jean—close enough for Jean to glimpse her hilltop house. One day, wrapped in furs, Clara even swept by Jean's place in an open carriage. With black humor, Twain said 21 Fifth Avenue had been transformed into "the House of Gayety! Miss Lyon left for Hartford day before yesterday . . . Jean's gone, Clara's gone—there'll be nobody on the premises but the servants and more for a fortnight."[10] Everyone in his life was now stricken with *something*, and the peculiar confluence of events deepened his pessimistic outlook. When he learned of the death of an old friend, he reflected, "It is another tragedy. Apparently, broadly speaking, life is just that, simply that—a tragedy; with a dash of comedy distributed through it, here and there, to heighten the pain and magnify it, by contrast."[11]

Hobbled by gout, Twain roused himself to battle an issue that had always enlisted his strongest passion: copyright protection. For years, he had been robbed of royalties by pirated editions of his work and repeatedly lobbied Congress to combat that. As early as 1876, after the widespread piracy of *Tom Sawyer,* he had bemoaned the toothless copyright law in effect. Lacking an international copyright law, American authors enjoyed no legal protections overseas. In 1891 Congress enacted the first international copyright agreement—a "lame, poor bill," said Twain, who supported it—giving authors limited protection in a handful of countries.[12] From that point on, Twain focused his attention on another front in the copyright war: extending the time an American author enjoyed copyright protection. When his Hartford neighbor Harriet Beecher Stowe lost copyright protection on *Uncle Tom's Cabin* several years before she died, Twain, both as an author and a friend, grew indignant. "Her daughters receive nothing from the book," he wrote. "Years ago they found themselves no longer able to live in their modest home and had to move out and find humbler quarters."[13]

Now, with two sickly daughters, Twain wanted to safeguard their financial security after his death, but was stymied by copyright protection that lapsed after forty-two years; this meant that within five years, such protection would start to expire on his earliest books, and the government "will begin to steal from my children the bread which I have earned for them."[14] He hoped to extend the copyright of his works by inserting into them excerpts from his autobiography, but he also wanted to stretch the forty-two-year limit to fifty. In Twain's humble opinion, he was the only person with suitable talent to persuade the president and Congress to enact such reform. On December 7, he settled into the New Willard Hotel in D.C. and prepared to take the White House and Capitol Hill by storm. "I shall stay here several days & work for the bill," he wrote to Jean, "in your interest and Clara's."[15]

When Twain showed up at Congress with other authors, he startled the reporters by pulling off a long overcoat and dazzling them with his "snow-white clothes. The others all wore black, & looked gloomy & funereal."[16] Even his shoes, collar, and cravat were blinding white—not your typical lobbying outfit—and this sealed the association of Twain and white suits in the public mind. One reporter wrote that Twain needed only "a palm-leaf fan to complete his personification of the tropics."[17] When journalists asked about his unusual white garb, he explained it was "the uniform of the American Association of Purity and Perfection," of which he was president and sole member.[18]

In committee testimony, Twain asserted that the copyright extension was not for him but for his daughters, "who can't get along as well as I can because I have carefully raised them as young ladies, who don't know anything and can't do anything"—a gauche attempt at humor that would not have sat well with Jean and Clara.[19] Twain pressed Speaker Joseph Cannon for access to the House floor so that he could accost members, but since rules forbade that, Cannon set up Twain in his private dining room and gave him a servant to steer interested parties in his direction. As word got out that Twain was there, a parade of legislators streamed in until the air grew "blue with tobacco smoke," said Albert Paine.[20] When Twain strolled over to the White House, he told the presidential doorkeeper, "I want the usual thing. I'd like to see the President."[21] After a five-minute chat with Teddy Roosevelt, Twain emerged to announce, "The President is one with us on the copyright matter."[22] The proposed bill didn't pass in 1906, but a new copyright law was enacted in March 1909, with TR signing it on his last day in office. Because it lengthened the royalty period by fourteen years, an elated Twain touted it as "the only sane & clearly defined & just & righteous copyright law that has ever existed in the United States."[23]

MAN IN THE WHITE CLOTHES

When he returned to New York on December 12, Isabel Lyon, back from Hartford, was ecstatic to glimpse her King again. "He seemed sweeter & mellower than ever before. He can go away from me, but I shall not go away from him again unless he sends me."[24] It delighted her that Albert Paine planned to move into 21 Fifth Avenue and become Twain's regular billiards partner. "Strength is flowing back into my veins & I am glad to be alive."[25] Despite the dark undercurrents she experienced with the Clemens daughters, Isabel sounded calmer after her rest. "We receive very encouraging news from Santissima, sweet Santissima, although we cannot see her, and we can only hope that her condition is as encouraging as the reports are. Jean is recovering a little from her homesickness . . . and has begun her studies—Italian, French and German in the Berlitz School."[26] It was the first time in a long while that Isabel had been alone with Twain, minus his daughters, and that may have accounted for her hopeful mood.

That December, Isabel became further enmeshed in the tangled web of family affairs when Twain confided that he projected a sharp drop in his annual income, based on his Harper contract. "Next year," Isabel wrote in her diary, "will begin the 40% of the previous year's income from the books—which this year has been $40,000.00 and the children must begin to realize that if they have only $25,000 a year to live on—they must manage to live on that."[27] With Isabel bouncing back from a nervous collapse, it was curious that Twain expanded her array of powers yet again, this time thrusting her into the midst of family finances, a move that threatened to bring her into more direct conflict with his daughters, especially Clara, who insistently demanded more money for her career.

As viewed through Jean's diary, the Katonah residence was scarcely a gloomy place, and she was able to lead a vigorous life, whether playing croquet or ice skating or dancing. She spent time carving mahogany and hoped to sell her handiwork to stores or an art association. Famished for love, she swooned over any eligible men in the vicinity and developed a close attachment to a young Dr. Hibbard, who allowed her to escort him on his medical rounds in the neighborhood, and their conversations acquired an increasingly personal tone. As with Gerry Brush, Jean pined for someone who didn't reciprocate her feelings. Though they spent four or five hours daily together, Jean was saddened by rumors that Dr. Hibbard was engaged to a woman in Buffalo. "He seems so outspoken and frank that it is hard for me to believe [it], even though I have seen so many letters addressed to Grace Carpenter."[28] When Dr. Hibbard mentioned that he might leave Katonah in June, Jean feared that, without him, the place would be an "absolute Hades to me . . . and I shall have to drag my useless, empty life out by itself."[29]

The day after Dr. Hibbard told Jean of his departure plans, she committed a violent, seemingly uncontrolled act when they played squash together. She was exasperated by a good play he made and "forgot myself so completely that I hit him in the back with the flat of my racket. Of course the minute I had done it, I realized what a disgusting thing I had done and apologized . . . It was a dreadful, lawless, thing to have done and I feel terribly about it."[30] This impulsive act lends credence to the idea that she had struck Katy Leary in a fleeting fit of anger, and it was also reminiscent of her flicking her fingers at Isabel's cheeks in Dublin. The episode likely cost Jean her coveted relationship with Dr. Hibbard, who afterward sat only briefly at her table. "He said he was not hurt on that dire occasion," Jean lamented, "but I very much feel that he was scared & meant to stop any such feeling developing" toward her, which was "a pretty sharp blow" to her emotions.[31]

Twain opted out of direct supervision of Jean and, shockingly, visited her only three times during her fifteen months in Katonah. At Christmas, he sent her a beautiful volume of *Birds of North America* and wrote tender letters, but otherwise he dispatched Isabel as his official emissary. Clara, with an imperious side to her nature, decided to assume responsibility for Jean. When she admonished her sister that frequent drives with Dr. Hibbard might prompt harmful gossip, Jean grew enraged. "Her attitude made me feel cold & that her one idea was to stick to all rules &

not regard—where it concerned me—my comfort or pleasure . . . Clara probably fears that I may fall in love with Dr. H and . . . feels, as mother did, that I must never marry."[32] As Dr. Hibbard drew away, Jean discovered that Clara had sneakily complained to Dr. Sharp about the liaison. "Her action was *low*, I think, & I don't feel that she had any right to do as she did. And I told her too, that she wasn't my mother & that I didn't consider that she had the privilege of doing as she had done."[33] In her view, Clara had robbed her of her one real pleasure. Nevertheless, yielding to convention, Jean told Dr. Hibbard that he could no longer come to her room for private chats.

As Jean suffered grand mal seizures in Katonah and up to three petit mals per day, she knew that no sudden, miracle cure would materialize. Dr. Sharp gave her painful hypodermic injections in her shoulder and hip to stave off attacks, but to no avail. She was gravely disappointed when doctors informed her that she would have to stay on through the following summer, dashing any hopes for a return to Dublin. When Clara said their father might be willing to summer in Katonah, Jean laughed at the very notion. "If he was lonely up in Dublin, where there are at least some very nice & interesting people, what under heaven would he be in this mud-hole containing not a soul."[34] When Isabel visited, she concurred. "Lioness looks better," Jean wrote, "but not well yet. She was very nice indeed & came out to watch Dr. H[ibbard] ski after lunch."[35] On another visit, Isabel brought plans for the Redding house and told Jean how she had argued for a bigger room for her.

Although the sanitarium had no walls, Jean lacked any semblance of adult freedom and hated the subtle atmosphere of restraint. Finding Dr. Sharp gruff and overbearing, she grew hotly confrontational when he objected to her dining with her friends, insisting that he alone reserved the right to seat patients. Strangely enough, he thought eating together might make patients too excitable. Jean went to him "fairly boiling over" with rage and accused him of repeatedly lying. As a parting shot, she said sarcastically, "Of course it's a charming thing to do to make one statement one day & change it the next!"[36] In a short time, the residence had become distasteful, even nightmarish, to her. It would

SHIPWRECK

have made a huge difference had her father interceded as her protector. Meanwhile, as Clara put it, Jean "chafed at the chains in her life which could not be entirely removed."[37]

The only person who could truly act as Jean's guardian was her father, who found the whole situation too distressing. Recently Emilie Rogers had given him a billiards table as a gift, and he now spent hours daily playing with Albert Paine, yet another symptom of his regression to childhood. He also felt a certain wanderlust. Right after Christmas, Jean was dismayed to learn that a party consisting of her father, Paine, Lyon, and Twichell would sail to Bermuda and that her father might even rent a house there for February and March, his doctors hoping to cure his bronchitis. "Before long I shall be deserted so far as family goes," Jean wrote plaintively. "If only I had one of my own!"[38] Ever since his 1877 trip with Twichell, Bermuda had served as Twain's Brigadoon, a place of pastoral simplicity and spotless white houses surrounded by masses of flowers, a preindustrial paradise. As he wrote, "Bermuda is the right country for a jaded man to 'loaf' in."[39] It seemed a spot without poverty, detached from the busy outside world and free of "the triple curse of railways, telegraphs & newspapers."[40]

On January 4, 1907, the group checked into the Princess Hotel in Hamilton, the main city of the Bermuda islands. On the boat, Isabel fiercely protected Twain's privacy, and when a woman tried to accost him, she fended off the intruder, saying, "The King wished to be let alone, *must* be let alone, because he had come away exhausted."[41] According to Isabel, Twain was irritated by Twichell's growing deafness and empty chatter, but still managed to squeeze laughter from his large brood of children. Had they stayed two days longer on the boat, Twain quipped, "he'd have had a child. He's been on the verge of it several times."[42]

Once installed at the hotel, the group drove in a carriage to a coastal spot, Devil's Cave, where Twain could feast his eyes on the array of colorful tropical fish, especially the magnificent angelfish. Touring the island, Isabel was ecstatic at being a fixture at his side. "I was in heaven as I sat beside the King and drove along those beautiful roads."[43] Lest people imagine he sinned against propriety, Twain explained why he was escorted by a single lady. "I have brought my Secretary with me because she knows everything; and I find that I don't know anything."[44] Isabel doted on him in matrimonial style, cleaning his pipes, knotting his necktie, and brushing off his clothes. "I'm glad I can spoil the King," she told Twichell, "that is all my meat and drink and life in these days."[45] Twain was pleased that Isabel fussed over him, removing worldly cares from his shoulders. "A daisy—a bouquet of daisies—a bushel of 'em, is she!" he told Twichell. He started to feel lost without her—"alone in the dark, as it were"—yet he didn't stop to speculate where all this might be heading.[46]

The stay in Bermuda proved brief. When the Clemens party left on January 7, Twain socialized on the way home with Paddy Madden, nineteen, a pretty girl from the Upper West Side.[47] He followed up by sending her a copy of *Christian Science* and a photograph of himself, binding her closer to him. When the ship docked in New York, reporters, avid for quotable witticisms, formed their usual scrum around Twain. "Please don't say I have been away for my health," he advised. "I have plenty of health. Indeed, I'll give some of it away."[48]

Doubtless feeling guilty that he had gallivanted while his daughter was shut up in a sanitarium, Twain and Isabel visited Katonah three days after returning from Bermuda. Though Jean was tremendously excited, the visit turned into a disaster. "His visit was a pleasure only in that I saw him," Jean wrote, "because he brought bad news"—that she couldn't go horseback riding.[49] Enraged, Jean denounced the deceitful doctors who had promised her that she could ride. To placate her, Twain shipped to the residence her favorite horse, Scott, as well as a carriage and a coachman named George. Jean had a stack of grievances awaiting her father, and Twain could barely tolerate her demands. As Isabel said, Jean "was in a torrent of impossible moods & distressed her wonderful father until he was ready to weep," and his ensuing depression lasted for days.[50] Jean's diary contains many examples of her berating people, and she took a dagger to another new maid: "She has such a disgusting smell that it makes me positively sick to pass through the hall after she has been there. She must be filthy!"[51] Twain got accurate reports about Jean, who saw everything through a glass darkly and found the company of "coarse & common" people unbearable.[52]

Writing to Jean after his visit, Twain reprised an old theme: that she should try to recapture the sweetness of her younger days. "Bear with the situation as well as you can, dear Jean, & call back the gentle spirit you were born with, & believe that all those people mean you well, for it is indeed so. It is your disease that makes you see ill intentions in them—they mean well by you."[53] By stressing how lovable Jean had once been, her father implicitly conveyed how much he disliked the way she was now—a dispiriting message, to be sure. He gave Panglossian advice to a young woman cursed with an incurable disease. "As a whole the letter was sweet," Jean wrote, "but the statement of my having been born with a sweet nature surprised me. I had always supposed that as a small child, I had been regarded as a young devil."[54]

Jean's keen outrage and feelings of paranoia toward authority figures were reminiscent of her father, who could also fly into prolonged rages against the powerful. After writing to her father, she set down an astonishingly clear-eyed appraisal of her family and assumed they must be relieved to be rid of her:

> I don't for a minute believe that I was sent out here for any such reason, but since it is better for me to be here it at the same time must be a relief to them. Also, the idea that they miss me is absurd. Clara's & my interests are too absolutely different for us to be necessary to one another even if we are fond of each other & Father can't possibly find any entertainment or interest in me. I am sure he is fond of me but I don't believe that he any more than Clara, really misses me. It seems a heartless thing to say, but now that I am accustomed to this place, I don't really miss either of them. I far more often feel a desire to see Father, than I do to see Clara, which is only right & natural. I do often have a sort of hunger to get hold of him & hug him but if I were to say I missed him or Clara steadily, I should be lying.[55]

MAN IN THE WHITE CLOTHES

Jean had clearly inherited her father's capacity to step back and coldly dissect her motivations.

While it is easy to fault Twain, Lyon, and Clara for their response to Jean's plight, there was no simple solution for what to do with someone with an extreme case of epilepsy who could not live on her own. What happened to the Clemenses often happens with a seriously ill person in a family: there is emotional burnout, a sense of being overwhelmed by sacrifice, and worry about being swallowed up by the sick person's needs—followed by an inevitable revulsion and a temptation to cut loose from the person. With no good treatment at the time, epilepsy tended to create tragic, unresolved tensions within afflicted families.

Jean remained a danger to herself. On February 1, she suffered four attacks and fell and bruised her nose and lips during one of them. "My face is very sore—my nose skinned & swollen and one of my eyes is steadily getting blacker."[56] Fortunately, by mid-February, these attacks had abated, and she managed three normal weeks without an episode, as she skied, tobogganed, played squash, and took long walks. Aside from the forbidding Dr. Sharp, Jean liked the place again. "Dr. Hunt seems as much amazed as I have been," Jean noted. "He says I am becoming his best patient!"[57] Her father, overjoyed, wrote to Jean that "Dr. Hunt gives us a splendid report of your health in a letter to Miss Lyon."[58] It is clear from such letters that Twain communicated directly with Jean, but equally clear that he assigned Isabel to monitor Jean's condition and consult with doctors, a situation fraught with peril. To spare Twain worry, Isabel volunteered to present him with summaries of Jean's letters, and the accuracy of her reports would emerge as a major issue.

At 21 Fifth Avenue, Twain was no less a prisoner of loneliness than Jean. "The King talks so much about his death in these days," Isabel wrote.[59] With Clara on tour, Twain felt alone in the large, vacant house. To combat the solitude, he formed the Human Race Club, made up of Howells, Colonel Harvey, and the humorist Finley Peter Dunne, of "Mr. Dooley" fame. Of course, Twain named himself President Pro Tem, and Isabel Honorable Secretary. He was obviously proud of her and incorporated her into every aspect of his life. Among other things,

SHIPWRECK

Isabel was now his therapist and nursemaid. Whenever he grew lonely, she scurried about to round up club members, like a protective mother lining up playmates for a shy, solitary child. Isabel continued to regard him as a figure of godlike stature and simply couldn't bear to be without him. When he spent a night with Henry Rogers, she lingered in Twain's "tobaccoed room" at 21 Fifth Avenue and thought it "better to be there than to be in a thousand chapels heavy with incense."[60] That winter, Twain also launched "doe" luncheons made up solely of ladies—and himself, of course: as with the Saturday Morning Club, the Juggernaut Club, and the Aquarium Club, Twain was again the lone male situated at the center of a harem. He had not forgotten nineteen-year-old Paddy Madden, the girl whom he met on the boat back from Bermuda, and invited her to a dinner party where Isabel sized her up scornfully as "pretty and absolutely empty-headed."[61]

That March, searching for solace, Twain fled to Bermuda for five days of escape from home—four aboard the ship and one overnight there. "I have lost interest in everything, & am in deadly need of a change," Twain explained to Clara. "We invited Paddy, by telephone, to go along with us, & her father has given his consent."[62] Isabel again mocked Paddy's vacuous talk and adolescent chatter, but admitted that she served as "delightful bait for the very nicest men on board," including the president of Harvard, Charles W. Eliot, whom she "seemed to delight . . . with her empty little remarks."[63] The trip served its main purpose of distracting Twain, although upon his return, he learned of the death of his dear friend, the poet and author Thomas Bailey Aldrich. He wrote to his widow, pleading exhaustion and a long train ride as his reason for missing the Boston funeral, but the truth was that he loathed the self-centered Mrs. Aldrich. "I do not believe I could ever learn to like her," he said, "except on a raft at sea with no other provisions in sight."[64] As happened after their January escape to Bermuda, Twain and Isabel made a trip of atonement to see Jean, who dismissed the visit as pro forma and insufficient. "Father & Lioness came . . . Father seemed very well indeed but the visit was again disgustingly short."[65]

CHAPTER FIFTY-NINE

"A Real American College Boy"

Upon his return from Bermuda, Twain, for once in his life, wasn't courting publicity. When Brander Matthews invited him to a formal dinner, he fired back that he wouldn't "go to any banquet not even the Last Supper."[1] In fact, Twain stood on the eve of the most prolonged spurt of showmanship of his later years, which took an unexpected shape. Through the good offices of Moberly Bell of the London *Times,* Twain was offered an honorary degree at Oxford University in June. "If only Livy could have known of this triumph!" he exclaimed upon learning the news. He was already at his summer house in Tuxedo, New York, when the cablegram came, and for someone who had skipped college, nothing appealed to his imagination more than this signal accolade. He knew his worth in the literary world and felt that, for too long, major universities had snubbed him in conferring degrees. "Privately I am quite well aware that for a generation I have been as widely celebrated a literary person as America has ever produced, and I am also privately aware that in my own peculiar line I have stood at the head of my guild during all that time, with none to dispute the place with me."[2] This was as full-throated an expression of confidence, even conceit, as Mark Twain ever allowed himself. Now Oxford healed a hurt that had lingered quietly for years.

Before leaving for England he made a point of visiting Jean in Katonah and expressed hope that this would be "the last far journey I shall ever have to take."[3] After a satisfying visit—"Father came & we had a

SHIPWRECK

real visit this time," she wrote, "without Miss Lyon & over an hour in length"—Jean was heartbroken that she couldn't accompany him, another reminder of her unwanted confinement. On June 8, as Twain was about to board the *Minneapolis* for England, the two spoke by telephone. "It was fearfully painful to hear his voice," Jean said, "& not be able to see or squeeze him. To think of his going abroad without one is horrible."[4] Concerned that her father would behave outlandishly, Clara urged him to eschew white clothing on the trip. Isabel, who was abashed to be left behind—there had been too much scuttlebutt about their relationship to risk it—also worried about Twain's "inclinations for the unconventional."[5]

Once out on the Atlantic, Twain found his attention arrested by a sweet, pretty girl of seventeen named Carlotta Welles, who sat at a nearby table. She attended the Baldwin School in Bryn Mawr and was sailing back to see her parents in France. Twain approached her chaperones with a request that she dine with him the next day. As she recalled, "I was forthwith installed with him and really spent every waking moment with him."[6] He nicknamed her "Charley." She evidently bore a resemblance to Susy, and Twain wooed her with all the charm at his disposal. To summon her on deck, he wrote, "There's more than two thousand porpoises in sight, and eleven whales, and sixty icebergs, and both Dippers, and seven rainbows."[7] At a concert one evening, still wallowing in grief, he gave a talk about Susy's diary "and he almost broke down," said Carlotta. "There was a heart-broken quality about him but . . . there were also effervescent spirits and at any moment, his eyes were ready to twinkle with mischief and out would come the most unexpected & picturesque remarks!"[8] Unlike many angelfish, Carlotta grew restless with Twain's unrelenting interest and sometimes wished to bolt and race around the ship. There was something warm and tender but also possessive about him that made her eager to escape.

Twain's rapturous reception in England was previewed as soon as he docked: he was cheered by stevedores as he strolled down the gangplank and lifted his hat in salute. He told a swarm of reporters that he was already planning his funeral and that it was "going to be a great thing. I shall be there."[9] By an extraordinary coincidence, he had sailed on the

"A REAL AMERICAN COLLEGE BOY"

same boat as Archibald Henderson, the biographer of George Bernard Shaw, and when they arrived at St. Pancras Station in London, Shaw himself was there to greet them, forewarned by reporters that Twain would come. "He is by far the greatest American writer," Shaw observed. "America has two great literary assets—Edgar Allan Poe and Mark Twain." While Poe was often ignored, "Mark Twain does not give you the chance of ignoring him."[10] Shaw expressed to reporters the literary affinity he felt with Twain in making iconoclastic ideas palatable. "He has to put matters in such a way as to make people who would otherwise hang him believe he is joking."[11] Amid a heap of luggage, Twain and Shaw enjoyed only a brief moment to chat, but they would have a chance to engage more fully when they lunched at Shaw's house two weeks later, even though Twain conceded to reporters that he had not yet read much of Bernard Shaw.

Twain checked into Brown's Hotel in Mayfair, which he preferred to fancier hostelries such as the Hotel Cecil and the Savoy; something old-fashioned and elegantly understated about Brown's pleased him. The moment he arrived, the hotel was deluged with affectionate letters from fans, and Twain was transported into a dreamlike state by all the attention. Instead of having Isabel to handle letters, he had brought along Ralph W. Ashcroft, a thirty-two-year-old Englishman who had grown close to Twain through the young gentleman's post at the Plasmon Company of America. Ashcroft was a slim, elegant man with spectacles, a mustache, and a carefully trimmed goatee. At this stage of their relationship, Twain idealized Ashcroft's cool efficiency, saying that "whatever he undertakes to do he does promptly, and in the best and most effective way . . . I have long thought of him privately in my mind as Ashcroft the Infallible."[12] Unfortunately, Twain's judgment would prove highly fallible, and he later came to deplore him as "obsequious, watchful, attentive, and looking as if he wanted to lick somebody's boots."[13] Aided by hindsight, he would notice Ashcroft's extreme penchant for secrecy, his way of cloaking his past in silence. But now the trusted Ashcroft and an assistant worked faithfully around the clock to answer the tidal wave of fan letters swamping the hotel.

SHIPWRECK

Clara had intuited correctly that Twain would cause a commotion in London through his flamboyant behavior. One day, he descended to the hotel lobby in a blue bathrobe and slippers, then shuffled across the street to the Bath Club as "pretty shop girls on their way to work" stared in shock.[14] Reporters descended in droves, with the London *Times* reporting that "after his bath Mark Twain returned to his hotel in his three-piece costume of one bathrobe and two slippers, and had the pleasure of making a lot more people open their eyes very wide."[15] Clara, who had assumed a motherly, slightly bossy attitude with her father, cabled him in concern: "Much worried remember proprieties." Twain, unapologetic, shot back, "They all pattern after me."[16] More terse banter bounced across the Atlantic. "Try not to be jealous," he admonished Clara, who retorted, "More worried than ever doctor, remember the proprieties."[17] Jean, who could be prudish and judgmental, was no less alarmed by the bathrobe episode and hoped that, if untrue, the *Times* would "correct its misstatement because most of the people, not knowing you, would be likely to believe it & be horrified—disgusted."[18] Clearly Twain's straitlaced daughters identified much more with their mother's gentility than with their father's notoriety.

On the ship over, Twain had met a second teenage girl, Frances Nunnally, the sixteen-year-old daughter of an Atlanta candy manufacturer, who also stayed at Brown's Hotel. Twain quickly enlisted "Francesca," as he named her, to escort him to many English homes, where she "got a world of petting homage," Twain recalled, "which pleased me as much as it pleased her."[19] Francesca—"a dear grave girl of 16, with the most wonderful little slender hands," Isabel was to observe—was destined to become a member of the Aquarium Club, and she was seen at Twain's side throughout his British visit, where she called him "Grandpa."

Before going to Oxford, Twain enjoyed himself at a garden party at Windsor Castle thrown by King Edward VII and Queen Alexandra. En route to the castle, outfitted in a frock coat and silk hat, he was applauded by crowds lining the route as if he were royalty himself. At the castle, Twain, a student of British history, stood transfixed by "the most imposing and majestic pile of picturesque old architecture in Great Britain."[20]

"A REAL AMERICAN COLLEGE BOY"

Even with such august personages as the King of Siam and Indian princes there, Twain was the cynosure of all guests as he chatted with the prime minister, Sir Henry Campbell-Bannerman, and the noted actress Ellen Terry (who, at sixty, arrived with her much younger thirty-one-year-old American husband). "She came charging down upon me with both hands extended, and looking as young as her husband, and twice as vivacious."[21] Some in the press wanted to portray Twain as a rube in his fifteen-minute encounter with the King, but he wittily corrected this misconception: "One newspaper said I patted his Majesty on the shoulder—an impertinence of which I was not guilty; I was reared in the most exclusive circles of Missouri, and I know how to behave."[22] The Queen was charmed when Twain humorously inquired if he could purchase Windsor Castle; evidently, she declined. In reporting to Jean, Twain observed that he had climbed all the social rungs in England, "from the stevedores on up to king & queen."[23] Clara summed up the English visit thus far when she told her father, "You certainly are having an eminent time and couldn't feel more important I suppose if you were a distinguished archangel from Heaven visiting the Earth"—exactly the sort of joke Twain himself would have made.[24]

In accepting the Oxford degree, Twain had planned on a more modest and less sociable trip than the extravaganza it now burgeoned into. It seemed as if every celebrity in London turned out at one function after another to honor him. When American ambassador Whitelaw Reid threw a high-class dinner for him at Dorchester House, Sir Arthur Conan Doyle and Sir Lawrence Alma-Tadema came to pay homage. A few days later, the Society of the Pilgrims held a luncheon for Twain at the Savoy Hotel, its guests including Joseph Duveen, Rider Haggard, and Sir Herbert Beerbohm Tree. Right around the time that Twain arrived in London, the thoroughbred racing trophy for the Ascot Cup had been stolen. Going to the Pilgrims luncheon, he noticed a sandwich man with a newspaper placard that read "Mark Twain Arrives Ascot Cup Stolen"—with no comma separating the two headlines. For the Pilgrims, Twain spun humor from the mix-up. "I suppose I ought to defend my character, but how can I defend it? I can say here and now . . . that I speak the

SHIPWRECK

truth. I have never seen that cup. I have not got the cup—I did not have a chance to get it."[25] On a more serious note, he talked about how startled he was by the outpouring of hundreds of letters he received, and "that is the last and final and most precious reward that any man can win."[26] Deeply moved, he said he would always associate England with learning of Susy's death while staying there. "So I must sometimes lay the cap and bells aside . . . I cannot always be cheerful . . . When a man stands on the verge of 73, you know perfectly well that he never reached that plane without learning what this life is—heart-breaking bereavement."[27]

Such festivities were mere curtain-raisers to the honorary doctor of letters degree at Oxford, whose students sent beforehand an exuberant telegram that promised, "Even if the weather is in Clement our welcome will be warm."[28] Once in Oxford, Twain wasted no time in amusing reporters, telling them that he came to the ancient university to show "what a real American college boy looks like."[29] In this banner year for Oxford honorees, Twain shared the spotlight with Rudyard Kipling, Auguste Rodin, Camille Saint-Saëns, Henry Campbell-Bannerman, and Foreign Secretary Edward Grey, but Twain grabbed the lion's share of adulation. The night he arrived, when he tried on the resplendent scarlet and gray gown he would wear the next morning, it was love at first sight. "I was born for a savage," he later said. "There isn't any color that is too bright and too strong for me, and the red . . . There is no such red as that outside the arteries of an archangel that could compare with this."[30] Even the decorous Jane Clemens herself had an extreme fondness for this riotous shade.

The next day, Lord Curzon, Oxford's chancellor, clad in a black and gold gown, led the double-file procession of honorary doctorate recipients through the narrow, crooked lanes of the university town. As Twain marched down thoroughfares thick with excited spectators, he was astounded by the thunderous reception reserved for him, dwarfing even that for Rudyard Kipling, who captured the moment well. "All the people cheered Mark Twain. And when they weren't cheering and shouting, you could hear the Kodak shutters click-clicking like gun locks . . . The

"A REAL AMERICAN COLLEGE BOY"

street literally rose at him—men cheered him by name on all sides."[31] Drinking in the spectacle, Twain smiled and waved to the crowd.

As honorees waited outside the circular Sheldonian Theatre to be summoned for their degrees, Twain and Kipling, dying for tobacco, ducked aside to smoke cigars, "like naughty boys under a big archway," said Kipling.[32] When Twain entered the packed tiers of the Sheldonian, he was engulfed by applause that continued for a quarter-hour, Kipling noting that "even those dignified old Oxford dons stood up and yelled."[33] The ovation eclipsed that accorded anyone else, and Twain was vain enough to savor that distinction. His presence triggered a wild tumult of joy such as that solemn old hall had probably never witnessed. One student shouted, "What have you done with the Ascot Cup, Mark?" and the audience burst into laughter. "Have you got that jumping frog with you, Mark?" another student shouted amid more peals of laughter.[34] To further guffaws, a student hollered, "Where are the rest of the Innocents?"[35] In his tribute to Twain, Lord Curzon said, "Most amiable and charming sir, you shake the sides of the whole world with your merriment." By the end of the ceremony, a massive throng of students clustered around Twain and escorted him to a luncheon at All Souls College.

Nobody was more enamored of ancient spectacles than the author of *The Prince and the Pauper* and *A Connecticut Yankee*. The next day, he occupied a box with Lord Curzon and Rudyard Kipling to view the famous Oxford Historical Pageant in which thirty-five hundred locals, outfitted in period costumes, depicted scenes from British history. On the nearby River Cherwell, "state barges leaving kings, and war-barges bearing pirate-raids of the legendary days" floated by, Twain wrote.[36] He descended from the box to exchange cordial handshakes with Henry VIII, Charles I, Queen Elizabeth, and other worthies. "Once I turned a corner, & came suddenly upon an ecclesiastic of A.D. 710 & up went his two fingers in prelatic blessing, & he called me by name & made me welcome to his long-vanished day."[37] For four hours, throngs marched and rode on horseback through dramatized scenes, and the climax occurred when all thirty-five hundred people gathered together in a meadow. For Twain, the day left him "convinced that Pageantry is the most instructive & most impressive way of portraying history."[38]

Notwithstanding his excessive attachment to his scarlet gown, he was misinformed about the dress for a college dinner that evening and arrived in formal black only to find everyone arrayed in their gaudy costumes from the graduation ceremony. "I was fairly within the place before I noticed that it was just one wide and flaming conflagration of crimson gowns—a kind of human prairie on fire." He felt conspicuous as he made a speech garbed in a black suit and "looked as out of place as a Presbyterian in hell."[39] In the future, Twain would find many occasions to sport his Oxford gown, and one scholar has detected a psychological message at work. "He seemed hypersensitive about having been taken from school in his early teens and put to work in a print shop. Wearing his Oxford gown . . . at every conceivable opportunity became his final defense against the lifelong deficiency he had always felt."[40] On the other hand, a college education might have crushed Twain's originality and turned him into a hothouse bloom; without it, he had been able to grow as free and wild as he liked.

Back in London, Twain lunched with George Bernard Shaw at his flat in Adelphi Terrace, overlooking the Thames. The two men were superbly matched: both were ubiquitous wits and publicity hounds, keen to share with reporters often radical views, wrapped in disarming humor. Both were willing to defy middle-class morality and pay the price for it, and at lunch they enjoyed the instant rapport of kindred spirits. "He had a complete gift of intimacy," Shaw observed of Twain, "which enabled us to treat one another as if we had known one another all our lives, as indeed I had known him through his early books, which I read and reveled in before I was twelve years old."[41] Twain reciprocated this high regard: "Shaw is a pleasant man; simple, direct, sincere, animated; but self-possessed, sane, and evenly poised, acute, engaging, companionable, and quite destitute of affectations."[42] Twain was especially touched when

Shaw wrote to him that his late friend William Morris—artist, poet, and socialist activist—had so revered Twain that he ranked him as a greater master of the English language than William Makepeace Thackeray and counted himself "an incurable Huckfinnomaniac."[43] Shaw capped the meal by sending Twain a generous letter of appreciation that said "the future historian of America will find your works as indispensable to him as a French historian finds the political tracts of Voltaire. I tell you so because I am the author of a play [*John Bull's Other Island*] in which a priest says, 'Telling the truth's the funniest joke in the world,' a piece of wisdom which you helped to teach me."[44]

The lunch's afterglow faded quickly when a troublesome report surfaced on the other side of the Pond about Twain and Isabel Lyon. Twain had vetoed Clara's attending the Oxford ceremony, telling her that if she came, "Miss Lyon would then have to go too which of course was out of the question."[45] Despite such regard for propriety, the *New York Herald* ran an article on July 4 that Twain and Isabel were engaged to marry. Twain, aghast, issued a categorical denial in the next day's paper. "I have not known, and shall never know, any one who could fill the place of the wife I have lost. I shall never marry again."[46] The story must have aroused guilty feelings in Twain that he had somehow betrayed Livy's memory.

Exactly who planted this mischievous story remains a mystery. At the time, Twain and Isabel blamed it on a vengeful Charlotte Teller, who had been infuriated by reports of Isabel branding her "an adventurer" who was "planning to marry Mr. Clemens."[47] Later on, Twain claimed that Isabel had launched the rumor in connivance with Ralph Ashcroft, which seems far-fetched, given that Ashcroft was then new to his retinue. Twain also professed to remember a scene before leaving for England in which Isabel grew flirtatious, gave him a little "love-pat," and said people whispered they were going to get married. At this she burst out with "girly-girly stage-laughter to indicate how killingly funny & wildly absurd an idea it was." When Twain asked who could have uttered such preposterous things, she answered, "Everybody. It's all over the town!"[48] It seems surprising that Twain didn't realize that Isabel's constant presence at his side would spawn such rumors. In response to the episode, Twain began showing far greater caution by having other companions around whenever he appeared in public with Isabel.

Later on, Clara, by then with a huge ax to grind, told her father that Isabel had long been scheming to capture him. "We knew—& so did the friends—that she was aiming to marry you, & she seemed to have gotten such a hold upon you that she could make you do whatever she pleased. She was supreme. She had everything her own way in the house. She had stopped making requests, she only gave orders. You never denied her anything . . . Mary Lawton, the psychist, said she had hypnotised you, & it certainly looked like it."[49]

Isabel always insisted that Twain had been "an old man"—he was seventy-one; she was forty-three—and she could never have fallen in love with him.[50] Her abundant journals suggest otherwise. On the eve of his Oxford trip, she described Twain as "the most wonderful creature in the world."[51] She was thrown into a solitary, aching depression every time he left and then miraculously revived when he reappeared. "I'm not sleeping any of these nights along here," she wrote as Twain sailed to England. "I'm groping along to Something, with an indescribable loneliness. It's the terrible loneliness that always comes over me with the King so far away."[52] It's hard to imagine that an unmarried woman of her age, smitten with a world-famous author and fully sharing his life, did not fantasize about marriage. Before departing for England, Twain had signed over to Isabel a deed for a farmhouse and twenty acres of the Redding property, further intertwining their lives. (Twain later claimed he offered her ten acres and she artfully wheedled another ten.) That summer, without consulting his daughters, Twain gave Isabel a power of attorney that enabled her to buy and sell property, stocks, and bonds for him, and to write checks or withdraw money from his bank accounts. He also gave her a supervisory role in constructing his new Redding house. In fact, he ceded so much authority to her that he declared he didn't even wish to see the new house until the last detail was completed. How could his bestowing such major powers upon her not have fed Isabel Lyon's most florid fantasies about a married life with Mark Twain? She was already very near to being his wife in all but name.

"A REAL AMERICAN COLLEGE BOY"

The toast of London, Twain decided to extend his stay, addressing a Savage Club dinner and appearing in white for the only time on his trip. His image was in such demand that in a single day he sat for twenty-two photographs and four drawings—to the point of exhaustion. He lunched with a phalanx of dignitaries at the House of Commons, including Arthur Balfour, the former prime minister, and was greeted by a former acquaintance, Winston Churchill, now a young MP. He appreciated the singular honor of being hosted by *Punch* at a lunch in its private dining room—the inner sanctum usually shielded from outsiders. *Punch* had run a cartoon showing an elderly gent drinking to Twain's health, and during the meal eight-year-old Joy Agnew, the publisher's daughter, sprang into the room, "a little fairy decked out in pink, like a rose, and came tripping toward me, her face all alive with smiles and excitement; and she bore in her hands the framed original of the *Punch* cartoon."[53] She made a lovely speech in Twain's honor, curtsied, then disappeared. "This is the prettiest incident of my long life, I think," Twain said, "and I cannot think of it yet without a thrill at my heart and quickened pulse-beat."[54] The final honor Twain received came when he traveled to Liverpool aboard a private car formerly reserved for the Prince of Wales and was received by the Lord Mayor of Liverpool, who told a large banquet audience, "There was no man in the world to-day . . . who had brought so much mirth and happiness to the citizens of this Empire and of the United States" as Mark Twain.[55]

When he departed for New York on July 13, Twain was sure that his four-week stay in England had been the pinnacle of his career, an unmistakable sign of the adoration that he had inspired in millions of readers. The British now enjoyed an unalloyed love affair with Twain, while in America he had ruffled feathers with controversial political stands. Beyond question, he valued the Oxford degree as his life's foremost honor, telling a reporter as he left England that it was "the most enjoyable holiday I have ever had, and I am sorry the end of it has come."[56] Aboard the boat home, the *Minnetonka*, Twain recruited a new angelfish, ten-year-old Dorothy Quick of Plainfield, New Jersey, then traveling with her mother and grandparents. One day on deck she saw Twain scanning the

SHIPWRECK

horizon in a gray tweed coat and gray cap with a "great shock of snowy white hair and a keen, kindly observant face," she recalled.[57] She had seen him mobbed by admirers at a London train station and tiptoed past him five or six times before he said, "Aren't you going to speak to me, Little Girl?" As with all the angelfish, she was an impressionable young girl flattered by his unexpected attention. "It was too wonderful; and I shall never forget how proud and happy I was." He inquired if she knew his identity. "Of course, you're Mark Twain, and I've read all your books." When she reeled them off, an amused Twain remarked that Dorothy "knew more about his books than he did himself."[58]

In enlisting angelfish, Twain was strategic in winning over their mothers. At one point, Dorothy grew concerned that her mother would be worried by her absence. "We'll go find her together," Twain rejoined, "and I'll tell her she needn't ever be worried about you when you're with me. She might as well know it now, for we're going to be together a lot, you and I."[59] One notes how charmingly aggressive Twain was. Hand in hand, he and Dorothy walked the deck until they found her mother reclining in a steamer chair. Like all angelfish mothers, Dorothy's was delighted by her daughter's new pal and doubtless startled when Twain moved his steamer chair to her group. When Twain heard that Dorothy wore a white sailor suit to dinner, he insisted that she wear it daily; he would don his white suit and together they would "match and present a perfect picture as we pace the decks."[60] Dorothy was starstruck. "We were inseparable for the rest of the voyage; he literally wouldn't let me out of his sight."[61] After Twain was invited to speak on a concert program, he replied that he never made such decisions without his business manager's approval. "So you'll have to ask her." Dorothy joyously gave permission. "Imagine my pride and delight when I saw printed on the concert program . . . S.L. Clemens (Mark Twain) *by courtesy of Miss Dorothy Quick.*"[62] One can imagine the dreamlike effect of this doting attention on girls who, within minutes, evolved from total strangers to surrogate daughters, and Dorothy described their nine days together as "the most thrilling and eventful" of her life.[63]

When the *Minnetonka* docked in New York on July 22, at least a

"A REAL AMERICAN COLLEGE BOY"

dozen journalists lay in wait. Far from hiding his relationship with Dorothy, Twain flaunted it. Whatever else one can say about them, there was nothing furtive or secretive about his dealings with these young girls. After obtaining permission from Dorothy's mother, he insisted that any photographs he took had to be with Dorothy. With reporters, he referred to Dorothy as *"mon amie"* and stood with his left arm "thrown paternally around the child's shoulder," wrote a reporter.[64] At one point, Dorothy sat on his lap, leaning her head against his shoulder. Dorothy must have blinked with amazement as she turned into a national news story. "I had never looked into so many cameras at once. They all clicked merrily, with the result that there was not a paper in New York the next day that didn't carry a photograph of 'Mark Twain and Dorothy Quick.'"[65] One newspaper ran the headline: "Mark Twain Home—Captive of Little Girl."[66] The press presented the story, not as a disturbing case of deviance, but as the heartwarming romance of an old man with a little girl. After all, wasn't Mark Twain beloved by children the world over?

In a robust mood, Twain engaged in his usual repartee with reporters and talked about how the eventful trip had shaved years off his life. With age, he said, came "a greater capacity for enjoyment. Maybe that's the only advantage of second childhood, but it isn't a bad one."[67] Among those musing on this second childhood was Isabel Lyon, who spotted Twain on the lower deck "with a little girl snuggling up against him."[68] Before they parted, Twain secured a promise from Dorothy and her mother to visit him in Tuxedo Park, where he would spend the summer. Mrs. Quick encouraged Dorothy to go. Once this promise was made, Clara, who jealously guarded her father's reputation, packed Twain into a taxi and whisked him off to 21 Fifth Avenue, and they left for Tuxedo Park the next day.

CHAPTER SIXTY

"All the Wonders That Are Occurring"

Bent on leaving Manhattan and with the Redding house not yet ready, Twain had leased a lakeside house in Tuxedo Park, thirty-five miles north of New York, for his summer sojourn. It was an aristocratic enclave originated by tobacco heir Pierre Lorillard IV, who had created a playground for the rich, studded with two lakes, a golf course, tennis courts, and a clubhouse for social gatherings. Twain was captivated by the beauty of this plutocratic paradise, which was barred to plebeian outsiders: one entered by a granite gateway manned by uniformed guards. "The whole population of the miniature republic probably does not exceed fifty families," Twain said proudly, "with an average of four members and five servants to the family."[1] Along with her husband, Harry, the young and delightful Mary Rogers had urged Twain to come there, and her presence doubtless served as a major incentive.

Deprived of Twain, Isabel had felt lonely and overwhelmed with responsibilities that left her in a sleepless, anxious state. Twain had placed her in charge of the New York house while she also had to preside over Tuxedo Park and develop plans for Redding. In addition, he left her with stacks of autobiographical dictations to comb through and file in chronological order. All the while, she had to tend to Clara with her chronic vocal problems and consult with Jean's doctors. For performing the labor of several people, Twain paid this capable woman a pittance, and since she adored the King, she dared not protest. "Miss Lyon runs Clara, and Jean, and me, and the servants, and the housekeeping, and the house-building, and the secretary work, and remains as extraordinarily competent as ever," Twain said in May, not quite aware of the problems inherent in vesting so much power in an underpaid employee.[2]

Among her manifold duties, Isabel served as Clara's confidante, the repository of her secrets, and she wrote about Clara in a breathless, enraptured tone. When Clara returned from a tour in March, Isabel seemed enthralled. "She is a made over creature with happiness & Success & music running rampantly through her veins. What a creature she is, & how beautiful."[3] If the tour qualified as a critical success, Twain lost $2,500 in financing it, but he was happy, at least for the moment, stating that his daughter was "winning her way to success and distinction with sure and steady strides. By all accounts she is singing like a bird."[4] For all her intimacy with Clara, Isabel oversaw the tour finances and was forced to write checks for a money-losing venture.

Later on, Twain accused Isabel of having acted seductively around him, but at Tuxedo they were both guilty of crossing the line of impropriety. One day, both Twain and Isabel appeared on the staircase—she on the third floor, he on the second—and listened as Clara played the piano down below. As Isabel described the scene, "I slipped down a flight, I had on a long thin black silk gown that made a little swish, just enough for the King who stood in his underdrawers in the 2nd hall, to hear and make him look up at me with his eyes shining with delight . . . There he stood in the hall listening to Santa. He had slipped off his trousers and stockings and he had his yellow calabash pipe in his hand."[5] Two days later, Isabel wrote: "Here at 6:15 the King came slipping up to my room with just his silk underclothes on—such a beautiful man he is."[6] It all boiled down to the old quandary of Isabel's undefined status: Was she Twain's mistress-in-waiting or his secretary? Was she Clara's bosom friend or just a glorified employee?

Clara grew so intimate with Isabel that she spilled secrets into her ear—too many, it later turned out. "Santa was bursting with glee tonight," Isabel wrote, "and called me Nan-Pan-Pete-Pan, and snuggled her darling head in my neck. I *wish* I could write of all the wonders that are occurring in all the lives about me."[7] One wonders if this referred to

"ALL THE WONDERS THAT ARE OCCURRING"

Clara's relationship with her new piano accompanist, Charles E. "Will" Wark. "I like Mr. Wark & his honest blue eyes ever so much," Twain told Clara. "I think you are fortunate to be in his guardianship."[8] Unfortunately, the blue eyes were not so very honest, and Clara would shortly engage in a clandestine romance with Will, a married man. With Twain in England, Wark dined nightly with Clara and Isabel at Tuxedo Park, making Isabel privy to this secretly unfolding drama. "Santa Clara and I. I have been dreaming a wonderful love story in these days," wrote Isabel. "A story all of beautiful colors, and it makes me so very lonely and so sad."[9] One wonders whether this alluded to Clara and Will, or was it even Isabel fantasizing about an affair with Clara—a woman she romanticized as "made all of fire and dew"?[10]

Debilitated by Tuxedo Park's heat, Clara and Isabel decided to embark on a bracing two-week cruise to Nova Scotia and Newfoundland before the King returned from England. Their ship was involved in a fogbound collision in Halifax Harbor, so they never made it to Newfoundland. While they awaited a new vessel, Isabel learned of the reported rumors alleging that Twain and she were engaged to be married. Stunned, Isabel wrote in her journal that "the King would be as pained as his secretary to hear of any such report," and she issued stern denials to the press.[11] She and Clara cut short their voyage to return to Tuxedo, and by the time Isabel reached Boston and checked into a hotel, she had a throbbing headache that "robbed me of my sense of being human."[12] For an entire day she couldn't rise from her bed, while Clara checked herself back into her rest cure in Norfolk, Connecticut. When Twain returned from England, he was so shaken up by the newspaper report about Isabel that he insisted upon having chaperones along whenever the two went out for carriage rides.

In his isolation, Twain needed the bluff company of Henry Rogers, who suffered a stroke on July 22, which early on was kept private. He had been targeted by antitrust actions against Standard Oil, a major source of stress that may have induced the attack. One day he went to 26 Broadway, slumped at his desk, and found his left arm paralyzed. Given his lofty stature on Wall Street, his office floated a false statement

SHIPWRECK

that he was recuperating from overwork and excessive heat, and even his redoubtable secretary, Katharine Harrison, minimized the situation to Twain. "Good," Twain told Rogers, "I was uneasy at first."[13] By mid-August, Emilie Rogers broke down and confessed what had happened. Though Rogers would recover and he and Twain would travel again, he never regained the red-blooded vigor of his earlier days.

With Jean in Katonah, Twain relied on Clara for attention, but he again felt her pulling away, telling Isabel that "he didn't get much good out of Clara. When she is in N.Y. he never sees anything of her & when he goes to her rooms he feels like a stranger making an untimely & unwelcome visit. Poor King! It is all Too True."[14] Disappointed by his family, Twain indulged, as compensation, in his late-in-life madness: the angelfish. In late July, he wrote to ten-year-old Dorothy Quick and pleaded with her to visit him in Tuxedo Park for a week. He sent a parallel letter to her mother, promising that Isabel, a former governess in her forties, would pick up Dorothy and deliver her home safely. As further reassurance, Isabel wrote to Mrs. Quick to attest that "both Mr. Clemens & I want Dorothy to be happy, and I too shall love to have her here, as I do love little girls."[15] So Isabel, among her varied duties, was now enlisted as special agent for the angelfish and deployed as protective camouflage to show the world that nothing untoward could happen.

During his five days with Dorothy, Twain posed with her for photographs, listened to Orchestrelle music, played cards, and trotted her around to social events. A photo shows them standing side by side: Twain has his right arm around her and she clings tightly to him, tilting her head against his chest. He read aloud to her from *Tom Sawyer* and paused to supply the personal anecdotes behind it. He also let Dorothy listen to his autobiographical dictations, and she was mesmerized as he paced back and forth, expatiating, hands folded behind his back. She saw flashes of temper when Twain proofread the stenographer's work and broke out "into fiery explosions of rage because she had left out something he had particularly wanted in the manuscript," telling Dorothy the stupidity of stenographers was the bane of his life.[16] Because Dorothy wanted to be a writer, Twain made her commit her stories to paper so

"ALL THE WONDERS THAT ARE OCCURRING"

that he could have them in "her own brisk and tumultuous handwriting, adorned with her own punctuation—I mean the absence of it—and steeped in the charm of her incomparable spelling." He noted that Dorothy was "even a more desperate speller than ever Susy was"—confirming that Twain labored to re-create the world that he had once known when his daughters were young girls.[17]

For the entire week, Twain was buoyed by Dorothy's company, and the second she was gone, he wrote to her in the most extravagant spirit of flattery. "I went to bed as soon as you departed, there being nothing to live for after that, and the sunshine all gone . . . Aren't you sorry for me, you fresh breeze blown from fragrant fields of flowers? I thought this was a home. It was a superstition. What is a home without a child? Particularly a house that's had such a child as you in it."[18] To Clara he wrote a lugubrious note lamenting that Dorothy had taken "the sun & the moon & the constellations with her, & left silence & solitude & night & desolation behind her."[19]

What did Clara think about this strange child who had suddenly usurped her place in her father's life? She immediately interpreted Dorothy's presence as a slap in the face, a rebuke of her desire to have an independent life, and she replied to his letter in a frosty tone, brittle with thinly veiled mockery. "Dear little Mark I am sorry that that child has gone away if you miss her so much. It makes me feel that I ought to drop my career & trot right home except that I am not a sun or a moon or perhaps even a firefly . . . A *great deal* of love to you poor little Marcus & a hard hug. Are you very lonely? P.S. Thank you for the child's picture of you which will do nicely 'till I find something better."[20] The letter artfully blended love with the most potent sarcasm.

Jean's dawning awareness of the angelfish phenomenon was no less bitter. As Twain prepared for a second visit from Dorothy, he wrote to Jean: "I am droopy & lazy; I need the turmoil & tumultuousness of that tumultuous child, to wake me up—& wear me out."[21] For Jean, who had complained early in the summer that her father's hour-long visit was "disgustingly short," the realization that her father now spent entire weeks with an unknown child came as an unpleasant shock. "One letter from Father makes me rabid... No word of regret about my unhappiness—nothing. Then a lot of *stuff* about the maids & a child—all three absolute strangers to me! A truly sympathetic Father," she added caustically.[22]

That summer, Jean showed astonishing improvement as her seizures abated, and she had every hope of joining her father when the Redding house was ready. Now armed with the power of the purse, Isabel practiced a series of petty economies that Jean found punitive, including the refusal to pay board for her dog, Prosper. When Jean reminded her father that Prosper was her mother's last gift to her, he acquiesced. When Isabel and Clara set sail for the expensive Nova Scotia trip, Jean felt the inequitable treatment, scoffing in her diary, "That's nice economy!"[23] She desperately wanted her father's love and attention. "While playing tennis, soon after five Father telephoned me! It was fearfully upsetting. Oh, I do so want to get to him. The tears would come, I couldn't keep them back & Father's voice broke, too."[24] After he returned from England, she eagerly sought the illustrated articles about his trip and begged him to visit her in Katonah. "I don't want you to tire yourself, dear little Herr Doktor, but when you do feel up to a hard trip, *please* come out here & give me a squeeze. I sometimes feel as though I could not endure it much longer to stay away from you."[25] Such letters are hard to read when one realizes how much time and affection Twain was lavishing on Dorothy Quick. Right around the time that Twain invited Dorothy to Tuxedo Park, he managed to forget Jean's twenty-seventh birthday altogether. "I don't think he has ever failed to remember it," Jean wrote in her diary, "or be reminded of it so that he gave something."[26]

In early September, Dorothy returned to Tuxedo Park, a visit that stretched to ten days, "and during the entire time," Dorothy recalled, Twain "never went anywhere that he couldn't take me with him."[27] He lured her into his world of enchantment, proposing that he and Dorothy start an Authors' League—"two authors together. We will work hard, and I shall teach you what I know—and you will teach me too." Dorothy protested that she could not teach him anything, and he corrected her: "You can teach me how to be young, dear."[28] Suddenly Dorothy Quick had America's most famous writer serving as her personal tutor. Each

"ALL THE WONDERS THAT ARE OCCURRING"

day she wrote a short story, Twain reviewed it, and then she revised it, and sometimes he read his stories aloud to her for reactions. Were it not for the start of the school year, he would gladly have had Dorothy extend her stay beyond ten days. After she left, Twain rushed off a personal note to her, asking if she still remembered how Isabel looked, then sketched a little caricature of her. "The way she looks. Good-bye, I love you very much."[29] Just like that, Mark Twain had added a new daughter, one getting far more attention than his own biological and very needy daughters.

In mid-September, Twain left Tuxedo to visit Henry Rogers in Fairhaven, and around this time Emilie Rogers revealed the true damage that her husband's stroke had caused, disclosing to Isabel by phone that it had "muffled his speech so that he could not be understood for a week, and his left arm and leg were affected."[30] Twain stayed at the Rogerses' mansion three days before traveling with young Mary and Harry Rogers aboard the *Kanawha* to the Jamestown Exposition in Virginia for a celebration of Robert Fulton. Twain had tried to wriggle out of a speaking engagement there until organizers insisted that his presence had been a major draw, and he complied. He received a warm reception from the crowd, but a planned parade of boats was foiled by heavy seas and gale-force winds to the point that Twain ridiculed the event as "the completest & perfectest fiasco in history."[31]

The tempo of Twain's meetings with the angelfish accelerated, and he was no sooner back at Tuxedo Park than Francesca Nunnally, who had escorted him around London, arrived for a two-day visit with her mother, which was mostly spent playing hearts. Isabel professed to be charmed by the angelfish and in her journal praised how Twain was "so gay & sweet & pretty in his ways with 'Francesca.'"[32] Like Dorothy, Francesca took extreme pride in her relationship with Mark Twain, and when Twain mentioned that he would be traveling to Annapolis, she extracted a promise that he would stop by her prep school in Baltimore. "I should so love to have you come out here to our school," she wrote to him afterward, "and all the other girls are crazy to have you come too."[33] Twain promised he would time his trip "to kiss you & the rest of the 70" girls at the school. "You, anyway, shipmate! With love, SLC."[34]

Again, it is important to note that while Twain adopted an unhealthily flirtatious tone with the angelfish, presenting himself as their lovesick swain, he was never accused of acting on such impulses or engaging in predatory behavior. Though, heaven knows, his actual behavior was odd enough. Even from afar, Jean sensed something peculiarly disturbing in his references to these strange girls. As she said of a letter received from her father in early November, "He wrote of two little girls wishing him to kiss them on the street because he had kissed their sister in public at Jamestown. He did it & to me, it's not pleasant. I don't know how old the girls are, but it seems a trifle queer, even if he is very old."[35]

As Twain took refuge with his angelfish, Jean found the Katonah residence more dreary than ever. "I don't see *how* I can endure it here much longer," she told her diary.[36] She couldn't find like-minded people and was scathing in her judgments of most. "I hate, no, I despise the heads of this establishment & one of the chief patients," she complained to Nancy Brush. "All three are liars & wholly despicable."[37] As she sank deeper into depression, she craved adult freedom and dreamed of having a farm of her own. Jean and her father had bickered about the growing power that Isabel Lyon wielded over her life, and she wondered why her father did not assume responsibility for her treatment himself. When Jean sent an angry complaint to her father, Isabel showed no sympathy whatever and worried only about Twain's reaction. "Terrible that his children cannot come under the spell of his glories, his subtleties, his sweetnesses," she wrote with a strange blindness. "For this morning there was a cruel letter from Jean damning me—finding fault with him—with *him*."[38] Isabel had such an exalted view of the King that any criticism of him was unthinkable—lèse-majesté.

"ALL THE WONDERS THAT ARE OCCURRING"

Responding to Jean's complaints, Twain showered unstinting praise on Isabel and had nothing but censure for his daughter. "Jean dear, if your mother were here she would know how to think for you and plan for you and take care of you better than I do; but we have lost her, and a man has no competency in these matters. I have to have somebody in whom I have confidence to attend to every detail of my daily affairs for me except my literary work. I attend to not one of them myself . . . I give Miss Lyon instructions—she does nothing of her own initiative. When you blame her you are merely blaming me—she is not open to criticism in the matter." He flatly insisted that Isabel did everything superbly and never made any enemies. "All Tuxedo likes Miss Lyon—the hackmen, the aristocrats and all. She has failed to secure your confidence and esteem and I am sorry. I wish it were otherwise, but it is no argument since she has not failed in any other person's case. One failure to fifteen hundred successes means that the fault is not with her."[39] It was a harsh, pitiless message that Twain later regretted, or perhaps chose to forget. He was calling his daughter a misfit for failing to appreciate the many virtues of the incomparable Isabel Lyon. His letters grew increasingly tone-deaf: Jean was looking for love and understanding, not the reprimands and condescending lectures he gave her.

When Jean first went to Katonah, she had gone voluntarily and was eager to go. As time went on, she felt more like an inmate than a resident. When she consulted with her doctors, they then had to consult with Isabel Lyon. With Isabel functioning as her surrogate guardian, Jean had lost all control over her own fate. Nobody seemed to fathom the depth of her despair as she squirmed in a fearful dilemma: If she got worse, then she would have to stay at the sanitarium because she needed more treatment. If she did better, she would have to stay because she was doing so well there—Dr. Peterson's position of late. While Jean dreamed of rejoining her family in Redding, Dr. Peterson told Isabel something privately that made Isabel determined to keep her away. "I didn't tell the King how he said that the epileptic temperament rarely improved, but that it grew worse, & that Jean must never live with her father again, because her affection might easily turn into a violent & insane hatred and

SHIPWRECK

she could slay, just by the sudden & terrible & ungovernable revulsion of feeling."[40] This was a critical turning point for Isabel, who decided that, for medical reasons, she had to keep Jean at bay and safely away from her father. But she also knew, after their clashes in Dublin, that if Jean returned home, Isabel herself would be responsible for the patient's welfare and have to contend with her seizures. A home setting had not worked for Jean in the past; she needed professional care. Dr. Peterson was reasonably sympathetic to Jean's mental state, allowed her to make short trips away from Katonah, and gave thought to trying another sanitarium, if it might make Jean happier, but he was unable to offer a solution there. All the while, Jean wished that Clara or her father was dealing with the doctors who exercised such a giant influence over her life.

Never lucky with money when he acted on his business instincts, Mark Twain had profited handsomely from the counsel of Henry Rogers and his assistant, Katharine Harrison, who had advised him to deposit his money with the Knickerbocker Trust Company at Fifth Avenue and 34th Street. Supposedly a blue-chip bank at a prestige address, it paid hefty interest rates until its president, Charles T. Barney, squandered millions with Wall Street speculators in a failed attempt to corner United Copper. As its stock price collapsed, depositors besieged Knickerbocker Trust, clamoring to get their savings out. In the absence of deposit insurance, Twain stared at a massive loss. He was at Tuxedo Park and hastily dispatched Isabel and Ralph Ashcroft to empty out his bank account. The two were shocked by the panicky scene they found, with mounted police seeking to contain a disorderly crowd, among them high-toned people in "finely appointed carriages" with "bank books in their quivering hands."[41] They arrived too late: the bank had shut its doors and suspended payments, and the contagion of fear spread to other banks as total panic gripped the city. "Oh, it's too dreadful," Isabel wrote privately. "Every penny the King has, fifty one thousand dollars, is in the Knickerbocker trust co." She was surprised, upon returning to Tuxedo,

"ALL THE WONDERS THAT ARE OCCURRING"

to find "the King in bed and so cheerful and beautiful and brave, and trying not to show his anxiety."[42] Twain knew that he still had ample stocks and bonds to keep him afloat, and a guaranteed $25,000 annual income from book royalties. "The King does need some one to love him and pet him," Isabel wrote.[43]

The Knickerbocker soon announced that it had sufficient assets to pay depositors and reopen for business, but it would be a lengthy process before Twain was eventually made whole on his money. As he prepared to leave Tuxedo Park and return to 21 Fifth Avenue, he had to usher in a period of financial stringency for his entire family. However much Clara rebelled at being Mark Twain's daughter, her entire career was subsidized by his largesse. "Clara's expenses this summer have been extremely great," Isabel wrote after the Knickerbocker failure. "We thought they were heavy other years, but this year has exceeded the others, and she has all her plans made for another costly concert tour."[44] Jean first heard about the Knickerbocker bust from Clara, who thought their father had lost all his money. Jean reacted with deep sympathy for her father and "the misery of imagining poor Father at 72 losing everything. Everything that he had built up with such hard work since his kind nephew-in-law [Charles Webster] had lost everything for him when he was 58, was utterly horrible."[45] It pained Jean that she could not earn any money to relieve the financial pinch.

That November, the editor of the *New York World* asked Twain if he had a Thanksgiving message for public consumption, and he seized the opportunity to vent his rage against the Knickerbocker bankers. "I am thankful—thankful beyond words—that I had only fifty-one thousand dollars on deposit in the Knickerbocker Trust, instead of a million; for if I had had a million in that bucket shop I should be nineteen times as sorry as I am now."[46] To the president and bank directors, he drafted a stinging letter, likely never sent: "Next time you will bring up in jail, where you probably ought to have been many & many a year ago. At large, you are a common danger, whereas in jail you would be useful—useful as an example."[47]

That December, Twain suffered yet another financial indignity when the Plasmon Company of America, with Twain still its acting president, went bankrupt. Though he had never lost his evangelical zeal for the dried milk supplement, he lost his original $25,000 investment and another $12,500 that he felt had been swindled from him. When a reporter asked if he had been swindled before, Twain assured him, "Why, I have been swindled out of more money than there is on this planet."[48] Twain had banked some handsome dividends from the English Plasmon shares, but its American cousin, despite Twain's proselytizing, had never prospered.

In dealing with the Knickerbocker Trust and American Plasmon, Twain drew heavily on the services of Ralph W. Ashcroft, who functioned as his proficient secretary in England and was slowly turning into his business manager. Isabel Lyon, always susceptible to eligible men in the vicinity, warmed to Ashcroft when he visited Tuxedo Park, and found him "pleasant, bright, considerate & properly appreciative."[49] Ashcroft began to suggest some innovative business ideas to Twain as he faced the expiration of copyrights on his early books. With Twain endorsing many products, ranging from cigars to whiskey, Ashcroft suggested that he trademark these endorsements in the name of Samuel L. Clemens. "Mr. Clemens likes that idea," Isabel wrote in the margin of Ashcroft's suggestion. "How shall he proceed?"[50] Just as Livy's death had created a huge void for Isabel Lyon to fill, so did Henry Rogers's stroke open a large vacuum that Ralph Ashcroft attempted to occupy. That Isabel and Ralph got on so swimmingly, seemingly united in their loyalty to Twain, only strengthened their presence in the household of the famous but solitary and quite unsuspicious author.

CHAPTER SIXTY-ONE

A Holiday from Life's Woes

Once back in Manhattan, Twain dedicated himself to a multitude of good causes that he had championed. Though he tended to hobnob in patrician circles, he had a special feeling for the masses of Russian and Polish Jews who had gravitated to the Lower East Side and relied on philanthropy for cultural enrichment. As early as January 1901, shortly after returning from Europe, Twain assisted with drumming up money for the Hebrew Technical School for Girls on Henry Street, the sole institution in the city offering free vocational education for Jewish girls. At a fundraiser for the school at Temple Emanu-El, he made a spirited plea for female suffrage, hoping it would purge municipal corruption. "Why, I've been in favor of women's rights for years. I see in this school a hope for the realization of a project I have always dreamed of."[1]

In April 1907, Twain gave a curtain speech at a performance of *The Prince and the Pauper* staged by the Children's Educational Theatre, a project of the Educational Alliance, a settlement house on the Lower East Side supported by many posh Jewish families. The play was acted mostly by Jewish children in front of an audience largely populated by children, and Twain claimed not to have "enjoyed a play so much, so heartily" since he played Miles Hendon many years earlier. Sheepishly he confessed that he had only recently learned about the Educational Alliance. "It's like a man living within thirty miles of Vesuvius and never knowing about a volcano."² After the performance, the young cast gathered around Twain as he signed copies of their programs backstage. A month later, he devoted his services to the Actors' Fund Fair, which raised money for ailing actors. "When you have been weary and downcast [the actor] has lifted your heart out of gloom and given you a fresh impulse," Twain reminded the audience in his solicitation pitch. "This is your opportunity to be his benefactor—to help provide for him in his old age and when he suffers from infirmities."³

By November, with Twain elevated to honorary president of the Children's Educational Theatre, he hosted another performance of *The Prince and the Pauper,* one brimming with elite uptown donors, Andrew Carnegie among them. Twain presented himself as the "ambassador of the children" and eloquently described how the theater introduced knowledge into immigrant families as young performers rehearsed their parts at home. He advocated a children's theater for every American school, noting how drama instilled in young actors a passion for literature along with a high-minded sense of justice. Theater, he contended, was the most effective history teacher, for it made "the dead heroes of the world rise up & shake the dust of the ages from their bones & live & move & breathe & speak."⁴ Of his involvement with the theater and the Jewish immigrant children, Twain informed reporters, "It is the most important work of my life."⁵

In these days, Twain suddenly had time to spare. Much of the fire had gone from his autobiographical dictations, which he padded with newspaper clippings, and he believed that he could now slacken the pace. "My Autobiography has reached 400,000 words at last," he told Jean in February, "& now I have no more solicitudes about it & can go slow & easy & take my time henceforth if I choose."⁶ His main objective with the autobiography had been to provide fresh snippets to lengthen copyright protection of his existing books, and he had now accomplished that goal. To reporters Twain boasted that the full autobiography, set to be published a hundred years after his death, would record "all the caustic and fiendish and devilish things I want to say."⁷ In fact, he learned that he was wrong in thinking dictations would represent his uncensored thoughts. "A stenographer is a lecture-audience; you are always conscious of him... You are not talking to yourself; you are not thinking aloud."[8]

Twain spent an inordinate amount of time playing billiards and hearts with Isabel Lyon, Ralph Ashcroft, and Albert Bigelow Paine, and listening to Orchestrelle selections. With Twain, Paine detected a loneliness stemming from his awareness that his creative brilliance now belonged to the past. Paine would have found confirmation for this view in a letter Twain wrote to Clara from Tuxedo Park, stoking her musical ambitions: "I am very very glad you are profoundly absorbed in your art & your labors, & care for no other pleasures, no other dissipations. It is as I used to be with the pen, long ago, & it is *life*, LIFE, LIFE!—there is no life comparable to it for a moment. Genius lives in a world of its own, in palaces of enchantment, & has dominion over the slaves of the ring & the lamp ... Everybody lives, but only Genius lives richly, sumptiously [*sic*], imperially."[9] It was his most fervent statement about the creative joy that had once inspired him—and his frankest acknowledgment that he knew his own genius.

In Lyon's voluminous journals, there is a noticeable increase in mentions of Twain's drinking problem in his final years, likely a symptom of depression. With her own weakness for the bottle, Isabel told of one occasion when she, Paine, and Twain emptied a whole quart of Scotch "and the King got drunk. He sailed around the room trying to reach the door ... He cast a gay little eye over at me in his unsteady gait, and said 'I'm just practicing,' as he sailed with light footsteps over to the door, and up to the bath room."[10] Twain often treated his inebriated state with levity. Once, when Isabel awakened to billiard noises at two-thirty in the morning, she found "the King playing in a drunken haze ... It was wonderful to see the King pick up a ball and fondle it, and then try to hit it with his cue and be unable to touch it; but he swore splendidly." Like a tender wife, Isabel gently led him back to his bedroom. "He staggered and hit his head against one of the little angels on his bed post, and grabbed his dear head with a volley of oaths."[11]

SHIPWRECK

For much of the year, Clara was nagged by tonsillitis and stage fright—"She certainly seems doomed to have something *always* the matter with her," Jean remarked—and spent comparatively little time with her father, but she reached an important career plateau when she performed at Chickering Hall in Boston in November, aided by the pianist Charles Wark and the violinist Marie Nichols, winning press plaudits.[12] The *Boston Transcript* gave her an enthusiastic notice: "Clara Clemens's voice may without exaggeration be termed unusually beautiful and individual . . . The personality of Miss Clemens became a potent factor in her performance."[13] But, as often was the case with Clara, she was handicapped by technical failures. While the *Mobile Register* conceded that her singing was "enjoyable and often brilliant," it faulted her voice as "at times badly placed, the tones falling too close to the foot lights."[14]

To a small extent, Jean was emancipated from the sanitarium that fall and made three trips to New York. Significantly, Dr. Peterson allowed her to visit her father only once at 21 Fifth Avenue, fearing he was too upsetting a presence. "I should be used to his peculiarities, by now, I suppose," Jean wrote, "but I can never wholly reconcile myself to some of them."[15] Twain's letters show enormous affection for Jean, even if he never fully fathomed her complex needs. When she attempted to earn money translating from French and German, he warmly encouraged her, and when she made him a special birthday gift of a copper tray with a frog smoking a pipe (as "Grenouille"—French for "frog"—was her pet name for him), he could not have been more touched, posting it on his billiard room wall. "You have put a world of patient & careful work upon it, dear child, & the result is a high credit to you. How delighted your mother would be with it if she could see it!"[16]

Twain had committed a serious error in allowing Isabel to supervise family finances, a decision that bred resentment in both daughters. To save money, Jean had asked if she could purchase a sleigh for her horse instead of renting it. Both Isabel and Clara criticized it as an immoderate expense, even though Jean argued that it would be a cheaper alternative. Jean felt Clara's reproach bitterly: "I tore her letters to shreds and I hope I can forget its brutality."[17] She felt so insulted in the matter, which was symbolic of her dependency, that she didn't care to see Clara or her father until after Christmas. Since all money requests were now routed through Isabel, Twain had placed her smack in the middle of acrimonious family squabbles. More and more, Jean felt Isabel as an insurmountable hurdle separating her from her distant, uncomprehending father. "He never hurts anyone knowingly," she wrote in her diary, "& his part of this trouble must be due to some extraordinary non-comprehension."[18]

Jean spent an exceedingly happy Christmas Eve with friends in Westchester while feeling estranged from her own family at 21 Fifth Avenue. "How awful it is to feel that you don't at all want to go home especially at Christmas-time!" she wrote. "I am racked by the thought & the realization of how different all would be if Mother's sweet heart were only here to understand all."[19] In January, her lobbying with Dr. Peterson paid off when he granted her tentative permission to leave the sanitarium and move into a cottage in Greenwich, Connecticut, with another patient, Mildred Cowles; her sister Edith; and a Frenchwoman named Marguerite "Bébé" Schmitt, who would act as Jean's nurse and companion. Jean had found Mildred a bright, attractive personality, and liked Edith, and she declared her "indescribable" joy at leaving Katonah.[20]

Before the Greenwich move could be finalized, the Cowles sisters visited 21 Fifth Avenue to secure Twain's permission and necessary financial support. Isabel said that when Twain heard the proposal, he "could not speak for a moment, & with his dear voice shaking he said, 'Anything, anything you can do to make that dear child happy first, & then comfortable, you are privileged to do. I am a man. I can do so little for her.'"[21] This was consistent with his self-serving theme that caring for Jean was women's work and hence lay in Isabel's realm. When Isabel telephoned her father's approval of Greenwich, Jean was elated. "Dr. Peterson is glad," Jean wrote, adding that Isabel and her father were "*delighted* with the cottage idea & Clara is overjoyed, too. She said she

SHIPWRECK

didn't see how I had stood it as I had."[22] Up until this point there had been no sinister plot to bar Jean from her own home and no sense that she was eager to go back, her main wish being to return to Dublin the following summer.

The history of Jean Clemens and her epilepsy was always a case of high hopes knocked down by the cruel reality of an insoluble illness. The day she moved to Greenwich in January, Twain and Isabel met her at the train station in New York City, where she had to change trains, and Isabel found her looking "very very ill. She is so white & her once beautiful face is so drawn; her fingers have a curious movement. She is like a drooping lily."[23] Those strange finger movements were always a prelude to attacks and the next day she had five of them, so severe that she was all but oblivious to them. Only the bitten tongue from a grand mal seizure alerted her afterward as to what had happened. Jean found the Greenwich cottage warm and cozy, with plenty of domestic help, but the cluster of attacks must have confirmed that the loathed sanitarium had at least been good for her health. Isabel shielded the King from knowledge of Jean's setback. "I have not told him that Jean has had a serious return of her malady since making the change [from Katonah to Greenwich], for it depresses him for days," she told a correspondent, noting that Jean sent her father notes "full of complaints of me and cruel accusations."[24] Under the guise of protecting the King, Isabel Lyon had now initiated a systematic effort to cut him off from his own daughter.

Unaware of Jean's plight, Twain assured Charlie Langdon that she was "much happier than she was in that desolate sanitarium."[25] As had happened with Jean in Katonah, Twain seldom visited her in Greenwich, knew little of what went on there, and seemed to some a sadly negligent parent. One of Jean's close Dublin friends, Gerald Thayer, wrote to Isabel to protest Twain's treatment of Jean. "We have been sore, though, at your King, for what has looked from outside like indifference about lonesome and afflicted & often misunderstood (??) brave pitiable beautiful Jean."[26] Of course, Isabel rushed to the King's defense, claiming that Jean's "misrepresentations" about her father were "a part of Jean's malady," but Twain had clearly distanced himself from his daughter's illness

A HOLIDAY FROM LIFE'S WOES

and some people spotted that.[27] However much Twain might have loved her inwardly, his outward actions often failed to reflect that.

Understandably, Jean banked high hopes on returning to Dublin that summer, for it was the only place where she had experienced a quasi-normal social life among congenial friends. With her impatience and short temper, the Cowles sisters began to prey on her nerves. Mildred wasn't an epileptic, though she was a patient of Dr. Peterson's and had made several suicide attempts. It didn't help Jean to be cooped up with someone with severe psychiatric troubles. "Mildred has times of being most desperately melancholy & cynical & disagreeable to her saint of all saints sister," Jean told Nancy Brush. "At such times I get desperately nervous, too."[28]

To Jean's chagrin, Dr. Peterson vetoed her plans for a Dublin summer and suggested instead that she and the Cowles sisters move in May to Gloucester, Massachusetts, where he spent the summer and had a relationship with a local doctor who could oversee their care. While Twain had expressly asked for Jean to be close to New York to facilitate his visits (however rare they were), a Gloucester residence made that scenario highly unlikely. Jean, now twenty-seven, continued to be stuck in a prolonged adolescence, like a teenager kept on a short leash through a skimpy allowance. "I have been very much troubled lately," Jean told Nancy Brush, "and perfectly furious at my helplessness caused by my inability to earn my own living. You can't imagine how enraged I get, at times, at my stupidity & uselessness."[29]

The crux of the problem with Jean Clemens wasn't simply the wiles of Isabel Lyon, who was trying to protect her boss and herself, but that Mark Twain had declared that he was taking a final vacation from life's everyday woes. As he explained to Jean, "I am taking my holiday, now after 60 years of work and struggle and worry and vexation, and am willing to know nothing, ever any more, of what Susy used to call 'the wars of life.'"[30] He decided to coast along in a carefree existence, shunting parental responsibilities onto Isabel Lyon and Ralph Ashcroft. But with such a woefully ill daughter—not to mention Clara's psychological problems—Twain could not afford the luxury of this holiday from real life.

The most dramatic expression of this septuagenarian's vacation was, of course, his angelfish obsession. One day, when discussing the collecting instinct with Isabel, Twain told her that he was "collecting school girls."[31] With these schoolgirls, he portrayed himself as a morose father abandoned by his daughters, not the other way around. When Clara went on a European concert tour in May, he told Francesca Nunnally: "This isn't a bright day—it is the other way: my daughter is leaving tonight, to be gone a good while, & she will be missed—nobody left but Miss Lyon & me."[32] Of all the schoolgirls, Dorothy Quick gave him exactly the adoration he craved and entered wholeheartedly into his mischief. In her later memoir, *Enchantment,* she recorded very adult perceptions of Twain's flaws—his self-centeredness, his vain desire for attention, his need always to be right in arguments. Still, in general, she was thrilled by his overwhelming attention and never found anything odd about all the time he devoted to her. Every little thing Dorothy did, Twain doted on, as if this magical little being could perform no wrong.

At Christmas 1907, Dorothy came for an extended stay at 21 Fifth Avenue and occupied a third-floor bedroom right next to Isabel's and one floor above Twain's. Far from being secretive, he loved to exhibit Dorothy in public, and when he spoke at a banquet for the Pleiades Club, she sat next to him at the speaker's table. Ever since the deaths of Susy and Livy, Twain had refused to exchange holiday gifts, but he broke that rule with Dorothy, accepting her gift of a silver Tiffany knife to cut cigar ends. One day, Dorothy sat entranced on the stairway, listening to Clara singing one floor below. (She said Clara treated her sweetly.) When Dorothy suddenly expressed a desire to be a singer as well as an author, Twain scowled and lectured her that they were "different aims and to achieve a goal one must devote every atom of his being to it." Only when Dorothy said, apologetically, "I'd rather be an author like you than anything in the whole world," did his scowl relax and his face resume its fond expression.[33]

When Dorothy left, Twain instantly felt the need to woo her back. "I miss you so, you dear child—I miss you all the time, you little rascal. Your mother said you could come again, before the end of January—you will be very welcome, honey. With love SLC."[34] Whatever else was going on psychologically with the angelfish, part of their attraction for Twain came from his unmitigated dread of solitude. And there were constant echoes of past happiness, as when he and Dorothy made a great fuss over a cat named Tammany that brought back memories of Twain and Susy and a beloved cat named Sour Mash.

Bermuda remained Twain's chief remedy for all ailments, and along with Ralph Ashcroft he set sail there on January 25, 1908, for a weeklong stay at the Princess Hotel, hoping to cure his chronic bronchitis. Stung by the false press reports that he was engaged to Isabel Lyon, he dared not go there with her. At the last minute, he strove futilely to get Dorothy to tag along, assuring her of Bermuda's healing powers. "In Bermuda a sick person gets well in 3 days & strong in a week."[35] Already staying in the Princess, a large wooden hotel with beautiful harbor views, was Elizabeth Wallace, an instructor of French literature at the University of Chicago, with whom Twain formed a steadfast friendship. It came about quickly since Wallace had already befriended a twelve-year-old girl named Margaret Blackmer, who was staying at the hotel with her fashionable mother. As Wallace wrote of this future angelfish, "The child was tall and slim and dark with a very straight nose and very straight hair. Her dresses were all made alike . . . They were very short and exposed a pair of very long slender legs."[36] In this dawn of Twain's angelfish mania, Isabel Lyon observed that his "first interest when he goes to a new place is to find little girls," and Margaret Blackmer at once became that girl.[37]

In a memoir, Elizabeth Wallace recorded how Twain established rapport with Margaret by stopping at her table and saying offhandedly, "Why, how do you do? I am very much ashamed of myself, but I believe I've forgotten your name."[38] There ensued sprightly exchanges about his

SHIPWRECK

supposedly knowing her but having to guess her name. Twain later took a pink shell and gave Margaret half of it, so they could produce their respective shells when they met and humorously confirm their identities. After her first encounter with Twain, Margaret came over to Wallace's table, "her sweet face beaming," and described her extraordinary new friend. "That nice old gentleman is Mr. Clemens, and he is *so* funny. He pretended to know me, and he wants me to ride with him in the donkey-cart this afternoon, but I told him I had an engagement with you, and couldn't go." Wallace exhorted her to go with the humorous Mr. Clemens instead. "I told her I would release her from her engagement with me, for it was an honor to be invited to go with Mr. Clemens, an honor which she ought not lightly to forego."[39]

It is revealing how even intelligent adults became unsuspecting accomplices with the angelfish. Elizabeth Wallace found something brave, honest, and poignant about Twain's adoration of children and threw an air of wondrous enchantment about it. "He has a yearning fondness for children and especially for young girls between ten and sixteen for it was during those years that he had as his constant companion his little daughter Susie—whose loss still seems an open wound after all these years."[40] This must have been Twain's explanation, but it begged the fact that Susy died at twenty-four, not sixteen. With Margaret, Twain replicated the games that he had played with his daughters, teaching her the reigns of English kings by sketching cartoon figures, their arms and legs meant to indicate years. Wallace viewed Twain as a "gentle charming courteous gentleman," and far from finding anything shady about his interest in Margaret, she wrote that his "sweet affection for children" would be enough "to win away our heart without the prestige" of his name.[41] It was Margaret who introduced Wallace to Twain, she said, but he soon "turned his attention to Margaret & became her faithful attendant. I felt that I had a formidable rival, and to preserve my own dignity I retired from the field."[42]

Dressed in a white serge suit, with brown cigars stacked neatly in his breast pocket (Ashcroft, by contrast, would dress formally in black, ex-

A HOLIDAY FROM LIFE'S WOES

cept for a white shirt and boater hat), Twain rode around the island with Margaret in a donkey cart drawn by a creature named Maude. Occasionally he devoted his time to adult conversation. He had a memorable encounter with Upton Sinclair, fresh from his success with *The Jungle,* an exposé of the Chicago slaughterhouses, a work that Twain admired. "He chatted about past times, as old men like to do," Sinclair recalled. "I saw that he was kind, warm-hearted, and also full of rebellion against capitalist greed and knavery, but he was an old man, and a sick man and I did not try to probe the mystery of his life."[43] Twain also dined with the president of Princeton University, Woodrow Wilson, and his friend Mary Peck, a longtime visitor to the islands with whom Wilson was temporarily smitten. Isabel called the unhappily married Mrs. Peck "a bewitching woman, and a snare for men folk."[44] Wilson would later be derided as "Peck's bad boy."[45] Wilson and Twain enjoyed playing billiards together and teamed up on a petition to ban private motorcars from the islands—a ban that survived until 1946.

Aside from reading Kipling poems aloud to Wallace in the evening, Twain spent the bulk of his time with Margaret, who adored him and felt protective toward this aging, comical gent. Right before Twain sailed back to New York, Margaret asked Elizabeth Wallace if Twain had a Mrs. Clemens back home. When she delicately explained that Twain was a widower, Margaret pursued the subject. "Has Mr. Clemens any little girls?" Wallace explained that he had lost a daughter and that's why he loved other little girls, for they made him less lonely. At this Margaret broke out feelingly, "I wish *I* was Mrs. Clemens, and then I would just care for him and care for him, and love him awfully!"[46] It says much about Twain's winning ways with these schoolgirls that they developed such protective emotions toward him.

Twain's glorification of childhood, expressed through his angelfish fixation, stood in stark contrast to the darkling mood of his late-life philosophy. Sitting with Twain in the hotel dining room, Wallace got an earful of his saturnine reflections. "He wondered why the Almighty had ever created us. It was bad enough to have concocted the house-fly, or to have imagined rats and mice . . . And then, to conceive of the idea that this same Almighty who had created us wanted to have our company through all eternity!"[47]

When the King returned to New York on February 6, he bore a piece of jewelry for Francesca Nunnally that was adorned with a Bermuda angelfish. Isabel Lyon was pleased to see his happy mood and pink cheeks and the fresh spring in his step, thanks to his week with Margaret Blackmer, who had not sated his insatiable appetite for angelfish. Twain now wanted a continuous string of girls at his side. The day after his return, he had Isabel telephone Dorothy Quick and ask her to visit him right away. The next day she came, and as he awaited her arrival, he grew fidgety and impatient with excitement, "pacing up & down the big rooms & going to the front door whenever the bell rang, & standing there in his white clothes in an icy blast of wind."[48] When Dorothy left after two days of cards, billiards, and Shakespeare, Twain felt tired and lonely. Like Elizabeth Wallace, Isabel professed to find nothing odd in his behavior. "The King's interest in children increases—his interest in little girls. He can spend hours & hours with them & finds them such good company."[49] For Isabel, Twain was a superior being, exempt from any criticism that might apply to other mortals. "If you could know the King just a little," she wrote, "you'd find in him all the exquisite colors of the world. You'd find in him an ice storm & a thunderstorm, & the deeps of night, & the granite crags, & the great song of the wind, & the sweetest flower."[50] One has to remember that this wasn't a psychotherapeutic age, so few contemporaries examined Twain's odd behavior with even a modicum of critical scrutiny.

Right before his next voyage to Bermuda, Twain attended a party on Washington Square bursting with celebrities, including Enrico Caruso. His attention was arrested by a "bright and engaging and untamed young Virginian," Nancy Langhorne Astor, with whom he shared a middle name. She had moved to England, married the fabulously wealthy Waldorf Astor, and was destined to become the first woman to enter the House of Commons. As Twain told the story, Astor at midnight dragged him "into the middle of the room and commanded the music to strike up and then she required me to dance with her. I was willing; I had never danced, but I always knew I could do it if I wanted to."[51] They created such a sensation on the dance floor that the audience demanded several encores, and Twain and Astor happily obliged them to great ovations.

On February 22, Twain departed again for Bermuda for an extended stay of forty-seven days. His entourage this time had expanded: in addition to Ralph Ashcroft, he was escorted by Isabel Lyon and an ailing Henry Rogers. In fact, the trip's purpose was to nurse Rogers back to health. Mr. Rogers stepped onto the boat, Isabel wrote, "a sick, sick man."[52] Nevertheless, Twain and Rogers lapsed into their usual ad lib comedy routine for the reporters who showed up to see them off. "Well, I see that we're discovered," Twain said. "That's what I get for being in bad company," Rogers replied, deadpan. "Well, you've got no edge on me. Some of my methods may be bad. The public says so, at least. But they are no worse than your jokes."[53]

In Bermuda, Elizabeth Wallace was reunited with Twain and cast an attentive eye on his new retinue. She found Rogers tall, distinguished-looking, and quietly amusing. On the previous trip, she had mocked the obsequious Ashcroft as Twain's "Pilot Fish," but now she saw he was replaced by a "black eyed black haired Italian looking little woman who hovers about [Twain] with the tender care of a mother and daughter combined. This is the Little Secretary of the King and my heart's doors were open for her."[54] Elizabeth Wallace was very much in the Isabel Lyon mold: she started referring to Twain as the King and viewed him in idealized terms. Soon Wallace and Lyon were fast friends, taking tea and going on shopping expeditions together. Wallace left a marvelous vignette of Twain's boyish hijinks when he hopped, skipped, ran, and danced crazily down an empty hotel corridor before assuming "a supernaturally grave aspect" when a stranger appeared.[55] Twain had instructed Wallace to find a successor to Margaret Blackmer, and she dug up a new angelfish, Irene Gerken. By the first day, Twain had promptly set off on an island tour with Irene, drawn by the sturdy but fickle Maude. Wallace described Irene as a "pretty graceful child," while also criticizing her failure to "fully appreciate what a wonderful thing was happening to her."[56]

The Bermuda sojourn helped to rejuvenate the health of Henry Rogers, nicknamed "the Rajah" by the group. When they gathered to play hearts in the evening, Twain kidded Rogers. "Now, I sincerely hope you are not going to make any display of your disagreeable disposition tonight. Do try to show us some pleasant sides of your character."[57] Refreshed by the stay, Twain badgered Dorothy to come down to Bermuda with her mother, arguing for its health benefits. "I am now so strong that I suppose I could pull up one of these islands by the roots & throw it half way to New York."[58] Yet he experienced, for the first time, medical symptoms of a far graver nature. One day, Isabel came upon him in the billiard room of the hotel, "pale as death" and bending over the table as a young German rubbed his head. While Twain brushed it off as just a "crick in his neck," Isabel was haunted by this potent reminder of an old man's mortality, and no less of her own tenuous place in the world without him.

For Twain, the high point of his stay was a Sunday morning visit with Rogers and Wallace to the local aquarium, where he stood in awe of the blues and yellows of the angelfish. On the spot he dreamed up the idea that he would convert his own angelfish into members of an Aquarium Club. The name was (inadvertently) well chosen: the girls were beautiful, exotic, and trapped in a tank. Twain had continued to bolster his collection in Bermuda, including thirteen-year-old Jean Spurr. Isabel gave a curious description of her: "Jean wears a blond wig and has no eye brows or lashes, but the King doesn't care about a detail like that. He sees into her fair young soul and is very glad."[59]

Soon Twain was busily issuing official invitations to his angelfish to join the Aquarium Club, explaining to Dorothy Quick that he would be the Shad; Clara, the Mother Superior; and Isabel, the Chatelaine of the group. For his M.A.s—Members of the Aquarium—he had Tiffany & Company manufacture small enameled angelfish pins to be worn like brooches on a garment, while he wore one representing a shad. Twain scouted fresh prospects as the club's count swelled to a dozen members. What made the angelfish obsession so disturbing was the strange intensity of his involvement with the girls. In 1908 he sent ninety-four letters to his M.A.s, or more than half of all the notes he wrote that year. Something profound had been unleashed in his mind that he could not seem to control.

Twain took enormous pride as he stocked his Aquarium with pretty young girls. His own life, of course, had been rife with wounds, bitterness, and tears, and the angelfish were there to vault him back into the vanished happiness of his youth. Far from feeling any guilt or embarrassment about this most curious hobby, he exulted about "my worship of schoolgirls—if worship be the right name, and I know it is."[60]

Before leaving Bermuda, Twain added one more schoolgirl to his coterie, the teenage Helen Allen, daughter of the American vice-consul to Bermuda. Their home, Bay House, near the Princess Hotel, became a frequent hideaway for Twain when he stayed on the island. He grew close to Helen's mother, Marion Schuyler Allen, who would leave an insightful memoir about her friendship with the author. Twain confided in her, telling her that "he thought that at his time of life he ought to be entitled to doing only the things he enjoyed, and only knowing people who interested him."[61]

Twain wrote to Francesca Nunnally from Bermuda, entreating her to stay at his house when he returned to New York on April 13. He was prepared to send Isabel Lyon down to Baltimore to fetch Francesca and bring her back to the city. "There is a comfortable room for you, & I would give you two if I could—or a dozen, if I had them. You will give us this pleasure, won't you?"[62] As always, Twain was aggressive to the point of being pushy with the girls. When he docked in New York in mid-April and was greeted by curious reporters, he stood at the stern rail with the latest addition to his gallery, sixteen-year-old Dorothy Sturgis from Boston. He told the press how he and Dorothy had survived the wintry gusts at sea and how they were drenched by a giant wave that washed over them. "I never knew the ocean was so wet before," he observed.[63]

Once back at 21 Fifth Avenue, Twain demanded a continuous stream of angelfish to lighten up his lonely days and continued to present himself to them as an unfortunate father ditched by his daughters. As he wrote to Helen Allen, "I miss you ever so much, you dear Helen . . . But I'm desolate now. My youngest daughter came yesterday, but she could only stay an hour or two, then hurry away. My other daughter (Clara) will arrive this evening . . . the Aquarium is empty."[64] As news of Twain and his platoon of teenage girls spread through New York society, people weren't appalled but charmed, regarding it as an amusing, if slightly zany, development, another version of Mark Twain's delirious high spirits. Margaret Illington, the actress wife of theater impresario Daniel Frohman, applied for membership in the Aquarium, but her being an adult, Twain turned her down cold. Then she showed up unexpectedly for dinner, Twain told Dorothy Quick, "dressed for 12 years, & had pink ribbons at the back of her neck & looked about 14 years old; so I admitted her as an angel-fish, & pinned the badge on her bosom. There's lots of lady-candidates, but I guess we won't let any more in, unless perhaps [the actress] Billy Burke."[65] He then enlisted Daniel Frohman as "legal staff" of the Aquarium Club, adding to the jocular air about the whole affair.

CHAPTER SIXTY-TWO

Innocence at Home

As Isabel Lyon and John Howells worked tirelessly to prepare the Redding house for a June 1908 occupancy, Twain wanted the house, as by some conjuring trick, to materialize in a fully furnished state, so that he could just stroll in and start living there. In his colorful phrasing, he elected not to see the house "until the cat is purring on the hearth."[1] He refused to glance at any plans or hear progress reports, and cared only that his new abode contain a living room big enough for his beloved Orchestrelle and a red billiard room. In this heedless state, Twain laid himself open to abuse. A serious rift had opened up between Isabel and Clara, who believed that Isabel was conniving to steal her place as head of the household. "My anxiety over the finishings," wrote an exhausted Isabel, suffering from headaches, "my interest in my search for the right thing for the King's house has all been misinterpreted, and the child says I am trying to ignore her . . . Somebody has put all these sickening ideas into Santa's head and I feel that my interest in the house is dead forever."[2] The central problem arose from Twain's fatal detachment and the ever perilous ambiguity of Isabel Lyon's status in his life. Livy had always supervised home furnishings and now a stranger was doing that—which may have triggered Clara's hostility. Isabel could function as a surrogate wife to Twain (minus the sex), but she could never act as a surrogate mother to Clara and Jean, who were, after all, grown women.

On June 18, 1908, Twain donned his white suit and Panama hat, and set out from Grand Central Terminal for Redding, accompanied by

SHIPWRECK

Paine's daughter Louise, a future angelfish returning from boarding school. He approached a town he didn't know and a house he had never seen. At the Redding train station, he was greeted by a gathering of local farmers in flower-bedecked vehicles, then drove three miles by carriage through scenic Saugatuck valley to his hilltop house. "This is the kind of a road I like," Twain said, "a good country road through the woods."[3] When he reached the house, with its gray stucco walls and a red shingled roof, Isabel; Claude, the butler; and other servants stood at the door to meet the King. There were also six cats on hand to greet him: Tammany—"much the handsomest cat on this planet," according to Twain—with her two children and three grandchildren.[4]

John Howells had done his work with such artistry that the Italianate villa seemed perfectly natural in this Yankee setting. As soon as Twain entered the house, draped with exquisite curtains and covered with elegant rugs, he stared agog at its splendor. Isabel had decorated with a loving hand and intimate knowledge of her master. There stood his Orchestrelle against the wall of a forty-foot living room lined with comfortable armchairs and couches for easy listening. Through arched rear windows, he could see a brick terrace and steps descending through a lane of cedars to a pergola with wooded hills in the distance. A vagabond for seventeen years, Twain could hardly believe this stylish place was his new home. "How beautiful it all is! I did not think it could be as beautiful as this."[5] When he entered the billiard room, his satisfaction was complete. "It is a perfect house—perfect, so far as I can see, in every detail. It might have been here always."[6] To top off his pleasure, he stood on the terrace that evening as neighbors set off fireworks in his honor, and he stared with pleasure at rockets streaking across the sky.

Initially, Twain thought the Redding house and its 248 acres would serve as a weekend or summer getaway, but he was so bowled over that he soon decided to abandon 21 Fifth Avenue—"that crude & tasteless New York barn"—and make Redding his full-time domicile.[7] In loveliness and comfort the house surpassed even the old Hartford home. "Miss Lyon has achieved wonders," he told Clara, then in London on a concert tour.[8] Set back from the road, secluded from other dwellings, the house lay wrapped in a deep woodland hush that was a tonic to his troubled spirit after Manhattan's hectic roar. In New York, he had been a ubiquitous toastmaster at banquets, constantly serving up funny lines, and now he reflected that "when a humorist rises to speak he is expected to simply bubble humor, and there are times when one does not feel the bubbling process as strongly as at others. I felt that I needed rest, and here I am going to get it."[9]

Twain puzzled over ingenious names for the new house. Because excerpts from his dictations had paid for it, Isabel favored "Autobiography House." Then Twain dreamed up "Innocence at Home," an echo of his first and best-selling book. Although people would be unaware of it, the name would also pay homage to the angelfish, expected as frequent and honored visitors. "My house is named Innocence at Home, and it is the angel-fishes that are to furnish the innocence though the public don't know that. It isn't the public's affair."[10] Clara, when she saw "Innocence at Home" on her father's stationery, grew alarmed and pleaded with him to delete it. As Paine later said, Clara "never quite liked her father's attentions to young girls (or old ones either, for that matter) in public."[11] In fact, Clara later sought to scrub the angelfish from the historical record altogether, telling Marion Schuyler Allen that anything her father wrote to little girls was personal and should never be published. At Clara's behest, the Redding house took the name "Stormfield" for two reasons: it sat on an exposed hilltop, vulnerable to approaching storms, and the final payment for the Redding house came from a magazine publication of an "Extract from Captain Stormfield's Visit to Heaven."

Privately, Twain retained the name "Innocence at Home" for his schoolgirl friends since the house would serve as official headquarters of the Aquarium. On his first day in residence he wrote to Dorothy Quick that "'Innocence at Home' is the right name for this house, because it describes me, & describes the Aquarium Club."[12] He declared his intention to have at least one angelfish on the premises at all times, his obsession having grown even crazier. The next day, two angelfish, Dorothy Harvey and Louise Paine, arrived for stays. He converted the billiard room into Aquarium Headquarters, garlanding its walls with photos of

SHIPWRECK

each girl. Faced with this picture gallery, Clara and Jean must have felt ousted from their own home by their father's bizarre predilection. At the same time, Twain sounded his self-pitying theme of being abandoned by his daughters. To Jean he regretted that "it was just *too* bad that there wasn't a solitary junior member of the family here to help me christen the house."[13] Explaining the Redding move to Emilie Rogers, he wrote, "It was always lonesome & home-sicky in New York, with Clara & Jean seldom in sight & no guests but 2-hour & 3-hour luncheonites & dinnerites, but is not lonesome here."[14] He planned to pack the Redding house with a steady procession of guests who would stay for days.

There was much truth to Twain's complaint that Clara avoided him. Where Jean was kept away, Clara *stayed* away. Yet whenever Clara came home, she immediately assumed superior airs and wanted to run the household, much as her mother had. Now on the warpath, she thought that Isabel, as an employee, should have a room outside the house, to which Twain snapped, "No, I want her here. She's like an old pair of slippers to me."[15] The image was revealing: Isabel had taken on so many assignments—spared him so many worldly cares—that she had made herself indispensable. There was no task too personal for her to perform. When she cut the King's hair that summer, he told her she had "beaten the barber at his own trade," and she crowed in her notebook, "How much of happiness that means."[16]

While Clara occupied her own pretty wing of the house—an apartment, known as the "Nightingale's Cage," right above the loggia—complete with a practice piano, there was no such special place reserved for Jean. At Katonah, Jean had dreamed that, if she were better, she might someday live in the Redding house. "Jean improving," Isabel wrote in March 1907, "and is full of plans for the future home in Redding."[17] Isabel now seemed to be the big winner. Twain was so grateful for everything that she had done that he gave her a small cottage, "The Lobster Pot," visible from his house, along with twenty surrounding acres. Isabel adored the Lobster Pot, with its old oak ceiling and splendid exposed beams, and poured all her talents into fixing it up. She knew that no corner of Twain's house belonged to her and began to dream that this little dwelling would guarantee her future salvation and keep her in close proximity to the King.

・——・——・

When Jean left Katonah to share the Greenwich cottage with the Cowles sisters, she had viewed it as a hopeful first step, albeit one that still left hanging the question of her future home. Visiting her in Greenwich, Twain professed to find her in excellent spirits. He had constantly reminded her of how much nicer she was when she was younger, before epilepsy distorted her personality, and he now claimed to have rediscovered that older, nicer Jean. After she arrived in Gloucester, Massachusetts, she received a letter reinforcing that message: "Jean dear, welcome to your new home, & happiness therein! In earlier days I would not have expected you to be otherwise than unhappy in a new strange home, but your spirit & your philosophy have undergone great & beneficent improvement in these latter days . . . I am aware that you are sweet, & forgiving, & helpful, now, & not fretful & not given to complaining, & faultfinding. In a word, that the fine & fortunate disposition you were born with is again in the ascendant—& long may it keep its supremacy!"[18] The message was crystal-clear: Jean wasn't allowed to complain, and if she did, it signified dangerous backsliding into her former pathology. In a hurt reply, Jean told her father that "your letter both delighted and pained me. Of course I am infinitely glad that you consider my character better and less disagreeable than of recent years, but I am equally sorry that I should ever have seemed complaining. The quality is one I detest, & always have."[19]

The next day, Twain wrote Jean a second letter, expressing relief that she was so satisfied with Gloucester and its outdoor delights. Evidently, Jean had complained that information about her situation was being withheld from him, and in his response lay the seeds of a tragic confusion. Far from being upset at not being told of Jean's condition, he expressed approval, saying, "That is right, & as it should be, unless it is something that I could remedy. Clara, Miss Lyon & Mr. Paine keep all sorts of distresses from me, & I am very thankful for it—distresses which they are aware I could not remedy, I mean . . . But whenever there is anything that depends upon *me & my* help, I want to know all about it."[20]

This was the crux of a problem that would fester and, within a year, shatter Mark Twain's life. He simply did not want to know about Jean's plight and allowed—nay, insisted—that Isabel keep unpleasant news from him and that she make decisions for him. It wasn't just a scheming Isabel who wanted to keep a disruptive Jean from his doorstep. Isabel and the canny Ashcroft saw that Twain's renunciation of responsibility made him an easy mark, oblivious to what was happening under his nose. This was no accidental blindness, but a tragic blindness, a *willed* blindness. As in a Greek tragedy, Twain made himself a party to his own undoing.

The Gloucester cottage was never a happy hearth for Jean, who had to deal with the Cowles sisters, and she painted a hellish picture of their emotional turmoil. "Mildred is ill," she told Nancy Brush. "That is she is really ill through love of *herself*." Edith "slaves for her, thinks for her . . . as though Mildred were the sun & she the miserable little earth following her around." As soon as she saw the house, Mildred declared, "It is hideous and I'm not staying here," and she went and locked herself in her room until the local Dr. Knowles came to treat her.[21] The doctor told Jean of Mildred's several suicide attempts at Greenwich. Mildred now displayed irrational rage at her bed, ripped it open to see what it was made of, and refused to sleep in it for a week. "Also," Jean wrote, "for four or five days she kept bolting her doors & refusing to eat or to see anyone . . . Since then there has been little peace."[22] Jean described vividly Mildred's "snake look": "She lowers her lids, looks at you sideways with a gleam of loathing in the eyes themselves, & frequently says that she despises everybody & everything, even her sister!"[23]

At the end of June, Twain spoke at the dedication of the Aldrich Memorial in Portsmouth, New Hampshire, giving him an opportunity to see Jean in Gloucester. She wanted him to stay overnight, but Twain insisted that the doctor had forbidden that. "Indeed I should like to tarry with you a considerable spell, but Dr. Peterson will not allow that," he

INNOCENCE AT HOME

told Jean. "For your good he will restrict me to hours, not days."[24] Twain invariably made excuses for not spending time with Jean. It seems hard to fathom that Dr. Peterson saw no trouble with Jean sharing a residence with the disturbed Mildred Cowles, yet denied her father an overnight visit. Twain, so baldly cynical about most doctors, completely trusted this one. Jean placed great faith in her doctor, assuring her father that "of Dr. Peterson's treatment, I cannot say enough."[25] With his treatment working, Jean was gradually returning to a more normal life. "I am very grateful to him for the wonderful work he has done for you," Twain told Jean, "& I feel that you & I ought to testify our thankfulness by honoring his lightest desire."[26]

On his visit, Twain found, to his astonishment, that Jean looked tanned and healthy and free of major seizures. This came as a revelation. The salt air and outdoor life had done wonders to boost her physical state and morale. "We were charmed & surprised to see how well she was, how sound & vigorous in mind & body," Twain recalled.[27] When Jean left Katonah, she had not wanted to return to her father, preferring the Greenwich setting. Now, in Gloucester, appalled by the Cowles sisters, she longed to join her father in Redding. In jubilation, Twain talked about bringing Jean home and buying her an old farmhouse near his new home.

When he returned to Redding, however, things at once took an unexpected turn. As Twain recalled, "When we got home to Stormfield I broke the good news to Miss Lyon in an outburst of enthusiasm, & said Dr. Peterson must cancel her exile & let her come home at once. Miss Lyon did her best to look glad, & said she would write the doctor, but there was frost upon her raptures, even I was able to notice it."[28] Evidently Isabel convinced Twain to revoke his promise to Jean, because he immediately sat down and sent her a guilt-ridden letter, squashing the farmhouse idea. Suddenly he claimed that the contemplated farmhouse was small, shabby, and uninhabitable. As if crestfallen, he wrote, "I am so sorry. I wish I could situate you exactly to your liking, dear child, how gladly I would do it. And I wish I could take your malady, & rid you of it for always. I wish your mother were here; she could help us. I will not try to write any more. I love you dear, dear, dearly, & I am so so sorry, so sorry. What can I do?"[29]

It seems hard to draw any conclusion other than that Isabel had talked him out of his decision, and helped by hindsight, Twain thought that he had been duped. "The minute my back was turned [Isabel] sent a telegram to Dr. Peterson telling him to absolutely refuse his consent to Jean's removal to Stormfield! . . . That evening Ashcroft & Miss Lyon walked the hall in agitated conversation, & Paine heard Miss Lyon say, with emphasis: 'This is the *last time!* He shall never leave this place again without one of us *with* him!'" Paine never said a word of this to Twain, knowing he would countenance no criticism of Lyon or Ashcroft. Belatedly, Twain agreed. "I would not have allowed any one to say a word in criticism of those worshiped pets of mine . . . Everybody was laughing at me, but I didn't know it."[30] This was Twain's version a year later, but it tallies with the extreme protectiveness toward Twain that Isabel expressed in her journals—"the high moral obligation of never leaving the King alone." For years, she had served him with nunlike devotion and come to see herself as his savior, shielding him from Jean's temper and epilepsy. But self-serving reasons intermingled with her altruism. She disliked Jean, feared she could be violent, and effectively banished her from her father's life. As she had declared of the King the year before, "He mustn't be with Jean."[31] Jean was the one thing standing between Isabel and an ideal existence alongside her hero. Through the years, her reverential concern for Twain had imperceptibly metamorphosed into an extreme and self-righteous form of control over him, often fanatical in its intensity.

For the remainder of the summer, it was difficult for Jean to stomach the "petty little lies & prevarications" of the Cowles sisters.[32] She escaped their company by going sailing, even as she was haunted by time passing, a sense that epilepsy had stolen her youth and trapped her in a remote house with two lunatic sisters while separating her from her father. As she told Nancy Brush, "I am almost twenty-eight and it makes me feel desperately aged . . . It makes me boil when I think of how the best years of my life were spoiled by disease & how that same disease affected my mind & rendered me unable to appreciate the beauty of the character of one now gone"—a reference to Susy's death.[33]

That Jean's fate was governed by Isabel Lyon was dramatically shown at the end of July when she received a letter from Isabel telling her that she would spend the fall and winter in Berlin to consult a renowned epilepsy doctor who had helped the daughter of a friend of the Clemens family. At first, a thunderstruck Jean was overjoyed at the prospect of sailing to Berlin in October. "I had hoped to spend the winter with father in Redding," she confessed to Nancy Brush. "For that reason I feel rather badly about going. Of course I am wildly excited at the idea of going abroad again & of seeing Berlin—I saw it last when I was only eleven years old."[34] After a few days, however, Jean began to rebel against a decision so unilaterally imposed upon her. "Is it positively *settled* that I must go to Berlin?" she asked Isabel. "I have a dread of it. I did so want to be in Redding."[35] When Dr. Peterson told Jean that she might have to stay in Berlin for six or eight months, the timetable alarmed her. "Now don't scare me, dear, into believing it may be longer!" she told Isabel. "I can't stay away from Father longer than that."[36] Jean also protested hotly Isabel's decision to fire George O'Conners, her groom and driver for two years. "To me it is the most horrible injustice . . . We haven't ever treated our servants so before."[37] Jean added a comment that testified to her knowledge of the total control that Isabel now exercised over her father. "You are the planner & arranger & you can do what I beg & can make Father see the justice of it if you only will."[38] Without telling Isabel, Jean had silently resolved to move to Redding in May or June.

All the while, Twain worked to cheer up Jean about her stay in Germany, sending naive notes that exuded an almost Panglossian optimism. "Be happy, dear love, & put all disturbing solicitudes away from you, & bury yourself in cheerful books & pleasant thoughts. Oh, yes, dear Jean, dear heart, shut your eyes & your heart to the burden of life, & be happy. Your loving Father."[39]

CHAPTER SIXTY-THREE

"Mark Twain's Daughter"

In his self-declared holiday from life—"a holiday whose other end is in the cemetery," he noted—Twain had scant incentive to work on his various unfinished manuscripts.[1] When it came to creativity, a certain lassitude had crept over him. He continued to dictate his autobiography at a more leisurely pace, sometimes as few as fifteen minutes per day, and his new stenographer, Mary Louise Howden, left some lion-in-winter impressions of Twain dictating from his bed in the morning. "Sometimes there were four or five minute pauses between sentences. But the phrase when it came was always perfectly formed. He put in the punctuation himself. His stenographer was not ever allowed to add so much as a comma."[2] She saw his wit, fire, and fury intermixed with considerable kindness and viewed him as "rather a tragic figure, lonely in his fame. To a casual observer he seemed just a kindly, gentle, rather sad old man with a courteous Old World dignity all his own."[3]

Stormfield was a gentleman's farm, and the only crops it produced, Twain said wryly, were "sunsets and scenery."[4] He loved to slump in a wicker chair and rejoice in the scenic splendor from the loggia, which framed the wooded hills perfectly, and he was simply swept away by the autumn colors. Of that ever-changing medley of hues he observed, "It was heaven & hell & sunset & rainbows & the aurora all fused into one divine harmony, & you couldn't look at it & keep the tears back."[5] For all his cynicism about life, Twain was more transported than ever by the natural beauty at his doorstep.

SHIPWRECK

Billiards, long a passion with Twain, became a craze after he got a pool table as a gift from Emilie Rogers. Since Albert B. Paine lived within walking distance of Stormfield, he came over at three o'clock each afternoon, and the two men played together. When he first started playing pool with Twain in 1906, he protested that he was a poor player. "The poorer you play," Twain encouraged him, "the better I shall like it."[6] The pair played for hours at a time, sometimes well past midnight, and Twain would exhibit "superhuman" endurance.[7] When kittens jumped on the table, Twain never chased them away. One might be tucked into a corner pocket of the billiard table "as snugly as a hand fits a glove," Twain said, and would spoil "many a shot by putting out his paw and changing the direction of a passing ball."[8]

In Bermuda, Isabel Lyon had found Twain looking ashen as he leaned over a billiard table. Now at Stormfield, Paine witnessed a similar episode, likely brought on by the game's exertion. "I feel a little dizzy," Twain said. "I will sit down a moment." After cooling off with a glass of water, he made an effort to resume playing but seemed disoriented. "I have lost my memory," he said. "I don't know which is my ball. I don't know what game we are playing."[9] If only a passing fright, it signaled the onset of a more serious medical condition.

Shortly afterward, Twain's health received another hammer blow when he learned on August 1 of the sudden death of his forty-eight-year-old nephew, Samuel E. Moffett, an editor at *Collier's Weekly,* who had drowned in full view of his son while struggling in rough surf off the Jersey shore. Twain had long admired Pamela's son. When they had labored together on the history game, Twain came to value Moffett's knowledge and memory, combined with a spotless integrity. As a journalist, Moffett had exhibited a crusading streak on causes ranging from preserving American forests to fighting tuberculosis.

On August 4, a sweltering day, Ralph Ashcroft escorted Twain to the funeral in Mount Vernon, which exacted a heavy toll on him. As he told Jean, "The shock of the tragedy, & the blistering heat, & the heavy black clothes & the pathetic sight of the broken-hearted family, was a heavy drain upon me & struck me down."[10] Depleted by the heat, Twain suf-

"MARK TWAIN'S DAUGHTER"

fered a "bilious collapse" after returning to Stormfield. Isabel sat up with him during a long grueling night of vomiting and discomfort, and then at dinner "he was so silent that several times I spoke to him to see if he were conscious."[11] The two doctors who treated him, Twain said, "had half an idea that there is something the matter with my brain . . . Doctors do know so little and they do charge so much for it."[12] The physicians treated the episode seriously and exhorted their patient not to "stir from here before frost."[13] Twain also noticed that he had recently grown "humpshouldered" and was told it was due to "bad circulation, lack of exercise, & excessive smoking."[14] Although Twain stopped drinking, he was wedded, as ever, to his evil-smelling cigars, old pals whom he refused to renounce.

It was this medical crisis that led Isabel to inform Harriet Whitmore that the doctors and Colonel Harvey "have vested me with the high moral obligation of never leaving the King alone again."[15] This expanded her ever-multiplying duties to include acting as Twain's nursemaid and made her feel as though she had a sacred trust to serve as his guardian, now endowing herself with an even more noble motivation to exclude Jean from the house. Twain's signs of aging would also have profound repercussions for Lyon and Ashcroft, raising the specter that he might not be around much longer. They may have wondered how, in such an event, they could guarantee their own future security. A photo of Isabel from this period shows a sad, earnest woman, moving into middle age, still attractive but with gray frosting the edges of her hair. At forty-four, she was still unmarried, leaving her in a highly vulnerable position, and Twain's mortality would naturally have weighed on her.

Stormfield was an ideal place to entertain guests, and Twain had hoped this would relieve his loneliness, with Isabel serving as his model hostess for visitors. "She made them happy, she made them cheerful, she made them gay, she delighted them . . . My paths have never been pleasanter than they were during her reign," Twain later admitted.[16] The New

SHIPWRECK

Haven Railroad, thrilled to have Twain and his friends as passengers, made special stops in Redding to unload them, and Twain hosted up to twenty visitors per month, running a small-scale hotel. Tired of the social swirl of dinners and banquets, he preferred to stay at home, letting people flock to him. "I don't ever want to be so lonesome & dreary again," he told Emilie Rogers, recalling how starved he had been for home company in New York.[17]

Twain received a stream of well-known personalities at Stormfield, including the actress Billie Burke—"as good as she is pretty"—and the writer Ida Tarbell, renowned for her Standard Oil exposé.[18] His most astute visitor was Helen Keller, who homed in on Twain's showmanship, noting that he did "all the talking in his own house . . . He talked delightfully, audaciously, brilliantly. His talk was fragrant with tobacco and flamboyant with profanity."[19] Her overwhelming impression was of a man who had suffered greatly. "Whenever I touched his face his expression was sad, even when he was telling a funny story."[20] Helen came with her teacher, Anne Sullivan Macy, and could "listen" to Twain either by laying her fingers gently on his lips or having Anne tap out the words into her hand. One night, Twain proudly donned his Oxford robe, sat before a blazing fire, and read aloud to Helen from *Eve's Diary*. She cried openly when Twain read Adam's farewell tribute at Eve's grave: "Wheresoever she was, there was Eden."[21] To Anne Sullivan Macy, Twain inscribed a photo of himself with these memorable words: "To Mrs. John Sullivan Macy with warm regard & with limitless admiration of the wonders she has performed as a miracle-worker."[22] This phrase later turned into the title of a renowned Broadway show and Hollywood film about Helen and her teacher.

Twain thought nothing could compete with the natural views from the windows of Stormfield, so he hung no pictures throughout much of his home. Still, there were Mark Twain touches galore, surprises that sneaked up on guests, including special instructions on how to obtain hot water. "Turn the starboard faucet & trust in God . . . Do not try to hurry this water. Just wait. Do not try to assist by flattery, persuasion, compulsion, nor by any other of the usual expedients."[23] A group of Ha-

"MARK TWAIN'S DAUGHTER"

waiians had shipped to Twain a special mantelpiece carved from exotic koa wood, featuring the welcoming word "Aloha," and he prized this memento of his stay on "the loveliest fleet of islands that lies anchored in any ocean."[24] Of course, nobody could miss the billiard room, where Twain planned for Jean to craft a wooden sign over the door saying "The Aquarium." In addition to photographs of the dozen angelfish on the walls, each girl selected a picture of an actual angelfish to accompany her portrait. Louise Paine, now age thirteen, could walk over from her house, but it was not unusual for most of the teenagers to stay as long as a week at Stormfield, and while there they had to abide by rules drawn up by Twain for the Aquarium Club. One example: "The Billiard Room is the Aquarium's Private Headquarters. Members may exclude non-members from that room at any time they choose, & for as long as they choose."[25] How could Clara and Jean not feel as if their family had been invaded by aliens?

Involved in arranging angelfish visits, Isabel was now assisted by Albert Paine in writing to them and meeting them at the train station. Perhaps never in history has a biographer performed such unorthodox tasks for his subject. In his influential authorized volumes on Twain, Paine breezily dismissed any notion of something peculiar about the angelfish hobby. "It was just another of the harmless and happy diversions of his gentler side. He was always fond of youth and freshness. He regarded the decrepitude of old age as an unnecessary part of life."[26] For Paine, the angelfish testified to Twain's perpetual glorification of adolescence, perhaps not unexpected from the creator of Tom Sawyer and Huck Finn. The girls ranged in age from eleven to sixteen, and Twain claimed that once admitted, they remained lifetime members, but he gradually shed interest as they grew older. In Twain's mind, he likely did this to shield himself from accusations that he planned to sleep with the girls as they matured; to modern eyes, however, it only reinforces the impression of an unhealthy interest in young girls. As part of their club membership, each girl was required to write often to Twain, who was first "Curator" and then "Admiral" of the Aquarium, and more than half of his general correspondence was exchanged with them. As he told Margaret Blackmer,

SHIPWRECK

"I watch the mails, for [the] Aquarium is one of my life's chiefest interests."[27] He fussed over the girls, showering them with profuse flattery. After a visit from Dorothy Sturgis, he praised the "contenting charm" of her presence, which had "pervaded this house like a fragrance, & refreshed its mouldy and antique atmosphere with the 'unbought grace of youth.'"[28] During visits, he kept the girls busy playing cards, shooting pool, taking hikes, or listening to him read aloud. The whole experience struck them as innocent fun with an endearing old gentleman. "He never made us feel that he was an elderly man whose good manners included being kind to children," Louise Paine recalled. "On the contrary, he seemed to be having such a genuinely good time himself that age differences were forgotten."[29]

The bountiful archive of angelfish letters begins to thin after September 1908, and their editor conjectures that Clara, "who strongly disapproved of the Aquarium Club, disposed of many of the angelfish letters after her return home from European travels in September 1908."[30] Clara's displeasure probably had several roots. She had inherited Livy's role as protector of her father's reputation and feared it could be tarnished by the schoolgirls. In all likelihood, she found something creepy about this side of his life. Twain's blatant adoption of these surrogate daughters would also have been construed as a not-so-subtle slap at the inattention of his real daughters and their failure to produce granddaughters. Clara would have understood that the Aquarium Club was partly Twain's pathetic attempt to re-create their bygone Hartford world and bring back the departed Susy. She may also have felt uncomfortable with what she interpreted as a regression to childhood by her father, an all-out, desperate flight from adult reality.

Clara was a mercurial, high-strung woman who flitted nervously in and out of her father's life. She was talented, but never talented enough, her singing hampered by vocal problems and lengthy sanitarium stays. In early 1908, her career seemed to progress in performances with the pianist Charles Wark and the violinist Marie Nichols. That spring, she was ready to hazard a London debut, then kept changing her mind about whether to go. This left Isabel, whose duties included making travel arrangements for Clara, exhausted. "Santa is never sure for 24 hours if she will be able to make this trip to London . . . My days are terrible."[31]

On May 16, Clara sailed for England with her two collaborators, and when she arrived was met by a throng of reporters, one of whom asked why she hadn't brought her father along. Taking a well-aimed shot, Clara said, "Well, I had him with me for two years in America, accompanying me, but I found he was so anxious to get on the platform and make a speech before I had finished singing and the people seemed to want to hear him so much, that I thought it safer to leave him behind me."[32] This was a funny, if rather graceless, comment, considering that Twain financed Clara's trip and that she only received press attention due to his celebrity. Clearly, she viewed the British tour as her chance to break free from his smothering shadow.

That June she performed at Queen's Hall and Bechstein Hall (later Wigmore Hall) in London along with Wark and Nichols. In what she may have thought a playful mood, she gave an interview to the *London Express* in which she aired many grievances against her father. She complained of "the glaring injustice of having to go about labelled 'Mark Twain's daughter' when I am doing my best to pursue a musical career." She allowed that her father was a genius, "and that is what makes me so tired. My fatigue is directly caused by the incessant strain—prolonged over some years and induced by trying to find a secret hiding-place where I can shroud my identity, and find a comfortable bed."[33] She talked about the family's stay in Berlin, where she would be ignored at receptions until she was pointed out as Mark Twain's daughter and then people swooped down on her en masse. "At social gatherings graced by his presence, my existence was on the level of a footstool—always an unnecessary object in a crowded room. Father, fresh from bed, would completely flood the place with his talk."[34] There is no doubt that Twain saw the interview, which was reported in full in the *New York Times*. He couldn't have been pleased by this portrait of a vain man who dominated the spotlight, little caring how this overshadowed his daughter.

What lay behind Clara's odd outburst? Perhaps she believed she was boldly establishing her independence from her father, but she had traded on his fame to get publicity for her performances. After all, the entire interview revolved around her anger with her father; the reporter showed little curiosity about her musical career. At the time her father was moving to Redding, and Clara was seething about Isabel Lyon's influence over the household. Was she feeling displaced and did she see this as a form of revenge? Now that Isabel controlled family finances, there arose mounting friction over money, with Isabel persuaded that Clara was a self-indulgent spendthrift and that "the more money she had on hand the more careless & squanderous [sic] she would be with it."[35] She and Ashcroft later stated that "Clara Clemens traveled about like a prima donna, with a violinist, accompanist, and maid in her train." They alleged that she had received $13,220.48 over a two-year period (or $453,000 in contemporary dollars) while also borrowing heavily from Dr. Edward Quintard and others.[36]

Despite the troubled undercurrents roiling their relationship, Clara still professed enormous affection for Isabel. From London she wrote, "I am *sorry, sorry* that you have been depressed . . . You poor dear good sweet kind courageous faithful Nana!" In closing, she added, "Dearest Nana here is a huge big enveloping velvet hug for you & a million good wishes. We love you very deeply & I have missed *you many* times. Devotedly C."[37] What strengthened their bond was that Isabel had spent time with Clara and Will Wark, and knew of their secret love affair, even though Will had been married for almost five years and had young twins. Clara hoped they would soon be able to disclose their love affair and confided to Isabel in June that "Dear old W. is more wonderful all the time but I can't bear to think of the many many months still . . . that separate us from freedom and frank expression of the truth."[38] So, potentially, Isabel exercised two forms of power over Clara: first through control of the family purse strings and second by her knowledge of this illicit affair.

For the moment, however, Clara overflowed with love and gratitude, telling Isabel that "I feel like thanking you in every letter for all you do, but you know how I *do* thank you in my heart, don't you?"[39]

Clara's surreptitious affair surfaced in a form different from what she had imagined. Two days before she and Wark arrived in New York Harbor, the *New York World* announced: "Miss Clemens will give a reception in her old home on Saturday to many friends. It is expected that at the reception her engagement to Mr. Wark will be announced. After his daughter's marriage, a friend of Clemens said yesterday, the novelist will be virtually alone; and this, it was said, influenced him strongly in deciding to make Redding his home throughout the year."[40] Ashcroft alerted Isabel to the story, and she categorically denied its truth to journalists. Some Twain biographers have fingered Ashcroft as the source of the story, claiming that he wanted to diminish Clara's power in order to elevate his own. But he was still relatively new to Twain's entourage, and it is hard to believe, at this point, that he would have risked Clara's wrath had his hand been exposed. In fact, he and Isabel greeted Clara when she and Will docked in New York. The article had no immediate impact, and the day after his arrival in New York, Will showed no qualms about traveling up to Stormfield to be with Clara and Isabel.

On September 18, 1908, shortly after midnight, Isabel was awakened by confused sounds downstairs and discovered two burglars outside, rifling through furniture and silverware they had looted. Clara remembered being awakened by "eerie muffled-sounding cries," then hearing Isabel say "in a blood curdling unnatural voice 'people have been in the house.'"[41] Roused by the racket, Claude, the butler, came charging in and fired at the fleeing burglars while Isabel contacted the police. Unable to resist a witticism, Twain explained the next day that he, too, had heard gunfire, but "thought Clara was giving a champagne supper & the popping corks did not interest me, since I was not invited, so I went off to sleep again."[42] By the next morning, the sheriff had nabbed the burglars on a departing train, taking a bullet in the leg as he did so, and the criminals were soon carted off to a Bridgeport jail.

Crime always played to Mark Twain's strong suit, and when a reporter

SHIPWRECK

arrived the next day, he found the humorist "in rare good humor" as he settled into an easy chair, puffing on a black cigar and dispensing comic commentary. He was quick to point out that "he was very, very glad to receive burglars—that he had always found them to be most amiable people, and that he had had so much experience with them in his lifetime that he had come to like them greatly."[43] With suspicious haste, he had drafted a warning that he would paste on the front door for future interlopers: "There is nothing but plated ware in this house, now and henceforth. You will find it in that brass thing in the dining-room over in the corner by the basket of kittens. If you want the basket, put the kittens in the brass thing. Do not make a noise—it disturbs the family. You will find rubbers in the front hall, by that thing which has the umbrellas in it, chiffonier, I think they call it, or pergola, or something like that. Please close the door when you go away."[44] Milking the moment, Twain even took Claude's gun and posed for photographers, aiming the pistol to show his superior crime-fighting prowess. The burglars were sentenced to four and nine years in prison, respectively, leading Twain to predict: "Now they are in jail, and if they keep on they will go to Congress."[45] He bore no malice, he claimed, toward the burglars, "for it is only circumstances & environment that makes burglars, therefore anybody is liable to be one. I don't quite know how I have managed to escape myself."[46]

For all of Twain's humorous sallies, the crime threw a fright into the entire household at Stormfield, shattering its aura of secluded harmony. A jittery Isabel stayed in bed for two days, and Clara swore she would never sleep there again. "Clara has the shudders every time she thinks of that night, & so does Miss Lyon," Twain wrote.[47] Of more lasting consequence was the impact upon the skittish domestic help, with one Irish maid suffering nightmares in which "a swarm of masked burglars" shredded her with bullets.[48] The fright was so general that the entire staff—butler, cook, and maids—quit in early October, hurling Isabel into a state of crisis as she had to hire a brand-new staff on short notice. Later Twain claimed, "It wasn't the burglars that scared the former servants away. They couldn't stand Miss Lyon."[49] But this view came with hindsight.

| 944 |

"MARK TWAIN'S DAUGHTER"

In her perplexity, Isabel learned to rely on Ralph Ashcroft, who now spent weekends at Stormfield, taking the affectionate nickname of "Benares." In her journal, Isabel stated that she was "unafraid, for always there is Benares to be near me, and to help me. And not merely to help me, but to *do* the many things I cannot do."[50] Always prone to hero worship, Isabel, in her anxious state, began to describe Ashcroft in glorified terms. "He is strong, and by his calm judgment he carries me through difficulties, he gives me a support and a knowledge of the value of things."[51] With the departure of Clara and the staff, Lyon and Ashcroft were now well positioned to tighten their hold over the lonely, isolated Twain.

To Clara's chagrin, newspaper accounts mentioned that Charles Wark was a guest at Stormfield the night of the burglary, which came as their adulterous affair took a momentous step forward. On September 17, Wark had rented an apartment on fashionable Stuyvesant Square in Manhattan, and on October 2 Clara followed suit, taking a nearby flat on the same square, installing a piano and decorating it with furniture left from 21 Fifth Avenue. Clara had chosen a tony, expensive building that also housed publisher George Putnam and Elizabeth Custer, widow of General George Armstrong Custer. Clara and Isabel talked about the apartment in intimate, conspiratorial tones, and it seems clear that Clara wanted to keep her father far from the flat, lest he perceive it as a love nest. "When father goes off on visits you can come and stay with me," Clara told Isabel, "for I shall have a nice little room for you but don't ever send father in to me unless you accompany him! You can always *make* some excuse for coming too."[52]

Despite her loving, thankful tone toward Isabel, Clara increasingly resented that when she returned to Stormfield, Isabel lorded over the household staff. When Clara sought to interfere with servants, Isabel complained bitterly in her journal, "The servants do not want more than one head—hence the wearying wearying confusion."[53] Isabel moaned of needing to get away "from the gloom that misunderstandings frequently put into my heart."[54] Of course, by her frequent absences, Clara had ceded the status of house mistress to Isabel, and now when she wanted it back, it seemed too late. Clara could be bossy and quick to assert her prerogatives, and Isabel was distraught over tension with her beloved Santa. In her journal, she proclaimed that her soul was "over its ears in mud—the mud of criticism—no, misunderstandings fired by C.C. [Clara]."[55] Isabel's charm masked her underlying fears about her future, which drove her further into the waiting arms of Ralph Ashcroft. In her melodramatic style, she said she drank in Ashcroft's "sweet philosophy that we must pay for what we have. And to hold so great a treasure as the King means that the price one must pay can never be too high a one."[56]

The sharpest disagreements between Clara and Isabel arose over money, especially now that Clara was touring and had taken an expensive apartment in a ritzy section of Manhattan. Twain, who closely tracked the expiration of his early copyrights, projected that his income would drop 20 percent once copyright lapsed on *The Innocents Abroad.* Since he had deputized Isabel to manage the family budget and exact necessary economies, it was Isabel who had to inform Clara that her monthly allowance was being slashed to "only 800 [dollars] a month instead of 2000." Such economies did not sit well with Clara, who retorted that "she had supposed that her father was very rich & that he had a million saved."[57] The self-indulgent Clara had expended money on her career with a free hand and wasn't inclined to make any sacrifices.

On Thanksgiving Day, Clara and Will Wark came to Stormfield for the holiday celebration, which marked the end of their relationship. The reason remains a mystery. Some biographers have speculated that Twain learned of Wark's marital status and ended the affair. Perhaps he discovered that Clara and Will had apartments near each other and that he was subsidizing their trysts. Another possibility is the arrival of Ossip Gabrilowitsch at Stormfield on December 18. The Russian pianist and Clara had twice been engaged, never lost touch, and saw each other periodically over the years. As recently as April 1907, Ossip had performed at 21 Fifth Avenue, with Isabel noting, "Gabrilowitsch was here this evening and played for a long time—played that great Schubert sonata."[58] Just as Clara had gotten mixed up with a married man, so had Ossip fallen for a married woman. While in Vienna in 1907, he had become in-

"MARK TWAIN'S DAUGHTER"

fatuated with Alma Mahler, the wife of Gustav Mahler, a composer and conductor whom he revered. "I must confess something terrible to you," Ossip told Alma. "I am in the process of falling madly in love with you . . . I like Mahler and would hate to upset him."[59] During the summer of 1908, when Ossip saw Alma in the South Tyrol, they exchanged a moonlight kiss that ended their affair. So both Clara and Ossip had dabbled in risky, extramarital liaisons and perhaps saw the wisdom of being with each other instead.

The burglary, the staff departures, the quarrels with Clara—all had exacted a terrible toll on Isabel, who consulted Dr. Quintard and was advised that she "was badly in need of rest & change."[60] In November she was traumatized by the "trying and terrible day" she spent at the burglary trial and "went to pieces" at dinner that night, after which she couldn't get out of bed for several days.[61] Isabel had a theatrical personality and only later did Twain attribute her erratic behavior to a drinking problem, saying that "she got her illness out of a whisky bottle & was drunk a good half of her time, but I didn't know it. All the servants & some of the guests knew it, but I never suspected it . . . She always came out of a 3-day drunk sound & strong. When she used to lose her temper & carry on like a maniac, I took it for hysterics."[62] Katy Leary told him that Isabel could polish off a bottle of Scotch in a day and secreted a "bottle of cocktails" in her bedroom cupboard for daily use.[63] If such things were true, it is puzzling that Twain, in daily contact with Isabel, could have been so blind to such glaring misbehavior. But he was blind to the many emotional dramas playing out around him, all of which thrived on his ignorance.

CHAPTER SIXTY-FOUR

The Death of Tammany

In the aftermath of the Stormfield burglary, Mark Twain had a visitor who reminded him of far happier times: Laura Hawkins, one of the imperishable figures from Hannibal days, who had married a physician named Dr. James W. Frazer while Sam Clemens was learning the piloting trade on the Mississippi. With her white summer dresses and pigtails, she had provided the pattern not only for Becky Thatcher in *Tom Sawyer*, but for the school of angelfish later on. Laura was now a widow, managed a home for orphaned children in Hannibal, and arrived with a granddaughter in tow. In inviting her to Stormfield, Isabel Lyon made a point of saying that "Mr. Clemens wishes me to say that he would not miss seeing your granddaughter for a good deal."[1]

When Laura knocked at the Stormfield door, it was answered by Clara, who warmly embraced her and exclaimed, "I know you, for I've seen your picture, and father has told me about you. You are Becky Thatcher, and I'm happy to see you."[2] So many women had laid claim to being the original for that character—some twenty-five by Paine's estimate—that only now did Laura know with absolute certainty that she was the true Becky. A short, stout woman with a round, kindly face, Laura strolled down to the rustic bridge at Stormfield with Twain as they exchanged Hannibal memories. "Mr. Clemens had that rare faculty of loyalty to his friends which made the lapse of fifty years merely an interim," she said. "It was as if the half century had rolled away and we were there looking on the boy and girl we had been."[3] Laura came away from the visit with a valued souvenir, a photo of Twain with the (misspelled) inscription, "To Laura Fraser, with the love of her earliest sweetheart Mark Twain."[4]

Hoping to bequeath a lasting legacy to Redding, Twain thought that a "public library is the most enduring of memorials." He hated to see books housed in bleak, utilitarian spaces and wanted them "bestowed in a heaven of light and grace and harmonious color & sumptuous comfort."[5] Hardly had he arrived in Redding than he leaped into creating the Mark Twain Library, temporarily located in an unused chapel, with Twain as president, Isabel Lyon as vice president, and Paine joining the committee for the constitution and bylaws. When the small library opened its doors that October, with two angelfish present, clad in Japanese kimonos and shaded by paper parasols, Twain personally presented it to the grateful townspeople. Like many prominent authors, he had a surfeit of books sent to him by strangers, and these were packed off to the new library. Contributions from his personal literary trove—including Kipling, Booth Tarkington, Victor Hugo, Lewis Carroll's *Alice's Adventures in Wonderland*, Louisa May Alcott's *Little Women*, and George Bernard Shaw's *John Bull's Other Island*—tell us something about his tastes. Those that came from Clara are conspicuously heavy in authors—Jane Austen, Sir Walter Scott, Bret Harte, George Eliot—whom Twain loathed, another sign of Clara's not-so-secret ambivalence toward her father. In the end, the Clemenses enriched the library with 1,751 books, many annotated by family members, and they would circulate publicly for years.

Donated books poured in from publishers Twain knew—all these "without coercion, indeed upon the merest hint," he facetiously noted—and he extorted similar contributions from magazines that he wrote for.[6] To raise money for a library building, he levied a guest tax of one dollar upon male visitors to Stormfield, posting a written notice: "Guests of the valuable sex are tax-free, and shall so remain; but guests of the other sex must pay, whether they are willing or not."[7]

THE DEATH OF TAMMANY

Redding children remembered that when they visited Stormfield, Twain ushered them into the billiard room and proudly showed off his beautiful cat Tammany, enthroned with her kittens in a bay window basket. Twain would station himself in a large armchair and narrate tales of the kittens as the children fondled them. Since Tammany shared space with the Aquarium Club, she held a place of honor in all its activities, and when she was killed by a dog that November, Twain grieved as though he had lost a dear friend. As he informed Louise Paine:

> Tammany is dead. I am very sorry. She was the most beautiful cat on this western bulge of the globe, and perhaps the most gifted. She leaves behind her, inconsolable, two children by her first marriage—Billiards and Babylon; and three grandchildren by her second—Amanda, Annanci and Sinbad. She met her death by violence, at the hands of a dog.
>
> She was buried by Miss Lyon with the honors due her official rank—for by appointment she was Mascot to the Aquarium, and brought it good luck as long as she lived. She took great interest in the M.A.'s, and went to the billiard room every day to look at their pictures. Requies Cat in Pace
>
> As a token of respect and regret, it is requested that each M.A. wear black head ribbons during one hour on the 30th of this month—Tammany's birthday.[8]

Behind the air of jollity that Twain generated, even on sad occasions, there was an atmosphere of byzantine intrigue at Stormfield, with the King unaware that he presided over a house full of scheming courtiers. In making Albert Paine his authorized biographer in December 1906, Twain had also chosen him as the executor of his literary remains, a

SHIPWRECK

move Clara vigorously contested, seeing herself as the high priestess of her father's reputation. Twain confided in Isabel about this piece of estate planning, and she spent two hours convincing him to side with Clara. A few weeks later, Paine was dropped as literary executor, with Clara granted "full authority over all literary remains."[9] Jean was not mentioned, as if she never existed. In her journal, Isabel effused: "Oh King— you are so wonderful, as you sit in bed leaning on one elbow, & reading the new clause of your will—the clause making C.C. library executrix."[10] It was the first crack in Paine's relationship with Isabel, one that he was not likely to forgive or forget.

At first, Isabel had believed that she and Paine marched forth as comrades-in-arms, a pair of holy warriors protecting the King. When Twain's dictations began, Isabel wrote that it was "such a comfort to have Mr. Paine full of the love of the daily dictation, missing not a gesture— not a word—not a glance, but treasuring it all."[11] Like Isabel, Paine saw himself as saving Twain from his own folly, a role long assumed by Livy. Isabel recalled that "Paine used to say that the King had to be protected, forcibly if there was no time for tact, from the indiscretions that Mrs. Clemens was always warning him away from."[12] In those halcyon early days, Paine and Lyon even engaged in a romantic flirtation in Dublin as they shared long walks together.

Insuperable conflicts soon arose, though. Before Paine came on the scene, Twain had granted Isabel and Clara the right to posthumously publish his letters, with Isabel performing most of the work and collecting one-tenth of the royalties. Both women counted on the income. Twain knew the biggest batch of correspondence resided with Twichell, Howells, and Rogers. Obviously, these would form the basis of any authorized biography, but Paine encountered repeated obstacles in using them. Isabel and Clara put up stiff resistance to Paine's unrestricted use of these documents, many of which sat in a Stormfield trunk. One day, Isabel discovered a bunch of letters missing, suspected Paine of having purloined them, and confronted him by phone. "He was cross & answered in a burst of ill temper that he had many letters & would take them when he wanted to."[13] If denied access to such letters, Paine protested indignantly,

THE DEATH OF TAMMANY

he would "become not *the* biographer but simply *a* biographer—one of a dozen groping, half-equipped men."[14] Paine promised to quote only brief excerpts from the letters and to use them discreetly. Quite naturally, Paine thought it his right as a biographer to rummage through letters, make copies, and quote them in his book. Jealously guarding the right to publish the letters, Isabel began to undermine Twain's faith in Paine to the point that Twain warned Howells, "If Paine should apply to you for letters, please don't comply. I must warn Twichell, too."[15] Such was Isabel's growing power over Twain that she banned Paine from the Bermuda trip in January 1908. "Somehow all my confidence is gone, & I do not greatly want to see him," she wrote. "My anxiety over the Howells letters incident seems almost to be making me ill. My philosophy is gone."[16] Once again, Twain's blind passivity created a dangerous tension between Paine and Lyon, since there was clearly some overlap in their projects. With Paine now marked as her enemy, Isabel needed a powerful new ally in the household, and she found it in Ralph Ashcroft, who approved of how she had handled the clash over the letters.

Years later, Isabel claimed that Katy Leary found Paine going through Twain's private letters to Livy, which he kept in his room. Twain then asked Isabel to lock up his manuscript trunk and box and hand the keys to him. What is more certain is that Twain contacted Colonel Harvey, who was to publish the authorized biography, to make sure that each volume would limit extracts from letters to no more than ten thousand words altogether. Only two or three short letters would be quoted in their entirety per volume. "I also ask that Galley-proofs shall be sent to Clara," he wrote, "so that she can edit the extracts, & suppress such parts of them as she is not willing to see printed."[17] This indicated that Isabel and Clara had routed Paine in their internecine battle and guaranteed that the authorized biography would be a bowdlerized version of Twain's life. Twain was starving his authorized biography of the very thing that would give it truth and vitality. He had now imposed so many restrictions on Paine that his biography would be Twain's preferred version of reality, not Paine's independent vision founded on extensive research.

SHIPWRECK

Soon after the burglary, Isabel discovered from Sue Crane that Paine had harbored letters between Livy and her sister for more than a year. With her taste for intrigue, Isabel seized the opportunity to retaliate against Paine instead of hashing out a reasonable solution. Isabel said that the "King's anger burned so furiously, so he bade me go to the telephone and demand those letters. I did so—with Benares (Ashcroft) standing beside me to encourage me up."[18] As Twain later scoffed, "She made me believe Paine was always spying around; always clandestinely reading letters he hadn't any business to read; always dishonorably slipping away with important letters & papers, & leaving behind him no list of them & no receipt."[19] Later on, Paine made the same point when he alleged that Isabel had "never missed an opportunity for poisoning his [Twain's] mind against me" and that such harassment had led him to think of resigning as Twain's biographer several times.[20]

That Isabel and, for a time, Twain himself feared what Paine might write is rather laughable, as it was obvious that Paine saw his hagiographic enterprise as not just preserving Twain's memory but burnishing it at every turn. As he told Isabel, "I have no desire to parade the things he would wish forgotten . . . but it is absolutely necessary that I should know all there is to know, whatever it may be, in order that I may build a personality so impregnable that those who, in years to come, may endeavor to discredit and belittle will find themselves forestalled at every point."[21]

By fall 1908, Ralph Ashcroft was a fixture at Stormfield, spending every weekend there, and he and Isabel were entrusted with many confidential matters for Twain, including handling stock certificates and depositing manuscripts in his safety deposit vaults. By this point, Ashcroft had evolved into Twain's business manager and boon companion, and he and Isabel often sat up late with the King, drinking heavily and playing hearts. Their intimacy was reflected in Ashcroft's nickname of "Benares," taken from the holy Hindu city of Benares, and plucked from a popular

THE DEATH OF TAMMANY

drama. Twain also called him "Ashcot," "Ashpan," and "Ashhopper." In testimony to his high standing at Stormfield, Twain now listed Ashcroft as a member of the Legal Staff of the Aquarium Club.

Like Isabel, Ashcroft was not averse to making mischief or retailing vicious gossip to Isabel to drive a wedge between her and Paine. That July, Ashcroft told her that "coming up in the train on Friday Paine sat with him and talked against me," Isabel recorded in her journal. "Said that I am ruining my mentality, etc. with drugs, fenascetine—Why I can't even spell the word."[22] Later spelled "phenacetin," the drug was introduced in 1887 as an analgesic and fever treatment, but was subsequently taken off the market. Isabel claimed that Paine never shrank from making accusations against Ashcroft behind his back. "Ashcroft drank terribly, but did not take dope, as Mr. Paine told Sam."[23]

Having developed a proprietary feeling toward her boss, Isabel enlisted Ashcroft in her sacred mission of acting as Centurion Guard for the King. "Benares and I have a moral obligation now in looking after the King. I shall not leave him for an hour unless Benares or another as good is here to look after him, and together we must uphold him in our spiritual arms. The plan was for me to take Jean to Germany, but I must not go away from the King, ever. He is too wonderful."[24] It was a very strange assertion—that Mark Twain was such a helpless child that she had a solemn duty to oversee every aspect of his life. In his loneliness, Twain had developed a total, myopic dependence upon this new palace guard. "Miss Lyon is now in New York for a day or two, & Mr. Ashcroft went away this morning," he told one angelfish in October. "So I am a solitary. I don't like being a solitary. However, it isn't for long: Miss Lyon will return this evening, & Mr. Ashcroft tomorrow!"[25]

There is intriguing evidence that Isabel and Ashcroft may have hatched a secret romance as early as June 1908, long before Twain knew anything was afoot. Isabel had evidently written to Clara that she had received a marriage proposal—we don't have the original letter—and Clara replied from England: "Well, if you *had* gone off and married you certainly would have been starting a march. I am not surprised at the offer of marriage—only *who* was it? The Bermuda man?"[26] As Ashcroft had visited Bermuda with Twain in January, it seems likely that he was the person whom Clara hinted at as the suitor.

Isabel would have feared disclosing any affair with Ashcroft, lest she arouse the King's jealousy or displeasure—probably why she rebuffed the marriage proposal. That October, she and Benares wandered down to the pergola at twilight, and Isabel described the moment in dreamily romantic terms. "The soft light and the dim trees put a spell over the place, like that of Debussy music . . . The only pin was the sound of Benar's [sic] voice, in the still green greyness, and now I know why the earth was so lonely when he was in Canada and it seemed as if he would never come back."[27] That month, Clara had started leveling accusations at Isabel related to the Stormfield staffing disputes after the burglary. Facing criticism from Paine and Clara, Isabel must have felt threatened and isolated, making Ashcroft's support the more necessary.

At this stage of Twain's business affairs, the ailing Henry Rogers had largely faded from the scene, superseded by Ralph Ashcroft. Twain believed wholeheartedly in his business acumen and admired how he had fought to save the Plasmon company. Of Ashcroft's personal loyalty, Twain was reluctant to entertain any doubt. Only later did he say cynically, "What I always admired about Ashcroft, was his diligence & single-mindedness in looking out for Number One."[28] Finding nothing sly or calculating about the man, Twain was delighted that he and Isabel now comprised his intimate social circle, the people devoted to protecting him from harm.

Then, on November 14, 1908, Ashcroft and Lyon got Twain to sign a sweeping power of attorney that gave the couple the right to buy and sell securities and property for him, write checks or draw money from financial institutions in his name, make investments for him, and receive payments—interest, dividends, and royalties—due to him. The document was signed and notarized, then placed for safekeeping in a safety deposit box in New York. "It makes a body gasp to read it!" Twain would

THE DEATH OF TAMMANY

later say. "It takes possession of everything belonging to me except my soul."[29] The remarkable thing is that Twain had no recollection of ever signing this all-powerful document. He thought Ashcroft had slipped it in with a batch of other documents for him to sign, masking its significance. By his own admission, Twain had a long history of signing things without reading or understanding them. Fred Hall noted that Twain had forgotten having signed loan papers for Webster & Company. "I am a pretty versatile fool when it comes to contracts, and business and such things," he wrote in October 1904. "I have signed a lot of contracts in my time, and at sometime I probably knew what the contracts meant, but six months later everything had grown dim and I could be *certain* of only two things, to wit: One, I didn't sign any contract. Two, the contract meant the opposite of what it says."[30] The power of attorney was one such case where he had played a pretty versatile fool. All his life he had been scattered and absentminded, and this was a particularly egregious example.

Why on earth did Isabel Lyon, after years of worshiping her King, become a party to this sneaky maneuver? She was in love with Ashcroft, who promised to rescue her from "old maid" status, and probably didn't question his judgment. The power of attorney probably seemed a self-protective measure in case Twain died and Clara attempted to banish her and Ashcroft. Perhaps Isabel's motives were less predatory than self-protective. We do know that she didn't then realize how dishonest and devious Ashcroft was. Asked years later if Twain had liked Ashcroft, she answered, "Yes, very much . . . He was a great help in every way . . . But all the time he was laying his own plans."[31] If Isabel was duped by Ashcroft, she would pay a very heavy price for it.

Far from being suspected, in the following weeks Ashcroft soared to new heights in Twain's estimation thanks to a brainstorm he had: the creation of something called the Mark Twain Company, with Twain's literary properties transferred to it. It struck Twain as an ingenious solution to copyright problems that had long beset him. Twenty-five years earlier, he had brought a lawsuit in Chicago claiming that his Mark Twain pen name was his trademark and should protect his books from being pirated when not copyrighted. Twain lost that case, but Ashcroft took that concept and enlarged it. Twain would register his pen name at the patent office and could then, at least in theory, sue anyone who published his books without permission or exploited his image without compensation. (Such trademark protection is today commonplace among celebrities.) Twain called Ashcroft's creation "a stroke of genius" and was especially pleased that it seemed to protect Clara's and Jean's rights to his royalties after his death.[32] Ashcroft cleverly played on the idea of protecting Twain's daughters. "When this name is the property of a perpetual corporation," he told the press, "Mr. Clemens's heirs will be in a position to enjoin perpetually the publication of all of the Mark Twain books not authorized by the Mark Twain Company," even after book copyrights had expired.[33]

But while Clara and Jean owned all stock in the new company, they wouldn't exercise all power since Twain would serve as the firm's president, Ashcroft as its business manager, and Isabel as a director along with Clara and Jean. Significantly, Ashcroft would receive a small percentage of royalties earned from Twain's books.[34] Twain later speculated that Ashcroft got him to sign the notorious power of attorney by describing the document as the charter for the Mark Twain Company. Ashcroft had now cunningly crafted a perpetual structure that would outlast Twain's life and safeguard his and Isabel's investment in the King after his demise. Twain was happy to be free of further business concerns, and the Mark Twain Company, officially registered on December 23, 1908, formed another part of his late-in-life vacation from worldly care and return to his evergreen boyhood. "He seemed to find a relief in this," Paine wrote, "as he always did in dismissing any kind of responsibility."[35]

———

That Christmas at Stormfield was seemingly a festive one, despite press rumors about his poor health, which Twain was glad to squelch. As Isabel and Benares decorated the loggia with green branches and holiday paraphernalia, Twain felt as if he had recaptured the warm, cozy feeling

THE DEATH OF TAMMANY

of Hartford days, and Isabel expressed pride that "every room smelt of Christmas & of a sweet suppressed excitement."[36] In her private writings, she still sounded as though she and Ashcroft were purehearted acolytes of the King, united in adoring and safeguarding him. "Around through the rooms of that blessed house we wandered & then sat down to talk of the King & of ourselves & the joy we find in living with him & in loving him."[37]

When Twain sent out a holiday card that December, it didn't show him with Clara and Jean, but with Isabel Lyon and Ralph Ashcroft. Twain sits in the center at an open window of Stormfield, smoking a pipe and staring out at the camera. Isabel stands in front of the window, a shy Madonna with downcast eyes, while the goateed Ashcroft stands behind Twain and leans attentively toward him. Were Lyon and Ashcroft protecting the author, or trapping him in their talons? Through these holiday cards Twain conveyed his trust in the pair, how proud he was of their association, and how the three of them now formed a close-knit new family.

Adding to the holiday spirit was that a week before Christmas, the publisher Robert Collier telephoned Isabel to announce that he would be sending a baby elephant to Twain as a present. Thunderstruck, she lapsed into a "near-apoplectic fit," said Mary Howden, who wondered whether it was a practical joke. Isabel dismissed the idea, certain that Collier "was a man of his word, and if he asserted that an elephant was forthcoming, an elephant undoubtedly would arrive."[38] Lyon and Ashcroft strove to guard Twain from the disastrous news, which only kept getting worse. Two days before Christmas, Collier sent over giant heaps of food for the creature—ten bales of hay and twenty bushels of carrots and fruit. Then, on Christmas Day, a Professor May arrived, an elephant trainer from the Barnum & Bailey Circus, who came to teach them how to care for the baby elephant. The next day it became clear that Lyon and Ashcroft had been snookered by a practical joke: when the elephant arrived, it was a small stuffed animal, two feet long, mounted on casters, and Professor May turned out to be Collier's butler. Twain, of course, relished the entire caper.

CHAPTER SIXTY-FIVE

"An Insane Idea"

On September 26, 1908, Twain, Isabel Lyon, and Dorothy Quick had trooped down to the dock in New York to see off Jean when she sailed for Germany with her maid Anna and nurse-companion Marguerite Schmitt, with Isabel noting that Jean appeared "pathetic and wan."[1] Jean had been both excited and apprehensive about the trip, and was mildly optimistic as she began treatment in Berlin under Dr. Hofrath von Renvers. She found him quiet, kind, and candid, although she was annoyed by restrictions that he placed on her studies and cultural outings. She also had to mind her money carefully and complained that Isabel kept her on a tight budget that prevented her from attending operas. Twain, as usual, piled onto Isabel the handling of Jean's expenses. "She will know what to do," he told Charlie Langdon. "(I protect myself from having to do things myself by always being able to plead that I don't know how.)"[2] It was yet another decision that estranged and distanced Twain from his youngest daughter.

Jean's life underwent another abrupt turn that December when she sent one of von Renvers's prescriptions to Dr. Peterson in New York, who grew alarmed by what he saw. "This will not do; order her home at once," he informed the folks at Stormfield.[3] On December 17, Jean, out of the blue, was stunned to receive the following cable: "You sail January ninth steamer Pennsylvania passage prepaid. Send Marguerite home. Don't cable. Father."[4] It was another dramatic illustration of how Jean was kept frozen in a childlike state, and she knew it was pointless to

SHIPWRECK

flout her father. She told Marguerite that she did certain things only so that "my father shall not grow too angry and tell me to go to the devil."[5]

Jean's premature return from Europe meant that Isabel had to deal with the one crucial dilemma she could never resolve: where Jean Clemens should live. As evidenced by the Christmas photo of her posing with Benares and Twain, not to mention the power of attorney and the Mark Twain Company, Isabel felt fully entrenched and empowered at Stormfield. According to Albert Paine, Isabel had told an acquaintance, "Jean Clemens and I can never live under the same roof, which means that she can never come home."[6] Isabel had feared that Jean was violent and difficult, and believed that she was protecting both the King and herself by keeping Jean at bay. After her firsthand exposure to Jean's worst bouts of epilepsy, she knew she was ill-equipped to deal with these attacks. But Jean had now spent several months successfully living in Berlin, and it grew unreasonable to contend that she couldn't live at home. She was, after all, Mark Twain's daughter, a status Isabel could never achieve.

On the last day of the year, Isabel began to search for housing that would keep Jean at a safe distance from Stormfield. She found a group home with paid caretakers in Babylon, Long Island, a choice that at once proved disastrous. Jean bristled at the boring, monotonous setting—"a few bushes and small ponds used as ice ponds"—and found the company "unendurable." The house, she asserted, contained a "crazy woman," two nurses, and a friendly but tiresome couple. "I hadn't been there ten minutes when I telephoned Clara & told her I could not stay there."[7] This was a turning point, for Clara informed Isabel that she thought her sister should come home to Stormfield. Isabel invoked Dr. Peterson, claiming that he didn't think Jean was well enough, but Clara remained adamant. The conflict over this issue aggravated Isabel's already frayed relationship with Clara and landed her, under doctor's orders, in bed for ten days. "It is a sort of nervous break-down, attributable to too much work & care," Twain told an angelfish.[8] Though Isabel was high-strung and unstable, Twain heaped on her more work than anyone could handle; now came the insoluble complication of Jean's return. There was also the

"AN INSANE IDEA"

grave risk posed by Isabel's secret romance with Ashcroft, soon to come to light.

Jean wound up in a lovely home in Montclair, New Jersey, a residence full of trained nurses, surrounded by hills and woods. "You don't know how glad I am to be here!" she wrote her father. "The country is beautiful."[9] She had waited to tell him about Babylon, lest he think she was again complaining—a factor that helped to keep Twain in the dark about her true situation. Evidently, he failed to visit the new residence, for he refers to a photograph Jean sent of the house. Its name was Wahnfried, and Twain told Jean it "suggests healing rest and refuge and peace for tired and worried and overworked brains; ships at anchor after hard and stormy voyages."[10] Jean began to flourish in Montclair and started her own Jean Clemens Humane Society, which protested mistreatment of birds and animals, and also wrote a fiery, eloquent letter to the *New York Times*, condemning cruelty practiced by a sheriff against a Native American prisoner. Meanwhile, she remained in exile from Stormfield, the family's true home port.

On February 23, Isabel went off to the Heublein Hotel in Hartford for ten days to recuperate from mental strain, having already decided to wed Ralph Ashcroft, "this dear & wonderful man."[11] She had yet to divulge the news to Twain—"the psychic moment hasn't come yet for telling the King," she informed a friend—but she was convinced her marriage "won't make any difference in my life with the King—I'll stay right here, & Benares will come when he can to be with us both."[12] That Isabel knew the marriage would be controversial was confirmed when she decided to forgo an engagement announcement or public wedding. "It will be quiet as a whisper."[13]

Mark Twain was a volatile figure, and Isabel must have dreaded his reaction to her wedding announcement and the potential threat to her job security. From the Hartford hotel, she drafted a carefully worded letter to the King, explaining her reason for the marriage and why it would actually benefit him—a major case of trying to foist wishful thinking upon someone. "Together we can work for you . . . And you won't ever know anything different from the present plan, except that I will have one [Benares] with the right to watch me & keep me from breaking down . . . Dear King, I shall feel so much securer & of more value to you, & I'm so grateful to you for your sweet sanction."[14] Isabel laid it on pretty thick, making it seem as if the overriding purpose of the marriage was to serve the King in joint humility with Benares.

Twain refused to confer his sweet sanction on the union and reacted with scathing language when Ashcroft apprised him of the shocking decision. "It was as amazing as if he had said they had concluded to hang themselves . . . I said it was an insane idea, & unbelievable . . . He was of the opinion that the marriage would not inconvenience me, & would change nothing." The plan, Ashcroft explained, was for him to live with his sisters in Brooklyn during the week, then spend weekends with Isabel and Twain at Stormfield. "That seemed to me to be the wildest proposition of all, & I said so. I said I wouldn't have any married people in the house, nor any babies." Ashcroft assured him there would be no babies and suggested he was marrying Isabel not for love, but from benevolent protective feelings. Twain retorted that "a marriage without love was foolish & perishable" and would last only two years.[15] That Ashcroft was thirty-four and Isabel was forty-five would only have strengthened Twain's suspicion of an implausible match.

The crux of the problem was that Isabel was Twain's substitute wife as well as his employee, and she now tried to merge her two lives, to straddle two men. For years she had lived under Twain's roof, catering to his every whim, and he wasn't eager to share her with anyone. Years later, Isabel admitted that it was a loveless marriage with Ashcroft, struck for practical purposes: to silence insidious rumors that she was Twain's mistress and to dispel Clara's and Jean's suspicions that she had designs on their father. In short, marriage would protect both her and the King. When Isabel told Twain that she was saving his reputation, he remained furious; ultimately, he would agree to attend the wedding.

"AN INSANE IDEA"

Instead of keeping the engagement "quiet as a whisper," Lyon and Ashcroft grandly announced it in the *Hartford Courant* of March 11, 1909, the notice stating that Isabel had worked as Twain's private secretary for seven years and "expects to make no change in her professional duties. Mr. Ashcroft is an Englishman and a warm personal friend of Mr. Clemens."[16] This announcement seemed designed to placate Twain and reassure him of the undying loyalty of the Lyon-Ashcroft duo. In retrospect, he mocked the pretentious cards that trumpeted the engagement and other "imitation aristocratic pomps & glories."[17]

The day after the wedding announcement, Jean wrote a warm congratulatory letter to Isabel. Clearly startled by the news, she was unsure what tone to adopt. "Mr. Ashcroft is practically a stranger here, consequently I can congratulate him on *his* luck with all my heart much more readily than I can *you* on what I can but hope will be yours. It is too weird for words and so sudden unexpected!" Jean wished Isabel great happiness and ended: "Much love to you, dear; how I should like to see you and have a long talk. Yours affect. Jean L. Clemens."[18]

Though Twain fumed over the engagement notice and impending marriage, he did something mystifying on March 13. Ashcroft presented him with four contracts that bound him and Isabel more tightly to him than ever before. Ashcroft would be his universal business agent, collecting all monies owed him and receiving a commission for that service. He would supervise all household affairs and expenditures. Isabel would be transformed into Twain's social and literary secretary, and would "invite my guests for me, & preside at table & in the drawing-room & entertain them."[19] Her salary would be doubled to $100 per month, and she would be exempt from housekeeping duties and involvement in Clara's and Jean's expenses. Later on, Twain ruefully admitted that these contracts converted him into "Miss Lyon's slave & also Mr. Ashcroft's slave."[20] So why was he foolish enough to sign them? The answer was that he desperately needed their services and, in his solitude, craved their obsequious company. They had filled the large vacuum left by Livy's death. "I was happy. I still had my Ashcroft, my precious, & we should now get back into the old delightful comradeship again right away."[21] In signing these contracts, Twain consulted no lawyers, made no copies, and summoned no witnesses. He showed no business prudence or common sense. Like Ulysses S. Grant, he was the most lovable great child in the world, all the while pretending to be a shrewd businessman.

When Lyon and Ashcroft got married on March 18 at the Episcopal Church of the Ascension, just one block north of 21 Fifth Avenue, there were a mere nine people present. Jean was absent, Paine was in Egypt, and it is unclear whether Clara attended. A disgruntled Twain said the "church was cold clammy" and found that symbolic of the marriage. "Miss Lyon acted the happy young bride to admiration. She almost made it look real."[22] Afterward Twain said to Ashcroft, "The first one of you people who gets pregnant is going to get fired."[23] On this happy note, he, Isabel, and Ashcroft went back to Stormfield, where Ashcroft spent days at the Lobster Pot with Isabel and evenings with Twain, and as the King had hoped, the trio resumed their old boozy camaraderie. "The Ashcrofts & I were soon very friendly & sociable again, & I hoped & believed these conditions would continue."[24] Of their marriage, he said mordantly, "They could not have been a colder pair if they had been on the ice a week."[25]

While Isabel had been recuperating in Hartford, Clara found herself in a better position to delve into the daily doings at Stormfield. It was perhaps predictable that there would be a blowup between the two women. Isabel had exercised the power of a mother over Clara without the love and authority a real mother commanded, and Twain had foolishly ceded control to Isabel of his daughter's finances. Clara returned to a home where Lyon and Ashcroft had camped out and monopolized Twain's life—it seemed a complete takeover—and where he had launched a cuckoo obsession with young girls. She would have felt her own home as an alien place, whatever her own responsibility in the matter. That Jean had been locked away in Germany, then Babylon, and now Montclair further destroyed any sense of the family she had known. Clara resented that Isa-

"AN INSANE IDEA"

bel stinted on her allowance and concert expenses, and may also have believed that she had gossiped maliciously about her adulterous affair with Charles Wark.

With Isabel away, Clara took the extreme step of resorting to a lawyer and presented her father with a lengthy list of serious grievances against Lyon and Ashcroft, accusing them of financial irregularities and demanding an audit. She was also outraged that Jean was still banned from home and insisted that her father speak directly to Dr. Peterson instead of fobbing this off on Isabel. At this point, Twain still reflexively defended Lyon and Ashcroft, though he did ask Ashcroft to draw up a report outlining income and expenditures for the previous two years. When this was requested, Ashcroft "floundered, hesitated, stammered," then grudgingly agreed that all checkbooks and bank deposits would be examined.

On March 11, on the eve of the Lyon-Ashcroft wedding, at 2:30 in the morning, Twain spent four hours composing a long, tortured letter to Clara, marked "Strictly PRIVATE," that began, "Clara dear, I am losing sleep again over this matter." He said he refused to confront Lyon and Ashcroft without proof and before the two financial reports were completed. "To put them on the work now, argues suspicion of Miss Lyon's honesty, & Ashcroft's—*charges it,* substantially. I have no such charge to offer, there being no evidence before me to found it on, & there being no suspicions in my own mind to base it on."[26] He thought Clara was wasting money on a lawyer and argued that she should dismiss him. "In my belief, you will not need a lawyer's services again."[27]

Twain then paid tribute to the wide-ranging duties Isabel had performed for $50 a month (just $21,000 a year in today's dollars) as she became an integral part of his household and a priceless social asset. "She could not have been replaced at any price, for she was qualified to meet our friends socially & be acceptable to them. This service has been beyond computation in money, for its like was not findable."[28] He paid well-merited tribute to Isabel for her monumental labors in furnishing the Redding house. "There isn't a decorator in New York who can compare with her for taste & talent. These services of hers have been very

SHIPWRECK

valuable; but she has charged nothing for them."[29] While conceding that she may have been "loose & unmethodical" in her business practices, he bluntly defended her honesty. Moreover, she had replaced Livy as his in-house reader and "developed literary capacities which are distinctly remarkable. She has served me with a tireless devotion, & I owe her gratitude for it . . . I have the highest regard for her character."[30] Whatever her flaws, he implied, Isabel had labored for him with exemplary love and devotion.

Twain turned next to Ralph Ashcroft and gave a no less superlative appraisal, telling of his four-year campaign to resuscitate the Plasmon company, pulling "that great property out of what seemed to me & to others a disastrous & hopeless hole."[31] He hailed the creation of the Mark Twain Company as "a stroke of genius" and said it might "supersede copy-right law some day."[32] Twain paid Ashcroft the highest compliment by stating that "his services have been absolutely endless—& they are daily, & constant." He referred to Isabel as "a sick & broken-down woman" whom he didn't care to expose to humiliation without solid evidence. In summation, Twain made a startling assertion: "I know Ashcroft & Miss Lyon better & more intimately than I have ever known any one except your mother, & I am quite without suspicion of either their honesty or their honorableness."[33]

It was an altogether remarkable letter: Twain had sided with his two employees against the fervent criticism of his own daughter. The letter not only bespeaks Twain's dependence upon Lyon and Ashcroft, but his suspicion of Clara's motives. As Twain said of his older daughter, Clara was "a very dear little ashcat, but has claws."[34] In giving Lyon and Ashcroft the benefit of the doubt, Twain could not have mounted a finer defense. But he also revealed, quite unwittingly, how stingy he had been with Isabel. Even as he threw more burdens upon her and her health broke down, she never asked for more money. In sketching out her talents, he had only touched on a tiny fraction of the manifold services she had performed, from taking care of his health to handling his correspondence to fending off reporters to shepherding angelfish to Stormfield. She formed the very infrastructure of his life. It had been a hellish week

"AN INSANE IDEA"

for Twain, and with Albert Paine off doing research in Europe, his wife wrote to him that Twain was "almost crazy" from the upheaval and that the "poor old man," who thought he was happy three weeks before, told her that "if things did not get better he would cut his G— D— throat."[35]

It is amazing that while Ashcroft and Lyon languished under a pall of suspicion, Twain signed the four contracts with them on March 14 that only deepened his reliance on them. He believed that he had erred in mingling business and pleasure, and somehow fancied that he had now established things on a more businesslike basis. "Nothing is as it was," he told Clara proudly. "Everything is changed. Sentiment has been wholly eliminated."[36] Perhaps the one good reform Twain instituted was that henceforth he would sign all checks and be less aloof from household finances. Real-world responsibility was encroaching ineluctably on the author's second childhood.

When Isabel returned to Stormfield, she took up her new salaried position as hostess, and things superficially reverted to some semblance of normality. She felt security in being married and having binding contracts. "She was the liveliest of the lively, the gayest of the gay," Twain said.[37] An uneasy truce prevailed with Clara, who now supervised the housekeeping. Outwardly, things were so calm that when William Dean Howells visited Stormfield in late March, he told his wife that Twain was lucky to have the newlyweds at his service. "The Ashcrofts watch over him with tender constancy."[38]

In early April, Twain enjoyed such cordial terms with Ashcroft that he brought him along on a trip to Norfolk, Virginia, for the official opening of the Virginian Railway, financed by Henry H. Rogers. The occasion gave Twain a chance to pay homage to the friend who had rescued him from bankruptcy and saved his copyrights. Twain and Ashcroft were inseparable on the trip: they sat together at meals, and Ashcroft almost functioned as Twain's devoted manservant. "We were together, & ever so content & comfortable until midnight," Twain recalled of one evening, "when he tucked me in, placed my books, tobacco, pipes, cigars, matches, & hot-whiskey outfit conveniently, then went his way."[39] Twain's peace of mind was disrupted when Ashcroft revealed

SHIPWRECK

that Horace Hazen, Stormfield's butler, had been unjustly fired by Clara and proclaimed "he would not serve under Miss Clemens for any wages in the world."[40] On the way back to Connecticut, Twain stopped by Clara's apartment on Stuyvesant Square and discovered that Ashcroft had fudged the truth. Clara had not fired the butler, and Ashcroft had pressured him into blaming Clara. While Twain was with Clara, they spoke by telephone with Jean, who sounded so healthy that they thought it high time for her return home. For the first time, Twain allowed Clara, not Isabel, to contact Dr. Peterson about Jean's future.

When Twain reached Stormfield on April 7, he disclosed to Isabel that Jean would come home, throwing his secretary into a state of panic. "Miss Lyon flushed, her eyes spewed fire," Twain wrote, "& she was hysterical in a moment."[41] Isabel heatedly disputed Twain's decision: "It isn't to be thought of for a moment; [Jean] is far worse than she looks; she has convulsions two & three times a month."[42] This was an exaggeration; Jean had had only three grand mal seizures since returning from Germany. While Twain was in New York at one of Clara's concerts on April 13, the Ashcrofts huddled with Dr. Peterson at Stormfield and convinced him that Jean should never come home, as it would hurt Twain's delicate constitution. When Twain himself finally went to see Dr. Peterson—something he had so long resisted—and pleaded for Jean's return, he found that the doctor, fresh from "listening to Miss Lyon's falsities," refused to believe his description of Jean's improved condition or his desire to have her at home. Twain and Clara did get the doctor to agree to a one-week trial stay at Stormfield. Isabel Lyon's total control over Jean Clemens had at last been broken. "Dear child," Twain wrote to her on April 19, "you will be as welcome as if it were your mother herself calling you home from exile!"[43]

In retrospect, Twain decided that Isabel had acted "to shut Jean out of her home permanently" and that Jean had probably been healthy enough to come home when she moved to Greenwich, "if there had been no Lyon in the path."[44] He came to believe that Isabel's blackest crime had been "keeping Jean exiled in dreary & depressing health institutions a whole year & more after she was well enough to live at home." And how

"AN INSANE IDEA"

had she accomplished this? "Mainly by keeping me persuaded that the cure of Jean's pathetic malady—epilepsy—would be disastrously interrupted if she came home, where there would be company & distractions & excitements, & where she would lack the strict control & the exacting regime so necessary to her improvement."[45]

Twain engaged in a round of breast-beating, noting that Jean had "made many an imploring & beseeching appeal to me, her father, & could not get my ear; that I, who should have been her best friend, forsook her in her trouble to listen to this designing hypocrite." Of course, Twain preferred to blame Isabel rather than himself. He had farmed out responsibility for Jean to Isabel, seldom wrote or visited her, and never himself evaluated her condition. He pretty much washed his hands of his youngest daughter and spent entire days and weeks frolicking with his angelfish. It was simply not true that Isabel had cut Twain off from all of Jean's "imploring & beseeching" appeals. Twain had read many letters and rebuffed Jean. When she squawked, he lectured her and made her feel guilty, chalking it up to an unfortunate personality change induced by epilepsy. If he had been duped by Isabel, it was because, for all his genuine love for Jean, he did not care to know what was happening with her. On April 26, when Jean Clemens moved into Stormfield, her long exile from the family hearth would end.

By the time Twain returned home after his Virginia trip, total warfare had broken out between Isabel and Clara, who wanted Isabel fired and expelled from the house. "Clara wanted Miss Lyon's trunks, in the attic, searched for stolen goods," Twain recalled. "This astonished me! Did she think Miss Lyon *that* kind of a thief? Yes, she thought she was."[46] Even though Twain had just signed a fresh contract with her, Twain did a volte-face and decided to end Isabel's employment on April 15, and "I would then give her a month's notice & let her retire to her own house."[47] It was a shocking turn of events after Isabel's years of reverential service to the man she had dubbed "the King." It was perhaps inevitable, in any final showdown, that Twain would side with his own daughters and not the hired hand, Isabel.

On April 15, Twain sent a formal notice to Isabel Lyon, terminating

SHIPWRECK

her services with two months' pay, and had a maid deliver it. Isabel's reply, that same day, was also carried by a maid. "Dear Mr Clemens Thank you so much for doing in so kind a way, the thing that I have been expecting... And I now accept my dismissal from your service, to take place at any time you shall cho[o]se within the month, with thanks inexpressable, [sic] for the wonder & beauty you have brought into my life. I am with great respect & homage, Your secretary Isabel V. Lyon."[48] It was hard to say whether this was a gracious letter, acknowledging her rapturous years with Twain, or a fearful one, designed to mollify Twain and impede him from taking further legal action against her. She might also have worried that Twain would scare off future employers.

Throughout his life Twain had a habit of placing excessive trust in people, but once he lost faith in them and felt betrayed, he would turn the full blast of his anger on them—think Bret Harte or Charles Webster or Ned House—and this is exactly what happened with Isabel Lyon. Before, she could do no wrong; now she could do no right. For a week after her official firing on April 15, she still came over from the Lobster Pot and hung about Stormfield—"still infested it with her unwelcome presence," Twain snarled—and hoped a show of good cheer would mend relations with Twain.[49] When she told him that she and Ashcroft had married to give him the loving and watchful care he needed, Twain cut short this malarkey and said, "I had had enough of that offensive nonsense already from Ashcroft, & didn't want any more of it."[50] Flattery, served up successfully in heaping portions for years, no longer worked.

One of many flashpoints for Clara concerned Isabel's clothing, which Clara claimed had been bought with her father's money. Twain had often hinted to Isabel the importance of proper dress as his hostess and that he wished her to be an ornament of his entourage. He once went to her room with $50 for a new dress, and when she asked him, "Brown? Gray? Blue?" he answered, "I'd like you to get all the colors of the rainbow."[51] At other times, Clara invited her to get new clothes using house money. Isabel was distraught over Clara's charges and the mixed messages. "Please read this," she wrote to the King, "for Mr. Ashcroft tells me that there has been some misunderstandings about the few garments I've bought, but which I never would have bought if Miss Clemens [i.e., Clara] in all sweetness & generosity did not tell me to buy."⁵² As Twain's rage at Isabel gathered steam, he ridiculed her claims of possessing only a modest wardrobe. "I am aware, myself, that her closets overflowed with gowns, & jackets, & silken shawls . . . Why, bless you, she had a whole milliner's outfit in her trunks & closets!"⁵³ Another bitter dispute concerned Isabel wearing jewelry that had belonged to Livy and that Clara had thought was stolen. One day Katy Leary and Clara spotted Isabel wearing a brooch that Livy had owned; after they grimaced at the sight, the brooch was quietly returned to its cabinet. Something similar happened with a set of carnelian beads that had belonged to Livy. For both Katy and Clara, such items possessed huge symbolic importance. Isabel, in her dream world, might have fantasized about becoming the second Mrs. Clemens. For Clara, Isabel wearing the jewelry would have crystallized her fear that her mother's place was being usurped by an interloper.

Perhaps the chief allegation leveled against Isabel was that she had secretly diverted Twain's money to pay for her Lobster Pot renovations. In December 1908, he had extended her a $1,500 loan for work on her house and expected to forgive all that debt in $500 increments. Then the construction foreman, Harry Lounsbury, told Twain that Isabel had, in fact, spent $3,500 on her house, the extra $2,000 having come from his own household account *before* he offered this loan. (The excess $2,000 would amount to about $68,000 in present-day money.) "This was plain, simple, stark-naked *theft*," Twain thundered.⁵⁴ In his wrath, he insisted that Isabel deed the house and grounds back to him.

Naturally, Twain appealed to the sound judgment of Henry H. Rogers, whose devotion to Twain was always beyond reproach. When Clara went to the Standard Oil building and asked for Rogers's help in producing an audit of the accounts, he promised to "take up the matter" and "straighten it out."⁵⁵ He then wrote to Twain that he had always harbored doubts about the Ashcrofts. "In the last two or three years I had my suspicions of things, which you in your good natured way have overlooked."⁵⁶ Twain was relieved to have Rogers's knowledgeable cooperation. "The check-books & vouchers which Ashcroft will have to place before your expert are my property, & I would be glad if you will keep possession of them for me, when the inquiry is finished. I don't want them to go back into Ashcroft's hands."[57]

Ashcroft also visited Rogers, then sent a self-serving letter to Twain claiming that Rogers had deplored his "ghastly treatment" of Isabel after all she had done for him. He appealed to Twain's sense of fairness and made an allusion to Clara that could only have infuriated her father. "As you have already stated, the charges emanated from a brain diseased with envy, malice and jealousy."[58] Here Ashcroft must have drawn on private criticisms Twain had made of Clara. On the envelope, Twain scrawled angrily, "Letter from a sniveling hypocrite—who is also a skunk, & a professional liar. It is precious, it has no mate in polecat literature—don't let it get lost."[59] Why would Ashcroft have expected Twain to disavow his own daughter? Twain was outraged that Ashcroft dared to address him as a peer. "I am nearly 74 & a figure in the world, yet he blandly puts himself on an equality with me, & insults me as freely . . . as if I were his fellow-bastard & born in the same sewer."[60] On May 2, Twain began writing a voluminous account of this colossal blowup in his life, "The Ashcroft-Lyon Manuscript," which would run to more than four hundred pages. He hated being hoodwinked, and Lyon and Ashcroft joined a long line of villains who had wronged Twain and had to face his stinging pen. As had happened before, his disappointment with people would curdle into hatred, and he had no Livy on hand to curb his vengeance, salve his wounded feelings, or guide his errant judgment.

On the morning of May 19, Twain traveled to Manhattan to confer with Henry Rogers. Alas, Rogers awoke that morning with a violent headache and a numbness in his arms, and he dropped dead of a stroke at age sixty-nine. Emilie Rogers alerted Clara, who headed to Grand Central Terminal to break the news to her father before he heard it from the press. One reporter recorded his pathetic reaction as Clara conveyed the news. "Tears filled his eyes and his hands were trembling. 'This is terrible, terrible, and I cannot talk about it. I am inexpressibly shocked and grieved. I do not know just where I will go.'"[61] With tears streaming down his face, Twain seemed a broken old man as he shuffled off to the

"AN INSANE IDEA"

exit, leaning on Clara and staring forlornly at the ground. Clara shepherded him to a hotel room, where, she said, "he looked so delicate, enveloped in this shadow of sorrow. He could think of nothing else for many days."[62] The death came at a punishing moment for Twain, robbing him of the clear-eyed counsel of Rogers when he most needed it. The Lyon-Ashcroft audit was put into the hands of an independent accountant.

The feud with Lyon and Ashcroft entered a new phase when the latter boasted to young Harry Lounsbury of his power over Twain. "I can sell his house, over his head, for a thousand dollars, whenever I want to!"[63] Albert Paine was now back in Connecticut, and on June 1 he went to Twain's safety deposit box at the Liberty National Bank and discovered the blanket power of attorney that Twain had signed in mid-November. "By it I transferred all my belongings, down to my last shirt, to the Ashcrofts, to do as they pleased with. So this was what they had up their sleeve all the time!"[64] This was, for Twain, the final proof of deep-dyed villainy. He called the power of attorney the "most amazing document that has seen the light since the Middle Ages," and from now on he would engage in all-out warfare with Lyon and Ashcroft.[65] He sent them both cold legal notices, revoking the power of attorney, and Ashcroft feigned a breezy air of nonchalance. "Of course we both cheerfully acquiesce in your request, in fact, neither of us has used or had cause to use the same recently."[66]

The way the couple acted at this point suggests either fear or guilt: they decided to flee the country. On June 3, Ashcroft wrote to Twain: "Mrs. Ashcroft's health has been seriously undermined, owing to the unjust and unfounded accusations made against her, and she is on the verge of a breakdown. Her doctor orders immediately a complete change."[67] He said they would travel to London in a few days. After Twain's lawyer, Charles Lark, warned Ashcroft that they should stay in the United States pending completion of the audit, he ignored the warning, and the couple sailed to England on June 8. "They are in disgrace—in irremediable disgrace—& nothing to blame for it but their own greed & treachery," Twain gloated.[68] He thought they had planned to be "indisputably

SHIPWRECK

supreme" at Stormfield, leaving Twain "another stripped & forlorn King Lear."[69] Now, he said, Ashcroft and "his wench surreptitiously fly the country."[70]

Faced with this defiance, Twain's lawyers suggested that he attach the Lobster Pot and the surrounding twenty acres to reclaim the money he had lost in its renovation. They would also put a lien on a property Isabel owned in Farmington, Connecticut. The arrival of the Ashcrofts in London led to a media circus, and when a reporter telephoned Stormfield, Jean picked up the phone and blurted out that Isabel had stolen money from her father to fix up her cottage. In response, Isabel announced that she would return to the United States to clear her name.

In mid-June, Jean sent Joe Twichell a lengthy, confidential letter about the scandal. It was doubtless cathartic to disgorge her pent-up anger at Isabel. "Miss Lyon took large quantities of whiskey & bromide, reducing herself pretty close to insanity—at times. She and Mr. Ashcroft so worked Father that he was as clay in their hands . . . Several years ago Miss Lyon began to say that Clara was insane & she told everybody about here that I was, last summer."[71] She wondered how Isabel had spent $3,000 on her house on a $50 monthly salary, although she said the investigation was ongoing and final proof was lacking. Jean complained that Isabel had left behind chaotic paperwork and unpaid bills, and noted how she sometimes intercepted letters she had sent to her father. "She read them & if she didn't like them, tore them up without even mentioning them!"[72] Jean closed by saying how blissfully thankful she was to be back with her family. "In fact, I don't know when I have been as happy & absolutely contented as now."[73] She at last was home, occupying her own farmhouse near Stormfield, complete with barns and livestock, with permission to go riding again, and she gloried in Redding's rustic beauty. She also began to perform secretarial duties for her father that had been the exclusive preserve of Isabel Lyon. "It's fine to have Jean at home again!" an elated Twain told Twichell. "Damn that reptile Miss Lyon for keeping her out of her natural home so long."[74] On June 26, with the independent audit completed, Twain believed it vindi-

"AN INSANE IDEA"

cated his suspicions. "The result proves that Miss Lyon did well & wisely to travel for her health."[75]

In mid-July 1909, when Isabel returned to New York, she was met at the dock by her mother and a bevy of reporters feeding off the turmoil in Mark Twain's private life. One reporter described the five-foot-tall Isabel as "a pretty, Quakerish-looking little woman, the kind you expect to wear a folded kerchief over her shoulders and dove-colored frocks."[76] Newspaper photos show a sad, downcast woman, biting her lips, looking crestfallen. She had decided to return to the United States, she stated, when she read that the Lobster Pot was being attached. "I have come back to vindicate myself," she said, teary-eyed. "It is a terrible shock to me. I loved Mr. Clemens like a father and he treated me like a daughter. No one was closer to him for years, I believe, and I don't think the bringing of this suit was his doing. It was his daughter who did it [i.e., Clara], . . . and I think that back of her action there are enemies of mine [i.e., Paine] who persuaded her . . . I am going right up to Redding to-day and will see Mr. Clemens. I am sure that he will treat me fairly and justly and that I can disprove every one of these charges."[77] Isabel wasn't content to slam only Clara and Paine, but took a swipe at Jean as well: "It is my firm belief that the whole trouble has been caused by his younger daughter, Miss Jean Clemens. She is of a highly artistic temperament that is apt to lead her at times in a wrong direction."[78] This was a misguided way to appease her former boss and accuser, and it recapitulated the same mistake that Isabel had made in attempting, through innuendos and blatant manipulation, to turn Mark Twain against his daughters and authorized biographer, all under the specious guise of protecting him.

Amid press clamor, Twain didn't deign to respond to Isabel's insinuations. "I did not care to make important people of the Ashcrofts, & they couldn't do it themselves, without my help."[79] Clara, however, was terrified that Isabel would seem like a sympathetic figure, one who knew how to wring pathos from the situation and win a newspaper war. She pleaded with her father to "make a simple statement for all the papers saying that you were grateful to me & my friends for discovering Miss Lyon's

SHIPWRECK

dishonest" behavior.[80] Her chief concern, however, seemed narrowly selfish: that Isabel's comments might harm her singing career and winter concerts. "If any reporters telephone me here I shall ask them to speak to you, provided you have no objection."[81] Instead of a public statement, Twain decided to dispatch Paine to meet with Adolph Ochs, the publisher of the *New York Times,* who promised to play down the coverage. In the meantime, Twain was out for blood against Isabel, with Paine telling lawyer Charles Lark that "he is rapidly arriving at a point where he wants her in jail, and would willingly put her there if the evidence will warrant."[82] Paine was also developing evidence that Isabel had misused so-called house money from Twain's account—anywhere from $1,500 to $4,000.

Once Isabel returned to Redding, she stayed secluded with her mother at the Lobster Pot and didn't see Twain. Twain sent Charles Lark to meet with her and present a simple proposition: that Twain would take legal action against her unless she handed over the deed to her house and its twenty acres. Since Lark required a witness, Jean was deputized to accompany him, and she left a detailed narrative of the extraordinary drama that unfolded. Isabel's mother was dressed in funeral black while Isabel appeared all in white, as if to connote innocence. She made no eye contact with Jean, who sat between her and the lawyer. When Isabel pleaded ignorance as to why her house was being attached, Lark cited a $400 check she had written on Twain's account to a plumber named Hull for work there, although she put down "Stormfield" on the check. "That silenced her for a moment and she changed her tack," wrote Jean, "trying to look Mr. Lark out of countenance with a long, pathetic, absolutely unwinking gaze. She failed, of course, and wearily said she was 'very sorry,' if she had done wrong."[83] If Isabel repaid Twain's $1,500 loan, Lark explained, he would still have lost $3,000, but "what he most wanted, was to get her out of the neighborhood."[84] Isabel, distraught at losing her house, defended herself by stating that she had always intended to repay Twain's loan. As to using Twain's funds to buy herself clothing, Isabel "responded that Father had given her permission to buy such clothing as she needed, because she had several times declined a higher salary."[85]

"AN INSANE IDEA"

Jean pointed out that permission was only granted the previous winter in Redding, whereas Isabel had been buying clothing earlier in New York.

Lark brought up the $4,000 in checks drawn for house money that Isabel had supposedly misused. Isabel insisted that much of this cash had been applied to Stormfield's furnishings, which elicited a stern rebuke from Lark, who said Twain was increasingly angry, realizing "the ingratitude of her conduct, after being treated practically as a member of the family for nearly seven years."[86] If Isabel refused to cooperate, Lark warned, a complaint would be filed with the county's prosecuting attorney. "Mrs. Ashcroft repeated that she was very sorry, at least four times and twice that she would raise the money to pay everything back with."[87] Jean handled herself with dignity and restraint despite her anger stored up against the woman who had so cruelly barred her from her own home.

Finally, Isabel agreed to surrender the house deed, although not without some theatrics. She and her mother broke down and wept in each other's arms, Isabel maintaining that she had never written false checks and asking Mrs. Lyon, "You know I wouldn't do such a thing, don't you, Mother?" To which Mrs. Lyon replied: "No, dear, of course you wouldn't." Lark put an end to the histrionics. "Mrs. Lyon, you were not a witness on those occasions, the checks are the witnesses of that fact."[88] Isabel was given six weeks to vacate the premises. The whole proceeding infuriated Ralph Ashcroft, who accused Lark of stooping to "threats and intimidations" to bully Isabel into giving up her house. Twain was pleased that justice had been done and reviled Isabel as "a brute; just a plain, simple, heartless brute, & rotten to the spine."[89] Yet he was also aware of the terrible human tragedy that had befallen Isabel and even predicted to Clara that "God will punish Paine. I know it. Because he is so intemperately glad over yesterday's tragedy."[90]

There was more high drama to come when Charles Lark, this time with Clara, went to give Isabel a lease that would allow her to stay in the house until September 1. Mrs. Lyon, after informing them that Isabel lay ill in bed, began to berate Lark until she was almost shouting. "My daughter does not even *know* what she signed, and we are both of us *crazy;* you intimidated her into giving her signature by threatening to arrest her if she didn't—and you *never* would have *dared* to do such a thing if there had been a *man* in the house."[91] Mrs. Lyon said she and Isabel had no desire to stay in this horrible place and were packing as fast as they could. She wasn't through expressing her outrage. "How could you accuse her of such things after her seven years of devotion to your family, she *lived* for you all and worked so hard in your interest . . . looking after the Servants and the household."[92] Clara replied that Isabel had refused their offer to get a housekeeper or raise her salary. "We tried to make her feel that she was one of us and when she did not wish to accept a higher salary for her increased services I told her to at least buy herself dresses now and then which she was willing to do."[93] This ambiguity struck at the heart of the matter: had Isabel been merely an employee or was she "one of them," someone who fancied herself the doyenne and mistress of the house, and hence entitled to take certain liberties with the money as if she had been Twain's second wife?

When Clara told Mrs. Lyon that Isabel had been guilty of stealing, Mrs. Lyon started to scream so loudly that her wails could be heard up at Stormfield. "Do you hear what Miss Clemens says? She says my daughter has been guilty of stealing—of *stealing*."[94] Faced with the pathetic spectacle of a mother unsettled by the scandal and seeking desperately to assert her daughter's innocence, Clara helped Mrs. Lyon to sit down on the sofa. At the close, Clara wrote, Mrs. Lyon "in the midst of sobs drew me down still nearer and whispered in my ear, 'if she ever did anything wrong it was because she was ill.'"[95] Isabel had once said that if she ever lost the Lobster Pot and her job, "all the bleeding heart of me would be torn out with it," and now that very thing had happened.[96]

After Ashcroft returned from England in late July, Twain expected him to meet with Charles Lark and arrange an amicable settlement. Instead, Ashcroft wrote a smarmy letter to Twain's lawyer mentioning the $3,000 in cash paid to Clara for her concert tours, some of which went to Charles Wark. Clearly, he was intimating that he would expose Clara's extravagance and her adulterous affair. He also said that Isabel had been browbeaten and turned over her house under duress. Then, on August 4, Ashcroft unleashed a vicious press attack against the Clemens family,

"AN INSANE IDEA"

published in the *New York Times*, and packed with every vile innuendo he could muster. He launched especially cruel attacks on Clara and Jean, mentioning their sanitarium stays and how "Miss Lyon naturally became Mr. Clemens's hostess and person of affairs . . . Both daughters, however, became jealous of her, were afraid that Mark Twain would marry her, and often indeavored [sic] to destroy his confidence in her." He zeroed in on Clara, saying that she thought more of her career "than of taking care of her old father and filling her mother's place. One's vocal ambitions, however, sometimes exceed one's capacities in that direction, and the bitter realization of this . . . caused the baiting of a woman who has earned and kept the admiration and respect of all of Mark Twain's friends."[97] That there was some truth to Ashcroft's diatribe didn't lessen the brutality of this public attack.

Ashcroft's statement got still uglier when he claimed that the missing money had actually gone to Clara, not to Isabel, to pay for her concerts and "paper" empty halls. He then had the gall to quote the letter in which Twain had once defended Isabel from Jean's criticism—the one in which he wrote, "When you blame her you are merely blaming me—she is not open to criticism in the matter"—and said that Isabel had secured the esteem of everybody but Jean. This was a blatant violation of Twain's private correspondence. That Isabel had provided Ashcroft with this letter was, for Twain, "a crime of such baseness, too, that it puts the final stamp of treachery upon her character."[98] It also grew clear that Isabel had betrayed private talks with Twain in which he had complained of feeling neglected by Clara. No blow or falsehood was too low for Ashcroft, who said, nonsensically, that he would remain manager of the Mark Twain Company for two years.

Ashcroft was indeed a smooth and practiced liar. In the *New York Times* of September 13, he made the absurd claim that he and Isabel had withdrawn their (nonexistent) defamation suits against Twain; that reparation had been made by Twain and Clara for their statements; and that Twain had signed a document "acquitting Mrs. Ashcroft of all blame for her conduct of affairs while she was in his employ as his secretary."[99] Although Twain and the Mark Twain Company board had asked for

SHIPWRECK

Ashcroft's resignation two days earlier, he distorted the truth and claimed that Twain had asked him to stay on. In the future, Paine would become the new company manager. Twain only corrected stories in the press at Clara's behest and sent a terse note to an Associated Press editor: "I caught Miss Lyon stealing money (she had been at it more than two years), & I bounced her. That is the whole of the dispute."[100] On September 10, Twain and his lawyers reached a settlement with the Ashcrofts, and Ralph stepped down from the Mark Twain Company. It would now be Albert B. Paine, not Isabel, who would edit Mark Twain's letters with Clara.

Twain had exhibited a lifelong tendency to hold implacable grudges against people who disappointed him. Of that tendency, Howells wrote that "it was always in him to be faithful to any trust, and in proportion as a trust of his own was betrayed he was ruthlessly and implacably resentful."[101] When struggling to contain her husband's bottomless rage against someone, Livy had trained him to find a safe outlet for his anger by writing unsent letters. Perhaps seizing on that concept, Twain began to compose the unpublished "Ashcroft-Lyon Manuscript," in which he not only sated his appetite for revenge with withering tirades against the couple, but struggled to figure how he had been so gullible and easily conned. He devoted an extraordinary amount of time to documenting the scandal, painting Lyon and Ashcroft as a diabolical couple spinning evil plots against him.

Twain asked how he had allowed Isabel to insinuate herself into every crevice of his life. The short answer, which he could never admit, was that he had enjoyed having a worshipful woman fawning over him and serving his every need. Lyon and Ashcroft had spotted Twain's vanity, his susceptibility to flattery, and how self-absorbed he was, how much he loved being coddled. Twain had prized Isabel's social skills and lectured Jean and Clara on her popularity with guests. Now, feeling bruised, he rewrote history: "I greatly liked to have Miss Lyon around, yet I had never much liked her; she was artificial, insincere, vain, gushy, & full of foolish affectations—& I had an aversion for these things; she was an old, old virgin, & juiceless, where my passion was for the other kind. To nearly everybody but me she was a transparent fraud, but to me

"AN INSANE IDEA"

she was not. I believed utterly in her honesty & in her loyalty to me & to my interests. She was master, & I was slave. She could make me do anything she pleased."[102]

Twain was startled to discover that many people—Jean, Clara, house servants, Emilie Rogers, young Harry Rogers, and others—had been convinced that Isabel was scheming to marry him, and he was scandalized that anyone could imagine her as a successor to the sainted Livy. "Miss Lyon compares with her as a buzzard compares with a dove."[103] But while claiming to have been blind to Isabel's seductions, he described her provocative acts in vivid detail: She would give him "arch girly-girly pats on the back of my hand & playful little spats on my cheek with her fan—& these affectionate attentions always made me shrivel uncomfortably."[104] Her attempts at seduction were still more blatant: "She would get herself up in sensuous oriental silken flimseys of dainty dyes, & stretch herself out on her bepillowed lounge in her bedroom, in studied enticing attitudes, with an arm under her head & a cigarette between her lips, & imagine herself the Star of the Harem waiting for the eunuchs to fetch the Sultan."[105] It is hard to imagine that Twain wasn't titillated by this self-styled enchantress with her Orientalist fantasies. And if Twain hadn't cared for such overt flirtation, why hadn't he said something and stopped it?

Twain dwelled at length on Isabel's alcohol abuse. Many friends and employees now dispensed anecdotes about her craving for whiskey and dependence on bromides to sleep. Twain alleged that "she was drunk. Drunk daily. On cocktails, on whisky, & on bromides. I did not know it, I never even suspected the whisky part of it—which was the main part. Everybody on the place knew it but me."[106] He now wondered how many of her breakdowns were alcoholic binges or disguised hangovers and recalled that she "often came to my room away in the night, both here & in New York, to get whisky—she being sick again." Twain once even badgered her, "Why in the nation don't you keep whisky in your room, when you are so often ill & need it in the night?"[107] Somehow Twain, who spent far more time with Isabel than anybody else, failed to see her glaring, chronic drinking problem.

SHIPWRECK

Of course, the most painful part of the story concerned the treatment of Jean. Clara reminded her father that he would write letters to Jean and allow Isabel to expunge any expressions of true feeling and affection. Isabel had convinced Twain that such sentiments would upset Jean and delay her medical progress. The hard truth was that Twain had been a willing accomplice in banning Jean from his home for a year or two beyond any medical need for it. For Twain it was wrenching to hear this. "By God I can't stand it, Clara! it makes me feel like a dog—like the cur I was; if I could land Miss Lyon in hell this minute, I hope to be damned if I wouldn't do it—& it's where I belong, anyway." To Clara, he also wrote, "Oh, the irony of it! that reptile Lyon mistress of our house these several years & Jean barred out of it."[108] The entire situation would have been resolved had he just bothered to meet with Dr. Peterson, as any good father would have done.

How does one square Isabel's fanatical devotion to Twain with the petty thefts uncovered? Given her paltry salary and vast duties, she might have seen this as a way to balance the books with nobody the wiser, and Ashcroft may well have convinced her that she was grossly underpaid (too true) and that the money was owed to her. Most probably she became so enmeshed in Twain's life, so almighty in his household, that she developed a sense of entitlement. Some of her thefts may have been spontaneous and haphazard, possibly influenced by depression and alcohol. Since her embezzlement came partly from unspecified house money, it is difficult to document the extent of her misdeeds.

Twain's sense of betrayal with Isabel was much deeper than with Ashcroft because of her lengthy service, yet Ashcroft was hardly spared the venom of his pen. Twain portrayed him as Uriah Heep, a cringing hypocrite who professed loyalty while plotting the downfall of his master, who remained blind to the situation until Uriah held a stranglehold over him. "And look at Ashcroft!" Twain wrote. "A sneaky little creature, with beady, furtive, treacherous little eyes, & *all* the ways of a lackey . . . I was never able to get to my room in time to take my clothes off unassisted—he was always at my heels, he always stripped me, he put my night-shirt upon me, he laid out my clothes for next day, & there was

"AN INSANE IDEA"

no menial service which he omitted. I despised him, yet I liked him, & liked his company."[109] As with Isabel, Twain never halted such servile behavior, which he claimed to find so loathsome in retrospect. Around this time, Clara was sitting in her New York apartment when a shot crashed through the window, missing her only by inches. She was sure, she later said, that Ashcroft had ordered her shot.[110]

The Ashcroft-Lyon fiasco occurred because Twain, with a truant disposition that had lingered since boyhood, had hired two people to free him from earthly cares. This strategy had boomeranged, creating an atmosphere in which chaos thrived and machinations went undetected, while he played billiards and gallivanted with angelfish. One day, after the scandal broke, Twain read in a periodical the following passage: "Old people, though in all appearance still independent and responsible, are often entirely under the suggestive influence of some masterful or interested person . . . who had succeeded in mastering the master's mind. In such cases the intriguer knew how to apply his suggestions so as to rule at last the whole household." Twain sat thunderstruck as he pondered this. "It describes my case minutely, exactly, vividly, & with most humiliating truthfulness."[111]

Twain believed that Isabel Lyon and Ralph Ashcroft had married only because they knew each other's crimes, which seems excessive. He was probably right that Isabel's crimes remained minor until she met Ashcroft. Her love for the King had been genuine, and even after the scandal arose, she could still write, "I miss the King so terribly, terribly . . . There is no one now whose voice breaks into a sob over a sonorous line of prose or poetry . . . There is no one to teach me those beauties; no one with the leisure or the wit to think literature."[112] There was a grand if sometimes twisted love for Twain inside Isabel Lyon, and some of the wrongs she had committed, especially with Jean Clemens, had stemmed from wanting to have him all to herself. Her job, Twain remarked, had elevated her from a chicken coop to an airplane, and she had grown giddy with the dizzying heights of her boss's fame, making her lose her bearings.

Twain's final revenge against Isabel was that she lost her job and home and was forced to marry Ashcroft, a decision she called a mistake. As she said forty years later, "Her husband was very unsatisfactory. He drank, and was fundamentally dishonest. He even accused her of doing some of the things he had done . . . He never could keep a job."[113] Married to Ashcroft, she came to realize that she had "taken a viper unto her bosom," and he had "proceeded to make her life a living hell."[114] After they separated and divorced in the 1920s, Ashcroft remarried and worked in advertising in Canada, while Isabel wound up working for an insurance company and residing in a small basement apartment in Greenwich Village in New York, where she died in 1958. Ralph Ashcroft emerges from the Twain saga as a pure rascal, as depraved as Twain portrayed him, while Isabel Lyon comes across as a far more complex and tragic figure. She had lovingly served Twain for many years and provided endless service at low cost. Her reverence for him was unfeigned, but she had proved pliant in the crafty hands of Ralph Ashcroft. Even Twain, in his outrage, was forced to admit: "Without a doubt it was Ashcroft who turned Miss Lyon into a thief. The check-stubs show that up to 1907 she was honest . . . I think she had been protected from dishonesty by fear until he beguiled her & showed her how to cover up her tracks."[115]

CHAPTER SIXTY-SIX

Grandpa Twain

Once Mark Twain was convinced of something, his mind betrayed a tenacity that seldom brooked disagreement. Flying in the face of bardolatry, he stuck to a fervent belief that William Shakespeare had never written the plays attributed to him and that credit likely belonged to Francis Bacon. His contrarian conviction was buttressed in January 1909 when Helen Keller visited Stormfield with Anne Sullivan Macy and her husband, John, who gave Twain the galleys of a book titled *Some Acrostic Signatures of Francis Bacon.* Its author, William Stone Booth, aimed to show that Shakespeare's work was shot through with coded messages pointing to Bacon's secret authorship. A second book, *The Shakespeare Problem Restated,* by George Greenwood, added to Twain's pro-Bacon ardor. Such was his zeal on the subject, wrote Isabel Lyon, that one would have thought he "had Shakespeare by the throat righteously strangling him for some hideous crime."[1] For two months, from January through March 1909, Twain beavered away at his next to last published book, *Is Shakespeare Dead?,* with bullheaded certainty about the correctness of his thesis. "I *know* that Shakespeare did not write those plays, and I have reason to believe he did not touch the text in any way," he told Paine. "It is the great discovery of the age."[2] Twain, it should be noted, had also identified John Milton, not John Bunyan, as the actual author of *Pilgrim's Progress.*

Twain cherished Shakespeare's plays, viewed them often, and only questioned their authorship. His fifty-year faith in Bacon dated back to his Mississippi River days when steamboat pilot George Ealer, "an idolater of Shakespeare," read the plays aloud to him and bashed Bacon supporters royally.[3] In the 1870s, Twain and Livy visited Stratford-upon-Avon, and Twain backed the creation of a Shakespeare Memorial Theatre there. He had researched Shakespeare while preparing *The Prince and the Pauper* and even tinkered with a burlesque version of *Hamlet*, told from the standpoint of an invented character, Hamlet's country cousin. In *Huckleberry Finn*, the King and Duke try to palm themselves off as Shakespearean actors and offer hilariously garbled versions of the Bard to backwoods audiences. The Shakespeare-Bacon controversy had long been a hot dinner topic in the Clemens household, with Livy defending Shakespeare and Susy lining up on Bacon's side with her father. After one performance of *Romeo and Juliet*, Twain even told a companion, "That's one of the greatest things Bacon ever wrote."[4]

Why did Twain attack Shakespeare with such gusto? Partly it stemmed from his extreme disillusionment with people in his later years, his belief that the planet was chock-full of fools and frauds, such as Mary Baker Eddy. "I think he [Shakespeare] & Mother Eddy are just about a pair—a pair of humbugs."[5] The Shakespeare cult, as he saw it, confirmed his view that people were merely sheep who followed a herd instinct and echoed what they heard.

Twain's main error was using his own career as a frame of reference in analyzing Shakespeare. In his final years, he had devoted enormous time to his autobiographical dictations, now amounting to 450,000 words, and he couldn't believe that Shakespeare had left behind no manuscripts or letters. With an extreme paucity of original documentation, Shakespeare biographers had relied on a handful of moldy anecdotes about Shakespeare, many recorded long after he was gone. Twain extrapolated from his own literary fame and the myriad stories told about him versus the glaring emptiness of Shakespeare's record. Had Shakespeare been truly famous, he argued, "his notoriety would have lasted as long as mine has lasted in my own village out in Missouri . . . a really celebrated person cannot be forgotten in his village in the short space of sixty years."[6] He mentioned his Hannibal schoolmates who regularly retailed legends about him to reporters. Of course, Twain lived in a very different media environment from Shakespeare, one where newspapers published features, profiles, and interviews, and where a celebrity culture had already taken root. Unwittingly he applied these assumptions to distant, publicity-shy Elizabethan times.

Like many Shakespeare deniers, Twain observed that the playwright was curiously well versed in law courts and legal proceedings. Nobody, thought Twain, could master "the *argot* of a trade at which he has not personally served."[7] Some scholars have speculated that Shakespeare clerked in a law office before starting his theater career in London, but that still begs Twain's larger point that Shakespeare plays betray knowledge that only a highly educated person like Bacon might have known. Twain was an unlikely messenger for this thesis: he was an uneducated young man from the provinces who had absorbed information from many sources, an autodidact with an eclectic mind that soaked up everything. Twain was also misled about Shakespeare because his own writings were so autobiographical that he couldn't imagine another author's purely inventive powers. In writing about Joan of Arc, Twain had accepted without question her miraculous mastery of law and military science at age sixteen, but with Shakespeare he evinced a thoroughgoing skepticism.

Despite the vigor of his argument, Twain failed to confront many obvious objections to his theory. How could Francis Bacon's imposture have remained hidden during his lifetime and after? Did he confide in no one? How did he know so much about stagecraft—something only an actor and manager like Shakespeare would have known? How did Bacon make needed changes to plays during rehearsals? Did Shakespeare have to rush off to Bacon's home each night for secret, emergency revisions? And what about cases where we know that Shakespeare collaborated with other authors? Twain also never dealt with the problem of the First Folio, the fact that his fellow actors thought so highly of William Shakespeare that they assembled this legacy for posterity seven years after he died.

Even Twain's heartiest admirers, Paine and Lyon, appealed to him not to publish the Shakespeare screed, and Colonel Harvey at Harper agreed it would be ill-advised, showing intellectual slippage on Twain's

SHIPWRECK

part and dealing another blow to his humorist image. Nonetheless, Twain was hell-bent on publishing it and wanted to beat the William Stone Booth book to press. As a result of this rushed editing process, the book appeared on April 8, 1909, a mere month after the manuscript was completed. It may have been this haste that landed Twain in an embarrassing imbroglio with George Greenwood, who claimed that Twain had quoted freely from *The Shakespeare Problem Restated* without crediting him—an awkward position for Twain, a militant on copyright issues. In the *New York Times,* Greenwood's publisher accused Twain of "literary larceny," but it turned out that Harper's staff had contacted the publisher and gotten permission to quote from Greenwood. Somehow the necessary footnote had been accidentally dropped. Twain apologized, the fugitive footnote was inserted in future editions, and the kerfuffle ended. *Is Shakespeare Dead?* was greeted with something less than acclaim, and nobody endorsed it, then or later, as "the great discovery of the age."

The Greenwood controversy blew up in June 1909, right around the time Twain traveled to Baltimore with Paine for the graduation of a favored angelfish, Francesca Nunnally, the Atlanta schoolgirl whom he met en route to Oxford in 1907. The day he checked into the Belvedere Hotel, one newspaper carried the incendiary headline "Is Mark Twain a Plagiarist?" Feeling worn out, Twain shunned newspapermen who came to elicit his reaction and lay down in the hotel room with a book. When he arose and paced the room, he suddenly paused with one hand clutching his chest. "I think I must have caught a little cold yesterday on that Fifth Avenue stage," he told Paine. "I have a curious pain in my breast."[8] He lay down again and seemed to doze, but when he resumed walking, he stopped with his hand again pressed to his chest. "That pain has come back," he said. "It's a curious, sickening, deadly kind of pain. I never had anything just like it."[9] Twain's instincts were accurate: at seventy-three, he was suffering from angina pectoris, with a reduced blood flow to the heart muscle producing sharp, frightening attacks.

GRANDPA TWAIN

Twain rallied enough to address the six graduates at St. Timothy's School in Catonsville, Maryland, a tiny, elite, and very proper all-female boarding establishment. On his way to the graduation, he chomped on a cigar and glanced admiringly at the parade of Baltimore girls traipsing down the sidewalk. "Pretty girls—and you almost have a monopoly of them here—are always an inspiration to me," he told a reporter.[10] When he arrived at St. Timothy's, looking dapper in white flannels and a Panama hat, Francesca was there to greet him as "Grandpa Twain." In addressing the graduates, Twain's eyes sparkled, and he spiced his remarks with trademark mischief. He advised the girls not to smoke or drink to excess, then delivered his punch line: "Don't marry—I mean, to excess."[11] It was to be his last speech, culminating a forty-year career. After the ceremony, Twain hung around to take pictures with Francesca and her classmates.

In terms of health, Twain knew that he had passed a watershed, and a sense of malaise from the Baltimore trip lasted. He didn't venture out again when he got back to Stormfield and in late June informed Twichell that "Dr. Quintard came up today & examined me, gave very positive orders that I am not to stir from here upon any account before autumn."[12] Among many restrictions the doctor placed on his activities, the most onerous, by far, was his exhortation to cut smoking down to heal his "tobacco heart." Since boyhood, Twain had remained defiant on this score. "It isn't going to happen," he insisted. "I shan't diminish it by a single puff."[13] In the end, Twain drastically slashed his consumption from forty cigars per day to only four, and he felt, if not happy, at least virtuous for a time.

With his health impaired, Twain's fascination with the angelfish began to wither. He wrote to them less often and recruited no new candidates. With Lyon and Ashcroft exiled and Jean and Clara restored to their rightful place at Stormfield, he presided over a real family again instead of a fictitious one. After Jean returned on April 26, he comprehended

SHIPWRECK

what this meant to her after her lonely odyssey, staying in a sanitarium and group homes. "How eloquently glad & grateful she was," he later wrote, "to cross her father's threshold again!"[14] Thrilled by the reunion, Jean never punished her father for his failings, and he admitted that he was "deeply grateful to Jean for that unearned love."[15] At first Dr. Peterson had allowed Jean to move to Stormfield on a one-week trial basis, but it proved such an obvious success that the move became permanent. The guilt-ridden Twain rediscovered the lost daughter he had loved so much as a little girl and now attributed to her every conceivable virtue. As he told Clara, "Jean is a surprise & a wonder. She has plenty of wisdom, judgment, penetration, practical good sense—like her mother—& character, courage, definiteness, decision; also goodness, a humane spirit, charity, kindliness, pity . . . she is everything that Miss Lyon isn't."[16]

With her own farmhouse near Stormfield, Jean had a rustic setting that well suited her. She fixed up the house and barn, supplied them with chickens and ducks, and led an active, woodland life. She would rise early, gather mail at the post office, then proudly help her father with bills and correspondence, plugging the vacuum left by Isabel Lyon. After an afternoon of farm labor, she would return to Stormfield for more secretarial duties and accounting work before having dinner and sometimes playing billiards with her father, toward whom she felt tender and protective. Twain drowned himself in a sea of mea culpas. "I could have had her at home two years ago . . . but for the schemings of that pitiless pair & my own inexcusable stupidity!" he wrote.[17] The malicious Ralph Ashcroft insisted that Stormfield had fallen apart without him and Isabel. "'This house has gone to hell,'" he falsely reported Twain saying, blaming the situation on Twain and "his two semi-insane daughters."[18] Isabel denied that Jean could replace her, telling people, "*You see, Paine was really his secretary—that crazy girl never was.*"[19]

Not nearly as remote as her father, Jean became a popular figure around Redding. When she rode her horse or took long walks with her dog, she stopped and chatted with the town children, who grew to adore her. Jean's keen environmental awareness came as a revelation to her neighbors. One of them, Coley B. Taylor, remembered her love for all living creatures. "I had just killed a garter snake in the fields one day when she came by and protested, very reasonably but firmly, that the snake was harmless and had a right to live. Just as good a right as we had."[20] She pointed out rocks to the children and gave them lectures on geological epochs. For once, Jean was perfectly happy, with only a single source of irritation: "the thought of what has happened in the past & the necessity of passing the charming little house still in Miss Lyon's possession, every time I leave the house."[21]

Where Twain had underrated Jean for years, he now transformed her into a paragon of goodness, overstating her virtues. She could still be blunt and meddlesome, bossy and intrusive. That summer, as her friend Nancy Brush prepared to wed, Jean offered unwanted advice, telling her that she shouldn't "begin right off to have a lot of children." She barged into other private matters. "Am I impudent when I ask how you are suddenly able to marry, from the financial point of view."[22] If her epilepsy was briefly in remission, it never went away. To attend the wedding, Jean told Nancy she would have to bring an escort. "They would not want me to go so far alone."[23] Whatever his daughters' flaws, Twain wanted to project an image of a contented family and permitted the Edison Company to shoot a brief film at Stormfield that summer using a Kinetograph camera. At first the viewer sees Twain, costumed in white and puffing a cigar, shambling along a path outside the house. Then he sits down in a wicker chair in the loggia with Jean and Clara as they sip tea together in a genteel, refined manner. The butler brings Clara a hat, which she pins securely to her hair. It is a cozy film of a harmonious clan, an advertisement that peace had been restored after the expulsion of Lyon and Ashcroft.

In that Stormfield summer, one senses that Twain grappled with a final reckoning about life and death, with his disappointments leading to a bleak verdict. "Life is too long and too short," he told Paine. "Too long for the weariness of it; too short for the work to be done."[24] And that was one of his sunnier conclusions. "Anybody that knows anything knows that there was not a single life that was ever lived that was worth living. Not a single child ever begotten that the begetting of it was not a crime."

SHIPWRECK

He insisted that "the man who *isn't* a pessimist is a d——d fool."[25] Life's sadness registered so much more deeply for him than love and laughter that he eagerly awaited his death. "I came in with Halley's comet in 1835," he said. "It is coming again next year, and I expect to go out with it. It will be the greatest disappointment of my life if I don't go out with Halley's comet."[26]

Twain's medical condition and high blood pressure gave him a pretty fair shot at his hoped-for rendezvous with Halley's Comet. With mounting frequency and severity, he had recurrences of the sharp chest pains first experienced in Baltimore. Such seizures, brought on by billiards, walking, and other forms of exertion, could persist for up to an hour and a half. "It must have been a deadly, sickening, numbing pain," said Paine, "for I have seen it crumple him, and his face became colorless while his hand dug at his breast; but he never complained, he never bewailed."[27] For a time, Twain cut back on smoking, after Dr. Quintard said it would kill him, but he now decided to resume his habit. "I don't care for death," he wrote, "& I do care for smoking."[28] After a lifetime of chasing medical panaceas, he refused to renounce the one habit harming him most. As with everything, Twain displayed a fine sense of humor about his mortality. When Jean told him of a visitor awaiting him in the living room, he declined to see her. "Jean, I can't see her. Tell her I am likely to drop dead any minute and it would be most embarrassing."[29]

Although Twain stopped making notebook entries, he remained mentally active, scribbling on pads, and Paine, ever the dutiful biographer, collected them. One poignant jotting described Livy. "She was always a girl, she was always young because her heart was young; & I was young because she lived in my heart & preserved its youth from decay."[30] Twain read voraciously in a wide range of disciplines. He read about astronomy and spent time computing the vast distances between stars and planets and galaxies. Paine escorted him to the American Museum of Natural History in Manhattan so he could "look at the brontosaurus and the meteorites and the astronomical model in the entrance hall," wrote Paine. "To him these were the most fascinating things in the world."[31]

GRANDPA TWAIN

Ever since Twain had sailed as a passenger on a Pacific Coast steamer in 1866, his imagination had been bewitched by Edgar "Ned" Wakeman, the brawny, unschooled pilot. A garrulous character with a colorful way of talking about the Bible, he was a spellbinding narrator of tall tales. He employed many of the same literary devices—burlesque, exaggeration, and bluster sprinkled with profanity—that Twain himself used. During their second voyage together in 1868, Wakeman recounted to Twain in vivid detail a dream he had of visiting heaven. That same year, Elizabeth Stuart Phelps had published a best-selling novel, *The Gates Ajar,* about a young woman whose brother died in the Civil War. Twain was eager to satirize its saccharine vision of heaven, which presented it as an improved version of life on earth. Inspired by Wakeman and Phelps, Twain wrote the first draft of what became *Captain Stormfield's Visit to Heaven,* a project that germinated in his mind for the next forty years.

Every now and then, Twain would fish out "that rusty old manuscript" to tweak it.[32] He knew his satirical treatment of the Christian heaven might offend the faithful—"laws bless you, it can't ever be published," he told Howells in 1881—but he kept returning at intervals to savor this guilty pleasure.[33] At one point, Susy said, the taboo manuscript was "locked up in the safe, down stairs," too controversial to be left lying around unattended.[34] Twain delighted dinner parties with the forbidden story, and people pleaded with him to commit it to print. In 1902 he asked his Hartford business agent, Franklin G. Whitmore, to dredge it up from a safety deposit vault, only to discover that it wasn't there. "However, it *must* be in the safe if still in existence," Twain told him. "That is where I kept it so many years."[35]

While Twain never hesitated to destroy writing he disliked, he had a sneaking fondness for *Captain Stormfield's Visit to Heaven,* which saved it from the flames. "Secretly and privately I liked it, I couldn't help it."[36] Livy's death emboldened him to scour more freely the subversive side of his mind, especially with religion, as he waded deeper into waters he had

SHIPWRECK

once deemed too treacherous. He published two excerpts from *Captain Stormfield* in *Harper's Magazine*—one in December 1907, a second in January 1908—using the money to build the loggia at his Stormfield residence. Twain's mockery of the Christian afterlife wasn't quite as explosive as he had imagined, and readers even reacted with mild enthusiasm. In October 1909, he published the unfinished story as a Christmas gift book, marking the final volume in the Mark Twain corpus to appear in his lifetime.

Captain Stormfield's Visit to Heaven opens with the captain streaking through space and racing other comets. "I judged I had some reputation in space," he boasts, "and I calculated to keep it."[37] Having been dead thirty years, he still doesn't know whether he's bound for heaven or its hotter counterpart. Then he espies "a tremendous long row of blinking lights away on the horizon" and knows he is heading to the heavenly gates, where a head clerk interviews him.[38] When Stormfield says he's from America, the clerk draws a blank and consults an under clerk, who snaps, "There's ain't any such orb." Stormfield clarifies that he's from "the world," only to have the clerk sneer, "*The* world! H'm! there's billions of them! . . . Next!"[39] It is Twain's familiar theme of human vanity, a reminder that the Earth is one speck among many in the universe. Only man's pride places him at the center of things, endowing him with undeserved cosmic significance. When the clerk tracks down the Earth on a giant map, he dismisses it as the Wart.

From boyhood on, Twain had mocked hackneyed depictions of heaven. As Captain Stormfield moves into heaven, he encounters hordes of disappointed souls streaming out, chucking aside in disgust their haloes, harps, and palm branches. When he samples his own harp, he gives up after sixteen or seventeen hours of plucking out the same tune, then starts fanning himself with his palm branch. He finds his wings clumsy to wear until he is reassured that they are merely for show. In despair, Stormfield says, "This *ain't* just as near my idea of bliss as I thought it was going to be, when I used to go to church."[40] Stormfield had imagined that everyone in heaven would be young and beautiful. Now he befriends a bald old angel, Sandy McWilliams of New Jersey, who had died at seventy-two, experimented with youth in heaven for a while, then exchanged it for a bald head and a pipe. "Think of the dull sameness of a society made up of people all of one age and one set of looks, habits, tastes and feelings," he informs Stormfield.

Sandy tells Stormfield that a Brooklyn preacher named Talmage will soon arrive, eager to embrace and weep over Abraham, Isaac, and Jacob, like sixty thousand other newcomers each day. If these biblical patriarchs obliged all the new arrivals, he said, they would be tired and "wet as muskrats all the time."[41] The demands on Adam's time were especially oppressive. "Why, if Adam was to show himself to every new comer that wants to call and gaze at him and strike him for his autograph, he would never have time to do anything else but just that."[42] Sandy recalls that the biggest turnout of holy figures came when a murderer named Charles Peace appeared. "Abel was there—the first time in twelve hundred years. A report got around that Adam was coming; well, of course, Abel was enough to bring a crowd, all by himself, but there is nobody that can draw like Adam."[43]

It is not surprising that, after forty years, *Captain Stormfield's Visit to Heaven* was unfinished. It has no real plot, no dramatic conflict, no character development. When Sandy McWilliams enters the scene, Stormfield becomes a mere spectator of the heavenly doings. A machine without a motor, the story is premised upon a single comic conceit: that the heaven of conventional Christian thought is a tedious, humdrum place. Yet the story contains some of the best comic passages Twain ever wrote and must have thrust him back into the blasphemous fun he had enjoyed as a teenager in Hannibal, snickering through Sunday services.

CHAPTER SIXTY-SEVEN

Letters from the Earth

During the winter of 1908–09, Clara Clemens had gradually begun to phase out her relationship with Charles Wark and ease into rekindling the old romance with Ossip Gabrilowitsch, whose standing had only grown in the classical music world with his Carnegie Hall recitals. Although Ossip spent time at Stormfield during the holidays, rumors of Clara's liaison with Wark trailed her, and when the Twichells came to visit, Harmony warned Isabel that "all the Hartford world is talking about Clara's reported engagement to Wark—saying that she is only waiting for Mrs. Wark to get a divorce from him, when the marriage will take place." Isabel confirmed this: "It is a sickening report. The Country people around here have got hold of a similar Tale."[1] Ossip had his own extramarital entanglement to resolve. With Gustav Mahler now in New York, conducting at the Metropolitan Opera, he confronted Alma and Ossip with suspicions about their relationship, and she reassured him that he had nothing to fear. Ossip clearly could not afford to antagonize a conductor of Mahler's standing.

On April 13, 1909, Clara sang at Mendelssohn Hall before a large audience—Twain gave her an enormous bouquet of roses—but the critical reaction punctured her always inflated hopes of a career. The pitiless commentary echoed earlier assessments. "Her tones last night were too often uneven and muffled," the *New York Times* complained, while other reviews cited fundamental technical flaws with her singing.[2] Her lack of progress, combined with unending vocal problems, made her whole career seem like a vanity project sustained by Mark Twain's fame and largesse. By the fall, she would cancel her entire concert tour. The demise of her ambitions coincided with an ever greater appreciation of Ossip's outstanding concert achievements. Twain, never enthusiastic about Clara's career, was grateful to Ossip for performing an important service: "He has squelched Clara's 'career.' She is done with the concert-stage—permanently, I pray. I hate the word. I never want to hear it again."[3] That he surrounded the word "career" with damning quotation marks confirms that he thought Clara had deluded herself with her singing career and that he had encouraged her only with reluctance. Her checkered experience on the platform brought back memories of his own stage performances, and for all his brilliance, he did not remember them fondly.

Ossip suffered a medical crisis in the summer of 1909 when he had three operations in Manhattan to treat an infection of the mastoid bone. This gruesome ordeal likely left him with hearing loss in one ear, and he ran such a high fever that Clara, during "terrible days of fright and helplessness," thought he might not live.[4] "There he lay, white, still—no light in his eyes; no movement of recognition when I laid my hand on his."[5] When he survived, Clara attributed it to the glorious power of her love, and he recuperated that summer in a guest room at Stormfield, with Clara nursing him back to health. The situation perhaps made Clara realize how much she cared for him, and she now informed him she was ready to consider marriage.

On September 21, a huge swarm of vehicles—scores of motorcars and carriages, plus farmers straggling on foot—descended on Stormfield for a library fundraiser to finish the building and gather books for it. Twain recruited Ossip, Clara, and the celebrated baritone David Bispham to entertain guests with a medley of Chopin, Saint-Saëns, Dvořák, and Brahms. Three hundred programs were printed but more than five hundred guests showed up, overflowing into the loggia and billiard room and terrace beyond the dining room door. Standing in the piano's curve, Twain was in his element. "My daughter has not been singing long before the public and is not as famous as either of these gentlemen," he assured the crowd, "but I am sure you will agree with me that she is much better-looking."[6] The audience roared its approval. Jean was elated to form part of this family event and turned pages as Ossip played. As Paine recalled, "Jean Clemens, fine and handsome, apparently full of life and health, danced down that great living-room as care-free as if there was no shadow upon her life."[7] The new library had become a deeply personal cause for Jean, who searched out books for it and donated many works from Stormfield. To acknowledge her contribution, she was elevated to third vice president of the library, a position formerly held by her nemesis, Isabel Lyon.

When the event ended, Ossip and Clara drifted into the garden and by starlight decided to marry. They had been engaged twice before, so when Twain heard the news, he couldn't restrain a sarcasm. "What! Again? Well, anyway, any girl could be proud to marry him. He is a man—a real man."[8] Though Twain was very fond of Gabrilowitsch, he felt a large twinge of regret when he learned that he and Clara would live in Europe. The sense of distance grated on him and doubtless stirred old memories of Clara's neglect.

With his philo-Semitic bent, Twain was happy to have a Russian Jewish son-in-law and approved of Ossip as a "refined, gentle-mannered young man, quite modest and unaffected and not at all foreign in mien."[9] With suspicious speed and secrecy, Clara and Ossip decided to wed two weeks later, on October 6. The alleged motive for the rush was that Ossip had to sail for Europe on October 12 and couldn't cancel his concert engagements; the couple then planned to live in Potsdam or Berlin. The reason given for the secrecy was that Ossip didn't want his parents to read about the marriage in the press before receiving his letter announcing it. Clara, at thirty-five, had dated so many men over so many years that the haste of this wedding seemed peculiar. She quickly roped "Uncle Joe" Twichell into hurrying to Stormfield to officiate at the wedding. "Don't say that you can not come," she told him, "for we expect you both here Tuesday night on the fifth & I couldn't get married without you."[10] To Clara's tour manager, Twain offered an entirely different explanation for the overly hasty marriage: Ossip hadn't healed fully from

SHIPWRECK

the mastoid operation, had canceled his European engagements, and Clara would nurse him in Italy for two or three months. The contradictory explanations seemed to mutate with each new letter. It made no sense that Clara would marry Ossip right away in order to nurse him in Italy. It all sounded like some botched cover story that nobody could keep straight.

Twain's medical difficulties may have lent urgency to the timing of the wedding. However much he made light of his difficulties—"During 23 hours out of 24 I am as comfortable as anybody"—the angina attacks, with their acute chest pains, left him in a weakened state.[11] With his period of banquets and speeches now behind him, he spent hours every day in endless rounds of billiards with Paine. Only to a minor extent did he participate in the wedding plans, as he selected those slated to receive announcement cards. For the most part, however, the rest of the household coped with the insanely compressed wedding schedule. Katy Leary recalled the "awful rush" to get things ready on time. "There wasn't a minute to spare," she said. Clara "went to Altman's and ordered dresses and hats and all kinds of beautiful clothes, and Miss Jean and I, we ordered all the rest, all the linen and silver and everything for her house. We had only a week, and oh, my! how we hustled!"[12]

On the eve of the wedding, when the rehearsal took place, Twain seemed moody and detached and refused to cease his billiard games upstairs. Never averse to attention, he had already decided to wear his Oxford graduation gown at the wedding. Clara sent her colleague, violinist Marie Nichols, upstairs to fetch him for the rehearsal, but he was adamant that he wished to continue playing billiards. Nichols recalled that she "argued with him in vain, and finally he put the mortar board on my head and the robe over my arm and told me to go in and take his place."[13] Perhaps Twain felt miffed that Clara, having expelled Lyon and Ashcroft from his life, was now deserting him and leaving him with an empty house, save for Jean. Clara had a way of sweeping into his life, taking command, turning things topsy-turvy, then sweeping out again. He also feared that he would never see her again. As the story of the marriage leaked out, press accounts acquired a puzzled tone. "News of the wedding will come as somewhat of a surprise to most persons except the close friends of the family," said the *New York Herald*, "for although the names of the pianist and Miss Clemens have been linked at various times, no formal announcement of the engagement has been made."[14]

With only thirty-two people there, the wedding was light, quick, and breezy. Claude decorated the living room with fall foliage and flowers harvested from nearby woods. In a white silk dress edged with lace, Jean served as bridesmaid and their cousin, Jervis Langdon, as the best man. In his flaming scarlet robe from Oxford, Twain came down the stairs with Clara resting on his arm as a pianist played the "Grand March" from *Tannhäuser*. "She did look so sweet and so little!" said Katy Leary. "She looked like a little cherub."[15] Stationed by the bay window, Joseph Twichell stood ready to marry Clara and Ossip as he had married Sam and Livy thirty-nine years before. This was followed by a wedding buffet and group photographs before Clara and Ossip jumped into a car and made a rapid getaway in a "cloud of dust."[16] Asked to provide a press statement, Twain expressed pleasure at the marriage and noted that Livy always had warm affection for Ossip, but he couldn't refrain from more somber reflections. "There are two or three solemn things in life and a happy marriage is one of them, for the terrors of life are all to come."[17] True to Twain's words, marriage didn't begin smoothly for the newlyweds. They decided to take a brief honeymoon in Atlantic City, which was interrupted when Ossip had an attack of appendicitis and had to hurry back to New York for an operation.

The true motive for the breakneck wedding likely surfaced a week later when a mysterious notice popped up in a New York newspaper: "Mrs. Edith Wark, wife of Charles E. Wark (formerly accompanist to Miss Clara L. Clemens) is requested to send her present address to Charles J. Campbell, attorney, 346 Broadway, New York City."[18] The next day, another New York newspaper clarified this in a story headlined "Clara Clemens in a Mysterious Case." It explained that the published notice had disclosed a lawsuit that would involve "a number of prominent people in sensational developments . . . it was reported that Mrs. Wark, who is now establishing a residence in a Western State, has started a suit against

SHIPWRECK

the former Miss Clemens."[19] The gist of the legal action was that Clara had alienated her husband's affections. When a reporter called Stormfield for clarification, Jean blamed Isabel: "I do not believe the story about the starting of a suit, and if such a story is in circulation it is probably the work of malicious persons. I have one woman in particular in mind who is taking every opportunity she can get to trouble us and who would be likely to start such a rumor."[20] Ossip sounded no less categorical. "There has been no suit for alienation against [Clara], nor is she engaged in any other litigation. Mr. Wark is a personal friend of both of us, and I am sure he has nothing to do with it."[21] The *Oakland Tribune* ran a story saying that Edith Wark had launched a suit against Clara.[22] One of the most damaging comments came from Clara's old tour manager, who said of Charles Wark: "He is an excellent man, but until I saw the advertisement I did not know he was married."[23] We do not know if Clara was the object of a legal action or whether the matter was privately settled by Twain. The fear of an imminent lawsuit and being served papers might explain the unseemly rush by Clara and Ossip to wed and flee to Europe. Or perhaps Clara believed that as a married woman, she might be less susceptible to such press innuendo. The Warks ended up getting divorced, and Charles remarried in 1912.

The cold weather sped up the frequency of Twain's chest spasms. That he bore a secret grievance against Clara was confirmed by a hurt letter that he wrote to a granddaughter of Henry Rogers, who had just gotten married, telling her that he couldn't go down to see her in New York. "If I should go down to see you off I should naturally have to stay over a day, & see my married daughter off, too, whereas at bottom I do not wish to do that, as the chances are against my ever seeing her again, for the reason that she will be in Europe a long while, & I am not willing to go abroad again—at least until I can go *sound*."[24] The letter underscored why Twain seemed less than gleeful about Clara's marriage, for it would precede her departure to Europe and a life spent far away from him, perhaps forever. He must also have felt that Clara would be nursing her husband back to health while he was in no less need of such treatment.

LETTERS FROM THE EARTH

After the wedding, Twain undertook one last literary project and produced a small gem, which would be published posthumously. In *Letters from the Earth,* he had satirical fun poking holes in the Bible and the Ten Commandments. As he told Elizabeth Wallace, "This book will never be published . . . because it would be felony to soil the mails with it . . . Paine enjoys it, but Paine is going to be damned one of these days, I suppose."[25] In this red-hot polemic, Twain doesn't merely try to expose the folly and hypocrisy of conventional religious belief but enters into a full-throated diatribe against God, accusing him of cruel, pitiless behavior toward his creatures. He keeps returning to the idea that a father should shelter his children and argues that God does the reverse, subjecting them to unspeakable punishments on earth.

When Satan (Twain's favorite alter ego) is temporarily expelled from heaven, he visits the earth and sends back eleven reports to the Archangels Gabriel and Michael. He finds it risible that deluded Man imagines he is loved and admired by the Creator. "He prays to Him, and thinks He listens. Isn't it a quaint idea? . . . I must put one more strain upon you: he thinks he is going to heaven! He has salaried teachers who tell him that."[26] Satan is especially savage in ridiculing the racial discrimination rampant upon earth. "All white nations despise all colored nations, of whatever hue, and oppress them when they can . . . All the world hates the Jew, and will not endure him except when he is rich."[27]

Usually bashful about sex, Twain is shockingly frank here, with Satan mocking that humanity's imagined heaven has omitted "the supremest of all his delights . . . sexual intercourse!"[28] As Satan points out: "From youth to middle age all men and all women prize copulation above all other pleasures combined . . . At its very best and longest the act is brief beyond imagination."[29] Sex may be the supreme joy, but Twain suggests disappointment after its heated anticipation. After a career spent avoiding female sexuality, Twain now argued that woman was far more fertile and sexual than man. As Satan says of man: "His procreative competency is limited to an average of a hundred exercises per year for fifty years, hers is good for three thousand a year for that whole time—and as many years long as she may live. Thus his life interest in the matter is five thousand refreshments, while hers is a hundred and fifty thousand."[30] Women, not men, should have harems, Satan suggests. In a passage that Livy would have banned, but that may say much about her sex life with Twain, Satan observes: "During twenty-three days in every month . . . from the time a woman is seven years old till she dies of old age, she is ready for action, and *competent*. As competent as the candlestick is to receive the candle . . . Also, she *wants* that candle—yearns for it, longs for it, hankers after it, as commanded by the law of God in her heart." Man is a poor wilting specimen in comparison. "He is competent from the age of sixteen or seventeen thenceforward for thirty-five years. After fifty his performance is of poor quality, the intervals between are wide, and its satisfactions of no great value to either party . . . Her candlestick is as firm as ever, whereas his candle is increasingly softened and weakened by the weather of age, as the years go by, until at last it can no longer stand."[31] This gives us a graphic picture of Twain's late sex life, or lack thereof, and makes the reader wonder why he had never dared to write of such things before. He also notes that people over seventy are praised for abstaining from adultery when, in fact, "if the oldest veteran there could get his lost heyday back again for an hour he would . . . ruin the first woman he came across, even though she were an entire stranger."[32]

In his later years, Twain was steeped in astronomy, and its unimaginable distances confirmed his sense of Earth's insignificance. Satan wonders sardonically why God has created twenty million suns and eighty million planets. "To furnish light for this little toy-world. That was his whole purpose; he had no other."[33] In a footnote, Twain records how many years it takes the light of distant stars to reach humanity, dispelling the biblical notion that the Earth is only six thousand years old. "It is only within the last hundred years that studious, inquiring minds have found out that it is nearer a hundred million."[34]

Satan next turns to biblical stories that had been perennial fodder for Twain's humor. Noah had long been a favorite butt of his jokes, and Satan computes that the Ark had to collect 146,000 birds, beasts, and fish and 2 million insect species. If Noah "had known all the requirements in the beginning, he would have been aware that what was needed was a fleet of Arks." For lack of cargo space, Noah had to block the entry of animals of monstrous size. "All these facts were suppressed, in the Biblical account. You find not a hint of them there. The whole thing is hushed up."[35]

Twain and his family had been beset by so many ailments that it is no surprise that Satan is appalled by the ubiquity of diseases upon Earth. For Adam and Eve's descendants, the Creator has served up a Pandora's Box of medical woes. "They are multitudinous; no book can name them all . . . Disease! That is the main force, the diligent force, the devastating force! It attacks the infant the moment it is born."[36] Satan lays blame for these horrors at the throne of God and stresses that microbes formed the most important part of Noah's cargo. "There were typhoid germs, and cholera germs, and hydrophobia germs, and lockjaw germs, and consumption germs, and black-plague germs, and some hundreds of other aristocrats."[37] He also observes that Noah and his family had to endure the hellish stench of the animals and the cacophony of their roaring, not to mention their wild copulation.

At the end of *Letters,* Twain sums up his dour view of life versus death, with death winning the contest hands down: "Life was not a valuable gift, but death was. Life was a fever-dream made up of joys embittered by sorrows, pleasure poisoned by pain . . . but death was sweet, death was gentle, death was kind."[38] In a passage that would have shocked contemporary readers, Twain viewed Catholic priests as hypocritical lechers. Satan says: "The confessional's chief amusement has been seduction—in all the ages of the Church. Père Hyacinthe testifies that of a hundred priests confessed by him, ninety-nine had used the confessional effectively for the seduction of married women and young girls. One priest confessed that of nine hundred girls and women whom he had served as father confessor in his time, none had escaped his lecherous embrace but the elderly and the homely."[39] In this last book-length work, Mark Twain confronted a litany of taboo subjects and exhibited in full the fearless, uncompromising nature that had served as the main source of his humor.

SHIPWRECK

Letters from the Earth was a valedictory statement of his bitterness and disillusionment with life itself. That fall, he read Charles C. F. Greville's *A Journal of the Reigns of King George IV and King William IV,* and in its margins he penned a comment that traces the genesis of this pessimism back to self-hatred. He wrote "that what a man sees in the human race is merely himself in the deep and honest privacy of his own heart. Byron despised the race because he despised himself. I feel as Byron did, and for the same reason."[40]

Twain was probably right that the public would have damned him had he published *Letters* during his lifetime. After his death, Clara objected to its publication on the grounds that it misrepresented her father's views on religion. More likely she feared it represented his views all too well. She managed to delay publication until September 1962, then died two months later. The book's belated appearance was so startling and ran contrary to so many people's view of a benign, avuncular Mark Twain that it jumped straight onto the *New York Times* bestseller list, some fifty-two years after the author's death, attesting to his enduring place in the American imagination.

CHAPTER SIXTY-EIGHT

"An Old Bird of Paradise"

Despite the steep drop in angelfish letters in 1909, Twain's peculiar hobby by no means petered out altogether. As he explained to Elizabeth Wallace, "the angel-fishes are not 'company.' They are part of the family."[1] He was quite open with the girls on two subjects: the medical problems that made him a prisoner at Stormfield and his grim sense of abandonment by his older daughter. His letters were now more sober, and he dropped the former air of mock-romance and fake chivalry, and talked far more candidly, telling Francesca Nunnally that he had a "tobacco heart"—coronary heart disease with a rapid, irregular pulse, and spikes of blood pressure that caused anginal pain twice daily, largely confining him to his bedroom. "This will move even the wise to laugh at me, for in my vanity I have often bragged that tobacco couldn't hurt me."[2] As Clara and Ossip made plans to sail to Europe, he grew mournful. "So I shall be here alone in an empty house," he wrote to Helen Allen, "& nobody but myself to welcome you & your mother."[3] It is not clear why he edited Jean out of the picture.

In *Harper's Bazaar,* Twain published an extended encomium to a Scottish child prodigy who died in 1811, at age eight, having written poems and diaries—"Marjorie Fleming, the Wonder Child." Twain doted on this deceased girl, who clearly reminded him of Susy. "I have adored Marjorie for six-and-thirty years; I have adored her in detail, I have adored the whole of her."[4] Twain shivered with delight at her precocious sayings on assorted subjects. As with the angelfish, he had an idealized image of this long-ago girl, but the reader is not likely to be nearly as ravished by the quotes as Twain.

Twain somehow managed to keep up correspondence with young foreign women from the Juggernaut Club, his earlier iteration of the Aquarium, and occasionally ventured with them into controversial territory. One day, Jean opened a letter that Twain had written to Hélène Elisabeth Picard and was shocked to see him argue that the Virgin Mary was not white. "The idea of saying the Mother of the Saviour was *colored!*" Jean protested, aghast. "It's sacrilegious."[5] Twain lectured her that at the time of Christ's birth, the globe held only a billion souls. "Not *one-tenth* of them were *white* . . . It most powerfully suggests that *white was not a favorite complexion with God* . . . There was not a white person in Nazareth, when I was there, except a foreign priest. The people were very dark. Don't you suppose they are the descendants of Mary's townsmen?" Neither swayed nor mollified, Jean persisted. "Well, I can't help it, papa; the idea of a colored Mother of the Saviour is still *revolting,* & you must change it."[6] Still fiery on the subject of race, Twain was willing to contemplate realities tolerated by few other white contemporaries. After Livy died, he had labored over a satirical sketch mocking the "universal brotherhood of man," saying "it couldn't ever be, not even in heaven—for there are only white angels there."[7] He continued to feel so keenly the Belgian Congo atrocities that when Sir Arthur Conan Doyle sent him his tract on the abuses, Paine advised him that Twain couldn't respond because the issue "excites and distresses him to a degree which we think dangerous."[8]

While Twain blamed his November 20 trip to Bermuda on doctor's orders, he confided to Marion Schuyler Allen that the true reason was his desire to skip Thanksgiving at Stormfield and "avoid the sorrow of leave taking of his married daughter, who was going to live abroad and who sailed a few days after he left New York."[9] Indeed, when Clara and Ossip sailed for Europe in December, Twain, by design, hid out in Bermuda. "My father detests adieux," Jean had rightly predicted, "and I have an idea that he won't come back till after their departure."[10]

Twain's official Bermuda residence was the Hamilton Hotel, the base he and Paine used for touring the island. "Paine & I drive in a light vic-

"AN OLD BIRD OF PARADISE"

toria about 3 hours every day," he told Clara, "over these smooth hard roads, with the dainty blues & greens & purples of the sea always in sight."[11] A short walk from the hotel, down a curving path and ringed by oleander hedges, was Bay House, the white stone waterfront home of Charles and Marion Schuyler Allen and their fifteen-year-old angelfish daughter, Helen. Twain's final years seemed full of surrogate families, and the Allens functioned as the final one, of which Mrs. Allen was fully aware. Before long, Twain had moved into the Allen home, thankful for their hospitality. "For you *can't* make a home out of a hotel," he explained, "& I can't be completely satisfied outside of a home."[12] He spent Thanksgiving with the Allens, bringing Helen an inscribed copy of the newly published *Extract from Captain Stormfield's Visit to Heaven.* To foster the illusion of home, he even had his own bedroom at Bay House, where he kept writing materials strewn across the bed, as in every residence he had ever occupied. He celebrated his seventy-fourth birthday there, reading aloud to Helen, before slicing his birthday cake, the whitewashing scene from *Tom Sawyer.* While at Bay House he was also preoccupied with the last magazine article Howells ever solicited from him: "The Turning Point of My Life" for *Harper's Bazaar.* Twain presented his life as an intricate chain of turning points that he ultimately traced back to Adam and Eve taking a bite from the forbidden apple.

Twain had always been immersed in his era, avidly tracking current events. Now, as if intuiting death's stealthy approach, he drifted off into another dimension, where he disengaged from worldly affairs. Newspapers accumulated unread at his elbow—"The sight of a newspaper stirs not a single quiver of interest in me"—and he even lost interest in billiards, his all-purpose therapy.[13] His fury over the Ashcrofts subsided briefly, and the chest pains seemed to moderate. He likely would have stayed in Bermuda for Christmas had he not promised Jean that, for the first time in several years, they would celebrate the holiday together.

On the day he left Bermuda, December 18, Twain inscribed for Helen copies of his work. He showered her with profuse flattery and feigned (or maybe not) jealousy of her boyfriend Arthur, writing in *Tom Sawyer Abroad:* "Lend this book to Arthur, Helen. There is a page in it which is

SHIPWRECK

poisoned."[14] Other inscriptions hinted at a cheerless vision of life that must have chilled young Helen's heart. In *The Prince and the Pauper*, he wrote, "Up to 18 we don't know. Happiness consists in not knowing."[15] And he vented his personal sadness, telling Helen to take to heart this maxim from *Pudd'nhead Wilson:* "Consider well the proportions of things: it is better to be a young junebug than an old bird of paradise."[16]

On the ship back to New York, as the vessel tumbled through rough seas in damp, blustery weather, Paine grew very seasick, and pangs of sharp chest pain kept Twain awake at night. When they landed in New York, Jean met them at the dock and stood "blue and shivering with cold," said Paine.[17] The voyage seemed to wipe out all the gains Twain had registered in Bermuda, and reporters who met him said he "did not look well" and struggled with a "severe pain in his chest," which he attributed to indigestion.[18]

Whether running her farm or keeping accounts for her father, Jean threw herself into her new Redding existence with a zest that suggested what had been missing in her life, and she took special delight in being her father's secretary. Twain, Katy Leary, and Albert Paine all worried that she exerted herself too much and that the strain might tax her system, bringing on epileptic seizures. As Katy put it, "You see, poor Miss Jean wanted to make up for all the lost time she'd had to be away from home, and sick."[19] To resurrect the spirit of bygone Hartford days, she undertook extensive holiday preparations, assuming the supervisory role once occupied by Livy. She set up a Christmas tree in the loggia, trimmed in silver foil, while heaping a lovely assemblage of bright gifts on tabletops, including a globe for her father. Much in her mother's philanthropic vein, she made up a gift list of fifty recipients and arranged for the village children to sing carols at Stormfield on Christmas Day.

Upon his return from Bermuda, Twain's sickly appearance sparked press rumors that he was struggling in critical condition. If he was inclined to laugh it off, Jean worried that Clara would read these errone-

"AN OLD BIRD OF PARADISE"

ous reports and take them seriously. To assuage Jean, Twain issued a statement to the Associated Press, which she telephoned in for him. "I hear the newspapers say I am dying. The charge is not true. I would not do such a thing at my time of life. I am behaving as good as I can. Merry Christmas to everybody! Mark Twain."[20] Twain and Jean held a long, cozy chat in the library the night before Christmas Eve. Because she had a cold, Jean didn't kiss her father good night. "I bent and kissed her hand," Twain said. "She was moved—I saw it in her eyes—and she impulsively kissed my hand in return."[21]

Jean had a routine of taking a cold bath every morning before mounting her horse and galloping to the village post office. The next morning, a maid named Jennie found it odd when Jean didn't emerge from her ablutions and summoned Katy to investigate, who opened the door and found Jean lying submerged in a tub full of water. "I picked her up, and then her head fell right over on my shoulder, against my cheek; and I knew the worst!" She shouted to Jennie: "Oh, come! Come! Miss Jean is dead!"[22] They spread Jean out on towels on the bathroom floor and worked in vain to resuscitate her. As he awoke, Twain heard a commotion and thought it was Jean en route to the post office. "Then Katy entered, stood quaking and gasping at my bedside a moment, then found her tongue: *'Miss Jean is dead!'* Possibly I know now what the soldier feels when a bullet crashes through his heart."[23] Twenty-nine-year-old Jean had suffered a grand mal seizure in the bathtub. At first it was assumed she had drowned, but an autopsy showed no water in her lungs, leading to the conclusion that she had suffered a heart attack triggered by the cold water. It is now known that seizures can cause serious irregularities in heart rhythms.[24] Twain had feared that Jean might have an epileptic attack on horseback and be crushed by horse's hooves. This was a fresh form of horror, one he had never contemplated.

Twain threw on a robe and went to the bathroom, where he found Jean stretched upon the floor, "looking so placid, so natural, and as if asleep."[25] A large reserve of love welled up inside him, and he was struck by her sweetness and dignified repose. That night, when Jean was laid out on her bed, Twain kept tiptoeing into the room, drawing back the sheet that

SHIPWRECK

covered her and planting a kiss on her cold brow. Memories flooded back of kissing Livy's dead face in Florence. "And last night I saw again what I had seen then—that strange and lovely miracle—the sweet, soft contours of early maidenhood restored by the gracious hand of death!"[26] After Livy's death, Twain had sworn that he would never again stand by a grave and watch a loved one being lowered into the earth, and as preparations were made for Jean's funeral in Elmira, Twain, true to his word, decided to stay behind in Redding.

When Paine arrived, he did not find Twain in the throes of hysterical grief so much as numb with philosophic resignation. "Well," Twain said, "I suppose you have heard of this final disaster."[27] Since Jean had not had a major attack in months, Twain blamed the fatigue of her Christmas preparations—an attack stemming from a surplus of goodness as she strove to re-create those long-lost Hartford holidays. For two days, Twain worked on his last printed article, the magnificently tender "The Death of Jean," published in *Harper's Monthly Magazine* that January. This elegiac piece marked the end of his autobiography and was the best balm for his tortured soul. With Jean dead and Clara prosperously married, he no longer needed to fret unduly about the book royalties he would leave to his daughters after his death. When he cabled Clara and Ossip about Jean's death, he urged them not to rush back—their boat would arrive after the burial. He composed a beautiful message to Clara:

> O, Clara, Clara dear. I am so glad she is out of it & safe—safe! I am not melancholy; I shall never be melancholy again, I think.
>
> You see, I was in such distress when I came to realize that you were gone far away and no one stood between her & danger but me—and I could die at any moment, and *then*—oh then what would become of her! For she was wilful, you know, & would not have been governable.
>
> You can't imagine what a darling she was that last two or three days; and how *fine*, & good & sweet & noble—and *joyful*, thank Heaven!—and how intellectually brilliant. I had never been acquainted with Jean before. I recognized that.[28]

"AN OLD BIRD OF PARADISE"

On December 26, with snow flurries filling the sky, Jean's body, dressed in the white silk gown she wore at Clara's wedding, was laid out in a coffin in the library before being transferred to Elmira. Jean had a German shepherd named Fix, her constant companion, who moped around bereft after she died. "They told me the first mourner was the dog," said Twain. "He came uninvited, and stood up on his hind legs and rested his forepaws upon the trestle, and took a long last look at the face that was so dear to him, then went his way as silently as he had come. *He knows.*"[29] When the hearse arrived, Twain requested that Paine play on the Orchestrelle the selections he associated with his three lost women: a Schubert impromptu for Jean, the "Intermezzo" from *Cavalleria Rusticana* for Susy, and Handel's "Largo" for Livy, and he had lanterns posted outside so that he could watch the coffin depart from Stormfield. "From my windows I saw the hearse and the carriages wind along the road and gradually grow vague and spectral in the falling snow, and presently disappear. Jean was gone out of my life, and would not come back any more."[30] Twain had been interested in paranormal phenomena, though not in spirits, but that night, in the bathroom, he felt a brisk wave of cold air brush past him. "I thought the door must be open; but it was closed. I said: 'Jean, is this you trying to let me know you have found the others?' Then the cold air was gone."[31] Katy was surprised, but also gratified, when Twain said, "Oh, Katy! She's in heaven with her mother."[32] For Jean's tombstone in Elmira, Twain chose a poetically apt tribute from *Macbeth*:

> IN MEMORY OF JEAN LAMPTON CLEMENS
> A MOST DEAR DAUGHTER.
> HER DESOLATE FATHER
> SETS THIS STONE.
> "AFTER LIFE'S FITFUL FEVER
> SHE SLEEPS WELL."[33]

America's funniest man, having outlived his wife and three of his four children, found his world burdened again with unimaginable sorrow.

SHIPWRECK

"How poor I am, who was once so rich!" he wrote.[34] Fate, as if on cue, had ratified his view of life as a swindle. Joe Twichell pleaded with him to stay with them in Hartford. "We feel that you are [the] lonesomest man in the world. Can't we somehow help you a little, poor fellow? We cannot bear to think of you sitting there solitary amid your ruins."[35] Twain, however, refused to budge. Stormfield had become dearer than ever because of its association with Jean, and he even kept her dog in his room. He contemplated Jean's memory with the uncritical veneration bestowed on the dead. "I miss Jean so!" he told Clara. "She was utterly sweet & dear those last days; & so wise, & so dignified, & so good."[36] After all the many mistakes he had made with her, "the love Jean manifested for me astonished me daily."[37]

It was difficult for Twain to make peace with Jean's loss because he had discovered her virtues much too late. Paine later printed an important passage from "Closing Words of My Autobiography" that Twain chose to delete. "Did I know Jean's value? No, I only thought I did. I knew a ten-thousandth fraction of it, that was all. It is always so, with us, it has always been so."[38] He found it hard to admit that he had pushed Jean away, passed up numerous chances to rescue her from lonesome residences. Whenever she complained about her plight, he had chided her for a personality grown defective from epilepsy. Not surprisingly, Twain found it easier to sublimate his guilt over Jean into self-righteous wrath against Isabel Lyon. "Jean had a fine mind, a most competent brain," he told Twichell. "That shit [i.e., Isabel] said she was insane! She & her confederate told that to everybody around here. Jean's last act, Thursday night, was to defend her when I burst out upon her!"[39] Twain never used obscenities, and it was a measure of his extreme anger that he applied one to Isabel. She had been guilty, as charged, in her treatment of Jean, but Twain had refused to visit his daughter or consult with her doctors to ascertain the truth of her situation. He had been an unwitting accomplice in what had happened, guilty of grave sins of omission.

In "The Death of Jean," he paid homage to his youngest daughter and expressed the profound meaning family had for him. "When Clara went away two weeks ago to live in Europe, it was hard but I could bear it, for

"AN OLD BIRD OF PARADISE"

I had Jean left. I said *we* would be a family. We said we would be close comrades and happy—just we two. That fair dream was in my mind when Jean met me at the steamer last Monday; it was in my mind when she received me at the door last Tuesday evening. We were together; *we were a family!* the dream had come true—oh, precisely true, contentedly true, satisfyingly true! and remained true two whole days. And now? Now Jean is in her grave!"[40] This poignant writing breathed a heartfelt eloquence. Twain had always viewed death as life's saving grace and felt this especially with Jean. "For sixteen years," he wrote, "Jean suffered unspeakably, under the dominion of her cruel malady, & we were always dreading that some frightful accident would happen to her . . . but now she is free, & harm can never come to her more."[41]

Overwhelmed with condolence letters, Twain detected a curious omission: a dearth of letters from Hartford, where Isabel Lyon remained very popular. The night before Jean's death, when she had defended Isabel, she had asked her father to write to Harriet E. Whitmore, who had first recommended Isabel, and give her his side of the story. She warned him not to do so in a heated vein, and if he could not keep his temper, to wait and present his case in person—very Livy-like advice. Instead, Twain wrote Harriet a vituperative letter, saying of Jean, "She has been shamefully & criminally abused for three years, through the plots & lies & malignities of that unspeakable person," then he bitterly mentioned that Hartford was "substantially unrepresented" in the condolence mail he received.[42] Twain was implacable: Isabel had become for him the embodiment of evil. In reply, Harriet confirmed his suspicion that many people in Hartford saw the scandal through a very different lens. "Do not try to revive the past issues about Isabel Ashcroft . . . Here, she is on her own ground and reaps that advantage."[43]

The whole rationale for building the large Stormfield house was to create a space for family gatherings, and now Twain had been left alone. Clara, having pressed to obtain her own wing of the house, had retired with Ossip to Switzerland. Albert B. Paine, now secretary and general manager of Twain's affairs, vacated his Redding house and moved into Jean's apartment with his wife and daughter. "They will constitute my

SHIPWRECK

family henceforth," Twain wrote to Mary Rogers, "and be a wholesome change from Miss Lyon and the confederate whom she married to keep him from turning State's evidence against her."[44] Jean lingered in the town's memory in a particularly lovely spirit. After Twain sold her farm, he directed that the proceeds be used to construct the Mark Twain Library in Redding, with the building to be named the Jean L. Clemens Memorial Building.

CHAPTER SIXTY-NINE

Halley's Comet

On Twain's last night alone with Jean, they had talked of making a trip to Bermuda together and renting a house on the island. As Twain now decided to return there alone, he felt a sense of peace that Jean had been released from her misery, and he asserted, quite improbably, that he would never be melancholy again. Wincing with chest pain, he sailed for Bermuda on January 5 and boarded the ship with a black mourning band on his arm. When asked by reporters why he had no companion, he waved his cigar at them. "This is my only companion and solace," he said. "I detest the idea of shaking him though, for he and myself have been companions such a long time."[1] He never breathed a word of his angina pectoris in public and employed the handy euphemism of "digestive pain" as his cover story for the deadly disease that ailed him.[2]

Twain planned to stay with the Allens while his butler, Claude, took a room at the nearby Hamilton Hotel. To foster the illusion of a make-believe family, Twain asked the Allens to address him with the fond nickname Clara and Jean had applied: "Marcus." He used Helen Allen as his amanuensis, replacing Jean. "It was pathetic and unreal to see Mark Twain crushed!" wrote Marion Schuyler Allen. "It was as though Jean's death made him realize anew the death and irreparable loss of his wife."[3] With his ankles swollen from circulatory problems, Twain shuffled around the house in slippers and kimono and could step straight from his ground-floor bedroom onto the veranda. He enjoyed tea on the little

SHIPWRECK

beach outside the house, told stories to children, and reread *A Connecticut Yankee* for the first time in twenty years. "I am prodigiously pleased with it—a most gratifying surprise," he notified Clara.[4]

Shockingly, Mark Twain was ending his days among comparative strangers—he likened himself to a shipwrecked sailor—yet this castaway accepted his sorry distance from his former life. He never wanted to return to Stormfield with its dark harvest of baleful memories. Writing to Paine, he portrayed his Bermuda stay as easy and restful. "There isn't a flaw in it. Good times, good home, tranquil contentment all day & every day, without a break."[5] Still, as Livy had known, he could never make peace with those people who had disappointed him, and his mind kept circling back to Lyon and Ashcroft, spewing venom over their memory.

In sending Paine "The Death of Jean" manuscript, he included a poem called "Who?" that began: "*Who* loves to steal a while away / From sinful joys & foolish play / And fold her holy hands & pray? / The Bitch. *Who* loves to watch while *others* pray / And hog their assets, night & day, / Wherewith to fat her Ashcroft—*say?* / *The Bitch.*"[6] Instead of soothing his vengeance, Paine inflamed it, sending Twain more Isabel-baiting verse: "Who feeds on bromide and on Scotch / To keep her nerves at highest notch? / Who makes of business-books a botch? The Bitch."[7] Even in the last months of life, Twain still demonized the Ashcrofts, saying "that putrescent pair cost me $50,000 . . . Each was familiar with the other's crimes against me, they have to marry & shut each other's mouths on the witness stand."[8] Although Ralph Ashcroft had acted with more malice and craft, Twain reserved his hottest temper for the personal betrayal by Isabel. "He is a reptile—yes, but not so slimy a one as his wife," he wrote. "*She* was intended for an insect—capturable with a fine-tooth comb."[9] Isabel herself was dazed by the nightmarish convulsions that had turned her life topsy-turvy. "No more association with the King," she wrote, "except as a strange white weak ghost. And here I am married to Ralph Ashcroft."[10]

Twain's medical condition was hardly conducive to measured judgments about people. He was visited by his old familiar complaint, bronchitis, for two or three weeks, and his health was far worse than he conceded in letters. Twain evaded reporters, but a journalist managed to trace him to the Allen residence and showed up unannounced as he lay in bed, surrounded by books; the interloper wrote: "His face looked small and pinched and ill. And then he started to cough, a miserable nerve-wracking cough that shook the whole of his slight frame, and left him nervous and trembling, and a trifle irritated."[11] Twain urged the reporter not to reveal his whereabouts to curiosity-seekers. "I'm too old a bird to be caught. Besides, I'm going to charge an admission fee. It's a shilling a look."[12] No matter what his health, Twain's mind was still a factory for manufacturing one-liners, and when a New York paper inquired about reports of ill health, he replied, "I am able to say that while I am not ruggedly well, I am not ill enough to excite an undertaker."[13]

Much of the magic went out of his favorite avocation: the angelfish. When Dorothy Quick came down to Bermuda for a brief stay with her mother, she was startled by Twain's haggard appearance. "He looked his age for the first time. In fact, he seemed suddenly to have grown years older and very worn. The once erect figure was a little stooped."[14] As always, he urged her to persevere in her writing. "A trade that is once taken up must be followed to the bitter end."[15] Dorothy, a smart girl, saw her idol sliding off into another sphere of existence. "His eyes were half-closed as he spoke, and it seemed as though he were talking more to himself than to me."[16] Although Twain usually sought to prolong angelfish encounters, he wrapped up dinner with Dorothy early and apologized, "I'm not as young as you, dear, and I have to keep my hours."[17] When he wrote to angelfish Margaret Blackmer, now at Rosemary Hall, he joked that a couple of years earlier, she and Helen Allen could have both been weighed on a grocer's scale. "Well, now it's a job for the hay-scales. Oh, stop growing, Margaret dear!"[18] It was his old plaintive plea, in the Peter Pan spirit, that she should promise never to grow up or grow old.

From the time he had first hatched his obsessive angelfish fantasy, Twain had posed as their gallant, elderly lover. There still remained some faux-wooing with Helen Allen, and on Valentine's Day he sent her a verse: "I know a precious little witch, / And Helen is her name, / With eyes so blue, the asters say, / 'They bring our blue to shame.' The poem ended: "I am hers, though she's not mine, / I'm but her loyal Valentine."[19] He again feigned jealousy of her small, quiet boyfriend—"the bloody-minded bandit Arthur, who still fetches and carries Helen. Presently he will be found drowned."[20] At moments, he lifted Helen high on a pedestal. "Yours is the best disposition & the patientest I have met with, Helen. A rare compliment, a good strong compliment, but I could add to it & keep within the facts."[21] In his notebook, in secret code, he addressed Helen amorously. "I think you are very pretty and sweet and dear and cute, Helen—in fact, I *know* it. I wish I could trade places with Teddy [her toy bear?]."[22] Twain wrote these words when he was in a great deal of pain and possibly delirious, but they may suggest his true feelings about Helen.

In private, however, he also began to compose a scalding portrait of Helen Allen and her parents in which he dispensed with all the ludicrous romantic posturing and, for once, got real. First he vehemently denounced Charles and Marion Allen for their cruel treatment of Helen. "All her life her parents have scolded her in the hearing of persons not entitled to hear. A frightful insult, an inexcusable insult . . . No parent has a right to insult a child. No parent can do it & not damage the child."[23] As a result of such treatment, whenever Helen resisted her parents, "she retorts (right before people) with language & manner which must be heard & seen to be believed, so far do they go beyond the bounds of anything resembling ladylike manners & speech."[24]

Helen was now fifteen, while Twain was ailing and elderly, and she may have felt him as an intrusive presence in her home. Like any adolescent, she had limited time for a much older companion, and Twain futilely sought to win her attention. He then rendered a harsh judgment on this once-beloved girl: "She is (substantially) destitute of curiosity," he wrote. "It is astonishing—stunningly, bewilderingly astonishing . . . she has a passion for romance-literature, but reads no poetry, & falls silent the moment you mention a poem . . . You may try to stir her up with the latest splendid news from the observatories—you are wasting your time: astronomy does not interest her, Halley's comet & the Martian canals are nothing to her, you cannot coax even a whisper out of her."[25] Twain attempted to inspire her by reading aloud a passage of great literature, and when he asked afterward if it was good, she simply replied, "Yes." "That is all. It is her entire opinion. You will get nothing more. Only just that one little word—little frosty word ... lifeless, colorless, indolently uttered."[26] No longer a magnetic figure for Helen, Twain said he felt as if he had been slapped in the face by her cold response.

The so-called Helen Allen manuscripts are remarkable documents in what they reveal: Twain was forced to spend an extended period of time with an angelfish whom he found anything but angelic. He was also composing this acid sketch of Helen and her parents while he was their guest and taking advantage of their generosity. It is clear that Helen no longer responded to Twain's gambits, and when she rebuffed him, he felt powerless. With a sense of horror, he listed the things Helen *was* interested in. "Takes a strong interest in clothes & dancing & the theatre, & riding & canoeing & picnicking, & a prodigious interest in any & all members of the male sex, under 45, married or single."[27] In short, Helen was a normal teenage girl. One senses that Twain felt slighted by her disapproval, even though he was a world-renowned author. Albert B. Paine made every effort to suppress the Helen Allen manuscripts, knowing that Twain's invective was unbecoming, casting him in an unattractive light.

Marion Schuyler Allen was a very bright woman who enjoyed discussing a broad range of topics with the author. She found him a firm believer in equal suffrage for women and quite visionary about race relations. "The Millennium will only come," Twain told her, "(when all races of men are blended, thus making a race of supermen) when this comes, all men will be able to look each other in the face and *speak the truth*."[28] Marion heard all about Twain's early life, including his guilt-ridden recounting of his brother Henry's death in a boiler explosion on the Mississippi. Twain, she said, thought he had "brought sorrow to all whom he loved ... he felt a certain responsibility, and a conviction that had they not been *his* loved ones they would have escaped." This desolate, guilt-laden viewpoint "colored his whole life."[29]

Twain's one remaining family link was Clara, who wrote to him expressing fear that he would "disclaim" their relationship because of her

SHIPWRECK

marriage. This was a sad misreading of her solitary father, who felt an urgent need to strengthen that tie, telling her, "You are nearer & dearer to me now than ever; of my fair fleet all my ships have gone down but you; you are all my wealth; but while I have you I am still rich."[30] He added that "I shall live as long as I may, for your sake—not my own, for I believe I was born indifferent to this silly life—in fact I can't see how a person in his right mind can refrain from laughing at it & making fun of it."[31] It was a paradoxical attitude for a man who had treasured his wife and three daughters, who had crafted such beauty on the printed page, and created such joy onstage. Clara deviated sharply from her father's stern view of human existence, and her future life would be marked by a search for spiritual and religious meaning. When Clara and Ossip wanted to attend Easter services at St. Peter's in Rome, Twain's publisher, George Harvey, was recruited to help. Twain refused to appeal to an archbishop friend, explaining that "I can't bring myself to personally ask a favor of that odious Church, whose history would disgrace hell, & whose birth was the profoundest calamity which has ever befallen the human race except the birth of Christ."[32] It was his final shotgun blast, not at religion per se, but at organized Christianity. In his depressed state, Twain sank deeper into a black hole of despair, seeing no consolation anywhere in the universe.

Luckily for Clara, she had Ossip, who helped to soften the terrible blow of losing her mother and two sisters. In the aftermath of Jean's death, Clara experienced a sympathy with her sister "which had not existed before & which I miss so much."[33] She was tortured with guilt over Jean's death and their quarrels. Still, she saw no redeeming features in Jean's life and no lost future. "She chafed at the chains in her life which could not be entirely removed and she had absolutely *nothing* to look forward to."[34] Clara had spent so many years darting in and out of her father's life, seeking to escape his influence, that she was defensive about any insinuations of having deserted him. When Marion Schuyler Allen later published an article about Twain's final days, an aggrieved Clara wrote in protest: "It seems to me that you give rather a one-sided picture of the last weeks of my fathers [sic] life, in leaving the impression that he had no blood relatives to call upon."[35] Her father might well have endorsed Marion Allen's impression.

That February, Woodrow Wilson, president of Princeton University and soon to be governor of New Jersey, checked into the Hamilton Hotel and was eager to renew his acquaintance with Twain. When the two played miniature golf and Twain lost, he issued an accurate prediction: "Wilson, you will be the next president of the United States."[36] "If that is so, Mr. Clemens," Wilson retorted, "I must be the choice of a party of one."[37] Wilson enjoyed a fine rapport with Twain, who spoke to him about personal matters. "He speaks of the tragical death of his daughter with touching simplicity," wrote Wilson. "He is certainly one of the most human of men . . . He evidently wants me to call on him and I shall of course do so."[38]

The Bermuda days drifted by slowly for Twain, enlivened by the occasional band concert and weekly dinner out. This relative serenity ended on March 22 when Mrs. Allen accompanied him to the aquarium, and he doubled over with a stabbing angina attack. She managed to shepherd him home, but he was tormented by a lack of sleep and shortness of breath. "I am losing enough sleep to supply a worn-out army," he said.[39] For three days he stayed in his room and for the first time resorted to morphine. During one sleepless night, he told Mrs. Allen, "Now I know what poor 'Livy' suffered."[40] The day after the aquarium attack, Twain alerted Paine that he would come home sooner than expected from the Islands of the Blest, as he termed them. "I don't want to die here, for this is an unkind place for a person in that condition. I should have to lie in the undertaker's cellar until the ship would remove me & it is dark down there & unpleasant."[41] It was a curious comment from someone who lacked belief in an afterlife and deemed death a reprieve from life's misery. No less odd was that he had young Helen Allen write out this morbid message for him.

Alarmed, Paine boarded a boat to Bermuda on April 2, having stopped by the New York office of Dr. Quintard, who gave him opiates and a crash course in injecting them with a hypodermic needle. Paine also cabled Clara and Ossip, then in Italy, advising them to sail posthaste to America. In Bermuda, Paine found Twain frail and thin and forced to sit

SHIPWRECK

up to mitigate his chest pain. Even as Paine, the biographer-turned-nurse, administered daily doses of morphine, the narcotics could not blunt the edge of Mark Twain's wit. He had received a poorly timed cable from the clowns of the Barnum & Bailey Circus, who wanted to honor him as "the world's great laugh-maker" at a Madison Square Garden luncheon. By the time Twain got this, the proposed date had already passed. "I am very very sorry," he wrote back, "but all last week's dates are full. I will gladly come week before last, if that will answer."[42] Waiting for the return ship to New York, Twain read Thomas Hardy's *Jude the Obscure*—the last complete book he read, and he was most impressed.

Though he knew the end was fast approaching, Twain's creative mind still whirred into action as he sat in an armchair, clad in his dressing gown, and wrote for his amusement "Etiquette for the Afterlife," a brief manual of advice on the deportment to be adopted with Saint Peter at the pearly gates. "Upon arrival do not speak to St. Peter until spoken to. It is not your place to begin . . . You can ask him for his autograph—there is no harm in that—but be careful and don't remark that it is one of the penalties of greatness. He has heard *that* before . . . Leave your dog outside. Heaven goes by favor. If it went by merit you would stay out and the dog would go in."[43] Even a knowledge of imminent death couldn't snuff out his humorous bent. He told Paine that when he entered heaven, he would be kind and forgiving, but couldn't help this dig at his former employees, whom he pictured in hell: "Send the Lyon-Ashcrofts a fan."[44] Before leaving Bermuda, Twain gave Helen Allen a copy of *What is Man?*, "but she refused to accept it," said Mrs. Allen, "as she said she did not like it and did not wish to believe it."[45]

On April 12, Twain, Paine, and Claude sailed for New York. Having visited the place eight times, leaving Bermuda for the last time counted as a small death for Twain. "You go to heaven if you want to," he had told Elizabeth Wallace, "I'd druther [sic] stay here."[46] A special tugboat came to fetch him at Bay House, and he was hoisted onto the ship while seated in a little chair, dressed in nightclothes and an overcoat, sucking on a pipe. The two-day voyage home was so harrowing that he once gasped for breath and sighed, "I am going—I shall be gone in a moment," and requested a hypodermic needle.[47] "It has been a ghastly trip for all of us," Paine wrote, "and I thank God we will soon be ashore."[48] Twain doubted that he would live to see Clara again at Stormfield. "It is a losing race," he moaned, "no ship can outsail death."[49] Still, his humor never failed him, and when his hat tumbled off a hook and rolled around his cabin, he remarked, "The ship is passing the hat."[50]

In New York, a group of friends awaited him at the dock as Claude and a porter toted him down the gangplank before an ambulance took him to the train station where he was rushed back to Stormfield in a special compartment. Although Twain tottered into his house without help, he immediately had to sit and recuperate before being raised in a canvas chair to his upstairs bedroom. As always, he had books at hand, including Suetonius and Carlyle, even if he was heavily sedated and showed little inclination to read.

On April 17, Clara and Ossip arrived at Stormfield and had an emotional reunion with a smiling Twain, who had held on till their arrival, crying out, "Oh, Clara, I'm so glad you're back again!"[51] Although Clara was now five months pregnant with Twain's first and only grandchild, she had not mentioned her pregnancy, an inexplicable decision since Twain's whole rationale for the angelfish was to experience grandfatherly feelings. Clara was distressed by her father's condition, which made conversation all but impossible. During a fleeting interval of lucidity, Twain asked her to sing, and she chose three soothing Scottish ballads, including "Flow Gently, Sweet Afton," which she delivered with fervor. "Her voice trembled so, it was full of tears, but she sang it all through for him, and oh, he was so glad to have her!" said Katy Leary.[52] Clara had embraced religion as passionately as her father had rejected it, and this tinged her view of unfolding events. "The early freshness of spring gave me waves of absolute conviction *that there can be no death*," she wrote, "and still, deepest gloom surrounded this sorrowful transformation."[53]

In the self-mythology in which he specialized, Twain had always claimed that he whirled in with Halley's Comet in 1835 and hoped it would reappear at his departure and round out his life. "The Almighty has said, no doubt: 'Now here are these unaccountable freaks; they came

SHIPWRECK

in together, they must go out together.' Oh! I am looking forward to that."[54] Astoundingly enough, right on time, Halley's Comet streaked across the Redding sky on the eve of his death. "We watched the comet with great admiration and excitement those summer evenings, for to us it was Mark Twain's star," a neighborhood child thought. "It seemed to be traveling towards a very bright star low on the far horizon. That, we decided, must be Miss Jean's."[55] Twain did not know the comet burned brightly above him or that he had shown one last prophetic touch of showmanship.

From Ossip, Twain learned that he and Clara were expecting a child, and on his last day he scratched an unfinished note to his daughter: "Dear—You did not tell me, but I have found out that you—"[56] Mostly he dozed that day, although at one point he blinked open his eyes, took Clara's hand, and whispered his last words. "Goodbye dear, if we meet—"[57] Knowing Twain's history, one suspects he emphasized the word "if." He had asked for a copy of Thomas Carlyle's *The French Revolution*, a book he had reread closely for many years.

On the evening of April 21, 1910, toward sundown, he emitted a sigh and peacefully expired at age seventy-four, perhaps dreaming of being afloat on the biggest river of them all—eternity. Katy Leary may have spoken for many Americans when she lamented, "I had lost the best friend I'd had in the world . . . Never to hear that voice again! Never to hear him talk any more—nor laugh!"[58] After Twain's death, Katy said his bedroom was still so strongly impregnated with a tobacco smell that she kept thinking he must be nearby sneaking a smoke. Later on, Clara said that, most of the time, Twain "felt sure of a life beyond," but that hopeful view probably mirrored her own needs far more than her father's fatalistic philosophy.

It is testimony to Twain's comedic genius that he had been able to squeeze laughter even from the subject of dying. Eight years earlier, he had addressed a high school class, and telling them of contracting measles as a boy, he said he had trembled in terror on the verge of death. "I did not know what an easy thing it is to die. I have since learned that it is like falling asleep. The hands and the feet grow cold, but you do not know it.

Then you are in a kind of dream or trance, and you do not understand that you are dead at all until you begin to investigate the matter."[59]

Albert B. Paine may have been correct that "perhaps never before had the entire world really united in tender sorrow for the death of any man."[60] Mark Twain had not only moved people to laughter and tears with his books, but had challenged them with unorthodox views as he ventured out from his safe cubbyhole as the avuncular humorist. He had dared to state things that others only thought. He had impressed himself upon the world as a personality as much as an author, a singular, salty, colorful figure who was instantly recognizable, defining a new form of celebrity. He had elevated himself into a character superior to any of his creations. Howells was right when he told Clara that in death Twain was "set apart from all other men in a strange majesty. Death had touched his familiar image into historic grandeur."[61] Nobody needed to await history's verdict: Twain had already earned his place in the literary pantheon. Only those close to him knew just how radically his own life deviated from the funny-man image. "With all his brilliant prosperities," Twichell wrote in the *Hartford Courant*, "he had lived to be a lonely, weary-hearted man, and the thought of his departure hence was not unwelcome to him."[62]

Twain had always deprecated funerals as second-rate entertainments. "I am not meaning to say anything *against* funerals—that is, as occasions . . . for as diversions I don't think they amount to much."[63] Two farewells were held for Twain: the first, a huge memorial gathering at the Brick Presbyterian Church on Park Avenue in Manhattan. If one counted the mourners crammed inside along with grieving Twain fans standing outside, three thousand people showed up to bid him farewell. In honor of Twain, everything that day was dressed in a blinding white: Twain's coffin was transported from Stormfield to the Redding train station behind a team of white horses, he lay dressed in a white suit, as if late to a performance, and his coffin at the church was flanked by white flowers. Katy Leary remembered "his beautiful hair that I had massaged every day for years, it looked like silver—it shone so."[64] The brief service featured statements from pastor Dr. Henry van Dyke and Joseph Twichell, the latter stooped beneath unbearable sadness since his wife, Harmony,

SHIPWRECK

lay dying. "Throughout the short service," one newspaper reported of Twichell, "he had sat with bowed head to conceal the fact that tears had found their way to the surface."[65] After speaking some broken, muffled words to honor his famous friend, Twichell hurried off to be with his wife, who died just after midnight. For the Twichells and Clara Clemens, calamity was now piled atop calamity.

Mark Twain once wrote: "Let us endeavor to so live that when we come to die even the undertaker will be sorry."[66] It is safe to say that, for all his flaws, Twain's death was mourned by undertakers across the country. The most profound tributes were probably silent ones. As William Dean Howells studied Twain, resting placidly in his coffin, he reflected on the enigmatic face, which held "something of puzzle, a great silent dignity, an assent to what must be from the depths of a nature whose tragical seriousness broke in the laughter which the unwise took for the whole of him."[67] That humor had taken root in a rich but extremely dark soil, giving it staying power. Howells knew that Samuel Langhorne Clemens was sui generis, having smuggled the rowdy side of American culture into the straitlaced halls of American letters. "Emerson, Longfellow, Lowell, Holmes—I knew them all and all the rest of our sages, poets, seers, critics, humorists; they were like one another and like other literary men; but Clemens was sole, incomparable, the Lincoln of our literature."[68]

Amid a steady patter of rain, Twain's mahogany casket arrived in Elmira and was placed in the Langdon parlor that had witnessed so many rites of passage, gay and somber, for the Clemens clan. Here it was that Sam and Livy had wed, and here it was that the dead family members—Langdon, Susy, Livy, and Jean—had preceded Twain to the grave. Twain had always seen death as a lucky exit from life, and his peaceful, slumbering form seemed to attest to that. One reporter couldn't help but notice that the cadaver still bore tobacco stains. "The stained moustache told of the one joy of his declining years, outside of his only living daughter, his cigar."[69] The Reverend Samuel E. Eastman, pastor of Park Church, delivered the simple eulogy that Twain wanted. On that Sunday afternoon, he was buried at Woodlawn Cemetery, the downpour so heavy that a tent had to be erected to shelter mourners, while the grounds were strewn with flowers sent from around the country. Veiled in black, Clara stood in a state of shock. "Every single member of my dear family gone!" she wrote. "It is overwhelming."[70]

Twain's small tombstone was simplicity itself: It said "Samuel Langhorne Clemens" and "Mark Twain" underneath, with just the dates of his birth and death. The most quotable man in American history wasn't memorialized with a famous saying or jest, and his democratic stone rose no higher than those of other family members. Later on, Clara constructed for her father a granite shaft twelve feet high—the two "fathoms" that had lent Mark Twain his pen name. With Ossip's death, she turned this into a Mark Twain–Gabrilowitsch Monument with a bronze bas-relief of her husband that was the exact size as that of her father and placed immediately below it. The clear message was that Ossip Gabrilowitsch, the pianist, was no less important than Mark Twain, the writer, and worthy of equal billing—a final act of rebellion by Clara against her father.

After the funeral, Clara and Ossip returned to Stormfield and adopted Jean's favorite German shepherd. They still resided there in mid-August when their daughter, Nina Gabrilowitsch—Mark Twain's sole grandchild—was born in Clara's old room. Six weeks later, the Gabrilowitsch family left for Europe, severing their ties forever with the house that had witnessed so much happiness but also such bitter dissension. "Regretfully," Clara wrote, "I left behind me a home which in two short years had seen a robbery, a wedding, two deaths and a birth."[71] To complete the dramatic picture, Stormfield burned to the ground in 1923. The one affirmative way in which Twain's spirit soldiered on in Redding was the opening of the Mark Twain Library a year after his death with its central building named after Jean. After a troubled life marred by alcohol problems and a failed career as an actress, Nina Gabrilowitsch, who may have committed suicide, died childless in 1966, at age fifty-five, ending the Clemens line.

The ghost of the Ashcroft-Lyon controversy never died. In a final surge of paranoia, Twain had predicted before his death, "At this very day Ashcroft is manufacturing forgeries to rob Clara with when I am dead,"

SHIPWRECK

and he advised that she keep lawyers on retainer.[72] Once the revered "Santa" of Isabel's journals, Clara still simmered over the explosive events. Poor Harriet Whitmore, who had innocently recommended Isabel Lyon to the Clemens family, was again pummeled with Isabel's misdeeds. "I do of course feel most bitterly about her," Clara wrote, "because I think her and Mr. Ashcroft's dishonesty were more than anything the cause of my father's death and consequently I myself am the cause for being such a *fool* all these years."[73] In her vengeance, she made sure that Albert B. Paine made only a single reference to Isabel in his 1,587-page biography of Twain. She was summarily expunged from the King's life.

Clara soon learned that Lyon and Ashcroft had purloined Twain documents and were hawking the manuscript of *Is Shakespeare Dead?* to dealers. She also received what she described as a "blackmailing letter" from the couple, likely rehashing the Charles Wark affair.[74] Twain had written the voluminous Lyon-Ashcroft Manuscript, chronicling the drama, as a posthumous weapon that Clara could wield in case the couple tried to extort anything from her. She now played that card and had her lawyer threaten the Ashcrofts "with the publication of this M.S. if they did not give back to me all the manuscripts of father's that they had in their possession & desist from annoying me in any way. It was successful. A paper was signed before a notary & I believe that we may for a time lead a peaceful private life," Clara told Harriet.[75] While she accused Isabel of slandering her behind her back, Clara returned the favor with pretty brutal judgments, saying the Isabel whom she once knew no longer existed because "her whole character has been changed by the constant use of drugs & stimulants."[76] In Clara's view, the cascading crises that crashed upon Stormfield were "so terrible that they seem to belong to one long hair-raising nightmare."[77] In a bold, posthumous act of defiance against her father, Clara became an adherent of Christian Science—"Mother Eddy deserves a place in the Trinity as much as any member of it," she wrote—before dying in San Diego, California, on November 19, 1962.[78]

By his death, Mark Twain's niche in the literary firmament seemed secure to many observers. In H. L. Mencken's view, he was "by great odds, the most noble figure America has ever given to English literature. Hav-

HALLEY'S COMET

ing him, we may hold up our heads when Spaniards boast of Cervantes and Frenchmen of Molière."[79] Upon learning of Twain's death, William Phelps, an eminent English professor at Yale University, termed it "a very great loss to American letters. I regarded him as our foremost representative in literature at the present day."[80] The press also recognized that Twain embodied something more than a great writer, that he had come to personify, at home and abroad, the country that had spawned him and of which he stood as such a unique specimen. He incarnated the best and sometimes the worst of America, all rolled into one. In eulogizing him, the *New York Times* wrote that Twain's death "meant to Americans everywhere and in all walks of life what the death of no other American could have meant. His personality and his humor have been an integral part of American life for so long that it has seemed almost impossible to realize an America without him."[81]

Beyond literary immortality, Twain had wondered where exactly he would wind up in the hereafter, heaven and hell having been staples in his repertoire of jokes. His rational side denied there could be any life after death. "As to a hereafter," he once told Paine, "we have not the slightest evidence that there is any—*no* evidence that appeals to logic and reason. I have never seen what to me seemed an atom of proof that there is a future life." But being the most contradictory of men, he qualified this observation with an afterthought: "And yet—I am strongly inclined to expect one."[82] He enjoyed another kind of afterlife, one that he had studiously planned. In November 2010, after a century-long embargo following his death, the University of California Press began to publish the first of three jumbo volumes of the *Autobiography of Mark Twain*. His clever tongue, full of vinegar and wit, suddenly spoke from beyond the grave. Even in death, he refused to yield the spotlight and showed with a flourish his posthumous mastery of public relations. The boy from Hannibal, who had always craved attention, was once again turning his old handsprings and cutting capers, only this time for the applause of posterity.

Acknowledgments

For a man who professed to be chronically lazy, Mark Twain bequeathed to his biographers a vast portfolio of writings that other authors would be hard-pressed to match. He produced more than thirty books and several thousand magazine articles. Thanks to a bequest from Clara Clemens, the chief repository of her father's work has long been the Bancroft Library of the University of California, Berkeley. Under the expert supervision of Robert H. Hirst, its general editor and resident genie, the Mark Twain Papers and Project has gathered from global archives some twelve thousand letters written by Mark Twain and his immediate family and nineteen thousand written to them or about them. Where the collection lacks originals, it has gleaned duplicates from dozens of libraries and private collections. Add to this a trove of forty-six out of fifty extant Twain notebooks, at least three hundred original photographs, and six hundred manuscripts left unpublished at his death, and any biographer with the requisite stamina can take a fresh look at Twain's life and reconstruct it with a fine-grained detail denied to earlier generations. Perhaps no other American author can boast such a richly documented record, and I was the lucky beneficiary of the assiduous efforts of many earlier scholars.

With its learned editions and digitized website, the Mark Twain Papers ranks as one of the foremost scholarly achievements of our era. As I approached the time when I planned to explore the collection in person,

ACKNOWLEDGMENTS

the Covid pandemic struck, and I was loath to travel by plane from my home in New York City to Berkeley. With exceptional generosity, Robert Hirst and associate editor Kerry Driscoll saved the day, sending me, via email, massive amounts of unpublished material that allowed me to soldier on. I cannot thank them enough for their unfailing kindness and helpfulness. Ditto for their able staff, including Benjamin Griffin, Terence Catapano, and Blake Bronson-Bartlett, who retrieved much wonderful material and engaged in stimulating chats when I visited.

In Hannibal, Missouri, the heartland of Mark Twain's world, I enjoyed the incomparable assistance of Henry Sweets, former director of the Mark Twain Boyhood Home & Museum. A tireless cicerone with an unrivaled mastery of local lore, he took me from home to hilltop, graveyard to evening cruise on the Mississippi River. I am no less grateful to James Lundgren, then CEO and executive director of the boyhood home and museum. Todd Curry, the co-owner of the Mark Twain Cave Complex, gave this claustrophobic author a limited tour that spared him 260 dreaded passageways. At the Mark Twain Birthplace State Historic Site in Florida, Missouri, I profited from the firsthand knowledge of Marianne Bodine, its historian and resource interpreter.

In Hartford, Connecticut, I very much appreciated the enthusiastic support of Pieter Roos, then executive director of the Mark Twain House & Museum, and his energetic staff. Sincere thanks to Steve Courtney, who gallantly saved me from some embarrassing errors, and Jennifer Larue; especially big thanks to Mallory Howard, who dug up important documents and many of the photos used in this book. Her assistance was invaluable. Across the lawn at the Harriet Beecher Stowe Center, I was aided by Elizabeth G. Burgess, the director of Collections and Research, and former executive director Briann Greenfield.

I got a warm reception from the folks in Elmira, New York, including Joseph Lemak, the director of the Center for Mark Twain Studies; Nathaniel Ball, the archivist and curator of the Mark Twain Archive; Matt Seybold, the associate professor of American literature and Mark Twain studies; Steve Webb, the caretaker of Quarry Farm; and Walter G.

ACKNOWLEDGMENTS

Ritchie, Jr., an expert on the design of Nook Farm and Quarry Farm. I also enjoyed the courtesy of Dr. Charles Lindsay, the president of Elmira College; Charles Mitchell, a professor of American studies; Jenny Monroe, the church council president of the Park Church; and Rachel E. Dworkin, archivist of the Chemung County Historical Society.

With enormous pleasure I retraced Mark Twain's footsteps in Bermuda. I wish to thank Susan and Richard Butterfield for a glimpse of Bay House, where the author spent some of his final days. I also received help from Karla Ingemann and Elizabeth Walter at the Bermuda Archive, Ellen Jane Hollis at the Bermuda National Library, and Margie Lloyd at the Bermuda National Trust. Judith Wadson, a resident of the island, regaled me with reminiscences of her grandmother, one of the young girls whom Twain befriended in Bermuda.

I was fortunate in being able to tour both houses rented by Mark Twain in Dublin, New Hampshire—the summer of 1905 house, with its incomparable views, now owned by Coleman and Susan Marshall Townsend, and the 1906 house, owned by David Godine and Sara Eisenman. Along with my cousin Martha Stearn and my friend Nancy Norton, we spent a week in the latter house, where we were attentively cared for by neighbor Neil Cotoni. Nancy Campbell of the Dublin Historical Society alerted me to relevant newsletters about Mark Twain's time there.

Redding, Connecticut, takes justifiable pride in being Twain's last stomping ground. At the Mark Twain Library, then director Beth Dominianni guided me through dozens of books with Twain's marginalia and markings. I am indebted to trustees Jen Wastrom and Pam Robey for hosting my visit along with library president Eric Rubury and vice president Michael Shinall. The rare hospitality of Marc Mellon and Babette Bloch facilitated my visit. Jake and Erika DeSantis and Cindy and Brian Meehl opened to me their "Stormfield" homes on the site of Twain's former house. Susan Durkee kindly invited me to her "Lobster Pot" home, once Isabel Lyon's place, and shared her enthusiasm for its erstwhile resident. Brent Colley imparted his wide knowledge of Mark Twain during his Redding years.

ACKNOWLEDGMENTS

At Wave Hill, Carolyn Liv, the director of corporate partnerships and conferences, provided vintage photos of the house Twain occupied in Riverdale. Alyssa Ritch-Frel was my genial companion for the journey.

Many individuals furnished insights that enriched these pages. Dr. Lauren Gorman offered pertinent insights about Twain's personality and the possibility that he suffered from attention deficit disorder. Stacy Schiff, wise as ever, shared valuable insights about the angelfish and Twain's psychosexual life in general. Brenda Wineapple was no less sage in discussing how to deal with various controversial aspects of the story. Matthew Aucoin and Michael Pressman offered keen insights into the angelfish phenomenon. As with my previous books, my brother, Dr. Bart Chernow, walked me through many maladies visited upon the Clemens family. Dr. Kirsten Healy helped me to understand the likely course of Livy's heart troubles. Dr. Rebecca Robbins gave her scholarly perspective on Mark Twain's sleepwalking. Editor Dean Baquet offered cogent comments on dealing with the recurring N-word problem in Mark Twain's life and how to be true to the period without offending readers. Karen Nielsen and Mark Tanenbaum brought to my attention Twain's will and Surrogate Court papers.

Susan Jaffe Tane laid out the many riches of her Mark Twain collection. I thank her and Gabriel McKee for the use of the photo of a bowler-hatted Twain for the frontispiece. Many thanks to rare book collector and dealer Kevin Mac Donnell for making available to scholars priceless items, including Isabel Lyon's annotations of Albert B. Paine's biography of Twain. He also gave me permission to use his newly discovered photo of George Griffin, Twain's Black butler—an exciting find indeed. David H. Fears has performed a spectacular feat in tracking Mark Twain's daily activities, and I thank him for enabling me to obtain a complete set of his four-volume masterwork. Alan Gribben and Irene Wong have led the way in resurrecting Mark Twain's extensive reading.

My emphasis on Mark Twain and race relations owes a special debt to the outstanding scholarship of Shelley Fisher Fishkin. In 2010 the Morgan Library and Museum mounted an exhibition titled "Mark Twain: A Skeptic's Progress," and library president Lawrence Ricciardi and cura-

ACKNOWLEDGMENTS

tor Philip S. Palmer gave me access to items from that show. I also received aid from Dean M. Rogers, a special-collections assistant at the Vassar College Library.

Other people who provided timely help: Joe B. Fulton, the editor of the *Mark Twain Journal;* David Richards, who brought to my attention Rudyard Kipling materials that had eluded me; Harold Holzer, who relayed several useful articles; Benjamin Shapell and Ariane Weisel Margalit, who gave me access to unpublished Twain manuscripts from the Shapell Manuscript Foundation; Madeline Myers, who provided information on Delia Bacon, who set Twain off on his mad Shakespeare escapade; and Lauren Belfer, who cleared up a critical mystery about Twain's time in Buffalo.

When I stop and count my many blessings as an author, I am especially grateful to the superb team that has now guided me for many years. Melanie Jackson is simply in a class by herself as an agent and friend. At the Penguin Press, my astute longtime editor, Ann Godoff; my publicist, Sarah Hutson; and Casey Denis and Victoria Laboz have given me exemplary editorial support through a string of books. Writing a biography is a long, arduous hike to a very high mountain peak, and these folks have formed my indispensable base camp. I am grateful for their affection, their talent, and their steadfast faith in my projects.

Abbreviations

Unless otherwise specified, all letters are written by or to Mark Twain. After the library call letters is the catalog number for that same letter at the Mark Twain Papers, the Bancroft Library, University of California, Berkeley.

ALM	Ashcroft-Lyon Manuscript.
AMT	*Autobiography of Mark Twain.*
BmuHA	Bermuda Archives, Hamilton, Bermuda.
CBev3	Charles Sachs, The Scriptorium, Beverly Hills, California.
CCamarSJ	St. John's Seminary, Camarillo, California.
CLjC	The James S. Copley Library, La Jolla, California.
CSmH	Henry E. Huntington Library, Art Collections and Botanical Gardens, San Marino, California.
CtHMTH	Mark Twain Memorial, Hartford, Connecticut.
CtHSD	Stowe-Day Memorial Library and Historical Foundation, Hartford, Connecticut.
CtY	Yale University, Sterling Memorial Library, New Haven, Connecticut.
CtY-BR	Yale University, Beinecke Rare Book and Manuscript Library, New Haven, Connecticut.
CtHT-w	Trinity College, Watkinson Library, Hartford, Connecticut.
CU-MARK	Mark Twain Papers, the Bancroft Library, University of California, Berkeley.
DLC	United States Library of Congress, Washington, D.C.
DSI	Smithsonian Institution, Washington, D.C.
DSI-AAA	Smithsonian Institution, Archives of American Art, Washington, D.C.
GEU	Robert W. Woodruff Library, Emory University, Atlanta, Georgia.

ABBREVIATIONS

ICN	Newberry Library, Chicago, Illinois.
IGK	Knox College, Galesburg, Illinois.
InU-Li	Indiana University, Lilly Rare Books, Bloomington, Indiana.
IVL	Isabel V. Lyon.
JCD	Jean Clemens Diary.
LaBrUHM	Hill Memorial Library, Louisiana State University, Baton Rouge, Louisiana.
LEP	Langdon Estate Papers, Chemung County Historical Society, Elmira, New York.
LNT	Tulane University, New Orleans, Louisiana.
MB	Boston Public Library and Eastern Massachusetts Regional Public Library System, Boston, Massachusetts.
MCo	Concord Free Public Library, Concord, Massachusetts.
MeWC	Colby College, Waterville, Maine.
Mfai	Millicent Library, Fairhaven, Massachusetts.
MH-H	Harvard University, Houghton Library, Cambridge, Massachusetts.
MiD	Detroit Public Library, Detroit, Michigan.
MnHi	Minnesota Historical Society, St. Paul, Minnesota.
MoCgS	Southeast Missouri State University, Cape Girardeau, Missouri.
MoFIM	Mark Twain Museum, Mark Twain State Park, Florida, Missouri.
MoFuWC	Westminster College, Fulton, Missouri.
MoHi	Missouri State Historical Society, Columbia, Missouri.
MoHM	Mark Twain Museum, Hannibal, Missouri.
MoKiU	Truman State University, Kirksville, Missouri.
MoSW	Washington University, St. Louis, Missouri.
MT	Mark Twain.
MTL	Mark Twain Library, Redding, Connecticut.
MTP	Mark Twain Papers, the Bancroft Library, University of California, Berkeley.
MWA	American Antiquarian Society, Worcester, Massachusetts.
NBuHi	Buffalo and Erie County Historical Society, Buffalo, New York.
NCH	Hamilton and Kirkland Colleges, Clinton, New York.
NHyF	Franklin D. Roosevelt Library, Hyde Park, New York.
NIC	Cornell University, Ithaca, New York.
NjP	Princeton University, Princeton, New Jersey.

ABBREVIATIONS

NMh	Library of Poultney Bigelow, Bigelow Homestead, Malden-on-Hudson, New York.
NN	New York Public Library, New York, New York.
NN-BGC	New York Public Library, Henry W. and Albert A. Berg Collection, New York, New York.
NNC	Columbia University, New York, New York.
NNGLI	The Gilder Lehrman Institute of American History, New York, New York.
NNPM	Pierpont Morgan Library, New York, New York.
NPV	Vassar College, Poughkeepsie, New York.
NSyU	Syracuse University, Syracuse, New York.
NzW2	National Library of New Zealand, Alexander Turnbull Library, Wellington, New Zealand.
OCHP	Cincinnati Historical Society, Cincinnati, Ohio.
ODa2	Collection of Benjamin Shapell.
OFH	Rutherford B. Hayes Library, Fremont, Ohio.
OrHi	Oregon Historical Society, Portland, Oregon.
PH	Profiles in History catalogs, Beverly Hills, California.
RuM2	Russian State Archives of Literature in Art, Moscow, Russia.
Salm	Collection of Peter A. Salm.
Tane	Private collection of Susan Jaffe Tane.
TXFTC	Texas Christian University, Fort Worth, Texas.
TxU-HU	Harry Ransom Humanities Research Center, University of Texas, Austin.
UkOxU	Oxford University, Bodleian Library, Oxford, England.
UkReU	University of Reading Library, Whiteknights, Reading, Berkshire, England.
ViMim	Middlebury College, Middlebury, Vermont.
ViU	University of Virginia, Charlottesville, Virginia.
WU-MU	Madison Memorial Union Library, University of Wisconsin, Madison, Wisconsin.

Notes

PRELUDE: THE PILOT HOUSE

1. *Life on the Mississippi*, 160.
2. *Love Letters of Mark Twain*, 166.
3. CU-MARK, 02202. Letter to Olivia L. Clemens, April 19, 1882.
4. *Mark Twain's Notebooks & Journals*, II:522. Notebook 21, April 19, 1882.
5. Ibid., 521. April 18, 1882.
6. CU-MARK, 02203. Letter to Olivia L. Clemens, April 21, 1882.
7. *Mark Twain's Notebooks & Journals*, II:523. Notebook 21, April 20, 1882.
8. Ibid., 534. April 21–22, 1882.
9. Ibid., 524–25. April 21, 1882.
10. CU-MARK, 02203. Letter to Olivia Langdon Clemens, April 21, 1882.
11. *Mark Twain's Notebooks & Journals*, II:530. Notebook 21, April 21, 1882.
12. Ibid.
13. CU-MARK, 02205. Letter to Olivia L. Clemens, April 25, 1882.
14. *Mark Twain's Letters*, 1:390.
15. Shelden, *Mark Twain: Man in White*, 358.
16. NPV (no number). Letter to Pamela A. Moffett, July 15, 1886.
17. Howells, *My Mark Twain*, 35.
18. Budd, *Mark Twain: Social Philosopher*, 189.
19. Kaplan, *Mr. Clemens and Mark Twain*, 123.

CHAPTER ONE: LOVELESS MARRIAGE

1. *Mark Twain Day by Day,* 2:534.
2. Blair, *Mark Twain's Hannibal, Huck & Tom*, 47.
3. NSyU, 04255. Letter to Chatto & Windus, November 22, 1891.
4. MTP. Orion Clemens. Unfinished draft about his mother.
5. Doris and Samuel Webster, "Whitewashing Jane Clemens."
6. Blair, *Mark Twain's Hannibal, Huck & Tom*, 47.
7. Ibid., 39. "Villagers of 1840–3."
8. Wecter, *Sam Clemens of Hannibal*, 30.
9. *AMT*, 1:469.
10. Ibid., 209. "Random Extracts."
11. CU-MARK, 47198. Letter from Jane L. Clemens to Orion and Mollie Clemens, May 5, 1880.
12. *AMT*, 1:62. "The Tennessee Land."
13. Wecter, *Sam Clemens of Hannibal*, 34.
14. Honce, "Twain Recollections," *Richmond Times-Dispatch*, June 4, 1944.
15. Gregory, "Orion Clemens on Mark Twain's Birthplace," *Mark Twain Journal*, Summer 1980.
16. Fanning, *Mark Twain and Orion Clemens*, 5.
17. *AMT*, 1:209. "Random Extracts."
18. CU-MARK, 47336. Letter from Jane Lampton Clemens to Samuel L. Clemens and Olivia L. Clemens, January 7, 1885.

NOTES

19. Wecter, *Sam Clemens of Hannibal*, 44.
20. CU-MARK, 47196. Letter from Jane L. Clemens to Orion Clemens, April 25, 1880.
21. *AMT*, 1:62. "The Tennessee Land."
22. Wecter, *Sam Clemens of Hannibal*, 60.
23. Fanning, *Mark Twain and Orion Clemens*, 7.
24. CU-MARK, 46928. Letter from John M. Clemens to Jane Lampton Clemens and Family, January 5, 1842.
25. Paine, *Mark Twain*, 1:44.
26. Wecter, *Sam Clemens of Hannibal*, 77.
27. Fanning, *Mark Twain and Orion Clemens*, 6.
28. CU-MARK, 50391. Letter from Orion Clemens, December 5, 1887.
29. *New York Times*, March 11, 1883.
30. Wecter, *Sam Clemens of Hannibal*, 66.
31. Ibid., 83 and 86.
32. Ibid., 67.
33. MnHi, 02833. Letter to Return I. Holcombe, September 4, 1883.
34. Trombley, *Mark Twain's Other Woman*, 53.
35. "Mark Twain's Boyhood," *Chicago Inter-Ocean*, April 5, 1885.
36. Paine, *Mark Twain*, 1:156.
37. *AMT*, 1:350. Autobiographical Dictation for February 12, 1906.
38. Paine, *Mark Twain*, 1:36.
39. *Mark Twain's Letters to Will Bowen*, 13.
40. Webster, *Mark Twain, Business Man*, 40.
41. Scharnhorst, *Twain in His Own Time*, 1.
42. Doris and Samuel Webster, "Whitewashing Jane Clemens."
43. Courtney, *The Loveliest Home That Ever Was*, 13–14.
44. *Mark Twain's Satires & Burlesques*, 201.
45. Doris and Samuel Webster, "Whitewashing Jane Clemens."
46. Webster, *Mark Twain, Business Man*, 225.
47. Blair, *Mark Twain's Hannibal, Huck & Tom*, 46.
48. Ibid., 50.
49. Wecter, *Sam Clemens of Hannibal*, 123.
50. *AMT*, 2:297. Autobiographical Dictation for November 30, 1906.
51. Paine, *Mark Twain*, 1:41.
52. Fanning, *Mark Twain and Orion Clemens*, 3.
53. CU-MARK, 46928. Letter from John M. Clemens to Jane Lampton Clemens and Family, January 5, 1842.
54. Wecter, *Sam Clemens of Hannibal*, 74–75.
55. MTP. Notebook 36, December 1895–March 1896. January 22, 1896, entry in Bombay.
56. Blair, *Mark Twain's Hannibal, Huck & Tom*, 39.
57. Ibid., 50.
58. Scharnhorst, *The Life of Mark Twain*, 1:17.
59. Blair, *Mark Twain's Hannibal, Huck & Tom*, 39.
60. MTP. Notebook 36, entry for January 22, 1896.

CHAPTER TWO: A WILD AND MISCHIEVOUS BOY

1. *Life on the Mississippi*, 63.
2. Fatout, *Mark Twain Speaking*, 458.
3. Blair, *Mark Twain's Hannibal, Huck & Tom*, 35.
4. Ibid.
5. *AMT*, 1:401. Autobiographical Dictation for March 9, 1906.
6. Crawford, *How Not to Get Rich*, 167.
7. *New York Times*, November 11, 1899.
8. Scharnhorst, *The Life of Mark Twain*, 1:42.
9. CtHMTH, 02867. Letter to Jervis Langdon II, December 19, 1883.
10. TxU-HU, 02464. Letter to William Bowen, February 6, 1870.
11. *Mark Twain's Letters to Will Bowen*, 19.
12. Paine, *Mark Twain*, 1:35.
13. *AMT*, 2:232. Autobiographical Dictation for September 10, 1906.
14. Lion Heart Autographs, 13863. Letter to John Tatlock, February 21, 1899.
15. Tuckey, *Which Was the Dream?*, 459.
16. *AMT*, 1:421. Autobiographical Dictation for March 16, 1906.
17. Honce, "Twain Recollections," *Richmond Times-Dispatch*, June 4, 1944.
18. Paine, *Mark Twain*, 3:1592.
19. Wecter, *Sam Clemens of Hannibal*, 149.
20. MTP. Notebook 36. December 1895–March 1896.
21. *Mark Twain Day by Day*, 2:861.
22. *AMT*, 1:399. Autobiographical Dictation for March 8, 1906.
23. *Life on the Mississippi*, 64–65.

NOTES

24. Ibid., 169.
25. Ibid., 68.
26. Ibid., 42.
27. *The Gilded Age*, 60.
28. Cooley, *Mark Twain's Aquarium*, 215.
29. *Hannibal Courier Post*, April 22, 1910.
30. Shelden, *Mark Twain: Man in White*, 285.
31. "Mark Twain's Childhood Sweetheart Recalls Their Romance," *Literary Digest*, March 23, 1918.
32. DeVito, *Mark Twain's Notebooks*, 249.
33. Wecter, *Sam Clemens of Hannibal*, 182.
34. Ibid.
35. *Mark Twain Day by Day*, 2:393.
36. Scharnhorst, *The Life of Mark Twain*, 1:27.
37. Paine, *Mark Twain*, 1:84.
38. Kaplan, *Mr. Clemens*, 14.
39. *AMT*, 1:159. "Scraps . . . from Chapter IX."
40. Scharnhorst, *The Life of Mark Twain*, 1:17
41. *AMT*, 1:212. "Random Extracts."
42. Paine, *Mark Twain*, 1:41.
43. *New York World*, December 10, 1899.
44. Neider, *Complete Essays of Mark Twain*, 517–18.
45. Blair, *Mark Twain's Hannibal, Huck & Tom*, 51.
46. *AMT*, 1:210. "Random Extracts."
47. Ibid.
48. Ibid., 211.
49. Paine, *Mark Twain*, 1:33.
50. *AMT*, 1:211. "Random Extracts."
51. GEU, 01997. Letter to Joel Chandler Harris, August 10, 1881.
52. *AMT*, 1:211–12. "Random Extracts."
53. Ibid.
54. Blair, *Mark Twain's Hannibal, Huck & Tom*, 49.
55. *Adventures of Huckleberry Finn*, xxiii.
56. Ibid.

CHAPTER THREE: PRINTER'S DEVIL

1. Fanning, *Mark Twain and Orion Clemens*, 12.
2. *AMT*, 1:61. "The Tennessee Land."
3. Paine, *Mark Twain*, 1:73.
4. *AMT*, 1:61. "The Tennessee Land."
5. Paine, *Mark Twain*, 1:73.
6. Blair, *Mark Twain's Hannibal, Huck & Tom*, 40. "Villagers of 1840–3."
7. NPV, 00027. Letter to Orion and Mary E. "Mollie" Clemens, February 6, 1861. Editorial note.
8. Scharnhorst, *The Life of Mark Twain*, 1:34.
9. Wecter, *Sam Clemens of Hannibal*, 118.
10. *AMT*, 1:63. "The Tennessee Land."
11. Trombley, *Mark Twain's Other Woman*, 53.
12. Wecter, *Sam Clemens of Hannibal*, 82.
13. Fanning, *Mark Twain and Orion Clemens*, 13.
14. *Chicago Inter-Ocean*, April 5, 1885.
15. Paine, *Mark Twain*, 1:76.
16. Wecter, *Sam Clemens of Hannibal*, 202.
17. Ibid.
18. Paine, *Mark Twain*, 1:77.
19. *Roughing It*, 271.
20. Fatout, *Mark Twain Speaking*, 201.
21. *Hannibal Courier-Post*, April 22, 1910.
22. Scharnhorst, *The Life of Mark Twain*, 1:47.
23. Wecter, *Sam Clemens of Hannibal*, 195.
24. MTP. Orion Clemens. Autobiographical Fragments.
25. Wecter, *Samuel Clemens of Hannibal*, 232.
26. Ibid., 235.
27. Ibid.
28. MTP. Orion Clemens. Autobiographical Fragments.
29. Fanning, *Mark Twain and Orion Clemens*, 23.
30. Scharnhorst, *The Life of Mark Twain*, 1:61.
31. Wecter, *Sam Clemens of Hannibal*, 250.
32. Ibid.
33. Paine, *Mark Twain*, 1:90.
34. Scharnhorst, *The Life of Mark Twain*, 1:70.
35. *Early Tales & Sketches*, 1:68.
36. Paine, *Mark Twain*, 1:85.
37. Wecter, *Sam Clemens of Hannibal*, 237.
38. Fanning, *Mark Twain and Orion Clemens*, 28.
39. *Mark Twain Day by Day*, 1:1030
40. Wecter, *Sam Clemens of Hannibal*, 263.
41. Ibid., 262.
42. Fulton, *The Reconstruction of Mark Twain*, 7.
43. *Mark Twain Day by Day*, 3:740.
44. Hoffmann, *Mark Twain in Paradise*, 3.
45. Paine, *Mark Twain*, 1:93.

NOTES

46. NPV, 00030. Letter to Pamela A. Moffett and Jane Lampton Clemens, October 25, 1861.
47. Blair, *Mark Twain's Hannibal, Huck & Tom,* 36.
48. Ward, *American Heritage,* September/October 1966.
49. New York *Graphic,* April 22, 1873.
50. Fulton, *The Reconstruction of Mark Twain,* 8.
51. *Hannibal Journal,* September 5, 1853.
52. Ibid.
53. Ibid.
54. Ibid., September 10, 1853.
55. Ibid.
56. Ibid.
57. Scharnhorst, *The Life of Mark Twain,* 1:78.
58. CU-MARK, 00001. Letter to Pamela A. Moffett, October 8, 1853.
59. NPV, 00002. Letter to Orion and Henry Clemens, October 26?–28, 1853.
60. NPV, 00003. Letter to Orion Clemens, November 28, 1853.
61. Ibid.
62. Ibid.
63. *Muscatine Journal,* December 4, 1853.
64. Ibid., February 17 and 18, 1854.
65. Fanning, *Mark Twain and Orion Clemens,* 36.
66. *Muscatine Journal,* August 5, 1854.
67. MoCgS. 01384. Letter to Jacob H. Burrough, November 1, 1876.
68. NPV, 00011. Letter to Jane Lampton Clemens and Pamela A. Moffett, June 10, 1856.
69. Scharnhorst, *The Life of Mark Twain,* 1:90.

CHAPTER FOUR: "DARLING EXISTENCE"

1. Crawford, *How Not to Get Rich,* 12.
2. Ibid., 12.
3. Ibid., 14.
4. NPV, 00012. Letter to Henry Clemens, August 5, 1856.
5. *Life on the Mississippi,* 70.
6. Crawford, *How Not to Get Rich,* 15–16.
7. Ibid., 17.
8. *AMT,* 1:461. Autobiographical Dictation for March 29, 1906.
9. Scharnhorst, *The Life of Mark Twain,* 1:94.
10. *Chicago Inter-Ocean,* April 5, 1885.
11. Paine, *Mark Twain,* 1:121.
12. *Life on the Mississippi,* 111.
13. *New Zealand Mail* (Wellington), December 12, 1895.
14. Paine, *Mark Twain,* 1:146.
15. Ibid., 123.
16. Bassford, *Saturday Evening Post,* December 16, 1889.
17. NPV, 00018. Letter to Orion Clemens, June 27?, 1860.
18. Webster, *Business Man,* 33.
19. Honce, "Twain Recollections," *Richmond Times-Dispatch,* June 4, 1944.
20. NPV, 10893. Letter to Pamela A. Moffett, July 15, 1886.
21. Blair, *Mark Twain's Hannibal, Huck & Tom,* 40. "Villagers 1840–43."
22. Scharnhorst, *The Life of Mark Twain,* 1:68.
23. NPV, 10893. Letter to Pamela A. Moffett, July 15, 1886.
24. *AMT,* 3:245. Autobiographical Dictation for July 7, 1908.
25. Lawton, *A Lifetime with Mark Twain,* 345.
26. Fatout, *Mark Twain Speaking,* 294.
27. NPV, 00014. Letter to Orion and Mary E. "Mollie" Clemens, March 9, 1858.
28. Scharnhorst, *The Life of Mark Twain,* 1:114.
29. Ibid., 103.
30. Ibid.
31. Ibid., 102.
32. *Mark Twain's Notebooks & Journals,* 1:22. June–July 1855.
33. *Love Letters of Mark Twain,* 66. Letter to Olivia Lewis Langdon, February 13, 1869.
34. *AMT,* 1:458. Autobiographical Dictation for March 29, 1906.
35. Wecter, *Sam Clemens of Hannibal,* 130.
36. *Life on the Mississippi,* 228.
37. CU-MARK, 02711. Letter to Mary E. "Mollie" Clemens, June 18, 1858.
38. Paine, *Mark Twain,* 1:138.
39. *Life on the Mississippi,* 236.
40. Paine, *Mark Twain,* 1:139.
41. *Life on the Mississippi,* 241.
42. CU-MARK, 02711. Letter to Mary E. "Mollie" Clemens, June 18, 1858
43. Memphis *Eagle and Enquirer,* June 16, 1858.

NOTES

44. *Life on the Mississippi,* 243.
45. Scharnhorst, *The Life of Mark Twain,* 1:110.
46. *AMT,* 1:561. "Explanatory Notes."
47. Paine, *Mark Twain,* 1:142.
48. Ibid.
49. CU-MARK, 02711. Letter to Mary E. "Mollie" Clemens, June 18, 1858.
50. *AMT,* 1:561. Editorial note.
51. *The Stolen White Elephant,* 112–13.
52. Kaplan, *Mr. Clemens,* 195.
53. *AMT,* 2:211. Autobiographical Dictation for August 31, 1906.
54. Scharnhorst, *The Life of Mark Twain,* 1:105.
55. TxU-Hu, 01772. Letter to David Watt Bowser, March 20, 1880.
56. Webster, *Business Man,* 51.
57. Ibid., 52.
58. NPV, 00027. Letter to Orion and Mary E. "Mollie" Clemens, February 6, 1861.
59. Ibid.
60. NPV, 00087. Letter to Jane Lampton Clemens and Pamela A. Moffett, September 25, 1864.
61. Kaplan, *Singular Mark Twain,* 130.
62. Scharnhorst, *The Life of Mark Twain,* 1:107.

CHAPTER FIVE: "A RAGGED AND DIRTY BUNCH"

1. Bassford, *Saturday Evening Post,* December 16, 1889.
2. Marsh, St. Louis *Missouri Republican,* December 8, 1878.
3. NPV, 00018. Letter to Orion Clemens, June 27?, 1860.
4. *Life on the Mississippi,* 246.
5. Griffin, *Mark Twain's Civil War,* 79.
6. Ibid., 80.
7. MTP. Notebook 48, 1905–8. Undated notebook entry.
8. CU-MARK, 13746. Letter to George William Beaman, January 27, 1861.
9. Griffin, *Mark Twain's Civil War,* 11.
10. Webster, *Business Man,* 60.
11. NPV, 46956. Letter from Jane Lampton Clemens to Samuel Langhorne Clemens, Orion Clemens, and Mary E. "Mollie" Clemens, October 12 and 14, 1862.
12. *Saturday Evening Post,* December 16, 1899.
13. Paine, *Mark Twain,* 1:161.
14. Fanning, *Mark Twain and Orion Clemens,* 56.
15. Webster, *Business Man,* 61.
16. Ibid., 60.
17. Scharnhorst, *The Life of Mark Twain,* 1:129.
18. *The Gilded Age,* 169.
19. Griffin, *Mark Twain's Civil War,* 11.
20. Ibid., 22.
21. Scharnhorst, *The Life of Mark Twain,* 1:130.
22. Rasmussen, *Dear Mark Twain,* 123.
23. St. Louis *Missouri Republican,* April 28, 1874.
24. CtHMTH, 05571. Letter to Francis E. Bliss, March 31–April 2, 1899.
25. Anderson, *Pen Warmed Up,* 20.
26. Griffin, *Mark Twain's Civil War,* 42, and Webster, *Business Man,* 72.
27. Griffin, *Mark Twain's Civil War,* 44.
28. Anderson, *Pen Warmed Up,* 32.
29. Ibid., 37.
30. Ibid., 38.
31. Ibid., 40.
32. Griffin, *Mark Twain's Civil War,* 32.
33. Anderson, *Pen Warmed Up,* 43.
34. Ibid., 41.
35. Pettit, *Mark Twain & the South,* 184.
36. *San Francisco Chronicle,* March 30, 1919.
37. *AMT,* 1:453. Autobiographical Dictation for March 28, 1906.
38. Scharnhorst, *The Life of Mark Twain,* 1:38.
39. NPV, 00027. Letter from Orion Clemens, January 7, 1861. Editorial note.
40. Fanning, *Mark Twain and Orion Clemens,* 51.
41. *Roughing It,* 1.
42. Fulton, *The Reconstruction of Mark Twain,* 29.
43. *Roughing It,* 4.
44. Ibid., 1.
45. *Lansing State Republican* (Michigan), December 14, 1871.
46. *Roughing It,* 6.
47. Scharnhorst, "Additional Mark Twain Contributions." *American Literary Realism,* Fall 2014.
48. *Roughing It,* 50.
49. Ibid., 126.

NOTES

50. Ibid., 129.
51. Ibid.
52. Ibid., 107.
53. Ibid., 105–6.
54. Ibid., 107.
55. *Mark Twain's Letters*, 772. Letter to Robert Fulton, May 24, 1905.
56. CU-MARK, 00031. Letter to Jane Lampton Clemens, October 26, 1861.

CHAPTER SIX: "THE MOST LOVABLE SCAMP"

1. Paine, *Mark Twain*, 1:178.
2. CU-MARK, 07048. Letter to Robert Fulton, May 24, 1905.
3. CU-MARK, 12811. Letter to William F. Cody, September 19, 1884.
4. *Roughing It*, 63.
5. Ibid., 66.
6. Ibid., 67.
7. Rasmussen, *Mark Twain A to Z*, 432.
8. *Roughing It*, 142.
9. Ibid., 147.
10. NPV, 00045. Letter to Orion Clemens, April 24 and 25, 1862.
11. *Roughing It*, 175.
12. Ibid., 184–85.
13. CU-MARK, 00034. Letter to Jane Lampton Clemens, January 30, 1862.
14. Ibid.
15. *Roughing It*, 182.
16. Paine, *Mark Twain*, 1:186.
17. NPV, 00036. Letter to Jane Lampton Clemens and Pamela A. Moffett, February 8 and 9, 1862.
18. NPV, 00036. Letter to Jane Lampton Clemens and Pamela A. Moffett, February 8 and 9, 1862.
19. Kaplan, *Singular Mark Twain*, 96.
20. ViU, 00037. Letter to William H. Clagett, February 28, 1862.
21. CU-MARK, 00043. Letter to Orion Clemens, April 17, 1862.
22. Scharnhorst, *The Life of Mark Twain*, 1:156.
23. Kaplan, *Singular Mark Twain*, 98.
24. NPV, 00048. Letter to Orion Clemens, May 11, 1862.
25. Crawford, *How Not to Get Rich*, 48.
26. NPV, 00045. Letter to Orion Clemens, April 24 and 25, 1862.
27. Sacramento *Union*, July 6, 1870.
28. Fanning, *Mark Twain and Orion Clemens*, 91–92.
29. Paine, *Mark Twain*, 1:195.
30. CU-MARK, 00035. Letter to Mary E. "Mollie" Clemens, January 29, 1862.
31. *Roughing It*, 148.
32. Ibid., 149.
33. NPV, 00021. Letter to Jane Lampton Clemens, September 18–21, 1861.
34. NPV, 00030. Letter to Pamela A. Moffett and Jane Lampton Clemens, October 25, 1861.
35. Scharnhorst, *The Life of Mark Twain*, 1:168.
36. *Roughing It*, 274.
37. CU-MARK, 00058. Letter to Pamela A. Moffett, August 15, 1862.
38. *Roughing It*, 357.
39. Ibid., 283.
40. Ibid., 282.
41. Ibid.
42. Scharnhorst, *The Life of Mark Twain*, 1:40.
43. Ibid.
44. *Roughing It*, 275.
45. Ibid., 276.
46. NPV, 00060. Letter to Orion and Mary E. "Mollie" Clemens, October 21, 1862.
47. Paine, *Mark Twain*, 1:212.
48. *Early Tales & Sketches*, 1:245.
49. Fanning, *Mark Twain and Orion Clemens*, 73.
50. Stewart, *Reminiscences*, 220.
51. *Life on the Mississippi*, 497.
52. CU-MARK, 02021. Letter to John B. Downing, August 18?, 1881.
53. Mac Donnell, *Mark Twain Journal*, Spring 2019.
54. Scharnhorst, *The Life of Mark Twain*, 1:191.
55. *Mark Twain Day by Day*, 2:363.
56. Shelden, *Mark Twain: Man in White*, 313.
57. CU-MARK, 00065. Letter to Jane Lampton Clemens and Pamela A. Moffett, May 18?, 1863.
58. NPV, 00061. Letter to Jane Lampton Clemens and Pamela A. Moffett, February 16, 1863.
59. CU-MARK, 00067. Letter to Jane Lampton Clemens and Pamela A. Moffett, June 4, 1863.

NOTES

60. Fanning, *Mark Twain and Orion Clemens*, 88.
61. Ibid., 89.
62. Kaplan, *Singular Mark Twain*, 115.
63. NPV, 00072. Letter to Jane Lampton Clemens, January 2, 1864. Editorial note.
64. Ibid.
65. NPV, 00072. Letter to Jane Lampton Clemens, January 2, 1864.
66. NPV, 00071. Letter to Jane Lampton Clemens and Pamela A. Moffett, August 19, 1863.
67. Ibid.
68. Ibid.
69. Tuckey, *Which Was the Dream?*, 161.
70. CU-MARK, 00070. Letter to Jane Lampton Clemens and Pamela A. Moffett, August 5, 1863.
71. *AMT*, 1:453. Autobiographical Dictation for March 28, 1906.
72. Ibid., 2:393. Autobiographical Dictation for January 28, 1907.
73. Ibid., 26. Autobiographical Dictation for April 9, 1906.
74. Scharnhorst, *The Life of Mark Twain*, 1:137.
75. *AMT*, 2:6. Autobiographical Dictation for April 2, 1906.
76. Ibid., 20. Autobiographical Dictation for April 5, 1906.
77. Ibid.

CHAPTER SEVEN: "HEAVEN ON THE HALF SHELL"

1. Scharnhorst, *The Life of Mark Twain*, 1:188.
2. NPV, 00076, Letter to Pamela A. Moffett, March 18, 1864.
3. CU-MARK, 00035, Letter to Mary E. "Mollie" Clemens, January 31, 1862.
4. ViU, 00037. Letter to William H. Clagett, February 28, 1862.
5. ViU, 00039. Letter to William H. Clagett, March 8, 1862.
6. CU-MARK, 12723. Letter to Orion Clemens, July 28, 1862.
7. Fulton, *The Reconstruction of Mark Twain*, 67.
8. Pettit, *Mark Twain & the South*, 28–29.
9. Fulton, *The Reconstruction of Mark Twain*, 74.
10. CU-MARK, 00078. Letter to Mary E. "Mollie" Clemens, May 20, 1864. Editorial note.
11. Ibid.
12. Ibid.
13. Scharnhorst, *The Life of Mark Twain*, 1:251.
14. Kaplan, *Singular Mark Twain*, 117.
15. Pettit, *Mark Twain & the South*, 31.
16. Fulton, *The Reconstruction of Mark Twain*, 80
17. CU-MARK, 00082. Letter to Orion Clemens, May 26, 1864.
18. *Roughing It*, 382.
19. *Gold Hill Evening News*, May 30, 1864.
20. Kaplan, *Singular Mark Twain*, 121.
21. Scharnhorst, *The Life of Mark Twain*, 1:281.
22. Ibid., 261.
23. *Mark Twain's Notebooks & Journals*, 1:64.
24. *AMT*, 2:115. Autobiographical Dictation for June 13, 1906.
25. *Early Tales & Sketches*, 2:11.
26. Kaplan, *Singular Mark Twain*, 123.
27. Anderson, *Pen Warmed Up*, 6.
28. MH-H, 01829. Letter to William Dean Howells, September 3, 1880.
29. *Roughing It*, 369.
30. Ibid., 375.
31. Ibid., 369.
32. Anderson, *Pen Warmed Up*, 6.
33. *AMT*, 2:115. Autobiographical Dictation for June 13, 1906.
34. Scharnhorst, *Twain in His Own Time*, 47.
35. *Roughing It*, 405–6.
36. Kaplan, *Singular Mark Twain*, 127.
37. NPV, 00087. Letter to Jane Lampton Clemens and Pamela A. Moffett, September 25, 1864.
38. NPV, 10993. Letter to Jane Lampton Clemens, August 12, 1864. Editorial note.
39. Scharnhorst, *The Life of Mark Twain*, 1:277.
40. *Early Tales & Sketches*, 2:57.
41. TxU-HU, 00106. Letter to William Bowen, August 25, 1866.
42. NPV, 00087. Letter to Jane Lampton Clemens and Pamela A. Moffett, September 25, 1864.
43. CU-MARK, 00088. Letter to Orion and Mary E. "Mollie" Clemens, September 28, 1864.

NOTES

44. *Early Tales & Sketches*, 2:31.
45. *AMT*, 2:119. Autobiographical Dictation for June 14, 1906.
46. Kaplan, *Singular Mark Twain*, 126.
47. *AMT*, 2:119. Autobiographical Dictation for June 14, 1906.
48. CU-MARK, 00094. Letter to Jane Lampton Clemens and Pamela A. Moffett, January 20, 1866.
49. *Mark Twain's Notebooks & Journals*, 2:76. Notebook entry for January 23, 1865.
50. Paine, *Mark Twain*, 1:271.
51. *Mark Twain's Notebooks & Journals*, 1:80.
52. *Mark Twain's Notebooks*, 30.
53. *Mark Twain Day by Day*, 1:133.
54. *Early Tales & Sketches*, 2:265.
55. Kaplan, *Singular Mark Twain*, 136.
56. CU-MARK, 00094. Letter to Jane Lampton Clemens and Pamela A. Moffett, January 20, 1866.
57. The San Francisco *Dramatic Chronicle*, October 18, 1865.
58. Heidig, *Known to Everyone*, 26.
59. CU-MARK, 00092. Letter to Orion and Mary E. "Mollie" Clemens, October 19, 1865.
60. Ibid.
61. Ibid.
62. Fanning, *Mark Twain and Orion Clemens*, 107–8.
63. MTP. Marginal comment made on April 21, 1909, in Mark Twain's copy of *The Letters of James Russell Lowell*.

CHAPTER EIGHT: "LAND OF INDOLENCE AND DREAMS"

1. *Roughing It*, 421.
2. TxU-HU, 00100. Letter to William Bowen, May 7, 1866.
3. NPV, 00096. Letter to Jane Lampton Clemens and Pamela A. Moffett, March 5, 1866.
4. Kaplan, *Singular Mark Twain*, 142.
5. Paine, *Mark Twain*, 1:474.
6. *AMT*, 2:21. Autobiographical Dictation for April 5, 1906.
7. NPV, 00101. Letter to Mary E. "Mollie" Clemens, May 22, 1866.
8. Paine, *Mark Twain*, 1:478.
9. Kaplan, *Singular Mark Twain*, 140.
10. Ibid., 141.
11. *Mark Twain–Howells Letters*, 378. Letter to William Dean Howells, October 26, 1881.
12. *Mark Twain's Notebooks & Journals*, 1:125.
13. Neider, *Mark Twain: Life As I Find It*, 184.
14. Ibid.
15. Kaplan, *Singular Mark Twain*, 152.
16. Ibid., 144.
17. *Roughing It*, 494–95.
18. Neider, *Mark Twain: Life As I Find It*, 183–84.
19. *Roughing It*, 459.
20. *Mark Twain's Notebooks & Journals*, 1:150. Notebook 5, March–September 1866.
21. *Roughing It*, 510.
22. *Mark Twain's Notebooks & Journals*, 1:133.
23. NPV, 00102. Letter to Jane Lampton Clemens and Pamela A. Moffett, June 21, 1866. Editorial note.
24. Ibid.
25. Neider, *The Complete Essays of Mark Twain*, 260. "My Debut as a Literary Person," *Century Magazine* 59 (November 1899), 76–88.
26. Kaplan, *Singular Mark Twain*, 151.
27. Neider, *The Complete Essays of Mark Twain*, 260. "My Debut as a Literary Person," *Century Magazine* 59 (November 1899), 76–88.
28. NPV, 00103. Letter to Jane Lampton Clemens and Pamela A. Moffett, June 27, 1866. Editorial note.
29. Ibid.
30. Neider, *Mark Twain: Life As I Find It*, 188.
31. MWA, 04155. Letter to Thomas L Gulick, January 8, 1891.
32. *Mark Twain's Notebooks & Journals*, 1:163.
33. *Roughing It*, 533.
34. Paine, *Mark Twain*, 1:290.
35. Scharnhorst, *The Life of Mark Twain*, 1:349.
36. Ibid., 384.
37. *Roughing It*, 533.
38. Kaplan, *Singular Mark Twain*, 163.
39. *Roughing It*, 535.

NOTES

40. Scharnhorst, *Twain in His Own Time,* 59.
41. CU-MARK, 02284. Letter to Charles T. Palmer, October 3, 1882.
42. *Early Tales & Sketches,* 1:36.
43. *Roughing It,* 537.
44. Scharnhorst, *The Life of Mark Twain,* 1:356.
45. *AMT,* 1:153. "Ralph Keeler."
46. Ibid.
47. Fitch, *San Francisco Chronicle,* March 30, 1919.
48. Kaplan, *Singular Mark Twain,* 167.
49. NPV, 00110. Letter to Jane Lampton Clemens and Family, November 2, 1866. Editorial note.
50. NPV, 00116. Letter to Jane Lampton Clemens and Family, December 15, 1866.
51. CU-MARK, 01493. Letter to Minnie Wakeman-Curtis, October 5, 1877.
52. *Mark Twain's Notebooks & Journals,* 1:240.
53. *Alta California,* February 23, 1867.
54. *Mark Twain's Notebooks & Journals,* 1:301.
55. Kaplan, *Singular Mark Twain,* 174.
56. Ibid., 175.
57. Scharnhorst, *The Life of Mark Twain,* 1:375.
58. Kaplan, *Singular Mark Twain,* 181.
59. Ibid.
60. Ibid., 182.
61. Scharnhorst, *The Life of Mark Twain,* 1:385.
62. *Roughing It,* 542.
63. Kaplan, *Singular Mark Twain,* 182.
64. Crawford, *How Not to Get Rich,* 57.
65. ViU, 00123. Letter to Jane Lampton Clemens and Family, April 19, 1867.
66. CtY-BR, 00128. Letter to Francis Bret Harte, May 1, 1867.
67. Crawford, *How Not to Get Rich,* 57.
68. NPV, 00126. Letter to Jane Lampton Clemens and Family, May 1, 1867. Editorial note.
69. MTP. "Concerning the scoundrel Edward H. House." March 1890. Unfinished manuscript.
70. Kaplan, *Singular Mark Twain,* 184.
71. Paine, *Mark Twain,* 3:1603.
72. Kaplan, *Singular Mark Twain,* 185.
73. Paine, *Mark Twain,* 1:314–15.
74. MTP. "Concerning the scoundrel Edward H. House." March 1890. Unfinished manuscript.
75. Scharnhorst, *The Life of Mark Twain,* 1:391.
76. Paine, *Mark Twain,* 1:316.
77. *New York Tribune,* May 11, 1867.
78. Ibid.
79. Scharnhorst, *The Life of Mark Twain,* 1:392.

CHAPTER NINE: "GRAVE OF A BLOOD RELATION"

1. TxU-HU, 00133. Letter to William Bowen, June 7, 1867.
2. Scharnhorst, *The Life of Mark Twain,* 1:380.
3. ViU, 00122. Letter to Jane Lampton Clemens and Family, April 15, 1867.
4. *Brooklyn Eagle,* March 4, 1876.
5. *New York World,* February 14, 1877.
6. Scharnhorst, *The Life of Mark Twain,* 1:397.
7. *Mark Twain's Notebooks & Journals,* 1:306.
8. Fanning, *Mark Twain and Orion Clemens,* 121.
9. Ibid.
10. *Mark Twain's Notebooks & Journals,* 1:344.
11. NPV, 00132. Letter to Jane Lampton Clemens and Family, June 1, 1867.
12. Hodgson, *The Bermudian,* September 1983.
13. LEP, CL 151. Langdon Estate Papers. Letter from Charles Langdon, August 21, 1867.
14. *Mark Twain's Notebooks & Journals,* 1:331.
15. *AMT,* 1:376. Autobiographical Dictation for February 23, 1906.
16. *Mark Twain's Notebooks & Journals,* 1:334.
17. CtY-Br, 01796. Letter to Miss Perkins, April 30, 1880.
18. Scharnhorst, *The Life of Mark Twain,* 1:399.
19. Hoffmann, *Mark Twain in Paradise,* 23.
20. Scharnhorst, *The Life of Mark Twain,* 1:406.
21. CU-MARK, 00407. Letter to Olivia L. Langdon, January 10, 1870.

NOTES

22. Fairbanks, *Chautauquan* No. 14, January 1892.
23. Ibid.
24. NPV, 00171. Letter to Jane Lampton Clemens and Family, December 10, 1867.
25. Paine, *Mark Twain*, 1:328.
26. *Mark Twain's Notebooks & Journals*, 1:342.
27. NPV, 00139. Letter to Jane Lampton Clemens and Family, June 30, 1867.
28. *Mark Twain's Notebooks & Journals*, 1:310.
29. NPV, 00139. Letter to Jane Lampton Clemens and Family, July 1, 1867.
30. *Mark Twain's Notebooks & Journals*, 1:364 and 368.
31. *The Innocents Abroad*, 650.
32. Ibid., 112.
33. Ibid., 112–13.
34. Ibid., 151.
35. NPV, 00141. Letter to Jane Lampton Clemens and Family, July 15,1867.
36. *The Innocents Abroad*, 164.
37. Ibid., 165.
38. Ibid.
39. Ibid., 361.
40. Ibid., 191.
41. Scharnhorst, *The Life of Mark Twain*, 413.
42. *The Innocents Abroad*, 194.
43. Ibid., 195.
44. Ibid., 221.
45. Ibid., 237.
46. Ibid., 236.
47. Ibid., 241–42.
48. Ibid., 258.
49. Ibid., 259–60.
50. MTP. Notebook 32, May 1892–January 1893.
51. Kaplan, *Mr. Clemens*, 46.
52. *Mark Twain's Notebooks & Journals*, 1:388–389. Notebook 9, entry for August 15, 1867.
53. Ibid., 389.
54. Kaplan, *Singular Mark Twain*, 201.
55. *The Innocents Abroad*, 368.
56. Ibid., 369.
57. Ibid., 379.
58. Ibid.
59. Scharnhorst, *The Life of Mark Twain*, 1:422.
60. NPV, 00145. Letter to Jane Lampton Clemens and Family, August 26, 1867.
61. *Mark Twain's Notebooks & Journals*, 1:407. August 25, 1867. Twain's speech to the emperor of Russia.
62. NPV, 00145. Letter to Jane Lampton Clemens and Family, August 26, 1867.
63. *Mark Twain's Notebooks & Journals*, 1:376.
64. *The Innocents Abroad*, 394.
65. *Mark Twain's Notebooks & Journals*, 1:411. Notebook 9, entry for August 18, 1867.
66. Ibid.
67. *Love Letters of Mark Twain*, 2.
68. Scharnhorst, *The Life of Mark Twain*, 1:430.
69. *Mark Twain's Notebooks & Journals*, 1:421.
70. Kaplan, *Mr. Clemens*, 54.
71. *Mark Twain's Notebooks & Journals*, 1:426. Notebook 9. Entry for September 20, 1867.
72. Kaplan, *Singular Mark Twain*, 208.
73. *The Innocents Abroad*, 571.
74. Ibid., 567.
75. Paine, *Mark Twain's Letters*, 1:330.
76. *Mark Twain's Notebooks & Journals*, 1:438. Notebook 9. Entry circa September 24, 1867.
77. Scharnhorst, *The Life of Mark Twain*, 1:430.
78. Scharnhorst, *The Complete Interviews*, 15–16.
79. Fairbanks, *Chautauquan* No. 14, January 1892.
80. *Cleveland Herald*, December 14, 1867.
81. NPV, 00156. Letter to Jane Lampton Clemens and Family, November 20, 1867. Second of two letters.
82. NPV, 00201. Letter to Jane Lampton Clemens and Family, March 15, 1868.

CHAPTER TEN: A BRANCH OF HELL

1. CU-MARK, 00144. Letter to Jane Lampton Clemens and Family, August 9, 1867.
2. CU-MARK, 00156. Letter to Jane Lampton Clemens and Family, November 20, 1867.
3. Stewart, *Reminiscences*, 219–20.
4. NPV, 00162. Letter to Jane Lampton Clemens and Family, November 25, 1867.
5. Stewart, *Reminiscences*, 223.
6. NPV, 00197. Letter to Jane Lampton Clemens and Family, February 21, 1868.

NOTES

7. Scharnhorst, *The Life of Mark Twain*, 1:450.
8. CSmH, 00196. Letter to Mary Mason Fairbanks, February 20, 1868. Editorial note.
9. CSmH, 00183. Letter to Mary Mason Fairbanks, January 24, 1868.
10. Paine, *Mark Twain*, 1:361.
11. Kaplan, *Mr. Clemens*, 69.
12. Ibid., 162.
13. Paine, *Mark Twain*, 2:724.
14. *Mark Twain's Notebooks & Journals*, 1:492. Notebook 10, circa December 1867.
15. Ibid., 492–93.
16. Ibid., 494.
17. Rogers, *Satires & Burlesques*, 463.
18. *Mark Twain's Notebooks & Journals*, 1:491. Notebook 10, circa December 1867.
19. *Alta California*, February 14, 1866.
20. CU-MARK, 12725. Letter to Jane Lampton Clemens and Pamela A. Moffett, January 20, 1868.
21. Fulton, *The Reconstruction of Mark Twain*, 140.
22. Kaplan, *Mr. Clemens*, 68.
23. Fulton, *The Reconstruction of Mark Twain*, 145. Virginia City *Territorial Enterprise*, March 13, 1868.
24. DLC, 00270. Letter to John Russell Young, March 8–10, 1869. March 1869. Editorial note. "The White House Funeral."
25. Fulton, *The Reconstruction of Mark Twain*, 120.
26. Kaplan, *Mr. Clemens*, 64.
27. *AMT*, 3:165. Autobiographical Dictation for October 11, 1907.
28. Ober, *Mark Twain and Medicine*, 125.
29. *Love Letters of Mark Twain*, 43.
30. Lawton, *A Lifetime with Mark Twain*, 62.
31. Fisher, *Abroad with Mark Twain*, 60.
32. *Alta California*, February 5, 1868.
33. *AMT*, 3:165. Autobiographical Dictation for October 11, 1907.
34. NPV, 00175. Letter to Jane Lampton Clemens and Pamela A. Moffett, January 8, 1868.
35. Nissen, *Bret Harte*, 145.
36. Paine, *Mark Twain*, 1:350.
37. CU-MARK, 00165. Letter to Elisha Bliss, Jr., December 2, 1867.
38. *AMT*, 1:372. Autobiographical Dictation for February 21, 1906.
39. TxU-HU 00184. Letter to William Bowen, January 25, 1868.
40. NPV, 00182. Letter to Jane Lampton Clemens and Pamela A. Moffett, January 24, 1868.
41. Ibid.
42. CSmH, 00183. Letter to Mary Mason Fairbanks, January 24, 1868.
43. Paine, *Mark Twain*, 1:359–60.
44. CSmH, 00200. Letter to Mary Mason Fairbanks, March 10, 1868.
45. WU-MU, 02731. Letter to Elisha Bliss, Jr., May 5, 1868.
46. Kaplan, *Mr. Clemens*, 70.
47. CSmH, 0735. Letter to Mary Mason Fairbanks, June 17, 1868.
48. San Francisco *Morning Call*, May 20, 1868.
49. Ibid.
50. MH-H, 00567. Letter to Thomas Bailey Aldrich, January 27, 1871.
51. Benfy, *Kipling's American Years*, 124.
52. Courtney, *The Loveliest Home*, 17.
53. CtY-BR, 00327. Letter to Elisha Bliss, Jr., July 22, 1869.
54. Scharnhorst, *The Life of Mark Twain*, 1:502.
55. CU-MARK, 00400. Letter to Horace E. Bixby, February [6?], 1870.
56. *The Innocents Abroad*, iii.
57. Paine, *Mark Twain*, 1:503.
58. CU-MARK, 01547. Letter to Orion Clemens, March 23, 1878.
59. NN-BGC, 09218. Letter to unidentified person, November 6, 1886.
60. CU-MARK, 50531. Notes by Samuel & Doris Webster on talk with Mrs. Lyon, March 5, 1948.
61. Scharnhorst, *The Life of Mark Twain*, 1:504.
62. Ibid., 555.
63. Ibid.
64. Paine, *Mark Twain*, 1:383.
65. NN-BGC., 02495. Letter to William Dean Howells, October 19, 1875.
66. Lawton, *A Lifetime with Mark Twain*, 92.
67. Clemens, *My Father Mark Twain*, 102.
68. *Mark Twain-Howell Letters*, 391.
69. *Mark Twain's Notebooks*, 244.
70. Butcher, *Southern Literary Journal*, Spring 1969.
71. Howells, *My Mark Twain*, 35.

| 1055 |

NOTES

CHAPTER ELEVEN: "MY HONORED 'SISTER'"

1. CU-MARK, 02746. Letter to Charles J. Langdon, August 21, 1868. Editorial note.
2. Ibid.
3. CU-MARK, 02750. Letter to Olivia L. Langdon, September 7 and 8, 1868. Editorial note.
4. NPV, 02747. Letter to Jane Lampton Clemens and Family, August 24, 1868.
5. Scharnhorst, *The Life of Mark Twain*, 1:473.
6. CU-MARK, 02750. Letter to Olivia L. Langdon, September 7 and 8, 1868.
7. CSmH, 02755. Letter to Mary Mason Fairbanks, October 5, 1868.
8. CU-MARK, 02759. Letter to Olivia L. Langdon, October 18, 1868.
9. Ibid.
10. Ibid.
11. CU-MARK, 02760. Letter to Olivia L. Langdon, October 30, 1868.
12. Courtney, *Joseph Hopkins Twichell*, 129.
13. *Love Letters of Mark Twain*, 317.
14. Tuckey, *Which Was the Dream?*, 170.
15. Courtney, *Joseph Hopkins Twichell*, 129.
16. NN-BGC and CSmH, 02767. Letter to Mary Mason Fairbanks, November 26, 1868.
17. Ibid.
18. CU-MARK, 02768. Letter to Olivia L. Langdon, November 28, 1868.
19. Ibid.
20. Scharnhorst, *The Life of Mark Twain*, 1:481.
21. Bush, *Letters of Mark Twain and Joseph Hopkins Twichell*, 18.
22. Scharnhorst, *The Life of Mark Twain*, 1:481.
23. NPV, 02766. Letter to Jane Lampton Clemens and Family, November 20, 1868. Editorial note.
24. Bush, *Letters of Mark Twain and Joseph Hopkins Twichell*, 16.
25. CLjC, 00212. Letter to Jervis Langdon, December 29, 1868.
26. CU-MARK, 00249. Letter to Olivia Lewis Langdon, February 13, 1869.
27. CU-MARK, 00340. Letter to Charles Warren Stoddard, August 25, 1869.
28. *AMT*, 1:359. Autobiographical Dictation for February 14, 1906.
29. CU-MARK, 00249. Letter to Olivia Lewis Langdon, February 13, 1869. Editorial note.
30. CU-MARK, 00245. Letter to Jane Lampton Clemens and Family, February 5, 1869.
31. CU-MARK, 02752. Letter to Mary Mason Fairbanks, September 24, 1868.
32. CU-MARK, 00322. Letter to Jane Lampton Clemens and Pamela A. Moffett, June 26, 1869. Editorial note.
33. Clemens, *My Father Mark Twain*, 20–21.
34. CtHMTH, 01627. Letter from Olivia Clemens to Olivia Lewis Langdon, February 2, 1879.
35. Fishkin, *Lighting Out*, 78.
36. *AMT*, 1:356. Autobiographical Dictation for February 13, 1906.
37. Willis, *Mark Twain Journal*, Spring 1986.
38. Ibid.
39. NPV, 02762. Letter to Jane Lampton Clemens, November 4, 1868. Editorial note.
40. Fanning, *Mark Twain and Orion Clemens*, 127.
41. CU-MARK, 00388. Letter to Olivia L. Langdon, December 15, 1869. Editorial note.
42. CU-MARK, 00737. Letter to Elisha Bliss, Jr., March 20, 1872. Editorial note.
43. CU-MARK, 00388. Letter to Olivia L. Langdon, December 15, 1869.
44. Elmira *Saturday Evening Review*, August 13, 1870.
45. Eastman, *Harper's Magazine*, May 1938.
46. William Still, *The Underground Railroad*. Copy in the collection of Susan Jaffe Tane.
47. Fishkin, *Lighting Out*, 81.
48. Ward, *American Heritage*, September/October 1990.
49. NPV, 00262. Letter to Elisha Bliss, Jr., March 30, 1869.
50. CU-MARK, 00264. Letter to Olivia L. Langdon, March 2, 1869.
51. Ibid.
52. CSmH, 00219. Letter to Mary Mason Fairbanks, January 7, 1869.
53. CU-MARK, 00289. Letter to Pamela A. Moffett, April 10?, 1869.
54. *North American Review*, December 1903.

NOTES

55. *AMT*, 1:321. Autobiographical Dictation for February 1, 1906.
56. Clemens, *My Father Mark Twain*, 85.
57. Ibid., 16.
58. NPV, 00336. Letter to Pamela A. Moffett, August 20, 1869.
59. Harnsberger, *Mark Twain Family Man*, 57.
60. CtHMTH, 05845. Letter from Olivia Langdon to Mary Mason Fairbanks, January 9, 1870.
61. CU-MARK, 00315. Letter to Jane Lampton Clemens and Family, June 4, 1869.

CHAPTER TWELVE: WEDDING PRESENT

1. CU-MARK, 00252. Letter to Joseph H. Twichell and Family, February 14, 1869.
2. NPV, 10893. Letter to Pamela A. Moffett, July 15, 1886; CU-MARK, 00394. Letter to Olivia L. Clemens, December 27, 1869.
3. CSmH, 00332. Letter to Mary Mason and Abel W. Fairbanks, August 14, 1869.
4. *Mark Twain's Notebooks*, 16–17.
5. NBuHi, 00331. Letter to Elisha Bliss, Jr., August 14, 1869.
6. Kaplan, *Mr. Clemens,* 113.
7. CtHMTH, 00419. Letter from Olivia Clemens to Jervis and Olivia Lewis Langdon, February 6, 1870. Editorial note.
8. Paine, *Mark Twain,* 1:394.
9. Ibid., 396.
10. Sloane, *Mark Twain's Humor,* 446.
11. CtHMTH, 00419. Letter from Olivia Clemens to Jervis and Olivia Lewis Langdon, February 6, 1870.
12. NPV, 00428. Letter to Joel Benton, February 20, 1870.
13. TxU-HU, 02464. Letter to William Bowen, February 6, 1870.
14. CtHMTH, 00427. Letter from Olivia Clemens to Olivia Lewis Langdon, February 16, 1870.
15. CtHMTH, 00419. Letter from Olivia Langdon to Jervis and Olivia Lewis Langdon, February 6, 1870.
16. Scharnhorst, *The Life of Mark Twain,* 1:532.
17. TxU-HU, 02464. Letter to William Bowen, February 6, 1870.
18. CtHMTH, 00423. Letter to Jervis and Olivia Lewis Langdon, February 9, 1870.
19. Scharnhorst, *The Life of Mark Twain,* 1:512.
20. Ibid., 513.
21. CSmH, 00448. Letter to Mary Mason Fairbanks, March 22, 1870.
22. Budd, *Mark Twain: Social Philosopher,* 43.
23. Kaplan, *Mr. Clemens,* 96.
24. Neider, *Mark Twain: Life As I Find It,* 40.
25. Vogelback, *PMLA,* March 1955.
26. Reigstad, *Mark Twain Journal,* Fall 2018.
27. Ibid.
28. Scharnhorst, *The Life of Mark Twain,* 1:542.
29. CU-MARK, 00488. Letter to Olivia L. Clemens, July 8, 1870.
30. Ibid. Editorial note.
31. Fishkin, *Lighting Out,* 82.
32. Duskis, *Forgotten Writings,* 94.
33. Fishkin, *Lighting Out,* 222. "Life on the Isthmus," *Buffalo Express,* October 4, 1870.
34. Fishkin, *Lighting Out,* 231.
35. Neider, *Complete Essays,* 7.
36. Ibid., 8.
37. Ibid.
38. *New York Tribune,* August 28, 1868.
39. Neider, *Mark Twain: Life As I Find It,* 105.
40. CU-MARK, 00679. Letter from Olivia L. Clemens, November 20, 1871.
41. *AMT,* 2:256. Autobiographical Dictation for October 11, 1906.
42. Scharnhorst, *The Life of Mark Twain,* 1:527.
43. Heidig, *Known to Everyone,* 12.
44. Paine, *Mark Twain,* 1:441.
45. CCamarSJ, 00174. Letter to Emeline B. Beach, January 8, 1868.
46. Kaplan, *Mr. Clemens,* 98.
47. Scharnhorst, *The Life of Mark Twain,* 1:522.
48. Kaplan, *Mr. Clemens,* 87.
49. Ibid.
50. NN-BGC, 00547. Letter to John H. Riley, December 2, 1870.
51. *Love Letters of Mark Twain,* 53.
52. Ibid., 49.
53. *AMT,* 1:153. "Ralph Keeler."
54. Webster, *Business Man,* 113.

NOTES

55. Ibid., 106.
56. CU-MARK, 00480. Letter to Jervis and Olivia Lewis Langdon, June 19, 1870.
57. Lawton, *A Lifetime with Mark Twain*, 240.
58. CtHMTH, 00454. Letter from Samuel Langhorne and Olivia Clemens to Susan L. Crane, April 16, 1870.
59. CU-MARK, 11723. Letter to the Buffalo Street Commissioners, May 26, 1870.
60. CU-MARK, 00462. Letter to Elisha Bliss, Jr., May 7, 1870.
61. DLC, 31922. Letter from Susan L. Crane to Anna E. Dickinson, June 14, 1870.
62. *AMT,* 1:360. Autobiographical Dictation for February 14, 1906.
63. CtHSD, 00474. Letter from Olivia Clemens to Alice Hooker Day, May 1870.
64. Scharnhorst, *The Life of Mark Twain,* 1:543.
65. NPV, 00498. Letter to Pamela A. Moffett, August 3, 1870.
66. NPV, 02795. Letter to Alice Hooker Day, January 25, 1871.
67. CU-MARK, 00503. Letter to Ella Wolcott, September 7, 1870.
68. *AMT,* 1:362. Autobiographical Dictation for February 15, 1906.
69. CtY-BR, 00533. Letter to Joseph H. and Harmony C. Twichell, November 12, 1870.
70. CtHSD, 00534. Letter to Jesse C. Haney, November 14, 1870.
71. CSmH, 00551. Letter to Mary Mason Fairbanks, December 17, 1870.
72. CU-MARK, 00576. Letter to Elisha Bliss, Jr., February 15, 1871.
73. CU-MARK, 00579. Letter to Orion Clemens, February 22, 1871.
74. NN-BGC, 02455. Letter to Elisha Bliss, Jr., March 17, 1871.
75. NN-BGC, 00582. Letter to John Henry Riley, March 3, 1871.
76. CLjC, 00631. Letter to James N. Gillis, July 2, 1871.
77. CtHMTH, 11006. Letter to Samuel S. Cox, March 9, 1871.
78. NN-BGC, 02455. Letter to Elisha Bliss, Jr., March 17, 1871.
79. Neider, *Mark Twain: Life As I Find It,* xiv.
80. MH-H, 00627 and 00626. Letter to James Redpath, June 28, 1871.
81. CSmH, 00606. Letter to Mary Mason Fairbanks, April 26, 1871.
82. CU-MARK, 00649. Letter to Orion Clemens, August 31, 1871.
83. CU-MARK, 00677. Letter from Olivia Clemens to Robert M. Howland, November 20, 1871.
84. CU-MARK, 00681. Letter from Olivia L. Clemens, November 28, 1871.
85. CU-MARK, 00691. Letter from Olivia L. Clemens, December 20, 1871.
86. CU-MARK, 00744. Letter to Charles Dudley and Susan L. Warner, April 22, 1872.
87. CU-MARK, 00747. Letter to Orion and Mary E. "Mollie" Clemens, May 15, 1872.
88. *AMT,* 1:433. Autobiographical Dictation for March 22, 1906.
89. Howells, *My Mark Twain,* 11–12.
90. CU-MARK, 47767. Letter from Susan L. Crane to Albert Bigelow Paine, May 25, 1911.
91. Snedecor, *American Literary Realism,* Fall 2012.
92. Ibid.
93. Ibid.

CHAPTER THIRTEEN: CHURCH OF THE HOLY SPECULATORS

1. Snedecor, *American Literary Realism,* Fall 2012.
2. Ibid.
3. *Alta California,* March 3, 1868.
4. Ibid.
5. *AMT,* 1:369. Autobiographical Dictation for February 20, 1906.
6. Neider, *Complete Essays,* 241.
7. NPV, 02759. Letter from Samuel Langhorne and Olivia L. Clemens to Mary E. "Mollie" Clemens, January 5, 1871.
8. MoCgS, 01384. Letter to Jacob H. Burrough, November 1, 1876.
9. CU-MARK, 02759. Letter to Olivia L. Langdon, October 18, 1868. Editorial note.
10. CU-MARK, 00254. Letter to Olivia Clemens, February 15, 1869.
11. CU-MARK, 00681. Letter to Olivia L. Clemens, November 28, 1871.
12. Andrews, *Nook Farm,* 69.
13. Clemens, *North American Review,* November 1930.

NOTES

14. Courtney, *Joseph Hopkins Twichell,* 221.
15. Ibid., 104.
16. Ibid., 106.
17. MH-H and DLC, 01068. Letter to Thomas Bailey Aldrich, March 24, 1874.
18. Ober, *Mark Twain and Medicine,* 249.
19. *Mark Twain–Howells Letters,* 407. Letter to William Dean Howells, June 22, 1882.
20. CU-MARK 12168. Letter from Clara Clemens, July 25, 1906.
21. *AMT,* 2:156. Autobiographical Dictation for July 31, 1906.
22. *Hartford Courant,* May 20, 1875.
23. Bush, *Letters of Mark Twain and Joseph Hopkins Twichell,* 108.
24. CtY-BR, 03342. Letter to Joseph H. and Harmony C. Twichell, December 24, 1885.
25. *Mark Twain's Letters to Will Bowen,* 24.
26. NN-BGC, 00523. Letter to Elisha Bliss, Jr., November 5, 1870.
27. Webster, *Business Man,* 116.
28. CU-MARK, 12784. Letter to Pamela A. Moffett, April 28, 1873.
29. CU-MARK, 00587. Letter to Orion Clemens, March 11 and 13, 1871. Editorial note.
30. Ibid.
31. CU-MARK, 00644. Letter to Olivia L. Clemens, August 10, 1871.
32. CU-MARK, 00730. Letter to Orion Clemens, March 7, 1872.
33. CU-MARK, 12784. Letter to Pamela A. Moffett, April 28, 1873.
34. Scharnhorst, *The Life of Mark Twain,* 1:548.
35. CU-MARK, 47097. Letter from Jane Lampton Clemens to Orion Clemens, November 23, 1873.
36. NPV, 01087. Letter to Jane Lampton Clemens, May 10, 1874.
37. Paine, *Mark Twain,* 1:507.
38. CU-MARK, 00489. Letter to Orion Clemens, July 15, 1870.
39. CU-MARK, 00587. Letter to Orion Clemens, March 13, 1871.
40. Heidig, *Known to Everyone,* 29.
41. CU-MARK, 00502. Letter to Elisha Bliss, Jr., September 4, 1870.
42. Paine, *Mark Twain,* 1:435.
43. Ibid., 438.
44. *Roughing It,* 841.
45. Howe, *Memories of a Hostess,* 246.
46. NHyF, 11405. Letter to David Gray, June 10, 1880.
47. ViU, 00881. Letter to Elisha Bliss, Jr., March 4, 1873.
48. CU-MARK, 00872. Letter to Olivia L. Clemens, February 2, 1873.
49. *Roughing It,* 875.
50. Kruse, *New England Quarterly,* June 1999.
51. *Love Letters of Mark Twain,* 176. Letter to Olivia L. Clemens, August 29, 1872.
52. MTP. Introduction, 1872–73.
53. *South London Press,* September 14, 1872.
54. Ibid.
55. CU-MARK, 00805. Letter to Olivia L. Clemens, September 11, 1872.
56. CU-MARK, 00815. Letter to Olivia L. Clemens, September 28, 1872.
57. CSmH, 00825. Letter to Mary Mason Fairbanks, November 2, 1872.
58. *New England Quarterly,* June 1999.
59. CU-MARK, 00488. Letter to Olivia L. Clemens, July 8, 1870.
60. NPV. Clemens. 20.4. Lyon Howe 1933. 1872–73. *The Gilded Age.*
61. NN5, Private Collection, 00554. Letter to Joseph H. Twichell, January 3, 1871.
62. Kaplan, *Mr. Clemens,* 158.
63. *AMT,* 1:364. Autobiographical Dictation for February 16, 1906.
64. CtHMTH, 00859. Letter from Olivia Clemens to Olivia Lewis Langdon, January 9, 1873.
65. CU-MARK, 02356. Letter to George MacDonald, March 9, 1883.
66. *The Gilded Age,* 74.
67. *AMT,* 1:207. "Random Extracts."
68. *The Gilded Age,* 111.
69. CU-MARK, 00909. Letter to Olivia L. Clemens, April 26, 1873.
70. CU-MARK, 01130. Letter to R. Shelton Mackenzie, September 23, 1874.
71. *The Gilded Age,* 184.
72. Ibid., 322.
73. Kaplan, *Mr. Clemens,* 166.
74. Warner, *Education of the Negro,* 5.
75. Ibid., 7.
76. Ibid., 19.
77. Ibid., 20.
78. Ibid., 25.
79. *The Gilded Age,* 64.
80. Ibid., 316.
81. Webster, *Business Man,* 58.
82. Scharnhorst, *The Complete Interviews,* 214.
83. CU-MARK, 00909. Letter to Olivia L. Clemens, April 26, 1873.

NOTES

84. Chicago *Tribune*, February 1, 1874.
85. MH-H and DLC, 01068. Letter to Thomas Bailey Aldrich, March 24, 1874.
86. CU-MARK, 00917. Letter to Charles Dudley Warner, May 17, 1873. Editorial note.
87. Ibid.
88. MTP. CLjC, 11429. Letter to Andrew Chatto, March 10, 1890.
89. NPV. Clemens. 20.4. Lyon Howe 1933. 1872–73. *The Gilded Age*.

CHAPTER FOURTEEN: MISSISSIPPI STEAMBOAT AND A CUCKOO CLOCK

1. CU-MARK, 00917. Letter to Charles Dudley Warner, May 17, 1873. Editorial note.
2. CSmH, 00947. Letter to Mary Mason Fairbanks, July 6, 1873.
3. *AMT*, 1:330. Autobiographical Dictation for February 5, 1906.
4. IGK, 04137. Letter to Thomas W. Knox, September 10, 1873.
5. CU-MARK, 00994. Letter to Olivia L. Clemens, December 9, 1873.
6. IGK, 04137. Letter to Thomas W. Knox, September 10, 1873.
7. Paine, *Mark Twain*, 1:480.
8. CtHMTH, 00859. Letter from Olivia Clemens to Olivia Lewis Langdon, January 19, 1873.
9. MH-H, 01192. Letter to H. O. Houghton and Company, February 12, 1875.
10. *Architectural Digest*, July 1982.
11. Kaplan, *Mr. Clemens*, 181.
12. Paine, *Mark Twain*, 1:521.
13. *The $30,000 Bequest*, 344.
14. Duquette, *Adirondack Daily Enterprise*, March 31, 1990.
15. Courtney, *The Loveliest Home*, 104.
16. Ober, *Mark Twain Journal*, Spring 2018.
17. Scharnhorst, *Complete Interviews*, 58.
18. CtY-BR, 02040. Letter to "Ignoramus" (pseud.), September 19, 1881.
19. Courtney, *The Loveliest Home*, 89.
20. Crawford, *How Not to Get Rich*, 79.
21. CU-MARK, 01133. Letter to Olivia Lewis Langdon and Family, September 24, 1874.
22. CU-MARK, 01105. Letter to Olivia L. Clemens, July 3, 1874.
23. Ibid.
24. Holzer, *Architectural Digest*, July 1982.
25. Andrews, *Nook Farm*, 83.
26. Hill, *God's Fool*, 89.
27. *Mark Twain's Notebook*, 314.
28. Rasmussen, *Dear Mark Twain*, 172.
29. Howe, *Memories of a Hostess*, 246.
30. MTP. Excerpts from Annie Field's Diary: Entry for April 27–29, 1876.
31. Paine, *Mark Twain*, 1:505.
32. Tuckey, *Which Was the Dream?*, 167.
33. Neider, *Selected Letters*, 189.
34. *Mark Twain's Notebook*, 396. Letter to Orion Clemens, November 29, 1888.
35. CSmH, 00426. Letter to Mary Mason Fairbanks, February 13, 1870.
36. MTP. Excerpts from Annie Field's Diary: Entry for April 6, 1876.
37. Courtney, *The Loveliest Home*, 50.
38. Clemens, *North American Review*, November 1930.
39. Neider, *Selected Letters*, 136.
40. Webster, *Business Man*, 140.
41. Hill, *God's Fool*, xxiv. Circa July 1904, letter to T. R. Lounsbury.
42. CtHMTH, 02185. Letter from Olivia L. Clemens, May 3, 1882.
43. Paine, *Mark Twain*, 2:730.
44. CtHMTH, 01730. Letter from Olivia Clemens to Olivia Lewis Langdon, November 30, 1879.
45. CU-MARK, 03476. Letter from Olivia L. Clemens, October 27, 1886.
46. CU-MARK, 00683. Introduction, 1871–72. Letter from Olivia Clemens, December 3, 1871.
47. Courtney, *The Loveliest Home*, 98.
48. *AMT*, 1:413. Autobiographical Dictation for March 15, 1906.
49. Lawton, *A Lifetime with Mark Twain*, viii.
50. Ibid., 27.
51. Griffin, *A Family Sketch*, 18.
52. *Love Letters of Mark Twain*, 350.
53. CU-MARK, 03572. Letter to Jeannette L. Gilder, May 14, 1887.
54. Jerome and Wisbey, *Mark Twain in Elmira*, 10.
55. *AMT*, 1:333. Autobiographical Dictation for February 5, 1906.
56. CtY-BR, 01097. Letter to Joseph H. and Harmony C. Twichell, June 11, 1874.

NOTES

57. Clemens, *My Father Mark Twain*, 78.
58. Scharnhorst, *Complete Interviews*, 94.
59. Clemens, *My Father Mark Twain*, 84.
60. Dolmetsch, *Our Famous Guest*, xvii.
61. *AMT*, 1:349. Autobiographical Dictation for February 9, 1906.
62. Scharnhorst, *Complete Interviews*, 156.
63. NMh, 04672. Letter to Poultney Bigelow, January 14, 1894.
64. Brooks, *Ordeal of Mark Twain*, 151.
65. Eastman, *Harper's Magazine*, May 1938.
66. Zacks, *Chasing the Last Laugh*, 339.
67. Krause, *American Literature*, November 1967.
68. Clemens, *My Father Mark Twain*, 68.
69. Howells, *My Mark Twain*, 48.
70. NN-BGC, 02515. Letter to William Dean Howells and Elinor M. Howells, August 25, 1877.
71. Griffin, *A Family Sketch*, 45.
72. Ibid., 50.
73. Ibid., 43.
74. Fishkin, *Journal of American Studies*, August 2006.
75. *Mark Twain's Notebooks*, 57.
76. NN-BGC, 02473. Letter to William Dean Howells, September 2, 1874.
77. New York *Evening Post*, May 16, 1876.
78. NN-BGC, 01473. Letter to John Brown, August 25, 1877.
79. Chadwick-Joshua, *The Jim Dilemma*, 20.
80. Ibid.

CHAPTER FIFTEEN: CHARTERING A COMET TO MARS

1. *Mark Twain Day by Day*, 1:693.
2. Kaplan, *Mr. Clemens*, 146.
3. *Mark Twain's Notebook*, 181.
4. Andrews, *Nook Farm*, 103.
5. Paine, *Mark Twain*, 1:541–42.
6. Budd, *Mark Twain: Social Philosopher*, 24.
7. Neider, *Complete Essays*, 666–67.
8. Ibid., 667–68.
9. Trombley, *Mark Twain Journal*, Fall 1996.
10. *Following the Equator*, 300.
11. MTP. Notebook 34, March–December 1895.
12. CU-MARK, 02163. Letter to Mary C. Noyes, February 23, 1882.
13. Ibid.
14. Driscoll, "Mr. Clemens and the Saturday Morning Club of Hartford."
15. Ibid.
16. *Mark Twain to Mrs. Fairbanks*, 218.
17. Driscoll, "Mr. Clemens and the Saturday Morning Club of Hartford."
18. *AMT*, 1:336. Autobiographical Dictation for February 6, 1906.
19. *Hartford Courant*, January 29, 1872.
20. NjP2, Private Collection, 00886. Letter to Tom Hood and George Routledge and Sons, March 10, 1873.
21. CU-MARK, 01205. Letter to Theodore F. Seward, March 8, 1875.
22. Lawton, *A Lifetime with Mark Twain*, 213.
23. TxU-HU, 01188. Letter from P. T. Barnum, January 19, 1875.
24. Ibid.
25. TxU-HU, 01188. Letter to P. T. Barnum, February 3, 1875.
26. IC4, Private Collection, 01051. Letter to P. T. Barnum, February 19, 1875.
27. Crawford, *How Not to Get Rich*, 86.
28. MTP. William Seaver's Squibs about Clemens, 1874–75.
29. *AMT*, 2:55. Autobiographical Dictation for May 24, 1906.
30. Kaplan, *Mr. Clemens*, 303.
31. *Mark Twain's Notebooks & Journals*, 2:56.
32. Courtney, *Joseph Hopkins Twichell*, 215.
33. Paine, *Mark Twain*, 3:1368.
34. Powers, *Smithsonian*, September 2003.
35. Kaplan, *Mr. Clemens*, 63.
36. Shelden, *Mark Twain: Man in White*, 154.
37. Crawford, *How Not to Get Rich*, 71.
38. NHyF, 11406. Letter to David Gray, Sr., September 23, 1880.
39. Paine, *Mark Twain*, 2:726.
40. DLC, 12069. Letter to Gardiner Hubbard, December 27, 1890.
41. CSmH, 01528. Letter to Mary Mason Fairbanks, February 5, 1878.
42. Ibid.
43. NN-BGC, 02476. Letter to William Dean Howells, October 24, 1874.
44. Heidig, *Known to Everyone*, 56.
45. TxU-HU, 02464. Letter to William Bowen, February 6, 1870.
46. CU-MARK, 01122. Letter to John Brown, September 4, 1874.
47. MCo, 07872. Letter to Florence Benson, December 1, 1907.

NOTES

48. NN-BGC, 01247. Letter to William Dean Howells, July 5, 1875.
49. NN-BGC, 02496. Letter from William Dean Howells, November 23, 1875.
50. Ibid.
51. *The Adventures of Tom Sawyer*, 33.
52. Ibid., 49.
53. Ibid., 117.
54. Ibid., 59.
55. Ibid., 165.
56. Ibid., 73.
57. Ibid., 73–74.
58. Ibid., 233.
59. *Atlantic Monthly*, May 1876.
60. *Cincinnati Commercial*, June 26, 1876.
61. NNC, 01386. Letter to Moncure D. Conway, November 2, 1876.
62. MH-H, 01774. Letter to William Dean Howells, March 24, 1880.
63. CU-MARK, 01798. Letter to Rollin M. Daggett, May 1, 1880.
64. CU-MARK, 01349. Letter to Elisha Bliss, Jr., July 22, 1876.
65. NNC, 01394. Letter to Moncure Conway, December 13, 1876.

CHAPTER SIXTEEN: "INVERTEBRATE WITHOUT A COUNTRY"

1. *Mark Twain's Notebooks & Journals*, 2:303. Notebook 18, February–September 1879.
2. *1601, and Is Shakespeare Dead?*, 1. Afterword.
3. Ibid., v–vi.
4. Ibid., vii.
5. Courtney, *Joseph Hopkins Twichell*, 186.
6. *Mark Twain's Notebooks & Journals*, 2:303. Notebook 18, February–September 1879.
7. Paine, *Mark Twain*, 2:580.
8. OrHi, 12541. Letter to George H. Himes, February 16, 1886.
9. ViU, 02161. Letter to Charles Erskine Scott Wood, February 21, 1882.
10. NIC, 06992. Letter to Michael Monahan, February 4, 1905.
11. ViU, 01110. Letter to William Dean Howells, July 22?, 1874.
12. *New York World*, September 17, 1874.
13. Fisher, *Abroad with Mark Twain*, 99.
14. Ibid.
15. *AMT*, 1:207. "Random Extracts."
16. Kaplan, *Mr. Clemens*, 168.
17. *Buffalo Express*, January 14, 1871.
18. NN-BGC, 00582. Letter to John Henry Riley, March 3, 1871.
19. CU-MARK, 31811. Letter from Bret Harte, June 17, 1872.
20. Paine, *Mark Twain*, 2:587.
21. NN-BGC, 02508. Letter to William Dean Howells, October 11, 1876.
22. *AMT*, 2:420. Autobiographical Dictation for February 4, 1907.
23. CU-MARK, 32473. Letter from Bret Harte, March 1, 1877.
24. ViU, 01409. Letter to Pamela A. Moffett, February 27, 1877. Editorial note.
25. Paine, *Mark Twain*, 2:589.
26. *Mark Twain's Notebooks & Journals*, 2:10.
27. Ibid., 40.
28. Ibid., 10.
29. CU-MARK, 12739. Letter to Jane Lampton Clemens, July 12, 1877.
30. CU-MARK, 01457. Letter from Olivia L. Clemens, July 28, 1877.
31. CU-MARK, 01459. Letter from Olivia L. Clemens, July 29, 1877.
32. CU-MARK, 01066. Letter to William Dean Howells, June 21, 1877.
33. MH-H, 01573. Letter to William Dean Howells, June 27, 1878.
34. Scharnhorst, *Twain in His Own Time*, 124.
35. CU-MARK, 01066. Letter to William Dean Howells, June 21, 1877.
36. CU-MARK, 11173. Letter to William Dean Howells, June 21, 1877. Editorial note.
37. Ibid.
38. MH-H, 01568. Letter to William Dean Howells, April 15, 1879.
39. *AMT*, 2:424. Autobiographical Dictation for February 4, 1907.
40. CU-MARK, 01415. Letter to Susan L. Crane, April 23, 1877.
41. *Mark Twain's Notebooks & Journals*, 2:9.
42. Ibid., 36.
43. Ibid., 18–19.
44. CtY-BR, 01444. Letter to Joseph H. Twichell, June 27, 1877.
45. OFH, 01366. Letter to Charles Warren Stoddard, September 20, 1876.

NOTES

46. NPV, 01530. Letter to Jane Lampton Clemens, February 17, 1878.
47. Boston *Evening Transcript*, December 18, 1877.
48. Paine, *Mark Twain,* 2:605.
49. Ibid., 606.
50. MH-H, 01184. Letter to Ralph Waldo Emerson, December 27, 1887.
51. Paine, *Mark Twain,* 2:607.
52. CSmH, 01528. Letter to Mary Mason Fairbanks, February 5, 1878.
53. *Mark Twain's Notebooks & Journals,* 2:41.
54. MB, 01546. Letter to Charles Warren Stoddard, March 20, 1878.
55. NN-BGC, 02523. Letter to William Dean Howells, May 4, 1878.
56. CU-MARK, 12744. Letter from Olivia Clemens to Susan L. Crane, May 7, 1878.
57. *Mark Twain's Notebooks & Journals,* 2:81.
58. CU-MARK, 12745. Letter to Susan L. Crane, June 2, 1878.
59. *A Tramp Abroad,* 83–84.
60. *Mark Twain's Notebooks & Journals,* 2:86.
61. MH-H, 01573. Letter to William Dean Howells, June 27, 1878.
62. *A Tramp Abroad,* 200.
63. *Mark Twain's Notebooks & Journals,* 2:147. Notebook 15, entry for August 26, 1878.
64. Ibid.
65. Ibid., 149. Notebook 15, entry for August 27, 1878.
66. Ibid., 165. Entry for August 28, 1878.
67. Ibid.
68. *Letters of Mark Twain and Joseph Hopkins Twichell,* 100.
69. Paine, *Mark Twain,* 2:631.
70. CtY-BR, 02800. Letter to Joseph H. Twichell, September 9, 1878.
71. *Mark Twain's Notebooks & Journals,* 2:154.
72. Ibid., 177.
73. Ibid., 182. Notebook 16, entry for September 13, 1878.
74. Ibid., 156.
75. Ibid., 191.
76. Ibid., 157.
77. Ibid., 221. Notebook 17, entry for October 14, 1878.
78. Ibid., 230.
79. CtY-BR, 01603. Letter to Joseph H. Twichell, November 3, 1878.
80. CU-MARK, 01610. Letter to Jane Lampton Clemens and Pamela A. Moffett, December 1, 1878.
81. CtHMTH, 01621. Letter to Olivia Lewis Langdon, January 19, 1879.
82. Ibid. Letter from Olivia Clemens to Olivia Lewis Langdon, January 19, 1879.
83. NIC, 01614. Letter to Bayard Taylor, December 14, 1878.
84. CU-MARK, 01794. Letter to Lucius Fairchild, April 28, 1880.
85. CtHMTH, 01645. Letter to Olivia Lewis Langdon, March 30, 1879.
86. *Mark Twain's Notebooks & Journals,* 2:309.
87. Ibid., 2:319.
88. Ibid., 297.
89. Ibid., 320–22. Notebook 18, February–September 1879.
90. Ibid., 320.
91. Ibid., 319.
92. CU-MARK, 01640. Letter from Olivia Clemens to Olivia Lewis Langdon, March 16, 1879.
93. Ibid.
94. *Mark Twain's Notebooks & Journals,* 2:486.
95. Ibid., 337.
96. Ibid., 348.
97. Ibid.
98. Ibid.
99. Ibid., 289.
100. Ibid.,
101. Howells, *My Mark Twain,* 31.
102. CU-MARK, 12746. Letter from Olivia L. Clemens to Susan L. Crane, June 16, 1878.
103. Paine, *Mark Twain,* 2:650.
104. CU-MARK, 02877. Letter to Olivia L. Clemens, November 27, 1879.
105. *Mark Twain's Notebooks & Journals,* 2:4.
106. ViU, 01792. Letter to Hjalmar H. Boyesen, April 23, 1880.
107. CBev3, 02814. Letter to John Brown, August 14 and 15, 1880.

CHAPTER SEVENTEEN: TOAST TO THE BABIES

1. Budd, *Mark Twain: Social Philosopher,* 86.
2. Ibid., 59.
3. Moser, *Mark Twain Journal,* Summer 1982.
4. Cohn, *Mark Twain Journal,* Fall 2015.
5. Ibid.

NOTES

6. McCord, *American Literary Realism*, Autumn 1983.
7. NN-BGC, 02505. Letter to William Dean Howells, September 14, 1876.
8. *AMT*, 2:424. Autobiographical Dictation for February 4, 1907.
9. OFH, 02198. Letter to Rutherford B. Hayes, April 10, 1882.
10. *Letters of Mark Twain and Joseph Hopkins Twichell*, 127.
11. CU-MARK, 32413. Letter from Sherrard Clemens, September 2, 1876.
12. Paine, *Mark Twain*, 2:581.
13. Scharnhorst, *Complete Interviews*, 6.
14. CU-MARK, 01702. Letter to William E. Strong, October 28, 1879.
15. CU-MARK, 01708. Letter to William E. Strong, November 6, 1879.
16. *AMT*, 1:68. "The Chicago G.A.R. Festival."
17. CtHMTH, 01713. Letter to Olivia L. Clemens, November 11, 1879.
18. Ibid.
19. CU-MARK, 01714. Letter to Olivia L. Clemens, November 12, 1879.
20. Ibid.
21. Chernow, *Grant*, 888.
22. CU-MARK, 01715. Letter to Olivia L. Clemens, November 14, 1879.
23. Ibid.
24. MH-H, 01718. Letter to William Dean Howells, November 17, 1879.
25. MH-H, 01812. Letter to William Dean Howells, June 15, 1880.
26. Paine, *Mark Twain*, 2:693.
27. Ibid.
28. Fulton, *The Reconstruction of Mark Twain*, 163–64.
29. CU-MARK, 09943. Letter to Herbert E. Hill, November 3, 1880.
30. ViU, 01891. Letter to James A. Garfield, January 12, 1881.
31. CU-MARK, 40678. Letter from Frederick Douglass, January 22, 1881.
32. CtHMTH, 09007. Letter to Franklin G. Whitmore, August 18, 1881.
33. CU-MARK, 02012. Letter to Charles Eliot Norton, August 23, 1881.
34. *Mark Twain's Notebooks & Journals*, 1:549.
35. CtHMTH, 16521. Letter from Olivia L. Clemens to Olivia Lewis Langdon, April 27, 1879.
36. Wheeler, *Yesterdays in a Busy Life*, 325.
37. MB, 10064. Letter to Karl Gerhardt, May 30, 1881.
38. NPV, 01928. Letter to Pamela A. Moffett, March 16, 1881.
39. MB, 02049. Letter to Karl and Hattie J. Gerhardt, October 9, 1881.
40. Holzer, *Architectural Digest*, July 1982.
41. Andrews, *Nook Farm*, 94.
42. CU-MARK, 32732. Letter from David Watt Bowser, March 16, 1880.
43. TxU-HU, 01772. Letter to David Watt Bowser, March 20, 1880.
44. Ibid.
45. Ibid.
46. TxU-HU, 02124. Letter to David Watt Bowser, December 22, 1880.
47. TxU-HU, 02147. Letter to David Watt Bowser, January 10, 1882.
48. *Mark Twain's Notebook*, 183. Notebook entry, May 26, 1885.
49. *Mark Twain's Notebooks & Journals*, 2:49.
50. NPV. Clemens. 20.7. Lyon Howe 1935. 1881. *Prince & Pauper*.
51. *New York World*, May 11, 1879.
52. MH-H, 01767. Letter to William Dean Howells, March 5, 1880.
53. NN-BGC, 02539. Letter to William Dean Howells, March 11, 1880.
54. *The Prince and the Pauper*, xvi.
55. CU-MARK, 01899. Letter to Annie E. Lucas, January 31, 1881.
56. CU-MARK, 32889. Letter from William Dean Howells, December 13, 1880.
57. NN-BGC, 02546. Letter to William Dean Howells, December 24, 1880.
58. *The Prince and the Pauper*, 237.
59. Ibid., 166.
60. Kaplan, *Mr. Clemens*, 237.
61. CU-MARK, 12460. Letter to Page M. Baker, October 3, 1882.
62. MH-H, 02159. Letter to James R. Osgood, February 12, 1881.
63. ViU, 02149. Letter to Hjalmar H. Boyesen, January 11, 1882.
64. MoSW, 02112. Letter to James R. Osgood, December 8, 1881.
65. CU-MARK, 02108. Letter to Olivia L. Clemens, December 2, 1881.
66. CU-MARK, 02811. Letter to Rollin M. Dagett, May 24, 1880.
67. MoSW, 02112. Letter to James R. Osgood, December 8, 1881.
68. *Mark Twain Day by Day*, 1:730.

NOTES

69. ViU, 02164. Letter to Edward H. House, February 23, 1882.
70. *Pall Mall Gazette,* January 8, 1882.
71. *Mark Twain's Notebooks & Journals,* 191.
72. Rasmussen, *Dear Mark Twain,* 89.
73. CU-MARK, 41003. Letter from Joseph T. Goodman, January 29, 1882.

CHAPTER EIGHTEEN: "INSPIRED BUGGER OF A MACHINE"

1. CU-MARK, 12812. Letter to Charles Hopkins Clark, November 9, 1884.
2. Ibid.
3. *Mark Twain's Notebook,* 188. Notebook entry, October 3, 1885.
4. *Mark Twain's Notebook,* 193. Notebook entry circa October 4, 1887.
5. *Mark Twain's Letters,* 2:664.
6. Clemens, *My Father Mark Twain,* 82.
7. NPV, 00201. Letter to Jane Lampton Clemens and Family, March 15, 1868.
8. ViU, 01970. Letter to Charles Webster, June 5, 1881.
9. NPV, 02285. Letter to Charles L. Webster, October 3, 1882.
10. Crawford, *How Not to Get Rich,* 84.
11. NPV, 01763. Letter to Orion Clemens, February 26, 1880.
12. *Mark Twain Day by Day,* 1:745.
13. NPV, 01934. Letter to Dan Slote, March 31, 1881.
14. CU-MARK, 40761. Letter from Charles L. Webster, April 26, 1881.
15. NPV, 01940. Letter to Charles L. Webster, April 29, 1881.
16. NPV, 01948. Letter to Charles L. Webster, May 6, 1881.
17. CU-MARK, UCLC, 40773. Letter from Charles L. Webster, May 18, 1881.
18. CSmH, 02162. Letter to Mary Mason Fairbanks, February 21, 1882.
19. NPV, 02008. Letter to Charles Webster, August 17, 1881.
20. CSmH, 02162. Letter to Mary Mason Fairbanks, February 21, 1882.
21. CU-MARK, 41073. Letter from Mary Mason Fairbanks, March 13, 1882.
22. *AMT,* 1:102. "The Machine Episode."
23. Neider, *Selected Letters,* 186.
24. *AMT,* 1:103. "The Machine Episode."
25. NPV, 02055. Letter to Charles L. Webster, October 18, 1881.
26. DLC, 01941. Letter to John Russell Young, April 29, 1881.
27. NPV, 02066. Letter to Charles L. Webster, October 25, 1881.
28. Courtney, *The Loveliest Home,* 117.
29. CU-MARK, 40935. Letter from Charles L. Webster, December 3, 1881.
30. CU-MARK, 40939. Letter from Charles L. Webster, December 6, 1881.
31. CU-MARK, 39322. Letter from Alexander & Green to Charles L. Webster, December 24, 1881.
32. CU-MARK, 40973. Letter from Charles L. Webster, January 5, 1882.
33. NPV, 02876. Letter to Charles L. Webster, April 8, 1883.
34. Lawton, *A Lifetime with Mark Twain,* 104–5.
35. *Mark Twain's Notebooks,* 230. 1899. "How to Make History Dates Work for Children."
36. *Mark Twain's Letters,* 1:435.
37. *Europe and Elsewhere,* 352.
38. NPV, 02845. Letter to Charles Webster, October 3/4, 1883.
39. NPV, 02413. Letter from Charles Webster, July 1, 1884.
40. NN-BGC, 02572. Letter to William Dean Howells, August 22, 1883.
41. ViU, 02844. Letter to Edward H. House, October 1, 1883.
42. CU-MARK, 41642. Letter from Joseph H. Twichell, September 8, 1883.
43. Courtney, *Joseph Hopkins Twichell,* 215.
44. Kaplan, *Mr. Clemens,* 253.
45. Crawford, *How Not to Get Rich,* 107.
46. Paine, *Mark Twain,* 2:702.
47. NN-BGC, 02549. Letter to William Dean Howells, February 21, 1881.
48. Ibid.
49. Ibid.
50. Ibid.
51. Paine, *Mark Twain,* 2:703.
52. Ibid., 704.
53. CU-MARK, 40712. Letter from Augustus Saint-Gaudens, March 2, 1881.
54. MH-H, 01918. Letter from Olivia L. Clemens to Elinor M. Howells, February 28, 1881.
55. CU-MARK, 40715. Letter from Hattie J. Gerhardt to Samuel L. and Olivia L. Clemens, March 4, 1881.

| 1065 |

NOTES

56. CU-MARK, 02881. Letter to the Gerhardts, June 14–25, 1883.
57. CU-MARK, 40777. Letter from Hattie J. Gerhardt, May 24, 1881.
58. MH-H, 02150. Letter to William Dean Howells, January 18, 1882.
59. CU-MARK, 02302. Letter to Karl and Hattie J. Gerhardt, December 4 [?], 1882.
60. CU-MARK, 41597. Letter from William Dean Howells, July 10, 1883.
61. CU-MARK, 41364. Letter from Karl Gerhardt to Samuel L. and Olivia L. Clemens, October 31, 1882.
62. Cummings, *Charles Ethan Porter*, 53.
63. CtHMTH, 02818. Letter to Karl and Hattie J. Gerhardt, August 1, 1883.
64. CtY-BR, 02969. Letter to Karl and Hattie J. Gerhardt, May 4, 1884.
65. *Hartford Daily Times*, December 18, 1877.
66. Cummings, *Charles Ethan Porter*, 42.
67. MB, 02083. Letter to Karl and Hattie J. Gerhardt, November 7, 1881.
68. CU-MARK, 41048. Letter from Charles Ethan Porter to Samuel L. and Olivia L. Clemens, March 1, 1882.
69. Hawkins, *African American Agency*, 146.
70. CU-MARK, 02380. Letter to Karl and Hattie J. Gerhardt, May 1, 1883.
71. Ibid.

CHAPTER NINETEEN: "HALLELUJAH JENNINGS"

1. Griffin, *A Family Sketch*, 131.
2. CU-MARK, 01455. Letter to Olivia Susan "Susy" Clemens, July 19, 1877.
3. CU-MARK, 01454. Letter to Clara Clemens, July 19, 1877.
4. *AMT*, 1:336–37. Autobiographical Dictation for February 6, 1906.
5. Ibid., 337.
6. Scharnhorst, *Twain in His Own Time*, 99.
7. Griffin, *A Family Sketch*, 73–74.
8. CU-MARK, 01451. Letter to Olivia Susan "Susy" Clemens, July 16, 1877.
9. Clemens, *Awake to a Perfect Day*, 16.
10. Ibid., 117.
11. Ibid., 52.
12. CU-MARK, 08513. Letter from Jean Clemens to Marguerite Schmitt, December 21, 1909.
13. MH-H, 03496. Letter to William Dean Howells, December 12, 1886.
14. Harnsberger, *Mark Twain Family Man*, 61.
15. *Mark Twain Day by Day*, 1:1043. Diary of Olivia L. Clemens, June 12, 1885.
16. Paine, *Mark Twain*, 2:638.
17. *Mark Twain's Notebooks*, 90. "Advice to Youth."
18. Willis, *Mark and Livy*, 150–51.
19. Neider, *Mark Twain: Life As I Find It*, 210.
20. ViU, 03427. Letter to Koto House, July 26, 1886.
21. Griffin, *A Family Sketch*, 93. "A Record of the Small Foolishnesses."
22. *AMT*, 1:338. Autobiographical Dictation for February 7, 1906.
23. Griffin, *A Family Sketch*, 157. "Mark Twain by Susy Clemens."
24. Ibid., 77. "A Record of the Small Foolishnesses."
25. Paine, *Mark Twain*, 2:577.
26. MH-H, 07538. Letter to Witter Bynner, October 5, 1906.
27. Griffin, *A Family Sketch*, 68. "A Record of the Small Foolishnesses."
28. Harnsberger, *Mark Twain Family Man*, 49.
29. Griffin, *A Family Sketch*, 15.
30. Ibid., 13.
31. Ibid., 65–66. "A Record of the Small Foolishnesses."
32. *AMT*, 2:224. Autobiographical Dictation for September 5, 1906.
33. CtHMTH, 01595. Letter to Olivia Lewis Langdon, September 13, 1878.
34. Clemens, *Awake to a Perfect Day*, 24.
35. Courtney, *The Loveliest Home*, 45.
36. Clemens, *My Father Mark Twain*, 85.
37. Griffin, *A Family Sketch*, 76.
38. CU-MARK, 03686. Letter from Clara Clemens to Grace E. King, December 28, 1887.
39. Harnsberger, *Mark Twain Family Man*, 123.
40. CU-MARK, 03857. Letter from Clara Clemens to Grace E. King, February 3, 1889.
41. CU-MARK, 01870. Letter to Pamela A. Moffett, December 11, 1880.
42. NHyF, 11407. Letter to Martha G. Gray, November 17, 1880.

NOTES

43. CU-MARK, 02822. Letter to Jane Lampton Clemens, August 16, 1883.
44. Wheeler, *Yesterdays in a Busy Life*, 326.
45. NPV, 03602. Letter to Pamela A. Moffett, July 12, 1887.
46. Griffin, *A Family Sketch*, 95.
47. CSmH, 04101. Letter to Mary M. Fairbanks, October 13, 1890.
48. NPV, 03611. Letter to Jane Lampton Clemens, July 24, 1887.
49. ViU, 03015. Letter to Edward H. House, October 31, 1884.
50. NPV. Clemens. 20.1. Lyon Howe. Jean as a child.
51. CLjC, 02177. Letter to Karl and Hattie J. Gerhardt, March 21, 1882.
52. CU-MARK, 02230. Letter to John Garth, July 3, 1882.
53. CU-MARK, 02289. Letter to Jane Lampton Clemens, October 9, 1882.
54. CU-MARK, 01632. Letter to James R. Osgood, January 21, 1883.
55. CLjC, 02803. Letter to James R. Osgood, April 6, 1883.
56. CU-MARK, 02380. Letter to Karl and Hattie J. Gerhardt, May 1, 1883.
57. CSmH, 02384. Letter to Mary Mason Fairbanks, May 7, 1883.
58. CU-MARK, 13781. Letter to Thomas Bailey Aldrich, March 28, 1883.
59. ViU, 03015. Letter to Edward H. House, October 31, 1884.

CHAPTER TWENTY: TWINS OF GENIUS

1. DLC, 02146. Letter to John Russell Young, January 9, 1882.
2. Budd, *Mark Twain: Social Philosopher*, 91.
3. Ibid., 89.
4. Davis, CivilWarNews.com, September 2022.
5. CU-MARK, 02208. Letter to Olivia L. Clemens, April 29, 1882.
6. Fatout, *Mark Twain Speaking*, 295.
7. CU-MARK, 02190. Letter to Olivia L. Clemens, May 17, 1882.
8. Budd, *Mark Twain: Social Philosopher*, 89.
9. Chicago *Tribune*, July 9, 1886.
10. *Life on the Mississippi*, 119.
11. MTP. CU-MARK, 02251. Letter from Olivia L. Clemens to Samuel E. Moffett, August 13, 1882.
12. CtY-BR, 02271. Letter to Joseph H. Twichell, September 19, 1882.
13. *Mark Twain's Notebooks & Journals*, 2:501. Notebook 20, January 1882–February 1883.
14. ViU, 02331. Letter to James R. Osgood, January 6, 1883.
15. *Mark Twain's Notebooks & Journals*, 2:435. Letter to Charles Webster, January 3, 1883.
16. CU-MARK, 01845. Letter to Orion Clemens, October 24, 1880.
17. GEU, 02114. Letter to Joel Chandler Harris, December 12, 1881.
18. CtY-BR, 02270. Letter to George MacDonald, September 19, 1882.
19. Cardwell, *New England Quarterly*, June 1973.
20. NPV, 02330. Letter to Charles L. Webster, January 5?, 1883.
21. ViU, 02292. Letter to James R. Osgood, October 18, 1882.
22. NPV, 02330. Letter to Charles L. Webster, January 5?, 1883.
23. *Mark Twain's Notebooks & Journals*, 2:506.
24. NPV, 02837. Letter to Charles L. Webster, 1883 [n.d.].
25. MH-H, 02372. Letter to James R. Osgood, April 17, 1883.
26. *Mark Twain Day by Day*, 1:893.
27. New Orleans *Times-Democrat*, May 20, 1883.
28. Kaplan, *Mr. Clemens*, 248.
29. CU-MARK, 41714. Letter from Joseph T. Goodman, December 8, 1883.
30. MH-H, 02872. Letter to James R. Osgood, December 21, 1883.
31. NN-B, 02573. Letter to William Dean Howells, January 7, 1884.
32. MH-H, 02914. Letter to William Dean Howells, February 9, 1884.
33. NPV, 02876. Letter to Charles L. Webster, April 8, 1883.
34. LNT, 08821. Letter to George Washington Cable, June 4, 1883.
35. Turner, *Mark Twain and George W. Cable*, 7.
36. LNT, 01985. Letter to George Washington Cable, July 17, 1881.
37. *Mark Twain–Howells Letters*, 392.

NOTES

38. NN-BGC, 02568. Letter to William Dean Howells, November 4, 1882.
39. LNT, 02336. Letter to George Washington Cable, January 15, 1883.
40. *Hartford Courant,* March 30, 1883.
41. LNT, 41510. Letter from George Washington Cable to his wife, April 3, 1883.
42. *Hartford Courant,* April 5, 1883.
43. LNT, 41516. Letter from George Washington Cable to his wife, April 5, 1883.
44. *AMT,* 3:166. Autobiographical Dictation for October 11, 1907.
45. MH-H, 02858. Letter to William Dean Howells, November 21, 1883.
46. CU-MARK, 02910. Letter to Francis E. Bliss, February 7, 1884.
47. *Mark Twain Day by Day,* 1:931.
48. ViU, 02923. Letter to Edward H. House, February 27, 1884.
49. CLjC, 02926. Letter to Karl and Hattie J. Gerhardt, March 5, 1884.
50. CU-MARK, 41785. Letter from George Washington Cable, February 16, 1884.
51. Lawton, *A Lifetime with Mark Twain,* 259.
52. ViU, 04894. Letter to John Horne, June 19, 1895.
53. Kaplan, *Mr. Clemens,* 258.
54. NPV, 01499. Letter to Charles L. Webster, July 15, 1884.
55. Webster, *Business Man,* 270–71.
56. NN-BGC, 02958. Letter to James B. Pond, October 23, 1884.
57. Cable, *Century Magazine,* January 1885.
58. Ibid.
59. Ibid.
60. Turner, *Mark Twain and George W. Cable,* 47.
61. ViU, 03020. Letter to Chatto & Windus, November 5, 1884.
62. *New York Sun,* November 19, 1884.
63. Turner, *Mark Twain and George W. Cable,* 50.
64. CU-MARK, 03024. Letter to Olivia L. Clemens, November 12, 1884.
65. Turner, *Mark Twain and George W. Cable,* 51–52.
66. Ibid., 58.
67. NN-BGC, 03025. Letter to James B. Pond, November 15, 1884.
68. Turner, *Mark Twain and George W. Cable,* 60.
69. CU-MARK, 42337. Letter from George Washington Cable to his wife, November 25, 1884.
70. Fatout, *Mark Twain Speaking,* 210.
71. *Baltimore Morning Herald,* November 29, 1884.
72. Turner, *Mark Twain and George W. Cable,* 134.
73. NN-BGC, 02601. Letter to James B. Pond, December 22, 1884.
74. MTP. Notebook 40, January 1898–July 1899. Entry for March 11, 1899.
75. CU-MARK, 03029. Letter from Olivia Langdon Clemens, November 21, 1884.
76. Paine, *Mark Twain,* 2:784.
77. Turner, *Mark Twain and George W. Cable,* 66.
78. *AMT,* 1:392. Autobiographical Dictation for March 6, 1906.
79. Scharnhorst, *Twain in His Own Time,* 147.
80. Ibid.
81. *Love Letters of Mark Twain,* 230.
82. CU-MARK, 03078. Letter to Olivia L. Clemens, December 30, 1884.
83. CU-MARK, 03059. Letter to Olivia L. Clemens, December 14, 1884.
84. NN-BGC, 02631, Letter to James B. Pond, January 15, 1886.
85. Scharnhorst, *Complete Interviews,* 57.
86. Ibid.
87. CU-MARK, 03097. Letter to Olivia L. Clemens, January 1, 1885.
88. CU-MARK, 03104. Letter to Olivia L. Clemens, January 7, 1885.
89. CU-MARK, 03107. Letter to Olivia L. Clemens, January 8, 1885.
90. Turner, *Mark Twain and George W. Cable,* 83.
91. Ibid., 84.
92. Ibid., 94.
93. CU-MARK, 03104. Letter to Olivia L. Clemens, January 7, 1885.
94. CU-MARK, 03150. Letter to Olivia L. Clemens, February 3, 1885.
95. CtHMTH, 03142. Letter from Olivia L. Clemens, January 9, 1885.
96. CU-MARK, 03116. Letter to Olivia L. Clemens, January 14, 1885.
97. Ibid.
98. CU-MARK, 03148. Letter to Olivia L. Clemens, February 1, 1885.
99. CU-MARK, 03153. Letter to Olivia L. Clemens, February 4, 1885.

NOTES

100. CU-MARK, 03148. Letter to Olivia L. Clemens, February 1, 1885.
101. CU-MARK, 03135. Letter from Olivia L. Clemens, January 25, 1885.
102. CU-MARK, 03166. Letter to Olivia L. Clemens, February 15, 1885.
103. Turner, *Mark Twain and George W. Cable,* 107.
104. CU-MARK, 03171. Letter to Olivia L. Clemens, February 17, 1885.
105. CU-MARK, 03158. Letter to Olivia L. Clemens, February 28, 1885.
106. NN-BGC, 02605. Letter to William Dean Howells, February 27, 1885.
107. NPV, 03134. Letter to Charles L. Webster, January 25, 1885.
108. Cardwell, *Twins of Genius,* 107–8.
109. Ibid., 108.
110. LNT, 03229. Letter to George Washington Cable, May 17, 1885.
111. Griffin, *A Family Sketch,* 122.
112. Harnsberger, *Mark Twain Family Man,* 81.
113. NN-BGC, 02606. Letter to James B. Pond, March 14, 1885.
114. CtHMTH, 10660. Letter from Olivia L. Clemens, April 9, 1885.

CHAPTER TWENTY-ONE: "A SOUND HEART & A DEFORMED CONSCIENCE"

1. *AMT,* 1:372. Autobiographical Dictation for February 21, 1906.
2. Ibid.
3. Webster, *Business Man,* 217.
4. NPV, 02888. Letter from Olivia L. Clemens to Charles L. Webster, January 11, 1884.
5. Webster, *Business Man,* 259. Letter to Charles L. Webster, June 6, 1884.
6. NPV, 01293. Letter to Charles L. Webster, September 1, 1884.
7. Ibid.
8. NPV, 02098. Letter to Charles L. Webster, November 24, 1881.
9. Webster, *Business Man,* 284.
10. NPV, 03068. Letter to Charles L. Webster, December 23, 1884.
11. CU-MARK, 03100. Letter from Olivia L. Clemens, January 3, 1885.
12. Scharnhorst, *Complete Interviews,* 69.
13. GEU, 01997. Letter to Joel Chandler Harris, August 10, 1881.
14. NN-BGC, 02503. Letter to William Dean Howells, August 9, 1876.
15. MB, 02300. Letter to the Gerhardts July 2, 1883.
16. CU-MARK, 02616. Letter to Jane, Mary E. "Mollie" and Orion Clemens, July 21, 1883.
17. NN-BGC, 02571. Letter to William Dean Howells, July 20, 1883.
18. *AMT,* 1:397. Autobiographical Dictation for March 8, 1906.
19. Blair, *Mark Twain's Hannibal, Huck & Tom,* 31. "Villagers of 1840–3."
20. Driscoll, *Mark Twain Among the Indians,* 13.
21. *AMT,* 2:413. Autobiographical Dictation for February 1, 1907.
22. GEU, 01997. Letter to Joel Chandler Harris, August 10, 1881.
23. Fishkin, *Was Huck Black?,* 16.
24. "Sociable Jimmy," *New York Times,* November 29, 1874.
25. *Adventures of Huckleberry Finn,* "Notice."
26. Ibid., xxii.
27. Ibid., 52–53.
28. MTP. Notebook 35, May–October 1895. Entry for late August 1895.
29. *Adventures of Huckleberry Finn,* 34.
30. *Times Literary Supplement,* August 21, 2020.
31. *Adventures of Huckleberry Finn,* 279.
32. Ibid., 40.
33. Ibid., 158.
34. Ibid., 201.
35. Ibid.
36. Ibid., 202.
37. Ibid., 105.
38. Ibid., 183.
39. Ibid., 146.
40. Ibid., 147.
41. Ibid., 190.
42. Ibid., 362.
43. Als, *New Yorker,* February 11, 2002.
44. Sloane, *Mark Twain's Humor,* 228.
45. Jackson, *The Jim Dilemma,* xi–xii.
46. Fishkin, *Lighting Out,* 112.
47. Fishkin, *Was Huck Black?,* 80.
48. Lester, *Mark Twain Journal,* Fall 1984.

NOTES

49. National Public Radio interview, March 22, 2024.
50. Paine, *Mark Twain*, 2:771.
51. Ibid., 773.
52. Willis, *Mark and Livy*, 157.
53. *Mark Twain Day by Day*, 1:951.
54. Paine, *Mark Twain*, 2:793.
55. *AMT*, 1:372. Autobiographical Dictation for February 21, 1906.
56. NPV, 03190. Letter to Charles L. Webster, March 16, 1885.
57. *Mark Twain Day by Day*, 3:30.
58. Ibid., 705.
59. *Mark Twain's Letters*, 2:643. Letter to William Dean Howells, February 23, 1907.
60. TxU-HU, 05814. Letter to Dora C. Bowen, June 6, 1900.
61. *Mark Twain Day by Day*, 2:590.
62. Boston *Evening Traveler*, March 5, 1885; Shannon, *The Mark Twain Annual*, 2021.
63. Shannon, *The Mark Twain Annual*, 2021.
64. NPV, 03205. Letter to Charles L. Webster, April 4, 1885.
65. NPV, 03207. Letter to Charles L. Webster, April 5, 1885.
66. Powers, *Mark Twain*, 490.
67. London *Saturday Review*, January 31, 1885.
68. *Adventures of Huckleberry Finn*, xxv.
69. Powers, *Mark Twain*, 494.
70. *The Tragedy of Pudd'nhead Wilson*, xi.
71. Kaplan, *Mr. Clemens*, 268.
72. Boston *Transcript*, March 17, 1885.
73. CU-MARK, 03192. Letter to Charles L. Webster, March 18, 1885.
74. NPV, 03219. Letter to Pamela A. Moffett, April 15, 1885.
75. GEU, 03319. Letter to Joel Chandler Harris, November 29, 1885.
76. CU-MARK, 03179. Letter to Frank A. Nichols, March 28, 1885.
77. CU-MARK, 33500. Letter to Fred L. Silvers, July 16, 1902.

CHAPTER TWENTY-TWO: PURE MUGWUMP

1. Scharnhorst, *Complete Interviews*, 10.
2. Courtney, *The Loveliest Home*, 94.
3. Courtney, *Joseph Hopkins Twichell*, 203.
4. Neider, *Complete Essays*, 580.
5. BGC, 02586. Letter to William Dean Howells, August 31, 1884.
6. *Mark Twain's Notebooks & Journals*, 3:52.
7. NN-BGC, 02587. Letter to William Dean Howells, September 17, 1884.
8. Fulton, *The Reconstruction of Mark Twain*, 164.
9. ViU, 03020. Letter to Chatto & Windus, November 5, 1884.
10. McCord, *American Literary Realism*, Autumn 1893. Speech before the Monday Evening Club, 1887.
11. MTP. Notebook 43, 1900. Entry for August 29, 1900.
12. *Europe and Elsewhere*, 405. "Corn-Pone Opinions."
13. Duskis, *Forgotten Writings*, 42.
14. Howe, *Memories of a Hostess*, 252–53.
15. NN-BGC, 02511. Letter to William Dean Howells, July 4, 1877.
16. Paine, *Mark Twain*, 2:691.
17. Fisher, *Abroad with Mark Twain*, 42.
18. MH-H, 01843. Letter to William Dean Howells, October 19, 1880. Twain reproduces a tribute he gave for General Grant.
19. ViU, 01910. Letter to Edward H. House, February 19, 1881.
20. Howells, *My Mark Twain*, 36.
21. Perry, *Grant and Twain*, 85.
22. Ibid.
23. *AMT*, 1:77. "About General Grant's Memoirs."
24. Ibid., 2:62. Autobiographical Dictation for May 28, 1906.
25. Paine, *Mark Twain*, 2:801.
26. *AMT*, 2:61. Autobiographical Dictation for May 28, 1906.
27. NPV, 03071. Letter to Philip H. Sheridan, December 26, 1884.
28. Webster, *Business Man*, 302.
29. Ibid., 307.
30. *Mark Twain's Notebooks & Journals*, 3:96. Notebook 23, September 1884–April 1885. Entry for February 26, 1885.
31. Ibid.
32. Ibid.
33. *AMT*, 1:84. "About General Grant's Memoirs."
34. NPV, 03228. Letter to Orion Clemens, May 16, 1885.
35. *Mark Twain's Notebooks & Journals*, 3:275.

| 1070 |

NOTES

36. Krass, *Business Adventures*, 146.
37. Ibid., 146–47.
38. Griffin, *Mark Twain's Civil War*, 49.
39. CU-MARK, 42610. Letter from Robert Underwood Johnson, August 10, 1885.
40. Paine, *Mark Twain*, 2:915.
41. CU-MARK, 03254. Letter to the Editor of the Boston *Herald*, July 6, 1885.
42. Ellsworth, *Golden Age*, 239.
43. *AMT*, 1:82. "About General Grant's Memoirs."
44. Ibid., 83.
45. Krass, *Business Adventures*, 143.
46. *Mark Twain's Letters*, 2:454. Letter to William Dean Howells, May 5, 1885.
47. *AMT*, 2:71. Autobiographical Dictation for June 1, 1906.
48. Ibid., 72.
49. NPV, 03221. Letter to Frederick T. Grant, April 30, 1885.
50. NPV, 03085. Letter to Charles L. Webster, May 3, 1885.
51. *Mark Twain's Notebooks & Journals*, 3:152. Notebook 24, April–August 1884. Entry for May 26, 1885.
52. Ibid.
53. CU-MARK, 42159. Letter from Karl Gerhardt, May 27, 1884.
54. CU-MARK, 00586. Letter to Karl Gerhardt, September 21, 1884.
55. *Mark Twain's Notebooks & Journals*, 3:135. Notebook 24, April–August 1885.
56. *AMT*, 1:86. "About General Grant's Memoirs."
57. *Mark Twain's Notebooks & Journals*, 3:110. Notebook 23, September 1884–April 1885. Entry for March 23, 1885.
58. Ibid., 3:127. Notebook 24, April–August 1885. Entry for April 4, 1885.
59. Ibid.
60. ODa2 (Private collection), 03522. Letter to William Smith, February 3, 1887.
61. *Love Letters of Mark Twain*, 243. Letter to Olivia L. Clemens, July 1, 1885.
62. CU-MARK, 03266. Letter to Olivia L. Clemens, July 24, 1885.
63. Mark Twain, *Who Is Mark Twain?*, 27.
64. *New York Sun*, August 1, 1885.
65. *Mark Twain Day by Day*, 1:1060.
66. *New York Sun*, July 30, 1885.
67. TxU-HU, 03281. Letter to unidentified person, August 30, 1885.
68. *Mark Twain Day by Day*, 1:1057.
69. OCHP, 03278. Letter to Richard S. Tuthill, August 11, 1885.
70. *Mark Twain's Notebooks & Journals*, 3:215. Notebook 25, August 1885–March 1886.
71. *AMT*, 3:58. Autobiographical Dictation for May 26, 1907.
72. *Mark Twain's Notebooks & Journals*, 3:163. Notebook 24, April–August 1885.
73. DLC, 13117. Letter to William Tecumseh Sherman, February 13, 1891.
74. CU-MARK, 03323. Letter to Olivia L. Clemens, December 3, 1883.
75. *New York Evening Post*, December 18, 1885.
76. *Mark Twain's Notebooks & Journals*, 3:217. Notebook 25, August 1885–March 1886. Entry for December 11, 1885.
77. Webster, *Business Man*, 314.
78. NPV, 03245. Letter to Jane Lampton Clemens, June 26, 1885.
79. NN-BGC, 02621. Letter to William Dean Howells, October 18, 1885.
80. CU-MARK, 04698. Letter to Pamela A. Moffett, February 25, 1894.
81. *Mark Twain Day by Day*, 2:152.
82. *AMT*, 2:73. Autobiographical Dictation for June 1, 1906.
83. CtHMTH, 03260. Letter to Karl Gerhardt, July 18, 1885.
84. *New York Times*, October 25, 1885.
85. NPV, 03334. Letter to Charles L. Webster, December 16, 1885.
86. TwainQuotes.com.
87. Dolmetsch, *Our Famous Guest*, 257.

CHAPTER TWENTY-THREE: REPARATION DUE TO EVERY BLACK MAN

1. CtHMTH, 03398. Letter from Olivia L. Clemens, May 5, 1886.
2. CtHMTH, 03381. Letter from Olivia L. Clemens, April 3, 1886.
3. CU-MARK, 03149. Letter to Olivia L. Clemens, February 2, 1885.
4. NN-BGC, 02656. Letter to Jenny S. Boardman, March 25, 1887.
5. MTP NN-B, UCCL 02619. Letter to William Dean Howells, July 21, 1885.
6. Griffin, *A Family Sketch*, 133–35.

NOTES

7. NNGLI, 11278. Letter to Francis Wayland, December 24, 1885.
8. CU-MARK, 42826. Letter from Francis Wayland, December 25, 1885.
9. CU-MARK, 42834. Letter from Francis Wayland, December 30, 1885.
10. Scharnhorst, *Twain in His Own Time*, 108.
11. CU-MARK, 43074. Letter from Francis Wayland, October 6, 1886.
12. Fishkin, *Lighting Out*, 106.
13. *Mark Twain Day by Day*, 2:80.
14. *Mark Twain's Notebooks & Journals*, 3:255, note 93.
15. *Mark Twain Day by Day*, 2:45.
16. CU-MARK, 42922. Letter from Prudence Crandall Philleo, April 14, 1886.
17. Joe B. Fulton, *Mark Twain in the Margins*.
18. *The New Princeton Review*, January 1888.
19. *Mark Twain's Notebooks & Journals*, 3:414. Notebook 28, July 1888–May 1889.
20. Fatout, *Mark Twain Speaking*, 163.
21. *Mark Twain's Notebook*, 166.
22. DLC, 03371. Letter to President Grover Cleveland, February 23, 1886. Editorial note.
23. Ibid.
24. *Mark Twain Day by Day*, 1:1001.
25. *Letters to His Publishers*, 181.
26. NPV, 10312. Letter to Charles L. Webster, January 19, 1885.
27. NPV, 03190. Letter to Charles L. Webster, March 16, 1885.
28. NPV, 03271. Letter to Annie M. Webster, July 30, 1885.
29. DLC, 01606. Letter to William T. Sherman, September 19, 1885.
30. *Mark Twain's Notebooks & Journals*, 3:312.
31. Ibid., 3:313.
32. NPV, 03304. Letter to Charles L. Webster, November 11, 1885.
33. *Mark Twain's Notebooks & Journals*, 3:260.
34. Ibid., 304.
35. *Mark Twain Day by Day*, 1:1085.
36. Howells, *My Mark Twain*, 73.
37. Scharnhorst, *The Life of Mark Twain*, 2:490.
38. *Love Letters of Mark Twain*, 247. Twichell diary entry, May 5–7, 1886.
39. CU-MARK, 03389. Letter to Olivia L. Clemens, May 5, 1886.
40. NPV, 03411. Letter to Charles L. Webster, June 17, 1886.
41. Paine, *Mark Twain*, 2:833–34.
42. Ibid., 834.
43. Crawford, *How Not to Get Rich*, 127.
44. NPV, 03434. Letter to Charles L. Webster, August 6, 1886.
45. NPV, 03534. Letter to Charles L. Webster, March 1, 1887.
46. Howells, *My Mark Twain*, 74.
47. Christie, Manson, and Woods catalog, 11721. Letter to William Dean Howells, August 7, 1886.
48. CU-MARK, 43173. Letter from Charles L. Webster, December 24, 1886.
49. NPV, 03313. Letter to Charles L. Webster, June 11, 1886.
50. ViU, 03416. Letter to Frederick J. Hall, July 14, 1886.
51. Ibid.
52. NN-BGC, 02639. Letter to Frederick J. Hall, July 21, 1886.
53. NN-BGC and ViU, 02640. Letter to Frederick J. Hall, August 6, 1886.
54. Fatout, *Mark Twain Speaking*, 217.
55. Scharnhorst, *Complete Interviews*, 87.
56. *Mark Twain Day by Day*, 2:96.
57. *Letters to His Publishers*, 17.
58. NN-BGC, 02637. Letter to Frederick J. Hall, July 16, 1886.
59. CU-MARK, 03498. Letter to Calvin H. Higbie, December 16, 1886.
60. CU-MARK, 43188. Letter from Charles L. Webster, January 3, 1887.
61. NPV, 03528. Letter to Charles L. Webster, February 15, 1887.
62. Webster, *Business Man*, 378.
63. Crawford, *How Not to Get Rich*, 134.
64. *Letters to His Publishers*, 215.
65. Ibid.
66. CU-MARK, 43262. Letter from Charles L. Webster, April 8, 1887.
67. NPV, 03412. Letter to Charles L. Webster, April 17, 1887.
68. NPV, 03534. Letter to Charles L. Webster, March 1, 1887.
69. *Mark Twain's Notebooks & Journals*, 3:320. Notebook 27, August 1887–July 1888.
70. Ibid.
71. *Mark Twain's Notebooks & Journals*, 3:125.

NOTES

72. Webster, *Business Man*, 376.
73. *Mark Twain Day by Day*, 2:186.
74. NPV, 03602. Letter to Pamela A. Moffett, July 12, 1887.
75. NN-BGC, 02667. Letter to Charles L. Webster, August 3, 1887.
76. *Mark Twain's Notebooks & Journals*, 3:316. Notebook 27, August 1887–July 1888.
77. *Mark Twain's Notebook & Journals*, 3:351. Notebook 27, August 1887–July 1888.
78. Webster, *Business Man*, 391.
79. Paine, *Mark Twain*, 2:858.
80. *Letters to His Publishers*, 241.
81. Krass, *Business Adventures*, 165.
82. *AMT*, 2:78. Autobiographical Dictation for June 2, 1906.
83. CU-MARK, 08699. Letter to an unidentified person, April 26, 1891.
84. Crawford, *How Not to Get Rich*, 137.
85. *Mark Twain's Notebooks & Journals*, 3:181. Notebook 25, August 1885–March 1886.
86. NPV, 03206. Letter to Charles L. Webster, April 4, 1885.
87. Webster, *Business Man*, 330.
88. *Mark Twain's Notebooks & Journals*, 3:176.
89. Ibid., 219. Notebook 25, August 1885–March 1886. Entry for January 20, 1886.
90. Ibid., 215. Notebook 25. Entry for November 19, 1885.
91. *AMT*, 1:103. "The Machine Episode."
92. Paine, *Mark Twain*, 2:906.
93. ViU, 03437. Letter to Edward House, August 11, 1886.
94. CU-MARK, 03626. Letter to Franklin G. Whitmore, August 13, 1887.

CHAPTER TWENTY-FOUR: "NO POCKETS IN THE ARMOR"

1. Griffin, *A Family Sketch*, 119.
2. CLjC, 03672. Letter to Cordelia Welsh Foote, December 2, 1887.
3. Donner, *Quarterly Journal of Speech*, 1947.
4. Wheeler, *Yesterdays in a Busy Life*, 333.
5. *Mark Twain Day by Day*, 2:175.
6. MoKiU, 43313. Letter from Grace King to May McDowell, June 7, 1887.
7. Ibid.
8. *Mark Twain's Notebooks & Journals*, 3:293.
9. Harnsberger, *Mark Twain Family Man*, 95.
10. CtHMTH, 03413. Letter to Franklin G. Whitmore, July 12, 1886.
11. NPV, 03436. Letter to Jane Lampton Clemens, August 7, 1886.
12. *Mark Twain Day by Day*, 2:55.
13. Ibid.
14. NPV, 10893. Letter to Pamela A. Moffett, July 15, 1886.
15. Fanning, *Mark Twain and Orion Clemens*, 205.
16. Ibid.
17. Ibid., 206.
18. Ibid.
19. *Mark Twain Day by Day*, 2:131.
20. Ibid., 182–83.
21. Ibid., 183.
22. Fatout, *Mark Twain Speaking*, 244.
23. Barber, *Chemung Historical Journal*, March 1967.
24. Jerome and Wisbey, *Mark Twain in Elmira*, 71.
25. MTP. IVL Journals 1903–06. Daily Reminder for February 15, 1906.
26. Griffin, *A Family Sketch*, 139.
27. CtHMTH, 02867. Letter to Jervis Langdon II, December 19, 1883.
28. *Mark Twain's Notebooks & Journals*, 3:78. Notebook 23, September 1884–April 1885.
29. Jerome and Wisbey, *Mark Twain in Elmira*, 12.
30. CSmH, 03480. Letter to Mary Mason Fairbanks, November 16, 1886.
31. CU-MARK, 03607. Letter to Franklin G. Whitmore, July 21, 1887.
32. Ibid.
33. NN-BGC, 02668. Letter to Frederick Hall and Charles L. Webster, August 15, 1887.
34. *Mark Twain's Notebooks & Journals*, 3:392. Notebook 27, August 1887–July 1888.
35. *Mark Twain's Notebook*, 198.
36. *Mark Twain's Notebooks & Journals*, 3:392. Notebook 27, August 1887–July 1888.

NOTES

37. CU-MARK, 03782. Letter to Theodore Crane, October 5, 1888.
38. Hoffman, *Inventing Mark Twain,* 352.
39. MH-H, 03924. Letter to William Dean Howells, August 5, 1889.
40. *Mark Twain's Letters,* 2:513.
41. NN-BGC, 02693. Letter to William Dean Howells, August 24, 1889.
42. NN-BGC, 02695. Letter to William Dean Howells, September 22, 1889.
43. MTP. UkReU, 03913. Letter to Andrew Chatto, July 16, 1889.
44. *Mark Twain's Notebooks & Journals,* 3:173.
45. UkReU, 03913. Letter to Andrew Chatto, July 16, 1889.
46. *A Connecticut Yankee,* 4.
47. Ibid., 100–101.
48. Ibid., 54.
49. Ibid., 64.
50. Ibid.
51. Ibid., 65.
52. Ibid., 114.
53. Ibid., 111.
54. Ibid., 191.
55. Ibid., 199.
56. Ibid., 239.
57. Ibid., 347.
58. Ibid., 353–54.
59. Ibid., 389.
60. Ibid., 393.
61. Ibid., 400–401.
62. Ibid., 430.
63. *Mark Twain's Notebooks & Journals,* 3:419. Notebook 28, July 1888–May 1889.
64. Neider, *Selected Letters,* 199.
65. Kaplan, *Mr. Clemens,* 287.
66. Hoffman, *Inventing Mark Twain,* 357.
67. Paine, *Mark Twain,* 2:850.
68. NN-BGC, 02705. Letter to Sylvester Baxter, December 19, 1889.
69. Scharnhorst, *Complete Interviews,* 103.
70. *Mark Twain's Notebook,* 209.
71. *Mark Twain's Notebooks & Journals,* 3:399. Notebook 28, July 1888–May 1889.
72. Fatout, *Mark Twain Speaking,* 258.
73. Hartford *Times,* December 11, 1889.
74. *Mark Twain Day by Day,* 2:451.
75. Ibid., 460.
76. Ibid., 465.
77. *Mark Twain's Letters,* 2:526.
78. Ibid., 527–28.
79. Ibid., 528.

CHAPTER TWENTY-FIVE: "THE DERIDING OF SHAMS"

1. *Hartford Courant,* June 29, 1888.
2. Ibid.
3. CU-MARK, 03728. Letter to Charles H. Clark, July 2, 1888.
4. CtY-BR, 13312. Letter to Robert Louis Stevenson, June 3, 1888. CU-MARK, 43968. Letter from Robert Louis Stevenson, April 13, 1888.
5. Paine, *Mark Twain,* 2:859.
6. *Mark Twain Day by Day,* 2:268.
7. Benfy, *Kipling's American Years,* 16.
8. Jerome and Wisbey, *Mark Twain in Elmira,* 104.
9. Ibid., 104.
10. Ibid., 106.
11. Ibid., 107.
12. Ibid., 107–8.
13. Ibid., 108.
14. Ibid., 110.
15. Langdon, *Some Reminiscences,* 18.
16. *Mark Twain's Letters,* 2:747.
17. Langdon, *Some Reminiscences,* 18.
18. Jerome and Wisbey, *Mark Twain in Elmira,* 12–13.
19. *AMT,* 2:177. Autobiographical Dictation for August 13, 1906.
20. CU-MARK, 05568. Letter to Annette Hullah, March 23, 1899.
21. Fisher, *Abroad with Mark Twain,* xviii.
22. Benfy, *Kipling's American Years,* 3.
23. MTP. "Concerning the Scoundrel Edward H. House." March 1890.
24. Huffman, *A Yankee in Meiji Japan,* 35.
25. Ibid., 34.
26. Ibid., 89.
27. Ibid., 146.
28. MTP. "Concerning the Scoundrel Edward H. House." March 1890.
29. ViU, UCCL, 01910. Letter to Edward H. House, February 19, 1881.
30. ViU, 02126. Letter to Edward H. House, December 27, 1881.
31. ViU, 02889. Letter to Edward H. House, January 14, 1884.

NOTES

32. ViU, 03227. Letter to Edward H. House, May 13, 1885.
33. Huffman, *A Yankee in Meiji Japan*, 201.
34. CLJC, 04012. Letter to Dean Sage, February 5, 1890.
35. ViU, 03484. Letter to Edward H. House, November 26, 1886.
36. ViU, 03405. Letter to Edward H. House, June 5, 1886.
37. ViU, 03499. Letter to Edward H. House, December 17, 1886.
38. *AMT*, 3:499. CU-MARK, 43434. Letter from Edward H. House. December 24, 1886.
39. *Hartford Courant*, January 18, 1890.
40. *AMT*, 3:115. Autobiographical Dictation for August 18, 1907.
41. Fatout, *American Literature*, March 1959.
42. Ibid.
43. *AMT*, 3:499. Fatout, *American Literature*, March 1959.
44. MTP. "Concerning the Scoundrel Edward H. House." March 1890.
45. Fatout, *American Literature*, March 1959.
46. Ibid.
47. *Mark Twain Day by Day*, 2:328.
48. Ibid., 329.
49. CU-MARK, 03867. Letter from Edward H. House, February 26, 1889.
50. Fatout, *American Literature*, March 1959.
51. CLjC, 02176. Letter to Edward H. House, March 2, 1889.
52. NNPM, 03946. Letter to Elsie Leslie, October 5, 1889.
53. Sales catalog: Parke-Benet Galleries, May 21, 1957. Inscribed copy of *Connecticut Yankee*, February 2, 1890.
54. Fatout, *American Literature*, March 1959.
55. *New York Times*, January 21, 1890.
56. Fatout, *Mark Twain Speaking*, 256–57.
57. Ibid.
58. *New York Times*, January 21, 1890.
59. Hoffman, *Inventing Mark Twain*, 358.
60. CCamarSJ, 04010. Letter to Daniel Frohman, February 2, 1890.
61. Ibid.
62. *Mark Twain's Notebooks & Journals*, 3:544.
63. LaBrUHM, 04021. Letter from Olivia L. Clemens to Grace E. King, February 25, 1890.
64. Fatout, *American Literature*, March 1959.
65. Huffman, *A Yankee in Meiji Japan*, 220.
66. Ibid.
67. Fatout, *American Literature*, March 1959.
68. *New York Times*, March 9, 1890.
69. MH-H, 04036. Letter to William Dean Howells, April 1, 1890.
70. Fatout, *American Literature*, March 1959.
71. CU-MARK, 04102. Letter to Daniel Whitford, October 16, 1890.
72. CU-MARK, 09176. Letter to Moncure D. Conway, April 25, 1890.
73. CtHMTH, 04038. Letter to John J. McCook, April 8, 1890.
74. MTP. "Concerning the Scoundrel Edward H. House." March 1890.
75. *Mark Twain's Correspondence with Henry Huttleston Rogers*, 238.

CHAPTER TWENTY-SIX: DEATH AND DELUSION

1. *Mark Twain's Notebooks & Journals*, 3:374. Notebook 27, August 1887–July 1888.
2. Crawford, *How Not to Get Rich*, 137.
3. *AMT*, 2:78. Autobiographical Dictation for June 2, 1906.
4. *Mark Twain's Notebooks & Journals*, 3:430.
5. *Mark Twain Day by Day*, 2:289. Note written by MT, July 14, 1888.
6. *Mark Twain's Notebooks & Journals*, 3:431. Notebook 28, July 1888–May 1889.
7. CU-MARK, 03812. Letter to Frank Fuller, December 29, 1888.
8. CU-MARK, 44019. Letter from Frederick Hall, May 12, 1888.
9. Crawford, *How Not to Get Rich*, 136.
10. CU-MARK, 43566. Letter from Edmund C. Stedman, October 23, 1888.
11. VtMiM, 03850. Letter to Frederick J. Hall, January 11, 1889.
12. *Mark Twain's Notebooks & Journals*, 3:465. Notebook 28, July 1888–May 1889.
13. CU-MARK, 03904. Letter to Orion Clemens, July 1, 1889.
14. MTP. CU-MARK, 03904. Letter to Pamela A. Moffett, July 1, 1889.
15. Fisher, *Abroad with Mark Twain*, xvii.
16. CU-MARK, 03782. Letter to Theodore W. Crane, October 5, 1888.
17. Paine, *Mark Twain*, 2:908.

NOTES

18. CtHMTH, 03804. Letter to Olivia Lewis Langdon, December 14–19, 1888.
19. *Mark Twain Day by Day*, 2:311.
20. Ibid., 272.
21. *Mark Twain's Notebooks & Journals*, 3:431.
22. CtHMTH, 03750. Letter to Franklin G. Whitmore, August 10, 1888.
23. TxU-HU, 03810. Letter to Olivia L. Clemens, December 31, 1888.
24. CU-MARK, 03847. Letter to Orion Clemens, January 5, 1889.
25. Ibid.
26. Paine, *Mark Twain*, 2: 909.
27. *Mark Twain's Notebooks & Journals*, 3:464.
28. MTP. MoHM, 03944. Letter to Clara L. Spaulding, September 29, 1889.
29. *Mark Twain's Notebooks & Journals*, 3:514. Notebook 29, May 1889–August 1890.
30. Neider, *Selected Letters*, 196.
31. CtY-BR, 03948. Letter to Joseph T. Goodman, October 7, 1889.
32. CU-MARK, 44772. Letter from Dean Sage, November 19, 1889.
33. *Mark Twain Day by Day*, 2:442.
34. *Mark Twain's Letters*, 2:522.
35. CU-MARK, 03708. Letter to Susan L. Crane, April 12, 1888.
36. CtHMTH, 02437. Letter to Candace Wheeler, May 25, 1888.
37. CtHMTH, 03837. Letter to Olivia L. Clemens, November 27, 1888.
38. CU-MARK, 03856. Letter to Susan L. Crane, March 1, 1889.
39. *Mark Twain Day by Day*, 2:388.
40. PH, 03912. Letter to Susy Clemens, July 16, 1889.
41. *Mark Twain Day by Day*, 2:393.
42. NPV, 03299. Letter to Jane Lampton Clemens, October 30, 1885.
43. MTP. CU-MARK, 50559. Letter from Annie Moffett, August 27–28, 1882.
44. NPV, 02843. Letter to Mary E. "Mollie" Clemens, August 16, 1883.
45. Neider, *Selected Letters*, 161.
46. Ibid.
47. CU-MARK, 47432. Letter from Orion Clemens, May 29–30, 1887.
48. *Mark Twain Day by Day*, 2:485.
49. MTP. CU-MARK, 03727. Letter to Orion Clemens, July 2, 1888.
50. Tane, 08604. Letter to William Winter, November 5, 1890.
51. Courtney, *The Loveliest Home*, 74.
52. CU-MARK, 03797. Letter to Olivia Lewis Langdon, December 1, 1888.
53. *AMT*, 2:354. Autobiographical Dictation for December 28, 1906.
54. MH-H, 04115. Letter to William Dean Howells, November 27, 1890.
55. CU-MARK, 12825. Letter to Olivia L. Clemens, November 28, 1890.
56. NN-BGC, 04560. Letter to James B. Pond, November 29, 1890.
57. LaBrUHM, 04159. Letter from Olivia L. Clemens to Grace E. King, January 14, 1891.

CHAPTER TWENTY-SEVEN: "ONE OF THE VANDERBILT GANG"

1. CtHMTH, 04107. Letter to Olivia Lewis Langdon, October 26, 1890.
2. CU-MARK, 04049. Letter from Olivia L. Clemens, May 20, 1890.
3. *Mark Twain's Letters*, 2:539.
4. NN-BGC, 04574. Letter to Frederick J. Hall, February 27, 1891.
5. ViU, 04186. Letter to Joseph T. Goodman, April 1891 [n.d.].
6. *Mark Twain Day by Day*, 2:499.
7. CU-MARK, 44867. Letter from Joseph T. Goodman, January 3, 1890.
8. Lawton, *A Lifetime with Mark Twain*, 108.
9. *Mark Twain Day by Day*, 2:514.
10. CU-MARK, 04033. Letter to Joseph T. Goodman, March 31, 1890.
11. CtY, 04053. Letter to Joseph T. Goodman, June 23, 1890.
12. CU-MARK, 12239. Letter to Senator John P. Jones, August 3, 1890.
13. CU-MARK, 12241. Letter to Senator John P. Jones, September 11, 1890.
14. *Mark Twain's Notebooks & Journals*, 3:590.
15. CU-MARK, 04090. Letter to Orion and Mary E. "Mollie" Clemens, August 31, 1890.
16. CU-MARK, 45202. Letter from Franklin G. Whitmore, August 19, 1890.
17. *Mark Twain's Notebooks & Journals*, 3:596. Notebook 30, August 1890–June 1891. Entry for December 20, 1890.

NOTES

18. *AMT*, 1:106. "The Machine Episode."
19. MTP. CU-MARK, UCLC, 45340. Letter from Joseph T. Goodman, December 4, 1890.
20. Hoffman, *Inventing Mark Twain*, 366.
21. NN-BGC, 04573. Letter to Joseph T. Goodman, February 22, 1891.
22. CU-MARK, 04164. Letter to Senator John P. Jones, February 14–28, 1891.
23. *AMT*, 2:80. Autobiographical Dictation for June 2, 1906.
24. NN-BGC, 04590. Letter to Frederick J. Hall, June 17, 1891.
25. Clemens, *My Father Mark Twain*, 65. Letter from Olivia Susan "Susy" Clemens to Sue Crane, March 24, 1890.
26. CU-MARK, 03752. Letter from Olivia Susan "Susy" Clemens to Samuel E. and Mary E. Moffett, December 25, 1889.
27. *Mark Twain Day by Day*, 2:363.
28. LaBrUHM, 04093. Letter from Olivia L. Clemens to Grace E. King, September 10, 1890.
29. Ibid.
30. CU-MARK, 11281. Letter to Joseph T. Goodman, October 4, 1890.
31. CU-MARK, 04100. Letter to Pamela A. Moffett, October 12, 1890.
32. CSmH, 04101. Letter to Mary M. Fairbanks, October 13, 1890.
33. CtHMTH, 04104. Letter from Olivia Susan "Susy" Clemens to Olivia Lewis Langdon, October 20, 1890.
34. CU-MARK, 04106. Letter to Olivia L. Clemens, October 24, 1890.
35. Andrews, "An Incident at Bryn Mawr," MTL, Redding, Connecticut.
36. CtHMTH, 04112. Letter from Olivia L. Clemens to Olivia Lewis Langdon, November 8, 1890.
37. CU-MARK, 08630. Letter to Olivia L. Clemens, November 27, 1890.
38. Smith-Rosenberg, *Disorderly Conduct*, 276.
39. MH-H, 04169. Letter to William Dean Howells, February 10, 1891.
40. Andrews, "An Incident at Bryn Mawr," MTL, Redding, Connecticut.
41. Ibid.
42. Ibid.
43. Ibid.
44. Ibid.
45. *Mark Twain's Notebook*, 320.
46. Hoffman, *Inventing Mark Twain*, 395.
47. Lystra, *Dangerous Intimacy*, 16.
48. Scharnhorst, *The Life of Mark Twain*, 2:619.
49. NCH, 090128. Letter from Olivia Susan "Susy" Clemens to Louise Brownell, April 20, 1891.
50. Scharnhorst, *The Life of Mark Twain*, 2:619.
51. RuM2, 06149. Letter to Sergei M. Stepniak-Kravchinsky, April 23, 1891.
52. CtY-BR, 11039. Letter from Olivia L. Clemens to Sarah A. Trumbull, May 31, 1891.
53. ViU, 03468. Letter from Olivia L. Clemens to Miss Beach, October 17, 1886.
54. NN-BGC, 04588. Letter to William Dean Howells, May 20, 1891.
55. NN-BGC, 04581. Letter to William Dean Howells, April 4, 1891.
56. InU-Li, 04165. Letter to James W. Riley, February 2, 1891.
57. NN-BGC, 04588. Letter to William Dean Howells, May 20, 1891.
58. CtHSD, 00444. Letter from Olivia L. Clemens to Alice Hooker Day, March 17, 1889.
59. Clemens, *My Father Mark Twain*, 88.
60. Boston *Journal Supplement*, May 15, 1891.

CHAPTER TWENTY-EIGHT: "PARADISE OF THE RHEUMATICS"

1. *Europe and Elsewhere*, 94.
2. Ibid., 103.
3. Ibid., 105–6.
4. *Illustrated London News*, November 1891.
5. *Letters to His Publishers*, 279.
6. CtHMTH, 04220. Letter to Robert Underwood Johnson, July 10, 1891.
7. CSmH, MTP. Clemens Family Papers. Box 1. Jean Clemens European Diary.
8. Scharnhorst, *The Life of Mark Twain*, 1:293.
9. *Mark Twain's Notebooks & Journals*, 2:139.
10. MTP. Notebook 35, May–October 1895.
11. Lawton, *A Lifetime with Mark Twain*, 115.
12. Harnsberger, *Mark Twain Family Man*, 131.
13. CU-MARK, 40114. Letter to unidentified person, August 11, 1891.

NOTES

14. Paine, *Mark Twain,* 2:922.
15. Scharnhorst, *Complete Interviews,* 390.
16. *AMT,* 2:294. Autobiographical Dictation for November 30, 1906.
17. CU-MARK, 04423. Letter to Susan L. Crane, July 9–10, 1893.
18. Clemens, *My Father Mark Twain,* 89.
19. *Mark Twain Day by Day,* 2:635.
20. LaBrUHM, 04224. Letter from Olivia L. Clemens to Grace E. King, August 23, 1891.
21. *Europe and Elsewhere,* 121.
22. Ibid., 124–25.
23. *AMT,* 2:398.
24. Gribben, *Mark Twain's Literary Resources,* 81.
25. CU-MARK, 04227. Letter to Olivia L. Clemens, September 20, 1891.
26. Neider, *Selected Letters,* 211.
27. CU-MARK, 04230. Letter to Olivia L. Clemens, September 22, 1891.
28. CtHMTH, 04231. Letter to Charles Dudley Warner, September 22, 1891.
29. CU-MARK, 04234. Letter to Olivia L. Clemens, September 25, 1891.
30. CU-MARK, 04235. Letter to Olivia L. Clemens, September 26, 1891.
31. CU-MARK, 11719. Letter to Olivia L. Clemens, September 28, 1891.
32. *Letters of Mark Twain and Joseph Hopkins Twichell,* 167.
33. NCH, 09136. Letter from Olivia Susan "Susy" Clemens to Louise Brownell, October 31, 1891.
34. Willis, *Mark and Livy,* 193.
35. CU-MARK, 04245. Letter to Francis D. Finlay, October 16, 1891.
36. NN-BGC, 04603. Letter to Frederick J. Hall, November 27, 1891.
37. *Chicago Daily Tribune,* April 3, 1892.
38. Paine, *Mark Twain,* 2:939.
39. Ibid., 938.
40. MTP. Notebook 31, 1891–July 1892. Circa October 1891.
41. MTP. Notebook 31, 1891–July 1892. December 1891.
42. *Mark Twain's Notebook,* 220.
43. MTP. Notebook 31, Transcript 20–21. January 1892.
44. MTP. Notebook 31, Transcript 20–21. January 1892.
45. *AMT,* 1:190. "Something About Doctors."
46. Paine, *Mark Twain,* 2:939.
47. *Mark Twain's Notebook,* 221.
48. NN-BGC, 04613. Letter to Frederick J. Hall, April 24, 1892.
49. Paine, *Mark Twain,* 2:940.
50. MTP. Notebook 39, September 1896–January 1897.
51. *AMT,* 2:431. Autobiographical Dictation for February 11, 1907.
52. Harnsberger, *Mark Twain's Clara,* 109.
53. *Mark Twain's Notebook,* 224.
54. CU-MARK, 10864. Letter to Samuel S. McClure, February 26, 1892.
55. *AMT,* 2:432. Autobiographical Dictation for February 11, 1907.
56. CtHSD, Katharine S. Day Collection. Letter from Olivia L. Clemens to Alice H. Day, March 7, 1892.
57. *Mark Twain Day by Day,* 2:692.
58. NPV, 04275. Letter to Pamela A. Moffett, March 21, 1892.
59. Neider, *Selected Letters,* 217.
60. *Mark Twain's Notebook,* 225.
61. NCH, 09140. Letter from Olivia Susan "Susy" Clemens to Louise Brownell, April 21, 1892.
62. *Mark Twain Day by Day,* 2:701.
63. Clemens, *My Father Mark Twain,* 113.
64. CU-MARK, 04296. Letter to Clara Clemens, June 10, 1892.
65. CU-MARK, 04302. Letter to Orion Clemens, June 28, 1892.
66. CSmH, 01649. Letter to William W. Phelps, August 5, 1892.
67. CtHMTH, 11865. Letter from Olivia L. Clemens, June 18, 1892.
68. Clemens, *My Father Mark Twain,* 113.
69. *Mark Twain Day by Day,* 2:635.
70. Vranken, *The Wildean,* July 2014.
71. Ibid.
72. *AMT,* 2:181. Autobiographical Dictation for August 27, 1906.
73. MTP. Notebook 32, May 1892–January 1893.
74. *Letters of Mark Twain and Joseph Hopkins Twichell,* 160.
75. *Europe and Elsewhere,* 187.
76. CU-MARK, 01912. Letter to Orion Clemens, September 2, 1892.
77. NN-BGC, UCCL 04599. Letter to Frederick J. Hall, November 7, 1891.
78. CU-MARK, 12829. Letter to Frederick J. Hall, August 7, 1892.
79. CU-MARK, 01912. Letter to Orion Clemens, September 2, 1892.
80. Willis, *Mark and Livy,* 196.

NOTES

81. CU-MARK, 02117. Letter to Franklin G. Whitmore, September 17, 1892.
82. NCH, 09148. Letter from Olivia Susan "Susy" Clemens to Louise Brownell, September 25, 1892.
83. NCH, 09135. Letter from Olivia Susan "Susy" Clemens to Louise Brownell, October 6–7, 1891.
84. NCH, 09141. Letter from Olivia Susan "Susy" Clemens to Louise Brownell, April 29, 1892.
85. Clemens, *Papa: An Intimate Biography*, 15.
86. LaBrUHM, 04159. Letter from Olivia L. Clemens to Grace E. King, January 14, 1891.
87. CSmH, 11569. Letter from Clara Clemens to Olivia L. Clemens, June 19, 1892.

CHAPTER TWENTY-NINE: "A LADY ABOVE REPROACH"

1. Blair, *Mark Twain's Hannibal, Huck & Tom*, 48.
2. MH-H, 01922. Letter to William Dean Howells, March 4, 1881.
3. NN-BGC, 02551. Letter to James R. Osgood, March 31, 1881.
4. *New York Times*, September 24, 1887.
5. *Mark Twain's Notebooks & Journals*, 3:609.
6. NN-BGC, 04572. Letter to Orion Clemens, February 25, 1891.
7. *The American Claimant*, unnumbered page, following 277.
8. *The American Claimant*, ix.
9. Ibid., 36.
10. Ibid., 18.
11. Ibid., 22.
12. Ibid., 103.
13. Budd, *Mark Twain: Social Philosopher*, 148.
14. *Mark Twain's Notebooks & Journals*, 3:606. Notebook 30, August 1890–June 1891.
15. TxFTC, 04617. Letter to Frederick J. Hall, August 10, 1892.
16. DLC, 04653. Letter to Frederick J. Hall, September 4 and 5, 1892.
17. *Tom Sawyer Abroad*, 265.
18. Pettit, *Mark Twain & the South*, 161.
19. *Tom Sawyer Abroad*, 308.
20. Ibid., 312.
21. *Mark Twain's Letters*, 2:569.
22. Paine, *Mark Twain*, 2:956–57.
23. *AMT*, 1:245. "Villa di Quarto."
24. CU-MARK, 04662. Letter to Susan L. Crane, September 30, 1892.
25. Scharnhorst, *Twain in His Own Time*, 178.
26. MTP. CU-MARK, 04358. Letter from Olivia Susan "Susy" Clemens to Clara Clemens, March 23, 1893.
27. NN-BGC, 04619. Letter to Frederick J. Hall, October 5, 1892.
28. Clemens, *My Father Mark Twain*, 120.
29. MTP. CU-MARK, 00777. Letter to Franklin G. Whitmore, December 2, 1892.
30. *AMT*, 1:248. "Villa di Quarto."
31. Ibid., 249.
32. CU-MARK, 02406. Letter to Clara Clemens, November 16, 1892.
33. CU-MARK, 49874. Letter from Susan L. Crane to Elizabeth Ford Adams, December 5, 1892.
34. NCH, 09148. Letter from Olivia Susan "Susy" Clemens to Louise Brownell, September 25, 1892.
35. CU-MARK, 08922. Letter from Olivia Susan "Susy" Clemens to Clara Clemens, October 7, 1892.
36. NCH, 09150. Letter from Olivia Susan "Susy" Clemens to Louise Brownell, November 7, 1892.
37. MTP. CU-MARK, 02722. Letter from Olivia Susan "Susy" Clemens to Clara Clemens, November 4, 1892.
38. CU-MARK, 04307. Letter to Clara Clemens, December 15, 1892.
39. *Mark Twain Day by Day*, 2:754.
40. CtHMTH, 04322, Letter from Olivia L. Clemens to Harriet E. Whitmore, January 5, 1893.
41. CU-MARK, 04333. Letter from Olivia Susan "Susy" Clemens to Clara Clemens, February 2, 1893.
42. CSmH, 11593. Letter from Clara Clemens to Olivia Susan "Susy" Clemens, February 14, 1893.

NOTES

43. CU-MARK, 04345. Letter from Olivia Susan "Susy" Clemens to Clara Clemens, February 28, 1893.
44. Ibid.
45. CU-MARK, 04346. Letter from Olivia Susan "Susy" Clemens to Clara Clemens, March 2, 1893.
46. CU-MARK, 04346. Letter from Olivia Susan "Susy" Clemens to Clara Clemens, March 2, 1893.
47. CU-MARK, 04358. Letter from Olivia Susan "Susy" Clemens to Clara Clemens, March 23, 1893.
48. CU-MARK, 04360. Letter from Olivia Susan "Susy" Clemens to Clara Clemens, March 26, 1893.
49. CU-MARK, 04376. Letter from Olivia Susan "Susy" Clemens to Clara Clemens, April 15, 1893.
50. CU-MARK, 00382. Letter from Olivia L. Clemens to Clara Clemens, October 7, 1892.
51. CU-MARK, 04306. Letter from Olivia L. Clemens to Clara Clemens, December 11, 1892.
52. *London Express,* June 3, 1908.
53. Clemens, *My Father Mark Twain,* 93–94.
54. Hoffman, *Inventing Mark Twain,* 381.
55. Harnsberger, *Mark Twain Family Man,* 140–41.
56. Ibid., 141.
57. Harnsberger, *Mark Twain Family Man,* 141.
58. CU-MARK, 04329. Letter from Olivia Susan "Susy" Clemens to Clara Clemens, January 24, 1893.
59. CSmH, 48927. Letter from Mary B. Willard, January 23, 1893.
60. CU-MARK, 04330. Letter from Olivia L. Clemens to Clara Clemens, January 26, 1893.
61. Willis, *Mark and Livy,* 199.
62. CSmH, 04327. Letter to Mary Mason Fairbanks, January 18, 1893.
63. CU-MARK, 04311. Letter from Olivia L. Clemens to Clara Clemens, December 20, 1892.
64. Willis, *Mark and Livy,* 199.
65. Scharnhorst, *Twain in His Own Time,* 181.
66. NjP, 04337. Letter to Laurence Hutton, February 5, 1893.
67. CU-MARK, 45838. Letter from William James to Josiah Royce, December 18, 1892.
68. Willis, *Mark and Livy,* 180.
69. NNPM, 04315. Letter to Dr. William Wilberforce Baldwin, December 28, 1892.
70. CU-MARK, 04326. Letter from Olivia L. Clemens to Clara Clemens, January 15, 1893.

CHAPTER THIRTY: "BOSS MACHINE OF THE WORLD"

1. CU-MARK, 00786. Letter to Frederick J. Hall, December 2, 1892.
2. *AMT,* 2:78. Autobiographical Dictation for June 2, 1906.
3. CLjC, 04318. Letter to Frederick J. Hall, January 1, 1893.
4. CtHMTH, 04368. Letter from Olivia L. Clemens, April 9, 1893.
5. Ibid.
6. Ibid.
7. CU-MARK, 04372. Letter from Olivia L. Clemens, April 12, 1893.
8. NN-BGC, 04363. Letter to Andrew Carnegie, April 5, 1893.
9. Paine, *Mark Twain,* 2:964.
10. NN-BGC, 04365. Letter to Andrew Carnegie, April 7, 1893.
11. MTP. Notebook 33, March 1893–July 1894. Entry for April 10, 1893.
12. CU-MARK, 04377. Letter to Olivia L. Clemens, April 18, 1893.
13. Fanning, *Mark Twain and Orion Clemens,* 206–7.
14. Ibid.
15. MTP. Notebook 33, March 1893–July 1894. Entry for April 23, 1893.
16. CU-MARK, 04382. Letter from Olivia L. Clemens, April 23, 1893.
17. CtHMTH, 04388. Letter from Olivia L. Clemens, April 28, 1893.
18. *Mark Twain Day by Day,* 2:793. Notebook entry for May 24, 1893.
19. Neider, *Selected Letters,* 219.
20. Ibid., 220.
21. Ibid.
22. Ibid., 345.
23. NN-BGC, 04645. Letter to Frederick J. Hall, June 26, 1893.
24. CU-MARK, 04419. Letter from Olivia L. Clemens to Frederick J. Hall, June 28, 1893.

NOTES

25. CU-MARK, 45931. Letter from Charles J. Langdon, July 3, 1893.
26. NN-BGC, 04647. Letter to Frederick J. Hall, July 18, 1893.
27. CU-MARK, 04420. Letter to Franklin G. Whitmore, July 3, 1893.
28. NN-BGC, 01633. Letter to Frederick J. Hall, July 26, 1893.
29. NN-BGC, 04437. Letter to Frederick J. Hall, August 14, 1893.
30. TxFTC, 04427. Letter to Frederick J. Hall, July 30, 1893.
31. NN-BGC, 01633. Letter to Frederick J. Hall, July 26, 1893.
32. NN-BGC, 04648. Letter to Frederick J. Hall, August 6, 1893.
33. CU-MARK, 04439. Letter from Jean Clemens to Clara Clemens, August 27, 1893.
34. CU-MARK, 04441. Letter to Olivia L. Clemens, September 7, 1893.
35. Ibid.
36. CU-MARK, 04442. Letter to Clara Clemens, September 10, 1893.
37. CU-MARKS, 04453. Letter to Olivia L. Clemens, September 17, 1893.
38. CLjC, 04461. Letter to Olivia L. Clemens, September 26, 1893.
39. Paine, *Mark Twain*, 2:970.
40. CU-MARK, 04450. Letter to Clara Clemens, September 15, 1893.
41. CU-MARK, 04693. Letter to Olivia L. Clemens, February 15, 1894.
42. Kaplan, *Mr. Clemens*, 321.
43. Crawford, *How Not to Get Rich*, 152.
44. Shelden, *Mark Twain: Man in White*, 51.
45. *Mark Twain's Correspondence with Henry Huttleston Rogers*, 5.
46. *Love Letters of Mark Twain*, 274.
47. CU-MARK, 04462. Letter to Olivia L. Clemens, September 28, 1893.
48. CU-MARK, 05448. Letter to Clara Clemens, October 16, 1893.
49. CU-MARK, 04473. Letter from Olivia L. Clemens, October 15, 1893.
50. CU-MARK, 04490. Letter to Olivia Susan "Susy" Clemens, November 6, 1893.
51. Christie's East catalogs, 04476. Letter to Olivia L. Clemens, October 18, 1893.
52. CU-MARK, 04490. Letter to Olivia Susan "Susy" Clemens, November 6, 1893.
53. Paine, *Mark Twain*, 2:972.
54. CU-MARK, 04693. Letter to Olivia L. Clemens, February 15, 1894.
55. Fatout, *Mark Twain Speaking*, 265.
56. *Mark Twain Day by Day*, 2:842.
57. CLjC, 04461. Letter to Olivia L. Clemens, September 26, 1893.
58. Fishkin, *Was Huck Black?*, 124.
59. CLjC, 04461. Letter to Olivia L. Clemens, September 26, 1893.
60. Clemens, *My Father Mark Twain*, 212.

CHAPTER THIRTY-ONE: "TOO MUCH OF A HUMAN BEING"

1. Clemens, *Papa: An Intimate Biography*, 18. Letter from Olivia Susan "Susy" Clemens to Louise Brownell, June 12, 1893.
2. NCH, 09154. Letter from Olivia Susan "Susy" Clemens to Louise Brownell, December 31, 1892.
3. MTP, Notebook 33, March 1893–July 1894. Notebook entry circa June 1893.
4. *Mark Twain Day by Day*, 2:805.
5. CU-MARK, 04465. Letter from Olivia Susan "Susy" Clemens to Clara Clemens, October 1–14, 1893.
6. NCH, 09164. Letter from Olivia Susan "Susy" Clemens to Louise Brownell, September 3, 1893.
7. CU-MARK, CTH. Letter from Olivia Susan "Susy" Clemens to Clara Clemens, November 14, 1893.
8. CU-MARK, 04531. Letter from Olivia L. Clemens, December 17, 1893.
9. CtY, 10999. Letter from Olivia L. Clemens to Annie E. Trumbull, January 25, 1894.
10. *Love Letters of Mark Twain*, 285.
11. MTP, Notebook 33, March 1893–July 1894. Entry for December 29, 1893.
12. CtHSd, 10520. Letter from Olivia L. Clemens to Alice Hooker Day, February 4, 1894.
13. Kaplan, *Mr. Clemens*, 327.
14. CtHSD, 10520. Letter from Olivia L. Clemens to Alice Hooker Day, February 4, 1894.

NOTES

15. CU-MARK, 04500. Letter from Olivia L. Clemens, November 14, 1893.
16. Ibid.
17. Harnsberger, *Mark Twain Family Man,* 104.
18. CU-MARK, 04692. Letter to Olivia L. Clemens, February 13, 1894.
19. *Letters of Mark Twain and Joseph Hopkins Twichell,* 183.
20. CU-MARK, 04698. Letter to Pamela A. Moffett, February 25, 1894.
21. CU-MARK, 04699. Letter to Olivia L. Clemens, February 25, 1894.
22. CU-MARK, 04523. Letter to Olivia L. Clemens, December 9, 1893.
23. CU-MARK, 04517. Letter to Olivia L. Clemens, December 4, 1893.
24. CU-MARK, 04529. Letter to Olivia L. Clemens, December 15, 1893.
25. Early American Auction catalog, 04536. Letter to Olivia L. Clemens, December 25, 1893.
26. Ibid.
27. MTP. Notebook 33, March 1893–July 1894. Entry for January 15, 1894.
28. *Love Letters of Mark Twain,* 293.
29. Paine, *Mark Twain,* 2:979.
30. MTP. Notebook 33, March 1893–July 1894. Entry for February 2, 1894.
31. CU-MARK, 04677. Letter to Olivia L. Clemens, January 24, 1894.
32. *Mark Twain Day by Day,* 2:874.
33. CU-MARK, 04688. Letter to Clara Clemens, February 5, 1894.
34. Paine, *Mark Twain,* 2:978.
35. *Mark Twain's Correspondence with Henry Huttleston Rogers,* 16. Letter to Olivia L. Clemens, January 30, 1894.
36. CtHMTH, 08839. Letter to Bram Stoker, February 2, 1894.
37. CU-MARK, 04689. Letter to Olivia L. Clemens, February 7 or 8, 1894.
38. CU-MARK, 04693. Letter to Olivia L. Clemens, February 15, 1894.
39. Ibid.
40. CU-MARK, 04701. Letter to Olivia L. Clemens, March 2, 1894.
41. CU-MARK, 04698. Letter to Pamela A. Moffett, February 25, 1894.
42. Ibid.
43. Salm, 05342. Letter to Henry H. Rogers, February 5–6, 1898.
44. *The Twainian,* November 1947. Letter from Frederick J. Hall to Albert Bigelow Paine, January 4, 1909.
45. ViU, 04737. Letter to Frederick J. Hall, June 1, 1894.
46. Fatout, *Mark Twain Speaking,* 272.
47. Ibid.
48. Salm, 04703. Letter to Henry H. Rogers, March 4, 1894.
49. Zacks, *Chasing the Last Laugh,* 413.
50. CtHMTH, 10489. Letter to Olivia L. Clemens, April 13, 1894.
51. *Love Letters of Mark Twain,* 301. Letter to Olivia L. Clemens, May 4, 1894.
52. Paine, *Mark Twain,* 2:984.
53. CU-MARK, 04724. Letter to Olivia L. Clemens, April 22, 1894.
54. Ibid.
55. CU-MARK, 04726. Letter to Orion and Mary E. "Mollie" Clemens, April 23, 1894.
56. CU-MARK, 12079. Letter from Olivia L. Clemens to Susan L. Crane, April 22, 1894.
57. CtHMTH, 11867. Letter from Olivia L. Clemens, April 26, 1894.
58. *Brooklyn Eagle,* April 18, 1894.
59. *Love Letters of Mark Twain,* 299.
60. Edwin H. Chubby, *Stories of Authors: British and American,* 352.
61. Kaplan, *Mr. Clemens,* 330.
62. Sotheby's Sales catalog, 10490. Letter to Olivia L. Clemens, May 16, 1894.
63. *Letters from the Earth,* 144. "Cooper's Prose Style."
64. *1601, and Is Shakespeare Dead?,* afterword, 10. "Fenimore Cooper's Literary Offenses."
65. Ibid.
66. CtHSD. Katharine S. Day Collection. Letter from Olivia L. Clemens to Alice Hooker Day, May 23, 1894.
67. CU-MARK, 04726. Letter to Orion Clemens, April 23, 1894.
68. CU-MARK, 04742. Letter to Orion Clemens, June 21, 1894.
69. CU-MARK, 04750. Letter from Olivia L. Clemens to Clara Clemens, July 1, 1894.
70. CtHSD, 10599. Letter from Olivia L. Clemens to Alice Hooker Day, July 1, 1894.
71. MTP. CU-MARK, 04752. Letter to Clara Clemens, July 4, 1894.

NOTES

72. CU-MARK, 04757. Letter from Olivia L. Clemens to Clara Clemens, July 18, 1894.
73. CU-MARK, 04761. Letter to Olivia L. Clemens, July 25, 1894.
74. *Love Letters of Mark Twain*, 309.
75. Crawford, *How Not to Get Rich*, 162.
76. *Mark Twain Day by Day*, 2:935.
77. MTP. CU-MARK, 04775. Letter to Orion Clemens, August 17, 1894.
78. Willis, *Mark and Livy*, 220.
79. Pfeffer, *A New Orleans Author*, 237.
80. *New York Sun*, August 15, 1894.
81. NN-BGC, 04913. Letter to Henry H. Rogers, August 25, 1894.
82. CU-MARK, 04779. Letter from Olivia Susan "Susy" Clemens to Clara Clemens, August 10, 1894.
83. Ibid.
84. NCH, 09167. Letter from Olivia Susan "Susy" Clemens to Louise Brownell, July 29, 1894.
85. Ibid.
86. MTP. IVL Journals 1903–06. Daily Reminder for December 13, 1906.
87. Salm, 04791. Letter to Henry H. Rogers, September 24, 1894.
88. Ibid.
89. *Mark Twain's Correspondence with Henry Huttleston Rogers*, 83.
90. Salm, 04805. Letter to Henry H. Rogers, November 2, 1894.
91. Paine, *Mark Twain*, 2:991.
92. CU-MARK, 04815. Letter to Henry H. Rogers, November 29–30, 1894.
93. CU-MARK, 04821. Letter to Henry H. Rogers, December 9, 1894.
94. NN-BGC, 04916. Letter to Henry H. Rogers, December 22, 1894.
95. Ibid.
96. CU-MARK, 04829. Letter to Henry H. Rogers, January 2, 1895.
97. NN-BGC, 04917. Letter to Henry H. Rogers, December 27, 1894.
98. Kaplan, *Mr. Clemens*, 284.
99. *AMT*, 2:80. Autobiographical Dictation for June 2, 1906.
100. Paine, *Mark Twain*, 2:996.

CHAPTER THIRTY-TWO: "PARIS THE DAMNABLE"

1. NCH, 09157. Letter from Olivia Susan "Susy" Clemens to Louise Brownell, March 1893 [n.d.].
2. Neider, *Complete Essays*, 119. "In Defense of Harriet Shelley."
3. Ibid., 121.
4. Ibid., 131–32.
5. Ibid., 147.
6. Ibid., 148.
7. Ibid., 153.
8. Shelden, *Mark Twain: Man in White*, 312.
9. *AMT*, 1:465. Autobiographical Dictation for March 30, 1906.
10. Ibid., 466.
11. Ibid., 2:375. Autobiographical Dictation for January 17, 1907.
12. Ibid., 376.
13. *Love Letters of Mark Twain*, 314.
14. *New York Times*, September 7, 2020.
15. Shelden, *Mark Twain: Man in White*, 313.
16. Scharnhorst, *Twain in His Own Time*, 308.
17. Ibid.
18. Ibid., 309.
19. *AMT*, 2:279. Autobiographical Dictation for November 20, 1906.
20. *AMT*, 1:466. Autobiographical Dictation for March 30, 1906.
21. Stojiljkovic, *Mark Twain Journal*, Fall 2014.
22. Ibid.
23. Ibid.
24. DLC, 04653. Letter to Frederick J. Hall, September 4, 1892.
25. Neider, *Mark Twain: Life As I Find It*, 233. "Talk About Twins."
26. *Mark Twain Day by Day*, 2:749.
27. Sloane, *Mark Twain's Humor*, 365.
28. *The Tragedy of Pudd'nhead Wilson*, 58.
29. Ibid., 62–63.
30. Ibid., 67.
31. Ibid., 77.
32. Ibid., 300.
33. *Mark Twain's Letters*, 2:591. Letter to Frederick J. Hall, July 30, 1893.
34. Fishkin, *Was Huck Black?*, 122.
35. Sloane, *Mark Twain's Humor*, 376.
36. Pettit, *Mark Twain & the South*, 149.
37. Sloane, *Mark Twain's Humor*, 375.
38. Fishkin, *Lighting Out*, 73.
39. *Southern Magazine*, February 1894.
40. Richmond *Dispatch*, March 10, 1895.

| 1083 |

NOTES

41. *Paris Review,* Fall 1993.
42. Ober, *Mark Twain and Medicine,* 135.
43. *Mark Twain Day by Day,* 3:870. October 2, 1897.
44. Clemens, *My Father Mark Twain,* 127.
45. CtHMTH, 04811. Letter to Franklin G. Whitmore, November 16, 1894.
46. *Mark Twain's Correspondence with Henry Huttleston Rogers,* 103.
47. MTP. Notebook 30, September 1896–January 1897. Entry for January 6, 1897.
48. *AMT,* 1:387. Autobiographical Dictation for March 5, 1906.
49. Ibid., 387–88.
50. CU-MARK, 01794. Letter to Lucius Fairchild, April 28, 1880.
51. Budd, *Mark Twain: Social Philosopher,* 73.
52. MTL, Accession No. 0024. *Dictionary of Miracles,* by Ebenezer Cobham Brewer, 1884.
53. Gribben, *Mark Twain's Literary Resources,* 52.
54. Ibid.
55. Scharnhorst, *Complete Interviews,* 146.
56. MTP. Notebook 41, January–July 1897. Entry for February 19, 1897.
57. Ibid. Entry for January 29, 1897.
58. Kaplan, *Mr. Clemens,* 222.
59. *Mark Twain's Notebooks & Journals,* 2:439.
60. Ibid, 3:173. Notebook 24, April–August 1885.
61. Ibid., 271. Notebook 26, March 1886–June 1887.
62. *Europe and Elsewhere,* 217. "Letters to Satan. Swiss Glimpses."
63. CtHMTH, 04834. Letter to Franklin G. Whitmore, January 8, 1895.
64. Ibid.
65. Salm, 04836. Letter to Henry H. Rogers, January 21, 1895.
66. NN-BGC, 04988. Letter to Henry H. Rogers, January 29, 1895.
67. CU-MARK, 04851. Letter to Olivia L. Clemens, March 20, 1895.
68. Ibid.
69. CU-MARK, 04852. Letter to Olivia L. Clemens, March 21, 1895.

CHAPTER THIRTY-THREE: "'COLOSSAL' IS A TAME WORD FOR HIM"

1. Salm, 04859. Letter to Henry H. Rogers, April 3, 1895.
2. CU-MARK, 04866. Letter to Henry H. Rogers, April 14, 1895.
3. NMh, 04870. Letter to Poultney Bigelow, April 25, 1895.
4. CU-MARK, 04880. Letter to Orion Clemens, May 26, 1895.
5. ViU, 04882. Letter to Robert Underwood Johnson, May 30, 1895.
6. *AMT,* 1:189. "Something about Doctors."
7. Ibid., 190.
8. NN-BGC, 04997. Letter to James B. Pond, June 19, 1895.
9. CtHMTH, 04903. Letter to Henry H. Rogers, June 26, 1895.
10. Salm, 02717. Letter to Henry H. Rogers, June 29, 1885.
11. Gribben, *Overland with Mark Twain,* 2.
12. CU-MARK, 04933. Letter to Henry H. Rogers, July 20–22, 1895.
13. CU-MARK, 04930. Letter to Henry H. Rogers, July 14, 1895.
14. Powers, *Mark Twain: A Life,* 66.
15. *New York Sun,* circa July 15, 1895.
16. Jerome and Wisbey, *Mark Twain in Elmira,* 72.
17. Zacks, *Chasing the Last Laugh,* 54.
18. Lawton, *A Lifetime with Mark Twain,* 130.
19. CtY-BR, 05120. Letter to Henry C. Robinson, September 28, 1896.
20. Kaplan, *Mr. Clemens,* 333.
21. *Letters to His Publishers,* 212.
22. NN-BGC, 05616. Letter to William Dean Howells, July 3, 1899.
23. Gribben, *Overland with Mark Twain,* 1.
24. Scharnhorst, *Twain in His Own Time,* 190.
25. Fatout, *Mark Twain Speaking,* 280. July 15, 1895. Music Hall in Cleveland.
26. Ibid., 280.
27. Ibid., 284.
28. Ibid., 286.
29. Gribben, *Overland with Mark Twain,* 3. July 17, 1895. Major Pond Journal.
30. MTP. Notebook 35, May–October 1895. Entry for July 17, 1895.
31. *Minneapolis Journal,* July 23, 1885.
32. *Detroit Journal,* July 18, 1895.
33. Scharnhorst, *Twain in His Own Time,* 191.

NOTES

34. *Mark Twain Day by Day*, 2:1018.
35. Petoskey *Daily Reporter*, July 21, 1895.
36. *Minneapolis Penn Press*, July 23, 1895.
37. Gribben, *Overland with Mark Twain*, 5. July 23, 1895. Major Pond Journal.
38. Ibid., 6. July 25, 1895.
39. MTP. Notebook 35, May–October 1895. Entry for July 26, 1895.
40. MTP. Notebook 35, May–October 1895. Entry for July 30, 1895.
41. Scharnhorst, *Twain in His Own Time*, 193. July 30, 1895. Major Pond Journal.
42. *Mark Twain's Notebook*, 247. August 1, 1895. Butte, Montana.
43. Gribben, *Overland with Mark Twain*, 10. August 8, 1895. Spokane, Washington.
44. MTP. Notebook 35, Transcript 25. May–October 1895. Entry for August 7, 1895.
45. Gribben, *Overland with Mark Twain*, 11. August 8, 1895. Major Pond Journal.
46. Scharnhorst, *Twain in His Own Time*, 196. August 7, 1895. Major Pond Journal.
47. Portland *Oregonian*, August 10, 1895.
48. CU-MARK, 04943. Letter to Samuel E. Moffett, August 14–15, 1895.
49. Seattle *Post-Intelligencer*, August 14, 1895.
50. CU-MARK, 04943. Letter to Samuel E. Moffett, August 14–15, 1895.
51. *Mark Twain Day by Day*, 2:1048.
52. San Francisco *Examiner*, August 17, 1895.
53. *Mark Twain's Correspondence with Henry Huttleston Rogers*, 181.
54. Gribben, *Overland with Mark Twain*, 15. August 21, 1895. Major Pond Journal.
55. Ibid., 14. August 15, 1895.
56. *Mark Twain's Correspondence with Henry Huttleston Rogers*, 186.
57. *Mark Twain Day by Day*, 2:1053.
58. Gribben, *Overland with Mark Twain*, 15. August 21, 1895. Major Pond Journal.
59. Harnsberger, *Mark Twain Family Man*, 151.
60. CU-MARK, 04941. Letter from Olivia Susan "Susy" Clemens to Clara Clemens, August 10, 1895.
61. Ibid.
62. Ibid.
63. Gribben, *Overland with Mark Twain*, 15. Major Pond Journal.
64. Ibid., 14.
65. Clemens, *My Father Mark Twain*, 84.

CHAPTER THIRTY-FOUR: "CLOWN OF THE SEA"

1. *Following the Equator*, 27.
2. Clemens, *My Father Mark Twain*, 142.
3. MTP. Notebook 35, May–October 1895. Entry for August 28, 1895.
4. *Following the Equator*, 48.
5. Ibid., 59.
6. Ibid., 60.
7. MTP. Notebook 35, May–October 1895. Entry for August 30–31, 1894.
8. CU-MARK, 04972. Letter from Clara Clemens to Samuel E. Moffett, November 12, 1895.
9. *Mark Twain's Notebook*, 251. Notebook 35, May–October 1895. Entry for September 2, 1895.
10. MTP. Notebook 35, May–October 1895.
11. CU-MARK, 04958. Letter from Olivia L. Clemens to Susan L. Crane, September 5, 1895.
12. MTP. Notebook 35, May–October 1895. Entry for September 4, 1895.
13. Scharnhorst, *Complete Interviews*, 224. *Evening News* (Melbourne), September 26, 1895.
14. Fisher, *Abroad with Mark Twain*, 90.
15. Scharnhorst, *Twain in His Own Time*, 204.
16. Ibid., 203–4.
17. Salm, 04965. Letter to Henry H. Rogers, September 25, 1895.
18. *Daily Telegraph* (Sydney), September 17, 1895.
19. *Evening News* (Sydney), September 16, 1895.
20. *Following the Equator*, 161.
21. Fatout, *Mark Twain Speaking*, 298. October 3, 1895. Dinner Speech, Yorick Club, Melbourne.
22. MTP. Notebook 35, May–October 1885. Entry for October 4, 1895.
23. MTP. Notebook 34, March–December 1895. Entry for October 17, 1895.
24. MTP. Notebook 34, March–December 1895. Entry for October 31, 1895.
25. CU-MARK, 04968. Letter from Olivia Langdon Clemens to Olivia Susan "Susy" Clemens, October 20, 1895.
26. *Courier* (Ballarat, Australia), October 21, 1895.

NOTES

27. MTP. Notebook 34, March–December 1895. Entry for October 26, 1895.
28. MTP. Notebook 34, March–December 1895.
29. Ibid. Entry for November 28, 1895.
30. Ibid. Entry for November 1, 1895.
31. *Following the Equator,* 265.
32. *Press* (Christchurch, New Zealand), November 13, 1895.
33. MTP. Notebook 34, March–December 1895. Entry for November 7, 1895.
34. Ibid. Entry for November 6, 1895.
35. *The New Zealand* (Auckland), November 31, 1895.
36. MTP. Notebook 34, March–December 1895. Entry for November 6, 1895.
37. *Following the Equator,* 290.
38. NzW2, 04975. Letter to Sarah G. Kinsey, November 23, 1895.
39. *Following the Equator,* 302.
40. NzW2, 04975. Letter to Sarah G. Kinsey, November 23, 1895.
41. ViU, 04976. Letter from Olivia L. Clemens to Susan L. Crane, November 24, 1895.
42. Budd, *Mark Twain: Social Philosopher,* 169.
43. MTP. Notebook 34, March–December 1885. Entry for December 7, 1895.
44. *Following the Equator,* 322.
45. Ibid., 287.
46. ViU, 04983. Letter from Olivia L. Clemens to Susan L. Crane, December 16, 1895.
47. MTP. Notebook 37, January–April 1896. Entry for January 6, 1896.
48. *Mark Twain's Notebook,* 265. January 4, 1896.
49. MTP. Notebook 37, January–April 1896. Entry for January 8, 1896.
50. Ibid. Entry for January 11, 1896.
51. *Following the Equator,* 336.
52. ViU, 05012. Letter from Olivia L. Clemens to Susan L. Crane, January 17, 1896.
53. Ibid.
54. MTP. Notebook 36, December 1895–March 1896. Entry for January 18, 1896.
55. Ibid.
56. *Following the Equator,* 339. January 14, 1896.
57. Clemens, *My Father Mark Twain,* 155–56.
58. *Following the Equator,* 345.
59. MTP. Notebook 36, December 1896–March 1896.
60. *AMT,* 1:190. "Something about Doctors."
61. Ibid., 191.
62. MTP. Notebook 36, December 1895–March 1896. Entry for January 20, 1896.
63. *Mark Twain Day by Day,* 2:1104.
64. *Following the Equator,* 351. January 20, 1896.
65. Ibid., 351–52.
66. Ibid., 352.
67. Ibid., 345.
68. Ibid., 346.
69. Ibid., 403.
70. Ibid., 347–48.
71. Ibid., 398.
72. Ibid., 381.
73. ViU, 05012. Letter from Olivia L. Clemens to Susan L. Crane, January 24, 1896.
74. *Bombay Gazette,* January 25, 1896.
75. *Mark Twain's Notebook,* 274. Entry for January 31, 1896.
76. *Mark Twain Day by Day,* 2:1106.
77. MTP. Notebook 36, December 1895–March 1896. Entry for February 4, 1896.
78. Ibid. Entry for February 2, 1896.
79. *Mark Twain Day by Day,* 2:1110.
80. *Following the Equator,* 480.
81. Ibid., 486.
82. Ibid., 497.
83. Salm, 05020. Letter to Henry H. Rogers, February 8, 1896.
84. *The Englishman* (Calcutta), February 8, 1896.
85. Ibid.
86. *Mark Twain's Notebook,* 276.
87. Clemens, *Mark Twain Journal,* Spring 1996.
88. MTP. Notebook 36, December 1895–March 1896. Entry for February 13, 1896.
89. *The Englishman* (Calcutta), February 8, 1896.
90. MTP. Notebook 36, December 1895–March 1896. Entry for February 14, 1896.
91. *Mark Twain's Correspondence with Henry Huttleston Rogers,* 195.
92. ViU, 05022. Letter from Olivia L. Clemens to Jean Clemens, February 16, 1896.
93. MTP. Notebook 36, December 1895–March 1896. Entry for February 27, 1896.
94. *Following the Equator,* 570.
95. *Mark Twain's Notebook,* 279.

NOTES

96. Salm, 05026. Letter to Henry H. Rogers, March 6, 1896.
97. Clemens, *Mark Twain Journal,* Spring 1996. Letter from Olivia L. Clemens to Jean Clemens, March 10, 1896.
98. *Following the Equator,* 582.
99. Ibid.
100. MTP. Notebook 36, December 1895–March 1896. Entry for March 21, 1896.
101. Ibid.
102. Ibid., Entry for March 26, 1896.
103. *Following the Equator,* 617.
104. Paine, *Mark Twain,* 2:1015.
105. Clemens, *Mark Twain Journal,* Spring 1996. Letter from Clara Clemens to Samuel E. Moffett, April 7, 1896.
106. *Mark Twain's Notebook,* 290. Notebook circa March 28, 1896.
107. MTP. Notebook 37, January–April 1896. Circa April 11, 1896.
108. ViU, 05034. Letter from Olivia L. Clemens to Susan L. Crane, March 30, 1896.
109. CtHSD, Katharine S. Day Collection. Letter from Olivia L. Clemens to Alice Hooker Day, April 13, 1896.
110. CtHMTH, 05038. Letter from Olivia L. Clemens to Harriet E. Whitmore, April 19, 1896.

CHAPTER THIRTY-FIVE: "CIRCUMNAVIGATION OF THIS GREAT GLOBE"

1. ViU, 05034. Letter from Olivia L Clemens to Susan L. Crane, March 30, 1896.
2. *Mark Twain Day by Day,* 2:1137.
3. Paine, *Mark Twain,* 2:1017.
4. MTP. Notebook 38, May–July 1896. Entry for May 4, 1896.
5. MTP. Notebook 38, May–July 1896. Entry for May 11, 1896.
6. *Following the Equator,* 645. Entry for May 7, 1896.
7. *Mark Twain Day by Day,* 2:1139.
8. CU-MARK, 12692. Letter from Clara Clemens to Martha Pond, February 18, 1896.
9. *Mark Twain Day by Day,* 2:1140.
10. CU-MARK, 05048. Letter from Olivia L. Clemens, May 19, 1896.
11. CU-MARK, 05050. Letter to Olivia L. Clemens, May 15, 1896.
12. CU-MARK, 05054. Letter to Olivia L. Clemens, May 20, 1896.
13. *Mark Twain Day by Day,* 2:1146.
14. Scharnhorst, *Twain in His Own Time,* 207.
15. *Mark Twain's Notebook,* 294.
16. Paine, *Mark Twain,* 2:1019.
17. Ibid.
18. Scharnhorst, *Complete Interviews,* 355.
19. CU-MARK, 05055. Letter to Olivia L. Clemens, May 25, 1896.
20. Salm, 05207. Letter to Henry H. Rogers, April 26–28, 1897.
21. MTP. Notebook 38, May–July 1896.
22. Ibid. Entry for June 12, 1896.
23. *Following the Equator,* 693.
24. MTP. Notebook 38, May–July 1896. Entry for June 1, 1896.
25. *Mark Twain's Notebook,* 298. Entry circa May 28, 1896.
26. *Following the Equator,* 691.
27. MTP. Notebook 38, May–July 1896. Entry for May 28, 1896.
28. Ibid.
29. MTP. Notebook 38, May–July 1896. Entry for June 1, 1896.
30. CU-MARK, 05069. Letter to Olivia L. Clemens, June 8, 1896.
31. *Mark Twain Day by Day,* 2:1154.
32. ViU, 11891. Letter from Olivia L. Clemens to Susan L. Crane, June 19, 1896.
33. Kaplan, *Mr. Clemens,* 335.
34. *Mark Twain's Notebook,* 301. Entry for June 18, 1896.
35. *Following the Equator,* 701.
36. Ibid., 704.
37. Ibid., 707.
38. MTP. Notebook 39, September 1896–January 1897. Entry for December 3, 1896.
39. Ibid.
40. MTP. Notebook 41, January–July 1897. Entry for April 13, 1897.
41. *Mark Twain Day by Day,* 2:1165.
42. NN-BGC, 08205. Letter to Major James B. Pond, September 14, 1900.
43. Salm, 05133. Letter to Henry H. Rogers, October 20, 1896.
44. Clemens, *My Father Mark Twain,* 170.
45. *Following the Equator,* 712.

| 1087 |

NOTES

46. Wallace, *Mark Twain and the Happy Island*, 44.
47. Neider, *Complete Essays*, 625. "The Finished Book."
48. Harnsberger, *Mark Twain's Clara*, 124.
49. Willis, *Mark and Livy*, 197.
50. Paine, *Mark Twain*, 2:996–97.
51. Scharnhorst, *Twain in His Own Time*, 181.
52. Ibid., 180.
53. CU-MARK, 04362. Letter to Olivia L. Clemens, April 4, 1893.
54. CU-MARK, 04720. Letter to Olivia L. Clemens, April 16, 1894.
55. *Mark Twain Day by Day*, 2:976.
56. Ibid., 977.
57. *Mark Twain's Correspondence with Henry Huttleston Rogers*, 216.
58. CtY, 04797. Letter to Lloyd S. Bryce, October 13, 1894.
59. MTP. Notebook 32, May 1892–January 1893.
60. Jenn and Morris, *Mark Twain Journal*, Spring/Fall 2017.
61. MTP. Notebook 34, March–December 1895.
62. Harnsberger, *Mark Twain's Clara*, 125.
63. *Mark Twain's Correspondence with Henry Huttleston Rogers*, 73.
64. *Mark Twain Day by Day*, 3:22.
65. *Hartford Courant*, April 11, 1895.
66. *Petoskey* (Michigan) *Reporter*, July 21, 1895.
67. Scharnhorst, *Twain in His Own Time*, 200.
68. NjP, 05123. Letter to Laurence Hutton, October 5, 1896.
69. *Personal Recollections of Joan of Arc*, 461.
70. *Mark Twain's Notebooks*, 24. Entry for November 30, 1908.

CHAPTER THIRTY-SIX: "THE ONLY SAD VOYAGE"

1. CtHMTH, 04893. Letter from Olivia L. Clemens to Franklin G. Whitmore, June 18, 1895.
2. CtHMTH, 05087. Letter to Henry H. Rogers, July 22, 1896.
3. CSmH, 04841. Letter to Mary Mason Fairbanks, February 9, 1895.
4. CU-MARK, 04937. Letter from Olivia Susan "Susy" Clemens to Clara Clemens, July 30, 1895.
5. CU-MARK, 04960. Letter from Olivia Susan "Susy" Clemens to Clara Clemens, September 13, 1895.
6. CU-MARK, 05018. Letter to Olivia Susan "Susy" Clemens, February 7, 1896.
7. CU-MARK, 04979. Letter from Olivia L. Clemens to Olivia Susan "Susy" Clemens, December 2, 1895.
8. CU-MARK, 04828. Letter from Olivia Susan "Susy" Clemens to Clara Clemens, undated letter, circa late 1895 or early 1896.
9. CU-MARK, 46101. Letter from James B. Pond, July 3, 1896.
10. Lawton, *A Lifetime with Mark Twain*, 135.
11. CU-MARK, 04962. Letter from Olivia Susan "Susy" Clemens to Clara Clemens, September 16, 1895.
12. Ibid.
13. CU-MARK, 04985. Letter from Olivia Susan "Susy" Clemens to Clara Clemens, December 30, 1895.
14. MoHM, 12446. Letter to Anna Goodenough, August 14, 1896.
15. *AMT*, 1:323. Autobiographical Dictation for February 2, 1906.
16. CU-MARK, 05095. Letter to Olivia L. Clemens, August 16, 1896.
17. Ibid.
18. Lawton, *A Lifetime with Mark Twain*, 137.
19. Courtney, *Joseph Hopkins Twichell*, 246.
20. CU-MARK, 31106. Letter from Samuel E. Moffett to Mary E. Moffett, August 20, 1896.
21. *Mark Twain's Notebook*, 319.
22. Kaplan, *Mr. Clemens*, 337.
23. Clemens, *Papa: An Intimate Biography*, 45–46. Writing of Olivia Susan "Susy" Clemens, August 15, 1896.
24. *Love Letters of Mark Twain*, 319.
25. Ibid.
26. *AMT*, 1:324. Autobiographical Dictation for February 2, 1906.
27. Ibid.
28. Clemens, *My Father Mark Twain*, 171.
29. Courtney, *Joseph Hopkins Twichell*, 246.
30. Clemens, *My Father Mark Twain*, 171.
31. *New York Times*, August 23, 1896.

NOTES

32. CtHMTH, 46113. Letter from Susan L. Crane to Harriet E. Whitmore, September 8, 1896.
33. *AMT*, 1:324. Autobiographical Dictation for February 2, 1906.
34. DSI-AAA, 12076. Letter from Jean Clemens to Mittie Taylor Brush, May 20, 1908.
35. Clemens, *My Father Mark Twain*, 171–72.
36. *AMT*, 2:619.
37. NCH, 37478. Letter from Elizabeth Ware Winsor to Louise Brownell, September 16, 1896.
38. *Love Letters of Mark Twain*, 320.
39. Ibid., 321–22.
40. CU-MARK, 05098. Letter to Olivia L. Clemens, August 21, 1896.
41. MTP. Notebook 39, September 1896–January 1897. Entry for January 6, 1897.
42. CU-MARK, 05100. Letter to Olivia L. Clemens, August 26–28, 1896.
43. Ibid.
44. CU-MARK, 05102. Letter to Olivia L. Clemens, August 29–30, 1896.
45. Ibid.
46. CU-MARK, 05100. Letter to Olivia L. Clemens, August 26–28, 1896.
47. CU-MARK, 05102. Letter to Olivia L. Clemens, August 29–30, 1896.
48. CU-MARK, 05106. Letter to Franklin G. Whitmore, September 10, 1896.
49. Harnsberger, *Mark Twain Family Man*, 172.
50. CU-MARK, 05110. Letter to Orion and Mary E. "Mollie" Clemens, September 14, 1896.
51. NMh, 05122. Letter to Poultney Bigelow, October 1896 [n.d.].
52. Pfeffer, *A New Orleans Author*, 243.
53. Ibid.
54. CU-MARK, 05235. Letter from Olivia L. Clemens to Grace King, June 27, 1897.
55. CtHSD, 05108. Letter from Clara Clemens to Alice Hooker Day, September 1, 1896.
56. MFai, 05743. Letter to Henry H. Rogers, January 8, 1900.
57. NPV. Clemens. 20.4. Lyon Howe 1933. Isabel Lyon recollections.
58. MFai, 05153. Letter to Henry and Emilie R. Rogers, December 18, 1896.
59. DLC, 13257. Letter to Col. Andrew Burt, December 12, 1896.
60. CU-MARK, 05166. Letter to Pamela A. Moffett, January 7, 1897.
61. *Letters of Mark Twain and Joseph Hopkins Twichell*, 191. Letter to Joseph H. Twichell, January 18, 1897.
62. MTP. Notebook 39, September 1896–January 1897. Entry for January 6, 1897.
63. CU-MARK, 05117. Letter to Joseph H. Twichell, September 27, 1896.
64. *AMT*, 1:382–83. Autobiographical Dictation for February 26, 1906.
65. MTP. Notebook 39, September 1896–January 1897. Entry for January 6, 1897.
66. CU-MARK, 05102. Letter to Olivia L. Clemens, August 29, 1896.
67. CtHSD, 10606. Letter from Olivia L. Clemens to Alice Hooker Day, October 22, 1896.
68. Ibid.
69. *Mark Twain's Notebook*, 322.
70. Willis, *Mark and Livy*, 245.
71. CU-MARK, 05151. Letter to Olivia L. Clemens, November 27, 1896.
72. LaBrUHM, 47725. Letter from Clara C. Gabrilowitsch to Grace E. King, July 1, 1910.
73. DSI, 08059. Letter from Jean Clemens to Nancy D. Brush, July 23, 1908.
74. CSmH, 53346. JCD, Vol. 1. October 22, 1900.

CHAPTER THIRTY-SEVEN: "A BOOK WRITTEN IN BLOOD & TEARS"

1. MTP. Notebook 39, September 1896–January 1897. Entry for October 24, 1896.
2. CU-MARK, 04979. Letter from Olivia L. Clemens to Olivia Susan "Susy" Clemens, December 2, 1895.
3. NjP, l 05352. Letter to Laurence Hutton, February 20, 1898.
4. NN-BGC, 05601. Letter to William Dean Howells, April 5, 1899.
5. Salm, 05325. Letter to Henry H. Rogers, December 21, 1897.
6. Zacks, *Chasing the Last Laugh*, 339.
7. Krause, *American Literature*, November 1967.

NOTES

8. Paine, *Mark Twain*, 2:1040.
9. Powers, *Mark Twain: A Life*, 572.
10. *Following the Equator*, 207.
11. Ibid., 186.
12. Ibid., 212.
13. Fulton, *The Reconstruction of Mark Twain*, 167.
14. *Following the Equator*, 300.
15. Ibid., 184.
16. Ibid., *Equator*, 459.
17. Ibid., 195.
18. Ibid., 622.
19. Ibid., 241.
20. *Mark Twain's Correspondence with Henry Huttleston Rogers*, 270. Letter of April 14, 1897.
21. *Saturday Review* (London), January 29, 1898.
22. Boston *Daily Globe*, December 31, 1897.
23. *Harper's Monthly*, January 1898.
24. *Mark Twain's Notebooks & Journals*, 3:355. Entry for June 1, 1896.
25. MTP. Notebook 39, September 1896–January 1897. Entry for November 26, 1897.
26. Paine, *Mark Twain*, 2:1027.
27. Clemens, *My Father Mark Twain*, 179.
28. CU-MARK, 05173. Letter to J. Woulfe Flanagan, January 20, 1897.
29. LaBrUHM, 05185. Letter from Olivia L. Clemens to Grace E. King, March 9, 1897.
30. *Mark Twain's Notebook*, 323. Notebook circa January 1897.
31. MTP. Notebook 41, January–July 1897. Entry for January 29, 1897.
32. NN-BGC, 05243. Letter to Abraham (Bram) Stoker, November 2, 1896.
33. Ibid.
34. Clemens, *My Father Mark Twain*, 181–82.
35. *AMT*, 1:113. "Travel-Scraps I."
36. MTP. Notebook 41, January–July 1897. Entry for January 12, 1897.
37. Ibid.
38. MTP. Notebook 39, September 1896–January 1897. Entry for December 3, 1896.
39. MTP. Notebook 39, September 1896–January 1897. Entry circa October/November 1896.
40. MTP. Notebook 39, September 1896–January 1897. Entry for October 1896.
41. Kaplan, *Mr. Clemens*, 341–42.
42. NN-BGC, 05505. Letter to William Dean Howells, February 23, 1897.
43. Ibid.
44. Paine, *Mark Twain*, 2:1055.
45. MTP. Notebook 41, January–July 1897. Entry for March 28, 1897.
46. Gribben, *Mark Twain's Literary Resources*, 80.
47. MTP. Notebook 41, January–July 1897. Entry for June 2, 1897.
48. Ibid.
49. McCoy, *Mark Twain Journal*, Spring 2018.
50. Paine, *Mark Twain*, 2:711.
51. Zwonitzer, *Statesman and the Storyteller*, 180.
52. *Outlook*, December 1910.
53. Zwonitzer, *Statesman and the Storyteller*, 183.
54. Ibid.
55. Ibid., 184.
56. *Mark Twain's Correspondence with Henry Huttleston Rogers*, 283.
57. Ibid., 282.
58. Salm, 04684. Letter to Henry H. Rogers, June 16, 1897.
59. *Mark Twain's Correspondence with Henry Huttleston Rogers*, 284.
60. Salm, 05231. Letter to Henry H. Rogers, June 23, 1897.
61. Fanning, *Mark Twain and Orion Clemens*, 209.
62. *Outlook*, December 1910.
63. *Europe and Elsewhere*, 204.
64. Ibid., 210.
65. Ibid., 209.
66. Zwonitzer, *Statesman and the Storyteller*, 194.

CHAPTER THIRTY-EIGHT: "LETTERS TO SATAN"

1. Dolmetsch, *Our Famous Guest*, 21.
2. MTP. Notebook 42, June 1897–March 1900. Entry for August 18, 1897.
3. CU-MARK, 31202. Letter from Susan L. Crane to Samuel E. Moffett, July 22, 1897.
4. *Mark Twain Day by Day*, 3:66. Letter to Major James B. Pond, July 30, 1897.
5. CU-MARK, 05280. Letter to Wayne MacVeagh, August 22, 1897.

NOTES

6. ViU, 05284. Letter to Mr. Skrine, September 10, 1897.
7. CtY, 05219. Letter from Olivia L. Clemens to Eliza N. Robinson, January 28, 1898.
8. Paine, *Mark Twain*, 2:1047.
9. Tuckey, *Fables of Man*, 131. Circa August 18, 1897. "In My Bitterness."
10. MTP. Notebook 41, January–July 1897.
11. MTP. "Kellgren Cure." August 1892.
12. Rogers, *Satires & Burlesques*, 185–86. "Hellfire Hotchkiss."
13. Ibid., 197.
14. Ibid., 200.
15. Ibid., 199.
16. Blair, *Mark Twain's Hannibal, Huck & Tom*, 29. "Villagers of 1840–3."
17. Ibid., 37.
18. Ibid., 33.
19. Ibid., 32.
20. Powers, *Mark Twain: A Life*, 586.
21. *Europe and Elsewhere*, 212. "Letters to Satan. Swiss Glimpses."
22. Ibid., 219.
23. NjP, 00886. Letter to Tom Hood, March 10, 1873.
24. CU-MARK, 05279. Letter to Joseph H. Twichell, August 22, 1897.
25. Ibid.
26. Ibid.
27. CU-MARK, MTP. Notebook 42, June 1897–March 1900. Entry for August 13, 1897.
28. CU-MARK, 05291. Letter to Joseph H. Twichell, August 22, 1897.
29. Salm, 05291. Letter to Henry H. Rogers, September 18, 1897.
30. Dolmetsch, *Our Famous Guest*, 27.
31. *New York Times*, October 2, 1897.
32. *Mark Twain's Notebook*, 340.
33. Clemens, *My Father Mark Twain*, 203.
34. Dolmetsch, *Our Famous Guest*, 36.
35. CtHMTH, 05570. Letter from Olivia M. Clemens to Katharine Boland, March 29, 1899.
36. *ATM*, 3:479. Letter from Madame Laszowska to William Blackwood, November 7, 1897.
37. CLjC, 02019. Letter to Karl and Hattie J. Gerhardt, August 31, 1881.
38. MTP. MT. "Kellgren Cure." 1896.
39. Lystra, *Dangerous Intimacy*, 21–22.
40. CU-MARK, 05294. Letter to Heinrich Obersteiner, October 5, 1897.
41. MTP. MT. "Kellgren Cure."
42. Ibid.
43. Ibid.
44. Shelden, *Mark Twain: Man in White*, 30.
45. Lystra, *Dangerous Intimacy*, 34.
46. Clemens, *My Father Mark Twain*, 215–16.
47. Dolmetsch, *Our Famous Guest*, 136.
48. CtHMTH, 05378. Letter from Olivia L. Clemens to Charles J. Langdon, April 24, 1898.
49. CU-MARK, 12842. Letter from Olivia L. Clemens to Susan L. Crane, September 11, 1898.
50. *AMT*, 3:316. Autobiographical Dictation for December 24–26, 1909. "Closing Words of My Autobiography."
51. Trombley, *American Literary Realism*, Winter 2008.

CHAPTER THIRTY-NINE: "STIRRING TIMES IN AUSTRIA"

1. *Christian Science*, 4.
2. *A Connecticut Yankee*, 213.
3. Dolmetsch, *Our Famous Guest*, 40.
4. Scharnhorst, *Twain in His Own Time*, 162.
5. Dolmetsch, *Our Famous Guest*, 316.
6. Ibid., 317.
7. *The Man That Corrupted Hadleyburg*, 284.
8. Dolmetsch, *Our Famous Guest*, 64.
9. Clemens, *My Father Mark Twain*, 198.
10. Ibid., 200.
11. MTP. Notebook 42, June 1897–March 1900. Entry for November 24, 1897.
12. Dolmetsch, *Our Famous Guest*, 76.
13. MTP. Notebook 42, June 1897–March 1900.
14. Dolmetsch, *Our Famous Guest*, 76.
15. *Mark Twain's Correspondence with Henry Huttleston Rogers*, 308.
16. Dolmetsch, *Our Famous Guest*, 72.
17. *The Man That Corrupted Hadleyburg*, 340. "Stirring Times in Austria."
18. *Mark Twain Day by Day*, 3:139.
19. *AMT*, 1:420. Autobiographical Dictation for March 16, 1906.
20. Neider, *Mark Twain: Life As I Find It*, 125.
21. *Mark Twain's Notebooks & Journals*, 2:302. Notebook 18, February–September 1879.

NOTES

22. CU-MARK, 05301. Letter to Joseph H. Twichell, October 23, 1897.
23. Griffin, *A Family Sketch,* 162.
24. CU-MARK, 11487. Letter to Charles Erskine Scott Wood, January 22, 1885.
25. *Life on the Mississippi,* 368.
26. *Mark Twain's Notebooks & Journals,* 3:266. Notebook 26, March 1886–June 1887.
27. Fisher, *Abroad with Mark Twain,* 120.
28. *Mark Twain's Notebooks & Journals,* 3:443. Notebook 28, July 1888–May 1889.
29. Dolmetsch, *Our Famous Guest,* 270.
30. *Mark Twain Day by Day,* 2:950.
31. Clemens, *My Father Mark Twain,* 130.
32. MTP. Notebook 36, December 1895–March 1896. Entry for February 5, 1896.
33. Neider, *Mark Twain: Life As I Find It,* 214.
34. Dolmetsch, *Our Famous Guest,* 173.
35. Shelden, *Mark Twain: Man in White,* 82.
36. Dolmetsch, *Our Famous Guest,* 174.
37. *Mark Twain Day by Day,* 3:105.
38. ViU, 05346. Letter to Chatto & Windus, February 8, 1898.
39. Dolmetsch, *Our Famous Guest,* 165.
40. Salm, 05416. Letter to Henry H. Rogers, July 26, 1898.
41. *The Man That Corrupted Hadleyburg,* 254. "Concerning the Jews."
42. Ibid., 260.
43. Ibid., 263.
44. Ibid., 268.
45. Ibid., 269.
46. Ibid., 279.
47. Clemens, *My Father Mark Twain,* 204.
48. Dolmetsch, *Our Famous Guest,* 178.
49. *AMT,* 3:19. Autobiographical Dictation for March 28, 1907.
50. Shelden, *Mark Twain: Man in White,* 27.
51. Lawton, *A Lifetime with Mark Twain,* 163–64.
52. CtHMTH, 05445. Letter from Olivia L. Clemens to Mary B. Cheney, October 7, 1898.
53. Dolmetsch, *Our Famous Guest,* 94.
54. *Mark Twain's Notebook,* 342.
55. CtHMTH, 05353. Letter from Clara Clemens to James B. Pond, February 21, 1898.
56. MTP. Notebook 40, January 1898–July 1899. Entry for January 19, 1898.
57. Paine, *Mark Twain,* 2:1063.
58. NjP, 05352. Letter to Laurence Hutton, February 20, 1898.
59. Clemens, *My Husband Gabrilowitsch,* 4.
60. Ibid.
61. Ibid., 5.
62. *Mark Twain's Notebook,* 354.
63. Shelden, *Mark Twain, Man in White,* 93.
64. Clemens, *My Husband Gabrilowitsch,* 31.
65. Charbonnel, *Mark Twain Journal,* Spring 1964.
66. CSmH, 08487. Letter to Elizabeth Wallace, November 10, 1909.
67. Harnsberger, *Mark Twain's Clara,* 116.
68. CtHMTH, 05445. Letter from Olivia L. Clemens to Mary B. Cheney, October 7, 1898.
69. Ibid.
70. Dolmetsch, *Our Famous Guest,* 97.

CHAPTER FORTY: "THE EUROPEAN EDISON"

1. MTP. Notebook 41, January–July 1897. Entry for July 19, 1897.
2. *Mark Twain Day by Day,* 3:110.
3. *AMT,* 2:27. Autobiographical Dictation for April 6, 1906.
4. Fanning, *Mark Twain and Orion Clemens,* 211.
5. *The Letters of Mark Twain and Joseph Hopkins Twichell,* 211.
6. Salm, 05324. Letter to Henry H. Rogers, December 16, 1897.
7. Salm, 05277. Letter to Henry H. Rogers, August 6, 1897.
8. *Mark Twain's Correspondence with Henry Huttleston Rogers,* 306.
9. Kaplan, *Mr. Clemens,* 350.
10. Zwonitzer, *Statesman and the Storyteller,* 252.
11. Salm, 05361. Letter to Henry H. Rogers, March 7, 1898.
12. NN-BGC, 05499. Letter to William Dean Howells, December 30, 1898.
13. Salm, 05336. Letter to Henry H. Rogers, January 20, 1898.
14. *New York World,* March 13, 1898.
15. Sales catalog, Hamilton (Charles) catalog, 05364. Letter to Amelia S. Levetus, March 15, 1898.
16. MTP. Notebook 40, January 1898–July 1899.

NOTES

17. Salm, 05365. Letter to Henry H. Rogers, March 17–20, 1898.
18. Ibid.
19. Ibid.
20. MTP. Notebook 32, Transcript 14. Entry for March 18, 1898.
21. MTP. Notebook 40, January 1898–July 1899. Entry for March 19, 1898.
22. Ibid.
23. Salm, 05368. Letter to Henry H. Rogers, March 24, 1898.
24. Ibid.
25. Ibid.
26. CtY-BR, 05373. Letter to Richard Watson Gilder, April 2, 1898.
27. Salm, 38969. Letter from William Whitman to James Phillips, Jr., April 5, 1898.
28. Salm, 05377. Letter to Henry H. Rogers, April 21, 1898.
29. Ibid.
30. Ibid.
31. DLC, 05560. Letter to John M. Hay, March 11, 1899.
32. Ibid.
33. NjP, 05352. Letter to Laurence Hutton, February 20, 1898.
34. *Mark Twain's Notebook*, 342.
35. *The Man That Corrupted Hadleyburg*, 1.
36. Ibid., 50.
37. Ibid., 36–37.
38. Ibid., 63.
39. Ibid., 83.
40. Hill, *God's Fool*, 21.
41. Paine, *Mark Twain*, 2:1069.
42. *Mark Twain's Correspondence with Henry Huttleston Rogers*, 384.
43. Shelden, *Mark Twain: Man in White*, 170.
44. *Mark Twain's Notebooks*, 88.
45. *Mark Twain Day by Day*, 3:204.
46. *Mark Twain's Notebooks*, 108.
47. Ibid., 345.
48. Dolmetsch, *Our Famous Guest*, 80.
49. *Mark Twain's Notebook*, 368.
50. Ibid., 344.
51. Ibid.
52. MTP. Notebook 40, January 1898–July 1899. Entry for August 7, 1898.
53. *Mark Twain Day by Day*, 3:100.
54. *Mark Twain's Notebook*, 344.
55. Tane, 05348. Letter to Francis E. Bliss, February 11, 1898.

CHAPTER FORTY-ONE: DREAM SELF

1. Scharnhorst, *Complete Interviews*, 337.
2. *No.44, The Mysterious Stranger*, 192.
3. MTP. Notebook 40, January 1898–July 1899.
4. DSI-AAA, 03535. Letter to an unknown person, March 4, 1887.
5. MTP. Notebook 41, January–July 1897.
6. *Bulletin* (Sydney), January 4, 1896.
7. MTP. Notebook 40, January 1898–July 1899. Entry circa January 1898.
8. Tuckey, *Which Was the Dream?*, 50.
9. Ibid., 55.
10. Ibid., 60.
11. MTP. Notebook 40, January 1898–July 1899. Entry for August 10, 1898.
12. Tuckey, *Which Was the Dream?*, 104.
13. Ibid., 113.
14. MTP. Notebook 40, January 1898–July 1899. Entry for August 10, 1898.
15. Tuckey, *Which Was the Dream?*, 124.
16. Ibid., 125.
17. Ibid., 130.
18. WU, 05799. Letter to Francis D. Finlay, April 25, 1900.
19. *Who Is Mark Twain?*, 31.
20. Ibid., 33–35. "Conversations with Satan."
21. MTP. Notebook 40, January 1898–July 1899.
22. *AMT*, 3:127. Autobiographical Dictation for September 4, 1907.
23. NN-BGC, 05601. Letter to William Dean Howells, April 2, 1899.
24. MTP. Notebook 40, January 1898–July 1899. Entry for August 7, 1898.
25. NN-BGC, 05601. Letter to William Dean Howells, April 6, 1899.
26. NN-BGC, 05607. Letter to William Dean Howells, May 12, 1899.
27. *Harper's Magazine*, December 1912.
28. Ibid.
29. Ibid.
30. Ibid.
31. Ibid.
32. Ibid.
33. Ibid.
34. Ibid.
35. Ibid.

NOTES

36. CtY, 05459. Letter to Richard Watson Gilder, November 6, 1898.
37. ViU, 05446. Letter to Edward Bok, October 10, 1898.
38. *The Man That Corrupted Hadleyburg,* 147.
39. MTP. MT. "Kellgren Cure."
40. CtHMTH, 05445. Letter from Olivia L. Clemens to Mary B. Cheney, October 7, 1898.
41. Salm, 05411. Letter to Henry H. Rogers, July 10, 1898.
42. Ibid.
43. MH-H, 05406. Letter to Thomas Bailey Aldrich, June 29, 1898.
44. Salm, 05426. Letter to Henry H. Rogers, August 28, 1898.
45. Dolmetsch, *Our Famous Guest,* 242. Letter to Henry H. Rogers, October 14, 1898.
46. Ibid.
47. Zwonitzer, *Statesman and the Storyteller,* 338.
48. Paine, *Mark Twain,* 2:1072.
49. Clemens, *My Husband Gabrilowitsch,* 6.
50. MoHi, 05351. Letter to Bertha von Suttner, February 17, 1898.
51. CtHMTH, 05378. Letter to Charles J. Langdon, April 24, 1898.
52. MS Tane, 05401. (Private collection.) Letter to Major James B. Pond, June 17, 1898.
53. Paine, *Mark Twain,* 2:1063.
54. MoHM, 05384. Letter to Chatto & Windus, May 6, 1898.
55. *Mark Twain Day by Day,* 3:161.
56. *Europe and Elsewhere,* 223.
57. *The Letters of Mark Twain and Joseph Hopkins Twichell,* 219.
58. Dolmetsch, *Our Famous Guest,* 188.
59. Powers, *Mark Twain: A Life,* 593.

CHAPTER FORTY-TWO: "A HUNDRED CAPERING CLOWNS"

1. NjP, 05561. Letter to Laurence Hutton, March 12, 1899.
2. *Letters of Mark Twain and Joseph Hopkins Twichell,* 235. March 22, 1899. Speech to Hungarian Journalists' Association.
3. *Letters of Mark Twain and Joseph Hopkins Twichell,* 235.
4. *Mark Twain Day by Day,* 3:237.
5. MTP. Notebook 40, January 1898–July 1899. Entry for February 4, 1898.
6. Clemens, *My Father Mark Twain,* 208.
7. *AMT,* 1:126. "A Viennese Procession."
8. CU-MARK, 12842. Letter from Olivia L. Clemens to Susan L. Crane, September 11, 1898.
9. CU-05432. Letter to Joseph H. Twichell, September 13, 1898.
10. Neider, *Complete Essays,* 539. "The Memorable Assassination."
11. Ibid., 537.
12. *AMT,* 1:293. Autobiographical Dictation for January 18, 1906.
13. Neider, *Complete Essays,* 543. "The Memorable Assassination."
14. *Mark Twain's Notebook,* 367. Entry for September 17, 1898.
15. *Mark Twain Day by Day,* 3:195. Speech of October 18, 1898.
16. Paine, *Mark Twain,* 2:1072.
17. Dolmetsch, *Our Famous Guest,* 194.
18. DLC, 05586. Letter to John Hay, May 4, 1899.
19. CU-MARK, 05578. Letter to Annette Hullah, April 18, 1899.
20. CU-MARK, 05475. Letter to Henry H. Rogers, January 3, 1899.
21. Salm, 05590. Letter to Henry H. Rogers, May 10, 1899.
22. CU-MARK, 11310. Letter from Clara Clemens to James R. Clemens, December 23, 1898.
23. *Mark Twain Day by Day,* 3:253.
24. *Chronicle* (London), June 3, 1899.
25. Clemens, *My Father Mark Twain,* 214.
26. Dolmetsch, *Our Famous Guest,* 18.
27. Ibid.
28. CtY-BR, 05533. Letter to Joseph H. Twichell, January 3, 1899.
29. ViU, 05546. Letter to Charles Dudley Warner, February 15, 1899.
30. Salm, 05590. Letter to Henry H. Rogers, May 10, 1899.
31. *Chronicle* (London), June 3, 1899.
32. *Mark Twain's Notebook,* 371–72. Savage Club speech, June 9, 1899.
33. Fatout, *Mark Twain Speaking,* 321.
34. Ibid., 323.

NOTES

35. Ibid., 327.
36. MTP. MT. "Kellgren Cure."
37. Salm, 05644. Letter to Henry Rogers, June 25, 1899.
38. CU-MARK, 50531. Notes by Samuel C. and Doris Webster on talk with Mrs. Lyon, March 5, 1948.
39. *New York Times,* July 8, 1899.
40. Clemens, *My Father Mark Twain,* 214.
41. CU-MARK, 05653. Letter to Clara Clemens, July 12, 1899.
42. NIC, 11373. Letter to Willard Fiske, July 15, 1899.
43. CtY-BR, 05657. Letter to Richard Watson Gilder, July 23, 1899.
44. *Mark Twain's Notebook,* 344.
45. CU-MARK, 12851. Letter to Joseph H. Twichell, August 20, 1899.
46. MTP. MT. "Kellgren Cure." August 7, 1899.
47. Ibid., August 19, 1899.
48. CU-MARK, 05658. Letter to John Brisben Walker, July 30, 1899.
49. *Mark Twain Day by Day,* 3:278. Notebook 40, Transcript 58. Entry for July 20, 1899.
50. MTP. Notebook 42, June 1897–March 1900. Entry for July 25, 1899.
51. Zwonitzer, *Statesman and the Storyteller,* 382.
52. MTP. MT. "Kellgren Cure."
53. Ibid., August 20, 1899.
54. Salm, 05662. Letter to Henry H. Rogers, August 3, 1899.
55. CU-MARK, 05658. Letter to John Brisben Walker, July 30, 1899.
56. NMh, 05659. Letter to Poultney Bigelow, July 30, 1899.
57. CU-MARK, 12851. Letter to Joseph M. Twichell, August 20, 1899.

"CHAPTER FORTY-THREE: "THE BASTARD HUMAN RACE"

1. Salm, 05671. Letter to Henry H. Rogers, September 3, 1899.
2. CU-MARK, 05674. Letter to Samuel E. Moffett, September 15, 1899.
3. Ober, *Mark Twain and Medicine,* 163.
4. NjP, 0567. Letter to Laurence Hutton, September 18, 1899.
5. *AMT,* 3:110. Autobiographical Dictation for August 26, 1907.
6. CU-MARK, 05727. Letter to Rudoph H. Krause, November 1, 1899–June 26, 1900.
7. MeWC, 08915. Letter to Franklin G. Whitmore, October 1, 1899.
8. CtHMTH, 05695. Letter to Franklin G. Whitmore, October 26, 1899.
9. MTP. NN-BGC, 05624. Letter to William Dean Howells, October 19, 1899.
10. CtHMTH, 08943. Letter to a Dr. Sullivan, November 8, 1899.
11. *Mark Twain Day by Day,* 3:316.
12. CU-MARK, 05723. Letter to Susan L. Crane, December 2, 1899.
13. LaBrUHM, 05728. Letter from Olivia L. Clemens to Grace E. King, January–June 1900.
14. LaBrUHM, 05729. Letter from Olivia L. Clemens to Grace E. King, December 1899 [n.d.].
15. Pfeffer, *A New Orleans Author,* 257.
16. LaBrUHM, 05729. Letter from Olivia L. Clemens to Grace E. King, December 1899 [n.d.].
17. MoSW, 05685. Letter to H. F. Gordon Forbes, October 1, 1899.
18. Paine, *Mark Twain,* 2:1095.
19. MTP. Notebook 38, May–July 1896. Entry for June 4, 1896.
20. CtHT-W, 05769. Letter to Joseph H. Twichell, March 4, 1900.
21. Clemens, *My Father Mark Twain,* 216.
22. NN-BGC, 08197. Letter to William Dean Howells, January 25, 1900.
23. *Mark Twain's Letters,* 2:694.
24. *Mark Twain's Notebook,* 166. Entry for late 1882.
25. CLjC, 04776. Letter to Olivia Susan "Susy" Clemens, August 8, 1894.
26. CU-MARK, 32954. Letter from Frederic W. H. Myers to Olivia L. Clemens, May 30, 1900.
27. CtHMTH, 08868. Letter to Laura Fitch McQuiston, March 26, 1901.
28. Clemens, *My Father Mark Twain,* 185.
29. CU-MARK, 12508. Letter to Susan L. Crane, October 1880 [n.d.].
30. Salm, 05790. Letter to Henry H. Rogers, April 8–9, 1900.

| 1095 |

NOTES

31. NN, 05810. Letter to Margaret Carnegie, May 28, 1900.
32. Salm, 05775. Letter to Henry H. Rogers, March 11, 1900.
33. Hill, *God's Fool,* 10.
34. ViU, 05774. Letter to John Y. MacAlister, March 10, 1900.
35. ViU, 09426. Letter to John Y. MacAlister, March 24, 1900.
36. Crawford, *How Not to Get Rich,* 183.
37. MFai, 05757. Letter to Henry H. Rogers, February 5, 1900.
38. CU-MARK, 05762. Letter to Andrew T. Still, February 23, 1900.
39. ViU, 0597. Letter to Samuel E. Moffett, April 23, 1900.
40. MH-H, 05792. Letter to William James, April 17, 1900.
41. MTP. CU-MARK, 05800. Letter to Pamela A. Moffett, April 25, 1900.
42. MTP. Notebook 43, 1900. Entry for May 4, 1900.
43. CU-MARK, 05807. Letter to Samuel E. Moffett, May 17, 1900.
44. Ibid.
45. Ibid.
46. CU-MARK, 11225. Letter to Mary E. "Mollie" Clemens, May 18, 1900.
47. *New York World,* June 17, 1900.
48. UkOxU, 05818. Letter to Mrs. T. Douglas Murray, June 7, 1900.
49. MTP. Notebook 43, 1900. Entry for July 2, 1900.
50. Paine, *Mark Twain,* 2:1109.
51. CU-MARK, 05851. Letter to Mrs. T. Douglas Murray, August 14, 1900.
52. CtY, 05855. Letter to Joseph H. Twichell, August 18, 1900.
53. Clemens, *My Father Mark Twain,* 216.
54. Neider, *Selected Letters,* 261.
55. ViU, 05877. Letter to John Y. MacAlister, October 16, 1900.

CHAPTER FORTY-FOUR: "THE ANCIENT MARINER"

1. Powers, *Mark Twain: A Life,* 599.
2. *New York World,* October 16, 1900.
3. Paine, *Mark Twain,* 2:1110.
4. *New York World,* October 14, 1900.
5. *New York Herald,* October 16, 1900.
6. Scharnhorst, *Complete Interviews,* 357.
7. *New York Herald,* October 16, 1900.
8. Ibid.
9. *Hartford Courant,* October 26, 1900.
10. Paine, *Mark Twain,* 2:1112.
11. CSmH, 53346. JCD, Vol. 1, Box 1. Entry for October 23, 1900.
12. MH-H, 05888. Letter from Olivia L. Clemens to Thomas B. Aldrich, October 27, 1900.
13. CU-MARK, 43529. Letter from William Dean Howells to Thomas B. Aldrich, November 4, 1900.
14. Zwonitzer, *Statesman and the Storyteller,* 410.
15. *Mark Twain's Notebooks,* 226.
16. Lawton, *A Lifetime with Mark Twain,* 193.
17. Clemens, *My Father Mark Twain,* 217.
18. *Mark Twain's Letters to Mary,* 17.
19. Ibid.
20. Fatout, *Mark Twain Speaking,* 349. November 10, 1900. Lotos Club Dinner.
21. Ibid., 351.
22. Ibid., 352.
23. *New York Times,* November 23, 1900.
24. Ibid.
25. Fatout, *Mark Twain Speaking,* 364. December 6, 1900. St. Nicholas Society Dinner.
26. Ibid.
27. CSmH, 53346. JCD, Vol. 1. Box 1. Entry for November 6, 1900.
28. CSmH, 53346. JCD, Vol. 1. Box 1. Entry for November 3, 1900.
29. CSmH, 53346. JCD, Vol. 1, Box 1. Entry for November 12, 1900.
30. CSmH, 53346. JCD, Vol. 1, Box 1. Entry for October 27, 1900.
31. CSmH, 53346. JCD, Vol. 1. Box 1. Entry for November 10, 1900.
32. CSmH, 53346. JCD, Vol. 1. Box 1. Entry for October 22, 1900.
33. CSmH, 53346. JCD, Vol. 1. Box 1. Entry for October 26, 1900.
34. CSmH, 53346. JCD, Vol. 1. Box 1. Entry for November 27, 1900.
35. CSmH, 53346. JCD, Vol. 1. Box 1. Entry for November 16, 1900.
36. MTP. Notebook 43, 1900. Entry for December 10, 1900.
37. *New York Times,* February 28, 1901.
38. Ibid.

NOTES

39. Ober, *Mark Twain and Medicine,* 164. February 27, 1901. Twain testimony on osteopathy.
40. Fatout, *Mark Twain Speaking,* 385. February 27, 1901. Twain testimony on osteopathy.
41. Ibid., 387.
42. *New York Times,* February 28, 1901.
43. CSmH, 53346. JCD, Vol. 1. Box 1. Entry for October 27, 1900.
44. CSmH, 53346. JCD, Vol. 1. Box 1. Entry for November 12, 1900.
45. Ibid.
46. CSmH, 53346. JCD, Vol. 1. Box 1. Entry for November 5, 1900.
47. Zwonitzer, *Statesman and the Storyteller,* 420.
48. Hill, *God's Fool,* 20.
49. CU-MARK, 05999. Letter from Olivia L. Clemens to Grace E. King, February 15 and 24, 1901.
50. Ibid.

CHAPTER FORTY-FIVE: THE ANTI-DOUGHNUT PARTY

1. *AMT,* 3:1020. Autobiographical Dictation for August 17, 1907.
2. Fatout, *Mark Twain Speaking,* 368. Speech of December 12, 1900.
3. Ibid., 367.
4. Ibid., 368.
5. Ibid., 369.
6. Schwarz, *Finest Hour,* Winter 2010–11.
7. Zwonitzer, *Statesman and the Storyteller,* 413–14.
8. Scharnhorst, *Twain in His Own Time,* 237.
9. *AMT,* 1:442–43. Autobiographical Dictation for March 26, 1906.
10. Powers, *Smithsonian,* September 2003.
11. CU-MARK, 07863. Letter to Jean Clemens, November 15, 1907.
12. Quick, *Enchantment,* 45.
13. Shelden, *Mark Twain: Man in White,* 226.
14. Clemens, *My Father Mark Twain,* 217.
15. Quick, *Enchantment,* 96.
16. Kaplan, *Mr. Clemens,* 361.
17. *Baltimore American,* May 11, 1907.
18. Heidig, *Known to Everyone,* 35.
19. CSmH, 04056. Letter to Charles Fairbanks, June 25, 1890.
20. MTP. Notebook 45, 1902. Entry for October 1902.
21. *Who Is Mark Twain?,* 202. "The American Press." June–September 1888.
22. Ibid., 203–5.
23. Ibid., 201.
24. NPV, 01530. Letter to Jane Lampton Clemens, February 17, 1878.
25. NPV, 03240. Letter to Pamela A. Moffett, June 12, 1885.
26. Rasmussen, *Dear Mark Twain,* 4.
27. *AMT,* 1:184. "Reflections on a Letter and a Book."
28. Ibid.
29. Ibid., 182.
30. Paine, *Mark Twain,* 3:1421.
31. *St. Louis Post-Dispatch,* May 19, 1889.
32. Heidig, *Known to Everyone,* 68.
33. CU-MARK, 02849. Letter to Miller and Bingham, October 8, 1883.
34. Heidig, *Known to Everyone,* 68.
35. NN, 05376. Letter to Arthur E. Gilbert, April 15, 1898.
36. CtHMTH, 05447. Letter to Paul E. Wirt Fountain Pen Company, October 11, 1898.
37. CU-MARK, 46199. Letter from Francis E. Bliss to Henry H. Rogers, April 20, 1898.
38. NN-BGC, 05499. Letter to William Dean Howells, December 3, 1899.
39. *Chronicle* (London), June 3, 1899.
40. Salm, 05722. Letter to Katherine L. Harrison, December 22, 1899.
41. *Mark Twain Day by Day,* 3:851.
42. Ibid., 3:896.
43. *Mark Twain's Notebook,* 381. Entry for October 22, 1903.
44. CU-MARK, 04864. Letter to Samuel E. Moffett, April 9, 1895.
45. MTP. Notebook 39, September 1896–January 1897.
46. Fatout, *Mark Twain Speaking,* 372.
47. *New York Times,* January 5, 1901.
48. Zwonitzer. *Statesman and the Storyteller,* 415. January 4, 1901. City Club Speech.
49. *New York Times,* January 11, 1901.
50. ViU, 05969. Letter to George A. Gates, January 21, 1901.
51. MTP. Notebook 44, 1901. Entry for October 2, 1901.
52. *New York Evening Post,* October 8, 1901.
53. *New York Herald,* October 14, 1901.

NOTES

54. Ibid.
55. Fatout, *Mark Twain Speaking*, 408–9. October 17, 1901. Acorns Dinner.
56. *New York Times*, October 30, 1901.
57. Fatout, *Mark Twain Speaking*, 414. October 29, 1901. Meeting of the Order of Acorns.
58. Ibid.
59. *New York Tribune*, October 31, 1901.
60. MTP. Notebook 44, 1901. Circa 1901.
61. Fatout, *Mark Twain Speaking*, 415–16. November 6, 1901. Acorns Election Jubilee.

CHAPTER FORTY-SIX: "THE UNITED STATES OF LYNCHERDOM"

1. CU-MARK, 09237. Letter to George V. Duryee, June 14, 1901.
2. CU-MARK, 06079. Letter to Charles Erskine Scott Wood, June 24, 1901.
3. CtY-BR, 06132. Letter to Joseph H. Twichell, September 8, 1901.
4. *New York Times*, April 18, 1901.
5. Paine, *Mark Twain*, 3:1140. Log of cruise, August 16, 1901.
6. CU-MARK, 06114. Letter to Olivia L. Clemens, August 14, 1901.
7. Fatout, *Mark Twain Speaking*, 381. February 11, 1901. Lincoln Celebration.
8. Ibid., 381–82.
9. Ibid., 382.
10. *New York Times*, February 13, 1901.
11. Blight, *Frederick Douglass*, 722.
12. Clemens, *My Husband Gabrilowitsch*, 13.
13. Fisher, *Abroad with Mark Twain*, 59.
14. *The Man That Corrupted Hadleyburg*, 169. "My First Life, and How I Got Out of It."
15. Zwick, *Confronting Imperialism*, 132.
16. Ibid.
17. Fishkin, *Journal of American Studies*, August 2006.
18. TxU-HU, 06119. Letter to Francis E. Bliss, August 26, 1901.
19. Ibid.
20. TxU-HU, 06126. Letter to Francis E. Bliss, August 29, 1901.
21. Ibid.
22. CU-MARK, 06134. Letter to Joseph H. Twichell, September 10, 1901.
23. Eden, *Mark Twain Journal*, Spring 2018. "Corn-Pone Opinions."
24. Zwonitzer, *Statesman and the Storyteller*, 355.
25. CU-MARK, 05753. Letter to Joseph H. Twichell, January 27, 1900.
26. MTP. Notebook 48, 1905–08.
27. Anderson, *A Pen Warmed Up*, 46. "As Regards Patriotism."
28. Fatout, *Mark Twain Speaking*, 350. November 10, 1900. Lotos Club Speech.
29. Ibid., 361–362. November 23, 1900. Berkeley Lyceum Speech.
30. CtY-BR, 05849. Letter to Joseph H. Twichell, August 12, 1900.
31. *Who Is Mark Twain?*, 105. July 16, 1900. "The Missionary in World-Politics."
32. Ibid.
33. Paine, *Mark Twain*, 3:1127.
34. CU-MARK, 05985. Letter to Joseph H. Twichell, January 29, 1901.
35. Gibson, *New England Quarterly*, December 1947.
36. Ellsworth, *Golden Age of Authors*, 225.
37. CSmH, 11092. Letter from Olivia L. Clemens to Annie A. Fields, February 19, 1901.
38. Heidig, *Known to Everyone*, 49.
39. Twain, *North American Review*, February 1901. "To the Person Sitting in Darkness."
40. Ibid.
41. Ibid.
42. Ibid.
43. Paine, *Mark Twain*, 3:1129.
44. LaBrUHM, 05999. Letter from Olivia L. Clemens to Grace E. King, February 15 and 24, 1901.
45. CSmH, 11092. Letter from Olivia L. Clemens to Annie A. Fields, February 19, 1901.
46. Clemens, *My Father Mark Twain*, 220.
47. Paine, *Mark Twain*, 3:1133.
48. Rasmussen, *Dear Mark Twain*, 183.
49. *Mark Twain Day by Day*, 3:493.
50. *Mark Twain's Letters*, 2:719. Letter to Helen Picard, February 22, 1901.
51. *New York Times*, February 7, 1901.
52. Rasmussen, *Dear Mark Twain*, 193.
53. *Mark Twain Day by Day*, 3:452.
54. Ibid., 1133–34.
55. Gibson, *New England Quarterly*, December 1947.

| 1098 |

NOTES

56. Hill, *God's Fool*, 29.
57. Zwonitzer, *Statesman and the Storyteller*, 424.
58. CU-MARK, 06018. Letter to Judson Smith, March 10, 1901.
59. Neider, *Complete Essays*, 303. "To My Missionary Critics."
60. Scharnhorst, *Twain in His Own Time*, 308–9.

CHAPTER FORTY-SEVEN: "MAGNIFICENT PANORAMA OF THE MISSISSIPPI"

1. Paine, *Mark Twain*, 3:1142.
2. Clemens, *My Father Mark Twain*, 227.
3. *New York Journal and Advertiser*, October 11, 1901.
4. *New York Sun*, October 11, 1901.
5. CU-MARK, 33306. Letter from Joseph H. Twichell, October 15, 1901.
6. *AMT*, 3:54. Autobiographical Dictation for May 23, 1907.
7. CU-MARK, 06163. Letter to Olivia L. Clemens, October 22, 1901.
8. *AMT*, 3:257. Autobiographical Dictation for July 14, 1908.
9. CU-MARK, 06262. Letter to Henry H. Rogers, January 31, 1902.
10. CU-MARK, 06250. Letter from Samuel E. and Olivia L. Clemens to Clara Clemens, January 20, 1902.
11. ViU, 06212. Letter from Olivia L. Clemens to Clara Clemens, January 1, 1902.
12. Twain Family Papers. CU-MARK, 06142. Letter from Olivia L. Clemens to Clara Clemens, September 25, 1901.
13. *AMT*, 2:82. Autobiographical Dictation for June 4, 1906.
14. Hill, *God's Fool*, 41–42.
15. CU-MARK, 06300. Letter to Olivia L. Clemens, March 14, 1902.
16. CU-MARK, 06302. Letter to Olivia L. Clemens, March 16, 1902.
17. *Mark Twain Day by Day*, 3:643. Ship log, March 16, 1902.
18. Ibid., March 23, 1902.
19. CU-MARK, 06311. Letter to Olivia L. Clemens, March 24, 1902.
20. Clemens, *My Husband Gabrilowitsch*, 24.
21. CtHMTH, 06348. Letter from Olivia L. Clemens to Harriet E. Whitmore, May 27, 1902.
22. Clemens, *My Husband Gabrilowitsch*, 41–42.
23. Zwonitzer, *Statesman and the Storyteller*, 458.
24. Hill, *God's Fool*, 60.
25. Scharnhorst, *Complete Interviews*, 478.
26. MTP. Notebook 45, 1902. Entry for May 15, 1902.
27. CU-MARK, 06337. Letter to William R. Gillis, May 16, 1902.
28. CtHMTH, 08879. Letter from Olivia L. Clemens to Katharine B. Clemens, May 27, 1902.
29. *St. Louis Star*, May 29, 1902.
30. Ibid.
31. Ibid.
32. Ibid.
33. Powers, *Mark Twain: A Life*, 612.
34. Kaplan, *Mr. Clemens*, 365.
35. *AMT*, 2:152–53. Autobiographical Dictation for July 31, 1906.
36. *St. Louis Republic*, May 31, 1902.
37. Paine, *Mark Twain*, 3:1167.
38. Fatout, *Mark Twain Speaking*, 431.
39. Wecter, *Sam Clemens of Hannibal*, 150.
40. Fatout, *Mark Twain Speaking*, 457.
41. *Hannibal Courier-Post*, June 3, 1902.
42. *St. Louis Star*, June 6, 1902.
43. *St. Louis Republic*, June 7, 1902.
44. Fatout, *Mark Twain Speaking*, 438. June 4, 1902. University of Missouri Commencement speech.
45. Ibid., 435.
46. MoHM, 08881. Letter to W. H. Dulany, June 17, 1902.

CHAPTER FORTY-EIGHT: "SPIRIT OF A STEAM ENGINE"

1. CU-MARK, 11971. Letter to Henry H. Rogers, June 26, 1902.
2. *AMT*, 2:82. Autobiographical Dictation for June 4, 1906.
3. Salm, 06385. Letter to Henry H. Rogers, July 7, 1902.
4. *AMT*, 2:83. Autobiographical Dictation for June 4, 1906.

NOTES

5. CtHMTH, 08882. Letter from Olivia L. Clemens to James R. Clemens, July 27, 1902.
6. Fatout, *Mark Twain Speaking*, 672. August 5, 1902. 250th Anniversary, York, Maine.
7. *AMT*, 2:97. Autobiographical Dictation for June 6, 1906.
8. Ibid., 99.
9. Ibid.
10. Clemens, *My Husband Gabrilowitsch*, 27–28.
11. Hill, *God's Fool*, 46.
12. CU-MARK, 12058. Letter from Clara Clemens to Dorothea Gilder, December 31, 1902.
13. CU-MARK, 06407. Letter to Susan L. Crane, August 15, 1902.
14. MTP. Notebook 45, Transcript 27–8. Entry for September 22, 1902.
15. Scharnhorst, *Twain in His Own Time*, 243.
16. NN-BGC, 08229. Letter to Frederick A. Duneka, September 15, 1902.
17. CU-MARK, 11937. Letter to Howard E. Wright, September 6, 1902.
18. MTP. Notebook 45, Transcript 27–8. Entry for September 21, 1902.
19. Salm, 06434. Letter to Henry H. Rogers, September 18, 1902.
20. Salm, 06441. Letter to Henry H. Rogers, September 24, 1902.
21. CU-MARK, 10158. Letter to Elisabeth Brachmann, September 26, 1902.
22. Salm, 06458. Letter to Henry H. Rogers, October 11, 1902.
23. *AMT*, 2:99. Autobiographical Dictation for June 6, 1906.
24. CU-MARK, 06629. Letter to Dr. Wilson L. Hawkes, April 23, 1903.
25. CtHMTH, 06381. Letter from Olivia L. Clemens to Harriet Whitmore, June 30, 1902.
26. Trombley, *Mark Twain's Other Woman*, 20.
27. Lystra, *Dangerous Intimacy*, 15.
28. Ibid., 38.
29. MTP. IVL Journals. Daily Reminder for January 6, 1903.
30. CtHMTH, 06509. Letter from Clara Clemens to Harriet Whitmore, December 10, 1902.
31. CU-MARK, 06493. Letter from Isabel Lyon to Franklin G. Whitmore, November 24, 1902.
32. Ibid., 1902.
33. IVL. *Annotated Mark Twain's Autobiography*, edited by Albert Bigelow Paine.
34. MTP. IVL Journals. Daily Reminder for June 29, 1903.
35. IVL. *Annotated Mark Twain's Autobiography*, edited by Albert Bigelow Paine.
36. NjP, 06483. Letter to Eleanor V. Hutton, November 6, 1902.
37. Clemens, *My Father Mark Twain*, 227.
38. Harnsberger, *Mark Twain Family Man*, 193–194.
39. CU-MARK, 06485. Letter to Franklin G. Whitmore, November 9, 1902.
40. CU-MARK, 06484. Letter to Franklin G. Whitmore, November 5, 1902.
41. *Mark Twain Day by Day*, 3:808.
42. CU-MARK,12058. Letter from Clara L. Clemens to Dorothea Gilder, December 31, 1902.
43. CU-MARK, 06477. Letter to Joseph H. Twichell, October 31, 1902.
44. Zwonitzer, *Statesman and the Storyteller*, 467.
45. *Mark Twain's Notebooks*, 71.
46. Fatout, *Mark Twain Speaking*, 458. November 28, 1902. Metropolitan Club speech.
47. CU-MARK, 06495. Letter to Olivia L. Clemens, November 30, 1902.
48. *Harper's Weekly*, November 15, 1902.
49. Ibid.
50. CU-MARK, 11438. Letter to Carl Thalbitzer, November 26, 1902.
51. MTP. IVL Journals. Daily Reminder for January 1, 1903.
52. *AMT*, 2:100. Autobiographical Dictation for June 7, 1906.
53. Ibid., 107.
54. Clemens, *My Father Mark Twain*, 234.
55. MTP. Notebook 45, Transcript 35–6. Entry for December 30, 1902.
56. Clemens, *My Father Mark Twain*, 230.
57. *Mark Twain Day by Day*, 3:816.
58. CtY, 06534. Letter to Joseph H. Twichell, December 31, 1902.
59. Paine, *Mark Twain*, 3:1190.
60. CU-MARK, 06975. Letter to Louise W. Carnegie, 1905 [n.d.].
61. MH-H, 06218. Letter to William Dean Howells, January 3, 1902.

NOTES

62. CU-MARK, 06282. Letter to Hélène Elisabeth Picard, February 22, 1902.
63. Ibid.
64. Ibid.
65. CtY-BR, 06460. Letter to Muriel M. Pears, October 13, 1902.
66. CU-MARK, 06518. Letter to Hélène Elisabeth Picard, December 15, 1902.

CHAPTER FORTY-NINE: DIVINE HEALING

1. CU-MARK, 05018. Letter to Olivia Susan "Susy" Clemens, February 7, 1896.
2. *AMT*, 2:343. Autobiographical Dictation for December 27, 1906.
3. NPV. Clemens. 20.4. Lyon Howe 1933.
4. CU-MARK, 12847. Letter to Joseph H. Twichell, May 4, 1899.
5. *Christian Science*, 49.
6. CtY-BR, 07732. Letter to Florence D. Jones, May 27, 1907.
7. *Mark Twain Day by Day*, 3:842. Letter to John Y. W. MacAlister, April 7, 1903.
8. *Mark Twain's Letters*, 2:734.
9. Paine, *Mark Twain*, 3:1200.
10. MTP. Notebook 46, 1903–04. Entry for July 1, 1903.
11. CU-MARK, 06693. Letter from Olivia L. Clemens to Clara Clemens, July 5, 1903.
12. CU-MARK, 06718. Letter from Olivia L. Clemens, August 5, 1903.
13. CU-MARK, 06728. Letter to Olivia L. Clemens, September 20, 1903.
14. Ibid.
15. CU-MARK, 06729. Letter from Olivia L. Clemens, September 23, 1903.
16. CU-MARK, 06936. Letter to Sue Crane, October 23, 1904.
17. MTP. Notebook 46, 1903–04. Entry for October 3, 1903.
18. *Mark Twain's Correspondence with Henry Huttleston Rogers*, 546.
19. MTP. Box 3. Notebook 46, Transcript 29. Entry for November 1, 1903.
20. Hill, *God's Fool*, 70.
21. *The Critic*, June 1904.
22. Lawton, *A Lifetime with Mark Twain*, 224–25.
23. *AMT*, 1:242. "Villa di Quarto."
24. MTP. IVL Journals. Entry for January 17, 1904.
25. Clemens, *My Father Mark Twain*, 243.
26. MTP. Box 47. 1904. Entry for January 6, 1904.
27. Hill, *God's Fool*, 73.
28. Clemens, *My Father Mark Twain*, 244–45.
29. Hill, *God's Fool*, xxvi.
30. DSI, 07871. Letter from Jean Clemens to Nancy D. Brush, November 29, 1907.
31. Lystra, *Dangerous Intimacy*, 40.
32. MTP. IVL Journals. Entry for February 28, 1904.
33. *AMT*, 1:220. "Random Extracts."
34. Trombley, *Mark Twain's Other Woman*, 32.
35. *AMT*, 1:241. "Villa di Quarto."
36. Ibid., 244.
37. Ibid.
38. Zwonitzer, *Statesman and the Storyteller*, 500.
39. Trombley, *Mark Twain's Other Woman*, 35–36.
40. Ibid, 36.
41. Ibid.
42. *New York Times*, April 10, 1904.
43. *Mark Twain Day by Day*, 3:952.
44. MTP. Notebook 47. Entry for February 22, 1904.
45. Hill, *God's Fool*, 83.
46. MH-H, 06812. Letter to Thomas Bailey Aldrich, March 21, 1904.
47. CU-MARK, 34085. Letter to Joseph H. Twichell, June 8, 1904.
48. Clemens, *My Father Mark Twain*, 251.
49. *Mark Twain Day by Day*, 3:974.
50. Harnsberger, *Mark Twain Family Man*, 208.
51. ViU, 06825. Letter to John Y. MacAlister, April 25, 1904.
52. MTP. Box 47. 1904. Entry for May 8, 1904.
53. CU-MARK, 06834. Letter to Joseph H. Twichell, May 11, 1904.
54. CU-MARK, 06835. Letter to Richard Watson Gilder, May 12, 1904.
55. CU-MARK, 08599. Letter to Dr. William Wilberforce Baldwin, May 15, 1904.
56. NNPM, 06837. Letter to Dr. William Wilberforce Baldwin, May 18, 1904.
57. MH-H, 06868. Letter to William Dean Howells, June 12, 1904.
58. Lawton, *A Lifetime with Mark Twain*, 225–26.

NOTES

CHAPTER FIFTY: THE DREAD CAVALCADE OF DEATH

1. CU, 06942. Letter to Frank N. Doubleday, November 1904 [n.d.].
2. Paine, *Mark Twain,* 3:1217.
3. MiD, 06933. Letter to Muriel Pears, October 24, 1904.
4. Paine, *Mark Twain,* 3:1218.
5. CU-MARK, 06858. Letter to Susan L. Crane, June 6, 1904.
6. Lawton, *A Lifetime with Mark Twain,* 228–29.
7. Neider, *Selected Letters,* 287.
8. MTP. Box 47. Entry for June 6, 1904.
9. Ibid. Entry for June 5, 1904.
10. *Mark Twain's Correspondence with Henry Huttleston Rogers,* 569.
11. MH-H, 06868. Letter to William Dean Howells, June 12, 1904.
12. CU-MARK, 12059. Letter from Clara Clemens to Dorothea Gilder, June 17, 1904.
13. CU-MARK, 12060. Letter from Clara Clemens to Helena Gilder, between June 20–24, 1904.
14. MTP. Notebook 37, Transcript 13. Entry for June 20, 1904.
15. Hill, *God's Fool,* 107.
16. CU-MARK, 06900. Letter to Frank Mason, July 23, 1904.
17. CU-MARK, 06994. Letter to Moses Allen Starr, February 26, 1905.
18. *Mark Twain's Notebook,* 389. Entry for July 12, 1904.
19. Ibid., 389. Entry for July 2, 1904.
20. Ibid., 388. Entry for July 1, 1904.
21. Jerome and Wisbey, *Mark Twain in Elmira,* 149.
22. *New York Times,* July 13, 1904.
23. Lawton, *A Lifetime with Mark Twain,* 231–232.
24. CU-MARK, 11450. Letter to Susan L. Crane, July 25, 1904.
25. MTP. Box 47. 1904. Notebook entry, September 1, 1904.
26. *AMT,* 2:393. Autobiographical Dictation for January 28, 1907.
27. Ibid., 1:451. Autobiographical Dictation for March 28, 1906.
28. NCH, 06916. Letter to Louise Brownell Saunders, September 3, 1904.
29. NCH, 07548. Letter to Louise Brownell Saunders, October 16, 1906.
30. CU-MARK, 06862. Letter to Richard Watson Gilder, June 7, 1904.
31. Lawton, *A Lifetime with Mark Twain,* 233.
32. CU-MARK, 42970. Letter from Richard Watson Gilder to G. E. Woodberry, August 4, 1904.
33. MTP. IVL Journals. Entry for July 16, 1904.
34. Ibid. Entry for July 4, 1904.
35. Paine, *Mark Twain,* 3:1224.
36. *Mark Twain's Correspondence with Henry Huttleston Rogers,* 579–80.
37. MTP. IVL Journals. Entry for July 31, 1904.
38. Clemens, *My Father Mark Twain,* 256.
39. MTP. IVL Journals. Entries for August 3 and 4, 1904.
40. Shelden, *Mark Twain: Man in White,* 92.
41. CtHMTH, 06901. Letter to Charles J. Langdon, July 25, 1904.
42. CU-MARK, 06919. Letter to Susan L. Crane, September 9, 1904.
43. Salm, 06914. Letter to Henry H. Rogers, August 18, 1904.
44. TxU-HU, 06935. Letter to Muriel M. Pears, October 23, 1904.
45. CU-MARK, 06947. Letter from Clara Clemens, November 7, 1904.
46. *Mark Twain Day by Day,* 3:1031.
47. Shelden, *Mark Twain: Man in White,* 23.
48. Paine, *Mark Twain,* 3:1225.
49. Trombley, *Mark Twain's Other Woman,* 43.
50. MTP. IVL Journals 1903–06. Stenographic Notebook 1.
51. NPV. Clemens, 21.35. Sam and Doris Webster, January 5, 1950.
52. CtHMTH, 10951. Letter from Isabel V. Lyon to Harriet E. Whitmore, January 5, 1905.
53. Trombley, *Mark Twain's Other Woman,* 61.
54. MTP. IVL Journals. Entry for December 14, 1904.
55. Lawton, *A Lifetime with Mark Twain,* 280.
56. CU-MARK, 07050. Letter to John Larkin, May 31, 1905.

NOTES

CHAPTER FIFTY-ONE: "THE WAR PRAYER"

1. CtHMTH, 10986. Letter from Isabel Lyon to Harriet E. Whitmore, February 6, 1905.
2. Scharnhorst, *Twain in His Own Time*, 239.
3. NPV. Clemens, 20.4. Lyon Howe.
4. MTP. IVL Journals 1903–06. Daily Reminder for January 30, 1906.
5. CU-MARK, 04060. Letter to Editor of *Free Russia*, July 1, 1890.
6. Rasmussen, *Dear Mark Twain*, 216.
7. WU-MU, 07055. Letter to Joseph H. Twichell, June 1, 1905.
8. CU-MARK, 12721. Letter to *Boston Globe* editor, August 29, 1905.
9. *AMT*, 1:648. "Explanatory Notes."
10. *AMT*, 1:462–63. Autobiographical Dictation for March 30, 1906.
11. MTP. IVL Journals 1903–06. Daily Reminder for December 22, 1905.
12. Fatout, *Mark Twain Speaking*, 468. December 18, 1905. Benefit Matinee for Jewish Sufferers.
13. Ibid.
14. CU-MARK, 07405. Letter to Nikolai V. Chaykovsky, March 28–29, 1906.
15. CU-MARK, 09911. Letter to *New York Times*, April 13, 1906.
16. *New York Times*, March 5, 2021.
17. *Mark Twain's Letters to Mary*, 32.
18. NN-BGC, 08257. Letter to Charlotte Teller, May 6, 1906.
19. CU-MARK, 34197. Letter to Edmund D. Morel, October 10, 1904.
20. Neider, *Mark Twain: Life As I Find It*, xvi.
21. Hochschild, *King Leopold's Ghost*, 241–42.
22. Fishkin, *Was Huck Black?*, 106.
23. MTP. IVL Journals 1903–06. Daily Reminder for February 10, 1905.
24. Ibid. Daily Reminder for July 7, 1905.
25. CU-MARK, 07064. Letter to Frederick A. Duneka, June 16, 1905.
26. *King Leopold's Soliloquy*, 3.
27. Ibid., 10.
28. Ibid., 38.
29. *New York Sunday World Magazine*, November 26, 1905.
30. Ibid.
31. *Boston Globe*, November 6, 1905.
32. *New York Sunday World Magazine*, November 26, 1905.
33. MTP. NN-BGC, 08249. Letter to Thomas S. Barbour, January 8, 1906.
34. NN-BGC, 02274. Transcript by Isabel V. Lyon: Letter to *Success Magazine* editor, October 12, 1906.
35. Ibid.
36. Budd, *Mark Twain: Social Philosopher*, 182–83.
37. *Mark Twain's Notebook*, 395. Entry circa October 13, 1904.
38. *Europe and Elsewhere*, 394. "The War Prayer."
39. Ibid., 396.
40. Ibid., 398.
41. Ibid.
42. Paine, *Mark Twain*, 3:1234.
43. Shelden, *Mark Twain: Man in White*, 60.
44. *AMT*, 3:173. Autobiographical Dictation for October 18, 1907.
45. *Mark Twain Day by Day*, 3:933.
46. *Letters of Mark Twain and Joseph Hopkins Twichell*, 353.
47. MTP. IVL Journals 1903–06. Daily Reminder for November 28, 1905.
48. *AMT*, 3:136. Autobiographical Dictation for September 13, 1907.
49. Ibid., 187. Autobiographical Dictation for December 2, 1907.
50. Ibid., 257. Autobiographical Dictation for July 14, 1908.
51. Ibid., 258. Autobiographical Dictation for July 14, 1908.
52. Ibid., 1:268. Autobiographical Dictation for January 12, 1906.

CHAPTER FIFTY-TWO: "AN ARTIST IN MORALS AND INK"

1. *AMT*, 3:340. ALM.
2. MTP. IVL Journals 1903–06. Daily Reminder for March 14, 1905.
3. Ibid. Daily Reminder for February 14–15, 1905.
4. Hill, *God's Fool*, 94.
5. NPV. Clemens. 20.7. Lyon Howe 1935.
6. Ibid.
7. Ibid.
8. MTP. IVL Journals 1903–06. Daily Reminder for April 2, 1905.
9. Ibid. Daily Reminder for April 23, 1905.

NOTES

10. Ibid. Daily Reminder for March 30, 1905.
11. Ibid. Daily Reminder for May 10, 1905.
12. Harnsberger, *Mark Twain Family Man*, 217.
13. CU-MARK, 13348. Letter to Edmund D. Morel, April 11, 1905.
14. Morgan, *Monadnock Summer*, 77.
15. Scharnhorst, *Complete Interviews*, 514.
16. MTP. IVL Journals 1903–06. Daily Reminder for May 16, 1905.
17. CSmH, 53347. JCD, Vol. 2. Box 1. Diary entry for June 2, 1905.
18. CSmH, 53347. JCD, Vol. 2. Box 1. Diary entry for June 4, 1905.
19. CU-MARK, 07048. Letter to Robert Fulton, May 24, 1905.
20. CU-MARK, 07147. Letter to Susan L. Crane, September 24, 1905.
21. CtY, 07090. Letter to Muriel M. Pears, July 26, 1905.
22. MTP. IVL Journals 1903–06. Daily Reminder for July 16, 1905.
23. CtY, 07069. Letter to Joseph H. Twichell, June 24, 1905.
24. MTP. IVL Journals 1903–6. Daily Reminder for June 13, 1905.
25. Ibid. Daily Reminder for August 12, 1905.
26. Ibid. Entry for July 9, 1905.
27. CU-MARK, 07060. Letter to Clara Clemens, June 8, 1905.
28. *Mark Twain's Letters to Mary*, 27.
29. Hill, *God's Fool*, 109.
30. MT. Notebook entry for August 12, 1883.
31. Tuckey, *Which Was the Dream?*, 433. *Three Thousand Years Among the Microbes*.
32. Ibid., 435.
33. Ibid., 438.
34. Ibid., 535.
35. Ibid., 536.
36. Trombley, *Mark Twain's Other Woman*, 74.
37. Rasmussen, *Mark Twain A to Z*, 2.
38. Scharnhorst, *Complete Interviews*, 494.
39. *The Diaries of Adam and Eve*, 29.
40. Ibid., 39, 45, 49.
41. Ibid., 89.
42. MTP. IVL Journals 1903–06. Daily Reminder for July 12, 1905.
43. MoHM, 07084. Letter to Clara Clemens, July 15, 1905.
44. *The Diaries of Adam and Eve*, 37.
45. Ibid., 71.
46. Ibid., 73.
47. Ibid., 89.
48. Ibid., 103.
49. Ibid., 109.
50. Heidig, *Known to Everyone*, 45.
51. *The Diaries of Adam and Eve*, 11 of afterword.
52. MTP. IVL Journals 1903–06. Daily Reminder for July 22, 1905.
53. *No. 44, The Mysterious Stranger*, 101–2.
54. Ibid., 186.
55. *Mark Twain's Notebooks*, 261.
56. *How Nancy Jackson Married Kate Wilson*, 132–33. "A Horse's Tale."
57. Ibid., 143.
58. Ibid., 178.
59. *Mark Twain's Letters*, 2:779.
60. CU-MARK, 35546. Letter from Lillian R. Beardsley, August 25, 1906.

CHAPTER FIFTY-THREE: "THE SWINDLE OF LIFE"

1. Ober, *Mark Twain and Medicine*, 141.
2. Hill, *God's Fool*, 116.
3. Harnsberger, *Mark Twain Family Man*, 219.
4. MTP. IVL Journals 1903–06. Daily Reminder for September 25, 1905.
5. CU-MARK, 07125. Letter to Clara Clemens, September 2, 1905.
6. CU-MARK, 07179. Letter to Clara Clemens, October 18, 1905.
7. CU-MARK, 07184. Letter to Clara Clemens, October 20, 1905.
8. NNC, 07509. Letter to Mary B. Rogers, August 28, 1906.
9. MTP. IVL Journals 1903–06. Daily Reminder for November 1, 1905.
10. *AMT*, 3:316. Autobiographical Dictation for December 24–26, 1909.
11. MTP. IVL Journals 1903–06. Daily Reminder for December 23, 1905.
12. Ibid. Daily Reminder for December 1, 1905.
13. Ibid. Daily Reminder for January 5, 1906.
14. Ibid.
15. DSI, 07302. Letter from Jean Clemens to Nancy D. Brush, January 11, 1906.
16. MTP. IVL Journals 1903–06. Daily Reminder for January 13, 1906.

NOTES

17. Ibid. Daily Reminder for January 24, 1906.
18. Ibid. Daily Reminder for January 27, 1906.
19. Ibid. Daily Reminder for November 26, 1905.
20. Trombley, *Mark Twain's Other Woman*, 83.
21. Shelden, *Mark Twain: Man in White*, 439.
22. Devinsky, *Epilepsy*, 105.
23. DSI, 07339. Letter from Jean Clemens to Nancy D. Brush, February 11, 1906.
24. Ibid.
25. NPV. Clemens. 12.24. Lyon Howe.
26. Ibid.
27. Ibid.
28. DSI, 08059. Letter from Jean Clemens to Nancy D. Brush, July 23, 1908.
29. DSI, 08094. Letter from Jean Clemens to Nancy D. Brush, August 27, 1908.
30. MTP. IVL Journals 1903–06. Daily Reminder for February 2, 1906.
31. Trombley, *American Literary Realism*, Spring 2005.
32. Trombley, *Mark Twain's Other Woman*, 98–99.
33. DSI, 07339. Letter from Jean Clemens to Nancy D. Brush, February 11, 1906.
34. Trombley, *Mark Twain's Other Woman*, 100.
35. Lystra, *Dangerous Intimacy*, 67.
36. Ibid.

CHAPTER FIFTY-FOUR: PIER 70

1. NPV. Clemens. 20.3. Lyon Howe 1933.
2. *Hartford Courant*, November 25, 1905.
3. CU-MARK, 35026. Letter from Helen Keller, December 8, 1905.
4. Fatout, *Mark Twain Speaking*, 462–63. Delmonico's Speech, December 5, 1905.
5. Ibid., 463.
6. Ibid., 464.
7. Paine, *Mark Twain*, 3:1252.
8. Trombley, *Mark Twain's Other Woman*, 90.
9. Lawton, *A Lifetime with Mark Twain*, 256.
10. Clemens, *My Father Mark Twain*, 258.
11. *New York Sunday World Magazine*, November 26, 1905.
12. CU-MARK, 06577. Letter to Samuel M. Bergheim, February 6, 1903.
13. CU-MARK, 06788. Letter to John B. Stanchfield, January 29, 1904.
14. *AMT*, 3:588. "Explanatory Notes."
15. *Mark Twain Day by Day*, 3:1051.
16. *AMT*, 3:270. Autobiographical Dictation for October 31, 1908.
17. Crawford, *How Not to Get Rich*, 184.
18. Lawton, *Living with Mark Twain*, 238–39.
19. *AMT*, 2:249. Autobiographical Dictation for October 8, 1906.
20. Kaplan, *Mr. Clemens*, 380.
21. MTP. IVL Journals 1903–06. Daily Reminder for October 8, 1906.
22. *AMT*, 3:253. Autobiographical Dictation for July 10, 1908.
23. CLjC, 07720. Letter to Jean Clemens, May 14, 1907.
24. Clemens, *My Father Mark Twain*, 268.
25. Harnsberger, *Mark Twain's Clara*, 136.
26. NPV, 03676. Letter to Orion Clemens, December 8, 1887.
27. NN-BGC, 08202. Letter to William M. Clemens, June 6, 1900.
28. CU-MARK, 05840. Letter to Samuel E. Moffett, July 28, 1900.
29. Gribben, *Mark Twain's Literary Resources*, 19.
30. *Mark Twain's Notebook*, 373.
31. Paine, *Mark Twain*, 3:1257.
32. Ibid., 1258.
33. Mac Donnell, *Mark Twain Journal*, Spring 2018.
34. MTP. IVL Journals 1903–06. Daily Reminder for January 9, 1906.
35. Mac Donnell, *Mark Twain Journal*, Spring 2018.
36. *AMT*, 1:25. "Introduction."
37. Mac Donnell, *Mark Twain Journal*, Spring 2018.
38. MTP. IVL Journals 1903–06. Daily Reminder for January 6, 1906.
39. *AMT*, 1:25. "Introduction."
40. MTP. IVL Journals 1903–06. Daily Reminder for January 9, 1906.
41. Kaplan, *Mr. Clemens*, 378.
42. *AMT*, 3:619. "Explanatory Notes: ALM."
43. Fanning, *Mark Twain and Orion Clemens*, 214.
44. Quick, *Enchantment*, 154.
45. Hoffmann, *Mark Twain in Paradise*, 144.

NOTES

46. Paine, *Mark Twain*, 3:1415.
47. *San Diego Reader*, May 8, 2003.
48. Lystra, *Dangerous Intimacy*, 57.
49. *AMT*, 1:7. "Introduction."
50. Jerome and Wisbey, *Mark Twain in Elmira*, 107.
51. Ibid.
52. *Times* (London), May 23, 1899.
53. Ibid.
54. MH-H, 05914. Letter to George Harvey, November 20, 1900.
55. *Mark Twain's Notebooks*, 50.
56. Clemens, *My Father Mark Twain*, 261.
57. Kaplan, *Mr. Clemens*, 379.
58. Paine, *Mark Twain*, 3:1268.
59. *AMT*, Ibid., 1299–1300.
60. Ibid., 2:136. Autobiographical Dictation for June 23, 1906.
61. Ibid., 138.
62. Ibid., 140.
63. Ibid., 158. Autobiographical Dictation for August 6, 1906.
64. NN-BGC, 08263. Letter to William Dean Howells, June 26, 1906.

CHAPTER FIFTY-FIVE: ANGELFISH

1. Hill, *God's Fool*, xxvii.
2. CU-MARK, 08444. Letter to Hélène Elisabeth Picard, August 26, 1909.
3. Clemens, *My Father Mark Twain*, 16.
4. *Mark Twain's Letters to Mary*, 80.
5. CU-MARK, 35123. Letter from Gertrude Natkin, December 27, 1905.
6. CU-MARK, 07278. Letter to Gertrude Natkin, December 28, 1905.
7. CUMARK, 07332. Letter to Gertrude Natkin, February 8, 1906.
8. CU-MARK, 07342. Letter to Gertrude Natkin, February 14, 1906.
9. MTP. IVL Journals 1903–06. Daily Reminder for March 4, 1906.
10. CU-MARK, 07401. Letter to Gertrude Natkin, March 24, 1906.
11. CU-MARK, 07393. Letter to Gertrude Natkin, March 18, 1906.
12. Shelden, *Mark Twain: Man in White*, 125.
13. CU-MARK, 07421. Letter to Gertrude Natkin, April 8, 1906.
14. CU-MARK, 07578. Letter to Gertrude Natkin, November 30, 1906.
15. *AMT*, 1:396. Autobiographical Dictation for March 7, 1906.
16. Ibid., 2:16. Autobiographical Dictation for April 4, 1906.
17. Ibid., 17. Autobiographical Dictation for April 4, 1906.
18. *New York World*, April 4, 1906.
19. Paine, *Mark Twain*, 3:1380.
20. CU-MARK, 08166. Letter to Nettie Brockley, December 7–10, 1908.
21. *AMT*, 3:213. Autobiographical Dictation for April 17, 1908.
22. Paine, *Mark Twain*, 3:1299–1300.
23. TxU-HU, 05814. Letter to Dora Bowen, June 6, 1900.
24. Scharnhorst, *Twain in His Own Time*, 253–54.
25. Scharnhorst, *The Life of Mark Twain*, 1:105.
26. Ibid.
27. MTP. IVL Journals. Annotated Copy of Paine biography of Twain.
28. Ibid. IVL Journals 1903–06. Stenographic Notebook #1. Entry for March 22, 1906.
29. Allen, *Our Friend Mark Twain*, 3.
30. Cooley, *Mark Twain's Aquarium*, 283.
31. Quick, *Enchantment*, 220–21.
32. Scharnhorst, *The Life of Mark Twain*, 1:106
33. Clemens, *My Father Mark Twain*, 274.
34. Cooley, *Mark Twain Journal*, Spring 1989.
35. *AMT*, 3:555. "Explanatory Notes." Isabel Lyon journal entry of April 1, 1908.
36. NN-BGC, 08254. Letter to Charlotte Teller, April 13, 1906.
37. MTP. NN-BGC, 08256. Letter to Charlotte Teller, May 4, 1906.
38. NN-BGC, 08261. Letter to Charlotte Teller, June 16–18, 1906.
39. Ibid.
40. Harnsberger, *Mark Twain's Clara*, 38.
41. MTP. IVL Journals 1903–06. Daily Reminder for June 25, 1906.
42. Ibid. Daily Reminder for October 24, 1906.
43. CU-MARK, 07316. Letter to Mr. and Mrs. William Gordon, January 24, 1906.
44. MTP. IVL Journals 1903–06. Daily Reminder for May 26, 1906.
45. *AMT*, 2:151. Autobiographical Dictation for July 30, 1906.
46. CU-MARK, 11451. Letter to Susan L. Crane, July 27, 1906.

NOTES

47. *AMT*, 2:150. Autobiographical Dictation for July 30, 1906.
48. Ibid., 151.
49. Ibid.

CHAPTER FIFTY-SIX: A FAN AND A HALO

1. NN-BGC, 07399. Letter to Kate W. Barrett, March 23, 1906.
2. CtY, 07523. Letter to Isabel Lyon, September 14, 1906.
3. Hawkins, *New England Quarterly*, June 1978.
4. *AMT*, 1:305. Autobiographical Dictation for January 23, 1906.
5. Ibid., 306.
6. Neider, *Complete Essays*, 475. Tuskegee Speech.
7. Ibid., 476.
8. *AMT*, 1:303. Autobiographical Dictation for January 23, 1906.
9. Hill, *God's Fool*, 129.
10. MTP. IVL Journals 1903–06. Daily Reminder for March 2, 1906.
11. Trombley, *Mark Twain's Other Woman*, 99.
12. Lystra, *Dangerous Intimacy*, 52.
13. Trombley, *Mark Twain's Other Woman*, 111–112.
14. MTP. IVL Journals 1903–06. Daily Reminder for February 28, 1906.
15. Hill, *God's Fool*, 122.
16. MTP. IVL Journals 1903–06. Daily Reminder for March 19, 1906.
17. Ibid. Daily Reminder for May 6, 1906.
18. CSmH, 53348. JCD. Vol. 3. Box 1. Entry for May 6, 1906.
19. Ibid. Entry for May 3, 1906.
20. Ibid. Entry for May 10, 1906.
21. Ibid. Entry for June 6, 1906.
22. Ibid.
23. Ibid. Entry for May 1906 [n.d.].
24. NN-BGC, 08259. Letter to Charlotte Teller, May 29, 30, 31, and June 2, 1906.
25. NN-BGC, 08260. Letter to Charlotte Teller, June 10, 1906.
26. MTP. IVL Journals 1903–06. Daily Reminder for May 17, 1906.
27. CU-MARK, 07902. Letter to Isabel Lyon, May 22, 1906.
28. CSmH, 53347. JCD. Vol. 2. Box 1. Diary entry for May 29, 1905.
29. Paine, *Mark Twain*, 3:1308.
30. MTP. IVL Journals 1903–06. Daily Reminder for April 7, 1906.
31. Ibid. Daily Reminder for June 16, 1906.
32. CSmH, 53348. JCD. Vol. 3. Box 1. Entry for June 9, 1906.
33. MTP. IVL Journals 1903–06. Daily Reminder for June 9, 1906.
34. CSmH, 53348. JCD. Vol. 3. Box 1. Entry for June 10, 1906.
35. MTP. IVL Journals 1903–06. Daily Reminder for June 13, 1906.
36. Hill, *God's Fool*, 140.
37. MFai, 07460, Letter to Henry H. Rogers, June 17, 1906.
38. Ibid.
39. Tuckey, *Fables of Man*, 15.
40. MTP. IVL Journals 1903–06. Daily Reminder for June 20, 1906.
41. CSmH, JCD. Vol. 3. Box 1. Entry for June 27, 1906.
42. NPV. Clemens. 12.3. Lyon Howe.
43. CSmH, 53348. JCD. Vol. 3. Box 1. Entry for June 1906 [n.d.].
44. CSmH, 53348. JCD, Vol. 3. Box 1. Entry for June 28, 1906.
45. Ibid.
46. Clemens, *My Father Mark Twain*, 182.
47. NN-BGC, 05601. Letter to William Dean Howells, April 2, 1899.
48. CU-MARK, 05985. Letter to Joseph H. Twichell, January 29, 1901.
49. Gewirtz, *A Skeptic's Progress*, 130.
50. MTP. IVL Journals 1903–06. Daily Reminder for August 31, 1905.
51. Ibid. Daily Reminder for August 8, 1906.
52. Ibid.
53. *AMT*, 3:130. Autobiographical Dictation for September 4, 1907.
54. *What is Man?*, 11.

CHAPTER FIFTY-SEVEN: WUTHERING HEIGHTS

1. MTP. IVL Journals 1903–06. Daily Reminder for July 12, 1906.
2. CU-MARK, 07478. Letter to Isabel Lyon, July 10, 1906.

NOTES

3. Hill, *God's Fool*, 146.
4. CSmH, 53348. JCD. Vol. 3. Box. 1. Entry for July 3, 1906.
5. Ibid., Vol. 4. Entry for July 22, 1906.
6. Ibid., Vol. 3. Box 1. Entry for July 3, 1906.
7. Ibid. Entry for July 21, 1906.
8. Lystra, *Dangerous Intimacy*, 74.
9. CSmH, 53348. JCD. Vol. 3. Box 1. Entry for July 6, 1906.
10. Ibid. Entry for July 19, 1906.
11. MTP. IVL Journals 1903–06. Daily Reminder for July 28, 1906.
12. CSmH, 53349. JCD. Vol. 4. Box 1. Entry for July 24, 1906.
13. Trombley, *Mark Twain's Other Woman*, 115.
14. Hill, *God's Fool*, 149.
15. NNC, 07490. Letter to Mary B. Rogers, August 4, 1906.
16. NNC, 07504. Letter to Mary B. Rogers, August 25, 1906.
17. *Mark Twain's Correspondence with Henry Huttleston Rogers*, 616.
18. CSmH, 53349. JCD. Vol. 4. Box 1. Entry for August 23, 1906.
19. MTP. IVL Journals 1903–06. Daily Reminder for August 24, 1906.
20. NNPM, 07511. Letter to Anne E. Benjamin, August 29, 1906.
21. CSmH, 53349. JCD. Vol. 4. Box 1. Entry for August 21, 1906.
22. Ibid. Entry for August 26, 1906.
23. Lystra, *Dangerous Intimacy*, 68.
24. NNC, 07507. Letter to Mary B. Rogers, August 28, 1906.
25. NNC, 07528. Letter to Mary B. Rogers, September 21, 1906.
26. Ibid.
27. *AMT*, 2:244. Autobiographical Dictation for October 4, 1906.
28. Harnsberger, *Mark Twain's Clara*, 118.
29. *New York Sun*, September 24, 1906.
30. Harnsberger, *Mark Twain Family Man*, 227.
31. CU-MARK, 07529. Letter to Jean Clemens, September 23, 1906.
32. Harnsberger, *Mark Twain's Clara*, 119.
33. MTP. IVL Journals 1903–06. Daily Reminder for September 15, 1906.
34. CSmH, 53350. Box 1. JCD. Vol. 5. Box 1. Entry for September 16, 1906.
35. MTP. IVL Journals 1903–06. Daily Reminder for September 20, 1906.
36. Ibid. Daily Reminder for September 24, 1906.
37. CU-MARK, 07531. Letter to Ralph W. Ashcroft, September 27, 1906.
38. CSmH, 53350. JCD. Vol. 5. HM 53350. Entry for September 27, 1906.
39. MTP. IVL Journals 1903–06. Daily Reminder for September 28, 1906.
40. Trombley, *Mark Twain's Other Woman*, 108.
41. CSmH, 53350. Box 1. JCD. Vol. 5. Box 1. HM 53350. Entry for September 29, 1906.
42. Ibid. Entry for October 1, 1906.
43. MH-H, 07534. Letter to Thomas Bailey Aldrich, October 1, 1906.
44. Ibid.
45. CLjC, 07533. Letter to Clara Clemens, October 2, 1906.
46. MTP. IVL Journals 1903–06. Daily Reminder for October 1, 1906.
47. Ibid. Daily Reminder for October 12, 1906.
48. MTP. CLjC, 07533. Letter to Clara Clemens, October 2 and 3, 1906.
49. CSmH, 53350. JCD. Vol. 5, Box 1. Entry for October 4, 1906.
50. Ibid. Entry for October 5, 1906.
51. MTP. IVL Journals 1903–06. Daily Reminder for October 16, 1906.
52. CU-MARK, 07539. Letter to Clara Clemens, October 9, 1906.
53. CSmH, 53350. JCD. Vol. 5. Box 1. Entry for October 10 or 11, 1906.
54. Hill, *God's Fool*, 154.
55. CSmH, 53350. JCD. Vol. 5. Box 1. Entry for October 20, 1920.
56. Ibid.
57. Hill, *God's Fool*, 160.
58. MFai, 07554. Letter to Emilie Rogers, October 24, 1906.
59. CSmH, 53350. JCD. Vol. 5. Box 1. Entry for October 25, 1906.
60. Hill, *God's Fool*, 152.
61. MTP. IVL Journals 1903–06. Daily Reminder for October 27, 1906.
62. CSmH, 53350. JCD. Vol. 5. Box 1. Entry for October 27, 1906.
63. MTP. IVL Journals 1903–06. Daily Reminder for October 27, 1906.
64. CSmH, 53350. JCD. Vol. 5. Box 1. Entry for November 1, 1906.

NOTES

CHAPTER FIFTY-EIGHT: MAN IN THE WHITE CLOTHES

1. CSmH, 53350. JCD. Vol. 5. Box 1. Entry for November 3, 1906.
2. CU-MARK, 07568. Letter to Jean Clemens, November 13, 1906.
3. MFai, 07561. Letter to Emilie Rogers, November 5, 1906.
4. CSmH, 53350. JCD. Vol. 5. Box 1. Entry for November 15, 1906.
5. Ibid. Entry for November 21, 1906.
6. MTP. IVL Journals 1903–06. Daily Reminder for November 8, 1906.
7. NPV. Clemens. 21.36. Lyon Howe. Notes from Samuel and Doris Webster, January 10, 1953.
8. Paine, *Mark Twain*, 3:1339.
9. MTP. IVL Journals 1903–06. Daily Reminder for November 24, 1906.
10. *Mark Twain's Letters to Mary*, 93. Letter to Mary Benjamin Rogers, November 28, 1906.
11. *AMT*, 2:277. Autobiographical Dictation for November 20, 1906.
12. Ibid., 284. Autobiographical Dictation for November 22, 1906.
13. CU-MARK, 12091. Letter to *Harper's Weekly*, January 24, 1905.
14. *AMT*, 2:285. Autobiographical Dictation for November 22, 1906.
15. CU-MARK, 07582. Letter to Jean Clemens, December 7, 1906.
16. Ibid.
17. *Washington Herald*, December 8, 1906.
18. Fatout, *Mark Twain Speaking*, 530.
19. Harnsberger, *Mark Twain's Clara*, 21.
20. *Mark Twain's Letters*, 2:802.
21. *Washington Times*, December 8, 1906.
22. Ibid.
23. CU-MARK, 08415. Letter to Champ Clark, June 5, 1909.
24. MTP. IVL Journals 1903–06. Daily Reminder for December 12, 1906.
25. Ibid. Daily Reminder for December 13, 1906.
26. Ibid. Daily Reminder for December 14, 1906.
27. Ibid. Daily Reminder for December 29, 1906.
28. CSmH, 53351. JCD. Vol. 6. Box 1. Entry for December 13, 1906.
29. Ibid. Entry for December 19, 1906.
30. Ibid. Entry for December 20, 1906.
31. Ibid. Entry for January 16, 1907.
32. Ibid. Entry for January 5, 1907.
33. Ibid. Entry for January 17, 1901.
34. Ibid. Entry for December 15, 1906.
35. Ibid. Entry for December 19, 1906.
36. Ibid. Entry for December 27, 1906.
37. Shelden, *Mark Twain: Man in White*, 392.
38. CSmH, 53351. JCD. Vol. 6. Box 1. Entry for December 28, 1906.
39. Hodgson, *The Bermudian*, November 1983.
40. Hoffmann, *Mark Twain in Paradise*, 54.
41. Ibid., 69.
42. Hill, *God's Fool*, 161.
43. MTP. IVL. Date Book for 1907. Entry for January 4, 1907.
44. Hoffmann, *Mark Twain in Paradise*, 75.
45. Lystra, *Dangerous Intimacy*, 102.
46. *The Letters of Mark Twain and Joseph Hopkins Twichell*, 391.
47. Hoffmann, *Mark Twain in Paradise*, 75.
48. *The New York Times*, January 10, 1907.
49. CSmH, 53351. JCD. Vol. 6. Box 1. Entry for January 10, 1907.
50. MTP. IVL. Date Book for 1907. Entry for January 10, 1907.
51. CSmH, 53351. JCD. Vol. 6. Box 1. Entry for January 11, 1907.
52. Ibid. Diary entry for January 20, 1907.
53. CU-MARK, 07625. Letter to Jean Clemens, January 11, 1907.
54. Lystra, *Dangerous Intimacy*, 90.
55. CSmH, 53351. JCD. Vol 6. Box 1. Entry for January 14, 1907.
56. Ibid. Entry for February 1, 1907.
57. Ibid. Entry for February 22, 1907.
58. CLjC, 07664. Letter to Jean Clemens, February 25, 1907.
59. Trombley, *American Literary Realism*, Winter 2008.
60. MTP. IVL. Date Book for 1907. Entry for January 20, 1907.
61. Hoffmann, *Mark Twain in Paradise*, 83.
62. CU-MARK, 07675. Letter to Clara Clemens, March 12, 1907.
63. Hoffmann, *Mark Twain in Paradise*, 78.
64. Ibid., 81.
65. Lystra, *Dangerous Intimacy*, 90.

NOTES

CHAPTER FIFTY-NINE: "A REAL AMERICAN COLLEGE BOY"

1. Hill, *God's Fool*, 182.
2. *AMT*, 3:54. Autobiographical Dictation for May 23, 1907.
3. CU-MARK, 07730. Letter to Jean Clemens, May 26, 1907.
4. CSmH, 53352. JCD. Vol. 7. Box 1. HM 53352. Entry for June 8, 1907.
5. Shelden, *Mark Twain: Man in White*, 102.
6. CU-MARK, Letter from Carlotta Welles Briggs to Dixon Wecter, November 4, 1947. [No catalog number.]
7. Cooley, *Mark Twain's Aquarium*, 40.
8. CU-MARK, Letter from Carlotta Welles Briggs to Dixon Wecter, November 4, 1947. [No catalog number.]
9. *Evening Dispatch* (Edinburgh), June 20, 1907.
10. *Westminster Gazette*, June 18, 1907.
11. Shelden, *Mark Twain: Man in White*, 105.
12. *AMT*, 3:72. Autobiographical Dictation for July 24, 1907.
13. Lystra, *Dangerous Intimacy*, 117.
14. MTP. IVL. Date Book for 1907. Entry for June 21, 1907, quoting a newspaper article from June 20.
15. Hill, *God's Fool*, 175.
16. CU-MARK, 07762. Telegram from Clara Clemens and to Clara Clemens, June 21, 1907.
17. Trombley, *Mark Twain's Other Woman*, 139.
18. CSmH, 11582. Letter from Jean Clemens, June 24, 1907.
19. *AMT*, 3:74. Autobiographical Dictation for July 25, 1907.
20. Ibid., 144. Autobiographical Dictation for October 1, 1907.
21. Ibid.
22. Ibid., 145.
23. CLjC, 07767. Letter to Jean Clemens, June 23, 1907.
24. CSmH, 11582. Letter from Clara Clemens, June 24, 1907.
25. *AMT*, 3:79. Autobiographical Dictation for July 25, 1907.
26. *Mark Twain's Notebooks*, 105.
27. Brittain, *Mark Twain Journal*, Fall 1961; Lanier, *Mark Twain Journal*, Spring 1986.
28. Brittain, *Mark Twain Journal*, Fall 1961.
29. Kaplan, *Mr. Clemens*, 382.
30. Fatout, *Mark Twain Speaking*, 610.
31. Shelden, *Mark Twain: Man in White*, 115.
32. Pinney, *The Letters of Rudyard Kipling*, 249.
33. Langdon, *Samuel Langhorne Clemens*, 18.
34. *AMT*, 3:84. Autobiographical Dictation for July 30, 1907.
35. Paine, *Mark Twain*, 3:1394.
36. CLjC, 07773. Letter to Clara Clemens, June 30, 1907.
37. Ibid.
38. CU-MARK, 07746. Letter to Louis N. Parker, June 18, 1907.
39. *AMT*, 3:86. Autobiographical Dictation for July 30, 1907.
40. Gribben, *Mark Twain's Literary Resources*, 1:50–51.
41. Scharnhorst, *Twain in His Own Time*, 282.
42. *AMT*, 3:109. Autobiographical Dictation for August 23, 1907.
43. Ibid., 494. "Explanatory Notes."
44. Shelden, *Mark Twain: Man in White*, 124.
45. CSmH, 11583. Letter from Clara Clemens, June 27, 1907.
46. Hill, *God's Fool*, 173.
47. Trombley, *Mark Twain's Other Woman*, 125.
48. *AMT*, 3:433–34. ALM.
49. Ibid., 434.
50. Shelden, *Mark Twain: Man in White*, 87.
51. Hoffmann, *Mark Twain in Paradise*, 68.
52. Lystra, *Dangerous Intimacy*, 103.
53. *AMT*, 3:124. Autobiographic Dictation for August 31, 1907.
54. Ibid.
55. Liverpool *Post*, July 11, 1907.
56. Fatout, *Mark Twain Speaking*, 637.
57. *North American Review*, September 1935.
58. Ibid.
59. Quick, *Enchantment*, 11.
60. Ibid., 14.
61. *North American Review*, September 1935.
62. Ibid.
63. Ibid.
64. Scharnhorst, *Complete Interviews*, 645.
65. Quick, *Enchantment*, 33.
66. Ibid., 34.
67. *New York Sun*, July 23, 1907.
68. MTP. IVL. Date Book for 1907. Entry for July 22, 1907.

NOTES

CHAPTER SIXTY: "ALL THE WONDERS THAT ARE OCCURRING"

1. *AMT*, 3:55. Autobiographical Dictation for May 24, 1907.
2. CU-MARK, 07735. Letter to Henry H. Rogers, May 29, 1907.
3. Trombley, *Mark Twain's Other Woman*, 132.
4. *Mark Twain's Letters to Mary*, 101.
5. MTP. IVL. Date Book for 1907. Entry for June 1, 1907.
6. Ibid. Entry for June 3, 1907.
7. Ibid. Entry for June 15, 1907.
8. CU-MARK, 07662. Letter to Clara Clemens, February 24, 1907.
9. MTP. IVL. Date Book for 1907. Entry for June 22, 1907.
10. Ibid. Entry for June 14, 1907.
11. Trombley, *Mark Twain's Other Woman*, 137.
12. MTP. IVL. Date Book for 1907. Entry for July 1907 [n.d.].
13. Shelden, *Mark Twain: Man in White*, 137.
14. Trombley, *Mark Twain's Other Woman*, 159–60.
15. CU-MARK, 07805. Letter from Isabel V. Lyon to E. Gertrude Quick, August 1, 1907.
16. Quick, *Enchantment*, 62–63.
17. *AMT*, 3:156. Autobiographical Dictation for October 5, 1907.
18. Quick, *Enchantment*, 79.
19. Cooley, *Mark Twain's Aquarium*, 51.
20. CSmH, 11549. Letter from Clara Clemens, August 13, 1907.
21. CU-MARK, 07818. Letter to Jean Clemens, August 25, 1907.
22. CSmH, 53352. JCD. Vol. 7. Box 1. Entry for September 30, 1907.
23. Ibid. Entry for June 28, 1907.
24. CSmH, 53352. JCD. Vol. 7. Box. 1. Entry for June 8, 1907.
25. CSmH, 11552. Letter from Jean Clemens, July 23, 1907.
26. CSmH, JCD. Vol. 7. Box 1. Entry for July 26, 1907.
27. Quick, *Enchantment*, 97.
28. Ibid., 75.
29. Cooley, *Mark Twain's Aquarium*, 67.
30. MTP. IVL Journals 1903–06. Date Book for 1907. Entry for September 17, 1907.
31. Salm, 07839. Letter to Henry H. Rogers, September 26, 1907.
32. MTP. IVL Journals 1903–06. Date Book for 1907. Entry for September 28, 1907.
33. CU-MARK, 37382. Letter from Frances Nunnally, October 27, 1907.
34. CSmH, 07858. Letter to Frances Nunnally, October 28, 1907.
35. CSmH, 53352. JCD. Vol. 8. Box 1. Entry for November 2, 1907.
36. Ibid. Vol. 7. Box 1. Entry for September 18, 1907.
37. CSmH, 07842. Letter from Jean Clemens to Nancy D. Brush, October 2, 1907.
38. MTP. IVL Journals 1903–06. Date Book for 1907. Entry for October 2, 1907.
39. CtHMTH, 07739. Letter to Jean Clemens, early October 1907 [n.d.].
40. Trombley, *American Literary Realism*. Isabel Lyon, Notebook 4, entry for October 5, 1907.
41. MTP. IVL Journals 1903–06. Date Book for 1907. Entry for October 22, 1907.
42. Ibid.
43. Ibid. Entry for October 23, 1907.
44. Ibid.
45. DSI, 07859. Letter from Jean Clemens to Nancy D. Brush, October 31, 1907.
46. CU-MARK, 07860. Letter to the *New York World* editor, November 22–26, 1907.
47. NN-BGC, 07915. Draft letter to the Knickerbocker Trust, President and Directors, November 22–26, 1907.
48. *New York American*, December 21, 1907.
49. Trombley, *Mark Twain's Other Woman*, 182.
50. Hill, *God's Fool*, 183.

CHAPTER SIXTY-ONE: A HOLIDAY FROM LIFE'S WOES

1. Fatout, *Mark Twain Speaking*, 375.
2. Ibid., 546–47. Curtain Speech, Educational Alliance, April 14, 1907.
3. Ibid., 548–49. Actors' Fund Fair, 6, 1907.
4. CU-MARK, 08096. Letter to Amelia D. Hookay, October 1908 [n.d.].
5. *Brooklyn Eagle*, November 24, 1907.
6. CU-MARK, 07649. Letter to Jean Clemens, February 14, 1907.

| 1111 |

NOTES

7. Scharnhorst, *The Complete Interviews*, 611.
8. MH-H, 08292. Unsent letter to William Dean Howells, April 17, 1909.
9. CtHMTH, 07790. Letter to Clara Clemens, July 27, 1907.
10. Hill, *God's Fool*, 194.
11. Ibid.
12. CSmH. Clemens Family Papers. Box 1. JCD, Vol. 7. HM 53352. Entry for June 23, 1907.
13. Harnsberger, *Mark Twain Family Man*, 237.
14. Ibid.
15. CSmH. Clemens Family Papers. Box 2. JCD, Vol. 8. HM 53352. Entry for November 1, 1907.
16. CU-MARK, 07878. Letter to Jean Clemens, December 2, 1907.
17. CSmH. Clemens Family Papers. Box 1. JCD, Vol. 7. HM 53352. Entry for December 7, 1907.
18. Ibid. Entry for December 11, 1907.
19. Ibid. Entry for December 15, 1907.
20. DSI, 07896. Letter from Jean Clemens to Nancy D. Brush, December 26, 1907.
21. Lystra, *Dangerous Intimacy*, 177.
22. CSmH. Clemens Family Papers. Box 1. JCD. Entry for December 25, 1907.
23. Trombley, *Mark Twain's Other Woman*, 177.
24. Hill, *God's Fool*, 197.
25. CtHMTH, 07934. Letter to Charles J. Langdon, February 11, 1908.
26. Trombley, *Mark Twain's Other Woman*, 178.
27. Ibid.
28. DSI-AAA, 07976. Letter from Jean Clemens to Nancy D. Brush, April 15, 1908.
29. DSI-AAA, 07966. Letter from Jean Clemens to Nancy D. Brush, March 29, 1908.
30. CLjC, 08005. Letter to Jean Clemens, May 22, 1908.
31. MTP. IVL Journals 1903–06. Date Book for 1907. Entry for October 14, 1907.
32. Cooley, *Mark Twain's Aquarium*, 82.
33. Quick, *Enchantment*, 126.
34. CU-MARK, 07897. Letter to Dorothy Quick, December 29, 1907.
35. CU-MARK, 07924. Letter to Dorothy Quick, January 21, 1908.
36. *Bermuda Journal*, 1908.
37. *The Bermudian*, December 1983.
38. Wallace, *Happy Island*, 5.
39. Ibid.
40. *Bermuda Journal*, 1908.
41. Ibid.
42. Ibid.
43. Hoffmann, *Mark Twain in Paradise*, 99.
44. MTP. IVL Journals 1903–06. Date Book for 1908. Entry for March 26, 1908.
45. Shelden, *Mark Twain: Man in White*, 212.
46. Wallace, *Happy Island*, 43–44.
47. Ibid., 16.
48. MTP. IVL Journals 1903–06. Date Book for 1908. Entry for February 8, 1908.
49. MTP. IVL Journals 1903–06. Date Book for 1908. Entry for February 7, 1908.
50. Trombley, *Mark Twain's Other Woman*, 77.
51. *AMT*, 3:211. Autobiographical Dictation for February 19, 1908.
52. Hoffmann, *Mark Twain in Paradise*, 103.
53. Shelden, *Mark Twain: Man in White*, 202.
54. *Bermuda Journal*, 1908.
55. Wallace, *Happy Island*, 80.
56. *Bermuda Journal*, 1908.
57. Wallace, *Happy Island*, 71.
58. CU-MARK, 07957. Letter to Dorothy Quick, March 10, 1908.
59. MTP. IVL Journals 1903–06. Date Book for 1908. Entry for March 20, 1908.
60. *AMT*, 214. Autobiographical Dictation for April 17, 1908.
61. Allen, *Our Friend Mark Twain*, 5.
62. Cooley, *Mark Twain's Aquarium*, 123.
63. Shelden, *Mark Twain: Man in White*, 220.
64. Cooley, *Mark Twain's Aquarium*, 144.
65. CU-MARK, 07997. Letter to Dorothy Quick, May 12, 1908.

CHAPTER SIXTY-TWO: INNOCENCE AT HOME

1. *AMT*, 3:556. "Explanatory Notes."
2. MTP. IVL Journals 1903–06. Date Book for 1908. Entry for May 2 and 4, 1908.
3. Paine, *Mark Twain*, 3:1449.
4. Harnsberger, *Mark Twain Family Man*, 245.
5. Paine, *Mark Twain*, 3:1450.

NOTES

6. Ibid.
7. *AMT*, 3:556. "Explanatory Notes."
8. CU-MARK, 08037. Letter to Clara Clemens, June 20, 1908.
9. Scharnhorst, *Complete Interviews*, 668.
10. Lanier, *Mark Twain Journal*, Spring 1986.
11. Hoffmann, *Mark Twain in Paradise*, 129.
12. Cooley, *Mark Twain's Aquarium*, 179.
13. CU-MARK, 08035. Letter to Jean Clemens, June 19, 1908.
14. Salm, 08076. Letter to Emilie Rogers, August 6, 1908.
15. NPV. Clemens, 21.36. Lyon Howe. Notes from Samuel and Doris Webster, January 8, 1953.
16. Trombley, *Mark Twain's Other Woman*, 114.
17. Shelden, *Mark Twain: Man in White*, 90–91.
18. CLjC, 08005. Letter to Jean Clemens, May 20, 1908.
19. CSmH, 11545. Letter from Jean Clemens, May 26, 1909.
20. CLjC, 08006. Letter to Jean Clemens, May 21, 1908.
21. Lystra, *Dangerous Intimacy*, 124.
22. DSI, 08045. Letter from Jean Clemens to Nancy D. Brush, June 29, 1908.
23. Ibid.
24. CLjC, 08028. Letter to Jean Clemens, June 14, 1908.
25. Shelden, *Mark Twain: Man in White*, 231.
26. CU-MARK, 08035. Letter to Jean Clemens, June 19, 1908.
27. *AMT*, 3:343. ALM for May 27, 1909.
28. Ibid.
29. Lystra, *Dangerous Intimacy*, 140.
30. *AMT*, 3:343. ALM for May 27, 1909.
31. Hill, *God's Fool*, 186.
32. DSI, 08059. Letter from Jean Clemens to Nancy D. Brush, July 23, 1908.
33. Ibid.
34. DSI, 08071. Letter from Jean Clemens to Nancy Brush, August 1, 1908.
35. CU-MARK, 08074. Letter from Jean Clemens to Isabel Lyon, August 4, 1908.
36. CU-MARK, 08075. Letter from Jean Clemens to Isabel Lyon, August 5, 1908.
37. Ibid.
38. Ibid.
39. Letter to Jean Clemens, August 10, 1908. Collection of Cindy and Brian Meehl.

CHAPTER SIXTY-THREE: "MARK TWAIN'S DAUGHTER"

1. NN-BGC, 08284. Letter to William Dean Howells, August 12, 1908.
2. *New York Herald*, December 13, 1925.
3. Ibid.
4. MTL, Redding, Connecticut. "Founding of Library" Folder.
5. CSmH, 08490. Letter to Elizabeth Wallace, November 13, 1909.
6. *Collier's Weekly*, January 1925.
7. Ibid.
8. CU-MARK, 08119. Letter to Mabel L. Patterson, October 2, 1908.
9. Paine, *Mark Twain*, 3:1458–59.
10. Salm, 08076. Letter to Jean Clemens, August 9, 1908.
11. MTP. IVL Journals 1903–06. Date Book for 1908. Entry for August 6, 1908.
12. *Mark Twain's Correspondence with Henry Huttleston Rogers*, 652.
13. Ibid.
14. Cooley, *Mark Twain's Aquarium*, 197–98.
15. CtHMTH, 10969. Letter from Isabel Lyon to Harriet Whitmore, August 17, 1908.
16. *AMT*, 3:348. ALM for June 19, 1909.
17. MFai, 08137. Letter to Emilie Rogers, October 12, 1908.
18. CSmH, 07898. Letter to Frances Nunnally, December 29, 1907.
19. *American Magazine*, July 1929.
20. Ibid.
21. Ibid.
22. Shelden, *Mark Twain: Man in White*, 316.
23. MTP. Pratt, 09389. Instructions "To Get Hot Water," March 13, 1909.
24. MTP. 09165. Walter Francis Frear. *Mark Twain and Hawaii*, 1947, facing p. 243.
25. Cooley, *Mark Twain's Aquarium*, 191.
26. Paine, *Mark Twain*, 3:1440.
27. Cooley, *Mark Twain's Aquarium*, 186.
28. NNC, 08113. Letter to Dorothy Sturgis, September 30, 1908.
29. Shelden, *Mark Twain: Man in White*, 247.
30. Cooley, *Mark Twain's Aquarium*, ix.
31. Shelden, *Mark Twain: Man in White*, 232.
32. Harnsberger, *Mark Twain Family Man*, 240.
33. *London Express*, June 3, 1908.
34. Ibid.
35. Lystra, *Dangerous Intimacy*, 137.

NOTES

36. MTP. Ashcroft-Lyon, Statement submitted on behalf of Mrs. Ashcroft.
37. Lystra, *Dangerous Intimacy,* 136–37.
38. CU-MARK, 08040. Letter from Clara Clemens to Isabel Lyon, June 24, 1908.
39. NPV. Clemens. 12.13. Lyon Howe. Letter from Clara Clemens to Isabel Lyon, August 4, 1908.
40. *New York World,* September 7, 1908.
41. CU-MARK, 12062. Letter from Clara Clemens to Dorothea Gilder, September 19, 1908.
42. Gewirtz, *A Skeptic's Progress,* 131.
43. *New York World,* September 19, 1908.
44. *AMT,* 3:269. Statement of September 18, 1908.
45. Paine, *Mark Twain,* 3:1472.
46. CU-MARK, 08167. Letter to Marjorie Breckenridge, December 1, 1908.
47. CU-MARK, 08126. Letter to Marjorie Breckenridge, October 7, 1908.
48. Ibid.
49. MTP. Manuscript items associated with ALM, 6.
50. MTP. IVL Journals 1903–06. Date Book for 1908. Entry for October 6, 1908.
51. Lystra, *Dangerous Intimacy,* 152. Isabel Lyon journal entry for October 18, 1908.
52. NPV. Clemens. 12.13. Lyon Howe. Letter from Clara Clemens to Isabel Lyon, August 4, 1908.
53. MTP. IVL Journals 1903–06. Date Book for 1908. Entry for October 20, 1908.
54. MTP. IVL Journals 1903–06. Date Book for 1908. Entry for October 21, 1908.
55. Lystra, *Dangerous Intimacy,* 151. Isabel Lyon journal entry of October 26, 1908.
56. Ibid., 152.
57. Trombley, *Mark Twain's Other Woman,* 171.
58. MTP. IVL Journals 1903–06. Date Book for 1907. Entry for April 7, 1907.
59. Giroud, *Alma Mahler,* 68–69.
60. Trombley, *Mark Twain's Other Woman,* 190.
61. Ibid.
62. CSmH, 08446. Letter to Elizabeth Wallace, August 27, 1909.
63. Lystra, *Dangerous Intimacy,* 153.

CHAPTER SIXTY-FOUR: THE DEATH OF TAMMANY

1. MoFuWC, 11251. Letter from Isabel Lyon to Laura Hawkins Frazer, October 10, 1908.
2. *Kansas City Star,* November 25, 1917.
3. Ibid.
4. MoFIM, 09536. Inscription to Laura Hawkins Frazer, October 14, 1908.
5. MFai, 04696. Address to the Millicent Library, February 22, 1894.
6. Heidig, *Known to Everyone,* 71. "To My Guests," October 7, 1908.
7. Ibid.
8. CU-MARK, 08151. Letter to Louise Paine, November 4, 1908.
9. Trombley, *Mark Twain's Other Woman,* 127.
10. Ibid.
11. MTP. IVL Journals 1903–06. Daily Reminder for February 9, 1906.
12. NPV. Clemens. 20.7. Lyon Howe 1935.
13. MTP. "Orion Clemens's Autobiography," by Benjamin Griffin. Isabel Lyon phone call to Albert Bigelow Paine, January 26, 1908.
14. CU-MARK, 50364. Letter from Albert Bigelow Paine to Isabel Lyon, January 28, 1908.
15. MH-H, 07925. Letter to William Dean Howells, January 22, 1908.
16. MTP. IVL Journals 1903–06. Date Book for 1908. Entry for January 23, 1908.
17. CU-MARK, 08065. Letter to George B. Harvey, July 30, 1908.
18. MTP. IVL Journals 1903–06. Date Book for 1908. Entry for October 15, 1908.
19. *AMT,* 3:334. ALM, May 1909.
20. CU-MARK, 50378. Letter from Albert B. Paine to Mrs. Lyon, July 21, 1909.
21. CU-MARK, 50378. Letter from Albert B. Paine to Isabel Lyon, January 28, 1909.
22. MTP. IVL Journals 1903–06. Date Book for 1908. Entry for July 26, 1908.
23. NPV. Clemens. 21.35. Lyon Howe. Notes from Samuel and Doris Webster, January 5, 1950.
24. MTP. IVL Journals 1903–06. Date Book for 1908. Entry for August 8, 1906.
25. CU-MARK, 08126. Letter to Marjorie Breckenridge, October 7, 1908.

NOTES

26. CU-MARK, 08040. Letter from Clara Clemens to Isabel Lyon, June 24, 1908.
27. MTP. IVL Journals 1903–06. Date Book for 1908. Entry for October 18, 1908.
28. *AMT*, 3:367. ALM for July 11, 1909.
29. Ibid., 391. ALM for July 1, 1909.
30. *Mark Twain's Notebook,* 393. Notebook entry for October 13, 1904.
31. Shelden, *Mark Twain: Man in White,* 295–96.
32. *AMT,* 3:398. ALM.
33. Shelden, *Mark Twain: Man in White,* 294.
34. MTP. Memorandum for Mr. Rogers, re: Clemens matter.
35. Paine, *Mark Twain,* 3:1485.
36. MTP. IVL Journals 1903–06. Date Book for 1908. Entry for December 24, 1908.
37. MTP. IVL Journals 1903–06. Date Book for 1908. Entry for December 27, 1908.
38. Shelden, *Mark Twain: Man in White,* 306.

CHAPTER SIXTY-FIVE: "AN INSANE IDEA"

1. MTP. IVL Journals 1903–06. Date Book for 1908. Entry for September 26, 1908.
2. CtHMTH, 08180. Letter to Charles J. Langdon, December 12, 1908.
3. *AMT,* 3:342. ALM for May 2, 1909.
4. CU-MARK, 08182. Letter to Jean Clemens, December 17, 1908.
5. CU-MARK, 08513. Letter from Jean Clemens to Marguerite Schmitt, December 21, 1908.
6. Hill, *God's Fool,* 215.
7. CU-MARK, 08363. Letter from Jean Clemens, March 5, 1909.
8. CSmH, 08344. Letter to Frances Nunnally, February 9, 1909.
9. CU-MARK, 0863. Letter from Jean Clemens, March 5, 1909.
10. Harnsberger, *Mark Twain Family Man,* 253.
11. CtHMTH, 10971. Letter from Isabel Lyon to Harriet W. Enders, February 16, 1909.
12. Ibid.
13. Trombley, *Mark Twain's Other Woman,* 203.
14. CU-MARK, 12719. Letter from Isabel Lyon, February 24–29, 1909.
15. *AMT,* 3:346. ALM for June 19, 1909.
16. *Hartford Courant,* March 11, 1909.
17. *AMT,* 3:348. ALM for June 19, 1909.
18. NPV. Clemens. 12.2. Lyon Howe. Letter from Jean Clemens to Isabel Lyon, March 14, 1909.
19. *AMT,* 3:349. ALM for June 19, 1909.
20. Ibid., 353.
21. Ibid.
22. Ibid., 354.
23. Trombley, *Mark Twain's Other Woman,* 209.
24. *AMT,* 3:354. ALM for June 1, 1909.
25. Lystra, *Dangerous Intimacy,* 171.
26. CU-MARK, 08370. Letter to Clara Clemens, March 11, 1909.
27. Ibid.
28. Ibid.
29. Ibid.
30. Ibid.
31. Ibid.
32. Ibid.
33. Ibid.
34. CtY, 07069. Letter to Joseph H. Twichell, June 24, 1905.
35. CSmH, 43438. Letter from Mercy C. Paine to Albert Bigelow Paine, March 8–9, 1909.
36. CU-MARK, 08370. Letter to Clara Clemens, March 14, 1909.
37. *AMT,* 3:354. ALM.
38. CU-MARK, 40179. Letter from William Dean Howells to Elinor M. Howells, March 24, 1909.
39. *AMT,* 3:355. ALM for June 19, 1909.
40. Lystra, *Dangerous Intimacy,* 174.
41. Ibid., 176.
42. Ibid.
43. CLjC, 08385. Letter to Jean Clemens, April 19, 1909.
44. CU-MARK, 12344. Letter to Mark Twain Company, Board of Directors, September 5, 1909.
45. *AMT,* 3:341. ALM.
46. Ibid., 341, 359.
47. Ibid., 366.
48. Ibid.
49. Ibid., 375.
50. Ibid., 376.
51. NPV. Clemens. 21.36. Lyon Howe. Notes from Samuel and Doris Webster, January 23, 1853.
52. *AMT,* 3:362. ALM.

NOTES

53. Ibid., 362–364.
54. Ibid., 379.
55. Shelden, *Mark Twain: Man in White*, 353.
56. Lystra, *Dangerous Intimacy*, 180.
57. Salm, 08396. Letter to Henry M. Rogers, May 4, 1909.
58. CU-MARK, 50365. Letter from Ralph Ashcroft, April 29, 1909.
59. *AMT*, 3:330, 613. ALM.
60. Lystra, *Dangerous Intimacy*, 184.
61. *New York Times*, May 20, 1909.
62. Clemens, *My Father Mark Twain*, 278.
63. Hill, *God's Fool*, 227.
64. *AMT*, 3:388. ALM for July 1, 1909.
65. CtHMTH, 08421. Letter to William R. Coe, June 16, 1909.
66. Shelden, *Mark Twain: Man in White*, 359.
67. CU-MARK, 50372. Letter from Ralph W. Ashcroft, June 3, 1909.
68. CSmH, 08148. Letter to Elizabeth Wallace, June 7, 1909.
69. *AMT*, 3:347. ALM.
70. CU-MARK, 12344. Letter to Mark Twain Company, Board of Directors, September 5–9, 1909.
71. CtHSD, 10610. Letter from Jean Clemens to Joseph H. Twichell, June 14, 1909.
72. Ibid.
73. Ibid.
74. CtY-Br, 08425. Letter to Joseph H. Twichell, June 23, 1909.
75. CtHMTH, 8428. Letter to William R. Coe, June 27, 1909.
76. *AMT*, 3:407. ALM.
77. Ibid.
78. Ibid., 410.
79. Ibid., 412.
80. CU-MARK, 08434. Letter from Clara Clemens, July 9, 1909.
81. Ibid.
82. CU-MARK, 50377. Letter from Albert B. Paine to Charles T. Lark, July 15, 1909.
83. *AMT*, 3:417. Jean Clemens Narrative for July 17, 1909.
84. Ibid.
85. Ibid.
86. Ibid., 418.
87. Ibid.
88. Ibid.
89. Ibid., 422.
90. CU-MARK, 08435. Letter to Clara Clemens, July 18, 1909.
91. *AMT*, 3:423. Clara Clemens Narrative for July 20, 1909.
92. Ibid., 424.
93. Ibid.
94. Ibid., 425.
95. Ibid., 426.
96. Hill, *God's Fool*, 207.
97. *New York Times*, August 4, 1909.
98. *AMT*, 3:432.
99. *New York Times*, September 13, 1909.
100. CU-MARK, 08451. Letter to Melville E. Stone, September 1909.
101. Scharnhorst, *Twain in His Own Time*, 106.
102. *AMT*, 3:437. ALM.
103. Ibid., 433.
104. Ibid.
105. Ibid., 338.
106. Ibid., 337–38.
107. Ibid., 420.
108. CU-MARK, 08435. Letter to Clara Clemens, July 18, 1909.
109. *AMT*, 3:438. ALM.
110. Harnsberger, *Mark Twain's Clara*, 36.
111. *AMT*, 3:438. ALM.
112. Lystra, *Dangerous Intimacy*, 240.
113. Clemens. NPV. 21.35. Lyon Howe. Notes from Samuel and Doris Webster, January 5, 1950.
114. Trombley, *American Literary Realism*, Winter 2008.
115. *AMT*, 3:393. ALM.

CHAPTER SIXTY-SIX: GRANDPA TWAIN

1. *AMT*, 3:604. "Explanatory Notes."
2. Paine, *Mark Twain*, 3:1480.
3. *1601, and Is Shakespeare Dead?*, 5.
4. Langdon, *Samuel Langhorne Clemens*, 12.
5. CU-MARK, 08355. Letter to Jean Clemens, February 26, 1909.
6. *AMT*, 3:303. Autobiographical Dictation for March 25, 1909.
7. *1601, and Is Shakespeare Dead?*, 15.
8. Paine, *Mark Twain*, 3:1497.
9. Ibid., 1498.
10. *Baltimore Sun*, June 11, 1909.
11. Fatout, *Mark Twain Speaking*, 645.
12. CtY-BR, 08425. Letter to Joseph H. Twichell, June 23, 1909.
13. CtHMTH, 08428. Letter to William R. Coe, June 27, 1909.
14. Lystra, *Dangerous Intimacy*, 252.

NOTES

15. NNPM, 08561. Letter to Clara Clemens, February 23, 1910.
16. CU-MARK, 08435. Letter to Clara Clemens, July 18, 1909.
17. *AMT*, 3:359. ALM for June 19, 1909.
18. Hill, *God's Fool*, 227.
19. BmuHA, Allen Papers. Letter from Albert B. Paine to Marion Schuyler Allen, November 6, 1910.
20. Taylor, *Mark Twain's Margins*, 18.
21. CtHSD, 10610. Letter from Jean Clemens to Joseph H. Twichell, June 14, 1909.
22. DSI, 08437. Letter from Jean Clemens to Nancy D. Brush, July 29, 1909.
23. Ibid.
24. Paine, *Mark Twain*, 3:1502.
25. Ibid., 1507–8.
26. Ibid., 1511.
27. Ibid., 1504.
28. NPV, 11242. Letter to Margery H. Clinton, August 27, 1909.
29. Paine, *Mark Twain*, 3:1529.
30. Ibid., 1514.
31. Ibid., 1519.
32. *AMT*, 2:194. Autobiographical Dictation for August 29, 1906.
33. MH-H, 02053. Letter to William Dean Howells, October 15, 1881.
34. *Mark Twain Day by Day*, 2:19.
35. Ibid., 3:747.
36. *AMT*, 2:195. Autobiographical Dictation for August 30, 1906.
37. *Extract from Captain Stormfield's Visit to Heaven*, 8.
38. Ibid., 14.
39. Ibid., 17–19.
40. Ibid., 38.
41. Ibid., 73.
42. Ibid., 73–74.
43. Ibid., 76–77.

CHAPTER SIXTY-SEVEN: *LETTERS FROM THE EARTH*

1. Trombley, *Mark Twain's Other Woman*, 201.
2. *New York Times*, August 14, 1909.
3. DLC, 08467. Letter to Augusta M. D. Ogden, October 13, 1909.
4. CU-MARK, 08434. Letter from Clara Clemens, July 9, 1909.
5. Clemens, *My Husband Gabrilowitsch*, 48.
6. Clemens, *My Father Mark Twain*, 280.
7. Paine, *Mark Twain*, 3:1522.
8. Clemens, *My Husband Gabrilowitsch*, 50.
9. Shelden, *Mark Twain: Man in White*, 379.
10. CtHSD, 10631. Letter from Clara Clemens to Joseph H. Twichell, September 26, 1909.
11. CSmH, 08548. Letter to Elizabeth Wallace, January 26–29, 1910.
12. Lawton, *A Lifetime with Mark Twain*, 310.
13. Trombley, *Mark Twain's Other Woman*, 227.
14. *New York Herald*, October 6, 1909.
15. Lawton, *A Lifetime with Mark Twain*, 312.
16. Clemens, *My Father Mark Twain*, 281.
17. Paine, *Mark Twain*, 3:1524.
18. *New York Herald*, October 13, 1909.
19. *New York American*, October 14, 1909.
20. Trombley, *Mark Twain's Other Woman*, 230.
21. Shelden, *Mark Twain: Man in White*, 381.
22. Trombley, *American Literary Realism*, Winter 2008.
23. *New York Herald*, October 14, 1909.
24. CU-MARK, 08482. Letter to Beatrice M. Benjamin, November 7, 1909.
25. CSmH, 08490. Letter to Elizabeth Wallace, November 13, 1909.
26. *Letters from the Earth*, 7.
27. Ibid., 9.
28. Ibid., 8.
29. Ibid., 10.
30. Ibid., 41.
31. Ibid., 40.
32. Ibid., 39.
33. Ibid., 15.
34. Ibid., 16.
35. Ibid., 23–24.
36. Ibid., 28–29.
37. Ibid., 30.
38. Ibid., 44.
39. Ibid., 52–53.
40. Paine, *Mark Twain*, 3:1539.

NOTES

CHAPTER SIXTY-EIGHT: "AN OLD BIRD OF PARADISE"

1. CSmH, 08457. Letter to Elizabeth Wallace, September 22, 1909.
2. CSmH, 08413. Letter to Frances Nunnally, July 15, 1909.
3. BmuHA, 11786. Letter to Helen S. Allen, October 12, 1909.
4. *Europe and Elsewhere*, 369.
5. CU-MARK, 08444. Letter to Hélène Elisabeth Picard, August 26, 1909.
6. Ibid.
7. Hill, *God's Fool*, 101.
8. Hawkins, *New England Quarterly*, June 1978. Letter from Albert B. Paine to Sir Arthur Conan Doyle, October 9, 1909.
9. Allen, *Our Friend Mark Twain*, 12.
10. CU-MARK, 08498. Letter from Jean Clemens to Marguerite Schmitt, November 20, 1909.
11. CU-MARK, 08500. Letter to Clara Clemens, November 26, 1909.
12. Hoffmann, *Mark Twain in Paradise*, 139.
13. CU-MARK, 08507. Letter to Jean Clemens, December 6, 1909.
14. BmuHA, Allen Papers. Mark Twain inscription, December 18, 1909.
15. Ibid.
16. Ibid.
17. Paine, *Mark Twain*, 3:1547.
18. *AMT*, 3:611. "Explanatory Notes."
19. Lawton, *A Lifetime with Mark Twain*, 320.
20. MoSW, 08516. Letter to the Associated Press, December 24, 1909.
21. *AMT*, 3:311. Autobiographical Dictation for December 25, 1909.
22. Lawton, *A Lifetime with Mark Twain*, 321.
23. *AMT*, 3:311. "Closing Words of My Autobiography."
24. Devinsky, *Epilepsy*, 53.
25. *AMT*, 3:311. Autobiographical Dictation for December 24, 25, 26, 1909.
26. Neider, *Complete Essays*, 492. Christmas Day, 1909. "The Death of Jean."
27. Paine, *Mark Twain*, 3:1548.
28. CSmH, 08527. Letter to Clara Clemens, December 29, 1909.
29. *AMT*, 3:318. Christmas Night, 1909. "Closing Words of My Autobiography."
30. Ibid.
31. Clemens, *My Father Mark Twain*, 285.
32. Jerome and Wisbey, *Mark Twain in Elmira*, 93.
33. Ibid., 164.
34. *AMT*, 3:312. December 25, 1908. "Closing Words of My Autobiography."
35. CU-MARK, 40534. Letter from Joseph H. and Harmony C. Twichell, December 25, 1909.
36. CU-MARK, 08574. Letter to Clara Clemens, March 24, 1910.
37. Hill, *God's Fool*, 255.
38. *AMT*, 3:613. December 27, 1909. "Closing Words of My Autobiography."
39. Bush, *The Letters of Mark Twain and Joseph Hopkins Twichell*, 414.
40. Neider, *Complete Essays*, 495. December 26, 1909. "The Death of Jean."
41. CtHMTH, 08524. Letter to Mai H. Coe, December 27, 1909.
42. CtHMTH, 08526. Letter to Harriet E. Whitmore, December 28, 1909.
43. Hill, *God's Fool*, 255. Letter from Harriet Whitmore, January 3, 1910.
44. *Mark Twain's Letters to Mary*, 130.

CHAPTER SIXTY-NINE: HALLEY'S COMET

1. Shelden, *Mark Twain: Man in White*, 399.
2. Scharnhorst, *Complete Interviews*, 693.
3. Allen, *Our Friend Mark Twain*, 29.
4. MoHM, 08569. Letter to Clara Clemens, March 12, 1910.
5. CLjC, 08546. Letter to Albert Bigelow Paine, January 24, 1910.
6. CU-MARK, 12583. Letter to Albert B. Paine, January 14, 1910.
7. Trombley, *Mark Twain's Other Woman*, 237.
8. CU-MARK, 12915. Letter to John Hays Hammond, March 22, 1910.
9. CSmH, 08548. Letter to Elizabeth Wallace, January 26, 1910.
10. Trombley, *Mark Twain's Other Woman*, 237.
11. Hoffmann, *Mark Twain in Paradise*, 150.
12. Ibid.
13. Harnsberger, *Mark Twain Family Man*, 265.
14. Quick, *Enchantment*, 213.
15. Hoffmann, *Mark Twain in Paradise*, 151.

NOTES

16. Ibid.
17. Shelden, *Mark Twain: Man in White*, 405.
18. CtY-BR, 08551. Letter to Margaret Blackmer, January 26, 1910.
19. Allen, *Strand Magazine*, August 1913.
20. Hodgson, *The Bermudian*, February 1984.
21. Cooley, *Mark Twain's Aquarium*, 278. April 1910. Helen Allen Manuscript number two.
22. Hill, *God's Fool*, 260–61.
23. Cooley, *Mark Twain's Aquarium*, 273.
24. Ibid.
25. Ibid., 274–75.
26. Ibid., 277.
27. Ibid., 276.
28. Allen, *Our Friend Mark Twain*, 32.
29. Ibid., 47.
30. NNPM, 08561. Letter to Clara Clemens, February 21, 1910.
31. NNPM, 08561. Letter to Clara Clemens, February 22, 1910.
32. Ibid.
33. CLjC, 1192. Letter from Clara Clemens to Mrs. Wilson, February 1–March 30, 1910.
34. Ibid.
35. BmuHA, Allen Papers. Letter from Clara Clemens to Marion Schuyler Allen, December 21, 1910.
36. Paine, *Mark Twain*, 3:1560.
37. Allen, *Our Friend Mark Twain*, 43.
38. Hoffmann, *Mark Twain in Paradise*, 148.
39. Paine, *Mark Twain*, 3:1569.
40. Allen, *Strand Magazine*, August 1913.
41. Paine, *Mark Twain*, 3:1562–63. Letter to Albert B. Paine, March 25, 1910.
42. BmuHA, 11112. Letter to the Clowns of Barnum and Bailey Circus, April 3, 1910.
43. Paine, *Mark Twain*, 3:1566–67.
44. Hill, *God's Fool*, 242.
45. Allen, *Our Friend Mark Twain*, 48.
46. Hoffmann, *Mark Twain in Paradise*, 1.
47. Paine, *Mark Twain*, 3:1570.
48. Shelden, *Mark Twain: Man in White*, 408.
49. Paine, *Mark Twain*, 3:1573.
50. Ibid., 1571.
51. Lawton, *A Lifetime with Mark Twain*, 328.
52. Ibid., 328–29.
53. Clemens, *My Husband Gabrilowitsch*, 53.
54. Clemens, *My Father Mark Twain*, 279.
55. Taylor, *Mark Twain's Margins*, 25.
56. Hoffmann, *Mark Twain in Paradise*, 156.
57. Clemens, *My Father Mark Twain*, 291.
58. Lawton, *A Lifetime with Mark Twain*, 331–32.
59. Scharnhorst, *Complete Interviews*, 466.
60. Paine, *Mark Twain*, 3:1579.
61. Clemens, *My Father Mark Twain*, 291.
62. Courtney, *Joseph Hopkins Twichell*, 267.
63. CU-MARK, 03664. Letter to Frances F. Cleveland, November 6, 1887.
64. Lawton, *A Lifetime with Mark Twain*, 332.
65. Bush, *The Letters of Mark Twain and Joseph Hopkins Twichell*, 415.
66. Lawton, *A Lifetime with Mark Twain*, 349.
67. Howells, *My Mark Twain*, 100–101.
68. Ibid., 101.
69. *Elmira Advertiser*, April 25, 1910.
70. MoKiU, 46305. Letter from Clara Clemens to Grace King, May 1910 [n.d.].
71. Clemens, *My Husband Gabrilowitsch*, 54.
72. Trombley, *Mark Twain's Other Woman*, 232.
73. CtHMTH, 47724. Letter from Clara Clemens to Harriet Whitmore, June 25, 1910.
74. CtHMTH, 47736. Letter from Clara Clemens to Harriet Whitmore, August 5, 1910.
75. Ibid.
76. Trombley, *Mark Twain's Other Woman*, 245.
77. Ibid.
78. Clemens, *Awake to a Perfect Day*, 15.
79. *Adventures of Huckleberry Finn*, xxxvii.
80. *New York Times*, April 22, 1910.
81. Ibid.
82. Paine, *Mark Twain*, 3:1431.

Bibliography

ARTICLES BY MARK TWAIN, BORN SAMUEL L. CLEMENS

"Blind Tom and His Performances." *Alta California* (San Francisco), August 1, 1869.
"Mark Twain on His Travels." *Alta California* (San Francisco), March 3, 1868.
"My Platonic Sweetheart." *Harper's Magazine*, December 1912.
"The Treaty with China, Its Provisions Explained." *New York Tribune*, August 28, 1868.
"To the Person Sitting in Darkness." *North American Review*, February 1901.

Secondary Sources: Articles

Alden, Henry M. "Mark Twain: Personal Impressions." *Book News Monthly,* no. 28 (April 1910).

Aldrich, Ian. "Mr. Twain Goes to Dublin." Dublin Historical Society. Newsletter no. 82 (Summer 2011).

Allen, Marion Schuyler. "Some New Anecdotes of Mark Twain." *The Strand Magazine* (London), August 1913.

Als, Hilton. "More Harm Than Good." *The New Yorker*, February 3, 2002.

Andrews, Evangeline W. "An Incident at Bryn Mawr." Mark Twain Library at Redding, CT, donated by her granddaughter.

Austin, Franklin H. "Mark Twain Incognito—A Reminiscence." *Friend,* no. 96 (September and October 1926).

Banks, Russell. "How a Clergyman from Hartford Freed Huckleberry Finn." *New York Times,* June 18, 1995.

Barber, W. Charles. "Mark Twain's Last Visit to Elmira." *The Chemung Historical Journal* 12, no. 3 (March 1967).

Barnes, George E. "Mark Twain as He Was Known during His Stay on the Pacific Slope." *San Francisco Morning Call,* April 17, 1887.

———. "Memories of Mark Twain." *Overland Monthly,* no. 66 (September 1915).

BIBLIOGRAPHY

Barr, Robert. "Samuel Clemens, 'Mark Twain.' A Character Sketch." *The Idler Magazine* (London) XIII, no. 1 (February 1898).

Bassford, Homer. "Mark Twain as a Cub Pilot: A Talk with Captain Horace Bixby." *Saturday Evening Post,* December 16, 1899.

Berkove, Lawrence I. "'Nobody Writes to Anybody Except to Ask a Favor': New Correspondence between Mark Twain and Dan De Quille." *Mark Twain Journal* 26, no. 1 (Spring 1988).

Blitz, Matt. "The Library Mark Twain Built." Smithsonian.com, June 30, 2015.

"Books: Twain at His Worst." *Time,* June 12, 1944. No Author.

Boomkamp, Leeuwen. "A Dutch Admirer Meets Mark Twain." *Mark Twain Journal* 10, no. 4 (Spring and Summer 1958).

Bosha, Francis J. "The Mark Twain–William James Friendship." *Mark Twain Journal* 21, no. 4 (Fall 1983).

Branch, Edgar M. "Three New Letters by Samuel Clemens in the Muscatine 'Journal.'" *Mark Twain Journal* 22, no. 1 (Spring 1984).

Branch, Mark Alden. "A Civil Rights Champion." *Yale Alumni Magazine,* January/February 2024.

Brittain, Harry. "My Friend Mark Twain." *Mark Twain Journal* 11, no. 3 (Fall 1961).

Brooks, Noah. "Mark Twain in California." *Century Magazine,* no. 570 (November 1898).

Burgess, Gelett. "A Famous Author Tells About His Meeting with Mark Twain." *Mark Twain Quarterly* 1, no. 1 (Fall 1936).

Bush, Jr., Harold K. "'The Pandemonium That Went On': An Unpublished Letter by Jean Clemens." *American Literary Realism* 44, no. 1 (Fall 2011).

Butcher, Philip. "Mark Twain's Installment on the National Debt." *Southern Literary Journal* 1, no. 2 (Spring 1969).

Cable, George Washington. "The Freedman's Case in Equity." *Century Magazine,* January 1885.

Cardwell, Guy A. "Mark Twain, James R. Osgood, and Those 'Suppressed' Passages." *New England Quarterly* 46, no. 2 (June 1973).

Charbonnel, Avis Bliven. "My Friend Clara Clemens." *Mark Twain Journal* 12, no. 2 (Spring 1964).

Clark, Charles H. "Mark Twain and Nook Farm (Hartford) and Elmira." *Critic,* January 17, 1885.

Clark, George P. "Joseph Conrad and Mark Twain." *Mark Twain Journal* 19, no. 2 (Summer 1978).

Clemens, Clara. "Letters from Olivia and Clara Clemens." *Mark Twain Journal* 34, no. 1 (Spring 1996).

———. "Recollections of Mark Twain: Part I: Her Childhood Memories." *North American Review* 230, no. 5 (November 1930).

———. "Recollections of Mark Twain: Part II: Love Letters of the Humorist." *North American Review* 230, no. 6 (December 1930).

Clemens, Cyril. "At Lunch with Hamlin Garland." *Mark Twain Quarterly* 4, no. 1 (Summer 1940).

BIBLIOGRAPHY

———. "Unpublished Recollections of Original Becky Thatcher." *Mark Twain Quarterly* 4, no. 4 (Summer–Fall 1941).

Clemens, Will M. "Mark Twain on the Lecture Platform." *Ainslee's*, no. 6 (August 1900).

Cohn, Henry S. "Mark Twain and Joseph Roswell Hawley." *Mark Twain Journal* 53, no. 2 (Fall 2015).

Conway, Moncure D. "Mark Twain in London." *Cincinnati Commercial*, October 10, 1872.

Cooley, John R. "Mark Twain's Aquarium: Editing the Samuel Clemens–Angelfish Correspondence." *Mark Twain Journal* 27, no. 1 (Spring 1989).

Coplin, Keith. "John and Sam Clemens: A Father's Influence." *Mark Twain Journal* 15, no. 1 (Winter 1970).

Cowan, Alison Leigh. "Scrawled in the Margins, Signs of Twain as a Critic." *New York Times*, April 18, 2010.

Cox, James M. "Walt Whitman, Mark Twain and the Civil War." *Sewanee Review* 69, no. 2 (April–June 1961).

Curley, Jane. "The Onteora Club." *The Magazine Antiques*, February 18, 2022.

Dam, Henry J. W. "A Morning with Bret Harte." *McClure's*, no. 4 (December 1894).

Davis, Stephen. "Mark Twain and the Civil War (1)." CivilWarNews.com, September 2022.

Donner, Stanley T. "Mark Twain as a Reader." *Quarterly Journal of Speech* 33, no. 3 (1947).

Dreiser, Theodore. "Mark the Double Twain." *The English Journal* 24, no. 8 (October 1935).

Driscoll, Kerry. "Mr. Clemens and the Saturday Morning Club of Hartford." (Manuscript courtesy of the author.)

Duquette, John. "Life on Lower Saranac: Mark Twain in SL." *Adirondack Daily Enterprise*, March 31, 1990.

Eastman, Max. "Mark Twain's Elmira." *Harper's Magazine* 176 (May 1938).

Eckman, Michael V. "Mark Twain and the American Civil War." *Mark Twain Journal* 51, no. 1/2 (Spring/Fall 2013).

Eden, Mary. "Albert Bigelow Paine's (Re)Vision of Mark Twain." *Mark Twain Journal* 56, no. 1 (Spring 2018).

Fairbanks, Mary Mason. "The Cruise of the Quaker City." *Chautauquan*, no. 14 (January 1892).

Fatout, Paul. "Mark Twain, Litigant." *American Literature* 31, no. 1 (March 1959).

Fishkin, Shelley Fisher. "Race and the Politics of Memory: Mark Twain and Paul Laurence Dunbar." *Journal of American Studies* 40, no. 2 (August 2006).

Fitch, Tom. "Fitch Recalls Mark Twain in Bonanza Times." *San Francisco Chronicle*, March 30, 1919.

Folsom, Ed, and Jerome Loving. "The Walt Whitman Controversy: A Lost Document." *Virginia Quarterly Review*, Spring 2007.

Fox, Margalit. "Putting a Happy Face on an Often Unhappy Twain." *New York Times*, April 22, 2000.

Gibson, William M. "Mark Twain and Howells, Anti-Imperialists." *New England Quarterly* 20, no. 4 (December 1947).

BIBLIOGRAPHY

Gregory, Ralph. "Orion Clemens on Mark Twain's Birthplace." *Mark Twain Journal* 20, no. 2 (Summer 1980).

Griffin, Benjamin. "Twins of Genius—Not!" www.twainquotes.com, February 2015.

Harding, Dorothy Sturgis. "Mark Twain Lands an Angel Fish." *Columbia Library Columns,* no. 16 (February 1967).

Hawkins, Hunt. "Mark Twain's Involvement with the Congo Reform Movement: 'A Fury of Generous Indignation.'" *New England Quarterly* 51, no. 2 (June 1978).

Hindley, Meredith. "Ulysses S. Grant: The Reluctant Memoirist." *Humanities,* Winter 2018.

Hirst, Robert H. "'He Trimmed & Trained & Schooled Me'—Bret Harte Edits *The Innocents Abroad.*" Microfilm Edition of Mark Twain's Literary Manuscripts Available at the Mark Twain Papers, 2001.

Hodgson, Tim. "Mark Twain Abroad—Part I." *The Bermudian* LIV, no. 8 (September 1983).

———. "Mark Twain Abroad—Part II." *The Bermudian* LIV, no. 9 (October 1983).

———. "Mark Twain Abroad—Part III." *The Bermudian* LIV, no. 10 (November 1983).

———. "Mark Twain Abroad—Part IV." *The Bermudian* LIV, no. 11 (December 1983).

———. "Mark Twain Abroad—Part V." *The Bermudian* LIV, no. 12 (January 1984).

———. "Mark Twain Abroad—Part VI." *The Bermudian* LV, no. 1 (February 1984).

Holzer, Harold. "Historic Houses: Mark Twain in Hartford." *Architectural Digest,* July 1982.

Honce, Charles. "More Twain Recollections." *Richmond Times-Dispatch,* June 4, 1944.

House, Edward H. "Mark Twain as a Lecturer." *New York Tribune,* May 11, 1867.

Howden, Mary Louise. "Mark Twain as His Secretary at Stormfield Remembers Him." *New York Herald,* December 13, 1925.

Jenn, Ronald, and Linda A. Morris. "The Sources of Mark Twain's 'Personal Recollections of Joan of Arc.'" *Mark Twain Journal* 55, no. 1/2 (Spring/Fall 2017).

Jones, Alexander E. "Mark Twain and Sexuality." *PMLA* 71:4, part 1 (September 1956).

"Jos. Goodman's Memories of Humorist's Early Days." *San Francisco Examiner,* April 22, 1910. (No author.)

Kane, Ivan P. "Elizabeth Wallace, the King, and I." *University of Chicago Magazine,* Fall 2017.

Kanellakou, Chris. "Mark Twain and the Chinese." *Mark Twain Journal* 12, no. 1 (Spring 1963).

Karlin, Daniel. "Mark Twain, Eccentric." *Times Literary Supplement,* October 17, 2018.

Keller, Helen. "Mark Twain." *American Magazine,* no. 108 (July 1929).

Kemble, E. W. "Illustrating *Huck Finn,*" *Colophon,* part 1 (1930).

Komroff, Manuel. "How I Shook Hands with Mark Twain." *Mark Twain Journal* 11, no. 1 (Summer 1959).

Krause, Sydney J. "Olivia Clemens's 'Editing' Reviewed." *American Literature* 39, no. 3 (November 1967).

Kruse, Horst H. "A Matter of Style: How Olivia Langdon Clemens and Charles Dudley Warner Tried to Team and to Tame the Genius of Mark Twain." *New England Quarterly* 72, no. 2 (June 1999).

BIBLIOGRAPHY

———. "Mark Twain's 'Nom de Plume' Some Mysteries Resolved." *Mark Twain Journal* 30, no. 1 (Spring 1992).

Lampton, Lucius Marion. "The Genealogy of Mark Twain: Being the Ancestors, Relatives, and Family of Samuel Langhorne Clemens." Diamond L. Publishing (1990).

Langdon, Ida. "My Uncle, Mark Twain." *The Chemung Historical Journal* 6, no. 2 (December 1960).

Lanier, Doris. "Mark Twain's Georgia Angel Fish." *Mark Twain Journal* 24, no. 1 (Spring 1986).

Larned, J. N. "Mark Twain." *Buffalo Evening Express,* April 26, 1910.

Larson, Thomas. "Decent Men Elude Mark Twain's Child—She Ends Up at Bahia in Mission Beach." *San Diego Reader,* May 8, 2003.

Leonard, James S., and James Wharton Leonard. "Mark Twain and the Anti-Doughnut Party." *The Mark Twain Annual* 9, no. 1 (November 2011).

Lester, Julius. "Morality and Adventures of 'Huckleberry Finn.'" *Mark Twain Journal* 22, no. 2 (Fall 1984).

Locher, Albert. "'This Is Paradise, Here': Mark Twain in Weggis in the Summer of 1897." *Mark Twain Journal* 40, no. 20 (Fall 2002).

Lucas, E. V. "E. V. Lucas and Twain at a *'Punch* Dinner.'" London *Bookman,* no. 38 (June 1910).

MacAlister, (Sir) George Ian. "Mark Twain, Some Personal Reminiscences," *Landmark,* no. 20 (March 1938).

Mac Donnell, Kevin. "George Griffin: Meeting Mark Twain's Butler Face-to-Face," *Mark Twain Journal* 62, no. 1 (Spring 2024).

———. "Mark Twain at Ten Paces: Facts Versus Fictions in the Origins of 'Mark Twain' as a Nom de Plume." *Mark Twain Journal* 57, no. 1 (Spring 2019).

———. "Mark Twain's Boswell; A Publication History of Albert Bigelow Paine's Biography of Mark Twain." *Mark Twain Journal* 56, no. 1 (Spring 2018).

———. "Mark Twain's Lost Sweetheart." *Mark Twain Journal* 53, no. 1 (Spring 2015).

———. "Who Killed Charlie Webster?" *Mark Twain Journal* 51, no. 1/2 (Spring/Fall 2013).

"Mark Twain Is Dead at 74." *New York Times,* April 22, 1910.

"Mark Twain's Boyhood: An Interview with Mrs. Jane Clemens." *Chicago Inter-Ocean,* April 5, 1885. (No author.)

"Mark Twain's Childhood Sweetheart Recalls Their Romance." *Literary Digest,* March 23, 1918. (No author.)

"Mark Twain's First Sweetheart, Becky Thatcher, Tells of Their Childhood Courtship." *Kansas City Star,* November 25, 1917. (No author.)

"Mark Twain's Speech for the Benefit of the Bermuda Hospital." *The Bermuda Historical Quarterly* XXXIV, no. 3 (Autumn 1977). (No author.)

Marleau, Michael H. "'Getting Along Tolerable Well': Captain Isaiah Sellers and Sam Clemens on the Steamer *William M. Morrison.*" *Mark Twain Journal* 61, no. 1 (Spring 2023).

Marsh, Grant. "Mark Twain." St. Louis *Missouri Republican,* December 8, 1878.

BIBLIOGRAPHY

McCord, Kay Moser. "Mark Twain's Participation in Presidential Politics." *American Literary Realism* 16, no. 2 (Autumn 1983).

McCoy, Max. "The Secret Life of Albert Bigelow Paine." *Mark Twain Journal* 56, no. 1 (Spring 2018).

McDowell, Edwin. "From Twain, a Letter on Debt to Blacks." *New York Times,* March 14, 1985.

McLaughlin, Bill. "Mark Twain: A Legend Shared by Our Village." *Adirondack Daily Enterprise,* July 2, 1960.

McNamara, Megan. "'Only Dead Men Can Tell the Truth in This World': The Growth of Mark Twain's Anger." *The Mark Twain Annual* 21 (2023).

Mendelsohn, Edward. "Mark Twain Confronts the Shakespeareans." *Mark Twain Journal* 17, no. 1 (Winter 1973–1974).

Moore, Louise Paine. "Mark Twain As I Knew Him." *Redding Times,* June 19, 1958.

Morris, Linda A. "Susy Clemens: The Final Years." *The Mark Twain Annual* 21 (November 2023).

———. "The Eloquent Silence in 'Hellfire Hotchkiss.'" *The Mark Twain Annual* 3 (September 2005).

Morrow, James B. "Mark Twain's Exclusive Publisher Tells What the Humorist Is Paid." *Washington Post,* March 3, 1907.

Moser, Kay R. "Mark Twain—Mugwump." *Mark Twain Journal* 21, no. 2 (Summer 1982).

Myers, Margaret. "Mark Twain and Melville." *Mark Twain Journal* 14, no. 2 (Summer 1968).

Ober, K. Patrick. "Mark Twain and Family Health in Nook Farm." *Mark Twain Journal* 56, no. 1 (Spring 2018).

Oggel, Terry. "Albert Bigelow Paine and Mark Twain." *Mark Twain Journal* 56, no. 1 (Spring 2018).

Ohge, Christopher. "'It Was a Mistake': Abolitionism, Revision, and Mark Twain's 'A Scrap of Curious History.'" *The Mark Twain Annual* 18 (2020).

Paine, Albert Bigelow. "Innocents at Home." *Collier's Weekly,* no. 3 (January 1925).

———. "Mark Twain at Stormfield." *Harper's Weekly,* no. 118 (May 1909).

Pettit, Arthur G. "Mark Twain's Attitude Toward the Negro in the West, 1861–1867." *The Western Historical Quarterly* 1, no. 1 (January 1970).

Pfeffer, Miki. "A Southern View of Twain's Hartford." *Connecticut Explored* 20, no. 3 (Summer 2022).

Powers, Ron. "Keeping Up with Mark Twain." *Smithsonian Magazine,* September 2003.

Quick, Dorothy. "A Little Girl's Mark Twain." *North American Review,* no. 240 (September 1935).

Railton, Stephen. "The Tragedy of Mark Twain, by Pudd'nhead Wilson." *Nineteenth-Century Literature* 56, no. 4 (March 2002).

Rasmussen, Frederick N. "A Little Help from Twain." *Baltimore Sun,* February 17, 2001.

R. C. B. "Mark Twain on the Platform." *Critic,* no. 25 (April 1896).

Reigstad, Thomas J. "The Coal Question." *Mark Twain Journal* 56, no. 2 (Fall 2018).

BIBLIOGRAPHY

Rideing, William H. "Mark Twain in Clubland." *Bookman*, no. 31 (June 1910).

Roark, Jarrod. "Teaching Racial Boundaries: How Mark Twain's Characters Expose Our 'Mental Attitudes' about Race and Racism." *The Mark Twain Annual* 18 (2020).

Sachs, Bernard. "In Memoriam. Frederick Peterson." *American Journal of Insanity* 95 (November 1938).

"Samuel L. Clemens To-day Lies Beside His Wife and Children in Woodlawn." *Elmira Advertiser*, April 25, 1910. (No author.)

Scharnhorst, Gary. "Additional Mark Twain Contributions to the Virginia City *Territorial Enterprise* 1863–66." *American Literary Realism* 47, no. 1 (Fall 2014).

———. "'Also, Some Gin': More Excerpts from Mark Twain's San Francisco Letters of 1865–66." *Mark Twain Journal* 26, no. 1 (Spring 1988).

———. "The Bret Harte–Mark Twain Feud: An Inside Narrative." *Mark Twain Journal* 31, no. 1 (Spring 1993).

———. "The End of a Friendship: Two Unpublished Letters from Twain to Howells About Bret Harte." *New England Quarterly* 58, no. 1 (March 1985).

Schmidt, Barbara. "Mark Twain & Karl Gerhardt." www.twainquotes.com/Gerhardt/gerhardt.html.

Schwarz, Christopher. "When the Twain Met: Winston Churchill and Samuel Clemens." *Finest Hour* 149 (Winter 2010–11).

Selby, P. O. "Me and the Clemenses." *Mark Twain Journal* 19, no. 3 (Winter 1978–79).

Shannon, Edward A. "'Trash of the Veriest Sort': Huck Finn's Missing Sex Life." *The Mark Twain Annual* 19 (2021).

Sharp, Luke. "Mark Twain: A Conglomerate Interview, Personally Conducted by Luke Sharp." *The Idler Magazine*, February 1892.

Shaw, George Bernard. "My Encounters with Mark Twain." *Mark Twain Journal* 9, no. 4 (Summer 1954).

Simboli, Raffaele. "Mark Twain from an Italian Point of View." *Critic* 44 (June 1904).

Simon, Linda. "Mark Twain's Disturbing Passion for Collecting Young Girls." *The Paris Review*, November 28, 2017.

Sloane, David E. E. "The N-Word in *Adventures of Huckleberry Finn* Reconsidered." *The Mark Twain Annual* 12, no. 1 (2014).

Slotta, Robert. "A Glimpse into Jean's World." *Mark Twain Journal* 45, no. 1 (Spring 2007).

Snedecor, Barbara E. "'He Was So Rarely Beautiful': Langdon Clemens." *American Literary Realism* 45, no. 1 (Fall 2012).

"Some New Twain Stories." *Kansas City Star*, October 6, 1907. (No author.)

Sorel, Edward. "The Very Brief Friendship of Maxim Gorky and Mark Twain." *New York Times*, March 5, 2021.

Stanfield, Bronx. "Where Are We with the Controversy over Isabel Lyon?" *Mark Twain Journal* 50, no. 1/2 (Spring/Fall 2012).

Stewart, Robert E. "The Carson City Mark Twain Knew." *Mark Twain Journal* 61, no. 1 (Spring 2023).

Stoddard, Charles Warren. "In Old Bohemia." *Pacific Monthly*, no. 19 (March 1908).

BIBLIOGRAPHY

Stojiljković, Bratislav, Dragoljub A. Cucic, and Zoran Pajic. "Nikola Tesla and Samuel Clemens: The Friendship Between Two Luminaries of the Gilded Age." *Mark Twain Journal* 52, no. 2 (Fall 2014).

Trombley, Laura Skandera. "'I Am Woman's Rights': Olivia Langdon Clemens and Her Feminist Circle." *Mark Twain Journal* 34, no. 2 (Fall 1996).

———. "Mark Twain's 'Annus Horribilis' of 1908–09." *American Literary Realism* 40, no. 2 (Winter 2008).

———. "'She Wanted to Kill': Jean Clemens and Postictal Psychosis." *American Literary Realism* 37, no. 3 (Spring 2005).

Turner, Arlin. "George W. Cable's Beginning as a Reformer." *Journal of Southern History* 17, no. 2 (May 1951).

Vogelback, Arthur L. "Mark Twain and the Tammany Ring." *PMLA* 70, no. 1 (March 1955).

Vranken, Thomas Lloyd. "Transatlantic Relations—The Convergence of Oscar Wilde and Mark Twain." *The Wildean*, no. 45 (July 2014).

Ward, Geoffrey C. "Yours Ever, Sam'l Clemens." *American Heritage* 41, no. 6 (September/October 1990).

Webster, Doris, and Samuel Webster. "Whitewashing Jane Clemens." *Bookman* LXI, no. 5 (July 1925).

White, Frank Marshall. "Mark Twain as a Newspaper Reporter." *Outlook*, no. 96 (December 1910).

Willis, Resa A. "'Quietly and Steadily': Olivia Langdon Clemens' Commonplace Book." *Mark Twain Journal* 24, no. 1 (Spring 1986).

Wineapple, Brenda. "'I Have Let Whitman Alone.'" *New York Review of Books* LXVI, no. 7 (April 18, 2019).

Wisbey, Jr., Dr. Herbert A. "Gabrilowitsch—Buried at Mark Twain's Feet." *The Chemung Historical Journal* 22, no. 1 (September 1976).

Yuran, Robin R. "Mark Twain at Norfolk, 1904–06." *Mark Twain Journal* 45, no. 1 (Spring 2007).

BOOKS AND LETTERS BY MARK TWAIN, BORN SAMUEL L. CLEMENS

A Connecticut Yankee in King Arthur's Court. Edited by Bernard L. Stein. Berkeley: University of California Press, 1983.

Adventures of Huckleberry Finn. Edited by Victor Fischer and Lin Salamo. Berkeley: University of California Press, 2001. Reprint.

A Pen Warmed-Up in Hell. Edited by Frederick Anderson. New York: Perennial Library, Harper & Row, 1979. Reprint.

A Tramp Abroad. Foreword by Shelley Fisher Fishkin. New York: Oxford University Press, 1996.

BIBLIOGRAPHY

Autobiography of Mark Twain. Volume 1. Edited by Harriet Elinor Smith. Berkeley: University of California Press, 2010.

Autobiography of Mark Twain. Volume 2. Edited by Benjamin Griffin and Harriet Elinor Smith. Berkeley: University of California Press, 2013.

Autobiography of Mark Twain. Volume 3. Edited by Benjamin Griffin and Harriet Elinor Smith. Berkeley: University of California Press, 2015.

Christian Science. Foreword by Shelley Fisher Fishkin. New York: Oxford University Press, 1996.

Complete Essays of Mark Twain. Edited by Charles Neider. Garden City, New York: Doubleday & Company, 1963.

Europe and Elsewhere. New York: Harper & Brothers, 1923.

Extract from Captain Stormfield's Visit to Heaven. New York: Oxford University Press, 1996.

Following the Equator: A Journey Around the World and Anti-Imperialist Essays. Foreword by Shelley Fisher Fishkin. New York: Oxford University Press, 1996.

How Nancy Jackson Married Kate Wilson and Other Tales of Rebellious Girls & Daring Young Women. Edited by John Cooley. Lincoln: University of Nebraska Press, 2001.

King Leopold's Soliloquy: A Defense of His Congo Rule. Boston: The P. R. Warren Company, 1905.

Letters from the Earth. Edited by Bernard DeVoto. New York: Harper & Row, 1962.

Life on the Mississippi. Foreword by Shelley Fisher Fishkin. New York: Oxford University Press, 1996.

Mark Twain–Howells Letters: The Correspondence of Samuel L. Clemens and William D. Howells 1872–1910. Edited by Henry Nash Smith and William M. Gibson. Cambridge, Massachusetts: The Belknap Press of Harvard University Press, 1960.

Mark Twain: Life As I Find It. Edited by Charles Neider. Garden City, New York: Hanover House, 1961.

Mark Twain's Aquarium: The Samuel Clemens Angelfish Correspondence 1905–1910. Edited by John Cooley. Athens and London: University of Georgia Press, 1991.

Mark Twain's Civil War: "The Private History of a Campaign That Failed." Edited by Benjamin Griffin. Berkeley: Heyday, The Bancroft Library, University of California, 2019.

Mark Twain's Correspondence with Henry Huttleston Rogers 1893–1909. Edited by Lewis Leary. Berkeley and Los Angeles: University of California Press, 1969.

Mark Twain's Fables of Man. Edited by John S. Tuckey. Berkeley: University of California Press, 1972.

Mark Twain's Hannibal, Huck & Tom. Edited by Walter Blair. Berkeley: University of California Press, 1969.

Mark Twain's Letters. Edited by Albert Bigelow Paine. Two Volumes. New York: Harper & Brothers, 1917.

Mark Twain's Letters to His Publishers, 1867–1894. Edited by Hamlin Hill. Berkeley: University of California Press, 1967.

Mark Twain's Letters to Mary. Edited by Lewis Leary. New York: Columbia University Press, 1963. Reprint.

BIBLIOGRAPHY

Mark Twain's Letters to Will Bowen: "My First, & Oldest & Dearest Friend." Austin: University of Texas Press, 1941.

Mark Twain's Notebook. Edited by Albert Bigelow Paine. New York: Harper & Brothers, 1935.

Mark Twain's Notebooks: Journals, Letters, Observations, Wit, Wisdom and Doodles. Edited by Carlo DeVito. New York: Black Dog & Leventhal Publishers, 2015.

Mark Twain's Notebooks & Journals: Volume I (1855–1873). Edited by Frederick Anderson, Michael B. Frank, and Kenneth M. Sanderson. Berkeley: University of California Press, 1975.

Mark Twain's Notebooks & Journals: Volume II (1877–1883). Edited by Frederick Anderson, Lin Salamo, and Bernard L. Stein. Berkeley: University of California Press, 1975.

Mark Twain's Notebooks & Journals: Volume III (1883–1891). Edited by Robert Pack Browning, Michael B. Frank, and Lin Salamo. Berkeley: University of California Press, 1979.

Mark Twain's Satires & Burlesques. Edited by Franklin R. Rogers. Berkeley: University of California Press, 1968.

Mark Twain Speaking. Edited by Paul Fatout. Iowa City: University of Iowa Press, 1976.

Mark Twain's Which Was the Dream? And Other Symbolic Writings of the Later Years. Edited by John S. Tuckey. Berkeley: University of California Press, 1967.

Mark Twain to Mrs. Fairbanks. Edited by Dixon Wecter. San Marino, California: Huntington Library, 1949.

No. 44, the Mysterious Stranger: Being an Ancient Tale Found in a Jug, and Freely Translated from the Jug. Berkeley: University of California Press, 1982.

Personal Recollections of Joan of Arc. Foreword by Shelley Fisher Fishkin. New York: Oxford University Press, 1996.

1601, and Is Shakespeare Dead? New York: Oxford University Press, 1996.

The American Claimant. Foreword by Shelley Fisher Fishkin. New York: Oxford University Press, 1996.

The Complete Short Stories of Mark Twain. Edited by Charles Neider. Garden City, New York: Doubleday & Company, 1957.

The Diaries of Adam and Eve. New York: Oxford University Press, 1996.

The Forgotten Writings of Mark Twain. Edited by Henry Duskis. New York: Philosophical Library, 1963.

The Gilded Age. With Charles Dudley Warner. Foreword by Shelley Fisher Fishkin. New York: Oxford University Press, 1996.

The Innocents Abroad or The New Pilgrims' Progress. Foreword by Shelley Fisher Fishkin. New York: Oxford University Press, 1996.

The Letters of Mark Twain and Joseph Hopkins Twichell. Edited by Harold K. Bush, Steve Courtney, and Peter Messent. Athens: University of Georgia Press, 2017.

The Love Letters of Mark Twain. Edited by Dixon Wecter. New York: Harper & Brothers, 1949.

The Man That Corrupted Hadleyburg and Other Stories and Essays. Foreword by Shelley Fisher Fishkin. New York: Oxford University Press, 1996.

BIBLIOGRAPHY

The Prince and the Pauper: A Tale for Young People of All Ages. Foreword and Notes by Victor Fischer and Michael B. Frank. Berkeley: University of California Press, 1983.

The Selected Letters of Mark Twain. Edited by Charles Neider. New York: Harper & Row, 1982.

The Stolen White Elephant and Other Detective Stories. Foreword by Shelley Fisher Fishkin. New York: Oxford University Press, 1996.

The Tragedy of Pudd'nhead Wilson and the Comedy Those Extraordinary Twins. Foreword by Shelley Fisher Fishkin. New York: Oxford University Press, 1996.

The War Prayer. New York: Perennial, HarperCollins, 2002. Reprint.

The Works of Mark Twain. Early Tales & Sketches. Volume 1, 1851–1864. Edited by Edgar Marquess Branch and Robert H. Hirst. Berkeley: University of California Press, 1979.

The Works of Mark Twain. Early Tales & Sketches, Volume 2, 1864–1865. Edited by Edgar Marquess Branch and Robert H. Hirst. With the Assistance of Harriet Elinor Smith. Berkeley: University of California Press, 1981.

The Works of Mark Twain. Roughing It. Edited by Harriet Elinor Smith and Edgar Marquess Branch. Berkeley: University of California Press, 1993.

The Works of Mark Twain. The Adventures of Tom Sawyer; Tom Sawyer Abroad; Tom Sawyer, Detective. Edited by John C. Gerber, Paul Baender, and Terry Firkins. Berkeley: University of California Press, 1980.

What is Man? Foreword by Shelley Fisher Fishkin. New York: Oxford University Press, 1996.

Secondary Sources: Books

Allen, Marion Schuyler. *Our Friend Mark Twain.* Typescript in Allen Papers, Bermuda National Trust, Bermuda Archives.

Andrews, Kenneth R. *Nook Farm: Mark Twain's Hartford Circle.* Cambridge, Massachusetts: Harvard University Press, 1950.

Baetzhold, Howard G. *Mark Twain and John Bull.* Bloomington: Indiana University Press, 1970.

Berg, A. Scott. *Wilson.* New York: G. P. Putnam's Sons, 2013.

Blight, David W. *Frederick Douglass: Prophet of Freedom.* New York: Simon & Schuster, 2018.

Bowditch, Nancy Douglas. *George de Forest Brush: Recollections of a Joyous Painter.* New Hampshire: Noone House, 1970.

Brooks, Van Wyck. *The Ordeal of Mark Twain.* New York: E. P. Dutton, 1970. Reprint.

Budd, Louis J. *Mark Twain: Social Philosopher.* Bloomington: Indiana University Press, 1962.

Cardwell, Guy A. *Twins of Genius.* London: Neville Spearman, 1962.

Chadwick-Joshua, Jocelyn. *The Jim Dilemma: Reading Race in Huckleberry Finn.* Jackson: University Press of Mississippi, 1998.

Cohen, Morton N. *Lewis Carroll: A Biography.* New York: Alfred A. Knopf, 1995.

Clemens, Clara. *Awake to a Perfect Day.* New York: The Citadel Press, 1956.

———. *My Father Mark Twain.* New York: Harper & Brothers, 1931.

BIBLIOGRAPHY

———. *My Husband Gabrilowitsch*. New York: Harper & Brothers, 1938.

Clemens, Susy. *Papa: An Intimate Biography of Mark Twain*. Edited by Charles Neider. Garden City, New York: Doubleday, 1985.

Conway, Moncure Daniel. *Autobiography: Memories and Experiences*. London: Cassell and Company, 1904.

Courtney, Steve. *Joseph Hopkins Twichell: The Life and Times of Mark Twain's Closest Friend*. Athens: University of Georgia Press, 2008.

———. *The Loveliest House That Ever Was: The Story of the Mark Twain House in Hartford*. Mineola, New York: Dover Publications, 2011.

Crawford, Alan Pell. *How Not to Get Rich: The Financial Misadventures of Mark Twain*. Boston and New York: Houghton Mifflin Harcourt, 2017.

Cummings, Hildegard. *Charles Ethan Porter: African-American Master of Still Life*. New Britain, Connecticut: University Press of New England, 2007.

Devinsky, Orrin. *Epilepsy: Patient & Family Guide*. Third Edition. New York: Demos Health, 2008.

Dolmetsch, Carl. *"Our Famous Guest": Mark Twain in Vienna*. Athens: University of Georgia Press, 1992.

Driscoll, Kerry. *Mark Twain Among the Indians and Other Indigenous Peoples*. Oakland: University of California Press, 2018.

Ellsworth, William Webster. *A Golden Age of Authors: A Publisher's Recollection*. Boston: Houghton Mifflin Company, 1919.

Evans, Jonathan Land. *Empire & Onion-Patch: A History of Bermuda from 1898 to 1918*. Copy in Bermuda National Library. No publisher given.

Everett, Percival. *James*. New York: Doubleday, 2024.

Fanning, Philip Ashley. *Mark Twain and Orion Clemens: Brothers, Partners, Strangers*. Tuscaloosa: University of Alabama Press, 2003.

Fears, David H. *Mark Twain Day by Day: An Annotated Chronology of the Life of Samuel L. Clemens. Volume One (1835–1885)*. Banks, Oregon: Horizon Micro Publishers, 2008.

———. *Mark Twain Day by Day: An Annotated Chronology of the Life of Samuel L. Clemens. Volume Two (1886–1896)*. Banks, Oregon: Horizon Micro Publishers, 2009.

———. *Mark Twain Day by Day: An Annotated Chronology of the Life of Samuel L. Clemens. Volume Three (1897–1904)*. Banks, Oregon: Horizon Micro Publishers, 2011.

———. *Mark Twain Day by Day: An Annotated Chronology of the Life of Samuel L. Clemens. Volume Four (1905–1910)*. Banks, Oregon: Horizon Micro Publishers, 2013.

Ferguson, DeLancey. *Mark Twain: Man and Legend*. New York: Charter Books, 1943. Reprint.

Fisher, Henry W. *Abroad with Mark Twain and Eugene Field: Tales They Told to a Fellow Correspondent*. New York: Nicholas L. Brown, 1922.

Fishkin, Shelley Fisher. *Lighting Out for the Territory: Reflections on Mark Twain and American Culture*. New York: Oxford University Press, 1997.

———. *Was Huck Black? Mark Twain and African-American Voices*. New York: Oxford University Press, 1993.

BIBLIOGRAPHY

Fulton, Joe B. *The Reconstruction of Mark Twain: How a Confederate Bushwacker Became the Lincoln of Our Literature.* Baton Rouge: Louisiana State University Press, 2010.

Gewirtz, Isaac. *Mark Twain: A Skeptic's Progress* with *A Century of Collecting Mark Twain at The Morgan Library & Museum and The New York Public Library* by Declan Kiely. New York: The New York Public Library, 2010.

Gilder, Richard Watson. *Letters of Richard Watson Gilder.* Edited by Rosamond Gilder. New York: Houghton Mifflin Company, Riverside Press, 1916.

Gill, Gillian. *Mary Baker Eddy.* Reading, Massachusetts: A Merloyd Lawrence Book, Perseus Books, 1998.

Giroud, Françoise. *Alma Mahler or the Art of Being Loved.* Translated by R. M. Stock. New York: Oxford University Press, 1991.

Goodman, Susan, and Carl Dawson. *William Dean Howells: A Writer's Life.* Berkeley: University of California Press, 2005.

Goodwin, Doris Kearns. *Team of Rivals: The Political Genius of Abraham Lincoln.* New York: Simon & Schuster Paperbacks, 2006. Reprint.

Gribben, Alan. *Mark Twain's Literary Resources: A Reconstruction of His Library and Reading. Volume One.* Montgomery, Alabama: NewSouth Books, 2019.

———. *Mark Twain's Literary Resources: A Reconstruction of His Library and Reading. Volume Two.* Montgomery, Alabama: NewSouth Books, 2022.

Gribben, Alan, and Nick Karanovich, eds. *Overland with Mark Twain: James B. Pond's Photographs and Journal of the North American Lecture Tour of 1895.* Elmira, New York: Center for Mark Twain Studies at Quarry Farm, Elmira College, 1992.

Griffin, Benjamin, ed. *A Family Sketch and Other Private Writings by Mark Twain, Livy Clemens, and Susy Clemens.* Berkeley: University of California Press, 2014.

Hall, Elton Wayland. *John Elton Wayland's and Isabel Scovill Wayland's Friendship with Mark Twain.* Dartmouth, Massachusetts: Brookside Press, 2014.

Harnsberger, Caroline Thomas. *Mark Twain Family Man.* New York: The Citadel Press, 1960.

———. *Mark Twain's Clara: Or What Became of the Clemens Family.* Evanston, Illinois: The Press of Ward Schori, 1982.

Harris, Susan K. *God's Arbiters: Americans and the Philippines, 1898–1902.* New York: Oxford University Press, 2011.

Hawkins, Cynthia. *African American Agency and the Art Object, 1868–1917.* Dissertation, State University of New York at Buffalo, conferred September 1, 2019. ProQuest Dissertations Publishing, 2019.

Hill, Hamlin. *Mark Twain: God's Fool.* New York: Harper & Row, 1973.

Heidig, Lance J., ed. *Known to Everyone—Liked by All: The Mark Twain Collection of Susan Jaffe Tane.* Ithaca, New York: Cornell University Library, 2010.

Hochschild, Adam. *King Leopold's Ghost: A Story of Greed, Terror, and Heroism in Colonial Africa.* Boston: Houghton Mifflin, 1998.

Hoffman, Andrew. *Inventing Mark Twain: The Lives of Samuel Langhorne Clemens.* New York: William Morrow, 1997.

Hoffmann, Donald. *Mark Twain in Paradise: His Voyages to Bermuda.* Columbia and London: University of Missouri Press, 2006.

BIBLIOGRAPHY

Holbrook, Hal. *Harold: The Boy Who Became Mark Twain.* New York: Farrar, Straus and Giroux, 2011.

Howe, M. A. DeWolfe. *Memories of a Hostess: A Chronicle of Eminent Friendships.* Boston: The Atlantic Monthly Press, 1922.

Howells, William Dean. *A Hazard of New Fortunes.* New York: The Modern Library, 2002. Reprint.

———. *My Mark Twain.* Mineola, New York: Dover Publications, 1997. Reprint.

Huffman, James L. *A Yankee in Meiji Japan: The Crusading Journalist Edward H. House.* Lanham, Maryland: Rowman & Littlefield Publishers, 2003.

Jasanoff, Maya. *The Dawn Watch: Joseph Conrad in a Global World.* New York: Penguin Press, 2017.

Jerome, Robert D., and Herbert A. Wisbey, Jr., eds. *Mark Twain in Elmira.* Elmira, New York: Mark Twain Society, 1977.

Kaplan, Fred. *The Singular Mark Twain: A Biography.* New York: Doubleday, 2003.

Kaplan, Justin. *Mr. Clemens and Mark Twain.* New York: Simon & Schuster Paperbacks, 2006. Reprint. Originally published 1966.

Krass, Peter. *Ignorance, Confidence, and Filthy Rich Friends: The Business Adventures of Mark Twain, Chronic Speculator and Entrepreneur.* Hoboken, New Jersey: John Wiley & Sons, 2007.

Langdon, Jervis. *Samuel Langhorne Clemens: Some Reminiscences and Some Excerpts from Letters and Unpublished Manuscripts.* Delhi, India: Pranava Books, 2020. Reprint.

Lawton, Mary. *A Lifetime with Mark Twain: The Memories of Katy Leary, for Thirty Years His Faithful and Devoted Servant.* Carlisle, Massachusetts: Applewood Books, 2015. Reprint.

Lyon, Peter. *Success Story: The Life and Times of S. S. McClure.* New York: Charles Scribner's Sons, 1963.

Lystra, Karen. *Dangerous Intimacy: The Untold Story of Mark Twain's Final Years.* Berkeley: University of California Press, 2004.

Macnaughton, William R. *Mark Twain's Last Years as a Writer.* Columbia: University of Missouri Press, 1979.

Morgan, William. *Monadnock Summer: The Architectural Legacy of Dublin, New Hampshire.* Boston: David R. Godine, 2011.

Nissen, Axel. *Bret Harte: Prince and Pauper.* Jackson: University Press of Mississippi, 2000.

Noyes, Rufus K. *Views of Religion.* Boston: L. K. Washburn, 1906.

Ober, K. Patrick. *Mark Twain and Medicine: "Any Mummery Will Cure."* Columbia: University of Missouri Press, 2011. Reprint.

Paine, Albert Bigelow. *Mark Twain. Volumes I, II, and III.* Broomall, Pennsylvania: Chelsea House, 1997. Reprint.

Perry, Mark. *Grant and Twain: The Story of an American Friendship.* New York: Random House Trade Paperbacks, 2005. Reprint.

Pettit, Arthur G. *Mark Twain & the South.* Lexington: University Press of Kentucky, 1974.

BIBLIOGRAPHY

Pfeffer, Miki, ed. *A New Orleans Author in Mark Twain's Court: Letters from Grace King's New England Sojourns*. Baton Rouge: Louisiana State University Press, 2019.

Pinney, Thomas, ed. *The Letters of Rudyard Kipling. Volume 3. 1900–10*. Iowa City: University of Iowa Press, 1996.

Pond, Major J. B. *Eccentricities of Genius: Memories of Famous Men and Women of the Platform and Stage*. New York: G. W. Dillingham Company Publishers, 1900.

Powers, Ron. *Mark Twain: A Life*. New York: Free Press, 2005. Reprint.

Quick, Dorothy. *Enchantment: A Little Girl's Friendship with Mark Twain*. Norman: University of Oklahoma Press, 1961.

Rasmussen, R. Kent. *Dear Mark Twain: Letters from His Readers*. Edited by R. Kent Rasmussen. Berkeley: University of California Press, 2013.

———. *Mark Twain A to Z: The Essential Reference to His Life and Writings*. New York: Facts on File, 1995.

Ryan, Ann M., and Joseph B. McCullough, eds. *Cosmopolitan Twain*. Columbia: University of Missouri Press, 2008.

Scharnhorst, Gary. *The Life of Mark Twain: The Early Years 1835–1871 (Volume 1)*. Columbia: University of Missouri Press, 2018.

———. *The Life of Mark Twain: The Middle Years 1871–1891 (Volume 2)*. Columbia: University of Missouri Press, 2019.

———. *The Life of Mark Twain: The Final Years 1891–1910 (Volume 3)*. Columbia: University of Missouri Press, 2022.

Scharnhorst, Gary, ed. *Mark Twain: The Complete Interviews*. Tuscaloosa: University of Alabama Press, 2006.

———. *Twain in His Own Time: A Biographical Chronicle of His Life, Drawn from Recollections, Interviews, and Memoirs by Family, Friends, and Associates*. Iowa City: University of Iowa Press, 2010.

Schiff, Karenna Gore. *Lighting the Way: Nine Women Who Changed Modern America*. New York: Miramax Books, Hyperion, 2005. Reprint.

Shelden, Michael. *Mark Twain: Man in White: The Grand Adventure of His Final Years*. New York: Random House, 2010.

Sloane, David E. E., ed. *Mark Twain's Humor: Critical Essays*. London and New York: Routledge, Taylor & Francis Group, 1993.

Smith-Rosenberg, Carroll. *Disorderly Conduct: Visions of Gender in Victorian America*. New York: Oxford University Press, 1986. Reprint.

Snedecor, Barbara E. *Gravity: Selected Letters of Olivia Langdon Clemens*. Columbia: University of Missouri Press, 2023.

Stewart, William M. *Reminiscences of Senator William M. Stewart*. Edited by George Rothwell Brown. New York: The Neale Publishing Company, 1908.

Taylor, Coley B. *Mark Twain's Margins on Thackeray's Swift*. New York: Gotham House, 1935.

Temkin, Owsei. *The Falling Sickness: A History of Epilepsy, from the Greeks to the Beginnings of Modern Neurology*. Second Edition. Baltimore: Johns Hopkins Press, 1971.

BIBLIOGRAPHY

Travis, Anthony S. *Dreamland: American Travelers to the Holy Land in the 19th Century.* The National Library of Israel: Shapell Manuscript Foundation, 2012.

Trombley, Laura Skandera. *Mark Twain's Other Woman.* New York: Alfred A. Knopf, 2010.

Turner, Arlin. *Mark Twain and George W. Cable: The Record of a Literary Friendship.* East Lansing: Michigan State University Press, 1960.

Wallace, Elizabeth. *Mark Twain and the Happy Island.* Chicago: A. C. McClurg & Company, 1913.

Warner, Charles Dudley. *The Education of the Negro.* Clifton, New Jersey: African Tree Press, 2015.

Webster, Samuel Charles, ed. *Mark Twain, Business Man.* Boston: Little, Brown and Company, 1946.

Wecter, Dixon. *Sam Clemens of Hannibal.* Boston: Houghton Mifflin Company, 1952.

Wheeler, Candace. *Yesterdays in a Busy Life.* New York: Harper & Brothers, 1918.

Willis, Resa. *Mark and Livy: The Love Story of Mark Twain and the Woman Who (Almost) Tamed Him.* New York: TV Books, 2000. Reprint.

Zacks, Richard. *Chasing the Last Laugh: Mark Twain's Raucous and Redemptive Round-the-World Comedy Tour.* New York: Doubleday, 2016.

Zwick, Jim. *Confronting Imperialism: Essays on Mark Twain and the Anti-Imperialist League.* West Conshohocken, Pennsylvania: Infinity Publishing, 2007.

Zwonitzer, Mark. *The Statesman and the Storyteller: John Hay, Mark Twain, and the Rise of American Imperialism.* Chapel Hill, North Carolina: Algonquin Books, 2016.

Illustration Credits

FRONTISPIECE

A seldom seen photo of Mark Twain from his final years. 1909. Courtesy of Susan Jaffe Tane.

PART TITLE PAGES

Page 1: The young Samuel Clemens, likely taken in his late teens. Courtesy of The Mark Twain House & Museum, Hartford, Connecticut.

Page 185: Mark Twain around the time he wooed and wed Olivia "Livy" Langdon. By J. Gurney & Sons. 1869. Courtesy of The Mark Twain House & Museum, Hartford, Connecticut.

Page 443: A rare photo of Sam and Livy. 1903. Courtesy of The Mark Twain House & Museum, Hartford, Connecticut.

Page 683: Mark Twain in an English garden in 1900, the year he returned to America from his European exile. Courtesy of The Mark Twain House & Museum, Hartford, Connecticut.

Page 869: Isabel Lyon with Mark Twain in Bermuda. Courtesy of Mark Twain Papers and Project, The Bancroft Library, University of California, Berkeley.

FIRST ILLUSTRATION INSERT

Page 1: Courtesy of Mark Twain Papers and Project, The Bancroft Library, University of California, Berkeley.

Page 2, top and bottom: Courtesy of Mark Twain Papers and Project, The Bancroft Library, University of California, Berkeley.

ILLUSTRATION CREDITS

Page 3, top, middle, and bottom: Courtesy of The Mark Twain House & Museum, Hartford, Connecticut.

Page 4, top, bottom left and right: Courtesy of The Mark Twain House & Museum, Hartford, Connecticut.

Page 5, top and bottom: Courtesy of Mark Twain Papers and Project, The Bancroft Library, University of California, Berkeley.

Page 6, top: Courtesy of The Mark Twain House & Museum, Hartford, Connecticut.

Page 6, middle: Photo by Thomas E. Marr. 1903. Courtesy of The Mark Twain House & Museum, Hartford, Connecticut.

Page 6, bottom: Photo by Daniel Camp. 1875. Courtesy of Kevin Mac Donnell, Austin, Texas.

Page 7, top: Courtesy of Mark Twain Papers and Project, The Bancroft Library, University of California, Berkeley.

Page 7, bottom left and right: Courtesy of The Mark Twain House & Museum, Hartford, Connecticut.

Page 8, top: Courtesy of The Mark Twain House & Museum, Hartford, Connecticut.

Page 8, bottom: Courtesy of Mark Twain Papers and Project, The Bancroft Library, University of California, Berkeley.

SECOND ILLUSTRATION INSERT

Page 1, top and bottom: Courtesy of Mark Twain Papers and Project, The Bancroft Library, University of California, Berkeley.

Page 2, top: Courtesy of The Mark Twain House & Museum, Hartford, Connecticut.

Page 2, bottom: Courtesy of Mark Twain Papers and Project, The Bancroft Library, University of California, Berkeley.

Page 3, top and bottom: Courtesy of Mark Twain Papers and Project, The Bancroft Library, University of California, Berkeley.

Page 4, top: Courtesy of The Mark Twain House & Museum, Hartford, Connecticut.

Page 4, bottom: Courtesy of Mark Twain Papers and Project, The Bancroft Library, University of California, Berkeley.

Page 5, top and bottom: Courtesy of The Mark Twain House & Museum, Hartford, Connecticut.

Page 6, top and bottom: Courtesy of Mark Twain Papers and Project, The Bancroft Library, University of California, Berkeley.

Page 7, top: Courtesy of the Library of Congress, Prints and Photographs Division, LC-USZ62-28786.

Page 7, bottom: Courtesy of Mark Twain Papers and Project, The Bancroft Library, University of California, Berkeley.

Page 8, top: Courtesy of Kevin Mac Donnell, Austin, Texas.

Page 8, bottom: Courtesy of the Mark Twain Archive, Elmira College, Elmira, New York.

Index

Titles of articles, books, essays, and plays refer to works by Mark Twain, unless otherwise noted.

abolitionists, 91, 120, 188, 227
  aid fugitive slaves, 42
  Hannibal, Mo.'s contempt for, 16, 25–26, 37
  Langdon family and, 162, 164
  on the lecture circuit, 174
  MT on, 42, 44, 139, 331
Acorns, Order of, 708–9
Actors' Fund Fair, 910
Adams, Maude, 832–33
Adirondacks, 578, 711, 715
Adventures of Huckleberry Finn, 107, 360, 939, 988
  admired by writers, 400
  autobiographical aspect of, 335
  banning of/criticism of, xx, 335–38, 340–42
  dialects in, 329–30, 335, 337, 342
  explanation of, 328–37
  first-person device in, 234, 330, 341
  Livy's editing of, 338
  lynchings in, 334–35
  and Mary Ann Cord's story, 221
  models for characters in, 330–31, 736
  and MT lecture tour, 313, 315, 317–19, 323
  MT on, 300, 328, 340, 342
  and MT's boyhood recollections, 27, 29, 329–31, 340
  MT's readings of, 388–89
  N-word in, xx, 314, 332–33, 335–36, 517

  pirated editions of, 326–27
  published by MT, 308, 326, 338–40, 348–50, 386
  reviews of, 340–41, 398
  slavery in, 328–29, 331–33, 336–38, 342
  success of, 339, 341–42, 349–50, 363, 386
  writing of, 284, 328
Adventures of Robin Hood, The, 20
Adventures of Tom Sawyer, The, 239, 401, 939, 1011
  autobiographical aspect of, 234
  Becky Thatcher character in, 24, 235, 464, 724, 736, 840, 949
  boyhood recollections in, 12, 234–35
  and *Huckleberry Finn*, 328, 335, 339
  Livy's views on, 234
  main themes in, 236
  models for characters in, 14, 24, 235, 949
  MT's readings of, 900
  pirated edition of, 237–38, 873
  positive reviews of, 237
  and *Prince and the Pauper*, 271
  product endorsements and, 703
  publishing/marketing of, 237, 338
  racial stereotypes in, 236–37
  sales of, 237–38, 241, 247, 257
  slavery in, 328–29
"Advice to Youth," 295
Age of Reason, The (Paine), 52
Aguinaldo, Emilio, 655, 715, 718, 725

INDEX

Ah Sin (play), 243–45, 247, 292
Aix-les-Bains, France, 445–48, 451
Alcott, Louisa May, 235, 341, 950
Aldrich, Thomas Bailey, 203, 310, 521, 652, 687, 700, 761, 764, 862, 882
Alexander & Green, 282, 373
Alexander II, Czar, 130–31, 782
Alexandra, Queen, 886–87
Alfred T. Lacey, 54, 61
Allen, Charles, 1011, 1019, 1022
Allen, Helen, 838, 923–24, 1009, 1011–12, 1019, 1021–23, 1025–26
Allen, Marion Schuyler, 836–38, 923, 927, 1010–11, 1019–26
Alonzo Child, 63
Amazonian adventure, 47–48
Ament, Joseph P., 34–35, 40, 723–24
Ament, William Scott, 721
American Claimant, The, 461–64
"American Press, The," 701
American Publisher, The, 192–93
American Publishing Company, 243, 311, 348, 704
  MT invests in, 196, 238
  and MT's contract, 705
  MT's criticism of, 148, 196, 238, 306, 308, 325
  MT's lawsuit against, 272
  publishes MT's books, 144–45, 148, 203, 238, 257, 517
"American Vandal Abroad, The" (lecture), 149, 156
Andrews, Evangeline, 434, 437–38
"angelfish," 866, 884, 949–51, 962, 971, 985, 990–91
  Isabel Lyon and, 836, 900, 903, 916–17, 923, 939–40
  MT corresponds with, 836–37, 858, 923, 939–40, 1009–10, 1021
  MT establishes club for, 922–23
  MT's daughters on, 837–38, 901–2, 904, 927–28, 940
  and MT's grandfatherly feelings, 834, 1027
  MT's idealized view of, 835, 919, 1009–10
  and MT's later years, 1009–12, 1021–23
  MT's obsession with, 833–40, 916–24
  MT's rationale for, 833–35, 862

recruitment of, 893–94, 917, 921
visit MT at Stormfield, 926–28, 939–40, 968
See also Aquarium Club
animals/animal welfare, 15, 801–2, 805–6, 850, 963. *See also* Clemens, Jean (daughter): love for animals
Anti-Imperialist League (N.Y.), 722, 749, 843
anti-Semitism, xix, 618, 620–25
antislavery, xx, 42, 174, 367, 514
Aquarium Club, 833–38, 866, 882, 886, 922–24, 927–28, 939–40, 951, 955, 1010
Arabian Nights, The, 20
aristocracy, xix, 198, 393–94, 397, 453, 514, 553, 599, 651
Arnold, Matthew, 392, 399, 701
Arthur, Chester, 266, 316
"As Regards Patriotism," 718–19
Ashcroft, Isabel Lyon. *See* Lyon, Isabel
Ashcroft, Ralph, 891, 911, 916, 930, 937
  in Bermuda with MT, 917–19, 921
  on Clara Clemens, 942–43, 980–82
  defends Isabel, 979–81
  escorts MT to funeral, 936
  flees to England, 975–77, 980
  intimacy with MT, 954–56, 959, 965–66, 968–69
  Jean Clemens on, 976
  Mark Twain Company and, 957–58, 968, 981–82
  marriage of, 962–67, 969, 985–86, 1020
  MT on, 819, 885, 957, 964–66
  MT signs contracts for, 965–66, 969
  as MT's business manager, 908, 954, 956–58, 965
  MT's feud with, 972–77, 982, 984–86, 993, 1018, 1020
  as MT's power of attorney, 956–58, 975
  as MT's secretary, 885, 906, 908
  at Plasmon Company, 819, 885, 956, 968
  publicly attacks Clemens family, 980–82
  purloins MT documents, 1032
  relationship with Isabel Lyon, 908, 932, 945–46, 953–58, 984
  and Stormfield, 954–55, 992
Astor, Nancy Langhorne, 920–21
astronomy, xviii, 994, 1006

INDEX

Asylum Hill Congregational Church (Hartford), 189, 227
Atlantic Monthly, 817
  MT's Mary Ann Cord story in, 221, 223, 330
  MT's "Old Times on the Mississippi" in, xiv, 233, 303, 307
  MT's "Some Rambling Notes" in, 246–47
  MT's unsigned articles in, 259
  reviews MT's books, 149–51, 237, 397
Aurora, Nevada Territory, 75–77, 80
Australia, 525, 540–44, 546, 588–89, 703
Austria, 645–48, 651–55, 804. *See also* Vienna
"Austrian Edison Keeping School Again, The," 637
Austro-Hungarian Empire, 618, 654, 657
Autobiography of Mark Twain, 21, 318, 1033. *See also* Twain, Mark: dictates autobiography
Autocrat of the Breakfast Table, The (Holmes), 164

"Babies, The," 261–63
Babylon, Long Island, 962–63, 966
Bacon, Delia Salter, 52
Bacon, Francis, 987–89
Bad Nauheim, Germany, 456–59, 464, 467
Badeau, Adam, 353–54
Baden-Baden, Germany, 250–51, 446
Badeni, Kasimir, 619–20
Baldwin, William Wilberforce, 468, 474, 766
Ball, Charles, 394
Baltimore, Md., 244, 366, 903, 990–91, 994
Bardi, Countess, 658–59
Barnard College, 833
Barnes, George, 95, 97, 100, 112
Barnum, Phineas, 228–30, 392
Barnum & Bailey Circus, 1026
Bates, Edward, 36, 68–69
Bavaria, 480, 612
Bayreuth Festival (Germany), 446–48
Beard, Dan, 392, 789
Beardsley, Lillian R., 806
Beecher, Henry Ward, 115, 119, 144, 163–64, 173–74, 190, 231, 312–13, 355, 375, 407
Beecher, Thomas K., 163–64, 166, 187, 421

Beethoven, 448, 630, 848
Belford Brothers, 237–38
Belgium, xix, 785, 788, 1010
Bell, Alexander Graham, 231–32, 512
Benton, Thomas Hart, 44
Berlin, Germany, 451–55, 460, 468, 470–73, 502, 933, 941, 955, 961–62, 966
Bermuda, 883, 936, 955–56
  Elizabeth Wallace's book on, 837
  MT visits aquarium in, 922, 1025
  and MT's angelfish, 882, 917–23, 1021
  MT's first trip to, 246–47
  MT's late-life trips to, 878–79, 953, 1010–12, 1019–21, 1025–26
  MT's series based on, 246–47
Bernhardt, Sarah, 783–84
Bible, 15, 26, 40, 71, 114, 133, 149, 173, 252, 307–8, 317–18, 384, 603, 647, 995, 1005–7
Bierce, Ambrose, 99, 374, 705
Bigelow, Poultney, 665–66, 669, 794
billiards, 101, 209, 217, 243, 343, 580, 824, 835, 862, 875, 878, 911, 919, 936, 1002, 1011
Bixby, Horace, 49–50, 61, 63, 148, 304, 734
Blackmer, Margaret, 917–21, 939–40, 1021
Blacks, 140, 260, 514, 549–50
  civil rights for, 345
  education of, 226–27, 364–67, 729, 843–44
  Langdon family support of, 162, 164
  lynchings of, 172, 334–35, 515, 714–18
  MT on, 115, 201–2, 304, 365, 562–63, 594–95, 729
  MT shares tales about, 220–22
  MT's fondness for, 27–28, 35, 43, 333, 559–60, 843–44
  and MT's political activism, 786, 791
  MT's racist language and, 27, 42–43, 125, 563
  MT's relationship with, 487
  MT's support of, 226–28, 364–67, 792
  MT's "white guilt" and, 290, 365
  music/songs of, 226–28, 376, 767
  and N-word, xx, 42–43, 314, 332–33, 335–36, 487, 517
  professionals, 515
  speech patterns of, 220–21, 329–30
  writers, 336–37

INDEX

Blaine, James G., 343–45
Blankenship, Benson, 29, 329
Blankenship, Tom, 22, 27, 29, 329–30, 736
Bliss, Elisha, Jr., 308, 704–5
   accusations against, 193, 196, 203, 238, 271, 325
   and Bret Harte, 243–44
   death of, 271
   hires Orion Clemens, 192–93
   MT confides in, 174, 180
   publishes MT's books, 144–49, 193–94, 196, 238
Bliss, Francis "Frank," 311, 597, 642, 704, 715–16
"Bloody Massacre Near Carson, A," 83, 86
Boers/Boer wars, 560–63, 674–75, 697–98
Booth, William Stone, 987, 990
Boston, 150, 208, 248–49, 304, 315–16, 330, 340, 850, 899, 912
Boston *Daily Globe*, 387, 590
Boston Herald, 323–24, 352, 370
Boston Lyceum Bureau, 174–76
Boston Transcript, 340, 912
Bowen, Will, 20, 63, 98, 105, 145, 169, 233
Bowser, David Watt "Wattie," 267–68
Brahms, 627, 1000
Brandt, Marianne, 629–30
Brewer, Ebenezer Cobham, 521
British Empire, 546, 552–53, 555–56, 561, 588–89, 599
British literature, 256
Brockway, Zebulon, 387–88
Brown, Dr. John, 205–6, 211, 234
Brown, John, 227, 403
Brown, William, 53–54
Brownell, Louise, 536
   career/marriage of, 505–6
   corresponds with MT, 772–73
   excluded from Susy's funeral, 580
   names child after Susy, 506, 772–73
   romance with Susy, 436, 439, 460, 468–69, 489, 520, 526, 584, 604, 772–73
   Susy's letters to, 448, 450, 456–57, 459–60, 468, 490
   Susy's visits to, 491, 575
Browning, Robert, 205, 383–84, 474, 786
Browning Society, 383–84
Brush, George de Forest, 795, 798, 810, 847

Brush, Gerome "Gerry," 847, 850, 856–58, 862, 864, 876
Brush, Nancy, 810, 812, 814, 904, 915, 930, 932–33, 993
Bryan, William Jennings, 686, 706
Bryn Mawr, 434–39, 459–60, 470, 489–90, 505, 568, 580, 772
Budapest, 657–58
Buffalo, N.Y., 168–70, 178, 180–81, 189, 194, 214
Buffalo Bill Cody, 73, 363
Buffalo Express, 167–68, 170–74, 177–78, 180, 218, 242, 247
Burke, Billie, 924, 938
Burlingame, Anson, 109, 188
Butes, Dorothy, 866
Butters, Henry A., 678, 819

Cable, George Washington, 309–24, 330, 348, 355, 363, 384, 388, 531, 817
Cadets of Temperance, 36
Cage, The (Teller), 838–40
Calaveras County, Calif., 101–4, 243
California
   gold rush, 19, 72
   MT's mining in, 100–101, 104
   MT's renown in, 102–4
Californian, 99, 102, 104
Campbell-Bannerman, Henry, 887–88
Canada, 162, 237, 272, 553, 986
Caprell, Madame, 59–60
Captain Stormfield's Visit to Heaven, 995–97, 1011
Carleton, George W., 102
Carlyle, Thomas, 159, 390, 394, 521, 1027–28
Carnegie, Andrew, 432, 475–77, 597, 678, 713, 722, 781, 818, 841, 910
Carnegie Hall, 694, 712, 831, 843–44, 999
Carson City, Nevada Territory, 70–75, 79, 83, 89, 93, 137
"Causes of Our Present Municipal Corruption, The," 706–7
Celebrated Jumping Frog of Calaveras County and Other Sketches, The, 116–17
"Celebrated Jumping Frog of Calaveras County, The," 100–104, 529

INDEX

celebrity, 21, 121, 243, 717
  culture of, xvii, 703, 820, 989, 1029
  of MT abroad, 197, 542
  MT capitalizes on, xvii, 232, 653, 699–701, 703, 908
  of MT in U.S., xiv–xvii, 83, 304, 529–30, 534, 688, 699–703, 820–21
  MT on, 820–21, 883, 988
  and MT's books, 148, 699
  and MT's *Quaker City* letters/lectures, 134, 146
Century Magazine, 314, 320, 486–87, 496, 513, 651, 715
  Civil War series of, 65–68, 347, 351–52
  and Grant's memoirs, 347–52
  Huckleberry Finn serialized in, 338
  MT's "Austrian Edison" article in, 637
  MT's Civil War article in, 65–68, 351–52
  Pudd'nhead Wilson serialized in, 482, 517
Ceylon (Sri Lanka), 525, 547–48
"Character of Man, The," 852
Charcot, Jean-Martin, 492
Charles L. Webster and Company, 358, 389
  bank loans for, 377, 479–82, 497, 499, 957
  bankruptcy of, 499–501, 517, 522–23, 526–29, 567, 583, 595, 633
  creditors repaid, 632
  debts of, 381, 427–28, 484, 494, 496–97, 566
  established by MT, 325–27
  failed projects of, 372–73, 375, 475, 484
  under Frederick Hall, 413–15, 433, 459, 475–76
  fund raising for, 475–77, 482–86
  Henry Rogers and, 493–503
  Livy loans money to, 424, 498
  MT disengages from, 496–97
  MT supplies capital for, 326, 360, 369, 374, 378, 414
  owes MT/Livy money, 476, 479, 497, 499
  publishes Civil War memoirs, 348–54, 372–74, 413–15, 496
  publishes MT's books, 326–27, 338–39, 499, 514
  publishes Pope Leo biography, 370–72, 418

undermines MT's health, 453
under Webster, 325–27, 373, 379, 413–16, 479, 496
Chatto, Andrew, 328, 392
Chatto & Windus, 237, 272, 279, 315, 328, 624, 654
Chaykovsky, Nikolai, 784
Chesnutt, Charles W., 817–18
Chester, J., 366–67
Chicago, 261–63, 322, 346, 477–78, 482, 494
Chicago *Herald*, 503, 506–7
childhood purity, cult of, 235
Children's Educational Theatre, 909–10
Chinese
  immigrants, 173, 242–45, 343–44, 719
  missionaries, 716–17, 719–24
Choate, Joseph H., 665, 844
cholera, 7, 114, 458, 539–40, 799–800, 1007
Chopin, 448, 533, 796, 848, 1000
Christian missionaries, 107–8, 545, 548, 720–24, 785
Christian Science, 491–92, 574, 577, 668, 753–55
Christian Science, 754, 850, 879
Christian Science, 1032
Christianity, 844
  MT's cynicism toward, 332, 641
  MT's final blast at, 1024
  MT's satirical treatment of, 754–55, 995–97, 1005–8, 1010
  See also religion
"Chronicle of Young Satan, The," 647, 680
Chronicle of Young Satan, The, 803
Church, Frederic E., 384–85
Churchill, Winston, 697–98, 893
Civil War, 190, 194, 227, 304
  Century's series on, 65–68, 347, 351–52
  MT flipped sides on, 62, 91–92, 161, 174
  MT on, 62–68, 346–47, 358–59, 397
  MT publishes memoirs on, 353, 372–74, 413–14, 428
  MT reviews Black troops in, 532
  MT serves in, 65–69, 261, 347, 349, 354, 643, 713–14
  MT's *Century* article on, 65–68, 351–52, 354
  secession and, 62–64, 66, 69, 92, 261, 347, 714

| 1143 |

INDEX

Clagett, Billy, 76, 91–92
Claude (MT's butler), 926, 943–44, 1003, 1019, 1026–27
Clemens, Benjamin (brother), 6, 11
Clemens, Clara (daughter), 213, 217, 219, 222, 424, 565, 658–59, 677, 751
  appearance of, 297, 626, 770, 993
  cares for mother, 591, 728–30, 732–33, 741, 746–47, 755, 763, 765, 769
  child of, 1027–28, 1031
  childhood of, 249, 441–42
  clashes with Isabel Lyon, 872, 925, 928, 942, 945–47, 955–56, 962, 966–68, 971–73
  concert tours of, 916, 926, 941–42, 946, 980–81
  cruise to Nova Scotia, 899, 902
  death of, 1008, 1032
  depression of, 846, 848–49, 865–66
  distant from MT, 928, 1024
  education of, 255, 294–95, 672, 732
  in England, 592–93, 599, 955
  in Europe, 253, 448, 451–52, 457, 460, 471, 489, 1024, 1031
  first American recital of, 694–95
  on George Griffin's death, 487
  health issues of, 481–82, 626, 664–65, 673, 695, 755–56, 763, 773–78, 814, 912, 916
  as heir to MT's royalties, 958, 1014
  and Henry Rogers's death, 974–75
  on her mother, 536, 733, 741
  her mother on, 298, 460, 470–73, 502–3, 580, 626–27, 630, 756–57
  her sister Jean on, 687, 694–95, 858, 865–66, 912
  on Isabel Lyon, 892, 964, 983, 1032
  Isabel Lyon on, 794, 798, 872, 875, 898
  lawsuit against, 1003–4
  on leaving Hartford for Europe, 441–42
  letters to MT, 774
  literary interests of, 794, 950
  and Lyon-Ashcroft scandal, 967–68, 977–82, 985, 1031–32
  marriage of, 1000–1004, 1009–10, 1014–15, 1023–24, 1031
  medical treatments of, 502–3, 666, 669, 673, 794, 871

  and money issues, 474, 942, 946, 952, 967, 972
  and mother's death, 768–71, 773–74
  and mother's final illness, 746–47, 755, 796
  on MT, 293, 452, 460, 467, 471, 584, 591–93, 623, 675, 688, 700, 760, 818, 827, 849, 855, 865–66, 941, 975, 1024–25
  MT on, 595, 627–28, 741, 746, 750, 765, 768–69, 776, 794–95, 797–98, 859–60, 865, 898, 911, 968, 974, 981, 1000–1001
  MT protective of, 592–93, 629, 857
  MT subsidizes singing career, 865, 875, 898, 907, 941–42, 946, 967, 1000
  and MT's books/writings, 268–69, 567, 720, 722, 800, 852, 949, 1008
  and MT's death, 1025, 1027, 1027–31
  on MT's global lecture tour, 526–27, 531–33, 536–37, 539–42, 545–49, 552–53, 557, 560, 566
  and MT's letters project, 799, 821, 824, 952–53, 982
  MT's letters to, 293, 457, 468, 469, 483, 485, 495, 502, 801, 808, 820–21, 862, 864, 882, 901, 911, 926, 967–68, 984, 992, 1011, 1014
  as MT's literary executor, 952
  MT's love for, xix, 1024, 1030
  music interests of, 447, 458, 460, 585, 632, 797
  on Oscar Wilde, 457
  overshadowed by MT, 297, 575, 694–95, 859–60, 941–42, 1024
  and parents' art patronage, 286
  personality of, 297–98, 460, 626, 629–30, 693–94, 872, 912, 940
  piano playing skills of, 533
  piano studies of, 468, 470–73, 502, 601, 609, 626–30, 941
  protective of MT, 884, 886–87, 895, 940
  relationship with her mother, 364, 730
  relationship with Isabel Lyon, 809, 845–46, 848–49, 851, 898–99, 942–43
  relationship with MT, 291–95, 297, 300, 471–72, 629, 746, 761, 763, 776–77, 834, 900, 928, 1023–24
  relationship with Ossip, 628–29, 653, 694, 732–33, 946–47, 999–1004, 1024

| 1144 |

INDEX

religious beliefs of, 795, 1024, 1027–28, 1032
reporter's description of, 541
"rest cure" of, 776–77
reviews of, 860, 912, 941, 999–1000
runs household, 808, 872, 925, 928, 945–46
sails to Europe, 1009–10, 1014, 1016–17
scandalous behavior of, 471–73, 502–3
secret affair of, 899, 942–43, 945–47, 967, 980, 999, 1032
shields mother from truth, 749–50
singing career of, 694–95, 834, 845–46, 859–60, 871, 898, 912, 916, 941, 978
singing lessons of, 629–30, 662, 669, 732
singing/vocal setbacks, 795, 807, 809, 845, 860, 897, 940, 999–1000
and sister Jean, 691, 693–94, 849, 878, 962, 967, 970
and sister Jean's death, 1014–16, 1024
and sister Jean's epilepsy, 614, 763, 865–66, 876–77, 906
and sister Susy's death, 576–77, 579–80, 582–85, 591–92, 595, 602, 687, 694
sister Susy's letters to, 468–71, 490–91, 536–37, 574–76, 578
social life of, 626–28, 632, 691, 693–94
"Tennessee land" and, 774–77
theater interests of, 298, 324
torn between career/family, 626, 732
trades on father's fame, 941–42
See also Norfolk sanitarium
Clemens, Henry (brother), 827
birth of, 9
death of, 54–58, 202, 423, 581, 735, 1023
in Keokuk, Iowa, 41, 45
and MT, 43, 48, 53–56, 235, 643
personality of, 53
as steamboat purser, 53–56
typesetting jobs of, 36, 38, 46
Clemens, James Ross (cousin), 596
Clemens, Jane Lampton (mother), 63–64, 66, 124, 200, 888
appearance of, 4, 13, 421
children of, 6, 8–9
death of, 423–24, 735, 820
and death of children, 11, 14, 57
dementia of, 422–23
earns income, 31, 36

and husband's death, 32–34, 57
influence on MT, 4, 13–15, 24, 321, 329
in Keokuk, Iowa, 45, 321, 421–24
language gifts of, 4, 15
lives with Moffetts, 50, 115
marriage of, 4–6, 11, 14
on MT, 8–9, 20–22, 34, 40–43, 49, 158, 423
MT dedicates book to, 148–49
MT gives Bible to, 133
MT inscribes book to, 116
MT models characters on, 14–15, 235, 606
MT names child after, 265
MT on, 4–5, 11, 13–16, 48, 176, 321
MT's estrangement from, 158, 166
MT's financial support of, 421–22
MT's letters to, 41–43, 72, 75–76, 85, 87, 98, 103, 213, 247, 301, 423
on MT's typesetter, 416
MT's visits to, 45, 115, 170, 304, 321, 385–86
personality of, 13–16
prints MT's letters, 72, 79
religion and, 14, 25, 115, 621
slavery and, 7, 15–17, 29
and son Orion, 41, 193, 423
Clemens, Jean (daughter), xix, 217, 265, 658, 756
affection for MT, 1016
Albert Paine on, 1001
anger/temper of, 807–8, 811–13, 871, 876, 879–80, 932
appearance of, 299, 808, 849, 993, 1001
appraisal of Clemens family, 880–81
attends MT's play, 409
banished by Isabel Lyon, 931–32, 937, 962–63, 966–67, 970–71, 976, 979
in the Berkshires, 773–76
clandestine liaison of, 775–76
clashes with Isabel Lyon, 850–51, 855–57, 863–64, 876, 902, 904–6, 914
clashes with parents, 692
death of, 1013–19, 1024, 1030
depression of, 812–13, 834, 846, 858–59, 904
diary of, 690–91, 875
on earning a living, 915
education of, 294–95, 299–300, 445, 492–93, 526

| 1145 |

INDEX

Clemens, Jean (*cont.*)
  epilepsy in remission, 993
  epilepsy of, 603–4, 612–15, 626, 647, 652, 662, 691, 694, 739–40, 749, 765, 768–69, 779, 796, 798, 914, 1013
  epilepsy treatments and, 665–69, 671–73, 677–81, 690–92, 729, 764, 809, 813–14, 877, 881, 905–6, 931
  epilepsy worsens, 807–12, 861, 881
  epilepsy's effects on, 774, 815, 847, 849, 855, 857, 859, 861, 932–33, 971, 1016
  estranged from family, 913
  farm/farmhouse of, 931, 976, 992, 1012, 1018
  on Gabrilowitsch's concert, 694
  on group homes, 962–63, 992
  as heir to MT's royalties, 958, 1014
  and her mother, 364, 492, 554, 615, 671, 747, 755, 765, 768–71, 796, 808, 902
  and her sister Clara, 614, 662, 691, 693–94, 970, 1002–4, 1015, 1024
  on her sister Clara, 687, 694–95, 849, 858, 871, 876–77, 913
  horse riding of, 774–75, 976, 1013
  illnesses of, 300–301, 424, 755
  on imperial invitation, 453–54
  improved health of, 742, 747, 902, 912–14, 928, 931, 971
  on Isabel Lyon, 964–65, 976–77, 983
  Isabel Lyon on, 798, 875, 879, 914, 933, 962, 977
  language studies of, 473, 604, 612, 798, 875
  letters to MT, 851, 963
  literary interests of, 864
  longs for love/marriage, 774
  love for animals, 299, 492–93, 802, 805, 808, 850, 864, 963, 993, 1015
  and Lyon-Ashcroft scandal, 976–79, 981
  and money issues, 416, 961
  on MT, 293–94, 300, 446, 692, 796, 815, 849, 857, 862, 865–67, 877, 883–84, 886, 901–2, 907, 913, 929, 962, 1010
  MT estranged from, 914–15, 961, 1016
  MT on, 298–300, 473, 595, 604, 612–14, 665, 667–68, 671, 692, 729, 739, 774, 798, 807–8, 862–64, 880, 912–14, 929–32, 976–77, 984, 992, 1016
  MT protective of, 592–93, 847–48, 858, 1012, 1017
  MT's affection for, 915, 992, 1013–14
  and MT's books/writings, 789, 800, 826, 852
  MT's homage to, 1014–18
  and MT's letters project, 799
  MT's letters to, 293, 503, 860, 874, 876, 880–81, 887, 901–2, 904–5, 910, 912, 928–33, 936, 963, 970–71, 984
  and MT's library, 1001
  and MT's private readings, 786, 789, 810
  as MT's typist/secretary, 744, 852, 976, 992, 1012–13
  MT's visits to, 929–31
  music interests of, 447, 796
  in New Hampshire, 795–96, 798
  osteopathic treatments of, 728–30
  personality of, 299–300, 473, 492, 604, 612, 668, 692, 807–10, 813, 929, 971, 977
  philanthropy of, 1012
  relationship with Clara, 808, 880
  relationship with Isabel Lyon, 796, 849
  relationship with MT, 291–95, 747, 777, 783, 808, 834, 849–50, 880, 971
  reunites with family, 573
  romantic attachments of, 847, 850, 856–58, 862, 864, 876–77
  sails to Berlin for treatment, 933, 955, 961–62
  and sister Susy's death, 578–81, 585, 595, 691, 694, 808, 933
  strikes Katy Leary, 811–13, 876
  telephone calls with MT, 884, 902, 970
  violent actions of, 876, 905–6, 932, 962
  wood carving of, 612, 747, 849–50, 864–65, 875, 939
  writing of, 963
  See also Katonah sanitarium
Clemens, John Marshall (father)
  appearance of, 12
  careers/jobs of, 5–7, 9–12, 31–32
  death of, 32–34, 423, 735
  and death of children, 11
  disapproves of MT, 61
  financial woes of, 10–11, 19–20, 31–33

INDEX

marriage of, 4–5
MT models character on, 7, 200, 235
MT on, 5, 7, 9–10, 12–13, 16–17, 32
personality of, 4, 7, 10–13, 27
relationship with MT, 12–14, 17, 20–21, 33, 39
religion and, 12, 25
slavery and, 4, 11, 16–17, 29, 549, 588
"Tennessee land" and, 6, 32
Clemens, Langdon (son), 179–83, 187, 292, 296, 300, 424, 827, 1030
Clemens, Margaret (sister), 6, 9
Clemens, Mary "Mollie" Stotts (sister in-law), 52
  in Carson City, 83, 89
  death of, 762
  and husband's death, 631–32
  in Keokuk, Iowa, 191, 421–22
  marriage of, 45–46, 50, 193
  on MT, 13
  MT's later visits to, 385–86
  MT's letters to, 53–57, 59, 78, 106, 182, 328, 422, 431, 631–32, 680
  Sanitary Commission and, 92–93
Clemens, Olivia "Livy" Langdon (wife), 60, 79, 233
  appearance of, 142, 212, 385, 745, 758, 831
  as art benefactor, 285–90
  attends literary club meetings, 224
  on bankruptcy, 499–501, 503–4, 527, 537, 540, 546, 597–98
  bedridden/sequestered, 728, 741–43, 746, 748–52, 755, 760–61, 765
  on Buffalo home, 168–69
  and Charles Warner, 198–99
  and Charles Webster, 326, 368–69
  children of, 177, 179–83, 187, 207, 213, 265, 298, 363
  chronic health problems of, 420, 467–68, 470, 474, 485, 499, 665, 673
  civilizes MT, 210–12, 520–21, 531, 537
  and Clara's singing career, 694–95
  coal business and, 161, 178, 214, 247, 254, 474, 564
  courted by MT, 153–65, 218
  criticism of, 218, 243–44
  and daughter Susy, 434–39
  and daughter Susy's death, 576–77, 579–82, 584–85

and daughters' education, 294–95, 302, 434–39
death of, xx, 767–74, 796, 827, 834, 852, 908, 965, 995, 1014, 1030
and death of Jane Clemens, 819–20
and death of mother, 423–25, 436
and death of son, 182–83, 187
declining health of, 739–52, 755–60, 762–66, 778, 1025
dislikes separations from MT, 174, 214, 315, 322, 324, 363, 504, 564, 734, 750
English psychic and, 675–77
family theatrical and, 324
and father's death, 177–78
fragile health of, 159–61, 179–83, 212–13, 301–2, 310, 322, 440–41, 452, 456, 459, 674, 729–30
at French spa, 502
and friendship with Twichell, 252
handles MT's letters, 743
heart troubles of, 302, 455, 457, 468, 479, 652, 665, 680–81, 728, 733, 740–43, 762
and her daughters, 452, 456, 460, 469–73, 476, 491, 502–3, 557, 585, 626, 774, 834
on her own death, 455, 459, 474, 500, 742, 757, 766
household run by, 212–15, 265, 302, 441–42, 474, 674
improved health of, 505, 519, 536, 549–52, 554, 756–57
on India, 550–51, 553–55
influence on MT, 142, 167, 177, 217–19, 218, 224, 228
inheritance of, 161, 178, 214, 416, 433, 501
and Jean's epilepsy, 613–15, 667, 671, 673, 678–80, 729–30, 739–40, 747, 749–50, 765, 774, 809
language studies of, 255, 452
letters to her mother, 253–55, 265, 423–24
letters to MT, 181, 476, 491
literary tastes of, 164–65, 217–18, 988
love for MT, 156, 165–66, 210, 213, 363, 427, 478, 750, 803
marriage of, 5, 168, 210–15, 256–57, 363–64, 441, 564, 611
medical treatments of, 505, 652, 692, 742–43

| 1147 |

INDEX

Clemens, Olivia "Livy" Langdon (*cont.*)
  money worries of, 255, 476, 478, 480, 485, 504, 519, 564
  mourns death of Susy, 592, 595, 602–4, 611–13, 615, 633, 675–76, 712
  on MT, 142, 206, 455, 547, 557, 559, 687
  MT inscribes book to, 570
  MT models character on, 645
  MT on, 160, 165–66, 177, 211–13, 218, 294, 301–2, 305, 310, 467–68, 595, 692, 729–30, 739–43, 747, 755, 764–66, 809
  MT's assets transferred to, 498, 504, 535
  MT's concern for, 485, 493, 502, 615
  MT's descriptions of, 994
  as MT's editor, 164, 217–19, 234, 240, 305, 338, 391–92, 506, 570–71, 588, 591, 640, 651, 762, 825
  and MT's fracas with Ned House, 410–11
  on MT's global lecture tour, 525–28, 531, 533, 536–37, 540–43, 545–52, 555, 557, 559, 587
  and MT's inventions, 231, 416, 418, 433, 478, 495, 507
  and MT's *Joan of Arc*, 506, 567–68, 570–71
  and MT's lectures/speeches, 315, 319, 542–43, 560, 740
  MT's letters to, xiv–xv, 175–76, 197, 209–10, 212–13, 262–63, 304, 318–24, 357, 449–50, 478, 482–84, 486–87, 491–92, 494–96, 500, 522–24, 577, 580, 584, 731–32, 757, 953
  as MT's literary agent, 219
  MT's love for, xv, xix–xx, 5, 132, 165, 171, 177, 196–97, 210–11, 213, 257, 268, 322, 363, 420, 450, 660, 771, 983, 1024
  MT's love notes to, 746, 748, 760, 763
  and MT's publishing firm, 479
  MT's reminiscences of, 772
  MT's tributes to, 748, 800–803, 1015
  on MT's writing, 198, 200, 218–19, 269, 305, 338, 647, 652, 720–22, 730–31, 852
  music interests of, 447
  as newlywed, 168–70, 176–78
  opulent lifestyle of, 476, 480, 501
  as parent, 291–92, 294–302, 473, 585
  as peacemaker, 312, 317, 319
  personality of, 142, 210, 294, 537, 742

  and politics, 654
  on *Prince and the Pauper* play, 410
  purchases Tarrytown home, 733
  relationship with Clara, 730, 756–57
  relationship with Jean, 692
  relationship with MT, xix, 53, 142, 164, 165
  religious beliefs of, 189, 257, 603, 765, 852
  on repaying creditors, 632–33
  reporter's description of, 541–42
  restrains MT's extreme views, 781, 794, 852
  rheumatism bouts of, 610, 652, 665
  sex life of, 240, 1006
  social life of, 212–13, 215, 217, 247, 302, 441, 452, 457
  spends money liberally, 214, 247, 250, 253–55, 265–67, 371, 467, 478
  tames MT's temper, xix, 245, 279, 294, 317, 327, 340, 770, 982
  trains MT on social graces, 210, 531, 560
  upbringing of, 159–61, 476
  on womanhood, 213
  See also Langdon, Olivia "Livy"
Clemens, Olivia "Susy" (daughter), 215–16
  appearance of, 433–34
  birth/childhood of, 182, 205–7, 243, 249
  Clara's letters to, 469, 473, 536
  death of, 576–82, 671, 757, 769, 827, 888, 1030
  education of, 294–95, 434–39, 466, 470, 485, 489
  in Europe, 253, 452, 456–57, 459–60, 505, 566
  family mourns death of, 587–93, 595, 647–48, 652, 675, 681, 687, 753, 918
  French governess of, 466, 468, 489
  health improves, 499, 505, 519
  health issues of, 312, 438–39, 489–93, 502, 527–28, 567, 573–74
  and her mother, 364, 456, 459, 468, 489
  her mother on, 485, 491, 493, 502, 543, 559, 574–75, 582, 585, 592
  infatuated with Italian count, 469–70, 536
  and Kipling's visit, 400–401
  literary interests of, 456, 468, 490, 505, 509, 520, 580–81, 584, 988
  Mental Science embraced by, 574–75, 577–78

1148

INDEX

on MT, 296, 324, 344, 383, 437–38, 467–68, 568, 575
MT models character on, 605, 645, 806
MT on, 187, 297, 438, 450, 456, 469, 490–93, 502, 520, 528, 574, 578, 580–81, 584, 827, 901, 915
MT's adoration of, xix, 295–96, 660
and MT's books/writings, 268–69, 338, 434, 506, 567, 569, 571, 995
MT's fond recollections of, 772, 917–18, 940, 1009
and MT's global lecture tour, 526, 528, 536, 574
MT's letters to, 293, 322, 421, 485, 574, 753
MT's tributes to, 603, 1015
personality of, 296–97, 434, 460, 489–90
relationship with MT, 291–301, 433–39, 575, 584, 834
romance with Brownell, 436, 439, 448, 450, 459–60, 468–69, 489–91, 505–6, 520, 526, 536, 575, 584, 604, 772–73
singing lessons of, 447, 468–69, 489–91, 505, 520
singing skills of, 575–76
theatrical interests of, 324, 434, 436–37, 473–74, 591
writes bio of MT, 296, 584, 827
Clemens, Orion (brother), 821
  appearance of, 68, 88
  in Carson City with MT, 74–75
  childhood/youth of, 5–6, 8, 10–12
  during Civil War, 68–70
  death of, 631–32, 735
  and his brother Henry, 53
  and his father, 11, 32–33, 36
  and his mother, 423
  July 4th presentation with MT, 385–86
  in Keokuk, Iowa, 321, 385–86, 421–23
  as lawyer, 50, 103, 191
  marriage of, 13
  on MT, 8, 22, 38–41
  MT models characters on, 88, 200, 604–6, 631
  MT on, 43, 48, 68–70, 76–77, 88–89, 106, 121, 631–32
  MT pays allowance to, 428, 632
  MT remains loyal to, 191–93

MT works for, 36–40, 45–46, 74
and MT's inventions, 417–18, 431, 502
MT's later visits to, 385–86
MT's letters to, 44, 50, 52, 59, 75, 92, 94–95, 146, 180–82, 193, 217, 328, 350, 387, 415, 457, 504, 526
as newspaper owner, 36–41, 45–46
personality of, 36, 38–39, 68, 88, 477, 631–32
politics of, 37, 45, 64, 68–69, 91, 106, 137
as a printer, 10, 32, 34, 36
prints MT's letters, 42, 44
relationship with MT, 37–41, 48, 51, 53, 58, 61, 76–78, 88, 137, 191–92, 477–78, 631–32
Sanitary Commission and, 92
as secretary of Nevada, 69–70, 72, 74–75, 80, 83, 87–89, 191
temperance crusade of, 106
"Tennessee land" and, 36, 38, 50, 106
writing skills of, 103
Clemens, Pamela Goggin (grandmother), 3–4
Clemens, Pamela (sister), 6, 32, 34. *See also* Moffett, Pamela Clemens (sister)
Clemens, Samuel B. (grandfather), 3–4, 8
Clemens, Samuel Langhorne. *See* Twain, Mark
Clemens, Sherrard, 260–61
Clemens, Will, 821
Clemens Gold and Silver Mining Company, 76–79
Clement, Gregory, 3
Cleveland, 525–29, 566
Cleveland, Grover, 318, 344–45, 368
Cleveland *Herald*, 123, 167
"Closing Words of My Autobiography," 1016
coca trade, 47–48, 75
Coggia's Comet, 228–29
Collier, Robert, 959
Colonel Sellers as a Scientist (play), 309, 326
Colonel Sellers character, 461–63, 636
Colonel Sellers (play), 226, 241–43
colonialism, xix, 543–46, 548, 550, 552–53, 589, 654–55, 719
Comstock Lode, 72, 80, 85, 230, 430, 532
"Concerning the Jews," 624–26

INDEX

"Concerning the Scoundrel Edward H. House," 412
Concord Public Library (Mass.), 341–42
Confederate militia, 65–68, 68, 261, 349, 354, 713
Congo, 785–88, 843, 1010
Congo Reform Association, 785–86
Connecticut Yankee in King Arthur's Court, A, 386, 409, 617, 659, 889
   and Arthurian legend, 388–90, 392–97
   British edition of, 392
   genesis of, 198, 318, 388–89
   humor in, 388, 396, 398
   illustrations in, 392
   Livy and, 389, 391–92, 730–31
   marketing of, 391–92
   MT pleased with, 1020
   and MT's politics, 396–98
   sales/reviews of, 397–98, 434
   slavery in, 393–95
   writing of, 377–78, 389–92
Conversation as It Was by the Social Fireside, in the Time of the Tudors. See *1601*
"Conversations with Satan," 646–47
Conway, Moncure, 237–38, 707
Coon, Ben, 101–2
Cooper, James Fenimore, 501
Cooper Institute (N.Y.C.), 117–18, 403
copyrights, 205, 404, 408, 853, 969, 990
   expiration of, 908, 946
   extension of, 828, 873–74
   MT lobbies Congress on, 873–74
   MT seeks better laws for, 237–38, 272–73
   and MT's *Quaker City* letters, 146
   and pirated books, 237–38, 272
   protection of, 237, 873–74, 957–58, 968
   transferred to Livy, 498, 504, 535
   violations of, 327
Cord, Mary Ann, 220–21, 223, 330, 333, 337, 516, 526
"Corn-Pone Opinions," 717–18
Cosmopolitan, 482, 651, 753
Count of Monte Cristo, The, 20
Cowles, Mildred and Edith, 913, 915, 929–32
Crane, Sue, 222, 257, 434, 436, 482, 500
   creates study for MT, 216–17
   and death of husband, 420–21
   in Europe, 451, 456

   inherits Quarry Farm, 178
   and Jean's epilepsy, 612, 615, 678, 811
   and Langdon's death/burial, 182–83, 187
   Livy on, 741
   and Livy's illness/death, 468, 741, 756, 803
   Livy's letters to, 546, 550, 557, 564, 566, 615
   on MT in Vienna, 602
   MT on, 216–17
   MT's letters to, 177, 246, 420, 673, 771, 841
   and MT's private readings, 786
   and Susy Clemens's death, 579–81
Crane, Theodore, 216–17, 222, 420–21
Croker, Richard, 706, 708–9
Cuba, 653–56, 675, 689, 718, 732
"Curious Republic of Gondour, The," 259
Curtis, Samuel, 91–92
Curzon, Lord, 888–89
Custer, George Armstrong, 372, 499
Cutter, Bloodgood H., 122–23
"Czar's Soliloquy, The," 781–82, 788

Daggett, Rollin M., 369–70, 476
Dake, Laura Wright. See Wright, Laura
Daly, Joseph, 411
Dana, Charles A., 370
Darwin, Charles, 163, 255–56, 727
Dawson, John D., 19, 34
Dawson, Theodore, 22–23
Day, Alice Hooker, 178, 187, 441–42, 455, 492, 501–2, 523, 557, 582, 584–85
De Beers diamond mines, 565
de Calry, Count, 469–70, 536
De Quille, Dan, 80–82, 84, 86–87, 91, 93
De Vinne Press, 853
"Death of Jean, The," 1014, 1016–17, 1020
Deerslayer, The (Cooper), 501
Delmonico's (N.Y.C.), 387, 817, 822
Democrats/Democratic Party, 34, 93, 189, 264, 303, 318, 345, 397, 454, 686, 706
Depew, Chauncey, 665, 688, 748
Dewey, George, 654–55, 721
dialects, 28, 74, 99, 220–21, 242–43, 309, 311, 329–30, 335, 339
Diary of Samuel Pepys, The (Pepys), 239, 269
Dickens, Charles, 46, 75, 99, 143, 271, 313
Dickinson, Anna, 157, 162, 376
Dictionary of Miracles (Brewer), 521

| 1150 |

INDEX

Dog's Tale, A, 757, 805
Don Quixote, 164, 218
"Double Barrelled Detective Story, A," 711
Doubleday, Frank, 853
Douglass, Frederick, xx, 42, 162, 264–65, 316, 376, 714
Dowden, Edward, 509–10
Doyle, Arthur Conan, 313, 817, 887, 1010
dreams/dream stories, 54–57, 60, 388, 393, 539, 594–95, 643–52, 797
Dreiser, Theodore, 340, 690
Dreyfus case, 622–24, 654
Dublin, N.H., 803, 914–15
  eminent figures of, 795–96
  Isabel Lyon in, 796, 798–801, 807–8, 849–50, 855–58, 861–63, 952
  Jean and Isabel clash in, 876, 906
  Jean Clemens in, 796, 798, 807–8, 847–50, 855–58, 861–64
  MT joins family in, 857–58, 862–64, 877
  MT on, 807, 848, 855
  MT seeks refuge in, 795–800, 846–52, 855
  MT's productivity at, 799–806
Duncan, Charles C., 120–21, 403
Duneka, Frederick, 786, 803, 850, 855

East Coast literary scene, 115, 146–47, 151, 188
Eastlake, Charles L., 207
Eddy, Mary Baker, 492, 574, 753–55, 988, 1032
Edison, Thomas, 231, 340, 637
Edison film, 993
Edward, Prince of Wales, 458
Edward VII, King, 886–87
Eliot, George, 218, 252, 950
Elisabeth, Empress, 659–60
Elizabeth, Queen, 240
Ellison, Ralph, 336, 518
Ellsworth, William Webster, 352, 720
Elmira, N.Y., 195, 326, 421, 525, 527–28, 825
  burials in, 183, 424, 579–80, 771, 1014–15, 1030–31
  Clemenses recuperate in, 265, 482, 729–30
  and death of Livy's father, 177–79
  Langdon Clemens dies in, 182–83
  Langdon family of, 122, 161–63
  Langdon home in, 144, 153, 400–401, 771, 1030

Livy and MT's wedding in, 165–66, 1030
Livy recuperates in, 180–83, 302
Livy's education in, 159
MT visits Livy in, 153–56
MT writes *Huckleberry Finn in*, 328
MT's speeches in, 387–88, 565
summer retreats in, 209, 301, 387, 523
Susy Clemens in, 536, 574, 576
See also Quarry Farm
Elmira Reformatory, 387–88
Emerson, Ralph Waldo, 174, 208, 218, 248, 795, 848, 1030
Enchantment: A Little Girl's Friendship with Mark Twain (Quick), 836, 916
England, 346, 387, 491, 525, 662, 718
  Arthurian legends and, 128, 390
  Ashcroft and Lyon sail to, 975–77, 980
  Clara Clemens's concerts in, 941
  Clemenses stay in, 255–56, 565–66, 573–74
  MT feted/honored in, 197, 884–90, 893
  MT's agent in, 237, 707
  MT's masters speech of, 239–40
  MT's novels about, 128, 196–98, 268–73, 307
  MT's pornographic sketch of, 239–41
  MT's trips to, 196–98, 883–93
  MT's views of, 198, 256, 269, 392, 397, 546
  sales of MT's books in, 339
"English as She Is Taught," 458
"Esquimau Maiden's Romance, The," 482
Estes & Lauriat booksellers, 327
"Etiquette for the Afterlife," 1026
Europe, 297
  Clara Clemens concert tour in, 916
  Clemens family in, 247–57, 269, 445–60
  Clemenses economize in, 445, 451, 491, 504, 519
  Clemenses' medical issues in, 457, 459
  Clemenses' spending sprees in, 250, 253–55
  Livy on, 249–50, 252–53, 440–42, 445, 448, 453, 455–56
  MT on, 127–29, 390, 397, 442, 445–46, 652
  MT writes in, 459, 506, 514
  MT's cruise to, 119–32, 134–35
  MT's eleven years in, 681–82

| 1151 |

INDEX

Europe (cont.)
    MT's illnesses in, 453–55
    and MT's politics, 686
    and MT's Rhône River trip, 449–51
    MT's royal invitations in, 453–55
    MT's self-imposed exile in, xviii, 439–42, 445–60, 567, 643, 652, 689, 767
    MT's travel letters of, 446, 448, 451
    Old Masters of, 127–29, 253, 255
    See also specific countries
Everett, Percival, 337
Eve's Diary, 800–803, 938
Exploration of the Valley of the Amazon, Made Under Direction of the Navy Department (Herndon), 47
Extract from Captain Stormfield's Visit to Heaven, 927, 1011
Extracts from Adam's Diary, 801

"Facts Concerning the Recent Carnival of Crime in Connecticut, The," 58
Fairbanks, Mary "Mother," 167, 209, 700
    friendship with MT, 123–24
    and MT's books, 218, 389
    on MT's fame, 134
    MT's letters to, 145–46, 154–56, 158, 164–65, 171, 181, 196, 226, 232, 249, 574
    and MT's marriage, 141, 157–58, 166
    on MT's temper, 279
Fairhaven, Mass., 484, 497–98, 712, 777, 855, 858–59, 903
Fields, Annie, 346
Fields, James T., 150, 346
Fifty Years in Chains (Ball), 394
Fisk Jubilee Singers, xx, 226–28, 608–9, 844
Florence, Italy, 489, 774, 819
    Clara Clemens in, 758, 760–61, 763
    Clara Clemens's concert in, 765
    Clemens family trip to, 456, 458–60, 465–76, 755–66
    Livy convalesces in, 759–66
    Livy on, 466–67
    Livy's death in, 767–70, 852, 1014
    MT writes in, 474, 514, 761
    MT's cruise to, 128–29
    Villa di Quarto in, 758–63, 769–70
    Villa Viviani in, 465–76, 479, 514, 568, 757

Florida, Mo., 7–10, 354, 734
Following the Equator, 544, 565, 587–91, 599, 633
Foote, Lilly, 294–95, 493
"Forty-Three Days in an Open Boat," 110
France
    Clemens family in, 445–46
    MT and Livy's holiday in, 455–56
    MT joins family in, 498, 501–2, 504–6
    MT on, 254–55, 521–22, 569, 623, 654–55
Franklin, Benjamin, 36–37, 46, 517
Franz Joseph I, Emperor, 659, 661–63
Franzensbad, Germany, 481–82, 490
Frazer, Laura Hawkins. See Hawkins, Laura
Free Russia, 782
"Freedman's Case in Equity, The" (Cable), 314, 320
Freedmen's Bureau, 140–41
French Revolution, The (Carlyle), 390, 1028
Freud, Sigmund, 492, 613, 622, 643
Frohman, Daniel, 407–8, 410–12, 924
Fugitive Slave Act, 42
Fugitive Slave Law, 37
Fuller, Frank, 117
"Funeral Oration Over the Grave of the Democratic Party," 264

Gabriel Conroy (Harte), 243–44
Gabrilowitsch, Clara Clemens. See Clemens, Clara (daughter)
Gabrilowitsch, Nina, 1031
Gabrilowitsch, Ossip, 714, 1024, 1031
    affair with Alma Mahler, 946–47, 999
    marriage of, 1001–4
    medical crises of, 1000–1003
    and MT's death, 1025, 1027–28
    MT's views of, 1000–1001
    pianist career of, 628–29, 653, 694, 1000
    relationship with Clara, 628–29, 653, 732–33, 999–1004
    sails to Europe, 1004, 1009–10, 1014, 1017
Galaxy magazine, 171, 173–74, 180–81
Garfield, James A., 139, 263–65, 343, 346, 404
Garrison, William Lloyd, 162, 320, 345
Genoa, Italy, 126–27, 478, 758
Gerhardt, Hattie, 285–90, 300–301, 324, 328, 355, 361
Gerhardt, Karl, 285–90, 300–301, 324, 328, 354–56, 360–61, 364

1152

INDEX

Germany, 247, 257, 612
Clemens family in, 249–51, 254, 451–59
   Clemenses attend operas in, 446–48
   language of, 35, 249–50, 254, 452, 617–19
   MT meets emperor of, 452–55
   politics of, 618–20, 718
   Twichell visits Clemenses in, 250–51
Gibraltar, 124–25
Gilded Age, xviii, 114–15, 150, 199–200, 207–8, 259, 280, 483, 795
Gilded Age, The, 81, 233, 800
   British copyright for, 205
   character models for, 7, 60, 200–202
   coauthor of, 198–99, 687
   Colonel Sellers archetype and, 200–201, 226
   critiques/reviews of, 203, 403
   genesis of/theme of, 198–202
   and MT's D.C. trip, 139, 198–99, 201
   MT's dislike of, 203–4
   play based on, 226, 241–43
   "Tennessee land" and, 200–204
Gilder, Richard Watson, 338, 348, 651, 773
Gilder, Rodman, 773–75
Gillette, Francis, 188, 226
Gillette, William, 226, 288, 408–9
Gillis, Jim, 100–101, 734
Gillis, Steve, 81, 95, 98, 100, 734
Gillis, William R., 734
Gloucester, Mass., 813, 915, 929–32
Gold Dust, xiv–xv
Gold Hill, Nev., 80, 113–14
"Golden Arm," 28, 437–38, 568
Golden Era, 95, 99
Goodman, Joseph T., 80, 83, 86–87, 91, 94, 194–95, 273, 307, 419, 428–33
Gorky, Maxim, 784–85, 840
Gould, Jay, 200, 392, 398, 432, 784
"Grand Coup d'Etat, The," 140
Grant, Fred, 348, 350, 353, 356
Grant, Julia, 348, 355–59, 361
Grant, Ulysses S., 404, 499, 645, 966
   biography on, 148, 407
   death of, 353, 356–61, 660
   memoirs of, 347–54, 356–60, 365, 369–71, 373–74, 377–78, 386, 392, 413, 428, 496, 633
   MT on, 68, 346, 352–54, 356–57
   MT's encounters with, 139–40, 172, 261–64

   portraits/death mask of, 355–56, 360–61
   presidential race of, 346
"Great Dark, The," 645–46
"Great Landslide Case, The," 83
Greenwich, Conn., 913–14, 929–31, 970
Greenwood, George, 987, 990
Greville, Charles C. F., 1008
Griffin, George, 215, 244, 291, 312, 331, 333, 343, 486–87
Guildford, England, 573, 579–80, 582

Hall, Frederick "Fred"
   and fundraising efforts, 428, 483
   and *Library of American Literature*, 414–15, 427–28
   manages Webster & Company, 373–74, 413–15, 451, 475–76, 479–80, 496–97, 957
   and MT's books, 391, 464
   MT's criticism of, 475–76, 480, 484, 496–97, 499–500
   and MT's inventions, 428, 477–78, 481
   MT's letters to, 433, 454, 467, 479, 480–81, 497
   MT's praise of, 413, 415, 459, 583
   on war literature, 413–14
Halley's Comet, 8, 994, 1022, 1027–28
Hamersley, William, 281, 380, 429
Hamilton Hotel (Bermuda), 1010–11, 1019, 1025
Hammond, John Hays, 561–62
Hannibal, Mo., 824
   during Civil War, 64–66
   Clemens burials/funerals in, 57, 423, 735
   Clemens homes in, 31, 36–37
   lynchings in, 40, 715
   MT departs from, 40–41
   MT on, 19–20, 23, 40, 588
   MT returns to, 304, 321, 423, 734–37
   MT's fond recollections of, 949–50
   MT's jobs in, 34–40
   MT's lectures in, 116, 321
   MT's writings about, 219, 233, 235, 237, 273, 328, 363–64, 606
   MT's youth in, xiii, xviii, 10–12, 19–23, 43, 113, 162, 188, 262, 363–64, 392, 508, 521, 529, 606, 735–36, 988–89, 997

INDEX

MT's youth in (*cont.*)
  slavery in, 15–18, 26–29, 40, 237, 262, 328, 588, 715
Hannibal Journal, 36–41, 42
Hardy, Thomas, 307, 340, 606, 817, 1026
Harper, J. Henry, 568, 570
Harper & Brothers, 581, 704, 747–48, 786, 817, 989–90
  declines *Christian Science* book, 754, 850
  gives MT annual income, 757, 875
  MT feuds with Duneka at, 850, 855
  MT's memoir and, 826
  publishes MT's articles/books, 568, 704–5, 803
  signs on Paine for MT bio, 824
Harper's, 229, 603, 748, 823
  Captain Stormfield excerpts in, 996
  Joan of Arc serialized in, 568, 570
  MT's articles in, 110, 620, 624, 676, 1014
  MT's speech in, 708
  MT's stories in, 640, 651, 750–51, 801, 803, 805–6
  publishes *Tom Sawyer*, 590–91
  reviews MT's Uniform Edition, 595
Harper's Bazaar, 790, 1009–11
Harris, Joel Chandler, 310, 330, 364
Harrison, Katharine, 900
Harte, Bret, 103, 226, 950
  books/poetry by, 242–44
  as *Californian* editor, 99–100
  collaborates on *Ah Sin*, 243–45
  edits MT's *Quaker City*, 147
  on MT, 100, 111–12
  MT competitive with, 194, 242–43
  MT falls out with, 149, 243–47, 402, 412, 971
  MT's friendship with, 99–100, 147, 149
  and MT's frog tale, 100, 102, 116
  MT's praise of, 99–100, 242, 246
Hartford, Conn., xiv, 330, 557
  Bret Harte's visits to, 243–44
  Cable's lecture in, 310–11
  Clara Clemens's recital in, 695
  and Clara Clemens's secret romance, 999
  Clemenses move to, 167, 180–83, 187–89

  Clemenses' theatrical in, 324
  diphtheria in, 182
  and Jean Clemens's death, 1017
  Jubilee Singers perform in, 227–28
  literary clubs in, 223, 311, 383, 647
  Livy much admired in, 524
  Lyon-Ashcroft scandal and, 1017
  MT criticized in, 344
  MT raises funds in, 482
  MT's admiration of, 145, 147, 187–89
  MT's political speeches in, 260–61, 264, 345–47
  MT's publisher in, 144–48
  See also Hartford house; Nook Farm, Hartford, Conn.
Hartford Accident Insurance, 230
Hartford Courant, 188, 198, 231
  interviews MT, 256
  on Jubilee Singers, 227
  Lyon-Ashcroft engagement in, 965
  MT seeks ownership of, 167, 199
  MT's comic ad in, 191
  on MT's death, 1029
  promotes Blaine's candidacy, 344–45
  reports on MT's doings, 284, 310–11, 345, 570
  reviews *Life on the Mississippi*, 307
Hartford Daily Times, 208, 289
Hartford house, 233, 277, 681, 777, 926
  billiard room in, 208–9, 214, 280, 343, 380
  Clemenses' attachment to, 674
  and Clemenses' bankruptcy, 500, 644
  Clemenses entertain in, 210, 267, 302
  closed for Europe trip, 247–49, 439–42
  curtailing expenses at, 522–23
  description of, 206–10
  European purchases for, 253–55
  expansion/decoration of, 265–67, 278
  family theatricals in, 208, 292, 324, 434, 591
  financial strain of, 206, 250, 255, 278, 288, 427, 433, 440, 504, 672, 674
  interior designers work on, 266, 384
  literary meetings in, 383–84
  Livy as owner of, 201, 206
  Livy plans design of, 207–9, 265–66, 523
  Livy's attachment to, 440, 546, 557, 573, 727

| 1154 |

INDEX

MT lures investors to, 429–30
MT on, 207–10, 421, 508, 522–24, 674
MT writes in, 209, 305, 391
MT's fond recollections of, 940, 959
Ned House's visits to, 404–7, 412
renting of, 573
selling of, 522, 727, 733, 742, 755
Susy Clemens on, 504
Susy Clemens's illness/death in, 575–80, 582–83
tied to Susy Clemens's memory, 663, 687, 727
Harvey, George, 705, 747, 777, 817, 826, 829, 881, 937, 953, 989–90, 1024
Harz Mountains (Germany), 452–53
Hawaii, 130, 476, 655, 938–39. *See also* Sandwich Islands
Hawkins, Laura, 24–25, 202, 235, 735–36, 831, 840, 949–50
Hawley, Joseph, 188, 199, 223
Hawthorne, Nathaniel, 256, 950
Hay, John, 195, 240–41, 312, 405, 638, 661, 748, 761, 790
Hay, Rosina, 215, 249, 254
Hayes, Rutherford B., 245–46, 259–61, 273, 343, 346
Hearst, William Randolph, 72, 598, 699, 784
"Helen Allen Manuscript," 1023
"Hellfire Hotchkiss," 15, 604–5
Hellmuth Ladies' College (Ontario), 322–23
Helmer, George J., 679–81, 690–92, 742–43
Hemingway, Ernest, 334, 341
Herndon, William L., 47
Herzl, Theodor, 618, 622
Hibbard, Dr., 876–77
Hillbourne Farms (Katonah), 864–67, 871–72
Hitchcock, Ethan Allen, 737, 795
Hobby, Josephine, 823, 826, 848, 850, 857
Holmes, Oliver Wendell, 109, 164, 248–49, 256, 312, 364, 495, 1030
Holmes, Sherlock, 226, 591, 711
Holy Land, 132–34, 146
Hooker, Alice, 144–45, 156, 167. *See also* Day, Alice Hooker
Hooker, Isabella Beecher, 187–88, 225
Hooker, John, 187–88
Hornet survivors, 109–10

"Horrors of the German Language, The," 617–18
"Horse's Tale, A," 805–6, 811, 819
Hotel Krantz (Vienna), 652–53, 660
Hotel Metropole (Vienna), 609–11, 615, 617, 619, 626–27, 633–38, 646, 652
House, Edward H. "Ned," 115, 118, 120, 203, 402–8, 410–12, 415, 971
Howard, Edward, 108–9
Howden, Mary Louise, 935, 959
Howells, John, 857, 871, 925–26
Howells, William Dean, xvi, xx, 226, 310–11, 323, 468, 700, 707, 757
and autobiography/biography of MT, 821, 824, 827–28
friendship with MT, 150–51
on Hayes campaign, 259
on imperialism, 655
Indian Summer novel by, 363–64
on Livy and MT, 219, 741–42
in Maine with MT, 740, 750
on MT and Civil War, 347
on MT and slavery, 365
MT confides in, 182, 231, 243, 245–46, 249–50, 257, 263, 284, 313, 346, 360, 373, 411, 422, 424, 437, 633, 647–48, 672, 704, 766, 778, 852, 855, 860, 995
MT correspondence and, 952–53
at MT dinners, 748, 817
MT on, 256, 462
on MT's appearance, 820
and MT's art patronage, 287–88
on MT's books, 234, 269–70, 273, 307–8, 328, 338, 391, 568
and MT's boyhood recollections, 40, 233
on MT's death, 1029–30
and MT's exile in Europe, 441
on MT's genius/legacy, 1030
and MT's global lecture tour, 588
and MT's Human Race Club, 881
and MT's letters project, 799
on MT's personality, 309, 416, 982
on MT's politics, 396–98, 720–23
on MT's Pope Leo biography, 370
on MT's return to America, 687
and MT's speeches, 248–49, 688
publishes MT's articles/stories, 221, 303, 1011
reviews Grant's *Memoirs*, 359

INDEX

Howells, William Dean (*cont.*)
  reviews MT's books, 150, 195, 237, 257, 397–98, 595
  supports Republican Blaine, 344–45
  and Susy Clemens's death, 585
  visits MT, 755, 969
  on Whittaker race case, 518
  writes play with MT, 309, 404, 461–62
Hugo, Victor, 117, 490, 950
human race, xviii, 544, 582, 593, 648, 659, 661, 675, 679, 702, 742, 800, 845, 853, 1008
Human Race Club, 881–82
Hunt, Frederick, 862, 864, 881
Hutton, Laurence, 510–11, 590, 664, 672, 724, 732

Ibsen, Henrik, 218, 617, 853
immigrants, 43–44, 96–97, 173, 909–10. See also Chinese: immigrants
imperialism, xix, 550
  of America, 109, 546, 654–55, 686, 693, 698, 715, 721, 724–25
  of Europe/Great Britain, 546, 697–98
  MT opposed to, 402, 552, 588–89, 654–55, 686, 693, 697–98, 715, 718–22, 724–25
  MT supportive of, 546, 599
  in MT's writings, 588–89, 719–22
"In Defense of Harriet Shelley," 509–10
"In Memory of Olivia Susan Clemens," 742
"In My Bitterness," 603
India, 17, 525, 546, 548–56, 559, 561, 588, 753
"Indiantown," 156, 211–12
Innocents Abroad, The, 130, 155, 554, 587, 800, 822
  and board game, 703
  copyright lapses on, 946
  edited by Livy, 164, 217
  irreverent tone of, 197, 233, 252
  MT's critical view of, 149
  MT's lectures for, 149, 156
  publishing/marketing of, 147–48
  and *Quaker City* cruise, 125–26, 135
  and *Quaker City* letters, 194
  religion in, 126
  reviews of, 218, 307
  success of, 148–50, 172, 194–95, 257
  See also *Quaker City*: MT's book on

inventions, xviii
  bed-clamp, 275, 326, 368, 378
  board games, 283–85, 326, 386–87, 428, 936
  Kaolatype Engraving, 276–81, 325
  MT on, 231, 256, 430, 432
  and Orion Clemens, 191–93, 284, 386–87
  Raster textile-printer, 634–38
  Self-Pasting Scrap Book, 232, 275–76, 279
  See also Paige typesetter invention
Irving, Henry, 298, 312, 429
Is Shakespeare Dead?, 987–90, 1032
Italy, 126–29, 252–54, 371–72, 456. See also specific cities

James (Everett), 337
James, Henry, 150, 306, 338, 340, 400, 468, 777
James, William, 474, 492, 650, 679
Jean Clemens Humane Society, 963
Jean L. Clemens Memorial Building (Redding, Conn.), 1018, 1031
Jennie (slave), 7, 16–17
Jewett, Sarah Orne, 306, 495
Jews, 620–26, 653, 655, 783–84, 909–10, 1005. See also "Concerning the Jews"
Jim Crow laws, 515, 714–15
Joan of Arc, 35–36, 39–40, 566–67, 660. See also *Personal Recollections of Joan of Arc*
Joan of Arc (play), 838
Johnson, Andrew, 140–41
Johnson, Robert Underwood, 351
Jones, A. W., 366–67
Jones, John Percival, 230–31, 419, 429–33
Jones, John W., 162–63
Journal of the Reigns of King George IV and King William IV, A (Greville), 1008
Juggernaut Club, 752, 831, 882, 1010

Kaltenleutgeben, Vienna, 647, 651–52, 659
Kanawha, 711–12, 731–33, 739, 777, 903
Katonah sanitarium
  Jean Clemens in, 861–67, 871–72, 875–84, 900–902, 904–6, 913–14, 928, 931
  MT on, 864, 871

| 1156 |

INDEX

MT visits Jean in, 871, 876, 879–80, 882–84, 901
Keller, Helen, 85, 510–12, 724–25, 817, 938, 987
Kellgren, Jonas Henrik, 665–69, 671–73, 678–81, 729, 742
Kentucky, 4, 7–8, 31, 319–20, 422–23, 461, 805
Keokuk, Iowa, 45–48, 50, 72, 115–16, 191, 193, 304, 321, 385–86, 421–24, 762
Keokuk *Gate City*, 72, 79
Kilauea volcano, 108–9, 112
King, Grace, 384–85, 410, 425, 434, 439, 448, 459, 466, 473, 491, 504, 567, 582, 592, 674, 695, 722
"King Leopold's Soliloquy," 786–88
Kinney, John, 79
Kipling, Rudyard, 400–402, 664, 817, 825, 848, 888–89, 919, 950
Kirch, G. W., 765, 770
Kleinberg, Ludwig, 634–38
Knickerbocker Trust Company, 906–8
Know-Nothing Party, 44, 52
Koto, Aoki, 403–5
Kruger, Paul, 561–62
Ku Klux Klan, xix, 140–41, 173, 334, 713–15

Laird, James L., 94
Lake Bigler, 79, 107, 133
Lampton, James J., 200–201, 461
Lampton, Jane. *See* Clemens, Jane Lampton
Lang, Andrew, 398
Langdon, Charlie, 222, 264, 914
　and family's coal business, 178, 216, 254, 480
　introduces MT to Livy, 132, 142, 153–55
　Livy's letters to, 654
　meets MT on cruise, 122, 132
　on MT, 122, 153
　MT confides in, 769, 776, 961
　MT on, 122, 157
　and MT's Paige typesetter, 418
　rescues Webster & Company, 481
　at Susy Clemens's deathbed, 578–79
　wedding of, 179
Langdon, Jervis, 156–64, 166–69, 171–72, 176–78, 195, 218, 368, 421, 424

Langdon, Jervis (MT's nephew), 771, 1003
Langdon, Olivia Lewis, 156–64, 166, 168–69, 206, 213, 253–55, 423–25, 427, 436
Langdon, Olivia "Livy"
　appearance of, 132, 142
　childhood/youth of, 159–63, 169, 771
　courted by MT, 153–65, 212
　meets MT, 142–44
　on MT, 169–70
　MT's letters to, 164, 424
　religious beliefs of, 160, 163–64
　wedding of, 165–66
　See also Clemens, Olivia "Livy" Langdon (wife)
Lark, Charles, 975, 978–80
Laszowska, Madame, 611–12
Leary, Catherine "Katy," 424, 566, 599, 689, 795
　on Clara Clemens, 626, 776, 872, 1002–3
　and Clemenses' Europe trip, 447, 451, 471
　as Clemenses' housekeeper, 212, 214–15, 523
　at Fifth Avenue house, 780, 808
　in Florence, 758–59
　on Isabel Lyon, 947
　and Jean Clemens's death, 1013, 1015
　and Jean Clemens's epilepsy, 691, 811–13, 876, 1012
　and Livy Clemens, 142, 755, 764, 766–68, 771, 777, 973
　as Livy's personal maid, 214
　on MT, 283, 429, 688, 818, 820, 1027–29
　MT on, 214
　and MT's correspondence, 953
　on Susy Clemens, 528, 575–79, 581
Leathers, Jesse M., 461–63
lecture circuit, 107, 330, 388, 844
　advertising of, 111, 113, 117, 316
　in America, 111–18, 196, 248–49, 497–98, 525–27, 601
　around-the-world tour, xviii, 484, 523, 525–37, 539–57, 559–66, 570, 573, 584, 587–89, 612, 685–86
　and Boston Lyceum Bureau, 174–76, 181
　and colleges, 383, 437–38, 833
　in England, 197, 206
　impact on MT's career, 112–13

INDEX

lecture circuit (*cont.*)
  and literary clubs, 688–89
  Livy on, 214, 560
  for making money, 111, 174–75, 196, 206, 214, 525, 534–35, 540, 564, 566
  MT on, 113, 118, 196, 317, 525, 534, 539, 541, 559, 609
  MT popular on, 141, 528–30, 533–34, 541, 543, 545, 551, 697–98
  MT successful on, 143, 174, 176, 206, 315–16, 321–23
  MT threatens to quit, 313, 315
  MT's dreams about, 643
  and MT's family, 383, 542–43
  MT's repertoire/strategies for, 175–76, 316–17, 527, 529, 531, 534, 536, 541, 547, 560
  and the press, 541–42
  takes toll on MT's health, 535
  "Twins of Genius" tour, 313–24, 348, 355, 363, 531
Leo XIII (pope), 370–72, 374, 418
Leopold II, King, xix, 785–88, 843
Leschetizky, Theodor, 627–28, 630, 654, 865
Leslie, Elsie, 407–10
Lester, Julius, 336–37
Letters from the Earth, 1005–8
"Letters to Satan," 607–8
Levetus, Amelia S., 633–34
Levy, M. S., 625–26
Lewis, John, 221–22, 331, 333
Liberty National Bank, 975
Library of American Literature, 376–77, 414–15, 427–28, 475, 480–81, 484, 497
"Life on the Isthmus," 173
Life on the Mississippi, xiv, 23, 53, 57, 233, 303–8, 400, 454, 621–22
Lincoln, Abraham, 52, 64, 68–69, 86, 89, 117, 139–40, 241, 261, 358–59, 712–14
literary criticism, 509–10
literary devices, xvii
  aphorisms, 516
  first-person, 234, 330, 341, 383
  narrator, 102, 233, 383
  stream-of-consciousness, 850
  used by MT, 114, 995
Liverpool, England, 205, 256, 819, 893
Logan, John A., 139, 262
London, England, 265, 805, 903
  Clara Clemens's concerts in, 926, 941
  Clara Clemens's singing lessons in, 662, 669, 680
  Clemens family in, 566, 582, 584, 590–99, 601–2
  Clemenses return to, 663–65, 672, 674–75, 680–81
  Diamond Jubilee in, 598–99
  Jean Clemens's treatments in, 672–73, 678, 680, 809
  Livy and MT's trip to, 205–6
  MT and politics in, 674–75
  MT meets Browning in, 383
  MT's celebrity in, 197, 205, 664–65, 885–86, 893–94
  MT's first solo trip to, 196–98
  MT's flamboyant behavior in, 886–87
  MT's lectures/speeches in, 197, 206
  and MT's moneymaking schemes, 232, 637–38, 677–78
  MT's secluded life in, 595–96, 610
  MT's social life in, 197, 205, 664–65
  MT's views of, 593–94
  MT's writings in, 672, 680–81
  osteopaths in, 693
  psychics in, 675–76
  and reviews of MT's books, 273, 341, 398, 590
London *Times*, 273, 674, 719, 883, 886
Longfellow, Henry Wadsworth, 248–49, 1030
Lost Cause advocates, 333, 338, 347, 714
Lotos Club (N.Y.C.), 486, 688–89, 719
Lounsbury, Harry, 973, 975
Low, Seth, 707–9
Lueger, Karl, 618–19
Lyon, Isabel, 583, 911
  affection for MT, 977
  ambiguous role of, 898, 925, 964, 980
  appearance of, 937, 977
  banishes Jean Clemens, 931–32, 937, 962–63, 970–71, 976, 979
  in Bermuda with MT, 921–22
  and burglary at Stormfield, 943–44, 947
  and Clara Clemens, 773, 775, 794, 798, 845, 851, 872, 898–99, 925, 942–43, 945–47, 955–56, 962, 966–67, 971–73, 976, 999, 1004

| 1158 |

INDEX

Clara Clemens on, 777, 892
and Clemens family, 744–46
control over MT, 932–33, 945, 953, 965–66, 976, 982–83
criticism of, 1032
cruise to Nova Scotia, 899, 902
descriptions of, 744–45, 793–94
devotion to MT, 984–86
drinking problem of, 911, 947, 976, 983–84
embezzlement/thefts of, 976, 978–80, 982, 984, 1020
emotionally frail, 809–10
expanding role of, 775, 777–79, 793–94, 798–99, 810, 857, 875, 937
in Fifth Avenue home, 808–9
fired by MT, 971–73
flees to England, 975–77
in Florence, 758–62
has to supplement income, 798–99
hero worship of MT, 778–79, 793, 803, 845, 863, 872, 879, 882, 892, 932
as hostess/secretary, 982
interferes with Jean and MT relationship, 984
intimacy with MT, 956, 959, 965–66, 968–69
on Jean Clemens, 796, 849–51, 879, 962, 977, 992
and Jean Clemens's epilepsy, 749, 779, 798, 807–15, 914, 962, 970–71
as Jean Clemens's main caretaker, 813–14, 833, 846–47, 849, 855–57, 861–64, 876–77, 881–82, 897, 904–6, 914, 933, 971, 1016
keeps news from MT, 929–30, 932
letters to MT, 963–64
and Livy Clemens, 756, 762, 775, 778
Lobster Pot house/property of, 966, 971–73, 976–80, 993
manages MT's finances, 875, 892, 906, 912–13, 942, 946, 954, 961
marriage of, 962–67, 969, 985–86, 1020
missing from MT's biography, 1032
on MT, 800, 813–14, 858, 866, 898, 911
MT confides in, 199, 754, 790, 850, 875, 952
MT defends her, 905, 928, 967–68, 981–82
MT on, 777–78, 793–94, 861, 879, 897–98, 944, 947, 962, 965–66, 969, 983, 985–86
on MT's appearance, 818, 820
as MT's assistant, 743–46, 760–62, 775
and MT's autobiography, 826, 897
and MT's books/writings, 149, 204, 800–801, 852–53, 989
MT's criticism of, 968, 970–73, 979, 981–84, 992, 1016, 1020
and MT's daughters, 779, 798–99, 875, 897
and MT's daughters' finances, 961, 966
as MT's editor, 761–62, 782, 803
MT's feud with, 971–86, 991, 993, 1017–18
and MT's angelfish, 831–33, 838–41, 882, 895, 920, 968
as MT's hostess/secretary, 857, 872, 965, 968, 972–73, 976, 981
as MT's in-house reader, 968
and MT's letters project, 799, 821, 824, 952–53
and MT's library, 950, 1001
and MT's litigious actions, 769, 780
on MT's mourning, 781
as MT's nursemaid, 937, 968
on MT's personality, 782, 794, 849, 920
as MT's power of attorney, 892, 956–58, 962
MT's praise of, 937, 967–68
and MT's private readings, 782, 786, 799–800, 848, 852
MT's reliance on, 798–99, 844–45, 851, 861, 879, 881–82, 897–98, 928, 955, 968–69
in New Hampshire, 796, 798
new salaried role of, 969
on Paine and bio of MT, 823–24
parental responsibilities of, 916
personality of, 779, 798, 861, 947
plays Orchestrelle for MT, 778, 845, 848, 900, 911
poor mental state of, 861–63, 897
poorly paid, 897–98, 965, 967–68, 976, 984, 986
protective of MT, 931–32, 955–56, 959, 964, 977
purloins MT documents, 1032
recuperates in Hartford, 963–64, 966
and Redding home, 857

| 1159 |

INDEX

Lyon, Isabel (*cont.*)
  relationship with Ashcroft, 908, 945–46, 953–58, 975, 984, 986
  relationship with Clara, 809, 845–46, 848–49, 981
  relationship with MT, 762, 861
  relationship with Paine, 849, 856–57, 952–59
  rumors about, 884, 891–92, 899, 917, 964
  sails to Bermuda with MT, 878–79
  schemes to marry MT, 845, 891–92, 964, 983
Lyon-Ashcroft audit, 975–77
"Lyon-Ashcroft Manuscript," 974, 982, 1032
Lyon-Ashcroft scandal, 971–86, 992–93, 1011, 1017–18, 1020, 1026, 1031–32

MacAlister, John Y. W., 678, 682
Macy, Anne Sullivan, 938, 987. *See also* Sullivan, Anne
Macy, John, 987
Madden, Paddy, 879, 882
Mahler, Alma, 947, 999
Mahler, Gustav, 618, 630, 643, 947, 999
Malory, Thomas, 318
"Man That Corrupted Hadleyburg, The," 638–40
"Man's Place in the Animal World," 589
Maori people, 546
Marchesi, Blanche, 662, 669
Marchesi, Mathilde, 489–91, 528
Maria Theresa, Archduchess, 658–59
Marienbad, 448–49, 451, 471
Marion Rangers, 65–69, 91
"Marjorie Fleming, the Wonder Child," 1009–10
Mark Twain Company, 957–58, 962, 968, 981–82
Mark Twain Library (Redding, Conn.), 950, 1000–1001, 1018, 1031
Mark Twain's Library of Humor, 850
Massiglia, Countess, 759–60, 762–63, 769–70
Matthews, Brander, 341, 704, 883
McAleer, Patrick, 169, 182, 214, 248, 796
McCarthy, Dennis, 113–14
McClellan, George B., 372, 428

McGuinn, Warner T., 364–66, 844
McKelway, St. Clair, 688
McKinley, William, 654–55, 686, 706–7, 717–18, 784
McReynolds, John, 42
"Memorable Assassination, The," 660
Memphis, 55–57, 63, 172
Mencken, H. L., 341, 1032–33
Mental Science, 574–75, 577–78, 582–83, 730, 753
"Mental Telegraphy," 676
Mental Telepathy/Telegraphy, 226, 673, 675–76
Menton, France, 455–56
Mergenthaler Linotype machine, 380–81, 416–18, 420, 431–32, 506–8
Milton, John, 52, 664, 987
Mind Cure, 491–93, 574
Minneapolis, 304, 530–31
minstrel shows, 16, 23, 27, 227, 336–37, 608
miscegenation, 93, 314
Mississippi River, xiii–xvi, 556
  Civil War and, 62–63
  in Hannibal, 10, 22–23, 49
  and MT's childhood, 22–23, 736
  MT's love for, 51–52, 62, 450, 734, 736
  and MT's pen name, 84–85
  MT's return trip to, 303–6
  MT's writings on, 233, 235, 303–5, 331–32, 363, 514–15
  steamboat disasters on, 54–55, 1023
  steamboats on, 9, 49–54, 61–64, 70, 84, 98, 107, 303–5, 736–37
Missouri State Guard, 65–66
Moffett, Annie, 41, 50–51, 57, 63–65, 166, 168, 277–78, 416, 422
Moffett, Pamela Clemens (sister), 75, 423, 797
  children of, 57, 115, 277, 936
  death of, 772
  marriage of, 41, 50–51
  moves to Fredonia, 170, 193
  MT on, 51, 772
  MT's letters to, 44, 51, 76, 80, 85, 98, 103, 115, 165, 342, 377, 391, 416, 421, 493, 496–97, 673
  MT's relationship with, 51, 53, 135
  MT's visits to, 115, 385–86
  at MT's wedding, 166

| 1160 |

INDEX

religious beliefs of, 78, 115, 135
Sanitary Commission and, 92
visits MT in Buffalo, 168, 170
See also Clemens, Pamela (sister)
Moffett, Samuel, 284, 534, 578, 671, 679–80, 705, 824, 936–37
Moffett, William, 41, 49, 170
Mommsen, Theodor, 451–52
monarchy, xix, 198, 396, 553, 620, 659–60, 701, 789
Monday Evening Club, 223–25, 345, 647, 687, 852
Montclair, N.J., 963, 966
Morel, Edmund Dene, 785–86
Morgan, J. P., 468, 484, 637, 712–13, 747
Mormons, 71–72
Morrison, Toni, 519
Morte d'Arthur, Le (Malory), 318, 359, 388–89
Moszkowski, Moritz, 460, 471
Mount Morris Bank, 414–15, 479–82, 497
Mount Olivet Cemetery, 423, 735
Mugwumps, 344–45, 686, 705–6, 709, 790, 844
Munich, Germany, 254, 479, 482
Muscatine Journal, 41, 45
"My Platonic Sweetheart," 60, 648–51, 660, 751, 840

Nast, Thomas, 822–23
Native Americans, 71–72, 82, 132, 173–74, 229, 236–37, 299, 367–68, 533, 553, 791–92, 963
Natkin, Gertrude, 831–33, 837
nature, sensitivity to, 79
Nevada Territorial Legislature, 82–84, 87, 89
Nevada Territory, xviii, 106
  anti-Black sentiment in, 91
  MT leaves in controversy, 91–95
  MT lives with Orion in, 74–75, 83, 335, 347
  MT nostalgic about, 797
  MT's descriptions of, 72–73, 80–81
  MT's life in, 70–75, 78, 83–88, 194
  MT's mining in, 75–80, 116, 194
  and MT's *Roughing It*, 70–74, 194
  Orion Clemens secretary of, 69–70, 72, 83, 87–89, 191
  Orion Clemens's mining in, 76–79
  See also Carson City, Nevada Territory;
Territorial Enterprise (Virginia City); Virginia City, Nevada Territory
New England Anti-Imperialist League, 720
New Haven, Conn., 315, 364
New Orleans, 13, 48, 54, 58–60, 62–63, 304, 307, 309, 320, 384, 648, 703, 840
New Orleans *Picayune*, 84, 309
New York City, 664
  Ah Sin performed in, 244–45, 292
  Clara Clemens convalesces in, 774–77
  Clara Clemens's apt. in, 945–46, 970, 985
  Clara Clemens's singing lessons in, 728
  Clemenses' 10th Street home in, 687–88
  Clemenses return to, 677, 681–82, 685–90
  Grant's tomb in, 357–58
  Jean Clemens's treatments in, 690–92, 864
  MT and daughters settle in, 770
  MT and politics in, 697–98, 705–9
  MT and reporters of, 685–87, 699–701, 895
  MT faces bankruptcy in, 499–500, 526–27
  MT feted/honored in, 486, 688
  MT meets Livy Langdon in, 142–44
  MT meets Stevenson in, 400
  MT on, 43–44, 690
  MT raises funds in, 476–77, 482–86
  MT seeks refuge in, 850, 855
  MT's bohemian days in, 402
  MT's first visits to, 42–44, 114–18
  and MT's inventions, 503–4
  MT's lectures in, 117–18, 196, 348, 387, 403
  MT's memorial in, 1029
  MT's publishing co. in, 326, 350–51, 358, 376
  MT's renown in, 685–86, 688, 699–701
  MT's speeches in, 697–98, 706–7, 747–48, 818, 832, 843–44, 916, 927
  osteopaths in, 673, 677, 679–81, 692–93
  Prince and the Pauper performed in, 408
  Russian revolutionaries in, 784–85, 838
  social whirlwind of, 495, 688, 690, 776, 809, 920–21
  Susy Clemens in, 575
New York *Evening Post*, 221, 359
New York *Herald*
  on Clara's marriage, 1002–3
  interviews MT, 597

| 1161 |

INDEX

New York Herald (cont.)
  on MT–Lyon engagement, 891
  MT's articles in, 119, 134–35, 139, 205
  on MT's mental/physical collapse, 596–97
  and MT's Paige typesetter, 282, 431
  on MT's return to America, 685
  promotes relief fund for MT, 597–98
  reviews MT's frog tale, 116
  Zola tribute in, 623
New York Sun, 357, 370, 373, 380, 446, 504, 527, 860
New York Times, 689, 712, 723, 840
  accuses MT of "literary larceny," 990
  Clara Clemens's interview in, 942
  on death of Susy Clemens, 579
  eulogizes MT, 1033
  Jean Clemens's protest letter in, 963
  and Lyon-Ashcroft scandal, 978, 980–82
  on MT as "defender of quacks," 693
  on MT at political rallies, 260, 708
  on MT–House feud, 411
  MT's best seller on, 1008
  and MT's Grant memoir, 351, 357
  on MT's return to America, 771
  on MT's "Swedish cure," 666
  reviews Clara Clemens concert, 999
  reviews MT's plays, 409, 462
  on sculptor Gerhardt, 361
New York Tribune, 115, 376, 407, 653
  MT's articles in, 119, 139, 223
  on MT's lectures, 118, 402–3
  Orion Clemens works for, 193
  refuses MT article, 141
  reviews MT's books, 195, 203
  uses Mergenthaler machine, 380, 416
New York World, 784
  on Clara Clemens's engagement, 943
  on Grant's memoir, 353–54
  interviews MT, 633, 680, 685–86, 907
  on MT's lectures, 833
  and MT's Paige typesetter, 417, 431
  reviews MT's *Huckleberry Finn*, 340
New Zealand, 525, 544–47, 589
Newton, James Rogers, 160–61
Nicholas II, Czar, 626, 661, 781–84, 788
Nichols, Marie, 912, 941
No. 44, The Mysterious Stranger, 803–5
Nook Farm, Hartford, Conn., 233, 384, 577, 744

  and Charles Dudley Warner's death, 687
  MT and Livy settle in, 188–89, 207, 209–12
  MT's active social life in, 212, 215, 217
  MT's eminent friends in, 188–89, 198–99, 210–11, 225–26, 273
  MT's friend Twichell in, 188–91
  Republican residents of, 188, 259, 343–44
  See also Hartford, Conn.
Norfolk, Conn., 776, 797, 807, 859, 872
Norfolk sanitarium
  Clara Clemens at, 776–78, 794–95, 845, 848, 860, 866, 872, 899, 940
  MT visits Clara at, 794–95, 797–98, 807
North American Review, 509, 720–24, 753, 772, 782, 822, 829
Nova Scotia, 899, 902
Nunnally, Francesca, 886, 903–4, 916, 920, 923, 990–91
Nye, Emma, 178–79
Nye, James W., 88, 92

Obersteiner, Heinrich, 613
Old Masters, 127–29, 253, 255
"Old Times on the Mississippi," xiv, 233, 303
"Only a Nigger," 172
Onteora Club (Catskills), 384
"On the Decay of the Art of Lying," 223
operas, 96, 250, 398, 436–37, 446–48, 469, 473, 485, 630, 632, 820, 961
Orchestrelle music, 778, 781, 845, 900, 911, 925–26, 1015
Osgood, James R., xiv, 198, 271–72, 279, 306–8, 325, 462
osteopathy, 665–67, 673, 677–79, 692–93, 728–30, 742–43
"Our Assistant's Column," 39–40
Overland Monthly, 149, 242
Oxford University, 198, 883, 887–90, 938

Paige, James W., 389, 507, 512, 634
  invents typesetter, 280–82, 477–78
  makes model of typesetter, 380–81, 417–20
  manipulates MT, 477–78, 494
  MT on, 280–81, 430–31, 464, 508, 636
  MT's deal with, 431–33, 494–95
  and testing of typesetter, 431, 506

| 1162 |

INDEX

Paige typesetter invention, 361, 389–90, 529
  defects in, 418, 429, 432, 506–7
  a failed venture, 508, 567, 633
  financial strain of, 282, 378, 381, 415–17, 430, 433, 440, 453
  Henry Rogers and, 485, 493–96, 502–3, 506–8
  investors in, 281–82, 418–19, 429–33, 476–77, 485, 493–96
  MT on, 387, 481–82
  MT's faith in, 281–83, 379–81, 386, 396, 417–20, 430, 501–3, 506–8
  MT's royalties from, 419, 431, 433, 485, 494, 498, 508
  testing of, 282, 431, 503, 506–7
Paine, Albert Bigelow, 874, 949, 966, 987, 993
  background of, 822–23
  in Bermuda with MT, 878, 1010–12, 1025–27
  collects MT's scribblings, 994
  Connecticut property of, 846
  on Isabel Lyon, 932, 1020
  Isabel Lyon on, 825, 952, 977, 992
  and Jean Clemens, 849, 1001, 1012, 1014–17
  and Lyon-Ashcroft scandal, 975, 977–79
  manages Mark Twain Company, 982
  moves to Jean Clemens's apt., 1017–18
  moves to MT's N.Y.C. house, 824–25, 875
  on MT, 821, 824, 911, 939, 958, 1010
  and MT's autobiography, 848, 857
  as MT's biographer, 640, 821–27, 939, 951–54, 994, 1026, 1032
  on MT's correspondence, 952–54
  and MT's death, 1029, 1033
  and MT's letters project, 982
  and MT's library, 950, 1001
  as MT's literary executor, 951–52
  as MT's nurse, 1025–26
  as MT's secretary/manager, 1017
  and MT's serious illness, 990, 994
  and MT's teenage girls, 833–36, 841, 927, 939
  on MT's writings, 640, 989, 1005
  plays billiards with MT, 875, 878, 911, 936, 1002

  protective of MT, 929–30, 952
  relationship with Isabel Lyon, 849, 856–57, 952–59
  research by, 824, 969
  suppresses "Helen Allen Manuscript," 1023
Paine, Louise, 835, 926–27, 939–40, 951
Paine, Thomas, 52
Paris, 485, 523, 584, 622
  Clara Clemens's voice lessons in, 732–33, 747
  Clemens family in, 254–55, 265, 499, 501, 519–22
  Livy and daughters in, 485, 490–93
  Livy's medical treatment in, 505
  MT's first trip to, 125–26
  and MT's global lecture tour, 525
  and MT's inventions, 232, 506
  sculptor Gerhardt in, 286–88, 356, 361
  Susy Clemens's singing lessons in, 489–93, 520
Parry, Angenette, 774–76
patriotism, 689–90, 718–19, 722, 788–89
Paul Jones, 48–49, 734
Pears, Muriel M., 751–52, 798
Pennsylvania, 53–55
Pepys, Samuel, 239, 269, 825
Perkins, Charles, 196, 272
Perry, Edward C., 96
Personal Memoirs of U. S. Grant (Grant), 347–54, 356–60, 363, 369–71, 373–74, 386, 392, 413
Personal Recollections of Joan of Arc, 509, 523, 610, 623, 989
  Livy and, 219, 338, 506, 730–31
  MT on, 340, 568–71
  MT's sources/research for, 506, 566–67, 569–71
  serialized in *Harper's*, 568, 570
  Susy Clemens's influence on, 567, 571
  writing of, 474, 503, 506, 525, 567–70, 757
Peterson, Frederick
  as epilepsy specialist, 813–14
  Isabel Lyon and, 932–33, 962, 967
  MT and, 970, 984
  sends Jean Clemens to Berlin, 933, 961–62
  sends Jean Clemens to Gloucester, 915, 930–31

| 1163 |

INDEX

Peterson, Frederick (cont.)
  sends Jean Clemens to sanitarium, 864, 905–6
  sends Jean Clemens to Stormfield, 992
  treats Jean Clemens, 814, 912–13
"Petrified Man, The," 82–83
Phelps, William Lyon, 764, 1033
Philadelphia, Pa., 44, 367, 373, 408, 437
Philippines, xix, 655–56, 686, 689, 698, 706, 715, 718–21, 724–25, 749, 790, 843
Philleo, Prudence Crandall, 367
Phillips, Wendell, 164, 320
Philosophy of the Plays of Shakespeare Unfolded, The (Bacon), 52
phonographs, 386, 390–91, 441, 462
Picard, Hélène, 751–52, 1010
pirated editions, 85, 237–38, 272, 326–27, 873, 957–58
Plasmon, 677–78, 682, 742, 807, 818–19, 885, 908, 968
Players Club, The (N.Y.C.), 482, 485–86, 499, 821–22, 839
plays
  Clemens family theatricals, 208, 292, 324, 434, 591
  by MT, 226, 241–45, 247, 292, 309, 326, 404–12, 461–62, 909–10
  See also specific titles
Plymouth Church (Brooklyn), 115, 119
Poe, Edgar Allan, 46, 885
poems
  by Bret Harte, 242–43
  by MT, 603, 742, 1020
  read aloud by MT, 383–84, 848, 919
politics, xix
  and Austro-Hungarian Empire, 618–20
  MT's activism in, 705–9, 781–90, 843–44, 1010
  MT's articles on, 52, 97, 141, 167–68, 259
  and MT's books, 391, 396–98
  MT's speeches on, 260–64, 345–47, 688–89, 719, 844
  MT's views on, 62–69, 139–41, 259–65, 343–47, 390–91, 396, 590, 658–59, 661, 893
  MT's writings on, 455, 705–7, 716–24, 730, 781–82, 828

  in South Africa, 560–63
  in Vienna, 653–56
  See also colonialism; imperialism; Republican Party
Pomeroy, Samuel Clarke, 198–200
Pond, James B., 601–2, 697
  on Livy Clemens, 536–37, 571
  on MT, 528–37
  MT on, 316–17, 528
  MT's letters to, 654
  runs MT's global lecture tour, 523, 566
  runs "Twins of Genius" tour, 313–14, 316–17, 319, 321, 324, 355, 523, 525, 527–37
  on Susy Clemens, 575–76
Porter, Charles Ethan, 289–90
"Postscript: The Jew as a Soldier," 626
Potter, Edward Tuckerman, 207
Pötzl, Eduard, 611
poverty
  MT on, 548, 550–51, 593, 731
  MT's fears of, 97, 103–4, 142, 231, 523, 559, 756
Presbyterian Church, 25–26, 51, 57, 163, 177, 239, 465, 1029
Price, Sterling, 65, 91
Prince and the Pauper, The, 279, 390, 395, 463, 514, 659, 889, 1012
  admired by MT's family, 268–69, 567
  and Clemens theatrical, 324
  genesis of, 198
  Livy and, 219, 226, 269, 338, 730–31
  MT's research for, 239, 268–69, 988
  and MT's Saturday Morning Club, 226
  pirated edition of, 272
  play based on, 404–12, 909–10
  published by MT, 271–72, 306, 338
  reviews of, 273, 307
  sales of, 272, 308
  theme of, 268–71
Prince of Wales Hotel (London), 664–65
Principles of Psychology, The (James, William), 650
"Private History of a Campaign That Failed, The," 65–68, 351, 354
psychics, 675–77
publicity/public relations, 195–96, 228, 323, 371, 513, 560, 570, 821, 890, 1033

| 1164 |

INDEX

Pudd'nhead Wilson, 362, 474, 481–82, 513–19, 589, 1012
Pudd'nhead Wilson's Calendar, 516–17
Pudd'nhead Wilson's New Calendar, 589–90
Pulitzer, Joseph, 699, 784

Quaker City, 142, 782
   MT's book on, 137–39, 141, 144–47
   MT's cruise on, 120–26, 129–32, 134–35, 144, 403
   MT's friends from, 122, 232, 276, 403
   MT's lecture tour on, 146–47
   See also *Innocents Abroad, The*
Quarles, John A., 7, 9, 27–28
Quarles farm, 27–28, 33, 35, 331, 437
Quarry Farm, 178, 268, 355, 526
   Clemenses' summer retreats in, 215–18, 420, 820
   Jean Clemens at, 299, 612
   Livy convalesces at, 756–57
   Mary Ann Cord and, 220–22
   and MT's board game, 283
   MT's productivity at, 217, 256–57, 305, 328, 387, 389, 757, 799
   MT's study in, 216–17, 234, 305, 757
   writers visit MT at, 400–401
Quick, Dorothy, 836, 893–95, 900–903, 916–17, 920, 922, 924, 927, 961, 1021
Quintard, Edward, 776, 797, 811, 813, 871–72, 942, 947, 991, 994, 1025

"Rabbi's Reply to Mark Twain, A" (Levy), 625–26
Rabelais, 239, 773
race
   equality and, 314
   inequality and, 128, 337–38, 560
   MT's views on, 128, 228, 653, 729, 1010, 1023
   MT's writings on, 172–74, 247, 514–19, 550, 556
   segregation and, 515
   stereotypes of, 27, 236–37, 563, 621–22, 625
racism
   condemnation of, 309, 320–21
   MT on, 334–35, 565, 715–16
   in MT's books, 27, 71, 335–36

   and MT's boyhood, xx, 27, 35, 42–45, 265
   in MT's writings, 92, 125, 173–74, 563
   See also Blacks: MT's racist language and
Raymond, John T., 241–42
Reconstruction, xix, 140–41, 201–2, 260, 314, 335, 337, 358, 515, 712–13, 715
Redding, Conn., 938, 1014
   Jean Clemens's life in, 976, 992–93, 1012–13, 1018
   and MT's death/funeral, 1028–29
   MT's house in. See Stormfield
   MT's lasting legacy to, 950
   Paine's home/land in, 846, 1017
   See also Mark Twain Library (Redding, Conn.)
Redeemer governments, 314, 337, 515
Redpath, James C., 174–76, 181, 196
Reed, Thomas B., 688–89, 712, 732, 748–49
Reid, Whitelaw, 195–96, 203, 405, 887
religion
   in MT's books, 71–72, 126, 155, 219, 236, 252, 332, 342, 569
   MT's boyhood training in, 12, 24–26, 78, 115, 164
   MT's controversial writings on, 146–47, 647, 995–97, 1005–8
   MT's rejection of, 1027
   MT's satirical treatment of, 995–97, 1005–8
   and MT's trip to Holy Land, 132–35
   and MT's trip to Italy, 252–53
   MT's views on, xix, 52, 123, 126, 155–57, 317–18, 552, 557, 641, 757, 1008, 1010
   MT's writings on, 132–35, 564, 603, 722, 730, 801, 804, 828
Renwick, James, Jr., 777
Republican Party, 93, 123, 707
   "black," 45, 91
   Liberal wing of, 259–60, 343
   MT breaks with, 318, 343–46, 790
   MT's support of, 139–41, 168, 171, 188, 259–61, 263, 343
   and MT's writings, 168, 171
   Orion Clemens and, 45, 68–69, 89, 91, 137
   Radical wing of, 137, 139–41
Rhodes, Cecil, 560–61, 563, 565, 608, 674
Rhône River, 449–51
Rice, Clarence, 482–83, 579, 732
Rice, Clement T., 82, 85, 95

| 1165 |

INDEX

Richardson, Abby Sage, 407–12
Richardson, Albert D., 148, 407
Riverdale home (Bronx, N.Y.), 739, 760, 834
  leased by Clemens family, 727–29
  Livy convalesces in, 743–45, 748–49, 755–56, 764, 766
  MT writes satire at, 754–55
  MT's room in, 745
Robinson Crusoe, 20
Rockefeller, John D., 496, 635, 637, 818
Rogers, Emilie, 865, 878, 900, 903, 928, 936, 938, 974, 983
Rogers, Harry, 897, 903, 983
Rogers, Henry H., 704, 755, 758, 761, 1004
  in Bermuda with MT, 921–22
  counsels MT on finances, 906, 969, 973–75
  death of, 974–75
  friendship with MT, 882, 899–900, 903
  MT confides in, 508, 520, 522–23, 525, 527, 564, 573, 583, 601, 614, 624, 632–33, 652–53, 664, 671, 729, 739, 741, 743, 850, 852
  MT correspondence and, 952
  MT on, 484–86, 662, 969
  on MT's business skills, 276
  and MT's debts/creditors, 498, 500–503, 540, 566, 595, 597–98, 632–33, 635
  and MT's *Following the Equator*, 590
  and MT's investments, 661–62, 733, 818–19, 956
  and MT's moneymaking schemes, 677–78
  and MT's Raster invention, 634–37
  at MT's speeches, 497–98, 688
  and Paige typesetter, 485, 493–96, 502–3, 506–7
  philanthropy of, 512
  as Standard Oil mogul, 482–85, 635
  stroke suffered by, 899–900, 903, 908
  and Webster & Company, 483, 493–503
  on yacht cruises with MT, 711–12, 731–33, 777, 850, 855, 858
  yacht of, 711–12, 739, 743, 756
Rogers, Mary Benjamin, 858–60, 864, 897, 903, 1018
Rome, Italy, 253, 371–72, 456, 754, 766, 1024
Roosevelt, Theodore, 689, 707, 723, 727–29, 770, 783–84, 790–91, 874

Rouen, France, 35, 506, 566
Roughing It, 107, 193
  advertising/marketing of, 195–97
  Chinese immigrants in, 96–97
  irreverent narrator of, 233
  MT's lectures on, 196–97
  sales/reviews of, 195–96, 400
  a sketch of MT's western adventures, 70–74, 194
  writing of, 179–80, 194–95
royalties, 214, 257, 440
  annual income from, 661, 705, 875, 907
  from *The Gilded Age*, 203
  inherited by MT's daughters, 958, 1014
  from MT's *Colonel Sellers*, 241–42
  and MT's debts, 480–81, 632
  MT's loss of, 237–38, 306
  from *Quaker City*, 145
  from *Roughing It*, 193–94, 196
  transferred to Livy, 498
royalty, 130–31, 390, 397, 453–55, 458, 463, 658–61
Russia/Russians, xix, 130–31, 626, 675, 718, 781–84, 838, 909, 1001
Russo-Japanese War, 782–83

Sacramento *Union*, 105, 110
Sage, Dean, 241, 419
Saint-Gaudens, Augustus, 254, 286, 354
San Francisco, 347, 446, 605, 649
  Chinese immigrants in, 173, 719
  MT lectures in, 111–13, 860
  MT lives/works in, 102, 104–5
  MT meets with editors in, 85, 146
  MT's correspondent/reporter jobs in, 94–99, 104–5, 110
  and *Roughing It*, 96, 194
San Francisco *Alta California*, 111, 146
  MT reviews Dickens for, 143
  MT's travel letters for, 114–15, 119, 124, 130–31, 134–35, 144
  reviews MT's frog tale, 102–3
  and *Roughing It*, 194
San Francisco *Morning Call*, 85, 95–99
Sandwich Islands, 91, 188, 194, 369, 483
  MT shops book on, 115
  and MT's global lecture tour, 525, 539–40

| 1166 |

INDEX

MT's lectures on, 107, 111–13, 117–19, 146
MT's travel letters on, 105–12, 121–22
Sanna, Sweden, 665–69, 671–72, 679–80
Satan, 755
   MT's writings on, 607–8, 646–47, 680, 803, 1005–7
   source of humor for MT, 25, 133
Saturday Morning Club, 225–26, 311, 752, 831, 882
Saunders, Louise Brownell, 506, 772. *See also* Brownell, Louise
Savage Club (London), 664, 893
Schlesinger, Siegmund, 611
Schmitt, Marguerite, 913, 961–62
Schubert, 448, 848, 860, 946, 1015
Science and Health, 753–54
Scott, Frank, 375
Scott, Walter, 52, 269, 303–4, 309, 501, 633, 950
Scroll and Key, 189–90
"Secret History of Eddypus, the World-Empire, The," 754–55
Sellers, Isaiah, 84
Sewall, G. T., 83, 92
Seward, William, 44
Shakespeare, William, 52, 239–40, 269, 333, 418, 434, 664, 853, 856, 987–90, 1015
Shakespeare Problem Restated, The (Greenwood), 987, 990
Sharp, Edward A., 871, 877, 881
Shaw, George Bernard, 457–58, 853, 885, 890–91, 950
Shelley, Harriet and Percy, 509–10
Sheridan, Philip H., 262, 349, 358–59, 372, 413–14, 428, 499
Sherman, William Tecumseh, 119–20, 262–63, 358–59, 369, 372, 428
Sinclair, Upton, 919
1601, 239–41
Slade, Jack, 74
slavery, xx, 261, 608–9
   Civil War and, 62, 67
   Jubilee Singers and, 226–28
   Langdon family opposed to, 162–63
   Mary Ann Cord's tale on, 220–22
   in Missouri, 26–27, 70
   MT on, xix, 26–29, 62, 67, 115, 128, 130, 150, 163, 227–28, 290, 365, 397, 549–50, 565

   and MT's books, 237, 328–29, 331–33, 336–38, 342, 393–95, 514–19, 546, 588–89
   MT's early experiences with, 16–18, 26–29
   and MT's family, 4, 7, 11, 15–17, 29, 227, 713
   MT's indignation toward, 365, 367
   and MT's lecture tours, 531, 549–50
   Orion Clemens on, 45, 68–69
   and post–Civil War ceremonies, 713–14
   runaway slaves and, 29, 37, 42, 115, 162–63, 328–29
Slote, Dan, 122, 134, 232, 276–79
Smith, Judson, 723–24
Smythe, Carlyle G., 560
Sneider, Charles, 277–78
Society for Psychical Research, 676
Society of the Pilgrims (England), 887–88
Some Acrostic Signatures of Francis Bacon (Booth), 987, 990
"Some Rambling Notes of an Idle Excursion," 246–47
"Some Thoughts on the Science of Onanism," 254
South Africa, 525, 555–56, 559–65, 608, 674–75, 697–98, 719–20
Spanish-American War, 653–56, 661, 675, 732
Spaulding, Clara, 205, 249–50, 253–54, 296
spiritualists/spiritualism, 576, 578, 582, 585
St. Louis, Mo.
   during Civil War, 63, 65
   Clemens family in, 50–51, 65, 115, 121, 158, 165
   MT on, 41
   MT returns to, 115, 121, 304
   and MT's honorary degree, 734, 736–37
   MT's lectures in, 115
   MT's printing jobs in, 41, 45
   Orion Clemens's printing jobs in, 10, 32, 34, 36
Standard Oil, 482–86, 496, 503, 635, 678, 754, 855, 899, 938, 973
Stanley, Henry Morton, 197, 587, 679, 762
Stanton, Edwin, 140–41
Starr, M. Allen, 612–13, 813
Stedman, Edmund C., 376, 415
Sterritt, Anna, 847–48, 861–62, 864, 866, 871
Stevens, Thaddeus, 139

| 1167 |

INDEX

Stevenson, Robert Louis, 341, 400, 643, 761
Stewart, William M., 83–84, 137–38, 172
"Stirring Times in Austria," 620
stock market
  and crash of 1893, 478–80, 482
  MT's insider trading and, 507, 662
  and MT's inventions, 502, 507–8
  MT's investments in, 85, 276–77, 325, 661–62, 733
Stoker, Bram, 429, 495–96, 587, 592–93
Stolberg-Wernigerode, Otto zu, 453
"Stolen Watermelon, The," 658
"Stolen White Elephant, The," 229–30
Stormfield (Redding, Conn.), 935
  Ashcroft at, 954–55, 964, 966–97, 992
  billiard room in, 925–27, 936, 939, 951
  burglary at, 943–44, 947, 949, 1031
  burns to the ground, 1031
  Christmas at, 958–59, 962, 1011–14
  Clara Clemens lives at, 928, 943–46, 966, 991, 1017, 1031
  Clara Clemens on, 857, 1031–32
  designed by John Howells, 857, 871, 925–26
  Edison film of, 993
  family tensions/crises at, 971, 1032
  furnishings by Isabel Lyon, 925, 967, 979
  Gabrilowitsch at, 946, 999–1000
  guests entertained at, 937–38, 949–50, 969, 987
  Isabel Lyon fired from, 971–73
  Isabel Lyon oversees building of, 877, 892, 897–98, 925–29
  Isabel Lyon runs, 942, 945–46, 959, 969, 978, 984
  Jean Clemens banished from, 962–63, 966–67, 970–71, 976, 979
  Jean Clemens comes home to, 962, 970–71, 976, 991–92
  Jean Clemens dreams of, 902, 905, 928, 931, 933
  MT buys land for, 846
  MT feels lonely at, 1009–10, 1016–17
  MT on, 925–28, 935, 938, 1020
  MT presides over, 969, 991
  MT's and daughter's Christmas at, 1011–14
  MT's correspondence stored at, 952–54
  MT's last days at, 1027–29
  and MT's library, 1001
  MT's writings pay for, 857, 927, 996
  naming of, 927
  staffing issues at, 944–45, 956, 970
Stotts, Mary. *See* Clemens, Mary "Mollie" Stotts
Stowe, Harriet Beecher, 148, 163, 188, 206, 210, 223, 273, 873
Strauss, Johann, 610, 627, 630
"Stupendous Procession, The," 715
Sturgis, Dorothy, 923, 940
subscription publishing, 704
  book reviews and, 150, 195
  by James Osgood, 306–8
  MT on, 144, 271, 348, 415, 632
  perils of, 369–70, 377
  popularity of, 144
  by Webster & Company, 327, 338, 348, 350–51, 356, 373, 389, 462
Sullivan, Anne, 510–12. *See also* Macy, Anne Sullivan
Sweden, 693, 742, 809. *See also* Sanna, Sweden
Swedish Movement Cure, 665–69, 673
Swift, Jonathan, 164, 239, 645
Switzerland, 17, 250–52, 445, 449, 502–3, 601–4, 606, 608–10, 613, 644–45, 1017
Sydney, Australia, 540–41
Szczepanik, Jan, 633–37, 677

Tarbell, Ida, 484, 938
Tarrytown, N.Y., 733, 742
Teller, Charlotte, 784, 838–40, 891
temperance, 106, 162, 201, 224–26
"Temperance Crusade and Woman's Rights, The," 224–25
Tennyson, 388, 390, 474, 602
Territorial Enterprise (Virginia City), 110, 113–14
  MT as local editor for, 80–87
  MT as San Francisco correspondent for, 97, 104
  MT's controversial articles in, 91–94
  MT's editor at, 83, 86, 91, 273
  and MT's *Roughing It*, 194
Terry, Ellen, 298, 312
Tesla, Nikola, 417, 512–13
Thayer, Abbott, 795, 798

INDEX

Thomas Nast: His Period and His Pictures (Paine), 822–23
Thomas Russell & Son, 526–27
Thoreau, Henry David, 174, 795
Those Extraordinary Twins, 513–14
Three Thousand Years Among the Microbes, 799–800, 819
Tiffany & Company, 226, 266, 326, 371, 916, 922
Tilden, Samuel J., 259–61
"To My Missionary Critics," 724
"To the Person Sitting in Darkness," 720–24
Tom Sawyer Abroad, 464–65, 486, 499, 590, 1011–12
Tom Sawyer, Detective, 590–91
trademark protection, 85, 957–58
Tramp Abroad, A, 250–51, 254, 256–57, 269, 317, 610, 617
"Trials and Rehabilitation of Joan of Arc," 567
"True Story: Repeated Word for Word as I Heard It, A," 220–21, 223
Turgenev, Ivan, 254
Turner, J. M. W., 256
"Turning Point of My Life, The," 1011
Tuxedo Park, N.Y., 883, 895, 897–903, 905–8, 911
Twain, Mark
  acting of, 292, 317, 324, 330
  affection for wife Livy, 177
  as American patriot, 397
  ancestors of, 3–5, 25
  antics of, 98, 113
  aphorisms of, xvii, 21–22, 255, 362, 401, 516–17, 589–90, 640–42, 686
  appearance of, xvi, 4, 13, 24, 35, 37, 49–51, 61, 73, 78, 83, 95, 100, 120, 124, 137–38, 153, 172, 256, 384, 401, 504, 530, 611–12, 685, 698, 771, 818, 1021, 1029
  as art benefactor, 285–90, 354–56, 360–61
  autobiography of, 761, 821, 825–29, 848, 873, 1016
  as autodidact, xviii, 20, 544–45
  bankruptcy/debts of, 20, 491, 498–501, 503–4, 522–23, 526–29, 534–35, 540, 566, 573, 582, 587, 595, 597–98, 601, 609, 643, 646–47, 689, 756, 969
  as baseball umpire, 387
  bigotry/prejudices of, 43, 96, 125, 132–33, 337
  biography of, 821–27, 939, 952–54, 1032
  birth of, 8
  boyhood antics of, 10, 12–14, 19–22, 24, 37–38, 83, 641
  boyhood recollections of, 232–35, 606, 733–34
  British agent of, 237
  as business man, xviii, 275–85, 360, 368–69, 381, 412, 479–80, 495, 633, 957, 965–66, 969
  cartoons of, 38
  and cats, 15, 177, 848, 917, 926, 936, 944, 951
  childhood/youth of, xiii–xvi, xviii, xx, 6–29, 92, 115–16
  chronic ailments of, 525–27, 535, 542, 545–50, 552, 555, 566, 574, 665, 667, 755, 764, 779, 871, 917
  collaborations of, 100, 198–204, 243–46, 309–10, 404
  comic gifts of, 78–79, 87, 103, 124, 175, 1028–29
  contempt for doctors, 504, 519, 526–27, 549, 555, 560, 583, 590, 673, 743, 937
  controversy and, 730
  on corruption, 97, 171, 199–202, 261, 269, 346, 663, 701, 705–7
  craves attention, 21, 24, 113, 123, 208, 455, 699, 791, 820–21, 836, 1033
  criticism of, 120, 123, 146–47, 157–58, 218, 374, 476, 722–24, 853
  cultivates/shapes his image, xvii, 73, 319, 513, 700, 703, 826, 958, 993
  darkness of later years, 806, 834–35, 845, 851–54, 873, 919–20, 1007–9, 1012, 1015–16, 1024
  and daughters' education, 283–85, 294–95, 434–39
  and daughter's financial security, 873–75, 907
  and daughter's inheritance, 958, 1014
  death of, 1027–33
  and death of brother, 55–58, 632
  and death of father, 32–34
  and death of Jean, 1013–19, 1025
  and death of mother, 423
  and death of nephew, 936–37
  and death of son, 181–83

1169

INDEX

Twain, Mark (*cont.*)
  and death of Susy, 576–85, 827
  dictates autobiography, 761, 823–24, 825–27, 841, 850, 857, 897, 900, 910–11, 927, 935, 952, 988
  dictates letters, 760, 823
  dislikes separations from Livy, 315, 322, 484, 494, 498, 560
  distrusts publishers, 116, 145, 148–49, 196, 271–72, 306, 325, 850
  drinking problem of, 911, 937
  early influences on, 25, 39
  early jobs of, 34–35
  education of, 20, 23–26, 34–35, 545, 735, 883, 890
  estranged from family, 158–59, 165–66, 209, 961, 984
  failed business ventures of, xviii, 275–85, 313, 429–30, 433, 481, 508, 584, 818–19, 908
  and family life, 324, 363–64, 855–58 1014, 1016–18
  fan correspondence of, 229, 701–2, 751–52, 778, 885
  film of, 993
  financial crises of, 429, 433, 440, 464, 475, 480, 485
  financial security of, 61–62, 69, 111, 178, 360, 371, 661–62, 705, 757, 907
  fires Isabel Lyon, 971–73
  first byline of, 221
  first forays in writing, 35, 37–40, 42, 44, 46, 82
  first published book of, 102, 116–17
  foreign languages and, 21–22, 35, 52, 249–50, 451, 617
  fortune teller seen by, 59–60
  guilt-ridden, 58, 121, 248, 317, 612, 652, 672, 768, 827, 931, 992, 1023
  and health fads, 665–69, 671, 742, 818–19, 994
  on himself, 45, 48, 52–53, 66, 100, 269, 911, 1020
  and his daughters, 485, 502–3, 557, 585, 589, 592–93, 626, 647, 834–35, 837, 860, 886, 901, 903, 940, 971, 991–92, 1024
  on his own death, 844, 881–82, 884, 993–94, 1025–30, 1033
  honorary degrees of, 399, 728–29, 733–34, 736–37, 883, 887–90, 938
  as humor editor, 171, 173–74, 180–81
  humorist beginnings of, 12–15, 21, 24–25, 38, 86–87, 102–3, 116
  as humorist, xvi–xviii, xxi, 103, 134, 149–50, 164–65, 174, 197, 219, 223, 260, 398, 399–400, 567–68, 590, 693, 827, 990, 997, 1007, 1026, 1029–30, 1033
  illnesses of, 305, 453–54, 477–78, 491–92, 519, 848
  impersonators of, 226, 702–3
  income of, 461, 595, 661, 705, 757, 828, 857, 875, 946
  interests, vast scope of, xviii, 52, 223
  interviewed in bed, 531, 560, 610, 822–23, 1021
  and Jean's epilepsy, 678–80, 729, 796, 807–9, 811, 813–14, 850, 859, 861, 862–64, 866, 871, 878, 880–81, 930, 932, 970–71, 1017
  journalism jobs of, 37–40, 46, 52, 80–87, 91–99, 104–10, 114–15, 119–35, 138–41, 143
  last days of, 1019–33
  last speech of, 991
  lawsuits against, 408, 410–12, 415
  lawsuits of, xix, 196, 272, 327, 763–64, 769–70, 818–19, 957–58
  as lecturer, 112–13, 141, 143, 316–17, 527, 529, 534, 697–98. *See also* lecture circuit
  legacy of, 341, 821, 1029–30, 1032–33
  letters project of, 799, 821, 824
  library of, 950, 1000–1001
  linguistic ingenuity and, 239–40
  literary tastes of, 20, 35–36, 46, 52, 109, 155, 164, 255, 318, 390, 400–402, 466, 477, 521, 650, 950, 994, 1008
  litigious nature of, 196, 271–72, 279, 327, 353–54, 373, 410, 412, 780
  love for animals, 15
  and Lyon-Ashcroft scandal, 985, 1011, 1020, 1031–32
  male friendships of, 190–91, 233, 245, 252, 411
  on marriage, 78–80, 98–99, 141–42, 153–54, 606

INDEX

marriage of, 363, 390, 440, 589, 768
medicine scorned by, 491–92, 742–43, 753
medium visited by, 57–58
as mentor, 226, 839, 900–903, 916–17, 1021
mercurial nature of, 52–53, 99, 170, 293, 680, 824
money worries of, 32, 97–98, 103–4, 106, 174, 206, 247, 250, 255, 267, 287–88, 359–60, 374–75, 416, 420, 458–59, 467, 474, 672, 677, 755–56
moneymaking schemes of, 6, 47–49, 75, 77, 111, 230–32, 590, 677–78, 818–19
mood swings of, xxi, 309, 416, 581, 849
as moralist, 86, 124, 640, 722–23
mourns death of Jean, 1019
mourns death of Susy, 587–93, 595, 602–4, 610–13, 615, 632, 647–48, 652, 671, 681, 687, 712, 742, 884, 888
mourns Livy's death, 767–74, 779, 781, 797, 891, 1019
music interests of, 50, 226–28, 250, 291, 446–48, 608–9, 630, 643, 767, 778, 781, 845, 848
as newspaper co-owner, 167–68, 170–74, 177–78, 180, 218
nicknames of, 103, 169, 300, 495, 575, 1019
northern sympathies of, xviii–xix, 70, 92, 120, 147, 188, 261, 263, 303–4, 316, 392
notebook jottings of, xvii, 52, 101, 246, 253, 268
as novelist, 198–99, 330, 495
opulent lifestyle of, 153, 253, 433, 480, 504, 547
oral output of, xvii–xviii, 24–25, 102
Oxford gown worn by, 888, 890, 938, 1002–3
as parent, 187, 291–302, 312, 339, 520, 585, 808–9, 834, 855, 914, 916
pays homage to Jean, 1014–18, 1020
pen names of, 46, 80, 84–85, 148, 511, 568–69, 853, 957–58, 1031
personality of, xv–xix, xix–xxi, 14, 20, 22, 24, 37–38, 50, 52–53, 58, 61, 70, 74, 81–82, 95, 108, 121, 126–27, 157, 170, 210, 397, 474, 509, 528, 611–12, 731, 935, 982, 1029, 1033

as philanthropist, 364–67, 512, 593, 844, 909–10
photographs of, 37, 513, 859–60, 893, 895, 900, 959, 962
poor investments of, 230–32, 288, 501, 633–38
portraits of, 288, 354–55, 652–53, 747, 818, 893
power of attorney and, 892, 956–58, 962
praise of, 103, 112, 149, 237, 269, 320, 340–41, 364, 702, 817, 834, 863
printing jobs of, xvii, 34–35, 37–38, 40–41, 43–47, 52, 566, 890
private readings by, 383–84, 615, 782, 786, 848, 852, 938, 940
pro-British sentiments of, 552–53, 561, 563, 599
product endorsements by, 703, 908
profanities used by, 124, 212, 218–19, 547, 582
professions/roles of, xvii, 52, 111
as publisher, 271–72, 306–8, 325–27, 338–40, 348–54, 356–60, 363, 368–79, 386, 389–90, 414–15, 424, 427–28, 433, 440, 475–77, 479–81, 496, 633
quartz mill job of, 78
record sales of, 305–6
relief fund for, 597–98
religious life of, 57, 189–91. *See also* religion
on repaying debts, 631–33, 686
revengeful nature of, 245–46, 279, 340, 373, 412, 639, 763, 769–70, 828, 974–75, 982
rheumatism bouts of, 251, 254, 300–301, 379, 441, 445–46, 449, 451, 454, 461–62, 665, 755
romantic life of, 58–60, 78–79, 131–32, 143, 203, 267–68, 831–32, 840–41
roving spirit of, 8, 41–43, 51, 70, 105, 119, 121, 252
rumors about, 839–40, 884, 891–92, 899, 917, 964
as satirist, 38, 121–23, 125, 127, 134–35, 148, 201, 230, 351, 365, 398, 560, 701, 707, 781
self-censorship of, 218

| 1171 |

INDEX

Twain, Mark (*cont.*)
  serious medical condition of, 863, 922, 936–37, 990–91, 994, 1002, 1004, 1009, 1011–13, 1019–22, 1025–27
  serious topics of, xvii, 221, 223–24, 269–70, 273, 307, 568, 638–40, 689, 707
  sexual reticence of, 132, 164, 218, 239–40, 255, 556, 594, 836
  on sexuality, 338, 593–95, 648, 651, 1005–6
  on the "shadow self," 826
  sleepwalking of, 9, 33, 81, 298
  smoking habits of, 78, 138, 195, 217, 543, 764, 779, 800, 889, 937, 991, 994, 1009, 1028, 1030
  social aspirations of, 79, 99, 153, 188–89
  southern sympathies of, 42, 64, 91–92, 319–20, 713–14
  speaking skills/style of, 28, 46, 86, 96, 102, 112, 118, 175–76, 197, 330, 384, 534, 541, 641, 823, 827
  spends money liberally, 206, 214, 247, 250, 253–55, 288, 467, 685
  stage fright of, 111–12, 860
  as steamboat pilot, xiii–xvi, 23, 25, 49–54, 61–65, 70, 79, 98, 103, 107, 116, 233, 303–5, 736–37, 949
  storytelling style of, 51, 102
  suffers from gout, 525–26, 610, 665, 680, 692, 755, 778–79, 807, 873
  superstitions/psychics and, 675–77
  taboo subjects and, 22, 105, 515, 723, 995, 1007
  teenage girls and, xx, 59–60, 131–32, 287, 322–23, 408–9, 509–10, 566, 604, 708, 751, 831–38, 879, 882, 886, 917–24, 949–50. *See also* "angelfish"
  temper of, xix, 13, 293–94, 309, 411, 468, 539, 591–91, 689, 900, 971
  "Tennessee land" and, 75, 106, 200–204, 242, 278
  theater interests of, 96, 226, 292, 643, 783, 833
  as toastmaster, xvii, 261–63, 688, 927
  trademarks of, 15, 85, 319, 531, 699, 819–21, 957–58, 991
  tributes to, 364, 702, 817–81, 822, 889, 1029–30
  typesetting skills of, 36, 41, 46, 280
  typewriter used by, 231, 234

  verbal dexterity of, 826–27
  vices of, 36, 123, 138, 156, 164, 195, 212
  voice of, xvii–xviii, 24–25, 330, 511, 761, 823
  wealth sought by, 267, 280, 478
  wedding of, 165–66, 168, 771
  white suits of, 217, 385, 803, 819–21, 848, 874, 894, 918, 920, 925, 993, 1029
  withdraws from life, 850, 855, 862–63, 915–16, 935, 958, 985, 1011
  women and, 14, 24–25, 123–24, 130, 141, 155, 164, 472, 648, 650–51
  working habits of, 138–39, 170–71, 208–9, 215–18, 234, 247, 249, 328, 389, 462, 474, 525, 604, 740
  writer's block of, 195
  yachting trips of, 711–12, 731–33, 777, 850, 855, 858, 862, 903
21 Fifth Avenue (N.Y.C.), 795, 882, 895, 945
  Albert Paine moves into, 824–25, 875
  angelfish stay at, 916, 920, 923–24
  and Clara Clemens, 776, 807–9, 872, 924
  designed by Renwick, 777, 779–80
  distinguished visitors to, 785, 810
  Gabrilowitsch performs at, 946
  and Jean Clemens, 777, 808–10, 864, 866, 912, 924
  MT abandons for Redding, 926–27
  MT dictates biography in, 822–24
  MT leases, 776–80
  MT on, 777, 846, 872, 881, 926
  MT's loneliness in, 938
  run by Isabel Lyon, 777–79, 793
Twichell, Harmony, 155–56, 191, 999, 1029–30
Twichell, Joseph H., 206, 227, 621, 632, 655, 1016
  in Bermuda with MT, 246–47, 878–79
  in Europe with MT, 250–52
  falls out with MT, 284–85, 720, 790
  as Hartford minister, 189–91, 344
  and Jean Clemens, 692, 976
  on Livy and MT, 210–11
  on MT and his death, 1029–30
  on MT and Prince of Wales, 458
  MT confides in, 179, 216, 305, 450, 658, 681, 718, 747, 783, 976
  MT correspondence and, 952–53
  MT models character on, 251

INDEX

MT's friendship with, 155–57, 189–91, 223, 233, 251–52
and MT's honorary degrees, 399, 728
and MT's letters project, 799
at MT's Metropolitan Club dinner, 747–48
and MT's serious illness, 991
and MT's writings, 239–40, 370–71
presides over Clemens burials, 771, 1029–30
presides over Clemens weddings, 166, 771, 1001, 1003
and Susy Clemens's death, 578–79, 581, 583
"Twins of Genius" lecture tour, 313–24, 348, 355, 363, 531
Tyringham, Mass., 773–76

Uncle Daniel (enslaved man), 28, 330–31, 333, 437
Uncle Tom's Cabin (Stowe), 148, 568, 873
Underground Railroad, 42, 162–63, 220, 289, 313
Uniform Edition of Twain's works, 595, 703–4
Union Army generals, 139–40, 261–63, 349, 358–59, 372, 428
"United States of Lyncherdom, The," 334, 716–17
United States Sanitary Commission, 92–95
University of California Press, 1033
University of Missouri, 733–34, 736–37
U.S. Congress, 44, 137, 139–41, 199, 201, 238, 638, 873–74

Van Vorst, Marie, 730
Vancouver, 525, 535
Vannuccini, Luigi, 468–69
Vassar College, 383, 437, 833
Venice, Italy, 127–28, 150, 252–54, 460, 476, 781
Verey, Joseph, 449
vernacular speech, xvii, 74, 329. *See also* dialects
Victoria, Queen, 283, 598–99
Vienna, 633, 686, 714, 946
    Clara Clemens's music training in, 601, 609, 626–30, 652, 662–63
    Clemens family in, 601, 609–12, 652–53

Clemenses and royalty in, 610, 658–60, 662–63
and Jean Clemens's epilepsy, 612–15, 662–63, 665
MT and culture of, 630, 643
MT and politics in, 618–20, 653–55, 658–59, 663, 675
MT on Jews in, 622–26
MT writes in, 645–48, 652, 852
MT's aphorisms and, 641–42
MT's "German Language" speech in, 617–18
MT's renown in, 610–11, 631, 653, 657
social whirlwind of, 610–12, 614–15, 626, 632
See also Hotel Metropole (Vienna); Kaltenleutgeben, Vienna
"Villagers of 1840-3," 606–7
Virginia City Daily Union, 82, 94
Virginia City, Nevada Territory, 80–87, 91, 94, 100, 114, 532
von Metternich, Pauline (princess), 610
von Versen, Frau, 471–72
von Versen, Maximilian, 453–54

Wagner, Richard, 446–48, 473, 520, 630
Wakeman, Ned, 114, 461, 995
Waldorf-Astoria (N.Y.C.), 697, 708
Wallace, Elizabeth, 837, 917–22, 1005, 1009, 1026
Wanamaker, John, 373
"War Prayer, The," 675, 788–90
Ward, Artemus, 86–87, 102–3, 111–12, 197, 399, 402–3
Ward, Ferdinand, 347, 352, 645
Ward, John Quincy Adams, 286, 354
Wardha, 556–57
Wark, Charles "Will," 899, 912, 941–43, 945–46, 967, 980, 999, 1003–4, 1032
Wark, Edith, 1003–4
Warner, Charles Dudley, 223, 226, 449
    books/articles by, 199, 201
    co-authors novel with MT, 198–204
    death of, 687
    on MT, 364
    Nook Farm home of, 188, 206
    sculptor Gerhardt and, 286
    and Susy Clemens, 575–76, 583–85
Warner, Lilly, 182–83, 493

| 1173 |

INDEX

Warner, Susan, 198, 226, 583–85
Warrimoo, 536–37, 539–41
Washington, Booker T., 688, 729, 786, 791, 843–44
Washington, D.C., 264–65, 429
    Ah Sin performed in, 244
    Clara Clemens's debut in, 695
    MT writes articles/books in, 137–41
    and MT's *Gilded Age*, 139, 198–99, 201
    MT's lobbying missions in, 172, 431–32, 874
    MT's secretary position in, 137–38
    "Twins of Genius" tour in, 316
Washington, George, 345, 498, 713
Watterson, Henry, 712
Wayland, Francis, 364–66, 368
Webb, Charles Henry, 99, 117
Webster, Annie, 277, 369, 371–72
Webster, Charles "Charley," 645, 828, 907
    Grant's memoirs and, 349–51, 357, 359–61, 377–78
    illness/death of, 377–79
    as manager of Webster & Company, 325–27, 373, 379, 413, 479, 496
    MT confides in, 305, 323, 327, 376
    MT falls out with, 375–79, 413–15, 971
    MT on, 369, 496–97, 583
    as MT's agent/publisher, 306–8, 325–27, 413–14, 500
    and MT's books, 272, 326–27, 338–40
    oversees MT's inventions, 277–79, 281–84, 325–26, 368–69, 378–80
    Pope Leo biography and, 371–72
    and *Prince and the Pauper* play, 405–6
    See also Charles L. Webster and Company
Weggis, Switzerland, 601–4, 606, 608–10, 613, 644–45
Welles, Carlotta, 884
Wells, Ida B., 714, 843
West, the, xvii, 45, 78, 103, 112–14, 157, 188, 219
West Point Academy Press, 241
Westinghouse, George, 417, 432, 512
Wharton, Edith, 340, 468, 606, 845
"What is Happiness?," 852
"What is Liberty?," 226
What is Man?, 224, 647, 851–54, 1026
Wheeler, Candace Thurber, 266, 384
"Which Was the Dream?," 644–45

White, Frank Marshall, 596, 598
White, Stanford, 495
"White House Funeral, The," 141
white superiority/supremacy, 260, 314, 331–34, 514, 548, 550
Whitefriars Club (London), 197, 665
Whitford, Daniel, 369, 411
Whitman, Walt, 102, 239, 306, 402
Whitmore, Franklin G., 381, 431, 480, 522, 573, 672, 733, 745, 747, 995
Whitmore, Harriet E., 557, 744–45, 762, 778, 937, 1017, 1032
Whittaker, Johnson, 518
"Who?," 1020
Wild West Show, 73, 363
Wilde, Oscar, 457–58
Willard's Hotel (D.C.), 139–40, 874
Wilson, Woodrow, 724, 919, 1025
women
    idealized by MT, xx, 59, 60, 660, 802, 835, 1009–10
    in MT's books/writings, 203, 516, 648, 650–51, 836
    nontraditional characters, 604–6
    sexuality of, 255, 1005–6
    See also Twain, Mark: women and; Twain, Mark: on sexuality
women's suffrage, 188, 366, 512
    endorsed by the Langdons, 162
    MT's advocacy of, xix, 108, 589, 1023
    MT's speeches on, 224, 909
    MT's writings on, 224–25, 259
Woodlawn Cemetery (Elmira, N.Y.), 183, 424, 580, 1030–31
Wright, Laura, 58–60, 132, 202, 267–68, 648, 660, 831, 840–41
Writings of Mark Twain, The, 704
Wydenbruck-Esterházy, Countess, 615, 651, 659

Yale Law School, xx, 364–66, 368, 844
Yale University, 189, 399, 728–29, 737, 764, 1033
Yonge, Charlotte M., 268
York Harbor, Maine, 739–43, 746–47, 750, 752

Zola, Émile, 623–24, 655